Lecture Notes in Computer Science 11877

More information about this series at http://www.springer.com/series/7408

Hervé Panetto · Christophe Debruyne ·
Martin Hepp · Dave Lewis ·
Claudio Agostino Ardagna ·
Robert Meersman (Eds.)

On the Move to Meaningful Internet Systems

OTM 2019 Conferences

Confederated International Conferences:
CoopIS, ODBASE, C&TC 2019
Rhodes, Greece, October 21–25, 2019
Proceedings

 Springer

Editors
Hervé Panetto
University of Lorraine
Vandoeuvre Les Nancy Cedex, France

Christophe Debruyne (iD)
Trinity College Dublin
Dublin, Ireland

Martin Hepp
Bundeswehr University Munich
Wilhelmshaven, Germany

Dave Lewis
Trinity College Dublin
Dublin, Ireland

Claudio Agostino Ardagna
Università degli Studi di Milano Crema
Crema, Italy

Robert Meersman
TU Graz
Graz, Austria

ISSN 0302-9743   ISSN 1611-3349 (electronic)
Lecture Notes in Computer Science
ISBN 978-3-030-33245-7   ISBN 978-3-030-33246-4 (eBook)
https://doi.org/10.1007/978-3-030-33246-4

LNCS Sublibrary: SL2 – Programming and Software Engineering

This Springer imprint is published by the registered company Springer Nature Switzerland AG
The registered company address is: Gewerbestrasse 11, 6330 Cham, Switzerland

General Co-chairs and Editors'
Message for OnTheMove 2019

The OnTheMove 2019 event held October 21–25 in Rhodes, Greece further consolidated the importance of the series of annual conferences that was started in 2002 in Irvine, California. It then moved to Catania, Sicily in 2003, to Cyprus in 2004 and 2005, Montpellier in 2006, Vilamoura in 2007 and 2009, in 2008 to Monterrey, Mexico, to Heraklion, Crete in 2010 and 2011, Rome 2012, Graz in 2013, Amantea, Italy in 2014, Rhodes in 2015, 2016, and 2017, and lastly in Valletta in 2018.

This prime event continues to attract a diverse and relevant selection of today's research worldwide on the scientific concepts underlying new computing paradigms, which of necessity must be distributed, heterogeneous, and supporting an environment of resources that are autonomous yet must meaningfully cooperate. Indeed, as such large, complex, and networked intelligent information systems become the focus and norm for computing, there continues to be an acute and even increasing need to address the software, system, and enterprise issues involved and discuss them face to face in an integrated forum that covers methodological, semantic, theoretical, and application issues. As we all realize, e-mail, the Internet, and even video conferences are not by themselves optimal or even sufficient for effective and efficient scientific exchange.

The OnTheMove (OTM) international Federated Conference series has been created precisely to cover the scientific exchange needs of the communities that work in the broad yet closely connected fundamental technological spectrum of Web-based distributed computing. The OTM program every year covers data and Web semantics, distributed objects, Web services, databases, information systems, enterprise workflow and collaboration, ubiquity, interoperability, mobility, as well as grid and high-performance computing.

OnTheMove is proud to give meaning to the "federated" aspect in its full title: it aspires to be a primary scientific meeting place where all aspects of research and development of internet- and intranet-based systems in organizations and for e-business are discussed in a scientifically motivated way, in a forum of interconnected workshops and conferences. This year's 18th edition of the OTM Federated Conferences event therefore once more provided an opportunity for researchers and practitioners to understand, discuss, and publish these developments within the broader context of distributed, ubiquitous computing. To further promote synergy and coherence, the main conferences of OTM 2019 were conceived against a background of their three interlocking global themes:

- Trusted Cloud Computing Infrastructures Emphasizing Security and Privacy
- Technology and Methodology for Data and Knowledge Resources on the (Semantic) Web
- Deployment of Collaborative and Social Computing for and in an Enterprise Context

Originally the federative structure of OTM was formed by the co-location of three related, complementary, and successful main conference series: DOA (Distributed Objects and Applications, held since 1999), covering the relevant infrastructure-enabling technologies, ODBASE (Ontologies, DataBases and Applications of SEmantics, since 2002) covering Web semantics, XML databases and ontologies, and of course CoopIS (Cooperative Information Systems, held since 1993) which studies the application of these technologies in an enterprise context through, e.g., workflow systems and knowledge management. In the 2011 edition, security aspects, originally started as topics of the IS workshop in OTM 2006, became the focus of DOA as secure virtual infrastructures, further broadened to cover aspects of trust and privacy in so-called Cloud-based systems. As this latter aspect came to dominate agendas in this and overlapping research communities, we decided in 2014 to rename the event as the Cloud and Trusted Computing (C&TC) conference, and it was originally launched in a workshop format.

These three main conferences specifically seek high-quality contributions of a more mature nature and encourage researchers to treat their respective topics within a framework that simultaneously incorporates (a) theory, (b) conceptual design and development, (c) methodology and pragmatics, and (d) application in particular case studies and industrial solutions.

As in previous years, we again solicited and selected additional quality workshop proposals to complement the more mature and "archival" nature of the main conferences. Our workshops are intended to serve as "incubators" for emergent research results in selected areas related, or becoming related, to the general domain of Web-based distributed computing. We were very glad to see that our earlier successful workshops (EI2N, META4eS, FBM, and SiANA) reappeared in 2019. The Fact Based Modeling (FBM) workshop in 2015 succeeded and expanded the scope of the successful earlier ORM workshop. The Industry Case Studies Program, started in 2011, under the leadership of Hervé Panetto, Wided Guédria, and Gash Bhullar, further gained momentum and visibility in its ninth edition this year.

The OTM registration format ("one workshop and/or conference buys all workshops and/or conferences") actively intends to promote synergy between related areas in the field of distributed computing and to stimulate workshop audiences to productively mingle with each other and, optionally, with those of the main conferences. In particular, EI2N continues to create and exploit a visible cross-pollination with CoopIS.

As the three main conferences and the associated workshops all share the distributed aspects of modern computing systems, they experience the application pull created by the Internet and by the so-called Semantic Web, in particular, developments of big data, increased importance of security issues, and the globalization of mobile-based technologies.

The three conferences seek exclusively original submissions that cover scientific aspects of fundamental theories, methodologies, architectures, and emergent technologies, as well as their adoption and application in enterprises and their impact on societally relevant IT issues.

- CoopIS 2019, Cooperative Information Systems, our flagship event in its 27th edition since its inception in 1993, invited fundamental contributions on principles and applications of distributed and collaborative computing in the broadest scientific sense in workflows of networked organizations, enterprises, governments, or just communities

- C&TC 2019 (Cloud and Trusted Computing) the successor of DOA (Distributed Object Applications), focused on critical aspects of virtual infrastructure for cloud computing, specifically spanning issues of trust, reputation, and security
- ODBASE 2019, Ontologies, Databases, and Applications of SEmantics covered the fundamental study of structured and semi-structured data, including linked (open) data and big data, and the meaning of such data as is needed for today's databases, as well as the role of data and semantics in design methodologies and new applications of databases

As with the earlier OnTheMove editions, the organizers wanted to stimulate this cross-pollination by a program of engaging keynote speakers from academia and industry and shared by all OTM component events. We are quite proud to list for this year:

- Elena Simperl, University of Southampton, UK
- Stefan Thalmann, Karl-Franzens University of Graz, Austria

The general downturn in submissions observed in recent years for almost all conferences in computer science and IT has also affected OnTheMove, but this year the harvest again stabilized at a total of 156 submissions for the three main conferences and over 45 submissions in total for the workshops. Not only may we indeed again claim success in attracting a representative volume of scientific papers, many from the USA and Asia, but these numbers, of course, allow the respective Program Committees to again compose a high-quality cross-section of current research in the areas covered by OTM. Acceptance rates vary but the aim was to stay consistently at about one accepted full paper for three submitted, yet as always these rates are subordinated to professional peer assessment of proper scientific quality.

As usual, we separated the proceedings into two volumes with their own titles, one for the main conferences and one for the workshops and posters. But in a different approach to previous years, we decided the latter should appear post-event and so allow workshop authors to eventually improve their peer-reviewed papers based on critiques by the Program Committees and on live interaction at OTM. The resulting additional complexity and effort of editing the proceedings were professionally shouldered by our leading editor, Christophe Debruyne, with the general chairs for the conference volume, and with Hervé Panetto for the workshop volume. We are again most grateful to the Springer LNCS team in Heidelberg for their professional support, suggestions, and meticulous collaboration in producing the files and indexes ready for downloading on the USB sticks. It is a pleasure to work with a staff that so deeply understands the scientific context at large and the specific logistics of conference proceedings publication.

The reviewing process by the respective OTM Program Committees was performed to professional quality standards: each paper review in the main conferences was assigned to at least three referees, with arbitrated e-mail discussions in the case of strongly diverging evaluations. It may be worthwhile to emphasize once more that it is an explicit OnTheMove policy that all conference Program Committees and chairs make their selections in a completely sovereign manner, autonomous and independent from any OTM organizational considerations. As in recent years, proceedings in paper form are now only available to be ordered separately.

The general chairs are once more especially grateful to the many people directly or indirectly involved in the setup of these federated conferences. Not everyone realizes a large number of qualified persons that need to be involved, and the huge amount of work, commitment, and the financial risk in the uncertain economic and funding climate of 2019, that is entailed by the organization of an event like OTM. Apart from the persons in their roles mentioned above, we therefore wish to thank in particular explicitly our main conference PC chairs:

- CoopIS 2019: Martin Hepp and Maria Maleshkova
- ODBASE 2019: Dave Lewis and Rob Brennan
- C&TC 2019: Claudio A. Ardagna, Ernesto Damiani, and Athanasios Vasilakos

And similarly we thank the Program Committee (co-)chairs of the 2019 ICSP and Workshops (in their order of appearance on the website): Hervé Panetto, Wided Guédria, Gash Bhullar, Georg Weichhart, Milan Zdravkovic, Peter Bollen, Stijn Hoppenbrouwers, Robert Meersman, Maurice Nijssen, Ioana Ciuciu, Anna Fensel, George Karabatis, and Aryya Gangopadhyay. Together with their many Program Committee members, they performed a superb and professional job in managing the difficult yet vital process of peer review and selection of the best papers from the harvest of submissions. We all also owe a serious debt of gratitude to our supremely competent and experienced conference secretariat and technical admin staff in Guadalajara and Dublin, respectively, Daniel Meersman and Christophe Debruyne. The general conference and workshop co-chairs also thankfully acknowledge the academic freedom, logistic support, and facilities they enjoy from their respective institutions: Technical University of Graz, Austria; Université de Lorraine, Nancy, France; Latrobe University, Melbourne, Australia – without which such a project quite simply would not be feasible. Reader, we do hope that the results of this federated scientific enterprise contribute to your research and your place in the scientific network, and we hope to welcome you at next year's event!

September 2019

Hervé Panetto
Robert Meersman

Organization

OTM (On The Move) is a federated event involving a series of major international conferences and workshops. These proceedings contain the papers presented at the OTM 2019 Federated conferences, consisting of CoopIS 2019 (Cooperative Information Systems), C&TC 2019 (Cloud and Trusted Computing), and ODBASE 2019 (Ontologies, Databases, and Applications of Semantics).

OTM Conferences and Workshops General Chairs

Hervé Panetto   University of Lorraine, France
Robert Meersman   TU Graz, Austria

CoopIS 2019 PC Co-chairs

Martin Hepp   Universität der Bundeswehr München, Germany
Maria Maleshkova   University of Bonn, Germany

ODBASE 2019 PC Co-chairs

Dave Lewis   Trinity College Dublin, Ireland
Rob Brennan   Dublin City University, Ireland

C&TC 2019 PC Co-chairs

Claudio A. Ardagna   Università degli Studi di Milano, Italy
Ernesto Damiani   Università degli Studi di Milano, Italy
Athanasios Vasilakos   Lulea University of Technology, Sweden

Publication Chair

Christophe Debruyne   Trinity College Dublin, Ireland

Logistics Team

Daniel Meersman

CoopIS 2019 Program Committee

Marco Aiello
Mehwish Alam
Joao Paulo Almeida
Eduard Babkin
Sebastian Bader
Ingmar Baumgart
Khalid Belhajjame
Narjes Bellamine
Salima Benbernou
Djamal Benslimane
Javier Berrocal
Xavier Blanc
Athman Bouguettaya
Uwe Breitenbücher
Richard Chbeir
Carlo Combi
Bruno Defude
Daniele Dell'Aglio
Elena Demidova
Giuseppe Desolda
Khalil Drira
Rik Eshuis
Javier A. Espinosa-Oviedo
Ernesto Exposito
George Feuerlicht
Walid Gaaloul
Chirine Ghedira Guegan
Mohamed Graiet
Daniela Grigori
Mohand-Said Hacid
Armin Haller
Karl Hammar
Anett Hoppe
Stijn Hoppenbrouwers
Stefan Jablonski
Manfred Jeusfeld
A. S. M. Kayes
Matthias Klusch
Agnieszka Lawrynowicz
Alexander Lazovik
Francesco Leotta
Jiangang Ma
Zakaria Maamar
Sanjay Madria
Amel Mammar

Maristella Matera
Raimundas Matulevičius
Simon Mayer
Massimo Mecella
Lionel Medini
Philippe Merle
Nizar Messai
Michele Missikoff
Sellami Mokhtar
Amira Mouakher
Juan Manuel Murillo Rodríguez
Giulio Napolitano
Alex Ng
Alexander Norta
Selmin Nurcan
Andreas L. Opdahl
Oscar Pastor Lopez
Olivier Perrin
Stefan Pickl
Gil Regev
Manfred Reichert
David Romero
Michael Rosemann
Shazia Sadiq
Gezim Sejdiu
Mohamed Sellami
Amartya Sen
Nicolas Seydoux
Michael Sheng
Pnina Soffer
Jacopo Soldani
Chengzheng Sun
Yehia Taher
Joe Tekli
Lucineia Heloisa Thom
Farouk Toumani
Maria-Esther Vidal
Tobias Weller
Lena Wiese
Guido Wirtz
Jian Yang
Jian Yu
Fouad Zablith
Amrapali Zaveri
Zhangbing Zhou

CoopIS 2019 Additional Reviewers

Tooba Aamir
Seun Adekunle
Abasi-Amefon Affia
Abdulwahab Aljubairy
Sabri Allani
Nour Assy
Etienne Begon
Matthias Börsig
Marius Breitmayer
Weiwei Cai
Karam Bou Chaaya
Bryden Cho
Jabed Chowdhury
Rajjat Dadwal
Hai Dong
Ghada El-Khawaga
Wissem Eljaoued
Vincent Emonet
Fairouz Fakhfakh
Hongfei Fan
Sheik M. M. Fattah
Ilche Georgievski
Simon Gottschalk
Roland Gröll
Marwa Hachicha
Hussein Hellani
Mubashar Iqbal
Klaus Kammerer
Akram Kamoun
Rihab Khemiri

Aleksandr Kormiltsyn
Tin Kuculo
Indika Kumara
Adnan Mahmood
Pavel Malyzhenkov
Kessentini Maroua
Edgard Marx
Fatma Masmoudi
Naija Mohamed
Pouya Ghiasnezhad Omran
Samir Ouchani
Madhawa Perera
Khouloud Salameh
Stefan Schestakov
Nicolai Schuetzenmeier
Feliks Praseta Sejahtera
Brian Setz
Babar Shahzaad
Sarah Ali Siddiqui
Christian Sturm
Romuald Thion
Imen Tounsi
Boris Ulitin
Qi Wang
Marek Wehmer
Qianli Xing
Aymen Yahyaoui
San Yeung
Munazza Zaib
Rita Zgheib

ODBASE 2019 Program Committee

Judie Attard
Sören Auer
Costin Badica
Christoph Bussler
Ademar Crotti Junior
Jeremy Debattista
Christophe Debruyne
Milan Dojchinovski
Vadim Ermolayev
Cristina Feier

Paul Fodor
Tiantian Gao
Guido Governatori
Harry Halpin
Sungkook Han
James Hodson
Carlos A. Iglesias
Jan Jürjens
Tomi Kauppinen
Jacek Kopecky

Kris McGlinn
Gary Munnelly
Nikolay Nikolov
Fabrizio Orlandi
Harshvardhan Pandit
Dimitris Plexousakis
Georg Rehm
Dumitru Roman

Harald Sack
Uli Sattler
Ahmet Soylu
Markus Stumptner
Evgenij Thorstensen
George Vouros
Guohui Xiao
Beyza Yaman

ODBASE 2019 Additional Reviewers

Hidir Aras
Maxim Davidovsky
Wolfgang Mayer

Matt Selway
Bjørn Marius Von Zernichow

C&TC 2018 Program Committee

Marco Anisetti
Rasool Asal
Valerio Bellandi
Adrian Belmonte
Michele Bezzi
Ashok Kumar Das
Scharam Dustdar
Nabil El Ioini
Stefanos Gritzalis
Patrick Hung
Meiko Jensen
George Karabatis

Miguel Vargas Martin
Weizhi Meng
Antonio Munoz
Evangelos Rekleitis
Julian Schuette
Stefan Schulte
Jun Shen
Shangguang Wang
Christos Xenakis
Jingwei Yang
Chia-Mu Yu

C&TC 2019 Additional Reviewers

Marios Anagnostopoulos
Aristeidis Farao

OnTheMove 2019 Keynotes

Qrowd and the City: Designing People-Centric Smart Cities

Elena Simperl

University of Southampton, UK

Short Bio

Elena Simperl is professor of computer science at the University of Southampton and director of the Southampton Data Science Academy. She is also one of the directors of the Web Science Institute and a Turing Fellow. Before joining Southampton in 2012, she was assistant professor at the Karlsruhe Institute of Technology (KIT), Germany and vice-director of the Semantic Technologies Institute (STI) Innsbruck, Austria. She has contributed to more than twenty research projects, often as principal investigator or project lead. Currently she is the PI on four grants: the EU-funded Data Pitch, which supports SMEs to innovate with data, the EU-funded QROWD, which uses crowd and artificial intelligence to improve smart transportation systems, the EPSRC-funded Data Stories, which works on methods and tools to make data more engaging, and the EU funded ACTION, which develops social computing methods for citizen science. She authored more than 100 papers in sociotechnical systems, knowledge engineering and AI and was programme/general chair of the European and International Semantic Web Conference and of the European Data Forum.

Talk

Smart cities are as much about the needs, expectations and values of the people they serve as they are about the underlying technology. In this talk, I am going to present several areas of system design where human and social factors play a critical role, from fostering participation to augmented intelligence and responsible innovation. I will present ongoing challenges, solutions and opportunities, drawing from recent studies in Qrowd, a Horizon 2020 programme proposing a humane AI approach for transport and mobility.

Managing Knowledge Risks in Data-Centric Collaborations

Stefan Thalmann

Karl-Franzens University of Graz, Austria

Short Bio

Stefan Thalmann is Professor and the Director of the Center for Business Analytics and Data Science of the Karl-Franzens University of Graz, Austria. Prior to that he was with the Graz University of Technology and lead the cognitive decision support group in the application-oriented research center Pro2Future. He managed several industry funded research projects as well as EU funded research projects and worked for universities in Austria, Germany, Italy, Finland and the UK. He holds a diploma in Information Systems from the University of Halle-Wittenberg, a PhD and a habilitation degree in Information Systems from the University of Innsbruck. His research interest includes industrial data analytics, data-driven decision support and the management of knowledge risks in digitized supply chains. Stefan authored more than 50 academic publications and a member of 40 conference and workshop program committees.

Talk

Due to digitization the exchange of data along the supply chain intensified over time and data-centric collaborations emerge. These data sets become more and more comprehensive as cheap sensors, affordable infrastructure and storage capacity intensified the data collection. Based on advanced data analytics it now more likely that supply-chain partners or even competitors discover valuable knowledge out of these data sets. Not sharing is however not an option in most cases and thus a suitable trade-off between sharing and protection needs to be found. Thus data-centric collaborations might be also the source of knowledge risks and need to be considered in an organisational knowledge protection strategy.

In this talk, I will analyze the challenges of data-centric collaborations from a perspective of knowledge risks. I will present examples and insights from current research projects and studies. Further, I will present solutions enabling companies to managing data-centric collaborations by finding a suitable tradeoff between the benefits arising from sharing data in such a collaboration on the one hand and the knowledge risks associated with the sharing of data.

Contents

Machine Learning and Knowledge Reconstruction and Discovery (Short Papers)

Semantic Web, Linked Open Data, and Knowledge Graphs

Security and Privacy

Security and Privacy (Short Papers)

Internet of Things

Human Aspects and Social Interaction

Services and Processes in Information Systems

Services and Processes in Information Systems (Short Papers)

**International Conference on Ontologies, DataBases,
and Applications of Semantics (ODBASE) 2019**

Cloud and Trusted Computing (C&TC) 2019

International Conference on Cooperative Information Systems (CoopIS) 2019

CoopIS 2019 PC Co-chairs' Message

The International Conference on Cooperative Information Systems (CoopIS) is an established international event for presenting and discussing scientific contributions to technical, economic, and societal aspects of distributed information systems at scale. The guiding theme of this 27th conference is "Information Systems in a Data Society", with a particular focus on the following areas:

- Data, Information, and Knowledge Engineering;
- Machine-Learning and Knowledge Reconstruction and Discovery;
- Semantic Web and Linked Open Data;
- Security and Privacy;
- Internet of Things;
- Architecture and Management of Information Systems;
- Human Aspects and Social Interaction; and
- Services in Information Systems.

Our call for papers attracted many submissions in that spirit of research. All in all, we received 121 submissions, of which we accepted 27 as full papers (22%), and eight additionally as short papers (6.6%), i.e. the total acceptance rate was a bit less than 29%. The review process was organized in a two-staged fashion. First, each paper was reviewed by two to four PC members. Then, we discussed every single submission in a PC chair meeting, partially soliciting additional reviews. All in all, we had to be very selective and had to reject many interesting submissions.

CoopIS 2019 would not have been possible without the hard work of many people. Our special thanks go to Robert Meersman and Hervé Panetto, the General Chairs of the On The Move umbrella conference series, for inviting us to chair this year's CoopIS conference, and for their continuous support throughout all phases of the preparation. We feel honored by their trust in our work.

Christophe Debruyne did a tremendous job in managing the EasyChair system and in preparing the proceedings for the entire conference. Thank you very much!

Our PC members took the majority of work. First, they helped distribute the call for papers in relevant communities and then put a lot of effort into the final selection of papers, reviewing up to six submissions each. They were supported by a large body of additional reviewers, whom we are also very thankful for their hard work.

Of course, all authors who submitted to the conference deserve a big thanks, too.

Finally, we would like to thank Springer for their professional support and guidance during the preparation of the proceedings.

September 2019

Martin Hepp
Maria Maleshkova

Towards a Reference Ontology of Trust

Glenda Amaral[1]([⊠]), Tiago Prince Sales[1,2],
Giancarlo Guizzardi[1], and Daniele Porello[2]

[1] Conceptual and Cognitive Modeling Research Group (CORE),
Free University of Bozen-Bolzano, Bolzano, Italy
{gmouraamaral,tiago.princesales,giancarlo.guizzardi}@unibz.it
[2] ISTC-CNR Laboratory for Applied Ontology, Trento, Italy
daniele.porello@loa.istc.cnr.it

Abstract. Trust is a key component of relationships in social life. It is commonly argued that trust is the "glue" that holds families, societies, organizations and companies together. In the literature trust is frequently considered as a strategic asset for organizations. Having a clear understanding of the notion of trust and its components is paramount to both trust assessment and trust management. Although much progress has been made to clarify the ontological nature of trust, the term remains overloaded and there is not yet a shared or prevailing, and conceptually clear notion of trust. In this paper we address this issue by means of an in-depth ontological analysis of the notion of trust, grounded in the Unified Foundational Ontology. As a result, we propose a concrete artifact, namely, the Reference Ontology for Trust, in which we characterize the general concept of trust and distinguish between two types of trust, namely, social trust and institution-based trust. We also represent the emergence of risk from trust relations. In addition, we make a comparative analysis of our Reference Ontology to other trust ontologies. To validate and demonstrate the contribution of our approach, we apply it to model two application examples.

Keywords: Trust · Ontological analysis · Unified foundational ontology

1 Introduction

Trust is a central component of social life. In the literature, trust is frequently referred to as the "glue of society", vital in economics, social cooperation, organizations, groups, etc. Because of its ubiquitous presence, the notion of trust appears in many contexts and has been defined in a wide number of ways throughout the years and across several areas [5,9,25,31].

The term trust has been used to refer to different types of relationships, such as the trust between individuals, as well as between individuals and organizations, individuals and autonomous agents, between software systems operating in a network, the trust in the context of offline or online commercial relationships,

© Springer Nature Switzerland AG 2019
H. Panetto et al. (Eds.): OTM 2019, LNCS 11877, pp. 3–21, 2019.
https://doi.org/10.1007/978-3-030-33246-4_1

and others. Regardless of the context, trust is generally the basis for decision making closely related to achieving a goal. Therefore, understanding the key factors that play a role in trust assessment is paramount to avoid exposing decision makers to the risk of loss from incorrect decisions due to misplaced trust. Since these factors are numerous, it is not trivial to select the key ones that maximize decision performance, and thus promote effective decision making. In technological contexts, many disciplines, such as human-computer interaction, distributed artificial intelligence, multi-agent systems and networked-computer systems, are working to integrate trust into technological infrastructures. In this scenario, the need for a technology able to deal with typical human cognitive and social features and phenomena, like trust, emerges. To support this, a precise and rigorous conceptualization, based on foundational ontologies, is needed, as well as some theoretical abstraction and some possible modeling of it.

Although much progress has been made to clarify the ontological nature of trust, the term remains overloaded and there is not yet a shared or prevailing, and conceptually clear definition for it [4,22]. In the light of the above, we advocate for the need of a reference ontology of trust to serve as a basis for communication, consensus and alignment among different approaches and perspectives, as well as to foster interoperability across the heterogeneous application domains. In this paper, we address this issue by means of an in-depth ontological analysis of the notion of trust, grounded in the Unified Foundational Ontology (UFO) [11,14]. As a result, we propose a concrete artifact, namely, the Reference Ontology of Trust, which we employ to harmonize different perspectives found in the literature. In our analysis, besides formally characterizing the concept of trust, we distinguish between two types of trust, namely, *social trust* and *institution-based trust*. Moreover, we clarify the relation between trust and risk and represent how risk emerges from trust relations.

This paper is part of a long-term research program that aims at developing ontological foundations for social and organizational modeling. In this context, we have analyzed the notions of *risk, value, economic preference, economic transaction, social roles, contracts, goal, capability*, among others [14]. These analysis, in turn, have been later employed to evaluate, integrate and redesign important organizational modeling languages such as ARIS, BPMN, and Archimate [1,16].

The remainder of this paper is organized as follows. First, in Sect. 2, we introduce the reader to the main notions of UFO. Then, in Sect. 3, we discuss the ontological nature of trust as discussed in the literature. In Sect. 4 we describe our view of Social System, an essential concept for the modeling of institution-based trust. In Sect. 5 we present our proposal, the Reference Ontology of Trust. In Sect. 6, to validate and demonstrate the contribution of our ontology to the modeling practice, we apply it to model two case illustrations: (i) an example of social trust; and (ii) an example of institution-based trust. We present some related work on Sect. 7 and conclude the paper in Sect. 8 with some final considerations.

2   Ontological Foundations

In this paper we provide an ontological analysis of *trust*, grounded on the Unified Foundational Ontology (UFO). UFO is an axiomatic domain independent formal theory, developed based on a number of theories from Formal Ontology, Philosophical Logics, Philosophy of Language, Linguistics and Cognitive Psychology. UFO is divided into three incrementally layered compliance sets: UFO-A, an ontology of endurants (objects) [11], UFO-B, an ontology of events (perdurants) [15], and UFO-C, an ontology of social entities built on the top of UFO-A and UFO-B, which addresses terms related to the spheres of intentional and social things [13,16]. For an in-depth discussion and formalization, one should refer to [11,15]. UFO is the theoretical basis of OntoUML, a language for Ontology-driven Conceptual Modeling that has been successfully employed in a number of academic and industrial projects in several domains, such as services, value, petroleum and gas, media asset management, telecommunications, and government [14]. Models created in OntoUML have a formal semantics, and a comprehensive support for model verification, validation and code generation, including in languages such as OWL [14]. The motivation for using UFO is to provide an accessible and sharable modelling of trust that may be applied across domains to foster the interoperability and the mutual understanding among modellers.

UFO distinguishes endurant types into *substantial types* and *moment types*. These are sorts of types whose instances are *substantials* and *moments* [11], respectively. *Substantials* are existentially independent objects such as Mick Jagger, the Earth, an organization, a car, a book. *Moments*, in contrast, are existentially dependent individuals such as (a) Alice's capacity to swim (which depends on her) and (b) the marriage between John and Mary (which depends on both John and Mary). Moments of type (a) are termed *modes*; those of type (b) are termed *relators*. *Relators* are individuals with the power of connecting entities. For example, an Enrollment relator connects an individual playing the Student role with an Educational Institution. Furthermore, there is a third sort of moments termed *qualities*. *Qualities* are individual moments that can be mapped to some quality space, e.g., an apple's color which may change from green to red while maintaining its identity [11].

In our analysis, we shall rely mainly on some concepts defined in UFO-C [13,16]. A basic distinction in UFO-C is related to *agents* and (non-agentive) *objects*. An agent is a specialization of a *substantial individual* that can be classified as *physical* (e.g., a person) or *social* (e.g., an organization, a society). *Objects* are non-agentive *substantial individuals* that can also be categorized in *physical* (e.g., a book, a table) and *social objects* (e.g., money, language). A *Normative Description* is a type of *social object* that defines one or more rules/norms recognized by at least one *social agent* and that can define nominal universals such as *social moment universals* (e.g., *social commitment types*), *social objects* (e.g., money) and *social roles* (e.g., president, PhD candidate or pedestrian). Examples of normative descriptions include the Italian Constitution, the

University of Bolzano PhD program regulations, and also a set of directives on how to perform some actions within an organization.

Agents can bear special types of *modes* (aspects, features, characteristics, objectified properties) named *intentional moments*. A common characteristic of all modes is that they are *existentially dependent* on their bearers. Intentionality should not be understood as the notion of "intending something", but as the capacity to refer to possible situations of reality [1]. Every *intentional moment* has an associated proposition that is called the propositional content of the moment. In general, the propositional content of an intentional moment can be satisfied (in the logical sense) by situations in reality. *Intentional moments* can be *social moments* or *mental moments*. *Mental moments* are specialized in *beliefs*, *desires* and *intentions* (internal commitments). The propositional content of a *belief* is what an agent holds as true. Examples include one's belief that Rome is the Capital of Italy and that the Earth orbits around the Sun. *Desires* and *intentions* can be fulfilled or frustrated. A *desire* expresses the will of an agent towards a possible situation (e.g., a desire that Italy wins the next World Cup), while an *intention* expresses desired states of affairs for which the agent commits to pursuing (internal commitment) (e.g., John's intention of going to Paris to see the Eiffel Tower). *Intentions* may cause the agent to perform *actions* (concept from UFO-B). The propositional content of an *intention* is termed a *goal*. *Social moments* are types of *intentional moments* that are created by *social actions* (e.g., an interaction composed of the exchange of communicative acts). *Social commitments* and *social claims* are types of *social moments*. A *social commitment* is a commitment of an agent A towards another agent B, which inheres in A and is externally dependent on B. The *social commitments* necessarily cause the creation of an internal commitment in A. Also, associated to this internal commitment, a *social claim* of B towards A is created. *Commitments* and *claims* always form a pair that refers to a unique propositional content.

3   On Trust

A wide number of definitions of trust have been proposed along the years, across several areas, such as psychology [25,29], sociology [2,7,19], economics [31], law [5], and more recently, computer science [9,23]. Although much progress has been made to clarify the nature of trust, the term remains semantically overloaded and there is not yet a shared or prevailing, and conceptually clear notion of trust [4].

A classic definition of trust, widely accepted in the literature, was proposed by the sociologist Diego Gambetta, who defines trust as "the subjective probability with which an agent expects that another agent or group of agents will perform a particular action on which its welfare depends" [7]. In his definition it is clear the existence of both a *trustor* and a *trustee*, as well a belief of the trustor about the behavior of the trustee. Gambetta also relates trust to an intention of the trustor regarding her welfare and the uncertainty about the trustee's behavior, which reveals the existence of a certain degree of risk. In fact, this idea that trust presupposes a situation of risk is ubiquitous in the literature. For instance, Luhmann [19] argues that when people trust others, they act "as if they knew the future", and uncertainty is transformed into risk. Also, Castelfranchi and Falcone [4] state that without uncertainty and risk there is no trust.

A similar concept of trust is proposed by Mayer, Davis, and Schoorman [20], who define trust as "the willingness of a party to be vulnerable to the actions of another party, based on the expectation that the other party will perform a particular action important to the trustor, irrespective of the ability to monitor or control that other party". Also here, the authors refer to the expectations (or beliefs) of the trustor regarding the trustee and correlates trust to the trustor's goals (the actions of the other party that are important to the trustor). According to the authors, by trusting another party, the trustor makes herself vulnerable and exposed to the occurrence of risk events.

Rosseau and colleagues relied on a large interdisciplinary literature and on the identification of fundamental and convergent elements to define trust as "a psychological state of a trustor comprising the intention to accept vulnerability in a situation involving risk, based on positive expectations of the intentions or behavior of the trustee" [26]. Note that, also in this definition, the authors reinforce the presence of the trustor's expectations regarding the trustee, as well as the relationship between trust and risk: by trusting, the trustor accepts to become vulnerable to the trustee in terms of potential failure of the expected action and result, as the trustee may not perform the expected action or the action may not have the desired result.

McNight and colleagues [22] compared sixty-five definitions of trust from different sources to propose an interdisciplinary model of conceptual trust types that takes into account several important aspects of trust and some of their mutual interactions. For example, the authors are able to distinguish between a belief and a behavioral component of trust, and to explain that the latter depends on the former. The belief component is related to cognitive perceptions about the attributes or characteristics of others, i.e., the trustor believes, with "feelings of relative security", that the trustee is willing and able to act in her interest. The behavioral component means that a person voluntarily takes actions that makes herself dependent on another person, with a feeling of relative security, even though negative consequences are possible. According to the authors, trust-related behavior comes in a number of subconstruct forms because many actions can make one dependent on another, such as cooperation, information sharing, informal agreements, decreasing controls, accepting influence, granting autonomy, and transacting business.

A further important aspect in the model of McKnight et al. [22] is the distinction between *interpersonal trust* and *institution-based trust*. This distinction is also made by Luhmann [19], who defines:

- **interpersonal trust** as that between individuals that frequently have face-to-face contact and become familiar with each other without substantially taking recourse to institutional arrangements; and

- **institution-based trust** as that in the reliable functioning of certain social systems, which no longer refers to a personally known reality, but is built on impersonal and generalized "media of communication", such as the monetary system and the legal system.

According to McKnight et al. [22], institution-based trust affects interpersonal trust by "making the trustor feel more comfortable about trusting others, as she securely believes that protective structures (such as guarantees, contracts, regulations, promises, legal recourse, processes or procedures) are in place that are conducive to situational success". For example, people believe in the efficacy of a bank to take care of their money because of the existence of laws and institutions that insure them against loss. Lewis and Weigert [18] argue that institution-based trust is indispensable for the effective functioning of "symbolic media of exchange", such as money and political power. They argue that "without public trust in the reliability, effectiveness, and legitimacy of money, laws, and other cultural symbols, modern social institutions would soon disintegrate".

More recently, Castelfranchi and Falcone [4] analyzed the concept of trust as a composed and "layered" notion, relying on some key aspects: (i) a mental attitude and a disposition towards another agent; (ii) a decision and intention to rely upon the other, which makes the trustor vulnerable; (iii) the act of relying upon the trustee's expected behavior; and (iv) the consequent overt social interaction and relation between the trustor and the trustee.

In their definition of trust, Castelfranchi and Falcone [4] emphasize the role of the trustor's goal by stating that an "agent trusts another only relative to a goal, i.e., for something she wants to achieve, that she desires or needs". They also reinforce the idea of trust consisting of beliefs about the trustee and his behavior: "the belief that the trustee is able and willing to do the needed action; the belief that the trustee will appropriately do the action, as the trustor wishes; and the belief that the trustor can make herself less defended and more vulnerable". As for the behavioral component of trust, Castelfranchi and Falcone [4] argue that there may be mental trust without the corresponding behavioral part (i.e., without an action). That may happen because the level of trust is not sufficient; the level of trust is sufficient, but there are other reasons preventing the action (e.g. prohibitions); or trust is just potential, a predisposition (e.g. "the trustor would, might rely on the trustee, if/when..., but it is not (yet) the case").

In summary, what can be extracted from these different proposals is that there is a conceptual core to be enlightened in order to properly define trust. Therefore, to conceptualize trust, one must refer to: (i) *agents and their goals*; (ii) *agents' beliefs*; (iii) possibly executable *actions* of a given type; and (iv) *risk*.

4   Defining Social Systems

A key aspect in the definition of institution-based trust is the reliance on Social Systems. This comes from the sociology tradition positing that people can rely on others because of structures, situations or assigned social roles that provide assurances that things will go well [2]. Institution-based trust refers to beliefs about those protective structures, not about the people involved. In this paper, we term these protective structures "Social Systems". We adopt the interpretation of Social Systems as orderly arrangements of social entities that interact with each other, based on established and prevalent social rules that structure social interactions. Social Systems create a shared world of clear rules and reliable standards, which no longer refers to a personally known reality, but is built on impersonal and generalized "media of communication" [19], such as the monetary system and the legal system.

A further important aspect, related to the nature of Social Systems, is that they can be seen as *integral wholes*, whose parts play particular *functional roles* that contribute in specific ways to the functionality of the whole [11,28]. UFO includes micro-theories to address different types of *part-whole relations* [11,28] generally recognized in cognitive science [8,24]. Social Systems embody one particular kind of such parthood relations, namely, *component-functional complex* [28]. In UFO's terminology, this "componentOf" relation is used to relate entities that are *functional complexes*. Some examples of functional complexes are an organization, a legal system or a monetary system and their corresponding "componentOf" relations (e.g., presidency-organization, law-legal system, currency-monetary system). Consequently, Social Systems can be defined as functional complexes composed of social entities like the ones mentioned in Sect. 2 (e.g. social roles, social objects, social relationships, normative descriptions and so on). An example of Social System is the legal system, which is an integral whole composed of a number of social entities, such as social roles (e.g. lawyer, judge, etc.), social objects (e.g. contract, court sentence), normative descriptions (e.g. laws, regulations) and others that contribute in complementary manners to the functionality of the whole.

5   The Ontology of Trust

In this section, we present a well-founded ontology that formalizes the concept of trust as discussed in the previous sections. We formalize the mental aspects of trust in the OntoUML[1] model depicted in Fig. 1, and the particular behavioral aspect of trust, as well as the relation between trust and risk in Fig. 2. In the OntoUML diagrams depicting the Reference Ontology of Trust, we represent types of substantials in pink, events in yellow, modes in blue and situations in orange.

We model TRUST as a complex mental state of a TRUSTOR agent, composed of a set of BELIEFS about a TRUSTEE and her behavior. TRUST is always about an INTENTION of the TRUSTOR regarding a goal, for the achievement of which she counts upon the TRUSTEE. Note that in the conceptualization of goal we propose here, the achievement of a goal does not necessarily require an action of the TRUSTEE. Also omissions may be relevant in this context as the TRUSTOR

---

[1] Once more, OntoUML is a conceptual modeling language whose primitives reflect the ontological distinctions put forth by the UFO ontology [11].

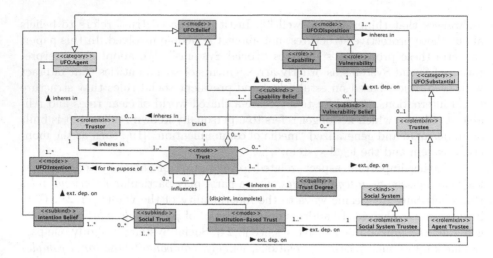

Fig. 1. Modeling the mental aspects of Trust

might precisely rely on the fact that the TRUSTEE will not do an specific action or, more generally, that the TRUSTEE will not do anything at all. The TRUSTOR is necessarily an "intentional entity", that is, a cognitive agent, an agent endowed with goals and beliefs. In UFO, a belief is a special type of mode, named mental moment, which is existentially dependent on a particular agent, being an inseparable part of its mental state. As for the TRUSTEE, it is an entity able to cause a positive impact on a TRUSTOR's goal by the outcome of its behavior, regardless if this involves an action or an omission (e.g. 'doing nothing', 'abstaining from doing X'). Moreover, note that the TRUSTEE is not necessarily aware of being trusted. An example, given in [4], is a person running to catch a bus. Even if this person is not seen by the bus driver and the people waiting for the bus at the stop, she may attribute to these people the intention to take the bus, and thus the intention to stop it. In such a case, the runner is trusting in the people at the bus stop to do so.

In our ontology, in accordance with [4], the TRUSTEE is not necessarily a cognitive system, or an animated or autonomous agent. It can also be a lot of things we rely upon in our daily activity: rules, procedures, conventions, infrastructures, technology and artifacts in general, tools, authorities and institutions, environmental regularities, as well as different types of social systems. Based on the nature of the TRUSTEE, we have modelled two specializations of TRUST, namely SOCIAL TRUST and INSTITUTION-BASED TRUST. The former stands for the "trust in another agent as an agent" [4]. Consequently, it is externally dependent of an AGENT TRUSTEE. For example, in a social trust relation between a mother that trusts a babysitter to take care of her kids, the babysitter is the AGENT TRUSTEE. The latter builds upon the existence of shared rules, regularities, conventional practices, etc. and is related to a SOCIAL SYSTEM TRUSTEE. An example of SOCIAL SYSTEM TRUSTEE is the monetary system: in the society, individuals provide something of value in return for a token they trust to be able to use in the future to obtain something else of value, as well as they trust that the value of the instrument will be stable in terms of goods and services. A third example, involving different types of trust, is the case of a person who buys a phone in an e-commerce platform. Here we can identify several trust relations: (i) the buyer's social trust in the seller about her delivering the phone in perfect state; (ii) the buyer's trust in the phone about it behaving as she expects; (iii) the buyer's and the seller's institution-based trust in the monetary system; (iv) the buyer's and the seller's institution-based trust in the legal system (in case of one of the parties does not fulfill its commitments); (v) the buyer's and the seller's trust in the online platform.

As shown in Fig. 1, we modeled TRUST as a complex mode composed of a TRUSTOR INTENTION, whose propositional content is a goal of the TRUSTOR, and a set of BELIEFS that inhere in the TRUSTOR and are externally dependent on the *dispositions* [1, 15] that inhere in the TRUSTEE. These beliefs include: (i) the BELIEF that the TRUSTEE has the CAPABILITY to perform the desired action (CAPABILITY BELIEF); and (ii) the belief that the TRUSTEE'S VULNERABILI-TIES will not prevent him from performing the desired action (VULNERABILITY BELIEF). The TRUSTEE'S VULNERABILITIES and CAPABILITIES are dispositions that inhere in the TRUSTEE, which are manifested in particular situations, through the occurrence of events [15]. In this paper we adopt the interpreta-tion of capability proposed by Azevedo et al. [1], who defined capability as the power to bring about a desired outcome.

SOCIAL TRUST is a specialization of TRUST in which the TRUSTEE is an AGENT. Therefore, this form of trust is also composed of the TRUSTOR's BELIEF that the TRUSTEE has the INTENTION to perform the desired action (INTENTION BELIEF). INSTITUTION-BASED TRUST is a specialization of TRUST in which the TRUSTEE is a SOCIAL SYSTEM. The relation INFLUENCES, holding between TRUST entities represents, as noted by Castelfranchi and Falcone [4], that "trust influences trust in several rather complex ways". McNight et al. [22] argues that INSTITUTION-BASED TRUST affects SOCIAL TRUST by making the TRUSTOR feel more comfortable about trusting others in a given situation. For example, regu-lations and institutions may enable people to trust each other not because they know each other personally, but because licensing, auditing, laws or governmen-tal enforcement bodies are in place to make sure the other person is either afraid to harm them or punished if they do so. This influence may also hold in the opposite direction. SOCIAL TRUST may influence INSTITUTION-BASED TRUST by generating positive beliefs about established social systems. For example, one's trust in the local police officer may increase one's trust in the "judiciary system".

The TRUSTS relation between the TRUSTOR and the TRUSTEE is a relation that is *non-symmetric, non-reflexive* and *non-transitive*. An example that evinces the non-symmetry is a child that trusts her father to lift a heavy object, but the father does not trust his child to do so. However, it is possible that the father trusts the mother to take care of their kids and vice-versa. Trust is non-reflexive because an agent may or may not trust herself to perform actions. For example, an athlete may trust herself to run one kilometer in ten minutes, but not to cook a sophisticated meal. Lastly, it is non-transitive because agents might have different evaluations about the same entity's trustworthiness. For instance, it is very well possible that Alice trusts Bob for performing certain actions and Bob trusts Charlie for performing the same actions, but it is not the case the Alice trusts Charlie to perform them.

We represent the quantitative perspective of trust by means of the TRUST DEGREE moment (*quality*) inhering in the TRUST entity. In UFO, a quality is an objectification of a property that can be directly evaluated (projected) into certain value spaces [11]. An example is a person's weight, which can be measured in kilograms or pounds. Thus, representing trust as a quality means that it can also be measured according to a given scale, such as a simple discrete scale like <Low,Medium,High> or a continuous scale (e.g. from 0.0 to 100.0).

We analyze the relation between trust and risk, based on the Common Ontology of Value and Risk (COVER) proposed by Sales et al. [27]. COVER proposes an ontological analysis of notions such as Risk, Risk Event (Threat Event, Loss Event) and Vulnerability, among others. This ontology characterizes and integrates different perspectives on risk. Given the objectives of this paper, we focus here on the perspective of risk as a chain of events that impacts on an agent's goals, which the authors named Risk Experience. Risk Experiences focus on unwanted events that have the potential of causing losses and are composed by events of two types, namely threat and loss events. A THREAT EVENT is the one with the potential of causing a loss, which might be intentional or unintentional. A THREAT EVENT might be the manifestation of a VULNERABILITY (a special type of disposition whose manifestation constitutes a loss or can potentially cause a loss from the perspective of a stakeholder). The second mandatory component of a Risk Experience is a LOSS EVENT, which necessarily impact intentions in a negative way (captured by a HURTS relation between LOSS EVENT and INTENTION) [27].

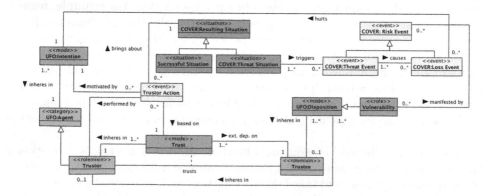

Fig. 2. Modeling the emergence of Risk from Trust relations

We represent the relation between trust and risk, together with its embedded concepts, in the OntoUML model depicted in Fig. 2. As part of the behavioral perspective of trust, the TRUSTOR may take some ACTIONS, motivated by her INTENTIONS and based on her TRUST in the TRUSTEE. These ACTIONS may involve the TRUSTEE or not (some examples are cooperation, information sharing, informal agreements, decreasing controls, accepting influence, granting autonomy, and transacting business [22]), however they are taken considering that the TRUSTEE will behave according to the TRUSTOR's BELIEFS. As previous mentioned, a TRUSTOR may *trust* in a TRUSTEE but not take any ACTION based on this TRUST. For this reason, the relationship between TRUST and the TRUSTOR's ACTIONS is optional.

An ACTION performed by the TRUSTOR based on her TRUST in the TRUSTEE brings about a RESULTING SITUATION, which may satisfy her goals (and in this case it is considered a SUCCESSFUL SITUATION) or, in the worst case, may not have the desired result and the TRUSTOR will not be able to achieve her goal. In this case, the RESULTING SITUATION stands for a THREAT SITUATION that may trigger a THREAT EVENT, which may cause a loss. The LOSS EVENT is a RISK EVENT that impacts intentions in a negative way, as it hurts the TRUSTOR's INTENTIONS of reaching a specific goal.

6   Use Case Illustrations

In this section, in order to illustrate the applicability of our proposal, we apply the Reference Ontology of Trust to model two examples. First, we model an instance of social trust using the case of a working mother who trusts a babysitter to take care of her children. Then, we model an instance of institution-based trust related to the trust of a person in the monetary system.

6.1   Social Trust Example: Babysitter

In this section we take the case of a mother who trusts a babysitter, to present an example of social trust. Firstly, we illustrate, in Fig. 3, the model regarding the mental aspect of trust, which is composed of a set of beliefs. In the example, the mother has the intention of "having an adult to take care of her kids while she is out" and she trusts in a specific babysitter to do this task. Her TRUST is composed of a set of BELIEFS regarding: (i) the CAPABILITIES of the babysitter (the babysitter has experience in caring for children and is First Aid trained); (ii) the babysitter's INTENTIONS (the mother believes that the babysitter is willing to take good care of her children); and (iii) the babysitter's VULNERABILITIES (the babysitter is well and probably is not going to have health issues).

Secondly, in Fig. 4, we illustrate the behavioral aspect of trust, i.e. the ACTIONS that the TRUSTOR performs relying on the behavior of the TRUSTEE. In the example, the mother believes that the babysitter is a good candidate and decides to count on her to take care of the kids. The mother arrives at a decision that is based on trust and eventually expresses her trust through an official delegation, which is the action of hiring the babysitter.

Finally, also in Fig. 4, we illustrate the emergence of risk from the trust relation. When the mother hires the babysitter, the latter commits to take care of the former's children. With the commitment of the babysitter, the mother becomes vulnerable and may be exposed to unanticipated risks. Considering a situation in which the babysitter gets sick during the term of the employment contract, it can be considered a THREAT SITUATION that may trigger a THREAT EVENT if, for example, the babysitter does not go to work because she is no feeling well. In this case, the babysitter not going work is a THREAT EVENT that may trigger a LOSS EVENT, which would be the children getting unattended while the mother was out. This LOST EVENT hurts the mother's INTENTION of having an adult to take care of her kids while she is out.

6.2 Institution-Based Trust Example: Monetary System

This section illustrates the trust of a person in the monetary system, which is a case of institution-based trust. In this example, a person has the INTENTION of "selling a house and use the money to buy an apartment" and she TRUSTS the monetary system as a protective structure, which assures that things will go well. Hinged on her INSTITUTION-BASED TRUST in the monetary system, the individual provides something of value in return for a "token" she trusts to be able to use in the future to obtain something else of value.

Figure 5 illustrates the model regarding the mental aspect of TRUST, which is composed of a set of BELIEFS about:

(i) the CAPABILITIES of the monetary system:

- **the function of money as a medium of exchange**: related to the capability of money (which is a social object and a component of the monetary system) to function as a means of payment with a value that everyone trusts.

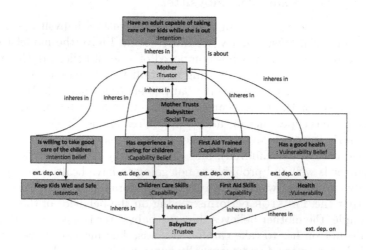

Fig. 3. Social Trust: Mother trusts a babysitter

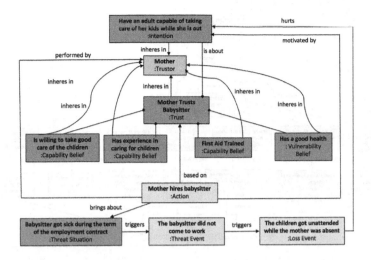

Fig. 4. The emergence of Risk from the Trust Relation

- **the function of money as a unit of account**: related to the capability of money to function as a standard numerical unit for the measurement of value and costs of goods, services, assets and liabilities.
- **the function of money as a store of value**: related to the capability of money that allows it to be saved and retrieved in the future.
- **inflation is controlled**: related to the capability of the monetary system to have structures and mechanisms to maintain price stability and inflation control.
- **the value of money is stable**: related to the capability of the monetary system to ensure the stability of the currency's purchasing power.

(ii) the VULNERABILITIES of the monetary system:

- **economy is healthy**: related to changes in the economy that may impact the monetary system.
- **the international scenario is favorable**: related to changes in the international scenario that may impact the monetary system.

In the sequel, Fig. 6 illustrates the behavioral aspect of trust, i.e. the ACTIONS that the TRUSTOR (the person) performs relying on the TRUSTEE (the monetary system). In the example, the person believes in the stability and efficiency of the monetary system and decides to sell the house to buy an apartment. The person arrives at a decision based on her INSTITUTION-BASED TRUST in the monetary system and eventually expresses her TRUST through the ACTION of selling the house.

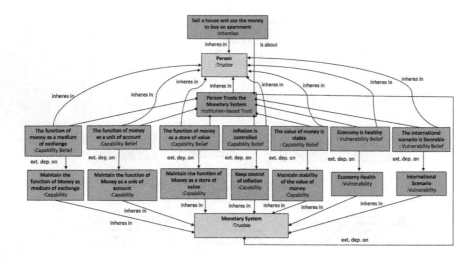

Fig. 5. Institution-based Trust: Person trusts the monetary system

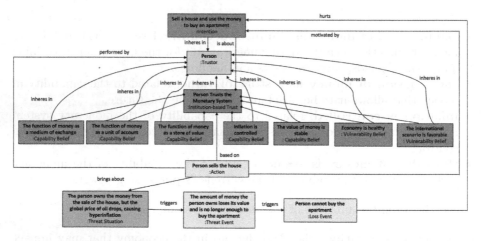

Fig. 6. The emergence of Risk from the Trust Relation

The person sells the house in exchange for an amount of money she trusts to be able to use in the future to buy an apartment. By selling the house, the person becomes vulnerable to the stability of the monetary system (which in turn has its own vulnerabilities) and may be exposed to unanticipated risks. In order to illustrate the emergence of risk, let us consider that in this example the economy is highly dependent on oil exports. Thus, the price of oil can be considered a VULNERABILITY of the monetary system regarding the international scenario. If the global price of oil falls to the point of causing a disruption in the economy, currency may lose value and the price of goods goes up. In this case, the situation in which "the person owes a large amount of money at the time when the global price of oil drops, causing hyperinflation" can be considered a THREAT SITUATION that may trigger a THREAT EVENT if, for example, the amount of money the person owns loses its value and is no longer enough to buy the apartment. In this case, the amount of money loosing its value is a THREAT EVENT that may trigger a LOSS EVENT, which would be the person no longer being able to buy the apartment. This LOST EVENT hurts the person's INTENTION of selling the house and use the money to buy an apartment.

7 Related Work

Several trust-modeling approaches have been proposed over the years. In the context of the semantic web and social networks, most approaches focused simply on the representation of trust relations. One example is the work of Golbeck et al. [10], which proposes an extension of the Friend of a Friend (FOAF) ontology to allow users to state and represent their trust in individuals they know. Another example is the Proof Markup Language Trust Ontology (PML-T) [21], which provides an extensible set of primitives for encoding trust information associated with information sources. PML-T was created as part of the Proof Markup Language, a standard developed by the Stanford University that defines primitive concepts and relations for representing knowledge provenance [21]. It defines trust and belief relations involving a trustor, a trustee (the information source), and pieces of information. Although providing a framework for encoding trust relations, PML-T does not prescribe a way for representing trust itself.

Moreover, Dokoohaki and Matskin [6] propose a trust ontology for the design of trust networks on semantic web-driven social systems. The main component of their ontology is the trust relation that represents the connection between entities on the network. Every relation has a set of main properties that describe its nature and purpose, such as a topic and a value that represents the trust level. The authors also define a set of auxiliary properties for the trust relation, such as a goal that stands for the reason for establishing the relation and a recommender, which is a person on the network that has recommended the trustee. Furthermore, the relation between trust and risk is not mentioned. An important difference between these ontologies and our proposal is that they are not based on foundational ontologies, but are built on semantic web languages that give precedence to computational tractability over expressiveness. As discussed in [12], a number of semantic interoperability problems that cannot be handled by semantic web languages, such as OWL and RDF, as their expressivity is purposefully limited so that they remain computationally tractable.

Huang and Fox [17] proposed a logical theory of trust in the form of an ontology that gives formal and explicit specification for the semantics of trust. The authors define two types of trust, namely, trust in belief and trust in performance. In the former, the trustor believes that something the trustee believes is true (for example: Mary wants to order a product and her friend John suggests she buys it from an online store he believes always delivers the orders on time. Mary does not know the online store at the time, but she believes what John believes, which is that the store delivers the orders on time). In the latter, the trustor believes in a piece of information created by the trustee or in the performance of an action committed by the trustee, both in a context within the trustor's context of trust. These two types refer to the general form of trust. The institution-based trust is not represented in Huang and Fox's ontology [17] nor is the relation between trust and risk.

Viljanen [30] surveyed and classified thirteen computational trust models to create an ontology of trust. In his proposal, trust is represented as a relation between a trustor and a trustee, which depends on the action that the trustor is attempting and on the competence of the trustee. Additionally, Viljanen defines an element of confidence attached to the trust relationship, as well as a set of third party opinions in the form of reputation information. The author uses the concept of business value to represent both value and risk associated to the trustor's action. By attaching business values to the action, the ontology is able to represent the potential impact, positive or negative, of the action that the trustor is attempting. However, the representation of the relation between trust and risk lacks a more detailed description. For example, the ontology does not make it explicit how risk events are triggered, nor how they affect the trustor.

Secure Tropos [9] is a security-oriented extension of the agent-oriented software development methodology Tropos [3] that adds both security and trust as part of the software development process. In Secure Tropos the concepts of trust and delegation are combined to represent dependence relations between agents. Their constructs for trust refer to existent trustworthiness between actors along trust relations rather than specify the nature of the concept of trust. Secure Tropos differs from our approach not only regarding this particularity, but also because it does not represent the close relation between trust and risk. Moreover, although supporting a role-based approach to trust [9], in which the trustee is represented by roles or positions rather than by individual agents, it does not address explicitly the notion of institution-based trust.

In [4], Castelfranchi and Falcone investigate what kind of beliefs and goals are necessary for trust to formulate several necessary conditions, such as the trustor having a goal and the belief that the trustee is competent and willing to achieve this goal. Moreover, the authors consider a behavioral aspect of trust, which is related to the notion of acting on trust. In our proposal we rely largely on their theory to formalize the general concept of trust, as well as the concept of social trust. As for the institution-based trust, Castelfranchi and Falcone [4] state that it "builds upon the existence of shared rules, regularities, conventional practices, etc. and relies on this, in an automatic, non-explicit, mindless way", however the authors do not formalize this aspect of trust. Likewise, the relation between trust and risk is emphasized in their theory, but is not formalized.

Table 1 summarizes some important aspects of our *Reference Ontology of Trust* and compare them to the other trust ontologies discussed in this section, such as: (i) the scope of the analysis of the trust concept; (ii) the types of trust modeled; (iii) the relation between trust and risk; (v) the language used to represent the ontology; and (vi) the ontological foundations adopted.

Table 1. The Reference Ontology of Trust and related trust ontologies

Ontology	Scope	Trust types	Relation to risk	Modeling language	Foundational ontology
Reference Ontology of Trust	Analyzes the nature of the concept of trust and trust relations	General trust, social trust, and institution-based trust	Models the emergence of risk from trust relations	OntoUML	UFO
Golbeck et al. [10]	Analyze the existence of trust relations between two agents	General trust	- - -	RDF/OWL	- - -
PML-T [21]	Analyzes the existence of trust and belief relations between agents and information sources	General trust	- - -	RDF/OWL	- - -
Dokoohaki and Matskin [6]	Analyze trust relations and some properties about them	General trust	- - -	RDF/OWL	- - -
Huang and Fox [17]	Analyze the nature of the concept of trust and trust relations	General trust	- - -	Situation calculus	- - -
Viljanen [30]	Analyzes the nature of the concept of trust and trust relations	General trust	Relates risk to actions on trusting, but does not detail how it emerges	UML	- - -
Secure Tropos [9]	Refers to existent trustworthiness between actors along trust relations	Socio-technical trust	- - -	Datalog	- - -
Castelfranchi and Falcone [4]	Analyze the nature of the concept of trust and trust relations.	Social trust (institution-based is only mentioned)	Emphasizes the relation between trust and risk, but does not model it	First-order Logic	- - -

8   Final Remarks

In this paper, we presented an initial proposal for a Reference Ontology of Trust. We first investigated the ontological nature of trust and formalized its general concept in an OntoUML model. This investigation lead to the identification and the formal characterization of two types of trust, namely social trust and institution-based trust. We also presented a description of our view of social system as it is an essential concept for the modeling of institution-based trust. Lastly, we leverage the analysis of the behavioral aspect of trust to explain the emergence of risk from trust relations.

As a next direction, we plan to further validate our ontology and expand our analysis to explain the factors that affect trust assessment, both under the perspective of the trustor and to the perspective of the trustee. We also plan to use the presented ontology to analyze and redesign existing modelling languages (e.g. Archimate) to enable them to consistently describe trust assessment.

Acknowledgment. CAPES (PhD grant# 88881.173022/2018-01) and OCEAN project (UNIBZ).

References

1. Azevedo, C.L.B., et al.: Modeling resources and capabilities in enterprise architecture: a well-founded ontology-based proposal for ArchiMate. Inf. Syst. **54**, 235–262 (2015)
2. Barber, B.: The Logic and Limits of Trust, 1st edn. Rutgers University Press, New Brunswick (1983)
3. Bresciani, P., Perini, A., Giorgini, P., Giunchiglia, F., Mylopoulos, J.: Tropos: An agent-oriented software development methodology. Auton. Agent. Multi-Agent Syst. **8**(3), 203–236 (2004)
4. Castelfranchi, C., Falcone, R.: Trust Theory: A Socio-Cognitive and Computational Model, vol. 18. Wiley, Hoboken (2010)
5. Cross, F.B.: Law and trust. Georgetown Law J. **93**, 1457 (2005)
6. Dokoohaki, N., Matskin, M.: Effective design of trust ontologies for improvement in the structure of socio-semantic trust networks. Int. J. Adv. Intell. Syst. **1**(1942–2679), 23–42 (2008)
7. Gambetta, D., et al.: Can we trust trust. In: Trust: Making and Breaking Cooperative Relations, vol. 13, pp. 213–237 (2000)
8. Gerstl, P., Pribbenow, S.: Midwinters, end games, and body parts: a classification of part-whole relations. Int. J. Hum.-comput. Stud. **43**(5–6), 865–889 (1995)
9. Giorgini, P., Massacci, F., Mylopoulos, J., Zannone, N.: Modeling social and individual trust in requirements engineering methodologies. In: Herrmann, P., Issarny, V., Shiu, S. (eds.) iTrust 2005. LNCS, vol. 3477, pp. 161–176. Springer, Heidelberg (2005). https://doi.org/10.1007/11429760_12
10. Golbeck, J., Parsia, B., Hendler, J.: Trust networks on the semantic web. In: Klusch, M., Omicini, A., Ossowski, S., Laamanen, H. (eds.) CIA 2003. LNCS (LNAI), vol. 2782, pp. 238–249. Springer, Heidelberg (2003). https://doi.org/10.1007/978-3-540-45217-1_18
11. Guizzardi, G.: Ontological foundations for structural conceptual models. Telematica Instituut/CTIT (2005)
12. Guizzardi, G.: The role of foundational ontologies for conceptual modeling and domain ontology representation. In: 7th International Baltic Conference on Databases and Information Systems, pp. 17–25. IEEE (2006)
13. Guizzardi, G., Falbo, R.A., Guizzardi, R.S.S.: Grounding software domain ontologies in the Unified Foundational Ontology (UFO). In: 11th Ibero-American Conference on Software Engineering (CIbSE), pp. 127–140 (2008)
14. Guizzardi, G., Wagner, G., Almeida, J.P.A., Guizzardi, R.S.S.: Towards ontological foundations for conceptual modeling: the Unified Foundational Ontology (UFO) story. Appl. ontology **10**(3–4), 259–271 (2015)
15. Guizzardi, G., Wagner, G., Falbo, R.A., Guizzardi, R.S.S., Almeida, J.P.A.: Towards ontological foundations for the conceptual modeling of events. In: 32nd International Conference on Conceptual Modeling (ER), pp. 327–341. Springer (2013)

16. Guizzardi, R.S.S., Guizzardi, G.: Ontology-based transformation framework from TROPOS to AORML. In: Social Modeling for Requirements Engineering, pp. 547–570. The MIT Press, Cambridge (2010)
17. Huang, J., Fox, M.S.: An ontology of trust: formal semantics and transitivity. In: Proceedings of the 8th International Conference on Electronic Commerce: The New E-commerce: Innovations for Conquering Current Barriers, Obstacles and Limitations to Conducting Successful Business on the Internet, pp. 259–270. ACM (2006)
18. Lewis, J.D., Weigert, A.: Trust as a social reality. Soc. Forces **63**(4), 967–985 (1985)
19. Luhmann, N.: Trust and Power. Wiley, Hoboken (2018)
20. Mayer, R.C., Davis, J.H., Schoorman, F.D.: An integrative model of organizational trust. Acad. Manag. Rev. **20**(3), 709–734 (1995)
21. McGuinness, D.L., Ding, L., Da Silva, P.P., Chang, C.: Pml 2: A modular explanation interlingua. In: ExaCt, pp. 49–55 (2007)
22. Harrison McKnight, D., Chervany, N.L.: Trust and distrust definitions: one bite at a time. In: Falcone, R., Singh, M., Tan, Y.-H. (eds.) Trust in Cyber-societies. LNCS (LNAI), vol. 2246, pp. 27–54. Springer, Heidelberg (2001). https://doi.org/10.1007/3-540-45547-7_3
23. Moyano, F., Fernandez-Gago, C., Lopez, J.: A conceptual framework for trust models. In: Fischer-Hübner, S., Katsikas, S., Quirchmayr, G. (eds.) TrustBus 2012. LNCS, vol. 7449, pp. 93–104. Springer, Heidelberg (2012). https://doi.org/10.1007/978-3-642-32287-7_8
24. Pribbenow, S.: Meronymic relationships: from classical mereology to complex part-whole relations. In: Green, R., Bean, C.A., Myaeng, S.H. (eds.) The Semantics of Relationships. Information Science and Knowledge Management, vol. 3, pp. 35–50. Springer, Dordrecht (2002)
25. Rotter, J.B.: A new scale for the measurement of interpersonal trust. J. Pers. **35**(4), 651–665 (1967)
26. Rousseau, D.M., Sitkin, S.B., Burt, R.S., Camerer, C.: Not so different after all: a cross-discipline view of trust. Acad. Manag. Rev. **23**(3), 393–404 (1998)
27. Sales, T.P., Baião, F., Guizzardi, G., Almeida, J.P.A., Guarino, N., Mylopoulos, J.: The common ontology of value and risk. In: Trujillo, J.C., et al. (eds.) ER 2018. LNCS, vol. 11157, pp. 121–135. Springer, Cham (2018). https://doi.org/10.1007/978-3-030-00847-5_11
28. Sales, T.P., Guizzardi, G.: "Is it a fleet or a collection of ships?": ontological anti-patterns in the modeling of part-whole relations. In: Kirikova, M., Nørvåg, K., Papadopoulos, G.A. (eds.) ADBIS 2017. LNCS, vol. 10509, pp. 28–41. Springer, Cham (2017). https://doi.org/10.1007/978-3-319-66917-5_3
29. Tyler, T.R.: Why People Obey the Law. Princeton University Press, Princeton (2006)
30. Viljanen, L.: Towards an ontology of trust. In: Katsikas, S., López, J., Pernul, G. (eds.) TrustBus 2005. LNCS, vol. 3592, pp. 175–184. Springer, Heidelberg (2005). https://doi.org/10.1007/11537878_18
31. Williamson, O.E.: Calculativeness, trust, and economic organization. J. Law Econ. **36**(1, Part 2), 453–486 (1993)

Personalised Exploration Graphs
on Semantic Data Lakes

Ada Bagozi, Devis Bianchini[✉], Valeria De Antonellis, Massimiliano Garda,
and Michele Melchiori

Department of Information Engineering, University of Brescia, Via Branze 38,
25123 Brescia, Italy
adabagozi@gmail.com, {devis.bianchini,valeria.deantonellis,
m.garda001,michele.melchiori}@unibs.it

Abstract. Recently, organisations operating in the context of Smart
Cities are spending time and resources in turning large amounts of data,
collected within heterogeneous sources, into actionable insights, using
indicators as powerful tools for meaningful data aggregation and exploration. Data lakes, which follow a schema-on-read approach, allow for
storing both structured and unstructured data and have been proposed
as flexible repositories for enabling data exploration and analysis over
heterogeneous data sources, regardless their structure. However, indicators are usually computed based on the centralisation of the data storage, according to a less flexible schema on write approach. Furthermore,
domain experts, who know data stored within the data lake, are usually distinct from data analysts, who define indicators, and users, who
exploit indicators to explore data in a personalised way. In this paper,
we propose a semantics-based approach for enabling personalised data
lake exploration through the conceptualisation of proper indicators. In
particular, the approach is structured as follows: (i) at the bottom, heterogeneous data sources within a data lake are enriched with Semantic
Models, defined by domain experts using domain ontologies, to provide a
semantic data lake representation; (ii) in the middle, a Multi-Dimensional
Ontology is used by analysts to define indicators and analysis dimensions,
in terms of concepts within Semantic Models and formulas to aggregate
them; (iii) at the top, Personalised Exploration Graphs are generated
for different categories of users, whose profiles are defined in terms of a
set of constraints that limit the indicators instances on which the users
may rely to explore data. Benefits and limitations of the approach are
discussed through an application in the Smart City domain.

Keywords: Semantic data lake · Data exploration · Smart City

1 Introduction

Modern organisations are spending time and resources in understanding their
Big Data, collected within heterogeneous sources, attracted by the opportunity

H. Panetto et al. (Eds.): OTM 2019, LNCS 11877, pp. 22–39, 2019.
https://doi.org/10.1007/978-3-030-33246-4_2

of turning it into actionable insights. A representative example is given by Smart Cities, whose infrastructures comprise both private and open data, legacy systems as well as new generation devices to collect city and citizens' consumption data, using different data formats, models and storage systems [5]. Data lakes, which follow a schema-on-read approach, have been proposed for storing both structured and unstructured data, regardless its structure. For end-users, data aggregation according to different analysis dimensions may help to take decisions in a more efficient manner. To this aim, indicators are powerful tools for meaningful data aggregation and exploration. However, they are usually computed based on the centralisation of data storage, according to a less flexible schema-on-write approach, and their definition in the context of data lakes deserves more investigation. Moreover, domain experts, who know data stored within the data lake, are usually distinct from data analysts, who define indicators, and users, who exploit indicators to explore data in a personalised way [15]. To this aim, Semantic Web technologies may come to the rescue, given their capability to enable interoperability over heterogeneous sources and improve data access; specifically, recent research efforts strove to combine the OBDA paradigm with data lakes, leading to the so-called *semantic data lakes*, with the development of semantic layers apt to uniformly access data lakes content [14]. In this context, the interest towards exploration techniques for multi-dimensional data (such as the ones collected within a Smart City), leveraging domain knowledge, is growing faster and faster [1]. Indeed, the objective is to capture users' analytical requirements, subject to a continuous and endless evolution over time.

Focusing on the exploratory aspect, the goal of this paper is to describe a semantics-based approach to enable personalised data exploration through the conceptualisation of proper indicators, built on top of a semantic data lake representation. In particular, the approach is structured over layers as follows: (i) at the bottom, heterogeneous data sources within a data lake are enriched with Semantic Models, defined by domain experts using domain ontologies; (ii) in the middle, a Multi-Dimensional Ontology is used by analysts to define indicators and analysis dimensions, in terms of concepts within Semantic Models and formulas to aggregate them, in order to extract what we call Smart City Exploration Graph; (iii) at the top, Personalised Exploration Graphs are generated for different categories of users, whose profiles are defined in terms of a set of constraints that limit the indicators instances on which the users may rely to explore data. The novel contribution of this approach mainly concerns the two upmost layers of the information model introduced above. These layers enable a progressive (and evolving) extraction of Smart City knowledge from the semantic data lake through the semantic modelling of indicators and the exploitation of users' profiles. Furthermore, the three layers enable the clear separation of roles, namely domain experts, data analysts and end-users.

The paper is organised as follows: in Sect. 2 a motivating example in the Smart City domain is provided; the approach overview is explained in Sect. 3, while Sects. 4, 5 and 6 describe in details the three layers of the information model; Sect. 7 reports personalised exploration scenarios over the semantic data lake; Sect. 8 discusses benefits and limitations of our approach; cutting-edge features of the approach with respect to the literature are discussed in Sect. 9; finally, Sect. 10 closes the paper.

2   Motivating Example

Different categories of users may be interested in exploring urban data: mobility managers, energy managers, utility and energy providers, building managers and citizens. As a motivating example, let's consider John, the manager of three buildings located in different districts of a Smart City. John is interested in monitoring the electrical energy consumption of the buildings, in order to plan saving policies and effective renovation interventions for the buildings with highest consumption. Among buildings administered by John, $Building_1$ and $Building_2$ are located in $District_1$, whereas $Building_3$ is located in a different district ($District_2$). In the example, energy consumption of a building is computed by defining an indicator ($EC_{building}$) obtained as the sum of the electrical consumption of the stairs (EC_{stairs}) and other common spaces of the building (such as gardens, $EC_{gardens}$) and the electrical consumption of building elevators ($EC_{elevators}$), that is $EC_{building} = EC_{stairs} + EC_{gardens} + EC_{elevators}$. Precisely, the factors in the aforementioned sum are in turn indicators that aggregate data stored within distinct data sources. For example, $EC_{elevators}$ is extracted from a relational database containing the electricity bills for all the three buildings. The other two indicators are measured in a different way, using new generation smart meters to extract a new value and store it within a JSON file. Given the quantity and heterogeneity of data in this motivating example, indicators are effective tools to provide John with meaningful aggregation of data of interest. Moreover, for privacy preservation issues, John should not be allowed to inspect data at the highest granularity level. He should explore data at building level (and only for administered buildings).

3   Approach Overview

The three-layered information model proposed in this paper organises knowledge about Smart City data sources through the following phases: (i) semantic modelling of data lake sources, which defines a Smart City Semantic Data Lake, (ii) semantic representation of indicators, which define a Smart City Exploration Graph, and (iii) selection of Personalised Exploration Graphs. Figure 1 shows the components of the information model, the involved roles, and architectural modules that implement the three phases.

Starting from the bottom, Smart City heterogeneous data sources (e.g., IoT devices, sensors, energy providers databases) are conveyed, through proper ELT (Extract, Load and Transform) processes, into the Data Lake, where raw data is stored as values of a set of attributes defined in the source. Semantic annotations of data in a source, based on the concepts of one or more domain ontologies, define a corresponding *Data Source Semantic Model*, which is stored in the *Smart*

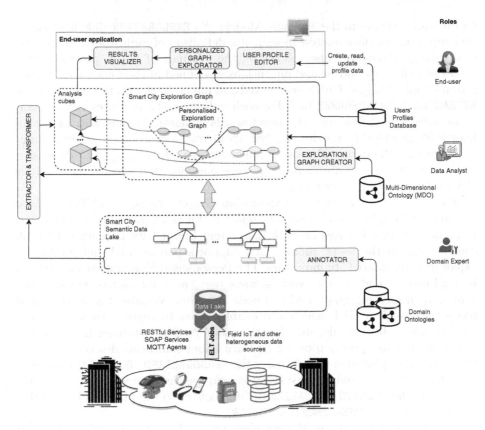

Fig. 1. Approach overview.

City Semantic Data Lake. Here, available data sources are described according to their meanings, rather than on their raw data attributes. Domain experts are in charge both to identify suitable domain ontologies and to use them for defining the Data Source Semantic Models, by adopting methodologies defined and validated in the literature [15]. A semi-automatic tool, ANNOTATOR, supports the domain expert in this task.

Semantic Models are the starting point for defining the *Smart City Exploration Graph*; in fact, by leveraging them, a data analyst can formally define Smart City indicators and detail their features (e.g., dimensions, computing formula, unit of measure). Base concepts and relationships required for modelling indicators are defined in a *Multi-Dimensional Ontology (MDO)*. Hence, the Smart City Exploration Graph contains knowledge about indicators, their dimensional characterisation and formulas. The semantic description of an indicator is obtained as an aggregation of other indicators (according to the formula) in a recursive way, until the most fine grained concepts are reached, corresponding to concepts in the Data Source Semantic Models. In this way, a set of mappings is established between concepts in the Smart City Exploration

Graph and concepts in the Semantic Models. An EXPLORATION GRAPH CREATOR tool supports the data analyst in semantic definition of indicators and creation of mappings. Analysis Cubes, shown on the left part of Fig. 1, provide actual values of indicators and related dimensions as defined in the Smart City Exploration Graph. Analysis Cubes are created and maintained with the support of an EXTRACTOR & TRANSFORMER tool. For each indicator, the tool uses both semantic definitions of indicators, mappings towards Semantic Models, and additional knowledge provided by the data analyst about transformation processes in order to materialise the cubes. Moreover, indicators (e.g., $EC_{building}$) and dimension levels (e.g., District) are mapped to corresponding attributes of the Analysis Cube schema (i.e., its star schema).

Portions of the Smart City Exploration Graph, the so-called *Personalised Exploration Graphs*, are dynamically selected, for different categories of users. Dynamic selection is based on both the current Smart City Exploration Graph content and on the users' profiles, and supports personalised and interactive exploration of Smart City indicators. The Personalised Exploration Graphs can be explored by end-users in various ways (e.g., as a interactive graph structure or by inspecting graph nodes, a node at a time, visualised as a structured record[1]) through a GUI, which also enables users to register themselves and create/update their profile, stored in the users' profiles database. In particular, end-users may use proper tools to: (i) learn about indicators description in the Personalised Exploration Graph (using the PERSONALIZED GRAPH EXPLORATOR); (ii) select indicators and dimension levels, and see their values in a tabular format (using the RESULTS VISUALIZER); (iii) register to the platform by creating a profile (using the USER PROFILE EDITOR).

In the following sections, the key elements of the approach will be detailed also with reference to the motivating example.

4   Smart City Semantic Data Lake

We represent the Data Lake DL as a set of *data sources*, namely $\langle \mathcal{S}_1, \mathcal{S}_2, \ldots, \mathcal{S}_n \rangle$. Each data source $\mathcal{S}_i$ is in turn composed of a collection of *data items*, whose definition is given as follows.

Definition 1 (Data item). *A data item $\mathcal{D}_j^i \in \mathcal{S}_i$ can be formalised as $\mathcal{D}_j^i = \langle \mathcal{A}_j^i, \mathcal{O}_j^i \rangle$ where: (i) $\mathcal{A}_j^i$ is a set of attributes and (ii) $\mathcal{O}_j^i$ is a set holding attribute-value pairs, with attributes belonging to $\mathcal{A}_j^i$, representing the content of the data item.*

Example 1. In the considered motivating example, a data item $\mathcal{D}_j^i$ may contain the electrical energy consumption sensed by a smart meter installed at a specific building. Coherently, for the data item, candidate attributes for the set $\mathcal{A}_j^i$ would be timestamp, smart meter configuration parameters (e.g., the physical

---

[1] http://vowl.visualdataweb.org/protegevowl.html.

position of the meter) and so forth, that is, $\mathcal{A}_j^i = \{\texttt{Electr\_Rdng}, \texttt{eMeter\_ID},$ $\texttt{building\_ID}, \ldots\}$, where $\texttt{eMeter\_ID}$ denotes the unique ID associated with a particular electricity meter, $\texttt{building\_ID}$ denotes the identifier of the building where the meter is located and $\texttt{Electr\_Rdng}$ denotes the electrical energy reading at a specific time on the meter. Given the attributes set $\mathcal{A}_j^i$, a sample of the content of set $\mathcal{O}_j^i$ is: $\{\langle\texttt{Electr\_Rdng}, 10023.5\rangle, \langle\texttt{eMeter\_ID}, RGO16 \rangle, \langle\texttt{building\_ID},$ $Building001\rangle, \ldots\}$.

4.1 Data Sources Semantic Models

Once data has been ingested in the Data Lake, domain experts are enabled to build proper *Semantic Models*, created during the addition of the data source into the Data Lake. These models serve as a semantic description of data attributes and their relationships, allowing data analysts, who might not be familiar with the data, to understand data meaning. In fact, concepts and relationships used within each Semantic Model represent the domain expert's view of the data source, based upon one or more (external) domain ontologies. In our approach, data lake sources are semantically annotated in order to define the *Smart City Semantic Data Lake* in terms of Semantic Models and their instances. For this purpose, we rely on techniques and models developed and tested in [15]. In particular, we design a Semantic Model for each data source $\mathcal{S}_i \in DL$ according to the following steps: (1) at the beginning, the domain expert considers all the attributes of the data source $\mathcal{S}_i$ and then seeks suitable semantic concepts and relationships amongst the ones available in the domain ontologies; (2) after that, the domain expert may specialise, if needed, the existing concepts and relationships in the domain ontologies by adding specific ones; (3) mappings are defined between concepts and attributes to automatically extract instances (i.e., individuals) of the aforementioned concepts from the underlying data sources.

A fragment of Semantic Model for the motivating example is depicted in Fig. 2. The domain ontologies chosen by the domain expert for this Semantic Model are: GeoNames[2], for representing spatial entities, SOSA[3] (acronym for Sensor, Observation, Sample and Actuator) containing concepts apt to describe sensors and measures produced by them, and Time[4], devoted to model temporal entities.

5 Smart City Exploration Graph

Semantic Models provided by domain experts are leveraged by data analysts to assure a formal definition of Smart City indicators. Specifically, data analysts are in charge of designing the aforementioned indicators (jointly with additional knowledge) by specialising concepts and relationships of a *Multi-Dimensional*

---

[2] http://www.geonames.org/ (prefix: GEO).

[3] http://www.w3.org/ns/sosa (prefix: sosa).

[4] http://www.w3.org/2006/time (prefix: time).

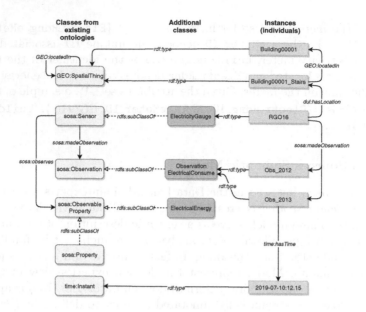

Fig. 2. Semantic Model designed for a data source in the motivating example.

Ontology (MDO, in brief) conceived as a modelling framework to provide a semantic representation of the indicators which have to be defined.

The semantic definition of indicators, obtained by specialising MDO concepts and relationships, weaves the *Smart City Exploration Graph*. In the following, the description of the MDO, emphasising its semantic areas, is provided, along with an example of indicator definition, related to the motivating example in Sect. 2.

5.1   The Multi-Dimensional Ontology

As shown in Fig. 3, the MDO contains baseline concepts and relationships regarding indicators and exploration personalisation aspects. Hereafter, the three conceptual areas of the MDO are described, emphasising the semantic role they fulfill.

Personalisation Concepts. Owing to the wide variety of data that can be explored, data exploration can be personalised taking into account user's category (e.g., building manager, citizen) and activities performed by users (e.g., building monitoring, check air pollution), the former abstracted through the `UserCategory` concept, whereas the latter through the `Activity` concept. An activity may involve one or more indicators to be observed, compatible with its purpose (`involves` relationship). Activities can be performed by users, according to their role inside the Smart City context (`hasPracticableActivity` relationship).

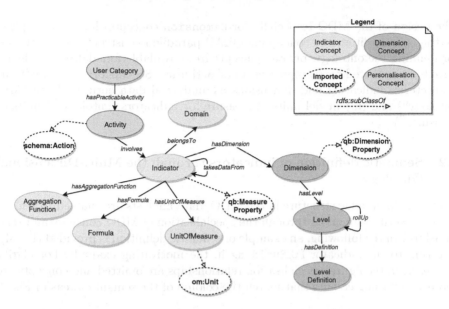

Fig. 3. TBox of the Multi-Dimensional Ontology (in the figure, the three semantic areas are highlighted with different colours).

Dimensions Concepts. Indicators can be segmented and calculated according to several dimensions (**hasDimension** relationship), which are in turn organised into levels, modelled through the **Level** concept. The **rollUp** semantic relationship enables a hierarchical organisation of levels, thus ensuring the navigability from the lowest to the highest aggregation level, resembling the renowned OLAP *roll-up* operator. Moreover, **Level** concept is linked in the MDO to **Level-Definition** concept through the **hasDefinition** relationship, in order to represent an abstraction for the procedure devoted to calculate level instances starting from their counterparts in the semantic models.

Indicators Concepts. Indicators are designed to aggregate urban data according to several perspectives and represent the ultimate target for data exploration, as their value may give valuable insights to users. In the ontology, indicators can be modelled as simple or compound, i.e. calculated exploiting other indicators (through **takesDataFrom** semantic relationship). Being measurable quantities, they are endowed with a unit of measure (abstracted through the **UnitOfMeasure** concept) and have a calculation formula (**Formula** concept). For an indicator, it is also possible to define an aggregation function (**AggregationFunction** semantic concept), adopted as standard operation to apply whenever switching from a dimensional level to another (through the **rollUp** semantic relationship). Finally, indicators may be associated with domains, such as environment, health, energy and so forth; this is represented inside the ontology through the **belongsTo** semantic relationship, connecting **Indicator** concept with **Domain** concept.

The design of the MDO (especially for Dimension concepts) has been inspired by the existing literature concerning OLAP paradigm constructs [6]. Moreover, for defining the ontology, pivotal concepts from available foundation ontologies have been exploited to: (i) represent users' activities (Schema.org ontology[5]), (ii) characterise indicators and dimensions as analytical data entities (Data Cube ontology[6]) and (iii) model units of measure for indicators (ontology of units of measures[7]).

5.2   Semantic definition of indicators through the Multi-Dimensional Ontology

Given the knowledge structure in the MDO, data analysts are enabled to semantically describe indicators through the specialisation of MDO concepts and relationships. In the following, an example of semantic definition is provided (Fig. 4), referring to the indicator EC_Building in the motivating example. For clarity purposes, in the figure, specialisation relationships are omitted and concepts are represented using colours that match the colours of the semantic areas in Fig. 3.

Example 2. According to the motivating example, the EC_Building indicator is compound, as it depends on (i.e., takesValueFrom) three indicators, namely EC_Stairs, EC_Gardens and EC_Elevators, whose sum contributes to produce the value for EC_Building. Indicators concepts are linked to a Spatial-Dimension, suitable for defining their spatial coverage, through the specialisation of Level concept. In the motivating example, the following levels of spatial dimensions are considered: City, District, Building and Electrical_Meter. Analogously to what happens for OLAP analysis, rollUp relationships ensure to establish a hierarchical organisation of levels concepts, assuring the navigability from the lowest (i.e., Electrical_Meter) to the highest (i.e., City) extent of aggregation. Focusing on Building concept, it is linked to BuildingLevel-Definition concept; this is exploited to formalise the calculation of Building instances starting from their conceptual counterpart in semantic models (that is, referring to Fig. 2, instances of SpatialThing concept). Noteworthy, different indicators concepts may share the same dimensional organisation (that is, EC_Building, EC_Stairs, EC_Gardens and EC_Elevator are all connected to SpatialDimension concept).

Mappings Towards Semantic Models and Analysis Cubes. We distinguish among two types of mappings, manually defined by data analysts, binding: (i) a concept in the Smart City Exploration Graph with a concept in a Semantic Model and (ii) a concept in the Smart City Exploration Graph with an attribute in a specific Analysis Cube.

---

[5] https://schema.org/ (prefix: schema).
[6] https://www.w3.org/TR/vocab-data-cube/ (prefix: qb).
[7] http://www.ontology-of-units-of-measure.org/resource/om-2/ (prefix: om).

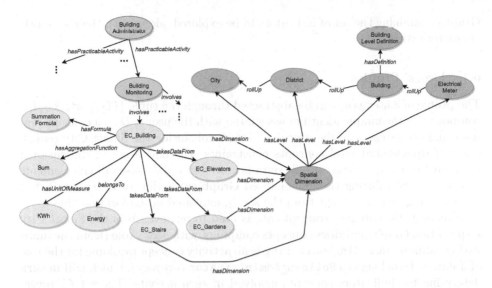

Fig. 4. Excerpt of the Smart City Exploration Graph for the description of $EC_{building}$ in the motivating example.

Specifically, the first kind of mapping is a tuple $\langle C_{EG}, C_{SM}, R \rangle$ binding a concept C_{EG} contained in the Smart City Exploration Graph to a concept C_{SM} belonging to a Semantic Model, through the relationship R (e.g., equivalence or subsumption relationship). In this case, data analysts may be supported in their definition by ad-hoc tools[8], which may be equipped with similarity-based matching algorithms, and ensure the possibility of exporting such mappings in various formats.

Similarly, mappings between concepts in the Smart City Exploration Graph and Analysis Cubes are expressed through the tuple $\langle C_{EG}, c_{ID}, c_{ATTR} \rangle$, where C_{EG} represents a reference to a concept in the Smart City Exploration Graph, c_{ID} is the Analysis Cube unique identifier and c_{ATTR} is an attribute contained in the Analysis Cube schema. These mappings are retained in a dedicated repository and processed by the **EXTRACTOR & TRANSFORMER** tool.

6   Personalised Graphs Extraction

In this section, we describe how to extract Personalised Exploration Graphs, containing a portion of the Smart City Exploration Graph targeted to a specific end-user. Specifically, the aim of this task is to assure a personalised exploration of Smart City indicators, achieved by considering users' profiles. In the following, a formalisation of users' profiles is given, together with the description of the stepwise procedure leading to the extraction of Personalised Exploration

---

[8] For instance, Protégé (https://protege.stanford.edu/) and COMA tool (https://dbs.uni-leipzig.de/Research/coma.html).

Graphs containing the set of indicators to be explored, along with their semantic characterisation.

6.1 Users' Profiles

The profile of a user $p(u)$ can be abstracted through the tuple $\langle ID_u, cat_u, C_l, I_l \rangle$, composed of: the unique identifier associated with the user (ID_u), a concept representing the category of the user, i.e. his/her role inside the Smart City (cat_u), a set of dimensional level concepts constraints (C_l) and a set of dimensional levels instances (I_l). Users' profile data is stored in a database; all the elements in $p(u)$ are used during the Personalised Graph extraction process, detailed in the following section, except from the set I_l, exploited at exploration time.

Precisely, the category concept cat_u is used to retrieve, from the Smart City Exploration Graph, activities concepts compliant with user's role (from the motivating example, BuildingMonitoring is an activity concept available for the role of John, as he belongs to BuildingAdministrator category), which will in turn determine the indicators concepts involved in such activity. The set C_l represent concepts deemed as constraints, applicable to delimit the dimensional levels to which the user is allowed to access. In this way, data privacy preservation is enabled, for instance granting building managers to visualise data up to building level (therefore not at lower levels, such as single electrical meters).

When users register themselves through the GUI, the registration wizard, starting from the user's category, prompts to the user proper masks to insert in C_l concepts references and in I_l instances references, which will be in turn validated by a third-party authority, in order to assure the exploration of indicators only for the dimensional levels the user has an explicit authorisation and for the buildings under his competency (e.g., buildings in the motivating example).

6.2 Personalised Graphs Derivation Procedure

As previously remarked, from the Smart City Exploration Graph, different personalised graphs can be derived, by considering users' profiles. The extraction process can be summarised by these two steps:

(1) *Activity-based indicators concepts selection*, in which, besides the user selects the activity he/she wants to perform, relying on his/her role, candidate indicators concepts (and related semantic knowledge) involved in the activity are identified and retrieved from the Smart City Exploration Graph;

(2) *Level-based dimension pruning*, in which concepts specialising the MDO Level concept, retained in the set C_l, are used to constrain the visibility of the dimensional organisation levels concepts only to those levels a user is allowed to access.

In the following, each step will be further described, considering the motivating example and with the support of Fig. 5.

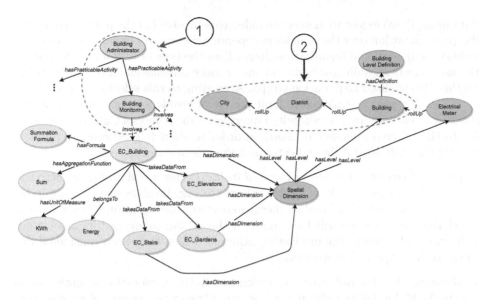

Fig. 5. Stepwise derivation of a Personalised Graph. In the figure, the focus is on a specific portion of the Smart City Exploration Graph (numbers in the circles represent the order of extraction steps).

Activity-based indicators concepts selection. Due to the fact that John is a building administrator, he must select only activity concepts compliant with his role. Amongst the available ones, he selects from the proposed ones Building-Monitoring. Such activity involves several indicators and EC_Building, as previously described, is one of them. Being EC_Building a compound indicator, the takesDataFrom relationship connects it to the concepts EC_Stairs, EC_Gardens and EC_Elevators. Noteworthy, the following dimensional pruning step is iterated over the aforementioned indicators. Overall, for these composing indicators and for the ancestor one, the related semantic characterisation (dimensional organisation, formula, aggregation function, domain and so forth) is retrieved from the Smart City Exploration Graph.

Level-based dimension pruning. Retained in John's profile data, the set C_l expresses the dimensional levels (that is, references to concepts specialising MDO Level concept) to which he may access. Referring to John, the set C_l in his profile holds the concepts {City, District, Building}. Furthermore, such elements are linked in a rollUp chain (starting from Building up to City), defining the dimension levels navigation path.

7 Personalised Graphs Exploration

Exploration within Personalised Graphs can be performed according to different perspectives (highlighted in Fig. 6), thus enabling the Explorative Search paradigm [4]: (a) exploration over the indicators involved in the performed activity, (b) exploration over the indicators dependencies and (c) exploration over the indicators dimensional organisation. Regardless the type of exploration scenario, the user selects an indicator node and one or more dimensional levels nodes from his/her Personalised Exploration Graph. According to this selection, the content of the set $I_l \in p(u)$ is exploited to limit the set of visible instances related to the selected levels concepts. As a result, a query over the Analysis Cube corresponding to the selected indicator is issued, in order to show (e.g., through a tabular layout) the instances of the indicator and the selected dimensions.

Exploration Over the Indicators Involved in the Performed Activity. An activity performed by a user, such as `BuildingMonitoring`, involves one or more indicators to be inspected (related to energy and water consumption). Nevertheless, for clarity purposes, we will focus only on the `EC_Building` and its associated indicators, adhering to the motivating example, which have been considered for the next two exploration scenarios.

Exploration Over the Indicators Dependencies. In this exploration scenario, John selects the `EC_Building` indicator and, starting from that, he can delve into other indicators by traversing the `takesDataFrom` semantic relationship, connecting a compound indicator concept with its dependencies (which in turn may be compound or not). In this respect, John can inspect the more specific indicators `EC_Stairs`, `EC_Gardens` and `EC_Elevators`. For instance, if John's focus is on evaluating the electrical consumption of the elevators of the building, he may select and inspect details about `EC_Elevators` indicator.

Exploration Over the Indicators Dimensional Organisation. This exploration scenario exploits the semantic relationships between an indicator and its dimensional organisation (through the `hasDimension` relationship). In particular, knowledge on dimensional organisation for indicators considers levels concepts (`hasLevel` relationship). Focusing on `EC_Building` indicator or one of its dependencies, John can position himself over one dimensional level (e.g., `Building`) and then he can change the granularity of the aggregation level for the chosen indicator, by exploiting the `rollUp` semantic relationship, thus switching to `District`. Therefore, John could choose to visualise at a higher aggregation viewpoint (in this case, district) the values of the `EC_Building` indicator; whenever such `rollUp` is performed, the aggregation function associated with the indicator, through the `hasAggregationFunction` relationship (e.g., "sum" in the case of `EC_Building`), is applied.

8   Preliminary Validation

Advantages on the use of a semantic layer on top of the data lake, composed of different Semantic Models managed by domain experts who know data stored within the data lake, have been already investigated in [15], both in terms of flexibility, expressiveness and expandability. Following the suggestions given

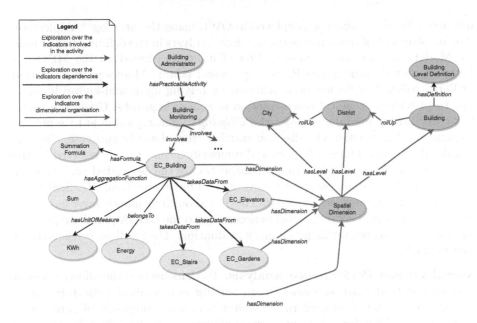

Fig. 6. Subset of a Personalised Graph on which exploration scenarios are considered.

in [15], possible inconsistencies and heterogeneity across different Semantic Models, already mitigated due to the adoption of reference domain ontologies, can be further reduced through the application of similarity-based alignment and reconciliation techniques. The goal of this section is to highlight pros and cons of the three-layered approach proposed in this paper. In particular, the focus will be on the preliminary proof that the Smart City Exploration Graph and Personalised Graphs are effective in supporting different categories of users for indicators exploration.

To this aim, a prototype implementation of the approach has been created, focusing on the GUIs designed to accomplish the exploration tasks. Specifically, a web-based dashboard has been built in order to: (a) let users register themselves to the exploration platform, specifying elements in $p(u)$ and (b) explore their Personalised Graphs, generated according to their profile data. In the prototype implementation, data sources containing energy consumption in the context of the Brescia Smart Living project[9], including sources considered in the motivating example, have been collected. A sample of users has been involved, including citizens without prior knowledge on Smart City indicators, representatives of Public Administration (in particular, the Municipality of Brescia, Italy), utility and energy providers. Citizens live in two districts of the city, a modern one (Sanpolino), where new generation smart meters have been installed, and a district in city downtown, more densely populated and presenting older buildings. Semantic Models, the Smart City Exploration Graph and Personalised Graphs

---

[9] https://www.bresciasmartliving.eu/index.php.

extracted for users have been deployed in OWL using the Stardog[10] Triplestore. The involvement of domain experts and data analysts in the definition of Semantic Models and semantic representation of indicators based on the MDO has been supported through the Protégé graphical editor. Moreover, visualisation of Personalised Graphs has been achieved by relying upon well-known libraries apt to provide a graphical representation of semantic graphs. Given the versatility of Stardog module, we used the *d3sparql*[11] library, suitable to represent dynamic and interactive visualisation starting from data (in this case, the Personalised Graphs). Once indicators and dimensions concepts are selected by the user from the Personalised Graph, the inspection of the associated analysis cube is achieved, in a tabular way, by means of the OpenCube Toolkit[12]. Scalability issues concerning the querying of data lake based on the semantic layer have been already studied in several approaches according to the OBDA paradigm [14] and are out of the scope of this preliminary evaluation. They will be considered for future work.

Workload and Performance Analysis. To demonstrate the effectiveness of three-layered information model in supporting personalised indicators exploration, we simulated an exploratory search scenario, composed of three tasks of increasing difficulty, where users were allowed to explore their Personalised Graphs according to the exploration methods introduced in Sect. 7. Specifically, the three aforementioned tasks included the exploration of: (i) a simple indicator, (ii) a compound indicator with a single level of dependencies (like the EC_Building of the motivating example) and (iii) a compound indicator with more than two nested levels of dependencies. Users attended an initial training of 30 min, in order for them to get acquainted with the GUI and, at the same time, let them create their profile. For evaluating the performance of our prototype, participants filled a likert scale NASA TLX questionnaire, a multidimensional assessment tool that rates perceived workload in order to assess a task or system. Questionnaires analysis has revealed that, for our proposal, the "Mental Demand" sub-scale has been rated with the highest score whereas "Performance" with the lowest. We impute such outcome to the fact that our proposal increases the success of users while accomplishing data exploration, despite a slight growth of mental and perceptual activity required to understand how to effectively navigate across Personalised Graphs.

Usability Tests. Usability experiments are being carried on within the Brescia Smart Living project until the end of 2019. Participants were assigned a task to be accomplished using the exploration tool, without imposing time-up or any particular exploration constraint. Specifically, the task was a broad exploratory search scenario for inspecting indicators in the Personalised Graph concerning the energy and the environmental domain (compliant with user's profile). Then, we asked participants to fill a standard System Usability Scale (SUS)

---

[10] https://www.stardog.com/.
[11] https://github.com/ktym/d3sparql.
[12] http://opencube-toolkit.eu/.

questionnaire, as an instrument to assess software usability. In this kind of questionnaire, for each statement, respondents can indicate the degree of agreement and disagreement on a five point scale. SUS scores a software in a range between 0 to 100, where 0 indicates the least usability and 100 represents a high usability, respectively. We averaged over all participants questions and the resulting mean score amounted to 87.5, which situates our prototype in the 90–95 percentile range in the curve matching SUS score with the corresponding rank. We also calculated the time participants spent to carry out their task. Using the prototype, participants accomplished their task in a shorter timer compared to a plain keyword-based interface. This relieves participants of a detailed knowledge about indicators definition, being guided in the exploration of indicators by the semantic relationships in the Personalised Graph.

9 Related Work

In the last decades, Semantic Web technologies have been suggested to effectively combine data from multiple heterogeneous sources, with the aim of providing a unified view of data resulting from integration processes. In this respect, in-depth studies concerning the renowned OBDA (Ontology-Based Data Access) paradigm have been applied in the field of data lakes, paving the way to the so-called semantic data lakes [14], wherein heterogeneous data is seamlessly accessed and queried through a proper semantic layer.

Generally speaking, the role of semantics in data lake approaches is manifold and goes beyond integration issues. For instance, in [3,11] semantic enrichment is exploited to link data with external knowledge bases, also envisaging probabilistic techniques [13]. Moreover, ontologies and knowledge graphs have been fostered in literature as a promising solution to offer a comprehensive view over the underlying data sources, modelling their relationships and dependencies [2,11]. Likewise, in [17] knowledge graphs store data fragments, represented as different typologies of nodes inside the graph. The tool presented in [14] embraces Semantic Web facilities to answer on-demand queries over heterogeneous data, ensuring high levels of scalability when treating significant data volumes. Nonetheless, in the former approaches, there is no mention about fostering such knowledge to achieve a personalised Data Exploration experience, and the focus is more on assessing the performance of the systems. Furthermore, the separation of roles and competencies of the actors involved in the aforementioned frameworks is less evident, with respect to our multi-layer approach. Sharing some issues with the proposal of this paper, the approach presented in [7] harnesses thematic views upon the datasources of the data lake, but again personalisation aspects are treated only at a high level of abstraction, without a fully-fledged semantic support. Lastly, a semantic data platform has been presented in [15], adopting a flexible data ingestion pipeline, but exploration aspects have been slightly neglected.

For what concerns approaches focused on Data Exploration tasks in data lakes, the starting point for users is almost always a GUI, where they can issue queries to perform a keyword-based search [3, 8] or where a direct interaction through ad-hoc visualisation tools can be achieved [9]. Other approaches, instead, focus more on favouring the user in getting acquainted with the exploration interface, taking into account his interaction waiting tolerance [12] or by implementing proper caching strategies, to ensure high responsiveness levels [16]. The ultimate goal of Data Exploration is also to provide suitable instruments to obtain actionable insights related to the observed data; in [10], for instance, current sensor data is compared against simulated data, computed from previously stored data, in order to predict future behaviours and trends.

In the majority of these approaches, the focus is more on the visualisation of data, instead of proposing techniques to detect and attract user's attention on data suitable and compliant with user's exploration interests, also suggesting effective exploration directions based on user's profile.

10 Concluding Remarks

In this paper, we described a semantics-based approach to extract Exploration Graphs for enabling personalised data lake exploration. In particular, the approach is structured over three layers: (i) at the bottom, heterogeneous data sources within a data lake are enriched with Semantic Models, defined by domain experts using domain ontologies, to provide a semantic data lake representation; (ii) in the middle, a Multi-Dimensional Ontology is used to describe indicators and their analysis dimensions, in terms of concepts within semantic models and formulas to aggregate them (iii) at the top, Personalised Exploration Graphs are generated for different categories of users, whose profiles are defined in terms of a set of constraints that limit the indicators concepts on which the user may rely to explore data. We presented the approach, discussing its benefits and limitations through an application in the Smart City domain.

Future efforts will be devoted to provide a full-fledged implementation of the approach, detailing the experimentation steps and the enabling technologies. In this respect, scalability issues, deriving from the potential vast amount of annotated data coexisting in the Smart City Semantic Data Lake, deserve a thorough dissertation and a comparison with other similar approaches (for instance, [14]) that will be under the lens of forthcoming research studies. Likewise, the impact of Personalised Exploration Graphs evolution (due to modifications in users' profiles) will be further investigated, focusing on the influence it has on the exploration tasks.

References

1. Abelló, A., et al.: Using semantic web technologies for exploratory OLAP: a survey. IEEE Trans. Knowl. Data Eng. **27**(2), 571–588 (2014)
2. Alserafi, A., Abelló, A., Romero, O., Calders, T.: Towards information profiling: data lake content metadata management. In: Proceedings of IEEE 16th International Conference on Data Mining Workshops (ICDMW 2016), Barcelona, Spain, pp. 178–185 (2016)

3. Beheshti, A., Benatallah, B., Nouri, R., Tabebordbar, A.: CoreKG: a knowledge lake service. PVLDB **11**(12), 1942–1945 (2018)
4. Buoncristiano, M., Mecca, G., Quintarelli, E., Roveri, M., Santoro, D., Tanca, L.: Database challenges for exploratory computing. SIGMOD Rec. **44**(2), 17–22 (2015)
5. Chauhan, S., Agarwal, N., Kar, A.: Addressing big data challenges in smart cities: a systematic literature review. Info **18**(4), 73–90 (2016)
6. Diamantini, C., Potena, D., Storti, E., Zhang, H.: An ontology-based data exploration tool for key performance indicators. In: Proceedings of 22nd OTM Conference on Cooperative Information Systems (CoopIS 2014), Amantea, Italy, pp. 727–744 (2014)
7. Giudice, P.L., Musarella, L., Sofo, G., Ursino, D.: An approach to extracting complex knowledge patterns among concepts belonging to structured, semi-structured and unstructured sources in a data lake. Inf. Sci. **478**, 606–626 (2019)
8. Hai, R., Geisler, S., Quix, C.: Constance: an intelligent data lake system. In: Proceedings of the 2016 International Conference on Management of Data (SIGMOD/PODS 2016), San Francisco, California, pp. 2097–2100 (2016)
9. Halevy, A.Y., et al.: Managing Google's data lake: an overview of the GOODS system. IEEE Data Eng. Bull. **39**(3), 5–14 (2016)
10. Kasrin, N., Qureshi, M., Steuer, S., Nicklas, D.: Semantic data management for experimental manufacturing technologies. Datenbank-Spektrum **18**(1), 27–37 (2018)
11. Lytra, I., Vidal, M., Orlandi, F., Attard, J.: A big data architecture for managing oceans of data and maritime applications. In: Proceedings of International Conference on Engineering, Technology and Innovation (ICE/ITMC 2017), Madeira, Portugal, pp. 1216–1226 (2017)
12. Maccioni, A., Torlone, R.: KAYAK: a framework for just-in-time data preparation in a data lake. In: Krogstie, J., Reijers, H.A. (eds.) CAiSE 2018. LNCS, vol. 10816, pp. 474–489. Springer, Cham (2018). https://doi.org/10.1007/978-3-319-91563-0_29
13. Malysiak-Mrozek, B., Stabla, M., Mrozek, D.: Soft and declarative fishing of information in big data lake. IEEE Trans. Fuzzy Syst. **26**(5), 2731–2747 (2018)
14. Mami, M.N., Graux, D., Scerri, S., Jabeen, H., Auer, S., Lehmann, J.: Squerall: virtual ontology-based access to heterogeneous and large data sources. In: Proceedings of 18th International Semantic Web Conference (ISWC 2019), Auckland, New Zealand (2019, in press)
15. Pomp, A., Paulus, A., Kirmse, A., Kraus, V., Meisen, T.: Applying semantics to reduce the time to analytics within complex heterogeneous infrastructures. Technologies **6**(3), 86–114 (2018)
16. Skluzacek, T.J., Chard, K., Foster, I.: Klimatic: a virtual data lake for harvesting and distribution of geospatial data. In: Proceedings of 1st Joint International Workshop on Parallel Data Storage and Data Intensive Scalable Computing Systems (PDSW-DISCS 2016), Salt Lake City, Utah, pp. 31–36 (2016)
17. Walker, C., Alrehamy, H.: Personal data lake with data gravity pull. In: Proceedings of 2015 IEEE Fifth International Conference on Big Data and Cloud Computing (BDCLOUD 2015), Dalian, China, pp. 160–167 (2015)

Characterizing Conceptual Modeling Research

Lois M. L. Delcambre[1], Stephen W. Liddle[2]($\boxtimes$), Oscar Pastor[3],
and Veda C. Storey[4]

[1] Portland State University, Portland, OR, USA
lmd@pdx.edu
[2] Brigham Young University, Provo, UT, USA
liddle@byu.edu
[3] Universitat Politècnica de València, Valencia, Spain
opastor@dsic.upv.es
[4] Georgia State University, Atlanta, GA, USA
vstorey@gsu.edu

Abstract. The field of conceptual modeling continues to evolve and be applied to important modeling problems in many domains. With a goal of articulating the breadth and depth of the field, our initial work focused on the many implicit and explicit definitions of conceptual modeling, resulting in the Characterizing Conceptual Modeling (CCM) framework. In this paper, we focus on *conceptual modeling research*, presenting a Characterizing Conceptual Model Research (CCMR) framework and a series of evaluations to assess the coverage and usability of CCMR, the utility and independence of the individual fields in the framework, and likelihood of consistent use.

Keywords: Conceptual modeling · Reference framework · Methods · Models

1 Introduction

There have been decades of work dedicated to making significant contributions to, and expanding the field of, conceptual modeling. Contributions have come from many computing fields such as database design, software development, business process articulation, and ontology. However, it is still difficult to describe the breadth and depth of the field in a short phrase or a single definition.

Previously, we synthesized many definitions of conceptual modeling from the literature and our colleagues to define a framework for Characterizing Conceptual Modeling (CCM) [5]. However, CCM focuses on conceptual modeling (as done by modelers) as opposed to conceptual modeling *research* with its rich and varied contributions.

The objective of this paper is to take steps toward the characterization of conceptual modeling research to enable researchers to easily articulate their contributions to conceptual modeling (CM). This may facilitate discussion and debate

© Springer Nature Switzerland AG 2019
H. Panetto et al. (Eds.): OTM 2019, LNCS 11877, pp. 40–57, 2019.
https://doi.org/10.1007/978-3-030-33246-4_3

among researchers and eventually promote more effective search of the literature. It might also acknowledge the various disciplines that contributed to CM
and contributed to the recognition of CM within the computing disciplines.

This paper provides a brief description of CCM in Sect. 2 followed by a description of the Characterizing Conceptual Modeling Research (CCMR) framework in
Sect. 3. We describe our evaluation of CCMR in Sect. 4 and provide discussion and
related work in Sect. 5. Conclusions and future work are given in Sect. 6.

2   Characterizing Conceptual Modeling Framework

Our initial framework focused on conceptual modeling. We first compiled a broad
set of definitions for conceptual modeling; this unearthed a number of purposes
for CM as shown in Fig. 1. These purposes allude to the various models, intents,
and people involved in conceptual modeling. Color indicates similar purposes:
blue—understanding/communicating a domain, phenomenon, or (future) system; purple—setting forth the meaning of terms/concepts; green—supporting
system building; red—eliciting and documenting conceptual models; and black—
supporting formalization and reasoning. The ideas for Fig. 1 are abundantly supported in the literature (e.g. [8,13,26,28,41]).

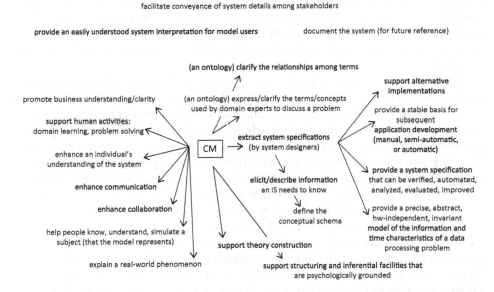

Fig. 1. The purpose of a conceptual model (drawn from the literature) (Color figure
online)

Our framework to characterize conceptual modeling, CCM [5], described
what was being modeled: information, events, processes, and/or interactions
and the activity of conceptual modeling, in addition to the purpose of conceptual modeling. CCM focused on when the activity of conceptual modeling

was done (*Timing*) and whether there was automated assistance (*Automation*) and whether the conceptual models (and conceptual modeling languages) were generic or domain-specific. However, when we applied the CCM framework to characterize CM papers, it was obvious that researchers engage in activities that lead to contributions that are not reflected in CCM. (E.g. does the paper contribute a new or extend an existing conceptual modeling language? does it contribute a conceptual model? or does it contribute a method or tool intended to improve the practice of conceptual modeling?).

3   The Characterizing Conceptual Modeling Research Framework

We used the following methodology as we developed the CCMR. We first tried to classify several papers from the CM literature using the CCM framework but we were able to characterize only the CMs that appeared in those papers, e.g. in examples. Based on our collective experience in the field of CM over the decades, we discussed the types of contributions made by papers in CM. This led us to the CCMR framework which we then applied in a series of experiments, as detailed in Sect. 4 below.

The CCMR framework consists of three parts (see Fig. 2). The first part provides the context for the conceptual modeling in a given project. The second and third parts expose the various types of research contributions that can be made in the field of conceptual modeling in two aspects: the use of conceptual models and/or conceptual modeling languages (CMLs), and the methods or tools provided.

The first part includes the intended purpose and intended domain (of the conceptual modeling activity considered in the paper), the domain used in any case studies or examples in the paper, and the intended users of the ideas/tools/ models etc. presented in the paper. Each field is optional. For example, a paper presenting a conceptual modeling language may be generic and thus would not have any particular intended application domain. But a paper might apply conceptual modeling to a new purpose (with existing conceptual modeling languages and processes) or identify a possible new class of intended users.

The second part of the framework accommodates significant new or extended conceptual models, conceptual model patterns, conceptual modeling languages; the evaluation of one or more modeling languages/models (often through comparison with other modeling languages/models); formalization of modeling languages, concepts, or perhaps even models; or the philosophical grounding that underlies modeling languages, concepts, or models.[1] The framework includes a level of modeling between a conceptual modeling language and a conceptual

---

[1] As examples of philosophical grounding, Wand and Weber take an ontological perspective to understanding information systems from a conceptual modeling perspective [44]. Guizzardi provides another kind of ontological foundation for conceptual models [11]. Guarino has long argued for the role of ontologies in conceptual modeling [10].

Conceptual Modeling Context					
Intended Purpose: circle one or explain other	DB design, SW development, BP articulation, Domain understanding, Knowledge representation, **Other:**				
Intended Domain:					
Domain of Case Study/Examples:					
Intended Users:					
Conceptual Models/Languages		**Contribute or Extend**	**Evaluate or Compare**	**Formalize**	**Philosophical Grounding**
Generic ... Domain-specific	Conceptual model(s): indicate CML(s) used				
	Conceptual model pattern(s), ideal/ seed model(s), metamodel(s): indicate CML(s) used				
	Conceptual Modeling Language(s): indicate what is modeled: information, events, business processes, interaction				
CM Tools and Processes		**Contribute or Extend**	**Evaluate or Compare**	**Formalize**	
Conceptual modeling methods/processes:					
Automated tools for CM: validation, simulation, "anti-patterns" check, translation (to lower-level/implementation) languages, reverse engineering (translation to higher-level) languages, mapping from one CM to another for integration/semantics					

Fig. 2. Characterizing conceptual modeling research framework

model for a conceptual modeling pattern or ideal model that could be adjusted, adapted, or extended in an actual conceptual model.

The third part of the framework captures the various activities involved in conceptual modeling through methodological support and automated tool support. As with part 2, a paper or research effort might contribute or extend, evaluate or compare, or even formalize methods or tools. Note that the portion on automated tools includes the use of mappings (from one conceptual modeling language to another conceptual or implementation-oriented language) and reverse engineering (i.e. developing a conceptual model from another, lower-level model). The philosophical perspective is not in this third part at this time because we suspect that the consideration of philosophical grounding would likely have influenced the conceptual modeling languages and models used as opposed to the methods, processes, or tools.

4   Evaluating the CCMR Framework

Over 15 months, we evaluated the CCMR framework with the results summarized in Table 1. In our experiments, we set out to evaluate the ease of use/feasibility/utility of the framework, correctness and consistency when using the framework, and the coverage of the framework for the field of CM. In our evaluation activities, we used various methods for selecting papers to characterize; this work could be viewed as an initial, small-scale step towards a systematic classification of CM.

We used the first version of CCMR (described in Sect. 3 above and referred to as CCM 2.0 in [6]) for the first three evaluation activities. Based on the results, we modified the framework slightly to include a fourth row in the second part (for *Metamodels of Conceptual Modeling Languages*), visually eliminated the vertical spectrum labeled *Generic ... Domain-specific* and eliminated the adjective *business* in front of *business process*, listed as one of the items that can be modeled. Thus, part 2 of the CCMR framework is not specific to a domain. Finally, we added a field in part 1 for *Intended Level of Abstraction* to delimit the focus of the conceptual modeling effort. Figure 3 shows the modified CCMR framework.

Table 1. Evaluation activities for the CCMR framework

Activity	Evaluation goal	Result
The researchers characterized 2 papers independently	(Initial) usability (Initial) consistency (Initial) correctness	Usable. Strong agreement/consistency Difference: minimalist vs. maximalist use of framework
We all characterized 3 papers; then we chose 6 of our own papers to characterize	(Initial) coverage of CM Utility of each field in the framework	All papers could be characterized. Papers exercised broad range of fields in framework. In 2nd and 3rd part, every square in 1st column was used; every row was used; every column was used
We led 2 workshops where CM experts each characterized 1 of their papers and presented to the group	Usability Coverage of CM Utility of each field in the framework	Lively discussion about terms used in framework Everyone characterized their paper with ease Difference: minimalist vs. maximalist use. Missing item (in coverage): metamodels in CM Significant use of most rows and columns in the framework
All four of us characterized 10 randomly selected ER2018 papers based on only title, abstract, and conclusions	Coverage of CM Consistency Feasibility of using (just) title, abstract, and conclusions potentially scale up the characterization of large numbers of papers) Independence of rows; independence of columns	All papers were characterized. In part 1: *intended purpose, intended domain*, and *intended level of abstraction* were very diverse. Regarding feasibility: *domain of case studies/examples* was generally not possible to fill in from only abstract and conclusions. In 2nd and 3rd parts, there was some inconsistency among our use of rows with: *method/tool* split; new *representation/tool or method* that uses the new representation split. In 2nd and 3rd parts, very strong agreement with use of columns indicating good independence

4.1   A Range of Papers Characterized in CCMR

We selected three papers from the CM literature and we independently characterized them. There was much agreement about the main contribution(s) of each paper. Our efforts differed in the amount of detail. At one extreme, two of us adopted a minimalist approach where we described the context of the conceptual modeling research, as appropriate, and then focused on the (typically one or possibly two) key, significant contribution(s) of the paper. The other two tended to provide more detail: adding a number of secondary contributions on the one hand and filling in nearly every square (to provide a detailed overview of the paper) on the other hand. The difference was trying to identify the main/significant contribution of the paper vs. considering the CCMR framework as a "checklist" that needed to be filled in.

We selected 6 additional papers on diverse topics to characterize; this selection intentionally included papers authored by one of us because we wanted to characterize papers that at least one of us was highly familiar with. Note that these were characterized by one of the four of us and then discussed with the others. We adopted a minimalist approach because a description of the main contribution is likely to be more helpful for discussion and literature search.

The first paper is Chen's classic ER paper [3] as Fig. 4 shows. (Note that the third part of the CCMR framework is omitted because the paper did not

Conceptual Modeling Context				
Intended Purpose: circle one or explain other	DB design, SW development, BP articulation, Domain understanding, Knowledge representation, Other:			
Intended Domain:				
Intended Level of Abstraction:				
Domain of Case Study/Examples:				
Intended Users:				

Conceptual Models/Languages	Contribute or Extend	Evaluate or Compare	Formalize	Philosophical Grounding
Conceptual model(s): indicate CML(s) used				
Conceptual model pattern(s), ideal model(s), seed model(s): indicate CML(s) used				
Conceptual Modeling Language(s): indicate what is modeled: information, events, processes, interaction				
Metamodeling language: to represent other CMLs				

CM Tools and Processes	Contribute or Extend	Evaluate or Compare	Formalize
Conceptual modeling methods/processes:			
Automated tools for CM: validation, simulation, "anti-patterns" check, translation (to lower-level/implementation) languages, reverse engineering (translation to higher-level) languages, mapping from one CM to another for integration/semantics			

Fig. 3. The complete CCMR framework after adjustments

contribute tools or methodological guidance). Figures 5 and 6 provide summaries of the characterizations of the contributions of the nine papers (3+6) by showing an iconified version of the framework and then describing contributions according to its indicated aspects. Primary contributions are marked by filling in the corresponding cells in dark gray; secondary contributions are marked by filling in cells using a cross-hatch pattern.

Conceptual Modeling Context					
Intended Purpose: circle one or explain other	(DB design,) SW development, BP articulation, Domain understanding, Knowledge representation, **Other:**				
Intended Domain:	Generic				
Domain of Case Study/Examples:	Company, employees, projects, parts, suppliers (fairly generic)				
Intended Users:	Database designers/developers				
Conceptual Models/Languages		Contribute or Extend	Evaluate or Compare	Formalize	Philosophical Grounding
Conceptual model(s): indicate CML(s) used					
Conceptual model pattern(s), ideal/ seed model(s), metamodel(s): indicate CML(s) used					
Conceptual Modeling Language(s): indicate what is modeled: information, events, business processes, interaction		Contribute a new CML: **ER Model**		Mathemat- ical relation theory and sets	

(left vertical label: Generic ... Domain-specific)

Fig. 4. Characterization of Chen's ER Paper [3] Using CCMR

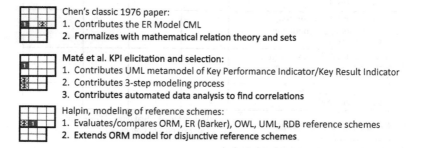

Chen's classic 1976 paper:
1. Contributes the ER Model CML
2. **Formalizes with mathematical relation theory and sets**

Maté et al. KPI elicitation and selection:
1. Contributes UML metamodel of Key Performance Indicator/Key Result Indicator
2. Contributes 3-step modeling process
3. **Contributes automated data analysis to find correlations**

Halpin, modeling of reference schemes:
1. Evaluates/compares ORM, ER (Barker), OWL, UML, RDB reference schemes
2. **Extends ORM model for disjunctive reference schemes**

Fig. 5. Summary characterizations of Chen [3], Maté et al. [25], and Halpin [15]

We were able to characterize all nine papers, demonstrating coverage of the framework. All fields in the first column of part 2 of the framework were used. Every column of parts 2 and 3 was used at least once, although for some fields it was only through secondary contributions, and every row in parts 2 and 3

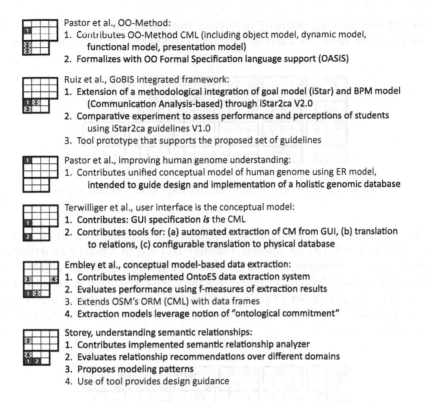

Pastor et al., OO-Method:
1. Contributes OO-Method CML (including object model, dynamic model,
        functional model, presentation model)
2. Formalizes with OO Formal Specification language support (OASIS)

Ruiz et al., GoBIS integrated framework:
1. Extension of a methodological integration of goal model (iStar) and BPM model
        (Communication Analysis-based) through iStar2ca V2.0
2. Comparative experiment to assess performance and perceptions of students
        using iStar2ca guidelines V1.0
3. Tool prototype that supports the proposed set of guidelines

Pastor et al., improving human genome understanding:
1. Contributes unified conceptual model of human genome using ER model,
        intended to guide design and implementation of a holistic genomic database

Terwilliger et al., user interface is the conceptual model:
1. Contributes: GUI specification *is* the CML
2. Contributes tools for: (a) automated extraction of CM from GUI, (b) translation
        to relations, (c) configurable translation to physical database

Embley et al., conceptual model-based data extraction:
1. Contributes implemented OntoES data extraction system
2. Evaluates performance using f-measures of extraction results
3. Extends OSM's ORM (CML) with data frames
4. Extraction models leverage notion of "ontological commitment"

Storey, understanding semantic relationships:
1. Contributes implemented semantic relationship analyzer
2. Evaluates relationship recommendations over different domains
3. Proposes modeling patterns
4. Use of tool provides design guidance

Fig. 6. Summary characterizations of Pastor et al. [29], Ruiz et al. [34], Pastor et al. [30], Terwilliger et al. [40], Embley et al. [7], and Storey [37]

was used at least once. Overall, this exercise provided an initial indication of usability, a very preliminary indication that it can be used consistently for the first three papers (albeit with differences between the minimalist/maximalist approach), an initial indication of coverage, and an indication of the utility of the fields in the framework.

4.2   Experience of Others Using the CCMR Framework

We organized two interactive workshops where CM experts tried our framework.

The first was at the ER2018 Conference [4], where 14 conference attendees selected a paper they had (co)authored and presented their characterization to the group. We offer the following anecdotal observations. All participants were able to complete the task and present to the group. No one gave up, as far as we were able to observe. Initially, some of the participants used the "maximalist" approach. But, with some prompting, all were able to identify the contribution they considered the most significant.

Papers evaluated by ER2018 workshop participants fit the patterns shown in Fig. 7 (some of which were repeated multiple times by different participants or for different papers). Figure 7 only gives the thumbnail of the actual characterization. Each field was filled in with textual descriptions of contributions.

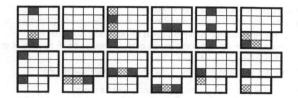

Fig. 7. Variety of patterns from the first workshop participants

At another research seminar, we repeated the exercise with approximately 24 experts and received 19 different characterizations of research contributions. Figure 8 shows a representative sample of the resulting evaluation patterns. The pattern in the upper-left corner represents the characterization of an entire book. The use of a large number of cells seems appropriate given the range of material in the book. Two others of the 19 evaluations used most of the cells in a "maximalist" approach.

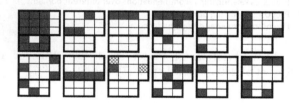

Fig. 8. Sample of patterns from research seminar participants

Through discussions and feedback from our colleagues, we were encouraged to: provide clear definitions for terms in the framework, introduce an additional level in part 2 for metamodels (of conceptual modeling languages), provide an MDA-oriented perspective where different levels of abstraction (e.g. CIM/PIM/PSM) are considered, and provide methodological guidance for using the framework. With the exception of metamodels, the framework provided reasonable coverage. The utility of the fields was demonstrated with significant use of most rows and columns in the framework. The *Philosophical Grounding* column tended to be used the least, but it was used repeatedly.

4.3 Assessing the Consistency of CCMR and Attempting to Scale Characterization

The final row of Table 1 summarizes our last assessment of CCMR. We selected 10 papers at random from the ER2018 Conference [12, 14, 18, 21–23, 27, 35, 36, 43].

We wanted to find out whether the four of us—with diverse backgrounds in conceptual modeling—could characterize these papers and do so consistently. For this evaluation, we used the CCMR framework shown in Fig. 3 and used only the paper titles, abstracts, and conclusions.[2]

The first part of the CCMR framework was problematic. The intended purpose was filled in a diverse manner. One of us described the intended purpose of the paper. Some of us attempted to describe the (apparent) purpose of the conceptual modeling that was being considered in the paper. We used the "Other" choice (for *Intended Purpose*) an average of 3.2 times per paper (out of 4 reviews). Sometimes, we used basically the same intended purpose but at different levels of detail. For example, one or two of us chose "Business process modeling" while one or two chose "Process extraction," which could be considered a subfield of business process modeling. The *Intended Domain* field was filled in a diverse manner for half of the papers. For the *Intended Level of Abstraction* field, there was a suggested controlled vocabulary: CIM (computation-independent model), PIM (platform-independent model), and PSM (platform-specific model) from the model-driven architecture (MDA) standard. One of us did not use that vocabulary; three of us selected values in diverse ways. Only one paper was described the same way by the three of us who used this vocabulary.

In parts 2 and 3, we exhibited strong consistency in the use of the columns. For approximately half of the papers, one of us (alone) indicated something in the *Evaluate or Compare* column: perhaps attributable to listing a secondary contribution (the "maximalist" approach). Our use of the rows in these two parts exhibited several interesting patterns; each occurred in approximately half of the papers characterized. A *method/tool* split occurred when some of us described a paper as contributing a method and the others, an automated tool. This is likely because a new tool is used in a method; a new method may have one or more tools. Also, using only the abstract and conclusions to characterize a paper made it difficult to discern if the paper was primarily contributing a method, a tool, or both. A similar pattern was the *representation/tool-or-method* split, where some of us described the paper as contributing a new representation (in the form of a new CML or CM pattern) whereas others described the paper as contributing a new method or tool (using the representation).

The following are some examples of these differences. When evaluating the paper of Ishikawa et al. [18], the excerpt in Fig. 9 from our combined reviews shows R2/R3 vs. R4 exhibiting a method/tool split and R1 vs. R2/R3/R4 exhibiting a representation/method-or-tool split.

As another example, the excerpt in Fig. 10 of our combined reviews of the paper by Leoni et al. [21] shows a representation/method-or-tool split, with Ra/Rb showing a new representation and Rb/Rc/Rd showing a new tool. There is also consistent use of the columns with every reviewer using the *Contribute*

---

[2] Note that our characterizations of these and the other 3 + 6 papers have not been vetted by the original authors of the research work. We, and not the original authors, are solely responsible for these characterizations.

Conceptual Models/Languages	Contribute or Extend
Conceptual model:	R1: MLQ framework
Conceptual model pattern, etc.:	
Conceptual Modeling Language:	
Metamodeling language:	
CM Tools and Processes	**Contribute or Extend**
Conceptual modeling methods/processes:	R2: MLQ framework for assessing the quality of ML components & ML-based systems R3: Framework for quality assessment of ML systems
Automated tools for CM:	R4: MLQ (ML quality) framework for assessing quality of ML components and ML-based systems

Fig. 9. Excerpt of the authors' combined reviews of Ishikawa et al. [18]

or Extend and *Formalize* columns. Three of four reviewers used the *Evaluate or Compare* column.

	Contribute or Extend	Evaluate or Compare	Formalize
CM:			
CM pattern:	Ra: Presented "technique"	Ra: Real world examples	Ra: Petri net-based process model
CML:	Rb: New rep. for process models (?) (Petri-net based) more expressive?		Rb: Formal def'n of models and their soundness
Metamodel.:			
	Contribute or Extend	**Evaluate or Compare**	**Formalize**
CM methods /processes:		Rc: Experiments on real-life reported	Rc: Holistic approach to verify the end-to-end soundness of a Petri net-based process model, enriched with case data and decisions
Automated tools:	Rb: Tool to translate Petri net to colored Petri net to validate soundness Rc: Tool that verifies soundness by translating the input into a colored Petri net with bounded color sets Rd: Method and tool to verify end-to-end soundness of Petri net-based process model enriched with case data & decisions		

Fig. 10. Excerpt of the authors' combined reviews of de Leoni et al. [21]

As a final example, when reviewing Santos et al. [36], there was perfect consistency among the four reviewers as Fig. 11 shows. (There were no entries in the *Formalize* or *Philosophical Grounding* columns).

The first part of the CCMR framework, the *Conceptual Modeling Context* definitely requires some modification for consistent use. The *Intended Purpose* field was inspired by our early review of conceptual modeling definitions, as Fig. 1 shows. Thus, it is not particularly appropriate for describing conceptual modeling research. The *Intended Level of Abstraction* field would likely benefit from defining additional controlled vocabularies for various contributing fields to conceptual modeling (e.g. MDA uses CIM/PIM/PSM; ontology could use *foundational/reference*, *upper*, and *domain*; database could use *conceptual*, *logical*, and *physical*). The *Domain of Case Study/Examples* field is unlikely to be filled in based only on the title, abstract, and conclusions of a paper.

	Contribute or Extend	Evaluate or Compare
CM:		
CM pattern:		
CML:	Rw: Alt. syntax for KAOS Rx: New notation for KAOS Ry: Syntax of KAOS Rz: Improve KAOS syntax	Rw: Evaluate new & original syntax Rx: Compare symbols Ry: Empirical analysis Rz: Compare old & new syntax—user test
Metamodel.:		
	Contribute or Extend	Evaluate or Compare
CM methods/processes:		
Automated tools:		

Fig. 11. Excerpt of the authors' combined reviews of Santos et al. [36]

For CCMR parts 2 and 3, we are cautiously optimistic. The various activities involved in research (as reflected in the major contributions), namely *Contribute or Extend, Evaluate or Compare, Formalize,* and (Provide) *Philosophical Grounding* were used in a consistent manner and offered major coverage of the field. For the rows in part 2, the *CM:CMPattern:CML:Metamodel for CML* spectrum is familiar to most researchers. It is often quite easy to describe a contribution as being in one of these areas. However, there are uses of these terms that blend across the levels of this spectrum. Still, this spectrum provides value. In the third part of CCMR, the description of methods or tools is very important; many papers were described as contributing one or both. The method/tool split in our evaluation of papers from ER may derive primarily from our use of (only) the title, abstract, and conclusions which, in general, may not be an effective way to characterize papers. This is the problem of classifying any scholarly work: how familiar does a librarian or other professional need to be with the work in order to characterize it correctly? However, this approach does give an effective starting point.

5   Discussion and Related Work

Our work seeks to define a knowledge structure that can be used to characterize and search the conceptual modeling literature. It may also provide a basis to compare existing bodies of work or help to articulate the contribution of various disciplines to the field.

CCMR comprises a set of metadata fields[3] (part 1) followed by a two-dimensional knowledge structure where each field can be filled with text (parts 2 and 3). One or more controlled vocabularies or taxonomies (from which to choose values) could be useful for the fields in part 1. Such a vocabulary may exist or be synthesized from the literature (e.g. lists of relevant topics from CM conference calls for papers). The fields in CCMR parts 2 and 3 are not

---

[3] We use the term *metadata fields* here as used in the digital library field: metadata describes the library item of interest. Typical metadata fields include such items as *author* and *subject*.

intended to be mutually exclusive; a paper may make several significant contributions. Reasonable independence of the columns (and rows) would be helpful because characterizations are likely to be more precise and thus more useful for characterizing papers and searching the literature. The *representation/tool-or-method* and *tool/method* splits do not necessarily reflect a misunderstanding of the row titles. Conceptual modeling experts undoubtedly understand the difference between a new representation scheme, a new method, or a new automated tool. Our analysis primarily indicates that it may be difficult to pinpoint the specific, significant contribution based only on the title, abstract, and conclusion of a paper—specifically for a topic unfamiliar to the reviewer. Overall, our assessment based on the various evaluations is that the CCMR framework is easy to use and exhibits very good coverage of the field.

In terms of related work, other efforts have tried to characterize CM, and this work has been ongoing for nearly four decades. For example, issues related to conceptual modeling from three reference disciplines is found in Brodie et al. [2]. Teorey et al. distinguish conceptual-versus logical-models [39]. Storey et al. provide a brief history and attempt to extract emerging research themes [38]. Thalheim argues that even the distinction between "model" and "conceptual model" is not clear [42]. These and other similar efforts are valuable and cover aspects that are significant in the conceptual modeling domain, but this coverage is partial and it neither allows delimiting in a general way the kind of CM research a paper involves nor comparing different papers in a precise way. In contrast, our proposed CCMR framework consists of a knowledge structure that provides a holistic perspective intended to succinctly characterize research contributions and facilitate literature searches.

More broadly, there is a significant amount of related work with respect to providing frameworks to characterize fields of study in computer science, information systems, and related disciplines. In some cases, broad frameworks explain a field of study and give guidance to researchers on how to go about the various research activities. Examples include movements toward design science [16,24,45] and evidence-based software engineering [19,20,32,33]. In other cases, frameworks are intended to provide a taxonomy for classifying work done in a field (e.g. [46,47]). Our approach fits somewhere between these two points, and is customized to the field of conceptual modeling.

The most distinctive aspect of our approach comes from the particularities of our working domain, namely, conceptual modeling research. We, therefore, focus on research that is strongly related to the process of conceptualizing and its associated results. For example, the analogous approach of March and Smith [24] states a similar problem, but for a different domain. They propose a research framework in information technology (IT). In their case, research in IT must address the design tasks faced by practitioners. IT is technology used to acquire and process information in support of human purposes.

In contrast, we are interested in research in conceptual modeling, so we must address how conceptualizations are faced by modelers, using CMLs to create CMs. This is why, even if the main goals are shared, the proposed dimensions are different, because they are adapted to the respective working domains. Considering the topic of a relevant research paper (in terms of conceptual modeling context, languages, tools, and processes), March and Smith [24] categorize the research outputs (constructs, model, method, instantiation). They identify the research activities (build, evaluate, theorize, justify) that are similar to the horizontal dimensions that we propose in Figs. 2 and 3.

These dimensions also have analogies in the framework of Wieringa et al. who propose classification and evaluation criteria for requirements engineering papers [46]. Under the claim that in requirements engineering much of what is called research is really design, they emphasize that while design produces an artifact, research produces new knowledge. Their classification scheme uses three top level aspects: research activities, design, and others. With a similar goal but in a different context (conceptual modeling research), our work proposes specific dimensions that focus on how to characterize the context for the conceptual modeling that is under consideration in a given paper, and the various types of research contributions that can be made in this field.

Wieringa extends that framework for design science research in terms of research goals [45], where design, mathematical analysis and empirical investigation correspond somewhat to our "contribute or extend," "formalize" and "evaluate or compare" dimensions. Our "philosophical grounding" dimension is additional evidence of the particularity of the CM domain: conceptualizing is strongly connected to the work on foundational ontologies; therefore this aspect must be explicit when characterizing research in conceptual modeling.

At a narrower scope, some frameworks describe a particular area succinctly and clearly in a way that helps other researchers position their work. An example is Flynn's description of approaches to computer architecture that included so-called SISD, SIMD, and MIMD types [9]. Research in computer organization and architecture since that point has generally accepted and used these labels.

Survey research also contributes considerably to the understanding of a field of interest by comparing specific primary research projects within the field. Well-known exemplars in conceptual modeling include surveys by Hull and King [17] and Peckham and Maryanski [31]. Batini et al. summarize approaches to view and schema integration [1]. A survey naturally requires the creation of a framework for comparison, but the scope of the framework is generally tailored to the immediate needs of the survey, and so is narrower than the kind of framework we propose. However, the CCMR framework should be useful for future researchers performing surveys within conceptual modeling.

6   Conclusion

This paper has presented and applied a framework for characterizing conceptual modeling research, with the results showing that it is, indeed, possible to provide a common way for researchers to characterize their work.

Future work will continue to evolve the CCMR framework by providing a glossary of (multiple versions of) standardized terminology, conducting more in-depth evaluations of the framework, and elaborating the labels for all parts of the framework with respect to their scope and intent. We also intend to develop guidelines for using the framework and to continue our evaluation and improvement of CCMR.

If the framework shows evidence of being a relatively complete, consistent, and reasonably stable way to characterize the field, we (or others) could consider providing tools to support the characterization of papers, search for similar papers, and so forth, which would be especially useful for scholars submitting their work for peer review. Finally, if the framework is deemed to be a relatively complete characterization of the field, we (or others) could provide a systematic review of (portions of) the literature using the CCMR framework as a guide.

Acknowledgments. We thank the participants of the interactive workshop at ER2018 and other research seminar participants who shared their characterizations of CM research papers using CCMR. We also thank Roel Wieringa for his comments on an earlier version of this paper. This work was supported in part by Brigham Young University, Georgia State University, and the Universitat Politècnica de València.

References

1. Batini, C., Lenzerini, M., Navathe, S.B.: A comparative analysis of methodologies for database schema integration. ACM Comput. Surv. **18**(4), 323–364 (1986)
2. Brodie, M., Mylopoulos, J., Schmidt, J. (eds.): On Conceptual Modelling, Perspectives from Artificial Intelligence, Databases, and Programming Languages. Topics in Information Systems. Springer, New York (1984). https://doi.org/10.1007/978-1-4612-5196-5
3. Chen, P.: The entity-relationship model–toward a unified view of data. ACM Trans. Database Syst. **1**(1), 9–36 (1976)
4. Delcambre, L.M.L., Liddle, S.W., Pastor, O., Storey, V.C.: Characterizing conceptual modeling workshop call for participation (2018). http://conceptualmodeling.org/er2018/ccm.pdf
5. Delcambre, L.M.L., Liddle, S.W., Pastor, O., Storey, V.C.: A reference framework for conceptual modeling. In: Trujillo, J.C., et al. (eds.) ER 2018. LNCS, vol. 11157, pp. 27–42. Springer, Cham (2018). https://doi.org/10.1007/978-3-030-00847-5_4
6. Delcambre, L.M.L., Liddle, S.W., Pastor, O., Storey, V.C.: A reference framework for conceptual modeling: focusing on conceptual modeling research. Technical report (2019). https://www.researchgate.net/publication/331653768
7. Embley, D.W., et al.: Conceptual-model-based data extraction from multiple-record web pages. Data Knowl. Eng. **31**(3), 227–251 (1999)
8. Embley, D., Thalheim, B. (eds.): Handbook of Conceptual Modeling-Theory, Practice, and Research Challenges. Springer, Heidelberg (2011). https://doi.org/10.1007/978-3-642-15865-0
9. Flynn, M.J.: Some computer organizations and their effectiveness. IEEE Trans. Comput. **21**(9), 948–960 (1972)
10. Guarino, N.: Formal ontology and information systems. In: Proceedings of FOIS 1998, pp. 3–15 (1998)
11. Guizzardi, G.: Ontological foundations for structural conceptual models. Ph.D. thesis, University of Twente (2005)

12. Guizzardi, G., Fonseca, C.M., Benevides, A.B., Almcida, J.P.A., Porello, D., Sales, T.P.: Endurant types in ontology-driven conceptual modeling: towards OntoUML 2.0. In: Trujillo, J.C., et al. (eds.) ER 2018. LNCS, vol. 11157, pp. 136–150. Springer, Cham (2018). https://doi.org/10.1007/978-3-030-00847-5_12
13. Guizzardi, G., Herre, H., Wagner, G.: On the general ontological foundations of conceptual modeling. In: Spaccapietra, S., March, S.T., Kambayashi, Y. (eds.) ER 2002. LNCS, vol. 2503, pp. 65–78. Springer, Heidelberg (2002). https://doi.org/10.1007/3-540-45816-6_15
14. Hai, R., Quix, C., Kensche, D.: Nested schema mappings for integrating JSON. In: Trujillo, J.C., et al. (eds.) ER 2018. LNCS, vol. 11157, pp. 397–405. Springer, Cham (2018). https://doi.org/10.1007/978-3-030-00847-5_28
15. Halpin, T.: Modeling of reference schemes. In: Nurcan, S., et al. (eds.) BPMDS/EMMSAD -2013. LNBIP, vol. 147, pp. 308–323. Springer, Heidelberg (2013). https://doi.org/10.1007/978-3-642-38484-4_22
16. Hevner, A.R., March, S.T., Park, J., Ram, S.: Design science in information systems research. MIS Q. **28**(1), 75–105 (2004)
17. Hull, R., King, R.: Semantic database modeling: survey, applications, and research issues. ACM Comput. Surv. **19**(3), 201–260 (1987)
18. Ishikawa, F.: Concepts in quality assessment for machine learning - from test data to arguments. ER 2018. LNCS, vol. 11157, pp. 536–544. Springer, Cham (2018). https://doi.org/10.1007/978-3-030-00847-5_39
19. Kitchenham, B.A., Brereton, P.: A systematic review of systematic review process research in software engineering. Inf. Softw. Technol. **55**(12), 2049–2075 (2013)
20. Kitchenham, B.A., Dybå, T., Jørgensen, M.: Evidence-based software engineering. In: 26th International Conference on Software Engineering (ICSE 2004), 23–28 May 2004, Edinburgh, United Kingdom, pp. 273–281 (2004)
21. de Leoni, M., Felli, P., Montali, M.: A holistic approach for soundness verification of decision-aware process models. In: Trujillo, J.C., et al. (eds.) ER 2018. LNCS, vol. 11157, pp. 219–235. Springer, Cham (2018). https://doi.org/10.1007/978-3-030-00847-5_17
22. Lin, L., Lin, C., Lai, Y.: Realtime event summarization from tweets with inconsistency detection. In: Trujillo, J.C., et al. (eds.) ER 2018. LNCS, vol. 11157, pp. 555–570. Springer, Cham (2018). https://doi.org/10.1007/978-3-030-00847-5_41
23. Maass, W., Shcherbatyi, I.: Inductive discovery by machine learning for identification of structural models. ER 2018. LNCS, vol. 11157, pp. 545–552. Springer, Cham (2018). https://doi.org/10.1007/978-3-030-00847-5_40
24. March, S.T., Smith, G.F.: Design and natural science research on information technology. Decis. Support Syst. **15**(4), 251–266 (1995)
25. Maté, A., Trujillo, J., Mylopoulos, J.: Key performance indicator elicitation and selection through conceptual modelling. In: Comyn-Wattiau, I., Tanaka, K., Song, I.-Y., Yamamoto, S., Saeki, M. (eds.) ER 2016. LNCS, vol. 9974, pp. 73–80. Springer, Cham (2016). https://doi.org/10.1007/978-3-319-46397-1_6
26. Mylopoulos, J.: Conceptual modeling and Telos. conceptual modelling. In: Databases and CASE: An Integrated View of Information Systems Development, pp. 49–68. Wiley, New York, NY (1992)
27. Nguyen, H., Dumas, M., La Rosa, M., ter Hofstede, A.H.M.: Multi-perspective comparison of business process variants based on event logs. In: Trujillo, J.C., et al. (eds.) ER 2018. LNCS, vol. 11157, pp. 449–459. Springer, Cham (2018). https://doi.org/10.1007/978-3-030-00847-5_32
28. Olivé, A.: Conceptual Modeling of Information Systems. Springer, Berlin (2007). https://doi.org/10.1007/978-3-540-39390-0

29. Pastor, O., Gómez, J., Insfrán, E., Pelechano, V.: The OO-method approach for information systems modeling: from object-oriented conceptual modeling to automated programming. Inf. Syst. **26**(7), 507–534 (2001)

30. Pastor, O., Levin, A.M., Casamayor, J.C., Celma, M., van der Kroon, M.: A conceptual modeling approach to improve human genome understanding. In: Embley, D., Thalheim, B. (eds.) Handbook of Conceptual Modeling - Theory, Practice, and Research Challenges, pp. 517–541. Springer, Heidelberg (2011). https://doi.org/10.1007/978-3-642-15865-0_16

31. Peckham, J., Maryanski, F.J.: Semantic data models. ACM Comput. Surv. **20**(3), 153–189 (1988)

32. Petersen, K., Feldt, R., Mujtaba, S., Mattsson, M.: Systematic mapping studies in software engineering. In: 12th International Conference on Evaluation and Assessment in Software Engineering, EASE 2008, 26–27 June 2008. University of Bari, Italy (2008)

33. Petersen, K., Vakkalanka, S., Kuzniarz, L.: Guidelines for conducting systematic mapping studies in software engineering: an update. Inf. Softw. Technol. **64**, 1–18 (2015)

34. Ruiz, M., Costal, D., España, S., Franch, X., Pastor, O.: GoBIS: an integrated framework to analyse the goal and business process perspectives in information systems. Inf. Syst. **53**, 330–345 (2015)

35. Sales, T.P., Baião, F., Guizzardi, G., Almeida, J.P.A., Guarino, N., Mylopoulos, J.: The common ontology of value and risk. In: Trujillo, J.C., et al. (eds.) ER 2018. LNCS, vol. 11157, pp. 121–135. Springer, Cham (2018). https://doi.org/10.1007/978-3-030-00847-5_11

36. Santos, M., Gralha, C., Goulão, M., Araújo, J.: Increasing the semantic transparency of the KAOS goal model concrete syntax. In: Trujillo, J.C., et al. (eds.) ER 2018. LNCS, vol. 11157, pp. 424–439. Springer, Cham (2018). https://doi.org/10.1007/978-3-030-00847-5_30

37. Storey, V.C.: Understanding semantic relationships. VLDB J. **2**(4), 455–488 (1993)

38. Storey, V.C., Trujillo, J., Liddle, S.W.: Research on conceptual modeling: themes, topics, and introduction to the special issue. Data Knowl. Eng. **98**, 1–7 (2015)

39. Teorey, T.J., Yang, D., Fry, J.P.: A logical design methodology for relational databases using the extended entity-relationship model. ACM Comput. Surv. **18**(2), 197–222 (1986)

40. Terwilliger, J.F., Delcambre, L.M.L., Logan, J.: The user interface is the conceptual model. In: Embley, D.W., Olivé, A., Ram, S. (eds.) ER 2006. LNCS, vol. 4215, pp. 424–436. Springer, Heidelberg (2006). https://doi.org/10.1007/11901181_32

41. Thalheim, B.: The science and art of conceptual modelling. Trans. Large-Scale Data Knowl.-Centered Syst. **6**, 76–105 (2012)

42. Thalheim, B.: Conceptual model notions–a matter of controversy: conceptual modelling and its Lacunas. Enterp. Modell. Inf. Syst. Architect. **13**, 9–27 (2018)

43. Tsoury, A., Soffer, P., Reinhartz-Berger, I.: A conceptual framework for supporting deep exploration of business process behavior. In: Trujillo, J.C., et al. (eds.) ER 2018. LNCS, vol. 11157, pp. 58–71. Springer, Cham (2018). https://doi.org/10.1007/978-3-030-00847-5_6

44. Wand, Y., Weber, R.: On the deep structure of information systems. Inf. Syst. J. **5**(3), 203–223 (1995)

45. Wieringa, R.J.: Design Science Methodology for Information Systems and Software Engineering. Springer, Heidelberg (2014). https://doi.org/10.1007/978-3-662-43839-8

46. Wieringa, R.J., Maiden, N.A.M., Mead, N.R., Rolland, C.: Requirements engineering paper classification and evaluation criteria: a proposal and a discussion. Requir. Eng. **11**(1), 102–107 (2006)
47. Zave, P.: Classification of research efforts in requirements engineering. ACM Comput. Surv. **29**(4), 315–321 (1997)

MapSDI: A Scaled-Up Semantic Data Integration Framework for Knowledge Graph Creation

Samaneh Jozashoori[1,2(✉)] and Maria-Esther Vidal[1,2]

[1] L3S Research Center, Leibniz University of Hannover, Hanover, Germany
`jozashoori@l3s.de`
[2] TIB Leibniz Information Center for Science and Technology, Hanover, Germany
`maria.vidal@tib.eu`

Abstract. Semantic web technologies have significantly contributed with effective solutions for the problems of data integration and knowledge graph creation. However, with the rapid growth of big data in diverse domains, different interoperability issues still demand to be addressed, being scalability one of the main challenges. In this paper, we address the problem of knowledge graph creation at scale and provide MapSDI, a mapping rule-based framework for optimizing semantic data integration into knowledge graphs. MapSDI allows for the semantic enrichment of large-sized, heterogeneous, and potentially low-quality data efficiently. The input of MapSDI is a set of data sources and mapping rules being generated by a mapping language such as RML. First, MapSDI pre-processes the sources based on semantic information extracted from mapping rules, by performing basic database operators; it projects out required attributes, eliminates duplicates, and selects relevant entries. All these operators are defined based on the knowledge encoded by the mapping rules which will be then used by the semantification engine (or RDFizer) to produce a knowledge graph. We have empirically studied the impact of MapSDI on existing RDFizers, and observed that knowledge graph creation time can be reduced on average in one order of magnitude. It is also shown, theoretically, that the sources and rules transformations provided by MapSDI are data-lossless.

Keywords: Knowledge graph creation · Semantic data integration · Transformation rules · Data integration system

1 Introduction

Knowledge graph creation as a method for knowledge representation has been through a significant progress with the development of semantic web technologies in recent years. The semantic web perspective of making the data and information more accessible to machines [1] by providing a unified view of data residing in different sources with heterogeneous structures, had made semantic web technologies desirable candidates to be used in semantic data integration systems

© Springer Nature Switzerland AG 2019
H. Panetto et al. (Eds.): OTM 2019, LNCS 11877, pp. 58–75, 2019.
https://doi.org/10.1007/978-3-030-33246-4_4

and knowledge graph creation. Coordinately, with the rapid growth of available big data in different domains, semantic data integration systems are required to be scaled up in order to transfer big data into an actionable knowledge represented in knowledge graphs. RDF[1] or Resource Description Framework, as a standard model on the web for describing the metadata of resources, is a common data model to create linked data and knowledge graphs. Nevertheless, in many domains such as biomedicine and biology, a massive amount of generated big data is not available in this format. To create a knowledge graph from non-RDF big data sources, it is required to define mapping rules for data model transformation along with semantic data integration. However, to scale up to big data, RDFizers need to be empowered with efficient processes for removing duplicates, and projecting and selecting only relevant attributes and data.

Problem and Objective: We tackle the problem of semantic big data integration into a knowledge graph and focus on scalability issues present in existing mapping rule-based RDFizers. As proof of concept, we concentrate on RML [5], a mapping language that expresses mappings from hierarchical sources into a RDF graph, and the RMLmapper and SDM-RDFizer as engines for RML triple maps. We show how dominant dimensions of big data, e.g., volume, variety, and veracity, negatively impact on the performance of these two engines and prevent them from scaling up to large datasets composed of duplicated data.

Our Proposed Approach: The main idea of this article is to present MapSDI, a framework for transforming big data into a knowledge graph. As traditional frameworks for knowledge graph creation, MapSDI resorts to semantification engines for creating RDF triples; however, to minimize the impact of big data dimensions, MapSDI performs transformations in the input datasets to eliminate irrelevant attributes and duplicates. MapSDI is able to exploit knowledge encoded in the triple maps to determine which attributes and data are required. It also falls back on well-known properties of the relational algebra operators, e.g., pushing down of the projections and selections, in order to pre-process the input datasets before the mappings are executed. First, by projecting out the attributes that are mentioned in a mapping rule, duplicates are eliminated and the size of the input data is reduced. Similarly, the projection of attributes positively impacts on the performance of joins between triple maps. We have empirically studied the performance of MapSDI framework on a testbed of real-world datasets. Observed results suggest that MapSDI framework is able to empower the performance of the studied RDFizers, reducing the semantification time by up to one order of magnitude (on average). While, we show theoretically that mentioned pre-processing of input datasets does not lead to any data lossness in the output i.e., generated knowledge graph remains the same.

Contributions: The main contribution of this work is MapSDI, a framework able to pre-process big datasets with the aim of empowering scalability of existing RDFizers. Another important contribution represents both theoretical and empirical evaluation of the effect of the MapSDI framework on the tasks of

---

[1] https://www.w3.org/RDF/.

knowledge graph creation; the testbeds are defined over real-world datasets of genomic data and show the benefits of the pre-processing step in the MapSDI framework.

This article is structured as follows: Sect. 2 motivates the problem of semantic data integration over a set of biomedical datasets, Sect. 3 describes the MapSDI framework, the main transformation rules and their correctness, and Sect. 4 reports on the results of the empirical study. Related work is presented in Sect. 5, and finally, Sect. 6 concludes and give insights for future work.

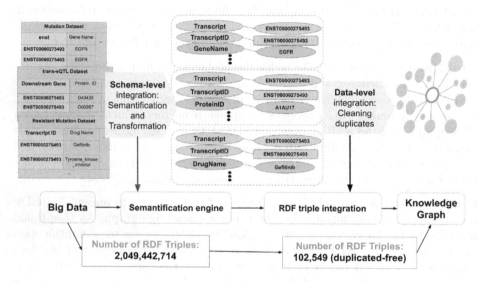

Fig. 1. Motivating example. A traditional framework where datasets characterized by big data dominant dimensions, i.e., volume, variety, and veracity, are semantically enriched and integrated into a knowledge graph. A semantification engine performs the schema-level integration by executing mapping rules, e.g., RML triple maps. Because data can be duplicated across the input datasets, a large number of RDF triples can be generated, e.g., 2,049,442,714 RDF triples. However, when duplicates are removed and cleaning techniques are performed, only 102,549 RDF triples (duplicated-free) are included in the knowledge graph.

2   Motivating Example

We motivate our work with a traditional pipeline for transforming three datasets into instances of a knowledge graph. The datasets contain information about mutations of genes, downstream genes, and drug resistances caused by mutations. These files are composed of up to 39 attributes (the mutation dataset), and their sizes are 186.4 MB, 71.9 GB, and 559 KB, respectively. The semantification of these datasets just for the concept transcript is performed using three RML triple maps. These triple maps consider only the attribute that represents *transcript* using a different name in each dataset (enst, downstream gene, transcript id). This process ends up producing 2,049,442,714 RDF triples. However, because of overlaps across the three files, a large number of duplicates are generated, being reduced the output to only 102,549 duplicate-free RDF triples when cleaning and duplicate elimination are performed. Figure 1 illustrates this pipeline; it receives the three datasets and outputs the RDF triples to be included in the knowledge graph. As observed, in this real-world example, the pipeline for this semantic integration task is performed via two separated steps including: (I) **Schema-level integration**: Ontology based data semantification and mapping rule-based data transformations. (II) **Data-level integration**: Redundancy elimination and cleaning. To explain the situation reported in this example, let us consider the meaning of these three datasets. A *transcript* refers to a ribonucleic acid via which a gene is expressed; it is used to synthesize a protein [11]. As it can be seen in Fig. 1, *transcript* as a concept, can be represented with different labels in various databases which means that it cannot be distinguished and treated as the same concept unless being semantified according to the unified schema. Therefore, the first step of integration in the framework is to unify all the concept representations residing in different datasets by defining RML triple maps while transforming the data into RDF. The data semantification allows for also detecting duplicated data that were not recognizable before. Consequently, in the second step, the redundant data that are now represented as RDF triples are eliminated. It should be noted that the overall number of generated triples from different sources are 16,445 times the number of non-redundant triples which means that there is a considerable amount of duplicated data that could not be detected in the raw files. Considering the fact that similarity-based comparisons between RDF triples are more expensive than between the relational data model, specifically in case of having huge amount of data, leaves room to think about providing a more efficient and low-cost approach to create knowledge graphs. In this paper, we address the problem of semantic data integration motivated in this example, and present MapSDI, a framework able to pre-process input datasets and avoid the generation of duplicated RDF triples. MapSDI is able to extract from the RML triple maps the knowledge required to pre-process the input datasets by means of the execution of basis relational algebra operations like the projection of attributes. Albeit simple, the transformations executed by MapSDI enable to project out only attributes that are utilized in the three triple maps, allowing the RDFizer to produce 102,549 duplicate-free RDF triples.

3 The MapSDI Framework

The MapSDI framework relies on a data integration system DIS_G which enables the transformation and integration of heterogeneous data in a knowledge graph G. The data integration system $DIS_G = \langle O, S, M \rangle$ is defined in terms of three components i.e., O a unified schema or ontology, S a set of data sources, and M a set of mapping rules [10].

- The unified schema O is defined as a triple, $O = (C, P, Axioms)$ where C and P correspond to the signature of O and represent the classes and properties of O. The set $Axioms$ denotes a collection of axioms staying the main characteristics of the properties of O; these asserted statements implicitly comprise knowledge describing the modeled universe of discourse.
- The data sources of DIS_G are represented by means of the set of signatures $S = \langle S_1^{A_1}, \ldots, S_n^{A_n} \rangle$ where each symbol S_j stands for a data source, e.g., a file or relational table, and A_j corresponds to the attributes of S_j:
- The transformation of the data collected from the sources in S into instances of the knowledge graph G is expressed using the Global As View paradigm (GAV), i.e., the classes and properties in O are described in terms of the sources S. The set M comprises mapping rules r_i where a class c_j is described as a *conjunctive query* on the sources and attributes in S.

$$r_i: \quad \underbrace{c_j(X, \overline{X})}_{\text{Head of the Rule}} \quad : - \underbrace{S_1(\overline{X_1}), S_2(\overline{X_2}), \ldots, S_m(\overline{X_m})}_{\text{Body of the Rule}}$$

- c_j is a class in C, X is a variable, and $\overline{X}$ is a set of pairs $(P_{i,j}, X_{i,j})$ where $P_{i,j}$ is a property of C, i.e., c_j is the domain of $P_{i,j}$, and $X_{i,j}$ is a variable. The variables $X_{i,j}$ and X appear all in the body of the rule, i.e., r_i is a *safe conjunctive rule*.
- The predicate $S_z(\overline{X_z})$ represents a source S_z in S and $\overline{X_z}$ is a set of pairs $(a_{i,z}, X_{i,z})$ where $X_{i,z}$ is a variable and $att_{i,z}$ is an attribute of S_z, i.e., $S_z^{A_z}$ and $att_{i,z}$ belong to S and A_z, respectively.

Given a data integration system $DIS_G = \langle O, S, M \rangle$, the evaluation of each of the rules r_i in M according to the data in the sources in S, generates the RDF knowledge graph G. The evaluation of r_i, $eval(r_i, \mu)$, is defined over a map μ of the variables in r_i to values in the sources in the body of r_i. A map μ corresponds to a function from variables V in the rules in M to the set D which denotes the union of all the data items in the data sources in S, i.e., $\mu : V \to D$.

Given a source predicate $S_z(\overline{X_z})$ in the body of a rule r_i, the evaluation of $S_z(\overline{X_z})$ on μ, $eval(S_z(\overline{X_z}), \mu)$, corresponds to a set μ_{S_z} of pairs, such that, for every pair $(att_{i,z}, X_{i,z})$ in $\overline{X_z}$, the following statements hold:

- The pair $(X_{i,z}, \mu(X_{i,z}))$ belongs to μ_{S_z} and
- If $\langle att_{1,z}, \ldots, att_{q,z} \rangle$ are the attributes of S_z in $\overline{X_z}$, then the tuple

$$\langle (att_{1,z}, \mu(X_{1,z})), \ldots, (att_{q,z}, \mu(X_{q,z})) \rangle \text{ belongs to the data extension of } S_z$$

The evaluation of a rule r_i on a map μ, $eval(r_i, \mu)$, corresponds to a set of RDF triples $t = (s\ p\ o)$ defined as follows:

- If the rule r_i is $c_j(X, \overline{X}) : -S_1(\overline{X_1})$ and the pair $(X, \mu(X))$ belongs to μ_{S_1}, then for each $(X_{i,1}, \mu(X_{i,1}))$ in μ_{S_1} and $(P_{i,1}, X_{i,1})$ in $\overline{X}$, the RDF triple $t = (\mu(X)\ P_{i,1}\ \mu(X_{i,1}))$ belongs to $eval(r_i, \mu)$.

– Suppose the rule r_i is $c_j(X, \overline{X}) : -Body$, μ is defined over all the variables of the sources S_Z in $Body$, and the pair $(X, \mu(X))$ belongs to at least one μ_{S_z}. Then for each $(X_{i,z}, \mu(X_{i,z}))$ in μ_{S_z} and $(P_{i,z}, X_{i,z})$ in $\overline{X}$, the RDF triple $t = (\mu(X)\, P_{i,z}\, \mu(X_{i,z}))$ belongs to $eval(r_i, \mu)$.

Given a data integration system $DIS_G = \langle O, S, M \rangle$ the function $RDFize(.)$ maps DIS_G with a knowledge graph G resulting from the evaluation of all the rules in M with the maps μ in the extensions of the sources in S. The result of the function $RDFize(.)$ only dependents on the mapping rules in M and the extensions of the sources in S over which these rules are evaluated. Nevertheless, in presence of data sources characterized with a large number of duplicates, the execution time of the function $RDFize(.)$ can be negatively impacted. In this paper, we tackle the problem of rewriting a data integration system $DIS_G = \langle O, S, M \rangle$ into another data integration system $DIS'_G = \langle O, S', M' \rangle$ whose evaluation produces the same results while the execution time is minimized.

Problem Statement: Given a data integration system $DIS_G = \langle O, S, M \rangle$, the *problem of knowledge graph creation* is defined as the problem of identifying a data integration system $DIS'_G = \langle O, S', M' \rangle$ such that:

– The results of evaluating the two data integration systems is the same, i.e., $RDFize(DIS_G - \langle O, S, M \rangle) = RDFize(DIS'_G - \langle O, S', M' \rangle)$.
– The execution time of the evaluation of $RDFize(DIS'_G = \langle O, S', M' \rangle)$ is *minimal*, i.e., there is no other DIS''_G different from DIS'_G that generates the same RDF knowledge graph G but in a lower execution time.

Proposed Solution: We propose MapSDI, an optimized alternative to traditional semantic data integration pipelines to create knowledge graphs. As it is shown in Fig. 2, MapSDI receives a data integration system $DIS_G = \langle O, S, M \rangle$ as input and generates an RDF knowledge graph that corresponds to the result of evaluating $RDFize(DIS_G = \langle O, S, M \rangle)$. Without lost of generality, MapSDI assumes that the mapping rules in M are represented in a mapping language, e.g., the RDF mapping language RML.

Before evaluating the function $RDFize(.)$, MapSDI applies transformations to the sources in S and the mapping rules in M in order to generate a data integration system $DIS'_G = \langle O, S', M' \rangle$ that corresponds to a solution of the *problem of knowledge graph creation*. MapSDI resorts to transformation rules applied to mapping rules and source depending on the attributes, variables, and sources that compose the mapping rules in M. That is, in a rule r_i, the attributes from the data sources in the $Body$ of r_i are detected, and the corresponding sources in S are transformed in order to have in S' only data sources associated with the attributes utilized in the mapping rules. Accordingly, mapping rules are also rewritten with the aim of reusing the attributes of the sources in S'. By projecting out only the attributes required in the mapping rules, duplicates from the extensions of the sources are removed, avoiding thus, the generation of the same RDF triple multiple times during the evaluation of the function $RDFize(.)$. Since only duplicates in the data sources are removed from the input, the resulting

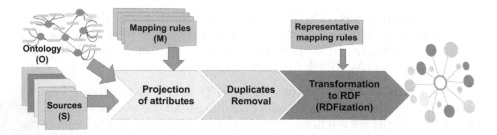

Fig. 2. The MapSDI framework. MapSDI receives as input a data integration system and produces as output RDF triples to be included in a knowledge graph. MapSDI extracts from the mapping rules information related to the attributes that are used from each file. Then, different operations are executed to project out the required attributes; projection eliminates duplicates inside each dataset. Next, datasets comprising equivalent attributes are merged and duplicates are eliminated. The mapping rules are rewritten accordingly in order to access the transformed files, and finally, the mapping rules are executed

knowledge graph remains being the same, while the time of producing duplicated RDF triples is reduced.

3.1 Transformations Performed in the MapSDI Framework

We present the transformation rules applied by the MapSDI framework in order to reduce duplicated data and speed up the execution time of the evaluation of a data integration system. The transformation rules are based on the axioms of the relational algebra [15] and in particular, the ones that stay when the project operator can be pushed down into the relations in a relational algebra

```
<TripleMap>
     rml:logicalSource [ rml:source "/data/gene/GenCode-Uniprot.csv";
     rml:referenceFormulation ql:CSV];
     rr:subjectMap [
          rr:template "http://project-iasis.eu/Gene/{ENSG}";
          rr:class iasis:Gene ];
     rr:predicateObjectMap [
          rr:predicate iasis:geneName;
          rr:objectMap [
               rml:reference "SYMBOL"];
     rr:predicateObjectMap [
          rr:predicate iasis:specieType;
          rr:objectMap [
               rml:reference "SPECIES"];
     rr:predicateObjectMap [
          rr:predicate iasis:uniprotID;
          rr:objectMap [
               rml:reference "ACC"]].
```

Fig. 3. Example of Transformation Rule 1- Projection of Attributes. Only four attributes of a data source are utilized in the RML rule; processing the values of these four attributes conduce to many duplicated RDF triples.

ID	ENSG	ENSGV	SYMBOL	SYMBOLV	ENST	SPECIES	ACC
1	ENSG00000187583	ENSG00000187583.10	PLEKHN1	PLEKHN1-203	ENST00000379410	HUMAN	Q494U1
2	ENSG00000187583	ENSG00000187583.10	PLEKHN1	PLEKHN1-202	ENST00000379409	HUMAN	Q494U1
3	ENSG00000187583	ENSG00000187583.10	PLEKHN1	PLEKHN1-201	ENST00000379407	HUMAN	Q494U1
4	ENSG00000187642	ENSG00000187642.9	PERM1	PERM1-202	ENST00000341290	HUMAN	Q5SV97
5	ENSG00000187642	ENSG00000187642.9	PERM1	PERM1-203	ENST00000433179	HUMAN	Q5SV97
6	ENSG00000131591	ENSG00000131591.17	C1orf159	C1orf159-204	ENST00000379339	HUMAN	Q96HA4
7	ENSG00000131591	ENSG00000131591.17	C1orf159	C1orf159-203	ENST00000379339	HUMAN	Q96HA4
8	ENSG00000131591	ENSG00000131591.17	C1orf159	C1orf159-205	ENST00000379325	HUMAN	Q96HA4
9	ENSG00000131591	ENSG00000131591.17	C1orf159	C1orf159-201	ENST00000421241	HUMAN	Q96HA4

(a) Portion of a Source File about Genes

ID	ENSG	SYMBOL	SPECIES	ACC
1	ENSG00000187583	PLEKHN1	HUMAN	Q494U1
2	ENSG00000187642	PERM1	HUMAN	Q5SV97
3	ENSG00000131591	C1orf159	HUMAN	Q96HA4

(b) Source File After the Transformation Rule 1

Fig. 4. Example of RML Triple Maps. Two RML Triple Maps connected by a join condition on the attribute `Genename`. Due to the number of duplicated values of the attribute `Genename`, the evaluation of the join condition generates a large number of duplicates. The projection of the relevant attributes reduce the number of duplicated values and RDF triples.

expression. Furthermore, MapSDI extracts information from the mapping rules to decide when two or more datasets have equivalent attributes while represented with different attribute labels and must be merged into one file; and in case the merging is conducted, the corresponding rules are also merged.

Transformation Rule 1: Projection of Attributes: A triple map may only use a subset of the attributes of a data source, generating thus high overhead whenever the number of attributes used in the triple map and the number of attributes in the data source differ considerably. To illustrate this situation consider the RML triple map in Fig. 3 whose evaluation produces many duplicates. Additionally, the data source in Fig. 5a comprises eight attributes but only four attributes are used in the rules. The values of the attributes ENSG, SYMBOL, SPECIES, and ACC are repeated, e.g., the rows 1, 2, and 3 have the same values in these attributes, and similarly rows 4 and 5, and 6, 7, 8, and 9, respectively.

```
<TripleMap1>
  a rr:TriplesMap;
  rml:logicalSource [
    rml:source "/home/data/Gene.csv";
    rml:referenceFormulation ql:CSV];
  rr:subjectMap [
    rr:template "http://project-iasis.eu/BioType/{Biotype}";
    rr:class iasis:BioType];
  rr:predicateObjectMap [
    rr:predicate iasis:isRelatedTo;
    rr:objectMap [
      rr:parentTriplesMap <TripleMap2>;
      rr:joinCondition [
        rr:child "Genename";
        rr:parent "Genename";]];].
```

```
<TripleMap2>
  a rr:TriplesMap;
  rml:logicalSource [
    rml:source "/home/data/output/Chromosome.csv";
    rml:referenceFormulation ql:CSV];
  rr:subjectMap [
    rr:template "http://project-iasis.eu/Chromosome/{Chromosome}";
    rr:class iasis:Chromosome].
```

Fig. 5. Example of Transformation Rule 1. Projection of Attributes: (a) RML Triple Map; only four attributes of the file are utilized in the rule; processing the values of these four attributes conduce to the generation of many duplicated RDF triples. (b) A file with information about genes; several values are duplicates across the file. (c) The file resulting of the projection of the attributes utilized in the triple map; the file does not have repeated attributes and the execution of the triple map does not produce duplicated RDF triples

Coincidentally, the evaluation of the triple map in Fig. 3 creates RDF triples from these four attributes and because during the execution of this triple map the data source is blindly traversed, several duplicated RDF triples are generated. *Transformation rule 1* reduces the overhead caused whenever a triple map utilizes only a subset of the attributes of a data source; it pushes down the projection of the triple map object attributes before the triple map is executed. Thus, during the execution of the triple map only three rows are processed and no duplicated RDF triples are generated. In the case reported in Fig. 5, processing the original file in Fig. 5a and the RML triple map (Fig. 3) generate five duplicated RDF triples. Contrary, when file in Fig. 5b is utilized, no duplicates are produced, thus the overhead during knowledge graph creation is considerably reduced. The time savings are reported in Sect. 4.

Transformation Rule 2: Pushing Down Projection into Joins: This rule is applied whenever a join exists between two triple maps r_1 and r_2 defined over data sources with a large number of attributes that are not utilized in r_1 and r_2. To illustrate this case, consider Fig. 4; the triple maps TripleMap1 and TripleMap2 are joined by the join condition highlighted in bold in TripleMap1. When this join is executed on datasets in Figs. 6a and b, 22 duplicated RDF triples are generated. Duplicate generation considerably impacts on the performance of a knowledge graph creation, particularly, whenever duplicates are blindly generated and then, eliminated. To reduce the effect of duplicates during the evaluation of join conditions between two triple maps, MapSDI pushes the projections of the relevant attributes down before the triple maps are executed. As observed in Fig. 7, this transformation considerably reduces the number of matches of the join condition and the resulting RDF triples.

Once the attributes mentioned in the triple maps in Fig. 4 are projected out (files in Figs. 7a and b), the execution of these triples maps still produces RDF triples that are duplicated. However, the number of duplicates is reduced from 22

ID	Gene name	HGNC ID	enst	enstv	ensg	Gene CDS length	Biotype
1	STAT5B	11367	ENST00000293328	ENST00000293328.7	ENSG00000173757	2364	protein_coding
2	STAT5B	11367	ENST00000498674	ENST00000498674.1	ENSG00000173757	2364	protein_coding
3	STAT5B	11367	ENST00000481253	ENST00000481253.2	ENSG00000173757	2364	protein_coding
4	STAT5B	11367	ENST00000468496	ENST00000468496.5	ENSG00000173757	2364	protein_coding
5	STAT5B	11367	ENST00000481517	ENST00000481517.1	ENSG00000173757	2364	protein_coding
6	KRAS	6407	ENST00000256078	ENST00000256078.8	ENSG00000133703	567	protein_coding
7	KRAS	6407	ENST00000557334	ENST00000557334.5	ENSG00000133703	567	protein_coding
8	KRAS	6407	ENST00000311936	ENST00000311936.7	ENSG00000133703	567	protein_coding
9	GAS7	4169	ENST00000437099	ENST00000437099.6	ENSG00000007237	1431	protein_coding

(a) Portion of a Source File about Genes (Outer Source File)

ID	Gene name	enst	Start	End	Chromosome	Sample name
1	STAT5B	ENST00000293328	42199168	42276406	chr17	16857
2	STAT5B	ENST00000498674	42202103	42202953	chr17	S52482
3	STAT5B	ENST00000481253	42207559	42210592	chr17	1148969
4	KRAS	ENST00000256078	25209431	25250803	chr12	CH-LA2
6	KRAS	ENST00000311936	25204789	25250931	chr12	1559296
7	EGFR	ENST00000342916	55019032	55168635	chr7	1479947
8	EGFR	ENST00000485503	55192811	55200802	chr7	1544875
9	GAS7	ENST00000437099	9946894	10059815	chr17	112146

(b) Portion of the Source File about Chromosomes (Inner Source File)

Fig. 6. Example of Transformation Rule 2. Pushing down Projections into a Join: (a) and (b) Files containing data to be considered as the outer and inner data sources of `TripleMap1` (Fig. 4), respectively. Duplicates in the join attribute conduce the generation of 22 duplicated RDF triples

ID	Gene name	Chromosome
1	STAT5B	chr17
2	KRAS	chr12
3	EGFR	chr7
4	GAS7	chr17

ID	Gene name	Biotype
1	STAT5B	protein_coding
2	KRAS	protein_coding
3	GAS7	protein_coding

(a) Projection on Genes　　　　　　(b) Projection on Chromosomes

(iasis:protein_coding, iasis:isRelatedTo, iasis:chr17)

(iasis:protein_coding, iasis:isRelatedTo, iasis:chr12)

(c) RDF triples with reduced duplicates

Fig. 7. Example of Transformation Rule 2. Pushing down Projections into a Join: (a) and (b) Projecting out from files in Figs. 6a and 6b the attributes mentioned in triple maps in Fig. 4. (c) RDF triples produced by the triple maps over the projected attributes; duplicates are reduced from 22 to four

to four. Considerably reducing thus, the workload required to generate, check, and eliminate duplicated RDF triples. Results of the experimental study will show the improvements of the MapSDI framework.

Transformation Rule 3: Merging Data Sources with Equivalent Attributes: This rule is applied whenever there exist two or more triple mapping rules that generate the same type of subjects associated with the same predicates, but the data is collected from different data sources with attributes that may have different names. This rule allows the MapSDI framework to first, project the relevant attributes, and then merge the data sources; duplicates are eliminated from the merged data source. Additionally, the triple maps are merged in one triple map that will access the merged data source and duplicated RDF triples are not generated (See Fig. 1).

MapSDI applies the transformation rules 1–3 over the input data integration system $DIS_G = \langle O, S, M \rangle$ in order to generate $DIS'_G = \langle O, S', M' \rangle$; these rules are applied until a fixed point over S' and M' is reached.

3.2   Correctness of the Transformation Rules

We demonstrate the correctness of the transformation rules 1–3 by proving that the application of each of these rules preserves the set of RDF triples produced during the evaluation of the original data integration system; these proofs are grounded on the axiomatic system of the Relational Algebra [13].

Transformation Rule 1: Projection of Attributes. For each mapping rule r_i in M with sources $S_z(\overline{X_z})$ in the body of r_i, the transformation rule 1, adds new sources S'_z to S', in the way, that S'_z is equal to $\prod_{Att} S_z$ and Att is the set of attributes utilized in $\overline{X_z}$. The rule r_i is removed from M' and a new mapping rule r'_i where all the sources $S_z(\overline{X_z})$ are replaced by $S'_z(\overline{X_z})$. Since the attributes from the sources S_z used in $\overline{X_z}$ are maintained in the new data sources S'_z and in the rule r'_i, the results of $RDFize(DIS_G = \langle O, S, M \rangle)$ and $RDFize(DIS'_G = \langle O, S', M' \rangle)$ are the same.

Transformation Rule 2: Pushing Down Projection into Joins. Transformation rule 2 is applied over a mapping rule r_i whenever there exist attributes and variables in the sources of the body of r_i that are not required to evaluate r_i, i.e., they are neither used to instantiate the head of r_i nor to join two or more data sources in the body of r_i. If so, transformation rule 2 projects out from the sources $S_z(\overline{X_z})$ in the body of r_i the attributes and variables that are required. Formally, the rewriting of r_i is defined as follows: Let $\overline{Z}$ be the set of variables in the head of r_i or in the join of at least two sources in the body. That is, $\overline{Z}$ is the union of variables in $\overline{X}$, X, and the variables that appear in more than one $S_p(\overline{X_p})$ and $S_q(\overline{X_q})$ in the body of r_i.

$$r_i : c_j(X, \overline{X}) : -S_1(\overline{X_1}), S_2(\overline{X_2}) \ldots S_m(\overline{X_m})$$

The application of the transformation rule 2, replaces r_i by the rule r'_i:

$$r'_i : c_j(X, \overline{X}) : -S_1(\overline{X'_1}), S_2(\overline{X'_2}) \ldots S_m(\overline{X'_m})$$

where each X'_j, $1 \leq j \leq m$, is defined as follows:

$$X'_j = X_j - \{(att_{i,j}, X_{i,j}) \mid (att_{i,j}, X_{i,j}) \in X_j \text{ and } X_{i,j} \notin \overline{Z}\}$$

The transformation 2 is grounded on the axiomatic system of the Relational Algebra, specifically, on the rule axiom that states the properties of distributing the Project operator over a Join (rule number 8 in [13]). Thus, after applying this transformation rule and replacing r_i by r'_i in M', the results of $RDFize(DIS_G = \langle O, S, M \rangle)$ and $RDFize(DIS'_G = \langle O, S', M' \rangle)$ are the same.

Transformation Rule 3: Merging Data Sources with Equivalent Attributes. This rule is applied over two mapping rules, r_i and r_j, whenever both rules share the same head but the bodies are composed of different data sources, i.e., $r_i : c_q(X, \overline{X}) : -S_i(\overline{X_i})$ and $r_j : c_q(X, \overline{X}) : -S_j(\overline{X_j})$. The result of applying the transformation rule 3 is a new data source $S_{i,j}$ that is populated with values of the attributes from S_i and S_j that are required for instantiating $c_q(X, \overline{X})$. Further, r_i and r_j are replaced by the rule $r_{i,j}$ in M', $r_{i,j} : c_q(X, \overline{X}) : -S_{i,j}(\overline{X_{i,j}})$

- $S_{i,j}$ is the union of $\prod_{Att_i} S_i$ and $\prod_{Att_j} S_j$ such that Att_i and Att_j, respectively, are the attributes in $\overline{X_i}$ and $\overline{X_j}$ related with variables in $c_q(X, \overline{X})$.
- The projected attributes in $S_{i,j}$ are renamed and these new attributes are used in $\overline{X_{i,j}}$ associated with the corresponding variables in $c_q(X, \overline{X})$.

The transformation 3 is also supported on the axiomatic system of the Relational Algebra, specifically, on the rule axiom that states the properties of distributing the Project operator over a Union (rule number 12 in [13]). Thus, after applying this transformation rule and replacing r_i and r_j by $r_{i,j}$ in M', and adding the data source $S_{i,j}$ to S', the results of $RDFize(DIS_G = \langle O, S, M \rangle)$ and $RDFize(DIS'_G = \langle O, S', M' \rangle)$ are the same.

4   Experimental Study

We compare the performance of MapSDI to the traditional framework for knowledge graph creation which we refer to as "T-framework" from now on in this paper. We aim to answer the following questions: (**Q**1) Does applying MapSDI lead to creation of the same knowledge graph? (**Q**2) Does MapSDI reduce the required time for knowledge graph creation compared to T-framework? (**Q**3) How influential is the performance of MapSDI framework, when data volume increases or data quality decreases? (**Q**4) Does MapSDI perform efficiently in case of having more complication in mapping rules e.g., join condition?

We set up the following testbeds:

Datasets. To prevent any bias that may arise due to using a specific database or data generated by a particular lab, several datasets have been combined. For the first experimental scenario, a dataset with an overall size of 312,1 MB and 19,503,200 records is created from the combination of three different datasets including mutations, drug-resistant mutations, and protein-RNA interaction predictions; they are collected from different data providers: (**i**) The datasets related to mutations and drug-resistant mutations are collected from COSMIC[2], an open source database of somatic mutations in human cancer diseases. (**ii**) A dataset defined by Lang et al. [9] at CRG[3], this dataset includes protein-RNA interaction predictions. The second studied dataset is generated by collecting different attributes from various publicly available datasets including the GENCODE reference annotation for the human and mouse genomes [6]. In this dataset, a large amount of selected data relates to exon, the sequence represented in the mature RNA whose mutations can directly affect the sequence of a protein [11]. Since there are overlaps between the data in these datasets, as we will explain later, there exist a large number of duplicates.

---

[2] https://cancer.sanger.ac.uk/cosmic.
[3] https://www.crg.eu/.

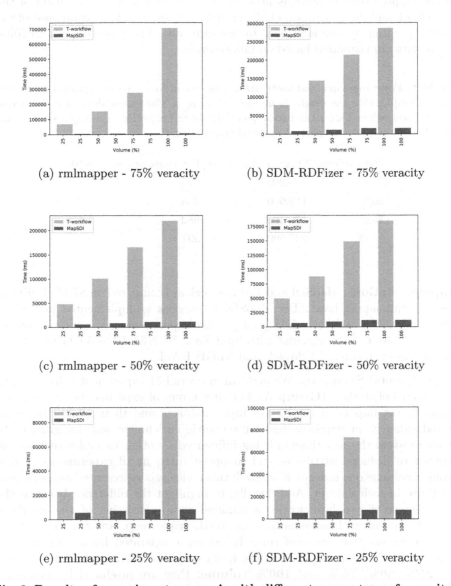

(a) rmlmapper - 75% veracity

(b) SDM-RDFizer - 75% veracity

(c) rmlmapper - 50% veracity

(d) SDM-RDFizer - 50% veracity

(e) rmlmapper - 25% veracity

(f) SDM-RDFizer - 25% veracity

Fig. 8. Results of experiment group A with different percentage of veracity. The performance of MapSDI and T-framework on four different sized datasets with 75% redundancy: (a) applying rmlmapper (b) using SDM-RDFizer. MapSDI is able to reduce duplicated and exhibits better performance independently of the data volume and RDFizer. But, the difference between the execution time of two frameworks is much higher when rmlmapper is evaluated

Metrics. Performance is measured in terms of execution time; it is computed as the elapsed time in seconds between the submission of an execution of the framework and the generation of all the RDF triples. The `time` command of the Linux operating system is utilized to measure time. The timeout is set to 500 s; the results are visualized based on milliseconds.

Table 1. Four instance datasets size. The size of four datasets applied in experiments group A with the results being shown in Fig. 8. The values show how the size of datasets are reduced after the two steps of attribute projection and duplicate removal have been applied on, as part of MapSDI framework.

Data volume	Original size (KB)	Pre-processed size (KB)
25%	59,200	895
50%	117,900	955
75%	176,400	982
100%	235,000	997

Implementations. MapSDI and T-framework are compared on SDM-RDFizer[4] and the rmlmapper-java[5]. The MapSDI framework is implemented in Python 3.6.3 and GNU bash 4.4.12(1) jointly. The experiments are executed on an Ubuntu 17.10 (64 bits) machine with Intel Xeon W-2133, CPU 3.6 GHz, 1 physical processor; 6 cores, 12 threads and 64 GB RAM.

Experimental Scenarios. We perform in overall 51 experiments; divided into two groups of studies. (**Group** A) The first group of experiments are designed to study the impact of the size of input datasets and their quality in terms of redundancy, on required time for semantic enrichment and integration. In order to avoid the experiments being influenced by other variables such as the number of included attributes and mapping rules, in all experiments of this group, the same one concept is utilized; this concept is represented as a different attribute in each dataset. Additionally, to highlight the difference between the performance of two frameworks, a minimal setup consisting of one attribute in each dataset and consequently one RML triple map, are evaluated. Each 12 experiments that are performed based on a separated framework using a different RDFizer, can be divided into four categories based on the data volume: the **25%, 50%, 75%,** and **100% volume**; they are produced by randomly selecting 25%, 50%, 75% and 100% of the records in created dataset, respectively. Subsequently, each mentioned category is divided into three subcategories based on data redundancy; from each generated dataset in the volume category, three datasets are produced by cleaning 25%, 50% and 75% of the data from duplicates. It should be noted that all selections of data have been performed randomly to avoid any sampling bias. (**Group** B) The second experiment setup is conducted to study the impact of data redundancy on performance of each framework in

---

[4] https://github.com/SDM-TIB/TIB-RDFizer.
[5] https://github.com/RMLio/rmlmapper-java.

case of join condition rules inclusion. Following the same objective, the minimum amount of required attributes are considered. Accordingly, three experiments are performed on joining two datasets: (a) No dataset with duplicates removal; (b) One dataset being duplicates-free; and (c) Both datasets being duplicates-free.

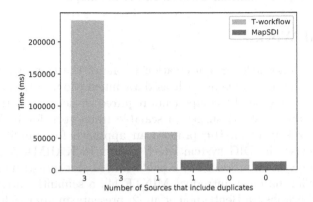

Fig. 9. Results of Experiment Group B. MapSDI and T-framework on two datasets joined by two triple maps. MapSDI performs *Transformation Rule 2 and Rule 3* and it is able to push down projection into the join. With the transformations conducted by MapSDI, the rmlmapper timed out at 500 s

4.1   Experimental Results

Experimental Results Group A: The results of the experiment group A are shown in Figs. 8. As it can be observed, MapSDI outperforms T-framework in terms of execution time in all the experiments independently of the RDFizers and percentage of duplicates. This instance of the MapSDI framework performs the *Transformation Rule 3*, i.e., the datasets are merged; while the *Transformation Rule 1* is performed in the two frameworks during the creation of the datasets. According to the results depicted in Figs. 8, regardless of the RDFizer, the more duplicated data in the datasets, the higher the execution time of the T-framework. It is also important to highlight, the diverse performance ratios of MapSDI and T-framework in terms of the growth of dataset size and data duplicates. MapSDI performs more stable than T-framework. These observations can be explained according to the two steps of pre-processing including attributes projection and duplicates removal that are executed former to the transformation step in the MapSDI framework. The mentioned steps decrease the size of the original datasets considerably. Table 1 reports on the reduced size of the input datasets after the pre-processing steps in the experiments conducted over the dataset with 25% data duplicates (Fig. 8).

Experimental Results Group B: Figure 9 illustrates the results of experiments in group B. The rmlmapper timed out in all experiments of group B, the results only refer to the performance of MapSDI and T-framework applying SDB-RDFizer. As it can be observed, the execution time of MapSDI is considerably lower than T-framework in case of having join condition in mapping rules independent of having data duplicates. This instance of MapSDI framework performs the *Transformation Rule 3* as well as *Transformation Rule 2*. The application of these two transformations considerably reduces the number of duplicates and enhances the performance of the SDM-RDFizer during the execution of the join condition between two triple maps.

5   Related Work

The problem of knowledge graph creation is one of the trending topics which also involves different problems such as data integration. Lenzerini et al. [10] provides an overview on the components required to define a data integration system. Gawriljuk et al. [7] suggest a scalable framework for building knowledge graphs. Szekely et al. [14] propose an approach for building knowledge graphs and devise the DIG system which resorts to KARMA [8], a semantic data integration system proposed by Knoblock et al., for integration at the level of schema. Collarana et al. introduce MINTE [4], a semantic integration technique for RDF graphs. In Benbernou et al. [2] presents an approach to integrate big RDF data. Although the mentioned approaches are effective, they either differentiate between the integration at the level of schema and the data-level integration or only focus on one of the two tasks. This distinction leads to a dramatic increase in the cost of semantic data integration in case of consuming big data. In contrast, in MapSDI both integration tasks are conducted simultaneously. Moreover, the semantics encoded in the schema and mapping rules is utilized in order to first, remove the data redundancy and then, transform the input data into RDF triples. Diverse mapping languages for transforming relational data into RDF have been introduced, reported in 2009 for the first time as a survey by W3C incubator group. Sequeda et al. explain the limitations of semantic technologies in relational databases integration in [12]. During the recent years several extension to R2RML have been proposed in order to represent mapping rules such as RML [5] by Dimou et al. or D2RML [3] by Chortaras et al. The same applies for the implementation of tools to execute mapping rules in different languages. In this work, we present MapSDI, a framework that is able to speed up the execution time of the task of knowledge graph creation independently of the mapping language or tools for knowledge graph creation. Experimentally, we have observed that MapSDI empowers the performance of the RDFizers regardless of the number of duplicates and size of the input data.

6   Conclusions and Future Work

We tackled the problem of optimizing semantically integrating data into a knowledge graph and presented MapSDI; it is devised for enabling the semantic enrichment of data characterized by the dominant dimensions of big data, i.e., volume, variety, and veracity. MapSDI resorts to the properties of the relational algebra operators and to the knowledge encoded in the mapping rules to identify the transformations that need to be performed to the input data to empower the performance of existing knowledge graph creation tools. Thus, our resource broadens the repertoire of techniques available to integrate heterogeneous datasets into a knowledge graph, and we hope that these techniques will help the community in the development of more scalable knowledge graph based applications. In the future, we will extend the MapSDI framework to include other transformations and mapping languages. Furthermore, the development of applications on top of the MapSDI framework is part of our future plans.

Acknowledgements. This work has been partially funded by the EU H2020 Program for the Project No. 727658 (IASIS).

References

1. Antoniou, G., Van Harmelen, F.: A Semantic Web Primer. MIT Press, Cambridge (2004)
2. Benbernou, S., Huang, X., Ouziri, M.: Semantic-based and entity-resolution fusion to enhance quality of big RDF data. IEEE Trans. Big Data (2017)
3. Chortaras, A., Stamou, G.: D2RML: integrating heterogeneous data and web services into custom RDF graphs. In: LDOW@ WWW (2018)
4. Collarana, D., Galkin, M., Traverso-Ribón, I., Vidal, M.-E., Lange, C., Auer, S.: MINTE: semantically integrating RDF graphs. In: Proceedings of the 7th International Conference on Web Intelligence, Mining and Semantics (2017)
5. Dimou, A., Vander Sande, M., Colpaert, P., Mannens, E., Van de Walle, R.: Extending R2RML to a source-independent mapping language for RDF. In: International Semantic Web Conference (Posters & Demos), vol. 1035 (2013)
6. Frankish, A., et al.: GENCODE reference annotation for the human and mouse genomes. Nucleic Acids Res. **47**(D1) (2018)
7. Gawriljuk, G., Harth, A., Knoblock, C.A., Szekely, P.: A scalable approach to incrementally building knowledge graphs. In: International Conference on Theory and Practice of Digital Libraries (2016)
8. Knoblock, C.A., Szekely, P.: Exploiting semantics for big data integration. AI Mag. **36**(1), 25–38 (2015)
9. Lang, B., Armaos, A., Tartaglia, G.G.: RNAct: Protein-RNA interaction predictions for model organisms with supporting experimental data. Nucleic Acids Res. **47**(D1), D601–D606 (2018)
10. Lenzerini, M.: Data integration: a theoretical perspective. In: Proceedings of the Twenty-First ACM SIGMOD-SIGACT-SIGART Symposium on Principles of Database Systems. ACM (2002)
11. Lewin, B., Krebs, J., Kilpatrick, S.T., Goldstein, E.S.: Lewin's GENES X (2011)
12. Sequeda, J.F.: Integrating relational databases with the semantic web: a reflection. In: Ianni, G., et al. (eds.) Reasoning Web 2017. LNCS, vol. 10370, pp. 68–120. Springer, Cham (2017). https://doi.org/10.1007/978-3-319-61033-7_4
13. Silberschatz, A., Korth, H.F., Sudarshan, S., et al.: Database System Concepts, vol. 4. McGraw-Hill, New York (1997)
14. Szekely, P., et al.: Building and using a knowledge graph to combat human trafficking. In: Arenas, M., et al. (eds.) ISWC 2015. LNCS, vol. 9367, pp. 205–221. Springer, Cham (2015). https://doi.org/10.1007/978-3-319-25010-6_12
15. Ullman, J.D.: Principles of Database and Knowledge-Base Systems, vol. 2. Computer Science Press, New York (1989)

A Contextual Approach to Detecting Synonymous and Polluted Activity Labels in Process Event Logs

Sareh Sadeghianasl[(✉)], Arthur H. M. ter Hofstede, Moe T. Wynn, and Suriadi Suriadi

Queensland University of Technology, Brisbane, Australia
sareh.sadeghianasl@hdr.qut.edu.au,
{a.terhofstede,m.wynn,s.suriadi}@qut.edu.au

Abstract. Process mining, as a well-established research area, uses algorithms for process-oriented data analysis. Similar to other types of data analysis, the existence of quality issues in input data will lead to unreliable analysis results (*garbage in - garbage out*). An important input for process mining is an event log which is a record of events related to a business process as it is performed through the use of an information system. While addressing quality issues in event logs is necessary, it is usually an ad-hoc and tiresome task. In this paper, we propose an automatic approach for detecting two types of data quality issues related to activities, both critical for the success of process mining studies: synonymous labels (same semantics with different syntax) and polluted labels (same semantics and same label structures). We propose the use of activity context, i.e. control flow, resource, time, and data attributes to detect semantically identical activity labels. We have implemented our approach and validated it using real-life logs from two hospitals and an insurance company, and have achieved promising results in detecting frequent imperfect activity labels.

Keywords: Data quality · Process event log · Activity label

1 Introduction

Process mining, as a relatively new research area, uses information in event logs, to discover, control and improve processes [3]. An event log is a record of events related to a business process, executed via an information system. Process mining has delivered promising results in discovering actual behaviors (i.e. *process discovery*), checking conformance of processes to organizational rules, analyzing process performance, and suggesting process improvements.

The starting point of process mining is an event log which contains data related to a *process*. A process is a series of tasks that are performed in a specific order to achieve a specific result. Each execution of a process is called a *case*. The records of the execution of these tasks are stored in a log as so-called *events*.

© Springer Nature Switzerland AG 2019
H. Panetto et al. (Eds.): OTM 2019, LNCS 11877, pp. 76–94, 2019.
https://doi.org/10.1007/978-3-030-33246-4_5

An event can be described by the type of *activity* (i.e. "a well-defined step in the process" [2]) that is executed as part of a case at a particular point in time (as represented by a *timestamp*). There may also be some supporting attributes for events e.g. *resources* (i.e. originator of activity), *transaction type* (e.g. start or complete), and *data attributes* (e.g. illness of a patient).

Unfortunately, in practice, event logs suffer from data quality issues, e.g. missing events (attributes) [6], imprecise timestamps [7], and duplicate events [22]. Analyzing an event log with plenty of data quality issues is not advisable as it will most likely lead to unreliable process mining results (*garbage in - garbage out*). Suriadi et al. [29] introduced 11 event log *imperfection patterns* as a systematic view of data quality issues in event logs, thus providing a pathway for subsequent (semi-)automated approaches to repair event logs. These patterns can be further categorized into timestamp, case, and activity label imperfection patterns. Existing approaches to detecting and repairing those event log imperfection patterns mainly focus on timestamp imperfection patterns [10,13,21]. Although activity label quality issues have been addressed at the process model level [1,5,12,15] and at the event log level [8,16,22,31], as will be discussed in Sect. 2, they are not well-suited to automatically detect synonymous and polluted activity labels in event logs.

In this paper, we focus on two activity label imperfection patterns, i.e. synonymous and polluted labels, both occurring in real-life logs, as reviewed by Suriadi et al. [29], and both critical for the success of process mining analysis. Synonymous activity labels are those that are semantically identical, but syntactically different, e.g. *"Dr. seen"* and *"Visited by doctor"*. They are most common when an event log is derived from multiple systems that use different names for the same concept. Polluted labels also refer to the same semantics but they have similar label structures where the differences further qualify their meaning, e.g. *"Notification of Loss XXXX Incident No. xxxx"*, *"Notification of Loss YYYY Incident No. yyyy"*, and *"Notification of Loss ZZZZ Incident No. zzzz"* as seen in an insurance log [29]. These labels are most common when the system records events from a free-text input providing an initial suggestion.

The existence of synonymous and polluted activity labels in event logs leads to unnecessarily large and confusing discovered process models which include behaviors that should have been merged. These patterns may also negatively affect performance analysis results since two or more activities that should be recognized as the same are considered as separate. Approaches to resolving such misclassifications mainly focus on activity labels and use domain ontologies or experts [8,16], however *our approach abstracts from labels and uses context information instead*, i.e. control flow, resource, time, and data to automatically detect semantically identical activity labels. Although using ontologies can be helpful, they might not always be available particularly when a specialized ontology is required for a specific domain, e.g. the medical domain where different names are used for the same test. Using label similarity metrics can also help in detecting synonymous and, mainly, polluted labels, but they can sometimes be misleading e.g. activities *"Admission IC"* and *"Admission NC"* regarding admission of a patient to intensive care and normal care in a hospital respectively [23].

Putting process mining into context leads to more qualified analysis results [4, 27]. In this paper, we provide a framework for activity context and use it, through some example distance measures, to investigate semantic distance between activities. We distinguished four perspectives (although flexible) for activity context: control flow, resource, time and data. In each of these perspectives, we have defined some principles and some example activity distance measures. We then use these measures to cluster activities and aggregate the results using configurable dimension and measure weights. We also guide the user by suggesting the best weights. Finally, we detect synonymous and polluted activity labels using a flexible context similarity threshold.

We have implemented and evaluated our approach using real-life logs from two hospitals and an insurance company. Our results show the approach detects frequent imperfect activity labels efficiently, e.g. it achieves an F-score of 1 in the Sepsis log. Furthermore, considering *multiple context dimensions* seems to be more helpful than looking at a single dimension as it might be misleading, e.g. control flow dimension when a flower model is discovered from the log.

This paper is organized as follows. Section 2 discusses the related work. In Sect. 3 we consider event log basics and formal notations. In Sect. 4 we describe a context framework for activities and distance measures for different context dimensions. Section 5 contains our approach to detecting synonymous and polluted labels. In Sect. 6 we present our evaluations using real-life logs and in Sect. 7 we summarize our findings and suggest future work.

2   Related Work

The subject of data quality of process event logs was initially proposed in the Process Mining Manifesto [3] where a 1 to 5 star rating was defined for the quality of an event log, where logs rated as 3, 4 or 5-star are ready for applying process mining analysis, whereas logs rated as 1 and 2-star are not. There are some works, e.g. [7,20,24,32], that provide a framework for event log quality, although they do not provide any method to detect such quality issues in logs. Bose et al. [6,7] identify four classes of process event log quality issues: missing data, incorrect data, imprecise data, irrelevant data, and how they may appear in different elements of an event log including cases, events, activity names, timestamps, resources, etc. Synonymous and polluted activity labels are manifestations of imprecise activity names in the classification of Bose et al. [7], where multiple names for (semantically) the same activity yields ambiguity in an event log. Mans et al. [24] define data quality for event logs as a two-dimensional spectrum, where the first dimension considers the abstraction level of events and the second considers the accuracy of timestamps, i.e. their granularity, currency, and correctness. Lu and Fahland [20] distinguish three concepts in event logs whose quality is important, i.e. events, ordering of events and labels of events. Each concept has two aspects: data (covering intrinsic qualities of event data) and analysis (determining whether a behavior is repeating across many cases). Synonymous and polluted labels threaten the quality of labels of events.

Suriadi et al. [29] classify common quality issues found in process event logs or raised when preparing event logs from raw data sources, as 11 generic imperfection patterns in logs thus paving the way for subsequent automatic approaches to cleaning event logs. These patterns can be further categorized into timestamp, case, and activity label imperfection patterns. Existing approaches mainly focus on detecting and repairing timestamp imperfection patterns in event logs [10,13,21], however, there are some methods, e.g. [22,31], that could be used for detecting and repairing duplicate tasks, i.e. *homonymous* labels [29], in event logs where multiple activities with different semantics have the same name. The notion of *label similarity* has been extensively discussed in the field of process model matching and similarity, which is reviewed in [5], however they mainly use syntactic and semantic similarity measures (using ontologies) [15] or control flow, duration and data attributes of activities [1,12] to match labels, ignoring other context dimensions, e.g. resources and timing patterns, that are typically found in event logs.

Synonymous activity labels are viewed as *semantic noise* by Gunther [14] who describes two possible types of noise in event logs: *syntactic noise* that occurs due to errors in logging (e.g. missing head or tail of traces) and *semantic noise* that is introduced to a log on purpose due to e.g. *customizations* of the same process, where for instance a company localizes activity names for each country. Gunther [14] indicates that customization noise can be resolved via *semantic pre-processing*, e.g. using an ontology. In the area of semantic process mining, ontologies are widely used to annotate tasks with the concept they represent [9, 26]. These annotations are further used to discover a conceptual process model [8] or to revise the vocabulary of process model elements [16]. However, our approach detects labels with the same semantics using context information provided in a log, i.e. control flow, resource, time and data, and abstracts from activity labels (hence e.g. it does not depend on access to an ontology).

3 Preliminaries

An event log L is formally defined as $L = (\mathcal{E}, \mathcal{A}, \mathcal{V}, \mathcal{T}, AN, \#, \mathscr{L})$, where $\mathcal{E}$ is the set of event identifiers, $\mathcal{A}$ is the set of activities, $\mathcal{V}$ is the set of values, $\mathcal{T}$ is the set of timestamps, AN is the set of attributes names, $\# : \mathcal{E} \rightarrow (AN \rightarrow \mathcal{V})$ gets the value of attribute $n \in AN$ recorded for an event $e \in \mathcal{E}$, i.e. $\#_n(e) \in \mathcal{V}$, and $\mathscr{L} \subseteq \mathcal{E}^*$ is the set of all traces over $\mathcal{E}$. A trace $\sigma \in \mathscr{L}$ is a sequence of events of a process instance such that each event occurs only once.

For any event $e \in \mathcal{E}$, $\#_{ac}(e)$, $\#_{ti}(e)$, $\#_{re}(e)$, $\#_{trans}(e)$, represent activity, timestamp, resource, and life-cycle transaction of event e. These attributes are referred to as *standard attributes*, among which activity and timestamp are mandatory. For any activity $a \in \mathcal{A}$, $AN_a \subset AN$ is the set of attribute names, excluding standard attributes, for events executing activity a, i.e. $AN_a = \{n \in AN \mid \#_{ac}(e) = a \wedge n \notin \{ac, re, ti, trans\} \wedge \#_n(e) \neq \perp\}$. We define $\mathcal{E}_{com} \subseteq \mathcal{E}$ as the set of *complete events*, i.e. $\mathcal{E}_{com} = \{e \in \mathcal{E} \mid \#_{trans}(e) = complete\}$. Similarly, $\mathcal{E}_{st} \subseteq \mathcal{E}$ consists of all *start events*, i.e. $\mathcal{E}_{st} = \{e \in \mathcal{E} \mid \#_{trans}(e) = start\}$.

A *directly before* relation $\sqsubset$ is derived over events, where for any $e_1, e_2 \in \mathcal{E}$, $e_1 \sqsubset e_2$ holds if and only if there exists a trace $\sigma \in \mathcal{L}$ such that $\sigma(i) = e_1$ and $\sigma(i+1) = e2$, $1 \leqslant i < |\sigma|$. Similarly, an *indirectly before* relation $\sqsubseteq$ is defined over events where for any $e_1, e_2 \in \mathcal{E}$, $e_1 \sqsubseteq e_2$ holds if and only if there exists a trace $\sigma \in \mathcal{L}$ such that $\sigma(i) = e_1$ and $\sigma(j) = e2$, $1 \leqslant i < |\sigma|$, $i < j \leqslant |\sigma|$.

For any activity $a \in \mathcal{A}$, we define its *events set* $\mathcal{E}_a = \{e \in \mathcal{E} \mid \#_{ac}(e) = a\}$ as the set of all events e that are executing activity a. The frequency $F : \mathcal{A} \to N$ for any activity $a \in \mathcal{A}$ is the size of its events set, i.e. $F(a) = |\mathcal{E}_a|$.

In the rest of this paper, we use the shorthands PDF and CDF to refer to probability density function and cumulative probability distribution function respectively. Here we also formulate the Manhattan distance measure [11] as it is used in defining distance measures in the rest of this paper. We use the Manhattan distance measure [11] because it integrates all the absolute differences between two PDFs, related to two activities, over the same domain and is suitable for comparing activities based on each of their attributes, e.g. resource, time, and data values. The normalized Manhattan distance between any two PDFs $p = (p_1, p_2, \cdots, p_n)$ and $q = (q_1, q_2, \cdots, q_n)$ is computed as[1]: $M(p, q) = \frac{\sum_{i=1}^{n} |p_i - q_i|}{2}$.

4 Activity Context Framework

The context in which activities are executed can provide meaningful insights into more qualified process mining analysis [4,27]. Our approach uses the activity context to identify synonymous and polluted activity label candidates. Figure 1 shows our activity context framework which includes four perspectives: (1) *The control flow perspective* (i.e. the ordering of activities), (2) *The resource perspective* (i.e. people, roles, or devices performing activities), (3) *The temporal perspective* (i.e. timing of activities), and (4) *The data perspective* (i.e. data attributes of activities). The principle is that the similarity of activities based on each perspective might be an indication of semantically identical activities even if they have different labels. As depicted in Fig. 1, context dimensions are assumed to be independent of each other, i.e. the absence or internal changes of one perspective does not influence the validity of others. In this section, we show some example distance measures for each dimension. Although one can replace them with other measures or even add other dimensions, the principles remain. The following sections discuss each perspective in terms of its principles and our example distance measure(s).

4.1 Control Flow Perspective

Principle. The control flow perspective is concerned with behavioral (ordering) relations between activities in an event log. Similar control flow contexts might

---

[1] The Manhattan distance between any two PDFs p and q lies in the interval $[0, 2]$, because in the best case, p and q are identical, then $M(p, q) = 0$, and in the worst case $\exists i, j \mid 1 \leqslant i, j \leqslant n, i \neq j$ such that $p_i = 1$ and $q_j = 1$, then $M(p, q) = 2$.

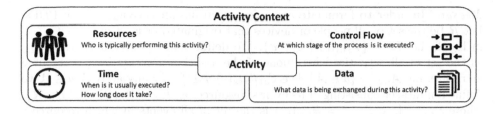

Fig. 1. Activity context framework

be an indication of identical activities i.e. activities that are following similar kind of work and are followed by similar kind of work, are more likely to be semantically identical than those with a different control flow context.

Measure. To formulate the control flow context, we use direct ordering relations between activities, as defined by van der Aalst [2], based on a primary "directly follows" relation. For any two activities $a, b \in \mathcal{A}$ executed in log L:

- $a >_L b$ (*directly follows* relation) if and only if $\exists e_1 \in \mathcal{E}_a, \exists e_2 \in \mathcal{E}_b \mid e1 \sqsubset e2$.
- $a \rightarrow b$ (*"Causes"* relation) if and only if $a >_L b$ and $b \not>_L a$.
- $a \leftarrow b$ (*"Caused by"* relation) if and only if $b >_L a$ and $a \not>_L b$.
- $a\#b$ (*"Exclusive"* relation) if and only if $a \not>_L b$ and $b \not>_L a$.
- $a \parallel b$ (*"Concurrent"* relation) if and only if $a >_L b$ and $b >_L a$.

For any pair of activities $a, b \in \mathcal{A}$, $a \rightarrow b$, or $b \rightarrow a$, or $a\#b$, or $a \parallel b$, i.e. exactly one of these relations holds. Therefore, we can capture ordering relations of a log in a *footprint* [2] matrix $F = [f_{i,j}], 1 \leqslant i, j \leqslant \mid \mathcal{A} \mid$, where $f_{i,j} \in \{\rightarrow, \leftarrow, \#, \parallel\}$ specifies ordering relations between any two activities $a, b \in \mathcal{A}$ such that $i = index(a)$, $j = index(b)$ and $index : \mathcal{A} \rightarrow \{1, 2, \cdots, \mid\mathcal{A}\mid\}$ is a function that assigns an index to each activity and forms a bijection. Equation 1 defines the control flow distance measure $D_{cf} : \mathcal{A} \times \mathcal{A} \rightarrow [0, 1]$ between any two activities $a, b \in \mathcal{A}$:

$$
D_{cf}(a, b) = \frac{\left| \{(i, j) \mid 1 \leqslant j \leqslant n \wedge (f_{i,j} \neq \# \vee f_{k,j} \neq \#) \wedge f_{i,j} \neq f_{k,j}\} \right|}{\left| \{(i, j) \mid 1 \leqslant j \leqslant n \wedge (f_{i,j} \neq \# \vee f_{k,j} \neq \#)\} \right|}, \quad (1)
$$

where $n = \mid \mathcal{A} \mid$, $i = index(a)$, $k = index(b)$ and we calculate the ratio of the different cells in rows i and k to the total number of cells in rows i and k of each matrix. We exclude *exclusive* relations $\#$, because the fact that two activities are excluded from many other activities does not mean that they are identical.

4.2 Resource Perspective

Principle. The resource perspective focuses on people, devices, or software involved in executing activities. Activities that are usually performed by similar groups of resources (roles) are more likely to be the same rather than activities executed by different groups of resources (roles).

Measure. In order to formulate resources executing an activity, we use PDFs. Let $\mathcal{R}$ be the set of all people or devices that originated at least one event $e \in \mathcal{E}$ in log L, i.e. $\mathcal{R} = \{\#_{res}(e) \mid e \in \mathcal{E}\}$. We define *null-resource* activities $\mathcal{A}_{R\perp}$ as the set of all activities where none of the associated events have a resource attribute, i.e. $\mathcal{A}_{R\perp} = \{a \in \mathcal{A} \mid \nexists e \in \mathcal{E}_a[\#_{res}(e) \neq \perp]\}$. For any activity $a \in \mathcal{A}$ we define a multi-set consisting of its events' resources as $\mathcal{R}_a = \{(r, |\mathcal{E}_{a,r}|) \mid r \in \mathcal{R}\}$, where $\mathcal{E}_{a,r} = \{e \in \mathcal{E}_a \mid r = \#_{res}(e)\}$ is the set of all events in which resource r executes activity a. The resource distance measure $D_{re} : \mathcal{A} \times \mathcal{A} \to [0,1] \cup \{\perp\}$ between any pair of activities $a, b \in \mathcal{A}$ is defined as:

$$D_{re}(a,b) = \begin{cases} M(PR_a, PR_b) & \text{if } a \notin \mathcal{A}_{R\perp} \wedge b \notin \mathcal{A}_{R\perp} \\ 1 & \text{if } a \notin \mathcal{A}_{R\perp} \oplus b \notin \mathcal{A}_{R\perp} \\ \perp & \text{otherwise,} \end{cases} \tag{2}$$

where $PR_a : \mathcal{R} \to [0,1]$ is a PDF estimated from multi-set $\mathcal{R}_a$. If activities a and b have resource information in the log, then their resource distance is computed as the normalized Manhattan distance between their corresponding PDFs, i.e. PR_a and PR_b. Otherwise if only one of the activities a and b has resource information, then they are assumed to be far apart $D_{re}(a,b) = 1$. Otherwise, if no resource information is available for neither a nor b, then no information is gained, i.e. $D_{re}(a,b) = \perp$.

4.3 Temporal Perspective

Principle. Timing information of activities, e.g. duration, waiting time, or point of time in which they are usually executed[2], is another perspective that can indicate the similarity or difference between types of work that have been performed.

Measure. We define two measures: one concerning the duration of activities and the other one concerning the point of time at which they are executed.

Life-Cycle Duration

We measure the distance between activities based on duration PDFs. We consider at most two life-cycle types for any event $e \in \mathcal{E}$ appearing in event log L: start and complete. Events with no transaction attribute (atomic events), i.e. $\#_{trans}(e) = \perp$, are assumed as *complete* events, i.e. $\#_{trans}(e) = $ complete. For any *complete* event $e_c \in \mathcal{E}_{com}$, we define its corresponding start event as $Start(e_c) = e_s \in \mathcal{E}_{st} \mid \#_{ac}(e_s) = \#_{ac}(e_c) \wedge e_s \sqsubseteq e_c \wedge \nexists e'_s \in \mathcal{E}_{st}[e'_s \sqsubseteq e_s \wedge \#_{ac}(e'_s) = \#_{ac}(e_s)] \wedge \nexists e'_c \in \mathcal{E}_{com}[e_s \sqsubseteq e'_c \sqsubseteq e_c \wedge \#_{ac}(e'_c) = \#_{ac}(e_c)]$, i.e. the earliest start event e_s that is not indirectly followed by another complete event e'_c before e_c, all with the same activity name. Event duration $\mathcal{D} : \mathcal{E}_{com} \to N$ for any *complete* event $e_c \in \mathcal{E}_{com}$ is defined as:

$$\mathcal{D}(e_c) = \begin{cases} \#_{ti}(e_c) - \#_{ti}(Start(e_c)) & \text{if } Start(e_c) \neq \perp \\ 0 & \text{otherwise.} \end{cases}$$

---

[2] However, it may not be helpful if activities are performed in batch processing mode.

With this formalization, we ignore start events where the corresponding complete event is not recorded in the log (i.e. incomplete events). Max event duration $\mathcal{D}_{max} \in N$, is the duration of the event which takes the longest time compared to other events in the whole log L, i.e. $\mathcal{D}_{max} = max_{e_c \in \mathcal{E}_{com}}(\mathcal{D}(e_c))$. We also define $\mathcal{A}_{at}$ as the set of all atomic activities in the log, i.e. $\mathcal{A}_{at} = \{a \in \mathcal{A} \mid \forall e \in \mathcal{E}_a \cap \mathcal{E}_{com}[\mathcal{D}(e) = 0]\}$. For any activity $a \in \mathcal{A}$ activity duration is defined as a multi-set $\mathcal{D}_a = \{(d, |\mathcal{E}_{a,d}|) \mid d \in [0, \mathcal{D}_{max}]\}$ where $\mathcal{E}_{a,d} = \{e \in \mathcal{E}_a \cap \mathcal{E}_{com} \mid \mathcal{D}(e) \div \beta = d\}$ and $\beta > 0$ is a bin width used for binning activity durations (as we are not interested in tiny differences in durations). The duration distance metric $D_{du} : \mathcal{A} \times \mathcal{A} \to [0,1] \cup \{\bot\}$ for any two activities $a, b \in \mathcal{A}$ is defined as:

$$D_{du}(a,b) = \begin{cases} M(PD_a, PD_b) & \text{if } a \notin \mathcal{A}_{at} \wedge b \notin \mathcal{A}_{at} \\ 1 & \text{if } a \notin \mathcal{A}_{at} \oplus b \notin \mathcal{A}_{at} \\ \bot & \text{otherwise,} \end{cases} \tag{3}$$

where $PD_a : [0, \mathcal{D}_{max}] \to [0,1]$ is PDF estimated using multi-set $\mathcal{D}_a$. If a and b are both non-atomic, their distance is computed as the normalized Manhattan distance between their corresponding PDFs PD_a and PD_b. If only one of the activities a and b has a duration, then they are assumed to be far away from each other, i.e. $D_{du}(a,b) = 1$. Otherwise if neither a nor b are non-atomic, then we can not judge their duration distance, i.e. $D_{du}(a,b) = \bot$.

Timing Pattern

The timing pattern measures how regularly an activity is executed, e.g. mornings or evenings, every Monday or every day. In order to formulate timing patterns of activities, we use PDFs. For any activity $a \in \mathcal{A}$ and any unit of time $U \in \mathcal{U} = \{h, dw, m\}$, referring to the part of a day[3](h), the day of a week (dw), or the month of a year (m), the activity execution pattern is a multi-set $\mathcal{T}_{U,a} = \{(u,n) \in N \times N \mid n = |\{e \in \mathcal{E}_a \mid \pi_U(\#_{ti}(e)) = u\}|\}$, where operator $\pi_U(t) : \mathcal{T} \to N$ extracts unit of time U from timestamp $t \in \mathcal{T}$. A complementary multi-set $\mathcal{T}_{U,a'} = \{(u,n) \in N \times N \mid n = |\{e \in \mathcal{E} - \mathcal{E}_a \mid \#_{ti}(e) = t \wedge \pi_U(t) = u\}|\}$, is defined for any activity $a \in \mathcal{A}$ concerning all activities in the log except a. Function $D_U : \mathcal{A} \times \mathcal{A} \to [0,1] \cup \{\bot\}$ measures the difference between timing patterns of any pair of activities $a, b \in \mathcal{A}$ based on any unit of time $U \in \mathcal{U}$:

$$D_U(a,b) = \begin{cases} M(PU_a, PU_b) & \text{if } CU_a \not\approx_{KS} CU_{a'} \wedge CU_b \not\approx_{KS} CU_{b'} \\ 1 & \text{if } CU_a \not\approx_{KS} CU_{a'} \oplus CU_b \not\approx_{KS} CU_{b'} \\ \bot & \text{otherwise,} \end{cases}$$

where for $x \in \{a,b\}$, PU_x is PDF estimated from multi-set $\mathcal{T}_{U,x}$, and CU_x, $CU_{x'}$ are CDFs estimated from multi-sets $\mathcal{T}_{U,x}, \mathcal{T}_{U,x'}$ respectively. Operator $\not\approx_{KS}$ checks whether two CFDs have statistically significant differences ($\alpha = 0.01$) under the Kolmog0rov-Smirnov test [25] or not. A statistical anomaly of an activity's execution times means that it has a significantly different timing distribution from all other activities in the log. Here we are only interested in

---

[3] A part of a day is a 4-hours period of a day.

activities that *have* a statistical anomaly, i.e. are executed only at *specific* times. If we see statistical anomalies in both the timing distributions of activities a and b then they need further checks and if they have similar timing patterns, e.g. they are both executed only on Mondays, then they are close. However, if a statistical anomaly is only observed in time CDF for one of the activities a or b, then they are assumed to be far from each other, i.e. their distance is 1. Otherwise, if none of the activities a and b have anomalies in their time distributions, then no information is gained (their distance is set to $\perp$).

The overall timing pattern distance $D_{tp} : \mathcal{A} \times \mathcal{A} \to [0,1] \cup \{\perp\}$ between any pair of activities $a, b \in \mathcal{A}$ is the minimum time distance for different time units U. We use the min function because we are going to use the distance measure D_{tp} for clustering, and we are interested in the smallest time distance between a and b. If such a small distance exists then a and b will be in the same cluster.

$$D_{tp}(a,b) = \min_{U \in \{h, dw, m\}} D_U(a,b) \tag{4}$$

4.4 Data Perspective

Principle. Data attributes and their values may also indicate similarity or difference between activities. Activities with different data attributes or, the same data attributes, but different distribution of values, are probably not identical[4].

Measure. In this paper, we focus only on event-level data, although case-level data attributes might also be helpful (they are left as future work). For any activity $a \in \mathcal{A}$ and any of its event data attributes $d \in AN_a$, we define a multi-set $\mathcal{V}_{a,d} = \{(v, |\mathcal{E}_{a,d,v}|) \mid v \in \mathcal{V}\}$, where $\mathcal{E}_{a,d,v} = \{e \in \mathcal{E}_a \mid \#_d(e) = v\}$ is the set of all events of activity a where event data attribute d has value v. The data distance measure $D_{ed} : \mathcal{A} \times \mathcal{A} \to [0,1] \cup \{\perp\}$ between any pair of activities $a, b \in \mathcal{A}$ is defined as:

$$D_{ed}(a,b) = \begin{cases} \frac{\Sigma_{d_1 \in AN_a \wedge d_2 \in AN_b \wedge d_1 = d_2} M(Q_{a,d_1}, Q_{b,d_2})}{|AN_a \cap AN_b|} & \text{if } AN_a \cap AN_b \neq \varnothing \\ 1 & \text{if } AN_a \cap AN_b = \varnothing \vee \\ & (AN_a \neq \varnothing \oplus AN_b \neq \varnothing) \\ \perp & \text{otherwise}, \end{cases} \tag{5}$$

where for $i \in \{1,2\}$, $Q_{a,d_i} : \mathcal{V} \to [0,1]$, is PDF defined using multi-set $\mathcal{V}_{a,d_i}$. The data distance between activities a and b is the average of the normalized Manhattan distances between the value distribution of data attributes $d_1 \in AN_a$ and $d_2 \in AN_b$ with the same name, i.e. $d_1 = d_2$. If activities a and b have no data attributes in common or only one of them has data attributes, then they are assumed to be far apart, i.e. $D_{ed}(a,b) = 1$. Otherwise, if none of the activities a and b have data attributes, then no information is gained, i.e. $D_{ed}(a,b) = \perp$.

---

[4] However, this principle may not hold for data attributes that take a wide range of values. One may be able to distinguish such attributes and informative ones via data-aware process mining [18]. The most informative attributes that indicate similarity or difference between activities are probably those involved in decision points.

5   Approach

Activities with similar contexts are candidates for synonymous or polluted labels. Here, context can be any of the aforementioned perspectives i.e. control flow, resource, time and data or any additional dimension. Let Φ be the context dimensions universe and $\mathcal{M} = \{m : \mathcal{A} \times \mathcal{A} \rightarrow [0,1] \cup \{\bot\}\}$ be the set of all context distance measures. Function $mrs : \Phi \rightarrow 2^{\mathcal{M}}$ assigns a subset of measures to each dimension $\varphi \in \Phi$. Weighting functions $W_\varphi : mrs(\varphi) \rightarrow [0,1]$ and $W_\Phi : \Phi \rightarrow [0,1]$ such that, $\Sigma_{m \in mrs(\varphi)} W_\varphi(m) = 1$ and $\Sigma_{\varphi \in \Phi} W_\Phi(\varphi) = 1$, set weights to measures within each dimension and to dimensions in Φ respectively. For any measure $m \in \mathcal{M}$, $G_m = (\mathcal{A}, E_m)$ is an activity distance graph where activities $\mathcal{A}$ are nodes and weighted edges $E_m = \{(a, b, w) \mid a, b \in \mathcal{A} \wedge w = m(a,b)\}$ represent the distance between activities based on m. We cluster activities using the minimum spanning tree (MST) clustering algorithm [30] which can be decomposed into two main steps: (1) computing a minimum spanning tree (MST) for the input activity distance graph, which is solved by the Kruskal algorithm [17], and (2) iteratively creating a new cluster by breaking an edge of MST with the largest weight, until the desired number of clusters is reached. In order to estimate the desired number of clusters, we use Silhouette analysis [28] where the maximum value of the average Silhouette score represents the optimal number of clusters. For any $m \in \mathcal{M}$, applying MST clustering on G_m yields a partition Ω_m and any pair of activities are similar based on measure m if and only if they belong to the same cluster in Ω_m, i.e. $a \sim_m b \equiv \exists \omega \in \Omega_m [\{a, b\} \subseteq \omega]$.

Algorithm 1 presents our approach for detecting synonymous or polluted activity labels in event logs. We initially perform a pre-processing phase (Line 1) to filter out case-level data attributes (i.e. event data attributes that have the same value across a case) and also id-like event data attributes (i.e. those where the number of distinct values in the whole log equals to the total number of events), as they can not give us useful information about the nature of an activity. In Lines 2–5, for each measure of each context dimension, we make a graph and perform MST clustering. For any pair of activities $a, b \in \mathcal{A}$, we compute the weighted average similarity score $avgSim$, (Line 22) which accumulates information about whether or not a and b are similar in each dimension. To do so, for any dimension $\varphi \in \Phi$, we compute $\varphi Sim_{a,b}$ as the weighted average of measures within φ (Line 20). If no information is available for comparing a and b based on distance measure $m \in mrs(\varphi)$, then we exclude this measure by setting its corresponding weight to 0 (Lines 12–13). Furthermore, if all the measures within a dimension have null values, then we ignore that dimension (Line 19). If average context similarity between activities a and b is more than a given threshold θ, then they are detected as synonymous or polluted activity labels (Line 23).

The time complexity of the algorithm depends on the time complexity of computing measures. For our defined context dimensions and measures, i.e. Eqs. 1–5, we break the algorithm into steps (assume n, m, k, v, r, d are the number of activities, events, data attributes, data values, resources, and binned durations in log L): The pre-processing step (Line 1) is $O(m \times k)$, making the activity distance graph (Lines 2–5) is $O(n^2 \times (m + n))^5$, $O(m + (n^2 \times r))^6$, $O(m + n^2 \times d)^7$, $O(m + n^2)^8$, and $O((m \times k) + (n^2 \times v))^9$ for control flow, resource, duration, time and data measures respectively, MST clustering is $O(n^3)$ [10], and finally the detection step (Lines 6–24) is $O(n^2)$. Therefore, the overall time complexity of our approach is $O(m \times (r + k) + n^2 \times (n + m + d + v))$.

Algorithm 1: Detect Synonymous and Polluted Activity Labels

Input: Event log $L = (\mathcal{E}, \mathcal{A}, \mathcal{V}, \mathcal{T}, AN, \#, \mathcal{L})$, context universe Φ, weighting
$\qquad$ functions W_φ and W_Φ, threshold θ

Output: $\mathcal{A}_{imperfect}$

1 $\quad L \leftarrow$ Preprocess(L) ;
2 $\quad$**foreach** $\varphi \in \Phi$ **do**
3 $\qquad$**foreach** $m \in mrs(\varphi)$ **do**
4 $\qquad\quad G_m \leftarrow$ makeGraph($\mathcal{A}, m$);
5 $\qquad\quad \Omega_m \leftarrow$ MST-Clustering(G_m);

6 $\quad$**foreach** $a, b \in \mathcal{A}$ **do**
7 $\qquad$**foreach** $\varphi \in \Phi$ **do**
8 $\qquad\quad allNull \leftarrow true$;
9 $\qquad\quad \varphi Sim_{a,b} \leftarrow 0$;
10 $\qquad\quad$**foreach** $m \in mrs(\varphi)$ **do**
11 $\qquad\qquad mSim_{a,b} \leftarrow 0$;
12 $\qquad\qquad$**if** $m(a, b) = \bot$ **then**
13 $\qquad\qquad\quad W_\varphi(m) \leftarrow 0$;
14 $\qquad\qquad$**else**
15 $\qquad\qquad\quad allNull \leftarrow false$;
16 $\qquad\qquad\quad$**if** $a \sim_m b$ **then**
17 $\qquad\qquad\qquad mSim_{a,b} \leftarrow 1 - m(a, b)$;

18 $\qquad\quad$**if** $allNull$ **then**
19 $\qquad\qquad W_\Phi(\varphi) \leftarrow 0$;
20 $\qquad\quad$**else**
21 $\qquad\qquad \varphi Sim_{a,b} \leftarrow \Sigma_{m \in mrs(\varphi)} mSim_{a,b} \times W_\varphi(m)$;

22 $\qquad avgSim_{a,b} \leftarrow \Sigma_{\varphi \in \Phi} W_\Phi(\varphi) \times \varphi Sim_{a,b}$;
23 $\qquad$**if** $avgSim_{a,b} \geq \theta$ **then**
24 $\qquad\quad \mathcal{A}_{imperfect} \leftarrow \mathcal{A}_{imperfect} \cup \{\{a, b\}\}$;

25 **return** $\mathcal{A}_{imperfect}$

---

^{5} $O(m + n^2)$ for the footprint matrix and $O(n^3)$ for the distance measure.
^{6} $O(m)$ for the resource multi-sets and $O(n^2 \times r)$ for the distance measure.
^{7} $O(m)$ for the duration multi-sets and $O(n^2 \times d)$ for the distance measure.
^{8} $O(m)$ for the time multi-sets and $O(n^2)$ for the distance measure.
^{9} $O(m \times k)$ for the data multi-sets and $O(n^2 \times v)$ for the distance measure.
^{10} $O(n^2 \log n)$ for the Kruskal algorithm and $O(n^3)$ for silhouette analysis.

6 Evaluation

We conducted three experiments to evaluate our approach using real-life logs. To perform these experiments, we implemented Algorithm 1 for the aforementioned distance measures[11] in Java and released a plug-in for the ProM framework[12]. Our design for four experiments is illustrated in Fig. 2. The first experiment (Fig. 2(a)) was aimed at assessing how our approach works with artificial imperfect activity labels. For this, we used a real-life log and generated other logs by incrementally renaming activity labels. These logs were provided as input to our detection approach. The next two experiments (Fig. 2(b)) aimed at investigating whether we can get the same performance in detecting real imperfect activity labels in real-life logs. We assessed the number of activity labels that could be detected by our method, by measuring precision, recall, and F-score.

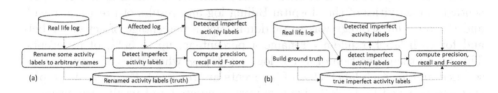

Fig. 2. Experiment setup for (a) artificial and (b) real imperfect activity labels

A summary of characteristics of real-life logs that we used for experiments can be found in Table 1, where the columns identify the number of traces, trace variants, events, activities, resources, event-level attributes, life-cycle, affected activities, affected events, and their percentage. Although none of these logs have activity duration information, we have tested our approach on simulated logs where activity duration is recorded. For the first experiment, we used the Hospital Billing log[13] which contains events related to billing of medical services provided by a Dutch hospital. We chose this log because it has a rich context, e.g. 18 event-level attributes, 1151 resources, and fine granular timestamps[14]. For the second experiment, we used the Sepsis log[15] [23] which contains events relates to the treatment process of sepsis cases from a Dutch hospital. It includes different attributes for events e.g. results of tests and some information from checklists. To the best of our knowledge, this was the only event log in 4TU Data Center that contains multiple activity labels with the same semantics that are frequently executed. As confirmed by Mannhardt and Blind [23], activity labels *"Release*

---

[11] We used the bin width of 1 min for duration binning, the number 2 for null-valued distances, and uniform weights for measures within the temporal dimension.

[12] https://svn.win.tue.nl/repos/prom/Packages/SynonymousLabelRepair.

[13] https://data.4tu.nl/repository/uuid:76c46b83-c930-4798-a1c9-4be94dfeb741.

[14] To access to logs, ground truths and results, refer to https://s3-ap-southeast-2.amazonaws.com/event-log-quality/CoopIS2019/ReadMe.docx.

[15] https://data.4tu.nl/repository/uuid:915d2bfb-7e84-49ad-a286-dc35f063a460.

C", "Release D", and "Release E" are different variants of discharging a patient. Therefore, our ground truth consists of any pair of these 3 activity labels. For the third experiment, we used an event log from an Australian insurance company[16] with existing true imperfect activity labels.

Table 1. Characteristics of real-life logs used for evaluation

Log	#Trc	#Trc vars	#Evt	#Act	#Res	#Dt attrs	Life-cycle	#Aff acts	#Aff evts	%Aff evts
Hospital Billing	100000	1020	451359	18	1151	18	complete	0	0	0%
Sepsis	1050	846	15214	16	26	27	complete	3	55	0.36%
Insurance	17153	2197	49950	506	62	8	complete	418	7542	15.10%

Table 2 shows the characteristics of logs generated by renaming different percentages of activities of the Hospital Billing log and results of precision, recall, and F-score. Our strategy was to randomly pick a percentage of activity labels and for each label, randomly rename a percentage, up to 50%, of its events. This led to the generation of a new log, e.g. $H_{40,30}$ where 40% of activities are selected and for each label, 30% of its events are renamed. For each of the percentages reported in Table 2, five logs were generated and results are averaged over the five logs. We aimed to simulate different levels of imperfect labels that can be present in real-life scenarios. In computations of Table 2 and Figs. 3 and 4 we assumed the final similarity threshold $\theta = 0.7$ and uniform weights for the timing pattern and duration measures within the temporal dimension. Then, in order to find the best weights of the four dimensions automatically[17], i.e. control flow, resource, temporal and data, we iterated Algorithm 1 where in each iteration, we set the weight of each dimension to an integer between 1 and 5 (inclusive), resulting in $5^4 = 625$ total weight settings, and we picked the first weight setting that maximizes the F-score and reported the results. As evidenced in Table 2, our approach achieves stable high precision, recall, and F-score, especially when renamed activities are frequent. However, when renamed activities are infrequent, e.g. in $H_{20,0.1}$ since only 0.017% of events of the log are affected, the approach gets a low F-score.

In Fig. 3, we compare our approach with four baselines, each considering only one of the context dimensions, control flow, resource, temporal and data, since we could not find any equivalent approach in the literature that detects synonymous or polluted activity labels in event logs without relying on any external data, e.g. an ontology or a thesaurus. As shown in Fig. 3, combining multiple context dimensions with the best weights, from 1 to 5 for each dimension, yields better F-scores than relying only on a single dimension. This is because when we rely solely on one dimension, e.g. data, then its quality highly influences

---

[16] We can't release the log due to the NDA agreement with the organization.

[17] Of course where domain knowledge is available, it can guide the user to set the weights, but we want our approach to be applicable even if domain knowledge is not available by finding the best weights automatically.

Table 2. Characteristics and results for the Hospital Billing log with artificial errors

Log	Traces variants	Affected activities	Affected events	Affected events%	Precision	Recall	F-score
$H_{20,0.1}$	1036	3	79	0.017%	0.4333	0.2833	0.3426
$H_{20,10}$	1448	4	11234	2.48%	0.8833	0.7833	0.8303
$H_{20,30}$	1741	4	38575	8.55%	1	0.8600	0.9247
$H_{40,30}$	2293	7	58308	12.91%	0.8560	0.9428	0.8973
$H_{40,50}$	2507	7	94378	20.91%	0.9250	0.9143	0.9196
$H_{60,50}$	3935	11	138396	30.66%	0.9333	0.8364	0.8822
$H_{80,50}$	4734	14	173395	38.41%	0.9703	0.8285	0.8938
$H_{100,50}$	6608	18	225684	50.00%	0.9889	0.8666	0.9238

the results, however, by investigating multiple dimensions, and assigning low priorities (weights) to low-quality ones, we can improve the outcomes. As evidenced in Fig. 3, for infrequent activity labels, i.e. below 3%, the resource and data dimensions are more informative than the control flow dimension, while for more frequent activity labels, the control flow dimension is more helpful. We can also see in Fig. 3 that, the temporal dimension is the least informative dimension for all the percentages of affected events, so assigning a low weight to this dimension would result in a better F-score. For instance, for the $H_{40,30}$ log with 12.91% affected events, the control flow and resource dimensions are more informative than the data and temporal dimensions. This fact is also evidenced in Fig. 4 where we show how F-score of our approach, applied on the $H_{40,30}$ log, varies with different dimension weights ranging from $(1, 1, 1, 1)$ to $(5, 5, 5, 5)$ for the control flow, resource, temporal, and data dimensions respectively. We can see that assigning low weights to the control flow and resource dimensions and high weights to the temporal and data dimensions, i.e. $(1, 1, 5, 5)$ yields the worst F-score of 0.57, while assigning high weights to the control flow and resource dimensions and low weights to the temporal and data dimensions, i.e. $(5, 4, 1, 1)$ yields the best F-score of 0.92.

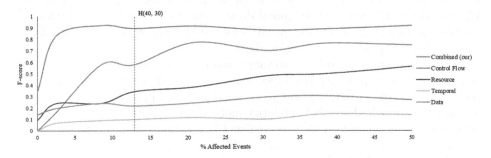

Fig. 3. F-score of our approach (combined) compared to single-dimension baselines for the Hospital Billing log with artificial errors

Table 3 reports the results obtained from the Sepsis, Insurance, and $H_{40,30}$ logs for different final similarity thresholds θ, i.e. 0.7, 0.8, and 0.9, with the

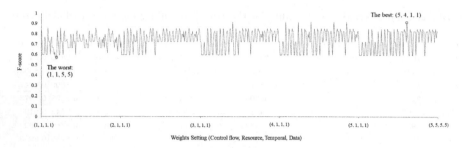

Fig. 4. F-score of our approach for different combinations of weights for the $H_{40,30}$ log

best weights[18], compared to the four single-dimension baselines. These results, same as the last experiments shown in Fig. 3, suggest that combining multiple dimensions with the best weights yields higher F-scores than single dimensions. We can see that increasing the threshold leads to higher precision and lower recall as the number of detections decreases. However, a too high threshold, i.e. $\theta = 0.9$ may result in detecting nothing, as e.g. for the $H_{40,30}$ log. Therefore 0.7 seems to be more suitable than other choices. For this threshold, applying our approach on the $H_{40,30}$ and Sepsis logs results in high F-scores of 0.89 and 1 respectively, however, for the Insurance log, we see a lower F-score of 0.36. This is because there are many activity labels with low frequency in the Insurance log, e.g. 324 of a total of 506 distinct activity labels have a frequency of 1, and our approach is better in detecting frequent imperfect activity labels as we are looking at probability distributions for different context dimensions. Furthermore, we can see that for the Insurance log, which contains infrequent activity labels, the data and especially the resource dimensions seem to be more informative than the control flow and temporal dimensions, while for the other two logs, which have more frequent activities, the control flow and resource dimensions seem to be more helpful than the data and temporal dimensions, as e.g. in the Sepsis log considering the data and temporal dimensions results in F-score of 0 for all thresholds. This is the same conclusion as for our last experiments with artificial imperfect activity labels depicted in Fig. 3.

Table 4 reports the results of our approach (context similarity with the best weights) on the Sepsis and Insurance logs[19] compared to the label similarity method and shows what happens if we combine our approach with the label similarity approach. The label similarity method assumes two activity labels to be synonyms or polluted if their normalized Levenshtein string distance [19] is

---

[18] We assigned weights 1, 2, 3, 4, 5 to each of the four dimensions and picked the first one that maximizes the F-score.

[19] We did not include the Hospital Billing logs in this experiment because their activity labels were artificially renamed to arbitrary names and therefore applying label similarity on those names would not result in meaningful outcomes.

Table 3. Results for different thresholds compared to four single-dimension baselines

Log	Approach	$\theta = 0.7$			$\theta = 0.8$			$\theta = 0.9$		
		Precision	Recall	F-score	Precision	Recall	F-score	Precision	Recall	F-score
$H_{40,30}$	Control flow only	0.8800	0.4333	0.5667	0.8000	0.2381	0.3543	0	0	0
	Resource only	0.2098	0.9714	0.3446	0.3592	0.9429	0.5180	0.4215	0.8000	0.5516
	Temporal only	0.0530	0.9429	0.1002	0.0566	0.9429	0.1068	0.0628	0.8762	0.1172
	Data only	0.1444	0.4619	0.2193	0.1356	0.2952	0.1847	0.1364	0.2333	0.1702
	Combined (Our)	0.8559	0.9428	0.8944	0.8714	0.9143	0.8788	1	0.5904	0.7388
Sepsis	Control flow only	0.2000	0.3333	0.2500	0.5000	0.3333	0.4000	0.5000	0.3333	0.4000
	Resource only	0.1579	1	0.2727	0.1579	1	0.2727	0.1579	1	0.2727
	Temporal only	0	0	0	0	0	0	0	0	0
	Data only	0	0	0	0	0	0	0	0	0
	Combined (Our)	1	1	1	1	1	1	1	1	1
Insurance	Control flow only	0.5468	0.0103	0.0202	0.5468	0.0103	0.0202	0.5468	0.0103	0.0202
	Resource only	0.2095	0.4614	0.2882	0.2098	0.4614	0.2885	0.2211	0.4612	0.2989
	Temporal only	0.0263	0	0.0001	0.0263	0	0.0001	0.0263	0	0.0001
	Data only	0.5351	0.0839	0.1451	0.6384	0.0112	0.0219	0	0	0
	Combined (Our)	0.3202	0.4098	0.3595	0.4468	0.2543	0.3241	0.6340	0.0053	0.0106

lower than a threshold θ_l[20]. The results suggest that the label similarity method gets lower F-scores than our approach, which relies on context similarity, for the Insurance log and much lower F-score for the Sepsis log. The reason is that the Sepsis log contains activity labels that are syntactically similar but semantically different, e.g. *"Admission IC"* and *"Admission NC"* regarding admission of a patient to intensive care and normal care in a hospital respectively. This also explains why the label similarity method gets a low precision for the Sepsis log. We can also see that the label similarity method has a neutral (no positive and no negative) effect on the results of our approach when it is added as another component[21] as we are already achieving the highest F-score of 1 by considering activity context only. However, for the Insurance log, combining our approach with label similarity yields an improvement of 0.04 of the F-score.

Table 5 reports the time performance, excluding the selection of the best weights, of our experiments with different logs. The results show that our approach works in a quite reasonable time since it looks at multiple context dimensions of each event. The time is increasing polynomially with the number of activities and linearly with the number of events. For the Insurance log, with 506 activities, the approach takes 7 to 8 min on average and the required time for deciding on each activity is 897 ms.

---

[20] We have considered final similarity threshold $\theta = 0.7$ and distance threshold $\theta_l = 0.3$ for the computations of Table 4 to compare methods under the same conditions.

[21] In combining our approach with label similarity we still select the best weights, i.e. from 1 to 5 for each dimension as well as the label similarity measure.

Table 4. Comparison of context similarity (our) and label similarity approaches

Log	Approach	Precision	Recall	F-score
Sepsis	Context similarity (our)	1	1	1
	Label similarity	0.2727	1	0.4216
	Context and label similarity	1	1	1
Insurance	Context similarity (our)	0.3202	0.4098	0.3595
	Label similarity	0.9525	0.1563	0.2685
	Context and label similarity	0.4818	0.3438	0.4012

Table 5. The time performance for experiments with different logs

Log	Time (sec)			
	Avg	StDev	Min	Max
$H_{40,30}$	28.345	2.739	24.345	31.223
Sepsis	2.060	3.126	1.634	2.432
Insurance	454.017	25.228	452.768	480.311

7   Conclusion

We have proposed a contextual approach for detecting synonymous and polluted activity labels since they manifest themselves in real-life event logs [29]. We have discussed different activity context dimensions, i.e. control flow, resource, time, and data, each with (a) dedicated distance measure(s). Synonymous and polluted labels are detected through the same approach which is looking at the overall context similarity. However, synonymous and polluted labels may need different treatments when it comes to repair, which is left as future work. We have evaluated our approach using real-life logs from two hospitals and an insurance company. The results show that we can detect frequent synonymous and polluted labels, which are more serious problems than infrequent ones, efficiently. The results also suggest that the control flow and resource dimensions are more informative for detecting frequent imperfect activity labels, while for detecting infrequent ones, the resource and data dimensions are more helpful. Furthermore, the temporal dimension seems to be the least informative perspective for detecting frequent and infrequent imperfect activity labels. Some possible future avenues of research are developing techniques for detecting infrequent imperfect activity labels more efficiently, repairing the detected labels, and considering other dimensions and measures, e.g. case data attributes.

References

1. van der Aa, H., Gal, A., Leopold, H., Reijers, H.A., Sagi, T., Shraga, R.: Instance-based process matching using event-log information. In: Dubois, E., Pohl, K. (eds.) CAiSE 2017. LNCS, vol. 10253, pp. 283–297. Springer, Cham (2017). https://doi.org/10.1007/978-3-319-59536-8_18
2. Van der Aalst, W.M.P.: Process Mining: Data Science in Action, 2nd edn. Springer, Heidelberg (2016)

3. van der Aalst, W., et al.: Process mining manifesto. In: Daniel, F., Barkaoui, K., Dustdar, S. (eds.) BPM 2011. LNBIP, vol. 99, pp. 169–194. Springer, Heidelberg (2012). https://doi.org/10.1007/978-3-642-28108-2_19
4. van der Aalst, W.M.P., Dustdar, S.: Process mining put into context. IEEE Internet Comput. **16**(1), 82–86 (2012)
5. Becker, M., Laue, R.: A comparative survey of business process similarity measures. Comput. Ind. **63**(2), 148–167 (2012)
6. Bose, R.J.C., Mans, R.S., van der Aalst, W.M.P.: Wanna Improve Process Mining Results - It's High Time We Consider Data Quality Issues Seriously. Technical Report BPM-13-02, BPM Center (2013)
7. Bose, R.J.C., Mans, R.S., van der Aalst, W.M.P.: Wanna improve process mining results - it's high time we consider data quality issues seriously. In: Computational Intelligence and Data Mining Symposium, pp. 127–134. IEEE (2013)
8. Cairns, A.H., et al.: Using semantic lifting for improving educational process models discovery and analysis. In: Symposium on Data-driven Process Discovery and Analysis. CEUR, vol. 1293, pp. 150–161 (2014)
9. Celino, I., de Medeiros, A.K.A., Zeissler, G., et al.: Semantic business process analysis. In: Workshop on Semantic Business Process and Product Lifecycle Management. CEUR, vol. 251, pp. 44–47. CEUR-WS (2007)
10. Conforti, R., La Rosa, M., ter Hofstede, A.H.M.: Timestamp Repair for Business Process Event Logs. Technical report, The University of Melbourne (2018)
11. Craw, S.: Manhattan distance. In: Shekhar, S., Xiong, H., Zhou, X. (eds.) Encyclopedia of Machine Learning and Data Mining, pp. 790–791. Springer, Cham (2017)
12. Dijkman, R., Dumas, M., van Dongen, B., et al.: Similarity of business process models: metrics and evaluation. Inf. Syst. **36**(2), 498–516 (2011)
13. Dixit, P.M., et al.: Detection and interactive repair of event ordering imperfection in process logs. In: Krogstie, J., Reijers, H.A. (eds.) CAiSE 2018. LNCS, vol. 10816, pp. 274–290. Springer, Cham (2018). https://doi.org/10.1007/978-3-319-91563-0_17
14. Günther, C.W.: Process Mining in Flexible Environments. Ph.D. thesis, Einhoven University Of Technology (2009)
15. Klinkmüller, C., Weber, I., Mendling, J., Leopold, H., Ludwig, A.: Increasing recall of process model matching by improved activity label matching. In: Daniel, F., Wang, J., Weber, B. (eds.) BPM 2013. LNCS, vol. 8094, pp. 211–218. Springer, Heidelberg (2013). https://doi.org/10.1007/978-3-642-40176-3_17
16. Koschmider, A., Ullrich, M., Heine, A., Oberweis, A.: Revising the vocabulary of business process element labels. In: Zdravkovic, J., Kirikova, M., Johannesson, P. (eds.) CAiSE 2015. LNCS, vol. 9097, pp. 69–83. Springer, Cham (2015). https://doi.org/10.1007/978-3-319-19069-3_5
17. Kruskal, J.B.: On the shortest spanning subtree of a graph and the traveling salesman problem. Am. Math. Soc. **7**(1), 48–50 (1956)
18. Leoni, M.D., van der Aalst, W.M.P.: Data-aware process mining: discovering decisions in processes using alignments. In: SAC, pp. 1454–1461. ACM (2013)
19. Levenshtein, V.I.: Binary codes capable of correcting deletions, insertions, and reversals. Soviet physics doklady **10**(8), 707–710 (1966)
20. Lu, X., Fahland, D.: A conceptual framework for understanding event data quality for behavior analysis. In: ZEUS. CEUR, vol. 1826, pp. 11–14 (2017)
21. Lu, X., et al.: Semi-supervised log pattern detection and exploration using event concurrence and contextual information. In: Panetto, H., et al. (eds.) OTM 2017. LNCS, vol. 10573, pp. 154–174. Springer, Cham (2017). https://doi.org/10.1007/978-3-319-69462-7_11

22. Lu, X., Fahland, D., van den Biggelaar, F.J.H.M., van der Aalst, W.M.P.: Handling duplicated tasks in process discovery by refining event labels. In: La Rosa, M., Loos, P., Pastor, O. (eds.) BPM 2016. LNCS, vol. 9850, pp. 90–107. Springer, Cham (2016). https://doi.org/10.1007/978-3-319-45348-4_6

23. Mannhardt, F., Blinde, D.: Analyzing the trajectories of patients with sepsis using process mining. In: CAiSE. CEUR, vol. 1859, pp. 72–80 (2017)

24. Mans, R.S., van der Aalst, W.M.P., Vanwersch, R.J.B., Moleman, A.J.: Process mining in healthcare: data challenges when answering frequently posed questions. In: Lenz, R., Miksch, S., Peleg, M., Reichert, M., Riaño, D., ten Teije, A. (eds.) KR4HC/ProHealth -2012. LNCS (LNAI), vol. 7738, pp. 140–153. Springer, Heidelberg (2013). https://doi.org/10.1007/978-3-642-36438-9_10

25. Massey Jr., F.J.: The kolmogorov-smirnov test for goodness of fit. J. Am. Stat. Assoc. **46**(253), 68–78 (1951)

26. de Medeiros, A.K.A., et al.: An outlook on semantic business process mining and monitoring. In: Meersman, R., Tari, Z., Herrero, P. (eds.) OTM 2007. LNCS, vol. 4806, pp. 1244–1255. Springer, Heidelberg (2007). https://doi.org/10.1007/978-3-540-76890-6_52

27. Rosemann, M., Recker, J., Flender, C.: Contextualisation of business processes. Int. J. Bus. Process Integr. Manage. **3**(1), 47–60 (2008)

28. Rousseeuw, P.J.: Silhouettes: a graphical aid to the interpretation and validation of cluster analysis. J. Comput. Appl. Math. **20**, 53–65 (1987)

29. Suriadi, S., Andrews, R., ter Hofstede, A.H.M., Wynn, M.T.: Event log imperfection patterns for process mining: towards a systematic approach to cleaning event logs. Inf. Syst. **64**, 132–150 (2017)

30. Tan, P.N., Steinbach, M., Kumar, V.: Cluster analysis: additional issues and algorithms. In: Introduction to Data Mining, pp. 569–650. Pearson (2005)

31. Tax, N., Alasgarov, E., Sidorova, N., et al.: Generating Time-Based Label Refinements to Discover More Precise Process Models. Technical report, Eindhoven University of Technology (2017)

32. Verhulst, R.: Evaluating Quality of Event Data within Event Logs: An Extensible Framework. Master's thesis, Eindhoven University of Technology (2016)

Automated Robotic Process Automation: A Self-Learning Approach

Junxiong Gao[1]([✉]), Sebastiaan J. van Zelst[1,2], Xixi Lu[3], and Wil M. P. van der Aalst[1,2]

[1] Chair of Process and Data Science, RWTH Aachen University, Aachen, Germany
{jx.gao,s.j.v.zelst,wvdaalst}@pads.rwth-aachen.de
[2] Fraunhofer Institute for Applied Information Technology (FIT), Sankt Augustin, Germany
{sebastiaan.van.zelst,wil.van.der.aalst}@fit.fraunhofer.de
[3] Department of Information and Computing Sciences, Utrecht University, Utrecht, The Netherlands
x.lu@uu.nl

Abstract. Robotic Process Automation (RPA) recently gained a lot of attention, in both industry and academia. RPA embodies a collection of tools and techniques that allow business owners to automate repetitive manual tasks. The intrinsic value of RPA is beyond dispute, e.g., automation reduces errors and costs and thus allows us to increase the overall business process performance. However, adoption of current-generation RPA tools requires a manual effort w.r.t. identification, elicitation and programming of the to-be-automated tasks. At the same time, several techniques exist that allow us to track the exact behavior of users in the front-end, in great detail. Therefore, in this paper, we present a novel end-to-end approach that allows for completely automated, algorithmic RPA-rule deduction, on the basis of captured user behavior. Furthermore, our proposed approach is accompanied by a publicly available proof-of-concept implementation.

Keywords: Robotic process automation · Information systems · User interaction · Data mining · Knowledge discovery

1 Introduction

Business process management [7] (BPM) revolves around the effective scheduling, orchestration and coordination of the different activities and tasks that comprise a (business) process. Indisputably, the end goal, or even holy grail, of any BPM practitioner is to design the most efficient process that achieves the highest possible quality for the end product and/or service. A natural question in this endeavor is related to *automation*, i.e., "What tasks are eligible for automated execution by a computer, rather than a human?".

Within BPM, the challenge of accurately automating a business process is known as *Business Process Automation* (BPA) [15]. Several researchers have

© Springer Nature Switzerland AG 2019
H. Panetto et al. (Eds.): OTM 2019, LNCS 11877, pp. 95–112, 2019.
https://doi.org/10.1007/978-3-030-33246-4_6

studied BPA, leading to various methodologies and techniques that enable automation in business processes. Techniques in BPA typically focus on the automation of activities and tasks from a *system perspective*, i.e., it requires a change of the configuration, or even redesign of, the information system supporting the process [6,16]. Therefore, applying BPA in practice is timely and costly, and, if applied incorrectly, can have a huge negative impact as well.

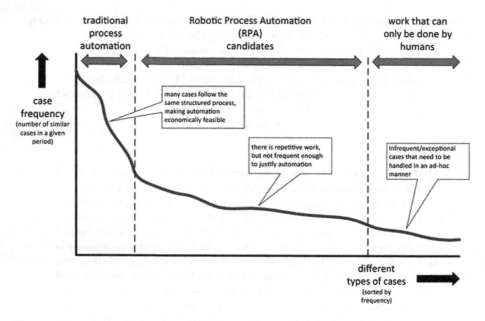

Fig. 1. Positioning of candidate processes for RPA [2]. The application of RPA is most effective in processes that comprise semi-similar execution flows.

For decades, techniques have been developed that allow us to apply automation on the *user interface (UI) level of computer systems*. More recently, these techniques were adopted by *Robotic Process Automation* (RPA) [17], allowing us to mimic user behavior within a process. Since RPA operates on the user interface level, rather than on the system level, it allows us to apply automation without any changes in the underlying information system [4,19]. Hence, the entry barrier of adopting RPA in processes that are already in place, is lower compared to conventional BPA [19]. Furthermore, as motivated in [2], there are ample opportunities for the application of RPA in the context of (business) processes. For example, the application of RPA thrives in processes and process instances that consist of a medium level of process similarity, cf. Fig. 1.

Current, (commercial) RPA techniques and products provide recorders and modelers that allow *manual construction of robotic behavior*. However, they are typically defined on low-level streams of user interactions (e.g., mouse clicks and keyboard strokes) [13,18]. Such techniques have three disadvantages: (1) *they require extensive domain knowledge* to identify, from the low-level interactions, which high-level tasks can be automated; (2) *such manual identification is labor intensive* [10]; (3) there is *no support for (semi-)automated learning* from these user interactions.

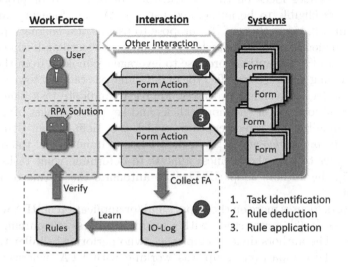

Fig. 2. The F2R approach presented in this paper, consisting of three steps.

In this paper, we propose a self-learning approach, i.e., the *Form-to-Rule (F2R) approach*, which automatically detects high-level RPA-rules, from captured historical low-level user behavior. Consider Fig. 2, in which we schematically present the F2R approach. In the first step, (1) *tasks are identified* by observing the user's interactions with the systems, on a collection of system forms that are defined. Next, it (2) *deduces rules* by learning relations between the different tasks performed. Such *rules* are defined as "if ... then ..." statements [17], which is a widely adopted definition in RPA. Finally, it (3) *applies the rules* by instantiating RPA on the basis of the deduced *rules*. The "then" part of the *rule* represents actions that can be automatically executed by the RPA solution. Hence, the RPA solution listens on *forms*, if certain triggering action is observed, it activates and executes the suitable *rule*.

The F2R approach allows RPA solutions to continuously and automatically learn from user behavior. Hence, it overcomes the main bottlenecks of adopting RPA, as mentioned before. A prototypical implementation of the F2R approach and a corresponding screencast are publicly available via https://github.com/FrankBGao/F2R_approach_RPA.

The remainder of this paper is structured as follows. In Sect. 2, we review related work. In Sect. 3, we present basic the notations used throughout the paper. Section 4 describes the core elements of the F2R approach. Section 5 presents the corresponding algorithm and implementation for the F2R approach. Section 6 concludes the paper and provides directions for future work.

2 Related Work

RPA has received much attention in recent work in the BPM community. Here, we provide a brief overview of related work in the field.

Some techniques focus on the identification of tasks and/or process properties that are eligible to be automated using RPA, i.e., focusing on *what to automate*. In [12], the authors of [12] propose to use natural language processing techniques to identify candidate tasks for automation, based on business process descriptions. In [8], the authors propose to leverage technology from the domain of process mining [1], i.e., a specific type of data analysis tailored towards analyzing execution logs of business processes, for RPA candidate task identification. In [10], the authors collect the mouse clicks and keyboard strokes of users combined with simultaneous screen captures, which they define as an UI-Log. They use *process discovery algorithms* [1] on the UI-Log to mine an end-to-end process model, in order to help the business analyst to determine what tasks to automate. In [5], the authors adopt UI-Logs to automate the testing of RPA tool deployment.

Other work focuses more on the impact and/or application of RPA w.r.t. business processes. In [3], a case study with a business process outsourcing provider is presented. The authors divided employees, who performed similar tasks, into two groups, the comparison group was working with RPA, whereas the control group was without RPA. The comparison group showed a 21% productivity improvement. In [14], the authors reflect on the impact of RPA, alongside with machine learning and blockchain technology, on the human perspective of business processes. In particular, the impact on individual tasks is discussed, i.e., repetitive tasks are identified as most suitable for RPA as well as the impact on the organizational/coordination perspective.[1]

The main deficiency of mainstream research in the domain of RPA is the lack of focus on *how to automate* RPA itself. Furthermore, it is difficult to deduce *how to automate* on the basis of the outcomes of the currently available studies. In this research, we try to fix these deficiencies by empowering RPA with the ability of self-learning.

3 Notation

In this section, we present the basic notation used throughout the paper.

Given an arbitrary set X, $|X|$ returns the size of set X, and, we let $\mathcal{P}(X) = \{X' \mid X' \subseteq X\}$ denote its *power set*. A *sequence* is an enumerated collection of objects. We write a sequence as $\langle a, b, c, a, c \rangle$, i.e., a is the first and fourth element of the sequence, d is the second element, etc. We write X^* to denote the set of all possible sequence over an arbitrary set X.

Given arbitrary sets X_1, X_2, ..., X_n, we let $X_1 \times X_2 \times \cdots \times X_n = \{(x_1, x_2, ..., x_n) \mid x_1 \in X_1, x_2 \in X_2, ..., x_n \in X_n\}$ denote the Cartesian product over

---

[1] Ref. [14] summarizes a panel discussion on the extent to which the emergence of recent technologies will reduce the "human factor" in business process management.

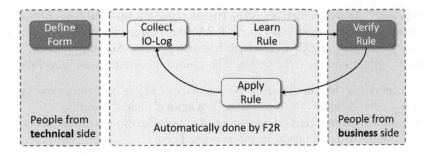

Fig. 3. The RPA lifecycle in the F2R approach: less human intervention in RPA by adopting the F2R approach.

sets X_1, X_2, ..., X_n, i.e., the set of all ordered pairs consisting of elements of X_1, X_2, ..., X_n.

Let X, Y be two no-empty sets, $f \in X \to Y$ is a total function, the domain $dom(f)$ of f is X, and the range $rng(f)$ of f is defined as $rng(f) = \{f(x) \mid x \in X\} \subseteq Y$. $f \in X \nrightarrow Y$ denotes a partial function, the domain of f is a subset of X, $dom(f) \subseteq X$. $\mathbb{B} = \{\texttt{True}, \texttt{False}\}$ represents the set of Boolean values, $\perp$ is the null value, $\mathbb{N}$ is the set of natural numbers. A multiset allows its elements to occur multiple times, e.g., $[a^2, b]$ consists of 2 times element a and one time element b. We let $\mathcal{B}(X)$ represent the set of all possible multisets for X.

4 The F2R Approach to Automate RPA

In this section, we discuss the F2R approach in detail. Section 4.1 describes the life-cycle of adopting the F2R approach and provides a running-example which is used in the remainder of this paper. Section 4.2 describes how to deduce user actions and tasks on the basis of inspecting form interactions. Section 4.3 defines the notion of a *rule* and details on how to apply multiple enabled *rules*. Section 4.3 provides examples of instantiation for *rule*'s components, it makes the definition concrete.

4.1 The F2R Lifecycle

By adopting the F2R approach, we enable RPA with an algorithmic self-learning ability. Consider Fig. 3, in which we present the new basic F2R life-cycle. In the life-cycle, there are only two points in which human interaction is required, i.e., *form definition* and *rule verification*. The *Form definition* step concerns identifying *forms* in the IT system, i.e., in order for F2R to be able to learn from users interacting with these forms. The *Rule verification* step concerns human validation of the rules learned by F2R, i.e., to determine whether a newly learned rule is in line with business/domain knowledge.

To ease the overall understanding of F2R and its definitions, we use a running example (the "SDAP scenario"), on the basis of the F2R life-cycle. We consider a "swivel chair" process, which concerns transferring information from one system to another. Such a process is a typical RPA adoption scenario [11]. Consider an imaginary company, SDAP Co., which has two systems for employment, i.e. an *interview system* and an *HR System*. The main business process is as follows.

1. An interviewee fills in the *Interviewee Form* (F_I) in the interview system. Form F_I has 4 fields: "Name", "Age", "Gender", and "Result".
2. The human resource (HR) department of SDAP Co. evaluates the interviewee, and updates the evaluation in Interviewee Form.
3. If the HR department's evaluation equals "Pass", an employee of the HR department subsequently fills in the *New Employee Form* (F_N) in the HR system. The F_N from has 3 fields, i.e., "Name", "Age", "Gender", which the employee copies from the F_I form. If the HR department's evaluation equals "Fail", the HR-department does not perform any action.

The conceptual description for adopting the F2R approach in the SDAP scenario is as follows:

1. Define two *forms* F_I and F_N, and collect the user interactions (captured in an *Input/Output (IO)-Log*) on these two *forms*.
2. Learn *rules* from the IO-Log. The rules represent statements of the form "if F_I's Result field is updated to "Pass", then copy the content of F_I's to F_N".
3. An employee verifies the *rule*. If the rule is verified, it is adopted into the RPA solution, i.e., the rule is applied automatically.

In the following sections, we provide more detailed descriptions and formal definitions of the F2R approach. Moreover, the algorithm for learning rules, i.e. instantiating F2R, is presented as well.

4.2   Task Detection Using Forms

The cornerstone concept of the F2R approach is the notion of a *form*. A form is an abstracted and standardized representation of any IT system's data container. For example, consider a simple excel sheet, a web form, a form in SAP, etc., all these data containers can essentially be seen as a form. A *form instance* represents a filled form. A form can be filled multiple times, hence, a form can be instantiated into one or multiple *form instances*. A form instance is distinguished by its *form instance identifier*. A *form state* is the set of values of a form instance at a point of time, i.e. it contains the filled information of the form instance. A *form action* describes a manipulation of a form's state, i.e. it describes two form states, collected at the points in time in which the user is starting to edit (enter) the form instance until the user closes (leaves) the form instance. Finally, an *IO-Log* represents a set of collected form actions. The F2R approach leverages the notion of an IO-Log to find behavioral rules that are eligible for automation through RPA.

As indicated, the notion of a form is the cornerstone of the F2R approach. For example, a purchase order form in SAP, in essence, is a simple form. However, the concept of a form is more general. Not only the actual forms in an IT system are defined as a form, but also any UI which has a fixed structure and position in the system, is represented by a form, e.g., tables, BI dashboards, etc. Any form has two elements, i.e., a *form name* and a set of *form fields*. The form fields refer to all the UI elements which are able to hold information.

Definition 1 (Form). *Let $\mathcal{U}_{frm}$ denote the universe of form names and $\mathcal{U}_{fld}$ the universe of form fields. A form F is a pair $F = (frm, Q) \in \mathcal{U}_{frm} \times \mathcal{P}(\mathcal{U}_{fld})$, where frm is the name of the form F and $Q \subseteq \mathcal{U}_{fld}$ is a set of form fields. Let $\mathcal{U}_F$ denote the set of all possible forms in the system, and $ID \in \mathcal{U}_{fld}$ be the form instance identifier, for which we enforce:*

$\forall F = (frm, Q) \in \mathcal{U}_F \, (ID \in Q)$, *i.e., every form has the form instance identifier in Q.*
$\forall F = (frm, Q), F' = (frm', Q') \in \mathcal{U}_F \, (frm = frm' \implies Q = Q')$, *i.e., the name of a form uniquely determines the set of fields associated with it.*

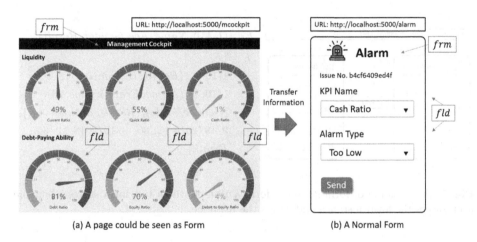

(a) A page could be seen as Form   (b) A Normal Form

Fig. 4. Two examples of a form, where *frm* points to the names of the forms and *fld* to the fields.

Figure 4 shows two examples of a form; Fig. 4(a) is a management dashboard, which is representable as a form, i.e., it is formalized as $F_{MC} = (MC, \{ID, CR, QR, CashR, DR, ER, DER\})$. Figure 4(b) is a more classical *form*, which is formalized as $F_A = (Alarm, \{ID, KPI, AlarmType\})$.

A *form instance* is a filled form with a unique id assigned to the omnipresent field ID. We assume that there always exists a unique form instance ID id $\in$ IID, which allows us to identify a single instance of a form. Observe that, in some cases, an IT system readily defines an instance identifier for a form. In other cases, such an instance identifier is derived, e.g., from the URL of a web form.

Definition 2 (Form Instance Identifier, Form Instance). *Let $\mathcal{U}_{Val}$ denote the universe of possible form-field values and let $IID{\subseteq}\mathcal{U}_{Val}$ denote the set of all possible form instance ids. A form instance $f = (F, id) \in \mathcal{U}_F \times IID$ of a form F is uniquely identified by $id \in IID$. Let $ids_F {\subseteq} IID$ denote all possible id values for form F. We assume $\forall F, F' \in \mathcal{U}_F \, (F{\neq}F' \Longrightarrow ids_F \cap ids_{F'} = \emptyset)$*

Since users typically do not fill out an instance of a form in one go, i.e., the user typically reopens the form and/or changes values, hence, the *state* of the form changes over time. Therefore, we define the notion of a *form state*, i.e., representing the actual information contained in a form instance at a specific point of time.

Definition 3 (Form State). *Let $\mathcal{U}_{Val}$ denote the universe of possible form-field values, and let $\mathcal{U}_T$ denote the universe of time. Let $F = (frm, Q) \in \mathcal{U}_F$ be a form, let $id \in ids_F$ and let $t \in \mathcal{U}_T$. A state of the instance of a form F, identified by instance-id id, at point t in time, is defined by a partial function $\phi_{(F,id,t)} \colon Q {\nrightarrow} \mathcal{U}_{Val}$, for which: $\phi_{(F,id,t)}(ID) = id, \forall t \in \mathcal{U}_T$, i.e., the instance-id is always present.*

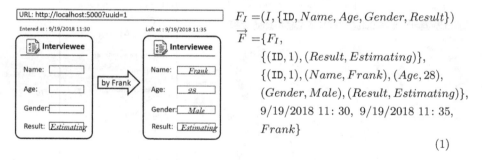

$$F_I = (I, \{\text{ID}, Name, Age, Gender, Result\})$$
$$\overrightarrow{F} = \{F_I,$$
$$\{(\text{ID}, 1), (Result, Estimating)\},$$
$$\{(\text{ID}, 1), (Name, Frank), (Age, 28),$$
$$(Gender, Male), (Result, Estimating)\},$$
$$9/19/2018 \; 11\colon 30, \; 9/19/2018 \; 11\colon 35,$$
$$Frank\}$$
$$(1)$$

Fig. 5. An example of form action, a form action captures two form states when the user enters the form instance and leaves the instance.

A *form action* (FA) records an interaction a user has performed on a form instance. More specifically, it records two form states at the points of time when the user is entering and leaving the form instance, respectively.

Definition 4 (Form Action, IO-Log). *Let $\mathcal{U}_U$ denote the universe of all possible users, let $F = (frm, Q) \in \mathcal{U}_F$ be a form, let $t_b, t_f \in \mathcal{U}_T$ s.t. $t_b{\leq}t_f$ be two timestamps, let $u \in \mathcal{U}_U$ be a user and $id \in IID$ be an instance ID. Furthermore, let $\overline{\phi}, \hat{\phi} \colon Q {\nrightarrow} \mathcal{U}_{Val}$. A form action $\overrightarrow{F} = (F, \overline{\phi}, \hat{\phi}, t_b, t_f, u)$ describes a manipulation of an instance of form F by user u, entering in the instance at time t_b and leaving it at time t_f. Observe that $\phi_{(F,id,t_b)} = \overline{\phi}$ and $\phi_{(F,id,t_f)} = \hat{\phi}$. We let $\mathcal{U}_{\overrightarrow{F}}$ denote a set of all possible form actions. An IO-Log $L \subseteq \mathcal{U}_{\overrightarrow{F}}$ is a set of form actions.*

The first step in the SDAP scenario is illustrated in Fig. 5, with an example of a form action. Moreover, a complete example of the SDAP scenario is illustrated using the IO-Log shown in Fig. 6.

4.3 Defining and Applying Rules

As an IO-Log is a collection of FAs, it records manipulations of form values corresponding to the tasks executed by users. We use the collection of FAs to deduce their relations, i.e., we identify whether certain input(s)/modification(s) in a form are likely to lead to other input(s)/modifications(s). We define such relations by using *rules*. For the notion of a rule we adopt a widely accepted RPA definition suggesting to describe RPA actions using "if ... then ..." statements [17]. When the if condition of a rule holds for an observed FA, our RPA solution applies the then part of the rule and generates a new FA as a response. Finally, the RPA solution translates this new FA into a sequence of low-level movements (e.g., mouse clicks or keyboard strokes) on the corresponding form instance.

An Instance of SDAP Scenario	**IO-Log**

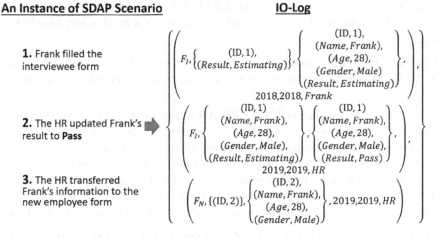

Fig. 6. An example of IO-Log, it is a set of FAs. This example describes that an interviewee Frank filled his form. HR updated Frank's result as "Pass", and copied Frank's information to an F_N instance.

A *rule* consists of two parts, a condition and a response. A *condition* checks whether an FA satisfies some requirements, i.e., it defines a function that maps an FA to true or false. For example, in the SDAP scenario, we have a condition that requires the Result field (of the Interview form) to be changed into a "Pass". The second FA shown in Fig. 6 satisfies this condition. Based on the condition, a *response* then generates a new FA, e.g., such an FA copies the current values in the "Name", "Age", and "Gender" fields to a form instance of the new employee form. In the following, we formally define the conditions, responses, and rules.

Definition 5 (Condition). *A condition* $\mathbf{c}$ *is a function* $\mathbf{c} \colon \mathcal{U}_{\overrightarrow{F}} \to \mathbb{B}$. *Let* $\mathcal{U}_{Cond}$ *be the set of all possible* conditions.

Definition 6 (Response). *A response* $\mathbf{r}$ *is a function* $\mathbf{r} \colon \mathcal{U}_{\overrightarrow{F}} \to \mathcal{U}_{\overrightarrow{F}}$, *which generates a new FA based on the observed FA. Let* $\mathcal{U}_{Resp}$ *be the set of all possible responses.*

Definition 7 (Rule). *Given a condition* $\mathbf{c} \in \mathcal{U}_{Cond}$ *and response* $\mathbf{r} \in \mathcal{U}_{Resp}$, *let* $\mathcal{U}_R$ *be the set of all possible* rules, *a rule* $\mathbf{R} \in \mathcal{U}_R$ *is characterized as:*

$$\mathbf{R}: \mathcal{U}_{\overrightarrow{F}} \nrightarrow \mathcal{U}_{\overrightarrow{F}}$$

$$\overrightarrow{F} \mapsto \begin{cases} \mathbf{r}(\overrightarrow{F}) & if\ \mathbf{c}(\overrightarrow{F}) \\ \bot & otherwise \end{cases}$$

Essentially, the RPA solution of our F2R approach learns a set of *rules*, which we refer to as a *rule base*. Moreover, we define a mechanism for selecting a set of suitable rules for one observed FA, this mechanism is called the *rule selector*. It is possible that a single, observed FA satisfies multiple conditions and, therefore, potentially triggers multiple rules present in a rule base. For example, consider the first FA of the SDAP scenario in Fig. 6, which satisfies the following two conditions: if the Age field is filled in, or if the Gender field is filled in. Therefore, we define a *rule selector*, which is a mechanism to select and apply a rule.

Definition 8 (Rule Selector). *A rule selector* $\zeta: \mathcal{P}(\mathcal{U}_R) \times \mathcal{U}_{\overrightarrow{F}} \nrightarrow \mathcal{U}_{\overrightarrow{F}}$, *selects and applies a rule present in a given rule base on an observed form action.*

Instantiating Conditions Using First-Order Logic. In order to make the concept of conditions more tangible, we provide a detailed example of how the conditions can be formally instantiated using First-Order Logic Conditions (FOLC). A FOLC is a set of propositions linked by logic connectives. A FOLC evaluates the values of the proposition variables and returns `True` or `False`. In our case, the propositions are defined on the observed FA. Each proposition describes the range of values that is acceptable for an observed FA's field value.

Definition 9 (First-Order Logic Condition). *Let* $F = (frm, Q) \in \mathcal{U}_F$, $\overrightarrow{F} = (F, \overline{\phi}, \hat{\phi}, t_b, t_f, u)$ *be an FA on an instance of form* F; *let* $\overline{\gamma}_1, ..., \overline{\gamma}_n, \hat{\gamma}_1, ..., \hat{\gamma}_m$ *be functions of the form* $Q \nrightarrow \mathcal{P}(\mathcal{U}_{Val}) \setminus \{\emptyset\}$. *And, let*

- $\overline{\mathbf{c}}_i \equiv \forall q \in dom(\overline{\gamma}_i) \left(q \in dom(\overline{\phi}) \wedge \overline{\phi}(q) \in \overline{\gamma}_i(q) \right)$, *for* $1 \leq i \leq n$;
- $\hat{\mathbf{c}}_i \equiv \forall q \in dom(\hat{\gamma}_i) \left(q \in dom(\hat{\phi}) \wedge \hat{\phi}(q) \in \hat{\gamma}_i(q) \right)$, *for* $1 \leq i \leq m$.

An FOLC function is formed by a Boolean expression over $\overline{\mathbf{c}}_1, ..., \overline{\mathbf{c}}_n, \hat{\mathbf{c}}_1, ..., \hat{\mathbf{c}}_m$.

For example, let us consider the third step in the SDAP scenario, where an FA, e.g., copying the field values, is performed, if the result field is changed from an "Estimating" to a "Pass" value. A corresponding FOLC $\mathbf{c}'_{\gamma}$ for this if condition is defined as follows. Let $F_I = (I, \{\text{ID}, Name, Age, Gender, Result\})$ be the interviewee form, and $\overrightarrow{F}' = (F_I, \overline{\phi}, \hat{\phi}, t_b, t_f, u) \in \mathcal{U}_{\overrightarrow{F}}$ be an arbitrary FA on a F_I's instance. Let $\overline{\gamma} = \{(Result, \{Estimating\})\}$ denote the range of the pairs of the fields and their values that are acceptable for the form-state $\overline{\phi}$, and $\hat{\gamma} = \{(Result, \{Pass\})\}$ the range of the pairs that are acceptable for $\hat{\phi}$. Using FOLC, we can define the if condition $\mathbf{c}'_{\gamma}$ as follows: $\mathbf{c}'_{\gamma}(\overrightarrow{F}') = (\overline{\phi}(Result) \in \{Estimating\}) \wedge (\hat{\phi}(Result) \in \{Pass\})$.

Instantiating Responses Using Transform Functions. To exemplify the concept of responses, we discuss a detailed type of response, namely the *transform* response. A transform response transforms, e.g., copies, the field values of an observed FA into the corresponding fields of a newly created form instance. Taking again the third step in the SDAP scenario as an example, the transform response in this case copies the "Name", "Age", and "Gender" values into a new form instance of the new employee form.

Definition 10 (Transform Response). *Let $F = (frm, Q)$, $F' = (frm', Q') \in \mathcal{U}_F$ be two forms, let $\lambda \colon Q \nrightarrow Q'$ be a field mapping, and, given $q \in Q$, let $\delta_q \colon \mathcal{U}_{Val} \rightarrow \mathcal{U}_{Val}$ be the transform function. Furthermore, let $\overrightarrow{F} = (F, \overline{\phi}, \hat{\phi}, t_b, t_f, u) \in \mathcal{U}_{\overrightarrow{F}}$ be an FA on an instance of form F. Let $\hat{\phi}_{F'} = \{(q', v) \in Q' \times \mathcal{U}_{Val} \mid \exists q \in dom(\lambda) \colon \lambda(q) = q' \wedge \delta_q(\hat{\phi}(q)) = v\}$. Let $t_r \in \mathcal{U}_T, t_r > t_f$, $id' \in IID$, the transform response function $\mathbf{r}_{tf}$ is characterized as:*

$$\mathbf{r}_{tf} \colon \mathcal{U}_{\overrightarrow{F}} \rightarrow \mathcal{U}_{\overrightarrow{F}}$$
$$(F, \overline{\phi}, \hat{\phi}, t_b, t_f, u) \mapsto (F', \phi(F', id', t_f), \hat{\phi}_{F'}, t_f, t_r, \mathcal{R}).$$

In essence, the transform response creates a new form instance (F', id') of the form F'. Moreover, it creates two states: state $\phi(F', id', t_f)$ is the default form state of the new form instance, and state $\hat{\phi}_{F'}$ is the state where its field values are transformed. These two states are then embedded in the returned FA. Besides, the entering time of this FA is t_f, which means it will be executed right after observing the previous FA. The leaving time would be t_f. Hence, the period between t_f and t_r allows the RPA solution to execute this new FA and the system latency. We use $\mathcal{R}$ to denote this new FA is done by the RPA solution.

A special case of the transform response is the *copy* response. If the transform function $\delta_q \colon \mathcal{U}_{Val} \rightarrow \mathcal{U}_{Val}$ returns the input itself for all fields $q \in Q$, it then basically copies the input values, which we called a *copy* response.

Considering the step 3 of the SDAP scenario, where the information of name, age, and gender is copied from the Interview form into the New Employee form, this can now be performed by applying a copy response $\mathbf{r}'_{tf}$. Let $F_N = (N, \{ID, Name', Age', Gender', Result'\})$ be the New Employee form. Let $t_r \in \mathcal{U}_T$ and $t_r > t_f$ be the two timestamps of the new FA. Let $id' \in IID$ be the id of the new form instance. Let $\lambda = \{(Name, Name'), (Age, Age'), (Gender, Gender')\}$ be the mapping. The response $\mathbf{r}'_{tf}(\overrightarrow{F'}) = (F_N, \phi(F', id', t_f), \{(q', v) \mid (q, q') \in \lambda \wedge \hat{\phi}(q) = v\}, t_f, t_r, \mathcal{R})$ is a copy response. A concrete example is shown by the second and the third FAs in Fig. 6, respectively as the input and the output of this copy response.

Simple Rules. We have explained that a rule consists of a condition and a response. We have shown a concrete instantiation of the conditions using FOLC and a concrete type of response defined as the transform response. Based on the SDAP scenario shown in Fig. 6, we can define a *rule* $\mathbf{R}'_{c.r}$ which given an input

FA $\overrightarrow{F}'$, it returns the new FA $\mathbf{r}'_{\text{tf}}(\overrightarrow{F}')$ (i.e., the result of the copy response) if the condition $\mathbf{c}'_{\gamma}(\overrightarrow{F}')$ on the FA $\overrightarrow{F}'$ holds, i.e., $\mathbf{R}'_{\text{c.r}} = \mathbf{r}'_{\text{tf}}(\overrightarrow{F}')$ if $\mathbf{c}'_{\gamma}(\overrightarrow{F}')$. We call this type of rules, which comprise a FOLC as its condition and a copy response, the *simple rules*.

5 Learning Simple Rules from IO-Logs

As discussed above, an RPA solution operates based on a rule base (i.e., a set of rules). Training such an RPA solution is basically learning a rule base from the IO-log and building up such a rule base. In this section, we discuss an algorithm to learn the simple rules. We call it the *simple rule learner (SRL)*.

The SRL algorithm consists of two phases, first learning the conditions and then learning the responses. Next, we explain the learning of conditions and responses in Sects. 5.1 and 5.2, respectively. In Sect. 5.3, we discuss how to use the obtained responses and conditions to construct the rule base and the rule selector for the RPA solution. In Sect. 5.4, we briefly explain the implementation of the RPA solution.

5.1 The Condition Learner in the SRL Algorithm

As discussed, based on the input IO-log, we propose the SRL algorithm to learn a set of rules in order to obtain our rule base. As defined in Def. 5, a condition of a rule checks whether an FA meets some properties. For learning such properties, we provide an algorithm which consists of 5 steps. An overview of these steps together with an example is shown in Fig. 7.

In step (1), we simply sort the input IO-Log $L \in \mathcal{P}(\mathcal{U}_{\overrightarrow{F}})$ to obtain a sequence $S \in L^*$ of FAs which is ordered by the timestamps t_b of the FAs. As shown by the output of step (1) in Fig. 7, where each rounded rectangle represents an FA, the sorted IO-log comprises $\langle \dots \overrightarrow{F}_A, \overrightarrow{F}_I, \overrightarrow{F}_I, \overrightarrow{F}_N, \overrightarrow{F}_I, \overrightarrow{F}_I, \overrightarrow{F}_N, \dots \rangle$.

In step (2), we find *cases* from the sorted IO-log S. A *case* $cs \in \mathcal{U}_{\overrightarrow{F}} \times \mathcal{U}_{\overrightarrow{F}}$ is a pair of FAs. In this paper, we assume there is a form field which captures the case identifier, i.e., the value in this field is the case ID. Every two FAs, which have the same case ID, are paired as a case. We define a function FC to find the cases, i.e., $FC \colon L^* \times \mathcal{U}_{\text{fld}} \nrightarrow \mathcal{P}(\mathcal{U}_{\overrightarrow{F}} \times \mathcal{U}_{\overrightarrow{F}})$.

For instance, in the SDAP scenario, let $F_I = (I, \{\text{ID}, Name, Age, Gender, Result\})$, $F_N = (N, \{\text{ID}, Name, Age, Gender\})$ be the two forms, the *Name* field in F_I and F_N could be the case identifier. Based on the values in the *Name* field, the second and the third FAs in Fig. 6 are grouped into one case, because they have the same name. In the output of step (2) in Fig. 7, the cases are highlighted in the original IO-log. For example, the third FA $\overrightarrow{F}_I$ is paired with the fourth FA $\overrightarrow{F}_N$.

In step (3), we use the set of cases to detect *patterns*. A *pattern* $p \in \mathcal{U}_F \times \mathcal{U}_F$ is a pair of forms. A pattern indicates that the FAs happened on the pattern's

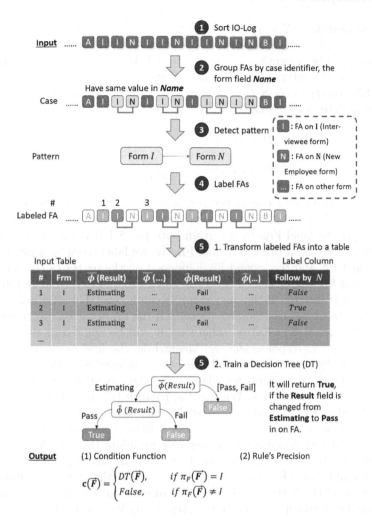

Fig. 7. Adopting learning algorithm of *condition* functions at the SDAP scenario.

forms are always paired as cases, and the order of these two FAs in a case is corresponding with the pattern. For example, in the SDAP scenario, the pattern could be $p = (F_I, F_N)$, it means after an arbitrary FA $\vec{F}$ happened on F_I, it is often observed that another FA, which has the same case ID with $\vec{F}$, happened on F_N. The main points of this step are (i) extracting candidates of patterns from cases; (ii) calculating the confidence for each candidate, if the confidence passes a threshold, the candidate will be selected as a pattern.

For the formal description, we define a function $mop\colon \mathcal{P}(\mathcal{U}_{\vec{F}} \times \mathcal{U}_{\vec{F}}) \to \mathcal{B}(\mathcal{P}(\mathcal{U}_F \times \mathcal{U}_F))$ for transforming a set of cases to a multiset of the pairs of forms, and a function $mof\colon \mathcal{P}(\mathcal{U}_{\vec{F}}) \to \mathcal{B}(\mathcal{P}(\mathcal{U}_F))$ for returning a multiset of forms by the same giving IO-Log, which is adopted to generate the set of cases. Let $q \in \mathcal{U}_{\mathtt{fld}}$

be the case identifier, $X = mop(FC(S, q))$ be a multiset of the pattern candidates, if $pc = (F, F') \in X$ is a pattern candidates, s.t. $F \in \mathcal{U}_F, F' \in \mathcal{U}_F, F \neq F'$. Let $Y = mof(L)$ be a multiset of forms; and let M be a multiset. The function $Count_M : M \to \mathbb{N}^+$ returns the counting number for an element in multiset M. The function $conf_{PT} : \mathcal{U}_F \times \mathcal{U}_F \to [0, 1]$ computes the confidence of a giving pattern candidate, its formula is Eq. 2.

$$pc = (F, F')$$
$$conf_{PT}(pc) = \frac{Count_X(pc)}{Count_Y(F)} \tag{2}$$

If the pattern candidate's confidence is greater than a certain threshold, it will be a pattern, and this threshold is set by the user.

In step (4), we label FAs by a certain pattern. A labeled FA $lfa \in \mathcal{U}_{\vec{F}} \times \mathbb{B}$ is a pair of an FA and a Boolean value. Firstly, we label cases by a pattern. If a case's the first FA and the second FA happened on the pattern's corresponding forms, the first FA will be signed the `True` label, otherwise, the `False` label, and the second FA is ignored in the next step. Secondly, we label all other FAs that do not belong to a case, by the same pattern. If the FA occurred on the pattern's first form, it is labeled as `False`, otherwise, it will be ignored in the next step and the steps in the response learner. Meanwhile, the first element of a case is labeled as `True` by a pattern, we call this case *is aligned* with this pattern.

As shown by the output of step (4) in Fig. 7, the rounded rectangle with the green background is labeled as `True` by the pattern (F_I, F_N), the one with rose color is labeled as `False`, and the one with white is ignored.

In step (5), we train a condition function from a sequence of *Labeled FAs*. This is a typical supervised learning scenario, we adopt the Decision Tree (DT) [9] algorithm in this research. There are two points in this step, (i) we transform the sequence of labeled FAs to the *input table* of DT, the attribute columns are the form fields in the "enter" and "leave" form states of FA, the label column is the Boolean label which is generated in step 4. (ii) We train a DT model based on the input table. The condition function will apply the trained DT model to giving the Boolean result if the input FA happened on the pattern's the first form; otherwise, it will return `False`. In this step, we not only gain the DT model, but also the precision of the model. And the DT model's precision is the rule's precision.

As illustrated in Fig. 7, each row of the input table corresponds a labeled FA in step (4). Based on this input table, we train a DT model. In the SDAP scenario, the DT model should able to represent the logic of "it will return `True` if the Result field is changed from Estimating to Pass".

5.2 The Response Learner in the SRL Algorithm

Using the SDAP scenario, we explained the *copy* response to illustrate one type of the response function. A copy response means that the function δ in Def.11 is an *identity function* (i.e., the input equals to its output). The main issue of this

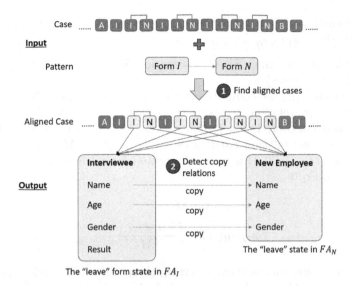

Fig. 8. Adopting learning algorithm of *response* functions at the SDAP scenario.

part is gaining the form field mapping λ, which is defined in Def.11. There are two steps in this part, and the learning process of the SDAP scenario's response function could be illustrated as Fig. 8.

In step (1), given all the cases found by the condition learner, we retain the set of cases that is aligned with a given pattern. Let $p = (F, F')$ be a pattern, and $ac = (\overrightarrow{F}, \overrightarrow{F'})$ a case. Case ac is aligned with p if and only if $\pi_F(\overrightarrow{F}) = F \wedge \pi_F(\overrightarrow{F'}) = F'$. The output is, thus, a set of cases $AC \subseteq \mathcal{U}_{\overrightarrow{F}} \times \mathcal{U}_{\overrightarrow{F}}$ that are aligned with p (i.e., $\forall ac \in AC : ac$ is *aligned* with p). For instance, as shown in Fig. 8, the cases that are aligned with the given pattern $p = (F_I, F_N)$ are highlighted after the step (1).

In step (2), we detect the *copy relation* between the form fields of a set of aligned cases. A *copy relation* $cr \in \mathcal{U}_{\texttt{fld}} \times \mathcal{U}_{\texttt{fld}}$ is a pair of form fields, where the values of these two fields are the same, i.e., is copied, and the two fields are not in the same form. This step is similar with the step (3) in the condition learner, which is for detecting the pattern. The two main substeps of this step are (i) extracting candidates for the copy relation from the set of aligned cases and (ii) computing a confidence for each candidate. If the confidence passes a threshold, the candidate is said to be a copy relation. A set of copy relations together with the identity function build a copy response.

For substep (i), a candidate is extracted from an aligned case, the first element of the candidate is a field in the aligned case's the first FA's "leave" state; similarly, the second element of this candidate is a field in the aligned case's the second FA's "leave" state. Moreover, these two fields are holding the same value. We define a function $fcr : \mathcal{P}(\mathcal{U}_{\overrightarrow{F}} \times \mathcal{U}_{\overrightarrow{F}}) \nrightarrow \mathcal{B}(\mathcal{P}(\mathcal{U}_{\texttt{fld}} \times \mathcal{U}_{\texttt{fld}}))$ which detects the candidates. Let $\overrightarrow{F} = (F, \overline{\phi}, \hat{\phi}, t_b, t_f, u) \in \mathcal{U}_{\overrightarrow{F}}$, $\overrightarrow{F'} = (F', \overline{\phi}', \hat{\phi}', t_b', t_f', u) \in \mathcal{U}_{\overrightarrow{F}}$ be two arbitrary FAs on F and F'. The multiset of candidates are generated as $fcr(AC) = \left[(q, q') \mid (\overrightarrow{F}, \overrightarrow{F'}) \in AC \wedge (q, q') \in dom(\hat{\phi}) \times dom(\hat{\phi}') \wedge \hat{\phi}(q) = \hat{\phi}'(q') \right]$. For instance, an output of the SDAP scenario is $[(\text{Name, Age})^2, (\text{Name, Name})^{97}, (\text{Name, Gender})^1]$.

For the substep (ii), we compute the confidence for each candidate to determine if it is a copy relation, by using the relative frequency of the candidate in the obtained multiset. For a formal description, let $MC = fcr(AC)$ be a multiset of the copy relation candidates; $cc = (q, q') \in MC$ be a candidate; $conf_{CR} : \mathcal{U}_{\texttt{fld}} \times \mathcal{U}_{\texttt{fld}} \to [0, 1]$ be a total function for calculating the confidence, its formula is in Eq. 3.

$$cc = (q, q') \in MC$$
$$conf_{CR}(cc) = \frac{Count_{MC}(cc)}{|MC|} \tag{3}$$

If a candidate's confidence is above a certain threshold, the candidate is selected as a copy relation. Meanwhile, this threshold is set by the user. For example, given the multiset returned by the previous step, $conf_{CR}$ (Name, Age) $= 0.02$, $conf_{CR}$ (Name, Name) $= 0.97$, $conf_{CR}$ (Name, Gender) $= 0.01$. If the user set the confidence to 0.9. The (Name, Name) is selected as a copy relation.

As illustrated in Fig. 8, the step (2) detects the copy relations from the set of aligned cases. The values, which are holding by the fields "Name", "Age", "Gender" in the "leave" state on F_I's FAs, are always equivalent to the values, which are in the fields "Name", "Age", "Gender" of the "leave" state in F_N's FAs. Thus, these threes copy relations are detected. Furthermore, the set of these threes copy relations is the field mapping λ, the identity function is the value transfer function δ, they build the copy response function for the SDAP scenario.

5.3 The Rule Base and the Rule Selector in the SRL Algorithm

In the rule selector, the rules are picked based on a certain criterion, in the SRL algorithm, we use the precision as the criterion. In principle, each rule classifies an observed FA `True` or `False`; since we are in the training phase, we know the true positive and false positive, which we use to calculate the precision measure [9]; as a result, if an observed FA satisfies multiple rules' condition, we will select the rule with the highest precision measures from the SRL rule base.

5.4 Implementation

The implementation is a proof of concept for the F2R approach and SRL algorithm, which supports the RPA solution to interact with web-pages. We developed a Chrome-extension (running in Chrome's back-end) that collects IO-Log and a web-service that receives IO-Log from the Chrome-extension, holds the rule base, and runs the SRL and the rule selector. We adopted Selenium (Web-page automation software) to translate each FA into a sequence of low-level movements on UI. The code together with screencasts for the F2R approach is publicly available at GitHub (https://github.com/FrankBGao/F2R_approach_RPA).

6 Conclusion and Future Work

In conclusion, this research provides the skeleton for our future studies in the area of RPA. We discussed the limitations in the current RPA techniques. For solving these issues, we provide the F2R approach, it formalizes the critical notions such as form, IO-Log, and rule. These notions allow the F2R approach to automatically identify tasks, deduce rules, and apply rules. We provided algorithms to learn FOLC as the conditions of rules and copy responses. It makes the concepts of the F2R approach much more concrete.

For future work, we consider dropping certain assumptions that are made in this paper. Firstly, in the definition of FA, an FA consists of two form states which are collected at the points in time at which the user enters and leaves the form instance. In the future, we will define the running FAs, which collects more form states at different timestamps.

Secondly, in the definition of Transform Response, we define $\lambda\colon Q \rightarrowtail Q', \delta_q\colon \mathcal{U}_{Val} \to \mathcal{U}_{Val}$, which are two "one to one" mappings. We plan to define other types of λ and δ, i.e., "one to many" or "many to one" mappings.

Thirdly, in learning simple rules, we assume there is a field that is the case identifier. However, this assumption does not always hold. Thus, detecting the case without the identifier is a research topic for the future.

Finally, in order to perform a response, we use the rule to check the condition and return an FA. For future work, we aim to develop a language to specify the rule's response. This language would extend the current definition of rule such that it can describe more complex tasks. The RPA solution can then be trained to execute this language to deliver more sophisticated FAs.

References

1. van der Aalst, W.M.P.: Process Mining - Data Science in Action, 2nd edn. Springer, Heidelberg (2016). https://doi.org/10.1007/978-3-662-49851-4
2. van der Aalst, W.M.P., Bichler, M., Heinzl, A.: Robotic process automation. Bus. Inf. Syst. Eng. **60**(4), 269–272 (2018)
3. Aguirre, S., Rodriguez, A.: Automation of a business process using robotic process automation (RPA): a case study. In: Figueroa-García, J.C., López-Santana, E.R., Villa-Ramírez, J.L., Ferro-Escobar, R. (eds.) WEA 2017. CCIS, vol. 742, pp. 65–71. Springer, Cham (2017). https://doi.org/10.1007/978-3-319-66963-2_7
4. Asatiani, A., Penttinen, E.: Turning robotic process automation into commercial success-case opuscapita. J. Inf. Technol. Teach. Cases **6**(2), 67–74 (2016)
5. Chacón-Montero, J., Jiménez-Ramírez, A., Enríquez, J.: Towards a method for automated testing in robotic process automation projects. In: Proceedings of the 14th International Workshop on AST, pp. 42–47. IEEE Press (2019)

6. Cichocki, A., Ansari, H.A., Rusinkiewicz, M., Woelk, D.: Workflow and Process Automation: Concepts and Technology, vol. 432. Springer, New York (2012). https://doi.org/10.1007/978-1-4615-5677-0
7. Dumas, M., La Rosa, M., Mendling, J., Reijers, H.A.: Fundamentals of Business Process Management, 2nd edn. Springer, Heidelberg (2018). https://doi.org/10.1007/978-3-662-56509-4
8. Geyer-Klingeberg, J., Nakladal, J., Baldauf, F., Veit, F.: Process mining and robotic process automation: a perfect match. In: BPM (Dissertation/Demos/Industry). pp. 124–131 (2018)
9. Han, J., Pei, J., Kamber, M.: Data Mining: Concepts and Techniques. Elsevier, New York (2011)
10. Jimenez-Ramirez, A., Reijers, H.A., Barba, I., Del Valle, C.: A method to improve the early stages of the robotic process automation lifecycle. In: Giorgini, P., Weber, B. (eds.) CAiSE 2019. LNCS, vol. 11483, pp. 446–461. Springer, Cham (2019). https://doi.org/10.1007/978-3-030-21290-2_28
11. Lacity, M., Willcocks, L.: Robotic process automation: the next transformation lever for shared services. Lond. Sch. Econ. Outsourcing Unit Working Papers **7**, 1–35 (2015)
12. Leopold, H., van der Aa, H., Reijers, H.A.: Identifying candidate tasks for robotic process automation in textual process descriptions. In: Gulden, J., Reinhartz-Berger, I., Schmidt, R., Guerreiro, S., Guédria, W., Bera, P. (eds.) BPMDS/EMMSAD -2018. LNBIP, vol. 318, pp. 67–81. Springer, Cham (2018). https://doi.org/10.1007/978-3-319-91704-7_5
13. Linn, C., Zimmermann, P., Werth, D.: Desktop activity mining - a new level of detail in mining business processes. In: Workshops of the INFORMATIK 2018-Architekturen, Prozesse, Sicherheit und Nachhaltigkeit (2018)
14. Mendling, J., Decker, G., Richard, H., Hajo, A., Ingo, W., et al.: How do machine learning, robotic process automation, and blockchains affect the human factor in business process management? Commun. Assoc. Inf. Syst. **43**(Art. 19), 297–320 (2018)
15. Scheer, A.W., Abolhassan, F., Jost, W., Kirchmer, M.: Business Process Automation. Springer, Heidelberg (2004). https://doi.org/10.1007/978-3-540-24702-9
16. Ter Hofstede, A.H., Van der Aalst, W.M., Adams, M., Russell, N.: Modern Business Process Automation: YAWL and Its Support Environment. Springer, Heidelberg (2009). https://doi.org/10.1007/978-3-642-03121-2
17. Tornbohm, C.: Market Guide for Robotic Process Automation Software. Gartner.com (2017)
18. Tripathi, A.M.: Learning Robotic Process Automation: Create Software Robots and Automate Business Processes with the Leading RPA Tool-Uipath. Packt Publishing Ltd. (2018)
19. Willcocks, L.P., Lacity, M., Craig, A.: The IT Function and Robotic Process Automation (2015)

iDropout: Leveraging Deep Taylor Decomposition for the Robustness of Deep Neural Networks

Christian Schreckenberger[1,2(✉)], Christian Bartelt[1],
and Heiner Stuckenschmidt[2]

[1] Institute for Enterprise Systems, University of Mannheim, Mannheim, Germany
{schreckenberger,bartelt}@es.uni-mannheim.de
[2] Data and Web Science Group, University of Mannheim, Mannheim, Germany
heiner@informatik.uni-mannheim.de

Abstract. In this work, we present iDropout, a new method to adjust dropout, from purely randomly dropping inputs to dropping inputs based on a mix based on the relevance of the nodes and some randomness. We use Deep Taylor Decomposition to calculate the respective relevance of the inputs and based on this, we give input nodes with a higher relevance a higher probability to be included than input nodes that seem to have less of an impact. The proposed method does not only seem to increase the performance of a Neural Network, but it also seems to make the network more robust to missing data. We evaluated the approach on artificial data with various settings, e.g. noise in data, number of informative features and on real-world datasets from the UCI Machine Learning Repository.

Keywords: Deep Neural Networks · Dropout · Explainability · Missing data

1 Introduction

Machine Learning in dynamic and unreliable environments, such as Wireless Sensor Networks, has many challenges. For one, new feature streams may appear, while other feature streams disappear, sometimes these feature streams come back and at other times they disappear for good [11]. While, this behavior heavily impacts the training and the prediction process, we want to focus on the latter in this work, i.e. unreliability in terms of missing data at prediction time.

As outlined by [3], Neural Networks are sensitive when it comes to missing inputs at prediction time [14], hence there is a need to propose methods to make Neural Networks more robust in this case. Recent advances have shown that using dropout at training time does, in fact, achieve this effect [3,4].

In this work, we make use of the recent advances in the community of explainability of Neural Networks [13]. Based on these methods the relevance for various

© Springer Nature Switzerland AG 2019
H. Panetto et al. (Eds.): OTM 2019, LNCS 11877, pp. 113–126, 2019.
https://doi.org/10.1007/978-3-030-33246-4_7

input neurons can be determined. Hereby, our hypothesis is, that if the Neural Network has more focus on the relevant inputs during the training, the connections of these inputs are strengthened more than they would be without this mechanism. In consequence, this leads to more robustness when some of the inputs are missing.

In the following we will elaborate on the background and related work, subsequently, we will introduce our approach. The approach is then evaluated empirically on artificial and real-world data. Finally, we will draw a conclusion based on the presented work.

2   Background and Related Work

In the following, we outline the background of the explainability of Neural Networks and in more detail Deep Taylor Decomposition, which is the method we make use of. Subsequently, we present related work from the areas of missing data and dropout.

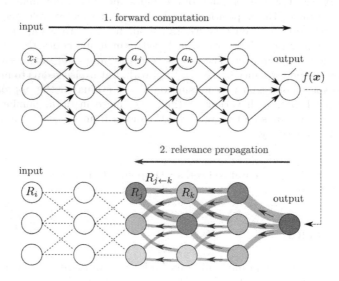

Fig. 1. Relevance computation for a Deep Neural Network. The figure is taken from Montavon et al. [13] (CC BY 4.0)

2.1   Explainability of Neural Networks

Neural Networks and especially Deep Neural Networks have become the go-to method for complex learning tasks such as image classification or natural language processing. However, in several domains, such as autonomous cars and medicine, it is not only essential to have a high accuracy representation of the domain, but also to have an understanding on which grounds the learned model is making its predictions. Due to these concerns, several efforts have been made to tackle this problem [13]. One of these methods is called Deep Taylor Decomposition [12].

Explanations methods, such as Deep Taylor Decomposition, need example data to compute the relevance. So the first step is to learn the Neural Network. After this is done the relevance of each input node is computed based on an example that is passed through the Neural Network. The computed relevance indicates the importance of the input nodes for the final prediction of the example. A visual representation of this procedure is shown in Fig. 1. On the top half of the figure, the data is passed forward through the network. In a second step (the bottom half of the figure), the relevances, which are based on the final output of the network, are propagated backward and flow through the network until they reach the input nodes, indicating which nodes had more relevance for the prediction and which had less relevance.

2.2   Missing Data

When dealing with missing data at either training or prediction time, the first method that comes to mind is imputation. A lot of work has gone into imputation methods and as of now it is still a quite active research field [10,15]. The most popular method is the mean-imputation, where the missing values are filled with the mean values of the respective feature [17]. Another, well known method is the imputation with kNN, hereby the missing value is filled based on the values of the k nearest neighbors, which are determined based on the distance of the available feature values [6].

Compared to the two presented methods, which are domain agnostic, there are also some domain-specific approaches for the imputation of values, e.g. in the domain of Wireless Sensor Networks: In [9] values are imputed based on the values of spatially close sensors and in [20] a similar idea is used to impute the values with a fuzzy artificial Neural Network and spatially close sensors.

2.3   Dropout

The initial form of dropout was presented by [16]. Hereby, it was shown that randomly setting some of the units in the input or the hidden layer to zero, can reduce overfitting and therefore boost the performance. This was done empirically on a wide range of datasets of various application domains, such as computer vision or speech recognition. As a follow-up DropConnect was introduced by [18]. Hereby, instead of setting a subset of units to zero, a less intrusive method was chosen by setting some of the weights to zero. An empirical evaluation showed that DropConnect often outperforms the conventional dropout method.

In [19], they introduce a defensive dropout mechanism against adversarial attacks, while there is no relation to missing data in this work, the main goal of them is to make the networks more robust. The defensive mechanism works in a way that the test dropout rate is adjusted based on the Neural Network model and the attacker's strategy.

The focus of [4] and [3] is on predicting with missing features. They propose DropIn, which makes use of the ensembling properties of dropout regularization to train a Neural Network as a committee machine of subnetworks. Due to this implementation the network is able to deal with up to 50% of missing features with barely a quality loss. Their proposed method is applied to a Recurrent Neural Network.

Further approaches that steer the dropout process and make it more adaptive exist. In [8] the dropout mechanism is guided in a way that high strength units of the Neural Network are more likely to be dropped and therefore low strength units are trained accordingly. The notion of high and low strength units are learned by the Neural Network itself.

In [2] another different way to adapt the dropout mechanism is applied. Hereby, they train a second Binary Belief Network that is used to regularize the hidden units by setting them to zero.

3   Approach

In this section, we present iDropout, which stands for informed Dropout. As opposed to traditional dropout in Neural Networks we make use of the relevance scores for each input node of the Neural Network that is provided by Deep Taylor Decomposition. Based on this relevance, the probabilities regarding the dropping of the input nodes are adjusted. Input nodes with a higher relevance are less likely to be dropped than input nodes with lower relevance.

First, we will introduce the iDropout layer and subsequently, we will present how iDropout can be incorporated in the learning process.

3.1   iDropout

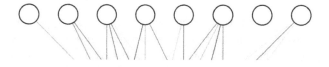

Fig. 2. The input layer of a Deep Neural Network with the respective relevance propagated from the lower layers to the input layer. For simplicity, we omitted the full network structure

Consider the input layer of the Deep Neural Network in Fig. 2, the red connections between the layers symbolize the relevance that is calculated with Deep Taylor Decomposition. More opaqueness means more relevance, less opaqueness means less relevance. It can be observed, that the first and second to last input have barely and no relevance respectively for the final decision of the Neural Network. With iDropout, we use this information to make the decision, which input nodes are dropped, less random than a conventional dropout layer, while still maintaining the advantages of it, when it comes to overfitting of the neural network.

To compute the dropout mask for iDropout, given our vector of relevance scores from the input node, we draw from a uniform distribution between zero and the maximum value ($\mathcal{U}(0, max(relevanceScores))$) of the relevance scores and check if the relevance is greater than the randomly drawn value. If it is the case, the neuron is kept for training, otherwise, the value will be zeroed out.

Example. Given a Neural Network with four inputs. After gathering the relevance for the input nodes, we get a vector with $(5, 8, 2, 10)$. For each value, we now draw a random value from a uniform distribution $\mathcal{U}(0, 10)$. Given the four drawn values $(1, 3, 7, 5)$, this would mean that the third input would get zeroed out, therefore creating a dropout mask of $(1, 1, 0, 1)$.

3.2   Learning with iDropout

While it is not uncommon to use Dropout before every layer, e.g. a fully connected layer, of the network, the described algorithm only considers iDropout as a first layer. However, depending on the explanation algorithm, relevance scores can also be computed for intermediate layers.

The process of learning with iDropout is described in Algorithm 1. The learning process requires labeled training data, a Neural Network that only has ReLU activation functions (as this is a requirement from Deep Taylor Decomposition), a grace period and the number of epochs used for training, and a number indicating after how many epochs the iDropout mask is to be recomputed.

We start with iterating for the number of epochs that were specified for the training. In the training process, we make use of a grace period. While within this grace period, we fit the model without iDropout. This is mainly done so that the various inputs are adjusted slightly before we start to use iDropout. If the grace period was set to zero, we would basically not be able to make an informed decision about the Dropout, so it would happen at random. When the point is reached, where we pass the grace period, we will start the calculations for iDropout. Since calculating the relevance is costly, we furthermore introduce the parameter *maskReset*. If this parameter is, for example, set to a value of ten, the mask based on the relevances of the iDropout layer is only calculated at every tenth step.

To calculate the relevance of the input neurons, we start by initializing a vector of the length of the input of the neural network, i.e. the features of the dataset. Then, we iterate over the output neurons of the model. This number depends on the number of classes, given a binary classification problem, then we would have to check the relevance of input nodes for two output neurons.

We start with analyzing a neuron based on the model and based on the training data that is being used within the learning process. Hereby, according

Algorithm 1. Learning with iDropout

Require: A labeled dataset *data*, a Neural Network with ReLU activation functions *model*, a grace period *gp*, the number of epochs *epochs* used for training, and a number of epochs for which the computed mask is reused until it is computed again *maskReset*

```
 1: i = 0
 2: for i to epochs do
 3:     if i < gp then
 4:         fit(model, data)
 5:     else
 6:         if i − gp mod maskReset == 0 then
 7:             summedRelevance = initializeZeroVector(model.input)
 8:             for neuron in model.output do
 9:                 relevance = analyze(model, neuron data)
10:                 relevanceOfNeuron = sum(relevance, axis = 0)
11:                 summedRelevance = summedRelevance + relevanceOfNeuron
12:             end for
13:             relevancePerInput = sum(summedRelevance, axis = 1)
14:             mask = createMask(relevancePerInput)
15:         end if
16:         fit(model, data.apply(mask))
17:     end if
18: end for
```

to the previously given explanation of Deep Taylor Decomposition, the data is sent through the network example-wise and then the relevance for the decision is propagated backward through the model. Therefore, we end up with a relevance score for each input neuron for each example that was passed through the network. In the next step, we sum the gathered relevance scores for each neuron (*relevanceOfNeuron*).

For each neuron, we collect the *relevanceOfNeuron* in the previously initialized vector *summedRelevance*. So in the end, we have a vector *relevancePerInput* with the size of the input indicating the relevance of each input based on the *data*.

Based on this information, we then calculate the *mask*, which is applied to the data. The calculation of the mask is described in Sect. 3.1.

4 Empirical Evaluation

The implementation of the experiments and iDropout was done in Python. For building the Neural Networks we used Keras, for the computation of the relevance we used iNNvestigate [1], which can be used on models built with Keras. We can subdivide the experiments into two parts. First, we thoroughly explore the method by using artificial data. This allows us to control the environment and make more reliable statements as to why and when iDropout is applicable and when not. In the second part, we used real-world datasets that were available from the UCI Machine Learning Repository [5].

The experiments are all based on the same Deep Neural Network architecture, an input layer according to the size of the features of the data. Two hidden layers with 32 and 16 units respectively both having a ReLU as the activation function. Finally, an output layer with the size of the number of classes in the dataset (always two) and a Softmax activation function. Since Deep Taylor Decomposition is not able to handle the Softmax activation function, this function is clipped from the model and the relevance is calculated based on the output without Softmax. As a loss function, we use cross-entropy and the optimization of the Neural Network is computed with Adam. The grace period is set to 20, i.e. iDropout is activated after 20 epochs of learning. The recalculation of the iDropout mask is set to 10, i.e. after 10 epochs of learning the mask is recomputed. The first variant for the baseline uses the exact architecture that is outlined $base_{FC}$ (without iDropout), while the other baseline, $base_{DO}$ makes use of a conventional dropout layer between the input layer and the first hidden layer. The dropout rate of $base_{DO}$ is set to 0.25, as this is roughly the dropout rate of iDropout in most settings.

4.1   Artificial Data

For the first part of the evaluation, we made use of artificially created data. We therefore make use of scikit-learns[1] *make_classification* function, which lets you manipulate certain parameters for the dataset to be created. The details behind the creation of the datasets are described in [7]. For each of the following experiments, we use 20% of the generated data as test data. The rest is used as training data. In total, we generate 5000 rows with 64 total features and run each process five times. The scores are reported as accuracy, which is determined as the mean of the accuracies of the five runs. We follow the evaluation method/idea of [16], they use the training set to fit the data and then evaluate on the test set for each epoch.

Noise in Data. In the first setting, we investigate how the noise in the data influences the performance of iDropout. Therefore, a specified fraction of the labels are flipped in the data. As a fixed parameter we set the number of informative features to eight, while the rest is uninformative.

In Fig. 3, we can see the accuracy scores for the respective noise levels after each epoch of learning. With no noise, the baseline $base_{FC}$ outperforms the second baseline $base_{DO}$. Until epoch 300 $base_{FC}$ also outperforms the network with iDropout but in the long run, iDropout overtakes $base_{FC}$ slightly. For a noise level of 10%, we can see that $base_{FC}$ and $base_{DO}$ perform roughly at the same level. However, a slightly better performance can be attributed to $base_{DO}$. iDropout crosses the two baselines after about epoch 250, however, since the performance varies more heavily than for $base_{DO}$, it can only be said at epoch

---

[1] https://scikit-learn.org/.

350, that iDropout outperforms the two baselines significantly. With a noise level of 20%, we can observe that iDropout reaches the same performance at roughly epoch 150. Similar to the noise level of 10%, the two baselines can be significantly outperformed at epoch 350. At a noise level of 30%, iDropout significantly outperforms the two baselines at epoch 100. While the two baselines reach an accuracy of roughly 0.57, iDropout reaches accuracy levels between 0.62 and 0.65.

In general, it can be observed that iDropout is preferably applied to noisy data, as with unnoisy data, the benefits of training the model with iDropout probably do not weigh up the disadvantage when it comes to the additional time needed for the training. It is also interesting to observe that when the grace period is over the performance first drops significantly until it recovers and then supersedes the two baselines.

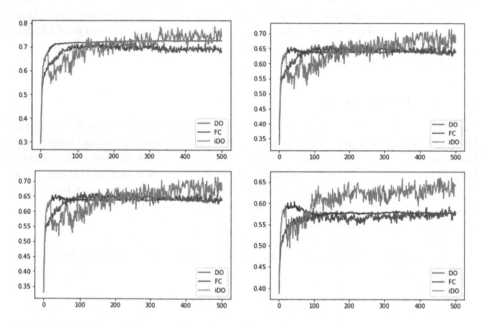

Fig. 3. From left to right and top to bottom, are the respective results for introducing 0, 10, 20, and 30% of flipped data. The lines show iDropout (green), and the two baselines, $base_{DO}$ (blue), and $base_{FC}$ (orange). (Color figure online)

Informative Features. The second setting is concerned with the influence of the number of informative features that are contained in the dataset. Therefore, we adjust the number of informative features within the dataset. We set the noise parameter to 0.3 (cf. the previous subsection).

On the top left graph in Fig. 4, where the data has four informative features, we can see that iDropout supersedes the two baselines quite quickly, at epoch 100. While it mostly outperforms the two baselines, due to its rather heavy fluctuations it drops below the two baselines in several epochs until it stabilizes at epoch 375 and then significantly outperforms the two baselines. With eight informative features, we have a similar behavior like with four informative features, iDropout supersedes the two baselines roughly at epoch 100. However, compared to the four informative features, iDropout has less fluctuation in its performance when we have a few more informative features. For 32 and 64 informative features, the two baselines beat iDropout in terms of training time until peak performance. While $base_{DO}$ and $base_{FC}$ reach the peak performance in both cases at epoch 50 to 100, iDropout needs until epoch 500 to achieve roughly the same performance.

So, in general, iDropout, seems to perform better with less informative features than more informative features in the dataset. This is due to the fact that if too many informative features are in the dataset it cannot pay attention to some very specific features. Furthermore, it could be observed that with more informative features iDropout seems to be more stable than with fewer informative features.

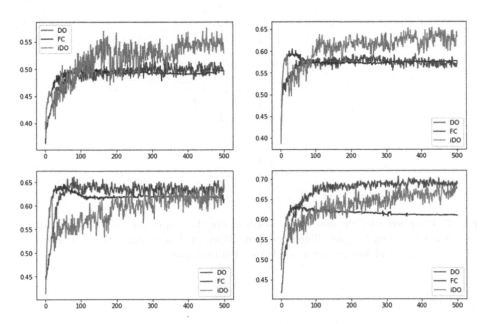

Fig. 4. From left to right and top to bottom, are the respective results for 4, 8, 32, and 64 informative features. The lines show iDropout (green), and the two baselines, $base_{DO}$ (blue), and $base_{FC}$ (orange). (Color figure online)

Missing Data. To evaluate the robustness when it comes to missing data in the test data, we used a setup similar to the two previous experiments, but instead of evaluating after every epoch, we now evaluate the model after every 100th epoch. Hereby, we simulate missing data by zeroing out a fraction of the inputs. To have reliable results, we repeat the process of zeroing out 20 times.

So, at every 100th epoch, we evaluate the model with 20 variations of simulated missing data for the test set. We repeat this for four different levels of missing data, i.e. 5, 10, 15, and 20% are missing. The model is learned for 900 epochs.

Figure 5 shows the results for the 5, 10, 15, and 20% of missing features respectively. Between the two baselines, $base_{FC}$ performs better than $base_{DO}$ in all four cases. iDropout outperforms the two baselines constantly after 200 training epochs when 5, 10, or 15% of the features are missing. However, it takes until epoch 500 when 20% of the features are missing. But in general, it can be observed that iDropout outperforms the two given baselines.

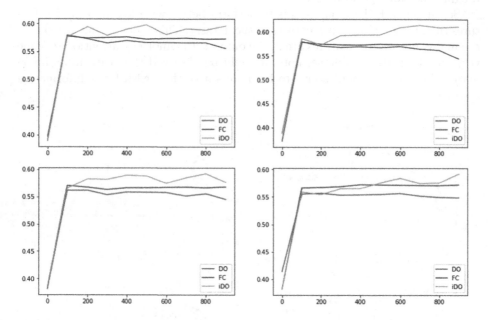

Fig. 5. From left to right and top to bottom, are the respective results for 5, 10, 15, and 20% of missing features. The lines show iDropout (green), and the two baselines, $base_{DO}$ (blue), and $base_{FC}$ (orange). (Color figure online)

4.2   Real Data

Experimental Setup. As real-world datasets we used spam, wbc and wdbc from the UCI Machine Learning Repository [5]. We trained each neural network for 300 epochs and then evaluated the model. Furthermore, we evaluated how missing data impacts the models by zeroing out 5 and 10% of the features. The zeroing out of the test data was repeated 20 times. The only preprocessing that was performed on the data was scaling the features to a standard normal distribution. The data is not shuffled and then split in the first 80%, training data, and the last 20%, test data. The evaluation metric is accuracy.

Table 1. Results for iDropout and the two baselines applied to the three datasets: spam, wbc, and wdbc.

	pmf.	spam	wbc	wdbc
iDropout	0	**0.928**	**0.985**	0.929
	5	**0.923**	0.985	0.926
	10	**0.917**	0.985	0.921
$base_{DO}$	0	0.818	**0.985**	**0.991**
	5	0.810	**0.986**	**0.982**
	10	0.810	**0.986**	**0.974**
$base_{FC}$	0	0.802	0.978	0.964
	5	0.784	0.976	0.948
	10	0.784	0.976	0.930

Results. The results of the experiments can be seen in Table 1. It can be observed that iDropout significantly outperformed the two baselines on the spam dataset. The accuracy, when no data is missing, is at 0.928, when five percent of the features are missing the accuracy drops by 0.005, and for another five percent of missing features by 0.006. Compared to $base_{DO}$ this is a less heavy drop for the first five percent of missing features but since $base_{DO}$ does not lose any more accuracy for the second five percent of dropped features, iDropout loses 0.003 more accuracy here. The second baseline $base_{FC}$ loses 0.018 accuracy points for either five or ten percent of missing features, compared to when no features are missing.

For the second dataset wbc $base_{DO}$ and iDropout have the same performance (0.985) when no features are missing. However, for five and ten percent of missing features $base_{DO}$ outperforms the scores of iDropout, as well as its own score for no missing features by 0.001. The second baseline $base_{FC}$ has the worst performance with an accuracy of 0.978 for no features missing, and 0.976 for five and ten percent of the features missing.

The third dataset is wdbc. Here, iDropout reached an accuracy of 0.929 for no missing features, which is significantly worse than $base_{DO}$, which achieved an accuracy of 0.991. For the third dataset $base_{FC}$ did not have the worst performance, an accuracy of 0.964 was achieved, which is better than iDropout by 0.035 accuracy points. The baseline $base_{DO}$ also achieved the best accuracies for five and ten percent of the missing features. However, while the difference of accuracy for iDropout between all features and ten percent of missing features is 0.008, the differences for $base_{DO}$ and $base_{FC}$ are 0.017 and 0.034 respectively.

5   Conclusion

In this paper, we have presented iDropout, which relies on the input of Deep Taylor Decomposition to determine relevant features to make an informed, rather than a purely random, decision on which features are to be kept. Based on this input we have shown an improvement for certain cases in terms of accuracy of the predictions, as well as more robustness when it comes to predicting with missing data.

However, a clear downside, that has to be noted, is that it takes additional computing resources for calculating the relevance of the input nodes, which is required by iDropout.

5.1 Limitations

Since Deep Taylor Decomposition and other similar methods were just published recently, more progress in this area is expected to be made soon. However, with the current state of the art in this field iDropout is only applicable to a very limited amount of Deep Neural Network architectures, i.e. the restriction of a ReLU as an activation function.

The artificial dataset provides features that are not dependent on each other and since we did not explore the feature space of the real-world datasets in detail it is hard to tell, which impact iDropout has if the classes are dependent on combinations of features.

Furthermore, the approach was evaluated on rather simple data. A conclusion, if the approach could also be applied to more complex data, such as images, cannot be drawn.

5.2 Future Work

As we only used Deep Taylor Decomposition to compute the relevance, further research could be done by applying other explanation methods to compute the relevance and make a decision based on this relevance.

Another open point is, as described in the limitations to evaluate iDropout on more complex tasks such as image classification.

More research should be attributed to computing the mask that is used for the informed Dropout. How often are updates necessary? And how much of the training data is needed? Having a good subset of data to determine the relevance of the input nodes would speed up the process of computing the dropout mask.

Acknowledgments. This research was supported by the German Federal Ministry for Economic Affairs and Energy (Grant No. 01MD18011D) and the German Federal Ministry of Transport and Digital Infrastructure (Grant No. 16AVF2139F).

References

1. Alber, M., et al.: iNNvestigate neural networks! arXiv:1808.04260 [cs, stat], August 2018
2. Ba, J., Frey, B.: Adaptive dropout for training deep neural networks. In: Advances in Neural Information Processing Systems, pp. 3084–3092 (2013)

3. Bacciu, D., Crecchi, F.: Augmenting recurrent neural networks resilience by dropout. IEEE Trans. Neural Netw. Learn. Syst. 1–7 (2019). https://doi.org/10.1109/TNNLS.2019.2899744. https://ieeexplore.ieee.org/document/8668686/
4. Bacciu, D., Crecchi, F., Morelli, D.: DropIn: making reservoir computing neural networks robust to missing inputs by dropout. arXiv:1705.02643 [cs, stat], May 2017
5. Dua, D., Graff, C.: UCI machine learning repository (2019). http://archive.ics.uci.edu/ml
6. Garca-Laencina, P.J., Sancho-Gmez, J.L., Figueiras-Vidal, A.R., Verleysen, M.: K nearest neighbours with mutual information for simultaneous classification and missing data imputation. Neurocomputing 72(7–9), 1483–1493 (2009). https://doi.org/10.1016/j.neucom.2008.11.026. https://linkinghub.elsevier.com/retrieve/pii/S0925231209000149
7. Guyon, I.: Design of experiments for the NIPS 2003 variable selection benchmark, p. 30 (2003)
8. Keshari, R., Singh, R., Vatsa, M.: Guided dropout. arXiv preprint arXiv:1812.03965 (2018)
9. Li, Y., Parker, L.E.: Nearest neighbor imputation using spatial-temporal correlations in wireless sensor networks. Inf. Fusion 15, 64–79 (2014). https://doi.org/10.1016/j.inffus.2012.08.007. https://linkinghub.elsevier.com/retrieve/pii/S1566253512000711
10. Liu, Z.G., Pan, Q., Dezert, J., Martin, A.: Adaptive imputation of missing values for incomplete pattern classification. Pattern Recogn. 52, 85–95 (2016). https://doi.org/10.1016/j.patcog.2015.10.001. http://arxiv.org/abs/1602.02617
11. Mahmood, M.A., Seah, W.K., Welch, I.: Reliability in wireless sensor networks: a survey and challenges ahead. Comput. Netw. 79, 166–187 (2015). https://doi.org/10.1016/j.comnet.2014.12.016. https://linkinghub.elsevier.com/retrieve/pii/S1389128614004708
12. Montavon, G., Lapuschkin, S., Binder, A., Samek, W., Mller, K.R.: Explaining nonlinear classification decisions with deep Taylor decomposition. Pattern Recogn. 65, 211–222 (2017). https://doi.org/10.1016/j.patcog.2016.11.008. https://linkinghub.elsevier.com/retrieve/pii/S0031320316303582
13. Montavon, G., Samek, W., Mller, K.R.: Methods for interpreting and understanding deep neural networks. Digit. Signal Process. 73, 1–15 (2018). https://doi.org/10.1016/j.dsp.2017.10.011. https://linkinghub.elsevier.com/retrieve/pii/S1051200417302385
14. Morris, A.C., Josifovski, L., Bourlard, H., Cooke, M., Green, P.: A neural network for classification with incomplete data: application to robust ASR. In: Proceedings of ICSLP, p. 4 (2000)
15. Singh, N., Javeed, A., Chhabra, S., Kumar, P.: Missing value imputation with unsupervised kohonen self organizing map. In: Shetty, N.R., Prasad, N.H., Nalini, N. (eds.) Emerging Research in Computing, Information, Communication and Applications, pp. 61–76. Springer, New Delhi (2015). https://doi.org/10.1007/978-81-322-2550-8_7
16. Srivastava, N., Hinton, G., Krizhevsky, A., Sutskever, I., Salakhutdinov, R.: Dropout: a simple way to prevent neural networks from overtting. J. Mach. Learn. Res. 15(1), 1929–1958 (2014)
17. Thirukumaran, S., Sumathi, A.: Missing value imputation techniques depth survey and an imputation algorithm to improve the efficiency of imputation. In: Fourth International Conference on Advanced Computing (ICoAC), pp. 1–5. IEEE, Chennai, December 2012. https://doi.org/10.1109/ICoAC.2012.6416805

18. Wan, L., Zeiler, M., Zhang, S., LeCun, Y., Fergus, R.: Regularization of neural networks using DropConnect. In: International Conference on Machine Learning, p. 9 (2013)
19. Wang, S., et al.: Defensive dropout for hardening deep neural networks under adversarial attacks. In: Proceedings of the International Conference on Computer-Aided Design - ICCAD 2018, pp. 1–8 (2018). https://doi.org/10.1145/3240765. 3264699. http://arxiv.org/abs/1809.05165
20. Li, Y., Parker, L.: A spatial-temporal imputation technique for classification with missing data in a wireless sensor network. In: IEEE/RSJ International Conference on Intelligent Robots and Systems, pp. 3272–3279. IEEE, Nice, September 2008. https://doi.org/10.1109/IROS.2008.4650774

A Case Study Lens on Process Mining in Practice

Fahame Emamjome[(✉)], Robert Andrews, and Arthur H. M. ter Hofstede

Queensland University of Technology, Brisbane, Australia
{f.emamjome,r.andrews,a.terhofstede}@qut.edu.au

Abstract. Process mining has a history of over two decades of published research papers and case studies started to appear a bit over a decade ago. In this paper we review these published process mining case studies to assess the maturity of the field from a practice point of view by considering (i) diffusion of tools and techniques into practice, and (ii) the thoroughness of the application of process mining methodologies. Diffusion is assessed by analysing the breadth of domains to which process mining has been applied and the variety of tools and techniques employed. We define measures of thoroughness for each of the various phases of a generalised process mining methodology and examine case studies identified from a literature search against these measures. We conclude that, despite maturing in terms of diffusion, application of process mining in practice has not seen an increased maturity over time in terms of thoroughness. One way to redress this situation is to pay more attention to the development of and adherence to methodological guidance.

Keywords: Process mining · Methodology · Case study

1 Introduction

Process mining has a history of over two decades of published research papers and case studies started to appear a bit over a decade ago. At the core of process mining (originally called workflow mining) is the use of logged traces from the execution of a business process to model the actual behaviour of the process. It is this data-driven approach that distinguishes process mining from other forms of process analysis which typically rely on developing an understanding of the process from people's perceptions of the way the process behaves (or should behave). The model-from-logged-data approach can be traced back to 1998 [2] where the authors "describe an algorithm that, given a log of unstructured executions of a process, generates a graph model of the process" [2]. The resulting process graph (capable of modeling any partial ordering of activities and of modeling loops) represents the control flow of the process.

Since 1998, process mining has received much attention from the research community. A search of the Scopus database for publications since 1998 which

© Springer Nature Switzerland AG 2019
H. Panetto et al. (Eds.): OTM 2019, LNCS 11877, pp. 127–145, 2019.
https://doi.org/10.1007/978-3-030-33246-4_8

mention "process mining", returns nearly 6,000 documents. In the research space, ProM[1] was developed as an open-source repository of process mining tools and techniques, and since then there have been many other tools, both open-source and commercial. In 2009, the IEEE CIS The Task Force on Process Mining was established, and in 2011 the Process Mining Manifesto [3] posed a number of challenges for the discipline including *C10: Improving Usability for Non-Experts* and *C11: Improving Understandability for Non-experts*, which can be interpreted as saying that, at the time of its (the Process Mining Manifesto) publication, process mining remained largely a research topic and still had some way to go to being accepted as a mainstream computing technology.

However, with the first process mining conference launched in June 2019, the field has reached an important milestone in the progress to become a mature academic field [10]. It is timely, thus, to assess just how far the discipline has matured to date in terms of application in practice.

There is a variety of definitions of the maturity of a field of study and different approaches to measuring it. From a literature survey, Keathley et al. [17] synthesizes criteria for assessing maturity and use the results to develop a generalized maturity assessment framework. Van der Aalst [1] refers to the maturity of the BPM field as its relevance, as acknowledged by practitioners and academics. Recker and Mendling [20] investigates the maturity of the BPM field based on academic impact (through measuring citations) and research methodologies (through measuring the presence of certain research components in a paper). In Information Systems research, Cheon et al. [9] examines maturity of IS research based on the diversity of variables, research approaches, and generalisability of research findings.

In this paper, we rely on the maturity assessment framework in Keathley et al. [17] to identify dimensions, criteria, and metrics relevant to assessing the maturity of the process mining field in practice. Consistent with [1], we consider *diffusion* in industry and among practitioners [17] as one of the relevant dimensions of maturity of process mining in practice. According to [17, Table 5], criteria associated with the diffusion dimension include adoption in industry which can be measured by the 'number of industries adopting findings from the research area'. Accordingly, the first research question this paper is interested in addressing is *RQ1: How widespread are process mining tools and techniques across different domains?*. To answer this question, we reviewed **all** published process mining case studies during the period 2007 to 2018 that are **directly related to practice**, i.e. that seek to address concerns raised by the industry partner, thus allowing us to assess the diffusion of process mining tools across different domains and different industries.

We also adapt the 'research design characteristics' maturity dimension from [17, Table 5] which is measured in terms of 'rigo[u]r'. In [17], rigour comprises the sub-criteria 'research objectives' and 'thoroughness'. In this paper we take thoroughness to refer to the combination of these two sub-criteria. Thus, the second research question in relation to maturity of the process mining field is *RQ2: How thoroughly are process mining methodologies applied in the case*

[1] promtools.org.

studies to address practical problems? To answer this question, we define measures of thoroughness for each of the various phases of a generalised process mining methodology and assess process mining case studies against these measures.

The remainder of the paper is organised as follows. In Sect. 2, we position our work against related work and then introduce our generalised process mining methodology. In Sect. 3 we describe the criteria and metrics we use in assessing process mining maturity in practice. In Sect. 4, we describe how we identified and coded case study papers for maturity analysis. In Sect. 5, we present the results of this analysis. In Sect. 6, we reflect on our analysis results and offer some thoughts on the maturity of the field of process mining as derived from our analysis and provide some thoughts on potential future work. In Sect. 7, we offer some conclusions and reflect on the limitations of our current work.

2 Background and Related Work

2.1 Related Work

In the field of process mining, there have been other literature review studies with the aim of providing an overall descriptive view (for a definition of descriptive review see [22]), though not many. Tiwari and Turner [26] reviews 50 papers in the field of process mining to show the distribution of different analysis techniques and to examine how various challenges in the field were addressed (e.g. noise, hidden tasks). In contrast, our paper focuses on the diffusion of process mining tools and techniques in practice.

Ghasemi and Amoyt [14] uses an extensive literature review to identify the distribution of process mining studies across six different search engines. The authors demonstrate a growing trend of process mining research over the last 10 years in general and in the healthcare domain in particular. They also conclude that Scopus and Google Scholar together cover 96% of the papers published in the field of process mining.

Rojas et al. [21] describes a systematic descriptive literature review on the application of process mining in healthcare. The authors reviewed 74 papers in this area and provide some observations in terms of the types of processes encountered and data used, process mining methodologies, tools and algorithms that were applied, and emerging research opportunities they identified in the field. The structured literature review in Kurniati et al. [18] includes 37 process mining studies in the oncology domain. The authors reviewed the research questions posed, the methodologies used, the findings and results presented, and suggest future research opportunities.

Thiede and Fuerstenau [24] explores the use and maturity of process mining as a technology in practice through a structured review of process mining research. The review analysed 68 papers published in 22 journals using a maturity model synthesised from maturity models in ERP and business analytics. They identified that cross-system and cross-organisational process mining is underrepresented in IS journals. Thiede et al. [25] continues this study, extending the search period to 2015 and 2016 and focusing more specifically on empirical studies. The study reviewed 144 papers in relation to their coverage of different types of systems in an organisational context with findings confirming the results of the earlier study. The main distinction between the two papers with Thiede as first author and our paper, is in the definition of process mining maturity. Unlike Thiede and Fuerstenau [24] which considers process mining as a technology and defines maturity based on technology maturity models, in our paper, we consider process mining as a field of study consisting of tools, techniques and research methodologies and define criteria for maturity based on the maturity definitions of a field of research [17].

Overall, existing related work has paid little or no attention to the degree of maturity of application of process mining techniques.

2.2 Process Mining Methodology

To be able to assess the thoroughness of process mining case studies, in this section, we introduce the common phases of a process mining methodology and the important considerations in relation to each phase. Process mining case studies, whether motivated by real world problems or by researchers' intentions to examine existing tools in a practical context, usually follow some kind of process mining methodology. While there is, as yet, no agreed standard process mining methodology, there are several process mining methodologies described in the literature, e.g. [3,7,12,15]. Each of these methodologies (i) is described in terms of phases, where each phase has an objective, some required inputs, and some defined outputs, (ii) is not prescriptive in terms of tools and techniques. For our analysis, a methodology would provide a standard against which each case study can be assessed. We therefore synthesised a set of methodology phases (and associated objectives and outputs) from the phases described in [3,7,12,15] that we use as the basis for analysing case study thoroughness. We do not see any objections to this approach as (i) few of the case studies we reviewed mentioned application of any specific methodology, and (ii) we assess each case study against the set of objectives and outputs (and then track these assessments using the relevant generalised methodology phase) not how closely the case study followed the generalised methodology. Thus no case study is penalised for not strictly applying the phases of the generalised methodology. Table 1 (Column 1) shows the phases of our generalized methodology lined up against synonymous phases of other published methodologies.

Phase 1 *(Defining research questions)*: In the first phase of a process mining project, objectives and research questions should be specified. This should be done in consultation with organisational stakeholders and domain experts.

Phase 2 *(Data collection)*: The objective of this phase is to understand the available data (as present in existing systems) and what can be extracted (event data and other attributes) and used (scope and granularity of data) to answer the research questions. According to the Process Mining Manifesto [3], the choice of data and data sources should be driven by the research questions. The outputs of this phase include (i) a conceptual data model (showing relationships between data sources and elements), and (ii) initial event logs.

Table 1. Generalised process mining methodology phases and semantically synony-mous phases from published methodologies.

Phase		Synonymous phase			
		PDM [7]	L* [3]	PMPM [15]	PM² [12]
Define research questions			Justification and planning	Scoping	Planning
Data collection		Log preparation	Extract	Data understanding	Extraction
Data pre-processing		Log inspection		Event log creation	Data processing
Mining & analysis	Discovery	Control flow analysis	Create control flow model and connect to event log; Create integrated process model	Process mining	Mining & analysis
	Conformance				
	Performance	Performance analysis			
	Social network analysis	Role analysis			
	Comparative analysis				
Results					
	Stakeholder evaluation		Evaluation deployment	Evaluation	
	Implementation	Transfer of results	Provide operational support		Process improvement and support

Phase 3 *(Data pre-processing)*: The objective of this phase is to ensure the extracted data is of high quality and is suitable for subsequent mining and analysis. Pre-processing may address missing data, incorrect data, or bringing data into the right or uniform format (e.g. timestamps), etc. A variety of process mining tools have been developed to transform data to the right format (e.g. [23]) and also to apply automated log cleaning methods on the extracted data. (e.g. [8,11]). However, data cleaning is an *ad hoc* task and usually depends heavily on domain knowledge [23]. It is therefore naive to rely solely on tools to automatically resolve data quality issues and not be mindful of the deeper underlying reasons as to why these quality issues emerge in the first place. They may result from the way systems have been configured (including both operational use and logging) or from organisational rules (e.g. [4,5,23]).

Phase 4 *(Mining and analysis of results)*: In this phase, process mining techniques are applied to the data prepared thus far in order to answer the research questions and to obtain process-related insights from analysis of the results. In our study, we consider a number of different types of process mining: process model discovery, conformance checking, performance checking, social network analysis, and comparative analysis. The form of analysis appropriate for a process mining case study is dependent on the research question(s) and the requirements of the context [12]. A variety of tools and techniques have been developed in the past 20 years in relation to different forms of process mining analysis. These algorithms and tools have different functionality, deal with different characteristics of input data, and produce different quality of outputs [11]. Accordingly, the appropriate choice of process mining analysis type, tools and techniques is crucial when conducting a process mining project. Similarly, the presentation of the results of an analysis is critical. Results should go beyond merely reporting the output of whichever tool was used, to include an interpretation of the findings with respect to the research question(s).

Phase 5 *(Stakeholder evaluation)*: This phase in our methodology is the presentation of the findings to the stakeholders with a view to gaining stakeholders' feedback as to the validity, accuracy, reasonableness and relevance of the findings. Interpretation and evaluation of the findings could occur more or less simultaneously and could also evolve through a number of iterations.

Phase 6 *(Implementation)*: In this phase of a process mining project, the insights derived from phases 4 and 5 are implemented with the objective of improving the process, and (possibly) providing further support through process mining. The actual implementation of a process mining project, however, often goes beyond the scope of the reported case study.

3   Process Mining Maturity Criteria

As discussed, to assess the maturity of the field of process mining we draw on the maturity framework in Keathley et al. [17] and adapt two maturity dimensions which suit process mining research: diffusion and research design characteristics. In this section we further define the measures that we apply in this paper to evaluate process mining maturity based on these two dimensions.

3.1   Diffusion of Process Mining

Keathley et al. [17] defines diffusion as one of the dimensions of maturity of a field of study. Diffusion can be related to three main criteria, (i) adoption in industry, (ii) communities of practice and, (iii) technology development [17]. In this paper, we focus on adoption in industry as the main diffusion criterion and define it as the application of process mining tools and methods in different practical domains. To measure diffusion, we consider (i) the frequency of application of different process mining tools across the published case studies, (ii) the range and frequency of domains to which process mining has been applied as revealed by our literature search, and (iii) how process mining tools and techniques have achieved traction across different domains.

3.2   Thoroughness of Process Mining Case Studies

This study refers to 'clarity of research questions' and 'thoroughness' of process mining approaches as sub-criteria of process mining methodological rigour in practice. In our view (see Sect. 2.2) defining clear research questions should be part of any process mining project methodology. Hence, in this paper, we use the term thoroughness to refer to both these sub-criteria. According to the Process Mining Manifesto [3], the impact of process mining tools in practical domains can suffer due to immaturity of existing tools and obliviousness of researchers/practitioners to process mining methodology i.e. a lack of knowledge of the limitations of process mining tools in the context of the study, and inattentiveness to research questions and domain knowledge. Accordingly herein, we define 'thoroughness' in relation to a process mining case study as thorough consideration of the stakeholders, their requirements and the study context, through different phases of a process mining methodology (Sect. 2.2) including: (i) unearthing the research questions of interest to the organisation involved, (ii) the way data is collected and pre-processed, (iii) the manner in which mining algorithms are applied and data is analysed, (iv) the attention that has been paid to presenting the results to the stakeholders and, (v) the way these results have been evaluated with the stakeholders. In evaluating the degree of thoroughness of a process mining case study, we assess the degree of thoroughness based on the above considerations in relation to each phase of our generalised process mining methodology. For each phase, the highest level of thoroughness is ranked as 3 and the lowest level is considered as 1. We rank a phase as 0 if that specific phase was not mentioned in the process mining case study at all. The details of our coding approach is described in Sect. 4.3.

4   Analysis of Process Mining Case Studies

In this section our approach to identifying relevant published process mining case studies, and the criteria used to assess them is described in detail.

4.1   Paper Extraction

According to Paré et al. [19] our work represents a combination of a descriptive and a critical review of the application of process mining techniques. Hence our review approach is influenced by a number of related guidelines [13,19,22]. In our approach we (i) extract process mining case studies of the last 18 years [22], (ii) determine a selection strategy [19], (iii) develop coding dimensions and related assessment criteria [19], and (iv) perform the coding and the analysis [6].

We aim to provide both a descriptive (research question 1) and a reflective (research question 2) review of process mining case studies. Rather than limiting the review to a selective or representative set of papers, we aim to be as comprehensive as possible in considering the corpus of process mining case studies [19]. According to Ghasemi and Amoyt [14], the combination of Google Scholar and Scopus covers 96% of the published process mining papers in any topic and domain. Consequently, for this paper we used these two search engines to find process mining case studies. We consider the search period used i.e. from 2000 to 2018, to be inclusive as the earliest process mining case study papers found were published in 2007. The search process was carried out in a number of phases [19, 22]. Firstly, the Scopus and Google databases were searched for papers (articles, conference papers and book chapters) containing the phrase "process mining" with a publication date after 1999. Secondly, the data set was scanned to remove duplicate papers. Thirdly, the articles were filtered to remove books, theses, literature reviews, position papers, state of the art papers, general BPM papers (which may mention process mining), data mining papers (which mention process mining) and 'citation only' references. Fourthly, the title, abstract and keywords were reviewed to exclude obviously irrelevant articles (for instance articles that relate to the process of minerals and ore mining). Lastly, the inclusion and exclusion criteria (explained in the next subsection) were applied to each of the articles. This resulted in a final set of 152 articles.

4.2 Inclusion and Exclusion Criteria

As our analysis concerns process mining case studies, we need to be specific about the criteria for a paper to be to considered a case study. A process mining case study is focused on reporting the application of **existing** process mining tools and techniques to a **specific domain** to provide **business value or address stakeholders' requirements**. To get a better picture of the application of process mining in a variety of contexts, we did not exclude any papers based on considerations of (perceived) quality [19].

We included, as case studies for our analysis, only those articles where process mining tools and techniques were the only forms of analysis used. We excluded the following articles: (1) articles where the principal contribution was a methodology, technique or tool, which was subsequently illustrated with a 'case study', (2) articles not written in English, (3) articles of which the full-text was not freely available to the authors, and (4) articles where process mining techniques were used for the purpose of data preparation as an input for data mining or statistical analysis rather than process discovery and analysis.

After initial filtering and subsequent application of inclusion and exclusion criteria, we identified 152 case study papers for analysis. Table 2 shows, by year, the number of published case studies.

Table 2. Articles published per year

	Number of case study papers per year											
Year	2007	2008	2009	2010	2011	2012	2013	2014	2015	2016	2017	2018
The paper reports on	3	4	6	1	7	6	6	15	27	18	40	19

4.3 Coding Dimensions and Analysis Approach

To answer the first research question in relation to diffusion of process mining case studies, we used literature review profiling techniques. Literature profiling is an effective approach to identify thematic trends and diffusion of interests in a field of study [13]. To evaluate the increase in the application of process mining in practice, we analysed the overall distribution of published case studies over the years. In order to evaluate the dissemination of process mining in different practical domains and the distribution of process mining techniques, the case studies were classified based on the domain of application and also the process mining tools applied to conduct the project.

To answer the second research question in relation to the thoroughness of application of process mining, case studies were evaluated, in each phase of process mining methodology, on a scale from 1 to 3. We assigned a coding value of 0 to any phase where, for one of a variety of legitimate reasons, the study authors skipped explaining the phase. Thus we were able to conduct our analysis without unduly penalising these studies. Table 3 shows the thoroughness criteria (Sect. 3.2) for this evaluation against each phase of process mining methodology (in Column 1) as discussed in Sect. 2.2.

To ensure coding reliability, two authors, using NVivo[2], coded the first 10 papers, resolved discrepancies and revised the coding criteria. Then the whole set of papers was coded by one author before being reviewed by all authors. Discrepancies were discussed and resolved, and, based on this feedback, the coding criteria were further revised. The whole set of papers was then coded a second time by the same author [16,20].

5 Analysis

In this section we present an in-depth analysis of the selected process mining case studies to assess the maturity of the field of process mining in practice. This analysis is guided by our coding efforts and provides both qualitative and quantitative insights. In Sect. 5.1, we address the first research question in relation to diffusion of process mining tools and techniques. In Sect. 5.2, we report on the thoroughness of process mining case studies.

5.1 An Overview of the Process Mining Field

The increasing interest in publishing case studies in the process mining discipline since 2014, a finding consistent with Thiede et al. [25], is a positive indicator of applicability of the field of process mining to practice [1].

Our survey of process mining case studies indicates that more and more researchers or practitioners from various domains are interested in practical applications of process mining tools and techniques. The 152 case studies reviewed in this paper cover 34 different domains, including healthcare and education (as the two most frequent application areas), manufacturing, banking, finance, customer service, audit and fraud detection, construction, cybersecurity, logistics, and even game playing. Figure 1 shows the number of case study

---

[2] https://www.qsrinternational.com/nvivo/home.

Table 3. Thoroughness coding values for each phase of process mining methodology

Phase	Thoroughness criteria and coding values			
	3	2	1	0
Defining research questions	A clear articulation of the research questions related to actual business needs, derived through consultation with relevant stakeholders	There are research questions but not explicitly linked to the stakeholders' concerns	The main intention is to test the applicability of process mining tools/techniques in a context	No research question or intention has been specified
Data collection	It is clearly explained what sort of data is needed to answer the research questions, and the different sources of data and methods of data collection are described	The limitations of available data sources in relation to the research question is recognized and data collection is based on these limited resources	Data sources are introduced but there is no discussion on data characteristics and suitability to address research questions	There is no description of the source of data
Data pre-processing	Data quality issues and the root causes of these issues in the data set are identified. Changes to the data set are justified in relation to the organisational context, research questions, and limitations of data cleaning activities	Data quality issues are identified, some possible root causes are mentioned and data cleaning activities are partially justified	Root causes of data quality issues are not considered, data cleaning methods are applied without justification and event logs are prepared assuming that the cleaned data is a faithful representation of reality	There is no description of any data cleaning activity
Mining and analysis	The choice of analysis type, tools and techniques are justified in relation to the research questions, the type of data at hand, strengths and limitations of available tools, and the desired outcomes	Analysis and tool choices are partially justified, but not clearly linked to the research questions, the data or the context	There is no justification for the use of a specific form of analysis and a choice for a particular (set of) tool(s)	The specific form of analysis (discovery, conformance, performance, social network analysis and comparative) is not used in the paper
Results	The findings are interpreted in relation to the context of the study and the actual reasons behind the findings are identified, supported by existing theories	There is some interpretation of the results, but this is not concretely linked to the context or supported by theoretical explanation	Only the outcome of analysis is presented without any interpretation	No explicit representation or discussion on results
Evaluation	The results are presented to different groups of relevant stakeholders and explanations are sought and documented	The results are presented to the stakeholders but no further explanation is provided	Rather than involving stakeholders, other evaluation methods have been applied	There is no evaluation of research findings
Implementation	The study reports on implementation and process improvements arising from the case study findings	The paper provides some recommendations on how to improve the process(es)	The paper provides some insights about the process(es) without any recommendations for improvements	The paper did not provide any recommendations for improvement or any insight into the process(es)

articles, by year of publication, that address the 7 most frequently mentioned domains. Figure 1 highlights that process mining has gained increasing traction in both the healthcare and education domains over time and suggests the suitability and potential of process mining to address problems in these complex domains. However,identifying the reasons behind these observations is not in the scope of this paper and could be investigated in future studies.[3]

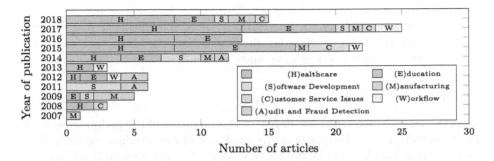

Fig. 1. Domains by year of publication - number of articles.

To better understand how advanced is the application of process mining tools and techniques in these top 7 domains, we investigated how the most developed process mining tools/techniques have been applied across the case studies conducted in these domains. Figure 2 shows, for the 7 most common domains, the process mining tools/techniques that were applied. We note the frequent use of Fuzzy Miner and Heuristic Miner and further note that Inductive Miner is used mostly in studies involving the healthcare and education domains.

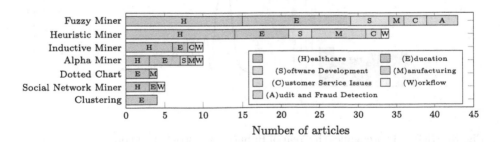

Fig. 2. Algorithms by domain - number of articles.

---

[3] The numbers of papers in each domain rather than traction of the field in these domains could also be representative of other factors such as the number of journals and conferences in that area, the review policy etc.

We further note that:

- Fuzzy Miner as one of the oldest, and simplest techniques, is overall the most commonly applied tool/technique, and has, on a year-by-year basis, been the most commonly applied tool/technique.
- The Heuristic Miner has shown a decline over time in usage.
- The Inductive Miner, since its release in 2016, has shown increasing usage.
- Despite its known limitations, the Alpha Miner algorithm remains a popular tool/technique.
- Even though Social Network Analysis is a common application area (19 articles include this form of analysis), the Social Network Miner tool/technique is infrequently mentioned by case study authors[4].

5.2   Process Mining Methodology

In this section we investigate the degree of thoroughness of the various case studies. To better present the trends in the whole set of case studies, we devised an aggregated thoroughness indicator for each paper. For any reviewed case study, c, we refer to T_c as the overall measure of the thoroughness of c where $0 \leq T_c \leq 1$ is calculated by summing the thoroughness value for each of the methodology phases and then dividing by 21 (the maximum possible value of thoroughness). To derive trends over time, the thoroughness values were averaged over year of publication (see Fig. 3A). It is clear that, over time, the number of case studies published per year generally increases. However, the degree of methodological thoroughness (average T_c per year) has significantly dropped.

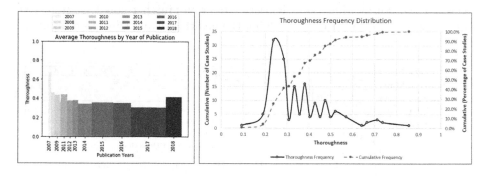

Fig. 3. A(left) - Thoroughness by Year of Publication, B(right) - Thoroughness (Cumulative) Frequency Distribution.

In Fig. 3A, the height of each bar shows average thoroughness per year. The x-axis represents year of publication with the width of each bar representing the number of case studies published in the indicated year.

---

[4] A detailed analysis of different process mining algorithms, their advantages and disadvantages is not within the scope of this paper.

Figure 3B shows a cumulative frequency for T_c. It can be observed that 53% of case studies in our survey achieved $T_c \leq 0.33$ thoroughness. Further, only 12.5% of case studies achieved $T_c \geq 0.5$ thoroughness. Finally, only 8 case studies (4%) of the 152 analysed, achieved $T_c \geq 0.67$ thoroughness (14 or better out of 21).

Based on a preliminary observation on the case studies' authorship, we hypothesised that a possible explanation of the downward trend in the level of thoroughness of the papers could be related to the changes in the patterns of authorship. Accordingly we conducted an analysis on the co-authorship of the top 8 most informed case studies. The results of this analysis show that (i) one author is involved in 4 of the 8 papers, (ii) there are groups of co-authors involved in multiple papers, e.g. the same set of authors wrote 2 of the case studies, one author is involved in 3 of the case studies with co-authors who are themselves involved in at least 2 of the case studies, and (iii) several of the case studies involve both process mining and domain experts[5] as co-authors. Further, each of these authors have research experience in multiple aspects of process mining. Further analysis of the (co-)authorship of case studies with lower levels of thoroughness is warranted to determine if (i) more domain experts are becoming involved in applying process mining techniques in practice, and (ii) if less experienced (from a process mining perspective) researchers are applying process mining methods and techniques in practice.

Year					Methodology Phases						
	1	2	3	4	5	6	7	8	9	10	11
2007	2.33	1.33	2.50	2.50	2.00	3.00	3.00	2.00	2.33	3.00	2.50
2008	1.25	1.75	1.33	1.33	2.50	1.33	2.00		1.75	2.50	1.50
2009	2.00	1.50	1.60	1.67	1.00				1.67	3.00	1.50
2010	1.00	1.00	1.00	1.00		2.00			2.00		1.00
2011	1.43	1.43	2.14	1.33	1.67	1.00	2.00		1.29	1.67	1.67
2012	1.80	1.67	1.20	1.25	2.00	2.00	1.50	1.00	1.60	2.00	1.00
2013	1.50	1.17	1.40	1.17	1.50			2.00	1.33	2.00	2.33
2014	1.33	1.33	1.53	1.20	1.40	1.20	1.67	1.50	1.40	2.00	1.43
2015	1.88	1.40	1.18	1.27	1.20	1.33	1.50	1.25	1.33	2.00	1.40
2016	1.85	1.32	1.36	1.33	1.00	1.00	1.00	1.33	1.16	2.00	1.56
2017	1.44	1.28	1.18	1.24	1.09	1.00	1.00	1.50	1.23	2.00	1.56
2018	2.06	1.61	1.64	1.28	1.00	1.50	2.00	1.33	1.28	1.00	1.58

Fig. 4. Thoroughness - Methodology Phases. 1 = Research Questions, 2 = Data Collection, 3 = Data Pre-processing, 4 = Process Discovery, 5 = Conformance Checking, 6 = Performance, 7 = SNA, 8 = Comparative Analysis, 9 = Results, 10 = Stakeholder Evaluation, 11 = Implementation.

Figure 4 shows the heat map representing the level of thoroughness for each phase of process mining methodology over the years. Each cell shows the average degree of thoroughness for the specific phase. The darker cells indicate higher levels of thoroughness of process mining phases (the columns) for the specific year (the rows). The darker colors on the top of the heat map, confirm our observation from Fig. 3A showing the overall downward trend in the level of

---

[5] Affiliation other than Computer Science or Information Technology department.

thoroughness of case studies over time. Looking in more detail, we can observe that phase 1 (formulation of the research questions) is one of the most thorough phases and, after an initial dip, has shown some progress in terms of methodological thoroughness. The level of thoroughness for phase 2 (data collection) is overall low (<2) and does not show much progress over the years. Thoroughness for phase 3, data pre-processing (column 3), also going down overall, shows few darker colors across the years, with only a high level of thoroughness for 2007 and 2011. For phase 4 (analysis, columns 4–8) the heat map shows the level of thoroughness in conducting these different forms of analysis, if present in the papers. The white cells show that we could not find instances of papers applying the related type of analysis in that year. We can observe that process discovery has a consistent downward trend in terms of its thoroughness. Conformance, performance, social network, and comparative analysis, also trend down, while showing a few peaks in thoroughness across the years. Phase 5, column 9 (results), shows a clear downward trend over the years. Column 10 (evaluation) shows that an evaluation, if present in the papers, is conducted mostly in a thorough way (>2). For phase 6, implementation (column 11), except in 2007 and 2013, the level of thoroughness is low (<2) and generally decreasing.

Our main criteria for assessing thoroughness includes consideration of the context and stakeholders' requirements as well as being reflective in the choice of methods. The downward trends in phases 4–8 together with the increasing penetration of process mining into different practical domains may be interpreted as researchers and practitioners (perhaps due to a lack of expertise and experience) putting little or no importance on reflecting or explaining the reasoning behind their choice of methods and analytical tools. In contrast, phases 1 (research question) and 5 (evaluation) show the highest level of thoroughness indicative of increased interaction with stakeholders leading to a deeper understanding of the problem context, and of the relevance of results and insights.

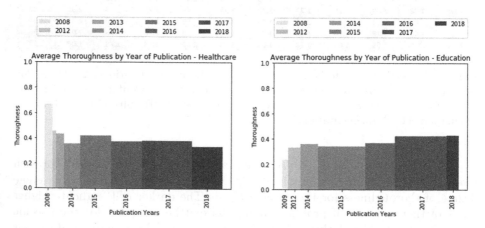

Fig. 5. A(left) - Thoroughness - Healthcare, B(right) - Thoroughness - Education.

As our analysis in Sect. 5.1 revealed that process mining has received much attention in the healthcare and education domains, we now analyse the case studies published in these domains to examine the respective levels of thoroughness and thus to investigate maturity of the application of process mining in these domains. Figure 5A and B respectively show the degree of methodological thoroughness for papers in the healthcare and education domains. We can observe that in healthcare, consistent with the whole set of process mining case studies analysed in this paper, there is a downward trend in terms of methodological thoroughness (from more than 0.6 to less than 0.4). However, this is not the case for case studies published in the education domain as they show a slightly upward trend, even though they are lower in the level of thoroughness (from 0.2 to 0.4) compared to studies in healthcare.

Year	1	2	3	4	5	6	7	8	9	10	11
2008	1.50	2.00	2.00	1.50		1.50	2.00			1.50	3.00
2012	2.00	2.00	1.00	2.00		2.00		1.00	2.00	2.00	1.00
2013	1.50	1.00	1.00	1.00	2.00				1.00		
2014	1.50	1.50	2.00	1.67	1.50	1.50	2.00	1.00	1.25		1.33
2015	1.88	1.50	1.25	1.00	1.00	1.00	1.00	1.50	1.14	2.00	1.00
2016	2.13	1.14	1.25	1.43	1.00		1.00	1.00	1.25	2.00	2.00
2017	1.42	1.38	1.10	1.36	1.00		1.00	2.00	1.08		1.00
2018	2.13	1.63	2.17	1.13	1.00		2.00	1.00	1.13	1.00	1.33

Year	1	2	3	4	5	6	7	8	9	10	11
2009	1.00	2.00			1.00	1.00			1.00		
2012	2.00	1.50	1.00	1.00					2.00		
2014	1.67	1.33	1.33	1.00			1.00	2.00	1.33		2.00
2015	2.00	1.38	1.00	1.43	1.00			1.00	1.50	1.67	
2016	1.80	1.80	1.60	1.20	1.00	1.00		1.00	1.00		1.00
2017	2.11	1.44	1.71	1.25	1.00		1.00		1.78	2.00	1.75
2018	2.00	1.50	1.50	1.50			2.00	2.00	1.50		1.50

Fig. 6. A(left) - Thoroughness - Methodology Phases Healthcare, B(right) - Thoroughness - Methodology Phases - Education.

To further understand these trends, we also looked to the heat maps, representing the thoroughness of process mining phases for these two domains. Figure 6A shows the heatmap for process mining phases in healthcare. Compared to the heatmap for the whole paper set, we can observe that the level of thoroughness in phase 1 (research questions) is always equal or higher than the level of thoroughness in phase 1 for the whole paper set (Fig. 4) across the years. This is consistent with the thoroughness of phase 1 in the education domain (except for 2009) with both domains showing an increasing trend in thoroughness of phase 1. These results suggest that over time, researchers in these two domains have developed their understanding of process mining and how it is related to the problems in these two domains. We also do not not observe any significant differences in the thoroughness of phase 1 between these two domains. There are no significant differences in relation to phase 2 (data collection) between the healthcare case studies and the whole paper set, but clearly we can see a higher degree of thoroughness in the application of process mining tools in healthcare compared to education. However, unlike healthcare case studies and the whole paper set, the level of thoroughness for phase 2, phase 3 (pre-processing), phase 5 (results in column 9 and evaluation in column 10), phase 6 (implementation in column 11), shows an increasing trend in the education domain. Different patterns in the level of thoroughness of process mining case studies in these two domains invites more investigation into the root causes of these variations; are process mining methods and techniques more suitable to specific domains and harder to apply in other domains? Do we need to tailor process mining methodologies according to the domain of application? Answering these questions is important in order to achieve higher levels of maturity and impact in practice. We will further discuss the analysis results in Sect. 6.

6 Discussion

To answer the question *how mature is the process mining discipline in terms of its application in practice?*, we assessed *diffusion* and *thoroughness* of process mining studies in practical domains by reviewing process mining case studies published between 2007 and 2018. In order to assess the diffusion of the process mining discipline in practice, we examined the dissemination of process mining tools and techniques across different domains through a literature review. The increasing number of process mining case studies and the broadening of domains in which these studies are conducted, imply a growing maturity of this field in relation to adoption in industry.

This paper also investigated maturity in terms of rigour (thoroughness of application of a process mining methodology). We consider a thorough application of a process mining methodology to be one where consideration of the organisational context and stakeholders' problems is reflected through all phases of the methodology. We firstly synthesised, from published methodologies, a generalised process mining methodology and defined measures of thoroughness for each phase of the methodology. We derived an overall thoroughness value for each case study by aggregating phase-thoroughness values. Our analyses revealed an overall decrease in the level of thoroughness of the case studies from 2007 to 2018. Furthermore, looking to the level of thoroughness for each phase of process mining separately, shows that even though the formulation of research questions has improved over the years, other phases, specifically analysis, results, evaluation and implementation are not showing any improvement in terms of thoroughness (in fact decline is evident). One plausible explanation is that case studies are increasingly being carried out by domain experts and novice researchers. This is supported by the growing number of domains in which process mining is being applied together with the continuing popularity of obsolete and limited tools and techniques such as the Alpha Miner[6]. This proposition can be further investigated by conducting a review on the authors of the paper set.

Unfortunately, the decrease in thoroughness of process mining case study approaches implies that, despite increasing adoption in industry, process mining is still not able to deliver the promised outcomes to real world problems. One way that the process mining research community can attend to this concern is by developing methodological guidelines (with emphasis on context and reflection through process mining phases) to support knowledge transfer from experienced process mining researchers to those that are relatively new to the field.

Future research is warranted to investigate other possible reasons behind this downward trend in the field. For instance, is the complexity of more advanced process mining tools and techniques hindering their application by

---

[6] Our analysis showed that since 2010, Alpha Miner has stayed among the three top algorithms used in process mining case studies.

non-process mining experts in practice?[7] Also, are more experienced process mining researchers moving away from publishing case studies (for example, as they are becoming harder to publish in good forums in the area) and do we thus see an increased number of case studies published by relative novices in the field (in lower quality forums)? If so, the aforementioned guidelines would help in increasing the thoroughness of published case studies.

7 Conclusion

The inaugural International Conference on Process Mining (Aachen/Germany June 2019) marked two decades of the existence of process mining as field of research and practice. Through a detailed analysis of 152 published process mining case studies, each involving an industry partner, we examined the maturity of process mining in practice by assessing the maturity dimensions of diffusion and thoroughness. Our analysis revealed a growth in diffusion of process mining tools and techniques across various domains, indicating maturation of the field in terms of usability for non-experts. However, we noted a continuing reliance on simple and outdated tools (such as Alpha Miner). We found an overall downwards trend in thoroughness of process mining case studies (with thoroughness differing across domains). We suggest the development of more accessible and suitable guidelines, possibly specific to individual domains, to help new researchers and domain experts as an area for future research.

Despite the limitations of our investigation in this paper; the subjective nature of the coding practice and being limited to what is recorded in publicly accessible papers, we believe that our observations pinpoint important considerations. However, future investigations such as authorship analysis or interviewing authors may shed further light on the progress of process mining in practice.

Acknowledgements. The contributions to this paper of R. Andrews were supported through ARC Discovery Grant DP150103356.

References

1. van der Aalst, W.M.: Business process management: a comprehensive survey. ISRN Softw. Eng. **2013**, 37 p. (2013). https://doi.org/10.1155/2013/507984. Hindawi Publishing Corporation, Article ID 507984
2. Agrawal, R., Gunopulos, D., Leymann, F.: Mining process models from workflow logs. In: Schek, H.-J., Alonso, G., Saltor, F., Ramos, I. (eds.) EDBT 1998. LNCS, vol. 1377, pp. 467–483. Springer, Heidelberg (1998). https://doi.org/10.1007/BFb0101003
3. van der Aalst, W., et al.: Process mining manifesto. In: Daniel, F., Barkaoui, K., Dustdar, S. (eds.) BPM 2011. LNBIP, vol. 99, pp. 169–194. Springer, Heidelberg (2012). https://doi.org/10.1007/978-3-642-28108-2_19

---

[7] The Process Mining Manifesto challenges C10: Improving Usability for Non-Experts and C11: Improving Understandability for Non-experts remain challenges to this day.

4. Andrews, R., Suriadi, S., Wynn, M., ter Hofstede, A.H.M., Rothwell, S.: Improving patient flows at St. Andrew's War memorial hospital's emergency department through process mining. In: vom Brocke, J., Mendling, J. (eds.) Business Process Management Cases. MP, pp. 311–333. Springer, Cham (2018). https://doi.org/10.1007/978-3-319-58307-5_17
5. Ash, J.S., Berg, M., Coiera, E.W.: Viewpoint paper: some unintended consequences of information technology in health care: the nature of patient care information system-related errors. JAMIA 11(2), 104–112 (2004)
6. Balijepally, V., Mangalaraj, G., Iyengar, K.: Are we wielding this hammer correctly? A reflective review of the application of cluster analysis in information systems research. JAIS 12(5), 375 (2011)
7. Bozkaya, M., Gabriels, J., van der Werf, J.M.: Process diagnostics: a method based on process mining. In: eKNOW 2009, pp. 22–27. IEEE (2009)
8. Cheng, H., Kumar, A.: Process mining on noisy logs - can log sanitization help to improve performance? Decis. Support Syst. 79, 138–149 (2015)
9. Cheon, M.J., Groven, V., Sabherwal, R.: The evolution of empirical research in IS: a study in IS maturity. Inf. Manag. 24(3), 107–119 (1993)
10. Culnan, M.J.: Mapping the intellectual structure of MIS, 1980–1985: a co-citation analysis. MIS Q. 11(3), 341–353 (1987)
11. De Weerdt, J., De Backer, M., Vanthienen, J., Baesens, B.: A multi-dimensional quality assessment of state-of-the-art process discovery algorithms using real-life event logs. Inf. Syst. 37(7), 654–676 (2012)
12. van Eck, M.L., Lu, X., Leemans, S.J.J., van der Aalst, W.M.P.: PM²: a process mining project methodology. In: Zdravkovic, J., Kirikova, M., Johannesson, P. (eds.) CAiSE 2015. LNCS, vol. 9097, pp. 297–313. Springer, Cham (2015). https://doi.org/10.1007/978-3-319-19069-3_19
13. Gaffar, A., Deshpande, A., Bandara, W., Mathiesen, P.: Importance of literature profiling: an archival analysis with illustrative examples for IS researchers. In: PACIS 2015: IT and Open Innovaton. AIS Electronic Library (AISeL), July 2015
14. Ghasemi, M., Amyot, D.: Process mining in healthcare: a systematised literature review. Int. J. Electron. Healthc. 9(1), 60–88 (2016)
15. van der Heijden, T.: Process Mining Project Methodology: Developing a General Approach to Apply Process Mining in Practice. Master's thesis, TUE. School of Industrial Engineering (2012)
16. Hruschka, D.J., Schwartz, D., St. John, D.C., Picone-Decaro, E., Jenkins, R.A., Carey, J.W.: Reliability in coding open-ended data: lessons learned from HIV behavioral research. Field Methods 16(3), 307–331 (2004)
17. Keathle, H., Van Aken, E., Gonzalez-Aleu, F., Deschamps, F., Letens, G., Orlandini, P.C.: Assessing the maturity of a research area: bibliometric review and proposed framework. Scientometrics 109(2), 927–951 (2016)
18. Kurniati, A.P., Johnson, O., Hogg, D., Hall, G.: Process mining in oncology: a literature review. In: ICICM 2016, pp. 291–297. IEEE (2016)
19. Paré, G., Trudel, M.C., Jaana, M., Kitsiou, S.: Synthesizing information systems knowledge: a typology of literature reviews. Inf. Manag. 52(2), 183–199 (2015)
20. Recker, J., Mendling, J.: Recommendations from analyzing the state-of-the-art of business process management research. In: EMISA Forum, vol. 36, pp. 16–21. Gesellschaft fuer Informatik (2016)
21. Rojas, E., Munoz-Gama, J., Sepúlveda, M., Capurro, D.: Process mining in healthcare: a literature review. J. Biomed. Inf. 61, 224–236 (2016)
22. Rowe, F.: What literature review is not: diversity, boundaries and recommendations. EJIS 23(3), 241–255 (2014)

23. Suriadi, S., Wynn, M.T., Ouyang, C., ter Hofstede, A.H.M., van Dijk, N.J.: Understanding process behaviours in a large insurance company in Australia: a case study. CAiSE **2013**, 449–464 (2013)
24. Thiede, M., Fuerstenau, D.: The technological maturity of process mining: an exploration of the status quo in top IS journals. MKWI **2016**, 1591–1602 (2016)
25. Thiede, M., Fuerstenau, D., Barquet, A.P.B.: How is process mining technology used by organizations? A systematic literature review of empirical studies. Bus. Proc. Manag. J. **24**(4), 900–922 (2018)
26. Tiwari, A., Turner, C.J., Majeed, B.: A review of business process mining: state-of-the-art and future trends. Bus. Proc. Manag. J. **14**(1), 5–22 (2008)

Initializing k-Means Efficiently: Benefits for Exploratory Cluster Analysis

Manuel Fritz[(✉)] and Holger Schwarz

Institute for Parallel and Distributed Systems, University of Stuttgart,
Universitätsstraße 38, 70569 Stuttgart, Germany
{manuel.fritz,holger.schwarz}@ipvs.uni-stuttgart.de

Abstract. Data analysis is a highly exploratory task, where various algorithms with different parameters are executed until a solid result is achieved. This is especially evident for cluster analyses, where the number of clusters must be provided prior to the execution of the clustering algorithm. Since this number is rarely known in advance, the algorithm is typically executed several times with varying parameters. Hence, the duration of the exploratory analysis heavily depends on the runtime of each execution of the clustering algorithm. While previous work shows that the initialization of clustering algorithms is crucial for fast and solid results, it solely focuses on a single execution of the clustering algorithm and thereby neglects previous executions. We propose Delta Initialization as an initialization strategy for k-Means in such an exploratory setting. The core idea of this new algorithm is to exploit the clustering results of previous executions in order to enhance the initialization of subsequent executions. We show that this algorithm is well suited for exploratory cluster analysis as considerable speedups can be achieved while additionally achieving superior clustering results compared to state-of-the-art initialization strategies.

Keywords: Exploratory cluster analysis · k-Means · Initialization

1 Introduction

Data mining addresses the gain of previously unknown knowledge from existing data. To this end, analysts typically follow an exploration cycle to explore various algorithms and parameters in order to find solid results. Existing reference models for data analysis like the KDD process [7] or CRISP-DM [4] illustrate this idea: analysts iterate over the steps of data selection, data pre-processing, data mining and finally conduct an evaluation. If the analysts are not satisfied with the result, they return to one of the previous steps and re-iterate the process using different algorithms or parameters in order to improve the final results. For supervised learning techniques, large portions of this exploration can be performed in an automated manner due to the recent advancements in the research area of automated machine learning (AutoML) [8,16,24].

© Springer Nature Switzerland AG 2019
H. Panetto et al. (Eds.): OTM 2019, LNCS 11877, pp. 146–163, 2019.
https://doi.org/10.1007/978-3-030-33246-4_9

For unsupervised learning techniques, domain knowledge is required for the evaluation, since training data lack information about the expected outcome, such as class labels for classification tasks. Hence, the exploration cannot be performed in an automatic manner. This is especially important for cluster analysis: Here, the number of clusters k often has to be provided as a parameter for the execution of the clustering algorithm. However, for an arbitrary dataset, the appropriate number of clusters is unknown in advance. As a consequence, analysts often execute the clustering algorithm multiple times with varying parameters in order to find the most appropriate number of clusters. This leads to time-consuming exploration processes.

Current approaches to accelerate exploratory cluster analysis mainly focus on the clustering algorithm itself but do not address the whole exploration process [6,9,21]. In particular, they ignore the results of previous executions of the clustering algorithm. Recent advancements like k-Means++ [2] or k-Means‖ [3] address a better initialization step of the clustering algorithm. This typically improves the runtime of the algorithm as it tremendously reduces the number of internal iterations that are needed for a single execution of the clustering algorithm. However, the initialization itself becomes rather time-consuming and, again, these approaches do not consider the results of previous executions of the clustering algorithm.

The goal of this work is to exploit the clustering results of previous executions of a clustering algorithm in order to accelerate repeated executions of the algorithm as they are typical in exploratory analysis. The overall goal is to significantly accelerate the exploration process that analysts typically follow to find solid parameters for clustering algorithms. In our work, we focus on k-Means, a broadly used clustering algorithm [26] and its initialization algorithms. Our contributions include the following:

- We investigate an exploratory process to estimate the number of clusters in a dataset and identify approaches to enhance this process.
- We examine commonalities across commonly used initialization strategies for clustering algorithms.
- We propose the Delta Initialization algorithm and detail on its improved initialization step compared to previous initialization algorithms.
- We discuss the advantages this new algorithm provides in an exploratory setting for cluster analyses.
- Our comprehensive evaluation unveils that tremendous runtime savings as well as an improved quality of clustering results can be achieved when using Delta Initialization.

The remainder of this paper is structured as follows: In Sect. 2, we discuss related work in this area. We show how analysts and existing approaches proceed when estimating the number of clusters in a dataset in Sect. 3. In Sect. 4, we investigate the commonalities of k-Means++ and k-Means‖, the current state-of-the-art algorithms for initializing the k-Means algorithm. We introduce our algorithm Delta Initialization and discuss its integration into the exploration process in Sect. 5. In Sect. 6, we evaluate our algorithm against existing initialization methods for k-Means. Finally, we conclude in Sect. 7.

2   Related Work

Nowadays, there are numerous approaches to accelerate partitioning clustering algorithms, such as k-Means. Several works aim to reduce the runtime of the algorithm by modifying the data structure or the runtime environment. For example, some works independently discovered that exploiting k-d-trees as data structure may lead to a shorter runtime [1,14,21]. Albeit exploiting k-d-trees as data structures may lead to performance improvements in some cases, they perform poorly in higher dimensions [12].

The rise of distributed analytic platforms, such as Apache Hadoop and Apache Spark led to new processing paradigms. MapReduce [5] or Spark's MLlib [19] are able to process voluminous datasets on multiple compute nodes, hence resulting in a shorter runtime [27]. Due to in-memory processing, Spark typically tends to perform better than the MapReduce framework [19]. This way, long runtimes of data mining algorithms are reduced due to faster data processing paradigms [10].

Regarding algorithmic improvements, prior work can be divided into two groups: Firstly, approaches to improve the initialization phase of k-Means. Secondly, approaches that accelerate the post-initialization phase of k-Means.

The acceleration approaches for the post-initialization phase mainly aim to (a) reduce the number of distance calculations, and (b) stop the algorithm, if an adequate level of quality is achieved. Elkan exploits the triangle inequality in order to avoid unnecessary distance calculations [6]. Thereby, the traditional k-Means algorithm can be executed up to 351 times faster than the standard algorithm, depending on the dataset and the number of clusters. Other works focus on the result of the clustering algorithm after each iteration and stop the algorithm, if the gain in quality between these iterations is below a certain threshold [9,20]. Thereby, these approaches lead to considerable time savings while trading off accuracy of the final result.

It is generally known, that the initialization phase is crucial in order to obtain high-quality clustering results [22]. The algorithm proposed by Lloyd [18] randomly selects k entities from the dataset as centroids. However, since the resulting quality can vary as shown by Pena et al. [22], more robust approaches were addressed by previous work. Hochbaum and Shmoys presented the so-called furthest-first strategy for the initial seeding of the centroids [13]. Here, the first centroid is selected randomly from the dataset, whereas the remaining $k-1$ centroids are selected in such a way that they are furthest away from already seeded centroids. However, this strategy tends to select outliers as initial centroids.

Further improvements, such as k-Means++ [2] or k-Means‖ [3] work in an iterative manner. In each round, they also take the position of previously sampled centroids into account. Furthermore, they aim to avoid outliers in contrast to the furthest-first strategy and thereby achieve more stable seedings and subsequently more stable clustering results. We defer the detailed discussion and analysis of these two algorithms to Sect. 4.

The aforementioned works mainly focus on improving the initialization step or the iteration step for a single execution of the k-Means algorithm. However, there is only one prior work, which addresses a repetitive execution with varying values for k. Karypis et al. proposed the so-called Bisecting k-Means algorithm [15]. The idea of Bisecting k-Means is similar to the principle of divisive hierarchical cluster analysis: The worst cluster is split in two clusters. Karypis et al. investigated several methods to identify the "worst" cluster, such as using the largest cluster or the cluster with the least overall similarity. Subsequently, they came to the conclusion, that various approaches perform similarly well. Albeit they re-use existing clustering results, Bisecting k-Means only performs local changes since they solely split one single cluster in two.

3   Exploration Cycle for Partitioning Clustering Algorithms

Finding the "correct" number of clusters in a dataset is a commonly known problem. There are several existing approaches, which draw on a repeated execution of the clustering algorithm with varying parameters, e.g., an increasing value for k for each execution of the clustering algorithm. Commonly used methods are for example the elbow method [11], the jump method [23] or the gap statistic [25]. However, the exploration can also be conducted by analysts in a very similar manner. Figure 1 shows the generic exploration cycle for partitioning clustering algorithms.

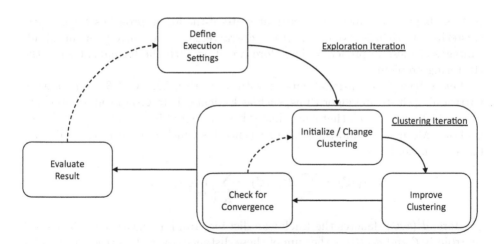

Fig. 1. Exploration cycle for partitioning clustering algorithms.

Firstly, the execution settings, i.e., the parameters are selected in order to initiate the first exploration iteration. For partitioning clustering algorithms, this is the value for k. Secondly, the clustering algorithm is executed. The algorithm follows 3 steps: (1) Initialize the clustering algorithm, i.e., seeding k centroids, (2) improve the clustering by assigning entities to the closest centroids, and (3) check, if the algorithm converges. If the convergence criterion is not met, the algorithm continues by moving the centroids to the next best location, e.g., to the center of the current clustering. These iterations are performed within the clustering algorithm itself (cf. clustering iteration in Fig. 1). Thirdly, once the convergence criterion of the clustering algorithm is met, the clustering result is evaluated. If the analyst is not satisfied with the result or a certain threshold of an estimation method is not yet met, another exploration iteration with a different set of parameters will be triggered.

Since multiple exploration iterations are typically performed in order to achieve solid results, also multiple clustering iterations are executed with varying parameters of the clustering algorithm. Especially when considering Big Data [17], it is clear that each clustering iteration and therefore each exploration iteration is very time-consuming. Furthermore, each clustering iteration is encapsulated and does not take previous results into account. Current approaches to accelerate the overall exploration cycle mainly focus on the execution step (cf. clustering iteration in Fig. 1) and thus ignore the exploration iterations.

In this work, we investigate how to exploit the results of previous exploration iterations. We show how clustering results of previous exploration iterations can be re-used in order to accelerate the next initialization step of the clustering iteration.

4   Initializing k-Means

In this chapter, we investigate current state-of-the-art approaches to initialize clustering algorithms. We discuss their characteristics and unveil certain disadvantages of these approaches. Therefore, we start with the formalization of the clustering problem:

Let $\mathcal{X}$ be a d-dimensional dataset with n entities, i.e., $\mathcal{X} \subset \mathbb{R}^d$. The idea of partitioning clustering algorithms, such as k-Means, is to group the dataset into k disjoint clusters, such that each cluster is represented by a centroid $c \in \mathcal{C}$. The goal of k-Means is to find the set $\mathcal{C}$ of k centroids which minimizes the objective function in Eq. 1.

$$\phi_{\mathcal{X}}(\mathcal{C}) = \sum_{x \in \mathcal{X}} d^2(x, \mathcal{C}) = \sum_{x \in \mathcal{X}} \min_{c \in \mathcal{C}} \|x - c\|^2 \tag{1}$$

Here, $d^2(x, \mathcal{C})$ denotes the Euclidean distance from an entity x to the closest centroid in $\mathcal{C}$ and $\phi_{\mathcal{X}}(\mathcal{C})$ is the sum of these distances over all entities in $\mathcal{X}$. This sum is also called the sum of squared errors (SSE). Algorithms like k-Means move these k centroids to a better position in each iteration, until their position converges, i.e., until no more changes occur. However, an initial placement of the centroids is required.

For the purpose of this work, we focus on k-Means++ [2] and k-Means∥ [3], since these are the two most commonly used initialization algorithms for k-Means. The authors of these algorithms showed, that their approaches significantly outperform previous initialization algorithms regarding runtime and quality of the clustering result. Hence, we investigated the commonalities of these two algorithms and show the steps they perform during the initialization phase. Figure 2 summarizes these commonalities. Both initialization algorithms require the number of centroids k that should be chosen as input parameter and return a set $\mathcal{C}$ of k centroids. The algorithms start with sampling *one* single centroid randomly from the dataset $\mathcal{X}$. Subsequently, the algorithms slightly differ throughout each round r (depicted with dashed lines in Fig. 2) in order to select the remaining $k - 1$ initial centroids. Hence, we focus on the explanation for k-Means++ first, before we explain k-Means∥ in detail.

Since k-Means++ doesn't rely on oversampling, the oversampling factor ℓ is set to 1, i.e., no oversampling is performed. Subsequently, in each round r, one point is sampled from $\mathcal{X}$ proportional to probability p_x, which is calculated as shown in Eq. 2. Hence, k-Means++ requires k rounds over the dataset and samples one centroid in each round.

$$p_x = \frac{\ell \cdot d^2(x, \mathcal{C})}{\phi_{\mathcal{X}}(\mathcal{C})} \tag{2}$$

The goal of the probability p_x is to neglect outliers, yet to choose centroids which are rather far away from previously chosen centroids. Note, that the probability is adjusted after each round, since a new centroid is added to C in each round. Subsequently, the k sampled points are returned.

k-Means++ is an improvement over the existing initialization algorithms we have discussed in Sect. 2 [2]. Similar to the furthest-first strategy, it takes the position of previously drawn centroids into account. This way, k-Means++ provides a stable initialization of the centroids, but it requires k rounds over the dataset. This is impractical for huge datasets or high values for k.

Bahmani et al. introduced k-Means∥ as a scalable enhancement of k-Means++ to tackle this problem of the potentially high number of rounds and thus high runtime of the k-Means++ algorithm [3]. Instead of requiring k rounds over the dataset, the authors show that less rounds are sufficient. According to their formal evaluation, $O(log\ \psi)$ rounds should be conducted, where ψ denotes the SSE of the clustering with the single aforementioned randomly chosen centroid. However, they also showed with various experiments that $r * \ell \geq k$ leads to solid results, where r is the total number of rounds during the initialization phase. Hence, a constant number of rounds suffices to achieve a high qualitative clustering result. Furthermore, Bahmani et al. showed how k-Means∥ can be parallelized and thus achieving even more runtime savings.

In each round, k-Means∥ samples more than just one centroid. To achieve this, probability p_x is adjusted by adding an oversampling factor $\ell > 1$ (see Eq. 2), which should be defined, e.g., as input variable. The points are chosen from $\mathcal{X}$ proportional to the probability p_x. Sampling ℓ points in each round leads

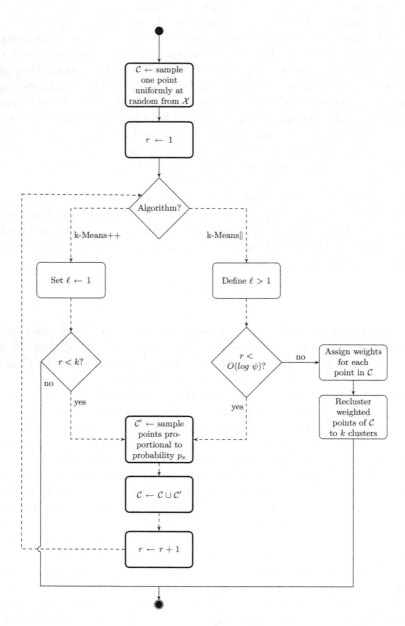

Fig. 2. Initialization steps of k-Means++ (left) and k-Means‖ (right). Identical steps are shown in bold. Dashed lines connect actions performed in each round of the initialization algorithm.

to a total of $\ell * O(log\ \psi)$ points, which due to the oversampling factor is typically more than k centroids. To this end, k-Means‖ proceeds by assigning weights to the sampled points. For each $c \in \mathcal{C}$, the corresponding weight w_c denotes the number of entities from $\mathcal{X}$ closer to c than to any other entity in $\mathcal{C}$. Finally, these weighted points are reclustered in order to achieve k centroids. For this step, k-Means‖ draws on k-Means++, which yields solid and fast results since the number of points in $\mathcal{C}$ is small.

As Fig. 2 shows, k-Means++ and k-Means‖ share two commonalities: (1) At the beginning, *one* initial centroid is chosen at random from $\mathcal{X}$. (2) During the initialization rounds, the centroids are sampled very similarly, i.e., according to the probability p_x (cf. Eq. 2), which takes already sampled centroids into account.

The main differences of these two initialization algorithms become evident, when regarding them in comparison with a random-based approach: A naive approach would be to perform one single round and to select k centroids within that round, e.g., the first k elements in a dataset. However, this strategy does not take the position of the chosen centroids into account and can therefore lead to long runtimes of the clustering algorithm and to bad final clustering results. k-Means++ performs k rounds and selects one centroid within each round according to p_x. While this allows to easily focus on the position of previously drawn centroids, the initialization algorithm is very time-consuming for huge datasets or a huge number of k. k-Means‖ is somewhere between both approaches. It requires less than k rounds and chooses $\ell * O(log\ \psi)$ centroids within each round, also according to p_x but with an oversampling factor $\ell > 1$. Since this is typically more than the demanded k centroids, further steps are necessary. Overall, we conclude, that the initialization steps of k-Means++ and k-Means‖ are still rather time-consuming.

5 Delta Initialization

Albeit k-Means++ and k-Means‖ lead to faster and more solid results than previous initialization algorithms, the number of clusters k is required prior to execution. However, the ground-truth value for k for an arbitrary dataset is typically unknown. Therefore, the analyst manually explores various values for k in order to find a promising solution. As shown in the previous section, the initialization step can become rather time-consuming and therefore impede the exploration for solid clustering results.

In this section, we propose Delta Initialization as initialization algorithm. The goal of this algorithm is to exploit the clustering result of previous executions in such an exploratory setting (cf. Fig. 1) in order to enhance subsequent executions of a clustering algorithm.

We assume, that k-Means is executed on the same dataset $\mathcal{X}$ with increasing values for k, e.g., k-Means with $k-1$ is executed before k. To preserve generality, we assume that Δk denotes the number of centroids that should be added to a previous clustering result $\mathcal{C}_{prev}$. The result of a previous result already contains a solid final position of the centroids as well as an assignment for each $x \in \mathcal{X}$

Algorithm 1: Delta Initialization for k-Means‖

Input: $\mathcal{X}$ - dataset, k - number of desired clusters, ℓ - oversampling factor, $\mathcal{C}_{prev}$ - set of centroids from a previous run, $\phi_{\mathcal{X}}(\mathcal{C}_{prev})$ - SSE from a previous run

Output: $\mathcal{C}_{result}$ - a set of k centroids

1 $\Delta k \leftarrow k - |\mathcal{C}_{prev}|$;

2 $\mathcal{C} \leftarrow \mathcal{C}_{prev}$;

3 $\mathcal{C}_{result} \leftarrow \mathcal{C}_{prev}$;

4 **for** $O(log\ \phi_{\mathcal{X}}(\mathcal{C}_{prev}))$ **do**

5 $\quad\big|\quad$ $\mathcal{C}' \leftarrow$ sample each point $x \in \mathcal{X}$ independently with probability p_x;

6 $\quad\big|\quad$ $\mathcal{C} \leftarrow \mathcal{C} \cup \mathcal{C}'$;

7 **end**

8 For $c \in \mathcal{C}$, set w_c to be the number of points in $\mathcal{X}$ closer to c than any other point in $\mathcal{C}$;

9 **for** Δk *times* **do**

10 $\quad\big|\quad$ $\mathcal{C}'' \leftarrow$ sample centroid according to w_c for each point $c \in \mathcal{C}$;

11 $\quad\big|\quad$ $\mathcal{C}_{result} \leftarrow \mathcal{C}_{result} \cup \mathcal{C}''$;

12 **end**

---

to the closest centroid $c \in \mathcal{C}_{prev}$. To this end, $\mathcal{C}_{prev}$ defines the set of centroids and $\phi_{\mathcal{X}}(\mathcal{C}_{prev})$ the SSE of a previous run (e.g., with $k-1$). These properties of a previous clustering result can be easily exploited for future executions, since not all k centroids need to be selected in the initialization process, but just Δk new centroids should be added to the previous clustering result. Algorithm 1 depicts the functionality of our proposed initialization algorithm Delta Initialization exemplified for k-Means‖. Note however, due to the striking resemblance between k-Means++ and k-Means‖ (see Fig. 2), Delta Initialization can also be applied to k-Means++ very similarly. That is, only Δk rounds have to be performed in lines 4–7 with $\ell = 1$. Also, the subsequent steps in lines 8–12 are not required for Delta Initialization with k-Means++.

The changes in contrast to k-Means‖ (see Fig. 2) mainly address the first and the last step (lines 1–4 and lines 9–12). Firstly, we calculate the number of clusters Δk that should be added to a previous clustering result (line 1). Since we already have the centroids of a previous clustering result, we use them as initial centroids instead of randomly sampling only a single centroid from $\mathcal{X}$ (line 2). Furthermore, the SSE $\phi_{\mathcal{X}}(\mathcal{C}_{prev})$ can also be employed from a previous run, which is required for determining the number of rounds in line 4. Hence, we replace ψ, which is the SSE of a clustering result with one single randomly chosen centroid (cf. Sect. 4) with $\phi_{\mathcal{X}}(\mathcal{C}_{prev})$, i.e., the SSE of a previous clustering result, which typically provides a more stable clustering. The procedure in each round (lines 5–6) remains unchanged compared to the procedure of k-Means++ and k-Means‖. That is, for k-Means‖, $\ell * O(log\ \phi_{\mathcal{X}}(\mathcal{C}_{prev}))$ points are chosen in total.

Similarly to k-Means‖ (cf. Sect. 4), when using Delta Initialization, further steps are required in order to reduce the number of centroids to the demanded

k centroids. Hence, we follow the process of k-Means$\|$. To this end, weights are assigned for each $c \in \mathcal{C}$, which are subsequently used to reduce $|\mathcal{C}|$ to k. We remember that the clustering result of a previous exploration iteration already provides local optima, i.e., the centroids have a solid position in the data space. Hence, we do not need to re-cluster the drawn data points. Yet, we solely sample Δk centroids from $\mathcal{C}$ according to their weights (lines 9–12). Note, that it is possible to draw duplicates, which are already contained in $\mathcal{C}_{result}$. Since the loop in lines 4–7 samples $\ell * O(log \ \phi_{\mathcal{X}}(\mathcal{C}_{prev}))$ points, it is possible to repeat the loop in lines 9–12 just as often to avoid potential duplicates. Hence, ℓ should be chosen in a way, that $\Delta k \geq \ell * O(log \ \phi_{\mathcal{X}}(\mathcal{C}_{prev}))$ in order to avoid duplicate centroids.

Consequently, we want to summarize the advantages of our proposed algorithm over the existing approaches of k-Means++ and k-Means$\|$: The latter two algorithms proceed by firstly choosing *one* centroid randomly from the dataset $\mathcal{X}$. Subsequent calculations base on this randomly chosen centroid, i.e., $k - 1$ are available after the initialization is performed. In each round, the probability p_x is calculated with regards to the first randomly chosen centroid, among later added centroids. In contrast to that, Delta Initialization exploits the clustering result of a previous run, i.e., the final position of $|\mathcal{C}_{prev}|$ centroids and the SSE. Subsequent calculations therefore solely add Δk centroids to a previous clustering result. Exploiting previous clustering results has two advantages: (1) The probability p_x is based on multiple centroids and (2) these centroids of a previous run are already at a (locally) optimum position due to the previous execution of the k-Means algorithm (cf. Eq. 1). Therefore, we aim for a faster and more solid initialization process, which ultimately results in a faster and also more solid clustering result.

Further, we argue that k-Means++ benefits from the Delta Initialization approach also in another way: Typically k rounds are required. However, when exploiting a previous clustering result, only Δk rounds in lines 4–7 have to be performed, i.e., less initialization rounds have to be performed.

Regarding k-Means$\|$, Bahmani et al. outlined how the algorithm can be parallelized [3]. Therefore, they used the generic MapReduce model [5] to demonstrate how the parallel computations can be performed. To this end, they assumed that $\mathcal{C}$ is small, thus it fits into each mapper's memory. Further, each mapper works on subsets of $\mathcal{X}$, i.e. $\mathcal{X}' \subseteq \mathcal{X}$. Hence, each mapper calculates the SSE $\phi_{\mathcal{X}'}(\mathcal{C})$ on its subset $\mathcal{X}'$. In the reducer, the overall SSE will be calculated by adding the aforementioned values. This overall SSE can further be exploited by each mapper to individually draw samples according to p_x. Since Delta Initialization doesn't address this point in particular, we argue that it still can be implemented in a parallel way.

Hence, the proposed algorithm maintains the properties of k-Means++ and k-Means$\|$, respectively. That is, a solid initialization of the centroids for the k-Means algorithm is performed.

6   Evaluation

In this section, we evaluate the proposed algorithm. We investigate the advantages of using Delta Initialization instead of k-Means|| as the initialization strategy for clustering in cases where the clustering algorithm is run for all values of k in a given range $\mathcal{R}$ of possible number of clusters. We focus on k-Means||, since it is very similar to k-Means++, yet scalable. Note however that the same effects can be achieved when using k-Means++ as explained in Sect. 5.

Furthermore, we also show that our approach is superior to Bisecting k-Means, which simply splits the worst cluster into two clusters. For the purpose of this evaluation, we consider the worst cluster to be the one with the highest sum of squared errors. This is a valid approach, since the variance of this cluster is the highest and the purpose of k-Means is to minimize this variance.

We structure the evaluation as follows: Firstly, we explain the setup, which we used throughout our experiments. Secondly, we unveil the results of the performance evaluation. Finally, we investigate the achieved quality of the cluster analysis when employing each initialization method.

6.1   Experimental Setup

In this section, we explain the hardware and software setup for our experiments. Furthermore, we describe how we implemented the investigated initialization methods. We explain the characteristics of the datasets that we used before we discuss the required parameters for the evaluation.

Hardware and Software. We conduct all of our experiments on a distributed Apache Spark cluster. This cluster consists of one master node and three worker nodes. The master node has a 12-core CPU with 2 GHz each and 128 GB RAM. Each worker has a 6-core CPU with 3.4 GHz each and 256 GB RAM. Each node in this cluster operates on Ubuntu 18.04. We installed OpenJDK 8u191, Scala 2.11.12 and used Apache Hadoop 3.1.0 as well as Apache Spark 2.3.1.

Implementation. Since we conduct our experiments on Spark, we used the current k-Means||[1] and Bisecting k-Means[2] implementations of Spark. Bahmani et al. showed, that only very few iterations are required in the second step of k-Means|| (cf. Algorithm 1, lines 4–7) [3]. Spark's current implementation sets this number per default to $r = 2$, which we also keep for Delta Initialization. Further, the oversampling factor is set to $\ell = 2k$ in the given Spark implementation of k-Means||, which we also keep unchanged.

---

[1] https://git.io/KMeansParallel.
[2] https://git.io/BisectingKMeans.

Datasets. We implemented a synthetic dataset generator. This tool generates datasets based on the following input parameters:

- n: number of entities in the dataset
- d: number of dimensions
- c: number of clusters in the dataset, where each cluster contains n/c entities
- r: additional noise ratio, which is added uniformly to the whole data space

Our tool generates datasets with values that lie within the range $[-10; 10]$ for each dimension. Each cluster has a Gaussian distribution with the mean at the center and a standard deviation of 0.5. The c centers are chosen randomly. The additional noise ratio adds uniformly distributed noise across the whole data. A noise ratio of 10% means that $0.1 \cdot n$ entities are added as noise.

For the purpose of the evaluation, we set r to 10%. That is, we consider datasets with some noise across the whole data space. However, we made similar observations for datasets with other noise ratios. The remaining parameters are subject to change. For our experiments, we used datasets having 10^6 or 10^7 entries, 10, 50 or 100 dimensions and the number of clusters set to 5, 15 or 25.

Parameters. Since Delta Initialization unfolds its potential in an exploratory setting (cf. Sect. 3), we assume that several values for k are executed sequentially. That is, k-Means with a specific value for k is executed after the execution of k-Means with $k-1$ is finished. That is, we set Δk to 1. We regard this assumption as realistic, since many automated approaches also proceed in such an iterative way.

Regarding the inherent characteristic of Delta Initialization and Bisecting k-Means, both approaches draw on clustering results which they subsequently use. Hence, we use k-Means|| as initialization method for $k = 2$ and employ this result for Delta Initialization and Bisecting k-Means. Therefore, we set the range $\mathcal{R}$ of values for k to execute throughout the experiments to $\mathcal{R} = \{2, ..., 2c\}$, where c denotes the actual number of clusters in the dataset. Hence, k-Means is executed with k-Means|| for $k = 2$ and for $2 < k \leq 2c$ with Delta Initialization, Bisecting k-Means and also with k-Means|| independently from another. Furthermore, we set the maximum number of iterations of each k-Means execution to 1,000 (cf. clustering iteration in Fig. 1).

We considered each combination of the three initialization algorithms (k-Means||, Bisecting k-Means, Delta Initialization), twelve datasets, and all values for parameter $k \in \mathcal{R}$. We executed our experiments for all these combinations three times, resulting in more than 1,000 runs.

6.2 Performance Evaluation

Table 1 summarizes the accumulated runtimes of our performance evaluation across several datasets. In general, we make three observations:

Firstly, both advanced initialization strategies lead to faster results than k-Means||. This observation becomes clear, when regarding the speedup. Solely

Table 1. Overview of the runtime results. Median values over 3 runs are depicted. Accumulated runtimes for $2 < k \leq 2c$ is shown in seconds for the initialization phase (Init) and the iterations of the k-Means algorithm (Iter). #Iter depicts the accumulated number of k-Means iterations until convergence. Speedup shows the acceleration in contrast to k-Means|| in regards to the total runtime. Bold values indicate the best performing results.

Dataset		k-Means||			Bisecting k-Means				Delta Initialization			
		Init (s)	Iter (s)	#Iter	Init (s)	Iter (s)	#Iter	Speedup	Init (s)	Iter (s)	#Iter	Speedup
I:	1×10^6n, 10d, 5c	8	**115**	**626**	2	156	842	**0.78**	3	169	929	0.71
II:	1×10^6n, 10d, 15c	23	1,103	6,226	**5**	**653**	**3,720**	1.71	8	851	4,888	1.31
III:	1×10^6n, 10d, 25c	51	2,853	11,238	**12**	**1,741**	**6,937**	1.66	17	1,937	7,704	1.49
IV:	1×10^6n, 50d, 5c	6	196	1,310	1	190	1,271	1.05	2	**137**	**919**	1.45
V:	1×10^6n, 50d, 15c	60	3,298	8,116	11	**2,027**	5,267	**1.65**	18	2,044	**5,150**	1.63
VI:	1×10^6n, 50d, 25c	87	6,208	16,665	16	**2,883**	**8,141**	**2.17**	26	3,274	9,278	1.91
VII:	1×10^6n, 100d, 5c	7	456	2,649	1	260	1,542	1.77	2	**4**	**24**	**70.98**
VIII:	1×10^6n, 100d, 15c	23	1,103	6,226	**5**	**653**	**3,720**	1.71	8	851	4,888	1.31
IX:	1×10^6n, 100d, 25c	185	13,211	18,029	29	5,185	8,069	2.57	60	**90**	**144**	**89.31**
X:	1×10^7n, 100d, 5c	48	1,632	2,055	**7**	1,440	1,812	1.16	13	**117**	**151**	**13.01**
XI:	1×10^7n, 100d, 15c	243	19,867	12,826	**39**	18,388	12,429	1.09	77	**849**	**560**	**21.72**
XII:	1×10^7n, 100d, 25c	616	56,293	24,113	**92**	47,383	21,811	1.20	184	**5,128**	**1,955**	**10.71**

on the smallest dataset I, Bisecting k-Means and Delta Initialization performed worse than k-Means||. For the remaining datasets, the speedups range from 1.05 to 89.31. These values can be achieved since the initialization time as well as the iteration time of the clustering algorithm itself are shorter for both methods compared to k-Means||.

Secondly, Bisecting k-Means is generally the fastest initialization method. The reason for this is the simple technique of splitting the worst cluster into two. Moreover, the runtime for the iterations until convergence is typically less than for k-Means||, since solely one cluster is split in two and the remaining clusters remain mostly unchanged. This leads to speedups ranging from 1.05 to 2.57 in contrast to k-Means||, when omitting dataset I.

Thirdly, Delta Initialization initializes slower than Bisecting k-Means, yet still considerably faster than k-Means||. Furthermore, Delta Initialization initializes the centroids closer to an optimum, since most often less iterations of k-Means are required. This leads to shorter overall runtimes. To this end, remarkable overall speedups from 1.31 to 89.31 in contrast to k-Means|| were achieved.

Hence, it is obvious that Bisecting k-Means and Delta Initialization significantly outperform the overall runtime of k-Means|| in an exploratory setting. While both initialization strategies are en par for lower dimensional datasets, Delta Initialization tends to perform significantly better than Bisecting k-Means for higher dimensional datasets. This observation becomes evident, if we observe the results of datasets with 100 dimensions (datasets VII-XII). Here, Delta Initialization is several orders of magnitude faster than Bisecting k-Means. There are two possible reasons for this observation: (1) Bisecting k-Means mainly focuses the assessment of the worst cluster, i.e., the calculation of the SSE for each cluster. Subsequently the cluster with the highest SSE is chosen and k-Means with $k = 2$ is applied solely on this cluster. To this end, Bisecting k-Means places these two centroids within this cluster symmetrically distant to the centroid of the previous iteration. Albeit this is a simple approach for the initialization of centroids, it neglects data characteristics, i.e., accumulation of data within the worst cluster. (2) Delta Initialization initializes the centroids closer to the optimum solution. The authors of k-Means|| have formally proven this property and it is also indicated by the significantly smaller accumulated number of the iterations Delta Initialization needs in comparison to the two other algorithms. In the next section, we will investigate the quality of the clustering results.

6.3 Quality Evaluation

For the qualitative evaluation, we base our observations on the generally accepted definition of a solid clustering result: A solid clustering result should have a high cohesion within each cluster and a high separation between the clusters. The separation between clusters can be measured as distance between the centroids. For the cohesion, we observe the SSE, since a low SSE indicates a high cohesion. To this end, we compare the SSE and the separation between both approaches in contrast to k-Means|| as baseline.

Figure 3 shows the results across all k-Means executions between $2 < k \leq 2c$. Here, *SSE Quotient* and *Separation Quotient* denote the quotient of the sum of squared errors, respectively the quotient for the separation, for Delta Initialization and Bisecting k-Means (dubbed as *incremental*) in contrast to the clustering result of k-Means||. Equations 3 and 4 present these observations in a formal way. Note, that we flipped dividend and divisor in a way, that values higher than 1 show a better result compared to k-Means|| and vice versa. This modification is required, since a low value for SSE describes compact clusters, whereas a high value for the separation describes better separated clusters.

$$SSE\ Quotient = \frac{SSE_{k-Means\|}}{SSE_{incremental}} \tag{3}$$

$$Separation\ Quotient = \frac{Separation_{incremental}}{Separation_{k-Means\|}} \tag{4}$$

The results in Fig. 3 show that both approaches produce different clustering results than k-Means||. Albeit the differences vary depending on the dataset, we observe that the clustering results are still comparable to the results of k-Means||, since the quotients are still very close to the baseline of k-Means||.

When considering Fig. 3a, it is clear that both approaches tend to create clustering results which are less compact than the baseline. However, the median values of both initialization approaches are very close to each other and also very close to the clustering result when using k-Means||. Especially for datasets IV-XII, the median values merely differ from the baseline. The median values for the *SSE Quotient* for Delta Initialization (Bisecting k-Means) range from 0.76 (0.99)

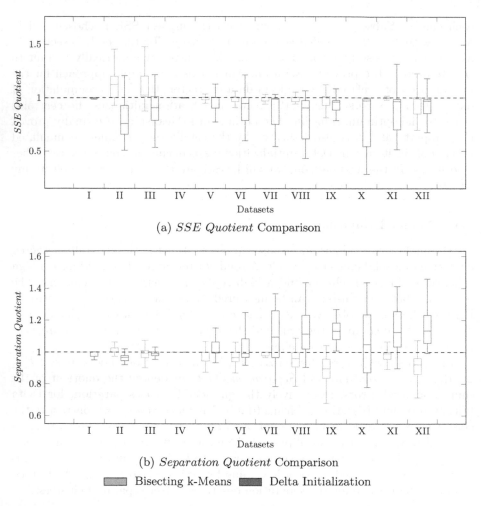

(a) *SSE Quotient* Comparison

(b) *Separation Quotient* Comparison

▭ Bisecting k-Means   ▬ Delta Initialization

Fig. 3. *SSE Quotient* and *Separation Quotient* for Bisecting k-Means and Delta Initialization in contrast to k-Means‖ (dashed line). Box plots show the minimum value, lower quartile, median, upper quartile and maximum value across all runs on the datasets. Note, that values greater than 1 indicate an improvement over k-Means‖ and vice versa.

to 1.00 (1.13). That is, Bisecting k-Means typically generates more compact clustering results than Delta Initialization. However, these differences are most often very small.

However, when considering the *Separation Quotient* in Fig. 3b, we make a different observation. Here, it is clear that Delta Initialization frequently creates better separated clusters than Bisecting k-Means and even k-Means‖. This becomes very evident, when regarding datasets V-XII. This observation can be traced back to the algorithm itself: Since $|\mathcal{C}_{prev}|$ centroids are used instead of

1 randomly chosen centroid (cf. line 2 in Algorithm 1), the entities in $\mathcal{X}$ are assigned to centroids with an optimal position. These optimal positions were achieved due to a previous execution of k-Means with another set of parameters. Subsequently, the calculated weight w_c per centroid $c \in \mathcal{C}$ provides a greater dispersion. Therefore, the sampled data points according to these weights provide a better separation due to the previous clustering result. The median values for the *Separation Quotient* for Delta Initialization (Bisecting k-Means) therefore range from 0.97 (0.90) to 1.37 (1.00).

Putting the observations from Fig. 3a and b together, we conclude that Delta Initialization creates clusters, which are almost as compact as clusters created by Bisecting k-Means and k-Means‖. However, the generated clusters are clearly better separated. When following the definition of a solid clustering result at the beginning of this section, these observations lead to the fact, that the overall clustering result is better than the clustering result achieved by Bisecting k-Means and k-Means‖. Furthermore, we argue that the separation between clusters is of paramount interest in a high-dimensional dataset. Since this enables the analyst to distinguish between the differences between the characteristics of the individual clusters, we argue that Delta Initialization is superior to Bisecting k-Means for an exploratory setting.

7 Conclusion

Data analysis is an exploratory process, which can be regarded as several iterations between different tasks. These tasks include the execution of a data mining algorithm and the evaluation of the result, until a satisfying result can be achieved. Especially for unsupervised learning techniques, this exploration can not be automated. Therefore, the exploration is often performed manually by analysts, since they need to contribute with domain knowledge in order to find solid results. However, each exploration iteration (cf. Fig. 1) is often performed independently from the others, i.e., there are no relations to previous iterations.

In this work, we presented Delta Initialization as initialization algorithm for k-Means in an exploratory setting. In order to estimate the number of clusters in a dataset, the k-Means algorithm is executed on this dataset with varying values for the number of clusters k. The goal of Delta Initialization is to exploit previous clustering results in order to enhance the initialization step of k-Means for previously unseen values for k. Therefore, our proposed algorithm tackles the problem of a high runtime overhead for the repeated initialization process in exploratory processes.

Our comprehensive evaluation unveiled, that in contrast to existing approaches tremendous overall runtime savings of several orders of magnitude are possible. Especially for high-dimensional datasets, which is of paramount interest of today's Big Data era, the investigated runtime savings are significant. At the same time, we showed that Delta Initialization provides high qualitative clustering results, which suggest that it is also very well suited to estimate the number of clusters in a dataset. Furthermore, the proposed algorithm generates

well-separated clusters, which may be of particular interest for analysts in order
to find differences between clusters.

Future work should address how Delta Initialization can be exploited for
approaches to estimate the number of clusters in a dataset. These approaches
typically perform k-Means and subsequent evaluations multiple times [11,23,25],
which can be seamlessly addressed by Delta Initialization.

Acknowledgments. This research was partially funded by the Ministry of Science of
Baden-Württemberg, Germany, for the Doctoral Program 'Services Computing'. Some
work presented in this paper was performed in the project 'INTERACT' as part of
the Software Campus program, which is funded by the German Federal Ministry of
Education and Research (BMBF) under Grant No.: 01IS17051. Finally, we thank Tim
Niederhausen for his implementation work.

References

1. Alsabti, K., Ranka, S., Singh, V.: An efficient k-means clustering algorithm. In:
   Proceedings of IPPS/SPDP Workshop on High Performance Data Mining (1998)
2. Arthur, D., Vassilvitskii, S.: k-means++: the advantages of careful seeding. In:
   Proceedings of the Eighteenth Annual ACM-SIAM Symposium on Discrete Algorithms, pp. 1027–1025 (2007)
3. Bahmani, B., Moseley, B., Vattani, A., Kumar, R., Vassilvitskii, S.: Scalable K-
   Means++. Proc. VLDB Endowment **5**(7), 622–633 (2012)
4. Chapman, P., Clinton, J., Kerber, R., Khabaza, T., Reinartz, T., Shearer, C.,
   Wirth, R.: CRISP-DM 1.0. CRISP-DM Consortium p. 76 (2000)
5. Dean, J., Ghemawat, S.: MapReduce: simplified data processing on large clusters.
   In: Proceedings of 6th Symposium on Operating Systems Design and Implementation, vol. 51, no. 1, pp. 137–149 (2004). https://dl.acm.org/citation.cfm?id=132749
6. Elkan, C.: Using the triangle inequality to accelerate k-Means. In: Proceedings of
   the Twentieth International Conference on Machine Learning, pp. 147–153 (2003)
7. Fayyad, U., Piatetsky-Shapiro, G., Smyth, P.: The KDD process for extracting
   useful knowledge from volumes of data. Commun. ACM **39**(11), 27–34 (1996)
8. Feurer, M., Klein, A., Eggensperger, K., Springenberg, J., Blum, M., Hutter, F.:
   Efficient and robust automated machine learning. Adv. Neural Inf. Process. Syst.
   28, 2944–2952 (2015)
9. Fritz, M., Behringer, M., Schwarz, H.: Quality-driven early stopping for explorative
   cluster analysis for big data. SICS Softw.-Intensive Cyber-Phys. Syst. **34**(2–3),
   129–140 (2019)
10. Fritz, M., Muazzen, O., Behringer, M., Schwarz, H.: ASAP-DM: a framework
    for automatic selection of analytic platforms for data mining. In: SICS Software-
    Intensive Cyber-Physical Systems, pp. 1–13 (2019)
11. Halkidi, M., Batistakis, Y., Vazirgiannis, M.: On clustering validation techniques.
    J. Intel. Inf. Syst. **17**(2–3), 107–145 (2001)
12. Hamerly, G., Drake, J.: Accelerating Lloyd's Algorithm for k-Means Clustering. In:
    Celebi, M.E. (ed.) Partitional Clustering Algorithms, pp. 41–78. Springer, Cham
    (2015). https://doi.org/10.1007/978-3-319-09259-1_2
13. Hochbaum, D.S., Shmoys, D.B.: A best possible heuristic for the k-Center problem.
    Math. Oper. Res. **10**(2), 180–184 (1985)

14. Kanungo, T., Mount, D., Netanyahu, N., Piatko, C., Silverman, R., Wu, A.: An efficient k-means clustering algorithm: analysis and implementation. IEEE Trans. Pattern Anal. Mach. Intel. **24**(7), 881–892 (2002)
15. Karypis, M.S.G., Kumar, V., Steinbach, M.: A comparison of document clustering techniques. In: Text Mining Workshop at KDD (2000)
16. Kotthoff, L., Thornton, C., Hoos, H.H., Hutter, F., Leyton-Brown, K.: Auto-WEKA 2.0: automatic model selection and hyperparameter optimization in WEKA. J. Mach. Learn. Res. **17**, 1–5 (2016)
17. Laney, D.: 3D data management: controlling data volume, velocity, and variety. In: META Group Research Note 6 (February 2001), 1–4 (2001)
18. Lloyd, S.P.: Least squares quantization in PCM. IEEE Trans. Inf. Theor. **28**(2), 129–137 (1982)
19. Meng, X., et al.: MLlib: machine learning in apache spark. J. Mach. Learn. Res. **17**, 1–7 (2016)
20. Mexicano, A., et al.: The early stop heuristic: a new convergence criterion for K-means. In: AIP Conference Proceedings. vol. 1738 (2016)
21. Pelleg, D., Moore, A.: Accelerating exact k-means algorithms with geometric reasoning. In: Proceedings of the Fifth ACM SIGKDD International Conference on Knowledge Discovery and Data Mining, pp. 277–281. ACM Press (1999)
22. Pena, J.M., Lozano, J.A., Larranaga, P.: An empirical comparison of four initialization methods for the k-means algorithm. Pattern Recogn. Lett. **20**(10), 1027–1040 (1999)
23. Sugar, C.A., James, G.M.: Finding the number of clusters in a dataset: an information-theoretic approach. J. Am. Stat. Assoc. **98**(463), 750–763 (2003)
24. Thornton, C., Hutter, F., Hoos, H.H., Leyton-Brown, K.: Auto-WEKA. In: Proceedings of the 19th ACM SIGKDD International Conference on Knowledge Discovery and Data Mining (2013)
25. Tibshirani, R., Walther, G., Hastie, T.: Estimating the number of clusters in a data set via the gap statistic. J. Royal Stat. Soc. Ser. B: Stat. Methodol. **63**(2), 411–423 (2001)
26. Wu, X., et al.: Top 10 algorithms in data mining. Knowl. Inf. Syst. **14**(1), 1–37 (2008)
27. Zhao, W., Ma, H., He, Q.: Parallel K-means clustering based on MapReduce. In: Jaatun, M.G., Zhao, G., Rong, C. (eds.) CloudCom 2009. LNCS, vol. 5931, pp. 674–679. Springer, Heidelberg (2009). https://doi.org/10.1007/978-3-642-10665-1_71

Exploiting EuroVoc's Hierarchical Structure for Classifying Legal Documents

Erwin Filtz[1]([⊠])(iD), Sabrina Kirrane[1](iD), Axel Polleres[1,2](iD),
and Gerhard Wohlgenannt[3](iD)

[1] Vienna University of Economics and Business, Vienna, Austria
{erwin.filtz,sabrina.kirrane,axel.polleres}@wu.ac.at
[2] Complexity Science Hub, Vienna, Austria
[3] ITMO University, St. Petersburg, Russia
gwohlg@itmo.ru

Abstract. Multi-label document classification is a challenging problem because of the potentially huge number of classes. Furthermore, real-world datasets often exhibit a strongly varying number of labels per document, and a power-law distribution of those class labels. Multi-label classification of legal documents is additionally complicated by long document texts and domain-specific use of language. In this paper we use different approaches to compare the performance of text classification algorithms on existing datasets and corpora of legal documents, and contrast the results of our experiments with results on general-purpose multi-label text classification datasets. Moreover, for the EUR-Lex legal datasets, we show that exploiting the hierarchy of the EuroVoc thesaurus helps to improve classification performance by reducing the number of potential classes while retaining the informative value of the classification itself.

Keywords: Document classification · EuroVoc · Eur-Lex · Legal domain · Word embeddings · Deep learning

1 Introduction

Handling unstructured data like text documents is easier for humans than for machines [4], however machines can help to make text accessible and searchable for example by classifying documents into several classes. Text or document classification can be attributed to the research area of text mining [12]. Applications of text classification in various domains range from text filtering, to document organization and to word sense disambiguation [25], etc. In general, text classification is defined as the process of the assignment of a category out of a set of categories to a document [25]. Text classification can be subdivided into binary classification, multi-class classification and multi-label classification [28]

© Springer Nature Switzerland AG 2019
H. Panetto et al. (Eds.): OTM 2019, LNCS 11877, pp. 164–181, 2019.
https://doi.org/10.1007/978-3-030-33246-4_10

tasks which generally exhibit an increasing level of difficulty. While binary classification aims at classifying documents into one out of two classes, multi-class classification aims at assigning one class out of a set of non-overlapping classes to a document. The hardest task is multi-label classification where the algorithm assigns a set of potentially overlapping labels from the whole label set to a document. Document classification tasks are typically approached with machine learning algorithms, in recent years in particular with deep learning systems. The choice of machine learning algorithms is dependent on the task and the classification problem at hand, and comprise, among others, for instance decision trees, probabilistic or rule-based classifiers [1,4,12], or variants of recurrent or convolutional neural networks [13,14].

Text classification is used in many domains (e.g. news, medical) to assign categories to documents, which are domain-specific in terms of the used vocabulary and length. There are many well-known datasets used by researchers to evaluate the performance of text classification approaches, for instance 20Newsgroups[1] or Reuters-21578[2] for the news domain or OHSUMED[3] for the medical domain. Highly interesting, but also challenging is the legal domain – as legal frameworks affect our daily life. Openly available datasets for document classification tasks in the legal domain are for instance the JRC-Acquis[4] and the EUR-Lex 4K[5] dataset [19], both containing legal documents from the EUR-Lex[6] legal database, which is available publicly and free of charge.

In the legal domain a multi-disciplinary and multi-lingual thesaurus called EuroVoc[7] is used to classify legal documents into a large number of overlapping categories, hence presenting a multi-label classification problem: indeed, EuroVoc contains more than 6,000 potential classes, which is a much higher number of classes than for many classic multi-label classification datasets used in previous research. Moreover, text documents are rich in semantic information which can be used in the classification task [5]. What makes the problem of classifying legal texts additionally challenging is the highly domain-specific language used in legal text corpora, with many abbreviations, as legal documents are primarily read by legal experts. We are therefore interested in

1. how standard document classification approaches perform on legal texts and
2. whether the class hierarchy of an external thesaurus can be exploited to improve the classification results.

Previous research carried out in this area with legal documents is treating the problem as a profile-based category ranking task [26], and focuses more on scalability issues of the classification problem than on classification quality [19].

---

[1] http://qwone.com/~jason/20Newsgroups/.
[2] http://www.daviddlewis.com/resources/testcollections/reuters21578/.
[3] http://disi.unitn.it/moschitti/corpora.htm.
[4] https://ec.europa.eu/jrc/en/language-technologies/jrc-acquis.
[5] http://www.ke.tu-darmstadt.de/resources/eurlex.
[6] http://eur-lex.europa.eu/.
[7] http://eurovoc.europa.eu/.

Others approach the task by transforming the problem into a simpler one by assuming that a multi-labelled document is a collection of different documents [8] or by choosing to classify documents according to another scheme which offers less classes [2]. All described approaches show that the main problem is the vast amount of different classes into which documents can be classified and the power-law class label distribution.

From our perspective, the key to approaching a document classification problem is to understand and incorporate the semantics of a document into the classification process. Furthermore, classifying documents into a given thesaurus hierarchy can also be supported by exploiting the hierarchy itself. Therefore, our contributions in this paper can be summarized as follows:

1. we show that legal documents have specific properties that can be exploited for the document classification task;
2. we demonstrate how the hierarchical structure of a thesaurus helps to boost the classification results;
3. we describe the influencing parameters of the legal document classification problem;
4. our results suggest that the advantage of using neural networks for the legal document classification problem at hand is lower compared to text classification in other domains.

The remainder of this paper is structured as follows: Sect. 2 summarizes previous work in this area. The specific properties of legal documents are discussed in Sect. 3, followed by a description of the EuroVoc thesaurus in Sect. 4. We then provide details of the evaluation datasets in Sect. 5. The approaches we used in this paper are presented in Sect. 6, evaluation results follow in Sect. 7. Finally, Sect. 8 concludes the paper.

2   Related Work

Previous research work on classifying legal documents in the EU mostly focuses on documents from the European legal database EUR-Lex, either based on the JRC-Acquis corpus, a multilingual aligned parallel corpus with 20+ languages containing documents taken from the European legal database [27] or another version provided by the Knowledge Engineering Group of the Technical University Darmstadt [19]. The Joint Research Centre (JRC) of the European Commission published the JRC EuroVoc Indexer JEX tool which treats the classification problem as a profile-based ranking task and reaches – on the former corpus – an F-score between 0.44 and 0.54 depending on the language by ranking the typical features of a class which form the profile [26].

One of the core findings in their work is that adjusting the stopwords to the domain (which is already a strong hint on the special nature of language of the legal domain) is the most efficient way to boost classification results. Another approach is proposed by Boella et al. [7] who transform the multi-label into a single-label problem in order to enable processing by a Support Vector Machine. The authors claim to reach an F-score of 0.75 for the Italian version of the

JRC-Acquis corpus, however, the algorithm description of Boella et al. in [8] was not reproducible and the results of an F-score of 0.75 on the classification task cannot be directly deduced from the paper. While details are vague, we suspect that the high F-score is due to the fact that the authors restrict themselves to only the most commonly used labels (above a certain threshold) which makes the classification task significantly easier: one of the main problems in the JRC and EUR-Lex 4K training corpora is that certain labels hardly appear in the training data and in general the label usage is extremely skewed. Other previous work on document classification in the legal domain also shows the common problem of classification tasks with a vast amount of classes and therefore either confirm the bad performance of classification algorithms [19] or approach the problem by reducing the number of classes to boost the results [2,23]. An exploratory excursion to an ontology-based training-less classification method by Alkhatib et al. [3] shows the same problems of having a skewed class distribution with a micro F-score of 0.29.

From a more general point of view, while text classification dates back to the 1960s, it started to gain a lot of interest from the information systems community in the 1990s with the large availability of digital documents and the rise of the machine learning (ML) paradigm [25]. Tsoumakas and Katakis [28] provide an early overview of multi-label document classification approaches, and the problem transformation strategies which enable classical methods like SVMs to be applied to the multi-label case, for example using binary classifiers for each class separately. In recent years, a lot of work has focused on *extreme classification*, a term which is used for multi-label classification in situations where there is a large number of classes, often with a skewed class distribution, and potentially a large number of documents [29]. Some benchmark datasets, and also real-world applications, contain hundreds of thousands of classes, therefore the focus of extreme classification is not only on prediction accuracy but also on computational performance. The datasets discussed herein (based on EUR-Lex and EuroVoc) fall into the category of *small* extreme classification datasets. Some extreme classification methods like SLEEC [6] reduce the effective number of classes by projecting the output space into a low-dimensional, continuous subspace [9] – similar to the idea of using word embeddings instead of one-hot encoding. Others use a tree hierarchy as a structural constraint, where trees or forests filter a fraction of classes on each node visited [22]. This leads to logarithmic prediction time. Finally, Yen et al. [29] present a greedy algorithm that combines the low runtime complexity of the primal-dual sparse approach with the simple parallelization of training and the small memory footprint of one-versus-all approaches.

Taking different routes, some authors exploit semantic methods [5] or specific sub-domains like sentiment classification [18]. Many surveys explore the area of text mining in general or describe classification methods in particular [1,4,12]. Our idea in the present work is – inspired by these related works – also attempting to take into account both the semantics and the hierarchical tree structure of the EuroVoc thesaurus and its keywords, in order to boost performance of multi-label document classification/labeling.

Table 1. Multi-label datasets

Dataset	Domain	# Doc	# Labels	Avg. # tokens	Std. Dev.	Skewness	Kurtosis
JRC-Acquis V3	Legal	17,519	3,563	3.065,90	8,931.94	8.61	112.82
EUR-Lex 4K	Legal	19,513	3,969	3,021.38	8,606.06	7.74	88.98
Reuters-21578	News	21,578	120	151,05	152.16	7.05	54.37

3   Legal Documents

We consider legal documents as documents with the purpose to transport legal information, from supra-national organizations like the European Union as well as from national governments, such as treaties, regulations or law gazettes. Compared to other corpora typically used for document classification [20], legal documents have linguistic features as they are written in a very domain-specific and typed language (e.g. specific terms are always used to indicate the same circumstances to avoid ambiguity problems) and structural features, hence legal documents from specific jurisdictions follow a known structure for each document type.

Table 1 presents some metrics of two legal datasets (JRC-Acquis V3 and EUR-Lex 4K) compared to the popular Reuters-21578 dataset from the news domain, which is comparable in the number of documents in the corpus, but it includes only 120 classes to classify the documents, which is less than 5% of the possible EuroVoc labels in legal datasets. In addition, the length of news documents is much shorter than the documents from the legal domain. The skewness describes the symmetry of the label distribution. A skewness value in the range -0.5 to 0.5 describes a symmetrical distribution and a high positive or negative skewness value indiciates highly asymmetrical, hence highly skewed data. Comparing the skewness values for all three datasets we can clearly see that label usage in all three datasets is highly skewed. The kurtosis of a dataset refers to the outliers in the distribution, with a value of 0 showing that the distribution follows the standard distribution. All three datasets have a positive kurtosis indicating larger tails, and a power-law distribution of labels usage.

4   The EuroVoc Thesaurus

The EuroVoc thesaurus (see Footnote 7) is published by the Publications Office of the European Union and has been updated regularly since 1982. The goal of the thesaurus is to standardize the language used by EU institutions and to provide a hierarchy of terms organized in 21 domains, 127 microthesauri and more than 500 top terms available in all EU member state languages. The most recent version of the thesaurus is version 4.9 which was released at the end of March 2019. The terms (also called descriptors, classes or labels) can have a hierarchical relationship to *broader* or *narrower* terms as well as an associative relationship to *related* terms. In the creation process of the thesaurus the creators tried to limit the polyhierarchy and all classes are assigned to a single domain or microthesaurus that seemed most logical for an average user [10].

Listing 1.1. EuroVoc example

```
@prefix ev: <http://eurovoc.europa.eu/> .
@prefix dcterms: <http://purl.org/dc/terms/> .
@prefix skos: <http://www.w3.org/2004/02/skos/core#> .

ev:100180
    dcterms:identifier ''100180'' ;
    skos:prefLabel ''1216 criminal law''@en ;
    skos:hasTopConcept ev:573 .
ev:573
    dcterms:identifier ''573'' ;
    skos:prefLabel ''criminal law''@en ;
    skos:topConceptOf ev:100180 .
ev:575
    dcterms:identifier ''575'' ;
    skos:prefLabel ''international criminal law''@en ;
    skos:broader ev:573 ;
    skos:inScheme ev:100180 .
```

The EuroVoc thesaurus contains around 6,900 concepts and is available for download as Resource Description Framework (RDF) or Extensible Markup Language (XML), as well as accessible via a SPARQL endpoint[8].

The thesaurus is organized using the *Simple Knowledge Organization System (SKOS)*[9] and *Dublin Core Metadata Initiative (DC)*[10] vocabularies to describe the above-mentioned hierarchical relationships and properties of the classes as illustrated in Listing 1.1, which shows an excerpt of the hierarchy and relationships used in EuroVoc. The identifier of each EuroVoc class is described using the **dcterms:identifier** and labels for the different languages (indicated with a language tag) of the EU member states are available as *preferred* using **skos:prefLabel** and *non-preferred* using **skos:altLabel** terms. Hierarchical relationships are expressed with **skos:topConceptOf** linking the top terms with the associated microthesaurus and **skos:inScheme** to link all concepts of lower hierarchies to the corresponding microthesaurus. The hierarchy below the top terms of the microthesaurus is described using **skos:broader** and **skos:narrower**. Hence the microthesaurus in the shown example is *1216 criminal law* (microthesauri are indicated with a four-digit number) and it has (among others) a top concept *573*, which is called *criminal law*, which itself has a narrower term *international criminal law*. It must be noted that **ev:573** does not have a predicate **skos:narrower** but instead the hierarchy must be approached in a bottom-up manner. The example also illustrates that the top term and the microthesaurus are linked via **skos:topConceptOf** and **skos:hasTopConcept** while the lower terms are only linked to the microthesaurus via **skos:inScheme**.

Due to the limited polyhierarchy (in almost all cases each class belongs to only one superclass) we can exploit the hierarchy to reduce the number of classes that a document can be assigned to. For instance, a document labelled with

---

[8] http://publications.europa.eu/webapi/rdf/sparql.

[9] https://www.w3.org/2004/02/skos/.

[10] http://www.dublincore.org/specifications/dublin-core/dcmi-terms/.

international criminal law can also be labelled with its top term *criminal law* or even the microthesaurus *criminal law.*

5   Datasets

We use two legal corpora for our experiments. The *EU Acquis Communautaire* is the collection of the legal documents and obligations within the European Union containing regulations, directives, decisions, treaties and many more. Version 3 of the JRC-Acquis corpus contains documents in various languages from institutions of the European Union dating from 1958 to 2006. The number of documents per language is around 20,000. The English version, which we use in this paper, contains 20,682 documents in XML format. The documents have been manually classified into the different EuroVoc classes and include the identifiers of the respective EuroVoc classes [27]. The JRC-Acquis corpus, which is the property of the European Commission, is available free of charge for commercial and non-commercial use under the provisions laid out in the Commission Decision of the 12th of December 2011[11]. Our second dataset, the EUR-Lex 4K dataset also consists of documents taken from the EUR-Lex database provided by the Technical University of Darmstadt [19]. Both datasets contain documents annotated with EuroVoc classes. The most important dataset properties, of the test datasets we created from these corpora are summarized in Table 2: we created two additional dataset versions from the original (*Full*) datasets, which contain the document and class assignments as they are provided. The *Topterms* and *Microthesauri* versions are based on the original EuroVoc class assignments but exploit the hierarchy to reduce the number of different classes. Note that, although as mentioned above there are 20,682 documents in the original JRC dataset, only 17,519 documents are actually annotated with EuroVoc classes. We pruned non-annotated documents from the dataset and kept only those documents which actually have EuroVoc classification labels. Furthermore, note that despite the fact that there are more than 6,000 EuroVoc classes available, only 3,563 are actually used by the documents in the full JRC-Acquis dataset. For the creation of the *topterms* version of the dataset we extracted all top terms from the EuroVoc thesaurus and replaced all EuroVoc leaf classes in the full JRC dataset with the top term classes (489) they belong to; similarly the *Microthesauri* version of the dataset is generated by replacing annotations with the unique microthesaurus which they belong to (126). The same approach reduces the number of classes of the EUR-Lex 4k dataset from 3,969 classes to 512 classes for the *Topterms* and again 126 classes for the *Microthesauri* version of the dataset.

The class reduction is based on the hierarchy of the classes in the EuroVoc thesaurus and works as follows: For each EuroVoc class for a given document the *top term* (*microthesaurus*) is looked up and replaced with the found *top term* (*microthesaurus*). Since multiple EuroVoc classes for a document can belong to the same microthesaurus we only take each result once, hence a set. For instance

---

[11] https://eur-lex.europa.eu/legal-content/EN/TXT/?uri=uriserv:OJ.L_.2011.330.01. 0039.01.ENG&toc=OJ:L:2011:330:TOC.

Table 2. Overview of dataset features

Dataset	Dataset version	# Doc	# Labels	Label cardinality	Avg. # Doc/Label
JRC-Acquis V3	Full	17,519	3,563	5.41	26.62
JRC-Acquis V3	Topterms	17,519	489	4.59	164.21
JRC-Acquis V3	Microthesauri	17,519	126	4.60	634.88
EUR-Lex 4K	Full	19,513	3,969	5.39	26.15
EUR-Lex 4K	Topterms	19,513	512	4.65	177.02
EUR-Lex 4K	Microthesauri	19,513	126	4.82	741.59
Reuters-21578	–	21,578	120	1.26	202.57

class 575 is a narrower term of class 573, hence we replace 575 with 573. This way we reduce the overall number of classes available for classification by 86% to 489 labels in total. For the *microthesauri* we apply the same procedure and are therefore able to reduce the number of classes to 126. Notice that the EuroVoc thesaurus has 127 microthesauri of which we use only 126. The 127th microthesaurus is a general microthesaurus to which every EuroVoc class belongs. Hence, this missing microthesaurus does not contribute to the classification problem and has therefore been removed.

The label cardinality describes the average number of EuroVoc classes assigned to each document. Documents from the original dataset have 5.41 class labels on average. The decrease of the label cardinality for the topterms (4.59) and microthesauri (4.6 classes per document) versions of the dataset is caused by going up the hierarchy in the EuroVoc thesaurus and reducing the number of classes. Moreover, some documents are annotated with multiple EuroVoc classes sharing the same top term or microthesaurus. The decrease in available EuroVoc classes also affects the number of documents per class. While in the orginal full dataset there are on average only 27 documents available per class, we have 164 documents per class in the topterms and 635 documents per class in the microthesauri version of the dataset.

Since the number of documents remains the same for all three versions of the dataset, the average number of tokens per document of 3,066 as well as the standard deviation of ±8,932.

For comparison we also use version 1.0 of the Reuters-21578 dataset available for research purposes. It contains documents that appeared in the Reuters Newswire which have been manually annotated with 120 classes. The label cardinality is also much lower compared to the two legal datasets, but the learning process can make use of around 200 documents per label.

6   Approach

As discussed before, most standard approaches proposed in the literature are often applied to datasets with only a few classes, but the EuroVoc thesaurus allows for the classification of documents by thousands of classes in a multi-label setting. In addition, as opposed to many other classification tasks, for many standard approaches we first have to transform the raw text into numeric representations. Afterwards the numeric representation can be used with many machine and particularly deep learning approaches for automatic document classification.

6.1   Preprocessing

The first step is to do the preprocessing of the raw text files not only to reduce the size of the documents but also to reduce the runtime of all subsequent processing steps. We opted to separate this preprocessing step from the actual classification process and runtime measurement. Preprocessing includes lowercasing as well as removing stopwords from the text using the standard English NLTK[12] stopword list. We also remove punctuation and special characters from the text as well as replacing all words with their lemma using the spaCy[13] lemmatizer to reduce the morphological variations of each word to their lemma. In addition to these standard preprocessing steps we also include specific preprocessing steps tailored to the legal documents, which include the removal of references to other legal documents (e.g. [..] amended by *Directive 83/191/EEC* [...]) and the removal of all brackets and their contents for the same reason. Also the structure of legal documents can be used in preprocessing in order to remove all headings contained in the documents (e.g. *Article* or *Appendix*).

6.2   Term Frequency - Inversed Document Frequency

The most basic approach used for classification is based on counting the numbers of term occurrences in documents. *Term Frequency (TF)* indicates the number of occurrences of each term in a document. Under the assumption that more important terms occur more often we could say that the higher frequency, the higher the importance (relevancy) of a term. However, there might be terms that occur many times, but are not unique to a particular document in a corpus. For instance, *regulation* might occur very often in legal documents from the European Union but rarely in tweets. To account for the descriptiveness of a term in relation to the entire corpus, term frequency is typically contrasted by *Inverse Document Frequency (IDF)* [15] to measure the descriptive power of a term in a corpus based on the assumption that a term is less descriptive and specific if it appears in a high number of documents. Terms that appear in only a fraction of documents are useful to distinguish those documents from others, and consequently are useful for classification. Finally, the TF-IDF score is the product of the TF and IDF scores. For our corpus this means that many of the generic domain-specific terms such as *regulation, directive, commission, EC, EEC* are considered to have low discriminative power and the remaining terms are weighted higher.

---

[12] https://www.nltk.org/.
[13] https://spacy.io/.

6.3 Word2Vec

In order to apply neural language modeling to large-scale text corpora in a run time-efficient manner, in recent years new methods based on simplified neural network architectures have been proposed. The first, and most well-known approach, in this area is Word2Vec [21]. Word2Vec trains a model on text in an unsupervised way, and as a result generates low-dimensional, dense, floating-point vector representations for each word in the corpus. There is the possibility to download pre-trained models which are trained on different corpora (e.g. from github[14]) or to train one's own corpus-specific model. Furthermore, Word2Vec includes two different algorithms for model training, the *Continuous Bag of Words (CBOW)* model and the *skip-gram* model. The former is primarily used to predict a word from a given context, while the latter aims at predicting the context given a word.

First, we tested large-scale pre-trained language models trained with general-purpose text corpora such as GoogleNews and the CommonCrawl, but as expected both performed badly on the legal dataset, for example the Common-Crawl model reached an F-score of 0.38 and the GoogleNews model an F-score of 0.31. Therefore, we opted to train our own model based on the JRC-Acquis corpus. Despite the fact that for using Word2Vec the corpus size typically has a large impact on model quality, we achieve better results by training a model on our 17,519 documents than reusing the large pre-trained models: at the very least, this seems to confirm our base assumption that generic language models do not work well on the domain-specific language used in legal documents. As for the training parameters we use the standard settings with a vector size of 300 and a minimum count of 1 due to the homogeneous corpus and in order to capture very specific words in legal documents. We use the CBOW model for the classification task because it outperforms skip-gram by more than 15% in terms of the F-score (0.4 for skip-gram vs 0.55 for CBOW). We employ a simple method to create the document vectors by summing up the vectors of all words contained in a document and computing an average vector. Our assumption is that these average vectors of documents specific to a given document topic (represented by their EuroVoc classifications) are similar.

6.4 Doc2Vec

While Word2Vec creates global word representations, Doc2Vec creates a vector for an entire document. Doc2Vec uses word vectors and extends the vectors by adding paragraph vectors which allows for the predictions of words in the context of a paragraph [16]. Similar to Word2Vec, Doc2Vec also allows the user to train two different kinds of models: *Distributed Bag of Words (DBOW)* and *Distributed Memory (DM)*. For our training we use a vector size of 300 and minimum count of 1.

---

[14] https://github.com/3Top/word2vec-api#where-to-get-a-pretrained-models.

6.5   TF-IDF Weighting Embeddings

In order to filter the domain corpora, and to exclude generic legal terms without discriminative power in the legal domain, we use the weighting approach as suggested in [17] to remove common words from the embeddings. We achieve this by combining the statistical TF-IDF approach mentioned above, with the word embeddings of Word2Vec and Doc2Vec. In the first step, we calculate the TF-IDF scores for all words in the corpus. Since the number of words varies from document to document and the TF-IDF scores are also different we do not set a hard limit for the TF-IDF scores, instead we calculate the TF-IDF scores for all words in a document and rank them according to these scores. Afterwards we set a threshold for the TF-IDF scores and remove all words with a score below the set threshold. The threshold is set as the top x percent of words, in particular experiments showed that the top 10% of the words are most descriptive and a setting of e.g. 25% of the top words decreases the results. We also cannot set the number of words to be considered to a fixed value (e.g. 10 words per documents) as we do not know the TF-IDF score distribution. The training parameters for Word2Vec and Doc2Vec are the same as in the individual approaches.

For all approaches mentioned above we tried Random Forest (RF) and a Support Vector Machine (SVM). For both algorithms we applied GridSearch to find the best training parameters. We mainly use the standard parameters, but set the *class_weight = balanced* to compensate for the skewed label distribution and $C = 100$ for the SVM. All machine learning tasks are performed using Python 3 and the Scikit-learn library[15].

6.6   fast.ai

As a representative of currently popular (deep) neural network training approaches, we also compared the above-mentioned approaches to the powerful fast.ai[16] framework: fast.ai is a library for training fast and accurate neural nets. It is based on deep learning research and tries to incorporate current best practices. The fast.ai framework provides support for different task types, such as computer vision, NLP, tabular data and recommender systems. As for input corpora we experimented both with the pre-processed dataset (see Sect. 6.1) and the original JRC dataset. In both cases, fast.ai also applies its own pre-processing on top, which includes lowercasing, marking the start and end of sentences, etc. Additionally, fast.ai applies an iterative model training process, which includes two basic steps: (i) fine-tuning a pretrained language model with the domain corpus, and (ii) learning the classifier. The process as well as additional techniques such as slanted triangular learning rates are explained in [13]. In training the models, we follow mostly the recommended architecture given in the fast.ai examples[17], which in the first basic step includes the finetuning of the provided

---

[15] https://scikit-learn.org/stable/.
[16] https://github.com/fastai/fastai.
[17] https://nbviewer.jupyter.org/github/fastai/course-v3/blob/master/nbs/dl1/lesson3-imdb.ipynb.

Table 3. Evaluation results for JRC corpus

Approach	Algorithm	Full			Topterms			Microthesauri		
		P	R	F	P	R	F	P	R	F
Baseline	–	0.44	0.52	0.47	–	–	–	–	–	–
TF-IDF	RF	*0.88*	0.24	0.37	*0.90*	0.30	0.45	*0.89*	0.39	0.55
Word2Vec	SVC	0.52	*0.59*	0.55	0.43	*0.80*	0.56	0.50	*0.85*	0.63
Doc2Vec	SVC	0.74	0.40	0.52	0.65	0.61	0.63	0.71	0.69	0.70
TF-IDF + Word2Vec	SVC	0.62	0.47	0.53	0.54	0.69	0.61	0.59	0.77	0.67
TF-IDF + Doc2Vec	SVC	0.62	0.45	0.52	0.46	0.71	0.56	0.53	0.78	0.63
fast.ai	LSTM	0.61	0.55	**0.58**	0.70	0.63	**0.67**	0.75	0.73	**0.74**

Table 4. Evaluation results for KED corpus

Approach	Algorithm	Full			Topterms			Microthesauri		
		P	R	F	P	R	F	P	R	F
Baseline	-	0.40	0.46	0.42	–	–	–	–	–	–
TF-IDF	RF	*0.84*	0.12	0.21	*0.86*	0.20	0.33	*0.88*	0.34	0.49
Word2Vec	SVC	0.29	*0.63*	0.40	0.34	*0.77*	0.47	0.44	*0.83*	0.57
Doc2Vec	SVC	0.53	0.41	0.46	0.60	0.52	0.56	0.69	0.63	0.66
TF-IDF + Word2Vec	SVC	0.15	0.26	0.19	0.20	0.38	0.26	0.29	0.50	0.36
TF-IDF + Doc2Vec	SVC	0.16	0.25	0.19	0.22	0.36	0.27	0.31	0.47	0.38
fast.ai	LSTM	0.54	0.49	**0.52**	0.64	0.59	**0.61**	0.73	0.69	**0.71**

AWD_LSTM RNN language model with the JRC corpus. When training the multi-label classifier, techniques such as gradual unfreezing of the network, weight decay (set to 0.1) and *momentum* are used. Further, we apply the default loss function for multi-label text classification, BCEWithLogitsLoss.

7   Evaluation and Discussion

In this section we present the experiment results. The experiments using embeddings were carried out on a 2.1 GHz machine with 24 cores and a memory of 246 GB. To run the fast.ai experiments we used a i7-8700 CPU with 3.76 GHz, 16 GB of memory and a GeForce GTX 1080 Ti graphics card. The code for the embedding experiments is available on Google[18] and the Jupyter notebooks with all fast.ai related experiments on Github[19].

We evaluate our approaches on three multi-label datasets. Two of these datasets contain legal documents (JRC-Acquis and Eur-Lex 4K), and the Reuters-21578 dataset, which contains news articles for comparison and because this dataset is used in many text classification tasks. The dataset properties

---

[18] https://drive.google.com/open?id=1Pl4H1pFNuFvcGQwHjkhcUJ9SMHrYjdQl.
[19] https://github.com/gwohlgen/JRC_fastai.

Table 5. Evaluation results for Reuters-21578 corpus

Approach	Algorithm	Full		
		P	R	F
TF-IDF	RF	*0.97*	0.63	0.76
Word2Vec	SVC	0.50	*0.94*	0.66
Doc2Vec	SVC	0.82	0.84	0.83
TF-IDF + Word2Vec	SVC	0.05	0.38	0.09
TF-IDF + Doc2Vec	SVC	0.14	0.27	0.18
fast.ai (no prep)	LSTM	0.90	0.87	0.88
fast.ai (w prep)	LSTM	0.92	0.88	**0.90**

are depicted in Table 1. The results for each dataset are presented in a separate table, Table 3 for the JRC-Acquis dataset, Table 4 for the results of the EUR-Lex 4K dataset and finally Table 5 contains the results of the Reuters-21578 dataset. Each result table contains a column indicating the chosen approach for the classification task. Furthermore, for each dataset version (full, topterms and microthesauri) we present the evaluation metrics *Precision*, *Recall* and *F-score*. A - means that there is no result available. The best result for each dataset version is highlighted in boldface while the best precision and the best recall for each dataset version are highlighted in italic. All results have been achieved using the preprocessed documents and a test set size of 20%.

The evaluation metrics *precision*, *recall* and *F-score* are calculated based on the classification results. *True positive (TP)* refers to the correctly predicted classes. *False positive (FP)* and *False negative (FN)* both indicate wrong prediction results, where a *FP* predicts a class that should not have been predicted and *FN* does not predict a class that should have been predicted [24]:

$$Precision = \frac{TP}{TP + FP}$$

Precision (p) is defined as the share of the *true positive (TP)* divided by the sum of the *true positive* and *false positive (FP)*.

$$Recall = \frac{TP}{TP + FN}$$

Recall (r) is defined as the share of the *true positive* divided by the sum of the *true positive* and *false negative (FN)*.

$$F\text{-}score = 2 * \frac{Precision * Recall}{Precision + Recall}$$

F-score (F) is defined as the harmonic mean of *precision* and *recall*. The Precision, Recall and F-score measures of our experiments are provided by the scikit-learn classification matrix.

For the baseline we used the JRC EuroVoc Indexer JEX tool as it can be downloaded with the pretrained english model to calculate the metrics for the JRC-Acquis and EUR-Lex 4K full legal datasets which is uses a profile-based ranking algorithm for text classification [26].

Although we tested Random Forest (RF) and Support Vector Machine (SVM) as learning algorithm, the results show that RF performs better only on TF-IDF while for all other machine-learning approaches SVM is the superior learning algorithm. Furthermore, the results clearly show that RF has the highest precision but also the lowest recall on all three versions of the dataset. The increase of the F-score with the TF-IDF approach also shows that a decrease of candidate classes by 87% leads to an increase of 10% of the F-score.

Looking at the result metrics we can say that using TF-IDF in combination with a Random Forest leads to a very high precision, independent of the number of candidate classes. In contrast, the recall is very low and only shows marginal improvement in the case of reduced classes.

The Word2Vec and Doc2Vec approaches and the combinations of both with TF-IDF show the best results using a SVM. However, there is no clear answer to which approach performs best. Having a look at the results for the full dataset the F-score ranges from 0.52 to 0.57 and therefore perform better than the baseline with the exception of TF-IDF with an F-score of only 0.37. Also the values for precision and recall are evenly distributed. Furthermore, the relation of precision and recall changes with the decreasing number of candidate classes. While the Word2Vec and Doc2Vec precision remains almost steady across all dataset versions (±0.09), the Word2Vec recall increases strongly from 0.59 to 0.85 (+0.26) for Word2Vec and from 0.40 to 0.69 (+0.29) for Doc2Vec on the JRC dataset. The increase of precision and recall on the EUR-Lex 4K is a little bit lower compared to the JRC dataset, but still shows a good increase over the different dataset versions.

The TF-IDF weighting approaches do not show an increase on the overall performance compared to the individual Word2Vec/Doc2Vec approach for both legal datasets. Only on the JRC dataset the TF-IDF + Word2Vec performs better than Word2Vec only, but solely on the dataset versions with the reduced number of classes. The performance of TF-IDF + Doc2Vec is always lower compared to Doc2Vec. For the EUR-Lex 4K dataset the TF-IDF weighting approach the metrics are much lower compared to the individual approaches.

Our approach using a neural network with language model transfer learning and the deep LSTM architecture of fast.ai delivers the best F-scores on all three versions of the dataset although it never has the best precision or recall values. Depending on the threshold value for label selection the precision and recall change, thus we used a threshold which provides a good F1 result. The results also demonstrate that the multi-label document classification with such a high number of classes and a strongly biased class distribution is very complex and very hard to handle even for deep neural networks which have proven to be very successful in recent year on a variety of NLP tasks. On the full dataset fast.ai performs only 3% better than the non-neural network approach using

Word2Vec. The advantage of fast.ai on topterms and microthesauri datasets the JRC dataset is 4% in both cases. The metrics for the EUR-Lex 4K dataset are lower in general, but fast.ai performs better by 6% on the full and 5% on the topterms and microthesauri dataset versions.

The Reuters-21578 results show the impact of the low number of classes in combination with the lower label cardinality. The best approach using embeddings is Doc2Vec with an F-score of 0.83, while the highest precision is achieved by TF-IDF and the highest recall by Word2Vec. Also fast.ai outperforms all other approaches with an F-score of 0.9.

Overall, we can say that prediction performance significantly increases with the reduction of the number of candidate classes by taking advantage of the hierarchy of terms, and that a neural network outperforms classic approaches. However, the differences in the results are small and therefore a final answer as to which approach performs best cannot be given. Particularly, predicting rare labels instead of resorting to the coarser, upper level prediction, is, as expected hardly possible, due to the lack of training data for rare labels. We hope, in the future to address this issue by investigating new methods to combine coarse-label and fine-label predictions and exploit other semantic connections to also enable predictions of these rare terms.

8   Conclusion

In this paper we investigate document classification approaches exemplified on the legal domain and contrast them with a dataset that is commonly used for such tasks. The results show that document classification in the legal domain is a very challenging task, which is also due to the legal datasets which are highly skewed and use a vast number of classes. We compared six different approaches encompassing a statistical method, methods using vector space embeddings and a neural network approach tested on two legal datasets (JRC-Acquis and EUR-Lex 4K), both domain-specific corpora from the legal domain containing legal documents published by the organizations of the European Union from 1958 to 2006. We classified the documents based on categories from the EuroVoc thesaurus, which contains more than 6000 candidate classes. The results of our experiments show that approaches taking the semantics into account work better than purely statistical approaches, but there is not much difference in the results among the remaining approaches. Furthermore we used the Reuters-21578 dataset containing around 20,000 news articles classified into 120 different classes to demonstrate the general applicability of our approach which shows very good results on a heterogeneous corpus with a low label cardinality. We are following a general approach which in theory should also work for other domains which provide a thesaurus that could be used for the classification task. For the same reason, an evaluation of the approaches we presented fails due to missing gold standard datasets for case laws or other legal documents like contracts. These kind of documents are usually not available to the public and if they are available they are not annotated.

In future work we will investigate the automatic creation of a domain-specific corpus to allow for additional training data in this field. The idea is to add additional documents specific for particular EuroVoc classes to get enhanced class descriptions. Another interesting avenue for exploration is to add external documents giving definitions of the EuroVoc classes and sharpen their semantic profile which could in turn be used for a semantic similarity comparison of documents with the individual EuroVoc classes.

Acknowledgment. The research leading to this work was partly funded by the Federal Ministry of Digital and Economic Affairs of the Republic of Austria and the Jubliaeumsfonds der Stadt Wien. Gerhard Wohlgenannt's work was supported by the Government of the Russian Federation (Grant 074-U01) through the ITMO Fellowship and Professorship Program.

References

1. Aggarwal, C.C., Zhai, C.: A survey of text classification algorithms. In: Aggarwal, C.C., Zhai, C. (eds.) Mining Text Data, pp. 163–222. Springer, Boston (2012). https://doi.org/10.1007/978-1-4614-3223-4_6
2. Alkhatib, W., Rensing, C., Silberbauer, J.: Multi-label text classification using semantic features and dimensionality reduction with autoencoders. In: Gracia, J., Bond, F., McCrae, J.P., Buitelaar, P., Chiarcos, C., Hellmann, S. (eds.) LDK 2017. LNCS (LNAI), vol. 10318, pp. 380–394. Springer, Cham (2017). https://doi.org/10.1007/978-3-319-59888-8_32
3. Alkhatib, W., Sabrin, S., Neitzel, S., Rensing, C.: Towards ontology-based trainingless multi-label text classification. In: Silberztein, M., Atigui, F., Kornyshova, E., Métais, E., Meziane, F. (eds.) NLDB 2018. LNCS, vol. 10859, pp. 389–396. Springer, Cham (2018). https://doi.org/10.1007/978-3-319-91947-8_40
4. Allahyari, M., et al.: A brief survey of text mining: classification, clustering and extraction techniques. CoRR abs/1707.02919 (2017). http://arxiv.org/abs/1707.02919
5. Altinel, B., Ganiz, M.C.: Semantic text classification: a survey of past and recent advances. Inf. Process. Manage. 54(6), 1129–1153 (2018). https://doi.org/10.1016/j.ipm.2018.08.001
6. Bhatia, K., Jain, H., Kar, P., Varma, M., Jain, P.: Sparse local embeddings for extreme multi-label classification. In: Advances in Neural Information Processing Systems, pp. 730–738 (2015)
7. Boella, G., et al.: Linking legal open data: breaking the accessibility and language barrier in European legislation and case law. In: Sichelman, T., Atkinson, K. (eds.) Proceedings of the 15th International Conference on Artificial Intelligence and Law, ICAIL 2015, San Diego, 8–12 June 2015, pp. 171–175. ACM (2015). https://doi.org/10.1145/2746090.2746106
8. Boella, G., Caro, L.D., Lesmo, L., Rispoli, D., Robaldo, L.: Multi-label classification of legislative text into EuroVoc. In: Schäfer, B. (ed.) Legal Knowledge and Information Systems - JURIX 2012: The Twenty-Fifth Annual Conference, University of Amsterdam, The Netherlands, 17–19 December 2012. Frontiers in Artificial Intelligence and Applications, vol. 250, pp. 21–30. IOS Press (2012). https://doi.org/10.3233/978-1-61499-167-0-21

9. Chen, Y.N., Lin, H.T.: Feature-aware label space dimension reduction for multi-label classification. In: Advances in Neural Information Processing Systems, pp. 1529–1537 (2012)
10. European Union: Eurovoc thesaurus user guide (2007)
11. Francesconi, E., Montemagni, S., Peters, W., Tiscornia, D. (eds.): Semantic Processing of Legal Texts: Where the Language of Law Meets the Law of Language. LNCS (LNAI), vol. 6036. Springer, Heidelberg (2010). https://doi.org/10.1007/978-3-642-12837-0
12. Hotho, A., Nürnberger, A., Paass, G.: A brief survey of text mining. LDV Forum **20**(1), 19–62 (2005). http://www.jlcl.org/2005_Heft1/19-62_HothoNuernbergerPaass.pdf
13. Howard, J., Ruder, S.: Fine-tuned language models for text classification. CoRR abs/1801.06146 (2018). http://arxiv.org/abs/1801.06146
14. Jacovi, A., Shalom, O.S., Goldberg, Y.: Understanding convolutional neural networks for text classification. arXiv preprint arXiv:1809.08037 (2018)
15. Jones, K.S.: A statistical interpretation of term specificity and its application in retrieval. J. Documentation **60**(5), 493–502 (2004). https://doi.org/10.1108/00220410410560573
16. Le, Q.V., Mikolov, T.: Distributed representations of sentences and documents. In: Proceedings of the 31th International Conference on Machine Learning, ICML 2014, Beijing, 21–26 June 2014. JMLR Workshop and Conference Proceedings, vol. 32, pp. 1188–1196. JMLR.org (2014). http://proceedings.mlr.press/v32/le14.html
17. Lilleberg, J., Zhu, Y., Zhang, Y.: Support vector machines and Word2vec for text classification with semantic features. In: Ge, N., et al. (eds.) 14th IEEE International Conference on Cognitive Informatics & Cognitive Computing, ICCI*CC 2015, Beijing, 6–8 July 2015, pp. 136–140. IEEE Computer Society (2015). https://doi.org/10.1109/ICCI-CC.2015.7259377
18. Liu, S.M., Chen, J.: A multi-label classification based approach for sentiment classification. Expert Syst. Appl. **42**(3), 1083–1093 (2015). https://doi.org/10.1016/j.eswa.2014.08.036
19. Loza Mencía, E., Fürnkranz, J.: Efficient multilabel classification algorithms for large-scale problems in the legal domain. In: Francesconi et al. [11], pp. 192–215. https://doi.org/10.1007/978-3-642-12837-0_11
20. Lu, Q., Conrad, J.G., Al-Kofahi, K., Keenan, W.: Legal document clustering with built-in topic segmentation. In: Macdonald, C., Ounis, I., Ruthven, I. (eds.) Proceedings of the 20th ACM Conference on Information and Knowledge Management, CIKM 2011, Glasgow, 24–28 October 2011, pp. 383–392. ACM (2011). https://doi.org/10.1145/2063576.2063636
21. Mikolov, T., Chen, K., Corrado, G., Dean, J.: Efficient estimation of word representations in vector space. In: Bengio, Y., LeCun, Y. (eds.) 1st International Conference on Learning Representations, ICLR 2013, Scottsdale, 2–4 May 2013, Workshop Track Proceedings (2013). http://arxiv.org/abs/1301.3781
22. Prabhu, Y., Varma, M.: FastXML: a fast, accurate and stable tree-classifier for extreme multi-label learning. In: Proceedings of the 20th ACM SIGKDD International Conference on Knowledge Discovery and Data Mining, pp. 263–272. ACM (2014)
23. Quaresma, P., Gonçalves, T.: Using linguistic information and machine learning techniques to identify entities from juridical documents. In: Francesconi et al. [11], pp. 44–59. https://doi.org/10.1007/978-3-642-12837-0_3
24. Rijsbergen, C.J.V.: Information Retrieval, 2nd edn. Butterworth-Heinemann, Newton (1979)

25. Sebastiani, F.: Machine learning in automated text categorization. ACM Comput. Surv. (CSUR) **34**(1), 1–47 (2002). https://doi.org/10.1145/505282.505283
26. Steinberger, R., Ebrahim, M., Turchi, M.: JRC EuroVoc indexer JEX - a freely available multi-label categorisation tool. In: Calzolari, N., et al. (eds.) Proceedings of the Eighth International Conference on Language Resources and Evaluation, LREC 2012, Istanbul, 23–25 May 2012, pp. 798–805. European Language Resources Association (ELRA) (2012). http://www.lrec-conf.org/proceedings/lrec2012/summaries/875.html
27. Steinberger, R., et al.: The JRC-Acquis: a multilingual aligned parallel corpus with 20+ languages. In: Calzolari, N., et al. (eds.) Proceedings of the Fifth International Conference on Language Resources and Evaluation, LREC 2006, Genoa, 22–28 May 2006, pp. 2142–2147. European Language Resources Association (ELRA) (2006). http://www.lrec-conf.org/proceedings/lrec2006/pdf/340_pdf.pdf
28. Tsoumakas, G., Katakis, I.: Multi-label classification: an overview. Int. J. Warehouse. Min. **3**, 1–13 (2007)
29. Zhang, W., Wang, L., Yan, J., Wang, X., Zha, H.: Deep extreme multi-label learning. CoRR abs/1704.03718 (2017). http://arxiv.org/abs/1704.03718

Fairness-Aware Process Mining

Mahnaz Sadat Qafari[(⊠)] and Wil van der Aalst

Rheinisch-Westfälische Technische Hochschule Aachen (RWTH), Aachen, Germany
{m.s.qafari,wvdaalst}@pads.rwth-aachen.de

Abstract. Process mining is a multi-purpose tool enabling organizations to improve their processes. One of the primary purposes of process mining is finding the root causes of performance or compliance problems in processes. The usual way of doing so is by gathering data from the process event log and other sources and then applying some data mining and machine learning techniques. However, the results of applying such techniques are not always acceptable. In many situations, this approach is prone to making obvious or unfair diagnoses and applying them may result in conclusions that are unsurprising or even discriminating. In this paper, we present a solution to this problem by creating a fair classifier for such situations. The undesired effects are removed at the expense of reduction on the accuracy of the resulting classifier.

1 Introduction

Motivation. Academic and commercial process mining tools aim to find the root causes of performance or compliance problems in processes. Mainly, a classifier, say a decision tree, is created using the data gathered from the process and then the rule mining is done using that decision tree [7]. However, this approach may lead to diagnoses that are not valuable. In some cases, the main cause of the problem is already known and essentially cannot be altered. Also, due to the strong correlation of the known main cause and the problem, it may become impossible to see the other minor but probably more practically valuable causes of the problem. Consider the following two scenarios: (i) there is a bottleneck in the process and it is caused by the busiest employee, or (ii) there are deviations caused by the most experienced resources taking the most difficult cases. In these scenarios, it is likely that the busiest employees or the most experienced resources are declared the main reasons for the bottleneck or deviations in the process. This is not just unfair but also does not provide novel insights (just stating the obvious). Even if we remove the attribute conveying the employee or the resource, still rules that proxy these attributes would be revealed as the result of the traditional rule mining [10]. In these cases, it is essential to make inference about the less trivial root-causes of the problem in the process.

As another application, consider that for a given process we are interested in questions which are related to investigating the process while ignoring the effect of different values of a particular attribute. "Following the progress of career paths while eliminating gender differences" is one example of these sorts

© Springer Nature Switzerland AG 2019
H. Panetto et al. (Eds.): OTM 2019, LNCS 11877, pp. 182–192, 2019.
https://doi.org/10.1007/978-3-030-33246-4_11

of situations where we need to remove the correlation between two attributes in the data.

Discrimination-Aware Data Mining. Each population can be partitioned into several subgroups according to the properties of its members, e.g., race, age, or academic degree. *Discrimination* means treating a subgroup of people, called *sensitive group*, in an unfair way merely because of being a member of that subgroup. There is a possibility that negligent usage of new advanced technologies, especially in the field of data mining and machine learning, inadvertently cause discrimination. To avoid these phenomena, detecting discrimination and designing fair predictors have been studied intensively.

Demographic parity indicates the portion of people in the sensitive subgroup who receive the desired result must be the same as the whole population. To maintain this criterion, in some approaches the training data is manipulated [3, 4, 10]. In another approach, [10], the representation of the data is changed, and the fairness is maintained as a side-effect of fair representations. In [5], demographic parity in a decision tree is retained by taking into account the information gain of the sensitive attribute as well as the class attribute as the criteria used for splitting the internal nodes. In [5], the relabeling technique is also used to further decrease the discrimination in the resulting decision tree. Besides demographic parity, other notions of fairness have been formalized in the literature. We refer the interested readers to [1] for a review of various fairness criteria.

Process Mining. Process mining is the link between model-based process analysis and data-oriented analysis techniques; a set of techniques that support the analysis of business processes based on event logs. In this context, several works have been dedicated to decision mining and finding the correlation among the process data and making predictions [2, 6, 7].

Ethical and legal effects of process mining can be considered in two categories; confidentiality and fairness issues. Confidentiality in the process mining has recently received attention [9]. To the best of our knowledge, there is no work in the area of process mining dedicated to investigating fairness issues. This is the first publication considering discrimination within a given process. The extended version of this paper is available in [8].

Our Results. We provide a solution for the previously mentioned problems. Specifying a problem in the process, we propose an approach by adopting the techniques available in data mining for removing discrimination from classifiers in the area of process mining to avoid unfair or obvious conclusions in such scenarios. We do that by declaring the attribute that indicates the existence of the problem in the given situation as the *class attribute* and the attribute that we want to decrease its dependency to the class attribute as the *sensitive attribute*. We consider the class attribute to be binary with the following two values: + indicates the desirable result conveying the problem of interest has not been faced while − has the opposite meaning. The sensitive attribute is also assumed to be binary, where ☹ convey belonging to the sensitive group while ☺ convey belonging to the rest of the population (favorable group). Now, we can consider the problem as a discriminatory case and remove the dependency of the class and the sensitive attributes in the resulting classifier by creating a fair classifier. Doing so, the resulting rules would not be discriminatory against the sensitive group. Also, this technique masks some of the causes of that problem and focus on the other ones.

The rest of the paper is organized as follow. In Sect. 2, we present the problem statement. A high-level overview of the proposed approach is presented in Sect. 3. The experimental results of applying the implemented method on a real event log are presented in Sect. 4. Finally, in Sect. 5, we summarize our approach and discuss directions for further research.

2   Problem Statement

To analyze conformance and performance problems, we use event data and process models (discovered or hand-made).[1] An event log is a collection of traces and each trace is a collection of events related to the same case. Also each trace may be associated with some attributes. Consider $\mathcal{U}_{act}$ as the universe of all possible *activity names*, $\mathcal{U}_{time}$ the universe of all possible *timestamps*, $\mathcal{U}_{att}$ the universe of all possible *attribute names*, $\mathcal{U}_{val}$ the universe of all possible *values*, and, $\mathcal{U}_{map} : \mathcal{U}_{att} \nrightarrow \mathcal{U}_{val}$. Also, let $values : \mathcal{U}_{att} \mapsto \mathbb{P}(\mathcal{U}_{val})$ be the function that returns the set of all possible values for each attribute name. We define an event log as follows:

Definition 1 (Event Log). *An* event *is an element of* $\mathcal{U}_{act} \times \mathcal{U}_{time} \times \mathcal{U}_{map}$ *and the universe of all possible* events *is denoted by* $\mathcal{E}$*. A* log *is an element of* $\mathbb{P}(\mathcal{U}_{map} \times \mathbb{P}(\mathcal{E}))$ *and the universe of all possible logs is denoted by* $\mathcal{L}$*. We call each* $t \in L$*, where* $L \in \mathcal{L}$*, a* trace*.*

stamp. To work with event logs, we need the following helper functions:

- Given an event $e = (act, time, map) \in \mathcal{E}$, $\pi_{act}(e) = act$, $\pi_{time}(e) = time$, and, $\pi_{map}(e) = map$.
- Given $t = (map, E) \in L$, where $L \in \mathcal{L}$, then $\pi_{map}(t) = map$ and $\pi_{events}(t) = E$.
- Given $E \in \mathbb{P}(\mathcal{E})$, then $\pi_{maxtime}(E) = \arg\max_{e \in E} \pi_{time}(e)$, $\pi_{act}(E) = \{e \in E | \pi_{act}(e) = act\}$, and, $E_{\leq time} = \{e \in E | \pi_{time}(e) \leq time\}$.

We assume that each event in a given log L has a unique timestamp.

If the problem in the process is about the traces, like delay in some cases, then for a given trace all the values of its trace and event-level attributes might be relevant. However, if the problem is related to a specific activity, like a bottleneck in activity *act*, then we need to extract the data from the trace attributes plus the attributes of a subset of its events that occur before the occurrence of that specific event. Also, the class attribute may occur several times in a given trace. We define the notion of a *situation* to handle such cases as follows:

---

[1] We assume the reader to be familiar with the concepts like set, multi-set, and function. Given a non-empty set X, we denote all the non-empty subsets of X by $\mathbb{P}(X)$. Given two sets A and B, a partial function $f : A \nrightarrow B$ is defined as a function $f : A' \mapsto B$ for some $A' \subseteq A$. We say $f(a) = \bot$ if $a \notin A'$.

Definition 2 (Situation). *We define a* situation *as an element in* $(\mathcal{U}_{map} \times \mathbb{P}(\mathcal{E}))$. *The set of all possible situations is denoted by* $\mathcal{U}_{sit}$. *Given a log* $L \in \mathcal{L}$, *we define the set of all situations derived from it as:*

$$S_L = \bigcup_{(map,E) \in L} \left(\bigcup_{e \in E} \{(map, E_{\leq \pi_{time}(e)})\} \right).$$

It is obvious that $L \subseteq S_L$. *Any* $S \subseteq S_L$ *is called a* situation subset *of* L. *For a given log* L, *there are two main types of situation subsets. The first one is the* trace situation subset *which is* $S_{L,\perp} = L$. *The second type is the* event specified situation subsets *which includes all* $S_{L,act} = \{(map, E) \in S_L | \pi_{act}(\pi_{maxtime}(E)) = act\}$, *where* $act \in \mathcal{U}_{act}$ *and* $S_{L,act} \neq \emptyset$.

To specify an attribute, besides the name of the attribute, we need to know if it is a trace or an event attribute and if it is an event attribute, we need to know to which events does it belong. To concretely specify an attribute, we use the *situation feature* notion defined as follows:

Definition 3 (Situation Feature). *For any given* $a \in \mathcal{U}_{act} \cup \{\perp\}$ *and* $att \in \mathcal{U}_{att}$, *we call* $sf_{a,att} : \mathcal{U}_{sit} \nrightarrow \mathcal{U}_{val}$ *a situation feature. Given a situation* (map, E), *we define* $sf_{a,att}((map, E))$ *as follows:*

$$sf_{a,att}((map, E)) = \begin{cases} map(att) & a = \perp \\ \pi_{map}(\pi_{maxtime}(\pi_a(E)))(att) & a \in \mathcal{U}_{act} \end{cases}.$$

We denote the universe of all possible situation features by $\mathcal{U}_{sf}$. *Given a situation feature* $sf_{a,att}$, *we define* $values(sf_{a,att}) = values(att)$. *Also, for a given* $n \in \mathbb{N}$, $EP \in \mathcal{U}_{sf}^n$ *is a* situation feature extraction plan *of size* n, *where* $\mathcal{U}_{sf}^n$ *is defined as* $\underbrace{\mathcal{U}_{sf} \times \cdots \times \mathcal{U}_{sf}}_{n \ times}$.

A situation feature extraction plan can be interpreted as the schema, the tuple composed of those situation features that are relevant to the given problem in the process.

The first step of solving any problem is concretely specifying the problem. We call such a problem description a *situation specification* which is defined as follows:

Definition 4 (Situation Specification). *A* situation specification *is a tuple* $SS = (EP, ssf, csf, \epsilon)$ *in which*

(i) $EP \in \mathcal{U}_{sf}^n$, *where* $n \in \mathbb{N}$, *is the situation feature extraction plan which includes all the situation features for which we are going to investigate their effect on the given problem.*

(ii) $ssf \in \mathcal{U}_{sf}$, *the* sensitive situation feature *where* $values(ssf) = \{\odot, \odot\}$ *and* $ssf \notin EP$.

(iii) $csf \in \mathcal{U}_{sf}$, *the* class situation feature *where* $values(csf) = \{+, -\}$, $csf \notin EP$, *and* $csf \neq ssf$.

(vi) $\epsilon \in [0,1]$, *indicating the acceptable level of discrimination against ssf (the amount of acceptable dependency between ssf and csf).*

For a given situation specification, we go through the following three steps: (1) Enriching the log, (2) Extracting the data, and (3) Learning fair classifier. The general approach of our method is depicted in Fig. 1.

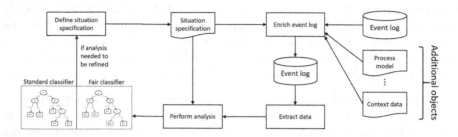

Fig. 1. The general framework proposed for fair root-cause analysis. First, according to the situation specification the event log is enriched by preprocessing the log and other sources of information. Then, the data is extracted from the enriched event log. Finally, two standard and fair classifier are created. Based on the analysis result, it is possible to adapt the situation specification to gather additional insights.

3   Approach

We go through every one of the steps for creating a fair classifier for a given situation specification, mentioned in the previous section, in more details.

1. Enriching the log. Let $SS = (EP, ssf, csf, \epsilon)$ be the given situation specification. If EP includes situation features that can not be directly extracted from the given log L, we enrich the log by augmenting each trace of it. In this step, we add some attribute values to the traces and its events. These added attributes can be related to any one of different process characteristics; time perspective, data flow-perspective, control-flow perspective, conformance perspective, or resource organization perspective. They may be driven from the given log, conformance checking results from replaying the traces on a given Petri-net model, or any external information resource like the weather information.

2. Extracting the data. To discover meaningful dependency results by the classifier, we need to capture the data such that the causality relations among them and the class attribute are not violated. To do so, given $csf = sf_{a,att}$, we apply the following two rules while extracting the data:

1. If $a \in \mathcal{U}_{act}$, each trace may map to several situations and the data should be extracted from that part of the trace that happens before the occurrence of csf. However, if $a = \bot$, then csf is related to a trace level attribute and the data should be extracted from the whole trace.
2. The value of the independent situation feature with the closest occurrence time to the occurrence of csf must be collected.

The second rule is valid assuming that if one of the independent situation features has happened several times before the occurrence of csf in a trace, the one that is chronologically closest to the occurrence of csf, has the most effect on it.

To follow the first rule, for the given log L and the situation specification $SS = (EP, ssf, csf, \epsilon)$, where $csf = sf_{a,att}$, we set $S = S_{L,\perp}$ if $a = \perp$ and we set $S = S_{L,act}$ if $a = act$.

The final step for extracting the data is creating a data table and annotating each row of the table by adding the values of sensitive and class situation feature to it.

Definition 5 (Situation Feature Table). *Given a situation feature extraction plan* $EP = (sf_{a_1,att_1}, \ldots, sf_{a_n,att_n})$, *and a situation set* $S \subseteq U_{sit}$, *a situation feature table is a multi-set which is defined as:*

$$T_{S,EP} = [(sf_{a_1,att_1}(s), \ldots, sf_{a_n,att_n}(s)) | s \in S].$$

For a log $L \in \mathcal{L}$, $S \subseteq S_L$, *we call* $T_{S,EP}$ *a situation feature table of* L.

For a given situation feature table $T_{S,EP}$ *and* $csf, ssf \in U_{ssf}$ *for which* $ssf \neq csf$ *and* $csf, ssf \notin EP$ *and* $\forall_{s \in S} (csf(s) \neq \perp \land ssf(s) \neq \perp)$, *we define an annotated situation table* $AT_{S,EP,ssf,csf}$ *as:*

$$AT_{S,EP,ssf,csf} = [(sf_{a_1,att_1}(s), \ldots, sf_{a_n,att_n}(s), ssf(s), csf(s)) | s \in S].$$

We call each element of $AT_{S,EP,ssf,csf}$ *an* instance. *For a given instance* $inst_s = (sf_{a_1,att_1}(s), \ldots, sf_{a_n,att_n}(s), ssf(s), csf(s))$ *we define* $\pi_{EP}(inst_s) = (sf_{a_1,att_1}(s), \ldots, sf_{a_n,att_n}(s))$, $\pi_{ssf}(inst_s) = ssf(s)$, *and,* $\pi_{csf}(inst_s) = csf(s)$.

Here, ssf is the sensitive and csf is the class (label) situation feature. Also, each member of $inst_s \in AT_{S,EP,ssf,csf}$ where $s \in S$ can be seen as a row of the data table in which $\pi_{EP}(inst_s) = (sf_{a_1,att_1}(s), \ldots, sf_{a_n,att_n}(s))$ is the tuple including independent attribute values and $\pi_{csf}(inst_s) = csf(inst_s)$ is the class attribute value of $inst_s$.

3. Learning fair classifier. We define a classifier as follows:

Definition 6 (Classifier). *Let* S *be a set of situations and* $EP = (sf_{a_1,att_1}, \ldots, sf_{a_n,att_n})$ *be a situation extraction plan and* $csf \in U_{sf}$ *such that* $\forall_{1 \leq i \leq n} sf_{a_i,att_i} \neq csf$, *then a classifier is a function class* $: T_{S,EP} \mapsto values(csf)$.

Given a classifier $class$ and an annotated situation table $AT_{L,EP,ssf,csf}$, then the accuracy of $class$ over $AT_{L,EP,ssf,csf}$ is measured as:

$$acc(class, AT_{L,EP,ssf,csf}) = \frac{|[inst \in AT_{L,EP,ssf,csf} | class(\pi_{EP}(inst)) = \pi_{csf}(inst)]|}{|AT_{L,EP,ssf,csf}|}.$$

For fairness, we use demographic parity as the main concept. To measure the discrimination in the data, we use the measure mentioned in [5], which is:

$$disc(AT_{L,EP,ssf,csf}) = \frac{|[inst \in AT_{L,EP,ssf,csf} | \pi_{ssf}(inst) = \odot \land \pi_{csf}(inst) = +]|}{|[inst \in AT_{L,EP,ssf,csf} | \pi_{ssf}(inst) = \odot]|}$$

$$-\frac{|[inst \in AT_{L,EP,ssf,csf}|\pi_{ssf}(inst) = \odot \wedge \pi_{csf}(inst) = +)]|}{|[inst \in AT_{L,EP,ssf,csf}|\pi_{ssf}(inst) = \odot]|}.$$

By replacing $\pi_{csf}(inst)$ with $class(\pi_{EP}(inst))$ in this equation, we can measure the discrimination imposed by the classifier $class$.

For the classifier, we use decision trees. It is worth mentioning that both the classifier and the measure of discrimination can be changed according to the given application.

The first step toward removing the discrimination has already been taken during the creation of the classifier by not considering the sensitive situation feature for the classification purpose (Definition 6). As mentioned in many works, e.g. [10], this is not enough due to the existence of correlation among different situation feature values in a given situation feature table. The discrimination in the classifier can be further eliminated by relabeling technique. In this paper, we relabel leaves in the decision tree to balance accuracy and fairness. However, other methods of creating a discrimination free classifiers can be used.

In the implemented plug-in two classifiers are generated. The first one is a tree classifier that is generated by J48 tree classifier implementation of C4.5 algorithm in WEKA package. Then, if the level of discrimination in the resulting decision tree is more than an acceptable threshold ϵ, the leaves of the decision tree are relabeled to create a fair classifier. For the relabeling, we use an algorithm similar to the one mentioned in [5]. In [5], the leaves of the tree are ordered in descending order of the ratio of the discrimination gain and accuracy lose of relabeling each leaf. Then according to this order, leaves are relabeled until the discrimination in the classifier tree is lower than ϵ. As mentioned in [5], the problem of finding the set of leaves to be relabeled such that the discrimination in the decision tree is lower than a given threshold ϵ with the lowest possible negative effect on the accuracy of the decision tree is equivalent to the knapsack problem. In the relabeling algorithm implemented in the ProM plug-in, we use dynamic programming and rounding to choose approximately the best possible set of leaves to be relabeled.

Note that in the context of process mining and root cause analysis, changing the class label from $+$ to $-$ and from $-$ to $+$ at the same time may not be desirable. So in some cases we may need to restrict the relabeling technique to just desirable or just undesirable labeled leaves of the tree. If we restrict the relabeling, there might be cases where the discrimination of the fair tree is higher than given ϵ.

4 Implementation and Experimental Results

The approach presented in Sect. 3 has been implemented as a plug-in of ProM which is an open-source framework for process mining. The implemented plug-in is available under the name *Discrimination aware decision tree*. The inputs of the plug-in are the event log, the Petri-net model of the process, and, the conformance checking results of replaying the given log on the given model. The current implementation focuses on three types of problems in a given process: (1) routing problems, (2) deviation problems, and (3) performance problems.

To illustrate the fair analysis of these problems we use one real data log, the *hospital billing*[2] event log. We use the last 20000 traces of hospital billing log in the experiments which include 71188 activities. In this initial evaluation, we created a controlled experiment with a known ground truth. In each experiment, the discrimination is added to the event log artificially and then the altered log is used to evaluate the method and investigate the effect of removing discrimination on the accuracy of the created fair decision tree. In all the experiments the same setting has been used. For example in all the experiments $\epsilon = 0.05$ and there was no limit for applying relabeling technique. Also for each event log, the same set of independent situation features has been chosen and all the parameters for creating the decision tree were the same. 60% of the data has been used for training, and 40% of the data has been used for testing the classifier. The results of our experiment are depicted in Fig. 2. The charts respectively show the results of applying our technique when there is (a) a performance problem, (b) a routing problem, and (c) a conformance problem in the hospital billing process.

As is depicted in Fig. 2, we can reduce the discrimination on the sensitive group at the expense of some reduction at the accuracy of the classifier. As expected, as the level of discrimination increases in the data, the amount of the accuracy of the classifier that needs to be sacrificed for removing the discrimination increases. We need to be careful using this technique, as there are occasions where discrimination may be put on the favorable group. This phenomenon is also unfair. Surprisingly, in some cases like Fig. 2(c), the fair decision tree outperforms the standard decision tree in terms of accuracy. This phenomenon has been reported in [5] as well.

The chart in Fig. 3, demonstrates the level of discrimination in the fair decision tree and its accuracy for different settings of parameter ϵ. As expected, the accuracy of the fair decision tree is lower when ϵ is smaller. Here, we use delay in traces as the class situation feature.

5   Conclusion

The first step toward enhancing a process by removing one of its performance or compliance problems is diagnosing the root causes of that problem. By using standard data mining techniques for detecting the causes, the results might be obvious and mainly regarding those parts of the process that can not be altered. To reveal other less vivid causes of the problem we need to mask the obvious ones. We did so by looking at the cause that we need to ignore its effect on the problem as the sensitive attribute. Then we remove the dependency between the sensitive and the class attributes from the created classifier. This is done at the expense of a small reduction in the accuracy of the resulting classifier.

This research has several applications; detecting the discrimination within a process, removing the discrimination from the process by replacing the fair

---

[2] https://data.4tu.nl/repository/collection:event_logs_real.

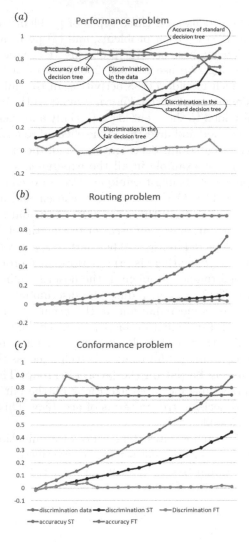

Fig. 2. The result of applying the implemented ProM plug-in on a real event log. In all these charts, the blue curve exhibits the level of discrimination in data (also by the x-axis.), the orange curve shows the level of discrimination in standard decision tree, the gray curve shows the level of discrimination in a fair decision tree, the yellow curve exhibits the accuracy of the standard decision tree, and, the green curve exhibits the accuracy of the fair tree. Chart (a) shows the results of applying our technique when there is a performance problem in the process for which we consider the delay in the traces. Chart (b) shows the results of applying our technique when there is a routing problem in the process for which we consider the choice between taking "BILLED" and skipping this transition in the hospital billing process. Chart (c) shows the results of applying our technique when there is a conformance problem in the process for which we consider the existence of deviation in the traces. In all these experiments $\epsilon = 0.05$. In all these experiments, the level of discrimination in the fair classifiers are less than the given threshold ϵ. Also, as the level of discrimination increases in the data, the difference between the accuracy of the fair decision tree and standard decision tree increases. In chart (c), the fair decision tree demonstrates a better performance than the standard decision tree in terms of accuracy. (Color figure online)

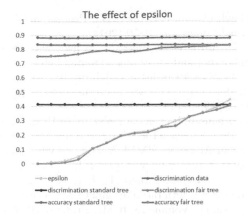

Fig. 3. The result of applying implemented plug-in with different values for parameter ϵ which is depicted in purple in the chart. In this chart, the value of ϵ shown by the pink curve. The level of discrimination in the data in all these experiments are the same. In all these experiments, the level of discrimination in the fair decision tree is lower than the given threshold ϵ. Also, the accuracy of the fair decision tree tends to be lower for the lower values of ϵ.

classifier with the current one, making more accurate and realistic judgments about the root causes of the problem at hand.

This research can be extended in several directions. The first one is to add new derived attributes to the log when enriching the log. The other one is altering the fairness criteria, the classification method, or the technique for creating the discrimination-free classifier depending on the application.

References

1. Berk, R., Heidari, H., Jabbari, S., Kearns, M., Roth, A.: Fairness in criminal justice risk assessments: the state of the art. Sociol. Methods Res. 0049124118782533 (2018)
2. Fani Sani, M., van der Aalst, W., Bolt, A., García-Algarra, J.: Subgroup discovery in process mining. In: Abramowicz, W. (ed.) BIS 2017. LNBIP, vol. 288, pp. 237–252. Springer, Cham (2017). https://doi.org/10.1007/978-3-319-59336-4_17
3. Kamiran, F., Calders, T.: Classification with no discrimination by preferential sampling. In: Informal Proceedings of the 19th Annual Machine Learning Conference of Belgium and The Netherlands, Benelearn 2010, Leuven, Belgium, 27–28 May 2010, pp. 1–6 (2010)
4. Kamiran, F., Calders, T.: Data preprocessing techniques for classification without discrimination. Knowl. Inf. Syst. **33**(1), 1–33 (2012). https://doi.org/10.1007/s10115-011-0463-8
5. Kamiran, F., Calders, T., Pechenizkiy, M.: Discrimination aware decision tree learning. In: Proceedings of the 2010 IEEE International Conference on Data Mining, ICDM 2010, pp. 869–874. IEEE Computer Society, Washington, DC (2010). https://doi.org/10.1109/ICDM.2010.50

6. Leemans, S., Fahland, D., van der Aalst, W.: Process and Deviation Exploration with Inductive Visual Miner. pp. 46–50 (2014)
7. de Leoni, M., van der Aalst, W.M., Dees, M.: A general process mining framework for correlating, predicting and clustering dynamic behavior based on event logs. Inf. Syst. **56**(C), 235–257 (2016). https://doi.org/10.1016/j.is.2015.07.003
8. Qafari, M.S., van der Aalst, W.: arxiv: Fairness-aware process mining (2019). https://arxiv.org/abs/1908.11451
9. Rafiei, M., von Waldthausen, L., van der Aalst, W.M.P.: Ensuring confidentiality in process mining. In: Proceedings of the 8th International Symposium on Data-driven Process Discovery and Analysis (SIMPDA 2018), Seville, Spain, 13–14 December 2018, pp. 3–17 (2018). http://ceur-ws.org/Vol-2270/paper1.pdf
10. Zemel, R., Wu, Y., Swersky, K., Pitassi, T., Dwork, C.: Learning fair representations. In: Proceedings of the 30th International Conference on International Conference on Machine Learning - Volume 28, ICML 2013, pp. III-325–III-333. JMLR.org (2013). http://dl.acm.org/citation.cfm?id=3042817.3042973

Model-Aware Clustering
of Non-conforming Traces

Florian Richter, Ludwig Zellner$^{(\boxtimes)}$, Janina Sontheim, and Thomas Seidl

LMU Munich, Munich, Germany
{richter,zellner,sontheim,seidl}@dbs.ifi.lmu.de

Abstract. Process deviations often are a difficult issue to deal with, revealing a concept in need of improvement. However, deviations are not equally interesting and focusing on each alike is probably not the most efficient approach in most applications. Our novel approach identifies groups of action sequences, called traces, with similar deviation characteristics. In contrast to trace clustering, we utilize a process model as a baseline, showing model awareness, to define conformance and establish a density-based anomaly aggregation regarding the process model as a map-like ground distance. Dense clusters of non-conform traces are collected as micro-processes, which might reveal itself as significant process variants from another perspective. Handling groups of deviating objects bears much more efficacy - either countermeasures or process augmentations - than dealing with singular objects individually.

Keywords: Trace clustering · Conformance checking · Process model adaption · Anomaly clustering

1 Introduction

Is your process running as intended? Conformance checking focuses on this very important question and offers valuable answers. Singular process instances are checked if they conform to a given or previously mined model.

Prominent techniques like token replay [7] and trace alignment [2] map traces to fitness scores between 0 and 1. Based on that, traces are classified into regular and abnormal process executions.

Various reasons for non-conformance exist and determining this root improves the process knowledge. Some traces might only be noise like aborted test cases or caused by defective recording. Extensive groups with similar behavior are interesting since they might emerge as a substantial process variant. Trace clustering covers the mining of those process variants. We focus on micro-processes, which are too small to be discovered as process variants regarding the number of contained traces. On the contrary, they contain enough traces with similar behavior and therefore form patterns, which are likely to have common root causes. Identifying micro-processes bears many opportunities. Unique deviations usually have a likewise unique reason to occur. A batch of traces in a

© Springer Nature Switzerland AG 2019
H. Panetto et al. (Eds.): OTM 2019, LNCS 11877, pp. 193–200, 2019.
https://doi.org/10.1007/978-3-030-33246-4_12

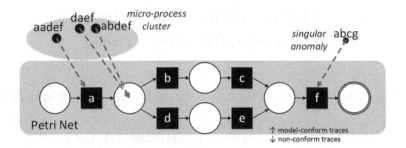

Fig. 1. Overview over our model-aware clustering of non-conform traces. It detects micro-process clusters, pictured in green, versus singular outliers, like abdg. (Color figure online)

micro-process is more likely to be caused by a common effect. If this deviation is undesirable, determining countermeasures is based on the commonalities and has a greater importance since further deviating traces of this kind can be expected. Micro-processes possibly yield new perspectives on the origin process and might induce a modification of the process model to encourage the emerging deviation.

Mining micro-processes requires a notion of similarity between traces. Simple sequence similarity measures like edit distance can not cope with this task due to process concurrency. Concurrency is a non-consecutive execution of actions and therefore edit distance is not reasonable. In this work we present our novel approach illustrated in Fig. 2 which uses a process model (Fig. 2 (1)) like a Petri net as a reference point cf. Fig. 1. To determine distances between deviating traces we refer to the distances of the deviations in the model (Fig. 2 (3)), which provides the clustering approach with a model-aware property.

Using the model as a map (Fig. 2 (4a)), we obtain a geodetic distance between non-conforming traces, detected by conformance checking (Fig. 2 (2)) to correlate pairs of traces regarding the characteristics of their deviation. A hierarchical clustering technique is applied afterwards to aggregate traces to clusters, which have a higher density within in contrast to singular outliers and noise (Fig. 2 (4b)). We refer to these clusters as micro-processes herein (Fig. 1). With our novel method we are able to detect emerging variants, which can not be detected by trace clustering due to their size and impact.

2   Related Work

The aggregation of traces with similar behavior is the main motive of trace clustering. Common approaches use vector embeddings of traces and apply traditional clustering methods on those vector spaces [6]. Song et al. [8] introduced more complex trace profiles to cover more behavior in the clustering result. In [4], Bose et al. presented a context aware approach for trace clustering. It is based on generic edit distance. They used trigrams and compared their context without the activity itself with other contexts to find out how similar these activities are. Trace clustering aims at clustering concurrent process variants. In contrast,

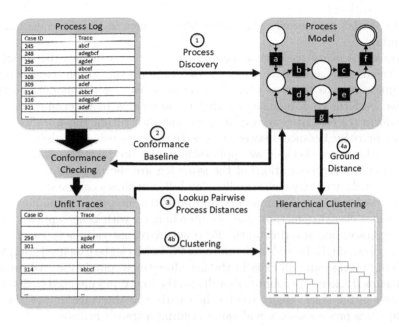

Fig. 2. Process steps of our approach exemplary shown on a small process log. The numbers at the arrows indicate the sequential order of the steps.

our approach mines small clusters of traces which have not yet emerged as an established variant considering their impact. Since those approaches focus on multiple processes, they rely on trace data only, while we introduce a model-aware clustering method. ActiTraC, as presented in [5], takes the process discovery perspective into account. Traces are not mapped into a vector space but are greedily aggregated to clusters until the fitness of the model for this cluster drops. It assumes clusters to be represented by proper models with good fitness. Because micro-clusters suffer from poor fitness, if considered as processes, active clustering does not aim at its detection. CTC [9] is a top-down hierarchical clustering approach that focuses on averaging the complexity of models of split logs. This is also not comparable with our method since the complexity of the micro-clusters would be very low due to the low number of contained traces and thus not in the scope of this clustering approach.

3   Preliminaries

Our novel anomaly trace clustering approach utilizes common process discovery and conformance checking to derive a geodetic distance measure. Process discovery starts with a log of process instances. Those cases are sequences of events. An event contains a reference to the case and an activity label, stating the type of this event. In many applications, additional information like execution time and resources enrich the event data. In this work we focus on the sequence of activity labels, which is known as the trace. A brief example of a log is seen in

Fig. 2 in the left top corner. The further steps shown in Fig. 2 are explained in the coming.

Process discovery uses event logs to create process models like Petri nets or equivalent representations. Our approach requires this graph-based model to determine distances between process deviations. We use the model two times: First we perform conformance checking on all traces to determine and filter the conform traces. Later we use the path distance within the workflow net to compute pairwise distances between traces. Here we are using the alpha miner [3].

For conformance checking we apply token replay on the Petri net model. This means that two representations of the same log are checked against each other (log vs. model), whereby commonalities and discrepancies can be discovered [1]. Our approach works as a framework and both the discovery technique and the conformance checking method can be interchanged with other approaches. By replaying traces one at a time in the Petri net, we count various types of tokens. Missing tokens might be added virtually, so the trace can be executed completely. Remaining tokens can still exist in the net after trace completion. All produced and consumed tokens are counted as well and the four types are used to determine the fitness of the trace. Hence the formula with σ as the trace and N the Petri net maps this process onto a real value yielding a trace's fitness:

$$fitness(\sigma, N) = \frac{1}{2} \cdot (1 - \frac{missing}{consumed}) + \frac{1}{2} \cdot (1 - \frac{remaining}{produced})$$

4   Clustering of Non-conform Traces

Traditional trace clustering identifies trace clusters that follow concurrent processes. Typically those variants are weighted equally or at least every variant contains enough traces to be considered a process. In the contrary, our approach assumes one large process to exist and identifies small groups of traces, that deviate from the process. Deviating traces can already be found using conformance checking. Instead we ignore singular deviating traces but look for clusters within the non-conform traces. Clusters are always an aggregation of objects using a similarity measure. In our case we utilize the main process as a reference model to determine similarities between outlier traces. Thus we can reveal process candidates before they emerge to valid variants. The complete procedure is sketched in Fig. 2.

4.1   Processing of the Event Log

Since we start with an event log as input instead of a process model, basically processes, which consist of an overall compliant main structure (excluding spaghetti processes) are suitable. We understand the main structure as the macro-process covering one specific core operation. However, if it is already clear that the process contains multiple significant variants instead of one common process, a traditional trace clustering should be applied as pre-processing for better results.

As it was mentioned before, for the event log conversion we are using the well-known alpha miner.

Given a model, traces can be marked as either conforming or non-conforming by applying conformance checking. They are hereby successively checked against the model. As previously sketched, this task is performed by token-replay [7]. However, other methods like alignments [2] can also be used. The important part is that the method returns not only a fitness value but has to highlight the points of deviation in the model.

Petri nets are a very useful representation of a process when it comes to aforementioned simulation and replay. However to compute distances between deviations, we transform the Petri net into an undirected graph of activity labels. The reason for additionally dropping directions is, that our distance computation does not depend on directions, because differences in a trace's activities are also not dependent on a sequence of activities e.g. assuming a temporal ordering. The graph connects two activities if both activities are connected in the Petri net by one place in-between. The distance between two activities is then the number of edges on the shortest path between the according nodes.

4.2 Clustering Procedure

So far we received a fitness value for each trace, which was calculated for conformance checking by token-replay. In detail, if $fitness(\sigma, N) < 1.0$, a trace can still be marked conforming, which is the case with problems depending on a *missing* or *remaining* token. But, if a trace is not conforming, then there is at least one transition, which can not be replayed in the right order, being marked and saved as problematic.

Thus on these non-conforming traces, we have the possibility to apply clustering, which helps to group similar traces together based on a specific distance function. Through this approach micro-processes emerge, which possess a relation to the main process model. There are many possibilities of choosing a clustering algorithm as well as deciding for a distance function. Every decision will lead to different results.

Since our approach should be seen as a framework, we exemplarily focus on average link as a distance function. Therefore every non-conforming trace is combined pairwise. Furthermore, among these pairs of traces, the cartesian product of every transition marked problematic is computed. By reference to this set we pick every combined pair of transitions and compute the distance between them. Finally the average of the cumulated distances yields our result for one combination of anomalous traces. The following formula of the unweighted pair group method with arithmetic mean describes the procedure given X and Y traces and x and y transitions:

$$\frac{1}{|X| \cdot |Y|} \cdot \sum_{x \in X} \sum_{y \in Y} distance(x, y)$$

Therefore, by combining every anomalous trace, the upper triangular of a distance matrix is pre-computed. Because the distance matrix is symmetrical, the remainder can be filled in easily.

In terms of interpretation, average link returns the mean distance of each pair of transitions regarding the number of hops which is covered by edges in between. As mentioned before, this gap is filled with edges by the main process model. In our approach e.g. the semantic value of maximal, i.e. minimum distances, is discarded, but it makes sense to substitute this measure to match ones goals.

For the clustering procedure we choose the hierarchical agglomerative (bottom-up) method which preserves the possibility to shift the splitting distance concerning the number of clusters. In other words, the resulting number of clusters depends on the choice of distance at which clusters are segmented. This is further illustrated in Fig. 3. Using hierarchical clustering is reasonable, because there are many adjusting screws such as process miners, distance functions and clustering algorithms, which can be changed leading to different results, hence different response strategies.

A popular way of visualizing hierarchical and especially agglomerative clustering is the usage of a dendrogram. It plots the particular traces against its distance between each other, cf. Fig. 3. Thereby it is evident, which traces are clustered. This can detected by referring to the distance value regarding the y-axis.

5 Experiments

For the experimental setup of our approach we compute the Manhattan distance based on unigrams and bigrams. The unit for our n-grams are activities. This means, that with unigrams solely the occurrences of each activity are counted. For bigrams the contiguous pairwise combination is considered. We compared the result of our approach experimentally with aforementioned generic trace clustering. For the setup of the comparison method we use classical trace clustering, which does not use any reference model, but relies on the relationship between traces. We use the activity profile for trace clustering, hence we vectorize each trace by counting the occurrences of each contained activity. Thus these vectorial representations are clustered (we use hierarchical clustering once more to support comparison), again based on a distinct distance function. Here we also use Manhattan-Distance calculated on n dimensions, where n is the number of unique activities in the log.

We use a random synthetic process with 15 activities and derive three deviating variants. A log is generated by simulating the processes with 1000 traces for the original one and 50 per deviation. Figure 3 shows the comparison between our approach and trace clustering with unigrams on the one hand and bigrams on the other. Since we are specifying a framework the actual interpretation and determination of clusters is the responsibility of the user. The dendrogram is a leverage point and indicates proper clusters by illustrating distances between groups of traces. A possible division is exemplified by different colors in the dendrogram on top.

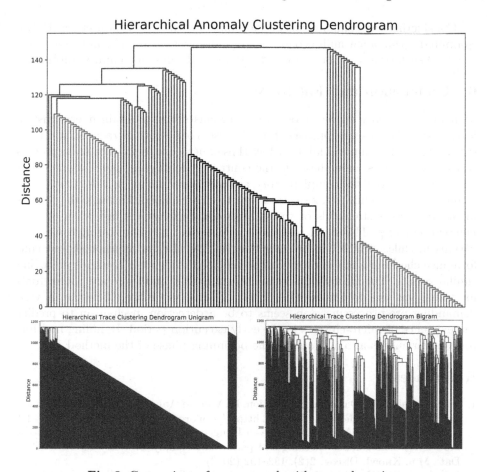

Fig. 3. Comparison of our approach with trace clustering

Using model-aware anomaly clustering, the corresponding upper dendrogram indicates the presence of three clusters, which is true according to the dataset generation. The plots below show dendrograms of the trace clustering procedure described earlier in Sect. 5. It is obvious, that this approach clusters traces independently from a reference model. For this process the result using unigrams is one large cluster as most of the activities occur in both the main process and the deviations. The structure of the activities is neglected and thus the control-flow does not influence the clustering. For the bigrams, the control-flow is partially contained in the vector embedding. Since the dimensions represent only local behavior in the traces, concurrency in the process causes many sequential variants to occur. Those variants are only caused by the limitations of sequential representation and the missing reference to the process model. Thus many deviations are identified and cause the dendrogram to become very noisy and difficult to interpret. Overall, our approach shows that using a reference model enables to cope with concurrency in trace clustering tasks.

Considering the computation performance, for the given dataset results are computed within a few milliseconds due to computation on solely unfit traces. Up to 500 of such traces can be processed with around 5 min of computation time.

6   Conclusion and Future Work

Utilizing a reference process model for trace clustering to obtain micro-clusters has shown to be a useful approach if small subsets of deviating traces exist. Traditional trace clustering will fail to detect those micro-clusters as the main process will cover those as anomalies. On the contrary, identifying them as anomalies only does not reveal the complete story, as there is system in their deviations and it might be worthwhile to take a closer look to either embed them into the process in future process standards or to establish countermeasures before an adverse behavior emerges. This novel reference-model-based micro-clustering consists of various modules, which can be interchanged. We already mentioned that conformance checking and discovery can be replaced with other methods achieving similar results. The clustering is also interchangeable and there are potent tools for visual analysis to explore the clustering structure more efficiently. A very demanding pre-processing step seems to be a detection mechanism to predict the existence of micro-clusters in the early execution period. Handling multiple process variants is also an issue for the beginning phase of the method.

References

1. Van der Aalst, W.: Data science in action. In: Van der Aalst, E. (ed.) Process Mining, pp. 3–23. Springer, Heidelberg (2016). https://doi.org/10.1007/978-3-662-49851-4_1
2. Van der Aalst, W., Adriansyah, A., van Dongen, B.: Replaying history on process models for conformance checking and performance analysis. Wiley Interdisc. Rev. Data Min. Knowl. Discov. **2**(2), 182–192 (2012)
3. Van der Aalst, W., Weijters, T., Maruster, L.: Workflow mining: discovering process models from event logs. IEEE Trans. Knowl. Data Eng. **16**(9), 1128–1142 (2004)
4. Bose, R.J.C., Van der Aalst, W.M.: Context aware trace clustering: towards improving process mining results. In: Proceedings of the 2009 SIAM International Conference on Data Mining, pp. 401–412. SIAM (2009)
5. De Weerdt, J., vanden Broucke, S., Vanthienen, J., Baesens, B.: Active trace clustering for improved process discovery. IEEE Trans. Knowl. Data Eng. **25**(12), 2708–2720 (2013)
6. Greco, G., Guzzo, A., Pontieri, L., Sacca, D.: Discovering expressive process models by clustering log traces. IEEE Trans. Knowl. Data Eng. **18**(8), 1010–1027 (2006)
7. Rozinat, A., Van der Aalst, W.M.: Conformance checking of processes based on monitoring real behavior. Inf. Syst. **33**(1), 64–95 (2008)
8. Song, M., Günther, C.W., Van der Aalst, W.M.P.: Trace clustering in process mining. In: Ardagna, D., Mecella, M., Yang, J. (eds.) BPM 2008. LNBIP, vol. 17, pp. 109–120. Springer, Heidelberg (2009). https://doi.org/10.1007/978-3-642-00328-8_11
9. Sun, Y., Bauer, B., Weidlich, M.: Compound trace clustering to generate accurate and simple sub-process models. In: Maximilien, M., Vallecillo, A., Wang, J., Oriol, M. (eds.) ICSOC 2017. LNCS, vol. 10601, pp. 175–190. Springer, Cham (2017). https://doi.org/10.1007/978-3-319-69035-3_12

Bank Branch Network Optimization Based on Customers Geospatial Profiles

Oleg Zaikin$^{(\boxtimes)}$ (iD), Anton Petukhov (iD), and Klavdiya Bochenina (iD)

ITMO University, Saint Petersburg, Russia
`zaikin.icc@gmail.com`

Abstract. In this study, the bank branch network optimization problem is considered. The problem consists in choosing several branches for closure based on the overall expected level of dissatisfaction of bank customers with the location of remaining branches. This problem is considered as a black-box optimization problem. We propose a new algorithm for determining dissatisfaction of customers, based on their geospatial profiles. Namely, the following geospatial metrics are used for this purpose: Loyalty and Diversity. Also, a method for comparison of algorithms aimed at solving the mentioned problem is proposed. In this method, data on really dissatisfied customers is employed. Using the method, the proposed algorithm was compared with its competitor on a data set from one of the largest regional banks in Russia. It turned out, that the new algorithm usually shows better accuracy.

Keywords: Branch network optimization · Branch closures · Spatial accessibility · Geospatial profile · Banking

1 Introduction

The problem of bank branch network optimization is usually considered in the following formulation: given a bank branch network, it is required to close a fixed number of branches to reduce the operational costs. Since this problem is very important and relevant, it has been widely studied during the last two decades. In particular, the problem was solved in application to bank branch networks in New Zealand [4], USA [7], Germany [5], and Russia [8].

In [3,6] it was shown that it is possible to reconstruct patterns of customers' behaviour and then predict their future actions using the history of bank transactions. In particular, in [6] two features were proposed: Loyalty and Diversity. The former is responsible for the variety of places visited by a customer, while the latter is responsible for the devotion of a customer to certain places. High Loyalty means that a customer very frequently visits his/her favorite places. High Diversity means that a he/she usually visits many different places.

In the present paper, we propose to employ Loyalty and Diversity to solve the bank branch network optimization problem. The idea is that high Loyalty and low Diversity of a customer would likely correspond to his/her dissatisfaction

© Springer Nature Switzerland AG 2019
H. Panetto et al. (Eds.): OTM 2019, LNCS 11877, pp. 201–208, 2019.
https://doi.org/10.1007/978-3-030-33246-4_13

with the closure of a branch that was frequently visited by him/her. On the other hand, low Loyalty and high Diversity of a customer would likely correspond to the opposite situation. We implemented the proposed approach and successfully applied it to a branch network of a large Russian regional bank. This approach is the main contribution of the present paper.

The outline of the paper is as follows. In the next section, the Loyalty and Diversity features are described. In Sect. 3, a new algorithm for determining dissatisfaction of customers is proposed that is based on the usage of Loyalty and Diversity. Also, it us proposed how such algorithms can be compared. Section 4 contains a description of the studied data set and the results of computational experiments. Finally, conclusions are drawn.

2   Loyalty and Diversity Features of Bank Customers

In [6], it was proposed to analyze bank customers' spatio-temporal behavior by the following features: *Diversity, Loyalty, Regularity*. In this section, the first two features are briefly described.

First, *bins* should be defined. In [6], four different definitions were proposed. In the present study, we use the *Spatial-Grid* definition: *bin* is a square with a side of 0.1 decimal degree units. Suppose that a grid structure of B bins is constructed within a city.

Diversity shows how equitably a customer spreads his/her bank transactions over various bins. Let p_{ij} denote the fraction of transactions that fall within bin j for customer i. The Diversity of customer c_i is then calculated as the normalized entropy of all transactions counted in all B bins with P of such bins being non-empty.

$$D(c_i) = \frac{-\sum_{j=1}^{B} p_{ij} \log p_{ij}}{\log P}. \tag{1}$$

The resulting values lie in the interval $[0, 1]$ with the larger numbers meaning higher spatial diversity. The normalization by $\log P$ in (1) is required to quantify the relative spread across bins. High spatial diversity of a customer means that he/she spreads transactions almost equitably across different locations.

Loyalty characterizes the fraction of bank transactions that occur in most frequently used bins. Let f_i denote the fraction of all transactions of customer i that occur in the top 3 (following [6]) most frequently used bins. The Loyalty of customer c_i is then calculated as follows:

$$L(c_i) = \frac{f_i}{\sum_{j=1}^{B} p_{ij}}. \tag{2}$$

The resulting values are also in the interval $[0, 1]$, with the larger numbers meaning higher spatial loyalty. High spatial loyalty of a customer means that he/she usually makes transactions within top 3 of the visited locations.

In the following section, it is proposed how Diversity and Loyalty can be useful for solving the bank branches optimization problem.

3   Using Loyalty and Diversity Features for Optimizing a Bank Branch Network

A bank with branch network of size M within a city is considered. Each of $b_1, \ldots, b_M$ branches is represented by two geo-coordinates. The bank has N customers $c_1, \ldots, c_N$, each of which is described with the following attributes: (i) place of living; (ii) place of work; (iii) visits to branches; (iv) transactions performed by a debit card. Transactions have the field "Address", and one can extract from this field geo-coordinates of a location where purchase was made.

Suppose that a bank decided to close $K << M$ branches for optimizing the expenses. The problem is to find K branches which closure leads to the lowest potential dissatisfaction of the bank's customers. In [8], this problem was considered as a problem of minimizing the number of potentially dissatisfied customers according to the spatial accessibility of the remaining branches. In particular, distances between customers' points of interest (home, work, payment clusters) and branches were taken into account. This function was minimized over the set of all possible combinations of K branches. A local search algorithm, a greedy algorithm, and their combination were used to perform the minimization.

In our earlier paper [8], customers' spatio-temporal features were not taken into account, while this would lead to more precise solution of the problem. In this section, we propose two new objective functions that are based on the Loyalty and Diversity features (see Sect. 2). These functions are described in Sect. 3.1. In Sect. 3.2, it is proposed how arbitrary objective functions aimed at solving the considered problem can be compared.

3.1   Objective Functions Based on Diversity and Loyalty

According to [8], the dissatisfaction score of a customer is equal to 1 if the distance to the closest branch is increased after branches closure, and 0 otherwise. The distance between a customer and a branch is the minimum distance between his/her points of interest (place of living, place of work, payment centers) and the branch. The objective function's value for a given set of branches is a summation of dissatisfaction scores of customers that visited at least one of the given K branches quite frequent. Hereinafter at least 2 visits of a customer within the last year are meant by the "quiet frequent visiting". Further we refer to the described objective function as F.

We propose two new objective functions, G and H, for solving the same problem. In both of them the dissatisfaction score of customer c_i is calculated using (1) and (2) as follows:

$$S(c_i) = \frac{L(c_i) - D(c_i) + 1}{2} \tag{3}$$

The resulting values of S lie in the interval $[0, 1]$, with the larger numbers meaning that a customer would more likely be dissatisfied. The intuition is that the higher Loyalty (and the lower Diversity), the more likely a customer would be dissatisfied with the closure of branches, which were frequently visited by him/her. On the other hand, low Loyalty and high Diversity of a customer would likely correspond to the opposite situation.

Suppose that the following data is given: a set of K branches $b_1, \ldots, b_K$; a set of T customers $c_1, \ldots, c_T$, each of which visited at least one of these K branches quite frequent; customers' transactions. Value of the objective function G is a summation of the dissatisfaction scores of all T customers:

$$G(b_1, \ldots, b_k) = \sum_{i=1}^{T} S(c_i). \tag{4}$$

The objective function H is also a summation of customers' dissatisfaction scores, calculated according to (3). The difference is that in H another set of customers is used. First, a set of T customers $c_1, \ldots, c_T$ that visited at least one of K branches quite frequent is formed. Second, their accessibility-based dissatisfaction scores are calculated (see the description of the function F above). Then, those of T customers that are marked as dissatisfied are taken, and for them a value of the function H is calculated. The idea is that we combine two approaches – as a result, we take into account both spatial accessibility of a branch network and spatio-temporal features of customers.

The objective functions G and H can be minimized by the same optimization algorithms, that were used in [8] for minimizing F.

3.2 On the Comparison of Two Objective Functions

We propose how the accuracy of two objective functions aimed at solving the bank branches optimization problem can be compared. Suppose that a set of K bank branches is closed, and we have a set of customers that visited at least one of them quite frequent. Following [2], a customer from this set is considered dissatisfied, if he/she has not performed any transactions within 3 months after the closure. Using this idea, the amount of really dissatisfied customers can be easily calculated for an arbitrary set of K branches.

Suppose that for a set of combinations of branches (say, a set of all possible combinations of K branches) the following three sets of values are known: the amount of really dissatisfied customers and values of two objective functions aimed at estimating dissatisfaction scores. To compare how the values of these objective functions correspond to the realty, they should be scaled. The simplest method of scaling is known as *min-max scaling* or *min-max normalization* (see, e.g., [1]). It consists in scaling the range of values using the following formula:

$$x' = \frac{x - min(x)}{max(x) - min(x)}. \tag{5}$$

For all three sets of values, the scaling is performed using formula (5). Then two objective functions are compared by the summation of residuals between their scaled values and the real amount of dissatisfied customers. The objective function with lower value of the summation is considered better.

4   Computational Experiments

The proposed objective functions G and H (see Sect. 3) were applied to optimize a bank branch network. A data set from one of the largest regional banks in Russia was considered. This set contains the following data: 58 bank branches; about 800 thousand customers; about 3 million customers' visits; about 150 billion of customers' transactions. Customers visits and transactions from May 2017 to January 2019 (21 months in total) were available in the data set.

Four closed branches were analyzed. Hereinafter they are called Branch 1, Branch 2, Branch 3, and Branch 4 respectively. The first two branches were closed in May 2018, the others were closed in October 2018. For each of these branches, customers visiting it at least twice during the last year before the closure were considered. Values of Loyalty and Diversity were employed to calculate dissatisfaction scores for the considered four closed branches and their combinations. Finally, the accuracy of two proposed objective functions is compared with the previously published function F using the method, proposed in Sect. 3.2.

First, Loyalty and Diversity were calculated for all customers from the data set. In Figs. 1 and 2, one can see distributions of probability density function of customers' average transaction amounts. Customers were split by quartiles corresponding to their values of Diversity and Loyalty. It turned out, that there are many customers with Loyalty equal to 0, so they formed an additional group.

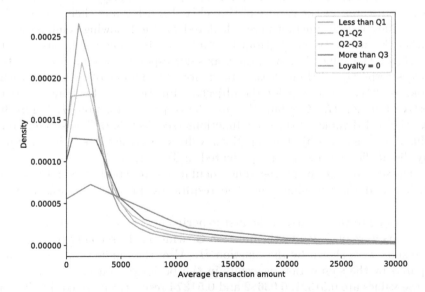

Fig. 1. Comparison of different classes of customers (split by values of Loyalty).

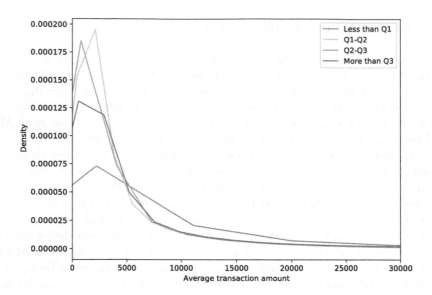

Fig. 2. Comparison of different classes of customers (split by values of Diversity).

Then, two computational experiments were performed. In the first one, the objective functions F, G and H (see Sect. 3) were employed to calculate dissatisfaction scores for the closure of Branch 1, Branch 2 and their combination. Three values of each function were calculated for the following combinations of branches: Branch 1; Branch 2; Branch 1 and Branch 2. The results are depicted in Fig. 3(a). The values 1, 2, 3 on the x-axis correspond to the mentioned sets of branches respectively. Here "Real" stands for the amount of really dissatisfied customers, "Access" stands for the objective function F, "LyalDiv" – for the objective function G, "Combined" – for the objective function H. Figure 3(b) shows the scaled values of the same functions (see Sect. 3.2). The summation of residuals between the objective functions' values and true values (the amount of really dissatisfied customers) are presented in Table 1.

In the second experiment, the same calculations were performed for Branch 3, Branch 4 and their combination. The results are presented in Fig. 4 and in Table 1.

According to the results, in the first experiment (i.e. for the first closure) the best results were obtained by the function G, while in the second experiment the best results were shown by the function H. Also, the studied functions can be compared by the summation of results in the both experiments. For F, G and H these values are 0.51321, 0.03682 and 0.51374 respectively. According to this, G showed the best results on average.

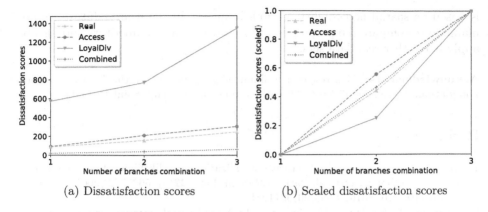

(a) Dissatisfaction scores   (b) Scaled dissatisfaction scores

Fig. 3. Dissatisfaction scores for the first set of closed branches

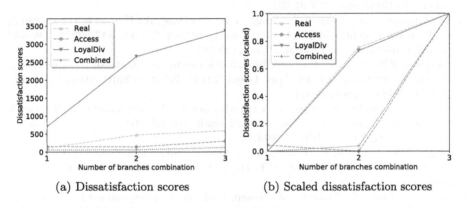

(a) Dissatisfaction scores   (b) Scaled dissatisfaction scores

Fig. 4. Dissatisfaction scores for the second set of closed branches

Table 1. Summation of residuals between values of objective functions and true values. The best result for each closure is marked with bold.

Function	Residual, first closure	Residual, second closure
F	0.013	0.5716
G	0.0363	**0.0005**
H	**0.0005**	0.5132

5   Conclusions

In the present study, it was proposed to use spatio-temporal features of bank customers in application to the bank branch network optimization problem. Also, it was proposed how two arbitrary functions aimed at calculating dissatisfaction scores can be compared. According to the computational results on a real data set, both proposed functions showed better accuracy than their competitor that is based on spatial accessibility of bank branches. In the nearest future we are planning to compare the proposed approach with other competitors and also to apply it to other real data sets.

Acknowledgments. This research is financially supported by the Russian Science Foundation, Agreement 17-71-30029 with co-financing of Bank Saint Petersburg.

References

1. Aksoy, S., Haralick, R.M.: Feature normalization and likelihood-based similarity measures for image retrieval. Pattern Recogn. Lett. **22**(5), 563–582 (2001). https://doi.org/10.1016/S0167-8655(00)00112-4
2. Haenlein, M., Kaplan, A.M., Beeser, A.J.: A model to determine customer lifetime value in a retail banking context. Eur. Manag. J. **25**(3), 221–234 (2007). https://doi.org/10.1016/j.emj.2007.01.004
3. de Montjoye, Y.A., Radaelli, L., Singh, V.K., Pentland, A.: Unique in the shopping mall: on the reidentifiability of credit card metadata. Science **347**(6221), 536–539 (2015). https://doi.org/10.1126/science.1256297
4. Morrison, P.S., Whitsed, R.: Bank branch closures in New Zealand: the application of a spatial interaction model. Appl. Geogr. **21**(4), 301–330 (2001). https://doi.org/10.1016/S0143-6228(01)00014-5
5. Schneider, S., Seifert, F., Sunyaev, A.: Market potential analysis and branch network planning: application in a german retail bank. HICSS **2014**, 1122–1131 (2014). https://doi.org/10.1109/HICSS.2014.145
6. Singh, V.K., Bozkaya, B., Pentland, A.: Money walks: implicit mobility behavior and financial well-being. PLoS ONE **10**(8), 1–17 (2015). https://doi.org/10.1371/journal.pone.0136628
7. Wang, Q., Batta, R., Bhadury, J., Rump, C.M.: Budget constrained location problem with opening and closing of facilities. Comput. Oper. Res. **30**(13), 2047–2069 (2003). https://doi.org/10.1016/S0305-0548(02)00123-5
8. Zaikin, O., Derevitskii, I., Bochenina, K., Holyst, J.: Optimizing spatial accessibility of company branches network with constraints. In: Rodrigues, J.M.F., Cardoso, P.J.S., Monteiro, J., Lam, R., Krzhizhanovskaya, V.V., Lees, M.H., Dongarra, J.J., Sloot, P.M.A. (eds.) ICCS 2019. LNCS, vol. 11537, pp. 332–345. Springer, Cham (2019). https://doi.org/10.1007/978-3-030-22741-8_24

Using Maps for Interlinking Geospatial Linked Data

Dieter Roosens[1], Kris McGlinn[2], and Christophe Debruyne[1,2](✉) iD

[1] WISE Lab, Vrije Universiteit Brussel, Brussels, Belgium
{dieter.roosens,christophe.debruyne}@vub.be
[2] ADAPT Centre, Trinity College Dublin, Dublin, Ireland
kris.mcglinn@adaptcentre.ie

Abstract. The creation of interlinks between Linked Data datasets is key to the creation of a global database. One can create such interlinks in various ways: manually, semi-automatically, and automatically. While quite a few tools exist to facilitate this process in a (semi-)automatic manner, often with support for geospatial data. It is not uncommon that interlinks need to be created manually, e.g., when interlinks need to be authoritative. In this study, we focus on the manual interlinking of geospatial data using maps. The State-of-the-Art uses maps to facilitate the search and visualization of such data. Our contribution is to investigate whether maps are useful for the creation of interlinks. We designed and developed such a tool and set up an experiment in which 16 participants used the tool to create links between different Linked Data datasets. We not only describe the tool but also analyze the data we have gathered. The data suggests the creation of these interlinks from these maps is a viable approach. The data also indicate that people had a harder time dealing with Linked Data principles (e.g., content negotiation) than with the creation of interlinks.

Keywords: Linked Data interlinking · Maps · Geospatial Linked Data

1 Introduction

Linked Data [1] is a set of best practices and guidelines to publish and interlink data on the Web. Those practices and guidelines prescribe how to cleverly combine several standardized technologies: the Resource Description Framework[1] (RDF) to describe things; URIs to identify those things and, in particular, HTTP URIs to retrieve these descriptions over the Web; and content-negotiation to retrieve the desired format (HTML for users and RDF for machines). We can observe the importance of geospatial data by the vast amount of geographic or geospatial datasets available on the Linked Data Web. The Linked Open Data cloud initiative tries to visualize the relations between such datasets that are both open and meet the inclusion criteria. While the image arguably only scratches the surface of the Linked Data available on the Web, it does indicate the importance of the datasets that contain geospatial information.

---

[1] https://www.w3.org/RDF/.

© Springer Nature Switzerland AG 2019
H. Panetto et al. (Eds.): OTM 2019, LNCS 11877, pp. 209–226, 2019.
https://doi.org/10.1007/978-3-030-33246-4_14

Key to the creation of a Linked Data Web is the creation of interlinks between resources both within and across Linked Data datasets. Moreover, as most datasets also have a geospatial dimension that is either explicit or implicit, it comes as no surprise that "location" is a convenient way for aligning and combining different datasets [21].

For the creation of interlinks, methods were proposed to create such Linked Data interlinks automatically. These methods often rely on subject matter experts to *validate* links. But what if interlinks have to be created manually by subject matter experts? Manual interlinking is essential when such interlinks need be authoritative. The study reported in [13] surveyed subject matter experts in the library field, and it indicated that there were challenges in tooling for creating authoritative interlinks. We believe that these challenges exist for other fields as well.

Geospatial information lends itself naturally to maps. Within the Semantic Web community, initiatives often limit the use of maps to displaying information or querying. To the best of our knowledge, no study has looked into the use of maps for the creation of links. As we were surprised by the lack of such tooling, we aim to answer the following question in this paper: "Can maps be used to create and manage interlinks of geospatial data on the Linked Data web?"

The remainder of this paper is organized as follows: Sect. 2 provides an overview of the related work; Sect. 3 introduces our requirements and elaborates how on the design and development of our tool; Sect. 4 describes the experiment we devised to evaluate our tool, the data we gathered, and an analysis of the data; and Sect. 5 concludes our paper.

2 Related Work

The State-of-the-Art often focusses on the creation of interlinks in a (semi-)automatic manner. In [20], the authors reported on declaring SILK rules [5] for generating interlinks between an Irish place names dataset and DBpedia [9]. Approaches such as SILK allow one to configure thresholds to classify pairs of entities as 'accepted', 'rejected', or 'to be validated'. The LIMES [15] interlinking platform, on the other hand, adopted EAGLE [16] and WOMBAT [23] to combine machine learning with geospatial functions for discovering interlinks. Others, such as [6], proposed semi-supervised approached in which users can guide the generation of rules that will generate the interlinks. While these approaches are valuable for the creation of a Linked Data Web, some interlinks need to be created manually [13]. While [13] reported on the challenges for authoritative Linked Data interlinking, we noticed that the state-of-the-art has not yet looked at the use of maps for creating interlinks between datasets that have a geospatial dimension. Within the Semantic Web community, however, the use of maps is often limited to displaying information or querying. Examples include:

– YASGUI [19] is a suite of tools that constitute a SPARQL editor and is entirely written in JavaScript. YASGUI has a plugin for displaying SPARQL query results on a map. Polygons and points on a map can be provided a label and a color if users follow a particular variable naming convention.

- Strabon [8] is a triplestore with support for GeoSPARQL^2 and allows the results of a GeoSPARQL query to be rendered on a map.
- FACETE [24] is a faceted browser for geospatial information. Unlike SPARQL in which one has to formulate a query, one is "guided" in searching for specific resources by constraining the selection criteria with so-called "facets". Each facet narrows down the results. Tools such as FACETE comprehend the facets by providing the right widgets depending on a facet's type –input validation for numbers, date and time pickers for `xsd:dateTime`,... Again, FACETE only uses map to display and engage with the results.
- GVIZ [11] is a tool that allows one to query GeoSPARQL triplestores by drawing search areas on a map. A user can achieve this by drawing the area as a polygon on a map. Their tool then translates that polygon into a GeoSPARQL query using Well-Known Text (WKT)^3 for representing that area.

The GeoKnow project was funded by the EU FP7 Programme and ran from 2013 to 2015. The project aimed to provide a suite of solutions to integrate and enrich external datasets with geospatial data using semantic technologies called the GeoKnow workbench [2]. The workbench provided support for the whole data lifecycle of projects involving geospatial datasets. This workbench integrated FACETE, which we have mentioned before, but also includes tools for transforming non-RDF into RDF with TripleGeo [18], automatic integration with LIMES [15], and discovery of implicit geospatial information with DEER [22]. The workbench does not, to the best of our knowledge, use maps to drive the interlinking process.

3   Design and Development

We observed from the State-of-the-Art that maps are mostly used to display results. Other studies have shown that the creation of Linked Data interlinks not always an automatic process and that appropriate tooling is lacking [13]. We wondered whether subject matter experts (e.g., historians, librarians, and archivists) could use maps for the creation of interlinks. Those subject matter experts will often seek resources to link and know what to look for. Our proposed solution should thus aid subject matter experts in creating Linked Data datasets. To design and develop a tool allowing one to create Linked Data interlinks on a map, we formulated the following requirements:

1. Search for geospatial resources in a Linked Data dataset;
2. Display the results on a map;
3. Engage with the resources on the map for the creation of interlinks;
4. Manage the created interlinks;
5. Keep track of provenance information.

---

^{2} https://www.opengeospatial.org/standards/geosparql, last accessed June 2019. GeoSPARQL is a standardized geospatial extension of the SPARQL query language. The extension consists of a vocabulary, geospatial functions, and query transformation rules to related predicates to geospatial functions.

^{3} https://en.wikipedia.org/wiki/Well-known_text_representation_of_geometry, last accessed June 2019.

Requirements 2, 3, and 4 are key to our study. The first requirement is necessary for the creation of an experiment as we need to simulate a realistic workflow; subject matter experts will first look for the resources that they want to relate with other datasets. The use of SPARQL to search for resources is indeed a possibility but would require users to know the language. Instead, we will adopt a suitable technique for searching resources in a dataset.

In [25], the authors stated that provenance information "provides information about [a resource's] origin, such as who created it, when it was modified, or how it was created." This type of information is useful to assess the trustworthiness of an interlink (e.g., by determining who has created an interlink, and why). The last requirement is essential to consider the integration of our tool into broader interlinking or governance frameworks.

As for the types of geospatial Linked Data datasets we want to support, we limit ourselves to such datasets that provide a SPARQL endpoint and use GeoSPARQL in combination with WKT to represent the geographic features and geometries. We can easily ingest a geospatial Linked Data dataset in their own (local) triplestore and endpoint if one wishes to avail of a dataset that has no (reliable) SPARQL endpoint. As for GeoSPARQL, we limit ourselves to GeoSPARQL to assess the viability of our approach. If viable, we will look into the other vocabularies for representing coordinates and geometries. GeoSPARQL also prescribes support for Geographic Markup Language (GML)[4] to represent geometries, but we will only consider incorporating GML once the approach is shown to be viable.

3.1   Searching for Geospatial Resources

While our study focuses on the use of maps for interlinking geospatial data on the Linked Data Web, a user would start by looking for the resources they want to interlink. A user can avail of GeoSPARQL and use tools such as YASGUI [19] or even adopt Faceted Search for RDF datasets with, for instance, Facete [24] and SemFacet [7]. We argue that it will be unlikely for subject matter experts to use SPARQL and deemed the adoption of faceted browsing more appropriate.

We initially wanted to reuse codebases of existing tools but were faced with a couple of challenges. Facete, for instance, was built for geospatial information, but we were unable to compile and run both versions of the tool.[5,6] Both versions required a convoluted setup using different programming languages and servers, and both – given the last commits were, at the time of writing, over four years ago – relied on deprecated libraries that were difficult to find or difficult to get working. SemFacet's codebase, referenced from their website, was unavailable.[7] We did find some branches hosted by others but were unable to run the project without problems.

---

[4] https://www.opengeospatial.org/standards/gml, last accessed July 2019.
[5] https://github.com/GeoKnow/Facete, last accessed June 2019.
[6] https://github.com/GeoKnow/Facete2, last accessed June 2019.
[7] http://www.cs.ox.ac.uk/isg/tools/SemFacet/, last accessed June 2019.

Given that the means for searching was subordinate to the use of maps for creating links, we decided to design and develop a minimalistic faceted browser solely for the evaluation (see Fig. 1). In this browser, there are two facets: type-facets based on rdf:type and property-facets (based on the other properties of the Linked Data dataset.

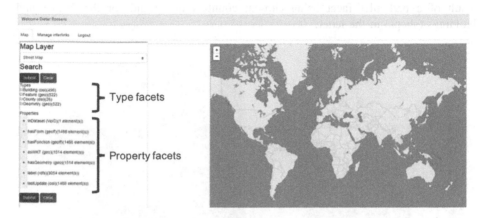

Fig. 1. Faceted browser built for the experiment

Property-facets are facets for property-value pairs, which are grouped by the property. For each selected facet, there is a new triple pattern added to the SPARQL query of the Linked Data dataset. Type-facets result in a triple pattern of the form ?this rdf:type *x* where *x* is the URI of the selected type. Property-facets result in a triple pattern of the form ?this *y* *z* where *y* is the URI of the predicate and *z* the value. The query furthermore retrieves:

1. An optional graph pattern, which looks for the geometries of ?this:

   OPTIONAL {?this geo:hasGeometry [geo:asWKT ?wkt]}

   We have chosen to make this graph pattern optional as the system would have otherwise only sought resources with a geometry. This approach furthermore allows us to inform of resources that meet all criteria but do not have a geometry. For this study, we have chosen to limit ourselves to GeoSPARQL.

2. Labels, by looking for triples using the rdfs:label, predicate, with a preference for English labels, followed by default and any other labels. We will use those labels for the interface elements of Requirements 2 and 3.

3.2 Displaying Information on a Map

Before one can engage with resources on a map, they need to be displayed. To this end, we drew inspiration from YASGUI [19]. YASGUI uses a particular variable naming convention to customize colors and add labels to the geometries (e.g., points and polygons). It is up to the person writing the query to manage those variable names. We did appreciate the visuals provided by the Leaflet[8] that YASGUI adopted. Since we have adopted GeoSPARQL and focus on WKT representations of geometries, we need to use Wicket[9] to translate WKT into a JSON representation supported by Leaflet. Figure 2 shows how multi-polygons and points are displayed on the map. Both are the result of a particular facet being chosen; counties in Ireland for the former and buildings (shops) in the latter.

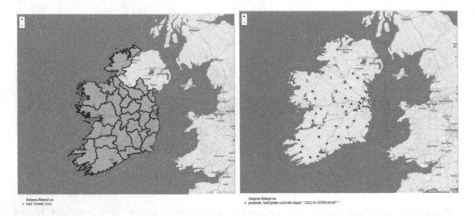

Fig. 2. Supporting the visualization of (multi)-polygons and point geometries.

3.3   Creating and Managing Interlinks

One creates interlinks by clicking on geometries, which result in a pop-up. The design of the popup was driven by ConcurTaskTrees [17]. ConcurTaskTrees allow one to model the tasks of users and systems. Those models can be used to drive the design of a user interface [14]. The algorithm outlined by [14] was used to create a mock-up, which was subsequently implemented (see Fig. 3). For managing and downloading the created interlinks, we created a separate tab displaying the information in a tabular manner. The table contains information on the triple constituting the interlink, the user, and the time it was created. Interlinks are stored in a local triplestore. Details on how we store the interlinks will be provided in Sect. 2.4.

---

[8] https://leafletjs.com/, last accessed June 2019.
[9] http://arthur-e.github.io/Wicket/, last accessed June 2019.

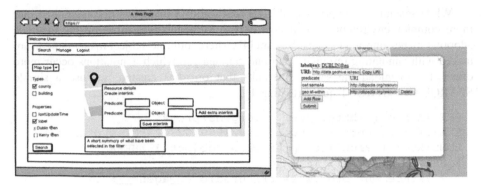

Fig. 3. From mock-up to implementation. Clicking on a polygon allows one to create interlinks

3.4 Knowledge Organization and Provenance

To facilitate storing interlinks and their metadata, we have chosen to save, for each interlink, the interlink as a reified RDF statement connected to its metadata in a separate named graph. Figure 4 depicts an example of such a reified RDF statement in a graph. We also avail of the PROV-O[10] ontology, a W3C Recommendation for capturing provenance information. We thus have a resource that is both an RDF statement and an instance of `prov:Entity`, and represent its creation, creator, and so forth using PROV-O.

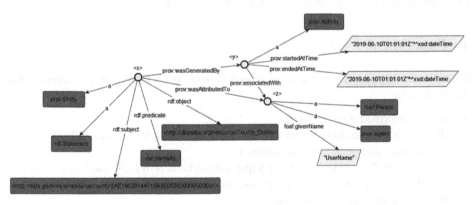

Fig. 4. Using reified RDF statements to treat interlinks as instances of `prov:Entity`. The RDF statement, the activity, and person are all identified by a URI, though we used x, y, and z for brevity.

---

[10] https://www.w3.org/TR/prov-o/, last accessed June 2019.

While seemingly complicated, this approach allows our tool to be integrated into more complex environments. Our approach to knowledge-organization fits methods adopting niche-sourcing (such as DaCura [4]) where multiple subject matter experts are tasked with annotating resources, and one can analyze which annotations occur more often. To download the set of interlinks that one has created, we use a simple SPARQL CONSTRUCT query (Listing 1).

```
PREFIX prov: <http://www.w3.org/ns/prov#>
PREFIX rdf: <http://www.w3.org/1999/02/22-rdf-syntax-ns#>
CONSTRUCT { ?subject ?predicate ?object } WHERE {
   GRAPH ?g {
      ?statement prov:wasAttributedTo <__agent__> .
      ?statement rdf:subject ?subject ;
                 rdf:object ?object ;
                 rdf:predicate ?predicate . } }
```

Listing 1. A SPARQL CONSTRUCT query to create a set of interlinks created by a particular user. Note that "__agent__" is replaced by the URI of the user.

3.5 Implementation

The prototype is available on GitHub.[11] It is a Java Web application and uses Apache Jena ARQ for communicating with the SPARQL endpoint of the Linked Data dataset to be linked and uses Apache Jena Fuseki for storing the interlinks.[12]

4 Experiment

To evaluate our approach, we devised an experiment. We recruited 16 participants and asked them to:

1. sign an informed consent form;
2. fill in a pre-questionnaire where they assessed their prior knowledge in Linked Data technologies and geospatial information;
3. look at a YouTube video providing a quick introduction to RDF and Linked Data[13];
4. consult at any time slides summarizing important points of the video as well as annotated screenshots of the tool;
5. perform the tasks in a think-aloud manner; and
6. fill in a post-questionnaire to assess the tool.

---

[11] https://github.com/dieterroosens/LinkedDataApplication.

[12] https://jena.apache.org/, last accessed June 2019.

[13] https://www.youtube.com/watch?v=zeYfT1cNKQg, until 5'45".

We have chosen to adopt the GeoHive [3] dataset for the experiment, as this dataset has not yet been included in the Linked Open Data cloud and contains very few interlinks to other Linked Data. As GeoHive has decided not to provide a SPARQL endpoint, we created a local endpoint that included – for the sake of the experiment – boundary information of Ireland's counties and some metadata of shops (part of [12]).

The eight tasks related to the tool were (note we provide the written instructions given to the participants for only a couple of the tasks):

1. To state that County Dublin is `owl:sameAs` its resource in DBpedia [16] and that County Dublin is `geo:sf-within dbpedia:Ireland`. We provided the URIs for both Dublin and Ireland in the document. I.e., participants could copy the URIs. We gave participants almost step-by-step instructions on how to achieve this task. The task was written as follows:
   (1) Go to the screen "Map" and search for the county with label "Dublin"
   (2) Select the element on the map and interlink it with "geo:sf-within" to the URI http://dbpedia.org/resource/Dublin
   (3) Do the same, but now with the predicate "owl:sameAs" and the URI http://dbpedia.org/resource/County_Dublin
2. To state that County Donegal is `owl:sameAs` as its corresponding resource in DBpedia, which participants had to look up. Now, participants were tasked with looking up County Donegal in DBpedia and copying it URI.
3. Given the URI for `dbpedia:Wicklow_Mountains`, to identify in which county they reside and create that relationship. Here, the trick was to look for the appropriate relation `geo:sf-contains`. It was up to the participant to identify the correct relation. The interface provided a list of predicates, but participants were able to provide their own.
4. To create interlinks within our dataset. Identify the counties that border cork and create one `geo:sf-touches` relations. It was up to the participant to identify the correct relation. The interface provided a list of predicates, but participants were able to provide their own. The task was written as follows:
   (1) Select all resources of the type County
   (2) Identify the counties that touch the border of County Cork
   (3) Create a relationship (interlink) between Cork and those counties. There are 2 possibilities: From Cork to that county, or From that county to Cork. It is not necessary to declare both for a county x and Cork, but we encourage you to try both approaches for different counties.

5. To look for the highest mountain on the map, which requires switching layers. Then find the DBpedia resource representing that mountain and create the relationship. We provided a hint that the mountain was 1039 m high.
6. To look for a specific shop and stating that its location is County Dublin using the representation of County Dublin in GeoNames[14]. Here, the participant had to use the facets to look for that shop. The task was written as follows:
   (1) Select the shop that has been last updated on "2014-01-16T13:14:52"
   (2) Interlink the shop with the county it is located in. Use the URI of the county that you can find in GeoName.
7. To look at the interlinks that the participant has created and correct any mistakes. We introduced one incorrect interlink which participants had to spot.
8. To download the interlinks.

The difficulty of the tasks increases from 1 to 6. We started by giving participants clear instructions and even the URIs to copy. From the second task onwards, participants had to look for the appropriate resources themselves. From the third task onwards, participants had to choose the predicate. Tasks 1 to 6 were related to searching for resources, displaying those resources, and interlinking resources. They thus correspond with the first three requirements. Tasks 7 and 8 were related to the fourth requirement, managing the created interlinks. We did not formulate tasks for using the provenance information, as that would have required more in-depth knowledge of SPARQL and PROV-O and is outside the scope of this study–creating interlinks from a map. The provenance graphs were used to display information for Task 7.

4.1 Prior Knowledge

Before the experiment, participants were asked to assess their knowledge on the Web Ontology Language (OWL), Resource Description Framework (RDF), the Terse Triple Language (TTL), and geospatial information (GEO) in "general". Participants were able to indicate their level of familiarity with 'none' (0), 'low' (1), 'medium' (2), and 'high' (3). Table 1 not only provides an overview of the answers, but we also computed a total for future analysis. From this table, we can conclude that only 4 of the 16 participants deemed themselves knowledgeable in these technologies (a score of 2 or more for at least one of the four technologies).

---

[14] https://www.geonames.org/, last accessed July 2019.

Table 1. Summary of the pre-questionnaire in which participants assessed their knowledge of the web Ontology Language, Resource Description Framework, the Terse Triple Language, and Geospatial information. Values range from 0 (none) to 3 (high).

Participant	OWL	RDF	TTL	GEO	Total
1	0	0	0	0	0
2	0	0	0	0	0
3	0	0	0	1	1
4	0	0	0	0	0
5	0	0	0	0	0
6	0	0	0	0	0
7	0	0	0	0	0
8	0	0	0	0	0
9	0	0	0	0	0
10	2	3	3	1	9
11	2	3	3	2	10
12	3	3	3	2	11
13	2	1	1	1	5
14	0	0	0	0	0
15	0	0	0	0	0
16	0	0	0	0	0

4.2   On Task Performance

All participants managed to download the interlinks, which were used to compare their results with that of a gold standard –the expected output. There were multiple correct answers for Task 4, so we manually checked those. When comparing the interlinks with the expected results, we noticed a couple of things:

– Many participants were unaware of the content-negotiation mechanism used by Linked Data datasets. Since participants were given the URI for the first interlink, many were able to execute the first task successfully. In other tasks where they had to look for DBpedia resources themselves, however, they looked for the resources in a browser and then copied the resource's page URI instead of the resource's URI.
– Only one participant was able to find the resource representing County Dublin in the GeoNames. The participant – in some capacity involved in the OSi projects – did state during the think-aloud experiment that the question was "tricky", and they knew how to find the resource. The other participants choose another URI, often referring to the city of Dublin.
– Some participants did not create interlinks within the dataset (Task 4) or an interlink with GeoNames (Task 6) and instead continued creating interlinks with DBpedia. We deem that this was due to haste, i.e., they read over those requirements.

Given the first two observations, we had decided to create a so-called "silver standard" in which we gave partial credit when the chosen URIs were either pointing to the page rather than the resource or when the city of Dublin was selected from

GeoNames. From Table 2, it is clear that participants had trouble with Tasks 2 and 6. The silver standard does provide a more nuanced view of the results. Most participants had difficulty with DBpedia's content negotiation (Task 2), and some participants were able to choose and link to a resource with the label "Dublin" in GeoNames (Task 6). While none of the participants were able to complete all tasks correctly, we believe that these errors were not due to the tool, but a lack of experience with Linked Data principles and the datasets we have adopted.

Table 2. Results of the participants' performance.

Participant	w.r.t. Gold Standard									w.r.t. Silver Standard								
	Task 1	Task 2	Task 3	Task 4	Task 5	Task 6	Task 7	Task 8	Percentage	Task 1	Task 2	Task 3	Task 4	Task 5	Task 6	Task 7	Task 8	Percentage
1	1.00	0.00	1.00	1.00	0.00	0.00	1.00	1.00	62.50	1.00	0.50	1.00	1.00	0.50	0.00	1.00	1.00	75.00
2	1.00	0.00	1.00	1.00	0.00	0.00	1.00	1.00	62.50	1.00	0.50	1.00	1.00	0.50	0.00	1.00	1.00	75.00
3	1.00	0.00	0.00	1.00	1.00	0.00	1.00	1.00	62.50	1.00	0.50	0.00	1.00	1.00	0.50	1.00	1.00	75.00
4	1.00	0.00	1.00	0.75	1.00	0.00	1.00	1.00	71.88	1.00	0.50	1.00	0.75	1.00	0.00	1.00	1.00	78.13
5	1.00	0.00	1.00	0.25	1.00	0.00	1.00	1.00	65.63	1.00	0.50	1.00	0.25	1.00	0.00	1.00	1.00	65.63
6	1.00	1.00	1.00	1.00	1.00	0.00	1.00	1.00	87.50	1.00	1.00	1.00	1.00	1.00	0.00	1.00	1.00	87.50
7	0.50	1.00	1.00	0.75	1.00	0.00	1.00	1.00	78.13	0.50	1.00	1.00	0.75	1.00	0.00	1.00	1.00	78.13
8	1.00	1.00	0.00	0.75	1.00	0.00	1.00	1.00	71.88	1.00	1.00	0.00	0.75	1.00	0.00	1.00	1.00	71.88
9	1.00	0.00	1.00	1.00	1.00	0.00	1.00	1.00	75.00	1.00	0.00	1.00	1.00	1.00	0.00	1.00	1.00	75.00
10	0.50	0.00	1.00	1.00	1.00	0.00	1.00	1.00	68.75	0.50	0.50	1.00	1.00	1.00	0.50	1.00	1.00	81.25
11	1.00	0.00	0.00	1.00	0.00	0.00	1.00	1.00	50.00	1.00	0.50	0.00	1.00	0.50	0.50	1.00	1.00	68.75
12	1.00	1.00	1.00	0.00	1.00	1.00	1.00	1.00	87.50	1.00	1.00	1.00	0.00	1.00	1.00	1.00	1.00	87.50
13	1.00	0.00	1.00	1.00	1.00	0.00	0.00	1.00	62.50	1.00	0.50	1.00	1.00	1.00	0.00	0.00	1.00	68.75
14	1.00	0.00	1.00	1.00	0.00	0.00	1.00	1.00	62.50	1.00	0.50	1.00	1.00	0.50	0.50	1.00	1.00	81.25
15	1.00	0.00	1.00	1.00	1.00	1.00	1.00	1.00	87.50	1.00	0.50	1.00	1.00	1.00	1.00	1.00	1.00	93.75
16	1.00	0.00	0.00	0.50	1.00	0.00	1.00	1.00	56.25	1.00	0.50	0.00	0.50	1.00	0.50	1.00	1.00	68.75
AVG:	0.94	0.25	0.75	0.81	0.75	0.13	0.94	1.00	69.53	0.94	0.56	0.75	0.81	0.88	0.28	0.94	1.00	76.95

4.3 On the Tool's Perceived Usability

Now we look into our tool's perceived usability. We have chosen to adopt the Post-study System Usability Questionnaire (PSSUQ) [10]. The survey consists of 19 questions using an invert Likert Scale from 1 (completely agree) to 7 (completely disagree). The questions are listed in Appendix A. Unlike other usability surveys, PSSUQ assesses three aspects of a system: the system's usefulness using questions 1 to 8; the information quality using questions 9 to 15; and the interface quality using questions 16 to 18. Question 19 asks a participant about their overall satisfaction and the average of questions 1 to 19 are used to compute the overall score. Participants were also able to indicate that a question was not applicable.

The results are shown in Table 3. A box plot of these values is shown in Fig. 5. Note that values closer to 1 are more positive and that a value of 4 is "neutral". With that in mind, we notice that there are four aspects worth investigating. Questions 5 and 6 – part of System Usefulness – were related to the tool's ability to help one efficiently

Table 3. Results of the PSSUQ questionnaire

#	Q1	Q2	Q3	Q4	Q5	Q6	Q7	Q8	Q9	Q10	Q11	Q12	Q13	Q14	Q15	Q16	Q17	Q18	Q19	SysUse	InfoQual	IntQual	Overall
1	3	3	2	3	3	3	2	3	3	3	3	3	3	3	3	3	2	2	2	2.75	3.00	2.33	2.74
2	3	3	3	3	3	3	3	3	3	3	3	2	3	2	3	3	3	3	2	3.00	2.71	3.00	2.84
3	3	2	3	2	4	2	2	3	3	5	2	3	3	3	2	2	2	2	2	2.63	3.00	2.00	2.63
4	2	2	4	5	2	2	2	2	2	2	2	3	2	2	2	2	2	2	2	2.63	2.14	2.00	2.32
5	4	4	3	4	4	4	3	3	5	3	5	4	5	5	4	3	3	3	3	3.63	4.43	3.00	3.79
6	2	2	3	2	3	3	2	3	4	4	3	2	3	3	3	3	3	3	2	2.50	3.14	3.00	2.79
7	3	2	3	3	3	3	3	2	3	3	3	2	3	2	4	3	3	2	3	2.75	2.86	2.67	2.79
8	6	5	4	2	5	5	5	5	7	5	6	5	5	4	5	4	4	4	5	4.63	5.29	4.00	4.79
9	1	2	2	3	4	5	2	2		3	2	3	2	2	1	1	1	2	2	2.63	1.86	1.33	2.11
10	2	3	2	3	3	2	2	1	2	2	2	2	1	2	2	2	2	3	2	2.25	1.86	2.33	2.11
11	2	3	2	3	3	2	2	2	5	2	2	2	2	2	2	2	2	4	2	2.38	2.43	2.67	2.42
12	3	3	2	3	2	1	3	4	7	2	7	4	2	2	4	5	4		3	2.63	3.71	3.00	3.11
13	4	4	5	5	5	5	3	4	6	5	3	2	5	3	6	6	6	2	3	4.38	4.29	4.67	4.32
14	2	2	2	1	2	1	1	1		1	1	1	1	1	2	1	1	1	1	1.50	1.00	1.00	1.21
15	2	2	1	1	2	2	1	1			3	2	3	3	2	3	2		2	1.50	1.86	1.67	1.68
16	7	7	4	5	6	7	6	6	7	5	5	4	5	6	5	5	7		7	6.00	5.29	4.00	5.47
AVG	3.06	3.06	2.81	3.00	3.38	3.13	2.63	2.81	4.38	3.29	3.25	2.75	3.00	2.81	3.13	3.00	2.94	2.54	2.69	2.98	3.05	2.67	2.94
STDEV	1.57	1.39	1.05	1.26	1.20	1.67	1.31	1.42	2.45	1.67	1.65	1.06	1.37	1.28	1.41	1.41	1.65	1.29	1.45	1.16	1.26	0.99	1.13

complete the tasks and how comfortable it was doing so. Questions 9 and 10 were associated with Information Quality: error messages and instructions to recover from mistakes. Faceted browsing was not the focus of our study; we merely adopted the technique as the starting point for the interlinking tasks. Problems with the faceted browsing may have harmed the overall perceived usability and thus also the interaction with the map. We do recognize that the system lacked clear error messages and documentation.

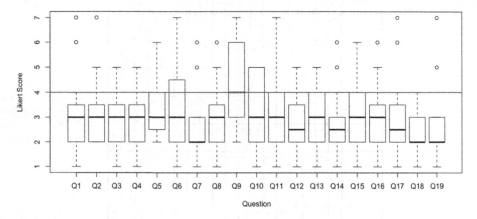

Fig. 5. Boxplot of the PSSUQ surveys

4.4 Analysis

There is a non-significant (p = 0.8) negative correlation (R = −0.068) between prior knowledge and the outcome (silver standard), from which we can conclude nothing. There were also no significant correlations between the four questions that stood out as having been problematic and task performance. If we analyze the correlations between the various PSSUQ dimensions and task performance, however, we see (from Fig. 6) that one correlation is significant (task performance vs. system usefulness with p = 0.0061) and one is almost significant (task performance vs. overall with p = 0.0019). The data thus seem to indicate that as task performance goes up, the perceived system's usefulness and overall usability are more appreciated.

If we look again at the PSSUQ in Table 3, we do notice that most values are close to 3, which is not terrific but leans towards a favorable impression. The only exception is Question 9, which has an average value of 4.38 (below 4). Three participants did not provide an opinion for that value, deeming it not applicable. Clear error messages and instructions on how to recover from errors are thus to be improved.

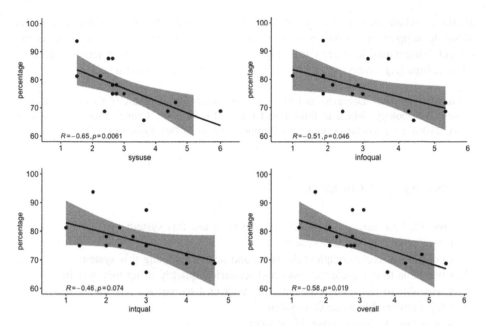

Fig. 6. Correlations between the PSSUQ dimensions and task performance according to the "silver" standard

5 Conclusions and Future Work

In this paper, we presented an approach to interlink geospatial Linked Data datasets using maps, which to the best of our knowledge has not been tried before and therefore constitutes a contribution. A second contribution is the experiment's protocol that was devised to validate the tool. From the analysis of the experiment, we can conclude that using maps for driving manual interlinking processes is a viable approach. We also noticed that participants had more trouble with certain Linked Data principles (content negotiation), which led them to create an interlink to the wrong URIs and is in itself an interesting observation.

Finally, we proposed an approach to organize and store the interlinks with provenance data using named graphs. While not validated in this study, this would provide an integration point for other initiatives in which such provenance data will be critical to assess the authoritativeness of an interlink. DaCura [4], for instance, is a platform that avails of niche-sourcing to collect annotations. DaCura keeps track of the annotations collected by annotators working on the same tasks to assess which inter-links are likely to be accurate. Our approach to knowledge organization would easily integrate with such methods.

There are a few limitations to this study. The first is the creation of our lightweight faceted browser, which may have had an impact on task performance and perceived usability. The second limitation is related to the geospatial vocabularies and types of interlinks our tool supports. The tool is only capable of processing GeoSPARQL data using WKT literals. Future work should thus look into the inclusion of GMLand other geospatial vocabularies. As for the links, the tool only supports the creation of interlinks, where the resource displayed on the map is the subject. We aim to extend the popup to support the inclusion of interlinks in which the resource on the map is the subject. That would leverage the problem of forcing users to think in terms of reverse relationships (e.g., `geo:sf-within` instead of `geo:sf-contains`).

Acknowledgements. Debruyne and McGlinn are funded by the ADAPT Centre for Digital Content Technology, which is funded under the SFI Research Centres Programme (Grant 13/RC/2106) and is co-funded under the European Regional Development Fund.

A. PSSUQ Questionnaire

1. Overall, I am satisfied with how easy it is to use this system
2. It was simple to use this system
3. I could effectively complete the tasks and scenarios using this system
4. I was able to complete the tasks and scenarios quickly using this system
5. I was able to efficiently complete the tasks and scenarios using this system
6. I felt comfortable using this system
7. It was easy to learn to use this system
8. I believe I could become productive quickly using this system
9. The system gave error messages that clearly told me how to fix problems
10. Whenever I made a mistake using the system, I could recover easily and quickly
11. The information (such as on-line help, on-screen messages, and other documentation) provided with this system was clear
12. It was easy to find the information I needed
13. The information provided for the system was easy to understand
14. The information was effective in helping me complete the tasks and scenarios
15. The organization of information on the system screens was clear
16. The interface of this system was pleasant
17. I liked using the interface of this system
18. This system has all the functions and capabilities I expect it to have
19. Overall, I am satisfied with this system

References

1. Bizer, C., Heath, T., Berners-Lee, T.: Linked data - the story so far. Int. J. Semantic Web Inf. Syst. **5**(3), 1–22 (2009). https://doi.org/10.4018/jswis.2009081901
2. Both, A., Wauer, M., Garcìa-Rojas, A., Hladky, D., Lehmann, J.: The geoknow generator workbench - an integrated tool supporting the linked data lifecycle for enterprise usage. In: Filipowska, A., Verborgh, R., Polleres, A. (eds.) Joint Proceedings of the Posters and Demos Track of 11th International Conference on Semantic Systems - SEMANTiCS 2015 and 1st Workshop on Data Science: Methods, Technology and Applications (DSci15) 11th International Conference on Semantic Systems - SEMANTiCS 2015, Vienna, Austria, September 15–17, 2015. CEUR Workshop Proceedings, vol. 1481, pp. 92–95. CEUR-WS. org (2015)

3. Debruyne, C., et al.: Ireland's authoritative geospatial linked data. In: d'Amato, C., et al. (eds.) ISWC 2017. LNCS, vol. 10588, pp. 66–74. Springer, Cham (2017). https://doi.org/10.1007/978-3-319-68204-4_6

4. Feeney, K.C., O'Sullivan, D., Tai, W., Brennan, R.: Improving curated web-data quality with structured harvesting and assessment. Int. J. Semantic Web Inf. Syst. 10(2), 35–62 (2014). https://doi.org/10.4018/ijswis.2014040103

5. Isele, R., Jentzsch, A., Bizer, C.: Silk server - adding missing links while consuming linked data. In: Hartig, O., Harth, A., Sequeda, J. (eds.) Proceedings of the First International Workshop on Consuming Linked Data, Shanghai, China, November 8, 2010. CEUR Workshop Proceedings, vol. 665. CEUR-WS.org (2010)

6. Isele, R., Bizer, C.: Active learning of expressive linkage rules using genetic programming. J. Web Semant. 23, 2–15 (2013). https://doi.org/10.1016/j.websem.2013.06.001

7. Kharlamov, E., Giacomelli, L., Sherkhonov, E., Grau, B.C., Kostylev, E.V., Horrocks, I.: Semfacet: making hard faceted search easier. In: Lim, E., et al. (eds.) Proceedings of the 2017 ACM on Conference on Information and Knowledge Management, CIKM 2017, Singapore, November 06–10, 2017. pp. 2475–2478. ACM (2017). https://doi.org/10.1145/3132847.3133192

8. Kyzirakos, K., Karpathiotakis, M., Koubarakis, M.: Strabon: a semantic geospatial DBMS. In: Cudré-Mauroux, P., Tudorache, T., et al. (eds.) ISWC 2012. LNCS, vol. 7649, pp. 295–311. Springer, Heidelberg (2012). https://doi.org/10.1007/978-3-642-35176-1_19

9. Lehmann, J., et al.: DBpedia - A large-scale, multilingual knowledge base extracted from Wikipedia. Semant. Web 6(2), 167–195 (2015). https://doi.org/10.3233/SW-140134

10. Lewis, J.R.: Psychometric evaluation of the PSSUQ using data from five years of usability studies. Int. J. Hum.-Comput. Interact. 14(3–4), 463–488 (2002)

11. McGlinn, K., Blake, D., O'Sullivan, D.: Gviz - an interactive webapp to support geosparql over integrated building information. In: Amer-Yahia, S., et al. (eds.) Companion of The 2019 World Wide Web Conference, WWW 2019, San Francisco, CA, USA, May 13–17, 2019. pp. 904–912. ACM (2019). https://doi.org/10.1145/3308560.3316536

12. McGlinn, K., Debruyne, C., McNerney, L., O'Sullivan, D.: Integrating Ireland's geospatial information to provide authoritative building information models. In: Proceedings of the 13th International Conference on Semantic Systems, SEMANTICS 2017, Amsterdam, The Netherlands, September 11–14, 2017. pp. 57–64 (2017). https://doi.org/10.1145/3132218.3132223

13. McKenna, L., Debruyne, C., O'Sullivan, D.: Understanding the position of information professionals with regards to linked data: a survey of libraries, archives and museums. In: Chen, J., Gonçalves, M.A., Allen, J.M., Fox, E.A., Kan, M., Petras, V. (eds.) Proceedings of the 18th ACM/IEEE on Joint Conference on Digital Libraries, JCDL 2018, Fort Worth, TX, USA, June 03–07, 2018. pp. 7–16. ACM (2018). https://doi.org/10.1145/3197026.3197041

14. Mori, G., Paternò, F., Santoro, C.: CTTE: support for developing and analyzing task models for interactive system design. IEEE Trans. Softw. Eng. 28(8), 797–813 (2002). https://doi.org/10.1109/TSE.2002.1027801

15. Ngomo, A.N., Auer, S.: LIMES - a time-efficient approach for large-scale link discovery on the web of data. In: Walsh, T. (ed.) IJCAI 2011, Proceedings of the 22nd International Joint Conference on Artificial Intelligence, Barcelona, Catalonia, Spain, July 16–22, 2011. pp. 2312–2317. IJCAI/AAAI (2011). https://doi.org/10.5591/978-1-57735-516-8/IJCAI11-385

16. Ngonga Ngomo, A.-C., Lyko, K.: EAGLE: efficient active learning of link specifications using genetic programming. In: Simperl, E., Cimiano, P., Polleres, A., Corcho, O., Presutti, V. (eds.) ESWC 2012. LNCS, vol. 7295, pp. 149–163. Springer, Heidelberg (2012). https://doi.org/10.1007/978-3-642-30284-8_17

17. Paternò, F., Mancini, C., Meniconi, S.: Concurtasktrees: a diagrammatic notation for specifying task models. In: Howard, S., Hammond, J., Lindgaard, G. (eds.) Human-Computer Interaction, INTERACT 1997, IFIP TC13 International Conference on Human-Computer Interaction, 14–18 July 1997, Sydney, Australia. IFIP Conference Proceedings, vol. 96, pp. 362–369. Chapman & Hall (1997)
18. Patroumpas, K., Alexakis, M., Giannopoulos, G., Athanasiou, S.: Triplegeo: an ETL tool for transforming geospatial data into RDF triples. In: Proceedings of the Workshops of the EDBT/ICDT 2014 Joint Conference (EDBT/ICDT 2014), Athens, Greece, March 28, 2014. pp. 275–278 (2014)
19. Rietveld, L., Hoekstra, R.: The YASGUI family of SPARQL clients. Semant. Web 8(3), 373–383 (2017). https://doi.org/10.3233/SW-150197
20. Ryan, C., Grant, R., Carragáin, E.Ó., Collins, S., Decker, S., Lopes, N.: Linked data authority records for Irish place names. Int. J. Dig. Libr. 15(2–4), 73–85 (2015). https://doi.org/10.1007/s00799-014-0129-8
21. Shadbolt, N., et al.: Linked open government data: lessons from datagovuk. IEEE Intel. Syst. 27(3), 16–24 (2012). https://doi.org/10.1109/MIS.2012.23
22. Sherif, M.A., Ngomo, A.-C.N., Lehmann, J.: Automating RDF dataset transformation and enrichment. In: Gandon, F., Sabou, M., Sack, H., d'Amato, C., Cudré-Mauroux, P., Zimmermann, A. (eds.) ESWC 2015. LNCS, vol. 9088, pp. 371–387. Springer, Cham (2015). https://doi.org/10.1007/978-3-319-18818-8_23
23. Sherif, M.A., Ngonga Ngomo, A.-C., Lehmann, J.: Wombat – a generalization approach for automatic link discovery. In: Blomqvist, E., Maynard, D., Gangemi, A., Hoekstra, R., Hitzler, P., Hartig, O. (eds.) ESWC 2017. LNCS, vol. 10249, pp. 103–119. Springer, Cham (2017). https://doi.org/10.1007/978-3-319-58068-5_7
24. Stadler, C., Martin, M., Auer, S.: Exploring the web of spatial data with Facete. In: Chung, C., Broder, A.Z., Shim, K., Suel, T. (eds.) 23rd International World Wide Web Conference, WWW '14, Seoul, Republic of Korea, April 7–11, 2014, Companion Volume. pp. 175–178. ACM (2014). https://doi.org/10.1145/2567948.2577022
25. Zhao, J., Hartig, O.: Towards interoperable provenance publication on the linked data web. In: Bizer, C., Heath, T., Berners-Lee, T., Hausenblas, M. (eds.) WWW2012 Workshop on Linked Data on the Web, Lyon, France, 16 April, 2012. CEUR Workshop Proceedings, vol. 937. CEUR-WS.org (2012)

A Conceptual Modelling Approach to Visualising Linked Data

Peter McBrien[1](✉)[iD] and Alexandra Poulovassilis[2][iD]

[1] Department of Computing, Imperial College,
180 Queen's Gate, London SW7 2BZ, UK
p.mcbrien@ic.ac.uk
[2] Birkbeck Knowledge Lab, Birkbeck, University of London,
Malet Street, London WC1E 7HX, UK
ap@dcs.bbk.ac.ukc

Abstract. Increasing numbers of Linked Open Datasets are being published, and many possible data visualisations may be appropriate for a user's given exploration or analysis task over a dataset. Users may therefore find it difficult to identify visualisations that meet their data exploration or analyses needs. We propose an approach that creates conceptual models of groups of commonly used data visualisations, which can be used to analyse the data and users' queries so as to automatically generate recommendations of possible visualisations. To our knowledge, this is the first work to propose a conceptual modelling approach to recommending visualisations for Linked Data.

1 Introduction

There are numerous Linked Open Datasets available on the web, and supporting their visual exploration and analysis by potential users is a pressing need. Conversely, there are many possible data visualisations that might be appropriate for a given user task, *e.g.* as provided by a typical visualisation library such as D3 or Google Charts. It may therefore be hard for users to select appropriate visualisations to meet their specific exploration or analysis needs with respect to a given dataset.

We propose an approach that addresses this problem by using "visualisation patterns" expressed in OWL that characterise each distinct (from a data representation capability) group of commonly-used data visualisations, and by generating SPARQL query templates corresponding to these visualisation patterns. Our starting premise is that users formulate SPARQL queries to extract the data that they wish to see visualised; this might be direct specification of a SPARQL query by a technically knowledgeable user, or indirect construction of a SPARQL query through a visual querying tool by a non-technical user. Our OWL visualisation patterns and SPARQL query templates are used to analyse the data and the users' queries, respectively, so as to automatically generate a more focussed set of recommendations of possible visualisations to the user. We

© Springer Nature Switzerland AG 2019
H. Panetto et al. (Eds.): OTM 2019, LNCS 11877, pp. 227–245, 2019.
https://doi.org/10.1007/978-3-030-33246-4_15

view our approach as being part of a broader set of solutions that can aid users in formulating queries and exploring Linked Data, *e.g.* it may be combined with browsing and exploration [4,6,17,19,31], faceted search [2,24,37] or structural summaries [5,23].

Current approaches to visualising linked data provide a limited set of data visualisations that are oriented specifically towards visualising RDF graphs or ontologies, or that support more general data visualisation capabilities but without the intermediate conceptual abstraction and recommendation process for the user that we propose here (see Sect. 2). In contrast, to our knowledge ours is the first work to propose a conceptual modelling approach to recommending visualisations for Linked Data to users.

We continue the paper with a review in Sect. 2 of related work on data visualisation in general and visualising linked data specifically, contrasting this with our approach. Section 3 describes an example use case motivating our approach. Section 4 presents OWL specifications characterising several groups of common data visualisations, as well as SPARQL query templates corresponding to the OWL visualisation patterns. Section 5 discusses transformations that can be applied to users' SPARQL queries so that they match the SPARQL query templates. Section 6 summarises our contributions and presents possible directions for further work.

2   Related Work

Data Visualisation. The field of data visualisation is a very active one (for reviews see *e.g.* [1,39,43]) and is continuing to expand with the advent of 'big data' arising from web-scale applications and the need to develop new techniques for exploring such data [15]. Current data visualisation tools (*e.g.* Tableau[1], D3[2], Google Charts[3]) require users to manually select from typically tabular data, apply transformations, and select appropriate visual encodings from a vast array of possibilities. The user may therefore find it hard to understand the meaning of the data, the transformations that may be applied to it, and the range of visualisation possibilities, and may easily fail to 'see the wood for the trees'.

For these reasons, there has been work towards automated recommendation of visualisation possibilities and for ranking recommendations [20,27,35,47]. The SemVis system [14] reduces the visualisation search space by using a domain ontology for mapping the source data into a visual representation ontology storing 'knowledge about visualisation tools', and a bridging ontology to map between the domain ontology and the visual representation ontology. Our work is similar in spirit to this, but we do not require the availability of a domain or a bridging ontology.

---

[1] https://www.tableau.com/products/desktop.
[2] https://github.com/d3/d3/wiki/Gallery.
[3] https://developers.google.com/chart/interactive/docs/examples.

Other recent work that is close to ours is the Voyager system [48] which provides techniques aiming to aid the user in selecting appropriate visualisations, including faceted browsing of visualisation recommendations, and automatic clustering and ranking of visualisations according to data properties and perceptual effectiveness principles. However, this work focusses on the visualisation of a single relational table of data. It also does not undertake matchings between the data and conceptual-level representations of visualisations.

Several works have derived taxonomies of classes of visualisation *e.g.* [11,36,41]. However, they focussed on properties of the data (dimensionality, dependent/independent variables, discrete/continuous, ordered/unordered) rather than capturing different visualisations as instances of a conceptual visualisation schema.

Finally, languages proposed for manipulating graphical data (*e.g.* Tableau's VizQL [38], Wilkinson's Grammar of Graphics [46], R's Tidyr package [33]) require programmers to manually select data, apply transformations, and select appropriate visual encodings.

Visualising Linked Data. Many research works and systems have addressed the visualisation of linked data (for reviews see *e.g.* [8,12,32]). There have been many proposals for visualising ontologies [13,25,26,45] and RDF graphs [3,7,10,22]. These proposals typically provide a fixed set of tree- or network-oriented data visualisations for viewing the graph structure of the data and/or the ontology, with little extensibility or customisation capability.

There are also proposals that support more general visualisation capabilities for linked data which allow end users to interactively select data and visualisations [9,18,34,40,42]. There has also been work on combining faceted search with data analytic visualisations, mainly in application-specific settings [21,24,28].

Graziosi et al. [16] discuss the difficulty of producing visualisations for linked data for users with little technical knowledge of semantic web technologies or programming. They present a reference model for building tools that generate customisable "infoviews" and conduct a survey of existing tools in terms of their customisation capabilities. Issues relating to the scalability of exploration and visualisation approaches in the face of large, distributed linked datasets are discussed by Bikakis and Sellis [8].

None of these works provide the conceptual abstraction of groups of visualisations nor a recommendation process for the user as we propose here.

Our own previous work [30] also proposed a conceptual modelling approach towards data visualisation. However, that was in the context of structured data sources with the assumption that strict schema information is available or inferable, and with schema-level matching being undertaken between the schema of the data on the one hand and the visualisation schema patterns on the other.

Finally, we note that our abstraction of *classes* of commonly used data visualisations generalises the visualisation capabilities of graph database systems such as GraphDB[4] which guide the user towards creating specific visualisations.

---

[4] http://graphdb.ontotext.com/.

3   Motivating Example

To motivate our approach we consider the Mondial database [29], which is available in RDF. A small fragment of it is illustrated in Fig. 1, with the relevant part of the OWL Schema illustrated in Fig. 2. In these figures, the directional arrows represent properties, with the arrow going from the domain to the range to the property.

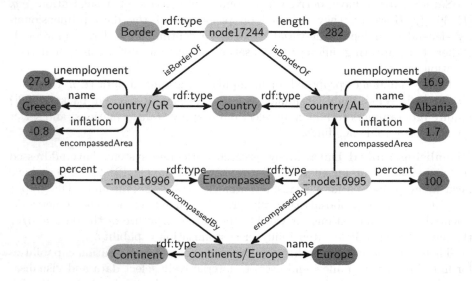

Fig. 1. RDF graph of countries and their borders from the Mondial database

The fragment of the Mondial database that we consider here contains countries, the continents they are within (some countries may span two continents), the length of the border between pairs of countries, and the population history of countries. Figure 3 shows a number of visualisations of this data. Each is presenting different information about the Country class, but in different ways according to the properties and datatypes being queried. In this paper we assume that users formulate SPARQL queries to extract the data they are interested in viewing, but then require guidance as to which visualisation method can be used, and we use OWL schema information such as that presented in Fig. 2 to guide that process.

4   OWL Patterns for Visualisation

In visualisation research, the various graphic elements of a visualisation are typically classified as **marks** (points, lines, areas, *etc*) or **channels** (colour, length, shape, coordinate, texture, orientation, movement, *etc*) of a mark [44]. We make two basic assumptions here: (1) instances of classes can be represented as a mark in a visualisation, so that a visualisation becomes a method of viewing the

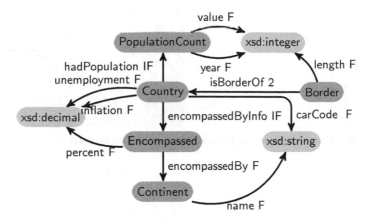

Fig. 2. Fragment of the OWL Schema for the Mondial Database. Functional properties are labelled F, inverse functional properties are labelled IF, and maximum cardinality two properties are labelled 2.

instances of one or more classes; and (2) each functional data property associated with a class can be used to alter a channel of the mark associated with that class — we refer to such properties as **dimensions** of the class instances.

Taking an approach similar to Tableau[5], and our previous work [30], we distinguish two major types of dimensions (we note that these are different to the 'discrete' and 'continuous' dimensions of [41]):

- **discrete dimensions** have a relatively small number of distinct values, that may nor may not have a natural ordering; they are used to label a mark or to vary a channel of a mark. Examples include the code associated with a country or the year associated with a population census.
- **scalar dimensions** have a relatively large number of distinct values with a natural numeric ordering (*e.g.* integers, real numbers, timestamps, dates); these are represented by a channel associated with a mark. Examples include the population of a country in a particular year, or the area of a country.

When a dimension is represented by a colour channel, then for a discrete dimension we assume that a colour key can be used, while for a scalar dimension we assume that a spectrum of colours can be used. Both discrete and scalar dimensions may have additional real-world characteristics, *e.g.* their data may be geographical, temporal, or lexical, which may suggest specific visualisations for their representation.

In the following subsections, we develop progressively more complex patterns of classes and properties, each characterising a group of possible alternative visualisations. Our approach aims to provide the user with assistance in selecting appropriate visualisations and should be viewed as being complementary to user interface design aspects such as interaction design and task-based visualisation design. To illustrate how the visualisation patterns could be applied in practice,

---

[5] https://www.tableau.com/products/desktop.

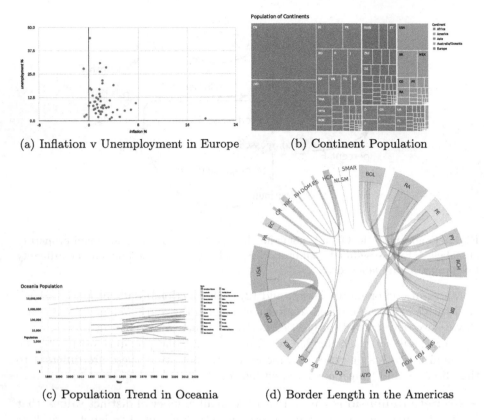

(a) Inflation v Unemployment in Europe   (b) Continent Population

(c) Population Trend in Oceania   (d) Border Length in the Americas

Fig. 3. Example visualisation of country data based on patterns

we conclude the description of each by listing the SPARQL query template that is implied by the visualisation pattern, together with the user queries matching this query template that have been used to generate the visualisations shown in Fig. 3.

4.1   Class with Data Properties

Starting from our two basic assumptions (1) and (2) above, we can identify the **graph pattern** illustrated in Fig. 4, showing a class, CA, with one or more functional data properties, DPA1... DPAn. This graph pattern can be formally specified by the following **visualisation pattern**, expressed in OWL:

DataPropertyDomain(DPA1 CA)   DataProperty(DPA1)
DataPropertyRange(DPA1 TA1)   FunctionalProperty(DPA1)
...   ...
DataPropertyDomain(DPAn CA)   DataProperty(DPAn)
DataPropertyRange(DPAn TAn)   FunctionalProperty(DPAn)

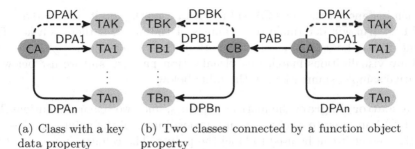

(a) Class with a key data property

(b) Two classes connected by a function object property

(c) Three classes connected by two functional object properties

Fig. 4. Graph patterns for visualisations

Note that here, and subsequently, we use variables CA, CB, ... to denote classes A, B, ...; variables DPA1, DPA2, ... to denote data properties of a class A; variables TA1, TA2, ... to denote the ranges of such data properties; variable DPAK to denote a data property of a class A that is a key; variable TAK to denote the range of such a data property; and variable PAB to denote an object property between classes A and B.

Some visualisations (such as scatter diagrams) do not require that each mark be labelled with a meaningful unique label, whilst others (such as bar charts) do require such labels if they are to be useful. We indicate such a key with a dashed line in the graph pattern, which adds the following additional statements to the OWL visualisation pattern:

DataPropertyDomain(DPAK CA)   HasKey(CA () (DPAK))
DataPropertyRange(DPAK TAK)   DataProperty(DPAK)
                                     FunctionalProperty(DPAK)

Each instance of the class CA will result in a mark, and its associated values of TA1... TAn will determine the channels of the mark. If there is a key TAK present, it may be used to label each mark of the visualisation.

Many visualisations match this visualisation pattern, and we list below an indicative sample, summarised in the table below:

- In a **scatter diagram** the marks are points, and two scalar dimensions TA1 and TA2 are used to alter the x and y coordinates of the points. If there is a TAK present it can be used to label the points. The colour, shape, *etc* of the point can be altered by additional optional dimensions TA3, ...
- In a **bubble chart**, the concept of a scatter diagram is refined to use a third scalar dimension TA3 to change the size of the point.
- In a **calendar chart** the marks are entries in a calendar, and hence the value of dimension TA1 must be a date to identify which slot on the calendar is used.
- Basic **bar charts** use each value of TAK to label one bar, and the scalar value of TA1 to change the length of the bar. There is a limit to the number of bars that can be displayed so that the chart remains comprehensible. In the table below, we therefore limit the cardinality of the class CA to be at most 100, constraining the selection of this type of visualisation to data that satisfies this constraint (the limit of 100 is of course subjective and would be tunable in an implementation).
- A **choropleth map** uses each value of TAK to identify regions on a map, and the scalar value of TA1 to change the colour of the region.
- In **word clouds**, the value of TAK is used to determine the word to be plotted, and the scalar value of TA1 to determine the size of the word.

The analysis above is summarised in the table below. All of these visualisations can support additional channels by altering the colour, texture, or other aspects of the mark. This is illustrated in the table by colour or texture dimensions in the optional column, which are extensible with additional dimensions of the data, mapping to additional channels in the visualisation. The notation |CA| is used to denote the number of instances of a class CA, so for example, we allow any number of instances to be visualised in a calendar chart, but restrict bar charts to have up to one hundred bars.

Visualisations for Classes with Data Properties			
Name	|CA|	mandatory	optional
Calendar Chart	1..*	TA1 temporal scalar	TAK,TA2 colour
Scatter Diagrams	1..*	TA1,TA2 scalar	TAK,TA3 colour
Bubble Charts	1..*	TA1,TA2,TA3 scalar	TAK,TA4 colour
Bar Chart	1..100	TAK, TA1 scalar	-
Choropleth Maps	1..*	TAK geographical, TA1 colour	TA2 texture
Word Clouds	1..*	TAK lexical, TA1 scalar	TA2 colour

A SPARQL query template to extract the values required for a visualisation that requires just TAK and TA1 is given below left; additional dimensions can be added to the query in the obvious way by adding :DPA2 ?TA2, *etc*. A typical user interaction scenario making use of the SPARQL query template and the OWL visualisation template is as follows. The user first formulates a SPARQL query to extract the data that they wish to see visualised; an example such query is given below right.

```
SELECT ?TAK ?TA1 ?TAn WHERE {
    ?CA rdf:type :CA ;
       :DPK ?TAK ;
       :DPA1 ?TA1 .
}
```

```
SELECT ?inflation ?unemployment WHERE {
    ?c rdf:type :Country ;
      :inflation ?inflation ;
      :unemployment ?unemployment ;
}
```

A system implementing our approach would match the user's query against the SPARQL query pattern corresponding to each group of visualisations (as presented here and in the following subsections); in this particular example, the user's query matches the SPARQL query template shown above left. The system would then validate that the OWL visualisation pattern is satisfied by matching it against the RDFS/OWL statements in the dataset that is being queried which relate to the classes and properties mentioned in the user's query. The group of visualisations that are satisfied (if any) would then be checked against the data for the additional constraints (see *e.g.* the above table) relating to individual visualisations. In our particular example, the Calendar Chart, Chloropeth Map and Word Cloud would be discounted due to the data type constraints on TA1 or TAK; and the Bar Chart would be discounted due to the cardinality constraint on CA. The remaining set of visualisations would finally be offered to the user as possible alternatives for generating their visualisation. In our particular example, a scatter diagram or bubble chart would be offered. If the user selects a scatter diagram, then the diagram shown in Fig. 3(a) is produced.

We assume here that users' SPARQL queries do not contain OPTIONAL clauses and therefore only full matches with respect to the data are returned. Exploring the interplay of OPTIONAL clauses with the recommendation techniques that we propose here is an interesting area of future work.

4.2   Two Classes Linked by a Functional Property

We now consider the case where in addition to having data properties and a key data property, a class CA is the domain of an object property PAB whose range is another class CB. This is illustrated in the graph pattern in Fig. 4(b) which can be specified by the OWL statements below being added to those of the previous subsection, giving an overall OWL visualisation pattern for this second group of visualisations:

ObjectPropertyDomain(PAB CA)   HasKey(CB () (DPBK))
ObjectPropertyRange(PAB CB)   FunctionalProperty(PAB)
DataPropertyDomain(DPBK CB)   DataProperty(DPBK)
DataPropertyRange(DPBK TBK)   FunctionalProperty(DPBK)
DataPropertyDomain(DPB1 CB)   DataProperty(DPB1)
DataPropertyRange(DPB1 TB1)   FunctionalProperty(DPB1)
. . .   . . .
DataPropertyDomain(DPBn CB)   DataProperty(DPBn)
DataPropertyRange(DPBn TBn)   FunctionalProperty(DPBn)

The fact that PAB is functional means the presence of a hierarchical pattern of data, with each instance of CA being associated with one instance of CB. Visualisations that represent two classes together rather than a single class are less common, but some examples are listed below:

- In a **tree map**, rectangles representing instances of class CB are divided into rectangles representing instances of class CA, the area of which is proportional to the value of a scalar dimension TA1. Typically it is a dimension TB1 of CB that is used to colour the rectangles, and additional dimensions such as TA2 are used for texture, *etc.*
- In a **hierarchy tree**, nodes represent instances of CB that are connected by lines to circles representing instances of CA. Since the nodes are at distinct levels, optionally it is possible to use TA1 to colour one level, and TB1 to colour the other level.
- A **circle packing** represents instances of CB by circles, with instances of CA placed as circles inside the circle of their parent instance of CB. A scalar dimension TA1 is used to determine the area of the circles of CA. Similarly to a hierarchy tree, distinct dimensions can be used to colour distinct levels of the circles.
- A **sunburst** represents instances of CB by segments of a central circle, with segments of an outer circle divided representing instances of CA, placed outside of the corresponding instance of CB. The relative size of the segment is determined by TA1. Similarly to a hierarchy tree, distinct dimensions can be used to colour distinct rings of the sunburst.

We note that all of these visualisations support additional levels in the hierarchy, such that one could add a third class CC connected by functional property PBC from CB giving an additional level to the hierarchy.

The table below summarises the above analysis, where |CA PAB CB| presents the number of instances in CA that are associated via PAB to each instance of CB. The upper cardinality figures given (such as 20 for the top level of a tree map) are there to guide the user towards selection of an uncluttered visualisation, and are not a rigid limit. The restrictions proposed are subjective, and aesthetics-driven, but serve to direct users to choosing appropriate visualisations so as to avoid situations where the amount of data would 'clutter' a particular type visualisation. In any implementation these limits should of course be user-configurable.

Name	|CB|	|CA PAB CB|	Visualisations for functional properties mandatory	optional
Tree Map	1..20	1..100	TAK,TBK,TA1 scalar	TB1 colour,TA2 colour
Hierarchy Tree	1..100	1..100	TAK,TBK	TA1 colour,TB1 colour
Sunburst	1..20	1..20	TAK,TBK,TA1 scalar	TA1 colour,TB1 colour
Circle Packing	1..20	1..20	TAK,TBK,TA1 scalar	TA1 colour,TB1 colour

A SPARQL query template to extract the labels and one attribute from each of the two classes is listed below left (again additional dimensions can be added in the obvious way). A possible user SPARQL query is shown below right. Although this does not directly match the SPARQL query template on the left, in Sect. 5 we discuss how the filter expression appearing in the user's query causes the concatenation of encompassedByInfo and encompassedBy to be functional, and hence match PAB in the query template. Following such a transformation, for the Mondial database the tree map and hierarchy tree are offered as alternative visualisations. If the user selects a tree map, then the diagram shown in Fig. 3(b) is produced.

```
SELECT ?TBK ?TAK ?TA1 ?TB1 WHERE {
    ?CA rdf:type :CA ;
        :DPAK ?TAK ;
        :DPA1 ?TA1 .
    ?CB rdf:type :CB ;
        :DPBK ?TBK ;
        :DPB1 ?TB1 .
    ?CA :PAB ?CB .
}
```

```
SELECT ?continent ?carcode ?population
WHERE {
    ?c  rdf:type :Country ;
        :carCode ?carcode ;
        :population ?population ;
        :encompassedByInfo ?en .
    ?en :encompassedBy ?con;
        :percent ?percent.
    ?con rdf:type :Continent ;
        :name ?continent .
    FILTER ( ?percent>50 )
}
```

4.3   Two Classes Linked by a Key Functional Property

A different set of visualisations are specified if we change the HasKey(CA () (DPAK)) definition in the previous subsection to

HasKey(CA () (DPAK PAB))

so that it is the combination of TAK and CB that identify instances of CA. In this case, instances of CA are in a sense dependent on instances of CB, and a number of visualisations naturally support such a dependency, a selection of which are listed below:

- In a **line chart** each line represents an instance of CB labelled with TBK; TAK represents a scalar dimension to be plotted along the x-axis; and TA1 must be a scalar dimension to be plotted along the y-axis. XY variations of line charts allow an additional dimension TA2 to be added to the y-axis. Optionally, additional dimensions TA3 could colour the points of the line, and TB1 colour the lines.

- In a **spider chart**, each ring represents an instance of CB, labelled by TBK, and each spoke a value of CA labelled by TAK; the intersection of the ring with a spoke is determined by TA1. Similarly to line charts, additional dimensions TA2 could colour the points of intersection, and TB1 colour the lines. For this visualisation type, we require CA to be **complete** with respect to CB, by which we mean that all instances of CB should appear with the same (or almost the same) set of values for TAK so that the different instances of TBK can be can be compared for each instance of TAK.
- In a **stacked bar chart**, instances of CB are represented by a bar labelled by TBK, with one of the elements in the stack representing an instance of CA, and the length of the bar determined by a scalar dimension TA1, and it being labelled and coloured by TAK. Optionally TA2 could alter the texture of the elements. For this visualisation type too, we require CA to be **complete** with respect to CB, so that the elements in each stack can be compared.
- A **group bar chart** is similar to a stacked bar chart, with one group labelled by TBK, and each bar in the group having its height determined by TA1 and labelled and coloured by TAK. There is no need for CA to be complete with respect to CB. Optionally TA2 could alter the texture of the bars.

The table below summarises the above analysis. Again the upper cardinalities shown for |CB| and |CA| are aesthetics-driven and would be user-configurable.

Visualisations of key functional properties					
Name	|CB|	|CA|	complete	mandatory	optional
Line	1..20	1..*	no	TAK scalar,TBK,TA1 scalar	TA2 scalar,TA3/TB1 colour
Spider	3..10	1..20	yes	TAK,TBK,TA1 scalar	TA2/TB1 colour
Stacked Bar	1..100	1..20	yes	TAK colour,TBK,TA1 scalar	TA2 texture
Grouped Bar	1..20	1..20	no	TAK colour,TBK,TA1 scalar	TA2 texture

The SPARQL query template for this group of visualisations listed below left is the same as in the previous subsection. Below right is a user's SPARQL query asking for the historical population trends of countries in Oceania that matches the query template and OWL visualisation pattern, and produces Fig. 3(c) if the user selects to view the data on a line chart.

```
SELECT ?TBK ?TAK ?TA1 ?TB1 WHERE {
    ?CA rdf:type :CA ;
        :DPAK ?TAK ;
        :DPA1 ?TA1 .
    ?CB rdf:type :CB ;
        :DPBK ?TBK ;
        :DPB1 ?TB1 .
    ?CA :PAB ?CB .
}
```

```
SELECT ?country ?year ?population
WHERE {
    ?c   rdf:type :Country ;
         :name ?country ;
         :encompassedByInfo ?en .
    ?py rdf:type :PopulationCount ;
        :year ?year;
        :value ?population .
    ?c   :hadPopulation ?py .
    # Filter conditions
    ?en  :encompassedBy ?con .
    ?con rdf:type :Continent ;
         :name "Australia/Oceania" .
}
```

4.4   Three Classes Linked by Functional Properties

As illustrated in the graph pattern in Fig. 4(c), suppose that we introduce a third class CC structured in a similar way to CB, through the following OWL statements:

ObjectPropertyDomain(PAC CA)	HasKey(CC () (DPCK))
ObjectPropertyRange(PAC CC)	FunctionalProperty(PAC)
DataPropertyDomain(DPCK CC)	DataProperty(DPCK)
DataPropertyRange(DPCK TCK)	FunctionalProperty(DPCK)
DataPropertyDomain(DPC1 CC)	DataProperty(DPC1)
DataPropertyRange(DPC1 TC1)	FunctionalProperty(DPC1)
. . .	. . .
DataPropertyDomain(DPCn CC)	DataProperty(DPCn)
DataPropertyRange(DPCn TCn)	FunctionalProperty(DPCn)

and that the HasKey on CA is changed to

   HasKey(CA () (PAB PAC))

so that instances of CA are identified by combinations of instances of CB and CC. With this visualisation pattern, we can regard CA as modelling a many-many relationship between the two classes CB and CC, leading to a group of visualisations that target a network view of data, such as the following:

- In **sankey** diagrams, the left hand elements of the diagram represent instances of CB, the right hand elements represent instances of CC, and the width of the flow between the left and right elements represents scalar dimension TA1. Optionally, a second attribute TA2 may be represented by varying the colour of the connection.
- In **network** charts, instances of CB and CC are represented by nodes in the graph, with an instance of CA that is connected to both an instance of CB and an instance of CC being represented by an edge between these two nodes. A optional scalar attribute TA1 can vary the colour of the line.
- In **chord** diagrams, instances of CB and CC are represented by points on the perimeter of the circle, with the value of TA1 varying the width of the connection between pairs of points. Again, a second attribute TA2 of the many-many relationship may be represented by varying the colour of the connection.
- In **heatmap** tables, instances of CB and CC are represented by cells of a table, with the colour of the cell varied using TA1. Optional attribute TA2, can be represented using texture.

We note that network charts, chord diagrams and heatmap tables can be used to represent **reflexive** relationships where CB and CC are the same class (let us say CB), so that the nodes/cells represent instances of CB, and CA has two properties associating it to CB.

The table below summarises the above analysis. Whilst most of this group of visualisations support optional dimensions being represented as a colour channel, an exception is heatmaps, which require the use of colour in a mandatory channel, and hence in this case we illustrate the optional dimensions by the use of texture.

	Visualisations for a non-functional property					
Name	|CB|	|CC|	reflexive	mandatory	optional
Sankey	1..20	1..20	no	TA1 scalar	TA2 colour
Network Chart	1..1000	1..1000	yes	-	TAK,TA1 colour
Chord	1..100	1..100	yes	-	TA1 size,TA2 colour
Heatmap	1..100	1..100	yes	TA1 colour	TA2 texture

A SPARQL query template to capture the keys of CB and CC and one attribute of CA is listed below left, and again additional attributes can be added in the obvious way. The SPARQL below right matches this template, and if the user selects a chord diagram, the diagram shown in Fig. 3(d) is produced.

```
SELECT ?TBK ?TCK ?TA1 WHERE {
    ?CA rdf:type :CA ;
        :PAB ?CB ;
        :PAC ?CC ;
        :DPA1 ?TA1 .
    ?CB rdf:type :CB ;
        :DPBK ?TBK .
    ?CC rdf:type :CC ;
        :DPCK ?TCK .
}
```

```
SELECT ?country1 ?country2 ?length WHERE {
    ?b rdf:type :Border ;
       :isBorderOf ?c1 ;
       :isBorderOf ?c2 ;
       :length ?length .
    ?c1 rdf:type :Country ;
        :carCode ?country1 .
    ?c2 rdf:type :Country ;
        :carCode ?country2 .
    # Filter conditions
    FILTER (?country1<?country2)
}
```

5 Transformations to Match Visualisation Patterns

It will often be the case that an RDF graph does not contain the precise structure required by a visualisation pattern. This is for two main reasons:

- The schema of the data is not fully defined, for example it is often the case that OWL hasKey properties are not specified (*e.g.* the original Mondial schema omits these, despite the keys being defined in the relational version of the database), and even RDFS functionalProperty declarations are sometimes not specified where they could have been (*e.g.* in YAGO, www.mpi-inf.mpg.de/yago-naga/yago/).
- The loosely structured nature of linked data results in inconsistency and variants of data, so that data may need to be filtered and restructured before being used for a particular visualisation or group of visualisations.

We therefore describe in this section two indicative transformations that can be applied to users' SPARQL queries to make them match a visualisation pattern.

Functional Subqueries: if a user SPARQL query can be rewritten to contain a subquery returning ?X and ?Y, such that the value of ?X functionally determines the value of ?Y, then we can regard the subquery as matching any pattern requiring a functional property of the form ?X :PXY ?Y.

Taking the example from Sect. 4.2 we can apply a rewriting as follows:

User Query

```
SELECT ?continent ?carcode ?population
WHERE {
    ?c   rdf:type  :Country ;
        :carCode ?carcode ;
        :population ?population ;
        :encompassedByInfo ?en .
    ?en :encompassedBy ?con;
        :percent ?percent.
    ?con rdf:type :Continent ;
        :name ?continent .
    FILTER ( ?percent>50 )
}
```

Transformed Query

```
SELECT ?continent ?carcode ?population
WHERE {
    ?c   rdf:type  :Country ;
        :carCode ?carcode ;
        :population ?population .
    ?con rdf:type :Continent ;
        :name ?continent .
    SELECT ?c ?con
    WHERE {
        ?c  :encompassedByInfo ?en .
        ?en :encompassedBy ?con;
            :percent ?percent.
        FILTER ( ?percent>50 )
    }
}
```

In general, we can determine that the variables of such a subquery obey the functional property if either the properties that bind them together are functional (which is not the case in this example), or if the subquery when executed obeys the functional property (which is the case in this example).

Denormalisation of Attributes: Suppose we wish to extend the scatter diagram in Fig. 3(a) to include information about the population of a country, and the continent it is within, with the user SPARQL query below left:

User Query

```
SELECT ?carcode ?inf ?unemployment
        ?continent ?population
WHERE {
    ?c   rdf:type  :Country ;
        :carCode ?carcode ;
        :inflation ?inf;
        :unemployment ?unemployment;
        :population ?population ;
        :encompassedByInfo ?en .
    ?en :encompassedBy ?con;
        :percent ?percent
    ?con :name ?continent .
    FILTER ( ?percent>50 )
}
```

Transformed Query

```
SELECT ?carcode ?inf ?unemployment
        ?continent ?population
WHERE {
    ?c   rdf:type  :Country ;
        :carCode ?carcode ;
        :inflation ?inf;
        :unemployment ?unemployment;
        :population ?population .
    SELECT ?c ?continent
    WHERE {
        ?c  :encompassedByInfo ?en .
        ?en :encompassedBy ?con;
            :percent ?percent.
            :name ?continent .
        FILTER ( ?percent>50 )
    }
}
```

The introduction of population matches the pattern for an additional dimension of Country, but the name property is not a dimension of Country. However we can 'denormalise' the name dimension of Continent by using a subquery, which relates the instances of the Country class with name of Continent.

6   Summary and Conclusions

In this paper we have proposed a conceptual modelling approach to matching linked data and visualisations. Our approach uses a set of "visualisation patterns" expressed in OWL each of which abstracts a group of potential visualisation alternatives. For each visualisation pattern, we define a corresponding SPARQL query template. The OWL visualisation patterns and SPARQL query templates are used to analyse the data and the users' queries, respectively, so as to make appropriate recommendations of groups of meaningful data visualisations to the user. We have also described transformations for denormalising data, handling non-functional properties as classes, and applying filters to use non-functional properties in visualisations that normally require functional properties.

By providing a set of OWL visualisation patterns each characterising the data representation capabilities of a group of common data visualisations, we make it easier for the user to select a visualisation that is meaningful in relation to their query and the data, narrowing their choice to a more focussed set of visualisations. An alternative scenario that would also be supported by our approach is where the user has a particular visualisation in mind to visualise a part of the data, in which case we can use the OWL visualisation pattern to validate that the data satisfies the requirements for generating that visualisation and we can instantiate the associated SPARQL query template in order to retrieve the data and populate the visualisation.

Future work includes implementing and empirically evaluating our approach with groups of users, investigating how the approach can be implemented as extensions of tools such as Tableau, and investigating the possibility of using it in a "top-down" approach, starting with a desired visualisation type, and using that to generate SPARQL queries and drill down into data.

We also need to perform an exhaustive analysis of the full range of visualisations supported by state-of-the art tools, and extend the indicative groups listed in Sect. 4 as necessary. This analysis may also give rise to additional visualisation groups, characterised by additional OWL visualisation patterns. Other directions of future work include investigating and providing customisation features for users, and exploring the scalability of our approach when applied to large distributed heterogeneous linked datasets that need to be accessed via query or API endpoints.

References

1. Andrienko, N., Andrienko, G., Gatalsky, P.: Exploratory spatio-temporal visualization: an analytical review. Vis. Lang. Comput. **14**(6), 503–541 (2003)
2. Arenas, M., Grau, B.C., Kharlamov, E., Marciuska, S., Zheleznyakov, D., Jimenez-Ruiz, E.: SemFacet: semantic faceted search over Yago. In: International Conference on World Wide Web, pp. 123–126. ACM (2014)
3. Atemezing, G.A., Troncy, R.: Towards a linked-data based visualization wizard. In: COLD (2014)

4. Auer, S., Dietzold, S., Riechert, T.: OntoWiki – a tool for social, semantic collaboration. In: Cruz, I., et al. (eds.) ISWC 2006. LNCS, vol. 4273, pp. 736–749. Springer, Heidelberg (2006). https://doi.org/10.1007/11926078_53
5. Benedetti, F., Bergamaschi, S., Po, L.: A visual summary for linked open data sources. In: ISWC, vol. 1272, pp. 173–176 (2014)
6. Berners-Lee, T., et al.: Tabulator: exploring and analyzing linked data on the semantic web. In: 3rd International Semantic Web User Interaction Workshop, p. 159 (2006)
7. Bikakis, N., Liagouris, J., Krommyda, M., Papastefanatos, G., Sellis, T.: graphVizdb: a scalable platform for interactive large graph visualization. In: ICDE, pp. 1342–1345. IEEE (2016)
8. Bikakis, N., Sellis, T.: Exploration and visualization in the web of big linked data: a survey of the state of the art. arXiv preprint arXiv:1601.08059 (2016)
9. Bikakis, N., Papastefanatos, G., Skourla, M., Sellis, T.: A hierarchical aggregation framework for efficient multilevel visual exploration and analysis. Seman. Web 8(1), 139–179 (2017)
10. Brunetti, J.M., Auer, S., García, R.: The Linked Data Visualization Model. In: ISWC (2012)
11. Card, S.K., Mackinlay, J.: The structure of the information visualization design space. In: Proceedings of Information Visualization, pp. 92–99. IEEE (1997)
12. Dadzie, A.-S., Rowe, M.: Approaches to visualising linked data: a survey. Seman. Web 2(2), 89–124 (2011)
13. Fu, B., Noy, N.F., Storey, M.-A.: Eye tracking the user experience - an evaluation of ontology visualization techniques. Seman. Web 8(1), 23–41 (2017)
14. Gilson, O., Silva, N., Grant, P.W., Chen, M.: From web data to visualization via ontology mapping. Comput. Graph. Forum 27(3), 959–966 (2008)
15. Gorodov, E.Y., Gubarev, V.V.: Analytical review of data visualization methods in application to big data. Electr. Comput. Eng. 2013, 22 (2013)
16. Graziosi, A., Di Iorio, A., Poggi, F., Peroni, S.: Customised visualisations of linked open data. In: VOILA@ISWC, pp. 20–33 (2017)
17. Harth, A.: VisiNav: a system for visual search and navigation on web data. Web Seman. 8(4), 348–354 (2010). Science Services and Agents on the World Wide Web
18. Heim, P., Lohmann, S., Tsendragchaa, D., Ertl, T.: SemLens: visual analysis of semantic data with scatter plots and semantic lenses. In: 7th International Conference on Semantic Systems, pp. 175–178. ACM (2011)
19. Heim, P., Ziegler, J., Lohmann, S.: gFacet: a browser for the web of data. In: International Workshop on Interacting with Multimedia Content in the Social Semantic Web, IMC-SSW 2008, vol. 417, pp. 49–58. Citeseer (2008)
20. Mackinlay, J.: Automating the design of graphical presentations of relational information. Trans. Graph. 5(2), 110–141 (1986)
21. Kämpgen, B., Harth, A.: OLAP4LD – a framework for building analysis applications over governmental statistics. In: Presutti, V., et al. (eds.) ESWC 2014. LNCS, vol. 8798, pp. 389–394. Springer, Cham (2014). https://doi.org/10.1007/978-3-319-11955-7_54
22. Klímek, J., Helmich, J., Nečaský, M.: Payola: collaborative linked data analysis and visualization framework. In: Cimiano, P., Fernández, M., Lopez, V., Schlobach, S., Völker, J. (eds.) ESWC 2013. LNCS, vol. 7955, pp. 147–151. Springer, Heidelberg (2013). https://doi.org/10.1007/978-3-642-41242-4_14
23. Kremen, P., Saeeda, L., Blaško, M.: Dataset dashboard - a SPARQL endpoint explorer. In: International Workshop on Visualization and Interaction for Ontologies and Linked Data, VOILA 2018 (2018)

24. Leskinen, P., Miyakita, G., Koho, M., Hyvönen, E., et al.: Combining faceted search with data-analytic visualizations on top of a sparql endpoint. In: International Workshop on Visualization and Interaction for Ontologies and Linked Data, VOILA 2018. CEUR-WS.org (2018)
25. Lohmann, S., Link, V., Marbach, E., Negru, S.: WebVOWL: web-based visualization of ontologies. In: Lambrix, P., et al. (eds.) EKAW 2014. LNCS (LNAI), vol. 8982, pp. 154–158. Springer, Cham (2015). https://doi.org/10.1007/978-3-319-17966-7_21
26. Lohmann, S., Negru, S., Haag, F., Ertl, T.: Visualizing ontologies with VOWL. Seman. Web **7**(4), 399–419 (2016)
27. Mackinlay, J., Hanrahan, P., Stolte, C.: Show me: automatic presentation for visual analysis. Trans. Visual Comput. Graph. **13**(6), 1137–1144 (2007)
28. Martin, M., Abicht, K., Stadler, C., Ngonga Ngomo, A.-C., Soru, T., Auer, S.: CubeViz: exploration and visualization of statistical linked data. In: International Conference on World Wide Web, pp 219–222. ACM (2015)
29. May, W.: Information extraction and integration with Florid: the Mondial case study. Technical report 131, Universität Freiburg, Institut für Informatik (1999)
30. McBrien, P., Poulovassilis, A.: Towards data visualisation based on conceptual modelling. In: Trujillo, J.C., et al. (eds.) ER 2018. LNCS, vol. 11157, pp. 91–99. Springer, Cham (2018). https://doi.org/10.1007/978-3-030-00847-5_8
31. Nuzzolese, A.G., Presutti, V., Gangemi, A., Peroni, S., Ciancarini, P.: Aemoo: linked data exploration based on knowledge patterns. Seman. Web **8**(1), 87–112 (2017)
32. Peña, O., Aguilera, U., López-de-Ipiña, D.: Linked open data visualization revisited: a survey. Seman. Web J. (2014)
33. R Core Team: R: a Language and Environment for Statistical Computing. R Foundation for Statistical Computing (2013)
34. Ristoski, P., Paulheim, H.: Visual analysis of statistical data on maps using linked open data. In: Gandon, F., et al. (eds.) ESWC 2015. LNCS, vol. 9341, pp. 138–143. Springer, Cham (2015). https://doi.org/10.1007/978-3-319-25639-9_27
35. Roth, S.F., Kolojejchick, J., Mattis, J., Goldstein, J.: Interactive graphic design using automatic presentation knowledge. In: Proceedings of CHI, pp. 112–117. ACM (1994)
36. Shneiderman, B.: The eyes have it: a task by data type taxonomy for information visualizations. In: The Craft of Information Visualization, pp. 364–371. Morgan Kaufmann (2003)
37. Stadler, C., Martin, M., Auer, S.: Exploring the web of spatial data with facete. In: International Conference on World Wide Web, pp. 175–178. ACM (2014)
38. Stolte, C., Tang, D., Hanrahan, P.: Polaris: a system for query, analysis, and visualization of multidimensional relational databases. Trans. Visual Comput. Graphics **8**(1), 52–65 (2002)
39. Telea, A.C.: Data Visualization: Principles and Practice. CRC Press, Boca Raton (2014)
40. Thellmann, K., Galkin, M., Orlandi, F., Auer, S.: LinkDaViz – automatic binding of linked data to visualizations. In: Arenas, M., et al. (eds.) ISWC 2015. LNCS, vol. 9366, pp. 147–162. Springer, Cham (2015). https://doi.org/10.1007/978-3-319-25007-6_9
41. Tory, M., Moller, T.: Rethinking visualization: a high-level taxonomy. In: Proceedings of Information Visualization, pp. 151–158. IEEE (2004)
42. Tschinkel, G., Veas, E.E., Mutlu, B., Sabol, V.: Using semantics for interactive visual analysis of linked open data. In: ISWC, pp. 133–136 (2014)

43. Ward, M.O., Grinstein, G., Keim, D.: Interactive Data Visualization: Foundations, Techniques, and Applications. CRC Press, Boca Raton (2010)
44. Ware, C.: Information Visualization: Perception for Design, 3rd edn. Morgan Kaufmann, Burlington (2013)
45. Weise, M., Lohmann, S., Haag, F.: Extraction and visualization of TBox information from SPARQL endpoints. In: Blomqvist, E., Ciancarini, P., Poggi, F., Vitali, F. (eds.) EKAW 2016. LNCS (LNAI), vol. 10024, pp. 713–728. Springer, Cham (2016). https://doi.org/10.1007/978-3-319-49004-5_46
46. Wilkinson, L.: The Grammar of Graphics. Springer, Heidelberg (2005)
47. Wills, G., Wilkinson, L.: AutoVis: automatic visualization. Inf. Visual. **9**(1), 47–69 (2010)
48. Wongsuphasawat, K., et al.: Voyager: exploratory analysis via faceted browsing of visualization recommendations. Trans. Visual Comput. Graphics **22**(1), 649–658 (2016)

S-RDF: A New RDF Serialization Format for Better Storage Without Losing Human Readability

Irvin Dongo[1,2(✉)] and Richard Chbeir[3]

[1] Univ. Bordeaux, ESTIA, Bidart, France
[2] Electrical and Electronics Engineering Department,
Universidad Católica San Pablo, Arequipa, Peru
`i.dongoescalante@estia.fr`
[3] Univ. Pau & Pays Adour, E2S/UPPA, LIUPPA, EA3000, Anglet, France
`richard.chbeir@univ-pau.fr`

Abstract. Nowadays, RDF data becomes more and more popular on the Web due to the advances of the Semantic Web and the Linked Open Data initiatives. Several works are focused on transforming relational databases to RDF by storing related data in N-Triple serialization format. However, these approaches do not take into account the existing normalization of their databases since N-Triple format allows data redundancy and does not control any normalization by itself. Moreover, the mostly used and recommended serialization formats, such as RDF/XML, Turtle, and HDT, have either high human-readability but waste storage capacity, or focus further on storage capacities while providing low human-readability. To overcome these limitations, we propose here a new serialization format, called *S-RDF*. By considering the structure (graph) and values of the RDF data separately, S-RDF reduces the duplicity of values by using unique identifiers. Results show an important improvement over the existing serialization formats in terms of storage (up to 71,66% w.r.t. N-Triples) and human readability.

Keywords: Serialization format · Semantic Web · Data representation · RDF

1 Introduction

For the Semantic Web, RDF is the *common format* to describe resources, which are abstractions of entities (documents, abstract concepts, persons, companies, etc.) of the real world. It was developed by Ora Lassila and Ralph Swick in 1998 [15]. RDF uses triples in the form of ⟨`subject`, `predicate`, `object`⟩ expressions, also named statements, to provide relationships among resources.

Currently, RDF data available on the Web is increasing rapidly due to the promotion of the Semantic Web and the Linked Open Data (LOD) initiatives [20]. Governments, organizations and research communities are part of the LOD initiatives, providing their data to have a more flexible data integration, increasing the data quality and providing new services [10]. Since RDF

© Springer Nature Switzerland AG 2019
H. Panetto et al. (Eds.): OTM 2019, LNCS 11877, pp. 246–264, 2019.
https://doi.org/10.1007/978-3-030-33246-4_16

does not restrict how data is converted, several RDF serializations are available in the literature [11]. For instance, RDF/XML is historically the first W3C standard which serializes the RDF graph (⟨subject, predicate, object⟩) into XML. Other serializations, such as Turtle and N3, are also highly recommended [18]. In the literature, several works have been proposed to convert different datasets to RDF/OWL. The works in [12,14,17,23,26] propose to convert XML data into RDF using XPath expressions, XSD Schemas, DTD[1], etc. Other works provided in [3,4,9,13,19,21,22,24] address RDF conversion of relational database models to publish huge quantity of information and linked to the Web. However, current adopted serialization formats are mainly focusing on document-centric view to increase human readability, while requiring important storage space and bandwidth resources [11]. In essence, these formats do not control the redundancy of data by definition which also affects the conceptual model. The authors in [25] address the syntactic redundancy of the data by applying a normalization methodology. Other authors as in [11] propose a binary representation format called HDT, reducing the redundancy of data, but decreasing the human readability of the information.

To overcome these limitations, we propose here a new serialization format called *S-RDF*, which represents the RDF graph structure and the values separately for a better human readability. This serialization is available to manage medium-large datasets by reusing identifiers (keys) extracted from several ones. Moreover, the storage is reduced and some graph properties (e.g., degree centrality measure[2]) can be easily analyzed. We validated our serialization format through several experiments. Results show an improvement over the existing serialization formats in terms of storage (up to 71.66% with respect to N-Triples) and human readability.

The rest of this paper is organized as follows. In Sect. 2, we present a motivating scenario to illustrate better the needs. Section 3 surveys the related literature. Terminologies and definitions are presented in Sect. 4. Section 5 describes our serialization format. In Sect. 6, we present the experiments conducted to evaluate the compression rate and the human-readability. Finally, we present conclusions in Sect. 7.

2   Motivating Scenario

As mentioned previously, RDF data can be represented in different ways (serializations), i.e., stored in a file system through several formats. In order to illustrate the limitations of existing serialization formats, we consider a scenario in which the information of Listing 1 is shared on the Web. This listing shows four Schools entities: S0991, S0992, S0993, and S0994, which have information such as rdf:type, ins:name, ins:postalCode, and ins:established.

---

[1] Document Type Definition (DTD) defines the structure and the legal elements and attributes of an XML document.

[2] Centrality identifies the most related nodes within a graph, which have a high number of relations.

```
@Prefix ins:http://institutions.com/0.2/
ins:S0991;
ins:name "Lycee du Parc"^^xsd:string ;
ins:postalCode "64600"^^xsd:string ;
ins:established 1985-05-19^^xsd:date ;
rdf:type http://www.w3.org/2002/07/owl#Thing.

ins:S0992;
ins:name "Napoleon Business"^^xsd:string ;
ins:postalCode "64100"^^xsd:string ;
ins:established 1986-12-19^^xsd:date .
rdf:type http://www.w3.org/2002/07/owl#Thing.

ins:S0993;
ins:name "Ecole national de l'energi"^^xsd:string ;
ins:postalCode "64500"^^xsd:string ;
ins:established 1984-11-21^^xsd:date .
rdf:type http://www.w3.org/2002/07/owl#Thing.

ins:S0994;
ins:name "Grande Ville School"^^xsd:string ;
ins:postalCode "64600"^^xsd:string ;
ins:established 1977-08-22^^xsd:date .
rdf:type http://www.w3.org/2002/07/owl#Thing.
```

Listing 1. School Information

Table 1 shows the serialization formats defined by the W3C (RDF/XML, Turtle, N-Triple, and N3). These formats are document-centric view since their data can be read and understood by humans; however, for a data that generates a graph with a considerable depth (more than three), the readability is reduced. For instance, according to our motivating scenario, one can easily observe the properties of the entity S0991 (`ins:name`, `ins:postalCode`, `ins:established`) and its respective values of the RDF/XML, Turtle, N-Triple and N3 serialization formats, since the depth of the generated graph is 2. If some blank nodes are added between the entity and the properties, the readability decreases by finding the properties in another part of the document, using the entity and blank nodes as references to search the values.

The RDFa, microdata and JSON-LD serialization formats are adopted as recommendation by the W3C. Table 2 shows and describes the three aforementioned formats. These formats are also document centric view as the previous ones; therefore, the same limitation is found. Moreover, since all serialization formats are document centric view, the storage is not taken into account by any of them. For small datasets, it is not a need, but for medium and large datasets, especially the ones obtained from relational databases, the storage represents a critical issue and has an impact on exchanging data.

In general, the first RDF serialization formats were proposed as document-centric view (RDF/XML, Turtle), since RDF data describes mainly Web Pages as resources (e.g., DBpedia from Wikipedia) and the number of properties to described them is limited (About: Eiffel Tower is describe by 156 triples); however, as the resources can be linked on the Web, the number of triples increases exponentially by considering datasets that use several resources. Therefore, a format able to describe a resource or a set of resources is needed considering the storage as a main requirement for medium-large datasets.

Table 1. Serialization formats defined by the W3C

S. Format	Description	Example of Listing 1

RDF/XML [18]	It is the first serialization format adopted by the W3C. This format serializes the RDF and XML files, where nodes and edges of the RDF document are represented using XML syntax. Their current media type is application/rdf+xml	```<?xml version="1.0"?>```
		```<rdf:RDF xmlns:rdf="http://www.w3.org/1999/02/22-rdf-syntax-ns#"```
		``` xmlns:dc="http://purl.org/dc/elements/1.1/"```
		```xmlns:ins="http://institutions.com/0.2/">```
		``` <rdf:Description rdf:about="http://institutions.com/0.2/S0991">```
		``` <ins:name rdf:datatype="xsd:string">Lycee du Parc</ins:name>```
		``` <ins:postalCode rdf:datatype="xsd:string">64600</ins:postalCode>```
		``` <ins:established rdf:datatype="xsd:date">1985-05-19</ins:established>```
		``` <rdf:type rdf:resource="http://www.w3.org/2002/07/owl#Thing" />```
		``` </rdf:Description>```
		``` ...```
		```</rdf:RDF>```

Turtle (Terse RDF Triple Language) [18]	It is a textual serialization format to encode RDF documents in a compact form and also readable for humans. Their current media type is application/x-turtle	```@prefix ns0: <http://institutions.com/0.2/> .```
		```@prefix xsd: <http://www.w3.org/2001/XMLSchema#> .```
		
		```<http://institutions.com/0.2/S0991>```
		``` ns0:name "Lycee du Parc"^^xsd:string ;```
		``` ns0:postalCode "64600"^^xsd:string ;```
		``` ns0:established "1985-05-19"^^xsd:date . ...```

N-Triple (Notation of Triples) [18]	It is simple serialization of RDF but not as compact as Turtle format. Their current media type is text/plain	```<http://institutions.com/0.2/S0991> <http://institutions.com/0.2/-```
		```postalCode> "64600"^^<xsd:string> .```
		```<http://institutions.com/0.2/S0991> <http://institutions.com/0.2/-```
		```name> "Lycee du Parc"^^<xsd:string> .```
		```<http://institutions.com/0.2/S0991> <http://institutions.com/0.2/-```
		```established> "1985-05-19"^^<xsd:date> . ...```

N3 (Notation 3) [18]	It is an extension format of turtle language expressing a superset of RDF and has been designed with human readability in mind. Their current media type is text/rdf+n3	```@prefix dc: <http://purl.org/dc/elements/1.1/> .```
		```@prefix ins: <http://institutions.com/0.2/> .```
		```@prefix rdf: <http://www.w3.org/1999/02/22-rdf-syntax-ns#> .```
		```@prefix rdfs: <http://www.w3.org/2000/01/rdf-schema#> .```
		```@prefix xml: <http://www.w3.org/XML/1998/namespace> .```
		```@prefix xsd: <http://www.w3.org/2001/XMLSchema#> .```
		
		```ins:S0991 ins:established "1985-05-19"^^<xsd:date> ;```
		``` ins:name "Lycee du Parc"^^<xsd:string> ;```
		``` ins:postalCode "64600"^^<xsd:string> . ...```

By regarding the limitations of existing serialization formats, we have identified three main requirements according to the challenges and objectives of this work:

- A high-human readability for easy understanding of data;
- A high radio compression for minimizing the storage space and reducing exchanging delays; and
- A format oriented to describe medium-large datasets.

The following section describes and compares the related work by using the identified requirements.

3 Related Work

To the best of our knowledge, several serialization formats have been also proposed in the literature other than the ones adopted or recommended by the W3C. The authors in [8] present a binary RDF representation for large datasets. They represent the RDF graph in three logical components: (i) Header, (ii) Dictionary, and (iii) Triples. The size of the datasets is reduced, improving the data sharing and the querying and indexing performance. In [11], the authors improve their previous work up to 2 times for more structured datasets, and a significant improvement for semi-structured datasets as DBpedia. Other works, as in [5], have focused on compressed representation for RDF Querying. The authors highlight that the improvement is around 50% to 60% of the original HDT. This format is proposed for the use of GPU.

Table 3 shows our related work classification. RDF/XML, Turtle, N3 and JSON-LD focus on human readability since their formats can be easily read by humans. HDT, HDT++ and TripleID-C have been designed to improve the

Table 2. Serialization formats recommended by the W3C

S. Format	Description	Example

RDFa (Resource Description Framework in Attributes)	It is a serialization format that adds structured data to HTML or XHTML documents by extending the attributes of elements	`<div xmlns="http://www.w3.org/1999/xhtml"`
		`  prefix="`
		`    owl: http://www.w3.org/2002/07/owl#`
		`    ns1: xsd:`
		`    rdf: http://www.w3.org/1999/02/22-rdf-syntax-ns#`
		`    ins: http://institutions.com/0.2/`
		`    rdfs: http://www.w3.org/2000/01/rdf-schema#"`
		`  >`
		`  <div typeof="owl:Thing" about="http://institutions.com/0.2/S0991">`
		`    <div property="ins:name" datatype="ns1:string" content=`
		`      "Lycee du Parc"></div>`
		`    <div property="ins:postalCode" datatype="ns1:string" content=`
		`      "64600"></div>`
		`    <div property="ins:established" datatype="ns1:date" content=`
		`      "1985-05-19"></div>`
		`  </div>  ...`
		`</div>`

Microdata [1]	It is a serialization format that describe a simpler way of annotating HTML elements with machine-readable tags	`<div>`
		`  <div itemtype="http://www.w3.org/2002/07/owl#Thing"`
		`  itemid="http://institutions.com/0.2/S0991" itemscope>`
		`    <meta itemprop="http://institutions.com/0.2/postalCode"`
		`      content="64600" />`
		`    <meta itemprop="http://institutions.com/0.2/established"`
		`      content="1985-05-19" />`
		`    <meta itemprop="http://institutions.com/0.2/name"`
		`      content="Lycee du Parc" />`
		`  </div>  ...`
		`</div>`

JSON-LD [16]	It is a concrete syntax format that extends the RDF data model to optionally allow JSON-LD to serialize Generalized RDF Datasets	`{`
		`  "@context": {`
		`    "ins": "http://institutions.com/0.2/",`
		`    "owl": "http://www.w3.org/2002/07/owl#",`
		`    "rdf": "http://www.w3.org/1999/02/22-rdf-syntax-ns#",`
		`    "rdfs": "http://www.w3.org/2000/01/rdf-schema#",`
		`    "xsd": "http://www.w3.org/2001/XMLSchema#"`
		`  },`
		`  "@id": "ins:S0991",`
		`  "@type": "owl:Thing",`
		`  "ins:established": {`
		`    "@type": "xsd:date",`
		`    "@value": "1985-05-19"`
		`  },`
		`  "ins:name": {`
		`    "@type": "xsd:string",`
		`    "@value": "Lycee du Parc"`
		`  },  ...`
		`}`

Table 3. Related work classification

Serialization format	Human readability	Storage (Compression)	Non-redundancy	Large-medium dataset	Media type
RDF/XML	Low+	Medium	Low	Low	RDF+XML
Turtle	High	Medium	Medium	Low	-
N-Triple	Low	Low	Low	Low	-
N3	High	Medium	Medium	Low	-
RDFa	Low	Low	Low	Low	HTML/XHTML
Microdata	Low	Low	Low	Low	HTML
JSON-LD	Medium	Medium	Medium	Low	JSON
HDT [8]	Zero	High	High	High	Binary
HDT++ [11]	Zero	High+	High	High	Binary
TripleID-C [5]	Low	High	High	Medium	GPU
RDF sequence	**High**	**Medium+**	**High**	**Medium+**	-

storage, affecting the human readability. Note that none of the works satisfies all the defined requirements; thus, a new RDF serialization format is required.

Before describing our serialization format, the following section introduces some common terminologies and definitions in the context of RDF.

4   RDF Terminologies and Definitions

RDF commonly uses triples in the form of ⟨subject, predicate, object⟩ expressions/statements, to provide relationships among resources. The RDF triples can be composed of the following elements:

- An **IRI**, which is an extension of the Uniform Resource Identifier (URI) scheme to a much wider repertoire of characters from the Universal Character Set (Unicode/ISO 10646), including Chinese, Japanese, and Korean character sets [7].
- A **Blank Node**, representing a local identifier used in some concrete RDF syntaxes or RDF store implementations. A blank node can be associated with an identifier (rdf:nodeID) to be referenced in the local document, which is generated manually or automatically
- A **Literal Node**, representing values as strings, numbers, and dates. According to the definition in [6], it consists of two or three parts:
  - A **lexical form**, being a Unicode string, which should be in Normal Form C[3] to assure that equivalent strings have a unique binary representation
  - A datatype **IRI**, being an IRI identifying a **datatype** that determines how the lexical form maps to an object value
  - A **non-empty language tag** as defined by "Tags for Identifying Languages" [2], if and only if the datatype IRI is http://www.w3.org/1999/02/22-rdf-syntax-ns#langString.

---

[3] It is one of the four normalization forms, which consists on a Canonical Decomposition, followed by a Canonical Composition -http://www.unicode.org/reports/tr15/.

Table 4 shows the sets of RDF's elements that we use in our formal approach description.

Table 4. Description of sets

Set	Description
I	A set of IRIs is defined as: $I = \{i_1, i_2, ..., i_n\} \mid \forall i_i \in I, i_i$ is an IRI.
L	A set of literal nodes is defined as: $L= \{l_1, l_2, ..., l_n\} \mid \forall l_i \in L, l_i$ is a literal node.
BN	A set of blank nodes is defined as: $BN = \{bn_1, bn_2, ..., bn_n\} \mid \forall bn_i \in BN, bn_i$ is a Blank Node

After the definition of sets of RDF'elements, we formally describe a triple in Definition 1.

Definition 1. Triple (t): *A Triple, denoted as t, is defined as an atomic structure consisting of a 3-tuple with a Subject (s), a Predicate (p), and Object (o), denoted as $t :< s, p, o >$, where:*

- *$s \in I \cup BN$ represents the subject to be described;*
- *p is a predicate defined as an IRI in the form* `namespace_prefix:predicate-_name`*, where namespace_prefix is a local identifier of the IRI, in which the predicate (predicate_name) is defined. The predicate (p) is also known as the* **property** *of the triple;*
- *$o \in I \cup BN \cup L$ describes the object.*   ◆

From Listing 1, one can observe the following triples with different RDF resources, properties, and literals:

- t_3: `<genid:S0991,rdf:type, http://www.w3.org/2002/07/owl#Thing>`
- t_4: `<genid:S0991,ins:name,"Lycée de la Plage">`
- t_5: `<genid:S0991,ins:established,1985-05-19>`

In this study, we also consider two types of properties (predicates):

- **Entity Property (ep):** A predicate is an entity property when it is related to an IRI or a blank node. It is also known as Object property. For example, the property `eni:locates` is an entity property since it is related to a blank node.
- **Value Property (vp):** A predicate is a value property when it is related to a literal node. It is also known as Datatype property. For example, the property `ins:established` is a value property since it is related to a literal node.

An RDF document is defined as an encoding of a set of triples, using a predefined serialization format complying with an RDF W3C standards, such as RDF/XML, Turtle, N3, etc. Additionally, we use the term *entity*, formally described in Definition 2, to identify an RDF resource (blank node and IRI).

Definition 2. Entity (e): *An entity in an RDF document, denoted as e, is represented as an IRI or a blank node (e.g., School, Power Plant).* ◆

For example, from Listing 1, the triple `<S0991,ins:name,"Lycée de la Plage">` has the entity `S0991`.

In Definitions 3, 4, 5, and 6, we formally describe the respective sets of entities, entity properties, value properties, and literal values of an RDF document.

Definition 3. Entity Set (E): *Given a set of triples $T = \{t_i \mid t_i :< s, p, o >\}$, the entities of each t_i define the set of all entities, denoted as $E = \bigcup_{i=1}^{n} t_i.s \cup t_i.o \iff t_i.o \in I \cup BN$, where n is the number of triples.* ◆

The entity set according to Definition 3 of Listing 1 is: E = {http://institutions.com/0.2/S0991, http://institutions.com.com/0.2/S0992, http://institutions.com/0.2/S0993, http://institutions.com/0.2/S0994, http://www.w3.org/2002/07/owl#Thing}.

Definition 4. Entity Properties (EP): *Given a set of triples $T = \{t_i \mid t_i :< s, p, o >\}$, the predicates of all t_i that are entity properties, define the set of entity properties, denoted as: $EP = \bigcup_{i=1}^{n} t_i.p \iff t_i.o \in I \cup BN$, where n is the number of triples.* ◆

The entity properties from Listing 1 are: EP = {rdf:type} or EP = {http://www.w3.org/1999/02/22-rdf-syntax-ns#type}.

Definition 5. Value Properties (VP): *Given a set of triples $T = \{t_i \mid t_i :< s, p, o >\}$, the predicate of all t_i that are value properties, define the set of value properties, denoted as: $VP = \bigcup_{i=1}^{n} t_i.p \iff t_i.o \in L$, where n is the number of triples.* ◆

According to Definition 5, the value properties obtained from the triples of Listing 1 are: VP = {http://institutions.com/0.2/name, http://institutions.com/0.2/postal-Code, http://institutions.com/0.2/established}.

Definition 6. Literal Values (LV): *Given a set of triples $T = \{t_i \mid t_i :< s, p, o >\}$, the literals of all t_i define the set of literal values, denoted as: $LV = \bigcup_{i=1}^{n} t_i.o \iff t_i.o \in L$, where n is the number of triples.* ◆

According to Definition 6, the literal values from Listing 1 are: VA={"Lycée de la Plage", "64600", "1985-05-19", "Napoleon Business", "64100", "1986-12-19", "École National de l'energie", "64500", "1984-11-21", "Grande Ville School", "64200", "1977-08-22"}.

Table 5 summaries the sets of entities, entity and value properties, and literal values of an RDF document.

The following section presents and describes our new serialization format S-RDF.

Table 5. Description of sets of data of an RDF document

Set	Description
E	A set of entities is defined as: $E = \bigcup_{i=1}^{n} \{t_i.s\} \cup t_i.o \iff t_i.o \in I \cup BN$.
EP	A set of entity properties is defined as: $EP = \bigcup_{i=1}^{n} t_i.p \iff t_i.o \in I \cup BN$.
VP	A set of value properties is defined as: $VP = \bigcup_{i=1}^{n} t_i.p \iff t_i.o \in L$.
LV	A set of literal values is defined as: $LV = \bigcup_{i=1}^{n} t_i.o \iff t_i.o \in L$

5   S-RDF: Our Proposal

Our proposal mainly relies on a three step process: (i) *Extraction of RDF elements*, where the input, an RDF document in any format, is analyzed in order to extract the set of entities (E), entity properties (EP), value properties (VP), and literal values (LV); (ii) *RDF Sequence-Value generation* where entities, properties, and literal values are represented by unique identifiers (e.g., primary keys); and (iii) *RDF Sequence-Structure generation* where relations among entities, which define the RDF graph structure, are expressed using the *Sequence-Value Representation*. Thus, our serialization format (*S-RDF*) consists in two parts: (i) Value Representation and (ii) Structure. Figure 1 shows the framework of our proposal composed by three modules that materialize the three respective phases.

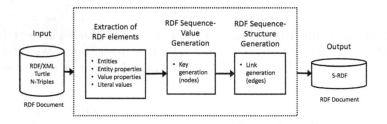

Fig. 1. Framework of our serialization format "S-RDF"

In Definition 7, we formally describe the Value Representation part of our RDF sequence, called RDF Sequence–Value. This representation associates to each entity, entity and value property, and literal value a unique identifier to be used in the structure representation of the sequence. We propose four different identifiers to easily recognize the type of data in the second part of our sequence. The entities are represented by numbers of the decimal numeral system (base 10), starting from 1. In the case of entity and value properties, both identifiers correspond to the hexavigesimal numeral system (base 26), with a domain of lowercase and uppercase alphabet letters, respectively. For the literal values, the identifiers belong to the decimal numeral system as the ones of entities, but a symbol "_" is added as a prefix. For instance, the 28th element of the entities is represented as "28", "AB" for entity properties, "ab" for value properties, while for literal values is "_28".

Definition 7. RDF Sequence–Value (S-RDF-V): *Given a set of triples* $T = \{t_i \mid t_i :< s, p, o >\}$, *its RDF Sequence-Value is defined as a 4-tuple of:*

$$S - RDF - V_T =<$$
$$Entities = \{\bigcup_{i=1}^{m} < pk_i, e_i, type_i >\},$$
$$Entity\_properties = \{\bigcup_{j=1}^{n} < pk_j, ep_j >\},$$
$$Value\_properties = \{\bigcup_{k=1}^{o} < pk_k, vp_k, datatype_k >\},$$
$$Literal\_values = \{\bigcup_{l=1}^{p} < \_pk_l, lv_l >\} >$$

where:

- *Entities is a set of 3-tuples, where:*
  * $m \in Z^+$, *is the size of E.*
  * $pk_i \in Z^+$, *is a key that represents e_i.*
  * $e_i \in E$ *is an entity.*
  * $type_i \in \{1, 2\}$, *is the type of the entity e_i (1=IRI, 2=blank node).*

- *Entity_properties is a set of 2-tuples, where:*
  * $n \in Z^+$, *is the size of EP.*
  * $pk_j \in \{A...Z\}$, *is a key that represents ep_j.*
  * $ep_j \in EP$ *is an entity property.*

- *Value_properties is a set of 3-tuples, where:*
  * $o \in Z^+$, *is the size of VP.*
  * $pk_k \in \{a...z\}$, *is a key that represents vp_k.*
  * $vp_k \in VP$ *is a value property.*
  * $datatype_k$ *is the datatype of the property.*

- *Literal_values is a set of 2-tuples, where:*
  * $p \in Z^+$, *is the size of LV.*
  * $\_pk_l$ *is a key that represents lv_l and $pk_l \in Z^+$.*
  * $lv_l \in LV$ *is a literal value.*   ◆

Tables 6, 7, 8 and 9 represent the Entities, Entity_properties, Value_properties, and Literal_values of Listing 1. The first element of the S-RDF-V is composed by the entities of Table 6. As only one relation among entities is shown in Listing 1, the second element (entity properties) of the 4-tuple is: $\{<A, \text{http://www.w3.org/1999/02/22-rdf-syntax-ns\#type}>\}$. The third and fourth elements are composed by the information in Tables 8 and 9, respectively. The set of triples (T), obtained from Listing 1, has the following RDF Sequence–Value:
S-RDF-V(T) = <
   Entities = {
   $< 1, http://institutions.com/0.2/S0991, 1 >,$
   $< 2, http://institutions.com/0.2/S0992, 1 >,$

Table 6. Entities

Key (pk_i)	Entity (e_i)	Type ($type_i$)
1	http://institutions.com/0.2/S0991	1
2	http://institutions.com/0.2/S0992	1
3	http://institutions.com/0.2/S0993	1
4	http://institutions.com/0.2/S0994	1
5	http://www.w3.org/2002/07/owl#Thing	1

Table 7. Entity properties

Key (pk_j)	Entity property (ep_j)
A	http://www.w3.org/1999/02/22-rdf-syntax-ns#type

Table 9. Literal values

Key (pk_l)	Value (lv_l)
_1	Lycée de la Plage
_2	64600
_3	1985-05-19
_4	Napoleon Business
_5	64100
_6	1986-12-19
_7	École National de l'energie
_8	64500
_9	1984-11-21
_10	Grande Ville School
_11	64200
_12	1977-08-22

Table 8. Value properties

Key (pk_k)	Value property (vp_k)	Datatype ($datatype_k$)
a	http://institutions.com/0.2/name	xsd:string
b	http://institutions.com/0.2/postalCode	xsd:string
c	http://institutions.com/0.2/established	xsd:date

$< 3, http : //institutions.com/0.2/S0993, 1 >,$
$< 4, http : //institutions.com/0.2/S0994, 1 >,$
$< 5, http : //www.w3.org/2002/07/owl#Thing, 1 >\},$
Entity_properties = {
$< A, http : //www.w3.org/1999/02/22 - rdf - syntax - ns#type >\},$
Value_properties = {
$< a, http : //institutions.com/0.2/name, xsd : string >,$
$< b, http : //institutions.com/0.2/postalCode, xsd : string >,$
$< c, http : //institutions.com/0.2/established, xsd : date >\},$
Literal_values = {
$< _1, "Lycée de la Plage" >, < _2, 64600 >, < _3, 1985 - 05 - 19 >,$
$< _4, "Napoleon Business" >, < _5, 64100 >, < _6, 1986 - 12 - 19 >,$
$< _7, "École National de l'energie" >, < _8, 64500 >, < _9, 1984 - 11 - 21 >,$
$< _10, "Grande Ville School" >, < _11, 64200 >, < _12, 1977 - 08 - 22 >\}$
$>$

The S-RDF-V represents the entities, properties, and values of an RDF document, but a document also has information about the relations among entities and literal values (node-edge-node); thus, the second part of our serialization is dedicated to represent the RDF graph structure, called RDF Sequence–Structure. It consists of a 3-tuple, where the first element is composed of an entity; the second element has all entities, which are related to the first element, preceded by its respective entity property; and the last element is used to represent value properties and its respective literal values. The RDF Sequence–Structure is defined in Definition 8.

Definition 8. RDF Sequence-Structure (S-RDF-S): *Given a set of triples $T = \{t_i \mid t_i :< s, p, o >\}$, its RDF Sequence-Structure is defined as a set of 3-tuples:*

$$S\text{-}RDF\text{-}S(T) = \{\textstyle\bigcup_{i=1}^{n} <$$
$$entity = e_i.pk,$$
$$entity\_property\text{-}entity = \{ep_j.pk, e_k.pk\},$$
$$value\_property\text{-}value = \{vp_l.pk, lv_m.pk\} >\}.$$

where:

− *entity*

  ∗ e_i *is an entity.*

− *entity_property-entity*

  ∗ ep_j, e_k *represents* $t :< e_i, ep_j, e_k >$, *such that* ep_j *is an EntityProperty where* e_i *is the subject and* e_k *the object.*

− *value_property-value*

  ∗ vp_i, lv_j *represents* $t :< e_i, vp_l, lv_m >$, *such that* vp_l *is a PropertyValue where* e_i *is the subject and* lv_m *the object.*   ◆

For example, the set of triples (T) obtained from Listing 1, has the following RDF Sequence–Structure:

S-RDF-S(T) ={
  $< 1, \{(A, 5)\}, \{(a, \_1), (b, \_2), (c, \_3)\} >$,
  $< 2, \{(A, 5)\}, \{(a, \_4), (b, \_5), (c, \_6)\} >$,
  $< 3, \{(A, 5)\}, \{(a, \_7), (b, \_8), (c, \_9)\} >$,
  $< 4, \{(A, 5)\}, \{(a, \_10), (b, \_11), (c, \_12)\} >$,
  $< 5, \{\}, \{\} >\}$,

representing: entity "1" (`http://institutions.com/0.2/S0991` according to Table 6), has an entity property " A" (`http://www.w3.org/1999/02/22-rdf-syntax-ns#type` according to Table 7), related to the entity "5" (`http://www.w3.org/2002/07/owl#Thing` according to Table 6). It also has a property value "a" (`http://institutions.com/0.2/name` according to Table 8) with a literal value "_1" ("Lycée de la Plage" according to Table 9), and so on.

Once values and structure of the RDF data are defined, we formalize the whole RDF Sequence in Definition 9.

Definition 9. RDF Sequence (*S-RDF*): *Given a set of triples* $T = \{t_i \mid t_i :<$ $s, p, o >\}$, *its RDF Sequence is a 2-tuple consisting of two parts, defined as:*

$$S - RDF(T) = <S - RDF - V(T), S - RDF - S(T)>$$

where:

- *S-RDF-V(T) is the set of values of T defined in Definition 7.*
- *S-RDF-S(T) is the structure of T defined in Definition 8.*   ◆

The S-RDF is built to represent triples considering the structure and values separately. Thus, an analysis over either the data or structure can be easily performed. Another benefit of this serialization format is the easy detection of some graph properties as the number of relationships (e.g., degree centrality measure) with respect to other serialization formats. Moreover, the storage space is reduced, since an IRI, which appears several times in an RDF document as a resource or property, is represented as a unique short key (e.g., `key:1` represents value: `http://institutions.com/0.2/S0991` or `key:A` represents value: `http://www.w3.org/2002/07/owl#Thing`, respectively). This new serialization format can be consider as part of RDF partition strategies where the models improve the storage and the querying; however, when the repository is exported/outsourced, the format is still the same (e.g., RDF/XML, Turtle). Our serialization is a new way to represent data to be shared on the Web, improving the storage without losing the readability.

In the following section, we evaluate our S-RDF with respect to the current serialization formats.

6   Experimental Evaluation

6.1   Experimental Environment and Datasets

In order to evaluate and validate our serialization format, we developed a desktop and online[4] prototype system based on Java and Jena[5] to manage the RDF data. Experiments were undertaken on a MacBook Pro, 2.2 GHz Intel Core(TM) i7 with 16.00 GB, running a MacOS Mojave and using a Sun JDK 1.7 programming environment.

Our prototype was used to perform several experiments to evaluate the viability and the compression rate of our approach in comparison with the works proposed in the literature. To do so, we considered two datasets:

---

[4] S-RDF: http://rdf-sequence.sigappfr.org.

[5] Jena is a Java framework for building Semantic Web applications. It provides a extensive Java libraries for helping developers develop code that handles RDF, RDFS, RDFa, OWL and SPARQL in line with published W3C recommendations - https://jena.apache.org/about_jena/about.html.

- **Data 1**: the *DBpedia person data*[6] with 16,842,176 triples; and
- **Data 2**: the *DBpedia geo coordinates*[7] with 151,205 triples.

Note that some of the serialization formats (e.g., RDFa, HDT++) described in the related work section were not evaluated since there are no tools available that can manage huge quantity of triples. They are mainly document oriented converters (e.g., Easy-RDF[8], RDF-Translator[9]). For our readability test, HDT and HDT+ formats were analyzed since they have a binary representation and cannot be read by humans.

We describe as follows the tests performed to evaluate our proposal.

6.2 Evaluation

Test 1: We chose randomly 50,000 triples from **Data 1** in order to measure the compression rate of the data with respect to the size of the input (6,102,029 bytes). Table 10 shows the results obtained for this test. HDT serialization format clearly overcomes the other ones (82.3936%), since it was created to minimize the storage. However, our serialization has also a good result (71.6564%) without losing the human readability criterion as the binary representation of HDT does. JSON-LD serialization has the biggest compression rate (39.0276%) among the W3C recommendation formats.

For **Data 2**, we also chose 50,000 triples from this dataset, having a size of 7,356,637 bytes. Table 11 shows similar results as the ones of *Data 1*. HDT obtained the best result with 75.6508%, while for our serialization format was 70.7767%. The JSON-LD serialization format has a 59.6130% of compression rate with respect to the input size.

Table 10. Related work comparison for **Data 1**

Serialization format	Triples	Size	Compression rate (%)
RDF/XML	50,000	3,828,810	37.2535
Turtle	50,000	4,650,993	23.7796
N-Triple	50,000	6,151,004	−0.8026
N3	50,000	4,650,993	23.7796
JSON-LD	50,000	3,720,552	39.0276
HDT	50,000	944,196 (HDT) 130,151 (Index)	82.3936
S-RDF	**50,000**	**1,729,533**	**71.6564**

---

[6] Information about persons extracted from the English and Germany Wikipedia, represented by the FOAF vocabulary - http://wiki.dbpedia.org/Downloads2015-10.

[7] Geographic coordinates extracted from Wikipedia - https://wiki.dbpedia.org/downloads-2016-10.

[8] Easy-Converte: http://www.easyrdf.org/converter.

[9] RDF-Translator: https://rdf-translator.appspot.com.

Table 11. Related work comparison for **Data 2**

Serialization format	Triples	Size	Compression rate (%)
RDF/XML	50,000	4,338,226	41.0298
Turtle	50,000	5,908,228	19.6885
N-Triple	50,000	7,356,638	−0.0001
N3	50,000	5,908,228	19.6885
JSON-LD	50,000	2,971,124	59.6130
HDT	50,000	1,665,119 (HDT) 126,163 (Index)	75.6508
S-RDF	**50,000**	**2,149,852**	**70.7767**

Test 2: Since there is no benchmark model for readability available in the literature to compare the existing serialization formats, we propose three questions which are related to several aspects of the RDF structure. (i) The first question is about relations, which can help to the end-user to recognize some important nodes according to the context, (ii) the second one is related to the terminal nodes, and (iii) the third one to literal values. The questions are presented as follows:

1. Is the resource X the most related one of the data?
2. Is the resource Y a terminal node in the data?
3. How many literal values has the resource Z?

where X, Y, and Z are resources that belong to the set of triples used to evaluate this test (see Listing 2).

```
@prefix ns0: <http://institutions.com/0.2/> .
@prefix xsd: <http://www.w3.org/2001/XMLSchema#> .
@prefix owl: <http://www.w3.org/2002/07/owl#> .
<http://institutions.com/0.2/S0991>
    ns0:validated ns0:N_1 ;
    ns0:invalidated ns0:N_2 ;
    ns0:expired ns0:N_3 .
ns0:N_1
    ns0:name "Lycee du Parc"^^xsd:string ;
    ns0:postalCode "64600"^^xsd:string ;
    ns0:established "1985-05-19"^^xsd:date ;
    a owl:Thing .
ns0:N_2
    ns0:name "Ecole du Parc"^^xsd:string ;
    ns0:postalCode "64100"^^xsd:string ;
    a owl:Thing .
ns0:N_3
    ns0:name "Universite du Parc"^^xsd:string ;
    ns0:postalCode "64200"^^xsd:string ;
    a owl:Thing .
```

Listing 2. List of triples used for **Test 2**, serialized in Turtle format

In this test, we evaluated our human readability criterion by surveying 40 people that have under- and post-graduate degrees in computer science[10]. The participants evaluated the serialization formats through the three previous questions, choosing an option to answer them: *Yes*, *No*, and *I do not know* for the two first questions, and a value among *1* to *5* and *"I do not know"* option for the third one.

To evaluate the results, we calculated the F-measure, based on the Recall (R) and Precision (PR). These criteria are commonly adopted in information retrieval and are calculated as follows:

$$\mathbf{PR} = \frac{A}{A+B} \in [0,1] \quad \mathbf{R} = \frac{A}{A+C} \in [0,1] \quad \mathbf{F\text{-}measure} = \frac{2 \times PR \times R}{PR+R} \in [0,1]$$

where A is the number of correct answers; B is the number of wrong answers; and C is the number of *"I do not know"* options selected by the participants.

Table 12 shows the results obtained for this evaluation. For *Question 1*, the N3 serialization format obtained the best Precision (84.62%), while the one for our serialization format was 84.00%. RDF/XML and JSON-LD obtained the lowest Precision (22.73% and 36.36%, respectively). By regarding the F-measure, we can observe that Turtle, N3, and our proposal (S-RDF) help user to identify some graph properties as the centrality measure, since they obtained a high result (over 68.00%). For *Question 2*, which is related to identify terminal nodes, most of the serialization formats obtained a similar F-measure ($\approx$61.00%), but for the RDF/XML format, the F-measure was 43.14% due to the low Recall (35.48%). A low Recall can be interpreted as the serialization format is not easy-readable for

Table 12. Number of correct, incorrect, and ambiguous values of each question per serialization format

Serialization Format	Question 1						Question 2					
	C	I	A	Precision	Recall	F measure	C	I	A	Precision	Recall	F measure
RDF/XML	5	17	18	22.73%	21.74%	22.22%	11	9	20	55.00%	35.48%	43.14%
Turtle	24	6	10	80.00%	70.59%	75.00%	17	5	18	77.27%	48.57%	59.65%
N-Triple	10	6	24	62.50%	29.41%	40.00%	15	6	19	71.43%	44.11%	54.55%
N3	22	4	14	84.62%	61.11%	70.97%	21	2	17	91.30%	55.26%	68.85%
JSON-LD	8	14	18	36.36%	30.77%	33.33%	18	9	13	66.67%	58.06%	62.07%
S-RDF	21	4	15	84.00%	58.33%	68.85%	19	8	13	70.37%	59.38%	64.41%

Serialization Format	Question 3					
	C	I	A	Precision	Recall	F measure
RDF/XML	15	6	19	71.43%	62.50%	66,67%
Turtle	23	14	3	62.12%	88.46%	73.02%
N-Triple	8	10	22	44.44%	26.67%	33.33%
N3	19	10	11	65.52%	63.33%	64.41%
JSON-LD	6	23	11	20.69%	35.29%	26.09%
S-RDF	21	12	7	63.63%	75.00%	68.85%
C = Correct						
I = Incorrect						
A = I do not know option (ambiguous).						

---

[10] The form is available here: https://forms.gle/DNMfsp5LL3nw1hW9A.

the user. For *Question 3*, Turtle obtained the best F-measure (73.02%), while for S-RDF the value was 68.85%. By analyzing the answers, we noticed that some people confused the entity property and its respective value as a literal value since they only counted the number of elements associated to the entity.

Table 13 shows the global results of this test. In this table, we can identify two groups: G1: RDF/XML, N-Triples, and JSON-LD with a F-measure around 43.00%, and G2: Turtle, N3, and S-RDF with a value around 68.00%. One of the reasons of the low F-measure obtained by G1, is that these formats were created to keep the interoperability among system, using XML and JSON formats for example. The results demonstrate that our serialization format (S-RDF) can improve the storage without losing the human-readability criterion.

Table 13. Total number of correct, incorrect and ambiguous values per serialization format

Serialization format	C	I	A	Precision	Recall	F-measure
RDF/XML	31	32	47	49.72%	39.91%	44.01%
Turtle	64	25	31	73.14%	69.20%	69.22%
N-Triple	33	22	65	59.46%	33.40%	42.63%
N3	62	16	42	80.48%	59.90%	68.08%
JSON-LD	32	46	42	41.24%	41.38%	40.50%
S-RDF	61	24	35	72.67%	64.24%	67.37%

C = Correct, I = Incorrect, A = I do not know option (ambiguous).

7   Conclusion

In this paper, we propose a new serialization format, called *S-RDF*, which represents the RDF graph structure and values, separately. This format is focused on human readability, storage, and data redundancy to represent medium and large datasets. We evaluated our serialization format in terms of compression rate and human readability with respect to the state of the art. Results show a high compression without losing human readability, which is an advantage over the serialization formats created to minimize storage. According to the survey evaluation, our S-RDF allows identify easily the resources with more relations in the RDF graph (degree centrality measure) by identifying the entity with the bigger number of entity properties.

We are currently working on normalization methods over the S-RDF in order to provide a unique and deterministic output for similar inputs.

References

1. Microdata to RDF - Second Edition - Transformation from HTML+Microdata to RDF. https://www.w3.org/TR/microdata-rdf/ (2014). Accessed 01 July 2019
2. Phillips, M.D.A.: Tags for identifying languages. https://tools.ietf.org/html/bcp47. Accessed 01 July 2019
3. Bornea, M.A., et al.: Building an efficient RDF store over a relational database. In: Proceedings of the 2013 ACM SIGMOD International Conference on Management of Data, SIGMOD 2013, pp. 121–132. ACM, New York (2013)
4. Būmans, G., Čerāns, K.: RDB2OWL: A practical approach for transforming RDB data into RDF/OWL. In: Proceedings of the 6th International Conference on Semantic Systems, I-SEMANTICS 2010, pp. 25:1–25:3. ACM, New York (2010)
5. Chantrapornchai, C., Makpaisit, P.: TripleiD-C: low cost compressed representation for RDF query processing in GPUs. In: Proceedings of the International Conference on High Performance Computing in Asia-Pacific Region, HPC Asia 2018, pp. 261–270. ACM, New York (2018)
6. Cyganiak, R., Wood, D., Lanthaler, M.: RDF 1.1 concepts and abstract syntax. Technical report (2014). Accessed 06 Dec 2016
7. Duerst, M., Suignard, M.: Internationalized resource identifiers (IRIs). Technical report, Microsoft Corporation (2004)
8. Fernández, J.D.: Binary RDF for scalable publishing, exchanging and consumption in the web of data. In: Proceedings of the 21st International Conference on World Wide Web, WWW 2012 Companion, pp. 133–138. ACM, New York (2012)
9. Goasdoué, F., Manolescu, I., Roatiş, A.: Getting more RDF support from relational databases. In: Proceedings of the 21st International Conference on World Wide Web, WWW 2012 Companion, pp. 515–516. ACM, New York (2012)
10. Hausenblas, M., Ding, L., Peristeras, V.: Linked open government data. IEEE Intell. Syst. 27, 11–15 (2012)
11. Hernández-Illera, A., Martínez-Prieto, M.A., Fernández, J.D.: Serializing RDF in compressed space. In: 2015 Data Compression Conference, pp. 363–372, April 2015
12. Huang, J.-Y., Lange, C., Auer, S.: Streaming transformation of XML to RDF using XPath-based mappings. In: Proceedings of the 11th International Conference on Semantic Systems, SEMANTICS 2015, pp. 129–136. ACM, New York (2015)
13. Konstantinou, N., Kouis, D., Mitrou, N.: Incremental export of relational database contents into RDF graphs. In: Proceedings of the 4th International Conference on Web Intelligence, Mining and Semantics (WIMS14), WIMS 2014, pp. 33:1–33:8. ACM, New York (2014)
14. Lacoste, D., Sawant, K.P., Roy, S.: An efficient XML to OWL converter. In: Proceedings of the 4th India Software Engineering Conference, ISEC 2011, pp. 145–154. ACM, New York (2011)
15. Lassila, O., Swick, R.R., Wide, W., Consortium, W.: Resource description framework (RDF) model and syntax specification (1998)
16. Kellogg, G., Lanthaler, M., Lindström, N., Sporny, M., Longley, D.: JSON-LD 1.0, A JSON-based Serialization for Linked Data, W3C Recommendation 16 January 2014 (2014). https://www.w3.org/TR/json-ld/. Accessed 27 Oct 2017
17. O'Connor, M.J., Das, A.: Acquiring OWL ontologies from XML documents. In: Proceedings of the Sixth International Conference on Knowledge Capture, K-CAP 2011, pp. 17–24. ACM, New York (2011)
18. Patel-Schneider, P.F., Hayes, P.J.: RDF 1.1 Semantics, W3C Recommendation 25 February 2014 (2014). https://www.w3.org/TR/rdf11-mt/#literals-and-datatypes. Accessed 01 July 2019

19. Salas, P.E., Marx, E., Mera, A., Viterbo, J.: RDB2RDF plugin: relational databases to RDF plugin for eclipse. In: Proceedings of the 1st Workshop on Developing Tools As Plug-ins, TOPI 2011, pp. 28–31. ACM, New York (2011)
20. Sandro Hawke, P.A., Herman, I.: W3C semantic web activity (2001). https://www.w3c.org/2001/sw/. Accessed 06 Dec 2018
21. Sequeda, J.F., Arenas, M., Miranker, D.P.: On directly mapping relational databases to RDF and OWL. In: Proceedings of the 21st International Conference on World Wide Web, WWW 2012, pp. 649–658. ACM, New York (2012)
22. Stefanova, S., Risch, T.: Scalable reconstruction of RDF-archived relational databases. In: Proceedings of the Fifth Workshop on Semantic Web Information Management, SWIM 2013, pp. 5:1–5:4. ACM, New York (2013)
23. Thuy, P.T.T., Lee, Y.-K., Lee, S.: DTD2OWL: automatic transforming XML documents into OWL ontology. In: Proceedings of the 2nd International Conference on Interaction Sciences: Information Technology, Culture and Human, ICIS 2009, pp. 125–131. ACM, New York (2009)
24. Thuy, P.T.T., Thuan, N.D., Han, Y., Park, K., Lee, Y.-K.: RDB2RDF: completed transformation from relational database into RDF ontology. In: Proceedings of the 8th International Conference on Ubiquitous Information Management and Communication, ICUIMC 2014, pp. 88:1–88:7. ACM, New York (2014)
25. Ticona-Herrera, R., Tekli, J., Chbeir, R., Laborie, S., Dongo, I., Guzman, R.: Toward RDF normalization. In: Johannesson, P., Lee, M.L., Liddle, S.W., Opdahl, A.L., López, Ó.P. (eds.) ER 2015. LNCS, vol. 9381, pp. 261–275. Springer, Cham (2015). https://doi.org/10.1007/978-3-319-25264-3_19
26. Vion-Dury, J.-Y.: Using RDFS/OWL to ease semantic integration of structured documents. In: Proceedings of the 2013 ACM Symposium on Document Engineering, DocEng 2013, pp. 189–192. ACM, New York (2013)

A Linked Open Data Approach for Web Service Evolution

Hamza Labbaci[1,3(✉)], Nasredine Cheniki[1], Yacine Sam[1], Nizar Messai[1],
Brahim Medjahed[2], and Youcef Aklouf[3]

[1] University of Tours, Tours, France
{hamza.labbaci,nasredine.cheniki,yacine.sam,nizar.messai}@univ-tours.fr
[2] University of Michigan - Dearborn, Dearborn, USA
brahim@umich.edu
[3] USTHB University, Algiers, Algeria
yaklouf@usthb.dz

Abstract. Web services are subject to changes during their lifetime, such as updates in data types, operations, and the overall functionality. Such changes may impact the way Web services are discovered, consumed, and recommended. We propose a Linked Open Data (LOD) approach for managing Web services new deployment and updates. We propose algorithms, based on semantic LOD similarity measures, to infer composition and substitution relationships for both newly deployed and updated services. We introduce a technique that gathers Web service interactions and users' feedbacks to continuously update service relationships. To improve the accuracy of relationship recommendation, we propose an algorithm to learn new LOD relationships from Web service past interaction. We conduct extensive experiments on real-world Web services to evaluate our approach.

Keywords: Web service evolution · Linked Open Data · Social feedback · Composition · Substitution

1 Introduction

Recent breakthroughs in service oriented computing have encouraged companies and organizations to export their functionalities as Web services. Deploying Web services guarantees a better exposure, visibility, and more market opportunities. Web services do not operate in silos; they usually interact through several relationships such as *Composition* and *Substitution*. *Composition* denotes collaboration between services with complementary functionality to provide an added-value service known as *composite service* [16]. It refers to the ability of services to be combined together (both syntactically and semantically) as parts of the same composite application [13]. *Substitution* [12] is defined as the possibility of replacing the invocation of a service (at compile or run-time) by another service. It may reflect competition between services offering comparable functionality

© Springer Nature Switzerland AG 2019
H. Panetto et al. (Eds.): OTM 2019, LNCS 11877, pp. 265–281, 2019.
https://doi.org/10.1007/978-3-030-33246-4_17

(e.g., Google Drive and Dropbox) or potential collaboration. For instance, an airline company may be unable to cope with the increasing number of requests before the vacation period. Instead of delaying these requests and penalizing customers, it may delegate some requests to partner services. In our previous work [9], we modeled Web service interactions as a multi-relation network where nodes are Web services and edges are composition and substitution that take place among services.

In dynamic environments such as service networks, new Web services are continuously deployed. Moreover, existing Web services are updated regularly. Providers improve their functionalities on a regular basis to keep services competitive in the market. Examples of updates include the addition, update, and deletion of operations and data types in the service interface [6]. Such updates are most of time associated with modifications to service description expressed in natural language. These updates affect operation results, and hence may lead to breach of contract between service providers and clients [5]. Therefore, it is mandatory to handle Web service changes that occur at run-time and accurately communicate these changes to the concerned peers in the network. Handling Web service continuous deployment and updates offers several advantages: First, it avoids brutal contract violation between providers and customers and maintains good relationships among entities in the network. Second, it speeds-up the exposure of new functionalities in the network, helps them gain more visibility, and hence improves the overall availability of new services. This is quite interesting for programmers who cannot devote too much time looking for new services as they are generally busy with their programming and maintenance duties. Mashup developers can easily retrieve new services when designing their mashups, and to find new services to replace unavailable ones. Third, building new relationships after acquiring new functionalities helps setting new partnerships among Web services. Service providers can establish new business interaction and gain more profits.

Managing the evolution of Web services is challenging for the following reasons. When initially deployed, Web service capabilities are described by means of keywords in natural language. Additionally, when a service undergoes an update, new acquired capabilities are also expressed in natural language. What is needed is a semantic approach to match service capabilities by matching their describing keywords. Moreover, Web service provided description may not match with service real capabilities. What is also needed is a technique to update service relationships according to service interaction experience and user feedbacks.

In this paper, we propose a novel approach based on Linked Open Data (LOD) for handling Web services deployment and evolution. LOD is a cloud of semantic, structured, and interconnected datasets. One of the most pioneering LOD datasets is DBpedia [1], the semantic mirror of Wikipedia. By extracting information from Wikipedia template instance, DBpedia reconstructs a graph of Knowledge that semanticizes and interconnects pieces of derived data. LOD consists currently in an extensive and evolutive global knowledge base. It provides interlinked knowledge for multiple domains; ontologies about persons, places, drugs, genetics, etc. The huge amount of data provided by LOD and its dynamic nature (i.e., data evolves constantly, new relationships are added continuously) makes it proper for handling services evolution. The key contributions of our research are summarized below:

- We introduce a three-phase process to deal with service continuous deployment and changes. (1) The *Bootstrapping Phase* performs two tasks: (i) Semantic Annotation associates a profile to each service and annotates it with LOD resources; (ii) Semantic Matchmaking bootstraps relationships for newly deployed and services undergoing updates by running LOD semantic matching of service capabilities. (2) The *Updating Phase* updates service relationships by gathering and analyzing Web service interactions and their user feedback. (3) The *Learning phase* leverages Web services interaction experience to learn new open data links that will be reused in further semantic matchmaking, hence improving the accuracy of relationship recommendation.
- We propose LOD semantic based heuristics and algorithms to infer potential relationships for both newly deployed and updated services. We adopt a technique to compute LOD similarity between groups of keywords that describe Web service capabilities. We leverage LOD similarity to assess composability, replacement, and interest that may take place among Web services.
- We introduce a technique that gathers and analyzes Web service interactions and user feedback for updating service relationships at run-time.
- We propose an algorithm that capitalizes on Web service interaction for learning new relationships in LOD. We show that learning new relationships in LOD increases the accuracy of relationship recommendation.
- We conduct experiments on real Web services to evaluate the accuracy of our relationship recommendation. We compare our LOD semantic approach with existing ones, and show substantial increase of relationship recommendation accuracy with our approach. We also illustrate that learning new LOD links increases relationship bootstrapping accuracy.

The remainder of this paper is organized as follows: Sect. 2 introduces a background, a motivating scenario, and provides an overview of the proposed approach. Section 3 presents our approach for bootstrapping relationships for newly deployed and updated services. Section 4 introduces our technic to update relationships according to service interaction with each other and with user. Section 5 describes our technic to learn relationships in LOD according to service interactions and feedbacks. Section 6 discusses the experimental study. Section 7 reviews related works. Section 8 concludes the paper.

2   Approach Overview

2.1   Background

Linked Open Data (LOD) - LOD is an initiative that aims at transforming traditional web of single hyperlink relation to a web of multidimensional semantic links [2]. The initiative launched by Time Berners Lee, WWW inventor, entourages disseminating open, semantic and interconnected data using semantic web standards (RDF, RDFS, SPARQL, etc). So far, a billions of LOD resources has been published by a myriad providers[1]. Published data are hence of divers domains such as people, books, medical, films, geography, media, biology, chemistry, economy, energy, tourism, etc. The semantic, structured and interconnection nature LOD data has enabled developers and researchers to build LOD-based applications on the top of provided LOD data. Most recent Semantic similarity measures [3,15] use LOD data to assess the similarity degree between two compared concepts. Such measure are commonly used in recent recommendation systems [4] to enable services/content recommendation based on LOD resources.

Multi-relation Network of Web Services - In previous research [9], we modeled Web service interactions using a multi-relation graph. Web services make-up the nodes of the graph, and the different invocations that occur between them such as composition, substitution, and subscription constitute its edges. Formally, a multi-relation network of Web services is a directed graph $G = (V, R)$ where V is a set of services, and $R = \bigcup_{k=1}^{k=3} R_k$ is a set of edges, where $R_k = \{(S_u, S_v) \in V \times V\}$ is the set of edges of the k-th relationship. Major services interaction relationships are: R_1 is the set of edges of the substitution relationship, R_2 is the set of edges of the composition relationship, and R_3 is the set of edges of the subscription relationship. An edge $(S_i, S_j) \in R_1$ indicates that there is a relationship of type substitution between Web services S_i and S_j, precisely it indicates that S_j is a substitute of S_i and clients can substitute the invocation of S_i by S_j if S_i is unavailable. Similarly, a composition edge $(S_i, S_j) \in R_2$ indicates that S_j can be composed with S_i and clients can invoke S_j and S_i in the same composite application. A subscription edge $(S_i, S_j) \in R_3$ indicates that S_i can subscribe to the news feed of a collaborator/competitor S_j to stay aware about its latest updates.

2.2   Motivating Scenario

The following scenario presents the example of two deployed Web services S_u and S_v in the network. Both S_u and S_v are e-learning services that offer free online courses covering various computer technology topics. When initially deployed, both services provided comparable functionalities. Hence being linked by substitution edge. As Web services interact with each other and with users, they start getting attention. S_u established a sound reputation for the pedagogical approach of its courses. S_v on another hand distinguished itself with a very active community that provides support to users facing technical issues. It is straightforward that service providers decide to evolve their services by adding new features that adapt to user needs and feedbacks.

---

[1] https://lod-cloud.net/datasets.

We notice that from one version to another S_u is acquiring appropriate tools and features to become a professional e-learning service platform. Providers capitalized on the pedagogy element and made it their central marketing priority. Examples of added features are *(1) tools to upload PDFs and Powerpoints, or to import them from Slideshare. (2) functionalities to upload videos or to import them from Youtube. (3) tools to organize content and course material, make podcasts, and live video conferencing.* The targeted audience also shifted as S_u offers Premium Plans to cover both end-users and professionals. Such an evolution is followed by the update of composition and substitution relationships. Examples of new composition partners are *Grammarly grammar checking API, Youtube API, Amazon streaming CloudFront API.* Examples of new substitution partners are *freeCodeCamp API, Coursera API.* In parallel, S_v provider decided to invest in the concept of active community that helps answering user technical questions/issues. S_v acquired new features such as *(1) a question answer Q&A platform that allows clients to collaborate with subject matter experts to tackle complex technical issues. (2) an extensive list of verified solution. (3) tool for hiring best talents.* New targeted clients are professionals. Examples of new composition partners are *Google Cloud Natural Language API, Google Cloud Storage API.* Examples of new substitution partners are *Quora API, Stackoverflow API.* Such changes are very frequent in distributed environments such as service networks. They may impact the way Web services interact. Indeed, in the latest version, S_u and S_v became no longer suitable to substitute mutually, or to interact with many other services they used to work with. In contrast, new acquired functionalities has led to new possibilities of interaction in the network.

2.3 Architecture

Figure 1 depicts the proposed architecture. The approach runs a three phases process to handle Web service deployment and evolution namely *Bootstrapping Phase, Updating Phase,* and *Learning Phase.* First, a service provider deploys the interface of his service, and provides a natural language description of service functionality and application domain. *Bootstrapping Phase* invokes then Annotation module on provided service information. Annotation module associates a profile to the service. A profile contains keywords describing service inputs, outputs, functionality, and application domain. Annotation module annotates profile keywords with LOD semantic resources. After that, *Bootstrapping Phase* invokes matchmaking module to match annotated service profiles and derive composition, substitution, and subscription relationships. This results in new weighted edges for newly deployed service and allows bootstrapping service relationships. This same process will be run when a Web service undergoes an update. Annotation module will annotate service new features in interface and description with LOD resources. Matchmaking module will match service new features with existing network features. This will result in new relationships and possibilities of collaboration for the updated service. The main research issues addressed by *Bootstrapping Phase* are summarized below:

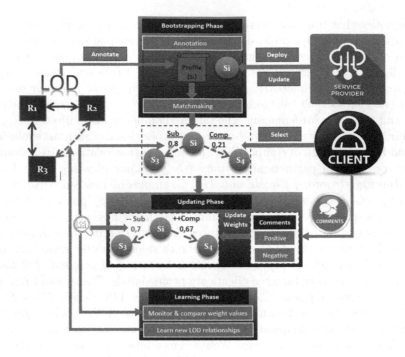

Fig. 1. Architecture of LOD management of service deployment and evolution

- **Research Question 1** - How do we bootstrap relationships for newly deployed services and for those undergoing updates? How do we figure out the most suited relationship type to link two services? Issues related to this research question are addressed in Sect. 3.

Updating Phase updates service relationships according to service interactions with each other and with users. As services record successful interactions, they receive high rating scores, this increases the weight of their relationships. The main research issues addressed by *Updating Phase* are summarized below:

- **Research Question 2** - How do we update service relationships? How do we ascertain whether two Web services are interoperable in practice? Issues related to this research question are addressed in Sect. 4.

Learning phase improves bootstrapping relationships accuracy by learning new relationships in LOD. When the *Updating phase* returns a higher weight than the *Boostraping phase* weight for the same relationship. This would mean new relationships should be added to LOD and viceversa. The main research issues addressed by *Learning Phase* are summarized below:

- **Research Question 3** - How does Web service interaction experience help learning new links in LOD? How does learning new links in LOD improve relationships recommendation accuracy? Issues related to this research question are addressed in Sect. 5.

3   Bootstrapping Phase

This section describes our approach for bootstrapping relationships for newly deployed services and those undergoing updates. We illustrate the use of LOD, particularly similarity measures, to infer composition, substitution, and interest relationships. The current phase runs a two steps process: (1) Semantic Annotation annotates service capabilities with LOD resources. (2) Semantic Matchmaking matches service capabilities, based on LOD similarity measure, to infer composition and substitution relationships.

3.1   Semantic Annotation

Semantic Annotation first associates a profile to each service in the network. A profile contains information about service inputs, outputs, functionality description, and application domain. Second, it annotates service profile with LOD resources. Annotation could be performed using specific tools that provide mappings between keyworks and LOD resources.

Definition 1. *A Web service profile is a couple of features (F, D) where:*

- F: *is a description in natural language of the service functionality.*
- D: *is a list of keywords that describe the service application domain.*

We perform preprocessing on service natural language functionality description. This gets rid of stop and empty words, and returns meaningful keywords that describe service functionality.

Annotating service profile consists in associating LOD resources to each keyword in service profile.

Figure 2 illustrates an example of a Web service annotated with resources from DBpedia LOD dataset. Service keywords are mapped to LOD resources to add semantics and meaning. Each resource is connected to semantic data such as ontology concepts and categories. More details concerning LOD architecture are provided in Sect. 3.2: **LOD Model**. Next, we show how does Semantic Annotation help Semantic Matchmaking of service capabilities to infer service relationships.

3.2   Semantic Matchmaking

This section proposes heuristics and algorithms, based on LOD similarity measures, to infer potential composition and substitution relationships. Semantic matching is invoked in two cases: (a) When a Web service joins the network. (b) When a Web service gets updated. It matches Web service capabilities (either the initial or the updated ones) to recommend the most appropriate relationship to link with two services. It also predicts the probability value to interact through the recommended relationship.

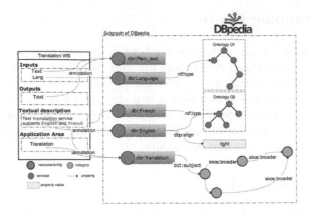

Fig. 2. Annotating web service profile keywords with DBpedia resources

In the following, we describe how to use LOD to match service profiles to infer relationships.

LOD Model - LOD model can be seen as a graph of resources that describe real-world entities and their relationships. Each LOD resource is described by semantic properties. For example the resource "Paris" has the semantic property "Location". LOD resources are linked to concepts in ontologies. Concepts denote a class of entities a resource belongs to. For example the resource "Paris" is associated to the ontology concept "Capital". Such an association is expressed in RDF *Paris rdf:type Capital*. In addition, resources may also be linked to a category information. For example "Hilton" has as a Category "Tourist Accommodations". Both ontology concepts and categories are defined in a hierarchical structure and are usually represented by the following relations: $(rdfs : subClassOf)$ for the ontology concept and $(skos : broader)$ for the category respectively. These relations put concepts or categories at specific levels of the hierarchy.

Relying on such semantic and structured description of LOD resources allows computing accurate similarity values. An example of LOD based similarity measure uses hierarchical positions of concepts and categories to estimate degree of similarity of resources.

Similarity between Service Features Annotated with LOD Resources - This section proposes a model to compute the semantic similarity among two service features annotated with LOD resources. Given two service features $feat_u$, $feat_v$ described each with a set of keywords $K_u = \{k_{u1}, k_{u2} \ldots k_{ui}\}$ and $K_v = \{k_{v1}, k_{v2} \ldots k_{vj}\}$ respectively, where each keyword can be attached to a subset of annotation resources $A_R \in LOD$, such that:
$\forall k_i, k_j \in K_u \times K_v, \exists r_i, r_j \in A_u | \langle k_i, r_i \rangle \times A_v | \langle k_j, r_j \rangle$. The similarity between features $feat_u$ and $feat_v$, annotated by a set of LOD resources A_u and A_v respectively is computed as follows:

$$Sim_{LOD}(feat_u, feat_v) = \frac{\sum_{a \in A_u} \sum_{b \in A_v} LODS^{\ell, \ell'}(a, b)}{|A_u| \cdot |A_v|}$$

This measure proceeds as follows :

- sums the scores obtained from applying $LODS$ similarity measure on each combination of the Cartesian product of the two compared sets.
- then, it divides the sum by the number of combinations to have a final score normalized in the interval $[0, 1]$.

This measure relies on $LODS$ similarity measure [3]. LODS exploits three aspects of LOD; *(i)* the hierarchical structure of ontology concepts; *(ii)* the hierarchical classification of categories; and *(iii)* the semantic properties used to describe LOD resources.

For concepts and categories, LODS proceeds by computing the portion of shared features in the hierarchy between compared LOD resources. For semantic properties, it computes the percentage of shared important ingoing/outgoing properties.

ℓ and ℓ' are two parameters to avoid used to avoid

Bootstrapping Composition Relationship - This phase assumes that two Web services S_u and S_v are composable and can be linked by a composition edge in the network if and only if: (i) S_u and S_v appear together in at least one mashup. We recall that a mashup is a composite application that leverages the invocation of many APIs. Moreover, (ii) the similarity values between S_u and S_v functional descriptions and application domains are higher than the following thresholds α_F and α_D respectively.

Algorithm 1. Composition Matching Algorithm

Input: $G(V, R)$: Graph of services. $S_u, S_v \in V$.

α_F, α_D : thresholds for similarities between functional descriptions and application domains respectively.

$Coef_F$, $Coef_D$: coefficient values for similarities between functional descriptions, and application domains respectively.

Output: $G(V, R)$: Updated graph of services.

    Begin

1: $Sim_F \leftarrow Sim_{LOD}(S_u.F, S_v.F)$;

2: $Sim_D \leftarrow Sim_{LOD}(S_u.A, S_v.A)$;

3: **if** $(Sim_F >= \alpha_F$ and $Sim_D >= \alpha_D)$ **then**

4:    $Comp(S_u, S_v) \leftarrow (Coef_F * Sim_F + Coef_D * Sim_D)/(Coef_F + Coef_D)$;

5:    **if** $((S_u, S_v) \in R_1)$ **then**

6:      $Comp(S_u, S_v) \leftarrow AVG(Comp(S_u, S_v), Weight(S_u, S_v))$

7:    **end if**

8:    $R_1 \leftarrow R_1 \cup (S_u, S_v, "Weight"=Comp(S_u, S_v))$;

9: **end if**

Algorithm 1 evaluates how likely are two services S_u and S_v to be part of the same composition. The algorithm computes (1) the similarity between their functional descriptions. And (2) the similarity between their application domains. If computed similarities are above given thresholds, then the algorithm computes a composability likelihood $Comp$ between Web services S_u and S_v. If the composition relationship (S_u, S_v) exists, the algorithm updates the composition likelihood as an average of the computed composition probability and the relationship current weight. Finally the algorithm adds a new composition edge (S_u, S_v) to the network of services with the composition likelihood as weight.

Bootstrapping Substitution Relationship - This phase assumes that two Web services S_u and S_v are candidates for substitution and can be linked through a substitution edge in the network if and only if: (i) They do not appear together as parts of the same mashup. In other words, there is no deployed mashup containing both S_u and S_v. Moreover, (ii) the similarities between S_u and S_u functional descriptions and application domains are higher given thresholds α_F and α_D respectively. Substitution Algorithm differs from Algorithm 1 in that: (1) It uses specific threshold and coefficient values. For instance, functional description similarity threshold should be higher for substitution than it is for composition.

The current phase allows bootstrapping relationships for, newly deployed services and those undergoing updates, based on LOD similarity measure. However, relying only on service profile data may lead to inconsistencies between service real capabilities and described ones in profiles. The next section proposes to continuously update service relationships according to user feedbacks.

4   Updating Phase

Although semantic matching of service profiles allows building relevant business relationships, it relies however entirely on Web service profile data. Such an approach considers Web services as isolated components and underlooks their interactive behaviour. In reality, Web services interact through various relationships such as composition, substitution, and subscription. *Bootstrapping Phase* may suggest that two services are composable while they struggle to interoperate in practice. Their record of successful interactions may be weak. Users will then give bad rating scores. The reason may be QoS limitations of some services that make them incapable to interoperate with network services. This may also be due to an incoherent service description with service real capabilities that led to biased semantic matching results. Gathering and analyzing Web service interactions and their user feedbacks allow assessing the real value/relevance of bootstrapped relationships. *The intuition is to update relationships weight values returned by semantic layer according to user rating scores.* A relationship (S_u, S_v) that keeps a high weight value after many service interactions means that S_u and S_v have collected a strong record of successful interactions. These interactions have been appreciated by users and consequently have been well rated. On the opposite, if a relationship will see its weight decreasing as services interact, this would mean that relation' services struggle to interoperate with each other. The relation did not get high rating scores and so even after semantic matchmaking returned a high weight value. This section catches Web service interactions and their user ratings and updates relation weight values accordingly. This allows keeping the network updated and eases identifying interoperable services and computing service reputation scores.

We extend the measure proposed in [8] to leverage user comments for updating relationship weights as follows:

$$WE_{t+\delta t}(S_u, S_v) \leftarrow AVG \left[\frac{|positiveFeedbacks(S_u, S_v)_{t+\delta t}|}{|allFeedbacks(S_u, S_v)_{t+\delta t}|}, WE_t(S_u, S_v) \right]$$

$WE_t(S_u, S_v)$ and $WE_{t+\delta t}(S_u, S_v)$ are the weights of the relation (S_u, S_v) observed at t and $t + \delta t$ respectively.

$positiveFeedbacks(S_u, S_v)_{t+\delta t}$ and $allFeedbacks(S_u, S_v)_{t+\delta t}$ designate the number of *positive comments* and *all comments* respectively that have been commented on the relation (S_u, S_v) in the time interval $[t, t + \delta t]$.

The updated weight depends on the previous weight (i.e., bootstrapped weight) and on user feedbacks on the relationship. The higher will be positive user feedbacks on the relationship, the higher will get the updated weight. The weight will decrease on the contrary case.

5 Learning Phase

This phase proposes an algorithm to learn new links in LOD according to Web service interaction experience. Keeping LOD up to date allows running accurate semantic matching of Web service capabilities, hence accurately identifying potential business relationships among Web services. Updating LOD is triggered when the gap between the updated weight value and the bootstrapped weight value gets above a given threshold for the same relationship. If the updated weight is greater than the bootstrapped one, this means that Web services are interoperable (i.e., have a strong record of interactions) in practice, while bootstrapping phase has not recommended them as such. This proves the lack of information in LOD. Thus, new relationships among resources describing these interoperable Web services should be added to LOD. On the opposite, if the updated weight is the lowest, this means that Web services struggle to interact. The cause can be either (i) Web service description is inadequate with service real capabilities, or (ii) Web service suffer from QoS limitations. For the first case, LOD relationships among resources describing such services should be destroyed. For the second case, LOD ontology structure will be preserved. But the service reputation score will be updated. Dealing with service reputation score is out of the scope of this paper and will be addressed in future work.

The following algorithm describes how to learn new relationships in LOD.

Algorithm 2 depicts how to learn new LOD relationships or to break existing ones. Learning algorithm derives (LearnLOD) and breaks (DestroyLOD) links among resources describing services according to a "Normal probability distribution". Such probability distribution is the most adequate to model phenomenon that consider the sum of many independent variables. In our case, LOD similarity measure of two service features is computed as the summation of atomic similarities of their LOD resources. By analogy, we learn or destroy new LOD relationships according to a "Normal probability distribution". As it is hard to overwrite exisiting LOD, we save new learned and broken relationships in

---

Algorithm 2. Learning New Relationships in LOD

Input: $G(V, R)_t$: Graph of services observed at t. $G(V, R)_{t+\delta t}$: Graph of services observed at $t + \delta t$. S_u, $S_v \in V$, gap: Learning gap.
Output: Updated LOD

    Begin
    $weightdiff \leftarrow weight(S_u, S_v)_{t+\delta t} - weight(S_u, S_v)_t$;
 1: **if** $(weightdiff - gap > 0)$ **then**
 2:    $LearnLOD(S_u.F, S_v.F)$
 3:    $LearnLOD(S_u.A, S_v.A)$
 4: **else if** $(weightdiff - gap \leq 0)$ **then**
 5:    $BreakLOD(S_u.F, S_v.F)$
 6:    $BreakLOD(S_u.A, S_v.A)$
 7: **end if**

---

local database. Such learning will serve further bootstrapping relationships that relies mainly on semantic matching of service features. Hence, future relationship bootstrapping will be more accurate. This allows a fast exploitation of new functionalities in the network and enhances their overall availability.

6   Experimental Study

6.1   Experimental Set-Up

We ran our experiments on a 64-bit Windows 10 environment, in a machine equipped with an intel i7 and 12 GB RAM. We collected APIs and their attributes from ProgrammableWeb. We used DBPediaSpotlight[2] for annotating Web service descriptions and categories. DBPediaSpotlight is a tool for automatically annotating mentions of DBPedia resources in text. We developed a Python client to invoke DBPedia REST API to annotate service attributes such as description with LOD resources. We collected 600 mashups from ProgrammableWeb[3]. We study Web service evolution over several time periods $[T_i, T_j]$ where $T_i \geq 2007$, $T_j \leq 2017$, $[T_j - T_j] = 2$ years. We first identify newly deployed services and those undergoing updates at T_i, after which we run our relationships recommendation. Then we observe each recommended relationship $[S_u, S_v]$ interaction history during the time interval $[T_i, T_j]$. Each mashup containing (S_u, S_v) that is deployed within $[T_i, T_j]$ means a successful composition interaction feedback on the relation (S_u, S_v). On the opposite, if no mashup containing S_u and S_v) is deployed within $[T_i, T_j]$, this is interpreted as a negative interaction feedback. Weight (S_u, S_v) is updated according to collected interaction feedbacks. We simulate interactions for substitution relationships.

---

[2] DBPediaSpotlight.
[3] www.ProgrammableWeb.com.

6.2   Results and Discussion

The goal of our experiments is to assess the ability of the proposed approach to correctly recommend relationships for newly deployed and updated services.

We compute recall, precision, average precision, and F-measure. Recall refers to the fraction of interaction relationships that occur within $[T_i, T_j]$ and that are accurately recommended to newly deployed and updated services at T_i. It is the number of Web service relationships that are successfully recommended divided by the number of all service interaction relationships (i.e., both correctly recommended relationships and ignored ones). It can be also seen as the percentage of relationships that are successfully recommended.

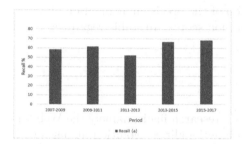 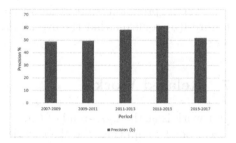

Fig. 3. Recall and Precision

Figure 3(a) shows the computed recall each time period. It is shown that up to 70% of service interactions are successfully recalled (i.e., recommended) by the proposed approach. The justification is that proposed relationships recommendation leverages both service semantic and service interaction history. Leveraging service interaction history shed the light on some relationships that should exist between LOD resources and that do not exist on the original LOD version. Considering those new relationships improves the relationship bootstrapping.

Precision checks the accuracy with which relationship are recommended for newly deployed and updated services. It is the number of precisely recommended

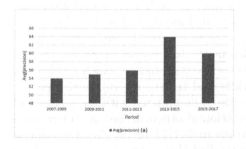 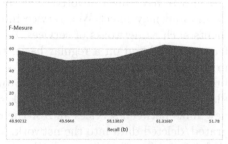

Fig. 4. Avg(Precision) and F-Mesure

relationships divided by all recalled relationships. It can be seen as the percentage of precisely recalled relationships. Precision compares the recommended relationship weights at T_i with real relationship weight at T_j. If the weight difference is less than a threshold value (0.2 in our case), the relationship is assumed to be precisely recommended. Figure 3(b) shows that our approach recommends relationships with up to 65% precision. The justification is that weight varies depending on service interaction feedbacks. As such, it gets challenging to predict with high accuracy future relationships weights.

F-Mesure denotes a trade-off between precision and recall. It is the harmonic mean between recall and precision. It is shown in Fig. 4(a) that precision varies from period to another which is predictable since the recall and precision scores also vary over time periods.

Average precision denotes the variation of the precision as function of recall. Figure 4(b) confirms that the overall precision scores are stable regardless recall scores.

7   Related Work

Our work is at the cross-road of three main research fields, namely the Web services social computing, the Web services functionalities evolution management, and linked open data semantic web. The new trend of the research community in service-computing is to exploit social technologies for a better discovery mechanism of services. In this trend, works in [8,10,11] propose to build a network of Web services with the purpose of addressing certain issues like Web services discovery. The particularity of such a network is that its main actors namely the nodes are Web services. The main addressed questions by Maamar et al. in [11] are: What kinds of relations link Web services, how to build a network of Web services. In [10], they propose a distributed approach using a referral system for trust-based service discovery in service networks using intelligent agents. We have shown in [8] how to infer a network of services from Web service Logs. The idea was first to identify itemsets of correlated invocations in Web service Logs, and then to input those itemsets to association rule algorithm with the purpose to learn weighted relationships among Web services.

Although related work above handled social interactions of Web services, few efforts have been devoted however to manage Web service evolution that occurs and may affect Web service interaction. Indeed, in distributed environments such as networks of services, data evolves constantly. Web service interfaces are updated on a regular basis, this may affect service operation results, in this case the functionality of the Web service will change, which can lead to break contract between the service provider and the client [5,6]. In this particular case, the topology of the network needs to be updated with the addition of new links between services and/or the deletion of others according to new integrated/deleted data into the network. Works in [5,7,14,18,20] aimed to address Web service functionality evolution. [20] studied the evolution of Amazon Web services and shows that service evolution comes at spike periods. The approach supports developers in their tasks of Web service selection and maintenance. [7] proposed an approach for managing services evolution by analyzing the co-occurences of their topics. A topic evolution graph is built according to the analysis of composition patterns in mashups. Resulting graph is used to recommend services for composition. [18] proposed a service evolution model to identify the changes that a Web service is subject to. They classified them into two major categories: Changes that concern Web service Operations and changes that concern Web Service DataTypes. [5] identified three types of changes with respect to their impact on client: (1) emphNo effect: These changes do not disrupt the Web service functionality, the semantics of the service will be preserved. *Adaptable:* These changes are about an adaptation of the existing parameters and/or operations of the Web service with the purpose to improve the Web service design. These changes do not affect the service functionality. And (3) *Non-recoverable:* We are particularly interested in this type of changes. These changes concern the functionality of the Web service itself. They need a review of the Web service's relationships according to the new updated data. Otherwise, the exploitation of this Web service functionality will be impacted. To handle efficiently Web service continuous deployment and evolution in service networks, We first annotate new Web service updates with LOD resources. Then we match Web service updates with existing service profiles to derive new relationships. We also take advantage from user feedbacks to evaluate recommended relationships and reorganize LOD relationships.

Web services evolution has been also at the center of interest of related fields such as IoT and service-based business processes. Tran et al. [17] proposed a framework to automatically capture and communicate services changes in IoT environment. The framework manages syntactic and semantic changes in IoT services capabilities described as RESTful services. In contrast to our work, ontologies have been used to add semantics to services definitions. Ontologies are generally domain-specific which limits management of services functional evolution. We rely instead on LOD that offers more resources to describe servcies semantic.

Xiu et al. [19] manages service evolution in service-based business processes (SBPs). The proposed approach relies on Petri-net modeling to detect predefined patterns. A change management framework was proposed to verify correctness of SBPs and to implement changes from change requirements.

Our proposed approach manages Web service evolution in service network dealing with continuous deployment and interface updates. We rely both on linked open data and Web social feedbacks to deal with Web service evolution.

8   Conclusion

In this paper, we proposed a LOD approach for managing service deployment and evolution. The proposed approach runs a three phase process. First phase recommends new relationships by matching service capabilities based on LOD. Second phase updates service relationships according to their interaction with each other and with users. Third phase increases recommendation accuracy by learning new relationships in LOD. Managing Web service evolution offers several advantages such as: setting long-lasting relationships between service providers and users, and increasing the visibility of newly added functionalities. Experiments conducted on real data returned promising results. In an ongoing research effort, we leverage big data real time brokers to allow real time evolution management. And we handle service reputation score evolution.

References

1. Auer, S., et al.: DBpedia: a nucleus for a web of open data. In: Aberer, K., et al. (eds.) ASWC/ISWC -2007. LNCS, vol. 4825, pp. 722–735. Springer, Heidelberg (2007). https://doi.org/10.1007/978-3-540-76298-0_52
2. Bizer, C., Heath, T., Berners-Lee, T.: Linked data-the story so far. Int. J. Seman. Web Inf. Syst. (IJSWIS) 5(3), 1–22 (2009)
3. Cheniki, N., Belkhir, A., Sam, Y., Messai, N.: LODS: a linked open data based similarity measure. In: 25th International Conference on Enabling Technologies: Infrastructure for Collaborative Enterprises (WETICE). IEEE (2016). https://doi.org/10.1109/WETICE.2016.58
4. Noia, T.: Recommender systems meet linked open data. In: Bozzon, A., Cudre-Maroux, P., Pautasso, C. (eds.) ICWE 2016. LNCS, vol. 9671, pp. 620–623. Springer, Cham (2016). https://doi.org/10.1007/978-3-319-38791-8_61
5. Fokaefs, M., Mikhaiel, R., Tsantalis, N., Stroulia, E., Lau, A.: An empirical study on web service evolution. In: 2011 IEEE International Conference on Web Services, pp. 49–56. IEEE (2011)
6. Fokaefs, M., Stroulia, E.: WSDarwin: studying the evolution of web service systems. In: Bouguettaya, A., Sheng, Q., Daniel, F. (eds.) Advanced Web Services, pp. 199–223. Springer, New York (2014). https://doi.org/10.1007/978-1-4614-7535-4_9
7. Gao, Z., Fan, Y., Wu, C., Tan, W., Zhang, J.: Service recommendation from the evolution of composition patterns. In: 2017 IEEE International Conference on Services Computing (SCC), pp. 108–115 (2017)
8. Labbaci, H., Medjahed, B., Aklouf, Y.: Learning interactions from web service logs. In: Benslimane, D., et al. (eds.) DEXA 2017. LNCS, vol. 10439, pp. 275–289. Springer, Cham (2017). https://doi.org/10.1007/978-3-319-64471-4_22
9. Labbaci, H., Medjahed, B., Aklouf, Y., Malik, Z.: Follow the leader: a social network approach for service communities. In: Sheng, Q.Z., Stroulia, E., Tata, S., Bhiri, S. (eds.) ICSOC 2016. LNCS, vol. 9936, pp. 705–712. Springer, Cham (2016). https://doi.org/10.1007/978-3-319-46295-0_50
10. Louati, A., El Haddad, J., Pinson, S.: Towards agent-based and trust-oriented service discovery approach in social networks. In: TRUST@ AAMAS, pp. 78–89 (2014)
11. Maamar, Z., Faci, N., Krug Wives, L., Yahyaoui, H., Hacid, H.: Towards a method for engineering social web services. In: Ralyté, J., Mirbel, I., Deneckère, R. (eds.) ME 2011. IAICT, vol. 351, pp. 153–167. Springer, Heidelberg (2011). https://doi.org/10.1007/978-3-642-19997-4_15
12. Maamar, Z., et al.: Using social networks for web services discovery. IEEE Internet Comput. 15(4), 48–54 (2011)
13. Medjahed, B., Malik, Z., Benbernou, S.: On the composability of semantic web services. In: Web Services Foundations, pp. 137–160 (2014)

14. Papazoglou, M.P., Andrikopoulos, V., Benbernou, S.: Managing evolving services. IEEE Softw. **28**(3), 49–55 (2011)
15. Piao, G., Breslin, J.G.: Measuring semantic distance for linked open data-enabled recommender systems. In: Proceedings of the 31st Annual ACM Symposium on Applied Computing, SAC 2016, pp. 315–320. ACM, New York (2016). https://doi.org/10.1145/2851613.2851839
16. Singh, M.P.: Physics of service composition. IEEE Internet Comput. **5**(3), 6 (2001)
17. Tran, H.T., et al.: DECOM: a framework to support evolution of IoT services. In: Proceedings of the 9th International Symposium on Information and Communication Technology, pp. 389–396. ACM (2018)
18. Wang, S., Higashino, W.A., Hayes, M., Capretz, M.A.: Service evolution patterns. In: 2014 IEEE International Conference on Web Services, pp. 201–208. IEEE (2014)
19. Xiu, P., Yang, J., Zhao, W.: Change management of service-based business processes. SOCA **13**(1), 51–66 (2019)
20. Zarras, A.V., Vassiliadis, P., Dinos, I.: Keep calm and wait for the spike! insights on the evolution of Amazon services. In: Nurcan, S., Soffer, P., Bajec, M., Eder, J. (eds.) CAiSE 2016. LNCS, vol. 9694, pp. 444–458. Springer, Cham (2016). https://doi.org/10.1007/978-3-319-39696-5_27

Security Risk Management in Cooperative Intelligent Transportation Systems: A Systematic Literature Review

Abasi-Amefon O. Affia$^{(\boxtimes)}$, Raimundas Matulevičius, and Alexander Nolte

Institute of Computer Science, University of Tartu, Tartu, Estonia
{amefon.affia,rma,alexander.nolte}@ut.ee

Abstract. The automotive industry is maximizing cooperative interactions between vehicular sensors and infrastructure components to make intelligent decisions in its application (i.e., traffic management, navigation, or autonomous driving services). This cooperative behaviour also extends to security. More connected and cooperative components of vehicular intelligent transportation systems (ITS) result in an increased potential for malicious attacks that can negatively impact security and safety. The security risks in one architecture layer affect other layers of ITS; thus, cooperation is essential for secure operations of these systems. This paper presents results from a comprehensive literature review on the state-of-the-art of security risk management in vehicular ITS, evaluating its assets, threats/risks, and countermeasures. We examine these security elements along the dimensions of the perception, network, and application architecture layers of ITS. The study reveals gaps in ITS security risk management research within these architecture layers and provides suggestions for future research.

Keywords: Cooperative intelligent transportation systems (ITS) · vehicular ITS · Internet of Things (IoT) · STRIDE · Information System Security Risk Management (ISSRM)

1 Introduction

Transportation is one of the cornerstones of human civilization, facilitating the mobility of people and goods. Intelligent transportation systems (ITS) provide such mobility through cooperative sensing, processing, and communication technologies [13]. To improve transportation efficiency in an ITS, sensors and objects have to interact to collect and exchange data over vehicular and infrastructure networks, and make intelligent predictions and decisions.

Due to the potential threat to critical business assets and the possible catastrophic physical effects that can endanger human lives [18,20] it is essential to consider ITS security covering all its components [20]. Security threats in this domain are multifaceted, including transportation, IoT, and distributed system type threats to ITS components and thus require security risk management.

© Springer Nature Switzerland AG 2019
H. Panetto et al. (Eds.): OTM 2019, LNCS 11877, pp. 282–300, 2019.
https://doi.org/10.1007/978-3-030-33246-4_18

ITS security risk management [28,41,42] is crucial to ensure the confidentiality, integrity, and availability of the data that is being collected and aggregated to ensure safe and efficient operation of transportation systems (e.g., speed management, navigation and traffic management [13]). There is thus a need to understand the current state of ITS security risk research related to the cooperative architecture of ITS. We seek to provide an overview of the current start-of-the-art in this field to foster continuous research and development of ITS security risk management by addressing the following main research question:

How can we manage security risks in ITS?

To answer this research question, we conducted a systematic literature review (SLR) (following the [26] guidelines) to aggregate existing analysis on security risk management in vehicular ITS [56]. We then analyze the results following the security risk management ontology [14].

The contribution of this paper is threefold. First, based on [30,51,52,54], we provide an overview of the ITS architecture and its protected assets. Second, we provide a state-of-the-art overview of security threats and their countermeasures within each ITS architecture layer. Third, we discuss the current state of security management research in ITS and highlight future research directions.

2   Background

In this section we ground our work in existing literature covering ITS, its structure, security risk management in information systems and secondary studies on IoT security risk management (Sect. 2.3).

2.1   Overview of ITS

ITS – based on the internet-of-things (IoT) paradigm [5] – utilize cooperative sensing and networking capabilities to manage people and goods for transportation via road, air, rail, and water. ITS encompass systems responsible for the collection, storage, transmission and manipulation of data involving vehicles, individuals (drivers, passengers, road operators, and managers), mobile devices and infrastructure (road units, video monitoring, traffic lights, internet) cooperating within each other and the environment [41]. System components include (*i*) systems that collect data (*ii*) systems that transmit collected data and (*iii*) systems that provide the data to end-users following predefined processes [41].

ITS can be perceived as IoT system since they consist of various objects that form a cooperative system to reach a common goal [2]. IoT systems consist of three architectural layers [30,51–55] as illustrated in Fig. 1:

– Perception: The perception layer consists of hardware and software components (sensors, actuators, visioning, and positioning devices), carrying out basic functions such as collecting, controlling, and storing data.

– Network: The network layer facilitates wireless or wired transmission (in-vehicle, vehicle to vehicle, and vehicle to infrastructure) of collected data from perception components.
– Application: The application layer connects the network layer with the end-user, application processes, computing, and storage, allowing high-level intelligent processing of the generated and transmitted data. These applications include speed and traffic management [17,23,43,48], navigation [6,36], and driver-related services [4,7,32,46,49] in the context of ITS.

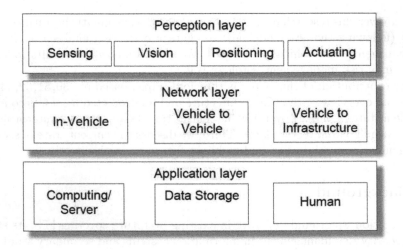

Fig. 1. Architecture layers of ITS

The layers are interconnected having a high impact on connected layers and collectively serving to deliver better mobility improvements for various forms of transport [13]. Dependencies between layers demand thorough security risk management consideration within all three layers to ensure confidentiality, integrity, and availability of data.

2.2 Security Risk Management

"*Security engineering* is concerned with lowering the risk of intentional unauthorized harm to valuable assets to a level acceptable to the system's stakeholders by preventing and reacting to malicious threats and security risks" [18]. Hence, security in the context of this paper deals specifically with intentional unauthorized threats and risks that explicitly pose harm to system assets. Security engineering is thus different from safety engineering dealing with unintentional risk, and privacy engineering dealing with accidental information leakage.

Previous work on security risk management methods [14] covers a number of standards and methods [9,16,25] to secure assets and manage security or security

risks. The review conducted by Dubois et al. [14] resulted in the development of
the ISSRM method and its domain model, compliant to the concepts and definitions we found in our review of security standards and methods. The ISSRM
domain model (see Fig. 2) consists of an ontology to compare, select, or improve
security risk management methods used in organizations. This domain model
suggests three conceptual parts covering *assets* (business and system assets),
security risks and *countermeasures*.

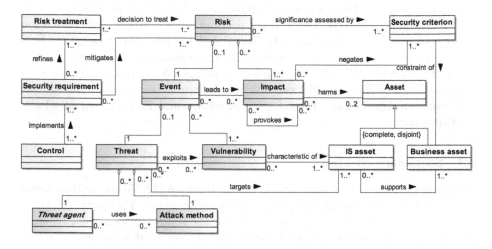

Fig. 2. ISSRM domain model adapted from [14,33]

- *Asset-related concepts*: *Business assets* are defined as information, data and
  processes that bring value to an organization. *System/IS assets* support *business assets*. *Security criteria* (confidentiality, integrity and availability) are
  constraints that define the security needs [14] of each *business asset*.
- *Security risk-related concepts*: A *security risk* is the combination of a security *event* and its *impact* (negation of the security criterion harming at-least
  a business and IS asset, c.f. Sect. 5.1 for an example scenario). A risk *event*
  is defined as the aggregation of a *threat* that exploits a *vulnerability* [33]. A
  vulnerability is a characteristic of a system asset, constituting its weakness.
  A *threat* targets a system asset by exploiting its vulnerability. It is a combination of a *threat agent* – an entity with interests to harm the assets – and
  an *attack method* – the means to carry out the threat. Methods of discovering this *threat* combination have been proposed and developed by security
  experts [24]. We selected the STRIDE method [44] for security threat analysis
  for this work due to its industrial usage, maturity, and high research concentration within the security community.
  The abbreviation STRIDE stands for *Spoofing (S)* – pretending to be something or someone, *Tampering (T)* – modifying something that you are not
  supposed to modify, *Repudiation (R)* – claiming you didn't do something
  (regardless of if this is true or not), *Information Disclosure (I)* – exposing

information to those who are not authorized to view it, *Denial of Service (D)* – attacks designed to prevent a system from providing its intended service by crashing it, slowing it down, or filling ts storage, and *Elevation of Privilege (E)* – when a program or user can to do things (technically) that they are not supposed to be able to do [44]. We use STRIDE to elicit and categorize security threats as well as for risk treatment.

- *Security risk treatment* concepts include *security requirements* that define conditions to be reached by mitigating the security risks and the *controls* implement the defined security requirements. Security requirements can be classified into different types [19] including identification, authentication, authorization, immunity, integrity, intrusion detection, non-repudiation. Each type of security requirement potentially corresponds and mitigates threats covered by STRIDE [44]: Spoofing can be mitigated by *Authentication*, Tampering - *Integrity*, Repudiation - *Non-repudiation*, Information Disclosure - *Confidentiality*, Denial of Service - *Availability* and Elevation of privilege - *Authorization*.

2.3   Secondary Studies

Secondary studies have been carried out in literature [53,55] to analyze assets, threats, and security solutions in IoT security architecture. This paper, however, presents a study of these cooperative architecture layers, focusing on ITS asset, risk, and risk treatment concepts. We assess ITS security risk management efforts following the ISSRM domain model [14].

3   Review Protocol

Figure 3 illustrates the review protocol used for this work. It is based on the proposed guidelines by Kitchenham *et al.* [26]. The review goal is to survey primary literature covering security risks in ITS.

Fig. 3. Systematic literature review protocol

3.1   Research Question Definition

We derived the following the sub-questions from our main research question to study security risk management in ITS:

RQ₁. *How are asset-related concepts in ITS addressed?*

RQ$_2$. *How are risk-related concepts in ITS addressed?*
RQ$_3$. *How are risk treatment-related concepts in ITS addressed?*

RQ$_1$ focuses on assets that are of high value to vehicular ITS. We thus focus on assets that will have a considerable impact in the event of a security threat and therefore pose a security risk. **RQ$_2$** focuses on known threats to ITS and their resulting risks. **RQ$_3$** focuses on countermeasures for risks to each ITS layer. We use the research questions to generate keywords used in the search process for relevant studies within the ITS domain (see Sect. 3.2).

3.2 Search Process

For our review, we used selected digital libraries, including IEEE Explorer, Science Direct, ACM Digital Library, and Springer. The search queries include *"Transport system, intelligent transportation systems, vehicles, smart car, connected vehicles, security threats, security vulnerabilities, security countermeasure"*. These search queries are connected using Boolean operators tailored to each digital library. Also, we conducted manual searches [3,50] to complement the search procedure. Table 2 shows the results of the search results from the sources. We identified a total of 134 results (see Table 2) from which we eventually selected 26 for analysis based on the following inclusion/exclusion criteria.

3.3 Paper Selection

We subjected the identified papers to an initial screening which covered title, keywords, abstract, results, and conclusion. To select relevant papers, we applied the following two filters based on our research questions:

1. **Filter 1:** Applying inclusion/exclusion criteria in Table 1 on the selected papers. Table 2 presents the results of applying the inclusion/exclusion criteria resulting in a total of 58 results.
2. **Filter 2:** Quality assessment of the papers that passed Filter 1 following the Kitchenham quality guidelines [27], with the questions:
   - Does the study cover the scope of work?
   - Does the study describe security risks on information transportation systems?
   - Does the study provide the countermeasures to mitigate security risks?
   The answers to above questions are scored as follows: 1 = Fully satisfied, 0.5 = Partially satisfied, 0 = Not satisfied. We included studies with 2.5 or more points, resulting in a total of 26 final paper for data extraction and further analysis (see Table 2).

Table 1. Inclusion/exclusion criteria on the selected papers

Inclusion criteria	Exclusion criteria
Papers in the area of IoT, research scope is cooperative ITS and sub-scope of vehicular ITS	Papers that focus on security in limited aspects of vehicular transportation systems
Papers that explicitly carry out security risk assessment or analysis	Papers that discuss safety – unintentional harm to systems
Papers that present security risk solutions	Non-English papers
Academic papers that are accessible in full text from the university	Duplicate works

Table 2. Selected sources and corresponding results for literature review

Sources	IEEE	ACM	Springer	ScienceDirect	Manual	Total
Returned	18	43	49	14	10	134
Filter 1	14	12	15	8	9	58
Filter 2 (Final selection)	6	7	4	2	7	26

3.4 Threats to Validity

There are multiple threats to the validity of this work. First, the derived keywords might not adequately address the scope defined by the research questions. Second, we might have missed relevant articles due to the quality of the keywords. Third, the studies selected might not meet scientific standards. To mitigate these threats, we conducted quality assessments based on the inclusion/exclusion criteria. Finally, the adoption of a three layers ITS model may pose a threat. Nonetheless, this work follows the IoT structure/layer state-of-art that propose these three layers as well.

4 Result Presentation

In this section, we summarize the results of our analysis. From 134 articles investigated, we discarded 108 papers while applying the filters from Sect. 3.3. The remaining 26 papers were analyzed to answer the research questions.

4.1 Protected Assets

Table 3 summarises ITS assets (system and business assets), classify these assets and in addition, illustrate basic functional areas of each layer.

Table 3. Architecture layer assets

Layer	System assets	Business assets
Perception [10]	Sensing	Light detection and ranging (LiDAR), visible light communication (VLC), ultrasonic ranging devices (URD), millimeter wave radar, thermometer and infrared ranging	Ultrasonic data, radio frequencies, heat measurement, traffic count, travel time, vehicle weight data
	Vision	Video cameras, HD cameras, stereo vision systems, and Closed-circuit television camera (CCTV)	Surveillance (picture and video) data, 3D imaging data, traffic count
	Positioning	Global positioning system (GPS) receiver and radars (doppler radar speedometers, radar cruise control, and radar based obstacle detection systems)	Pseudo-range measurements, travel speed, radar data, vehicle location data
	Actuating	Vehicle node, ECU, key/remote device, infotainment	Mileage measurement, error codes, event data records, traffic warning messages, key/remote signal, transaction information
Network [31]	In-vehicle network	Controller area network (CAN), automotive Ethernet, byteflight, FlexRay, local interconnect network (LIN), low-voltage differential signaling (LVDS), and media oriented systems transport (MOST)	Perception data (e.g., tire pressure monitoring system (TPMS) messages)
	Vehicle-to-vehicle (V2V) network	Dedicated short range communications (DSRC)/wireless access in vehicular environments	Perception data (e.g., travel direction, vehicle range data)
	Vehicle-to-infrastructure (V2I) network	(WAVE) LTE/5G, worldwide interoperability for microwave access (WiMAX)	Perception data (e.g., Traffic count, accident data, transaction information, vehicle range data)
Application [12]	Computing/Server	Web application server (parking space allocation server, central parking server)	Application service, application process, application data, perception data (e.g., key/remote signal, vehicle location data)
	Data Storage	Data center, Edge data center (Fog)	Perception data (e.g., vehicle location data)
	Human	User, Driver, Administrator	Application process

Perception Layer Assets are illustrated in Table 3. This layer consists of devices for sensing (e.g., ranging devices, thermometers), vision (e.g., Closed-circuit television camera (CCTV), HD camera), positioning (e.g., GPS receiver and Radars) and actuating (e.g., ECU, key/remote device). These devices are system assets that support data perception and primary actuating functions. The business assets are data generated or stored at this layer supported by its system assets. For example heat measurement (sensing – thermometers), surveillance data (vision – CCTV, HD camera), pseudo-range measurements (positioning – GPS receiver), and error codes (actuating – engine control unit (ECU)).

Network Layer Assets cover in-vehicle networks facilitating the transmission of data collected from the perception layer (e.g., controller area network (CAN), vehicle-to-vehicle (V2V) and vehicle-to-infrastructure (V2I)). Related business assets include, e.g., tire pressure monitoring systems (TPMS) messages (supported by CAN) and vehicle range data (supported by V2V or V2I).

Application Layer Assets collated in Table 3 cover computing/server devices (e.g., web application server), data storage devices (e.g., data center), and human assets (e.g., driver, administrator). Examples for business assets are smart application services (running on a web application server), vehicle location data (stored in a data storage) and application processes (executed by the driver).

4.2 Security Risks

We have defined security risk-related concepts in Sect. 2.2 which covers *vulnerability*, *threat*, *impact*, and the resulting *risk*. While not all risk-related concepts are fully covered in ITS security research, *threat* risk-related concept is widely covered. Tables 4, 5, and 6 summarize security threats at different architectural layers of ITS. We categorized these threats following the STRIDE threat model.

Perception Layer Threats (see Table 4) include threats to sensing, vision, positioning and actuating ITS components. The spoofing category (S) contains 6 threats (15 occurrences) with spoofing reported to be the most common. The tampering (T) presents 5 threats (6 occurrences) with tampering reported to be the most common. The repudiation (R) presents 1 threat – bogus messages. The information disclosure (I) contains 2 threats – stored attacks and eavesdropping each having 1 occurrence. The denial of service (D) presents 5 threats (6 occurrences) with jamming reported to be the most common. Lastly, the elevation of privilege (E) contains 5 threats (6 occurrences) with malware to be the most common.

Network Layer Threats are covered in Table 5. These threats affect the ability of system assets to transmit necessary data for ITS functions. ITS typically transmits data through in-vehicle, vehicle-to-vehicle (V2V), and vehicle-to-infrastructure (V2I) communication technologies. The spoofing category (S)

Table 4. Perception layer security threats

System Asset	Security Threats					
	S	T	R	I	D	E
Sensing, Positioning, and Vision Technologies	Spoofing (6), Node Impersonation (1), Illusion (3), Replay (3), Sending deceptive messages (1), Masquerading (1)	Forgery (1), Data manipulation (1), Tampering (2), Falsification of readings (1), Message Injection (1)	Bogus message (1)	Stored attacks (1), Eavesdropping (1)	Message saturation (1), Jamming (3), DoS (1), Disruption of system (1)	Backdoor (1), Unauthorised access (1), Malware (2), Elevation of privilege (1) Remote update of ECU (1)
Total	6 threats (15 occurrences)	5 threats (6 occurrences)	1 threat (1 occurrence)	2 threats (2 occurrences)	5 threats (6 occurrences)	5 threats (6 occurrences)

contains 12 threats (56 total occurrences) with spoofing threat reported to be the most common (13 occurrences). The tampering category (T) contains 7 threats (29 total occurrences) with injection (message, command, code, packet) and manipulation/alteration/fabrication/modification reported to be the most common (7 occurrences each). The repudiation category (R) contains 3 threats (5 total occurrences) with bogus messages reported to be the most common (3 occurrences). The information disclosure category (I) contains 11 threats (30 total occurrences) with eavesdropping reported to be the most common (10 occurrences). The denial of service category (D) contains 7 threats (29 total occurrences) with denial of service/distributed denial of service (DoS/DDoS) reported to be the most common (10 occurrences). Lastly, the elevation of privilege category (E) contains 7 threats (16 total occurrences) with malware reported to be the most common (7 occurrences).

Application Layer Threats (see Table 6) involve attacks to disrupt or corrupt high level ITS processes and services enabling intelligent transportation. In the application layer, the spoofing category (S) contains 3 threats (3 total occurrences) with spoofing, sybil and illusion attack, each having 1 occurrence in literature. The tampering category (T) contains 1 threat – malicious update (1 total occurrence) in literature. The repudiation category (R) contains no threats in literature for this layer. The information disclosure category (I) contains 3 threats (4 total occurrences) with eavesdropping reported to be the most common (2 occurrences). The denial of service category (D) contains 1 threat – DoS (2 total occurrences). Lastly, the elevation of privilege category (E) contains 4 threats (4 total occurrences) with malware, jail-breaking OS, social engineering and rogue data-center each reported to be the most common (1 occurrence each) in literature.

Table 5. Network layer security threats

System asset	Security threats					
	S	T	R	I	D	E
In-vehicle network, Vehicle-to-Vehicle (V2V), Vehicle-to-Infrastructure technologies (V2I)	Sybil (10), Spoofing (GPS) (13), Replay attack (11), Masquerading (7), RF Fingerprinting (1), Wormhole (6), Camouflage attack (1), Impersonation attack (2), Illusion attack (2), Key/Certificate Replication (1), Tunneling (1), Position Faking (1)	Timing attacks (1), Injection (message, command, code, packet) (7), Manipulation/Alteration/Fabrication/Modification (7), Routing modification/manipulation (5), Tampering(broadcast, message transaction, hardware) (6), Forgery (1), Malicious update (software/firmware) (2)	Bogus messages (3), Rogue Repudiation (1), Loss of event trace-ability (1)	Eavesdropping (10), Man-in-the-middle (5), ID disclosure (1), Location tracking (5), Data sniffing (1), Message interception (2), Information disclosure (1), Traffic analysis (1), Information gathering (1), TPMS tracking (1), Secrecy attacks (1)	DoS/DDoS (10), Spam (5), Jamming (5), Flooding (3), Message suppression (1), Channel interference (1), Black hole (4).	Malware (7), Brute Force (2), Gaining control (1), Social engineering (3), Logical attacks (1), Unauthorised access (1), Session Hijack (1)
Total	12 threats (56 occurrences)	7 threats (29 occurrences)	3 threats (5 occurrences)	11 threats (30 occurrences)	7 threats (29 occurrences)	7 threats (16 occurrences)

Table 6. Application layer security threats

System asset	Security threats					
	S	T	R	I	D	E
Application server, Edge data center, Human	Spoofing (1), Sybil (1), Illusion attack (1)	Malicious Update (1)		Eavesdropping (2), Location tracking (1), Privacy leakage (1)	DoS (2)	Jail-breaking OS (1), Social engineering (1), Rogue Data-center (1), Malware (1)
Total	3 threats (3 occurrences)	1 threat (1 occurrence)	0	3 threats (4 occurrences)	1 threat (2 occurrence)	4 threats (4 occurrences)

4.3   Security Countermeasures

We illustrate the security countermeasures proposed in surveyed literature to address security risks in ITS for each layer in Table 7. Security risks are classified into the following security requirements: confidentiality, integrity, availability, authentication, authorization, and non-repudiation. Our findings indicate that related work mainly covers network layer threats, e.g., spoofing by authentication controls and denial of service by availability controls. Repudiation category threats in the network and application layers and denial of service category threats in the perception and application layers are not as frequently covered. However, we did not identify non-repudiation and availability countermeasures to mitigate security threats.

Table 7. Security countermeasures in ITS layers.

Security Req types	Perception layer	Network layer	Application Layer
Authentication	Spoofing resistant positioning system [38], device level user authentication [40], digital certificates, digital signature of software and sensors [10,34], challenge/response mechanism [34], encrypted Precise Positioning System (PPS)	ID authentication [15], radio-frequency identification (RFID) tokens, public key infrastructure [8,47], WAVE security standard [29], secure routing protocol [45], reputation scoring [22], central validation authority (CVA) [21,34], secure location verification [34], digital certificates and digital signatures [10,22,34], bit commitment and zero-knowledge mechanisms [34], variable MAC and IP addresses, challenge/response mechanism [34]	Digital certificates and digital signatures [10,34]
Integrity	Restricted physical access [10], challenge/response mechanism [34], use trusted hardware piratically impossible to alter existing values unless authorised [34]	Public key infrastructure (PKI) [1,15], hashing function, cryptographic primitives [34], security protocol [15], plausibility validation network (PVN) [1]	Plausibility Validation [35]
Non-repudiation	Use trusted hardware piratically impossible to alter existing values unless authorised [34]		
Confidentiality	Encryption [47]	Vision integrated pseudorange error removal (VIPER) algorithm [34], encryption [15,34,47], secure routing protocol [45], key management [11,15,45], digital signatures [11,15], WAVE security standard [29], firewall [47]	Firewall [47], cryptography services [29]
Availability		Frequency hopping spread spectrum (FHSS) technique [21,22,34], secure routing protocol [22,45], time stamping mechanism [34], bit commitment and signature based authentication mechanisms [34], WAVE security standard [29], firewall [47]	
Authorization	Threat modelling [45], hardware and software access control [34], upgrading on-board diagnostics (OBD)-II port [11]	Variable MAC and IP addresses [34], WAVE security standard [29], intrusion detection system, honeypot system [11,45]	Firewall [47]

5   Discussion

This study presents results from a literature analysis on security risk management in ITS. From this study, we gained the following three distinct insights:

- the importance of defining security risk-related concepts in the ITS domain.
- research concentration in security risk management within layers of ITS.
- an evaluation of the ITS layer with the lowest research concentration.

This section will present a discussion of these concerns based on our results.

5.1   Security Risk-Related Concepts

The benefits of the ISSRM method, its domain model and domain model concepts for security risk management is highlighted in [14]. However, risk-related concept analysis, in combination with associated asset-related concepts to allow sufficient risk treatment analysis, is lacking in most papers. It is essential to understand the cause of risk, and its consequences on assets to deciding for appropriate countermeasures.

We provide security risk analysis in each ITS layer (Table 8) following the asset-related and risk-related concepts of the domain model. Common threats discovered in each layer were selected to form each scenario. As we consider security risk management concepts in the following examples, concepts relating to the measurement of risk is out of the scope of this work.

- *Perception layer risk example.* Spoofing threat is commonly mentioned in the reviewed literature for the perception layer. In Table 8-column 1, an attacker provides a vehicle GPS receiver with false information about its pseudo-range measurements. When such information is accepted by the vehicle GPS receiver and transmitted to the application layer, it misleads the application, sending wrong location information e.g., in case of an emergency.
- *Network layer risk example.* A common threat in this layer is the Sybil attack. In Table 8-column 2, an attacker can create multiple false identifications. One vehicle can send traffic data associated with multiple identities at the same time, creating the illusion that the same messages come from multiple vehicles. This threat leads to the loss of integrity of traffic data, and an attacker can deceive the traffic management application and other vehicles that there is e.g. a traffic jam.
- *Application layer risk example.* A common threat is the DoS attack. An application layer example is a driver-less valet application [12] where a human driver, having arrived at a parking garage, initiates a parking space allocation service. The vehicle communicates with the parking allocation server to autonomously navigate to the parking space allocated. In Table 8-column 3, an attacker can induce a traffic jam to freeze the driver-less valet application by launching a denial of service attack on the parking space allocation server which for example, does not protect against malicious connections. This attack can lead to a shutdown of the parking space allocation service.

Table 8. Security risk analysis examples in ITS layers

Risk Scenario	Perception Layer Spoofing [37]	Network Layer Sybil Attack [11]	Application Layer Denial of Service [12]
Business Asset	Pseudo-range measurements, location data	Traffic data	Parking space allocation service
Security Criteria	Integrity of Pseudo-range measurements, location data	Integrity of traffic data,	Availability of Parking space allocation service
System Asset	Vehicle GPS receiver	Communication medium V2I (Cloud)	Parking space allocation server
Vulnerability	Vehicle GPS receiver is not spoof resistant	Ease of generation of node identities	Parking space allocation server does not protect against malicious connections
Threat	An attacker carries out a spoofing attack to mislead a vulnerable vehicle GPS receiver and inject counterfeit pseudo-range measurements, disrupting the emergency response system of the vehicle	An attacker creates numerous false identities to create the illusion that the traffic data broadcasts come from multiple vehicles to deceive other vehicles that there is a traffic jam	An attacker induces a traffic jam or to freeze the driver-less valet service by launching a denial of service attack on the parking space allocation server
Impact	loss of integrity of Pseudo-range measurements, location data, the vehicle sends wrong location information in emergency	loss of integrity of traffic data	loss of availability of parking space allocation service
Risk	An attacker carries out a spoofing attack to mislead a vulnerable GPS receiver and inject counterfeit pseudo-range measurements leading to wrong location data transmitted and used by emergency response system	An attacker creates numerous false identities to create the illusion that the traffic data broadcast come from multiple vehicles to deceive other vehicles that there is a traffic jam leading to the loss of integrity of traffic data	An attacker induces a traffic jam to freeze the driver-less valet application by launching a denial of service attack on the parking space allocation server leading to the loss of availability of parking space allocation service

5.2 Security Risk Research Concentration

Research in ITS currently concentrates on vehicular network layers and perception layer devices. Security efforts thus tend to be focused on those layers. Only a few papers discuss security issues of the ITS application layer leading to an incomplete state-of-the-art about security risks in ITS in literature.

The application layer provides functions that connect ITS and end-users. However, this layer is also prone to security risks as it is primarily supported by system assets (web, internet, and cloud services) known for security vulnerabilities [39]. It is thus imperative to encourage risk analysis and to propose countermeasures for this layer. This section evaluates ITS application layer security risk and countermeasure dependencies requiring cooperative security efforts.

Security Risk Impact. Security risk impact in the application layer can stem from attacks within this layer or the perception and network layers forming a ripple effect [35]. A false GPS time originating in the perception layer can e.g., inhibit application processes. Sybil and illusion attacks can flood the application with incorrect information, hindering its service process.

Security Defence. ITS demands cooperative security defence. The application layer can provide defence for threats originating within its layer and perception or network layers. Attacks can be challenging to resolve on the perception and network layer, requiring a significant amount of time and resources to identify and revoke an attacker from negatively impacting ITS. Here, countermeasures can be implemented in the application layer as a last line of defence. To protect against spoofing threats (e.g., sybil, replay, and illusion threats), plausibility checks on information from vehicle nodes to validate the correctness of the data. The application layer can deal with ripple effect risks from other layers. It is also the last line of defence against threats to ITS. Future research within this layer is encouraged to realize its opportunities fully.

6 Concluding Remarks

The possibilities of making intelligent decisions and predictions through functional and operational cooperation within ITS components have created opportunities in the transportation industry, research, and development. This cooperative behaviour extends to security within its functions and operations. In this paper, we presented an extensive and comprehensive literature review on the current state of the art in ITS security risk management along with the layered architecture of IoT – perception, networking, and application layers. ITS stakeholders must ensure the required security criteria (i.e., confidentiality, integrity, and availability) within each architecture layer and its cooperative interactions. We explored in each architecture layer, asset-related concepts to elicit assets, risk-related concepts to document possible threats to these assets, and risk treatment-related concepts to provide security solutions. Also, our research revealed a lack of analysis for risk-related concepts with its connected asset-related concepts to allow risk treatment-related analysis. Results also reveal low research concentration for the application architecture layer despite its cooperative functional and security importance within ITS layers. Research in the field of ITS security risk management, especially the application layer needs to be explored further to develop innovative security solutions and applications.

Acknowledgments. This paper is supported in part by European Union's Horizon 2020 research and innovation programme under grant agreement No 830892, project SPARTA.

References

1. Al-Kahtani, M.S.: Survey on security attacks in vehicular ad hoc networks (VANETs). In: 2012 6th International Conference on Signal Processing and Communication Systems, pp. 1–9. IEEE (2012)
2. Atzori, L., Iera, A., Morabito, G.: The Internet of Things: a survey. Comput. Netw. **54**(15), 2787–2805 (2010)
3. Badampudi, D., Wohlin, C., Petersen, K.: Experiences from using snowballing and database searches in systematic literature studies. In: Proceedings of the 19th International Conference on Evaluation and Assessment in Software Engineering, p. 17. ACM (2015)
4. Barth, M., Boriboonsomsin, K.: Energy and emissions impacts of a freeway-based dynamic eco-driving system. Transp. Res. Part D: Transp. Environ. **14**(6), 400–410 (2009)
5. Bojan, T.M., Kumar, U.R., Bojan, V.M.: An Internet of Things based intelligent transportation system. In: 2014 IEEE International Conference on Vehicular Electronics and Safety, pp. 174–179. IEEE (2014)
6. Boriboonsomsin, K., Barth, M.J., Zhu, W., Vu, A.: Eco-routing navigation system based on multisource historical and real-time traffic information. IEEE Trans. Intell. Transp. Syst. **13**(4), 1694–1704 (2012)
7. Cervero, R., Tsai, Y.: City Carshare in San Francisco, California: second-year travel demand and car ownership impacts. Transp. Res. Rec.: J. Transp. Res. Board **1887**(1), 117–127 (2004)
8. Chen, Q., Sowan, A.K., Xu, S.: A safety and security architecture for reducing accidents in intelligent transportation systems. In: Proceedings of the International Conference on Computer-Aided Design, p. 95. ACM (2018)
9. DCSSL: Ebios: Expression of needs and identification of security objectives (2005)
10. De La Torre, G., Rad, P., Choo, K.K.R.: Driverless vehicle security: challenges and future research opportunities. Future Gener. Comput. Syst. (2018)
11. Den Hartog, J., Zannone, N., et al.: Security and privacy for innovative automotive applications: a survey. Comput. Commun. **132**, 17–41 (2018)
12. Dominic, D., Chhawri, S., Eustice, R.M., Ma, D., Weimerskirch, A.: Risk assessment for cooperative automated driving. In: Proceedings of the 2nd ACM Workshop on Cyber-Physical Systems Security and Privacy, pp. 47–58. ACM (2016)
13. D'Orey, P.M., Ferreira, M.: ITS for sustainable mobility: a survey on applications and impact assessment tools. IEEE Trans. Intell. Transp. Syst. **15**(2), 477–493 (2014). https://doi.org/10.1109/TITS.2013.2287257

14. Dubois, É., Heymans, P., Mayer, N., Matulevičius, R.: A systematic approach to define the domain of information system security risk management. In: Nurcan, S., Salinesi, C., Souveyet, C., Ralyté, J. (eds.) Intentional Perspectives on Information Systems Engineering, pp. 289–306. Springer, Heidelberg (2010)
15. Engoulou, R.G., Bellaïche, M., Pierre, S., Quintero, A.: VANET security surveys. Comput. Commun. **44**, 1–13 (2014)
16. ENISA: Inventory of risk assessment and risk management methods (2005)
17. Ferreira, M., D'Orey, P.M.: On the impact of virtual traffic lights on carbon emissions mitigation. IEEE Trans. Intell. Transp. Syst. **13**(1), 284–295 (2012)
18. Firesmith, D.: Engineering safety and security-related requirements for software-intensive systems. Carnegie-Mellon University Pittsburg PA Software Engineering Institute, Technical report (2007)
19. Firesmith, D., et al.: Engineering security requirements. J. Object Technol. **2**(1), 53–68 (2003)
20. Fries, R., Chowdhury, M., Brummond, J.: Transportation Infrastructure Security Utilizing Intelligent Transportation Systems. Wiley, Hoboken (2009)
21. Hamida, E., Noura, H., Znaidi, W.: Security of cooperative intelligent transport systems: standards threats analysis and cryptographic countermeasures. Electronics **4**(3), 380–423 (2015)
22. Hasrouny, H., Samhat, A.E., Bassil, C., Laouiti, A.: VANet security challenges and solutions: a survey. Veh. Commun. **7**, 7–20 (2017)
23. Huang, S., Sadek, A.W., Zhao, Y.: Assessing the mobility and environmental benefits of reservation-based intelligent intersections using an integrated simulator. IEEE Trans. Intell. Transp. Syst. **13**(3), 1201–1214 (2012)
24. Hussain, S., Kamal, A., Ahmad, S., Rasool, G., Iqbal, S.: Threat modelling methodologies: a survey. Sci. Int. (Lahore) **26**(4), 1607–1609 (2014)
25. ISO/IEC: 27001: 2013: Information technology-security techniques-information security management systems-requirements (2013)
26. Kitchenham, B., Brereton, O.P., Budgen, D., Turner, M., Bailey, J., Linkman, S.: Systematic literature reviews in software engineering - a systematic literature review. Inf. Softw. Technol. **51**(1), 7–15 (2009)
27. Kitchenham, B., Pretorius, R., Budgen, D., Brereton, O.P., Turner, M., Niazi, M., Linkman, S.: Systematic literature reviews in software engineering - a tertiary study. Inf. Softw. Technol. **52**(8), 792–805 (2010)
28. Kong, H.K., Hong, M.K., Kim, T.S.: Security risk assessment framework for smart car using the attack tree analysis. J. Ambient Intell. Humanized Comput. **9**(3), 531–551 (2018)
29. Laurendeau, C., Barbeau, M.: Threats to security in DSRC/WAVE. In: Kunz, T., Ravi, S.S. (eds.) ADHOC-NOW 2006. LNCS, vol. 4104, pp. 266–279. Springer, Heidelberg (2006). https://doi.org/10.1007/11814764_22
30. Li, L.: Study on security architecture in the Internet of Things. In: Proceedings of 2012 International Conference on Measurement, Information and Control, vol. 1, pp. 374–377. IEEE (2012)
31. Lu, Y., Maple, C., Sheik, T., Alhagagi, H., Watson, T., Dianati, M., Mouzakitis, A.: Analysis of cyber risk and associated concentration of research (ACR) 2 in the security of vehicular edge clouds. In: Living in the Internet of Things: Cybersecurity of the IoT - 2018, pp. 1–11. IET (2018)
32. Malakorn, K.J., Park, B.: Assessment of mobility, energy, and environment impacts of IntelliDrive-based cooperative adaptive cruise control and intelligent traffic signal control. In: 2010 IEEE International Symposium on Sustainable Systems and Technology (ISSST), pp. 1–6. IEEE, IEEE (2010)

33. Matulevičius, R.: Fundamentals of Secure System Modelling. Springer, Heidelberg (2017)
34. Mejri, M.N., Jalel, B.O., Hamdi, M.: Survey on VANET security challenges and possible cryptographic solutions. Veh. Commun. **1**(2), 53–66 (2014)
35. Moalla, R., Labiod, H., Lonc, B., Simoni, N.: Risk analysis study of its communication architecture. In: 2012 3rd International Conference on the Network of the Future (NOF), pp. 1–5. IEEE (2012)
36. Morris, B.T., Tran, C., Scora, G., Trivedi, M.M., Barth, M.J.: Real-time video-based traffic measurement and visualization system for energy/emissions. IEEE Trans. Intell. Transp. Syst. **13**(4), 1667–1678 (2012)
37. Mukisa, S.S., Rashid, A.: Cyber-security challenges of agent technology in intelligent transportation systems. In: Proceedings of the 1st International Workshop on Agents and CyberSecurity, p. 9. ACM (2014)
38. ben Othmane, L., Ranchal, R., Fernando, R., Bhargava, B., Bodden, E.: Incorporating attacker capabilities in risk estimation and mitigation. Comput. Secur. **51**, 41–61 (2015)
39. OWASP: Top 10 IoT Vulnerabilities (2014)
40. Pelzl, J., Wolf, M., Wollinger, T.: Automotive embedded systems applications and platform embedded security requirements. In: Markantonakis, K., Mayes, K. (eds.) Secure Smart Embedded Devices, Platforms and Applications, pp. 287–309. Springer, New York (2014). https://doi.org/10.1007/978-1-4614-7915-4_12
41. Perallos, A., Hernandez-Jayo, U., Zuazola, I.J.G., Onieva, E.: Intelligent Transport Systems: Technologies and Applications. Wiley, Hoboken (2015)
42. Ruddle, A.R., Ward, D.D., Perallos, A., Hernandez-Jayo, U., Onieva, E., Garcia-Zuazola, I.: Cyber security risk analysis for intelligent transport systems and in-vehicle networks. In: Intelligent Transport Systems Technologies and Applications, p. 83 (2015)
43. Servin, O., Boriboonsomsin, K., Barth, M.: An energy and emissions impact evaluation of intelligent speed adaptation. In: 2006 IEEE Intelligent Transportation Systems Conference, ITSC 2006, pp. 1257–1262. IEEE (2006)
44. Shostack, A.: Threat Modeling: Designing for Security. Wiley, Hoboken (2014)
45. Sun, Y., Wu, L., Wu, S., Li, S., Zhang, T., Zhang, L., Xu, J., Xiong, Y., Cui, X.: Attacks and countermeasures in the internet of vehicles. Ann. Telecommun. **72**(5–6), 283–295 (2017)
46. Tao, C.C.: Dynamic taxi-sharing service using intelligent transportation system technologies. In: 2007 International Conference on Wireless Communications, Networking and Mobile Computing, WiCom 2007, pp. 3209–3212. IEEE (2007)
47. Tbatou, S., Ramrami, A., Tabii, Y.: Security of communications in connected cars modeling and safety assessment. In: Proceedings of the 2nd International Conference on Big Data, Cloud and Applications, p. 56. ACM (2017)
48. Tielert, T., Killat, M., Hartenstein, H., Luz, R., Hausberger, S., Benz, T.: The impact of traffic-light-to-vehicle communication on fuel consumption and emissions. In: 2010 Internet of Things (IOT), pp. 1–8. IEEE (2010)
49. Tsugawa, S., Kato, S., Aoki, K.: An automated truck platoon for energy saving. In: 2011 IEEE/RSJ International Conference on Intelligent Robots and Systems (IROS), pp. 4109–4114. IEEE (2011)
50. Wohlin, C.: Guidelines for snowballing in systematic literature studies and a replication in software engineering. In: Proceedings of the 18th International Conference on Evaluation And Assessment in Software Engineering, p. 38. ACM (2014)

51. Yang, X., Li, Z., Geng, Z., Zhang, H.: A multi-layer security model for Internet of Things. In: Wang, Y., Zhang, X. (eds.) IOT 2012. CCIS, vol. 312, pp. 388–393. Springer, Heidelberg (2012). https://doi.org/10.1007/978-3-642-32427-7_54
52. Yang, Z., Yue, Y., Yang, Y., Peng, Y., Wang, X., Liu, W.: Study and application on the architecture and key technologies for IoT. In: 2011 International Conference on Multimedia Technology, pp. 747–751. IEEE (2011)
53. Yousuf, O., Mir, R.N.: A survey on the Internet of Things security: state-of-art, architecture, issues and countermeasures. Inf. Comput. Secur. **27**(2), 292–323 (2019)
54. Zhang, Z., Cho, M.C.Y., Wang, C., Hsu, C., Chen, C., Shieh, S.: IoT security: ongoing challenges and research opportunities. In: 2014 IEEE 7th International Conference on Service-Oriented Computing and Applications, pp. 230–234 (2014)
55. Zhao, K., Ge, L.: A Survey on the Internet of Things security. In: 2013 9th International Conference on Computational Intelligence and Security, pp. 663–667. IEEE (2013)
56. Zhou, H., Liu, B., Wang, D.: Design and research of urban intelligent transportation system based on the Internet of Things. In: Wang, Y., Zhang, X. (eds.) IOT 2012. CCIS, vol. 312, pp. 572–580. Springer, Heidelberg (2012). https://doi.org/10.1007/978-3-642-32427-7_82

Data Sharing in Presence of Access Control Policies

Juba Agoun$^{(\boxtimes)}$ and Mohand-Saïd Hacid

Université de Lyon, Université de Lyon 1, CNRS UMR 5205, Lyon, France
{juba.agoun,mohand-said.hacid}@univ-lyon1.fr

Abstract. In the context of data analysis and data integration, very often information from different and autonomous sources are shared. Sources use their own schema and their own access control policies. We consider the case where data sources decide to share information by specifying entity matching rules between their contents. A query to a given data source is rewritten to produce queries to other data sources that share information with that data source. This entity-matching oriented and policy-oriented rewriting preserves local data source policies. In this paper, we describe our methodology for data sharing between sources by ensuring the satisfaction of local access control policies.

Keywords: Data sharing · Data integration · Entity matching · Record matching · Access control · Query rewriting

1 Introduction

Large volumes of information are shared between several sources for data analysis purposes [6,8]. Data sharing is one of the configurations that allows sources hosting data sets complying to specific schemas to share information. Data in different and heterogeneous sources may overlap or may be closely associated. Entity matching is used to identify the same real-world object from different sources even if it is represented differently in the different sources (different formats, spellings, etc.) or containing errors. Data sharing uses data-level mappings which differs from data exchange and data integration [5]. The data heterogeneity problem arises when the same real world object is represented using different identifiers in different sources. For example, a patient may be uniquely identified using the social security number (SSN) in an admission hospital and by a local identifier ($donor\_id$) in a blood bank service.

Information that is protected against unwarranted disclosure is sensitive. Nonetheless, sharing data from different sources could potentially reveal sensitive information [2]. Indeed, each source enforces its own security policy to control

This research is performed within the scope of the DataCert (Coq deep specification of privacy aware data integration) project that is funded by ANR (Agence Nationale de la Recherche) grant ANR-15-CE39-0009 - http://datacert.lri.fr/.

H. Panetto et al. (Eds.): OTM 2019, LNCS 11877, pp. 301–309, 2019.
https://doi.org/10.1007/978-3-030-33246-4_19

the access to its content. Access control policies may also differ from one source to another since they are independent and autonomous. However, some of the information that are shared could be sensitive in a given source and not in another one. For some pieces of data that may be closely associated and similar[1], the access could be denied in one source, whereas it may be granted in another source. Hence, one of the collaborative sources faces a violation of a security policy.

In our work, we consider a data sharing framework in the presence of access control policies associated with the involved sources. Data sharing is computed by entity matching rules[2] considered at data-level rather than at schema-level. We describe a methodology that includes a set of transformation and verification steps to restrict, in the answer of a given query, the objects which do not satisfy the security policies of all involved sources. This paper is organized as follows. We give a motivating example in Sect. 2. In Sect. 3, we describe our framework. A posed query over a data source is translated into a equivalent query over a collaborative data source. The translated query is evaluated in such a way that the access control policies are preserved. We conclude in Sect. 4.

2   Motivating Example

Let us consider two institutions, a *hospital* and a *blood bank* that agree on sharing some subsets of their data sets.

The *hospital* stores data about patients in a relation we denote *patient(SSN, name_p, address_p, city_p, sex, blood_pressure, blood_glucose, height_weight, diagnosis)*. The *blood bank* institution stores in the relation *donor(id_d, donor _name, donor_address, donor_city, gender, blood_pressure, blood_glucose, h_w, number_donation)* information related to donors.

Table 1. Instance of *patient*

SSN	name_p	address_p	city_p	Sex	blood_pressure	blood_glucose	height_weight	Diagnosis
738-77-8987	Bob Tracy	3 rue emile zola	lyonn	M	120/79	73	162/71	Headache
358-87-9526	Smith, John	06 bis rue notre dame	paris 6	M	126/76	71	182/85	Stomachache
852-37-9526	Tim McCall	43 av. des Postes	Lille center	M	124/75	131	175/42	Diabetes
436-44-0945	Jeane Henri	48, rue du Four	75006 Paris	F	146/97	69	156/52	Hypertension

---

[1] Semantically equivalent, they denote the same real-world object.

[2] Entity matching rules specify under which conditions two records from different sources are considered as a *match* and represent the same real-world object [1,7].

Table 2. Instance of *donor*

id_d	donor_name	donor_address	donor_city	Gender	blood_pressure	blood_glucose	h_w	number_donation
455	Robert Tracy	03 rue emile Zola	lyon	Male	120/79	71	162/72	2
589	John A. Smith	06 bis rue notre dame	paris	Male	127/77	70	181/89	4
996	Timothy McCall	43 aveunue des Postes	lille	Male	121/73	136	176/53	0
195	Marine.P Jolio	48 B.v pierre marion	marseille	Female	116/77	72	163/55	1

The two relations *patient* and *donor* agree on an *attribute alignment* that maps the *patient* attributes *name_p, address_p, city_p, sex, blood_pressure, blood_glucose, height_weight* to *donor_name, donor_address, donor_city, gender, blood_pressure, blood_glucose, h_w* of the relation *donor*, respectively.

The two databases display entity heterogeneity as they do not share a common identifier (*see* Tables 1 and 2). Some information describing a donor might be associated with a given patient in the hospital database if both tuples refer to the same real-world individual. Indeed, a donor could have dealt with the hospital for a particular reason. For instance, a name can be spelled as John A. Smith in the blood bank database instance, whereas in the hospital database it can be spelled as Smith, John. Nevertheless, the patient and donor records, in this case, represent the same real-world person with similarities in name, address, city and sex. The similarities are computed according to an entity matching rule denoted by ϕ_{EM} (*more details will be provided later on*). Given two tuples $p \in patient$ and $d \in donor$ the entity matching rule in our scenario is expressed as follows:

$$\Phi_{EM} = p[name\_p] \approx_{(Jaro,78)} d[donor\_name] \wedge$$
$$p[address\_p] \approx_{(Levenshtein,72)} d[donor\_address] \wedge$$
$$p[city\_p] \approx_{(Smith-Waterman,77)} d[donor\_city] \wedge$$
$$p[sex] \approx_{(jaro,70)} d[gender].$$

The entity matching rule is computed over a subset of the aligned attributes where $\approx_{(f,\epsilon)}$ is the corresponding similarity function f and ϵ the threshold. Two records p and d *match* iff Φ_{EM} is evaluated to *true*.

Please note that there are some records that are similar since they satisfy Φ_{EM}, *see* Tables 1 and 2. For instance, the record *Tim McCall* with the *SSN* "852-37-9526", in the *patient* instance, has a similar record with the *id_d* "996" in the *donor* instance, as it satisfies Φ_{EM} when assessing:

$$Jaro(\text{Tim McCall, Timothy McCall}) = 90 \wedge$$
$$Levenshtein(\text{43 av. des Postes, 43 aveunue des Postes}) = 76 \wedge$$
$$Smith - Waterman(\text{Lille center, lille}) = 80 \wedge$$
$$jaro(M, Male) = 75.$$

In our setting, we consider the rules expressed as *forbidden views* [4], also called *secret views*. Each data source exposes a security policy expressed as a set of access control rules. On one hand, the hospital database denies access simultaneously to both attributes *SSN* and *diagnosis* (expressed in *rule r_1*), and it also denies access simultaneously to both attributes *name* and *diagnosis* (*rule r_2*) for all the patients. The rules r_1 and r_2 express the access control policy $\Pi_{patient}$ associated with the relation *patient*:

r_1 : **Deny** SSN, diagnosis
       From patient
r_2 : **Deny** name_p, diagnosis
       From patient

On the other hand, the blood bank database denies access to the combination of *name* and the *blood_glucose* (*rule r_1'*), and the association of the *donor_id* and the *blood_glucose* (*rule r_2'*) for all the donors living in *Lille*. The access control policy Π_{donor} associated with the relation *donor* is the set of the two rules:

r_1' : **Deny**   donor_name, blood_glucose
      From   donor
      Where donor_city = 'lille'
r_2' : **Deny**   id_d, blood_glucose
      From   donor
      Where donor_city = 'lille'

Now, assume we want to retrieve all the male patients with their *name, city, blood_pressure, blood_glucose* and their *height/weigh* from *patient*. Such a query can be expressed as:

q : **Select** name_p, city_p, blood_pressure, blood_glucose, height_weight
    From   patient
    Where sex = 'M'

The attribute alignment and the entity matching rule between *patient* and *donor* might provide sufficient information to translate the query q over *patient* in the hospital database to a query q' over the *donor* relation in the blood bank database. The derived query q' could be of the following form (*details will be given in the next section*):

q' : **Select** donor_name, donor_city, blood_pressure, blood_glucose, h_w
    From   donor
    Where gender = 'Male'

Next, we show the access control violation that could occur, when answering the previous queries, without any mechanisms for data sharing security policy compliance.

The tuples returned from the evaluation of q are displayed in Table 3.

Table 3. Retrieved records from q

name_p	city_p	blood_pressure	blood_glucose	height_weight
Bob Tracy	lyonn	120/79	73	162/71
Smith, John	paris 6	126/76	71	182/85
Tim McCall	Lille center	124/75	131	175/42

Table 4. Retrieved records from q'

donor_name	donor_city	gender	blood_pressure	blood_glucose	h_w
Robert Tracy	lyon	Male	120/79	71	162/72
John A. Smith	paris	Male	127/77	70	181/89

The results of the query q' are shown in Table 4. Please note that the tuple with the name **Timothy McCall** living in Lille is not returned because it is denied by the rule r'_1.

If we look at the both results in Tables 3 and 4, and based on the entity matching rule Φ_{EM}, the tuple corresponding to the record *"Tim McCall"* is returned by the evaluation of q. The latter matches with the donor record namely *"Timothy McCall"* which was not returned when evaluating q' due to the access control restriction.

Thus, the disclosure of a record with information from the hospital database (here *patient* relation) leads to the violation of the blood bank access control policy. This scenario highlights an access control policy violation in a data sharing context.

3   General Framework

The main objectives of our work are to: (1) guarantee the preservation of the source policies and (2) guarantee that for each record t subject to an access control (AC), if t has an equivalent record t' in the other sources, then t' should comply with AC during the query evaluation process.

We consider SQL queries and views without grouping and aggregation. For notational convenience, we modify the naming convention of standard SQL to guarantee unique attribute names for each of the attributes in a query. Let $R(A_1, A_2, ..., A_n)$ be a relation with $n > 1$ attributes denoted $att(R)$. Let t be a record (or *tuple*) from R instance. We use $Tables(q)$ to denote the set of tables in the FROM clause of a query q. The set of attributes in the SELECT clause of q, denoted by $Sel(q)$, consists of non-aggregation of attributes. The conditions in the WHERE clause of a query q, denoted $Conds(q)$, consists of a Boolean combination of constraints.

Please note that for the simplicity of the notation $Sel(r)$ appoints the set of attributes in the Deny clause of r, where r is an access control rule.

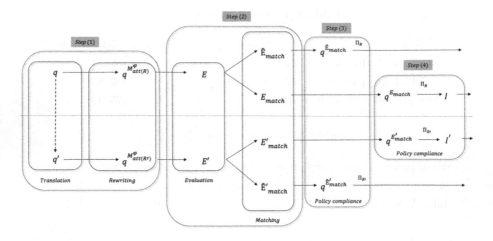

Fig. 1. General framework of for query evaluation in a data sharing setting

The general framework is shown Fig. 1. We consider two databases D and D' with $R \in D$ and $R' \in D'$ two relations without duplicates, an attribute alignment m between R and R', and an entity matching rule Φ. Each database provides its own security policy Π_R and $\Pi_{R'}$, attached to R and R', respectively.

We describe step by step, how to answer a posed query q over R by considering the collaborative source R'. From q, one generates q' over R'. If q could access and retrieve a given tuple $t \in R$ and q' is denied to access $t' \in R$, with $t \sim_\Phi t'$; then, the restriction should be applied to q.

Please note that our approach requires a trusted third party that must deal with partial results at a given stage.

Step 1. This step is mainly based on returning tuples from the sources aligned in such a way that we can perform an entity matching resolution. It consists, first, in translating the query q over R into q' over R'. For a correct translation, the query q must satisfy some conditions:

1. All the selection attributes $Sel(q)$ must appear in the set of aligned attributes $M_{att(R)}^{\Phi}$.
2. All the attributes involved in $Conds(q)$ must appear in the aligned attributes $M_{att(R)}$.

Please note that $Sel(q)$ might be not suitable for the entity matching since it needs all the attributes of matching from both sources. Therefore, based on the query q, construct in the database D a query $q^{M_{att(R)}^{\Phi}}$ where its clauses have the following properties:

1. $Sel(q^{M_{att(R)}^{\Phi}}) = M_{att(R)}^{\Phi} \cup Sel(q)$. We recall that $M_{att(R)}^{\Phi}$ is the set of attributes of R appearing in the matching rule Φ.
2. $Sel(q^{M_{att(R)}^{\Phi}}) = Conds(q)$.

Thereby, $q^{M^{\Phi}_{att(R)}}$ has the following form:

$$q^{M^{\Phi}_{att(R)}} : \quad \textbf{Select} \quad M^{\Phi}_{att(R)} \cup Sel(q)$$
$$\textbf{From} \quad \text{Tables(q)}$$
$$\textbf{Where} \quad \text{Conds(q)}$$

The same process is applied to the translated query q' in database D' to construct the query $q'^{M^{\Phi}_{att(R')}}$. The answers to $q^{M^{\Phi}_{att(R)}}$ and $q'^{M^{\Phi}_{att(R')}}$ will then be used to find matches according to Φ.

To sum up, this step returns the tuples satisfying the given query with the matching attributes of each source. Later on, the access control will be applied to these queries through a rewriting process.

Step 2. In this step, we proceed, respectively, to the evaluation of queries $q^{M^{\Phi}_{att(R)}}$ and $q'^{M^{\Phi}_{att(R')}}$ in the databases D and D'. Let E and E' be the results of $q^{M^{\Phi}_{att(R)}}$ and $q'^{M^{\Phi}_{att(R')}}$, respectively.

We apply the entity matching resolution to E and E' to identify the pairs of tuples that represent the same real world object $w.r.t$ the entity matching rule Φ.

As a result, we obtain the set E_{match} (*resp.* E'_{match}) consisting of the records in E that match to records in E' (*resp.* E). We also deduce $\overline{E}_{match}$ (*resp.* $\overline{E'}_{match}$) consisting of records in E (*resp.* E') for which there is no matching.

Step 3. In this step, we deal with the sets $\overline{E}_{match}$ and $\overline{E'}_{match}$. From each set, we remove those tuples that do not satisfy the local access control policies. We note that the tuples whose access is denied by one or more access control rules are considered as sensitive. Therefore, we consider the set $\overline{E}_{match}$ of the non matching records. We produce a query $q^{\overline{E}_{match}}$ of the following form:

$$q^{\overline{E}_{match}}: \quad \textbf{Select} \quad Sel(q)$$
$$\textbf{From} \quad \overline{E}_{match}$$

Then, $q^{\overline{E}_{match}}$ is evaluated in accordance to access control policy Π_R. The result of this query evaluation will be directly returned as a part of a final answer. The same process is also applied to set $\overline{E'}_{match}$.

Step 4. In this step, we consider the matching sets returned in *step 2*. For each set of tuples, we check the satisfiability of the access control policies.

Given the relation R and its corresponding access control policy Π_R, we apply Π_R to the returned matching records E_{match}. For that, we have to generate a query $q^{E_{match}}$ of the form:

$$q^{E_{match}}: \quad \textbf{Select} \quad *$$
$$\textbf{From} \quad E_{match}$$

The query $q^{E_{match}}$ is rewritten in accordance to the access control Π_R in order to return only the non-sensitive tuples. Thereby, in the AC query rewriting of $q^{E_{match}}$, the relevant rules[3] are selected relatively to $Sel(q)$ instead of $Sel(q^{E_{match}})$.

When proceeding to the query evaluation of $q^{E_{match}}$, it returns the set of tuples, we denote it $E_{match}^{\Pi_R}$, which contains only tuples that do not violate any access control rule Π_R.

The same is applied to the set E'_{match} leading to the set $E'^{\Pi_{R'}}_{match}$. Nevertheless, the set $E_{match}^{\Pi_R}$ may disclose some tuples that could violate the access control policy $\Pi_{R'}$. Indeed, some of the tuples in $E_{match}^{\Pi_R}$ may have a match in E'_{match} even they do not appear in $E'^{\Pi_{R'}}_{match}$. In this case, they need to be removed from $E_{match}^{\Pi_R}$ and it is performed by computing the following expression:

$$I = E_{match}^{\Pi_R} \setminus_{\Phi} (E'_{match} \setminus E'^{\Pi_{R'}}_{match})$$

$\setminus_{\Phi}$ is a set difference under entity matching rule ϕ, it is used as an operator to remove the tuples from a set having a similar. We introduce in the following definition the Set Similarity-based Difference.

Definition 1. *(Set Similarity-based Difference) Given S and S', two relations with the same arity and Φ an entity matching rule between S and S', the similarity-based difference is defined as: $S \setminus S' = \{t \mid t \in S \wedge \nexists\, t' \in S' : t \sim_\Phi t'\}$.*

Similarly to $E_{match}^{\Pi_R}$, we compute I' by evaluating the expression over the set $E'^{\Pi_{R'}}_{match}$ (see Fig. 1).

Finally, project the obtained results I and I' on the attribute $Sel(q)$ and $Sel(q')$, respectively. Since the translation conditions guarantee the mapping of $Sel(q)$ to $Sel(q')$, this means that we could merge the partial results of step 3 and step 4 as a one final answer.

4   Conclusion

In this work, we have considered the problem of data sharing between heterogeneous and autonomous data sources in the presence of access control policies. We described an approach where several sources could share their data according to their security policies. We used entity matching rules to link data from different sources and we have shown how the entity matching rules are used in

---

[3] Given a query q over R and a set of access control rules Π_R, a rule $r \in \Pi_R$ is relevant to a query q *iff* $Sel(r) \subseteq Sel(q)$.

the translation of structured queries. We wanted a restrictive approach, in the sense that in case of conflict, deny takes precedence. The reference architecture requires a trusted third party to manage the query translation and prevent from the disclosure of sensitive data.

Future work will address more complex data sharing scenarios: richer queries, data dependencies, data fragmentation etc. Also, another architecture of the solution to the problem could be addressed if it avoids the third party. Finally, since our proposal is applied to relational databases, we are interested in investigating other data models (e.g., RDF) and other access control principles with positive and negative access control rules [3].

References

1. Fan, W., Jia, X., Li, J., Ma, S.: Reasoning about record matching rules. Proc. VLDB Endow. **2**(1), 407–418 (2009)
2. Haddad, M., Stevovic, J., Chiasera, A., Velegrakis, Y., Hacid, M.-S.: Access control for data integration in presence of data dependencies. In: Bhowmick, S.S., Dyreson, C.E., Jensen, C.S., Lee, M.L., Muliantara, A., Thalheim, B. (eds.) DASFAA 2014. LNCS, vol. 8422, pp. 203–217. Springer, Cham (2014). https://doi.org/10.1007/978-3-319-05813-9_14
3. Jajodia, S., Samarati, P., Sapino, M.L., Subrahmanian, V.: Flexible support for multiple access control policies. ACM Trans. Database Syst. (TODS) **26**(2), 214–260 (2001)
4. Kaushik, R., Ramamurthy, R.: Efficient auditing for complex SQL queries. In: Proceedings of the 2011 ACM SIGMOD International Conference on Management of Data, SIGMOD 2011, pp. 697–708 (2011)
5. Kementsietsidis, A., Arenas, M.: Data sharing through query translation in autonomous sources. In: Proceedings of the Thirtieth International Conference on Very Large Data Bases, vol. 30, pp. 468–479 (2004)
6. Labrinidis, A., Jagadish, H.V.: Challenges and opportunities with big data. Proc. VLDB Endow. **5**(12), 2032–2033 (2012)
7. Singh, R., et al.: Synthesizing entity matching rules by examples. Proc. VLDB Endow. **11**(2), 189–202 (2017)
8. Wu, X., Zhu, X., Wu, G.Q., Ding, W.: Data mining with big data. IEEE Trans. Knowl. Data Eng. **26**(1), 97–107 (2014)

Library Usage Detection in Ethereum Smart Contracts

Alexander Hefele[✉], Ulrich Gallersdörfer, and Florian Matthes

Department of Informatics, Technical University of Munich, Munich, Germany
{a.hefele,ulrich.gallersdoerfer,matthes}@tum.de

Abstract. We analyze the usage of the SafeMath library on the blockchain with a data set of 6.9 million bytecodes of Ethereum smart contracts. This library provides safe arithmetic operations for contracts. In order to detect smart contracts that make use of the library from the bytecode alone, we perform the following five steps: download all available library versions, write test contracts that use the library, compile all test contracts with all compatible compiler versions, extract the internal library functions from the compiled bytecode, and search for contracts on the blockchain that use these library function bytecodes. In total, we detect usage of the SafeMath library in 1.34% of all smart contracts on the blockchain and in 27.52% of all distinct contract codes. To evaluate our approach, we use more than 50,000 verified contracts from Etherscan for which both the Solidity source code and the bytecode is available. Our algorithm correctly detects library usage for 86.34% of the smart contracts in the evaluation set.

Keywords: Blockchain · Ethereum · Library · SafeMath · Smart contract · Solidity

1 Introduction

The Ethereum system facilitates the execution of decentralized programs, called smart contracts [1]. This blockchain has been running since 2015 and since then, millions of smart contracts have been deployed to it. Most contracts are written in the Solidity programming language and are then compiled to Ethereum Virtual Machine (EVM) bytecode. The bytecode is deployed on the network and is executed by every full node. The contract is easily usable by anyone with knowledge of the interface of the smart contract.

While the bytecode of every smart contract is publicly accessible on the blockchain, the respective source code is usually not. This creates an information asymmetry, as the creator of a smart contract has information the (potential) user has not. This often leads to decreased counts of users, which are willing to engage with the respective smart contract and generally limits the potential insights into the ecosystem in whole. We develop methodologies to analyze any bytecode deployed in the network in order to gain information about the activities on the blockchain.

© Springer Nature Switzerland AG 2019
H. Panetto et al. (Eds.): OTM 2019, LNCS 11877, pp. 310–317, 2019.
https://doi.org/10.1007/978-3-030-33246-4_20

Previous research papers have analyzed the Ethereum blockchain with a focus on a wide variety of aspects. For example, network classification and clustering undergo extensive research [2,3]. These works group smart contracts based on different properties, e.g. their purpose. Another approach is to analyze only a subset of smart contracts, which implement some functionality. Two examples for that are token systems [4] and Ponzi schemes [5,6].

Similar to that, our approach is to investigate library usage, more specifically usage of OpenZeppelin's SafeMath library [7]. This library provides safe functions for basic arithmetic operations that cannot over- or underflow as Solidity itself does not protect against these errors. Several hacks of smart contracts exploited over- or underflows, e.g. the DAO attack in June 2016 [8]. It appears that SafeMath is one of the most used Solidity libraries, but this conjecture lacks concrete numbers. Therefore, the main question, which we answer in this paper, is: How many smart contracts actually use the SafeMath library? This information can for example be useful for security analyses, where the absence of the SafeMath library can indicate the presence of over- or underflow bugs.

2 Methodology and Data Set

The basis of our research is an extensive and complete data set. It contains all smart contracts that are deployed on the Ethereum blockchain until the block 6,900,000. That includes both contracts created by externally owned accounts and those created by other smart contracts. Moreover, our data set encompasses several verified contracts, for which we additionally have the Solidity source code. We run a full node using the Geth client for data acquisition.

2.1 Methodology

User-Created Contracts. Transactions that directly create a new contract can be easily identified, as their recipient is `null`. For each transaction, we determine the address of the newly created contract and leverage the `eth.getCode()` call in order to obtain the bytecode of the contract. The address of the new contract is only based on the address of the creating account and its nonce [9]. We can read both of these values directly from the contract-creation transaction.

If a contract is selfdestructed by the time we request the code, the `eth-call` will return an empty contract as the Ethereum node has already deleted the code. In that case, we apply a heuristic to try to extract the contract code from the `input` field of the contract-creation transaction. The heuristic detects several standard instructions that the Solidity compiler puts in the creation-code. It is not perfect, but is able to generate bytecode for the majority of contracts that are created using the Solidity compiler. Since we use it only for selfdestructed contracts and the number of those is very small in comparison to the total number of smart contracts, this heuristic is sufficient here.

Contract-Created Contracts. Smart contracts that are created by other contracts are instantiated through message calls, which are not explicitly stored in the block. Furthermore, only contracts containing the `CREATE` instruction can create new smart contracts.[1] Since the address of the created contract is deterministic, we can calculate the addresses of possible child contracts. We iterate over all user-created contracts from the previous step, which contain a `CREATE` instruction. Starting with nonce 0, we leverage the `eth.getCode()` call to see if the account behind the possible child address actually contains code. Then we increment the nonce and continue with the next possible child contract. We stop when 500 consecutive nonces return an empty contract in order not to stop prematurely when some child contracts have already selfdestructed. However, there is no heuristic to obtain these selfdestructed contract-created contracts.

Next, we iterate over the contract-created contracts that were found in this step to see if they, in turn, have created new contracts. We do this recursively until no more new contracts are found.

Verified Contracts. For the evaluation of our approach, we use verified contracts from the block explorer Etherscan.[2] The site allows users to upload the Solidity source code of their deployed smart contracts and verifies that it matches the bytecode on the blockchain. These verified contracts have been used by the authors of several other papers, e.g. [3,5,6].

2.2 Data Set Overview

We apply our data extraction techniques to the first 6,900,000 blocks of the Ethereum blockchain. In total, we are able to extract 6,980,654 smart contracts. More than two thirds (4,803,701) of all contracts on the blockchain are created by another smart contract, the rest is created by externally owned accounts. In addition, despite the existence of millions of contracts, our data set only contains 190,223 distinct codes, which is the result of code duplication. Our set of verified contracts from Etherscan encompasses 50,173 contracts.

The authors in [10] create a data set of smart contracts that is similar to ours. They investigate the first 5,000,000 blocks of the Ethereum blockchain and gather approximately 1.2 million user-created contracts and 3.5 million contract-created contracts. Their results show that 2.71% of the bytecodes in their data set are unique. These numbers coincide well with our findings, as the amount of unique contract bytecodes in our data set is only marginally higher: $\frac{190223}{6980654} = 2.73\%$.

3   Library Usage Detection

Our approach for detecting SafeMath library usage in smart contracts consists of five steps. To begin with, we download all official released versions of the library

---

[1] The `CREATE2` instruction was introduced only after our data collection process.
[2] https://etherscan.io.

and write a test contract for each library version that calls every function once. Next, we compile all these contracts with all compatible Solidity compiler versions. From the compiled bytecode, we extract the library functions and search for them in the bytecodes of all deployed contracts on the blockchain.

3.1 Obtaining All Library Versions

We only use the official SafeMath releases from OpenZeppelin's GitHub repository and do not consider other sources, like forked repositories. From version 1.0.0 until 2.1.1 of the library, there are 31 versions which we take into account. Note that some versions do not differ at all from their predecessors.

Early SafeMath versions contained max() and min() functions that were later outsourced into a separate Math library. We do not take these functions into account as we observed them in contracts whose programmers did not include the SafeMath library, but just happened to write the exact function themselves.

Lastly, it is important to say that all functions of the SafeMath library are declared internal. Because of that, these functions are not called via the DELEGATECALL instruction, but are at compile time copied into the bytecode of every contract that uses them.

3.2 Writing Test Contracts

The next step is to write one test contract for each SafeMath library and call every SafeMath function once. This is necessary because bytecodes of internal library functions are only included in the binary of the contract if they are called by the contract. We write test functions for all arithmetic functions that are provided by SafeMath. For example, in the function test_mul(), we call SafeMath's mul() function and set one of the parameters to 0x1111. The byte sequence 0x1111 is chosen in such a way that it does not appear anywhere else in the compiled binary and can therefore be used to recognize the call of the mul() function inside the test_mul() function. The functions for the other arithmetic functions are constructed analogously, but with different distinct parameters.

We write all test contracts manually because there is no simple way to automate this step, as every library has slight differences. For example, early versions of SafeMath are declared a contract, requiring different code to import it. However, due to only 31 existing versions, the contract creation can be done by hand.

3.3 Compiling All Libraries with All Compiler Versions

Next, we compile the test programs from the previous step with every compatible Solidity compiler version. To get the minimum compatible compiler version, we read the pragma solidity header of the SafeMath library. As maximum compiler version, we set 0.4.25 for all libraries with a minimum version of 0.4.x and 0.5.2 for all libraries with a minimum version of 0.5.x. At the time of our analysis, 0.5.2 was the latest compiler version released. Additionally, for every combination of test program and compiler, we compile the program both with optimization turned on and off. This approach produces 540 compiled binaries.

3.4   Extracting Library Functions

Zhou et al. [11] describe a sophisticated heuristic to detect internal functions in a general way. However, as we are able to control the environment of the internal function calls, we can take a simpler approach. To find the start of our internal functions, we search for the unique parameter that we call the internal function with (see Sect. 3.2). In case of our `mul()` function from before, we search for the instruction `PUSH2 0x1111`. Then, the next `PUSH2` instruction pushes the code location of the internal function that is about to be called onto the stack. Immediately afterwards, a `JUMP` to that location follows. From here, we search for the end of the function. Our investigations show that there are only three possible instruction sequences indicating the function's end. Either `JUMPI INVALID STOP` or `REVERT STOP` or `JUMP`, if the instruction directly preceding it is not a `PUSH2`.

The extracted bytecode needs to be sanitized next. The library functions contain several relative jumps within themselves whose destinations depend on the offset at which the function is located in the code. To be able to compare the bytecodes with others from the blockchain, we replace the parameter of every `PUSH2` instruction with a placeholder. That way, we eliminate all code destinations for relative jumps. We are able to extract 82 distinct function bytecodes.

3.5   Library Usage Results

Finally, we search through all smart contract bytecodes on the blockchain. We allow any byte to match the placeholder that we introduced in the previous step. If at least one library function is anywhere within the bytecode of a smart contract, we assume that this contract uses the SafeMath library.

In total, we detect 93,652 smart contracts that use the library, which is 1.34% of all contracts currently deployed on the blockchain. These contracts use 52,347 different contract codes, which is 27.52% of all distinct codes in our data set. This is a sign that many contract codes that make use of the SafeMath library are only deployed once or a few times on the blockchain. Lastly, 73,944 or 3.40% of contracts that are created by externally owned accounts use SafeMath.

4   Evaluation

In order to evaluate our approach, we use verified contracts from Etherscan because both the bytecode and the original Solidity source code is available for them. Our data set contains 50,173 verified contracts. However, these contracts are not labeled whether they make use of the SafeMath library or not. Therefore, we detect SafeMath usage if a source code contains a `contract` or a `library` named "SafeMath" or "SafeMathLib", which are the most commonly used names for the library. We consider this classification as the ground truth.

4.1   Evaluation Results

Table 1 shows the confusion matrix of our evaluation. In the rows are our predicted values, i.e. the results of the library detection from the bytecode. The columns represent the "true" condition, i.e. the results of the library detection based on the Solidity source code.

Table 1. Evaluation confusion matrix

	Source code uses SafeMath	Does not use SafeMath
Detected SafeMath in bytecode	22,549 true positives	731 false positives
Did not detect SafeMath	6,123 false negatives	20,770 true negatives

From the confusion matrix, we can read that 86.34% of all evaluated smart contracts are classified correctly (either true positives or true negatives). 1.46% are false positives, i.e. we detect SafeMath usage in the bytecode, but not in the Solidity source code. Manual inspection shows that most of these contracts do implement SafeMath functionality, but use unusual library names, like Utils.

Finally, 12.20% of the smart contracts are false negatives, meaning that we detect SafeMath in the source code, but not in the bytecode. That happens for example when a contract includes the library in the source code, but never calls any of its functions. Another reason for false negatives originates in our methodology for generating SafeMath function bytecodes. Apparently, there are more valid bytecodes for SafeMath functions, which can be created by using nightly compiler versions or pre-releases of the library or combinations of these. Additionally, we only consider zero and 200 optimizer runs in our analysis because these are the two standard settings. Though, it is possible to use any number of optimization runs and this might produce slightly different binaries, hence causing false negatives. It is left for future research to determine more SafeMath library function bytecodes and by that lower the number of false negatives.

4.2 Limitations and Advantages

The main limitation of our approach is that it is not yet generic for any library. Other libraries have other internal functions and for public functions, an entirely new approach needs to be implemented. Additionally, new test contracts need to be written by hand and the function extraction algorithm needs to be adapted manually for the test contracts. Our implementation is specifically tailored for the SafeMath library. However, to us, there are no libraries known that are as widely used as SafeMath. Therefore, this library is of the most interest and for other smaller libraries, usage statistics become relevant with increased adoption.

On the other hand, the biggest advantage of our approach is that by looking at all deployed smart contracts on the blockchain, we are able to get a much more accurate picture of the Ethereum system than by just looking at verified contracts. The evaluation of our approach shows a large discrepancy between verified contracts and the entirety of contracts that are actually deployed on the blockchain. Performing analyses solely on the small subset of verified contracts is not representative of all programs on the blockchain. Our approach of analyzing all contracts and then using verified contracts for evaluation results in the most precise library usage statistics of the Ethereum system possible.

5 Related Work

Many papers describe data extraction and analysis platforms for Ethereum. The authors of *"Osiris"* [12], a framework for finding integer bugs in Ethereum, state that one of the causes for these kinds of bugs is the negligble or incorrect use of safe arithmetic libraries like SafeMath. They run their analysis on 495 verified token contracts from Etherscan and find that 68.08% of them use SafeMath. This number is not far off from our results for SafeMath usage of verified contracts (57.15%). However, the authors do not describe how exactly they detect usage of the library from the source code. Their tool still detects integer over- or underflow bugs in 15.73% of the contracts that do use the SafeMath library. The reason for this is that some developers do not use SafeMath for every single arithmetic operation in their contract.

In [13], the authors extract different SafeMath libraries from Solidity source codes. In order to identify usage of the library, they strip comments from the source code and then search for the keywords `contract SafeMath` and `library SafeMath`. As data input they use verified token contracts from Etherscan and open source code repositories. In total, they identify about 90 different source code versions of the library and rank them by their occurrence count.

One study compares 27 analysis tools for Ethereum [14]. The authors compare the tools with each other regarding several different aspects, like their purpose, implementation details, and detection of security issues. The survey states that support for the detection of unchecked math is only provided by Mythril, Osiris, SmartCheck, and Manticore.

6 Conclusion and Future Work

In this paper, we measure the usage of the SafeMath library in EVM bytecode. With a five-step approach we extract and analyze `internal` library functions in bytecodes deployed to the Ethereum blockchain. Our findings show that about 1.34% of all contracts and 27.52% of all unique contract bytecodes use SafeMath. The library is used much more often by contracts created by externally owned accounts than by contracts created by other contracts.

A key finding of our research is that verified contracts are not representative for all smart contracts on the blockchain. The percentage of verified contracts that use SafeMath (57.15%) is much higher than when considering all contracts from the entire network (1.34%). Hence, we strongly suggest that further research on Ethereum smart contracts should always take all contracts deployed on the blockchain as a basis. Still, verified contracts are a good verification data set.

Our methodology can be extended to other libraries. It might be interesting to create a ranking of most-used Solidity libraries to learn more about which libraries are relevant. To add to that, some more investigations about internal functions in general could be performed. For example, extracting all internal functions from all smart contracts and comparing them could help us see if there is code reuse. If the bytecode of an internal function is used multiple times on the blockchain, that might suggest that this function is a library function. Previously unknown libraries could be discovered this way. Internal functions are of interest, because in a way, they hide information. Studying them might reveal more information about single smart contracts and the network in general.

References

1. Buterin, V.: A next-generation smart contract and decentralized application platform. white paper (2014)
2. Payette, J., Schwager, S., Murphy, J.: Characterizing the ethereum address space (2017)
3. Norvill, R., Awan, I.U., Pontiveros, B.B.F., Cullen, A.J.: Automated labeling of unknown contracts in Ethereum (2017)
4. Fröwis, M., Fuchs, A., Böhme, R.: Detecting Token Systems on Ethereum. arXiv preprint arXiv:1811.11645 (2018)
5. Bartoletti, M., Carta, S., Cimoli, T., Saia, R.: Dissecting Ponzi schemes on Ethereum: identification, analysis, and impact. arXiv preprint arXiv:1703.03779 (2017)
6. Chen, W., Zheng, Z., Cui, J., Ngai, E., Zheng, P., Zhou, Y.: Detecting ponzi schemes on ethereum: towards healthier blockchain technology. In: Proceedings of the 2018 World Wide Web Conference on World Wide Web, pp. 1409–1418 (2018)
7. OpenZeppelin: OpenZeppelin is a library for secure smart contract development. https://github.com/OpenZeppelin/openzeppelin-solidity. Accessed on 07 July 2019
8. Atzei, N., Bartoletti, M., Cimoli, T.: A survey of attacks on Ethereum smart contracts. IACR Cryptology ePrint Archive, vol. 2016, p. 1007 (2016)
9. Wood, G.: Ethereum: A secure decentralised generalised transaction ledger. Ethereum project yellow paper, vol. 151, pp. 1–32 (2014)
10. Kiffer, L., Levin, D., Mislove, A.: Analyzing Ethereum's Contract Topology. In: Proceedings of the Internet Measurement Conference, vol. 2018, pp. 494–499 (2018)
11. Zhou, Y., Kumar, D., Bakshi, S., Mason, J., Miller, A., Bailey, M.: Erays: reverse engineering ethereum's opaque smart contracts. In: 27th {USENIX} Security Symposium ({USENIX} Security 18), pp. 1371–1385 (2018)
12. Ferreira Torres, C., Schütte, J., State, R.: Osiris: Hunting for integer bugs in ethereum smart contracts. In: 34th Annual Computer Security Applications Conference (ACSAC 2018), San Juan, Puerto Rico, USA, 3–7 December 2018 (2018)
13. Reibel, P., Yousaf, H., Meiklejohn, S.: Short Paper: an exploration of code diversity in the cryptocurrency landscape (2019)
14. Di Angelo, M., Salzer, G.: A survey of tools for analyzing ethereum smart contracts. In: 2019 IEEE International Conference on Decentralized Applications and Infrastructures (DAPPCON) (2019)

JusticeChain: Using Blockchain to Protect Justice Logs

Rafael Belchior[1,2](✉), Miguel Correia[1,2], and André Vasconcelos[1,2]

[1] Instituto Superior Técnico, Universidade de Lisboa, Lisbon, Portugal
{rafael.belchior,miguel.p.correia,andre.vasconcelos}@tecnico.ulisboa.pt
[2] INESC-ID, Lisbon, Portugal

Abstract. The auditability of information systems plays an essential role in public administration. Information system accesses are saved in log files so auditors can later inspect them. However, there are often distinct stakeholders with different roles and different levels of trust, namely the IT Department that manages the system and the government ministries that access the logs for auditing. This scenario happens at the Portuguese judicial system, where stakeholders utilize an information system managed by third-parties. This paper proposes using blockchain technology to make the storage of access logs more resilient while supporting such a multi-stakeholder scenario, in which different entities have different access rights to data. This proposal is implemented in the Portuguese Judicial System through JusticeChain. JusticeChain comprises the blockchain components and blockchain client components. The blockchain components grant log integrity and redundancy, while the blockchain client component is responsible for saving logs on behalf of an information system. The client allows end-users to access the blockchain, allowing audits mediated by the blockchain.

Keywords: Blockchain · Auditing · Audit logs · Public administration

1 Introduction

Organizations have the responsibility of protecting their sensitive data, a valuable resource that often guides business decisions. *Access control* mechanisms aim to identify subjects that require access to resources and allow or deny them the access, based on the context of the request [7]. Users that utilize such systems leave digital traces recorded in *log files*. *Auditors* can later analyze such log files, for example, to assess that no parties are using the systems for illegal purposes or to gain an unfair advantage.

At the Portuguese judicial system, there is an information system to manage judicial processes at courts that supports several stakeholders. The entity that maintains that the system faces different incentives from the stakeholders that use it, leading to a multi-stakeholder scenario with uncertain trust among them. In such a scenario, separate entities have different access rights to data. Threats

© Springer Nature Switzerland AG 2019
H. Panetto et al. (Eds.): OTM 2019, LNCS 11877, pp. 318–325, 2019.
https://doi.org/10.1007/978-3-030-33246-4_21

to *log integrity*, like *data tampering*, have to be minimized, as they can invalidate audits because tampered data cannot be trusted [3]. This paper proposes the use of *blockchain* technology to overcome the problems with the integrity of logs and support auditing, by assuring that no entity or individual can tamper the logs, allowing to build a transparent and collaborative network. Blockchain technology has emerged as a vehicle for decentralization, transparency and trust while conserving security, privacy and control, which can leverage auditability and trust distribution [9], both critical requirements for information systems at public administration.

In particular, we introduce JusticeChain, a system to store, protect and decentralize applicational logs built on top of a permissioned private blockchain, *Hyperledger Fabric* [1]. JusticeChain receives log entries from a set of *oracles*, processes them at the Log Manager component, and acts as a client to the underlying Hyperledger Fabric infrastructure. The Audit Log Manager component can be used by authorized auditors to read logs from the blockchain.

2   Preliminaries on JusticeChain

Security risks such as data tampering, denial of service (DoS/DDoS), man-in-the-middle attacks, identity theft, and spoofing pose severe challenges concerning the security of any information system. We focus on the *data tampering* problem, for it is one of the most frequent security risks, and the one with the most impact on Portuguese public administration audits. We considered different blockchain infrastructures, both public and private. Public blockchains such as Bitcoin and Ethereum are not suitable, as sensitive information cannot be easily stored and retrieved efficiently. Private infrastructures, such as Quorum, Corda, and Multichain seem to be less stable and may lead to lower throughput rates than Fabric. Fabric was found to be the most appropriate blockchain, as it is backed by a large active community and has a significantive maximum throughput [1].

JusticeChain improves *log resilience* in two ways: it records applicational logs from information systems with different stakeholders and secures them on the blockchain; it decentralizes the storage of such logs, resulting in higher redundancy and availability. Therefore, it allows authorized auditors to analyze the usage of the system with integrity guarantees. The auditing process is decentralized and transparent for all participants on the network, due to programs (smart contracts, or *chaincode* in Fabric's lingo) that inspect logs. The threats to which logs are exposed and that are mitigated by JusticeChain are the following:

- **T1**: Log tampering from an external element.
- **T2**: Database tampering from an internal adversary
- **T3**: Log tampering by the system administrator
- **T4**: A participant tries to edit logs that are protected by the blockchain.
- **T5**: The majority of participants conspire and try to modify the logs.

The fact that Fabric allows the creation of a permissioned blockchain, where participants are vetted, allows reducing the risk of collusion. Fabric records updates to the configurations of the system and deployments of chaincode. This process enables the straightforward identification of the subject that initiated specific actions, being a demotivating factor for adversaries.

2.1 System Model

The use case addressed in this paper presents three characteristics: (i) the participants are willing to cooperate but have limited trust in each other, (ii) the trust and responsibility of managing the logs belong to all stakeholders and (iii) one organization should be able to administer the network, in accordance with the governance model. Regarding the first and second aspects, the use of a consensus algorithm to reach agreement ensures that no single entity controls the blockchain. Concerning the third characteristic, permissioned blockchains as Hyperledger Fabric allow the delegation of a different level of control to specific participants [1].

We assume a worst-case scenario in which participants have limited trust on each other (e.g., have different political incentives). Fabric supports sub-blockchains called channels; we use a single channel that is used by all participants. Participants control peer nodes which maintain the ledger and endorse transactions. JusticeChain allows data management, through Log pre-processing (i.e., standardization, automatic analysis and attribute checks), which is leveraged by distributed chaincode execution (i.e., the execution of programs in blockchain nodes). Although those are useful features, JusticeChain focuses on assuring data integrity and distribution, by storing logs by authorized loggers and retrieving them to authorized auditors. There are three actors (participants) who take part in the ecosystem:

- *Logger*: receives log entries from information systems and uploads them to the blockchain, belonging to a member participant. They act as blockchain clients and can be considered to be oracles (in blockchain lingo).
- *Auditor*: audits secured applicational logs on behalf of an organization. Auditors have a set of permissions, allowing for fine-grain permissions for auditing purposes.
- *Network Administrator*: manages the blockchain configurations. Responsible for creating and managing participants within the blockchain

2.2 Data Model

JusticeChain has a data model that addresses the business concerns about managing applicational logs. Participants defined in Sect. 2.1 interact with the data in the following ways:

- *Network Administrator (Admin)*: can see the whole ledger, the whole transaction history and update participants. However, they cannot create, update or delete applicational logs.

- *Auditor*: minimizes the risk associated to threat T5. An auditor member participates in the network, monitoring the flow. If the adversaries try to change their states, the auditor node would perceive such change, as there would be state inconsistencies across nodes. The auditor can be given permissions by the system administrator to enforce synchronization of the state of the ledger if needed. Auditors can only see part of the ledger – logs associated with the auditor's organization and the transaction history that affects the network configurations.
- *Logger*: can create logs associated with one information system. For instance, a Logger associated with System A can create an asset type *Log-A*, but cannot create an asset of type *Log-B*.

The ecosystem aims to protect an asset, the Log.

- *Log*: has a unique identifier, *timestamp*, *log creation timestamp*, an associated Logger and case-specific attributes. In the Portuguese justice, there are attributes which represent the universal unique identifier of the user, the audit and also the related court. A timestamp attribute is associated with each entry, as latency issues can place gaps between the log generation and log recording on the blockchain. Several log types can be defined, depending on how many information systems participate in the network. Only Loggers can create Logs, and no entity can update or delete logs.

The process of executing and validating chaincode can produce *Events*, which applications may listen and take actions upon.

Transactions are requests to the blockchain to execute a function on the ledger. Transactions can affect participants and assets. Chaincode written in *NodeJS* creates logs that are recorded on the immutable ledger, via a transaction. We defined a transaction to create a Log type asset, as logs are created through the issuing of such transaction, by an authorized logger.

3   JusticeChain Overview

This section presents an overview of JusticeChain. JusticeChain allows decentralizing trust concerning logging. The assets to be protected are applicational logs generated by an information system related to the judicial system, in our case. The proposed solution is scalable when it comes to supporting different organizations, different types of logs and different auditors. The architecture is represented in Fig. 1, using the Archimate modelling language [4].

The blockchain component stores applicational logs and enforces blockchain configurations concerning the different participants on the network. The blockchain client component ensures that participants can access the applicational logs via submitted transactions, and can audit logs, under certain circumstances.

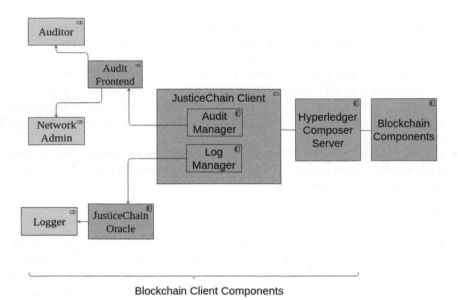

Fig. 1. JusticeChain architecture

3.1   Blockchain Components

JusticeChain leverages *Hyperledger Composer* (or simply Composer)[1] that, in its turn, uses Hyperledger Fabric to launch and operate a blockchain ecosystem. Composer is an abstraction built on top of Hyperledger Fabric that simplifies the development of blockchain solutions. Through the definition of endorsement policies, one can put more or less trust in a specific set of endorser peers, making the trust system independent from the consensus algorithm to be used [1]. Unlike the public ledger whose truthfulness is guaranteed by the design of consensus processes, it is the endorsement policy that guarantees consensus on the network. For instance, one can define that for a transaction to be valid, peers from organization A and organization B must yield the same result with respect to the execution of specific chaincode. A custom trust system allows an organization to administer the network, while assuring that it cannot take unfair advantages out of it, thus distributing trust.

In this use case, we use two different chaincodes (i.e., programs): chaincode that creates instances of applicational logs (*S1*) and chaincode that accesses the ledger (*S2*), regains logs and retrieves them to the end-user. Chaincode S1 receives the attributes necessary to create a Log from the Log Manager, validate them, apply pre-processing (if needed) and commit the new data to the ledger, by issuing a transaction. Chaincode S2 queries the blockchain for a specific type of Logs.

---

[1] https://www.hyperledger.org/projects/composer.

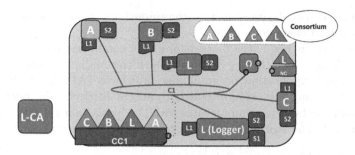

Fig. 2. JusticeChain blockchain architecture - example with a consortium composed of four organizations (A,B,C,L), five peers (Peer A, Peer B, Peer C, Peer L, Peer L (Logger)), one orderer (O), one certificate authority (L-CA), a channel CC1, and network configurations (NC).

A custom certificate authority (CA) is used to issue identities for each participant on the network. Each organization that participates in the network, and thus interested in auditing a specific information system should maintain at least a peer node that holds an instance of the ledger. As applicational logs should not be shared amongst different member organizations, one has to define access control rules that manage that flow (e.g., only Admins and Auditors from organization A can see applicational logs from A, only Loggers from organization A can create type A Logs). Composer allows the definition of such access control rules, by associating an operation (READ, UPDATE, CREATE, DELETE) and an action (ALLOW, DENY) to an Asset (e.g., Log). JusticeChain supports several stakeholders, which do not need to belong to the same organization. Fabric supports different solutions to ensure data privacy between organizations (e.g., Auditor from organization A cannot see logs from organization B): (i) create a different channel; (ii) use the private data functionality of Fabric; and (iii) tune access control rules via Composer. Private data can be used in this case[2], which allows a subset of organizations the ability to endorse, commit, and query private data.

Client application JusticeChain Audit Manager can use channel C1 to connect to A, B, C, L, L (Logger), and Orderer O. Client application JusticeChain Log Manager can use C1 to access L (Logger) and Orderer O (Fig. 2). Applications can only access the ledger L1 through the chaincode instantiated on their respective peers.

3.2 Blockchain Client Components

JusticeChain is a full-stack application that leverages Fabric to secure audit logs while providing support for automatized auditing techniques. The Composer

---

[2] https://hyperledger-fabric.readthedocs.io/en/release-1.4/private-data/private-data.html.

REST Server is used to interact with the underlying Fabric blockchain; hence, it is a blockchain client component.

As presented in Fig. 1, the blockchain client comprises mainly two entities: the *Audit Manager* and the *Log Manager*. Both the Audit Manager and the Log Manager expose application programming interfaces (APIs), which allow the *Audit Frontend* and *JusticeChain Oracle* to access JusticeChain functionalities. JusticeChain, on its turn, communicates with the blockchain via the Hyperledger Composer API. The JusticeChain blockchain client has several components:

- JusticeChain Client: is a collaboration between two components - Log Manager and Audit Manager that aims to problem exposed in this paper.
- JusticeChain Oracle (Oracle): overcomes the inability of communicating with the "outside" world. An oracle in the context of our problem is a component that retrieves applicational logs from an outward log repository.
- JusticeChain Log Manager (Log Manager): is connected to one or more oracles. When the Log Manager receives a log, preprocessing is applied, as anonymization or standardization. After that, the Log Manager submits a transaction to the blockchain, on the correspondent Logger's behalf.
- JusticeChain Audit Manager (Audit Manager): sends transactions to the blockchain on behalf of the corresponding Auditor or Admin who needs to audit logs. The transactions are, in fact, queries on the blockchain ledger.
- Audit Frontend: is a user interface that allows the stakeholders (Auditors or Network Admins) to retrieve the applicational logs, via the Audit Log Manager.
- Log Repository: corresponds to the repository that stores logs (i.e. database).
- Hyperledger Composer (REST) Server: is generated from a business network archive and exposes an API that the JusticeChain client can use to access the blockchain. Hyperledger Composer Server access Fabric using its API.

In addition to acting as a proxy between frontend applications and the blockchain, the JusticeChain Client, allows end-user authentication to the blockchain network. A local database stores local end user's credentials. This way, one can map local authentication credentials and the user's cryptographic identity on the blockchain network, providing traceability.

4 Related Work

In [2], a write-only logger creates log entries as a way to give integrity guarantees. More advanced solutions use a third-party notary service to prevent data-tampering, along with cryptographic hashing, and partial result authentication codes [8]. Such solutions, although efficient, have a single point of failure, where the centralized authority that grants integrity can collude with attackers. Several solutions support forward security but depend at least partially on a third-party [5]. Such solutions, although suitable, does not tackle the need for a trust distribution.

In [6], the authors propose Logchain, a blockchain-assisted log storage system. Logchain tries to decentralize trust on stakeholders that use a third party service. Cloud participants have access to logs but, unlike JusticeChain, fine-grain permissions related to audit are lacking.

5 Conclusion

This paper presented JusticeChain, a blockchain-based system which increases trust in information systems managed by third-parties, regarding logging and audits. In particular, JusticeChain aims to increase the resilience of applicational logs used in the Portuguese justicial system, by assuring integrity and redundancy. JusticeChain improves traditional logging systems by distributing logs, where stakeholders depend on a centralized information system to conduct their activities, which cause trust issues.

Acknowledgements. This work was supported by national funds through Fundação para a Ciência e a Tecnologia (FCT) with reference UID/CEC/50021/2019 (INESC-ID) and by the European Commission program H2020 under the grant agreement 822404 (project QualiChain).

References

1. Androulaki, E., et al.: Hyperledger fabric: a distributed operating system for permissioned blockchains. In: Proceedings of the 13th ACM EuroSys Conference (2018)
2. Bellare, M., Yee, B.S.: Forward Integrity For Secure Audit Logs. Technical report (1997)
3. Chen, Z., Yang, Y., Zhang, R., Li, Z.: An efficient scheme for log integrity check in security monitoring system. In: IET Conference Publications, vol. 2013, pp. 246–250 (2013). https://doi.org/10.1049/cp.2013.2026
4. Group, T.: ArchiMate® 3.0 Specification. Van Haren Publishing (2016)
5. Ma, D., Tsudik, G.: A new approach to secure logging. In: Atluri, V. (ed.) DBSec 2008. LNCS, vol. 5094, pp. 48–63. Springer, Heidelberg (2008). https://doi.org/10.1007/978-3-540-70567-3_4
6. Pourmajidi, W., Miranskyy, A.V.: Logchain: blockchain-assisted log storage. In: 2018 IEEE 11th International Conference on Cloud Computing (CLOUD), pp. 978–982 (2018)
7. Sandhu, R.S., Samarati, P.: Access control: principle and practice. IEEE Commun. **32**(9), 40–48 (1994)
8. Snodgrass, R.T., Yao, S.S., Collberg, C.: Tamper detection in audit logs. In: Proceedings of the Thirtieth International Conference on Very Large Data Bases, VLDB 2004, vol. 30, pp. 504–515. VLDB Endowment (2004)
9. Zheng, Z., Xie, S., Dai, H.N., Chen, X., Wang, H.: An Overview of Blockchain Technology: Architecture, Consensus, and Future Trends (2017). https://doi.org/10.1109/BigDataCongress.2017.85

Triage of IoT Attacks Through Process Mining

Simone Coltellese[1], Fabrizio Maria Maggi[2], Andrea Marrella[1(✉)],
Luca Massarelli[1], and Leonardo Querzoni[1]

[1] DIAG, Sapienza Universitá di Roma, Rome, Italy
`coltellese.1534700@studenti.uniroma1.it`,
`{marrella,massarelli,querzoni}@diag.uniroma1.it`
[2] University of Tartu, Tartu, Estonia
`f.m.maggi@ut.ee`

Abstract. The impressive growth of the IoT we witnessed in the recent years came together with a surge in cyber attacks that target it. Factories adhering to digital transformation programs are quickly adopting the IoT paradigm and are thus increasingly exposed to a large number of cyber threats that need to be detected, analyzed and appropriately mitigated. In this scenario, a common approach that is used in large organizations is to setup an attack triage system. In this setting, security operators can cherry-pick new attack patterns requiring further in-depth investigation from a mass of known attacks that can be managed automatically. In this paper, we propose an attack triage system that helps operators to quickly identify attacks with unknown behaviors, and later analyze them in detail. The novelty introduced by our solution is in the usage of process mining techniques to model known attacks and identify new variants. We demonstrate the feasibility of our approach through an evaluation based on three well-known IoT botnets, *BASHLITE*, *LIGHTAIDRA* and *MIRAI*, and on real current attack patterns collected through an IoT honeypot.

Keywords: IoT security · Process mining · Behavioral attack analysis

1 Introduction

The Internet of Things (IoT) is supposed to revolutionize, in the forthcoming years, the way we interact with the physical world. Nowadays, this interaction mainly happens through smartphones and connected gadgets, but, in the soon-to-come future, people will heavily rely on automated vehicles, wearable medical devices, and other connected items to avoid potentially harmful incidents.

In this scenario, cybercriminals are starting to grasp the opportunities of a new era where an impressively large number of connected devices can be exploited for criminal activities. Even if this phenomenon is still in its infancy, we already experienced the first glimpses of a glooming future: between 2016 and

H. Panetto et al. (Eds.): OTM 2019, LNCS 11877, pp. 326–344, 2019.
https://doi.org/10.1007/978-3-030-33246-4_22

2018, a large botnet, named *MIRAI*[12], was used to launch some of the most intense distributed denial of service (DDoS) attacks ever recorded, topping at more than 1Tbps [2]. The source code of the botnet was openly released to the public by the end of 2017, paving the way for new breeds of the same threat.

Three factors mainly justify the growing alarms surrounding the security of forthcoming IoT solutions:

- so far, most producers and system integrators have not paid enough attention to security issues in IoT devices. Most of them are designed to be sold to the masses at the lowest possible price, and consumers are still hardly willing to spend more to pay for security features against advanced functionalities;
- IoT devices are often built on dedicated HW/SW platforms; this results in a large heterogeneity of platforms to be defended, with a growing number of potentially exploitable vulnerabilities that are hardly patched by producers;
- IoT systems are growing in size and complexity, with boundaries that are sometimes difficult to define precisely, so that it becomes complex to identify their exposed attack surface.

A common approach used by large organizations to protect complex systems is to setup an internal structure (e.g., a Security Operations Center) to manage cyber incidents. Incident response processes are typically based on the acquisition of data from probes and sensors (firewalls, intrusion detection systems, AVs, etc.) that is then analyzed by security operators in order to characterize ongoing attacks. As the number of cybersecurity incidents increases, this approach needs to be supported by a filtering phase that quickly discards cases representing known attack patterns (for which remediation plans are already known and in-place) thus allowing security operators to concentrate their efforts on new attack patterns. This phase is known as *triage*[1] and its output is a prioritized list of attacks to be analyzed, where higher priority is assigned to attacks that do not resemble known patterns.

In this paper, we introduce a novel solution to support security operators during the triage of attacks that target IoT systems. Our solution leverages state-of-the-art process mining techniques [4] to recognize known attack patterns and identify new variants, providing the operators with information on the differentiating details. Process mining stands for techniques to analyze business process models and their execution traces (logs). It provides methods for reconstructing process models from logs (*process discovery*), checking the conformance of an existing model with logs (*conformance checking*), and enhancing process models based on the results of process analysis (*process enhancement*).

Specifically, our proposed approach analyzes logs of commands issued by a botnet against a IoT device during the fingerprinting phase[2], and discovers a

---

[1] The name comes from the process used by ER-units in hospitals to quickly prioritize incoming patients depending on the severity of their health status.

[2] In this phase, the botnet issues commands on the shell of a device found on the internet to identify its architecture before deploying the appropriate attack payload. See Sect. 2 for further details.

process model representing an up-to-date picture of the recorded attacks, i.e., of the behavior of the botnet. New observed traces (the new attacks) are prioritized by aligning them to the model and then calculating their *fitness* score: the smaller the score, the more the log contains actions that were not observed in previous attacks, and therefore the larger is the priority for the operator. The main finding of our research is that process mining techniques provide a powerful tool for the automated discovery of new IoT attacks and of their "anatomy". This allows our solution to provide detailed feedbacks of such unknown malevolent behaviors to support security operators in their identification and classification of new attack patterns. Differently from other solutions, commonly based on statistical models trained with machine learning algorithms, this system allows us to inspect the model, extract human-readable information from it, and use this information to notify the security operator about how a new attack differs from previous observations.

To demonstrate the feasibility of our approach, we evaluated our solution on attacks generated by three well-known IoT botnets, namely *MIRAI*, *LIGH-TAIDRA* and *BASHLITE*. The evaluation demonstrates that our solution is able to build a global attack model that correctly represents the various behaviors characterizing these botnets, identify their attack patterns and gracefully evolve as new variants are observed. We also evaluated our approach using current attack patterns in a real world environment. In particular, we show how our system correctly identifies new botnets, and how it supports security operators by providing precise information on the behavior of new attacks.

The rest of the paper is organized as follows. Section 2 provides a background on the security of IoT systems, with a specific focus on botnets. Section 3 introduces the process mining techniques used to realize our approach. Section 4 describes our system, while Sect. 5 discusses its evaluation. Section 6 presents related work and, finally, Sect. 7 concludes the paper.

2   Background on IoT (In-)Security

Even if the success of IoT is today a reality, the security of IoT devices remains a big challenge. In 2014, the OWASP Foundation [33] published a list of the top ten most dangerous vulnerabilities in IoT. At the first place, they listed insecure web interfaces that often permit to an attacker to login into a device using weak credentials or to capture plain-text password. Other sources of danger come from the insecurity of the network services exposed by devices and the lack of transport encryption. As evidenced by Hossain et al. [23], these security issues are sometimes due to HW (e.g., limited memory, constrained energy consumption, etc.) and SW (e.g., poor testing, unavailable security updates, etc.) constraints that characterize IoT devices.

Given the roles played by IoT devices, oftentimes the risks involved by the presence of such vulnerabilities cannot be easily mitigated. Indeed, these devices are often deployed in places where the most common form of connection is an internet link, which exposes their attack surfaces to remote threats. As a consequence, user's privacy is at high risk and operational safety cannot be guaranteed.

This scenario becomes even more worrying if we consider that an attacker can leverage the vulnerabilities of each device to enroll it into a malicious network of connected devices, namely a *botnet*, which respond to her commands.

2.1 IoT Botnets

IoT botnets are networks of infected devices (*bots*) that perform malicious actions issued as commands from a command and control (C2) server controlled by an attacker. Bertino et al. [15] discussed the several potential usages of a botnet: distributed denial of services (DDoS) attacks, crypto-mining, password cracking, email spam and key logging. One of the most well-known IoT botnets is *MIRAI*, which infected several hundreds of thousands devices [12] all over the world and was successfully used to launch strong DDoS attacks against several large companies. Other botnets, like *BASHLITE* [31] or *LIGHTAIDRA* [11] may present some technical differences, but most of them act similarly. The operations of an IoT botnet can be grouped into the following four phases:

Target Selection. Bots continuously scan the IPv4 address space searching for new vulnerable devices. They look for online devices that expose SSH/Telnet consoles or web interfaces, and try to get access by either brute-forcing the login using a dictionary of credentials or exploiting known vulnerabilities. When a new vulnerable device is found, the bot informs the C2 server.

Device fingerprinting and infection. Once a new vulnerable device is found, the botnet tries to infect it. In order to load the correct infection code on the target device, the botnet first needs to discover its architecture (e.g., x86 vs ARM). To do this, the target has to be fingerprinted by issuing a sequence of commands on its shell. After a matching fingerprint is found, the botnet uses shell commands to download and execute the infection code.

Detection evasion and persistence. The infection code uses detection evasion mechanisms to avoid being detected. *MIRAI*, for example, deletes the downloaded binary code and changes the bot process name using an alphanumeric string. In this particular case, the botnet software does not persist if the device is rebooted. Recent techniques try to avoid the blacklisting of C2 server IPs using domain fluxing [15]. Other botnets do not directly connect bots to the C2 server, but rather use proxies or *peer2peer* overlay network architectures to evade detection.

Activation. When the malicious code is running on the infected device, the new bot can be activated by the C2 server. Once activated, it starts performing the malicious actions requested by the attacker, like, for example, opening connections towards a targeted server in order to overload it.

3 Petri Nets and Process Mining

In this section, we present the process mining techniques that are the starting point of our attack triage approach. Preliminaries on Petri nets, which act as main artifacts to represent process models, and event logs are introduced as well.

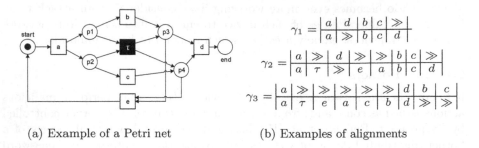

(a) Example of a Petri net

(b) Examples of alignments

Fig. 1. Examples of a Petri net and of trace alignments

3.1   Petri Nets and Event Logs

Many notations have been introduced to represent process models, such as BPMN, EPC or UML Activity Diagrams [22], and some of those are characterized by an ambiguous semantics. Since we need a simple language with clear semantics to explain our approach, we opted for Petri nets, which have proven to be adequate for representing process models [3]. This is especially true when the focus is only on the control-flow perspective, which is the case in this paper.

A *Petri net* $N = (P, T, F)$ is a directed graph with a set P of nodes called *places* and a set T of *transitions*. Places are represented by circles and transitions by rectangles. The nodes are connected via directed arcs $F \subseteq (P \times T) \cup (T \times P)$. Connections between two nodes of the same type are not allowed. Figure 1a illustrates an example of a Petri net. Given a transition $t \in T$, $^\bullet t$ is used to indicate the set of *input places* of t, which are the places p with a directed arc from p to t (i.e., such that $(p, t) \in F$). Similarly, $t^\bullet$ indicates the set of *output places*, namely the places p with a direct arc from t to p. At any time, a place can contain zero or more *tokens*, drawn as black dots. The state of a Petri net, a.k.a. *marking* m, is determined by the number of tokens in places, i.e., $m : P \to \mathbb{N}$.

In any run of a Petri net, the number of tokens in places (i.e., the marking) may change. A transition t is *enabled* at a marking m iff each input place contains at least one token, i.e., $\forall\, p \in {}^\bullet t,\ M(p) > 0$. A transition t can *fire* at a marking m iff it is enabled. As result of firing a transition t, one token is "consumed" from each input place and one is "produced" in each output place. This is denoted as $m \xrightarrow{t} m'$. In the remainder, given a sequence of transition firings $\sigma = \langle t_1, \ldots, t_n \rangle \in T^*$, $m_0 \xrightarrow{\sigma} m_n$ is used to indicate $m_0 \xrightarrow{t_1} m_1 \xrightarrow{t_2} \ldots \xrightarrow{t_n} m_n$.

An *event log* L is a multi-set of *traces* $\sigma_L \in T^*$. A trace is a sequence of transition firings and describes the execution of a *process instance* in terms of the executed *activities*.[3] Transition firings in an event log are known as *events*. Event logs may store additional information about events such as the *timestamp* when the activity was executed. Some transitions do not represent process activities but are necessary to correctly represent a process model through Petri nets.

---

[3] We use multisets because the same trace can appear multiple times in an event log.

These transitions are *invisible transitions* (the black-colored transition τ in the Petri net of Fig. 1a is invisible) and are not recorded as log events.

3.2   Process Discovery and Trace Alignment in Process Mining

Event logs are the starting point for any process mining technique. Typically, three types of process mining techniques can be distinguished [4]: (a) process discovery (learning a model from example traces in an event log), (b) conformance checking (comparing the observed behavior in the event log with a given modeled behavior), and (c) model enhancement (extending models based on additional information in the event logs, e.g., to highlight bottlenecks).

Process discovery techniques [13] automatically construct a representation of complex processes based on example executions in an event log, without using any a-priori information. In particular, we focus on online process discovery from event streams [16,17,29] as a way to deal with big amounts of data derived from IoT attacks. Events are processed on-the-fly, as they occur, and only information about the most relevant ones is stored in a limited budget of memory. The discovered process models are represented using Petri nets that change over time, as new events are processed.

Then, we perform conformance checking by constructing an *alignment* of an event log and a process model [4,9] to pinpoint where exactly deviations occur. To this aim, events in the log need to be matched with transitions in the model, and vice versa. In addition, to identify the alignment, we need to relate "moves" in the log to "moves" in the model. To represent moves in the log and moves in the model, we use the symbol $\gg$ to indicate "no moves", i.e., moves in the log that cannot be mimicked by the model and vice versa.

Definition 1 (Alignment Moves). *Let $N = (P, T, F)$ be a Petri net and L be an event log with events in E. A legal alignment move for N and L is represented by a pair $(s_L, s_M) \in (E \cup \{\gg\} \times T \cup \{\gg\}) \setminus \{(\gg, \gg)\}$ such that:*

- *(s_L, s_M) is a move in the log if $s_L \neq \gg$ and $s_M = \gg$,*
- *(s_L, s_M) is a move in the model if $s_L = \gg$ and $s_M \in T$,*
- *(s_L, s_M) is a synchronous move if $s_L = s_M$.*

An alignment is a sequence of alignment moves:

Definition 2 (Alignment). *Let $N = (P, T, F)$ be a Petri net with initial marking and final marking denoted with m_i and m_f and L be an event log. Let Γ_N be the universe of all alignment moves for N and L. Let $\sigma_L \in L$ be a log trace. Sequence $\gamma \in \Gamma_N^*$ is an alignment of N and σ_L if, ignoring all occurrences of $\gg$, the projection on the first element yields σ_L and the projection on the second one yields a sequence $\sigma'' \in T^*$ such that $m_i \xrightarrow{\sigma''} m_f$.*

A move in the log for a transition t indicates that t occurred when not allowed; a move in model for a visible transition t indicates that t did not occur when, instead, it was expected. Many alignments are possible for the same trace. For example, Fig. 1b shows three possible alignments for a trace $\sigma_1 = \langle a, d, b, c \rangle$.

Note how moves are represented vertically. For example, as shown in Fig. 1b, the first move of γ_1 is (a, a), i.e., a synchronous move of a, while the second and the fifth move of γ_1 are a move in the log and in the model, respectively.

We aim at finding an alignment of σ_L and N with minimal deviation cost. In order to define the severity of a deviation, we first introduce a cost function on legal moves and, then, generalize it to alignments. The alignments with the lowest cost are called *optimal alignments*.

Definition 3 (Cost Function). *Let $N = (P, T, F)$ be a Petri net and σ_L a log trace, respectively. Assuming Γ_N as the set of all legal alignment moves, a cost function κ assigns a non-negative cost to each legal move: $\Gamma_N \to \mathbb{N}_0^+$. The cost of an alignment $\gamma \in \Gamma_N$ between σ_L and N is computed as the sum of the cost of all constituent moves: $\mathcal{K}(\gamma) = \sum_{(f_\mathcal{L}, f_\mathcal{M}) \in \gamma} \kappa(f_\mathcal{L}, f_\mathcal{M})$.*

γ is an optimal alignment if, for any alignment γ' of N and σ_L, $\mathcal{K}(\gamma) \leq \mathcal{K}(\gamma')$. Consider the following cost function for the example in Fig. 1:

$$\kappa((s_L, s_M)) = \begin{cases} 1 \text{ if } s_M = \gg, \\ 1 \text{ if } s_L = \gg \text{ and } s_M \neq \tau, \\ 0 \text{ otherwise.} \end{cases} \tag{1}$$

With reference to the alignments in Fig. 1b, alignment γ_1 has cost 2, since it has 1 move in the model and 1 move in the log. Conversely, γ_2 has cost 4 and γ_3 has cost 6 (moves for invisible transitions τ have cost 0). Since no alignment exists with cost lower than 2, γ_1 is an optimal alignment. To quantify the amount of deviations between a trace and a model, we use the notion of *fitness* presented in [9] that takes into account the cost of the deviations. The outcome of the fitness is a score that may vary between 0 (very poor fitness) to 1 (perfect fitness between the trace and the model).

4   An Approach for Attack Triage

In this section, we introduce our solution and its approach for attack triage in IoT systems that leverages process mining to help prioritizing the analysis of new attack patterns. The output of our system is a prioritized list where unknown attacks have a higher priority with respect to known attacks. Moreover, a classification score for each attack is derived, which allows us to associate it to a specific botnet campaign. We first introduce an overview of the proposed approach and then move to describe the system.

4.1   Overview

The basic idea at the core of our approach is that operations performed by an attacker while infecting an IoT device can be logged, and this log can be analyzed to mine the infection processes. Therefore, the starting point of our approach is a log that contains *attack traces* each referring to a different IoT attack.[4]

---

[4] Note that distinguishing attack interactions from bening interactions, namely *detecting attacks*, is a different problem that is out of the scope of this paper. We assume that data fed as input only contains traces of attacks.

Since the same botnet often exhibits a repetitive behavior during the device fingerprinting phase, our intuition is that process mining techniques can shed light on that behavior and support security operators to automatically distinguish between known and unknown attacks. Our approach models commands issued by the attacker on the target device while fingerprinting it as events of a process, groups them into a trace representing the evolution of the attack and stores the trace in a log. Then, online discovery techniques are leveraged to provide security operators with a process model representing an up-to-date picture of the attacks recorded in the log. Note that the log becomes indefinitely large over time as new attacks are recorded. This is the reason why online discovery techniques allow us to keep the analysis of the log computationally feasible by "forgetting" obsolete attacks. New observed traces are prioritized by aligning them to the discovered model and then calculating their fitness score.

Figure 2 depicts the main steps in our approach. A target system keeps track of incoming connections from the internet and logs commands received on its interfaces (Raw log). The log is then filtered to get rid of spurious information and to prepare it for the subsequent model discovery phase. An online discovery algorithm is then applied to the filtered log in order to extract an up-to-date global *attack model*. When a new incoming *attack trace* is collected, we check its conformance with the global attack model using trace alignment and compute the fitness of the new attack trace with the model. According to the fitness, we can assign a priority to the attack and report it to the security operators. When we detect that a given trace does not belong to a new attack, the trace is fed into the classification sub-system that is described in Sect. 4.2 to update a set of local models representing different classes of attacks. Finally, the trace is used to feed the discovery algorithm to update the global attack model.

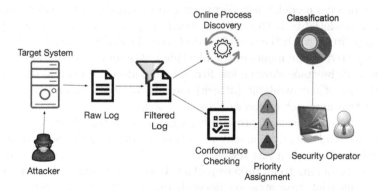

Fig. 2. Schematic overview of the proposed approach

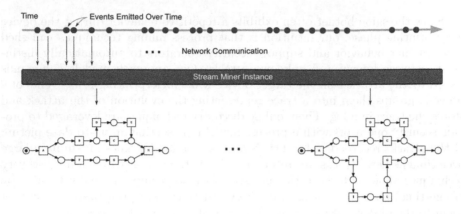

Fig. 3. Online process discovery [16]

4.2 Attack Classification

As already discussed in the previous section, given an attack trace, our approach is able to assign it a priority based on how much the trace differs from known behaviors. This information can be used to classify "similar" attack traces in the same class of (already seen) attacks. Attack classification is a well known practice in IT security that enables important threat intelligence activities. In particular, it allows security operators to identify common characteristics of a class of attacks, information that is fundamental when studying the provenance of attacks or their attribution (i.e., who is performing the attack).

We perform the classification task through process mining. Given a set of traces belonging to different classes of attacks, and representing each class with a different process model, trace alignment can be employed to understand which class (i.e., model) fits better with a recent captured trace. When a trace is particularly fitting with the model related to a class of attacks, its behavior can be later injected in the model of the identified class in order to keep it updated. Conversely, if the trace shows a low fitness value after performing the alignment task with any of the available (attack) models, then the trace is considered as belonging to a new, yet unknown class of attacks.

The above classification procedure requires an initial effort by the security operators to build the initial models reflecting the different classes of attacks; this is particularly true when just few attack traces have been collected and when a trace seems to belong to an unknown class. It is worth noting that the precision of the classification task strongly depends on the fitness threshold values used to state whether a trace belongs to a class of attacks or not.

4.3 Online Process Discovery

One of the main aims of process mining is *automated process discovery*, i.e., learning process models from example traces recorded in some event log. Many

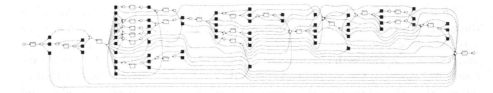

Fig. 4. Petri net representing the attack model

different process discovery algorithms have been proposed in the past [13]. Basically, all such algorithms have been defined for batch processing, i.e., a complete event log containing all executed activities is supposed to be available for their execution. However, when dealing with data coming from IoT attacks, we have to deal with large amounts of events so that it becomes impossible to store all of them. Moreover, even if it would be possible to store all event data, it is often impossible to process them due to the exponential nature of most discovery algorithms. Finally, the process evolves over time when new attacks are detected.

For these reasons our solution makes use of the *online discovery algorithm* presented in [16], which is able to mine process models based on streaming event data. The general representation of the online discovery problem is shown in Fig. 3: one or more sources emit events (represented as solid dots). Events are observed by the miner that keeps the representation of the discovered model up-to-date. Algorithms that are supposed to interact with event streams must respect some requirements, such as: (a) it is impossible to store the complete stream; (b) backtracking over an event stream is not feasible, so algorithms are required to make only one pass over data; (c) it is important to adapt the model to cope with unusual data values. The algorithm used in [16] is based on the Heuristics Miner [34], one of the most effective algorithms for practical applications of process mining [13]. Figure 4 shows the Petri net discovered from the event stream provided by our honeypot at a given point in time.

4.4   Conformance Checking

One of ours goals is to provide security operators with an effective tool that supports them in the analysis of incoming traces representing malicious attacks. One of the strengths of our approach based on process mining lies in the possibility of employing trace alignment to extend the range of the available security analysis features. In particular, with trace alignment, it is possible to "build" a relevant feedback for the security operators that are in charge of monitoring incoming attacks. This feedback includes the identification of unseen attacks and insights into their structure. This enables the security operator to have a prioritized list of malicious traces ranked according to their distance from known behaviors and pinpoint where these traces differ from the up-to-date global attack model.

After an initialization phase of 1 day, the global attack model discovered by the online discovery algorithm from the event stream provided by our honeypot was the one shown in Fig. 4. In Fig. 5, we show a trace containing a new attack and its discrepancies with the original attack model. In particular, the new attack requires 3 moves in the log to be aligned with the process model (the 3 activities indicated in the figure should be skipped according to the original model) and the new trace has a fitness of 0.97 with the model. This new behavior is taken into consideration by the online discovery algorithm that changes the process model into the one shown in Fig. 6.

It is important to observe that the cost of each legal alignment move depends on the specific application domain. Hence, the cost function κ needs to be defined specifically for each setting and cannot be automated. For instance, in our context, inserting an *ls* command should not be punished too hard, since this command is not too relevant in the context of an IoT attack, while inserting a *ping* command should lead to a lower fitness of the trace. While approaches could be researched to support security operators in the definition of the cost function, this is beyond the scope of this paper and left for future work.

5   Evaluation

We developed a prototype implementing our proposed approach using the ProM[5] framework. To evaluate our approach, we first collected data from three well-known botnets that we ran against an instance of a honeypot to test the ability of our solution to *recognize* unknown attacks and *classify* attack traces according to their behavior. Then, we tested how our system correctly identifies new botnets using a honeypot instance collecting real attacks over the web.

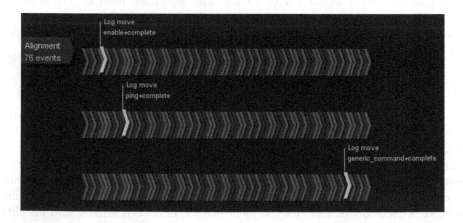

Fig. 5. Alignment for a non-compliant trace

---

[5] ProM (http://www.promtools.org/) is an open-source framework for implementing process mining tools and algorithms.

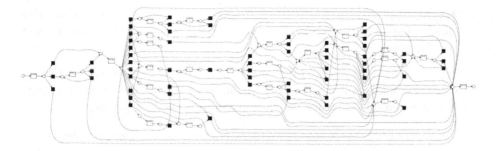

Fig. 6. Petri net modified with the addition of a non-compliant trace

5.1 Experimental Setup

In order to collect data to test our approach, we setup a honeypot to mimic the behavior of a target system. A honeypot is a software device that simulates the behavior of a real system to fool attackers in infecting it. Using a honeypot, it is possible to collect data about attacks without running the risk of compromising real systems. In addition, a honeypot includes security features that block the attacker as soon as s/he tries to execute dangerous commands (e.g., execute infection code). In particular, we setup an instance of *Cowrie* [1], a medium interaction SSH and Telnet honeypot. This software can be configured to mimic different linux-based environments.[6] We configured the honeypot to accept login attempts with user "root" and any password.

Data Filtering. When a new connection is received, Cowrie logs all the commands prompted by the attacker into a JSON file, also registering if the command is executed successfully or not. Since the logs produced by Cowrie are highly verbose, we filtered out all the events that were not related to an interaction between the attacker and the honeypot. For example, after each login, the honeypot logs the internal event *cowrie.client.size*; we discarded this event, since it does not provide interesting information about the attack behavior.

The commands prompted by an attacker into the shell represent the most important sources of information of a botnet. Hence, in some preliminary tests, we tried to model all the shell commands as activities. However, in this way, our logs recorded more than five thousands different commands (considering also their arguments). Since most process mining techniques have been tested with a smaller maximum number of activities, it has been required to reduce the number of possible activities by filtering out some of them. Therefore, we decided to ignore the arguments of each command. For example, if the attacker prompts the command $ *ls/usr/bin*, we modeled it as $ *ls*. After this first filter, we removed all front and back spaces in order to normalize all commands. From the resulting set of shell commands, we retained only the most frequent ones:

---

[6] Many commercial IoT devices are based on linux-like operating systems.

– /bin/busybox, rm, enable, shell, sh, system, cd, dvrHelper, cat, echo, tftp, uname, killall, ping, linuxshell, exit, ls,wget, chmod, /bin/busybox wget, /bin/busybox tftp.

Other commands were modeled with the activity *generic command*. Finally, we represented all shell commands starting with the symbol > with activity *redirect*. An example of attack trace obtained after the filtering step is:

$$\langle cowrie.session.connect, cowrie.login.success, enable, sh, /bin/busybox, rm,$$
$$cd, /bin/busybox, cowrie.session.file\_download, cowrie.session.closed \rangle.$$

Note that, together with shell commands, internal commands of the honeypot like *cowrie.session.connect* and *cowrie.login.success* can occur.

Data Collection. We collected data from the honeypot in two different setups: Controlled Environment (CE) and Not Controlled Environment (NCE).

CE: We put the honeypot into an isolated LAN network to enable it receiving "controlled" attacks from three different botnets whose source code has been leaked and publicly released: *BASHLITE, LIGHTAIDRA* and *MIRAI*. We triggered the botnets to generate new attacks; consequently, we exactly knew which specific botnet produced an attack trace. For the CE configuration, we collected 1000 different attack traces for each botnet.

NCE: The honeypot had an associated public address with ports 22 and 23 open (i.e., reachable by anyone over the internet). This has allowed us to test the feasibility of our approach when deployed in a real world environment. In this configuration, we collected a total of 122 complete attack traces in four days.

5.2 Detection of Unknown Attacks

We initially performed an experiment to test if our system was able to distinguish between a new attack and a known one. We used the data collected from the honeypot in the CE configuration. Results are shown in Fig. 7a.

First, we mined a global attack model using the first attack trace obtained with the *BASHLITE* botnet. After that, we computed the fitness of the model with the remaining 999 attack traces produced by the same botnet. Since this botnet exhibited the same behavior for any attack trace, the fitness score for each trace was 1.

Then, we computed the fitness of the previously discovered attack model with the first attack trace obtained with *LIGHTAIDRA*. In this case, we measured a fitness of 0.24, meaning that a new attack was discovered. Since the first attack trace of *LIGHTAIDRA* was unknown for the global attack model (i.e., the fitness score was lower than 1), we updated it to reflect the new recorded behavior. When we computed the fitness with the second trace obtained with *LIGHTAIDRA*, we measured a higher accuracy, i.e., a fitness of around 0.88, and we again updated the model (note that fitness scores greater than 0.8 refer to attack traces that are only partially unknown, as they represent variants of known attacks, cf. Sect. 5.4). We repeated this procedure for the first 20 attack traces obtained with *LIGHTAIDRA*, being the measured fitness lower than 1. After that, for the remaining attack traces, the measured fitness was 1.

Finally, as expected, when we computed the fitness with the first trace obtained with *MIRAI*, we registered a new drop in the fitness to 0.34. Repeating the same update procedure as before, we started to measure high fitness scores (around 0.97) after the first 20 traces produced by *MIRAI*.

The above results show that, with our approach, we can distinguish between new attacks and known ones just looking at the value of the fitness.

5.3   Attack Classification

The aim of this second experiment was to verify the ability of our system to classify the kind of attack underlying a recorded log trace. Leveraging again the CE configuration, for each botnet, we split the generated log in two sublogs including 500 traces each. For each botnet, we used the first sublog as training set to discover the attack model underlying the specific botnet. Then, we used the second sublog as test set computing the fitness of any trace in this set with respect to the attack models previously discovered.

The results of this experiment are summarized in the confusion matrix in Fig. 7b, which includes the mean of the fitness scores of traces in the test set with respect to the three attack models. The analysis of the matrix makes clear that our approach can classify attacks belonging to specific botnets very accurately. Moreover, we can notice that the fitness between the traces of *BASHLITE* and the *LIGHTAIDRA* model is high. This is because *LIGHTAIDRA* is an evolution of *BASHLITE* and includes most behaviors from *BASHLITE*.

5.4   Experiments with Real Attack Traces

The aim of this third experiment is to test the effectiveness of the proposed approach in a real world scenario. Leveraging the NCE configuration, which allowed us to collect data associated to real attack traces, we investigated the amount of new attacks that was possible to identify using our approach. The results of this experiment are reported in Fig. 8. Analysing such results, two considerations can be made: *(i)* looking at the drops in the fitness (and considering the first 20 attacks as an initialization phase), we distinguished 13 different types/classes of attacks; and *(ii)* the threshold of the fitness score for identifying new unknown attacks can be fixed to 0.8. This value, which is a result of this last empirical test, is useful to consider attacks having a fitness score greater than 0.8 but lower than 1 as variants of already known attacks, and not as totally new attacks.

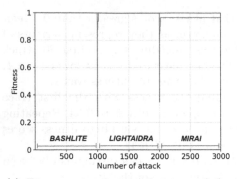
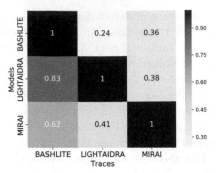

(a) Fitness score for attack traces of the three botnets. The arrow represent the fitness drop due to a new type of attack.

(b) Confusion Matrix for the classification experiment. The columns represent the traces of the 3 botnets and the rows represent the respective attack models.

Fig. 7. Experiments for the detection of unknown attacks and attack classification

6   Related Work

IoT Botnets – Research in the area of IoT security is recent by its nature, and only contains few important works that have been driven by the observation of attacks in the last 5 years. In particular, there are some works that aim at analyzing the evolution of the largest botnets based on IoT devices. We already cited the work by Antonakakis [12] that provides an in-depth analysis of *MIRAI*, while the evolution of *MIRAI* and *BASHLITE* was described by Marzano et al. in [31]. From a more general standpoint, Cozzi et al. [19] studied common characteristics of current linux malware, an important contribution for this research area, as a large number of IoT devices run on some form of linux-based platforms.

Attack Triage – The idea of applying the concept of triage to attacks comes from practitioners that first experimented it within security operation centers of large companies. In particular, it is often associated with the analysis of malware. Recent research contributions applied this concept to malware analysis for android-based platforms. Bitshred [25] proposes a probabilistic data structure created through feature hashing for large-scale correlation of malware samples. Bitshred was designed to efficiently identify samples of similar malware, but differently from us, its internal data structures are not designed to detail how two samples differ. SigMal [27] shares some similarities with Bitshred, but uses signal-processing-based analysis to improve resistance to noise. More recently, Calleja et al. [18] showed that confusing statistical classification systems may be easy for malware writers. More generally, the recent research trend on adversarial machine learning [24] cast a shadow on the robustness of triage solutions based on statistical models. Recently, Shen et al. have shown that it is possible to find similarities between attacks with temporal word embeddings [32]. If compared with our approach, the main difference is that the work in [32] relies on explicit

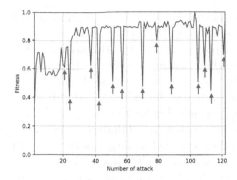

Fig. 8. Fitness score for the attacks in the NCE configuration. In red we report the values of fitness below 0.8 (from trace 20 and on) that represent a new attack. (Color figure online)

alerts given by an Intrusion Detection System (IDS) and requires a very large dataset of alerts to produce reliable results.

Process Mining and Security – In the research literature, there are some studies that advocate the use of process mining to analyse logs for the detection of security violations in business processes [5–8,26]. It is worth noting that such studies focus on investigating security aspects regarding the *execution* of business processes. Conversely, our work aims at applying process mining techniques directly to malicious traces extracted from event logs containing attacks. We found only two existing studies that go in our same direction [10,14].

In [10], the authors combine process mining techniques and visual features to help a network administrator analyzing the alerts (i.e., the amount of malicious events included in a trace) generated by IDSs. If this amount is greater than a predefined threshold, the alert is captured. Process discovery techniques have been also employed for studying and classifying malware and malicious code in [14]. In this work, by extracting a process model from the system logs of infected devices and comparing it against the normal execution of non-infected and similar devices, the authors create a classification of malware families.

Differently from the above studies, which employ offline process discovery algorithms coupled with ad-hoc attack detection techniques, our solution uses online discovery in combination with trace alignment. This ensures a more precise identification of malicious traces and gives insights about their potential impact at run-time.

7   Concluding Remarks

In this paper, we have presented a novel solution for attack triage support dedicated to IoT systems that, leveraging process mining techniques, can help security operators to quickly identify new attacks with unknown behaviors, to later analyze them in detail. We implemented and tested our solution with traces generated by running publicly available botnet code (*MIRAI, BASHLITE* and

LIGHTAIDRA) in a controlled environment, experimentally demonstrating the validity of the proposed approach. Furthermore, we validated the effectiveness of this system when deployed in a real world environment.

It is worth noting that current algorithms for online process discovery and trace alignment performs and scales very well with input models consisting of hundreds of transitions and logs including thousands of execution traces [13, 20, 21, 28], making them very suitable for the automated triage of IoT attacks.

Future work will be devoted to validate our approach against larger collections of attack traces characterized by larger botnet variability. Furthermore, we will investigate ways to automatically tune at run-time the cost function used for trace alignment and the alarm threshold applied to the fitness score.

Finally, we plan to investigate how our approach can be used to monitor systems and lock attacks as they unfold. To this aim, *predictive process monitoring* methods [30] can be employed to provide the user with predictions about the future of an ongoing trace. The forward-looking nature of predictive monitoring enables applications where evolving traces can be analyzed before completion, to predict how they evolve, and possibly identify them as malicious (and thus block them), before the infection vector is installed on the target system.

Acknowledgments. This work has been partially supported by the Estonian Research Council Grant IUT20-55, the Italian "Dipartimento di Eccellenza" grant for DIAG at Sapienza University of Rome, the Sapienza grants IT-SHIRT, ROCKET and METRICS, the PANACEA project under the grant agreement 826293, and a student grant from Vitrociset S.p.A.

References

1. Cowrie. https://github.com/cowrie/cowrie
2. The ddos that didn't break the camel's vac. https://goo.gl/p9kUCy (2017)
3. van der Aalst, W.M.P.: The application of Petri nets to workflow management. J. Circ. Syst. Comput. **8**(01), 21–66 (1998)
4. van der Aalst, W.M.P.: Data science in action. Process Mining, pp. 3–23. Springer, Heidelberg (2016). https://doi.org/10.1007/978-3-662-49851-4_1
5. van Aalst, W.M.P., van Hee, K.M., van Werf, J.M., Verdonk, M.: Auditing 2.0: using process mining to support tomorrow's auditor. Computer **43**(3), 90–93 (2010)
6. van der Aalst, W.M.P., Alves de Medeiros, A.K.: Process mining and security: detecting anomalous process executions and checking process conformance. Electron. Notes Theor. Comput. Sci. **121**, 3–21 (2005)
7. Accorsi, R., Stocker, T.: On the exploitation of process mining for security audits: the conformance checking case. In: SAC 2012, pp. 1709–1716 (2012)
8. Accorsi, R., Stocker, T., Müller, G.: On the exploitation of process mining for security audits: the process discovery case. In: SAC 2013, pp. 1462–1468 (2013)
9. Adriansyah, A., Sidorova, N., van Dongen, B.F.: Cost-based fitness in conformance checking. In: ACSD 2011 (2011)
10. de Alvarenga, S.C., Zarpel, B., Miani, R.: Discovering attack strategies using process mining. In: AICT 2015, pp. 119–125 (2015)

11. Angrishi, K.: Turning internet of things (iot) into internet of vulnerabilities (iov): Iot botnets. Technical report. arXiv preprint arXiv:1702.03681 (2017)
12. Antonakakis, M., et al.: Understanding the mirai botnet. In: 26th USENIX Security Symposium, pp. 1093–1110 (2017)
13. Augusto, A., et al.: Automated discovery of process models from event logs: review and benchmark. IEEE TKDE **31**(4), 686–705 (2018)
14. Bernardi, M.L., Cimitile, M., Distante, D., Martinelli, F., Mercaldo, F.: Dynamic malware detection and phylogeny analysis using process mining. Int. J. Inf. Secur. **18**(3), 1–28 (2018)
15. Bertino, E., Islam, N.: Botnets and internet of things security. IEEE Comput. **2**, 76–79 (2017)
16. Burattin, A.: Applicability of process mining techniques in business environments. Ph.D. thesis, University of Bologna, Italy (2013)
17. Burattin, A., Cimitile, M., Maggi, F.M., Sperduti, A.: Online discovery of declarative process models from event streams. IEEE Trans. Serv. Comp. **8**(6), 833–846 (2015)
18. Calleja, A., Martín, A., Menéndez, H.D., Tapiador, J., Clark, D.: Picking on the family: disrupting android malware triage by forcing misclassification. Expert Syst. Appl. **95**, 113–126 (2018)
19. Cozzi, E., Graziano, M., Fratantonio, Y., Balzarotti, D.: Understanding linux malware. In: 39th IEEE Symposium on Security and Privacy (SP), pp. 161–175 (2018)
20. De Giacomo, G., Maggi, F.M., Marrella, A., Patrizi, F.: On the disruptive effectiveness of automated planning for LTLf-based trace alignment. In: AAAI 2017, pp. 3555–3561 (2017)
21. van Dongen, B.F.: Efficiently computing alignments. In: BPM 2018 (2018)
22. Dumas, M., La Rosa, M., Mendling, J., Reijers, H.A., et al.: Fundamentals of Business Process Management, vol. 1. Springer, Heidelberg (2013). https://doi.org/10.1007/978-3-662-56509-4
23. Hossain, M.M., Fotouhi, M., Hasan, R.: Towards an analysis of security issues, challenges, and open problems in the internet of things. In: SERVICES 2015 (2015)
24. Huang, L., Joseph, A.D., Nelson, B., Rubinstein, B.I., Tygar, J.: Adversarial machine learning. In: AISEC 2011, pp. 43–58 (2011)
25. Jang, J., Brumley, D., Venkataraman, S.: Bitshred: feature hashing malware for scalable triage and semantic analysis. In: CCS 2011, pp. 309–320 (2011)
26. Jans, M., Alles, M., Vasarhelyi, M.: The case for process mining in auditing: sources of value added and areas of application. Int. J. Acc. Inf. Syst. **14**(1), 1–20 (2013)
27. Kirat, D., Nataraj, L., Vigna, G., Manjunath, B.: Sigmal: a static signal processing based malware triage. In: ACSAC 2013, pp. 89–98 (2013)
28. de Leoni, M., Marrella, A.: Aligning real process executions and prescriptive process models through automated planning. Expert Syst. Appl. **82**, 162–183 (2017)
29. Maggi, F.M., Burattin, A., Cimitile, M., Sperduti, A.: Online process discovery to detect concept drifts in ltl-based declarative process models. In: CoopIS 2013 (2013)
30. Maggi, F.M., Di Francescomarino, C., Dumas, M., Ghidini, C.: Predictive monitoring of business processes. In: CAiSE 2014, pp. 457–472 (2014)
31. Marzano, A., et al.: The evolution of Bashlite and Mirai IoT Botnets. In: ISCC 2018, pp. 813–818 (2018)
32. Shen, Y., Stringhini, G.: Attack2vec: Leveraging temporal word embeddings to understand the evolution of cyberattacks. In: 28th Usenix Security Symposium (2019)

33. The OSWAP Fundation: OWASP Internet of Things Project. https://tinyurl.com/yc3plqr9 (2014)
34. Weijters, A.J.M.M., van der Aalst, W.M.P.: Rediscovering workflow models from event-based data using little thumb. Int. Comp.-Aided Eng. **10**(2), 151–162 (2003)

An Automatic Emotion Recognition System for Annotating *Spotify*'s Songs

J. García de Quirós[1], S. Baldassarri[1], J. R. Beltrán[2], A. Guiu[1], and P. Álvarez[1(✉)]

[1] Department of Computer Science and Systems Engineering, University of Zaragoza, Zaragoza, Spain
{jgarciaqg,sandra,aguiu,alvaper}@unizar.es
[2] Department of Electronic Engineering and Communications, University of Zaragoza, Zaragoza, Spain
jrbelbla@unizar.es

Abstract. The recognition of emotions for annotating large-size music datasets is still an open challenge. The problem lies in that most of the solutions require the audio of the songs and user/expert intervention during certain phases of the recognition process. In this paper, we propose an automatic solution for overcoming these drawbacks. It consists of a heterogeneous set of machine learning models that have been developed from *Spotify*'s Web data services and miner tools. In order to improve the accuracy of resulting annotations, each model is specialized in recognizing a class of emotions. These models have been validated by using the *AcousticBrainz* database and have been exported to be integrated into a music emotion recognition system. It has been used to emotionally annotate the *Spotify* music database which is composed by more than 30 million songs.

Keywords: Emotion recognition · Affective annotation · Machine learning · Music and *spotify*

1 Introduction

The effect of the music as an emotional stimulus has been studied for elicited emotions [24,27] and for emotions perceived by the user while listening [5,15]. Traditionally, the user's emotional response has been recognized using different physiological sensors (heart rate, GSR, ANS or ECG sensors, for instance) [11, 25]. The processing of the low-level signals from these sensors allows to detect the users' reactions for different kinds of music. In the recent years, technological advances have reduced the cost of these sensors, improved their performance and even placed a wide range of the wearable devices to the market. Despite these advances, the recognition of emotions in music is still facing the critical problem of the low repetitiveness of experiments under the same conditions [13]. Music libraries are increasingly rich and varied, and each user reacts in a different way to the same song, preventing reaching significant conclusions.

© Springer Nature Switzerland AG 2019
H. Panetto et al. (Eds.): OTM 2019, LNCS 11877, pp. 345–362, 2019.
https://doi.org/10.1007/978-3-030-33246-4_23

Although music is still emotionally annotated through evaluations with real users [5], the trend is to automate this process. Some works apply Web crawling techniques over specialized music Websites or over social networks in order to obtain the users' opinion about particular songs [7,16,26]. Subsequently, these opinions are processed and converted into annotations that represent the emotion perceived by the listener. This solution is time-consuming, it requires to process large amount of information and, in general, the information obtained from the emotional point of view is scarce and is strongly conditioned by the user's musical preferences.

On the other hand, automatic annotation systems usually need to process the audio features of songs [29,31]. In these works, the idea is to determine those features that affect the user reactions and, later, to generate affective annotations. These solutions require the original audio of the song for extracting its audio features by using specialized tools. This requirement limits the applicability of the solution. For the reasons already given, regardless of the strategy, the automatic recognition solutions work on small music repositories (for example, MediaEval [2]).

Spotify is the reference online music provider, with an available data set of more that 30 million songs and 96 million paid Premium subscribers in 2018. In the late 2017, *Spotify* began to publish a set of Web APIs and tools for developers that enabled the access to songs' metadata and audio features and users' playlists with the aim to promote the development of new applications based on its music streaming services and to foster the power of their music recommender system.

The aim of this work is to develop an automatic recognition system of the emotions perceived by the users, integrated into the *Spotity*'s service platform. The solution will allow to emotionally classify and annotate the complete provider database without the necessity of evaluating it with users, by using as input the audio features of the songs and the descriptions published by the users about their playlists. Our solution offers a procedure suitable to be implemented on a large scale regarding the number of songs and users involved. The emotional recognition system has been developed applying different machine learning techniques and has been validated using *AcoustinBrainz*, a massive database of information about music [1]. The results are being used in the *DJ-Running* project with the aim of improving the sport performance of long distance runners.

The remainder of this paper is organized as follows. In Sect. 2, the related literature regarding techniques to automatically recognize emotions in music is reviewed. Section 3 introduces the proposal based on *Spotify* services. Sections 4 and 5 describe the development and validation of machine learning models for the massive recognition of perceived emotions. The system implementation and its integration in the *DJ-Running* infrastructure are presented in Sect. 6. Finally, Sect. 7 presents the paper's conclusions and makes suggestions for future research.

2   Related Works

2.1   Music Emotion Recognition Systems

There are many research works that propose automatic systems for *Music Emotion Recognition* (MER). In [29] a detailed review of these solutions is presented. More specifically, a comparative table of the different systems proposed between 2003 and 2017 is discussed (Table 4, pages 384–386). This table identifies the common features of these systems and helps us to highlight the contributions of our proposal.

Most of reviewed systems process directly the audio of songs (column "Formats") to extract their features (column "Music features"). This processing limits the applicability of solutions, being the maximum number of recognized songs around 1,500 (column "Songs(no)."). The input of the recognition function is the audio features of songs, and the output is an emotion mapped to a two-dimensional valence-arousal space (VA, column "Emotion models"). These functions have been implemented by using different machine-learning and deep-learning algorithms (column "Methods"). Finally, many works restrict their recognition capabilities to an unique musical genre.

Some other relevant MER systems that have not been included in [29] or are subsequent to 2017 are following reviewed. The input of these systems are still the audio features of the songs, but new combinations of them have been considered to improve the recognition of emotions. For example, [8] proposes the use of four music features from three different categories (pitch, volume and tempo). Besides, these solutions also recognize small-size datasets: 1,802 songs [17], 900 songs [20] or 300 songs [8], for instance. On the other hand, learning algorithms continue being the most popular techniques: machine learning algorithms (such as Support Vector Machines (SVM) [19,20], Regression Trees [8], or Random Forest (RF) [12]) or deep learning algorithms (in this case, different types of Neural Networks [17,19]). Therefore, the most recent approaches and their problems are similar to those described in [29].

Our music emotion recognition method addresses some of the drawbacks of the previous approaches, mainly: to avoid the necessity of having the audio of the songs, to process and annotate large-scale music datasets from an emotional perspective, and to improve the accuracy of learning-based recognition by applying a multi-method approach. Different net-accessible data services and music databases have been integrated in order to get these goals.

2.2   Music Recommendation Systems Based on *Spotify*

Most of the *Spotify* related works propose music recommendation systems for helping users to create their playlists. Recommendations are based on the user preferences (musical genres and artists, mainly) and the features of songs that she/he usually listens to. Users' profiles are determined by utilizing users' past interactions [9] or by processing the messages published by users in social networks, such as *Twitter* [22] or *Facebook* [10]. Internally, these recommendation systems are programmed integrating content and collaborative filtering techniques [9,10,22]. The first ones help to determine the similarity between songs based on their audio features, while the latter determine the similarity between users based on their preferences. The same approach is currently used by *Spotify* [18]. As a conclusion, these *Spotify*-based systems do not consider music emotions. Exceptionally, [9] adds a mood value to the set of songs' features which is obtained from the *Million Playlist Dataset*, released by *Spotify* in 2018 as part of the *Spotify RecSys Challenge*.

In this paper, our goal is to annotate emotionally the *Spotify* songs from the data services offered by that music provider. These annotations will be used in the future to recommend music from a different perspective than reviewed works, as it will be discussed in Sect. 6.

3   A Music Emotions Recognition System Based on *Spotify*

In this section, the automatic system developed for the recognition of emotions in music is presented. It interacts with the *Spotify* Web API for getting songs' metadata and audio features. Then, these data are used by a set of machine learning models to determine the emotion perceived by an user when listening to each one of these songs. These emotions are represented by means of labels that are stored jointly with song's metadata into a database. The system has been developed for automatically processing a massive collection of songs.

The process of *Building the machine learning models* used for the recognition (right side of Fig. 1) consists of four phases. The first stage extracts the input data from *Spotify*. More specifically, two of the Web data services offered by the music provider have been used:

- The *Spotify Web API for developers* that allows to access the music database of the provider (list of songs) and to get the metadata (author, album, musical genre, etc.) and audio features of each song.
- The *Spotify Playlist miner API* that aggregates the top songs from the most popular playlists on *Spotify*. These playlists have been previously created and published by registered users. The API allows the requester to specify search criteria based on keywords that will be used by the miner for creating the aggregations. These criteria are matched with names and descriptions of playlists.

The *Data extraction and preprocessing* phase combines the information provided by these two Web interfaces. The goal is to create an intermediate repository of annotated songs that will be used for the training of classification models. We have assumed that a song contained into a playlist called "Motivating music for running" is likely that conveys positive energy and emotions. Therefore, firstly, it searches for aggregations that contain songs that could match with certain perceived emotions of interest. The results are ranked and filtered in order to select the songs to be emotionally annotated. For example, some of the songs

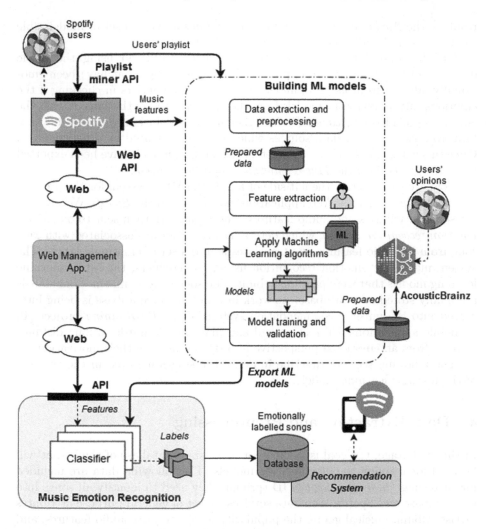

Fig. 1. System for recognizing music emotions

contained into the mentioned playlist could be annotates as *happy* or *excited*. Then, it gets the general attributes and audio features of these songs, and they are stored jointly the annotations into the intermediate repository.

The second stage of the process, called *Feature extraction*, consists of determining the set of audio features that are relevant to predict the perceived emotion of songs. This analysis is complex and requires expert intervention. However, some previous research works have already studied the influence of certain musical parameters on the emotional perception of users [20,29]. Once the selection of these features has been completed, different machine learning algorithms have been applied to find the most suitable ones from a predictive point of view. The result of the *Applying machine learning algorithms* stage is a set of models able to classify emotionally the songs from its audio features.

On the other hand, these models have been validated using the music database of the *AcousticBrainz* project. It contains songs that have been emotionally labelled from users' opinions. The validation consists in checking if the emotions calculated by the models from the *Spotify* data are the same as that the emotions provided by *AcousticBrainz*. Therefore, the solution combines information from two different data sources which were also created by different users. Once this validation has been complete, the resulting models have been exported to be integrated into the *Music emotion recognition system*.

Now, we will describe the left side of Fig. 1: the MER system for the processing of *Spotify*'s songs. A Web application interacts with the *Spotify* Web API to get songs' attributes and audio features. These data are then sent to our *Music emotion recognition system*, which determines the emotions associated with each song from its audio features and translates it into a set of emotional labels. The system makes the emotion recognition using, as classifiers, the set of machine learning models that were previously built. The song's data and emotional labels are finally stored in a database. As work in process, this database is being integrated into the music recommendation system of the *DJ-Running* project [4]. A mobile applications will recommend and play *Spotify* music to long distance runners from an emotional perspective in order to increase their motivation.

The following sections describe in detail the stages involved in the creation of the machine learning models.

4   Data Extraction and Preprocessing

In this first stage, the goal is to create a small-sized database of songs that will be used for training the classification models. The following data are included for each song: its unique *Spotify* ID (primary key used to identify all songs into the database and *Spotify* Web data services), a set of general purpose attributes (artist, album, musical genre, the popularity level, etc.), its audio features, and the emotional label that represents the users' perceived emotion when they listen to the song. All these data can be obtained from the *Spotify* Web data services except the emotional annotation that requires a complex recognition process. In any case, they are stored into a intermediate database, called *Prepared data* (see Fig. 1).

4.1   Representation and Processing of the Song's Emotional Label

Nowadays, the two main approaches in the field of emotional models are the categorical and the dimensional ones [31]. Our work is based on the Russell's circumplex model [23], one of the most popular dimensional models and widely used in affective computing. It represents affective states over a two-dimensional space that is defined by the *valence* (X-axis) and *arousal* (Y-axis) dimensions. The valence represents the intrinsic pleasure/displeasure (positive/negative) of an event, object or situation, and the arousal the feeling's intensity. The combination of these two dimensions (valence/arousal) determines four different quadrants: the *aggressive-angry* (negative/positive), the *happy* (positive/positive), the *sad* (negative/negative) and the *relaxed* (positive/negative) quadrant. Then, each emotion is mapped to a point in the two-dimensional space and, therefore, is also located into one of the mentioned quadrants.

As it was introduced before, we need to create an emotional annotation for each song that will be used in the training of the classification models. This annotation represents the emotion perceived by the listeners. In our proposal, in this first stage, we annotate regarding the Russell model's quadrants, instead of concrete emotions. Therefore, each song is annotated with one of these four values (representing in which of the four quadrants is located the emotion perceived by the listeners): *angry, happy, sad* or *relaxed.*

The *Spotify Playlist Miner* plays a relevant role in the process of creating these emotional annotations. This Web-accessible tool allows to search the most popular playlists created by *Spotify* registered users. For example, if the keyword *happy* is used as the search criterion, the tool returns a list of songs included in playlists matching that criterion. The matching is based on the word similarity between the search keywords and the terms used by users for naming and describing playlists. Besides, the tool also allows to specify unwanted keywords in order to filter the search results.

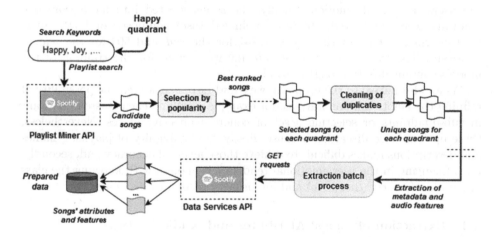

Fig. 2. Abstraction of the data preprocessing process

Figure 2 shows the process of selecting and annotating the songs recorded into the *Prepared data* repository. Firstly, the *Miner service* is invoked to get songs that could be located into a concrete Russell's quadrant. Therefore, four different requests are executed, one for each quadrant. The search criterion of each request is a set of affective states contained into the quadrant of interest. This criterion is refined adding as unwanted keywords a set of states from the other three quadrants. For example, *"Happy AND Joy NOT Sad NOT Relaxed NOT Angry NOT No"* is the search parameter configured for getting songs that are probably contained in the *happy* quadrant. Secondly, the returned songs are processed to select the most popular by applying the inverse frequency, a numerical statistic widely used in the field of information retrieval that is intended to reflect how important a song is in the returned playlists. We are interested in songs that have a low inverse frequency because it represents that a relevant number of users have perceived the same emotion when listening to each of these songs. It helps to guarantee the validity of source annotations. Finally, the best ranked songs are selected and emotionally annotated with an emotion label. In the case of the example, they will be annotated with the label *happy*.

Additionally, once the process of selecting the songs is completed for the four quadrants, the songs that appear in more than one quadrant are removed to avoid confusion in the creation and training of future classification models.

At the beginning of this processing stage, we obtained 83,078 *Spotify* songs from the *Playlist Miner*. More specifically, the number of songs for each of the four requests was: 17,661 songs probably conveying emotions located into the *angry* quadrant, 19,092 into the *happy* quadrant, 23,931 into the *sad* quadrant, and 22,394 into the *relaxed* quadrant. After applying the inverse frequency, we selected 1,817 songs for the *angry*, 3,055 for the *happy*, 2,943 for the *sad*, and 1,671 for the *relaxed* quadrants. This selection process reduces significantly the number of available songs, but increases confidence in results concerning the users' perceived emotion. Finally, the songs located into more than one quadrant were eliminated, obtaining a final dataset composed of 1,307 songs for the *angry*, 1,644 for the *happy*, 1,737 for the *sad*, and 504 for the *relaxed* quadrant. Therefore, the *prepared data* database used for the training of the models contained 5,192 songs in total.

As an alternative to the proposal, we could have considered the possibility of refining the emotional annotations, for example, dividing each Russell quadrant in sub-quadrants or selecting a set of concrete affective states. Nevertheless, these options were discarded because, firstly, the ambiguity of playlists' names and descriptions makes difficult to achieve those levels of accuracy and, secondly, for influencing in the user emotional tendency is enough with knowing the class of emotion (positive/negative) and intensity of recommended songs.

4.2   Extraction of Songs' Attributes and Audio Features

As it is shown at the bottom of Fig. 2, the next step of the preprocessing is to complete the data of annotated songs. The *miner service* responses also contained the unique *Spotify* IDs of selected songs. Now, these IDs are used to invoke the RESTful operations provided by the *Spotify* Web data services. More specifically, two different operations are invoked for each song: the *GET track* and the *GET audio-features* endpoints. The first returns the general purpose attributes of the requested song, such as the artist, the album, etc. On the other hand, the second endpoint returns its audio features, specifically, loudness, energy, tempo, acousticness, valence, liveness, speechiness, instrumentalness, danceability, key, duration, and mode. Finally, all these data are recorded jointly with the emotional annotation into the repository.

In the *Spotify* data model, the songs don't have an attribute that determines their musical genre. This attribute has to be obtained indirectly from the artist's metadata invoking the *GET artists* endpoint. As consequence, an extra processing is needed to add this information to each artist's songs.

The extraction of songs' metadata and audio features has been programmed as a batch application. Each batch job extracts the information of 50 songs. The application was executed in Intel Core 2 Quad Q8200 processor at 2.33 GHz with 8 GB of RAM, running the Windows 8.1 Pro x64 operating system, and connected through an Ethernet network at 100 Mbps. In this environment, the execution time of each job was 2.75 s (286.44 s in total for the 5, 192 annotated songs).

5   Building of *Spotify*-Based learning models

In this section the three stages directly involved in the building of the machine learning models are described: the extraction of the features of interest, the application of algorithms and the training and validation of the models. The result is a set of models that will be exported and integrated into the *Music emotion recognition system* to annotate the *Spotify* music database.

More specifically, four classification models have been built, one per each of the Russell quadrants. Each model predicts whether or not the emotions perceived by the listeners belong to the corresponding quadrant (a logical value) and the probability of belonging to it (a real value). Therefore, the emotional annotation of a *Spotify* song will consist of two vectors of four values. For example, the "I want to hold your hand" song by "The Beatles" will have the following emotional annotation ([*false, true, false, false*],[0.174, 0.765, 0.155, 0.006]) which represents that is a *happy* song with a 0.765 probability. The sad, angry and relaxed probabilities (0.174, 0.155 and 0.006, respectively) are lower than the classification threshold and, therefore, the song is also classified as not sad, not angry and not relaxed.

At the end of this section, the advantages of this classification approach and the obtained results will be also discussed.

5.1   Analysis and Feature Extraction

The decision of considering four different hypothesis, one for each Russell's quadrant, aims at creating more accurate models. Nevertheless, it is necessary to identify first the audio features that must be involved in the building of these models. We have decided to analyse these features from the perspective of each Russell's quadrant, that is, we are supposing that a feature may be significant to identify a class of emotions, but irrelevant to others. In the literature this analysis is usually carried out by applying three different approaches: by selecting the same features used in other similar research works, consulting the opinion of music experts, or evaluating and interpreting certain statistical tests frequently used in the machine learning field. We propose to use mainly tests and, then, to corroborate their results with previous works and expert opinions. Let us first review the features considered in other music emotion recognition systems. Most of these systems work with low-level features directly extracted from the audio of songs [8, 28–30]. In general, these works are mainly interested in extracting *timbral* and *rhythmic* features. Each solution uses a different audio processing tool, which makes it difficult to compare their results (it is even unknown how the features are calculated by *Spotify*).

On the other hand, we have also consulted some music experts. They have analysed the audio features provided by the *Spotify* Web data services and concluded that the most significant ones are energy, valence, danceability and tempo. Besides, they believe that the key and duration features are the least relevant ones. The rest of features could have a moderate influence depending on the emotion to be recognised.

Finally, three statistical tests have been calculated to evaluate the degree of features' relevance in each of the Russell quadrants, specifically, the *Chi cuadrado*, *ANOVA F-value* and *Mutual information* tests. These order the features from most to least relevant. Table 1 shows the result of combining the three tests. For each quadrant, the most significant features are represented in italic and the least in bold.

Table 1. Analysis of songs' audio features

Sad	Happy	Angry	Relaxed
Energy	*Valence*	*Acousticness*	*Instrumentalness*
Acousticness	*Acousticness*	*Energy*	*Energy*
Valence	*Danceability*	*Speechiness*	*Loudness*
Loudness	*Energy*	*Loudness*	*Acousticness*
Liveness	*Instrumentalness*	*Danceability*	*Valence*
Danceability	**Liveness**	**Key**	**Key**
Speechiness	**Mode**	**Valence**	**Liveness**
Key	**Key**	**Mode**	**Mode**

As it was concluded by experts, energy and valence features should be considered on the process of recognising any emotion, whereas key and duration could be dismissed. Besides, danceability, tempo and mode may not be as decisive as deduced from previous works. And, finally, acousticness and loudness seem to be more important than initially expected by the experts.

Therefore, here the proposal is to use different audio features in the building of each classification model (this type of approach was already considered by [20]) and to avoid working with a restricted number of features (most of the recognition systems based on classification techniques are built considering only between 3 and 5 features [29]). Following, we detail the audio features that have been finally selected for each classification model:

- *Sad* classifier: [acousticness, duration, energy, instrumentalness, liveness, loudness, mode, tempo, valence]
- *Happy* classifier: [acousticness, danceability, duration, energy, instrumentalness, loudness, speechiness, tempo, valence]
- *Angry* classifier: [acousticness, danceability, duration, energy, instrumentalness, liveness, loudness, speechiness, tempo]
- *Relaxed* classifier: [acousticness, danceability, duration, energy, instrumentalness, loudness, speechiness, tempo, valence]

5.2   Model Selection and Training

In this stage, the goal is to build a machine learning model for each Russell quadrant. The *target function* of these models is defined as: the input are the song's audio features, while the output is a pair of values (a logical value and a real value) that predicts whether the emotions perceived by the listeners are located into to the corresponding quadrant. For the building of the models we have considered three types of machine learning algorithms: *Support Vector Machine* (SVM), *K-Nearest Neighbours* (KNN) and *Random Forest* (RF). These have been widely used with good results in the recognition of emotions [16,28]. Nevertheless, we have also considered the possibility that the use of an unique algorithm is not the best option for building the different classification models. Therefore, the best machine learning algorithm for each quadrant (its model) is also studied.

Before comparing the algorithms we must define the positive and negative datasets that will be used in the training and testing of resulting models. The starting point is the dataset of annotated songs that was created during the pre-processing stage (described in Sect. 4). For each quadrant, this dataset has been been divided into two parts. On the one hand, the songs that were annotated with the emotional value of that quadrant and, on the other hand, the rest of songs. For example, for the *happy* quadrant, the first dataset is composed by the songs annotated as *happy* (positive class), and the second by those annotated as *sad*, *angry* and *relaxed* (negative class). This partitioning strategy has been replicated for the four quadrants.

Then, the three selected machine learning algorithms have been applied in the building and training of models. The choice of input audio features is determined by the results of the previous analysis. Besides, the range of input hyperparameters has been varied in order to find the best configuration. The library *Scikit randomized search* has been used for this evaluation because it provides an efficient procedure for the analysis of the possible permutations [6].

Table 2 shows the results for the different combinations of algorithms and quadrants. The best combinations has been highlighted in italic. Each of these has been configured with the optimal input of audio features and hyperparameters. Besides, the resulting models have been trained with the 70% of its corresponding dataset and tested with the remaining 30%. This partitioning allow us to evaluate the overfitting of models. As conclusions, *Random Forest* models offer good accuracy results for the four quadrants. These results contradict the initial assumptions (to apply different algorithms for building the model of each quadrant in order to improve the models' accuracy). The mean accuracy is 88.75%, a good result compared to other similar studies that obtained values near 80%, such as [17,20].

Table 2. Comparative of different models/quadrants

Algorithm	Tests	Sad	Happy	Angry	Relaxed
SVM	Accuracy	0.8036	0.767	0.872	0.929
	f1	0.783	0.752	0.821	0.733
K-NN	Accuracy	0.842	0.843	0.876	0.935
	f1	0.816	*0.822*	0.824	0.784
Random forest	Accuracy	*0.862*	*0.844*	*0.899*	*0.945*
	f1	*0.839*	0.820	*0.860*	*0.801*

5.3   Validation of the Models

The last stage is the validation of models. It has been carried out using the music database published by the project *AcousticBrainz* [1]. The repository contains over 11 million of songs, but the version that can be downloaded is only composed by half a million (songs released before 2015). Each song has an attribute that represents the emotion conveyed by it. More specifically, this attribute is a vector of four numerical values, where each of them determines the probability of conveying an emotion belonging to a Russell quadrant. These values have been generated from users' opinions published in the music Website *Last.fm*.

The downloaded dataset has been preprocessed for selecting those songs that have a high probability value in one emotion and a low probability value in the other three (in other words, a quadrant stands out from the others). After the preprocessing, the dataset size has been reduced to 60,000 songs (around 15,000 songs per quadrant). Then, the audio features of these songs has been obtained by invoking the *Spotify* Web data services. In this way, we have the features and an emotion for each song contained into the preprocessed dataset. The goal is now to validate the models using this set of annotated songs.

Table 3. Results of the model validation

Model	Test	Sad	Happy	Angry	Relaxed
SVM	Accuracy	*0.853*	*0.697*	0.685	*0.729*
	f1	*0.844*	*0.649*	0.683	*0.721*
K-NN	Accuracy	0.834	0.690	0.705	0.686
	f1	0.824	0.620	0.699	0.667
Random forest	Accuracy	0.771	0.694	*0.705*	0.729
	f1	0.745	0.623	*0.700*	0.719

Table 3 shows the validation results. In general, the model accuracy gets worse with respect to the results of the training and test stage (see Table 2). In any case, the most important is that the accuracy results are still quite good, with a mean accuracy over 75%, considering that we are "comparing" two different types of annotations: the emotions deduced from the *Spotify* playlists and the emotions extracted from *AcousticBrainz* users' opinions. These types of annotations were created by applying different procedures based on the users' perception and by involving different listeners. Also, it can be remarked that the *Support Vector Machine* models improve their accuracy when they work with the *AcousticBrainz* dataset (*happy*, *sad* and *relaxed* quadrants). Nevertheless, the *Random Forest* models are still the best option for recognising emotions related to the *angry* quadrant, and they present good results for the other three quadrants.

5.4 Brief Discussion About the Approach and the Results

As an alternative to the described approach of building four classification models, one per each of the quadrant, we have also considered the possibility of building only one model able to solve a multi-class classification problem. The *target function* of this multi-class model is defined as: the input are the song's audio features, while the output is a vector of four logical values ([*is_sad*, *is_happy*, *is_angry*, *is_relaxed*]) that determine in which Russell quadrants could be located the emotions perceived by users. In this way, the results of the two approaches are the same, but applying a different classification solution.

Table 2 showed the results obtained with the four classification models. The mean accuracy and f1 are 0.89 and 0.83, respectively. We have built and validated the multi-class model using the same datasets. For its building we have also considered different machine learning algorithms, obtaining the best results with the *Random Forest*. In this case, the accuracy and f1 that have been obtained are 0.78 and 0.75, respectively. Therefore, the results are slightly worse than our proposal. In our opinion, the good results of our approach are due to: the splitting of the classification problem into four subproblems, simplifying the classification constraints to be considered; and the adaptation of the building model stages (the selection of features and algorithms, and the training of models) to the characteristics and particularities of each quadrant. On the other hand, the four models were integrated into the *Music Recognition system*. The testing of this system consisted of downloading 5, 420, 271 songs from the *Spotify* Web data services and of classifying them emotionally using the models. Once the recognition was completed, we analysed the results paying particular attention to songs' logical vectors. Ideally, one of the values of logical vector should be true (it represents that emotions conveyed by that song belong to an only affective quadrant). If two logical values are true, then they should have the same valence (*happy-relaxed* or *sad-angry*) in Russell terminology (it represents that all the emotions conveyed by that song are positive -or negative-, but they can have different arousal). The rest of outcomes are undesirable and they should be improved.

The analysis concluded that 78.77% of the songs had an only value to true (4, 269, 244 songs). A 3.07% had two values to true (166, 546 songs), but most of them had the same valence (exceptionally, 22, 121 song had been annotated as *happy* and *sad*, and 8, 751 as *angry* and *relaxed*; these classifications should be reviewed). Additionally, only 12 songs had three or four values to true. Nevertheless, 18.1% of songs could not be classified (the four fields of vector were false). As future work, we are interested in analysing in detail this set of songs and studying the emotions perceived by the listeners (carrying out experiments with users, for instance). The models use by default a probability threshold of 0.5 to determine the belonging to a quadrant. One possibility is to customize the threshold for each of the quadrants in order to refine the model predictions and to reduce the number of unclassified songs.

6 Implementation Details and Integration into the DJ-Running System

In this section we describe the software technologies used to program the components and systems shown in Fig. 1. The process of building machine learning models has been mainly implemented in the Python programming language. It provides different libraries to interact with RESTful services and to store any type of data into MongoDB databases. All the databases designed as part of the solution have been created using this open-source storing and management technology. Besides, Python also facilitates the integration of *Scikit-learn* into the process, the data analysis tool that has been used for the extraction of features and the creation and testing of machine learning models [21]. Finally, these models have been exported by *Joblib* [3]. Both tools are included into *Python ecosystem's Scientific Computing tools* [14].

On the other hand, the *Music Emotion Recognition* system has been also implemented as a RESTful service. Internally, it is composed by a set of software components that have been also programmed in Python. These components integrate the classifiers exported from the machine learning models. The recognition service is remotely invoked by the *Web Management App.*, a Java application that is responsible for accessing to the *Spotify* music database and coordinating the emotional annotation process of songs. Finally, songs' data and emotional annotations are stored in a MongoDB database which currently contains more than 5 million of songs.

The resulting database is being used by the music recommendation system developed as part of the *DJ-Running* project. The goal of this research project is to use the music for increasing long-distance runners' motivation. A mobile application allows the runner to configure her/his musical preferences and to determine her/his mood in that moment. Besides, the application monitors the runner's location and some race parameters during the physical activity. These data are periodically sent to the *DJ-Running* recommendation system to determine the next song that will be played. The application also integrates the *Spotify player* and, therefore, is able to connect and serve music from the *Spotify* streaming service (a premium license is required) [4].

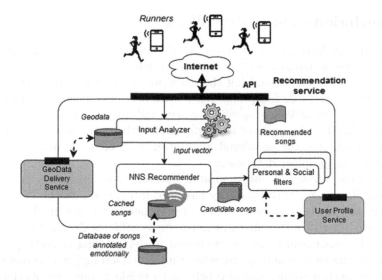

Fig. 3. *DJ-Running* recommendation system

Figure 3 shows the components of the music recommendation system. It is a Web-service that is currently deployed in the *Amazon EC2* cloud infrastructure. Internally, the service integrates three software components: an *input analyzer*, a *recommender*, and a set of *filters*. The analyzer is responsible for determining what kind of song (or songs) will be recommended to the runner considering the service request's input parameters (the runner location and mood, the type of training session, or the emotion to be induced to the runner, among others). A rule engine translates these parameters to an internal description of the song to find. On the other hand, the implementation of the recommender is based on a *Nearest Neighbor Search* algorithm (specifically, on the *Annoy* algorithm). This class of algorithms solves the problem of finding a point in a given set (a cached copy of the *Spotify* songs annotated emotionally) that is closest (or most similar) to a given point (the description of the song to be recommended). These points are numeric vectors created from the songs' audio features and emotional annotations. Finally, the list of candidate songs to be returned as part of the recommendation request is filtered using two class of filters. The *personal filters* score the candidate songs in accordance with the runner's profiles, whereas the *social filters* are based on the concept of similarity between runners. *Clustering* algorithms and *collaborative filtering* techniques have been combined to implement a prototype version of these filters.

Finally, we would like to remark that the *DJ-Running* system is currently being validated with real users (more specifically, with triathletes) in collaboration with the *Sports Medicine Centre* of the Government of Aragón which is located in Zaragoza, Spain.

7   Conclusions and Future Work

In this paper we have proposed an automatic system for music emotion recognition. The system integrates four learning models (a model for each one of the Russell quadrants) for recognising the emotions of the songs from their audio features. Unlike the existing proposals, the models have been built from data published by different Web-accessible services and are able to annotate without the need of having the audio of the songs and without the intervention of the user. This facilitates the emotional annotation of large-scale music data-sets, such as the *Spotify* music database.

The current version of our annotated database contains more than 5 million of popular songs. This repository has been integrated into the *DJ-Running* technological infrastructure as part of its recommendation system. The solution is being used to study the effects of music on triathletes during their training sessions. More specifically, we are interested in determining runners' perceived emotions and motivational response when they listen a song (or a type of songs). These experimental studies will also help us to validate songs' emotional annotations, but this part of the work is still under development.

On the other hand, as future work, we would like to use *deep learning* techniques to create other alternative models, and to compare them with those presented. It will probably provide us feedback for improving the audio feature selection stage and, therefore, the classifiers' accuracy. Besides, we are also interested in creating other emotional annotations, for example, annotations for each one of the song's segments (some research works propose to annotate only the first 30–45 s of songs [1,2]).

Acknowledgments. This work has been supported by the TIN2015-72241-EXP and TIN2017-84796-C2-2-R projects, granted by the Spanish Ministerio de Economía y Competitividad, and the DisCo-T21-17R and Affective-Lab-T25-17D projects, granted by the Aragonese Government.

References

1. AcousticBrainz (2015). http://acousticbrainz.org/
2. DEAM: Mediaeval database for emotional analysis in music (2016). http://cvml.unige.ch/databases/DEAM/
3. Joblib: Running python functions as pipeline jobs (2019). https://joblib.readthedocs.io/
4. Álvarez, P., Beltrán, J.R., Baldassarri, S.: Dj-running: wearables and emotions for improving running performance. In: Ahram, T., Karwowski, W., Taiar, R. (eds.) Human Systems Engineering and Design, pp. 847–853. Springer International Publishing, Cham (2019)
5. Ayata, D., Yaslan, Y., Kamasak, M.: Emotion based music recommendation system using wearable physiological sensors. IEEE Trans. Consum. Electron. **64**(2), 1–1 (2018). https://doi.org/10.1109/TCE.2018.2844736
6. Bergstra, J., Bengio, Y.: Random search for hyper-parameter optimization. J. Mach. Learn. Res. **13**(1), 281–305 (2012). http://dl.acm.org/citation.cfm?id=2503308.2188395

7. Cheung, W.L., Lu, G.: Music emotion annotation by machine learning. In; 2008 IEEE 10th Workshop on Multimedia Signal Processing, pp. 580–585 (2008)

8. Chiu, M.C., Ko, L.W.: Develop a personalized intelligent music selection system based on heart rate variability and machine learning. Multimed. Tools Appli. **76**, 15607–15639 (2016)

9. Fessahaye, F., et al.: T-recsys: A novel music recommendation system using deep learning. In: 2019 IEEE International Conference on Consumer Electronics (ICCE), pp. 1–6 (2019). https://doi.org/10.1109/ICCE.2019.8662028

10. Germain, A., Chakareski, J.: Spotify me: facebook-assisted automatic playlist generation. In: 2013 IEEE 15th International Workshop on Multimedia Signal Processing (MMSP), pp. 25–28, September 2013. https://doi.org/10.1109/MMSP.2013. 6659258

11. Girardi, D., Lanubile, F., Novielli, N.: Emotion detection using noninvasive low cost sensors. In: 2017 Seventh International Conference on Affective Computing and Intelligent Interaction (ACII), pp. 125–130, October 2017. https://doi.org/10. 1109/ACII.2017.8273589

12. Hastarita Rachman, F., Sarno, R., Fatichah, C.: Music emotion classification based on lyrics-audio using corpus based emotion. Int. J. Electr. Comput. Eng. (IJECE) **8**(3), 1720–1730 (2018). https://doi.org/10.11591/ijece.v8i3.pp1720-1730

13. Huang, W., Knapp, R.B.: An exploratory study of population differences based on massive database of physiological responses to music. In: 7th International Conference on Affective Computing and Intelligent Interaction (ACII 2017), pp. 524–530. San Antonio, TX, USA (2017). https://doi.org/10.1109/ACII.2017.8273649

14. Jones, E., Oliphant, T., Peterson, P., et al.: SciPy: Open source scientific tools for Python (2019). http://www.scipy.org/

15. Kim, J., André, E.: Emotion recognition based on physiological changes in music listening. IEEE Trans. Pattern Anal. Mach. Intell. **30**(12), 2067–2083 (2008). https://doi.org/10.1109/TPAMI.2008.26

16. Laurier, C., Sordo, M., Serrá, J., Herrera, P.: Music mood representations from social tags. In: Proceedings of the 10th International Society for Music Information Retrieval Conference (ISMIR 2009), pp. 381–386, Kobe, Japan (2009)

17. Liu, H., Fang, Y., Huang, Q.: Music emotion recognition using a variant of recurrent neural network. In: 2018 International Conference on Mathematics, Modeling, Simulation and Statistics Application (MMSSA 2018), vol. 164, pp. 15–18, Atlantis Press (2019)

18. Madathil, M.: Music recommendation system spotify - collaborative filtering, reports in Computer Music. Aachen University, Germany (2017)

19. Nalini, N., Palanivel, S.: Music emotion recognition: the combined evidence of mfcc and residual phase. Egypt. Inf. J. **17**(1), 1–10 (2016). https://doi.org/10.1016/j. eij.2015.05.004

20. Panda, R., Malheiro, R., Paiva, R.P.: Novel audio features for music emotion recognition. IEEE Trans. Affect. Comput. Early Access (2018). https://doi.org/10.1109/ TAFFC.2018.2820691

21. Pedregosa, F., et al.: Scikit-learn: machine learning in python. J. Mach. Learn. Res. **12**, 2825–2830 (2011)

22. Pichl, M., Zangerle, E., Specht, G.: Combining spotify and twitter data for generating a recent and public dataset for music recommendation. In: Proceedings of the 26th GI-Workshop Grundlagen von Datenbanken (GvDB 2014), Ritten, Italy (2015)

23. Russell, J.: A circumplex model of affect. J. Pers. Soc. Psychol. **39**(6), 1161–1178 (1980)

24. Scherer, K.R.: Which emotions can be induced by music? What are the underlying mechanisms? And how can we measure them. J. New Music Res. **33**(3), 239–251 (2004). https://doi.org/10.1080/0929821042000317822

25. Senachakr, P., Thammasan, N., Ichi Fukui, K., Numao, M.: Music-emotion Recognition Based on Wearable Dry-electrode Electroencephalogram, pp. 235–243 (2017). https://doi.org/10.1142/9789813234079_0018

26. Shao, X., Cheng, Z., Kankanhalli, M.S.: Music auto-tagging based on the unified latent semantic modeling. Multimed. Tools Appl. **78**(1), 161–176 (2019). https://doi.org/10.1007/s11042-018-5632-2

27. Tian, L., et al.: Recognizing induced emotions of movie audiences: are induced and perceived emotions the same. In: 7th International Conference on Affective Computing and Intelligent Interaction (ACII 2017), pp. 28–35, San Antonio, TX, USA, October 2017

28. Trohidis, K., Tsoumakas, G., Kalliris, G., Vlahavas, I.: Multi-label classification of music by emotion. EURASIP J. Audio, Speech Music Process. **2011**(1), 4 (2011). https://doi.org/10.1186/1687-4722-2011-426793

29. Yang, X., Dong, Y., Li, J.: Review of data features-based music emotion recognition methods. Multimed. Syst. **24**(4), 365–389 (2018). https://doi.org/10.1007/s00530-017-0559-4

30. Yang, Y., Lin, Y., Su, Y., Chen, H.H.: Music emotion classification: a regression approach. In: 2007 IEEE International Conference on Multimedia and Expo, pp. 208–211 (2007). https://doi.org/10.1109/ICME.2007.4284623

31. Yang, Y.H., Chen, H.: Machine recognition of music emotion: a review. ACM Trans. Intell. Syst. Technol. (TIST) **3**(3), 40:1–40:30 (2012)

An Approach for the Automated Generation of Engaging Dashboards

Ünal Aksu[1]([⊠])(iD), Adela del-Río-Ortega[2](iD), Manuel Resinas[2](iD),
and Hajo A. Reijers[1](iD)

[1] Department of Information and Computing Sciences,
Utrecht University, Utrecht, The Netherlands
{u.aksu,h.a.reijers}@uu.nl
[2] Dpto. de Lenguajes y Sistemas Informáticos,
Universidad de Sevilla, Sevilla, Spain
{adeladelrio,resinas}@us.es

Abstract. Organizations use Key Performance Indicators (KPIs) to
monitor whether they attain their goals. To support organizations at
tracking the performance of their business, software vendors offer dashboards to these organizations. For the development of the dashboards
that will engage organizations and enable them to make informed decisions, software vendors leverage dashboard design principles. However,
the dashboard design principles available in the literature are expressed
as natural language texts. Therefore, software vendors and organizations
either do not use them or spend significant efforts to internalize and
apply them literally in every *engaging dashboard* development process.
We show that engaging dashboards for organizations can be automatically generated by means of automatically visualized KPIs. In this context, we present our novel approach for the automated generation of
engaging dashboards for organizations. The approach employs the decision model for visualizing KPIs that is developed based on the dashboard
design principles in the literature. We implemented our approach and
evaluated its quality in a case study.

Keywords: Key Performance Indicators · Dashboard · Visualization

1 Introduction

To determine whether they attain their goals, organizations measure the performance of their business execution. To do so, they use Key Performance Indicators (KPIs). As a means to monitor KPIs, organizations use dashboards that are
either developed by themselves or offered by software vendors. A typical dashboard aims to inform decision makers by displaying the information that they

Supported by the projects NWO AMUSE (628.006.001), TIN2015-70560-R
(MINECO/FEDER, UE), and RTI2018-101204-B-C22 (MICINN/FEDER, UE). See
amuse-project.org for more information.

© Springer Nature Switzerland AG 2019
H. Panetto et al. (Eds.): OTM 2019, LNCS 11877, pp. 363–384, 2019.
https://doi.org/10.1007/978-3-030-33246-4_24

need to improve the business processes in their organization. In particular, such information is displayed mostly as a table or a graph. By doing so, it adds visual attractiveness to grab the attention of decision makers and enable them to make informed decisions at a glance.

However, most dashboards are poorly designed displays, although adequate technology is used while developing them. Therefore, most dashboards fail to communicate efficiently and effectively since they mainly focus on decoration rather than substance [7,9,12,21,25]. For example, the dashboard depicted in Fig. 1 is an incident management dashboard of an organization[1]. By analyzing this dashboard, one can see that the dashboard goes against the dashboard design principles in the literature. For example, pie charts have many slices that make them unreadable; also, their colors are distracting, which causes misleading associations. More importantly, this is a cluttered design that does not reflect the overall status of the related business processes in that organization. Since there is an overload of information displayed as a cluttered view, decision makers need to spend substantial effort to identify the messages that the dashboard designed to convey. As a result, the dashboard is "not engaging" decision makers to take relevant decisions for improving the performance of their organization.

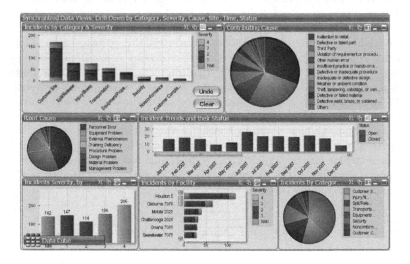

Fig. 1. An example of a non-engaging dashboard

Instead of providing only a fraction of the insight that is needed to monitor business, engaging dashboards communicate in a manner that enlightens decisions makers for informed decisions [4,9]. More specifically dashboards engage decision makers if the available dashboard design principles in the literature [7,11,12,17,19–21,23,25] are used when creating them. Moreover, engaging

---

[1] The example dashboard is taken from https://adniasolutions.com/dashboard-design-principles/introduction-to-dashboards/.

dashboards enable decision makers to sense and process the displayed information rapidly through the visualization elements, which can be quickly examined and understood without requiring any further interpretation. Not to distract decision makers with overloaded information, the right context for KPIs is visualized such a way that it inspires actions. Besides, "Are we on track?" and "How well is our organization performing its business?" are such questions in organizations to which complete answers can be obtained at a glance in engaging dashboards. Simply put, engaging dashboards do not require any investigation, analysis, or aggregation of the information, which is a must for informed decisions and is distributed inside an organization.

To overcome these issues in the field of dashboard development, several approaches are available in the literature. Within these approaches, mostly dashboards are either developed from scratch for each organization or a template is created and customized for organizations depending on their specific needs. This customization process is carried out by software vendors or by their client organizations. Although organizations may perform this customization process, it still requires a significant effort both from software vendors and organizations [7,9–12]. To deal with that, some approaches [5,13,14,22] focus on the automation of dashboard development. Creating a dashboard template and expressing the structure of a dashboard in terms of the elements of a descriptive dashboard design language are the two prominent ways in these approaches. However, these approaches either cover only a few of the state-of-the-art dashboard design principles [7,11,12,17,19–21,23,25] or require human intervention to incorporate each dashboard design principle consistently. Therefore, the KPIs that are visualized using these approaches still lead to misinterpretations.

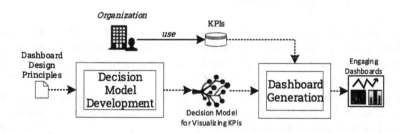

Fig. 2. Our Approach for the automated generation of engaging dashboards

With this paper, we propose a novel approach for the automated generation of *engaging* dashboards for organizations (See Fig. 2). The approach takes a set of KPIs with their attributes and values, as well as a decision model that is developed for visualizing those KPIs as inputs. As such decision models for visualizing KPIs are not readily available, we developed a decision model for visualizing KPIs, which is our second contribution in addition to the approach. The decision model that our approach uses is developed by analyzing the prominent dashboard design principles in the literature, and evaluated to show its common usability. Using the decision model, the approach determines which visualization element will be used to display each KPI on a dashboard. Depending on the attributes and the values of a KPI, a particular table or graph will be chosen as the visualization element. By means of the automatically determined visualization elements for each KPI, we automate the generation of engaging dashboards for organizations. Our approach sets itself apart from the state of the art in conveying relevant messages to decision makers via automatically generated engaging dashboards. Thus, decision makers can make informed decisions to improve the performance of their organizations.

In the evaluation of the approach, first, we check the common usability of the decision model developed for visualizing KPIs in two organizations with experts. Then, in one of the organizations, we execute the approach, and together with experts in that organization, we compare the newly created dashboard with an existing dashboard to see how our approach helps them at making informed decisions. The results that we obtained indicate that this new approach is able to fulfill the needs of organizations for improving their business.

We provide the background on dashboard design principles in Sect. 2. In Sect. 3, we present our approach for the automated generation of engaging dashboards. In Sect. 4, we evaluate the decision model for visualizing KPIs that our approach employs, and then present the results obtained while evaluating the dashboard generated using our approach in a case study. Section 5 is devoted to the discussion of the obtained results. In Sect. 6 an overview of the related work on developing dashboards for organizations is given. Finally, we present our conclusions and directions for future work in Sect. 7.

2   Theoretical Background

Dashboards are pervasive means to display important information at a glance, as needed to achieve objectives. Accordingly, much work has been conducted on developing the dashboards that are communicating important information and engaging. Notably, researchers developed guidelines [1,7,10–12,17–21,23,25,26]. Within these guidelines, they described principles for visualizing quantitative information in dashboards, i.e., dashboard design principles. Simply put, dashboard design principles describe what visual representations (e.g., various graphs) should be used and how they should be used. In this context, we list the dashboard design principles available in the literature.

2.1   Dashboard Design Principles

In the literature, numerous researchers provide various dashboard design principles [1,7,10–12,17–21,23,25,26] to develop dashboards that are communicating important information visually in the most informative way such that organizations can make informed decisions to improve their business. These dashboard design principles are mostly expressed as natural language texts in the form of rules and best practices. Some researchers [1,7,10–12,17–19,26] follow a more structured approach and provide mechanisms (e.g., a table consists of rules for selecting graphs or a diagram shows which graphs should be used in which condition) such that organizations can determine appropriate visualization elements while visualizing certain quantitative information in dashboards. In this context, we identify which of these dashboard design principles for visualizing quantitative information are more suitable to determine sense-making visual elements for displaying KPIs. Accordingly, we take the dashboard design principles that provide comprehensive guidance explained in [7,10–12,17,19–21,23,25] as the sources for developing a decision model for visualizing KPIs. In these sources, eight typical relationships that can be encoded in quantitative information are discussed. We explain each relationship by specifying the visualization elements, which are mostly recommended and used for visualizing that relationship.

Time Series: This relationship is about how a set of values change over time based on particular time units (intervals), e.g., by year, month, day, or hour. Line Graph is the graph that is well-know and mostly used for displaying this relationship. Bar Graphs and Area Graphs are also often used for displaying a time series relationship.

Ranking: How a set of values relate to each other in a particular order is described in ranking relationships. Since bars can be easily understood by any audience and best encode the values in a ranking relationship, Bar Graphs are mostly used to display a ranking relationship in dashboards.

Part-to-Whole: This relationship is about how much the parts of a whole contribute to the whole, i.e., expressing the proportions of a whole. As a common practice, Pie Graphs are used to display a part-to-whole relationship.

Deviation: In this relationship, the focus is on how one or more values in a set of values vary from a reference, e.g., forecast. This is achieved by comparing values with a reference and displaying the degree of that difference. The values that divert from a reference are represented as bars and displayed in Diverging Bar Graphs, i.e., Variance Graph in most of the time.

Distribution: This relationship expresses the way how a set of values are distributed across a particular range that is from lowest to highest. Histogram and Box-Plots are well-known graphs that are usually used for displaying a distribution relationship.

Correlation: How a set of values affect each other is expressed in a correlation relationship. Mostly, two-paired, i.e., categorized set of values are analyzed to see how they relate to each other: whether the values in one set increases or decreases based on the values in another set. Scatter Plot is the most used graph to display a correlation relationship.

Nominal Comparison: This relationship describes a set of values based on a categorical scale without an order. For instance, the revenue of each department in an organization. Bars best encode values on a categorical scale. Bars best encode values on a categorical scale and therefore Bar Graphs are the most common visualization elements used to display a nominal comparison in dashboards.

Geospatial: The values in a geospatial relationship are located based on their geographical location. Spatial Maps are always used for visualizing this relationship.

Although there are many types of graphs for visualizing quantitative information, most of them are not recommended and listed as the graph types to avoid [7,11,12,17,19–21,23,25], such as Pie, Donut, Radar, Funnel, Circle, Area Graphs, or 3D Graphs. The main reason for that is these graphs fail effectively communicating quantitative information and causing misinterpretations. Overlapping shapes, missing scales, hidden values, distracting decoration, and cluttered view are the problems these graphs commonly have.

Within the dashboard design principles available in the literature, researchers provide guidance on using colors, resizing visualization elements, and placing them in dashboards in addition to determining visualization elements. To decide how visualization elements should be placed in dashboards, layout patterns are devised. The most common layout pattern is the Z-diagram layout [3] where readers follow the shape of the letter z while scanning quantitative information. In this regard, we define our visualization element placement strategy in our approach. Moreover, to achieve the consistency in dashboards using colors and resizing visualization elements, there are guidelines in the literature [7,11,12, 19,21,23]. Since these visual aspects of dashboard development are not our the main focus of our approach, we use an embedded mechanism, i.e, a fixed set of colors and size values.

3   Approach

This section elaborates our approach for the automated generation of engaging dashboards. The procedure to automatically generate engaging dashboards consists of two tasks, as introduced in Sect. 1: (1) developing the decision model for visualizing KPIs and (2) generating dashboards automatically using the decision model. The second task is automated and takes a set of KPIs with attributes and the values of these KPIs as inputs in addition to the decision model itself. KPIs with attributes and values are taken as input in a "machine-readable" format. For this, human involvement is required. To reduce that human involvement, KPIs with attributes and values are desired to be defined such a "machine-readable" format that enables their automated analysis and computation as proposed in [6].

Unlike the second task, the first task is not automated in our approach. The reason for that is the available dashboard design principles in the literature are in the form of natural language texts. Thus, human interpretation is required to develop a decision model for visualizing KPIs using those principles [7,10–12,17,19–21,23,25]. However, this task only needs to be performed once. The decision model created as its output, and presented in this paper, can be reused in any scenario for the automated generation of engaging dashboards. In particular, it is possible to prune or extend the decision model for a given set of

KPIs of a certain organization, which is part of the second step, the automated dashboard generation. In this sense, the amount of human involvement required will highly depend on the way KPIs are defined, i.e., the amount of information provided for them in their definition and its correspondence with the attributes required by our approach. In this context, we now explain how we developed the decision model for visualizing KPIs, and then give the details of the automated dashboard generation task.

3.1   Developing the Decision Model for Visualizing KPIs

As explained in Sect. 2, we identified the most prominent sources [7,10–12,17,19–21,23,25] for dashboard design principles. Using these sources, we construct a decision model for visualizing KPIs, which is shown in Fig. 3 and encoded as such in our approach. We explain how we construct the decision model by listing our considerations below.

A typical KPI may have a single value or a set of values as quantitative information. For example, the total revenue of an organization or the total revenue of each department within an organization. We take this attribute of KPIs as the top decision point of the decision model (see ① in Fig. 3). Then, we determine how a KPI with a single value and a KPI with a set of values should be visualized using the most common types of visualization elements, namely tables and graphs.

When a KPI has a single value, bar graphs better convey the message of that KPI [7,10–12,19,21,25]. Since a KPI must have a *"target"*, that target needs to be displayed in a graph together with the value of the KPI. This can be achieved in the most informative way using a Bullet Graph [7,8,10,12,19,20] since it is a special, simplified bar graph and is designed for visualizing a value along with a comparative measure to enrich the meaning of the value.

If a KPI has a set a of values, then we need to determine the *"purpose"* of the KPI. That purpose can be taking the attention of a decision maker to *"look up"* the values or *"revealing the relationship"* between the values for the decision maker (see ② in Fig. 3). Tables are the visual elements that are designed to look up values [7,10–12,19,21,25]. While constructing a table, it is important to emphasize how individual values in a table relate to the target of the KPI, which is visualized. It is recommended to use a table where the values of the KPI represented are highlighted with colors according to the fulfillment of its target value, e.g. red if not fulfilled and green if fulfilled [7,10,12,19,21,25]. However, in addition to purpose, while looking up values, a KPI may require decision makers to focus on the *"changes of values"* rather than *"individual values"* (see ③ in Fig. 3). This can be achieved by using a Heat Map. In a Heat Map, values are represented by colors, and one can easily determine precise individual values using the color scheme if needed.

When the purpose of a KPI is to reveal the relationship between its values to decision makers, graphs are used. To determine what graphs are particularly useful for specific relationships (see ④ in Fig. 3), we take the relationships as the base that we listed in Sect. 2, and then describe how each relationship can be visualized such that decision makers will be engaged in.

Time Series: Although Line Graph is the commonly used graph for visualizing a time-series relationship [7,10,12,17,19–21,23,25], connecting the data points representing values as a line will cause a misleading communication when the values are not collected "*at a regular interval*". Dot Plot deals with that problem by displaying a time-series relationship in the form of points in which missing values are not displayed. Furthermore, a KPI may aim decision makers to "*focus on the history of changes in values*" over time instead of the values over time (see ⑤ in Fig. 3). To this end, there is a special graph, namely Sparkline [10–12], which provides a simple and quick view of the history of changes in values at a glance to determine whether there is anything unexpected. Although bar graphs and area graphs are commonly used for this relationship, they miserably fail to show changes over time [10–12], and they especially clutter the display when values are categorized or benchmarked against various comparative measures, e.g., target or forecast.

Ranking: Since a KPI must have a target, a Bullet Graph will perform better than classical Bar Graphs at displaying values along with a comparative measure [7,8,10,12,19,20]. If "*changes in rankings over time*" are important, Slope Graph outperforms among other graphs [10–12,23] since it focuses on the evaluation of rankings between two or more points in time (see ⑥ in Fig. 3).

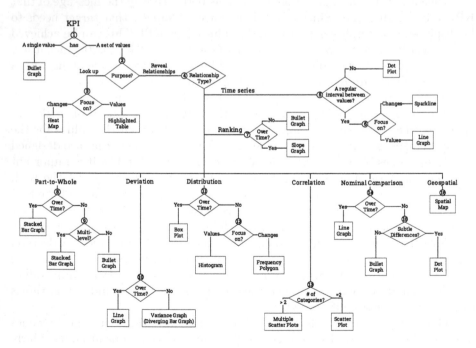

Fig. 3. The decision model used for visualizing KPIs within the approach

Part-to-Whole: Although Pie Graphs are quite often used for visualizing part-to-whole relationships, they are listed in the graphs to avoid [7, 10–12, 19 21, 23, 25] due to several reasons. One of the reasons for that is that view will be cluttered when there are many slices, and many of them have similar sizes. Another reason is the common practice of creating a slice named as "others," which mostly causes misleading interpretations [10–12, 19, 21]. In addition, as seen in many examples [7, 10–12, 19], the total of slices is not checked correctly, e.g., total does not add up to 100. To overcome these problems, bars are recommended to encode values [7, 10–12, 19–21, 23, 25]. While displaying a *"part-whole-relationship over time"* Stacked Bar Graphs outperform among other bar graphs since they will not require the duplication of each proportion for each time unit, which causes a cluttered view [10–12]. When a KPI is solely about a part-to-whole relationship with no time involvement, it is required to check whether a *"multi-level"* hierarchy exists between values (see ⑧ in Fig. 3). For example, the revenue of an organization may be the aggregation of the revenues of its branches, and even the revenue of each branch may be the total of the revenue of various departments. When there is a multi-level hierarchy in a part-to-whole relationship, we select Stacked Bar Graphs. Otherwise, Bullet Graph outperforms than classical Bar Graph displaying a KPI with its target. In Stacked Bar Graphs, the target of a KPI can be displayed using lines with a secondary axis.

Deviation: Since Diverging Bar Graphs perform well visualizing a deviation relationship [7, 11, 12, 21, 25] and there are no competing alternatives, we select them for visualizing the KPIs that reveal a deviation relationship. However, to see a *"deviation relationship from a time-perspective"*, i.e., how deviations evolve, the Line Graph stands out as the best option [10–12, 20, 21, 25] due to its power of showing things over time in a simple way (see ⑨ in Fig. 3).

Distribution: Although Box-Plots are common in visualizing distributions, interpreting Box-Plots requires specific statistic knowledge [10–12]. To take actions based on the displayed relationship, decision makers will prefer simple graphs that require less effort [7, 10–12, 19, 23]. As the Histogram is a special type of bar graphs and bars are easy to understand by everyone, we select the Histogram (see ⑫ in Fig. 3) as the graph to visualize KPIs when the focus is on values across the range of distribution. If the *"changes of the shape"* of distribution are the main focus, Frequency Polygon (see ⑫ in Fig. 3) outperforms than Histogram [7, 10–12, 19–21, 23, 25]. Moreover, when a distribution relationship needs to be displayed *"over time"* (see ⑩ in Fig. 3) we select to use Box-Plots (see ⑩ in Fig. 3) since others will cause a cluttered view [7, 10–12, 19–21, 23, 25] due to the duplication of the range of the distribution.

Correlation: Although Scatter plots perform quite well visualizing a correlation relationship, an increase in the number of categories will make a Scatter Plot very complex. As the biggest negative effect of this increase, the readability and interoperability of a Scatter Plot will dramatically decrease since adding categories will hinder some values beyond others. Although circles are used to support the added categories in scatter plots [10, 11, 20, 21, 25], they overlap and decrease the understandability when values are closer to each other. Multiple Scatter Plots can be used. In this way, when a correlation between two categories is to be displayed, scatter plots are used. Otherwise, we propose multiple scatter plots to be used. A Multiple Scatter Plot consists of a number of scatter plots where each scatter plot displays the correlation in the values of two categories (see ⑬ in Fig. 3). In each scatter plot, the target of a KPI can be visualized using lines.

Nominal Comparison: As discussed in ranking relationship, instead of Bar Graphs, we select the Bullet Graph due to its simplified and beneficial view where bars best encode a particular relationship. However, if bars become similar in length, detecting the subtle differences between them can become difficult. To capture these subtle differences, a Dot Plot is the most effective alternative in which the scale has no longer need to start at zero, which is a must [7,10–12] for Bar Graphs (see ⑭ in Fig. 3). When the aim is to display a set of values on a categorical scale over time, bars fail since they cause a cluttered view [7,10–12,19–21,23,25] by duplicating each discrete value for each time point. For that reason, we select the Line Graph to show a nominal comparison relationship over time, where a separate line represents each discrete value (see ⑮ in Fig. 3).

Geospatial: The de-facto way of displaying a geospatial relationship is using a map called Spatial Map (see ⑯ in Fig. 3) and no criticism have been found in this regard [7,10–12,17,19–21,23,25].

To execute the developed decision model, it is required to provide the KPI attributes that map to the decision points of the decision model and identify which visualization element needs to be used. In this regard, first, we identified what attributes of KPIs are taken into account while visualizing KPIs within the described dashboard design principles in the literature. Then, we transformed the identified KPI attributes into a single set. Finally, we checked the completeness of the identified KPI attributes against the developed decision model. This check is conducted by controlling the existence of mapping both from each KPI attribute to the decision points in the decision model and vice versa. The identified KPI attributes are listed in Table 1.

3.2 Generating Dashboards Automatically

To generate dashboards automatically in our approach, a set of KPIs with attributes, their values, and the decision model for visualizing KPIs are needed as inputs. These attributes are common attributes described when defining KPIs [6]. The approach determines what kind of visualization element will be utilized for each KPI by applying the given KPIs with their attributes on the given decision model. In particular, a mapping from the decision points in the given decision model is searched for the given KPIs with attributes. The approach completes this search when a visualization element for each KPI is determined. Then, each determined visualization element is created and placed in dashboards, as shown in Fig. 4.

Table 1. KPI attributes required by the decision model

KPI attribute	Definition
Relationship type of values	Describes how the values of the KPI are related. For example, time series, correlation, ranking, part-to-whole, nominal comparison, or distribution
Purpose	Whether the KPI is about looking up its values or revealing the relationship between its values
Focus	Describes what is the focus of the KPI with respect to its purpose attribute. Example values: look up-changes, look up-values, relationship-changes in a time series, relationship-values in a distribution
Time interval	Whether the KPI needs to be displayed over time
KPI values	Describe the quantitative information of the KPI
Categories	The discrete groups in which one or more values exist. For example, the total revenue is a KPI that has a single category, which contains a single value. However, the revenue per department is a KPI that will have a category for each department
Sort direction	Describes how the categories or the values in a category will be ordered, e.g., ascending or descending. This is especially important in ranking and distribution relationships
Multi-level hierarchy	Whether there is a hierarchy or main-sub grouping in the categories attribute of the KPI. For example, main group: region and sub-group: county
Regular interval between values	This will be determined using the attribute time interval. If there is any missing value in the values of the KPI based its time interval, the branch "No" will be selected in the related decision point of the decision model
Subtle difference threshold for the values of the KPI	Describes the limit of the difference between the values of the KPI that should be clearly detectable at a nominal comparison

In addition to the KPI attributes, listed above as required by the decision model, the approach uses a set of KPI attributes while creating dashboards and displaying according to the values of KPIs. Those KPI attributes are listed in Table 2.

To determine how many dashboards need to be created, we defined a strategy so-called Dashboard Creation Strategy in the approach. The strategy is based on the relations between the KPIs of an organization. More specifically, the KPIs that are related to the business processes in a particular process area will be grouped and placed onto a particular dashboard. For example, the KPIs related to the sales process and the KPIs involved in the purchasing process of an organization are combined into the dashboard, Order Management. In addition,

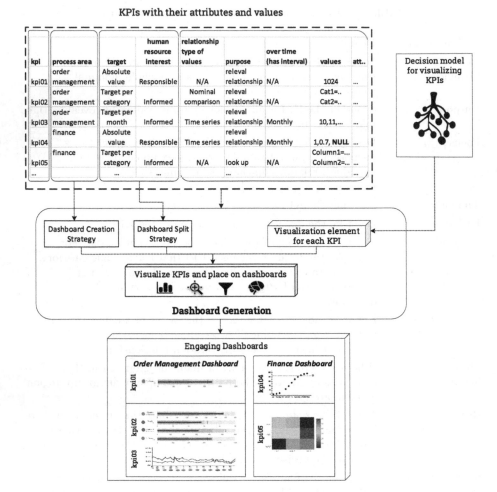

Fig. 4. Generating engaging dashboards for organizations

the KPIs about creditors and debtors are grouped into the dashboard, namely Finance dashboard.

The creation of each determined visualization element for a KPI consists of four tasks: (1) creating the visualization parts for the target thresholds of the KPI on the visualization element, (2) creating the visualization parts for the KPI values, (3) creating the visualization parts for the target of the KPI, and finally (4) combining all parts as a single visual element, e.g., graph or table. In the first task, the approach creates bars and arranges them with respect to the boundaries of target thresholds. Then, in the second task, the approach creates the visualization part in the form of bars, dots, or lines using the KPI values. These forms depend on the determined visualization element. Depending on the type of the target of the KPI (e.g., achievement, reduction, absolute, zero, or

Table 2. Additional KPI attributes required for visualizing dashboards

KPI attribute	Definition
Process area	The category of the business process that is related to the KPI. This attribute is used for determining the number of dashboards that will be created. Example values: order management, finance
Target	The value or value-range that needs to be achieved with respect to the related strategic goals of the organization. The target and its type may change over time for the KPI. Example target values: zero, at minimum €50K, a reduction of 10%, precisely 7 days, or within 1–3 days
Target Thresholds	The set of value-range that shows to what extent the target of the KPI is achieved. Each threshold has a lower and upper bound value. For example, good: [KPI target-10K, KPI target-30K], bad: [KPI target-30K, KPI target-50K]
Human resource interest	Represents the interest of the human resources in the KPI. It can have a value of Responsible or Informed. This attribute is used within the dashboard split strategy of the approach
Name	The textual description used to define the KPI
Unit	The quantity used as the standard for the measurement of the KPI's values. Although this is not important at determining visualization elements, it is essential to convey an informative message via KPIs

min-max), the visual signs that indicate the target are created as a visualization part in the third task. In addition, in the third task, noticeable alerts that indicate whether the KPI and its categories are on target or not (see the cross, check, and warning signs used as alerts in Fig. 5) are created. In the last task, the approach combines all these visualization parts as a single visualization element considering the embedded coloring[2], orientation, and resizing rules for visualization in it. How many categories should be visualized in graphs is determined using an implicit, configurable parameter in the approach. The reason for that is to determine the orientation (horizontal or vertical), which increases the readability. For example, a ranking relationship better reads when it is horizontal and has a maximum of 10 categories where the rest is grouped as "others."

Similarly, to determine how created visual elements will be placed on dashboards is determined using the strategy, Dashboard Split Strategy, that we defined in the approach. In this strategy, the approach creates a flow through a combination of visual weight and visual direction to take advantage of how people read through a design. The created flow splits a dashboard into two areas: top and bottom. By applying the most common layout pattern (the Z-diagram layout [3]), which is recommended for simple designs, the approach defines the route that the human eye travels on these areas: left to right and top to bottom. To determine the order of the KPIs that the human eye should read in this travel

---

[2] http://colorbrewer2.org is used as the source for color selection.

the approach uses the KPI attribute "human resource interest." The KPIs that have the value "Responsible" in their "human resource interest" attribute will be placed to the top area of dashboards. Then, the KPIs that have the value "Informed" in their "human resource interest" attribute will be placed to the bottom area of dashboards. The KPIs will be ordered in an ascending order based on their names in each area unless there is a particular ordering for displaying KPIs, such as the relevance of KPIs for decision makers.

In the next section, we give the details of the evaluation of both the approach[3] and the decision model for visualizing KPIs.

4 Evaluation

In this section, first, we explain how we evaluated the decision model for visualizing KPIs, which was described in Sect. 3. Then, we elaborate on the evaluation of the proposed approach in a case study.

4.1 Evaluation of the Decision Model

We evaluated the decision model within two organizations, A and B for confidentiality reasons. We did so by discussing our considerations and walking through each path in the decision model together with the experts in these organizations (for more details on their background, see Tables 3 and 4). The experts whom we worked together are actively involved in the dashboard development process in their organizations. We collected their opinions about the decision model using the three-points Likert-type scale (agree, somewhat agree, and disagree). While collecting experts' opinions in each organization, we had an open discussion meeting on the usefulness of the decision model to the needs of each organization at dashboard development. In particular, we gathered opinions related to two aspects of the decision model: (1) decision points, and 2 visualization elements. Then, an average value is calculated for each organization using the collected expert opinions. That average value shows to what extent the decision model is useful to the needs of an organization at visualizing KPIs.

Organization A: In order to automatically generate ERP software from a model, a Dutch ERP software vendor is developing a novel model-driven software generation approach. As part of that approach, a declarative modeling language is being developed that is aimed at modeling an organization's business in the form of an ontological enterprise model. In order to build dashboards automatically for its client organizations with the power of that declarative modeling language, this company is currently investigating how KPIs can be automatically visualized. Since this is highly related to the approach that we propose,

---

[3] The implementation of our approach for the automated generation of engaging dashboard is available at http://amuse-project.org/software/. In the implementation, two *Python* libraries are preferred: *Plotly* is for visualizing KPIs and *Dash* is for creating dashboards.

Table 3. Evaluation of the decision model in Organization A

Expert	Area of expertise	Years of expertise	Meeting duration (hours)	To what extent agree on the decision points in the decision model	To what extent agree on the visualization elements in the decision model
Software Architect-1	Dashboard development	>5	1	Agree: 13 Somewhat agree: 2 Not agree: 0	Agree: 20 Somewhat agree: 3 Not agree: 0
Software Architect-2	Product management and Information visualization	>20	1	Agree: 13 Somewhat agree: 2 Not agree: 0	Agree: 20 Somewhat agree: 3 Not agree: 0
Manager	Product management and Dashboard development	>15	1	Agree: 12 Somewhat agree: 3 Not agree: 0	Agree: 19 Somewhat agree: 4 Not agree: 0

in this company, we evaluated the decision model. The details of the evaluation of the decision model in this organization are listed in Table 3. As shown in the table, the experts on average *agree* on the decision points and also on the visualization elements in the decision model. Only for a minority of the decision points and the visualization elements in the decision elements they indicated their partial agreement, i.e., somewhat agree. In particular, the experts shared their partial agreement for the following decision points in the decision model: ⑥, ⑫, and ⑮. Similarly, for the visualization elements at these decision points, the experts shared their partial agreement. The experts did not mention any disagreement for the decision points or the visualization elements in the decision model.

Organization B: To monitor the usage of physical resources, the IT department of a Dutch bank uses a dashboard. This dashboard consists of a set of KPIs in which particular psychical resources are monitored with respect to their response rates. A performance management expert maintains that dashboard in accordance with the change requests coming from the performance monitoring chapter lead of the IT department. We followed the same procedure that we explained above as for the evaluation of the decision model in this organization. The details of the evaluation of the decision model in this organization are listed in Table 4. As depicted in the table, the experts agreed on average more than 70% of the decision points and also the visualization elements in the decision model. In addition, only for one visualization element in the decision model a disagreement is mentioned. This was for the Box Plot graph that is identified for visualizing a distribution relationship over time. As in the evaluation in Organization A, we received partial agreement feedback in Organization B for the decision points ⑥, ⑫, and ⑮ in the decision model.

Table 4. Evaluation of the decision model in Organization B

Expert	Area of expertise	Years of expertise	Meeting duration (hours)	To what extent agree on the decision points in the decision model	To what extent agree on the visualization elements in the decision model
Performance Management Expert	Dashboard development	>20	1.5	Agree: 12 Somewhat agree: 3 Not agree: 0	Agree: 18 Somewhat agree: 4 Not agree: 1
Performance Monitoring Chapter Lead	Dashboard design and monitoring	>15	1.5	Agree: 12 Somewhat agree: 3 Not agree: 0	Agree: 18 Somewhat agree: 4 Not agree: 1

In both organizations that we evaluated the decision model, the calculated average value of the usefulness of the decision model for the needs of the organizations is *agree*.

4.2 Evaluation of the Approach

The proposed approach was evaluated in the first organization, which we evaluated the decision model, namely Organization A. In that organization, the three aforementioned experts developed a finance dashboard template to create dashboards for the client organizations of the company. Together with the same three experts whom we worked in the evaluation of the decision model, we created a sample dashboard using that template. After that, the created sample dashboard was used as the *existing dashboard* in the evaluation of the approach. We executed our approach for the KPIs, in total 8, contained in the existing dashboard, and created a new dashboard. Then, together with the aforementioned three experts, we evaluated our approach by comparing the existing dashboard with the *newly generated dashboard*. The results that we obtained are explained below.

As shown in Fig. 5, the KPIs that have implicit target values on the existing dashboard, namely KPI-1, KPI-2, KPI-6, and KPI-7 are displayed differently in the newly generated dashboard than the existing dashboard. These KPIs are visualized as bullet graphs in the newly generated dashboard, since each of them has a single value. Moreover, the target values of these KPIs are also highlighted using a diamond shape; corresponding alerts are added next to each KPI based on those target values. Besides, the approach visualized KPI-4 as a dot plot as that KPI aims to display a nominal comparison relationship. To do so, whether the differences between values are subtle is checked with respect to the given subtle difference threshold by the experts.

Furthermore, the approach visualized 3 out of 8 KPIs, namely KPI-3, KPI-5, and KPI-8 slightly different than the existing dashboard. These KPIs are visualized in the newly generated dashboard in a way such that each KPI conveys its intended message clearly. More specifically, since KPI-3 is about a nominal

Fig. 5. The existing dashboard (left) in comparison to the newly generated dashboard (right)

comparison and has no subtle differences between its values, this KPI is visualized as a bullet graph. As KPI-5 presents values over time, the visualization element for that KPI has not changed. The only change is the addition of its target. KPI-8 reveals a ranking relationship, and it is visualized as bullet graphs accordingly. For each of these three KPIs, the approach added a noticeable alert next to each graph to indicate target achievement.

Since there were no defined values in the human resource interest attribute of the displayed 8 KPIs, the KPIs are displayed in the top area of the newly generated dashboard and placed in orange boxes, which is the assigned color for the value "responsible" of human resource interest attribute.

To determine the implications of the differences between the existing dashboard and the newly generated dashboard in the evaluation of the approach, we had an open discussion meeting with the experts who were involved in the evaluation of the approach. The experts confirmed that visualizing KPI-1, KPI-2, KPI-6, and KPI-7 as bullet graphs in the newly created dashboard helps them to observe a KPI along with its comparative measure, e.g., target. Similarly, the experts agreed on visualizing KPI-4 as a dot plot as the subtle difference become visible to make precise decisions. In addition, as KPI-1 and KPI-6 are visualized different in the newly generated dashboard than the existing dashboard and become noticeable, the experts decided to check the need for these KPIs. Besides, the experts agreed both on the usefulness of the displayed target thresholds (e.g., perfect, good) and the alerts (cross, check, and warning signs) that display whether the KPIs are on target and to what extent at a glance.

In the following section, we discuss the results that we obtained both in the evaluation of the decision model and also in the evaluation of the approach.

5   Discussion

Regarding the evaluation of the decision model we proposed, as listed in Tables 3 and 4, we obtained a partial agreement for the following decision points in the decision model: ⑥, ⑫, and ⑮. Similarly, for the visualization elements at these decision points, we obtained a partial agreement. The experts who are involved in the evaluation of the decision model expressed that the difference between the visualization elements at these decision points is not big since these decision points are rarely investigated in their organizations while developing dashboards. This shows that our decision model has a wide coverage of decision points, considering even the less common scenarios. Moreover, the experts mentioned that the visualization elements in those decision points, namely Slope Graph, Frequency Polygon, and Bullet Graph are very simple and useful. However, the experts noted that these graphs are not completely supported in most business intelligence software products although they are not very new. This means that our decision model helps organizations to determine simple and useful visualization elements for creating engaging dashboards.

Furthermore, there was no decision point that the experts neither in Organization A nor in Organization B disagree. However, only for one visualization element in the decision model, we received a disagreement in Organization B. This was about the Box Plot graph that is used for visualizing a distribution relationship over time. Since the Box Plot graph requires particular knowledge of statistics to interpret the message of it, especially for decision makers who are not familiar with the Box Plot graph grasping the conveyed message with it may not be easy. However, although there are alternatives, they have more drawbacks we think that required knowledge of statistics can be easily obtained.

As for the evaluation of the automated approach itself, since the newly generated dashboard enabled organizations to check and eliminate the KPIs that are not often a source for decision making in their organization, in that respect, the approach helps organizations to focus on the KPIs that are relevant to their business.

The results of the evaluation confirm that the approach proposed in this paper is of sufficient quality to show its practical usage. On the one hand, as we observed in the evaluation, the newly generated dashboard by the approach can help organizations to clearly observe KPIs along with their comparative measures. On the other hand, the approach enables organizations to focus on the message conveyed via KPIs with engaging visualizations, which is the main substance for wise decisions. Moreover, organizations can detect whether any KPI is not a good source for decision making and avoid misleading communications.

Software vendors that focus on automatically generating dashboards for their client organizations can apply our approach. To do so, these software vendors need to provide KPIs with attributes and the values of these KPIs to our approach in addition to the decision model, which is already encoded in the approach. For obtaining these required inputs, organizations may leverage formal notations for defining KPIs, such as PPINOT [6]. Using them, on the one hand, organizations can reduce their management efforts on KPIs since these formal KPI definitions enable their automated analysis and computation. On the other hand, formally defined KPIs can be integrated into our approach facilitating the automated generation of dashboards.

One of the limitations of the approach is the decision model development task since it is not automated. In addition, our approach is limited to visualizing KPIs as tables and graphs. However, in the literature, there are principles on how to combine multiple visual elements as a single visual element, e.g., multipanes for visualizing a KPI. Additionally, the visual aspects of visual elements such as fonts, coloring, responsiveness are not covered so far.

6 Related Work

In this section, we list some of the works that relate to the approach we proposed for the automated generation of engaging dashboards.

A model-driven dashboard development approach is proposed in [5] to automatically create dashboards with the code necessary for their deployment. To create a dashboard automatically, the approach requires a dashboard user to model both the dashboard and the related KPIs. Then, an engine executes the model and creates the dashboard with its code. To handle the change management of dashboards, the approach is enriched with the observers [22] who manage the maintenance of dashboards. However, to derive dashboards automatically using this approach, organizations need to have the intensive knowledge required to visualize KPIs in an effective way and should model each dashboard using the notation in the approach. Since these tasks are manual, the approach will require a significant effort of every organization that wants to apply it.

To create customized dashboards automatically considering the requirements of different users, Vázquez-Ingelmo et al. have proposed an approach that uses domain engineering practices [24]. Based on the analysis of the similarities and differences between users' requirements and existing dashboards, a feature model is constructed. The constructed feature model specifies what visualization will be created within a dashboard. Since the approach uses existing dashboards as a base, for each existing dashboard users' requirements need to be obtained. Therefore, using this approach, each organization will need to spend a great effort in addition to the effort for internalizing dashboard design principles.

To visualize KPIs for production planning on a BPMN model in the manufacturing domain, Heidema et al. [13] present an approach. Based on the dashboard design principles defined in [11], the applicability of visualizations are determined in the context of BPMN. Then, a set of KPIs for the manufacturing domain, which are listed in ISO 22400 are automatically visualized on a BPMN model. However, the visualization elements that are supported by the approach are limited. For example, the values in a time series relationship cannot be seen since only sparklines are used, which do not contain values. Moreover, some relationship types are not covered, such as part-to-whole, distribution, correlation, and geospatial. Displaying the values over time in a various relationship is not addressed comprehensively within the approach. Since the approach is dependent on BPMN models, adding visualization elements on the relatively large BPMN models with numerous elements will clutter the view and distract decision makers.

To automatically build a monitoring infrastructure, Koetter and Kochanowski [16] have proposed a modeling language, called ProGoalML for KPIs. The language enables organizations to model their KPIs in their business process models, i.e., annotate the business process models using the language components proposed. Kintz [14] has proposed a dashboard design methodology that can transform the inputs created by ProGoalML to formal KPI definitions, which are required as inputs to derive dashboards automatically by the dashboard engine—a component of the proposed methodology. Kintz et al. have extended the proposed methodology by adding support to create the dashboards that are customized to users [15]. To determine how KPIs should be visualized, from data types to visualizations 4 mappings are employed within the aforementioned methodology. However, in these mappings, it is unclear what the data types imply, i.e., how the data type of a KPI can be determined is not explained. Furthermore, some important relationships in quantitative information, e.g., correlation, ranking, are not covered. Additionally, a data type is mapped to two visualizations in a mapping, which causes ambiguity.

As explained above, to develop the dashboards that are communicating important information and are engaging, each organization, first, has to internalize dashboard design principles, and then apply them. However, this is time-consuming and costly. To provide a solution to these problems, we proposed an approach for the automated generation of engaging dashboards.

7   Conclusion and Future Work

In this paper, we presented a novel approach aimed at the automated generating of engaging dashboards for organizations by means of automatically visualizing KPIs. A set of KPIs with their attributes and values and a decision model developed for visualizing those KPIs are the required inputs by the approach. The approach determines which visualization elements (a table or a graph) will be used to visualize each KPI using the given decision model. The approach creates the dashboards based on the dashboard creating strategy encoded in it, and then places the built visualization elements on dashboards using the dashboard split strategy, which is also encoded in it. Since the available dashboard design principles are not in the machine-readable form, we described how a decision model for visualizing KPIs can be devised.

To evaluate our approach, we conducted two tasks: an evaluation of the developed decision model and the evaluation of the created dashboards using our approach. The former was carried out in two organizations: an ERP software vendor and a bank. The latter was done with the ERP software vendor. In both tasks, we conducted the evaluation by informal interviews with the experts in the organizations who are actively involved in dashboard development. As a result, we showed that the approach enables organizations focusing on the messages conveyed via KPIs with engaging visualizations to make informed decisions for improving the performance of their organizations. In most recent approaches, visualizing KPIs is a manual endeavor and needs to be carried out in every single organization. Thus, we feel confident to that our approach lowers the efforts of software vendors for developing engaging dashboards for their client organizations and the efforts of these organizations doing this themselves.

In future work, we want to extend our approach by adding predictive technologies. In particular, we want to predict the values of KPIs such that decision makers can take preventive actions instead of corrective actions, which costs more to improve the business processes in their organizations. Moreover, to provide insights for organizations by means of the benchmarks that are developed using the relevant KPIs for them, we plan to integrate this approach with the approach we presented in [2]. In addition, we will add the support for automatically providing the consistency of visual aspects (e.g., colors, size, and spacing) in dashboards.

References

1. Abela, A.V.: The Presentation: A Story About Communicating Successfully with Very Few Slides. CreateSpace Independent Publishing Platform, Middletown (2010)
2. Aksu, Ü., Schunselaar, D.M.M., Reijers, H.A.: An approach for automatically deriving key performance indicators from ontological enterprise models. In: Proceedings of the 7th International Symposium on Data-driven Process Discovery and Analysis, SIMPDA (2017)
3. Arnold, E.: Graphics overview. J. Appl. Commun. **62**(3), 6 (1979)
4. Barr, S.: Prove It!: How to Create a High-performance Culture and Measurable Success. Wiley, Milton (2017)
5. Chowdhary, P., Palpanas, T., Pinel, F., Chen, S.K., Wu, F.Y.: Model-driven dashboards for business performance reporting. In: Proceedings of the 10th IEEE International Enterprise Distributed Object Computing Conference, EDOC (2006)
6. del-Río-Ortega, A., Resinas, M., Cabanillas, C., Cortés, A.R.: On the definition and design-time analysis of process performance indicators. Inf. Syst. **38**(4), 470–490 (2013)
7. Eckerson, W.W.: Performance Dashboards: Measuring, Monitoring, and Managing Your Business, 2nd edn. Wiley, Hoboken (2010)

8. Few, S.: Bullet graph design specification. https://www.perceptualedge.com/articles/misc/Bullet_Graph_Design_Spec.pdf
9. Few, S.: Why most dashboards fail (2007). http://www.perceptualedge.com/articles/misc/WhyMostDashboardsFail.pdf
10. Few, S.: Now You See It: Simple Visualization Techniques for Quantitative Analysis. Analytics Press, Berkeley (2009)
11. Few, S.: Show Me the Numbers, 2nd edn. Analytics Press, Burlingame (2012)
12. Few, S.: Information Dashboard Design. Analytics Press, Oakland (2013)
13. Heidema, Y., Vanderfeesten, I., Erasmus, J., Keulen, R., Dizy, K.: Visualizing performance indicators for production planning in BPMN 2.0 in the manufacturing domain. Master's thesis, Eindhoven University of Technology (2018)
14. Kintz, M.: A semantic dashboard description language for a process-oriented dashboard design methodology. In: Proceedings of the 2nd International Workshop on Model-based Interactive Ubiquitous Systems, MODIQUITOUS (2012)
15. Kintz, M., Kochanowski, M., Koetter, F.: Creating user-specific business process monitoring dashboards with a model-driven approach. In: Proceedings of the 5th International Conference on Model-Driven Engineering and Software Development, MODELSWARD (2017)
16. Koetter, F., Kochanowski, M.: Goal-oriented model-driven business process monitoring using ProGoalML. In: Abramowicz, W., Kriksciuniene, D., Sakalauskas, V. (eds.) BIS 2012. LNBIP, vol. 117, pp. 72–83. Springer, Heidelberg (2012). https://doi.org/10.1007/978-3-642-30359-3_7
17. Kriebel, A.: Visualvocabulary. https://public.tableau.com/profile/andy.kriebel#!/vizhome/VisualVocabulary/VisualVocabulary
18. Lyons, J., Evergreen, S.: Qualitative chart chooser 3.0. https://stephanieevergreen.com/qualitative-chart-chooser-3/
19. McDaniel, E., McDaniel, S.: The Accidental Analyst: Show Your Data Who's Boss. Freakalytics, Seattle (2012)
20. McDaniel, E., McDaniel, S.: Rapid Graphs with Tableau Software 8: The Original Guide for the Accidental Analyst. CreateSpace Independent Publishing Platform (2013)
21. Nussbaumer, C.K.: Storytelling with Data: A Data Visualization Guide for Business Professionals. Wiley, Hoboken (2015)
22. Palpanas, T., Chowdhary, P., Mihaila, G.A., Pinel, F.: Integrated model-driven dashboard development. Inf. Syst. Front. 9(2–3), 195–208 (2007)
23. Tufte, E.R.: The Visual Display of Quantitative Information. Graphics Press, Cheshire (1992)
24. Vázquez-Ingelmo, A., García-Peñalvo, F.J., Therón, R.: Application of domain engineering to generate customized information dashboards. In: Zaphiris, P., Ioannou, A. (eds.) LCT 2018, Part II. LNCS, vol. 10925, pp. 518–529. Springer, Cham (2018). https://doi.org/10.1007/978-3-319-91152-6_40
25. Wexler, S., Shaffer, J., Cotgreave, A.: The Big Book of Dashboards: Visualizing Your Data Using Real-world Business Scenarios. Wiley, Hoboken (2017)
26. Zelazny, G.: Say It with Charts Workbook. McGraw-Hill, New York (2004)

Process-Based Quality Management in Care: Adding a Quality Perspective to Pathway Modelling

Peggy Richter[✉] and Hannes Schlieter

Faculty of Business and Economics, Chair of Wirtschaftsinformatik,
esp. Systems Development, Technische Universität Dresden,
Helmholtzstr. 10, 01069 Dresden, Germany
peggy.richter2@tu-dresden.de

Abstract. Care pathways (CPs) are used as a tool to organize complex care processes and to foster the quality management in general. However, the quality management potentials have not been sufficiently exploited yet, since the development, documentation, and controlling of quality indicators (QIs) for quality management purposes are not fully integrated to the process standards defined by CPs. To support the integration of a quality perspective in CPs, the paper addresses the questions which and how quality concepts can be integrated into the process documentation in order to support managers, health service providers, and patients. Therefore, we extended the widely accepted modelling language "Business Process Model and Notation" (BPMN) with a quality perspective. The conceptualization is grounded on a systematic literature review on (quality) indicator modelling. Together with previous work on the conceptualization of QIs in health care, it provided the basis for a comprehensive domain requirements analysis. Following a design-oriented research approach, the requirements were evaluated and used to design a BPMN extension by implementing the quality indicator enhancements as BPMN meta model extension. All design decisions were evaluated in a feedback workshop with a domain expert experienced in quality management and certification of cancer centres on national and international level. The approach is demonstrated with an example from stroke care. The proposed language extension provides a tool to be used for the governance of care processes based on QIs and for the implementation of a more real-time, pathway-based quality management in health care.

Keywords: Care pathways · Pathway modelling · Quality management · Integrated care · Systematic literature review · Conceptual modelling · BPMN extension

1 Introduction

Care pathways are recognized as an appropriate tool for the organization and stream-lining of complex integrated care processes for a well-defined patient population [1]. Especially against the background of demographic changes, skilled worker shortages, an increasing number of multimorbid people with chronic diseases, and economic

© Springer Nature Switzerland AG 2019
H. Panetto et al. (Eds.): OTM 2019, LNCS 11877, pp. 385–403, 2019.
https://doi.org/10.1007/978-3-030-33246-4_25

efficiency efforts in Western countries, the management of the care process is of high importance [2–4]. Besides the organization of the core clinical process, i.e. interactions between patients and health service providers, care pathways are also important for process governance and compliance purposes as well as for the establishment of an integrated process management. However, the potentials of defined process standards by care pathways has not been sufficiently exploited so far. This is particularly apparent in quality management, which supports health care organizations be more pro-active, improves operational efficiency and outcomes, increases patient safety, and reduces errors [5, 6]. Although care pathways are an important means to this end, especially in integrated care settings [4, 7], the development, documentation and controlling of quality indicators (QIs) for quality management purposes are yet not based on the process standards defined by care pathways. On the one hand, there are process modelling languages for the conceptual representation of care pathways (e.g. [8]). On the other hand, the issue of conceptualizing and modelling indicators, especially for performance management purposes is comprehensively addressed in the literature (e.g. [9]). However, the integration of both is yet not sufficiently supported.

This isolated view on quality management and care pathways hampers the comprehensive, process-based quality improvement intentions of healthcare organizations, e.g. the pathway-based identification of activities which reduce or enhance quality and the real-time monitoring of quality levels in care provision [10]. Annual quality reports do not allow quick reactions based on current quality levels. To address this shortcoming, the objective of the paper at hand is the integration of a quality perspective in care pathways represented as conceptual process models. The focus of this paper is on design decisions, i.e. the questions of which and how quality concepts shall be integrated in care pathways in order to support managers of health institutions, health service providers, and patients in terms of quality information and management tasks. The presented approach contributes as a tool for the governance of care processes based on QIs and for the development of real-time process-based quality dashboards complementing the pathway view and supporting continuous quality management.

The remainder of the paper is structured as follows: In Sect. 2 the applied methods are described. Section 3 addresses the current body of knowledge in the fields of indicator modelling in relation to process modelling. In Sect. 4 the integration of a quality perspective in conceptual care pathway models is described by extending the widely accepted and used Business Process Model and Notation (BPMN). This involves the definition and expert evaluation of user requirements for the integration of QIs in pathway models, the development and description of a domain ontology, and, building upon that, the extension design of the modelling language. The approach is demonstrated with an example from stroke care in Sect. 5. The paper closes with a conclusion and a discussion of open issues in Sect. 6.

2 Methods

The presented work comprises both the design and development as well as the demonstration phase of a design-oriented information systems (IS) research project [11, 12]. The general focus of this design science research (DSR) genre is the instruction of the design and operation of IS and of innovative IS concepts [13]. The addressed DSR artefact is a method in terms of the extension of a modelling language [14], intended to be used for pathway-based quality management in healthcare settings. This approach is reasonable since the adaption of an existing modelling language with domain-specific concepts is expected to be less expensive than the invention of a new one [15]. The relevance for the language extension is reasoned in additional requirements from the environment which are yet not addressed, i.e. pathway-related QIs required in the context of quality management initiatives in the stroke and cancer care context [16] (supporting the DSR relevance cycle according to Hevner [17]). We conducted interviews with domain experts to gain insights into these two care domains and to validate requirements for the language extension. The presented research contributes to the current knowledge base with a quality-integrating pathway ontology and a corresponding BPMN extension. The work is grounded in the theoretical knowledge base regarding meta modelling, modelling language (esp. BPMN) extensibility, and indicator modelling (supporting the DSR rigor cycle according to Hevner [17]). The applied DSR approach and their relation in the DSR framework are shown in Fig. 1. For the extension of an existing process modelling language with a quality perspective we follow the requirements-based extension procedure described by Braun and Schlieter [18]. This approach was chosen since it includes a deep consideration of the requirements resulting from the application domain, which is of high importance for design-oriented research. The extension procedure is outlined in Fig. 1 and detailed in Sect. 4.1.

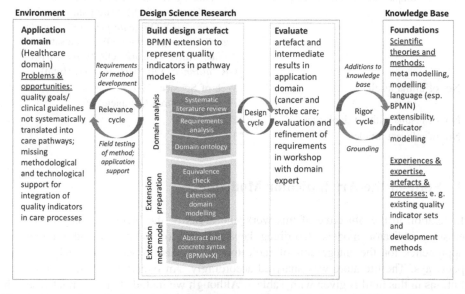

Fig. 1. Research methods in relation to DSR framework from Hevner et al. [14] and Hevner [17], artefact design applying the BPMN extension method proposed by Braun and Schlieter [18].

In order to reflect on the existing literature body in the field of indicator modelling as well as its feasibility and fitness in terms of the representation of QIs in care pathway models, we conducted a systematic literature review [19]. The search was based on the literature review on performance modelling conducted by Livieri et al. [9]. As represented in Table 1, we adapted their search string to also cover quality-related issues and the health care domain. The search was performed in February 2019. Only articles that described either a conceptual model of indicators or an approach (e.g. modelling language) to represent indicators in business process models or care pathways were included in the analysis. The database searches were complemented by backwards searches and hand search using google scholar.

Table 1. Search strategy (italic keywords taken from search string used by Livieri et al. [9]).

Reporting item	Description
Databases	Web of Science, Academic Search Complete
Keywords searched in titles	(("*enterprise monitoring*" OR "*performance monitoring*" OR "quality monitoring" OR "quality measurement" OR "*performance measurement*" OR *indicator* OR *KPI**) AND (*ontolog** OR *semantic* OR model* OR *formal**))
	AND
Keywords searched in abstracts (Academic Search Complete)/topic (Web of Science)	(("health care" OR "care network" OR "integrated care" OR "care process" OR "clinical pathway" OR "care pathway" OR "care process") OR (*enterprise* OR "*supply chain*" OR *organization* OR organisation OR "*collaborative network*" OR "*supply network*" OR "*alliance*" OR "*virtual enterprise*"))
No. of initial results	Web of Science: 270 Academic Search Complete: 56
No. of results without duplicates	285
No. of relevant articles	18

3   State-of-the-Art Indicator Modelling

In relation to the objective of this work, the focus of the literature analysis was on existing indicator models describing key concepts of indicators and on existing approaches for the integration of indicators in process models, especially in care pathways. The literature was analysed accordingly. An overview of the main contributions in this field is given with Table 2. Although we included quality-related search terms, the search did not result in work specifically addressing the modelling of QIs. The focus of existing literature is on the modelling of business goals and of organizational- and process performance. However, this literature provides a useful basis for the conceptualization and modelling of QIs, since business goals can equal quality goals and thus be reflected with QIs. Also, performance is a quality aspect, focusing on the business processes as means to improve outcomes [20].

Table 2. Overview of main contributions in the field of indicator modelling.

Reference	Indicator focus	Process model integration
Popova and Sharpanskykh [21]	Business goals, conceptualization of and relations between performance indicators	Not specified
Strecker et al. [22]	Modelling method METRICM for performance indicator systems; indicator meta model	Not specified
Staron et al. [23]	Quality model and relevant characteristics of key performance indicators	Not specified
Maté et al. [24]	Meta model for key performance indicators and key results indicators	Not specified
Amor and Ghannouchi [25]	Ontology model of key performance indicators in context of process improvement	Not specified
Ghahremanlou et al. [26]	Ontology design patterns to consistently represent indicators from multiple indicator sets	Not specified
del-Río-Ortega et al. [27]	Ontology defining process performance indicators	Ontology-based definition of relationships between indicators and BPMN elements
Silva and Weigand [28]	Monitoring metric ontology as part of an enterprise monitoring ontology	Not specified
Zeise [29]	Performance indicators	Proposal of graphic representation of indicators in BPMN
Ronaghi [30]	Performance management meta model including an indicator model	Not specified
Pourshahid et al. [31]	Extension of User Requirements Notation (URN) with key performance indicators to measure and align processes and goals	Relation between process models, goals and indicator models in URN
Rojas and Jaramillo [32]	Pre-conceptual schema for the representation of key performance indicators	Not specified
Braun et al. [33]	QIs and objectives in healthcare	BPMN extension, indicators and objectives annotated to clinical pathways
Jussupova-Mariethoz and Probst [34]	Ontology specifying business concepts for enterprise performance monitoring; focus: key performance indicators	Not specified

There are several ontology-based conceptualizations of indicators described in the literature. They define key attributes of indicators as well as the relations to other organizational elements such as policy, goals, processes, or roles. The identified indicator ontologies were mostly developed and used for enterprise monitoring purposes. In addition, literature addressing indicator modelling in the health care domain is scarce. Pourshahid et al. [35] as well as Amor and Ghannouchi [25] apply their approaches with example case studies in healthcare. Braun et al. [33] integrated QIs in BPMN models of care pathways by representing them as labelled circles, annotated as properties to activities, gateways, and processes. Still, the QI element is not further specified. Another, but domain-independent proposal for the process integration of indicators was made by Zeise [29] by drafting a graphical representation of indicators in BPMN models. However, there is no technical integration of their proposal to the BPMN meta model. In summary, there is no fully defined healthcare domain-specific process modelling language integrating a detailed perspective on QIs yet.

4 Development of the Extension

4.1 Extension Procedure and Language Selection

According to the requirements-based extension procedure described by Braun and Schlieter [18], we conducted a domain requirements analysis to understand the domain in detail and to derive necessary requirements for the intended modelling approach (see Sect. 4.2). Based on this, the next step was to select a modelling language to be used for the extension design. We decided on BPMN since it is a broadly accepted and established standard for business process modelling in economy and industry. Also, it provides a meta model, so that it can be modified and extended as needed for particular domain specificities. BPMN is already used for modelling care processes (e.g. [36, 37]) and thus, is a known approach in health care practice. Also, we include the existing BPMN extension for care pathway modelling (BPMN4CP) [38] and its revised version including a resource and document view [33] in our extension design. Within the step of language selection, a domain ontology based on the previously defined requirements is developed (see Sect. 4.3). The next step contains an equivalence check to determine whether a domain concept is already covered by existing BPMN elements, resulting in extension requirements (see Sect. 4.4). After this, Braun and Schlieter refer to the extension method of Stroppi et al. [39] for the domain modelling (see Sect. 4.5) and definition of the abstract syntax of the extension. Finally, the concrete syntax (graphical representation) of the BPMN extension shall be specified. In this paper, we focus on the presentation of the Conceptual Domain Model of the Extension (CDME) functioning as the basis for the BPMN meta model extension. Also, the graphical representation (concrete syntax) in a BPMN pathway model is outlined (see Sects. 4.5 and 5).

4.2 Requirements for the Integration of a Quality Perspective in Pathway Models

In order to identify underlying requirements for the integration of a quality perspective in care pathways, we conducted a user-centred requirements analysis. In general, pathways are used for patient information, documentation, monitoring and evaluation purposes [40]. As part of health operations management, care pathways are utilized within the following five main activity areas [1]:

- care planning and documentation for individual patients
- care planning and -controlling for specific patient groups
- care resource capacity planning (e.g. providers, materials, space) and controlling
- patient volume planning and -controlling
- strategic planning with regard to long-term policy of a health organization

These imply that care pathways are used by different stakeholder groups with different purposes. For example, management uses QIs to monitor and direct the organization's care policies and practices [20]. Based on the described activity areas above, we distinguished between the main user groups patients, health service providers engaged in care provision along the care pathway (e.g. physicians, nurses), and managers (especially quality management, controlling). We presented an initial list of requirements to an expert in the field of cancer care and certification of comprehensive cancer centres. She reviewed and revised the requirements on the basis of her many years of experience on national and European level. For example, she pointed out that it should be identifiable whether a quality indicator was developed based on existing evidence or on an experts' consensus. Table 3 represents the final, validated set of requirements for the representation of a quality perspective in care pathway models.

Table 3. Requirements for an integrated quality perspective in care pathways (HSP – health service provider, M – manager, P – patient).

No.	Requirement	User group
R_1	Information about relevant quality aspects along the care pathway	HSP, M, P
R_2	QIs as integrative part of the care pathway (represented at the relevant point in the pathway, i.e. decision point, activity, whole pathway or part of the pathway, time frame, outcome, structural unit)	HSP, M, P
R_3	Representation of the source of a QI	HSP, M, P
R_4	Representation of the recommendation level of a QI (e.g. evidence indicator or recommendation based on consensus report)	HSP, M, P
R_5	Representation of relevant QI attributes to describe and measure them	HSP, M
R_6	Representation only of those QIs to a user which are relevant for the user's work/purpose	HSP, M, P
R_7	Representation of data sources used for data provision	HSP, M
R_8	Representation of the relation of a QI to the corresponding quality- and business goals	M
R_9	Representation of deviations from defined QI target value and thus, of quality and process improvement potentials at corresponding points in the pathway	HSP, M
R_{10}	Representation of current QI values (status)	HSP, M
R_{11}	Representation of QI values over time to see quality development/trend	HSP, M

The user-related requirements are complemented by theory-based requirements [41], i.e. R_{12}: base development on multi-perspective modelling theory [42], R_{13}: procedural transparency of extension design [33, 43], R_{14}: evolution of existing BPMN extension [44], R_{15}: base development on classification and characteristics of QIs in care [45]. This theoretical basis ensures the rigorousness within the followed DSR approach [17].

4.3   Domain Ontology

Ontologies are used to deepen the understanding of a domain by explicating the domain knowledge, core concepts and their relationships [46]. Informal ontologies are a means to that end, functioning as a terminological and conceptual basis [47]. In order to conceptualize the quality perspective in relation to care pathways, the pathway ontology proposed by Braun et al. [38] was extended. Therefore, the identified indicator ontologies as described in Sect. 3, own previous research on the conceptualization of process quality in healthcare [16], and the user-centred requirements identified in Sect. 4.2 were used. The evolved domain ontology is depicted in Fig. 2.

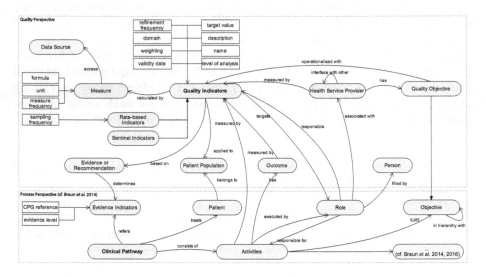

Fig. 2. Care pathway based on [38] and extended with a quality perspective, represented using the OWL Lite ontology [48].

Quality indicators are in the centre of the quality perspective. They are measures to assess particular health care structures, processes or outcomes [45]. This corresponds to the traditional classification of care quality by Donabedian, who distinguishes between the quality of structures (e.g. infrastructure, environment, employee qualification), processes (e.g. interventions, diagnosis activities), and outcomes (e.g. patient's health status, patient satisfaction) [49] (for examples see Table 4). This division is also represented in the domain ontology with QIs measuring structures of *health care providers* (corresponding to structural quality), pathway *activities* (corresponding to process quality and analogous to the process relation of indicators described in [25, 34]), and pathway activity *outcomes* (corresponding to outcome quality).

Table 4. Examples of QIs (identified from [45]).

Quality dimension	QI example
Structure	access to specific technologies/medical devices, proportion of specialists to other doctors
Process	proportion of patients assessed by doctor within 24 h after referral
Outcome	blood pressure, mortality

QIs operationalise *quality objectives*, being part of the goal hierarchy of a health care institutions [34]. Useful QIs need to be relevant, scientifically developed and feasible [50]. Thus, indicators are linked to *recommendation or evidence sources*. Typically, these are consensus reports, clinical studies, systematic literature reviews, or clinical practice guidelines (CPGs). The latter bundle the current evidence from clinical studies regarding the care for particular patient groups [51]. Mature CPGs already describe QIs to be used for assessing quality of care. If new evidence becomes available or the original source such as the corresponding CPG is updated, applied QIs may themselves need revision, updating or discontinuation. This lifecycle of QIs is specified by attributes such as a refinement frequency, responsible person and validity date. Other attributes of QIs as represented in the domain ontology are adapted from existing indicator-related meta models proposed in performance measurement literature (see [22, 52]). QIs are either *rate-based* (e.g. proportions, mean values) or *sentinel indicators* (identifying undesirable events such as number of patients who died during surgery) [45]. They are categorised with respect to their domain, e.g. the phase in care provision (prevention, diagnosis, treatment, follow-up), symptoms, comorbidities, side effects, documentation and communication, service availability and access, or team-work (examples for QI domains in [27, 53, 54]). Thus, they are generic or disease-specific, on patient level or institutional level [45].

QIs are used by *health service providers*, e.g. in a hospital, nursing home, or care network, and they refer to a specific *patient population*. Therefore, it needs to be specified for whom a QI is applicable, e.g. by detailing clinical situation, age, gender, comorbidities of the targeted patient group. However, QIs are applied to groups, not individuals and thus, there may occur exceptions.

To measure quality, QIs use particular *measures,* having a calculation formula depending on the type of the indicator. Rate-based indicators are represented as If-Then-statements, resulting in ratio calculations (with the then-part as numerator and the if-part as denominator) [45]. However, sentinel indicators are for example opera-tionalised into volumes, yes/no statements or time periods, e.g. waiting times for an appointment. The QI measurement results in an actual value for the analysed setting. It might deviate from a specified target or threshold value. It is possible to apply a weighting scheme to a QI set to differentiate the importance of the QIs. To assess a QI, the necessary *data sources* need to be accessible. These might be electronic or paper-based medical records, accounting databases, e.g. DRG (diagnosis related group) reporting systems, health insurance claims data, additional documentation on in- and outpatient care, or patient surveys.

4.4 Equivalence Check

In this section, we compare the identified domain concepts to original BPMN elements in order to identify the need for extension, adaption or reuse of elements. If applicable, the domain concepts are also compared to the already existing language extension BPMN4CP in order to reuse extension concepts. The results of the equivalence check are shown in Table 5. It includes the classification of the equivalence type for each domain concept and correspondingly, the classification either as *BPMN Concept* or *Extension Concept*. Therefore, each domain concept is analysed regarding semantic equivalence to existing BPMN elements as specified in [55] and BPMN4CP elements as described in [33, 38]. In case of equivalence, a domain concept is either represented by a valid composition of original BPMN elements (equivalence by composition) or as specification of original BPMN elements, i.e. adding domain-specific properties or semantics (equivalence by specification) [34].

Table 5. Equivalence check.

Req.	Concept	Description	Equivalence check	CDME
R_1, R_2, R_5	**Quality Indicator**	Measurement of quality bound to activities, decisions, process parts, entire processes, structural units, or outcomes	**Conditional equivalence:** BPMN4CP extension concept *Quality Indicator* (specification of BPMN *Property* element) but without further structuring or parametrization according to domain ontology attributes	Extension concept and specified BPMN4CP concept
R_8	**Quality Objective**	Quality goal of activities, decisions, process parts, entire processes, structural units, or outcomes in relation	**Conditional equivalence:** see *Quality Indicator*; BPMN4CP extension concept needs reference to *Quality Indicator*	Extension concept and specified BPMN4CP concept
R_5	**Measure**	Specification of how and when to calculate the value of a QI	**No equivalence**	Integrate as complex data type in *Quality Indicator* concept since each QI has one measure (1:1 relation)

(*continued*)

Table 5. (*continued*)

Req.	Concept	Description	Equivalence check	CDME
R$_7$	**Data Source**	Data source used for the provision of data to calculate value of a QI	**Conditional equivalence:** BPMN concept *Data Input* as mechanism to retrieve data; needs reference to *Quality Indicator*	Extension concept and specified BPMN concept
R$_6$	**Interest group**	Group of people (roles) for whom a QI is relevant	**No equivalence**	Integrate as complex data type in *Quality Indicator* concept
R$_3$	**Recommendation source**	Reference to specific source which was used to reason and derive the QI from	**Conditional equivalence:** BPMN4CP extension concept *CPG Reference* is too restricted since CPGs are not the only source for QIs	Extension concept and specification of BPMN and BPMN4CP concepts
R4	Recommendation	Statement of recommendation that a QI refers to	**Conditional equivalence:** see Quality Indicator; BPMN4CP extension concept Evidence Indicator needs reference to Quality Indicator; if QI is not evidence-based the recommendation strength shall be represented	Extension concept and specified BPMN4CP concept

It was assessed to be unnecessary to include the domain concept *Patient Population* in the quality perspective of a pathway model since it is already covered by patient inclusion and exclusion criteria of a pathway. Instead, the relevant patient population for ratio-based QIs is represented in the formula (e.g. "percentage of patients with postoperative radiation of the remaining breast/chest wall among all patients with breast-conserving surgery for invasive carcinoma"). Furthermore, the domain concepts Health Service Provider and Outcome are not specifically included in the language extension. The type of a QI (structural, process-, and outcome-oriented) is represented by the QI domain, which is an attribute of the *Quality Indicator* concept. Understandably, the focus of QI representation in pathway models is on process-related QIs.

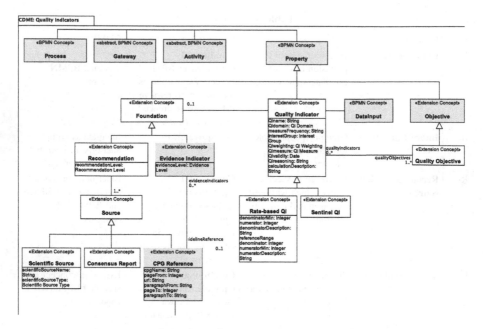

Fig. 3. Conceptual Domain Model of the Extension (CDME).

4.5 Extension Modelling – CDME and BPMN Extension Model

The CDME model is part of the extension preparation and was created based on the detailed analysis of the required quality concepts. The quality-related extension parts were embedded in the existing BPMN4CP CDME model and are depicted in Fig. 3. As assessed during the equivalence check (see Table 5), we added relevant QI concepts to be represented in BPMN pathway models. Extension elements are marked with the *Extension Concept* stereotype. For easier visual distinguishability all new, i.e. quality-related extension concepts, are coloured white whereas BPMN concepts and previous BPMN4CP extension concepts from [33, 38] are coloured grey. The CDME model shows the integration of the *Quality Indicator* concept, a detailed specification of the BPMN *Property* concept, in pathway models. The CDME informs the extension of the BPMN meta model, which we developed according to [18]. Therefore, new concepts were marked as *Extension Definitions* and *Extension Elements* and new relationships as *Extension Relationship* (example see Fig. 4a). An outline of the graphical representation (concrete syntax) of the added quality concepts is given in Fig. 4b. Picking up on the introduced symbols of circled *Quality Indicators* and *Objectives* in the revised BPMN4CP version [33], we detailed *Quality Indicators with Measures* and added QI *Data Inputs*.

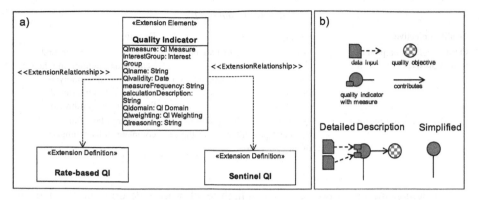

Fig. 4. (a) Example part of the BPMN extension model (BPMN+x), (b) extension of the concrete syntax by new graphical representations.

5 Demonstration

To demonstrate the application of the BPMN modelling language extension, we use a case example from integrated stroke care. Stroke is one of the most common causes of death globally. It holds a high risk of causing life-long, chronic disabilities in adults [56]. A coordinated stroke care, from acute care to rehabilitation and aftercare, aims to enable a quality-assured and evidence-based treatment to control risk factors and reduce recurrence rates, the need for long-term care and mortality [57]. Thus, managing quality in stroke care is an important issue and the proposed approach of integrated QIs in care process models shows high applicability for this case.

We gained insights to the process of stroke acute and aftercare via an expert interview with an experienced case manager. In the current flow chart-like integrated care pathway, objectives are already associated with QIs and individual pathway steps. They are depicted as circles near the corresponding process step [58]. The relation between a QI and an objective is shown by coherent numbering. A closer linkage between these concepts and their attributes shall be provided by applying the proposed BPMN extension.

Table 6. Exemplary quality indicators, related quality objectives and data inputs.

Quality objective	Quality indicator	Data input
O1: Increase the proportion of patients with stroke symptoms who receive adequate treatment within 3 h	QI1.1: proportion of patients admitted within 3 h after onset of symptoms in all patients with stroke or transient ischemic attack (TIA)	time interval stroke to admission (time_adm)
	QI1.2: proportion of patients with duration "admission - 1st imaging" under 30 min in all patients with stroke and duration of symptoms at the time of admission <4 h	time interval admission to first imaging (time_imag)

(continued)

Table 6. (*continued*)

Quality objective	Quality indicator	Data input
O2: Guideline compliant thrombolysis	QI2.1: percentage of patients with symptomatic cerebral haemorrhage in all patients with thrombolysis	complication: intracerebral hemorrhage (compl_intrahem); intravenous thrombolysis (iventhrom); intraarterial thrombolysis (iartthrom)
O3: Discharge management	QI3.1: Completely structured treatment plan aftercare in the set of all case charts	Treatment plan aftercare complete (tplan_compl)

For demonstration purposes, we use a high-level process description of acute care in the care pathway for stroke patients and four exemplary QIs as described in Table 6. The example representation in Fig. 5 shows the specification of QIs and their relation to activities in the care process. Also, it shows the connection to quality objectives and the input of data for measurement of a QI. QIs can either be represented in a simplified or more detailed description in the pathway. To not overload the process model, the QIs in the care process are further detailed in separate QI diagrams, representing a distinct view on the care pathway (see Fig. 5). Continuing to use the concrete syntax of the language extension BPMN4CP [33], the orange index finger now not only represents the evidence level of activities but also of quality indicators.

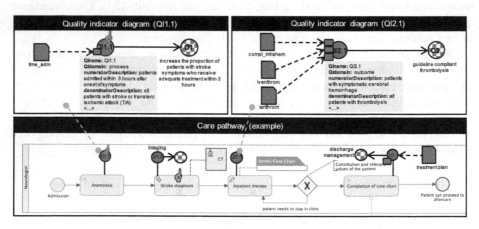

Fig. 5. Extended BPMN4CP demonstration model exemplarily presenting the integration of QIs in a process from stroke care.

6 Conclusion

Although care pathways are a commonly used tool to organize complex care processes and to increase care quality, their potentials in terms of quality management have not been sufficiently exploited yet. The development, documentation and controlling of QIs for quality management purposes are not fully integrated to the process standards defined by care pathways. Such integration could contribute to the governance of care processes and support continuous process-based quality management.

The purpose of this paper was to advance a common and widely used process modelling notation in order to integrate quality management information such as quality objectives, related QIs, and measure inputs. Therefore, we consolidated the characteristics of QIs as concept and QI modelling as method by conducting a systematic literature review. The results were implemented into an ontology connecting the concepts of care pathways with quality-related concepts such as QIs. This ontology served as mean to assess and describe the domain knowledge. For other researchers, the ontology provides an instrument to extend existing modelling approaches with that quality information. Based on the literature-based requirements analysis and a validation from a domain expert in the field of integrated cancer care, we developed a BPMN language extension to integrate a quality perspective in care pathway models. A separate QI view allows the description of structure-related information of the quality concepts. It also helps to inform and use the simplified QI description in the pathway diagram.

Critically reflecting on our own work, the validation of requirements for the BPMN language extension could be improved by interviewing more domain experts also outside of the cancer care domain. For example, discussing the requirements in a focus group would allow experts' interaction [59] and might result in additional or revised requirements. Also, the literature review could be broadened to also include work from other research fields. For example, Quality of Service literature provides modelling approaches of quality and quality indicators in process models. How such approaches could be adapted to the modelling of care pathways is a question to be addressed in future research.

Nowadays the interoperability between modelling tools is still not sufficient. Therefore, we concentrated our work on the specification of a meta model extension (abstract syntax) that can be incorporated in various tools or meta case tools and which can also be used to compare the proposed modelling extension with similar approaches. In addition, with the outline of the concrete syntax and the modelling example, the general applicability and utility of the approach were illustrated. However, for a better integration into the daily work processes the approach shall be linked to a documentation system (or to the clinical information system) so that the quality related documentation is directly derived and triggered by the pathway. The direct linkage of QIs to the process may also help to assess the documentation efforts in the process and can help the automated generation of quality-related data, e.g. to use inhouse tracking to collect time stamps that can be used to determine waiting times. Our approach is also a starting point for the integrated monitoring of QIs, which combines the quality performance of a concrete medical treatment process with historical data. In sum, the work contributes to an integrative quality management approach on the basis of care pathways. We showed how an existing general-purpose modelling language can be systematically extended to integrate the scope of quality information within care process models.

Acknowledgments. The work for this paper was funded by the European Social Fund (ESF) and the Free State of Saxony (Grant no. 100310385). We thank PD Dr. med. Simone Wesselmann, German Cancer Society for her valuable feedback from the domain of integrated cancer care and Uwe Helbig for providing us with his experience and knowledge with regard to integrated stroke care.

References

1. Schrijvers, G., van Hoorn, A., Huiskes, N.: The care pathway: concepts and theories: an introduction. Int. J. Integr. Care **12**(Special Edition Integrated Care Pathways), e192 (2012)
2. Antunes, V., Moreira, J.: Approaches to developing integrated care in Europe: a systematic literature review. J. Manage. Mark. Healthc. **4**(2), 129–135 (2011)
3. Nolte, E., Pitchforth, E.: What is the evidence on the economic impacts of integrated care? World Health Organization (2014)
4. Vanhaecht, K.: The Impact of Clinical Pathways on the Organisation of Care Processes. Katholieke Universiteit Leuven, Leuven (2007)
5. Sánchez, E., Letona, J., González, R., García, M., Darpón, J., Garay, J.: A descriptive study of the implementation of the EFQM excellence model and underlying tools in the Basque Health Service. Int. J. Qual. Health Care **18**(1), 58–65 (2006)
6. Stoimenova, A., Stoilova, A., Petrova, G.: ISO 9001 certification for hospitals in Bulgaria: does it help service? Biotechnol. Biotechnol. Equip. **28**(2), 372–378 (2014)
7. Minkman, M., Ahaus, K., Fabbricotti, I., Nabitz, U., Huijsman, R.: A quality management model for integrated care: results of a Delphi and concept mapping study. Int. J. Qual. Health Care **21**(1), 66–75 (2009)
8. Burwitz, M., Schlieter, H., Esswein, W.: Modeling clinical pathways - design and application of a domain-specific modeling language. In: Proceedings of the 11th International Conference on Wirtschaftsinformatik, Leipzig, pp. 1325–1339 (2013)
9. Livieri, B., Cagno, P.D., Bochicchio, M.: A bibliometric analysis and review on performance modeling literature. Complex Syst. Inf. Model. Q. **2**, 56–71 (2015)
10. Richter, P., Burwitz, M., Esswein, W.: Conceptual considerations on the integration of quality indicators into clinical pathways. Stud. Health Technol. Inf. **228**, 38–42 (2016)
11. Österle, H., et al.: Memorandum on design-oriented information systems research. Eur. J. Inf. Syst. **20**(1), 7–10 (2011)
12. Peffers, K., Tuunanen, T., Rothenberger, M.A., Chatterjee, S.: A design science research methodology for information systems research. J. Manage. Inf. Syst. **24**(3), 45–77 (2007)
13. Peffers, K., Tuunanen, T., Niehaves, B.: Design science research genres: introduction to the special issue on exemplars and criteria for applicable design science research. Eur. J. Inf. Syst. **27**(2), 129–139 (2018)
14. Hevner, A.R., March, S.T., Park, J., Ram, S.: Design science in information systems research. Manage. Inf. Syst. Q. **28**(1), 75–106 (2004)
15. Mernik, M., Heering, J., Sloane, A.M.: When and how to develop domain-specific languages. ACM Comput. Surv. **37**(4), 316–344 (2005)
16. Richter, P.: Bringing care quality to life: towards quality indicator-driven pathway modelling for integrated care networks. In: Proceedings of the 27th European Conference on Information Systems, Stockholm-Uppsala (2019)
17. Hevner, A.R.: A three cycle view of design science research. Scand. J. Inf. Syst. **19**(2), 87–92 (2007)

18. Braun, R., Schlieter, H.: Requirements-based development of BPMN extensions: the case of clinical pathways. In: Proceedings of the IEEE 1st International Workshop on the Interrelations Between Requirements Engineering and Business Process Management (REBPM), pp. 39–44 (2014)

19. vom Brocke, J. et al.: Reconstructing the giant: on the importance of rigour in documenting the literature search process. In: Proceedings of the 17th European Conference of Information Systems, Verona (2009)

20. McLellan, A.T., Chalk, M., Bartlett, J.: Outcomes, performance, and quality: what's the difference? J. Subst. Abuse Treat. **32**(4), 331–340 (2007)

21. Popova, V., Sharpanskykh, A.: Formal modelling of organisational goals based on performance indicators. Data Knowl. Eng. **70**(4), 335–364 (2011)

22. Strecker, S., Frank, U., Heise, D., Kattenstroth, H.: MetricM: a modeling method in support of the reflective design and use of performance measurement systems. IseB **10**(2), 241–276 (2012)

23. Staron, M., Meding, W., Niesel, K., Abran, A.: A Key Performance Indicator Quality Model and Its Industrial Evaluation. IEEE, New York (2016)

24. Maté, A., Trujillo, J., Mylopoulos, J.: Key performance indicator elicitation and selection through conceptual modelling. In: Comyn-Wattiau, I., Tanaka, K., Song, I.-Y., Yamamoto, S., Saeki, M. (eds.) ER 2016. LNCS, vol. 9974, pp. 73–80. Springer, Cham (2016). https://doi.org/10.1007/978-3-319-46397-1_6

25. Amor, E., Ghannouchi, S.A.: Toward an ontology-based model of key performance indicators for business process improvement. In: IEEE/ACS 14th International Conference on Computer Systems and Applications (AICCSA), pp. 148–153. IEEE, New York (2017)

26. Ghahremanlou, L., Magcc, L., Thom, J.A.: Using ontology design patterns to represent sustainability indicator sets. In: Dragoni, M., Poveda-Villalón, M., Jimenez-Ruiz, E. (eds.) OWLED/ORE -2016. LNCS, vol. 10161, pp. 70–81. Springer, Cham (2017). https://doi.org/10.1007/978-3-319-54627-8_6

27. del-Río-Ortega, A., Resinas, M., Ruiz-Cortés, A.: Defining process performance indicators: an ontological approach. In: Meersman, R., Dillon, T., Herrero, P. (eds.) OTM 2010. LNCS, vol. 6426, pp. 555–572. Springer, Heidelberg (2010). https://doi.org/10.1007/978-3-642-16934-2_41

28. de Alencar Silva, P., Weigand, H.: Enterprise monitoring ontology. In: Jeusfeld, M., Delcambre, L., Ling, T.-W. (eds.) ER 2011. LNCS, vol. 6998, pp. 132–146. Springer, Heidelberg (2011). https://doi.org/10.1007/978-3-642-24606-7_11

29. Zeise, N.: Modellierung von Kennzahlensystemen mit BPMN. In: Software Engineering (2010)

30. Ronaghi, F.: A modeling method for integrated performance management. In: Proceedings of the 16th International Workshop on Database and Expert Systems Applications (DEXA 2005), pp. 972–976 (2005)

31. Pourshahid, A., et al.: Business process management with the user requirements notation. Electron. Commer. Res. **9**(4), 269–316 (2009)

32. Rojas, L.F.C., Jaramillo, C.M.Z.: Executable pre-conceptual schemas for representing key performance indicators. In: Proceedings of the IEEE Computing Colombian Conference (8CCC) (2013)

33. Braun, R., Schlieter, H., Burwitz, M., Esswein, W.: BPMN4CP revised - extending BPMN for multiperspective modeling of clinical pathways. In: Proceedings of the 49th Hawaii International Conference on System Sciences, Koloa (2016)

34. Jussupova-Mariethoz, Y., Probst, A.-R.: Business concepts ontology for an enterprise performance and competences monitoring. Comput. Ind. **58**(2), 118–129 (2007)

35. Pourshahid, A., Amyot, D., Chen, P., Weiss, M., Forster, A.J.: Business process monitoring and alignment: an approach based on the user requirements notation and business intelligence tools. In: WER (2007)
36. Zerbato, F., Oliboni, B., Combi, C., Campos, M., Juarez, J.: BPMN-based representation and comparison of clinical pathways for catheter-related bloodstream infections. In: Proceedings of the International Conference on Healthcare Informatics, pp. 346–355 (2015)
37. Scheuerlein, H., et al.: New methods for clinical pathways-business process modeling notation (BPMN) and tangible business process modeling (t.BPM). Langenbeck's Arch. Surg. 397(5), 755–761 (2012)
38. Braun, R., Schlieter, H., Burwitz, M., Esswein, W.: BPMN4CP: design and implementation of a BPMN extension for clinical pathways. In: Proceedings of the IEEE International Conference of Bioinformatics and Biomedicine, pp. 9–16 (2014)
39. Stroppi, L.J.R., Chiotti, O., Villarreal, P.D.: Extending BPMN 2.0: method and tool support. In: Dijkman, R., Hofstetter, J., Koehler, J. (eds.) BPMN 2011. LNBIP, vol. 95, pp. 59–73. Springer, Heidelberg (2011). https://doi.org/10.1007/978-3-642-25160-3_5
40. Richter, P., Schlieter, H.: Understanding patient pathways in the context of integrated health care services - implications from a scoping review. In: Proceedings of the 14th International Conference on Wirtschaftsinformatik, Siegen, pp. 997–1011 (2019)
41. Braun, R., Benedict, M., Wendler, H., Esswein, W.: Proposal for requirements driven design science research. In: Donnellan, B., Helfert, M., Kenneally, J., VanderMeer, D., Rothenberger, M., Winter, R. (eds.) DESRIST 2015. LNCS, vol. 9073, pp. 135–151. Springer, Cham (2015). https://doi.org/10.1007/978-3-319-18714-3_9
42. Frank, U.: Multi-perspective enterprise modeling: foundational concepts, prospects and future research challenges. Softw. Syst. Model. 13(3), 941–962 (2014)
43. Braun, R., Esswein, W.: A generic framework for modifying and extending enterprise modeling languages. In: Proceedings of the 17th International Conference on Enterprise Information Systems, Barcelona (2015)
44. Schlieter, H., Stark, J., Burwitz, M., Braun, R.: Terminology for evolving design artifacts. In: Proceedings of the 14th International Conference on Wirtschaftsinformatik, Siegen (2019)
45. Mainz, J.: Defining and classifying clinical indicators for quality improvement. Int. J. Qual. Health Care 15(6), 523–530 (2003)
46. Happel, H.J., Seedorf, S.: Applications of ontologies in software engineering. In: Proceedings of 2nd International Workshop on Semantic Web Enabled Software Engineering (SWESE 2006) Held at the 5th International Semantic Web Conference (ISWC) (2006)
47. Uschold, M.: Building ontologies: towards a unified methodology. In: Proceedings of the 16th Annual Conference of the British Computer Society Specialist Group on Expert Systems (1996)
48. W3C: OWL 2 web ontology language - document overview; W3C recommendation. (2012). http://www.w3.org/TR/owl2-overview. Accessed 19 Nov 2018
49. Donabedian, A.: The quality of care: how can it be assessed? J. Am. Med. Assoc. 260(12), 1743–1748 (1988)
50. Reiter, A., et al.: QUALIFY: Ein Instrument zur Bewertung von Qualitätsindikatoren, Zeitschrift für ärztliche Fortbildung und Qualität im Gesundheitswesen. Ger. J. Qual. Health Care 101(10), 683–688 (2008)
51. Woolf, S.H., Grol, R., Hutchinson, A., Eccles, M., Grimshaw, J.: Potential benefits, limitations, and harms of clinical guidelines. BMJ 318(7182), 527–530 (1999)
52. Frank, U., Heise, D., Kattenstroth, H., Schauer, H.: Designing and utilising business indicator systems within enterprise models-outline of a method. In: Proceedings of Modellierung betrieblicher Informationssysteme (MobIS), Saarbrücken (2008)

53. Khare, S.R., et al.: Quality indicators in the management of bladder cancer: a modified Delphi study. Urol. Oncol. **35**(6), 328–334 (2017). Seminars and Original Investigations
54. Ludt, S., et al.: Evaluating the quality of colorectal cancer care across the interface of healthcare sectors. PLoS ONE **8**(5), e60947 (2013)
55. Object Management Group: OMG BPMN Version 2.0. (2011). https://www.omg.org/spec/BPMN/2.0/PDF/. Accessed 01 July 2019
56. Busch, M.A., Kuhnert, R.: 12-Month prevalence of stroke or chronic consequences of stroke in Germany. J. Health Monit. **2**(1), 64–69 (2017)
57. Barlinn, J., et al.: Koordinierte Schlaganfallnachsorge durch Case Management auf der Basis eines standardisierten Behandlungspfades. Nervenarzt **87**(8), 860–869 (2016)
58. SOS-NET. Das Neurovaskuläre Netzwerk Ostsachsen und Südbrandenburg: SOS-Care - Hilfe nach Schlaganfall. Akuttherapie bis Nachsorge. https://www.sos-net.de/das-netzwerk/struktur/sos-care/data/sos-care_behandlungspfad.pdf. Accessed 25 Feb 2019
59. Morgan, D.L.: Focus groups. Ann. Rev. Sociol. **22**(1), 129–152 (1996)

Preference-Based Resource and Task Allocation in Business Process Automation

Reihaneh Bidar$^{(\boxtimes)}$ (iD), Arthur ter Hofstede (iD), Renuka Sindhgatta (iD), and Chun Ouyang (iD)

Queensland University of Technology, Brisbane, Australia
{r.bidar,a.terhofstede,renuka.sr,c.ouyang}@qut.edu.au

Abstract. Preference plays an important role in organisational and human decision making as it may be a manifestation of proven practices or of individual working styles. The significance of the notion of preference has been recognised in a number of different disciplines. Unfortunately its potential does not seem to have been fully unlocked in the field of Business Process Automation (BPA), even though resource and task allocations play a pivotal role in process performance and these allocations could be guided by explicit formulations of preferences. In this paper, we examine the state of the art with respect to preference in the field of BPA and use this as the basis for a conceptual model capturing recognised manifestations of preference in the literature. We investigate how preferences may exhibit themselves in process automation through the notion of well-established (workflow) resource patterns. We then show that manifestations of preference may occur in real-life process event logs and how these can be extracted through the application of machine learning techniques. The findings from this research contribute towards establishing a rich understanding of preferences in the context of business processes, ways of specifying and deriving these preferences, and their more explicit incorporation in work allocation mechanisms, which can lead to a step change for realising better process performance and more effective work collaboration in today's organisations.

Keywords: Preference · Business Process Automation · Resource patterns · Resource allocation · Process mining

1 Introduction

In the context of Business Process Management (BPM), a resource is an entity that can perform an activity, either alone or in collaboration with other resources, including humans, software applications and cyber-physical systems (such as robots). Resources are requested at run-time to perform a specific activity towards the objective of a particular process instance [6,21]. Human resources can exhibit a variety of behaviours, depending on "their attentiveness in the task,

© Springer Nature Switzerland AG 2019
H. Panetto et al. (Eds.): OTM 2019, LNCS 11877, pp. 404–421, 2019.
https://doi.org/10.1007/978-3-030-33246-4_26

nature of the task and other personal preferences" [29]. This dynamic behaviour of human resources (or resources for short) can affect their performance and the process differently, while this does not hold for non-human resources [26].

From a future work perspective, the forces of technological advancement and resource empowerment are transforming the nature of work conducted and are compelling organisations to redesign their systems to consider resource autonomy and empowerment [12]. Resources are both more productive and more motivated when they have some degree of control over their work [24]. When designing (or redesigning) business processes, resource allocation is crucial for resource performance [20]. Current resource allocation strategies in BPM systems only consider general organisational information such as the role of a resource [6], and other resource attributes (e.g. experience or workload) are overlooked [30]. It is suggested that focusing on these other resource attributes will lead to the improvement of resource allocation and thus process performance [30].

An important resource attribute that has not received a lot of attention in the BPM literature is the notion of *preference*. The notion of preference has been captured in different areas such as task recommendation in crowdsourcing [31] and AI and decision making systems [4]. However, resource preferences have not been considered in a business process automation (BPA) context, an area which is uniquely positioned by the fact that resources are all identified, may play certain roles and be part of an organisational hierarchy, and participate through well-defined allocation rules in the performance of clearly delineated tasks. The focus of this paper is the forms that preferences of resources in a BPA context can take and how preferences can be derived from event logs, i.e. the process execution history. Preferences naturally present themselves in the conduct of work in the form of proven practices, established working relationships, or working styles suited to particular individuals. Resources have different preferences, which may affect their motivation [9] and overall process outcomes in the case of preference for certain activities [23]. Thus, understanding resource preference is important for managing task and resource allocation.

Preference has been defined in different ways in the BPM literature. Sohail, Dominic, and Shahzad [29] define preference as an inclination of human resources to use a non-human resource for executing the assigned task. Lee [19] on the other hand, only focuses on the preference of resources for tasks and defines resource preference as "the property that the resource likes to carry out some tasks more than others". We take a broader view on preference and we define preference as the degree to which a resource has a tendency for choosing particular types of work or for involving particular resources in the conduct of work.

The objective of this paper is to advance the state of the art in the field of BPM by examining the notion of preference in more detail and to set the stage for unlocking the potential of this notion in business process automation. This is achieved by exploring the current literature and formally capturing notions of preference that are retrieved in the form of a conceptual data model. Patterns related to the resource perspective in business process automation are then examined for the (implicit or explicit) presence of preferences. Preferences can also manifest themselves in execution logs and it is shown how some specific forms of preference can be discovered as this opens up the possibility of automatically detecting and updating preferences at runtime.

The key research questions we consider in this paper are RQ1) *What are current manifestations of preference in a BPA context?*, and (RQ2) *How can we derive certain forms of preference from event logs?*. To address the first research question, we develop a conceptual data model of preference which is informed by existing studies in the field of BPM. We then examine well-known resource patterns to determine to what degree they encapsulate various forms of preference. As these patterns have been used to assess workflow management systems, this also gives us an idea how preferences may be reflected in these systems. To address the second research question, we use machine learning applied to real-life publicly available event logs to show how certain forms of preference can be automatically derived and what factors in the logs may contribute to higher accuracy.

The main contributions of this paper are as follows: (i) synthesis of a rich notion of preference through the provision of a conceptual model of preference (preferences may be classified as resource-task, resource-resource, and task-resource), (ii) detection of implicit preferences by looking at what is encoded in resource patterns, which provides an indication of what workflow management systems offer, and (iii) an approach to derivation of preferences from event logs based on machine learning which can be used to guide resource allocation and task selection in business process automation.

The paper is organised as follows. A brief literature review (Sect. 2) is followed by a formal representation of preferences in the form of two ORM [13] models (Sect. 3). Manifestations of preferences in workflow resource patterns (Sect. 4) and real-life event logs (Sect. 5) are subsequently investigated. The paper concludes with a brief summary and avenues for future work.

2   Related Work

It has been stated that "[p]reference is inherently a multidisciplinary topic" [17] and "[t]he expression of preference by means of choice and decision making is the essence of intelligent, purposeful behavior" [27]. Preference has been found to be a fundamental attribute for decision making by agents and for supporting the decisions of users [10]. Preference has been used in an AI context to improve decision-making algorithms [4] and to improve planning [16]. In the context of recommender systems and crowdsourcing, preference is used to model and predict results for alternative options (c.f. Guo et al. [11] and Yuen et al. [31] resp.). The goal of preference-aware interactive systems is to help users perform tasks [22] by providing support for decision making by learning and reasoning over preferences [5]. While the aforementioned work is not targeted at resource allocation in the context of business process automation, the work of Yuen et al. [31] aims to support task selection based on preferences deduced from worker search history and thus illustrates that resource preferences can guide task allocation.

In the field of management, Shaw et al. [25] examined preference and its relationship between task interdependence, reward interdependence and preference for group work regarding performance and satisfaction of individuals. They found that the interaction of task interdependence and preference for group work was positively related to group-member performance. García et al. [8] proposed an ontological model for preference as a solution for discovery and ranking of scenarios in the context of user preferences and semantic web services.

Current research efforts related to the topic of preference in the field of BPM focus on determining the ontology of preference [3] and recognising preference as an underlying factor for resource allocation [26,30,32]. Preference is identified as an important criterion in Arias et al. [2] for the purpose of research allocation, but it is not further elaborated upon. Zhao et al. [32] proposed a method to support resource allocation by mining resource characteristics and task(-oriented) preference patterns. Sindhgatta et al. [26] suggested an approach to support resource allocation decisions by extracting information about process performance and process context that takes into account the aspect of preference. Huang et al. [14] proposed a resource allocation mechanism to measure resource behaviour from four perspectives consisting of preference, availability, competence and cooperation, and similarly Sohail et al. [29] found preference to be an important variable that should be measured for resource behaviour along with competencies and suitability.

In addition to the above, some studies considered preference an attribute of resource behaviour. For instance, Lee [19] proposed a resource scheduling method to model resource competence and preference in order to improve performance of workflow management systems and resource utilisation in workflows, while Pika et al. [23] developed a software framework that allows organisations to extract information about some resource characteristics including experience, preferences, and collaboration patterns from process event logs. Furthermore, compatibility of resources for task assignment has been considered [18], but it is different from preference as compatibility focuses on process and team outcome while preference focuses on choices resources make.

Although the existing literature recognises the importance of preference in understanding resource behaviour and, more specifically, the importance of preference in the context of resource allocation in business process automation, establishing a rich notion of preference in this context is largely unexplored in the BPM literature. Our research aims to contribute to removing this gap.

3   Conceptual Modelling

In this section, we design a conceptual model of preference which is informed by the existing studies on the topic of preference in the field of BPM. We use Object Role Modeling (ORM) to design our conceptual model. ORM is a fact-oriented method for modelling information systems at the conceptual level [13].

Findings from the literature review helped synthesise a current notion of preference in the context of business processes. Three typical scenarios can be found in the existing studies. First, a resource prefers one task to other tasks; second, a resource has preference to work with one specific resource among several resources; and third, when a task is to be allocated a resource, preference is given to one resource among several resources to perform the task. Hence, preference can be expressed as a (directed) relationship between resource and task (referred to as *resource-task preference*), a relationship between two resources (*resource-resource preference*), and a relationship between task and resource (*task-resource preference*).

We present two ORM models to capture the above notions of preference. The model shown in Fig. 1 specifies resource-task preference and resource-resource preference, and the model depicted in Fig. 2 specifies task-resource preference.

In the model of Fig. 1, it can be seen that a resource has a tendency for performing a particular task among some offered alternatives, or for involving certain other resources in the execution of a task. A human resource may prefer a particular type of task to other types of task [19,26,30]. He/she may prefer to use a particular non-human resource (e.g., a tool or instrument) to another non-human resource for executing an assigned task [28,29]. Sohail, Dominic, and Shahzad [29] give the example of a nurse who is assigned to measure blood pressure of a patient and may have a preference for either a clinical mercury monometer or a digital sphygmomanometer as the instrument (both are instances of non-human resources). A resource may also prefer a certain person over another for collaboration purposes [14].

In the model of Fig. 2, it is shown that for the execution of a task human resources with particular characteristics are preferred. In order to offer a task to a particular resource instead of to another resource (e.g., during automated resource allocation), resources can be ranked according to their characteristics [3, 32]. A number of resource characteristics to be considered include skills and specific knowledge, experience, workload, and execution of a certain task in the past [3]. For example, a human resource who has more task completions and longer work experience with a company is preferred over other resources to do a certain task [3].

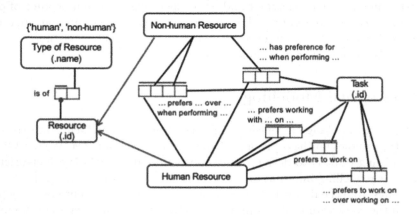

Fig. 1. An ORM model of resource-task preference and resource-resource preference

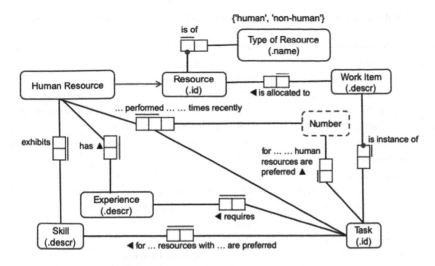

Fig. 2. An ORM model of task-resource preference (with resource characteristics)

4 Resource Patterns Analysis

In this section, we revisit the workflow resource patterns [24] from a preference perspective in order to understand to what extent preferences can be captured or facilitated through the mechanisms implied by these patterns. The workflow resource patterns (or resource patterns for short) were defined to provide a comparative insight into resource management capabilities of process-aware information systems. They have been used in the evaluation of various tools and languages (e.g. BPMN) and provided insights into their relative strengths and weaknesses and thus into opportunities for future improvements.

We use the conceptual model of preference proposed in Sect. 3 as the basis for the assessment of the resource patterns. Table 1 provides an overview of the assessment results between this notion of preference and the resource patterns. Preferences can be hard coded as part of the process definition at design time (**DT**), or they can manifest during the process execution at run-time (**RT**) through the application of a resource pattern. A resource pattern may involve some notion of preference but one that is outside the scope (**OS**) of our definition. Finally, a pattern is not applicable (**NA**) for assessment if it focuses on mechanism(s) irrelevant to preference. Below we discuss in more detail the assessment of the resource patterns that belong to the various groups.

Creation Patterns. A preference for a specific resource to perform a certain task can be expressed at design time through the use of the 'Direct allocation' pattern. Similarly, the 'Role-based distribution' pattern can be used to capture a preference for assigning a task to the resources playing a certain role at design time. We can also decide, at design time, that resource capability (e.g. demonstrated by possession of certain knowledge and skills) is used as a basis for the distribution of certain tasks to resources (i.e. 'Capability-based distribution'), or that

Table 1. Evaluation of resource patterns from a preference perspective

Nr	Resource patterns	Rate	Nr	Resource patterns	Rate
Creation Patterns			Push Patterns		
1	Direct allocation	DT	12	Dist. by offer - single resource	NA
2	Role-based distribution	DT	13	Dist. by offer - multiple resources	NA
3	Deferred distribution	NA	14	Dist. by allocation - single resource	NA
4	Authorization	OS	15	Random allocation	NA
5	Separation of duties	NA	16	Round robin allocation	NA
6	Case handling	NA	17	Shortest queue	NA
7	Retain familiar	NA	18	Early distribution	OS
8	Capability-based distribution	DT	19	Distribution on enablement	NA
9	History-based distribution	DT	20	Late Distribution	OS
10	Organizational distribution	DT			
11	Automatic execution	NA			
Pull Patterns			Detour Patterns		
21	Resource-init. allocation	RT	27	Delegation	RT
22	Resource-init. exec. - allocated WI	RT	28	Escalation	NA
23	Resource-init. exec. - offered WI	RT	29	Deallocation	NA
24	System-determ. work queue cont	DT	30	Stateful reallocation	RT
25	Resource-determ. work queue cont	RT	31	Stateless reallocation	RT
26	Selection autonomy	RT	32	Suspension/Resumption	NA
			33	Skip	RT
			34	Redo	NA
			35	Pre-do	NA
Auto-start Patterns			Visibility Patterns		
36	Commencement on creation	NA	40	Config. unallocated WI visibility	OS
37	Commencement on allocation	NA	41	Config. allocated WI visibility	OS
38	Piled execution	RT			
39	Chained execution	NA			
Multiple-resource Patterns					
42	Simultaneous execution	OS			
43	Additional resources	RT			

task execution history is to be considered (i.e. 'History-based Distribution') for example because a resource has acquired a certain amount of experience with a task. In addition, tasks can be distributed to resources that hold a certain position or that have certain relationships with other resources, and this can be formalised at design time through the use of the 'Organizational distribution' pattern.

The 'Authorization' pattern is concerned with privileges a resource may hold in terms of what work-related actions the resource is allowed to perform (e.g. delegation or skipping of work). This may be seen as a form of preference in a broad sense, but such preference is outside the scope of our model.

The remaining patterns in the group are not applicable for assessment as they focus on the mechanisms that are irrelevant to preference. For example, the 'Case handling' pattern focuses on having the same resource to work through an entire instance of a process regardless of preference.

Push Patterns. All the patterns in this group focus on the existence of a distribution mechanism (e.g. 'Random allocation' or 'Shortest queue') in a system rather than the ability to select certain specific resources due to preference. However, the 'Early Distribution' and 'Late Distribution' patterns are also concerned with whether the (predetermined) distribution of a task to a resource is made available at an earlier or a later stage, which might be seen as a weak form of preference and which is not considered in our model.

Pull Patterns. The 'Resource-initiated allocation' and 'Resource-initiated execution' patterns are concerned with the presence of mechanisms for resources to choose which tasks to commit during process execution and thus can be used to capture resource-task preferences at run-time. Through application of the 'System-determined work queue content' pattern one can capture the presentation of worklists (e.g. the order in which tasks are listed), and as such, this pattern can be applied to encapsulating resource preferences at design time (e.g. through the use of certain data attributes). Using the 'Resource-determined work queue content' and 'Selection autonomy' patterns, resource preferences can be captured that manifest at run-time, specifically their preference for how work is presented to them (which may influence what they choose to work on next) and what tasks to work on next.

Detour Patterns. The 'Delegation' pattern can be used to capture that, at run-time, preference may play a role in determining to whom work is delegated. Similarly, the 'Stateful reallocation' and 'Stateless reallocation' patterns may be applied when work is reallocated. Skipping of tasks by the 'Skip' pattern may be a manifestation of resource preference of not wishing to perform certain work at run-time. The remaining patterns are not applicable for assessment (e.g. the 'Suspension/Resumption' pattern is to allow a resource to pause/continue with a task that has already started rather than to capture its preference for a task).

Auto-start Patterns. These patterns are not applicable for assessment except for the 'Piled execution' pattern which can be used to capture that instances of a certain task should all go to a specific resource upon request by that resource. Piled execution should be enabled at design time, but resource preferences come to the fore at run-time.

Visibility Patterns. Both patterns are out of scope as they are concerned with the means to make work items visible ('Configurable allocated' or 'unallocated'), which may enable certain viewing preferences to be realised.

Multiple-resource Patterns. The 'Simultaneous execution' pattern is out of scope as it is concerned with the ability of a resource to work on multiple work items at the same time, which is not a preference in the model defined in this paper. Next, the 'Additional resources' pattern constitutes an important preference-related pattern as it allows multiple resources to be involved in performing a task. The run-time involvement of additional resources can be guided by preference.

Discussion. Insights learned from the above pattern-based analysis are two-fold. First of all, it shows that preferences are pervasive in resource mechanisms in process-aware information systems though their presence is not necessarily explicit. It seems worthwhile to make the role of preference more visible and this could be achieved by considering them an aspect of resource allocation (in the sense of aspect-orientation [15]). Hence any preference-related change can be facilitated through its own aspect.

Secondly, our analysis also reveals that the full richness of preference does not manifest itself in the resource patterns, which seems a consequence of the time in which these patterns were conceived. For example, at the time of concep-tion of the resource patterns, the idea of having multiple resources involved in carrying out a task was relatively novel and only limited support was offered by contemporary process-aware information systems. This explains the existence of only a single pattern with that focus and as our earlier analysis of preferences shows, additional and more sophisticated patterns (and associated mechanisms) can be envisaged. To this end, the emergence of research relating social media and BPM (e.g. [7]) could give rise to additional patterns as could mechanisms offered by modern process-aware information systems.

5   Detecting Preferences in Process Logs

In this section we look at real-life event data and how some forms of preference may manifest themselves and how they may be derived. The derivation of prefer-ences, especially if performed on an ongoing basis as to make sure they are up to date, can produce useful information for work allocation in the context of a busi-ness process automation environment. We should note upfront that preferences as they manifest themselves in real-life settings may have different support than what can be found in the literature as a combination of factors could influence these preferences. Hence, we take a broader view on log-derived preferences than what is supported by the literature.

An event log contains a set of events. We assume each event has the fol-lowing key attributes: *case_id, task, time_stamp, status, resource*. The *case_id* captures the case identifier of each unique case, *task* corresponds to the pro-cess' activity being performed by *resource* at a given *times_stamp*, and *status* $\in$ {*schedule, start, complete*} reflects the states in the life cycle of the task where a task is scheduled, started, and completed by a resource (note that other statuses may be recorded in an event log). Each event may further have process-specific attributes such as a loan amount for a loan application process.

The preference of a resource in performing a task or working with another resource can be influenced by factors such as the experience of the resource in performing a task, the number of tasks that need to be completed, and the workload of other resources. Computing preference as a frequency of a resource performing a certain task [14], while indicative may not be sufficient. Figure 3(a)

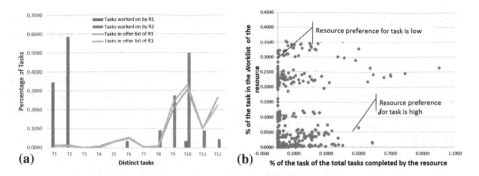

Fig. 3. (a) The percentage of tasks two resources work on and the percentage of tasks in their worklist. (b) Each point in the chart represents the percentage of a task available in the worklist for a resource vs. percentage of that task of the total tasks worked by that resource.

uses a real world event log to illustrate the dependence of resource preference on different factors. The frequency of tasks completed by two resources (R1 and R2) and frequency of tasks in the worklist of the resource is presented. Worklist of a resource contains all tasks that are 'scheduled' or not allocated at the time of the allocation of a task to the resource. From the figure, it can be deduced that Resource R1 has a high preference to work on task T2 which is infrequent on her worklist. Resource R2 prefers to work on tasks T9 and T10 which are the most frequent tasks in the worklist of R2. Figure 3(b) is a plot of the frequency of tasks completed by a resource and the frequency of tasks in the worklist of the resource. While one factor influencing resource preference is presented, there can be many such factors. Given the scenario of multiple factors impacting resource preference, our proposed approach (Fig. 4) uses supervised learning to examine manifestations of resource preferences. Supervised learning consists of arriving at a hypothesis by mapping the inputs (or features derived from the event log) to an output class (or label) that is interpretative of the preference of a resource. The assumption is that, if the learned hypothesis predicts the output values for unseen events (test data), then this hypothesis will be a good representation of the resource preference. Two classifiers, each using specific input features and corresponding output classes, are trained to learn two different resource characteristics that indicate a preference that resources may have. K-fold cross-validation is used to train and test the performance of these classifiers.

5.1   Predicting Next Selected Task in a Worklist

The preference of a resource for performing a certain task over other tasks available on its worklist, is explored by training a classifier with a set of input features comprising of the resource, and (work) list of work items (instances of tasks) available to the resource. The output label is the selected task the resource will work on next. As preference may be influenced by other resource characteristics, such as experience of the resource with the task, we add these additional features when building the model. These input features are computed for all events that are in the log where the status is *start*. The following input features for event e are used:

- **Resource**: As the objective is to learn the preference of a resource, this is an input feature. Binary encoding is used to create a resource feature vector $\boldsymbol{r} = (r_1, r_2, \ldots, r_n)$ corresponding to n resources in the log, where $r_i = 1$ for the resource of event e, and 0 otherwise.
- **Worklist**: There can be one or more work items available on the worklist at the time of event e for the resource for which we are interested in its choice of subsequent task. The worklist of a resource consists of all tasks that are 'scheduled' and not 'started' prior to the time of event e. The worklist feature vector $\boldsymbol{w}_{t_e} = (a_1, a_2, \ldots, a_m)$, corresponds to m tasks in the log (where t_e refers to the timestamp of event e). Frequency encoding is used where each feature represents the task, and the feature value is the frequency of the number of work items of that task in the worklist at time t_e.
- **Previous owner**: In certain scenarios, a work item of a task is placed back onto the worklist after being worked on by a resource. A feature vector using binary encoding is used to represent the resource that worked on that work item prior to the event ($case\_id, task$ are used to identify the work item). For newly scheduled or created tasks, this is a zero value vector.
- **Experience**: The number of completions of work items of a task a by a resource r, during a time slot $[t_1, t_2]$ is used as the indicator of experience of r in performing a: $exp(r, a, t_1, t_2)$ [23]. Linear scaling (or min-max normalisation) is used to normalise the experience of resources with a task to the [0,1] range. The experience vector for a resource r_i reflects its experience with all tasks considering a time slot $[t_1, t_2]$, and is given as:
$\boldsymbol{ex}_{r_i} = (exp(r_i, a_1, t_1, t_2), exp(r_i, a_2, t_1, t_2), \ldots, exp(r_i, a_m, t_1, t_2))$.

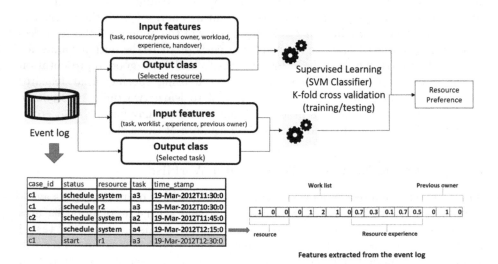

Fig. 4. Approach to learning preferences from event logs.

Figure 4 presents an overview of our approach and includes an example of a feature vector comprising of resource, worklist, resource experience and previous owner features.

5.2 Predicting the Resource for the Subsequent Task

Given a resource and a task that the resource has executed, in this section, we look at predicting which next resource will work on a subsequent task. We consider handover of task preference influenced by factors such as the workload of the resource the task is being handed over to, experience of the resources on the task being handed over, and frequency of handovers of tasks made by the resource to other resources. The preference of a resource for another resource to do upcoming work is explored by training a classifier on a set of input features for all events in the log where the status is *start*. The input features comprise the previous owner and the task itself. The output label is the (selected) resource of the event. Experience of resources with the task and an additional runtime factor of workload of resources are added when building the model. The following input features for event e concerning task a are used:

- **Previous Owner**: This feature represents the resource working on a work item of task a prior to the event. The objective is to learn the preference of this resource. Binary encoding is used to represent this feature as discussed in Sect. 5.1.
- **Task**: Binary encoding is used to create a task feature vector $a = (a_1, a_2, \ldots, a_m)$ corresponding to m tasks in the log, where $a_j = a = 1$ and 0 otherwise.
- **Experience**: The experience vector is computed during a time slot $[t_1, t_2)$ and the feature vector containing experience of n resources with task a is given as:
  $ex_a = (exp(r_1, a, t_1, t_2), exp(r_2, a, t_1, t_2), \ldots, exp(r_n, a, t_1, t_2))$.
- **Workload**: The workload $wl(r, t)$ is the number of tasks that are not yet completed by resource r at time t of event e. The feature vector for workload consists of the workload of n resources at the time of event e:
  $l_{t_e} = (wl(r_1, t_e), wl(r_2, t_e), \ldots, wl(r_n, t_e))$.
- **Handover**: The frequency of tasks handed over by a resource r_1 of event e_t to resource r_2 of event e_{t+1} computed during a time slot $[t_1, t_2)$ is used as the resource handover experience $hover(r_1, r_2, t_1, t_2)$ [1]. The handover vector for a resource r_1 is given as:
  $hd_{r_1} = (hover(r_1, r_1, t_1, t_2), hover(r_1, r_2, t_1, t_2), \ldots, hover(r_1, r_n, t_1, t_2))$.

5.3 Data Sets

The approach is evaluated on two Business Process Intelligence Challenge (BPIC) logs[1]. These logs contain resource and task life cycle information required for computing the input features of the model (Table 2).

---

[1] https://www.win.tue.nl/bpi/doku.php?id=2012:challenge, https://www.win.tue.nl/bpi/doku.php?id=2013:challenge.

Table 2. Event log statistics

Event log	# events	# cases	# resources	#tasks	# events considered	Case attr. used
BPIC 2012 W	262200	13087	69	7	10704	Loan amount
BPIC 2013 (Incidents)	65533	7554	1472	1	7436	Product, impact

1. **BPIC 2012 log**: From the BPIC 2012 logs we chose the work items log (or BPIC-W 2012 log). The data set contains events for a period of 6 months. The first three months of data is used to compute experience and handover experience of resources. The remaining three months of data is used to train and test the classifier. Tasks are categorised into two bins using the loan amount: ($\leq 10000, >10000$). Two types of ownership changes were considered: (i) events corresponding to newly scheduled work items where the corresponding task never had previous work items in the same case associated with a resource or with events where the scheduled work item had a previous work item of the same task in the same case but it was associated with a different resource, (ii) events corresponding to handovers where the work item of the task is completed by a resource and followed by a work item of the subsequent different task which is performed by a different resource.

2. **BPIC 2013 log**: From the BPIC 2013 logs we chose the BPIC 2013 (Incidents) log (or BPIC-I 2013). The log contains 1472 resources. However, only 40 resources have worked on at least 1% of the cases. As the event log contains only one task, domain attributes are used to further characterise tasks. A high impact 'PROD424' incident is considered as a task distinct from a low impact 'PROD660' incident. Characterising tasks using the attributes results in 20 distinct tasks.

5.4 Evaluation

For the purpose of evaluation, we experimented with Random Forest Classifier, K-Nearest Neighbour Classifier, and Support Vector Machine (SVM) Classifiers. Based on our experimental results, we chose SVM as it provided better results over the others. Two SVM Classifiers are trained and evaluate using 5-fold cross-validation. Experiments are performed by building SVM models using the Python library Scikit-learn[2].

Three commonly used performance measures are reported - classification accuracy, macro-averaged F1 and weighted F1 score. Accuracy is the ratio of correctly classified data points to the total number of data points. The F1 score is the harmonic mean of the precision and recall of a classifier. The F1 score is measured for each class and then the average is taken. This measure is known as the macro-averaged F1. The weighted F1 score is computed where the F1 score

---

[2] https://scikit-learn.org/stable/.

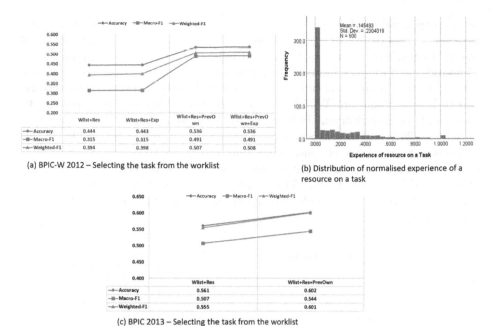

(a) BPIC-W 2012 – Selecting the task from the worklist

(b) Distribution of normalised experience of a resource on a task

(c) BPIC 2013 – Selecting the task from the worklist

Fig. 5. (a) Model performance for predicting the task from the resource worklist using BPIC-W 2012 event log, (b) Distribution of resource experience computed from BPIC-W 2012 event log, and (c) Model performance using BPIC 2013 event log

is measured for each class and the average is weighted by the number of data points of the class. The number of resources as an output class is lower than the total number of resources in the event log. We trained the model considering classes that had at least 15 data points in the test data set and hence resources with lower numbers of data points were not used.

The performance of the model predicting the next task on a resource's worklist is evaluated and presented in Fig. 5. In order to gain a detailed understanding of the proposed input features, we show experiments with a number of variants of the input features: (1) resource and its worklist, (2) resource, its worklist and resource experience on each of the tasks, (3) resource, its worklist and the previous owner, and (4) resource, its worklist, previous owner and its experience. For the BPIC-I 2013, the event logs cover a time period of one month. Hence experience of a resource was not included as a feature as the time interval of the log was too small to compute a measure of resource experience. Model performance is low with an accuracy of 0.444 for the BPIC-W 2012 event log when resource and worklist are used as input features (WList+Res in Fig. 5(a)). The model performance does not improve (for BPIC-W 2012) with the inclusion of resource experience (WList+Res+Exp). As resource experience would naturally be an important consideration in task selection, we further investigate the reason for its limited influence. It can be observed that in the BPIC-W 2012 data set, a large number of resources have very low levels of experience with a limited few having high levels of experience. This skewness in the distribution of resource experience results in its limited influence on the model performance. The model performance improves significantly when the previous owner is considered. Hence, manifestations of preference could consider resource (co-workers) and task in conjunction (WList+Res+PrevOwn). Addition of resource experience yields no improvement in accuracy of Macro-F1. The accuracy is 0.5612 for BPIC-I 2013 and increases to 0.6020 when previous owner is considered, further indicative of resources considering tasks and co-workers together (Fig. 5(c)). Given the high number of output classes (10 tasks in BPIC-W 2012, and 20 tasks in BPIC 2013), the accuracy of 53–60% provides a good indication that the classifier is able to learn the preference function and predict the right task with favourable accuracy.

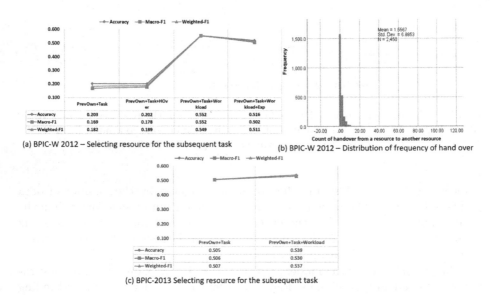

Fig. 6. (a) Model performance for predicting the next resource for BPIC-W 2012, (b) Distribution of past hand overs between resources (c) Model performance for predicting next resource for BPIC-2013

The second model is concerned with predicting who will perform instances of the next task. We show results with variants of the proposed features: (1) previous owner and task, (2) previous owner, task and past handovers made by the previous owner, (3) previous owner, task and workload of the available resources, and (3) previous owner, task, workload and experience of the resources with the task (BPIC-W 2012). Figure 6 presents the results for BPIC-W 2012 and BPIC-2013 for the variants of the features. Here again the accuracy for the BPIC-W 2012 event log is low when considering previous owner and task. Addition of past handovers made by a resource does not cause any improvements in the model accuracy (PrevOwn+Task+HOver in Fig. 6(a)). The long-tail distribution of handovers made by resources indicates that resources often work with many other resources while a select few have a high value of handovers to specific resources (Fig. 6(b)). Addition of resource workload significantly improves model performance. Addition of experience of resources on the task does not improve the model accuracy, which can be attributed to the distribution of resource experience on the tasks. Hence, model results show that resources consider workload when handing over tasks to other resources. Model performance for the BPIC 2013 log, improves by 3 points (6%) by addition of workload (Fig. 6(c)), confirming the influence of workload on the handover preference of one resource for another.

The model accuracy ranges from 53% to 60% in predicting the subsequent task or the resource indicating that the preference function can be learned from the event logs when information of workload, worklist and handovers are captured. The use of different features provides insights into the factors influencing resource preference such as frequency of the item in the worklist and workload of resources. Using a preference model to predict resource preferences would lead to 'preferred' resource and task allocation.

6   Conclusions and Future Work

While it has been recognised that preference can play a prominent role in resource behaviour and that this may guide resource allocation, there is only a small body of work in the BPM literature that touches upon this topic. Preferences can't take various forms and may influence resource allocation and choice of task in the context of business process automation. In this paper preference has been trated as an explicit concept in business process automation and various manifestations have been shown, some as mentioned in the literature and later formalised in the form of ORM models, some as (implicitly) present in workflow resource patterns and thus as mechanisms in process automation systems, and some as can be found in event logs. In the latter case it was shown how these could be discovered through the use of machine learning. This was illustrated using two real-life logs from the set of BPIC logs.

The present work provides a starting point for examining preference in greater detail in a business process automation context, in terms of the forms it can take, the way these forms can be used to support resource allocation and how they can automatically be derived from event logs in order to keep them up to date. All of these give rise to further work. Ideally, preferences are more explicitly represented in BPM systems so that their influence is more visible and they can be utilised better.

We would like to conclude by acknowledging some limitations. We recognise that one can think off-the-cuff of many forms of preference in the context of resource allocation for business process automation. However, we have consciously refrained from doing so and stuck to what we unearthed from the literature. Also, ideally, more publicly available logs will be made available in the future containing rich resource information. These logs could expose other forms of preference, provide more insight into the accuracy of the methods we presented in Sect. 5, and even give rise to new automatic preference derivation mechanisms.

References

1. van der Aalst, W.M.P., Song, M.: Mining social networks: uncovering interaction patterns in business processes. In: Desel, J., Pernici, B., Weske, M. (eds.) BPM 2004. LNCS, vol. 3080, pp. 244–260. Springer, Heidelberg (2004). https://doi.org/10.1007/978-3-540-25970-1_16
2. Arias, M., Munoz-Gama, J., Sepúlveda, M.: Towards a taxonomy of human resource allocation criteria. In: Teniente, E., Weidlich, M. (eds.) BPM 2017. LNBIP, vol. 308, pp. 475–483. Springer, Cham (2018). https://doi.org/10.1007/978-3-319-74030-0_37
3. Cabanillas, C., García, J.M., Resinas, M., Ruiz, D., Mendling, J., Ruiz-Cortés, A.: Priority-based human resource allocation in business processes. In: Basu, S., Pautasso, C., Zhang, L., Fu, X. (eds.) ICSOC 2013. LNCS, vol. 8274, pp. 374–388. Springer, Heidelberg (2013). https://doi.org/10.1007/978-3-642-45005-1_26
4. Canal, G., Guillem A., Carme, T.: A taxonomy of preferences for physically assistive robots. In: 26th IEEE International Symposium on Robot and Human Interactive Communication, pp. 292–297. IEEE (2017)
5. Doyle, J.: Prospects for preferences. Comput. Intell. **20**(2), 111–136 (2004)
6. Erasmus, J., Vanderfeesten, I., Traganos, K., Jie-A-Looi, X., Kleingeld, A., Grefen, P.: A method to enable ability-based human resource allocation in business process management systems. In: Buchmann, R.A., Karagiannis, D., Kirikova, M. (eds.) PoEM 2018. LNBIP, vol. 335, pp. 37–52. Springer, Cham (2018). https://doi.org/10.1007/978-3-030-02302-7_3
7. Batista, M.F., Magdaleno, A., Kalinowski, M.: A survey on the use of social BPM in practice in brazilian organizations. In: Brazilian Symposium on IS, June 2017
8. García, J.M., Ruiz, D., Ruiz-Cortés, A.: A model of user preferences for semantic services discovery and ranking. In: Aroyo, L., et al. (eds.) ESWC 2010. LNCS, vol. 6089, pp. 1–14. Springer, Heidelberg (2010). https://doi.org/10.1007/978-3-642-13489-0_1
9. Glasser, W.: Choice Theory: A New Psychology of Personal Freedom. Harper Collins, New York (1998)
10. Goldsmith, J., Junker, U.: Preference handling for artificial intelligence. AI Mag. **29**(4), 9–103 (2008)
11. Guo, Z., et al.: An enhanced group recommender system by exploiting preference relation. IEEE Access **7**, 24852–24864 (2019)
12. Hagel, J., Schwartz, J., Bersin, J.: Navigating the future of work: can we point business, workers, and social institutions in the same direction? In: Deloitte Review, Issue 21, pp. 27–45. Deloitte University Press (2017)
13. Halpin, T.: Temporal modeling and ORM. In: Meersman, R., Tari, Z., Herrero, P. (eds.) OTM 2008. LNCS, vol. 5333, pp. 688–698. Springer, Heidelberg (2008). https://doi.org/10.1007/978-3-540-88875-8_93
14. Huang, Z., Xudong, L., Duan, H.: Resource behavior measure and application in business process management. Expert Syst. Appl. **39**(7), 6458–6468 (2012)

15. Jalali, A., et al.: Supporting aspect orientation in business process management - from process modelling to process enactment. Softw. Syst. Model. **16**(3), 903–925 (2017)
16. Jorge, A.B., McIlraith, S.A.: Planning with preferences. AI Mag. **29**(4), 25 (2008)
17. Kaci, S.: Working with Preferences: Less Is More. Springer, Heidelberg (2011). https://doi.org/10.1007/978-3-642-17280-9
18. Kumar, A., Dijkman, R., Song, M.: Optimal resource assignment in workflows for maximizing cooperation. In: Daniel, F., Wang, J., Weber, B. (eds.) BPM 2013. LNCS, vol. 8094, pp. 235–250. Springer, Heidelberg (2013). https://doi.org/10.1007/978-3-642-40176-3_20
19. Lee, K.M.: Adaptive resource scheduling for workflows considering competence and preference. In: Negoita, M.G., Howlett, R.J., Jain, L.C. (eds.) KES 2004. LNCS (LNAI), vol. 3214, pp. 723–730. Springer, Heidelberg (2004). https://doi.org/10.1007/978-3-540-30133-2_95
20. Macris, A., Papadimitriou, E., Vassilacopoulos, G.: An ontology-based competency model for workflow activity assignment policies. J. Knowl. Manag. **12**(6), 72–88 (2008)
21. zur Muehlen, M.: Organizational management in workflow applications–issues and perspectives. Inf. Technol. Manag. **5**(3–4), 271–291 (2004)
22. Peintner, B., Viappiani, P., Yorke-Smith, N.: Preferences in interactive systems: technical challenges and case studies. AI Mag. **29**(4), 13–13 (2008)
23. Pika, A., Wynn, M.T., Fidge, C.J., ter Hofstede, A.H.M., Leyer, M., van der Aalst, W.M.P.: An extensible framework for analysing resource behaviour using event logs. In: Jarke, M., et al. (eds.) CAiSE 2014. LNCS, vol. 8484, pp. 564–579. Springer, Cham (2014). https://doi.org/10.1007/978-3-319-07881-6_38
24. Russell, N., van der Aalst, W.M.P., ter Hofstede, A.H.M.: Work-Flow Patterns: The Definitive Guide. MIT Press, Cambridge (2016)
25. Shaw, J.D., Duffy, M.K., Stark, E.M.: Interdependence and preference for group work: main and congruence effects on the satisfaction and performance of group members. J. Manag. **26**(2), 259–279 (2000)
26. Sindhgatta, R., Ghose, A., Dam, H.K.: Context-aware analysis of past process executions to aid resource allocation decisions. In: Nurcan, S., Soffer, P., Bajec, M., Eder, J. (eds.) CAiSE 2016. LNCS, vol. 9694, pp. 575–589. Springer, Cham (2016). https://doi.org/10.1007/978-3-319-39696-5_35
27. Slovic, P.: The construction of preference. Am. Psychol. **50**(5), 364–371 (1995). ISSN: 0003–066X
28. Sohail, A., Dominic, P.D.D.: Business process improvement: a process warehouse based resource management method. In: International Symposium on Technology Management and Emerging Technologies, pp. 291–296. IEEE (2015)
29. Sohail, A., Dominic, P.D.D., Shahzad, K.: Business process analysis: a process warehouse-based resource preference evaluation method. Int. J. Bus. Inf. Syst. **21**(2), 137–161 (2016)
30. Vanderfeesten, I., Grefen, P.: Advanced dynamic role resolution in business processes. In: Persson, A., Stirna, J. (eds.) CAiSE 2015. LNBIP, vol. 215, pp. 87–93. Springer, Cham (2015). https://doi.org/10.1007/978-3-319-19243-7_8
31. Yuen, M., King, I., Leung, K.: Task recommendation in crowdsourcing systems. In: Proceedings of the First International Workshop on Crowd- Sourcing and Data Mining, pp. 22–26. ACM (2012)
32. Zhao, W., et al.: An entropy-based clustering ensemble method to support resource allocation in business process management. Knowl. Inf. Syst. **48**(2), 305–330 (2016)

Scenario-Based Prediction of Business Processes Using System Dynamics

Mahsa Pourbafrani[1(✉)], Sebastiaan J. van Zelst[1,2],
and Wil M. P. van der Aalst[1,2]

[1] Chair of Process and Data Science, RWTH Aachen University, Aachen, Germany
{mahsa.bafrani,s.j.v.zelst,wvdaalst}@pads.rwth-aachen.de
[2] Fraunhofer Institute for Applied Information Technology (FIT),
Sankt Augustin, Germany
{sebastiaan.van.zelst,wil.van.der.aalst}@fit.fraunhofer.de

Abstract. Many organizations employ an information system that supports the execution of their business processes. During the execution of these processes, event data are stored in the databases that support the information system. The field of process mining aims to transform such data into actionable insights, which allow business owners to improve their daily operations. For example, a process model describing the actual execution of the process can be easily extracted from the captured event data. Most process mining techniques are "backward-looking" providing compliance and performance information. Few process mining techniques are "forward-looking". Therefore, in this paper, we propose a novel scenario-based predictive approach that allows us to assess and predict future behavior in business processes. In particular, we propose to use system dynamics to allow for "what-if" questions. We create a system dynamics model using variables trained on the basis of the past behavior of the process, as captured in the event log. This model is used to explore the effect of possibly applied changes in the process as well as roles of external factors, e.g., human behavior. Using real event data, we demonstrate the feasibility of our approach to predict possible consequences of future decisions and policies.

Keywords: Process mining · Scenario-based prediction · System dynamics · What-if analysis · Simulation

1 Introduction

Modern information systems allow us to track the execution of the business processes of an organization. *Process mining* techniques [2] have proven to be a valuable addition to the toolbox of modern-day process analysts. Process mining provides several data-driven algorithms and tools that allow us to gain a better understanding of, and insights in, the execution of the business processes at play. For example, in *process discovery* [3], techniques allow us to discover a process

© Springer Nature Switzerland AG 2019
H. Panetto et al. (Eds.): OTM 2019, LNCS 11877, pp. 422–439, 2019.
https://doi.org/10.1007/978-3-030-33246-4_27

model that accurately describes the process as captured in the data. Similarly, in *conformance checking* [4], techniques assess to what degree a given process model is in line with the captured data. Furthermore, a multitude of techniques exists, i.e., *process enhancement techniques* [8,9], that aim to increase the overall *view of the process*, e.g., projecting performance information in a process model.

The intrinsic value and premise of process mining are clear and widely accepted: *data does not lie*. At the same time, data-driven support for possible next steps to be taken by the organization, in order to improve the process performance, e.g., increasing workforce, is often missing. Undisputed, more advanced algorithms to predict the future behavior of a process, specifically with the aim of improving process performance, are of interest to many organizations. However, in process mining, existing work towards the prediction of future behavior w.r.t. performance of processes, typically depends on extensive knowledge about the process [13,14]. For example, the approach presented in [14] uses discovered process models as a basis and, therefore, implicitly, depends on the quality of the discovered process model. Other techniques do not require in-depth knowledge of the process [18,19], however, such techniques focus on short-term prediction. "What-if" analysis is different from existing techniques that try to predict at the case level. None of the existing techniques predict the effects of changes in the execution of the process on a large scale, without having explicit in-depth knowledge of the process. However, a decision maker of an organization often has a limited view and understanding of the global process, yet is interested in the prediction of global key process performance indicators by *explicitly taking the business context into account*. For example, to investigate whether replacing a resource in an assembly line reduces the overall service time.

In this paper, we present a novel approach that allows us to predict future behavior in business processes, subject to envisioned future scenarios. In particular, we exploit *system dynamics* [16], i.e., a modeling formalism designed to inspect the effects of changes within an organization. System dynamics is a widely used approach in the context of scenario-based analysis supported by software tools, e.g., `vensim` (http://vensim.com). An overview of the proposed approach, including its relation to conventional system dynamics and process mining, is depicted in Fig. 1.

Our approach starts with a data processing step in which we transform an event log into a collection of measurable aspects with an associated temporal ordering. Subsequently, we map these measurable aspects onto system dynamics model elements, which allows us to predict future behavior of virtually any measurable aspect of a process. To evaluate the proposed approach, we conducted a collection of experiments using both synthetic and real data sets and we mostly focus on the real data sets. Our experiments show that by using an aggregated view of the process performance by means of system dynamics, it is possible to predict the effects of changes on future process performance.

The remainder of this paper is organized as follows. In Sect. 2, we explain the motivation. In Sect. 3, we present related work. In Sect. 4, we introduce background concepts and basic notation used throughout the paper. In Sect. 5, we present our main approach. We evaluate the proposed approach in Sect. 6. Section 7 concludes our work and discusses interesting directions for future work.

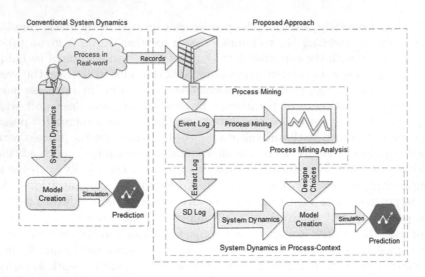

Fig. 1. Schematic overview of the proposed approach and its relation to conventional System Dynamics and Process Mining. In the proposed framework, we populate a system dynamics model with process performance statistics distilled from the previous execution of the process as captured in an event log.

2   Motivation

Business owners and decision makers are highly interested to improve the performance of their processes. However, considering the cost of changes in the process, it is required to have insights about the effects of the new changes in the processes before applying them in reality. Different techniques propose the simulation and prediction of the processes, e.g., discrete event simulation. Discrete event simulation techniques need extensive knowledge of the process, and are not able to take the context of prediction into account. Context is often neglected during future analysis in process mining [5]. Also, it is not possible to incorporate the effects of external factors in the models, e.g., human behaviors or environmental variables such as economic. Moreover, the level of detail in these types of approach does not allow for high-level modeling and long-term predictions.

As Fig. 2 represents, most of the prediction techniques in process mining focus in the center of the circle, i.e., instance level. As opposed to the existing simulation techniques, system dynamics allows us to assess the impact of changes in the process from a *global perspective* as well as the effects of *external factors*. Using different levels of granularity in the modeling, we can address major drawbacks of discrete event simulation techniques.

The motivation of our new approach is to move from the center of Fig. 2, i.e., instance level to the outside layers and providing "what-if" analysis at a higher level of abstraction which also takes the context into account. There is a trade-off between the amount of knowledge inside the process and the chosen

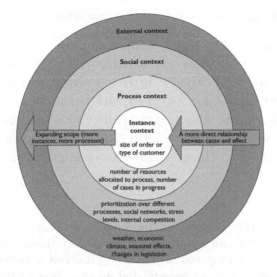

Fig. 2. Various contexts and levels of abstraction in process mining [5].

abstraction level. Also, freedom of considering the external factors influences the accuracy of the results. The detailed level of designed system dynamics models, i.e., benefiting from knowing the detail of a process will lead the simulation to be more similar to the discrete event simulation. However, we mainly focus on the roles of external variables and providing the missing bridge between the "as-is" state of the processes to the future state, i.e, "to-be" based on "what-if" analysis.

3   Related Work

To the best of our knowledge, this is the first work that proposes to combine the fields of process mining and system dynamics techniques for the purpose of scenario-based prediction. We refer to [2, 16] for an overview of system dynamics and process mining respectively.

Process mining research is mostly "backward-looking". Compared to the "backward-looking" approaches, a few "forward-looking" approaches exist. In [14] discrete event simulation on the basis of discovered process models is introduced. The approach in [15] is based on a combination of workflow management and simulation. Work using discrete event simulation requires many details. As a result, modeling and tuning models can be very time consuming. It is also impossible/difficult to simulate human behavior at a very detailed level as mentioned in [1]. There are approaches that focus on the prediction and recommendation, e.g., predicting the remaining process time or outcome of specific cases in [6]. The right abstraction level is very important for creating a model. These work are based on a detailed and case-based view and not at an aggregated level. A considerable number of methods have been put forward to address the problem of predictive process monitoring at the instance level [20]. Also, it

Table 1. A simple event log. Each row refers to an event.

Case ID	Activity	Resource	Start Timestamp	Complete Timestamp
1	Register	Rose	10/1/2018 7:38:45	10/1/2018 7:42:30
2	Register	Max	10/1/2018 8:08:58	10/1/2018 8:18:58
1	Submit Request	Eric	10/1/2018 7:42:30	10/1/2018 7:42:30
1	Accept Request	Max	10/1/2018 8:45:26	10/1/2018 9:08:58
2	Change Item	Eric	10/1/2018 9:45:37	10/1/2018 9:58:13
3	Register	Rose	10/1/2018 8:45:26	10/1/2018 9:02:05
...	...	...	...	...

is difficult to assess the reliability of the prediction results [1]. Moreover, some work generating models using statistical analysis. Considering time intervals in performance analysis is proposed in [17]. The proposed framework allows for a systematic approach to performance-related analysis beyond the capabilities of existing log-based analysis techniques.

In the field of system dynamics, different work focus on simulation and prediction. In particular, use of system dynamics in the context of business process management, e.g., using both Petri net models and system dynamics to develop a model for the same situation [7,12] can be mentioned. In [12], a standard SAP reference business process is used. The authors use system dynamics models to determine how the business process can be changed to achieve improvement in the employee productivity. Furthermore, [7] demonstrates how common problems, e.g., finding the average waiting time, are addressed with different models using a comparison of Petri net and system dynamics. In this work, the elements in Petri net (places and transitions) are considered as elements in the system dynamics models (stocks and flows).

The approach presented in this paper differs from existing approaches in various ways: (1) there is no need to model the process at a fine-grained level, i.e., our approach is based on an aggregated level (using system dynamics), (2) designing the system dynamics model at an aggregated level is relatively simple in comparison with methods such as Colored Petri Net tools (CPN) (which is complicated for the larger/complex processes and need complete knowledge of the processes), (3) the approach uses valid models which behave the same as reality, and, (4) the approach provides a platform, allowing us to involve the external factors/human behavior and their effects in the simulation results.

4 Background

In this section, we formalize concepts related to process mining and system dynamics.

Process Mining. Historic data, captured during the execution of a company's processes, play a central role in any process mining analysis. The execution of an *activity*, in the context of some process instance, identified by a unique *case ID*, is referred to as an *event*. Consider Table 1, in which we present a simplified example of an event log. Observe that, in the event log, there are events depicted of three different process instances, identified by Case IDs 1, 2 and 3. The first event in the event log describes that *Rose* started performing a *Register* activity at 10/1/2018 7:38:45 and completed the activity at 10/1/2018 7:42:30. Note that, as exemplified, multiple process instances run at the same time, i.e., the second event refers to Case ID 2, whereas the third event again refers to Case ID 1. Table 1 depicts the basic form of an event log. Typically, an event log includes more data attributes related to the process, e.g., the costs of an activity, account balance, customer id, etc.

Definition 1 (Event Log). *Let $\mathcal{C}$, $\mathcal{A}$, $\mathcal{R}$ and $\mathcal{T}$ denote the universe of case identifiers, activities, resources and the time universe respectively. The universe of events ξ is defined as the Cartesian product of the aforementioned universes, i.e., $\xi=\mathcal{C} \times \mathcal{A} \times \mathcal{R} \times \mathcal{T} \times \mathcal{T}$. Furthermore, we define corresponding projection functions $\pi_{\mathcal{C}}: \xi \rightarrow \mathcal{C}$, $\pi_{\mathcal{A}}: \xi \rightarrow \mathcal{A}$, $\pi_{\mathcal{R}}: \xi \rightarrow \mathcal{R}$ and $\pi_{\mathcal{T}}: \xi \rightarrow \mathcal{T} \times \mathcal{T}$, where, given $e=(c,a,r,t_s,t_e) \in \xi$, we have $\pi_{\mathcal{C}}(e)=c$, $\pi_{\mathcal{A}}(e)=a$, $\pi_{\mathcal{R}}(e) = r$ and $\pi_{\mathcal{T}}(e)=(t_s,t_c)$ where t_s and t_c represent the start and complete time of event e. $L \subseteq \xi$ is defined as an event log. Also, we consider T_s and T_c as the start and completion time of the event log respectively.*

Consider the first event depicted in Table 1. In the context of Definition 1, the first row (which we denote as e_1), describes: $\pi_{\mathcal{C}}(e_1)=1$, $\pi_{\mathcal{A}}(e_1)=Register$, $\pi_{\mathcal{R}}(e_1)=Rose$ and $\pi_{\mathcal{T}}(e_1)=(10/1/2018 \; 7:38:45, \; 10/1/2018 \; 7:42:30)$.

System Dynamics. System dynamics modeling describes a collection of approaches, techniques, and tools, that help in understanding how complex systems change over time [16]. It allows us to model complex, dynamic systems, in a structured manner and to capture the factors affecting the behavior of such a system by modeling the typically *nonlinear behavior* of such systems. Within system dynamics, we use a specific modeling notation, i.e., a *stock-flow diagram*, that allows us to simulate possible future behavior of a system [10], e.g., a (business) process. Such a diagram captures the different relations between a given collection of variables. Moreover, it allows us to calculate, subject to the aforementioned relations, the future values of these variables during different steps in time. The basic structure of a system dynamics model is a set of mathematical equations such as first-order differential (or integral) equations.

A stock-flow diagram consists of three basic elements, i.e., *stocks*, *flows* and *variables*. A stock represents any entity that is able to accumulate over time, e.g., the number of patients waiting in a hospital. A flow is either an *inflow* or *outflow*. An inflow increases the accumulated entity represented by a stock, whereas an outflow reduces the accumulated entity. Finally, any environmental factor that is able to influence the in-/outflow of a stock is modeled as a variable. A variable is also able to influence other variables. Furthermore, the value of a stock, in turn, is able to influence a variable. In Fig. 3, an example stock-flow

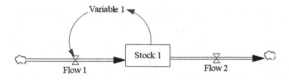

Fig. 3. A simple example stock-flow diagram and the underlying relation of Stock 1 (st_1) w.r.t. its in- and outflow (Flow 1 (f_1) and Flow 2 (f_2)).

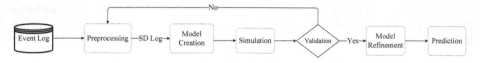

Fig. 4. General overview of the proposed framework. An event log is transformed into a *System Dynamics Log* (SD-Log), which describes the values of a collection of parameters of the process over time. The calculated values of the process parameters are used to populate a stock-flow diagram, which is used for simulation. After validation, model refinement and adding external parameters to the stock-flow diagram is possible. The model is used to predict future behavior of the process.

diagram is shown and the equation depicted on the right-hand side of Fig. 3 describes the underlying relation for the diagram. Consider t as time, Stock 1 is equal to the amount in Stock 1 at time t_0 plus the integral over the difference of the Flow 1 and Flow 2 over the time interval $[t_0, t_n]$.

In each step, values of stock-flow elements get updated based on the previous values of the other elements that influence them. For example, if the number of the patients arriving for a visit (pa) in a hospital is about 5 patients per hour (flow), and in one hour, 4 patients is being visited (pv), the number of patients waiting to be visited (pw) (stock) after 5 h is 5 patients (time step 1 h and at first there is no patient waiting ($pw_0 = 0$)) according to the equation $pw = pw_0 + \int_0^5 (+pa - pv)\mathrm{d}t.$

5   Approach

In this section, we describe the main approach presented in this paper, i.e., using system dynamics for scenario-based prediction of business processes, on the basis of past process executions. Consider Fig. 4, in which we present an overview of the proposed architecture. First, we transform a conventional event log into a *System Dynamics Log (SD-Log)*. An SD-Log describes the values of different process parameters over a predefined fixed set of time windows. Using an SD-Log the behavior of the process parameters, i.e., their patterns over time are identified. We use the SD-Log to populate the stocks, flows, and variables in a given stock-flow diagram. Ideally, the designed stock-flow model does not contain any external parameters from outside the SD-Log. External parameters which are not provided in the SD-Log, complicate the validation step. Having both the values/patterns of the process parameters in the SD-Log and the simulation results, we check the validity of the model. If the model is unreliable, we change the time window granularity and repeat the aforementioned steps. When we have a reliable model, we are able to refine the stock-flow diagram to represent a specific scenario, e.g., by adding external parameters outside the process into it. Subsequently, we generate predictions by simulating the model.

5.1 Preprocessing

We populate the elements in the stock-flow diagrams with values originating from the process execution, extracted from the event log. We translate the conventional event log into a sequence of process parameter values, e.g., the arrival rate of cases for the execution of the process, measured per window of time. Hence, we first transform the event log into an SD-Log, which describes the values of these parameters over a sequence of discrete time windows.

The first step in the transformation of an event log to be used in system dynamics is to find its *measurable aspects*. We refer to these measurable aspects as process parameters, which provide values for the stock-flow diagrams elements. To do so, we define *scopes* and *types*. A variable scope represents the entity that we measure whereas the type represents what we measure for a given scope. In principle, numerous scopes and associated types are possible, e.g., measuring how the number of patients waiting (type) to be visited (scope) in a hospital changes over time.

In the context of this paper, we define a collection of *standard scopes and types*. The scopes are defined based on the granularity of different perspectives of business processes. Particularly covering the *general process, organization level, control-flow/process milestones* and *roles/resources* perspectives of business processes. The type of a parameter can be a *rate*, a *duration* or a *number*. In Fig. 5b, we schematically present the aforementioned pre-defined types. Figure 5a shows an example set of possible process parameters for the general perspective which is at the instance level and resource perspective at the event level. By taking the possible scopes and types of the process, we are able to generate a log with all possible process parameters which are usable in a stock-flow diagram used for prediction.

Using a predefined time window δ, in which we have the most similar behavior of the process parameters, we calculate values of process parameters and structure SD-Log. The time window can be derived in multiple ways, however, in this work, we consider selecting the time window based on ground knowledge.

Definition 2 (SD-Log). *Let $\mathcal{V}$ be a set of process parameters, δ be the selected time window, and $k \in \mathbb{N}$. An SD-Log is a function $SD\colon \mathcal{V} \times \{1,...,k\} \to \mathbb{R}$, where $k = \lceil (T_c - T_s)/\delta \rceil$.*

We split the event log based on the selected time window (δ) and calculate the possible process parameters in each time window. Reconsider the example of number of patients waiting to be visited in the hospital,

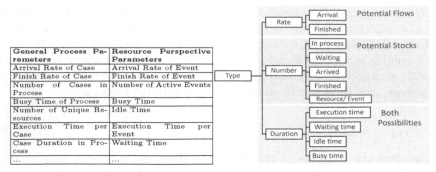

(a) An example set of process param- (b) Three types of process parameters regarding the general process eters. The possible detail parame-
and resource perspective, e.g., types ters regarding each type. The relation
of "Arrival Rate of Case" and "Wait- between the stock-flow diagram ele-
ing Time" are rate and duration re- ments and the types of parameters is
spectively.   shown.

Fig. 5. Different types of process parameters and an example set of process parameters.

assume that $L \subseteq \xi$ is an event log and $\delta=1$ h. Let v_1 and $v_2 \in V$ be
the *arrival rate of patients for the visit* and *number of patients waiting for
the visit* in each time window. Assume the duration of L is 10 h, imply-
ing $k = 10$. The SD-log regarding $\delta = 1$ h and the two parameters is:
$\{((v_1, 1), 12), ((v_1, 2), 11), ..., ((v_1, 10), 13), ((v_2, 1), 6), ..., ((v_2, 10), 8)\}$, i.e., representing that in the first hour, 12 patients arrived to be visited and 6 patients
were waiting to be visited, and so on.

Duration and rate based parameters occur multiple times in one time window,
we consider the average of the values in each time window. In some cases, the
information regarding calculation of specific parameters is not included in the
selected parts of the event log. If an activity or a resource does not appear in
some parts of the event log, we assign specific policies to tackle the situation.
For the duration based parameters, in the absence of a specific activity/resource
in one of the time window, we consider a value of 0. If it is running in more than
one time window, then in each time window the complete duration is taken into
account. For the number and rate based parameters, in the absence of specific
activity/resource in one of the time windows, we consider a value of 0.

Time Window Stability Test and Behavior Detection. The ultimate
goal of our approach is to have a model which is able to perform a scenario-
based analysis. For this reason we need to have a model which behaves same
as in reality. Therefore, the values, which represent the process parameters
in the stock-flow diagram should behave similar in the selected time window
δ. *Behavior Detection* provides insights inside the patterns of values and the
closest distribution which they can fit into. In *Behavior Detection*, we use

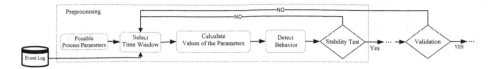

Fig. 6. Detailed view of preprocessing step in the approach (Fig. 4). *Time Window Stability* and *Behavior Detection* continue through the framework.

Kolmogorov-Smirnov test [11], to discover the closest distribution in the selected time window. The coefficient of variance is also used to define the accepted variance among values of a parameter which we refer to it as *Stability Test*. Stability test helps us to inspect whether the values of the process parameters behave similar enough in provided δ or not. The threshold for the distributions similarity (p-value) and for the coefficient of variation (less than 1) is customized based on the level of freedom for accepting the difference between values in reality and simulation. The time window selection in preprocessing step Fig. 6, is a repetitive process, i.e., it continues until the stability test is passed and finishes when validation is passed for the simulation results.

An event log represents the events up to the specific point in time, therefore, the model can be populated with the values of parameters until the event log is recorded. In order to have an aggregated model, the values can be replaced by a single value, e.g., mean or their behavior which are defined by discovered distributions and attributes using behavior detection.

It should be noted, in some cases, variables in the event log are not supposed to show a similar behavior in each time window. Therefore, we mainly focus on the aggregated level of the variables. For instance, it is difficult to find the small time window of hours or days for the event log of the emergency room in a hospital. The arrival rate or duration of activities are not similar enough, however we are able to extend the time windows to capture more similar behavior.

5.2 Designing Stock-Flow Diagrams

In the second step, we design a stock-flow diagram with the process parameters contained in the SD-Log. Such a stock-flow diagram is either given such as the aggregated model in Sect. 6 or, designed based on the scenarios of interests. The generated SD-Log based on the scenarios and the detected behavior from the prepossessing step are the inputs for designing the stock-flow diagram. Figure 5b provides some constraints on how to map the process parameters inside the SD-Log on the stock-flow diagram elements. The rate-based parameters are allowed to represent flows, the number-based parameters are allowed to represent stocks, and duration types are either flows, stocks or simple variables. For example, parameter "patient arrival rate for visit" per hour has the scope of activity-flow (visit) and type of arrival (rate), therefore in a stock-flow diagram it can act as an (in)flow for the activity "number of patients waiting for the visit".

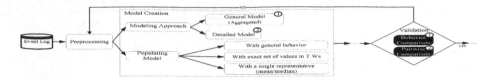

Fig. 7. The "model creation" step in the approach including "modeling approaches" and "populating approaches". Aggregated and detailed modeling regarding the abstraction level and three approaches for model population. The validation after simulation depends on the modeling approach of choice (labeled with 1 and 2).

This parameter can be a stock element since it has the same scope (activity-flow) and type of number (waiting).

As Fig. 7 shows, two approaches are possible for designing the models, designing general models or detailed models. In the general models, we are looking for the aggregated level of the process without having extensive knowledge from inside the process. For designing detailed models more knowledge of the process is required. Since modeling benefits from detail knowledge of the process, it is possible to perform the validation including pairwise comparison (labeled as 2 in Fig. 7), which is explained in Sect. 5.3.

The main steps for designing the stock-flow diagrams and simulation are: (1) identify related process parameters for the desired scenario/change, (2) identify the relationship between the parameters, and (3) define the mathematical relationship between the parameters (equations). The design choices in the scenarios and model creation can be addressed more effectively using contextual knowledge from the process mining, i.e., decide on diverting more cases to a specific resource based on the idle time that performance analysis reveals.

After determining the involved parameters (which affect the target of simulation) in the scenario, and their relations, adding the equations lead to a complete stock-flow diagram. Observe that, the values of some of the parameters are directly derived from the SD-Log whereas the values of the stocks are calculated by mathematical equations based on flows. Also, the values of flows are allowed to be based on the values of variables. After defining the equation, the values of the stock-flow diagram elements get updated automatically (simulation).

For the example of patients visiting the hospital, a sample scenario for the hospital is to decrease the *number of patients waiting (npw)* (stock) to be visited in each time window δ. It is clear that the *average arrival rate (aar)* of patients (flow) and the *average duration of the visit (ad)* (variable) are process parameters which directly influence the npw in δ. Also, the *average number of patients being visited* in δ (one hour) (*anp*) (flow) can be derived from (*ad*). Figure 8a shows the simple stock-flow diagram for the example scenario. The underlying equations for the designed stock-flow diagram which update the values for npw in each δ are mentioned in Fig. 8b. The values of ad and aar in each time window are calculated using the presented SD function. We can simulate the model and calculate the values of npw for k time window of δ.

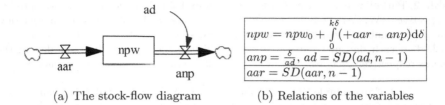

(a) The stock-flow diagram   (b) Relations of the variables

Fig. 8. Simple stock-flow diagram and equations representing underlying relations of the variables for predicting the number of patients waiting to be visited.

5.3   Simulation and Validation

The next step in the proposed approach is performing the simulation and validation, i.e., predicting and checking similarity of the values of the parameters in simulation and reality in each time window. We populate stock-flow diagrams with the values of the process parameters. Using the exact values of the parameters, for each element in the stock-flow diagram, current value gets updated by the value in the previous time window. From the specific point in time in which there is no value for the event log, we are able to use the most similar distribution derived from time window selection section. We generate the data based on the distribution and its features and populate our model with them. This is done based on the same time window as described by the SD-Log. Moreover, it is possible to use a representative for the values of parameters over time in the stock-flow diagram, i.e., the average of the values. Figure 7 includes three aforementioned approaches. Also, it illustrates the populating approaches in the modeling step which affect validation step. We refer to SD_l and SD_m as functions which return the values from SD-log (SD_l) and values from simulating the model (SD_m). We want to ensure that any prediction we perform is meaningful. Consider $v_1, v_2, v_3 \in V$, where $SD_l(v, n)$ represents the value of process parameters v in the SD-Log in time window n. Assume that v_3 is calculated based on the values of v_1 and v_2, $v_3 = F(v_1, v_2)$, where F represents the equation in the model. Performing simulation, $SD_m(v_3, n + 1) = F(SD_m(v_1, n), SD_m(v_2, n))$, where $SD_m(v_1, n)$ and $SD_m(v_2, n)$ can be provided directly from SD-Log, i.e., $SD_m(v_1, n) = SD_l(v_1, n - 1)$ or can be generated by their behavior, i.e., the distributions of the values in the SD_l. As Fig. 7 indicates the other possibility is to use a representative of values in SD_l such the average. Consider Tables 2a and b as examples of the SD_l and the peer SD_m. We used the exact set of values in each day to perform simulation. The values of "Number of Cases Arrived" and "Number of Cases Finished" are updated in the SD_m by their previous values in the SD_l. The values of "Number of Cases in the Process" is calculate in each day using values of two other parameters.

Table 2. Part of an example SD_1 and the generated simulated log SD_m for the process perspective. TW, Arrival Rate, Finished Rate, Cases in the process are time window (one day), number of cases arrived for the process in each day, number of cases that finished in each day and number of cases which remains unfinished per day in the process respectively.Notation "S" indicates that the values of the parameters are simulated.

(a) Part of an example SD_l, including three process parameters for general perspective.

(b) Part of the generated SD_m containing training results of simulation using the provided SD_l.

TW	Arrival Rate	Finished Rate	Cases in the Process	...	TW	SArrival Rate	SFinished Rate	SCases in the Process	...
0	42	41	1	...	0	42	41	1	...
1	54	49	6	...	1	42	41	2	...
2	51	55	2	...	2	54	49	7	...
3	46	45	1	...	3	51	55	3	...
...	...	...	...	...	...	...	...	...	...

In the validation step, the level of similarity of our simulation results with reality (SD-Log) is being investigated. Based on the populating approach in the simulation, we perform validation. We perform a pairwise comparison of values for each process parameter, which is defined as $SD_l(v, n) - SD_m(v, n)$, in the cases that we chose exact values from SD_l. In the cases that we use the aggregated level and the values are generated using SD_b, the validation comprises only similarity between the generated values for the process parameters in the simulation (their distributions). In fact, we compare whether simulated results are not significantly different from the SD-Log. Background knowledge allows us to define the maximum allowed difference considering the scale of variables, purpose of simulation and the underlying subject of simulation.

5.4   Prediction

In the prediction phase, we assess the effect of different scenarios, e.g., policy changes within the process, on the process performance characteristic of interest. We do so by systematically altering the values of the different parameters, i.e., elements in the stock-flow diagram, or changing the underlying equations. In the example of patients waiting to be visited, we are able to predict the change in the number of patients waiting to be visited, by changing the average patient arrival rate in the model. The results of the prediction (using **vensim**) are shown in Fig. 9. Assume the arrival rate is a normal distribution with a mean of 6 patients per hour and the average duration of visiting of each patient follows the normal distribution with the mean of 18 min. A change such as the arrival of 1 more patient per hour leads to a higher number of patients waiting over the sequence of time steps in 12 h.

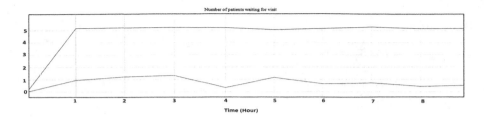

Fig. 9. The prediction result of a simple stock-flow diagram for the number of patients waiting for the visit. The green chart (bottom) shows the number of waiting patients in each time step when the average arrival rate is 6 and the blue chart (up) indicates the same variables with 7 as average arrival rate.

6 Evaluation

To validate the proposed approach, we performed different evaluations including real and synthetic event logs. In this section, we provide the results of evaluating our approach using real event logs. The purpose of the evaluation is to illustrate that our proposed approach is able to predict the result of specific changes in the process at an aggregated level without specific knowledge about the process model. Having the event log and generated SD-log, our model is able to simulate and show similar behavior to reality. After the validation, we are able to enrich our model for further change/policy analysis.

We applied our framework on the real event log *BPIChallenge2017* [21] to test the feasibility of the approach in reality. The event log includes different executions of processes for taking a loan by customers. Using our framework we assess different scenarios. Our goal is to achieve a stock-flow diagram which behaves same as reality and then perform further scenario-based analyses such as resource allocation. Note that, we have no explicit knowledge of any policy/change being applied in the process over the time period captured in the event log. We design a model at an aggregated level without having any information from the steps inside the process. Starting from the event log we choose the time window of one week and create the SD-Log regarding the *general process* perspective. The process parameters in a holistic view are case arrival rate, case finish rate and maximum capacity of the process in the time window. Figure 10 shows the designed model for a general process. After performing time stability test and identifying the behavior of the values of parameters (distributions), we populate the designed model with the existing behavior of process parameters in the SD-Log. Since the parameters in the model are generated using random functions following the identified distributions, specific conditions regarding reality should be considered. The sum of the numbers of arriving cases and the number of cases in the process in each time window should be always less than the sum of the number of cases that finished and maximum capacity of the process in the same time window. The equation below represents the aforementioned conditions: $Case\,in\,Process + Case\,Arrival\,Rate < Finish\,Rate + Max\,Process\,Capacity$. Also, the finish rate of the process in each time window cannot be bigger

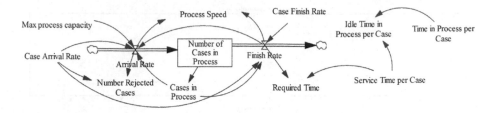

Fig. 10. Model designed based on the general process perspective. The generated behavior is similar to reality.

Table 3. Table of underlying equations in the general process perspective stock-flow diagram.

Stock-flow element	Value
Case Arrival Rate	Poisson distribution with mean 440 case per week
Case Finish Rate	Poisson distribution with mean 440 case per week
Number of Cases in Process	Arrival Rate - Finish Rate
Max process capacity	56
Number Rejected Cases	Case Arrival Rate - Arrival Rate
Time in Process per Case	Normal distribution with average of 8.30 h
Service Time per Case	Normal distribution with average of 7 h
Required Time	Finish Rate * Service Time per Case
Idle Time in Process per Case	Time in Process per Case - Service Time per Case

than the number of arrived cases and the number of cases in the process: $Finish\,Rate < Case\,Arrival\,Rate + Cases\,in\,Process$.

Table 3 shows the values and equations of the stock-flow diagram. As the result of validation shows the behavior of the elements in the model such as the number of cases in the process is similar to reality. Therefore our model as a valid model can be refined by inserting more external factors including resource efficiency in each time window.

Sample Scenario 1. Using the extended model in Fig. 11, we are able to predict several different scenarios, e.g., the effect of increasing in the arrival rate with the same finish rate on the number of rejected cases. Moreover, the effect of resource efficiency in the required time of resources can be predicted. For instance, in the process, 56 unique resources exist and in the case that they work 48 h per week for the current state of the process, variables *Resource Required Time* and *Resource Idle Time* show the needed and idle hours of the resources in the process. Inserting variable *Resource Efficiency* into the model, provides the possibility to manage the required time of resources realistically. Figure 12 shows the changes in required time per week with the efficiency of 85%. It reflects the reality more clear regarding the facts that resources does not work whole time with full efficiency. Benefiting from the result, the business owners are able to

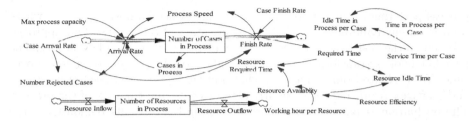

Fig. 11. Extended model based on the validated general model. The effect of changes in the resource aspects is predictable on the general aspect of the process. The effect of change in the aspects of process such as increase in arrival rate on the resources aspects is also predictable.

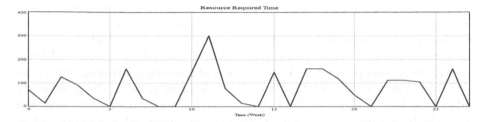

Fig. 12. The change in the required hours of resources based on the external factor, resource efficiency. Red chart (below) shows that with 100% efficiency the resource working hours regarding the current state of the process are enough. Blue chart indicates the required time after importing effect of resource efficiency of 85%. (Color figure online)

set policies such as providing more resources or setting more working hours in the current state of the process. There are variety of scenarios, e,g. effect of performing an activity such as "A_REGISTERED" in this event log using online forms instead of resources performing that manually. Changes in the service time in the process will influence the required hours of resources in the process.

This simple model illustrates the ability to perform scenario-based prediction regarding different aspects of a process and including external factors regardless of any knowledge inside the process. For the same purpose, existing techniques such as discrete event simulation need to know every step inside the process to simulate the behavior of the process even in aggregate level or the effect of changes. In long term policy analysis, the level of accuracy is highly different from the short term prediction such as discrete event simulation. Moreover, as the extended model shows the effects of different factors which may not explicitly exist in the process, e.g., resource efficiency can be considered in the results.

7   Conclusion

The approach presented in this paper provides a platform for organizations to inspect, in a scenario-based manner, the effect of changes in the process on process performance metrics of interest. We introduced a novel approach where we use system dynamics to predict the future state of the process. Our approach is based on the past behavior of a process captured in the form of event logs. The past behavior is transformed to a set of values of the process parameters over time. We evaluated our framework, choosing the aggregated level of a process and scenarios regarding changing arrival/finish rate and capacity of the process. The evaluation is based on a real event log, and the results demonstrate the ability of the proposed approach to predict the effects of changes similar to the way which would happen in reality. Moreover, presenting the stock-flow diagram of the specific scenario (the effect of increasing the arrival rate of cases and resource efficiency in the process), for the real event log, shows the feasibility of the approach.

Since this paper is the first work combining process mining and system dynamics, there are ample opportunities to extend our work. As a next step, we consider the automated generation of system dynamics models focusing on the general prospective. Furthermore, we aim to extend the scopes and types beyond the general perspective, control-flow and resource dimension, which exist in this work such as organization level. Using knowledge inside the process, the balance between aggregation level and the accuracy is also an interesting next step. Finally, we aim to investigate to what degree time window selection can be completely automated.

Acknowledgement. This work is partially funded by the German Research Foundation (Deutsche Forschungsgemeinschaft –DFG) in the context of the Cluster of Excellence Internet of Production (EXC 2023, 390621612).

References

1. van der Aalst, W.M.P.: Business process simulation survival guide. In: vom Brocke, J., Rosemann, M. (eds.) Handbook on Business Process Management 1. IHIS, pp. 337–370. Springer, Heidelberg (2015). https://doi.org/10.1007/978-3-642-45100-3_15
2. van der Aalst, W.M.P.: Process Mining - Data Science in Action. Springer, Heidelberg (2016). https://doi.org/10.1007/978-3-662-49851-4
3. Augusto, A., Conforti, R., Dumas, M., La Rosa, M., Bruno, G.: Automated discovery of structured process models from event logs: the discover-and-structure approach. Data Knowl. Eng. **117**, 373–392 (2018)
4. Carmona, J., van Dongen, B.F., Solti, A., Weidlich, M.: Conformance Checking - Relating Processes and Models. Springer, Switzerland (2018). https://doi.org/10.1007/978-3-319-99414-7
5. van Der Aalst, W.M.P., Dustdar, S.: Process mining put into context. IEEE Internet Comput. **16**(1), 82–86 (2012)
6. van Dongen, B.F., Crooy, R.A., van der Aalst, W.M.P.: Cycle time prediction: when will this case finally be finished? In: Meersman, R., Tari, Z. (eds.) OTM 2008. LNCS, vol. 5331, pp. 319–336. Springer, Heidelberg (2008). https://doi.org/10.1007/978-3-540-88871-0_22

7. Duggan, J.: A comparison of Petri net and system dynamics approaches for modelling dynamic feedback systems. In: 24th International Conference of the Systems Dynamics Society (2006)
8. Leemans, S.J.J., Fahland, D., van der Aalst, W.M.P.: Process and deviation exploration with inductive visual miner. In: Proceedings of the BPM Demo Sessions 2014 Co-located with the 12th International Conference on Business Process Management, Eindhoven, The Netherlands, 10 September 2014, p. 46 (2014)
9. Mannhardt, F., de Leoni, M., Reijers, H.A.: The multi-perspective process explorer. In: Proceedings of the BPM Demo Session 2015 Co-located with the 13th International Conference on Business Process Management, pp. 130–134 (2015)
10. Pruyt, E.: Small System Dynamics Models for Big Issues: Triple Jump Towards Real-world Complexity (2013)
11. Razali, N.M., Wah, Y.B., et al.: Power comparisons of shapiro-wilk, solmogorov-smirnov, lilliefors and anderson-darling tests. J. Stat. Model. Anal. **2**(1), 21–33 (2011)
12. Rosenberg, Z., Riasanow, T., Krcmar, H.: A system dynamics model for business process change projects. In: International Conference of the System Dynamics Society, pp. 1–27 (2015)
13. Rozinat, A., Mans, R.S., Song, M., van der Aalst, W.M.P.: Discovering colored Petri nets from event logs. STTT **10**(1), 57–74 (2008)
14. Rozinat, A., Mans, R.S., Song, M., van der Aalst, W.M.P.: Discovering simulation models. Inf. Syst. **34**(3), 305–327 (2009)
15. Rozinat, A., Wynn, M.T., van der Aalst, W.M.P., ter Hofstede, A.H.M., Fidge, C.J.: Workflow simulation for operational decision support. Data Knowl. Eng. **68**(9), 834–850 (2009)
16. Sterman, J.D.: Business dynamics: systems thinking and modeling for a complex world. No. HD30. 2 S7835 2000 (2000)
17. Suriadi, S., Ouyang, C., van der Aalst, W.M.P., ter Hofstede, A.H.M.: Event interval analysis: why do processes take time? Decis. Support Syst. **79**, 77–98 (2015)
18. Tax, N., Teinemaa, I., van Zelst, S.J.: An interdisciplinary comparison of sequence modeling methods for next-element prediction. CoRR abs/1811.00062 (2018). http://arxiv.org/abs/1811.00062
19. Tax, N., Verenich, I., La Rosa, M., Dumas, M.: Predictive business process monitoring with LSTM neural networks. In: Dubois, E., Pohl, K. (eds.) CAiSE 2017. LNCS, vol. 10253, pp. 477–492. Springer, Cham (2017). https://doi.org/10.1007/978-3-319-59536-8_30
20. Teinemaa, I., Dumas, M., Rosa, M.L., Maggi, F.M.: Outcome-oriented predictive process monitoring: review and benchmark. ACM Trans. Knowl. Discov. Data **13**(2), 171–1757 (2019). https://doi.org/10.1145/3301300
21. Van Dongen, B.F. (Boudewijn): BPI challenge 2017 (2017). https://doi.org/10.4121/UUID:5F3067DF-F10B-45DA-B98B-86AE4C7A310B

A Three-Layered Approach for Designing Smart Contracts in Collaborative Processes

Ada Bagozi, Devis Bianchini$^{(\boxtimes)}$, Valeria De Antonellis, Massimiliano Garda, and Michele Melchiori

Department of Information Engineering, University of Brescia,
Via Branze 38, 25123 Brescia, Italy
adabagozi@gmail.com, {devis.bianchini,valeria.deantonellis,
m.garda001,michele.melchiori}@unibs.it

Abstract. In collaborative environments, where enterprises interact each other's without a centralised authority that ensures trust among them, the ability of providing cross-organisational services must be enabled also between mutually untrusting participants. Blockchain platforms and smart contracts have been proposed to implement collaborative processes. However, current solutions are platform-dependent and deploy on-chain the whole process, thus increasing the execution costs of smart contracts if deployed on permissionless blockchain. In this paper, we propose an approach that includes criteria to identify trust-demanding objects and activities in collaborative processes, a model to describe smart contracts in a platform-independent way and guidelines to deploy them in a blockchain. To this aim, a three-layered model is used to describe: (i) the collaborative process, represented in BPMN, where the business expert is supported to add annotations that identify trust-demanding objects and activities; (ii) Abstract Smart Contracts based on trust-demanding objects and activities only and specified by means of descriptors, that are independent from any blockchain technology; (iii) Concrete Smart Contracts, that implement abstract ones and are deployed over a specific blockchain, enabling the creation of a repository where a single descriptor is associated with multiple implementations. The flexibility and reduced costs of the approach, due to the smart contracts abstraction and the use of blockchain only when necessary, are discussed with a case study on remote monitoring services in the digital factory.

Keywords: Blockchain · Smart contract · Collaborative processes

1 Introduction

In collaborative environments enterprises provide cross-organisational services to deliver integrated offerings of products and services, also known as servitization [15]. An example is given by anomaly detection services for remote monitoring

© Springer Nature Switzerland AG 2019
H. Panetto et al. (Eds.): OTM 2019, LNCS 11877, pp. 440–457, 2019.
https://doi.org/10.1007/978-3-030-33246-4_28

of Cyber Physical Systems in the digital factory. The Original Equipment Manufacturer (OEM) supplies the anomaly detection service, based on data streams collected from the machines of clients. In case anomalies have been identified before breakage events occur, the clients may be notified to avoid expensive repair operations, as well as costly down-times. Furthermore, insurance agencies may offer additional services to the OEM in order to limit the costs of maintenance operations under warranty, and external suppliers may know in advance scheduled maintenance interventions to prepare required spare parts. To ensure an additional value for the involved parties, servitization must be enabled also between mutually untrusting organisations. This is further true in open collaborative environments, where new enterprises might join or leave in every moment and it is not easy to find a centralised authority that ensures trust among them. From a data viewpoint, transactions performed on data objects, on which process activities are based, must be immutable and not repudiated for all participants. From an operational perspective, the way data objects are elaborated by software components (i.e., services) must be properly shared. For example, collected sensor data, used by the OEM for monitoring, should not be repudiated by clients. On the other hand, implementation of anomaly detection services must be accepted and transparently shared among all participants involved in the collaborative process.

Blockchain platforms, which maintain a distributed ledger of transactions without relying on any central authority, and smart contracts, i.e., programs transparently deployed on the blockchain, have been proposed to implement collaborative processes [2, 8, 10]. However, current solutions are platform-dependent and focus on the implementation of collaborative processes as a monolithic solution, where the whole process is deployed on-chain, thus increasing the execution costs of smart contracts on the blockchain. In [3] we proposed a preliminary approach where blockchain and smart contracts have been used to ensure trust in remote monitoring services. In this paper, we propose an approach that includes criteria to identify trust-demanding objects and activities in collaborative processes, a model to describe smart contracts in a platform-independent way and guidelines to deploy them in a blockchain. To this aim, a three-layered model is used to describe: (i) at the top, the collaborative process, represented using BPMN, where the business expert is supported to add annotations that identify *trust-demanding objects* and *activities*; (ii) *Abstract Smart Contracts* based on trust-demanding objects and activities only and specified by means of descriptors, that are independent from any blockchain technology; (iii) *Concrete Smart Contracts*, that implement abstract ones and are deployed over a specific blockchain, enabling the creation of a repository where a single descriptor is associated with multiple implementations. The flexibility and reduced costs of the approach, due to the smart contracts abstraction and the use of blockchain only when necessary, are discussed with a case study on remote monitoring services in the digital factory.

In the following, Sect. 2 introduces the three-layered approach overview; Sect. 3 describes the motivating case study and provides core definitions; Sect. 4 explains the semi-automatic steps to support Abstract Smart Contracts

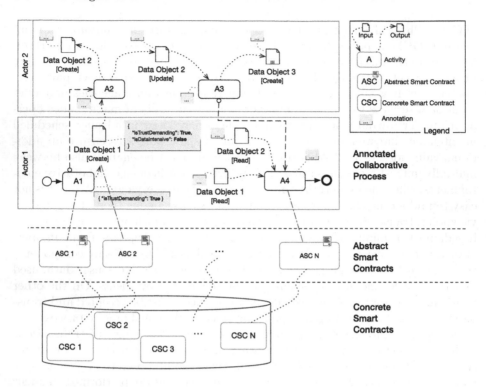

Fig. 1. Three-layered approach overview.

generation; Sect. 5 describes implementation and validation of the approach; Sect. 6 provides a comparison with related work; finally, Sect. 7 closes the paper and sketches future research work.

2   Three-Layered Approach Overview

Annotated Collaborative Process Layer. Figure 1 shows the three-layered approach proposed in this paper. At the top layer, the collaborative process is represented using BPMN. This standard represents, among the others, *activities*, that are organised into swimlanes, and different kinds of artefacts. Swimlanes can be *pools*, representing a participant in the process, and *lanes*, representing sub-partitions of a pool, such as different divisions within the same enterprise. Artefacts can be data objects, that is, data required (inputs) or created/updated/deleted by activities (outputs) and annotations, that is a mechanism for a modeler to provide additional text information on a BPMN diagram. Annotations can be associated to both activities and data objects. Using the annotations, the collaborative process is enriched in order to highlight *trust-demanding objects* and *trust-demanding activities*. The former ones represent data objects that are shared across different participants, and therefore transactions performed on these objects should be immutable and not repudiated by any participant. Transactions can be expressed through the well-known CRUD (Create, Read, Update, Delete) actions, as specified in Fig. 1 in the name of the object. In our approach, trust-demanding objects are candidates to be permanently stored within a blockchain. Among trust-demanding objects we distinguish those characterised by high volume and acquisition speed, denoted as *data-intensive*. Transactions on such objects, if stored within a blockchain, may require increased costs and will be properly managed as described below. Trust-demanding activities correspond to automated activities whose business logic must be non-repudiated and transparently shared among all the participants of the process. In our approach, they represent the candidates to be deployed as smart contracts within a blockchain.

Abstract Smart Contracts layer. In the middle layer, annotations are used to generated *Abstract Smart Contracts* (ASC). An ASC is generated: (a) for each BPMN activity annotated as trust-demanding, to represent its business logic that must be stored on-chain as shared code; (b) for each trust-demanding object, in which case the ASC includes as contract functions the CRUD actions performed on the object when stored on-chain. In the latter case, for data-intensive objects, in order to strike a trade-off between costs and tamper-proofness, the full data is kept off-chain, on top of an external Distributed File System (DFS) such as the InterPlanetary File System (IPFS)[1], while a link to it is stored on-chain.

Concrete Smart Contracts Layer. At the lower layer, ASC are deployed as *Concrete Smart Contracts* (CSC) over a specific blockchain. The development of CSC starting from ASC is in charge of the developer, who has the skills to deploy CSC over a specific blockchain. The developer provides the necessary platform-dependent code in order to implement the CSC functions. The proposed distinction between Abstract and Concrete Smart Contracts enables the creation of a repository where a single ASC descriptor may be associated with multiple CSC implementations. Moreover, it separates the role of business experts, who are in charge of designing the collaborative process and being supported during the identification of trust-demanding objects and activities, and the role of developers, who possess development skills for the specific blockchain technology on which CSC will be deployed.

In the next sections, formal definitions of trust-demanding objects and activities will be provided, as well as the description of semi-automatic steps that generate ASC/CSC starting from the annotated collaborative process. The deployment of CSC on a specific blockchain is out of the scope of this paper and will be treated only within the presentation of the remote monitoring service case study.

3 Motivating Case Study and Basic Definitions

3.1 Introduction of the Case Study

In Fig. 2 an example of BPMN for Remote Monitoring Services (RMS) in the digital factory is presented. Participants of the process are the OEM, one of

---

[1] https://ipfs.io.

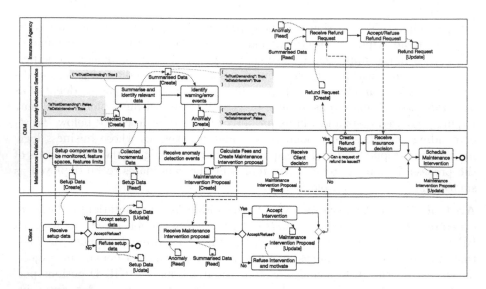

Fig. 2. BPMN of the remote monitoring services case study (only sample annotations are reported here).

its clients and the insurance agency, corresponding to three different BPMN pools, namely: OEM, Client and Insurance Agency. The OEM pool has been further organised in two sub-partitions, Maintenance Division lane and Anomaly Detection Service lane. In our model, we do not consider trust issues between participants associated with lanes within the same pool.

In the considered case study, the Anomaly Detection Service is used to monitor a CNC machine, produced by the OEM and installed within its client's factory. Monitoring is performed by measuring some variables thought sensors on the machine (features), and check if the detected measures exceed (or are going to) pre-defined thresholds. Monitored CNC machine, features and thresholds are denoted as *setup data*. Once the Maintenance Division of the OEM and the client agreed on setup data, the Maintenance Division starts to monitor the client machine by incrementally collecting data. On collected data, the Anomaly Detection Service applies summarisation and data relevance evaluation techniques, in order to identify relevant data. We refer to [4] for a definition of data summarisation and relevance evaluation techniques, as well as their use for anomaly detection. Relevant data are compared against thresholds in order to identify a warning (an anomaly is going to occur) or error events (anomaly is currently occurring). Whenever a *warning/error* event is identified, the Maintenance Division is notified about the detected event. A maintenance intervention proposal is prepared with calculated fees and sent to the client. If *warning* events are identified, the Maintenance Division may propose precautionary maintenance activities. Upon notification, the client may accept or decline the proposal from the Maintenance Division. If the client decides to refuse, a motivation about the decision must be provided. If the client accepts the proposal, the Maintenance

Division evaluates if it is possible to issue a refund request to the Insurance Agency, whose decision will be taken based on the way the machine has been used. Therefore, the Agency needs to access both detected events and summarised data on which events have been identified. Finally, the Maintenance Division can proceed with the maintenance procedure (not detailed here).

3.2   Trust-Demanding Objects and Activities

The annotations on the BPMN representation of the process are used to identify *trust-demanding activities* and *trust-demanding objects*, defined as follows.

Definition 1 (Trust-demanding activity). *A trust-demanding activity* $\hat{act}$ *is defined as a tuple*

$$\hat{act} = \langle n_a, IN_a, OUT_a, r_a, annot_a \rangle \tag{1}$$

where: (i) n_a is the name of the activity; (ii) IN_a is the set of activity inputs; (iii) OUT_a is the set of activity outputs; (iv) r_a is the participant who is responsible for the activity execution; (v) $annot_a$ is an annotation.

We use a JSON-based representation for annotations. In particular, for trust-demanding activities, $annot_a = \{$ *"isTrustDemanding"*$: True\}$. We denote with $\hat{ACT}$ the overall set of trust-demanding activities. Data objects used to represent inputs/outputs are defined as follows.

Definition 2 (Data object). *A data object obj is defined as a tuple*

$$obj = \langle n_{obj}, ATTR_{obj} \rangle \tag{2}$$

where: (i) n_{obj} is the name of the object; (ii) $ATTR_{obj}$ is the set of attributes of the object. Each attribute of the object is a tuple $\langle type_{attr}, name_{attr} \rangle$ composed of its type and its name. Type can be either primitive (e.g., string) or defined recursively as a data object.

Trust-demanding objects are defined as follows.

Definition 3 (Trust-demanding object). *A trust-demanding object $\hat{obj}$ is defined as a tuple*

$$\hat{obj} = \langle obj, R_{obj}, annot_{obj} \rangle \tag{3}$$

where: (i) obj is the corresponding BPMN data object; (ii) R_{obj} is the set of actors that execute CRUD operations on the object; (iii) $annot_{obj}$ is an annotation on the object.

For trust-demanding objects $annot_{obj} = \{$ *"isTrustDemanding"*$: True,$ *"isDataIntensive"*$: True|False\}$ where the second annotation is used to denote whether the object is data-intensive or not. We denote with $\hat{OBJ}$ the overall set of trust-demanding objects, either data-intensive or not.

Example 1. Considering the BPMN represented in Fig. 2, the `Identify Warning/Error Events` activity is annotated as a trust-demanding activity $\hat{act}^i \in \hat{ACT}$, where:

$n_{a^i} = $ "$IdentifyWarningErrorEvents$"
$IN_{a^i} = \{SummarisedData\}$
$OUT_{a^i} = \{Anomaly\}$
$r_{a^i} = AnomalyDetectionService$
$annot_{a^i} = \{$"$isTrustDemanding$" : $True\}$

Let's consider the output object $obj^v \in OUT_{a^i}$ of the aforementioned activity, described as follows:

$n_{obj^v} = $ "$Anomaly$"
$ATTR_{obj^v} = \{\langle string, $"$anomalyType$"$\rangle, \langle int, $"$componentId$"$\rangle\}$

In the same process, the `Anomaly` object is annotated as trust-demanding $\hat{obj}^v \in \hat{OBJ}$, but not as data-intensive, where:

$obj^v = Anomaly$
$R_{obj^v} = \{AnomalyDetectionService, MaintenanceDivision, Client,$
$InsuranceAgency\}$
$annot_{obj^v} = \{$"$isTrustDemanding$" : $True,$ "$isDataIntensive$" : $False\}$

In Sect. 4 criteria to be used for supporting the proper annotation of trust-demanding activities and objects and of data-intensive objects will be defined.

3.3   Abstract Smart Contracts

Once the trust-demanding activities and objects have been identified, the ASC can be generated. ASC are formally defined as follows.

Definition 4 (Abstract Smart Contract).   *An Abstract Smart Contract $asc \in ASC$ is modeled as a tuple*

$$asc = \langle n_{asc}, VAR_{asc}, P_{asc}, F_{asc} \rangle \tag{4}$$

where: (i) n_{asc} is the name of the asc; (ii) VAR_{asc} is the set of state variables of the asc, i.e., data structures (either primitive data types or objects) on which contract functions operate; (iii) P_{asc} is the set of nodes (i.e., users registered on the blockchain or other contracts) that are allowed to interact with the asc by invoking its functions; (iv) F_{asc} represents the set of functions of the asc expressed as $functionName(IN_f) : OUT_f$, where IN_f and OUT_f are the inputs and outputs of the function.

Example 2. Let's consider the trust-demanding object and activity described in Example 1. From the trust-demanding activity $\hat{act}^i$ we obtain the following $asc^j \in \overline{ASC}$:

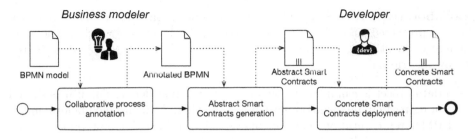

Fig. 3. Workflow of the Abstract/Concrete Smart Contracts generation process.

$$n_{asc^j} = \text{``}IdentifyWarningErrorEventsSC\text{''}$$
$$VAR_{asc^j} = \{summarisedDataHash, Anomaly\}$$
$$P_{asc^j} = \{AnomalyDetectionService, BPMNengine\}$$
$$F_{asc^j} = \{identifyWarningErrorEventsFunc([summarisedDataHash]) : [Anomaly]\}$$

where `summarisedDataHash` is a hash code pointing to an external DFS on which summarised data is saved, being annotated as data-intensive. The BPMN engine is the process execution engine that supports the creation and execution of instances of the collaborative process model. Considering that the execution logic of trust-demanding activities is deployed on the blockchain as smart contracts, the BPMN engine interacts with the smart contracts in order to fulfil his goals and it is therefore modelled as a node of the blockchain.

On the other hand, from the trust-demanding $\hat{obj}^v \in \hat{OBJ}$ we obtain the $asc^w \in \overline{ASC}$, described as:

$$n_{asc^j} = \text{``}Anomaly\text{''}$$
$$VAR_{asc^j} = \{Anomaly\}$$
$$P_{asc^j} = \{AnomalyDetectionService, MaintenanceDivision, Client, Insurance, BPMNengine\}$$
$$F_{asc^j} = \{read() : [Anomaly], update([Anomaly]) : [Anomaly], \dots\}$$

4 Abstract Smart Contracts Generation

Figure 3 reports the procedure to generate ASC/CSC starting from the BPMN model. Three steps are considered: (i) the collaborative process annotation, in which the business modeler is supported to add annotations; (ii) the automatic ASC generation, starting from annotated BPMN; (iii) the semi-automatic CSC deployment, where a platform specific skeleton of smart contract is automatically generated and a developer who possesses skills on the chosen blockchain technology is asked to complete the contract coding. In the following, we will focus mainly on the guidelines that support the modeler during the first step and on the rules to perform the ASC generation.

Collaborative Process Annotation. The annotation of the collaborative process, represented in BPMN, is performed by the business modeler, who is in charge of identifying trust-demanding objects and activities according to the following criteria:

- a data object is candidate to be annotated as trust-demanding if it is shared among participants who do not trust each other. As mentioned before, in the BPMN representation, participants associated with different pools can be seen as potentially untrusting in a collaborative environment. On the other hand, within the same pool, different lanes represent distinct divisions within the same participant. Therefore, different lanes do not identify untrusting divisions. According to these premises, a candidate trust-demanding object is a data object created/updated/deleted by a participant p_i (i.e., it is an output of an activity associated to p_i) and read as input of another activity associated with $p_j \neq p_i$, where p_i and p_j belong to different pools. For example, the Anomaly trust-demanding object introduced in Example 1 is created by the Anomaly Detection Service through the Identify warning/error events activity and read by the Client and the Insurance Agency, that represent different pools. Same considerations hold for Summarised Data object, while Collected Data is shared only within the same pool and therefore it is not candidate as trust-demanding;
- a data object is candidate to be annotated as *data-intensive* if it is characterised by high volume; in BPMN terms, such an object is expressed as a collection, that could potentially present high volume and needs to be properly treated in order to avoid higher costs before being stored on-chain. For example, the Summarised Data in the Fig. 2 is annotated as data-intensive, since it represents the stream of data collected from the monitored machine. On the other hand, Collected Data is not trust-demanding and therefore, even if it is annotated as data-intensive, there is no need to save it on-chain.
- an activity is identified as a candidate trust-demanding activity considering its inputs and outputs. In particular, a trust-demanding activity creates/updates/deletes trust-demanding objects. Indeed, activities that write trust-demanding objects may perform manipulations on them during their execution and the logic behind such manipulations should be transparently shared among untrusted participants. Therefore, such activities are selected as trust-demanding candidates as well. An example is given by Identify warning/error events activity in Fig. 2.

Abstract Smart Contracts Generation. Once the sets of trust-demanding objects $O\hat{B}J$ and activities $A\hat{C}T$ have been identified and the BPMN has been properly annotated, a set of Abstract Smart Contracts $\overline{ASC}$ can be generated, according to the following rules.

Given a trust-demanding activity $\hat{act}^i \in A\hat{C}T$, an $asc^j \in \overline{ASC}$ is generated as follows:

- the ASC name n_{asc^j} is obtained from the activity name n_{a^i};
- the set of ASC variables VAR_{asc^j} contains the activity inputs/outputs IN_a and OUT_a definitions;
- the set of ASC participants P_{asc^j} contains the participant of the activity and the BPMN engine;
- a function in F_{asc^j} is generated, whose signature is named as the activity name n_{a^i}, inputs correspond to the $\hat{act}^i$ inputs and outputs correspond to the $\hat{act}^i$ outputs; the signature of ASC function is given by $functionName(IN_{a^i})$: OUT_{a^i}.

Given a trust-demanding object $\hat{obj}^v \in \hat{OBJ}$, an $asc^w \in \overline{ASC}$ is generated as follows:

- the ASC name n_{asc^w} is obtained from the object name $n_{\hat{obj}^v}$;
- the set of ASC variables VAR_{asc^w} contains the object definition obj^v of $\hat{obj}^v$;
- the set of ASC participants P_{asc^w} contains the participant of the activity that reads the object and the BPMN engine;
- functions in F_{asc^w} are generated according to the CRUD actions on the object $\hat{obj}^v$.

Concrete Smart Contracts Deployment. Finally, the developer is guided to implement the set $\overline{CSC}$ of Concrete Smart Contracts starting from the set $\overline{ASC}$ generated in the previous step. Considering that ASC are independent from the adopted blockchain technology, the developer relies on a set of modules (one for each specific blockchain technology) that are able to automatically extract the skeleton of a CSC, starting from the ASC descriptors. Each module is able to transform an ASC descriptors into a skeleton CSC expressed in the language of the selected blockchain platform. For example, considering the Ethereum platform, the skeleton of CSC extracted from the `Identify warning/error events` trust-demanding activity is reported in Fig. 4. Once the skeleton of the CSC is generated, the developer is asked to implement the functions code, completing the CSC. In the example in Fig. 4 the developer is asked to implement the code of the `identificationWarningErrorEventsFunc` function, coding the business logic to identify the `anomalyType`. Functions within the smart contracts assess as a precondition what is the authorized actor, depending on the scope of the invoked function (applying the so-called *Authorization* design pattern [5]).

5   Implementation and Validation Issues

5.1   Architecture Overview

The approach architecture is shown in Fig. 5 and is organised into three levels. The level at the bottom is referred to as the *On-Chain level* and includes the real blockchain, on which CSC are deployed. For example, on an Ethereum network, all deployed CSC can be replicated on each client node, that hosts an Ethereum Virtual Machine (EVM). The On-Chain level also includes a *Log Repository*, that

```
contract IdentifyWarningErrorEventsSC{
    address AnomalyDetectionService; address BPMNengine;

    string summarisedDataHash;
    struct Anomaly{  // could be generated also as Ethereum library
            string anomalyType;
            uint componentId;
    };
    function identifyWarningErrorEventsFunc(uint _componentId, string _summarisedDataHash)
        public returns (Anomaly _anomaly) {
                // code provided by developer
```

Fig. 4. Concrete Smart Contract skeleton example.

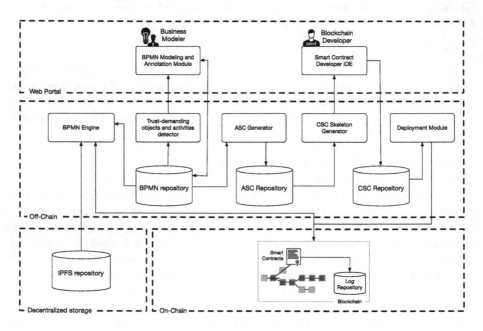

Fig. 5. Approach architecture

is used to store the results of CSC execution, to implement the communication channel from the smart contracts on the blockchain and external services of the collaborative process. In fact, smart contracts have no way to call external services. However, contracts can write information on a log space that is visible to external applications. A decentralised storage (e.g., IPFS) is also considered, not included within the On-Chain level, in order to store data-intensive information without impacting on the blockchain costs.

The middle layer, denoted as *Off-Chain level*, includes the modules that implement the identification of trust-demanding objects and activities, ASC and CSC skeleton generation and deployment. Specifically, the *Trust-demanding objects and activities Detector* implements criteria to support BPMN annotation.

The BPMN is stored within the *BPMN repository*. The *ASC Generator* extracts ASC descriptors and stores them into the *ASC Repository*. The *CSC Skeleton Generator* is in charge of generating skeletons, that are provided to the developer who complete them with platform-specific code insertion. Developed CSC are stored within a *CSC Repository* and deployed on the blockchain by the *Deployment Module*. ASC/CSC repositories will contribute to increase the reuse of generated contracts, as shortly suggested in the future work section. The middle layer also includes the *BPMN Engine*, that has to execute the collaborative process and must be able to invoke some activities as CSC deployed on the blockchain.

Finally, the top-most level (*Web Portal*) comprises a set of Web components, provided to the business modeler and the developer for editing BPMN processes, confirming or discarding suggested annotations, and editing CSC starting from the generated skeletons, respectively. Components at the top-most level use functionalities made available by other modules at the middle layer through RESTful APIs.

5.2 Remote Monitoring Services Case Study

The approach described in this paper has been applied in the context of Remote Monitoring Services in the digital factory, using Ethereum blockchain for deployment [16]. Remote Monitoring Services present recurrent functionalities, that can be summarised as follows:

- *monitoring setup service*, that allows the OEM and its client to agree upon the components to be monitored, the features to observe, the limits used to detect warning and error events (setup data);
- *relevance-based anomaly detection service*, that performs the anomaly detection, starting from measures collected and summarised from the monitored component, considering the setup data;
- *maintenance preparation service*, that manages the preparation of a maintenance intervention supplied by the OEM to the client and is in charge of computing the maintenance fee according to the history of past interventions and to the type of occurred warning/error events.

Starting from these services, proper smart contracts have been identified, as illustrated in the following.

Monitoring Setup Smart Contracts (MS). Suggested annotations to identify trust-demanding elements are reported in Table 1. Setup data is created by the Maintenance Division and read by the client, who is also in charge of accepting or declining by modifying the `Setup Data` object, that therefore is identified as trust-demanding. Therefore, an ASC is generated for the `Setup Data` trust-demanding object and all activities (associated with the Maintenance Division or the Client) that create or modify such objects are recognised as trust-demanding, bringing to the generation of corresponding ASC.

Table 1. Objects and activities annotations for the monitoring setup service.

Data objects and activities	isTrustDemanding	isDataIntensive
Setup Data [OBJ]	✓	
Setup components to be monitored, feature spaces, features limits [ACT]	✓	
Receive setup data [ACT]		
Accept setup data [ACT]	✓	
Refuse setup data [ACT]	✓	

Table 2. Objects and activities annotations for the relevance-based anomaly detection service.

Data objects and activities	isTrustDemanding	isDataIntensive
Collected Data [OBJ]		✓
Summarised Data [OBJ]	✓	✓
Anomaly [OBJ]	✓	
Collected Incremental Data [ACT]		
Summarise and identify relevant data [ACT]	✓	
Identify warning error events [ACT]	✓	

Anomaly Detection Smart Contracts (AD). Suggested annotations to identify trust-demanding elements are reported in Table 2. Anomaly Detection Service is in charge of summarising the collection of `Collected Data` objects and applying relevance evaluation in order to identify relevant data only, generating a collection of `Summarised Data` objects. Both `Collected Data` and `Summarised Data` objects are generated at high volumes, and for this reason can be considered as data-intensive. `Summarised Data` is then used by the Anomaly Detection Service to identify warning or error events, generating an `Anomaly` object. Considering that `Summarised Data` and `Anomaly` objects are read by the Client and by the Insurance Agency, both are recognised as trust-demanding. Therefore, two ASC are generated, one for `Summarised Data` object and one for `Anomaly` object. Moreover, all activities that create or modify such objects are recognised as trust-demanding, bringing to the generation of corresponding ASC.

Maintenance Intervention Preparation Smart Contract (MIP). Suggested annotations to identify trust-demanding elements are reported in Table 3. The `Maintenance Intervention Proposal` object is created by the Maintenance Division and modified by the Client to accept/decline it. Therefore, it is identified as trust-demanding. The same considerations hold for `Refund Request` object. All activities that create and modify these objects are denoted as trust-demanding.

Table 3. Objects and activities annotations for the maintenance preparation service.

Data objects and activities	isTrustDemanding	isDataIntensive
Maintenance Intervention Proposal [OBJ]	✓	
Refund Request [OBJ]	✓	
Receive anomaly detection events [ACT]		
Calculate Fees and Create Maintenance Intervention proposal [ACT]	✓	
Receive Maintenance Intervention proposal [ACT]		
Accept Intervention [ACT]	✓	
Refuse Intervention and motivate [ACT]	✓	
Receive Client decision [ACT]		
Create Refund Request [ACT]	✓	
Receive Refund Request [ACT]		
Accept/Refuse Refund Request [ACT]	✓	
Receive Insurance decision [ACT]		
Schedule Maintenance Intervention [ACT]	✓	

5.3   Experimental Evaluation and Cost Analysis

We validated the approach proposed in this paper using Ethereum permissionless blockchain. We run experiments on a MacBook Pro Retina, having an Intel Core i7-6700HQ processor, CPU 2.60 GHz, 4 cores, 8 logical cores, RAM 16 GB. Other examples of blockchain that could be used to deploy Concrete Smart Contracts in our approach could be permissioned ones, such as Hyperledger [1], where Concrete Smart Contracts can be developed using different languages such as Go[2], node.js and Java. Selecting the proper blockchain and its configuration is not trivial [14]. On the one hand, a permissioned blockchain ensures more confidentiality and privacy, as well as better performances in terms of response time, but also requires an ad-hoc implementation and configuration of the network infrastructure, that in the considered domain should be replicated for each client of the OEM. On the other hand, according to the "as-a-Service" paradigm, permissionless solutions allow to rely on off-the-shelf infrastructures, equipped with a Proof-of-Work consensus mechanism that is based on the resolution of a computationally complex problem to prevent malicious attacks. However, a permissionless blockchain takes more time to write and confirm a transaction to be added to the ledger. Finally, in a permissionless blockchain the execution of a smart contract and the validation of a new transaction are performed by nodes that are rewarded with a fee paid by the node that initiates the transaction. Since, to the best of our knowledge, there are no collaborative processes datasets to compare our implementation with similar efforts, we performed here

---

[2] https://golang.org.

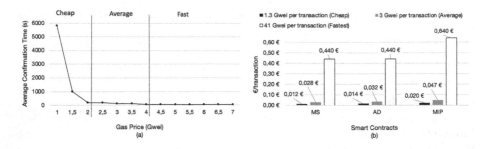

Fig. 6. Gas value required to execute all the functions of the smart contracts generated for each service in the considered case study.

a cost analysis, in order to evaluate the economic effort in using a permission-less blockchain. In Ethereum-based blockchains, the cost is expressed in *gas*, which is a value established for every basic operation invoked from within the smart contract and in turn translated into an elementary operation processed by the Ethereum Virtual Machine (EVM). Then, the fee paid for a transaction is expressed as the product between the gas used to process the transaction and the *gas price*, which is the amount that the node initiating the transaction is willing to pay for each gas unit.

Figure 6(a) illustrates the average time (in seconds) to confirm the transaction for each smart contract by varying the gas price, relying on the simulator provided by ETH Gas Station[3]. As expected, the more gas price a user is willing to offer, the faster the transaction will be added to the blockchain.

Figure 6(b) reports the cost per transaction required to execute each of the smart contracts implemented for the Remote Monitoring Services case study, using Ethereum simulator[4]. Results deserve some considerations to highlight the impact of an approach such as the one proposed in this paper. Reducing the cost of the collaborative process deployment on a permissionless blockchain can be obtained decreasing the performances of smart contract execution or limiting the elements that are deployed on the blockchain to trust-demanding objects and activity only. Indeed, our approach reduces the execution costs on the blockchain thanks to the deployment of a limited set of BPMN elements, only if necessary. In fact, only trust-demanding objects and activities will be converted in smart contracts to be deployed on the blockchain. According to the cost analysis learned by the application of our approach to the Remote Monitoring case study, as shown in Fig. 6(a) and (b), from a certain amount of gas price (4.5 *Gwei*) the average confirmation time remains quite the same. Assuming that the participants have access to IPFS nodes, there is no extra cost, in terms of gas, associated with storing data-intensive objects. However, for the same application scenarios such as the anomaly detection one considered in the case study, promptness in identifying warning/error events is directly related to

---

[3] https://ethgasstation.info/calculatorTxV.php (accessed: July 2019).
[4] Testrpc: https://github.com/trufflesuite/ganache-cli.

the validity of the supplied services. Therefore, this issue can be addressed by limiting the number of elements to be deployed on-chain. The proposed approach described in this paper is to meet these requirements by excluding non trust-demanding objects and activities.

6 Related Work

Several attempts have been made in literature to suggest possible applications of blockchain and smart contracts in various fields to safely exchange money, property, shares, or anything of value in a transparent and conflict-free way: agri-food [7,9], chemical and pharmaceutical applications [6,13], logistics [11], and other industry sectors [12]. Recently, approaches aimed at deploying collaborative processes using blockchain and smart contracts have been investigated. In a recent research, the Caterpillar system [10] introduces an abstraction layer over the Ethereum blockchain in order to support execution of collaborative business processes, represented in BPMN. Noteworthy, a collaborative process in Caterpillar is fully executed on the blockchain, in the sense that all the states of a process instance are recorded on-chain and all the control-flow logic is coded as smart contracts. The Caterpillar approach is a remarkable effort on the research topic addressed in this paper, but the proposed solution is platform dependent. Abstraction given by Abstract Smart Services increases the flexibility and reuse of generated smart contracts, while deployment of a limited set of BPMN elements, only if necessary, reduces the execution costs on the blockchain. The approach proposed in [11] underlines the importance of blockchains in multi-party business processes, presenting different application strategies. Nevertheless, the deployed smart contracts are not described in details and the proposed solution is application-dependent. Similarly, authors in [12] propose an application of blockchain in the material industry, focusing on the interaction flow between the OEM and clients, while smart contracts are not used. In [7] the focus is on the multi-agent perspective of the introduced blockchain solution. The explanation about how smart contracts have been deployed is reported in a coarse-grained manner and no distinction between Abstract and Concrete Smart Contracts is proposed.

Recent efforts also focused on the importance of conceptual modeling to demonstrate how business artefacts leverage the data-centric nature of blockchain [8] and to provide a user-centric framework to design rules deployed in smart contracts [2]. In this respect, collaborative activities involving many participants in supply chain processes are remarkably susceptible to flaws in trust management between the interacting parties, thus demanding the sophisticated properties offered by blockchains in assuring trustworthiness. Furthermore, in order to cope with possible network overloads, proper policies must be chosen to select which data should be stored on the blockchain. Again, the approach described in this paper is different, since it aims to rely on the blockchain and smart contracts to abstract from specific deployment technology and to provide a set of criteria and guidelines to convert trust-demanding activities and objects into Abstract Smart Contracts.

7   Concluding Remarks

In this paper, we proposed a three-layered model to describe: (i) the collaborative process, represented in BPMN, where the business expert is supported to add annotations that denote trust-demanding objects and activities; (ii) Abstract Smart Contracts, based on trust-demanding objects and activities only and specified by means of descriptors, that are independent from any blockchain technology; (iii) Concrete Smart Contracts, that implement abstract ones and are deployed over a specific blockchain technology, enabling the creation of a repository where a single descriptor is associated with multiple implementations. Results confirm the advantages of designing Abstract Smart Contracts regardless of specific blockchain technologies, bringing to increased flexibility and reuse and reduced deployment costs where applicable. Future efforts will be devoted to the design and implementation of an ASC/CSC repository, in which further annotations (e.g. adopting Semantic Web technologies) may be used to better support matchmaking of newly generated ASC against existing CSC or reconciliation of similar ASC to increase flexibility and reuse. Moreover, future work will be focused on further automating the process of CSC generation, already partially addressed through the generation of CSC skeleton code, studying techniques and methods to semi-automatically implement the functions code of the CSC in order to reduce as much as possible error-prone involvement of developers.

References

1. Androulaki, E., et al.: Hyperledger Fabric: a distributed operating system for permissioned blockchains. In: Proceedings of the 13th EuroSys Conference, EuroSys 2018, Porto, Portugal, pp. 30:1–30:15 (2018)
2. Astigarraga, T., et al.: Empowering business-level blockchain users with a rules framework for smart contracts. In: Proceedings of International Conference on Service Oriented Computing, ICSOC 2018, Hangzhou, China, pp. 111–128 (2018)
3. Bagozi, A., Bianchini, D., De Antonellis, V., Garda, M., Melchiori, M.: Services as enterprise smart contracts in the digital factory. In: Proceedings of 2019 IEEE International Conference on Web Services, ICWS 2019, Milan, Italy (2019, in press)
4. Bagozi, A., Bianchini, D., De Antonellis, V., Marini, A.: A relevance-based data exploration approach to assist operators in anomaly detection. In: Proceedings of 26th International Conference on Cooperative Information Systems, CoopIS 2018, Valletta, Malta, pp. 354–371 (2018)
5. Bartoletti, M., Pompianu, L.: An empirical analysis of smart contracts: platforms, applications, and design patterns. In: Proceedings of International Conference on Financial Cryptography and Data Security, FC 2017, Sliema, Malta, pp. 494–509 (2017)
6. Bocek, T., Rodrigues, B.B., Strasser, T., Stiller, B.: Blockchains everywhere-a use-case of blockchains in the pharma supply-chain. In: Proceedings of IFIP/IEEE 15th Symposium on Integrated Network and Service Management, IM 2017, Lisbon, Portugal, pp. 772–777 (2017)
7. Casado-Vara, R., Prieto, J., De la Prieta, F., Corchado, J.M.: How blockchain improves the supply chain: case study alimentary supply chain. Procedia Comput. Sci. **134**, 393–398 (2018)

8. Hull, R., et al.: Towards a shared ledger business collaboration language based on data-aware processes. In: Proceedings of International Conference on Service Oriented Computing, ICSOC 2016, Banff, AB, Canada, pp. 18–36 (2016)
9. Leng, K., Bi, Y., Jing, L., Fu, H.C., Van Nieuwenhuyse, I.: Research on agricultural supply chain system with double chain architecture based on blockchain technology. Future Gener. Comput. Syst. **86**, 641–649 (2018)
10. López-Pintado, O., García-Bañuelos, L., Dumas, M., Weber, I., Ponomarev, A.: Caterpillar: a business process execution engine on the Ethereum blockchain. Soft. Pract. Experience **49**(7), 1162–1193 (2019)
11. Meroni, G., Plebani, P.: Combining artifact-driven monitoring with blockchain: analysis and solutions. In: Proceedings of 30th International Conference on Advanced Information Systems Engineering, CAiSE 2018, Tallinn, Estonia, pp. 103–114 (2018)
12. Mondragon, A.E.C., Mondragon, C.E.C., Coronado, E.S.: Exploring the applicability of blockchain technology to enhance manufacturing supply chains in the composite materials industry. In: Proceedings of IEEE International Conference on Applied System Invention, ICASI 2018, Tokyo, Japan, pp. 1300–1303 (2018)
13. Sikorski, J.J., Haughton, J., Kraft, M.: Blockchain technology in the chemical industry: machine-to-machine electricity market. Appl. Energy **195**, 234–246 (2017)
14. Staderini, M., Schiavone, E., Bondavalli, A.: A requirements-driven methodology for the proper selection and configuration of blockchains. In: Proceedings of IEEE 37th Symposium on Reliable Distributed Systems SRDS 2018, Salvador, Bahia, Brazil, pp. 201–206 (2018)
15. Vandermerwe, S., Rada, J.: Servitization of business: adding value by adding services. Eur. Manage. J. **6**(4), 314–324 (1988)
16. Wood, G.: Ethereum: A secure decentralised generalised transaction ledger. Ethereum project yellow paper, vol. 151, pp. 1–32 (2014)

Towards Green Value Network Modeling: A Case from the Agribusiness Sector in Brazil

Juscimara Gomes Avelino[1], Patrício de Alencar Silva[1(✉)], and Faiza Allah Bukhsh[2]

[1] Programa de Pós-Graduação em Ciência da Computação, Universidade Federal Rural do Semi-Árido (UFERSA), Mossoró, Rio Grande do Norte, Brazil
{juscimara.avelino,patricio.alencar}@ufersa.edu.br
[2] Department of Computer Science, University of Twente, 7500AE Enschede, The Netherlands
f.a.bukhsh@utwente.nl

Abstract. The main purpose of a value network model is to prospect the sustainability of business strategies. However, much attention has been paid on the economic issues of value modeling, leaving critical environmental and social issues uncovered. On the environmental scope, this study proposes an ontology for modeling value networks to match Green Computing requirements. The ontology supports semi-automatic configuration of value network models to help business analysts deciding upon alternative value paths to satisfy market segments demanding products or services bundled with green accreditations or certifications. The ontology was built according to guidelines of Design Science in combination with specific methodologies for Ontology Engineering. For the ontology evaluation process, the acceptance, utility and usability of the ontology were evaluated by means of Technical Action Research (TAR) applied in a real-world case from the Brazilian agribusiness sector. Business expert opinion pointed to the viability of the models produced, from both the economic and environmental perspectives.

Keywords: Design Science · Green Computing · Ontology · Sustainability

1 Introduction

According to Normann and Ramirez (1993), a value network is referred to as *a system of business agents exchanging objects of economic value that are transformed into a final product or service demanded by a market segment of consumers* [1]. A value network "model" is a conceptual structure used to prospect the long-term sustainability of a cooperative business strategy model [2]. This type of modeling is currently supported, for instance, by the e^3value framework proposed by Gordijn and Akkermans [3, 4], which is aimed not only for analyzing the viability of businesses, but also for eliciting organizational requirements preluding the specification of business process models. In regards to business sustainability, many contributions of the Value Network Modeling community have been focused on purely economic issues, not to mention, monetary. However, business sustainability demands a harmonization of economic, environmental

© Springer Nature Switzerland AG 2019
H. Panetto et al. (Eds.): OTM 2019, LNCS 11877, pp. 458–475, 2019.
https://doi.org/10.1007/978-3-030-33246-4_29

and social restrictions pushed by societal needs. These two last dimensions have not yet been sufficiently addressed by the Value Network Modeling community.

Hevner and Chatterjee (2010) refer to *Green Computing* as a *set of guidelines or practices for the efficient use of computational resources to achieve business or organizational goals* [5]. The authors identify some critical requirements for Green Computing which ought to be considered during the design of Information Systems. These requirements include, for instance, disposal of electronic waste, end user satisfaction, energy use, management restructuring, regulatory compliance, return on investment (ROI), telecommuting, thin client solutions and virtualization of server resources. However, considering that modern Enterprise architectures are composed by a cross-functional blend of people, data, software, hardware and communication infrastructure, these requirements could be treated progressively, along managerial layers, i.e., from the business strategy level (business value models), along the tactical layer (business process models), to the operational layers (people, infrastructure, intelligent software and sensors). For instance, *end user satisfaction* and *regulatory compliance* are requirements that can be treated by design in value network modeling.

In response to the research agenda of Green Computing proposed by Hevner and Chatterjee (2010) [5], and in line with Wieringa's defense of Design Science as a research methodology to cope with problems of societal relevance [6], in this study are specially concerned with treating the problem of *how value network models could be designed to fill (prospected) consumers' needs for products or services that are bundled with environmental certifications*. From an organizational point-of-view, as proposed by Cameron (1980) [7] and according to the research problem decomposition suggested by Wieringa (2014) [6], this research problem can be decomposed into other questions such as: (1) *what green value network models are*; (2) *what concepts will ground such models*; and (3) *how these concepts will be related to satisfying consumers' needs in compliance with green certifications*.

To treat these questions, we propose an ontology to represent the so-called *green value network models*. These models are based on a Service-Dominant Logic, as proposed by Lusch, Vargo and Tanniru (2010) [8], which settles the consumers' view as dominant over the business actors that compose a value network. In other words, this logic dictates that business actors and corresponding capabilities ought to be arranged in a way that will optimally satisfy the needs of a market segment. Subordinated to the Design Science guidelines adopted, we have followed the formal Ontological Engineering methodology proposed by Uschold and King (1995) [9]. This approach was chosen due to its simplicity of use and its emphasis on the cognitive effort paid during the ontology capture phase – a common issue to be considered on designing new ontological propositions. For the ontology validation, we have combined guidelines proposed by Gómez-Pérez, Fernandez-Lopes and Corcho (2004) [10] and Vrandečić and Sure (2007) [11] into a single validation process comprising: (1) ontology *verification* of consistency, correctness and completeness; (2) ontology *conformance checking* regarding theoretical and practical requirements; and (3) ontology *evaluation* of acceptance, usability and utility. For this last phase, we have evaluated the ontology models based on a real-world case of a Brazilian agribusiness company by combining Technical Action Research with business expert opinion to assess the viability of the value network models inferred.

The rest of this paper is organized as follows. In Sect. 2, we provide a theoretical background in Value Network Modeling, Service-Dominant Logic and Green Computing requirements. In Sect. 3, we describe the ontology for *green value network modeling*. In Sect. 4, we report on the validity of the ontology by presenting the green value models generated for a real-world case from the agribusiness sector in Brazil. The most closely related studies are described in Sect. 5, along with critical assessment of how this proposal advances the current capabilities of value modeling. Conclusions and future research directions are discussed in Sect. 6.

2 Theoretical Background

The concept of a value network is not new. Norman and Ramirez (1993) [1] have introduced the term as an evolution of value chains. In a value network, economically independent actors exchange objects of economic value, which will be ultimately transformed into a product or service that will satisfy the needs of a certain market segment of consumers. Peppard and Rylander (2006) [2] to value networks as business ecosystems, as these structures may collapse or merge multiple value chains to satisfy markets' needs in a reliable way. However, in the Information Systems community, Gordijn and Akkermans (2003) [3] proposed a framework named e^3value for designing value network models. The framework is composed by an ontology of interorganizational exchange behavior, a graphical notation and a profitability calculation mechanism to prospect monetary return on the investment made by the actors cooperating in a value network. Since its initial proposal, the e^3value framework has been applied in several real-world case studies in European markets. Best practices for Value Network Modeling have been documented further by Gordijn and Akkermans (2018) [4]. According to Ionita et al. (2016), a value network model can be used to prelude the specification of a process model, by supporting risk analysis and prospection of profitability share [12].

Consumers' needs comprise the starting configuration point of a value network model. Certain consumers' needs may be complex and possibly filled by products or services of aggregated value, which will be provided not by an only business actor, but by a network of companies or organizations working in cooperation. The more demanding a consumers' need is, the more actors may be necessary to fill it. This is a typical case of market exploitation, which Lusch, Vargo and Tanniru (2010) refer to as Service-Dominant Logic, i.e. the perspective of a consumers' need driving the economic arrangement of business-to-business exchanges and transactions among economically independent actors willing to make profit out of it [8].

However, sustainability-aware markets have pushed the provision of products or services accompanied with evidence of proof of clean production. In Value Network Modeling, critical quests of any business case include "what" the consumer wants, "who" will provide it (i.e. actors and activities) and "how" it will be provided (i.e. how the actors will communicate by economic exchange). In the organic food market, for instance, products and corresponding evidences of clean production may be provided by different value paths. How these value paths could be analyzed, organized and merged into a single value network model is an organizational problem still open in the Value Network Modeling community.

The research agenda for Green Computing proposed by Hevner and Chatterjee (2010) include requirements that vary from efficient energy use in data centers to long-term business strategies of environmental preservation [5]. We believe those requirements ought to be treated progressively, by managerial layers, for the sake of simplicity. In this study, we analyze the requirements of satisfaction of consumers' needs for products and services that demand green regulatory compliance. Despite substantial contributions of the Value Network Modeling community in strategic business modeling, an organizational logic for structuring what would be called "green" value network models is still missing. In the next section, we describe an ontology that will possibly fill this research gap.

3 An Ontology for Green Value Network Modeling

The Green Value Network Ontology (GVNO) organizes the conceptual elements that will compose a *green value network* model. The ontology reconciles the original e^3value concepts proposed by Gordijn and Akkermans (2003) [3] with extensions proposed by Silva (2013) [13], which blends concepts of Enterprise Engineering proposed by Loucopoulos and Kavakli (1999) [14]; Dietz (2006), e.g. formation of business transactions based on coordination and production acts [15]; Multiple Agency Theory, e.g. Agency roles [16]; Speech Acts Theory, i.e. linguistic grounding of speech acts [17]; Contract Theory, e.g. accountability of value transactions [18]; and Principles of Economics, e.g. the notion of economic reciprocity [19].

The starting point of configuration is an assertion about the *business need* of the final consumer (i.e., a bundle of a core business object with a corresponding proof of green production) to be provided by actors playing multiply agency roles. These objects can be provided through different communication arrangements of roles for *actors*, *activities* and *value objects*. These combinations represent *policies* defining *who exchanges which object to whom* in a *green value network* model.

The ontology was built by following the method proposed by Uschold and King (1995) [9], which includes four steps: (1) *identify* the scope and modeling goal of the ontology; (2) *build* the ontology; (3) *evaluate* the ontology; and (4) *document* the concepts of the ontology. The ontology was formalized in OWL with the Protégé tool[1] to support semi-automatic configuration of *green value network* models. The original code of the ontology is available online for formal verification[2]. The consistency and correctness of the ontology model were checked with the support of the reasoners Fact ++[3], Hermit[4] and Pellet[5]. To facilitate the reader's comprehension, we present the ontology model here using a combination of Description Logics, natural language the OntoGraph[6] tool for ontology visualization (vide Fig. 1).

---

[1] https://protege.stanford.edu/.

[2] https://www.dropbox.com/s/2cm9rln73ee0r8t/GVN.owl?dl=0.

[3] http://owl.cs.manchester.ac.uk/tools/fact/.

[4] http://www.hermit-reasoner.com/.

[5] https://www.w3.org/2001/sw/wiki/Pellet.

[6] https://github.com/NinePts/OntoGraph

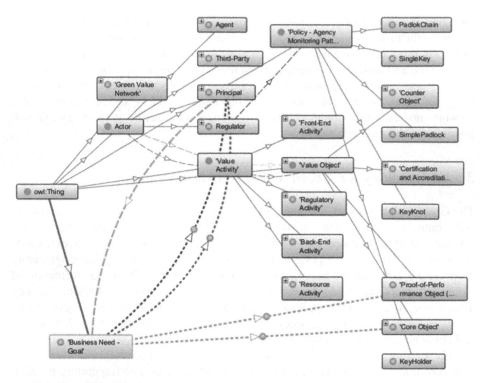

Fig. 1. General visualization of the Green Value Network Ontology in Ontograph

3.1 Defining Roles for Actors, Value Activities and Value Objects

The grounding concepts of a value network model are *actors, value activities* and *value objects*. An *actor* represents an economically responsible entity or organization [3]. An actor can be stereotyped by one among four disjoint Agency roles [16] that can be played inside a value network: (1) *principal*, i.e. the final consumer that declares a business need of a product or service, which in a *green value network* model, will be a bundle of a core business product and a proof of green production; (2) *agent*, i.e. an actor delegated by the principal to perform a business transformation activity; (3) *third-party*, i.e. has an indirect business relation with the principal, the role of which can be played by a primary producer operating at the back-end of the value network; and (4) *regulator*, i.e. an entity or organization with authority to grant accreditations or certifications that allow agents to operate in transformational activities.

A *value activity* is the core competency of a business actor. A green value activity aggregates or transfers a value object of environmental certification. A value activity is defined by how it is related to value objects by means of *production acts* [15], e.g. *consumes, produces, distributes, grants, bundles* or *transfers*. Each actor-role is assigned to one of four disjoint activity-roles: (1) the *front-end activity* is of competency of the *principal* (2) the *resource activity* is of responsibility of an *agent*; (3) the *back-end activity* is of responsibility of a *third-party*; and (4) the *regulatory activity* is of authority of a regulator. The transformations performed by these types of value activity are formalized below in Table 1.

Table 1. Ontology axioms of activity-role organization for *green value networks* modeling.

Class: FrontEndActivity ≡ ValueActivity
∩ ((*bundles* ∃ (CnAObject ∪ PoPObject)) ∪ (*consumes* ∃ CoreObject))
∩ (*isCompetenceOf* ∃ Principal)
∩ (*produces* ∃ CounterObject)
∩ (*bundles* ∀ (CnAObject ∪ PoPObject))
∩ (*consumes* ∀ CoreObject) ∩ (*isCompetenceOf* ∀ Principal)
∩ (*produces* ∀ CounterObject)

Class: ResourceActivity ≡ ValueActivity
∩ ((*bundles* ∃ (CnAObject ∪ CoreObject ∪ CounterObject ∪ PoPObject))
∪ (*consumes* ∃ CounterObject))
∩ ((*distributes* ∃ (CoreObject ∪ CounterObject)) ∪ (*grants* ∃ PoPObject)
∪ (*transfers* ∃ CnAObject))
∩ (*isCompetenceOf* ∃ Agent) ∩ (*bundles* ∀ (CnAObject ∪ CoreObject
∪ CounterObject ∪ PoPObject))
∩ (*consumes* ∀ CounterObject)
∩ (*distribute* ∀ (CoreObject ∪ CounterObject))
∩ (*grants* ∀ PoPObject) ∩ (*isCompetenceOf* ∀ Agent) ∩ (*transfers* ∀ CnAObject)

Class: BackEndActivity ≡ ValueActivity
∩ ((*bundles* ∃ (CnAObject ∪ CoreObject)) ∪ (*consumes* ∃ CounterObject))
∩ ((*grants* ∃ PoPObject) ∪ (*produces* ∃ (CoreObject ∪ CounterObject)))
∩ (*isResponsabilityOf* ∃ ThirdParty)
∩ (*bundles* ∀ (CnAObject ∪ CoreObject))
∩ (*consumes* ∀ CounterObject)
∩ (*grants* ∀ PoPObject) ∩ (*isResponsabilityOf* ∀ ThirdParty)
∩ (*produces* ∀ (CoreObject ∪ CounterObject))

Class: RegulatoryActivity ≡ ValueActivity
∩ ((*bundles* ∃ (CnAObject ∪ CoreObject ∪ PoPObject)) ∪ (*consumes* ∃ CounterObject))
∩ ((*grants* ∃ CnAObject) ∪ (*transfers* ∃ (CoreObject ∪ PoPObject)))
∩ (*isAuthorityOf* ∃ Regulator) ∩ (*bundles* ∀ (CnAObject ∪ CoreObject ∪ PoPObject))
∩ (*consumes* ∀ CounterObject) ∩ (*grants* ∀ CnAObject)
∩ (*isAuthorityOf* ∀ Regulator) ∩ (*transfers* ∀ (CoreObject ∪ PoPObject))

Value objects are products or services of economic value, which are transformed by value activities and exchanged among business actors in a value network [3]. A value object can be assigned to one of four disjoint roles: (1) *core business object*, i.e., the main object of a consumer's desire; (2) *proof-of-performance object* (PoPObject), i.e., an evidence that a core object was produced according to a regulation; (3) *certification & accreditation object* (CnAObject), i.e., a permission granted by a regulator to assess core or proof objects; and (4) *counter-object*, i.e., an object given in exchange of any other type of object to ensure economic reciprocity [19]. Objects can be transformed by four types of activities assigned to the Agency roles, as formalized in the Table 2.

Table 2. Ontology axioms of object-role organization for *green value networks* modeling.

Class: CoreObject ≡ ValueObject
∩ ((*isBundledBy* ∃ (BackEndActivity ∪ ResourceActivity))
∪ (*isConsumedBy* ∃ FrontEndActivity))
∩ ((*isDistributedBy* ∃ ResourceActivity) ∪ (*isProducedBy* ∃ BackEndActivity))
∩ ((*isBundledBy* ∀ (BackEndActivity or ResourceActivity))
∪ (*isConsumedBy* ∀ FrontEndActivity))
∩ (¬ (*isBundledBy* ∃ FrontEndActivity)) ∩ (¬ (*isConsumedBy* ∃ BackEndActivity))
∩ (*isDistributedBy* ∀ ResourceActivity) ∩ (*isProducedBy* ∀ BackEndActivity)
∩ (*isTransferredBy* ∀ RegulatoryActivity)
Class: PoPObject ≡ ValueObject
∩ (¬ (*isConsumedBy* ∃ (BackEndActivity ∪ FrontEndActivity
∪ RegulatoryActivity ∪ ResourceActivity)))
∩ (¬ (*isProducedBy* ∃ BackEndActivity))
∩ (*isBundledBy* ∃ (FrontEndActivity ∪ RegulatoryActivity ∪ ResourceActivity))
∩ (*isGrantedBy* ∃ (BackEndActivity ∪ ResourceActivity))
∩ (*isBundledBy* ∀ (FrontEndActivity ∪ RegulatoryActivity ∪ ResourceActivity))
∩ (*isGrantedBy* ∀ (BackEndActivity ∪ ResourceActivity))
∩ (*isTransferredBy* ∀ RegulatoryActivity)
Class: CnAObject ≡ ValueObject
∩ ((*isGrantedBy* ∃ RegulatoryActivity) ∪ (*isTransferredBy* ∃ ResourceActivity))
∩ (*isBundledBy* ∃ (BackEndActivity ∪ FrontEndActivity ∪ ResourceActivity))
∩ (*isBundledBy* ∀ (BackEndActivity ∪ FrontEndActivity ∪ ResourceActivity))
∩ (*isGrantedBy* ∀ RegulatoryActivity) ∩ (*isTransferredBy* ∀ ResourceActivity)
Class: CounterObject ≡ ValueObject
∩ ((*isBundledBy* ∃ ResourceActivity)
∪ (*isConsumedBy* ∃ (BackEndActivity ∪ RegulatoryActivity ∪ ResourceActivity)))
∩ ((*isDistributedBy* ∃ ResourceActivity)
∪ (*isProducedBy* ∃ (BackEndActivity ∪ FrontEndActivity)))
∩ (*isBundledBy* ∀ ResourceActivity)
∩ (*isConsumedBy* ∀ (BackEndActivity ∪ RegulatoryActivity ∪ ResourceActivity))
∩ (*isDistributedBy* ∀ ResourceActivity) ∩ (*isPriceOf* ∀ ValueObject)
∩ (*isProducedBy* ∀ (BackEndActivity ∩ FrontEndActivity)

3.2   Defining Organizational Policies

The concept of *policy* used here refers to an organizational arrangement of roles played by actors, activities and objects in a value network settled to fill a consumer's need. In other words, a value network policy defines *who exchanges which types of objects with whom* and is inspired in the NIST Role-Based Access Control models proposed by Ferraiolo et al. (2001) [22]. In a *green value network* model, a policy specifies alternative value paths whereby certifications and proof objects are transformed by the intermediary actors to fill a consumer's need. A policy is configured by connecting actor-roles of Agency to activity-roles via OWL object properties of *authority, competence* or *responsibility*, and then, by connecting activity-roles to object-roles via OWL object properties of production acts. In this study, five candidate policy models were identified through Technical Action Research applied on the business case described in Sect. 4: *simple padlock, key holder, single key, padlock chain* and *key knot*. The names of the models suggest different value network arrangements to organize actor-roles, activity-roles and object-roles of a *green value network* model to fill a consumer's (principal) business need of products or services bundled with green certifications. For simplicity, only the specification of the *key holder* policy model is shown in Table 3.

Table 3. Description logics of the *KeyHolder* organizational policy model.

Class: KeyHolder ≡ Policy
∩ (*isComponencyBy* ∃ (Regulator
∩ (*hasAuthority* ∃ (RegulatoryActivity
∩ ((*grants* ∃ (CnAObject
∩ (*isBundledBy* ∃ (BackEndActivity
∩ (*isResponsabilityOf* ∃ (ThirdParty
∩ (*hasResponsability* ∃ (BackEndActivity
∩ (*grants* ∃ (PoPObject
∩ (*isBundledBy* ∃ (ResourceActivity
∩ (*isCompetenceOf* ∃Agent))))))))))))
∩ (*grants* ∃ (CnAObject
∩ (*isBundledBy* ∃ (ResourceActivity
∩ (*isCompetenceOf* ∃ (Agent
∩ (*hasCompetence* ∃ (ResourceActivity
∩ (*grants* ∃ (PoPObject
∩ (*isBundledBy* ∃ (FrontEndActivity
∩ (*isCompetenceOf* ∃Principal))))))))))))
∩ (*grants* ∃ (CnAObject
∩ (*isBundledBy* ∃ (ResourceActivity
∩ (*isCompetenceOf* ∃ (Agent
∩ (*hasCompetence* ∃ (ResourceActivity
∩ (*grants* ∃ (PoPObject
∩ (*isBundledBy* ∃ (ResourceActivity
∩ (*isCompetenceOf* ∃Agent))))))))))))))))))

4 Ontology Validation and Evaluation: A Case from the Agribusiness Sector in Brazil

According to Gómez-Pérez, Fernandez-Lopez and Corcho (2004), after an ontology is formally verified according to its consistency and correctness, it can be validated via proof-of-concept tool (i.e., technological validation), via confrontation with a "standard" theory or upper-level ontology (i.e., theoretical validation) or with a case study (i.e., practical validation) [10]. In this study, we validated the ontology proposed with Technical Action Research (TAR) applied to a real-world case. In TAR, a researcher validates the utility of an artifact of Information Systems by working in close cooperation with a real-world organization to extract elements of practice that will be used to refine the design of the artifact. According to Wieringa (2014), with TAR it is possible to predict how organizational problems could be solved if the artifact was implemented in real life [6]. TAR is a specific type of single case study, but different from an observational case study. In TAR, the researcher intervenes in the context where the artifact is applied with transfer of knowledge. However, in an observational case study, the researcher analyzes a case from a distance, with no direct intervention with the stakeholders of the organization that circumscribes the case study. Moreover, in TAR, while the researcher obtains knowledge to refine the IS artifact, the client organization acquires knowledge about how to solve its operational problems.

The behavior of an ontology can be characterized by its input data (i.e., individuals that will populate the classes, properties and restrictions of the ontology) and its output knowledge (i.e., the ontology models). In this study, the input data was collected directly from the owners of the selected company by following the TAR protocol suggested by Wieringa (2014) [6]. The input data concerned organizational information about how the company operates in national and international markets of fresh tropical fruit trade. The output data comprised knowledge generated by automatic inference on the ontology to produce alternative green value models. Therefore, the main *validation question* comprised *to assess if the ontology models would be economically effective in practice*. To facilitate the understanding of the models by business analysts, the ontology models were translated into e^3value models. Hence, the main evaluation question comprised *how the inferred ontology models leveraged our clients' understanding about current and future state of adopted strategies for green value networking*.

4.1   Ontology Validation – Practical Conformance Checking

The company that participated in this research was **Vita+**, part of the **Ecofertil Group**[7], with its main office located in the city of Mossoró, State of Rio Grande do Norte, in the northeastern and semi-arid region of Brazil. The company operates the agribusiness sector, producing and exporting *fresh tropical fruit* to European and American markets. Its main products for exportation are melon (e.g. *yellow, galia* and *toadskin*) and watermelon (*seedless*, specially). Structured interviews were applied to collect data about the current business network in which the company operates, including business actors, activities and objects of economic interest (including aimed green certifications). In TAR, there are three types of knowledge inference: *descriptive* (to explain causes for phenomena of interest), *analogic* (to identify architectural patterns) and *abductive* (to prospect how the IS artifact would change the context of the case), which was the type of inference applied in this study. Such changes can be classified as: *expected effect* (i.e. the difference between current and future models of

---

[7] http://ecofertil.com.br.

the case), *expected value returned* (i.e. economic effectiveness and efficiency) and *trade-off* (i.e., structural differences among the different models produced for the same case). After populating the ontology with the contextual data from the case, five *green value network* models were produced, which are framed according to the organizational *policies* introduced in Sect. 3 (fully formalized in the OWL model available online). The models are explained textually and illustrated with the e^3value notation as follows.

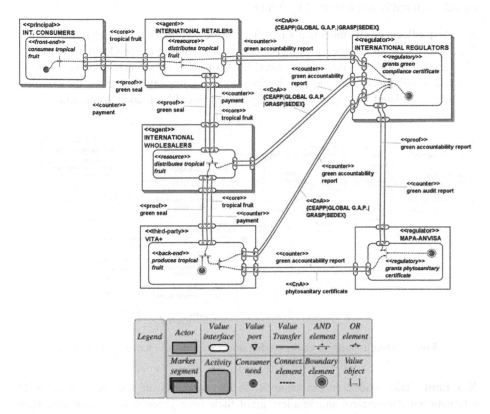

Fig. 2. Padlock chain model: compliance regulation shared between national and international regulators

Padlock chain model: in direct export via international wholesalers, the fruit produced by **Vita+** are checked by the Ministry of Agriculture Livestock and Food Supply (Ministério da Agricultura, Pecuária e Abastecimento – MAPA)[8], via the Brazilian Health Regulatory Agency (Agência Nacional de Vigilância Sanitária – ANVISA), which grants a phytosanitary document authenticated by a certified Agronomy engineer that releases a fruit container for exportation. As depicted in Fig. 2, the national regulator (MAPA-ANVISA) provides green accountability reports to foreign regulators in

---

[8] http://www.agricultura.gov.br/.

exchange of audit reports to certify that the Brazilian company complies to internal regulations. **Vita+** currently has GLOBAL G.A.P.[9], SEDEX[10], GRASP[11] and CEAPP certifications, which allows for exporting tropical fruit to England, Italy, Spain, Portugal and The Netherlands. Its main wholesaler partners are Jaguar, QPI, Barbosa and VidaFresh, which distributes their products to international retailers. According to the model, the proof-of-performance object (green seal) is produced by the back-end activity and transferred through wholesalers and retailers to the final consumer. This model is currently implemented by **Vita+**.

Simple padlock chain model: a simplification of the previous model is depicted in Fig. 3, which illustrates the case of a direct export involving the producer and retailers. This model is *not currently implemented* by **Vita+** due to some restrictions, as fractionated distribution is not the core business of the company. However, the board of managers validated the model as currently implemented by market competitors.

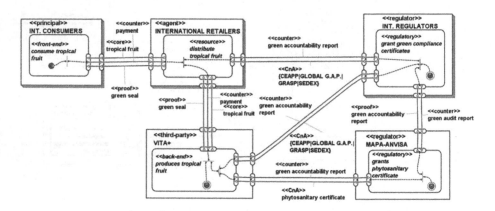

Fig. 3. Simple padlock chain model: direct exports to international retailers.

Key knot chain model: an extension of the first model is the specific case in which international wholesalers and retailers grant their own green certifications and standards, to which the products imported from foreign companies must comply (vide Fig. 4). In this case, retailers or wholesalers might operate as both agents and regulators. The final product has an aggregated value of green seals. As depicted in the model, the green seals flow originally from the producer, but each intermediary adds different seals to the products. **Vita+** currently implements this model.

Key holder model: to operate in the national market, **Vita+** needs to be granted by the only national regulator (MAPE-ANVISA), as depicted in Fig. 5. With this certification, the producer can sell fruit directly to the national wholesalers. **Vita+** cooperates with

---

[9] https://www.globalgap.org/uk_en/.

[10] https://www.sedexglobal.com/.

[11] https://www.globalgap.org/uk_en/for-producers/globalg.a.p.-add-on/grasp/.

many national wholesalers, such as Pilon, Casa da Uva, Benaci, Villalva and Canaã, which redistributes fruit to the local retailing supermarkets.

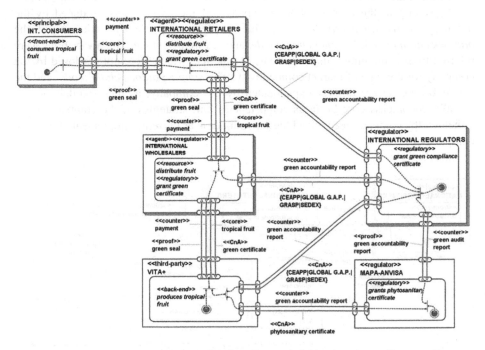

Fig. 4. Key knot chain model: international retailers and wholesalers demanding compliance to own green certifications from producers, in addition to global certifications.

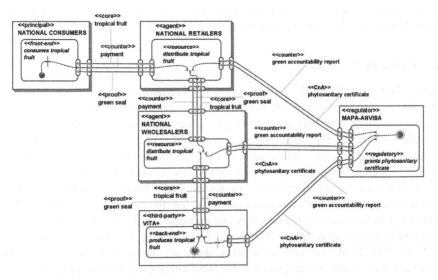

Fig. 5. Key holder model: national retailers and wholesalers obtain green certificates from a centralized national regulator.

Single key model: A simplification of the previous model is the case when the producer cooperates directly with national retailers (vide Fig. 6). **Vita+** does not implement this model currently, but validated the model as adopted by local competitors.

According to the owners of the company, all the five models produced by the
ontology are *economically feasible*. **Vita+** implements currently variations of the
padlock chain model, *key knot chain model* and *key holder model*. Such variations were
referred to as containing critical elements of practice, which were not disclosed by the
company for the sake of market competitivity. The *simple padlock chain model* and the
single key model are not yet implemented by the company, as these models do not
actually encompass core business competencies and strategies of the company. Nevertheless, the company recognized these two models as currently implemented by local
competitors.

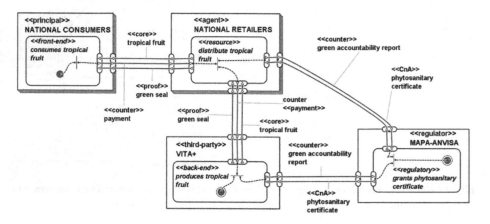

Fig. 6. Single key model: national retailers obtain the core object and the green certificate
directly from the producer and national regulator, respectively.

4.2   Ontology Evaluation

Adams, Nelson and Todd (1992) proposes a framework to evaluate information
technology in general, based on how the final user *accepts* a new technology and
perceives its *usefulness* and *ease of use* [23]. These requirements are also considered in
the evaluation phase of Ontological Engineering [10, 11]. As the ontology proposed by
this study was expressed with properties based on the Speech Acts Theory of Searle
(1969) [17], its original specification in OWL can be understood by IS scholars but
may be difficult to be apprehended by business analysts. Therefore, as Technical Action
Research normally demands business *expert opinion*, the ontology was evaluated based
on the models generated by the ontology and expressed in the e^3value notation (already
evaluated in related study as an effective tool to communicate business requirements)
[3, 4, 13, 21]. From our best knowledge, there are no strict standards to evaluate
usefulness, ease of use or acceptance of business ontologies. For this purpose, we have

adapted the TAR protocol proposed by Wieringa (2014) [14] to elaborate a survey that was submitted to the owners of **Vita+** with the following questions:

(1) *Is it necessary for your company to have value network models defining explicit business strategies to obtain green certifications?*
(2) *Do the green value models describe how the transactions are arranged in the markets where your company operates?*
(3) *Would these models support decision making in your company?*
(4) *Do the organizational policies expressed in the models make practical business sense?*
(5) *Is the decision-making problem of attempting to satisfy a consumer's need of products bundled with green seals and certifications through different value paths clearly formulated?*
(6) *Does the visualization of the green value models help explaining and prospecting opportunities for sustainable business strategies?*
(7) *Do the models generated in this study reflect the current state of green business practice adopted by your company?*
(8) *Do the complementary explanations of the models (i.e., modeling sessions, e^3value models, case documentation and interview reports) add knowledge to decision-making in your company?*

The questions were answered according to a value partition scale as: (1) *extremely*; (2) *a lot*; (3) *partially*; (4) *a little*; and (5) *not at all*. **Questions 2 to 7** were answered with **level 2** (a lot) and **question 1** with **level 3** (partially). The cause explanation given by the owners of **Vita+** for **question 1** is that there are conditions of practice and subjective values currently affecting the cost of transactions made by the company that are not present in the models and will be kept undisclosed for the sake of market differentiation and competitivity of the company. Moreover, it was pointed by the owners of the company that corporate values such as *availability, loyalty* and *trust* involved in component transactions of the *green value network* models could be assessed prior to actual calculation of cost of transaction. If aggregated, the values of each component transactions can provide Key Performance Indicators (KPIs) to assess the economic efficiency of each value model produced.

5   Related Study

There is a progression of studies in Value Network Modeling addressing the configuration of value models for development of long-term business relationships. These studies include the seminal e^3value framework of Gordijn and Akkermans (2003) [2], refined latter by Gordijn and Akkermans (2018) [3]; the $e^3control$ framework of Kartseva, Gordijn and Tan (2009) [21]; and the Value Monitoring Ontology of Silva (2013) [13], refined latter by Silva et al. (2017) [20].

The original e^3value framework proposed by Gordijn and Akkermans (2013) supports specification and analysis of networked business strategies that prelude business process modeling. One of the main strengths of the framework is its graphical notation, evaluated through several European business cases as "easy to understand", by business analysts. Nonetheless, in its original formulation, this framework does not support prospective analysis of opportunistic behavior that normally emerges in untrusted business networks. This limitation was treated latter with the $e^3control$ framework proposed by Kartseva, Gordijn and Tan (2009).

The $e3control$ framework extends the original e^3value with a set of design patterns and a methodology to configure preemptive controls against opportunistic behavior in value networks. Particularly, this framework allows the prospection of how value transactions of a value network could be negatively affected by contract violations, and which actors could be possibly involved in such violations. This study advances the current state of value network modeling with the consolidation of design patterns validated with multiple real-world case scenarios. Nevertheless, one limitation of this study is that its grounding ontology was not formally verified, and model inference is limited by the architectural *rigidity* of the design patterns expressed in the e^3value notation.

The Value Monitoring Ontology proposed by Silva (2013) and corresponding design patterns described in Silva et al. (2013) elaborates on preemptive monitoring of fraudulent behavior in value networks. This study extends the original e^3value ontology with concepts of Multiple Agency proposed by Eisenhardt (1989) [16], principles of Contract Theory, by Colton and Dewatripont (2004) [18], Dietz' Enterprise Ontology (2006) [15] and the linguistic framework of Speech Acts proposed by Searle (1969) [17]. The ontology was evaluated with real-world case scenarios in renewable energy markets in Europe, Intellectual Property Rights in the music industry and Customs Control in The Netherlands. However, as its preceding studies, this study does not address explicitly Green Computing requirements.

In general, the related study point to the importance of business *sustainability*, which demands expression of *social, economic* and *environmental* concerns. However, the treatment of monetary value was still dominant in these studies. In this research, we attempted to treat Green Computing requirements in the early design of value models in two ways: (1) by *extending* the concept of a *consumer's need* from a single core business object to a bundle of products, green certifications and proof-of-performance evidence; (2) *by proposing an organizational design* logic to configure value paths whereby green certified products will flow within a value network. The case in the Agribusiness sector in Brazil is only a starting point to raise elements of practice to develop and mature *green value network modeling*.

6 Conclusions and Future Research

This research was driven by a Design Science perspective, conforming to guidelines provided by Hevner and Chatterjee (2010) [5] and Wieringa (2014) [6], and thereby focused on treating problems of social relevance. We give account of the knowledge questions raised in Sect. 1 (Introduction) and Sect. 4 (Ontology validation) as follows.

(1) *What are green value network models?*

These models extend original value network models with concepts of environmental sustainability. The research agenda for Green Computing proposed by

Hevner and Chatterjee (2010) recommends leveraging Information Systems design to cope with issues of environmental conservation. This perspective demands the treatment of requirements such as disposal of electronic waste, end user satisfaction, energy use, management restructuring, regulatory compliance, return on investment (ROI), telecommuting, thin client solutions and virtualization of server resources. These requirements can be treated progressively, on different managerial layers. In this study, we extend the notion of a business need as the starting point of configuration of a value network model as a bundle of core business product and corresponding green certificates and proof of clean production.

(2) *What concepts ground these models?*

According to Gordijn and Akkermans (2003) [3] the grounding concepts of a value network model are: *business needs, actors, value activities* and *value objects*. In this study, actors, activities and objects are typified according to roles of Multiple Agency [16], organized in a communication model inspired in the Role-Based Access Control (RBAC) model [22] and connected by Speech Acts [17] – previously adapted to express business process models by Dietz (2006) [15].

(3) *How these concepts are related to consumers' needs of products that demand green certifications?*

The concept of a *policy* in a *green value network* model defines *who exchanges which type of object through which activity to whom*. This communication structure was translated as ontology properties to characterize *actor-roles, activity-roles* and *object-roles* within a *green value network* model. Each policy has a different economic efficiency, as green seals and corresponding certificates add value to the final product to be delivered to the final consumer. The e^3value framework already provides an internal mechanism to prospect distributed profit share among the actors willing to form value networks.

(4) *Would the green value models proposed in this research be economically effective if implemented in practice?*

According to the Technical Action Research protocol applied at **Vita+** company, all the green value models depicted in Sect. 4 were evaluated as *economically effective*. The *simple padlock chain model* (vide Fig. 3) and the *single key model* (vide Fig. 6) are not yet implemented by the company but were recognized as currently implemented by market competitors.

(5) *How the inferred ontology models leveraged our clients' understanding about current and future state of adopted strategies for green value networking?*

The *utility* of the ontology models was evaluated with **questions 1 to 4** of the questionnaire presented in Sect. 4, whereas its *ease of use* was evaluated with **questions 5 to 8**. The owners of **Vita+** indicated that the value network models are *useful* to support decision-making about the adoption of value paths necessary to obtain green certifications and are *easily communicated* and understood.

This study can be leveraged by at least three research directions: (1) to investigate if the organizational structures of the green value network models proposed in this study could be consolidated as design patterns, by application in multiple and similar case studies (i.e., for sensitivity analysis) or in related business domains (e.g., wind and solar energy trading companies); (2) to investigate how business values such as availability, loyalty and trust could be analyzed prior to the actual formation of transactions *in green value network* models; and (3) to extend the ontology with a taxonomy of *environmental resources* to classify and prospect the sustainability of the value activities to be included in a *green value network* model.

References

1. Normann, R., Ramirez, R.: From value chain to value constellation: designing interactive strategy. Harv. Bus. Rev. **71**(4), 65–77 (1993)
2. Peppard, J., Rylander, A.: From value chain to value network: insights for mobile operators. Eur. Manag. J. **24**(2–3), 128–141 (2006)
3. Gordijn, J., Akkermans, J.M.: Value-based requirements engineering: exploring innovative e- commerce ideas. Requir. Eng. **8**(2), 114–134 (2003)
4. Gordijn, J., Akkermans, H.: Value Webs, Understanding e-Business Innovation. The Value Engineers, B.V., Soest (2018)
5. Hevner, A., Chatterjee, S.: Design Research in Information Systems: Theory and Practice. Springer, Heidelberg (2010). https://doi.org/10.1007/978-1-4419-5653-8
6. Wieringa, R.J.: Design Science Methodology for Information Systems and Software Engineering. Springer, Heidelberg (2014). https://doi.org/10.1007/978-3-662-43839-8
7. Cameron, K.: Critical questions in assessing organizational effectiveness. Organ. Dyn. **9**(2), 66–80 (1980)
8. Lusch, R.F., Vargo, S.L., Tanniru, M.: Service, value networks and learning. J. Acad. Mark. Sci. **38**(1), 19–31 (2010)
9. Uschold, M., King, M.: Towards a methodology for building ontologies. In: Proceedings of Workshop on Basic Ontological Issues in Knowledge Sharing, held in conjunction with IJCAI-95, 13p. (1995)
10. Gómez-Pérez, A., Fernandez-Lopez, M., Corcho, O.: Ontological Engineering: With Examples from the Areas of Knowledge Management, e-Commerce and the Semantic Web. Springer, Berlin (2004). https://doi.org/10.1007/b97353
11. Vrandečić, D., Sure, Y.: How to design better ontology metrics. In: Franconi, E., Kifer, M., May, W. (eds.) ESWC 2007. LNCS, vol. 4519, pp. 311–325. Springer, Heidelberg (2007). https://doi.org/10.1007/978-3-540-72667-8_23
12. Ionita, D., Gordijn, J., Yesuf, A.S., Wieringa, R.: Value-driven risk analysis of coordination models. In: Horkoff, J., Jeusfeld, Manfred A., Persson, A. (eds.) PoEM 2016. LNBIP, vol. 267, pp. 102–116. Springer, Cham (2016). https://doi.org/10.1007/978-3-319-48393-1_8
13. Silva, P.A.: Value Activity monitoring, Ph.D. thesis, Tilburg University (2013). https://pure. uvt.nl/ws/portalfiles/portal/1522768/PhD_Thesis__Patr_cio_de_Alencar_Silva_.pdf. Accessed 14 July 2019
14. Loucopoulos, P., Kavakli, V.: Enterprise knowledge management and conceptual modelling. In: Goos, G., et al. (eds.) Conceptual Modeling. LNCS, vol. 1565, pp. 123–143. Springer, Heidelberg (1999). https://doi.org/10.1007/3-540-48854-5_11
15. Dietz, J.: Enterprise Ontology: Theory and Methodology. Springer, Heidelberg (2006). https://doi.org/10.1007/3-540-33149-2
16. Eisenhardt, K.M.: Agency theory: an assessment and review. Acad. Manag. Rev. **14**(1), 57–74 (1989)

17. Searle, J.R.: Speech Acts: An Essay in the Philosophy of Language. Cambridge University Press, Cambridge (1969)
18. Bolton, P., Dewatripont, M.: Contract Theory. The MIT Press, Cambridge (2004)
19. Mankiw, N.G.: Principles of Macroeconomics, 6th edn. South-Western Cengage Learning, Mason (2014)
20. de Alencar Silva, P., Allah Bukhsh, F., da Silva Reis, J., de Castro, A.F.: Agency monitoring patterns for value networks. In: Pham, C., Altmann, J., Bañares, J.Á. (eds.) GECON 2017. LNCS, vol. 10537, pp. 81–93. Springer, Cham (2017). https://doi.org/10.1007/978-3-319-68066-8_7
21. Kartseva, V., Gordijn, J., Tan, Y.-H.: Designing value-based inter-organizational controls using patterns. In: Lyytinen, K., Loucopoulos, P., Mylopoulos, J., Robinson, B. (eds.) Design Requirements Engineering: A Ten-Year Perspective. LNBIP, vol. 14, pp. 276–301. Springer, Heidelberg (2009). https://doi.org/10.1007/978-3-540-92966-6_16
22. Ferraiolo, D.F., Sandhu, R., Gavrila, S., Kuhn, D.R., Chandramouli, R.: Proposed NIST standard for role-based access control. ACM Trans. Inf. Syst. Secur. 4(3), 224–274 (2001)
23. Adams, D.A., Nelson, R.R., Todd, P.A.: Perceived usefulness, ease of use, and usage of information technology: a replication. MIS Q. 16(2), 227–247 (1992)

Business Object Centric Microservices Patterns

Adambarage Anuruddha Chathuranga De Alwis[1(✉)], Alistair Barros[1],
Colin Fidge[1], and Artem Polyvyanyy[2]

[1] Queensland University of Technology, Brisbane, Australia
{adambarage.dealwis,alistair.barros,c.fidge}@qut.edu.au
[2] The University of Melbourne, Parkville, VIC 3010, Australia
artem.polyvyanyy@unimelb.edu.au

Abstract. A key impediment towards maturing microservice architecture conceptions is the uncertainty about what it means to design fine-grained functionality for microservices. Under a traditional service-oriented architecture (SOA), the unit of functionality for software components concerns individual business domain objects and encapsulated operations, enabling desirable architectural properties such as high cohesion and loose-coupling of its components. However, at present it is not clear how this SOA design strategy should be refined for microservices nor, more generally, how design considerations for different degrees of granularity apply, in a consistent and systematic way, for large SOA systems to smaller microservices. This paper proposes *microservice patterns*, as a contribution to the maturity of microservice architectures, through the refinement of the functional structure of SOAs. The patterns are derived by considering the splitting of business object (BO) operations and salient types of BO relationships, which influence software structure (as captured in UML): object association, exclusive containment, inclusive containment and specialisation (i.e., subtyping). The viability of the patterns for evolving large SOA systems into microservices is demonstrated through automated microservices discovery algorithms, on two open-source enterprise systems used widely in practice, Dolibarr and SugarCRM.

Keywords: Microservices patterns · Microservice discovery · System re-engineering

1 Introduction

Microservice architectures are the latest development of distributed systems, evolving service-oriented architectures (SOAs) to enable high-performance, Internet-scale applications. Seen through the software transformations of Netflix[TM], Twitter[TM], eBay[TM] and Amazon[TM] among others, microservices are fine-grained software components which support individualised functionality of businesses, manage local and synchronised databases, and communicate via lightweight protocols.

© Springer Nature Switzerland AG 2019
H. Panetto et al. (Eds.): OTM 2019, LNCS 11877, pp. 476–495, 2019.
https://doi.org/10.1007/978-3-030-33246-4_30

To date, different ways of understanding microservices have emerged, notably from reported Internet player experiences [1] and more general software practitioner references [2,3]. The agile development community emphasises microservices as a *unit of continuous development*, which can be separately developed, deployed, composed, and ultimately accrued into a collective software solution, that can provide *high scalability, availability* (replication), and execution *integrity*, when compared with monolithic systems. However, these nonfunctional properties are insufficient for a full understanding of a microservice architecture, which also requires precise insights concerning the functional structure of software in terms of software components, relationships, composability and deployment constraints.

Domain-driven design principles of software [4] have been indispensable for understanding the functional structure of software components in SOA, aligning it with the functionality of business domains. In particular, SOA components are structured to manage distinct business objects (BOs) of domains (e.g., order, customer, payment), containing encapsulated CRUD (create, read, update, and delete) operations of the objects [5]. Designed this way, SOA components can exhibit high intra-functional dependencies, (i.e., high cohesion) and low inter-functional dependencies with other components, (i.e., low coupling), allowing a systematic composition for larger components and applications. Emerging principles and patterns for microservices [6], which likewise appeal to domain-driven design, recommend decomposing BOs for support of fine-grained functionality (e.g., from an order to order entry, order tracking and order delivery) [2]. However, by appealing to business design considerations only, the implications for a precise functional structure required of a microservice architecture are left open.

In this paper we consolidate emerging developments of microservices towards an architecture style that is refined from the functional structure of SOAs (background in Sect. 2). Specifically, we present *patterns for microservices* (in Sect. 3), aligning, as done for the SOA paradigm, software components with BOs. To address the requirement for refined decomposition of BOs, the patterns support the splitting of BO operations into microservices (i.e., subsets of business object operations). In addition, our patterns address overall architectural coherence, and how microservices can be related to each other and be potentially co-located in Cloud containers, given BO intra- and inter-relationships. Four important BO relationships that pertain to software component design are considered (as expressed in the widely used Unified Modelling Language) [7]: BO association (relationship), BO exclusive containment (composition), BO inclusive containment (aggregation) and subtyping (specialisation). Taken together, we claim a crucial first step towards maturing the field of microservices through microservice patterns, in a similar vein to other IT fields [8–10].

While presenting the patterns for "greenfield" (new) development of software, we also demonstrate the value of the patterns for "brownfield" (evolving) developments, whereby the patterns are used to identify prospective microservices from the most prominent form of software used in businesses and utilising SOAs, i.e., enterprise systems (algorithms and validation are presented in Sects. 4 and 5). Related works (Sect. 6) and a conclusion (Sect. 7) are provided towards the end of the paper.

2 Systems Architecture Context

This section describes a systems architecture context in which microservices operate and is relevant for our definition of the microservice patterns (in Sect. 3). The context assumes that microservices are aligned with larger SOA-based systems such that they are either refactored parts of the systems or new designs whose processes are connected to backend SOA systems. Enterprise systems are used as exemplar SOA system, given their widespread use, and the examples we use are drawn from this software domain. As depicted in Fig. 1, an enterprise system consists of self-contained modules drawn from different subsystems (e.g., production management), and is deployed on a "backend" platform. Modules consist of a set of functions (e.g., software classes) managing one or more BOs through CRUD operations. For example 'Software Module₁' consists of several functions with operations manipulating the data related to 'Shipment', 'Element' and 'User' BOs in the database system. In this case, we have illustrated reduced cohesion and increased coupling, as the modules manage multiple BOs, unlike the desirable design of SOA components which should manage a single BO [7]. Through the database, different types of BO relationships are illustrated. These are: subtyping, where 'At-Store Reclamation' and 'Generic Transport' are specialised from 'Shipment'; exclusive containment, where 'Shipment' is exclusively made up of 'Element' and controls its creation/deletion; inclusive containment, where 'Order' is inclusively made up of 'Product' but does not control its creation/deletion; and basic associations such as a 'User' has an 'Order'.

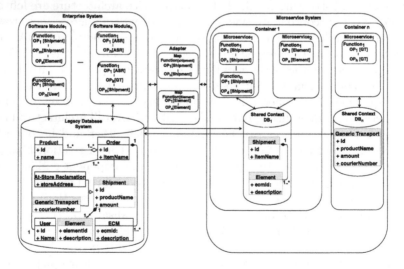

Fig. 1. Enterprise system integrated with a microservice system.

Through the microservice system (right-hand side of Fig. 1) aligned with the enterprise system, individual microservices, distributed in Cloud containers, have been introduced (in this case, refactored from the ES). They support subsets of individual BO operations. For example, Microservice$_1$ and Microservice$_2$ are responsible for subsets of 'Shipment' and 'Element' operations, respectively. In this example, the microservices are co-located on the same container because of the related BO exclusive containment relationship, which results in a dedicated coupling between them. The execution of operations across the enterprise and microservice systems are coordinated through business processes, which means that invocations of BO operations on the microservices trigger operations on enterprise system functions involving the same BOs and potentially related BOs through orchestration or choreography [11]. As per microservice systems, BO data is synchronised across databases managed by microservices and enterprise systems periodically.

Given this systems architecture context, we provide the following formalisation, which is used to define the microservice patterns (in Sect. 3) and pattern-based microservice discovery from enterprise systems (in Sect. 4). For this, we reuse the abstract representation of an enterprise system that we introduced previously [12].

Let $\mathbb{I}$ and $\mathbb{O}$ be *input* types and *output* types, respectively. Let $\mathbb{OP}$, $\mathbb{B}$, $\mathbb{T}$ and $\mathbb{A}$ be, respectively, a universe of *operations, BOs, database tables* and *attributes*. We characterize a *database table* $t \in \mathbb{T}$ by a collection of attributes, i.e., $t \subseteq \mathbb{A}$, while a *business object* $b \in \mathbb{B}$ is defined as a collection of database tables, i.e., $b \subseteq \mathbb{T}$.

An *operation op*, either of an enterprise or microservice system, is given as a triple (I, O, T), where $I \in \mathbb{I}^*$ is a sequence of *input types* the operation expects for input, $O \in \mathbb{O}^*$ is a sequence of *output types* the operation produces as output, and $T \subseteq \mathbb{T}$ is a set of *database tables* the operation accesses, i.e., either reads or augments.[1]

We define an enterprise system, or more precisely its abstract representation, as a finite automaton.

Definition 2.1 (Enterprise system, ES)
An *enterprise system* is a 5-tuple $(Q, \Lambda, \delta, q_0, A)$, where Q is a finite nonempty set of *states*, $\Lambda \subseteq \mathbb{OP}$ is a set of *operations*, such that Q and Λ are disjoint, $\delta : Q \times (\Lambda \cup \{\tau\}) \to \mathcal{P}(Q)$ is the *transition function*, where τ a is a special *silent operation* such that $\tau \notin Q \cup \Lambda$, $q_0 \in Q$ is the *start state*, and $A \subseteq Q$ is the *set of accept states*.[2]

We refer to computations of an enterprise system as *processes*, or *process instances* of the system. Finally, a microservice system is defined as follows.

Definition 2.2 (Microservice system, MS)
Let $\mathbb{C}$ and $\mathbb{M}$ be a universe of containers and a universe of MSs, respectively. A *MS* is a 4-tuple (C, M, σ, μ), where $C \subseteq \mathbb{C}$ is a set of *containers*, $M \subseteq \mathbb{M}$ is a set of *microservices*, $\sigma : C \to \mathcal{P}(M) \setminus \emptyset$ is a *deployment function* that maps each

---

[1] A^* denotes the application of the Kleene star operation to set A.
[2] Given a set A, by $\mathcal{P}(A)$ we denote the powerset of A.

container $c \in C$ onto a non-empty set of microservices $\sigma(c)$ that are deployed on c, and $\mu : M \to \mathcal{P}(\mathbb{OP}) \setminus \emptyset$ is a *microservice definition function* that maps each microservice $m \in M$ onto a non-empty set of operations.

3   Microservices Patterns

We present four Microservice (MS) patterns related to intra- and inter-BO relationships that form important design considerations for software components [7]. As detailed above, each pattern identifies a microservice as a collection of operations that manipulate data related to a single BO.

Pattern 3.1 (Microservice Subtyping)
A microservice is used to manage subsets of operations related to a BO subtype. Since there can be multiple BO subtypes of a supertype, a MS can apply to any given subtype, at any level of a subtype hierarchy and a subset of operations related to that subtype.

More formally, let $b_1, b_2 \in \mathbb{B}$ be two BOs such that b_2 is a subtype of b_1, at any level of the subtype hierarchy. A MS m reflects the *microservice subtype pattern* for b_2 and its supertype b_1, iff for each operation $(I, O, T) \in \mu(m)$ it holds that $b_2 \cap T \neq \emptyset$. Support of the other operations that relate to b_2 not covered by m, i.e., $(I, O, T) \notin \mu(m)$ where $b_2 \cap T \neq \emptyset$, is subject to systems architecture considerations, inclusive of the ES and other MSs. We distinguish two variants of the subtype pattern:

- *Data population partition:* MS m reflects the *data population partition* variant of the *subtype pattern* iff $b_1 \subseteq \bigcup_{(I,O,T) \in \mu(m)} T$. That is, m involves operations over all the tables b_1 has access to.
- *Data typing partition:* MS m reflects the *data typing partition* variant of the *subtype pattern* iff (i) $b_1 \subseteq \bigcup_{(I,O,T) \in \mu(m)} T$ and (ii) for every BO $b_3 \neq b_2$, such that b_3 is a subtype of b_1 at the same hierarchy level as b_2, it holds that $(b_3 \setminus b_1) \cap (\bigcup_{(I,O,T) \in \mu(m)} T) = \emptyset$. That is, m reflects the data population partition and, in addition, does not involve operations over the tables that are specific to other subtypes of b_1 at the same level of the subtype hierarchy as b_2.

Examples: As depicted in Fig. 1, BO 'Shipment' has two subtypes 'At-Store Reclamation' and 'Generic Transport' that have dedicated attributes *storeAddress* and *courierNumber*, respectively, and common attributes *id, productName,* and *amount*. Partitioning of the BOs occurs at the attribute level, to which the MS subtyping variant, *data typing partition*, can be applied (see the MS system in Fig. 1). If, on the other hand, a single attribute in shipment BO is used to indicate whether it is an 'At-Store Reclamation' or a 'Generic Transport', partitioning of the BOs occurs at the data level, to which the *data population partition* variant can be applied.

Problem: Developing a single microservice to manage subtype BOs will result in services which do not follow the single responsibility rule [2] in MS development. Furthermore, this can result in increased request processing time due to the fact that a request related to multiple subtypes are processed through the same service endpoint. Consequently, the unavailability of a single service endpoint may result in the unavailability of all subtype services.

Solution: The pattern addresses selective implementation through MSs of BO subtypes, with BOs abstracted over database tables. Implementations on the database level can vary, ranging from a single table storing the supertype and subtypes of BOs to individual tables per supertype and each subtype, to combinations of both. This in turn can give rise a considerable set of CRUD operations related to the supertype and each subtype of the BO, potentially resulting in software inconsistencies as to which operations are provided as part of the different MSs. Such a problem is compounded when the structure of BOs change, resulting in changes to the different operations. A way of handling is to include a standard set of operations for handling all the supertype and subtypes and allowing for a qualification (e.g. a special parameter) when the operations are called to indicate which subtype is required. Each operation then results in the calling of a data handling MS which contains logic for determining which parameters are required for each different subtype. This way, the BO attribute sets are mapped to different BO subtypes in the same, reusable core MS.

Pattern 3.2 (Microservice Exclusive Containment)

Description: Microservices manage subsets of operations of BOs which have an exclusive containment relationship. One MS relates to the parent (or composite) BO and other MSs manage child BOs, such that the existence (i.e., create, update and delete) of a child BO depends on the existence of the parent BO. MSs should be co-located to run on the same (execution) container, given their tight-coupling resulting from the existence of the corresponding parent and child BOs.

More formally, let $b_1, b_2 \in \mathbb{B}$ be two BOs such that b_2 is exclusively contained in b_1. MSs m_1 and m_2 reflect the *exclusive containment pattern* for b_1 and b_2 iff:

○ for each operation $(I, O, T) \in \mu(m_1)$ it holds that $b_1 \cap T \neq \emptyset$,
○ for each operation $(I, O, T) \in \mu(m_2)$ it holds that $b_2 \cap T \neq \emptyset$,
○ m_1 and m_2 includes object existence operations related to BOs of type b_1 and b_2 respectively,
○ BOs of type b_2 are created only after the corresponding BO of type b_1 is created,
○ a BO of type b_1 is deleted only after all the corresponding BOs of type b_2 are deleted, and
○ updates of a BO of type b_2 always come after that BO is created.

We distinguish two variant of exclusive containment pattern:

○ *Mandatory exclusive containment:* The invocation of create and delete operation related to the parent BO b_1 requires that the corresponding child BO's

b_2 operations (I, O, T) *must* also be done simultaneously, as part of the same process instance.

o *Optional exclusive containment:* The invocation of create and delete operation related to the parent BO b_1 does not requires that the corresponding child BO's b_2 operations (I, O, T) to be invoked.

Examples: When considering a 'Shipment' BO, as depicted in Fig. 1, the 'Element' BO is contained in the 'Shipment' and the creation of the 'Shipment' BO always requires creating one or more 'Element' BOs. Similarly, deleting the 'Shipment' BO requires deleting the 'Element' BO, resulting in mandatory exclusive containment. As such, the *mandatory exclusive containment* variant can be applied when designing MSs (see the microservice system in Fig. 1). If, on the other hand, creation of a 'Shipment' does not always require having an 'Element' (i.e., 'Shipment' and 'Element' have a zero or more relationship) then *optional exclusive containment* can be applied.

Problem: Developing separate microservices contained in separate microservice containers to manage exclusively contained BOs may result in increased communication overhead between services. In addition, separating the data related to parent BOs and child BOs into separate microservices may result in data inconsistencies and unavailability.

Solution: Given two variants of exclusive containment the development of the MS should be done while checking the last three conditions against all the processes the ES supports as below.

o *Mandatory exclusive containment:* This can be supported in three ways. Firstly, through the MS managing the parent object (i.e., m_1), the parent object b_1 is created and invocations are made on the child MSs (i.e, m_2) to create the child objects b_2 (i.e., concurrently). Secondly, through a process context, the parent object's b_1 creation using the parent MS m_1 and the child objects' b_2 creations using the child MSs m_2, occur in the same process. The process allows the latter to occur at some point following the former (i.e., eventually) but before the end of the process instance. Thirdly, if there are multiple instances of a child object b_2, then the instance after the first can be created through an update operation on the child MS m_2. In the case of object deletion, through the MS managing the parent object (i.e., m_1), invocations are made on the child MSs (i.e., m_2) to delete any child object b_2 as a part of parent's deletion process (i.e., concurrently) and to delete the parent object b_1.

o *Optional exclusive containment:* The same create and delete mechanisms described for mandatory inclusive containment (refer Pattern 3.3) also apply here, with the exception that the creation and deletion of child objects b_2 and therefore corresponding invocations of child MSs m_2 are optional.

Pattern 3.3 (Microservice Inclusive Containment)
Description: Microservices manage subsets of operations of BOs which have an inclusive containment relationship. One MS relates to the parent (or aggregate) BO and other MSs manage child BOs, such that the existence of children does

not depend on the parent's existence, i.e., the children exist independently but are used in the context of the parent. No dedicated tight-coupling, as such, exists between the MSs operating on parent and children objects, and therefore there is no requirement to strictly co-locate them for execution.

More formally, let $b_1, b_2 \in \mathbb{B}$ be two BOs such that b_2 is inclusively contained in b_1. MSs m_1 and m_2 reflect the *inclusive containment pattern* for b_1 and b_2 iff:

○ for each operation $(I, O, T) \in \mu(m_1)$ it holds that $b_1 \cap T \neq \emptyset$,
○ for each operation $(I, O, T) \in \mu(m_2)$ it holds that $b_2 \cap T \neq \emptyset$,
○ m_1 and m_2 includes create, read, update and delete operations related to BOs of type b_1 and b_2 respectively,
○ m_1 contains an operation for reading BOs of type b_2, and
○ each time a BO of type b_1 is created, it reads a BO of type b_2.

Variants:

○ *Mandatory inclusive containment:* The invocation of create and delete operations related to BO b_1 of parent MS m_1 requires that the corresponding child BOs b_2 *must* also exist and be used in the parent's aggregation, despite their independent existence. As such parent MS m_1 will call child MS m_2 for information retrieval.
○ *Optional inclusive containment:* The invocation of create and delete operations related to BO b_1 of parent MS m_1 does not require invocation of operations related to the child MS m_2 corresponding to child BOs b_2.

Examples: The 'Order' BO as depicted in Fig. 1 has an inclusive containment relationship with the 'Product' BO, because an order should contain a list of products which are ordered, which results in a mandatory inclusive containment relationship. As such the *mandatory inclusive containment* variant can be applied to design MSs. If, on the other hand, creating an 'Order' is not always require creating a 'Product' (i.e, 'Order' and 'Product' have a zero or more relationship), then the *optional inclusive containment* variant can be applied to design MSs.

Problem: Developing a single microservice to manage inclusively contained BOs will result in bigger services which does not follow the single responsibility rule in MS development and can result in difficulty of maintenance due to the fact that it is responsible for the operations related to multiple BOs. Furthermore, this can result in service unavailability of multiple BOs if the hosted microservice fails. When considering the scalability aspect, this will result in reduced scalability due to the fact that it requires more resources such as memory and CPU to provide the services.

Solution: Given two variants of inclusive containment the development of the MSs should be done while checking the last three conditions against all the processes the ES supports as below.

○ *Mandatory inclusive containment:* When the parent MS m_1's create operations are invoked, read operations are invoked on the child MS m_2 and corresponding object references are held in the parent MS m_1. These references can be created concurrently (as part of the parent's create operation) or sometime before the end of the process instance (as part of a process context which includes the creation of parent object b_1 and child object b_2 references). If there are multiple instances of a specific child object b_2, its object reference is used to update the list of instances in the parent aggregate using reads on the child MS m_2. When the parent MS m_1's delete operations are invoked, object references to the child BOs b_2 are thereby deleted.

o *Optional inclusive containment:* The same create and delete mechanisms described for mandatory inclusive containment also apply here, with the exception that the creation and deletion of child object b_2 references the parent b_1 and therefore corresponding invocations of child MS m_2 existence operations are optional.

Pattern 3.4 (Microservice Association)
Description: Two microservices manage operations of BOs which have an association relationship. One MS relates to one BO and the other MS manages another BO, such that the existence of both BOs are independent of each other. As there is no dedicated tight-coupling, there is no requirement to strictly co-locate them.

More formally, let $b_1, b_2 \in \mathbb{B}$ be two BOs in an association relationship. MSs m_1 and m_2 reflect the *association pattern* for b_1 and b_2 iff:

o for each operation $(I, O, T) \in \mu(m_1)$ it holds that $b_1 \cap T \neq \emptyset$,
o for each operation $(I, O, T) \in \mu(m_2)$ it holds that $b_2 \cap T \neq \emptyset$,
o m_1 includes operations over BOs of type b_1,
o m_2 includes operations over BOs of type b_2, and
o m_1 contains operations which reference m_2 for reading BOs of type b_2.

Examples: 'Order' and 'User' BOs can have an association relationship as depicted in Fig. 1. In this situation one 'User' can have one or more 'Orders' related to it. The create, read, update, and delete operations on the values related to each BO can occur independently of each other even though they are related. However, some create or update operations related to 'Order' might require the 'User' information which leads to a read execution of the BO 'User'.

Problem: Developing a single microservice to manage associated BOs will result in bigger services which result in difficulty of maintenance due to the fact that it is responsible for the operations related to multiple BOs. Furthermore, this can result in service unavailability of multiple BOs if the hosted microservice fails. When considering the scalability aspect, this will result in reduce scalability due to the fact that it requires more resources such as memory and CPU to provide the services.

Solution: Develop separate MSs m_1 and m_2 to manage associate BOs b_1 and b_2, such that the CRUD operation of one MS may invoke CRUD operations related to the other MS.

4   Utilisation of MS Patterns in ESs Re-Engineering

In this section, we demonstrate the added value of using our microservice patterns in the context of re-engineering parts of enterprise systems as microservices (i.e., "brownfield" development) (refer to Fig. 2).

In the first step, we identify the BOs in the given enterprise system by evaluating the SQL queries and relationships between database tables according to the method described by Nooijen *et al.* [13]. In the second step, we analyse the database tables and their cardinalities in order to derive the mandatory and optional containment relationships. In the third step, we derive the BO relationships based on the BOs derived from step one, cardinalities derived from step two and system execution logs, as detailed in Sect. 4.1. In the fourth step, we generate the call graphs based on the execution logs which were generated in the previous step. Finally, in the fifth step, all the structural and behavioural details generated are provided to an optimization algorithm (Non-dominated Sorting Genetic Algorithm (NSGA II)) which suggests the best splitting of subset of operations related to BOs, by considering the four major factors namely, operations' relationships with BOs, BO relationships, execution frequencies of operations and their execution patterns.

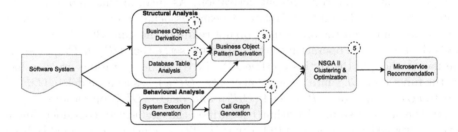

Fig. 2. Overview of the microservice discovery approach.

4.1   Business Object Pattern Derivation

As depicted in Fig. 2, to derive microservice recommendations, BO pattern derivation should be achieved in the third step. This is done using two algorithms. The first algorithm derives the subtyping patterns as detailed in our previous work [12]. The second algorithm (i.e., Algorithm 1) is detailed in this section. It derives inclusive containment, exclusive containment and association patterns using eight steps.

As described in Sect. 2, BOs are often stored across several database tables. Thus, in the first step, the *BOS* function is performed by Algorithm 1, which derives the set of all BOs *B* of the system through the analysis of the database table relationships and their data similarities, as described by Nooijen *et al.* [13]. In the second step, the algorithm extracts all the operations *OPS* related to the system through static analysis. This mainly involves the invocation of function

STATOPEX which uses Abstract Syntax Tree (AST) parsing to process the source code *SC* of the system to extract all the CRUD operations related to the system. Generally, in *join sql operations*, database tables are referred to by different names, other than their original names in the database (e.g., 'cus' is used to refer to the 'customer' database table). As such, the details (*TNM*) related to such tables (i.e., table names and alias names) are provided to the function for processing. Function *STATOPEX* extracts all the operations related to the given system and uses a mapping function to map table names to alias names (*TNM*) when there are join operations. In the third step of the algorithm, function *DYNOPEX* is executed to extract the operations from the execution logs (line 3). In the fourth step, function *DYNTM* computes the execution time of each dynamic operation as per the log. This allows to classify the operations which execute together, by analysing the execution sequences and execution times in the logs. According to Andrews *et al.* [14], such classification helps to derive relationships between operations. Apart from operation extraction, both functions *STATOPEX* and *DYNOPEX* identify and store the database tables related to each operation. In the fifth step, Algorithm 1 classifies the static operations extracted in step three into association create (OP_a^c) and association delete (OP_a^d) operations (lines 6–13). Generally, in a database, there can be foreign key relationships among the tables that relate to the same BO. Such relationships are not important for the containment derivation. As such, in this step, the *TBLS* function extracts the tables T_k related to each association operation op_k. Next, after confirming that the tables in T_k do not relate to the same BO, the algorithm adds the association operation to the respective set, either OP_a^c or OP_a^d. Using a similar method, in the sixth step (line 14), the dynamic operations are classified by the function *DCLS* into association create (OP_{da}^c), association delete (OP_{da}^d), create (OP_d^c), update (OP_d^u), read (OP_d^r), and delete (OP_d^d) operations.

In the seventh step, Algorithm 1 identifies the exclusively contained, inclusively contained and associated BOs (lines 15–22). Exclusively contained BOs (γ) are identified by verifying that two BOs are related by create (OP_{da}^c) and delete (OP_{da}^d) association operations, or related by update (OP_{da}^u) and delete (OP_{da}^d) association operations, or related by create (OP_d^c) and delete (OP_d^d) operations, or related by update (OP_d^u) and delete (OP_d^d) operations while not having any other operations in OP_a^c and OP_a^d that govern the relationship between b_i and b_j (lines 16–17). Similarly, inclusively contained BOs (β) are derived if there are two BOs b_i, b_j in which b_j is created or read before updating the values in b_i related to it while not having any delete association operations in OP_a^d and OP_{da}^d between them (lines 18–19). Note that in inclusive and exclusive containment derivation, the algorithm uses the time sequences related to the dynamic operations to identify the execution patterns of the operations. For example, if there is a create operation of a BO which is immediately followed by a create operation of another BO, there is a possibility of exclusive containment given that the other criteria match. The BOs which are not in the inclusive or exclusive containment relationships are categorised as associated BOs (δ) (lines 20–21).

In the final step of the algorithm, function $MANDOROP$ analyses the constructed inclusive and exclusive relationships and verifies which BOs have mandatory or optional relationship (line 23). Function $MANDOROP$ requires information about foreign keys and primary keys of database tables ($TDATA$), because different developers use different patterns to define foreign key and primary key relationships. Based on the given keys, mandatory relationship is identified if for every record in BO b_i there is at least one record in BO b_j. However, if there are no records related to items of b_i in b_j, it is considered as an optional relationship.

Algorithm 1: Computing BO relationship patterns

Input: Source Code SC, Execution Logs EL, Database Schema DB, Alias names TNM, Database Table Data $TDATA$ of an ES s.

Output: γ, β, δ are binary relations over BOs that capture exclusive containment, inclusive containment and association, respectively, α captures mandatory and optional types.

1   $B = \{b_1, \ldots, b_n\} := BOS(SC, DB)$;   // Identify BOs

2   $OPS = \langle op_1, \ldots, op_m \rangle := STATOPEX(SC, TNM)$;   // static analysis

3   $OPD = \langle opd_1, \ldots, opd_n \rangle := DYNOPEX(EL, TNM)$;   // dynamic analysis

4   $OPT = \langle opt_1, \ldots, opt_n \rangle := DYNTM(EL, TNM)$;   // dynamic operation time analysis

5   $OP_a^c := OP_a^d := OP_{da}^c := OP_{da}^d := OP_d^c := OP_d^u := OP_d^r := OP_d^d := \emptyset$;

6   **for** *each* $k \in [1..m]$ **do**

7   **if** op_k *is an association operation* **then**

8         $T_k := TBLS(op_k)$;

9   **if** $\nexists b \in B . T_k \subseteq b \wedge op_k$ *is a create operation* **then**

10           $OP_a^c := OP_a^c \cup \{op_k\}$;   // Identify an association create operation

11   **else if** $\nexists b \in B . T_k \subseteq b \wedge op_k$ *is a delete operation* **then**

12           $OP_a^d := OP_a^d \cup \{op_k\}$;   // Identify an association delete operation

13   **end**

14   $\langle OP_d^c, OP_d^u, OP_d^r, OP_d^d, OP_{da}^c, OP_{da}^d \rangle := DCLS(OPD)$;

15   **for** *each* $b_i, b_j \in B$ *where* $i \neq j$ **do**

16   **if** $((\exists op \in OP_{da}^c . op \in OP_{da}^d) \vee (\exists op \in OP_{da}^u . op \in OP_{da}^d) \vee$
        $(\exists op_d^i \in OP_d^c . \exists op_d^j \in OP_d^d . op_d^i = op_d^j) \vee$
        $(\exists op_d^i \in OP_d^u . \exists op_d^j \in OP_d^d . op_d^i = op_d^j)) \wedge (\nexists op \in OP_a^c \wedge op \in OP_a^d)$ **then**

17   Record in γ that b_i, b_j are exclusively contained;

18   **else if** $((\exists op_d^i \in OP_d^c \vee \exists op_d^i \in OP_d^r) \wedge \exists op_d^j \in OP_d^u \cup OP_d^c . op_d^i < op_d^j) \wedge$
        $(\nexists op \in OP_a^d \wedge \nexists op \in OP_{da}^d)$ **then**

19   Record in β that b_i, b_j are inclusively contained;

20   **else**

21   Record in δ that b_i, b_j are associated;

22   **end**

23   $\alpha := MANDOROP(TDATA, \gamma, \beta)$;

24   **return** $\gamma, \beta, \delta, \alpha$;

After obtaining the BO relationships using Algorithm 1 we provide that information with the call graphs generated from system executions (see step 4 in Fig. 2) to our genetic optimization algorithm, which is detailed in our previous work [15]. This algorithm clusters the executed operations in the graphs based on their relationships to the BOs while minimizing the communication overhead between different clusters (i.e., the number of calls between operations of different clusters would be minimal). These clusters are then provided to the users as recommendations to create microservices to optimize the system's performance.

5 Implementation and Validation

To demonstrate the applicablity of the patterns for re-engineering of legacy software systems, we developed a prototype[3] which uses the patterns to discover prospective microservices from two enterprise systems: Dolibarr[4] and Sugar-CRM[5]. The validity of the discovered microservices was evaluated by comparing their performance against the enterprise systems, considering five system characteristics, namely, scalability, availability, execution efficiency, cohesion and coupling.

A detailed description of the experiments conducted with Dolibarr is presented here. (The experimental details related to another case study using SugarCRM can be found in our technical report [20]). The Dolibarr system contains 10,735 files and around 3,000 attributes divided between 250 tables. We performed the static analysis of the Dolibarr source code and identified the BOs related to the system. Meanwhile, Selinium[6] scripts were used to perform dynamic analysis and generation of execution sequences. For Dolibarr we performed executions related to 'product purchase and sales', covering all the major functionalities. The execution logs were captured by customizing the log generation functionality of the system. The logs were then converted to XES file format and analyzed using the process mining tool Disco[7], as depicted in Fig. 3, to generate the call graph. The call graph generated for Dolibarr contained 301 unique nodes. Each node in the call graph represents a unique operation performed on database tables by the system and edges between the nodes represent the number of calls between the nodes. The execution graphs and the identified BOs were fed into our prototype to discover microservices and their interactions, as depicted in Fig. 3.

Discovered MSs: Based on the provided data, the prototype managed to identify 41 different business objects related to Dolibarr, for example 'User', 'Shipment', 'Element', 'ECM', 'Order', 'Third-party', 'Account', and 'Product'. Furthermore, system execution analysis led to the identification of *mandatory exclusive containment relationship* between 'Order' and 'ECM', and 'Element' and 'Shipment' and *mandatory inclusive containment relationship* between 'Order' and 'Thirdparty', 'Shipment' and 'Thirdparty', and 'Order' and 'Product' BOs.

---

[3] https://github.com/AnuruddhaDeAlwis/BORelationshipDerivation.git.
[4] https://www.dolibarr.org/.
[5] https://www.sugarcrm.com/.
[6] https://www.seleniumhq.org/.
[7] https://fluxicon.com/disco/.

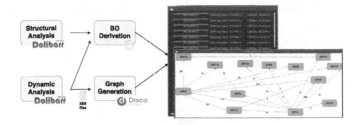

Fig. 3. Microservice discovery steps with related tools.

Also, the prototype identified two *subtypes* related to shipments named 'At-Store Reclamation' and 'Generic Transporter'. The relationship between 'User' and 'Order' was identified as an *association* relationship. Based on the containment and association relationship patterns and the execution sequences the prototype derived eleven microservice recommendations for Dolibarr.

Validation Process: The validation of the microservice recommendations was conducted in two steps. First, we evaluated the improvement of cohesion and coupling of different modules when clustering the classes based on recommendations provided by the prototype. This was achieved through measuring the Lack of Cohesion (LOC) and Structural Coupling (StrC) of the clusters, as described by Candela *et al.* [18]. We calculated the corresponding values for the enterprise system by clustering the classes into folders while preserving the original package structure, and then calculated the same values for the systtem with microservices. We have only considered six microservices in these calculations out of 11 recommendations. The obtained values are reported in Tables 1 and 2.

Then, we evaluated the system's performance improvement. In order to validate performance, we hosted the original Dolibarr system on a AWS cloud.[8] We used 2 EC2 instances which individually contained one virtual CPU and memory of 1 GB. The data related to the system was hosted in a MySQL relational database on AWS, which had one virtual CPU and storage of 20 GB. This implementation can be seen as the 'Enterprise System' depicted in Fig. 4. This system was then tested against 100 and 200 executions generated by 4 machines simultaneously, simulating customer requests, while recording their total execution time, average CPU consumption, and average network bandwidth consumption. For Dolibarr, we simulated the functionality related to *product purchase and sales*, using Selenuim[9] scripts which executed the system similar to a real environment. The values we obtained for Dolibarr enterprise system are detailed in Table 3.

Next, we introduced the microservices we have identified to the system to evaluate the effectiveness of the patterns. First, we evaluated the effectiveness of the 'Subtyping' pattern. We conducted two experiments. The first experiment was conducted by introducing a single microservice which contains both 'At-Store Reclamation' and 'Generic Transporter' BOs and a subset of the operations

---

[8] https://aws.amazon.com/.
[9] https://www.seleniumhq.org/.

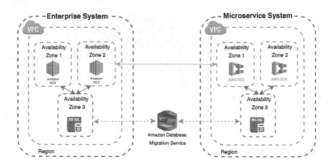

Fig. 4. System implementation in AWS.

related to them. The second experiment was conducted by introducing individual microservices for 'At-Store Reclamation' and 'Generic Transporter' BOs and the subsets of the operations related to them. Similarly two experiments were conducted regarding inclusive containment of 'Order' and 'Thirdparty' BOs and association of 'Product' and 'User', for which, firstly, a single microservice was created to manage both BOs and, secondly, separate microservices were created to manage each BO. The results obtained for these experiments are summarised in Tables 4, 6 and 7. Each microservice was hosted on an AWS elastic container service (ECS), which has two virtual CPUs and a total memory of 1 GB, as depicted on the right side of Fig. 4. The data related to the BOs of each microservice was stored in one MySQL relational database instance with one virtual CPU and total storage of 20 GB. Next, the executions were performed on ES again. Since microservices are extended parts of the enterprise system, in these executions, the enterprise system used API calls to pass the data to the microservices and the microservices processed and sent back the data to the enterprise system. The data in the microservice databases and enterprise system database was synchronized using the Amazon database migration service. Again, we recorded the total execution time, average CPU consumption, and average network bandwidth consumption for the entire system (i.e., enterprise system integrated with microservices). Since exclusive containment suggests co-locating contained BOs in a single MS, we evaluated the effectiveness of this using two experiments. First, we implemented one microservice to manage 'Order' and 'ECM' BOs with a subset of their operations in a single container and obtained the execution results. Then, we created a separate microservices to manage 'Order' and 'ECM' and conducted the experiment again. The results obtained for this experiment are summarised in Table 5.

Based on the attained values, we calculated the scalability, availability, and execution efficiency of the different combinations, the results are summarised in Tables 8, 9, 10 and 11. Scalability was calculated according to the resources and their usage over time, as described by Tsai *et al.* [16]. In order to determine availability, first we calculated the time taken to process 100 packets when a particular microservice is not available. Then, we measured the difference between

Table 1. Dolibarr ES vs MS system (Lack of Cohesion).

System type	Thirdparty	Order	ECM	Shipment	Product	User
Original ES	62	17	4	7	217	17
MSs	42	17	4	7	81	17

Table 2. Dolibarr ES vs MS system (Structural Coupling).

System type	Thirdparty	Order	ECM	Shipment	Product	User
Original ES	23	27	7	20	34	18
MSs	22	27	7	20	26	18

Table 3. Legacy enterprise system result for Dolibarr.

System type	No of executions	No of packets sent	Ex. time (s)	Avg CPU util (EC2)	Avg CPU util (DB)	Avg network (Kb/s)
Original ES	100	136452	8220	9.535	2.37	47.31
Original ES	200	163270	17400	8.805	2.13	45.31

Table 4. Dolibarr system. (1) All subtypes in one MS. (2) Subtypes in separate MSs.

System type	No of executions	No of packets sent	Ex. time (s)	Avg CPU util (EC2)	Avg CPU util (DB)	Avg network (Kb/s)
ES & single MS (1)	100	139860	8400	5.288	1.71	30.585
ES & single MS (1)	200	162099	16740	4.498	1.665	19.55
ES & multi MS (2)	100	124188	7860	8.543	1.597	28.73
ES & multi MS (2)	200	168990	15720	8.345	1.64	26.57

Table 5. Dolibarr system. (1) Exclusive BOs in one MS. (2) Exclusive BOs in separate MSs.

System type	No of executions	No of packets sent	Ex. time (s)	Avg CPU util (EC2)	Avg CPU util (DB)	Avg network (Kb/s)
ES & single MS (1)	100	110789	7980	5.045	1.67	26.75
ES & single MS (1)	200	181828	15720	5.228	1.55	21.71
ES & multi MS (2)	100	117912	8160	6.127	1.87	25.77
ES & multi MS (2)	200	165273	16020	5.613	2.11	18.48

the total uptime and total downtime, as described by Bauer *et al.* [17]. Efficiency gain was calculated by dividing the total time taken by the legacy system to process all requests by the total time taken by the corresponding microservice system.

Table 6. Dolibarr system. (1) Inclusive BOs in one MS. (2) Inclusive BOs in separate MSs.

System type	No of executions	No of packets sent	Ex. time (s)	Avg CPU util (EC2)	Avg CPU util (DB)	Avg network (Kb/s)
ES & single MS (1)	100	95499	7860	5.04	1.75	25.795
ES & single MS (1)	200	135182	15780	5.05	1.75	21.695
ES & multi MS (2)	100	105996	7920	3.702	1.907	25.81
ES & multi MS (2)	200	136371	15720	2.633	1.653	14.58

Table 7. Dolibarr system. (1) Association BOs in one MS. (2) Association BOs in separate MSs.

System type	No of executions	No of packets sent	Ex. time (s)	Avg CPU util (EC2)	Avg CPU util (DB)	Avg network (Kb/s)
ES & single MS (1)	100	109052	8220	5.123	1.71	26.655
ES & single MS (1)	200	124343	18060	3.1	1.415	13.275
ES & multi MS (2)	100	227010	8280	4.318	1.987	39.67
ES & multi MS (2)	200	252591	16140	3.017	1.837	21.14

Table 8. Legacy vs MS system characteristics comparison for subtyping.

Campaign type	Scalability [CPU EC2]	Scalability [CPU DB]	Scalability [network DB]	Availability [100]	Availability [200]	Efficiency [100]	Efficiency [200]
Original ES	3.458	3.366	3.586	99.27	99.31	1.000	1.000
ES & single MS	2.915	3.336	2.19	99.29	99.29	0.979	1.039
ES & multi MS	2.871	3.019	2.72	99.24	99.24	1.046	1.107

Table 9. Legacy vs MS system characteristics comparison for exclusive containment.

Campaign type	Scalability [CPU EC2]	Scalability [CPU DB]	Scalability [network DB]	Availability [100]	Availability [200]	Efficiency [100]	Efficiency [200]
Original ES	3.458	3.366	3.586	99.27	99.31	1.000	1.000
ES & single MS	2.45	2.195	1.919	99.25	99.24	1.03	1.107
ES & multi MS	2.511	3.103	1.972	99.27	99.26	1.007	1.086

Table 10. Legacy vs MS System characteristics comparison for inclusive containment.

Campaign type	Scalability [CPU EC2]	Scalability [CPU DB]	Scalability [network DB]	Availability [100]	Availability [200]	Efficiency [100]	Efficiency [200]
Original ES	3.458	3.366	3.586	99.27	99.31	1.000	1.000
ES & single MS	2.85	2.847	2.394	99.24	99.24	1.045	1.103
ES & multi MS	2.17	2.655	1.729	99.24	99.24	1.037	1.107

Table 11. Legacy vs MS system characteristics comparison for association.

Campaign type	Scalability [CPU EC2]	Scalability [CPU DB]	Scalability [network DB]	Availability [100]	Availability [200]	Efficiency [100]	Efficiency [200]
Original ES	3.458	3.366	3.586	99.27	99.31	1.000	1.000
ES & single MS	2.56	3.503	2.108	99.28	99.34	1	0.964
ES & multi MS	2.381	3.157	1.819	99.28	99.26	0.993	1.078

Experimental Results: As described by Tsai *et al.* [16], the lower the number the better the scalability. Thus, it is evident from Tables 8, 10 and 11 that developing separate microservices to manage BOs which have subtype, association and inclusive containment relationships achieve better scalability than creating single microservices to manage such BOs. When comparing availability, there is not much gain. However, better execution efficiency for subtypes, association and inclusively contained microservices were achieved when they are developed as separate microservices. When comparing scalability, availability and execution efficiency for exclusively contained BOs, it is evident that they achieved better results when the microservices were co-located in the same container (see results for single microservice and multiple microservices in Table 9). These results affirmed that the patterns that our work suggested for subtyping, association, inclusive containment and exclusive containment relationships work well when developing microservices.

The lower the lack of cohesion and structural coupling numbers the better the cohesion and coupling of the system [18]. As such, it is evident from Tables 1 and 2 that the microservices derived from the Dolibarr system achieved better cohesion and coupling values than the legacy system. Hence, the obtained results have affirmed that the microservices extracted based on the patterns described in Sect. 3 led to microservices which could provide the same services to users while preserving overall system behaviour and achieving higher scalability, availability, efficiency, and cohesion, and lower coupling.

6   Related Work

Architectural and design conceptions of microservices have emerged through practitioner reports [1] and the textbooks by Newman [2] and Fowler [3], and have contributed to ongoing developments of microservice architectures. To date, general properties which are widely accepted for microservices as distributed and fine-grained software components are high scalability, high availability, high integrity, strong cohesion, loose coupling, and eventual consistency [2]. Furthermore, microservices have been characterised through agile units of software development, which can be separately developed, deployed, and composed.

Concerning the essential structure of a microservice architecture, the domain-driven design principle (DDD) [4] has been popularized through the widely cited references by Newman [2] and Fowler [3]. According to DDD, each service-based software component encapsulates all operations of objects, which in SOA based enterprise systems corresponds to business objects (BOs). Accordingly, patterns have been proposed for microservices by Chris Richardson such as 'database per service' and 'saga' [19]. However, to date, there are no clear definitions that help to refine SOA components which manage distinct BOs of domains, containing encapsulated CRUD operations of the objects [5], into microservices which recommend decomposing BOs for support of fine-granular functionality. Our work presented a refinement of the design strategy for SOA components such that the system operations are split based on four fundamental object relationships, namely, subtyping, association, inclusive containment, and exclusive containment. Considering such BO relationships and system execution patterns, we have conducted research here and in previous work [12,15] and demonstrated that BO relationships could be used in the microservice derivation process to achieve prominent outcomes, such as high scalability, availability, and processing efficiency.

7   Conclusion

This paper presented four microservice patterns, namely object association, exclusive containment, inclusive containment and subtyping for 'greenfield' (new) development of software while demonstrating the value of the patterns for 'brownfield' (evolving) developments by identifying prospective microservices using prototypes we developed for two enterprise systems, Dolibarr (Sect. 5) and SugarCRM [20]. The conducted experiments confirmed that our patterns provide good suggestions for better microservice development while obtaining desirable characteristics such as high cohesion, low coupling, high scalability, high availability, and processing efficiency. The patterns presented herein could be used for further extended and refined pattern development, for example by taking into account the operation subtypes (i.e., create, read, update and delete). Furthermore, considerations for software modularization based on class clustering and method clustering should be considered as future work for microservice derivation.

References

1. Adopting Microservices at Netflix: Lessons for Architectural Design. https://www.nginx.com/blog/microservices-at-netflix-architectural-best-practices. Accessed 5 May 2019
2. Newman, S.: Building Microservices: Designing Fine-Grained Systems. O'Reilly, Sebastopol (2015)
3. Microservices a definition of this new architectural term. https://martinfowler.com/articles/microservices.html. Accessed 5 May 2019
4. Evans, E.: Domain-Driven Design: Tackling Complexity in the Heart of Software. Addison-Wesley Professional, Boston (2004)
5. Erl, T.: SOA Design Patterns (Paperback). Pearson Education, London (2008)
6. Taibi, D., Lenarduzzi, V., Pahl, C.: Architectural patterns for microservices: a systematic mapping study. In: CLOSER, pp. 221–232 (2018)

7. Barros, A., Duddy, K., Lawley, M., Milosevic, Z., Raymond, K., Wood, A.: Processes, roles, and events: UML concepts for enterprise architecture. In: Evans, A., Kent, S., Selic, B. (eds.) UML 2000. LNCS, vol. 1939, pp. 62–77. Springer, Heidelberg (2000). https://doi.org/10.1007/3-540-40011-7_5

8. Gamma, E.: Design Patterns: Elements of Reusable Object-Oriented Software. Pearson Education India, Chennai (1995)

9. van der Aalst, W.: Workflow patterns. In: Liu, L., Ozsu, M.T. (eds.) Encyclopedia of Database Systems, pp. 3557–3558. Springer, Boston (2009). https://doi.org/10.1007/978-0-387-39940-9

10. Barros, A., Dumas, M., ter Hofstede, A.H.M.: Service interaction patterns. In: van der Aalst, W.M.P., Benatallah, B., Casati, F., Curbera, F. (eds.) BPM 2005. LNCS, vol. 3649, pp. 302–318. Springer, Heidelberg (2005). https://doi.org/10.1007/11538394_20

11. Decker, G., Barros, A., Kraft, F.M., Lohmann, N.: Non-desynchronizable service choreographies. In: Bouguettaya, A., Krueger, I., Margaria, T. (eds.) ICSOC 2008. LNCS, vol. 5364, pp. 331–346. Springer, Heidelberg (2008). https://doi.org/10.1007/978-3-540-89652-4_26

12. De Alwis, A.A.C., Barros, A., Polyvyanyy, A., Fidge, C.: Function-splitting heuristics for discovery of microservices in enterprise systems. In: Pahl, C., Vukovic, M., Yin, J., Yu, Q. (eds.) ICSOC 2018. LNCS, vol. 11236, pp. 37–53. Springer, Cham (2018). https://doi.org/10.1007/978-3-030-03596-9_3

13. Nooijen, E.H.J., van Dongen, B.F., Fahland, D.: Automatic discovery of data-centric and artifact-centric processes. In: La Rosa, M., Soffer, P. (eds.) BPM 2012. LNBIP, vol. 132, pp. 316–327. Springer, Heidelberg (2013). https://doi.org/10.1007/978-3-642-36285-9_36

14. Andrews, R., Suriadi, S., Ouyang, C., Poppe, E.: Towards event log querying for data quality. In: Panetto, H., et al. (eds.) OTM 2018. LNCS, vol. 11229. Springer, Cham (2018). https://doi.org/10.1007/978-3-030-02610-3_7

15. De Alwis A.A.C., Barros A., Fidge C., Polyvyanyy A.: Discovering microservices in enterprise systems using a business object containment heuristic. In: Panetto H., et al. (eds.) OTM 2018 Conferences On the Move to Meaningful Internet Systems, OTM 2018. LNCS, vol. 11230. Springer, Cham (2018). https://doi.org/10.1007/978-3-030-02671-4_4

16. Tsai, W.T., Huang, Y., Shao, Q.: Testing the scalability of SaaS applications. In: IEEE International Conference on Service-Oriented Computing and Applications (SOCA), pp. 1–4 (2011)

17. Bauer, E., Adams, R.: Reliability and Availability of Cloud Computing, 1st edn. Wiley, Hoboken (2012)

18. Candela, I., Bavota, G., Russo, B., Oliveto, R.: Using cohesion and coupling for software remodularization: is it enough? In: ACM Transactions on Software Engineering and Methodology (TOSEM), p. 24 (2016)

19. A pattern language for microservices. https://microservices.io/patterns/. Accessed 5 Aug 2019

20. Technical report for SugarCRM. https://drive.google.com/file/d/1u0Ai0XNOx-3yGoz0Keycxj093_NyDrJl/view?usp=sharing

Availability and Scalability Optimized Microservice Discovery from Enterprise Systems

Adambarage Anuruddha Chathuranga De Alwis[1]([✉]), Alistair Barros[1],
Colin Fidge[1], and Artem Polyvyanyy[2]

[1] Queensland University of Technology, Brisbane, Australia
{adambarage.dealwis,alistair.barros,c.fidge}@qut.edu.au
[2] The University of Melbourne, Parkville, VIC 3010, Australia
artem.polyvyanyy@unimelb.edu.au

Abstract. Microservices have been introduced to industry as a novel architectural design for software development in cloud-based applications. This development has increased interest in finding new methodologies to migrate existing enterprise systems into microservices to achieve desirable performance characteristics such as high scalability, high availability, high cohesion and low coupling. A key challenge in this context is discovering microserviceable components with promising characteristics from a complex monolithic code base while predicting their resulting characteristics. This paper presents a technique to support such reengineering of an enterprise system based on the fundamental mechanisms for structuring its architecture, i.e., business objects managed by software functions and their interactions. The technique relies on queuing theory and business object relationship analysis. A prototype for microservice discovery and characteristic analysis was developed using the NSGA II software clustering and optimization technique and has been validated against two open-source enterprise systems, SugarCRM and ChurchCRM. Our experiments demonstrate that the proposed approach can recommend microservice design which improves scalability, availability and execution efficiency of the system while achieving high cohesion and low coupling in software modules.

Keywords: Microservice discovery · System reengineering · System optimization

1 Introduction

Microservices were introduced around 2011 to the software industry and interest in microservices has increased over the years due to the development and deployment advantages they provide over monolithic system architectures. A microservice architecture encourages development of applications as small independent services, each running its own process and while communicating with

H. Panetto et al. (Eds.): OTM 2019, LNCS 11877, pp. 496–514, 2019.
https://doi.org/10.1007/978-3-030-33246-4_31

other microservices via REST API calls [1]. Even though different industry giants such as Netflix^{TM}, and now Twitter^{TM}, eBay^{TM} and Amazon^{TM} have adapted their systems to microservices, they have not been adopted for the dominant form of software in businesses, namely enterprise systems, limiting such systems' evolution and their ability to exploit the full benefits of modern cloud-enabled platforms such as Google Cloud, Amazon AWS and IoT [2].

Enterprise systems, such as enterprise resource planning (ERP) and customer relationship management (CRM), are large and complex and contain complex business processes encoded in application logic managing business objects, in typically many-to-many relationships [3]. Restructuring such a system into microservices is an error-prone task due to several reasons. Firstly, it is difficult to identify the highly cohesive and loosely coupled functions and operations which could be usefully separated as microservices, by a vast code base. Secondly, it is challenging to figure out an optimal splitting of the system functionalities as fine-grained microservices while minimizing the communication costs (i.e., service calls) between them. Thirdly, it is difficult to predict the system's scalability and availability behaviour based on the components identified as microservices without implementing them. The third issue is a major concern because implementing a system to validate its scalability and availability performance incurs additional cost and time, and the developers might need to conduct several implementations to validate the best configuration for the microservice system's development.

Automated software re-engineering techniques have been proposed to improve the efficiency of transforming legacy applications and structures [4], into a Service-Oriented-Architecture (SOA) using static analysis techniques (i.e., source code analysis) [5] and dynamic analysis techniques (i.e., execution log and pattern analysis) [6]. However, these techniques have, to date, not been applied to the re-engineering challenges of microservices. More specifically, there has been no research conducted in the area of deriving microservices from enterprise systems while evaluating the scalability and availability of the resulting microservices.

This paper presents discovery techniques that support the identification of suitable consumer-oriented parts of enterprise systems which could be re-engineered as microservices based on knowledge gained through business object relationships and their execution patterns while analysing their scalability and availability characteristics to provide better microservice configurations. A microservice recommendation process was developed using the Non-dominated Sorting Genetic Algorithm (NSGA) II and was validated against two open source customer management systems, SugarCRM[1] and ChurchCRM[2]. Our experiments showed that our methodology can be used to discover microservices which improve system structure and achieve high scalability, availability and execution efficiency of the system while achieving high cohesion and low coupling in software modules.

---

[1] https://www.sugarcrm.com/.

[2] http://churchcrm.io/.

2   Related Work

Restructuring existing monolithic systems into new architectures has been an important branch in the software engineering research community. However, being a relatively new concept to the business-centric software industry, microservices have had very limited research conducted in the area of system re-engineering and restructuring. Even though there are some approaches for microservice discovery, a better understanding of monolithic to microservice migration can be obtained through the manual migration report of Balalaie et al. [7]. They describe the complexity associated with the system re-engineering process while pointing out the importance of considering business objects and their relationships in the system migration process. Further, Martin Fowler emphasizes the importance of adapting business object relationships in microservices [8] by mentioning Domain Driven Design (DDD) principles [9]. DDD specifically focuses on identifying business objects that are related to the same domain, which helps to develop software components that are highly cohesive and loosely coupled.

Even though there is research about discovering business objects in enterprise systems and analysing their complex relationships [10,11], research related to re-engineering enterprise systems while considering the enriched semantic insights available through the complex relationship of business objects is limited. As described by Fuguo et al., business objects in enterprise system play a major role in the overall system structure and their effect can even be seen at the API level of the system [12]. A proper evaluation of such relationships and identification of functions related to each business object leads to software components or microservices which align with the single responsibility principle [13], which makes the components highly cohesive and loosely coupled.

Apart from business object relationships, the number of execution calls between different microservices plays a major role in defining high performing microservices, because an excessive number of network calls can increase response times while decreasing the availability of the service [1]. Available research related to microservice discovery has considered the number of calls between different methods to suggest microservices for the developer by analysing system execution logs [14,15]. However, such research has not considered the possibility of evaluating scalability and availability to derive better microservice configurations from enterprise systems. Even though there is queuing theory based research about evaluating system scalability [16] and ways of suggesting system configurations while evaluating system workload [17], applying such theories to microservice discovery has yet to be done, and is the focus of our research herein.

3   Microservice Discovery and Optimization Model

To discover microservices with desirable characteristics we developed a three-step approach, which is illustrated in Fig. 1. First we perform static analysis on the system in order to derive the business objects it manipulates. To achieve this, we extract and evaluate all the SQL queries in the given enterprise system's code and identify the relationships between database tables. These relationships are then used to derive the business objects according to the approach described by Nooijen *et al.* [10]. In the second step, a behavioural analysis is performed in order to generate and extract data related to system execution. For this we execute the system, simulating the users' behaviour with the help of Selenium scripts. These simulations generate system execution logs which are then used to generate call graphs related to the executions. Finally, as the third step, all the structural and behavioural details generated are provided to an optimization algorithm in order to discover a high performing system partitioning for microservices. The optimization criteria were derived by answering the four research questions below.

RQ1: *How can we derive highly cohesive components out of a given enterprise system which will provide better microservices?*

In the microservice literature, the bounded context related to the DDD is presented as a promising design rationale for identifying microservices. According to this rationale, each microservice should correspond to a single and defined bounded context, such that all the operations in the microservice should correspond to the changes in that particular context [1]. Generally, each bounded context can be defined as an artifact or a business object in an enterprise system [7]. As such, discovering the business objects in an enterprise system and extracting the operations performed on each business object leads to the discovery of microservices with a proper bounded context. In this situation, each microservice is changed only for a single reason (i.e., each microservice is aligned with the single responsibility) which leads to a highly cohesive microservice system. As such, our optimization algorithm should group business objects and operations related to (i.e., performed on) each business object into different clusters. To evaluate the optimization level of such clustering we implemented the BO and operation clustering evaluation (i.e., 3a in Fig. 1) as the third step in our process.

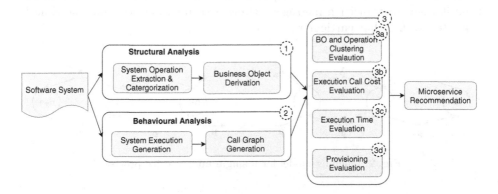

Fig. 1. Overview of our microservice discovery approach.

RQ2: *What is the criterion needed to evaluate the coupling between two microservice components?*

Coupling can be defined as the dependency evaluation criterion between two classes, packages or modules [18]. Given three software packages 'A', 'B', 'C', if there is a higher number of calls between 'A' and 'C' than 'A' and 'B', then one can define that 'A' and 'C' are more tightly coupled than 'A' and 'B', because the number of interactions between 'A' and 'C' is higher than the number of interactions between 'A' and 'B'. In fact this is one of the criteria used in software re-modularisation when clustering software packages to achieve better coupling [5,18]. If software packages are developed properly there should be low coupling between packages (i.e., a low number of inter-package calls) and high coupling between the classes in the same package (i.e., a high number of intra-package calls) [5,18]. Similarly, when defining microservices, one should choose the level of operation clustering to minimize inter-microservice communication while maximizing intra-microservice communication. As such, to evaluate the coupling in microservice discovery we implemented an execution call cost evaluation (i.e., 3b in Fig. 1) step in our process.

RQ3: *What is availability of a software system and how can we measure it?*

Availability of a system can be defined in two perspectives, namely the probability that a system is operational at a given time and the probability of the system providing a response to the customer within a given time limit. The basic method to measure the system's operation time is to calculate the ratio between the service up time and the total time [19]. This measure provides an idea about the probability of service unavailability experienced by a customer. However, sometimes systems take more time than expected to provide a response to the customer even though the system is available. If the response time is too long then customers tend to leave the system [20]. Generally, the service up time of a given system is based on the particular environment and the execution situation. As such, it is difficult to predict such behaviour without an implementation. However, when it comes to the response time one can predict it based on the time it takes to transfer a message between two microservices and the time it takes to execute that particular message.

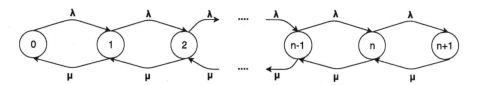

Fig. 2. Queuing model for a single microservice process.

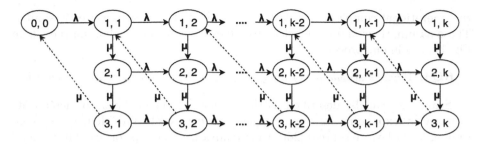

Fig. 3. Queuing model for a multiple microservices process.

In the literature, for different predictions related to system provisioning and performance, monitoring queuing theory has been used as reliable method [21, 22] and it has been clearly noted that such predictions can achieve solutions close to the corresponding real world scenarios [16]. In our work, we have considered two possible scenarios related to microservice execution. The first scenario would be where only a single microservice is processing customer requests. The second scenario would be the situation where there are multiple microservices in the system and they interact with each other to process a customer request. In Fig. 2 each circle with a number represents a microservice instance of the same microservice. As such, Fig. 2 showcases the scenario where multiple microservice instances will be created to support customer requests at a given time. Similarly, in Fig. 3, the circles represent the microservice instances. In this situation the first comma-separated number inside the circle represents the microservice and the second number represents the instance of that microservice. For example, if we take '1, 2', this represents the second instance of the first microservice. As such, in Fig. 3, we have depicted three microservices (1, 2, 3) with their related instances. The first scenario can be defined using a birth and death process in queue modeling as depicted in Fig. 2 while the second one can be defined using a matrix as in Fig. 3. In both Figs. 2 and 3 variable λ is the request arrival rate and μ is the execution rate of the system.

In order to derive the models needed, we assumed that requests arrive at a Poisson rate but they get processed in an exponential rate and the system is in a steady state. Given such a model, one can define the response time for a particular customer request to be the total of the message transfer time (i.e., $1/\lambda$) and execution time (i.e., $1/\mu$). However, there are several other variables which should be counted in this process such as the microservice provisioning time, CPU usage, Memory usage, IO and network bandwidth. In this work, we assume that all the microservices have the same CPU, Memory and IO configurations. However, when consider the provisioning time, microservices take time to start up when there are multiple services residing in the same container [23]. As such, we add the provisioning time for each microservice to the response time calculation. Furthermore, we assume that there is enough bandwidth such that an increase in the number of requests will not reduce the message transformation speed between clients and microservices [23,24]. Furthermore, we assume that the operational complexity of each process related to microservices is similar. These assumptions and models lead to the execution time evaluation (i.e., 3c in Fig. 1) step in our process.

RQ4: *What is scalability of a software system and how can we measure it?*

Scalability can be described as the ability of a cloud layer to increase its capacity by expanding its resource quantity (e.g., CPU and Memory) by consuming lower layer resources [26]. A more advanced concept of scalability would be elasticity which is a measure of resource provisioning and de-provisioning over time. According to Herbst *et al.*, one can calculate provisioning characteristics by monitoring the change in the amount of resources allocated and the time it takes to allocate those resources [27]. Generally, one can define the amount of memory required for request processing to be dependent on the data transferred into the system and the amount of data transferred within the system. As such, in order to derive the amount of memory allocated to each microservice, we use the number of inter-microservice and intra-microservice calls. The provisioning times are simply derived from the experimental results of Amaral *et al.* [23]. In this scenario we assume that the microservice allocates its total memory requirement in the provisioning time and until that the system is in an under-provisioned state. As such, the system which spends less time and uses fewer resources in an under-provisioned state provides better scalability. This leads to the provisioning evaluation (i.e., 3d in Fig. 1) step in our process.

A detailed overview of the algorithm used to implement the above four criteria is provided in Sect. 4.

4   NSGA II Optimization

In order to discover an optimal microservice configuration while evaluating the four criteria described in Sect. 3, we chose the Non-dominated Sorting Genetic Algorithm II (NSGA II) which is a multi-objective optimization algorithm which provides an optimal set of solutions while achieving global optima, when there are multiple conflicting objectives to be considered [28]. NSGA II can provide near optimal solutions when used to cluster software packages and classes to achieve high cohesion and low coupling [5].

Algorithm 1 provides microservice configuration solutions using three execution steps and requires the population size (n), number of generations (Gen), chromosome length (C_Len), crossover probability (Cr_Prob) and mutation probability (Mut_Prob) as input data. Apart from the above standard parameters, our algorithm requires further input, such as the BOs of the system (B), and execution graph nodes (N) and their relationships (R) extracted from the execution graphs. These details can be extracted from a software system based on the methodology described by De Alwis *et al.* [14]. The population size (n) defines how many chromosomes are populated in a single generation, while the number of generations (Gen) defines the number of times the algorithm generates different populations before it stops. The crossover probability (Cr_Prob)

and mutation probability (Mut_Prob) are responsible for defining the probability of performing crossovers and mutations on chromosomes. Interested readers can find further details about NSGA II elsewhere [28].

Here onwards we describe our algorithm variant based on the hypothetical execution graph depicted in Fig. 4. In the graph, each node illustrates an operation executing in the system and the 'BO's illustrate the business objects that each operation executes on.

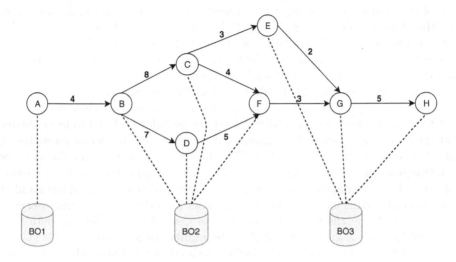

Fig. 4. Hypothetical execution graph of a system process.

The first step of the algorithm involves the $SYNPOP$ function which synthesizes a parent population of the given size n (see line 1). Function $SYNPOP$ uses a random number generator to generate chromosomes of length C_Len, where a chromosome is a sequence of numbers each representing a node in the execution graph. A chromosome generated for the execution graph in Fig. 4 can be represented as a sequence of numbers '0, 1, 2, 3, 4, 5, 6, 7', in which the numbers refer to the corresponding graph nodes 'A, B, C, D, E, F, G, H', such that 0 refers to A, 1 refers to B, etc. Apart from generating the parent population, $SYNPOP$ calculates and stores the fitness for each parent. The fitness calculation is preformed in two steps. First, the algorithm calculates the maximum cost (Max_c) for a chromosome as $\sum_{i=0}^{C\_Len} 2^i$ which can achieve a highest value of 255 (i.e., $1 + 2 + 4 + 8 + 16 + 32 + 64 + 128$). Then the algorithm calculates the costs for the four criteria that we described in Sect. 3. Since we need to achieve high cohesion as our first objective, the algorithm should be able to cluster system operations with their related business objects. To calculate such cohesion the cost function should be able to represent to which extent the nodes related to the same BO have been grouped together. As such, for each chromosome, the clustering cost ($Cost_c$) is calculated as $Cost_c = \sum_{i=0}^{Clus} \sum_{j=0}^{d} 2^d$, where d is the distance from the first occurrence of a node related to a particular BO to the next occurrence of the node related to the same BO within the chromosome and *Clus* is the number of business object clusters. When considering the scenario given in Fig. 4 high cohesion can be achieved by clustering the operations into three groups containing nodes 'A', 'B, C, D, F' and 'E, G, H' based on the business objects they execute on. This leads to a total clustering cost of 23 (i.e., $1 + 15 + 7$).

Similarly, to achieve low coupling (i.e., the second objective described in Sect. 3), the cost of execution calls ($Cost_e$) between clusters is computed as the sum of inter-cluster calls between the different clusters. For the running example, i.e., the chromosome '0, 1, 2, 3, 5, 4, 6, 7', this sum would be $4 + 3 + 3 = 10$, because the costs of calls between the pairs of clusters in '0', '1, 2, 3, 5', '4, 6, 7', are '4', '3' and '3'. Further details for calculating the first two objectives for the NSGA II algorithm can be found elsewhere [14].

Availability (i.e., the third objective described in Sect. 3) is dependent on the time it takes to provide a response to a customer. As such to derive a cost function to measure availability (Ava) we used data related to inter-cluster and the intra-cluster calls. For example, if we take the number of inter-cluster calls between '0', '1, 2, 3, 5', '4, 6, 7' it would be 4 and 6, and the number of intra-cluster calls would be 0, 24 and 7. We consider the number of inter-cluster calls as the number of requests sent to each microservice and the number of intra-cluster calls as the number of requests passed within the microservice. As such, we define the total amount of time needed to transfer the data to a microservice (i.e., λ in Figs. 2 and 3) as the number of inter-cluster calls ($Call_i$) multiplied by the data packet size ($Data_s$) divided by the bandwidth of the network ($Band$) (i.e., $(Call_i \times Data_s)/Band$). The execution time of a microservice (i.e., μ in Figs. 2 and 3) is calculated as the number of intra-cluster calls ($Call_e$) multiplied by the data packet size ($Data_s$) divided by the process complexity (Com) (i.e., $(Call_e \times Data_s)/Com$). In this calculation, we assumed that all the packets transferred have the same amount of data and each packet is of the maximum TCP packet size which is 64 kb. Furthermore, we assumed that the bandwidth is equal to the general Ethernet bandwidth of 10 Mbit/s. The time taken for internal data transfer is not taken into consideration because microservices have the same transfer speed as a native system which is negligible [29]. The process complexity is given a fixed value assuming that none of the operations are related to floating point executions [25]. Since provisioning time (Pro) also affects the response time of a microservice we add provisioning time values obtained from Amaral *et al.* [23] to the total response time. Since we evaluate two scenarios where only a single microservice responses to a customer request (as depicted in Fig. 2) and multiple microservices response to customer requests (as depicted in Fig. 3), two cost functions were defined and evaluated. For a single microservice with x number of operational instances we defined the cost function as $Ava = ((Call_i \times Data_s)/Band + (Call_e \times Data_s)/Com + Pro) \times x$. For a microservice system with y number of different microservices, in which each microservice has x number of operational instances we defined the cost function as $Ava = ((Call_i \times Data_s)/Band + (Call_e \times Data_s)/Com \times (y - 1) + Pro) \times x$.

Algorithm 1: NSGA II Algorithm adapted for microservice discovery

---

Input: n, Gen, C_Len, Cr_Prob, Mut_Prob, B, N, R
Output: A list of clustering of BOs and OPs for MSs

1 $Pop^p = \langle pop_1, \ldots, pop_n \rangle := SYNPOP(n, C\_Len, \gamma, B, N, R)$;
2 $Pop^c := Rank^f := \langle \rangle$;
    /* Perform crossover and mutation to generate child population   */
3 **while** $Pop^c.length() < n$ **do**
4   **if** $RANDOM(0,1) < Cr\_Prob$ **then**
5          $Pop^c := CROSSOVER(Pop^p, Pop^c)$;
6   **if** $RANDOM(0,1) < Mut\_Prob$ **then**
7          $Pop^c := MUTATION(Pop^p, Pop^c)$;
8 **end**
9 **for** each $i \in [1 .. Gen]$ **do**
10      $Pop^t := Pop^p + Pop^c$;
11      $Rank^f = \langle rank^f_1, \ldots, rank^f_m \rangle := FNDS(Pop^t)$;
12   **if** $i = Gen$ **then**
13   **break**;
        /* Identify the Pareto front of the generated population and rank them   */
14      $Pop^c := \langle \rangle$;
15   **for** $k \in [1 .. m]$ **do**
16   **if** $length(rank^f_k) < (n - length(Pop^c))$ **then**
17              $Pop^c := Pop^c + rank^f_k$;
18   **else**
19              $Pop^c := Pop^c + CCS(rank^f_k)$;
20   **end**
21      $Pop^p := Pop^c$;   // Initialize new parent population
22      $Pop^c = \langle pop^c_1, \ldots, pop^c_n \rangle := SYNCHD(Pop^p)$;
23 **end**
24 **return** $(Rank^f)$

As described in Sect. 3, to calculate scalability ($Scal$) we need to figure out the amount of resources used and the time taken to provision the resources. Here we assume that the total amount of memory required for each microservice is similar to the total number of packets it receives and processes. Thus we calculate the total memory requirement for a microservice as $(Call_i + Call_e) \times Data_s$ and the provisioning time values are obtained from Amaral *et al.* [23]. For a microservice system with x instances we defined the cost function as $Scal = (Call_i + Call_e) \times Data_s \times x$. The *fitness* for a given chromosome is finally obtained as $fitness = Max_c - (Cost_c + Cost_e + Ava + Scal)$.

The second step of the algorithm generates the child population by performing crossover operations and mutation operations on the parent chromosomes (see lines 3–8). In order to perform the crossover operation, the algorithm selects two parents using binary tournament selection [28]. This is performed by randomly identifying two parent chromosomes and extracting the chromosome with the highest fitness value out of them. After identifying two parent chromosomes for crossover, the algorithm splits the first parent chromosome from a predefined position (normally half of the chromosome's length) and includes it as the first part of the child chromosome. As the second part of the chromosome it includes the genes extracted from the second parent which are not in the first part of the child chromosome.

After generating the first child population, the algorithm generates Gen new populations, (refer to lines 9–23 in Algorithm 1) which constitutes the third (and last) step of the algorithm. First, the current total population Pop^t is computed at line 10 by concatenating the parent population Pop^p and the child population Pop^c. Next, the algorithm calculates the non-dominated fronts, or the Pareto fronts, of the total population. A non-dominated front contains the chromosomes which have the optimal values for the four objectives that were defined above, namely the clustering cost ($Cost_c$), cost of execution calls ($Cost_e$), availability cost (Ava) and scalability cost ($Scal$). The chromosome's optimization of node clustering is calculated as the difference between the maximum possible cost of the chromosome and cost of its node clustering (i.e., $Max_c - Cost_c$). Similarly, the chromosome's optimization of execution calls is calculated as the difference between the maximum possible cost of the chromosome and the cost between its cluster calls (i.e., $Max_c - Cost_e$). The chromosome's optimization of availability and scalability is similarly calculated by obtaining the difference between maximum possible cost of the chromosome and cost of scalability and availability (i.e., $Max_c - Ava$ and $Max_c - Scal$). The non-dominated chromosomes in Pop^t are extracted as the first front using function $FNDS$ (see line 11). After extracting the first non-dominated front, the algorithm evaluates the other chromosomes in Pop^t and identifies the second non-dominated front. This process is repeated until all the chromosomes are categorised into different fronts (2, ..., m), where each generated front may contain multiple non-dominated chromosomes.

Once the Pareto fronts are obtained, a new child population is created by concatenating the ranked fronts in several steps (see lines 14–20). First, the algorithm verifies that there is enough space in the child population to add all the chromosomes in each ranked front $rank_k^f$ by comparing the remaining space in the child population ($n - length(Pop^c)$) with the rank front size $length(rank_k^f)$ (see line 16). If there is enough space, the rank front is directly added to the child population (see line 17). If there is no space, then the algorithm identifies the most prominent chromosomes in the front using a crowd comparison sort [28] (see line 19, function CCS) and assigns them to the child population. Through the loop of lines 15–20, the algorithm filters out the chromosomes in the total population Pop^t with the highest objective fitness values. The new population is used as the next parent population and again synthesizes a new child population by performing crossover and mutation (see lines 21–22). Finally, the non-dominated front (the Pareto optimal solution) $Rank^f$ is returned to the user which constitutes the clustering of BOs and operation nodes in the system to develop MSs (see line 24).

5   Implementation and Validation

In order to validate our microservice discovery and optimization process, a recommender[3] was developed based on the algorithms presented in Sect. 4 and we experimented with it on the SugarCRM and ChurchCRM customer relationship management systems. A detailed description of the experiments conducted on both systems is presented in this section.

SugarCRM as a system contains 8116 source files and 600 attributes divided between 101 tables, while ChurchCRM contains 8039 source files and 350 attributes divided between 55 tables. We generated execution sequences for both systems covering major functionalities[4] such as campaign management, customer management, etc. The execution logs containing the details about execution sequences, operations and database tables were captured using the log generation functionality already available in the systems. These execution logs cannot be directly used by process mining tools to obtain call graphs. Instead we used our own code[5] to convert them into XES format which is accepted by the Disco process mining tool. These XES files were then analyzed using Disco[6] and call graphs were generated for SugarCRM with 178 unique nodes and for ChurchCRM with 58 unique nodes. Each node in a call graph represents a unique operation performed on database tables in the system and the edges between nodes represent the number of calls between the nodes, similar to Fig. 4.

Discovered MSs: As the initial step, the prototype identified 18 different business objects related to SugarCRM, such as 'action control lists', 'calls', 'contacts', 'campaigns', 'meetings', 'users', 'prospects', 'accounts', 'documents', 'leads', 'emails', 'projects' and 'email management', 11 different business objects related to ChurchCRM, such as 'calendar', 'locations', 'deposits', 'emails', 'events', 'family', 'group', 'property', 'query', 'users' and 'kiosk'. The identified BOs and the call graphs with execution details were given to the optimization algorithm described in Sect. 4 and tested against both scenarios depicted in Figs. 2 and 3. Both executions provided the same solution deriving 8 MSs for ChurchCRM and 11 MSs for SugarCRM.

Validation Process: Validation of the microservice recommendations was conducted in two steps. First, we evaluated the improvement of cohesion and coupling of different modules when clustering the classes based on recommendations provided by our prototype. This was achieved through measuring the Lack of Cohesion (LOC) and Structural Coupling (StrC) of the clusters, as described by Candela et al. [5]. We calculated the values for the enterprise system by clustering the classes into folders while preserving the original package structure, and then calculated the values for microservices. The LOC and StrC values calculated for ChurchCRM are summarized in Table 1 and Table 2, respectively, and

---

[3] https://github.com/AnuruddhaDeAlwis/NSGAIIFOROptimization.git.

[4] http://support.sugarcrm.com/Documentation/Sugar_Versions/8.0/Pro/
Application_Guide/.

[5] https://github.com/AnuruddhaDeAlwis/XESConvertor.git.

[6] https://fluxicon.com/disco/.

LOC and StrC values calculated for SugarCRM are summarized in Table 3 and Table 4, respectively.

Next we validated the performance of the systems by implementing the microservices suggested by the prototype. In order to achieve this, first we hosted the SugarCRM and ChurchCRM systems in AWS Cloud. For each system, we used 2 EC2 instances which individually contained one virtual CPU and memory of 1 GB. The data related to the systems were hosted in a MySQL relational database in AWS, which has one virtual CPU and storage of 20 GB. A clear idea of this implementation can be obtained through the 'Enterprise System' section depicted in Fig. 5. These systems were then tested against 200 and 400 executions generated by 4 machines simultaneously for ChurchCRM and 100 and 200 execution generated by 4 machines simultaneously for SugarCRM, simulating customer requests, while recording their total execution time, average CPU consumption, and average network bandwidth consumption. For Sugar-CRM, we simulated the functionality related to *Campaign management*, while for ChurchCRM we simulated the functionality related to *People management*. For the simulations, we used Selenuim[7] scripts which executed the system similar to a real user. The Average CPU consumption of EC2 instances and DB instances and Average Network usage for ChurchCRM and SugarCRM enterprise system are listed in the first two rows of Tables 5 and 9, respectively.

After obtaining the results for the enterprise systems, we needed to evaluate the effectiveness of introducing a single microservice (i.e., the scenario depicted in Fig. 2) to the system based on the suggestions provided the by the prototype. As such, for SugarCRM we introduced a microservice which manages 'prospect' BO with its subset of operations suggested by the prototype and for the ChurchCRM we introduced a microservice which manages 'family' BO with its subset of operations suggested by the prototype. Each microservice was hosted on an AWS elastic container service (ECS), which has two virtual CPUs and a total memory of 2 GB, as depicted on the right side of Fig. 5. The data related to the BOs of each microservice was stored in one MySQL relational database instance with

Table 1. ChurchCRM ES vs MS system lack of cohesion value comparison.

System type	1	2	3	4	5	6	7	8	9	10	11
Original ES	61	188	853	7	4	1065	31	378	3064	13	17
MSs	61	**77**	**666**	33	8	1453	73	**351**	3802	**3**	**10**

Table 2. ChurchCRM ES vs MS system structural coupling value comparison.

System type	1	2	3	4	5	6	7	8	9	10	11
Original ES	41	26	61	17	16	70	29	31	123	27	19
MSs	**41**	**25**	**8**	37	20	**64**	33	**31**	**121**	**3**	**7**

---

[7] https://www.seleniumhq.org/.

Table 3. SugarCRM ES vs MS system lack of cohesion value comparison.

System type	1	2	3	4	5	6	7	8	9	10	11	12
Original ES	42	342	229	65	63	581	53	26	64	14	64	33
MSs	**11**	**291**	**208**	65	**42**	**547**	53	**26**	64	14	**53**	**33**

Table 4. SugarCRM ES vs MS system structural coupling value comparison.

System type	1	2	3	4	5	6	7	8	9	10	11	12
Original ES	22	58	32	21	30	57	20	17	31	20	19	48
MSs	**12**	**57**	32	21	**29**	57	20	17	31	20	19	48

Table 5. Legacy vs Single MS results for ChurchCRM.

System type	No of executions	No of packets sent	Ex. time (s)	Avg CPU util (EC2)	Avg CPU util (DB)	Avg network (Kb/s)
Original ES	200	29768	2580	4.27	1.6	6.57
Original ES	400	37579	4440	5.14	1.68	4.06
ES & Single MS (1)	200	28490	2220	3.06	2.365	11.42
ES & Single MS (1)	400	39620	4200	2.945	2.26	9.26
ES & Single MS (2)	200	33462	2340	3.153	2.25	11.45
ES & Single MS (2)	400	36936	4380	3.04	2.125	11.322

Table 6. Legacy vs Single MS system characteristics comparison for ChurchCRM.

Campaign type	Scalability [CPU EC2]	Scalability [CPU DB]	Scalability [Network DB]	Availability [200]	Availability [400]	Efficiency [200]	Efficiency [400]
Original ES	2.819	2.459	1.448	97.727	97.368	1.000	1.000
ES & Single MS (1)	2.477	2.459	2.087	97.37	97.228	1.162	1.057
ES & Single MS (2)	3.061	2.998	3.138	97.5	97.33	1.103	1.014

Table 7. Legacy vs Multiple MS results for ChurchCRM.

System type	No of executions	No of packets Sent	Ex. time (s)	Avg CPU util (EC2)	Avg CPU util (DB)	Avg network (Kb/s)
Original ES	200	29768	2580	4.27	1.6	6.57
Original ES	400	37579	4440	5.14	1.68	4.06
ES & Multi MS (1)	200	25900	2100	2.397	2.567	7.46
ES & Multi MS (1)	400	35713	4260	2.737	2.29	8.521
ES & Multi MS (2)	200	26040	2100	2.313	2.14	7.72
ES & Multi MS (2)	400	35926	4260	2.325	2.15	7.118

Table 8. Legacy vs Multiple MS system characteristics comparison for ChurchCRM.

Campaign type	Scalability [CPU EC2]	Scalability [CPU DB]	Scalability [Network DB]	Availability [200]	Availability [400]	Efficiency [200]	Efficiency [400]
Original ES	2.819	2.459	1.448	97.727	97.368	1.000	1.000
ES & Multi MS (1)	3.407	2.662	3.408	97.222	97.26	1.229	1.042
ES & Multi MS (2)	2.997	2.992	2.751	97.222	97.26	1.229	1.042

Table 9. Legacy vs Single MS results for SugarCRM.

System type	No of executions	No of packets sent	Ex. time (s)	Avg CPU util (EC2)	Avg CPU util (DB)	Avg network (Kb/s)
Original ES	100	16417	2400	4.27	1.6	6.57
Original ES	200	20632	3900	5.14	1.68	4.06
ES & Single MS (1)	100	14318	2100	4.738	1.67	6.496
ES & Single MS (1)	200	19847	3540	2.42	1.58	5.717
ES & Single MS (2)	100	16099	2160	6.0175	1.64	6.465
ES & Single MS (2)	200	22426	3960	5.26	2.1	6.341

Table 10. Legacy vs Single MS system characteristics comparison for SugarCRM.

Campaign Type	Scalability [CPU EC2]	Scalability [CPU DB]	Scalability [Network DB]	Availability [200]	Availability [400]	Efficiency [200]	Efficiency [400]
Original ES	2.206	2.435	4.403	97.56	97.01	1.000	1.000
ES & Single MS (1)	1.0472	1.939	1.804	97.22	96.72	1.143	1.102
ES & Single MS (2)	2.109	3.089	2.366	97.29	97.05	1.111	0.984

Table 11. Legacy vs Multiple MS results for SugarCRM.

System type	No of executions	No of packets sent	Ex. time (s)	Avg CPU util (EC2)	Avg CPU util (DB)	Avg network (Kb/s)
Original ES	100	16417	2400	4.27	1.6	6.57
Original ES	200	20632	3900	5.14	1.68	4.06
ES & Multi MS (1)	200	16417	1920	3.905	2.167	5.716
ES & Multi MS (1)	400	20632	3900	3.861	2.067	5.097
ES & Multi MS (2)	200	41856	2160	4.521	1.73	5.190
ES & Multi MS (2)	400	52920	4140	4.526	1.723	5.899

Table 12. Legacy vs Multiple MS system characteristics comparison for SugarCRM.

Campaign type	Scalability [CPU EC2]	Scalability [CPU DB]	Scalability [Network DB]	Availability [200]	Availability [400]	Efficiency [200]	Efficiency [400]
Original ES	2.206	2.435	4.403	97.56	97.01	1.000	1.000
ES & Multi MS (1)	3.246	3.131	2.927	96.96	97.01	1.25	1.000
ES & Multi MS (2)	2.926	2.911	3.322	97.29	97.18	1.11	0.942

one virtual CPU and total storage of 20 GB. Next, the executions were performed on both enterprise systems again. Since microservices are extended parts of the enterprise systems in these executions, the enterprise systems used API calls to pass the data to the microservices and the microservices processed and sent back the data to the enterprise systems. The data in the microservice databases and enterprise system databases were synchronized using the Amazon database migration service replication instance. Then, we again conducted the same set of experiments while introducing operations to the 'prospect' BO microservice and 'family' BO microservice which contradicted the optimal suggestions given by the prototype. In this situation we introduced operations related to 'user'

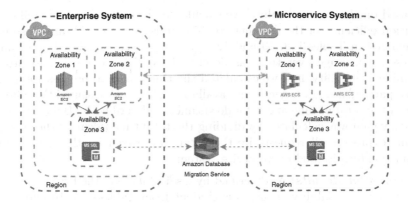

Fig. 5. System implementation in AWS for performance evaluation.

BO to both microservices. The objective of this is to validate the effectiveness of the suggestions provided by the prototype (i.e., to evaluate the effectiveness of clustering operations with BOs as suggested by the prototype). The results obtained for ChurchCRM and SugarCRM regarding this experiment are summarised in Tables 5 and 9, respectively. In the tables 'Legacy & Single MS (1)' stands for the implementation suggested by the prototype (i.e., the correct MS implementation) and the 'Legacy & Single MS (2)' stands for the implementation we did against the suggestion given by the prototype (i.e., the wrong MS implementation).

Next, we introduced two microservices to each system to experiment with the scenario depicted in Fig. 3. For SugarCRM, we introduced two microservices in which one manages 'prospect' BO with its subset of operations and the other manages 'user' BO with its subset of operations. Similarly for ChurchCRM we introduced two microservices in which one manages 'family' BO with its subset of operations and the other manages 'user' BO with its subset of operations. The configuration of the hardware and database properties of these microservices are similar to the ones we have set up for single microservices. Again, we executed the total system and obtained the results of 200 and 400 executions for ChurchCRM and 100 and 200 executions for SugarCRM. Then we again conducted the same set of experiments while introducing operations to 'prospect' BO, 'user' BO MSs of SugarCRM and 'family' BO, 'user' BO MSs of ChurchCRM which contradict the optimal suggestions given by the prototype. As detailed earlier, the objective of this is to validate the effectiveness of the suggestions provided by the prototype. The results obtained for ChurchCRM and SugarCRM regarding this experiment are summarised in Tables 7 and 11, respectively. In the tables, 'Legacy & Multi MS (1)' stands for the implementation suggested by the prototype (i.e., the correct MS implementation) and the 'Legacy & Multi MS (2)' stands for the implementation we did against the suggestion given by the prototype (i.e., the wrong MS implementation).

Based on the attained values, we calculated the scalability, availability, and execution efficiency of the different combinations, and the obtained results are summarized in Tables 6, 8, 10 and 12. Scalability was calculated according to the resources, usage over time, as described by Tsai *et al.* [30]. In order to determine availability, first we calculated the time taken to process 100 packets when a particular microservice is not available. Then, we measured the difference between the total uptime and total downtime, as described by Bauer *et al.* [31]. Efficiency gain was calculated by dividing the total time taken by the enterprise system to process all requests by the total time taken by the corresponding combined enterprise and microservice system.

Experimental Results: As described by Tsai *et al.* [30], the lower the number the better the scalability. Thus, it is evident from Tables 6, 8, 10 and 12 that most of the time the microservices developed based on the suggestions provided by the prototype achieve better scalability than the ones we implemented contrary to the suggestions. When comparing availability, the gain is not significant. However, when comparing the execution efficiency of the systems it is clear from Tables 6, 8, 10 and 12 that the microservices developed based on the suggestions managed to process user requests quicker than the other systems, thus providing the output to the users more quickly.

The lower the lack of cohesion and structural coupling values the better the cohesion and coupling of the system [5]. As such, it is evident from Tables 1 and 4 that the microservices derived from the ChurchCRM and SugarCRM systems achieved better cohesion and coupling values than the legacy system. Thus, the obtained results have affirmed that the microservices extracted based on the suggestions provided by our prototype developed based on the algorithm in Sect. 4 led to microservices which could provide the same services to users while preserving overall system behaviour and achieving higher scalability, availability, efficiency, high cohesion, and low coupling.

6   Conclusion

This paper presented a novel technique based on queuing theory and business object relationships to support re-engineering of an enterprise system as microservices while improving system characteristics such as scalability, availability, cohesion and coupling. A prototype was developed based on the presented technique and validation was conducted by implementing the microservices recommended by the prototype for SugarCRM and ChurchCRM. The experiments conducted proved that the microservices derived based on the suggestions provided by the prototype had the desired characteristics. In future work, the presented technique can be further improved by evaluating method level relationships of the system.

References

1. Newman, S.: Building Microservices: Designing Fine-Grained Systems. O'Reilly Media Inc., Sebastopol (2015)

2. Internet Of Things (IoT) Intelligence Update. https://www.forbes.com/sites/louiscolumbus/2017/11/12/2017-internet-of-things-iot-intelligence-update/#43aa6f4c7f31. Accessed 5 May 2018
3. Magal, S.R., Word, J.: Integrated Business Processes with ERP Systems, 1st edn. Wiley Publishing, Hoboken (2011)
4. Anquetil, N., Laval, J.: Legacy software restructuring: analyzing a concrete case. In: 15th European Conference on Software Maintenance and Reengineering (CSMR), pp. 279–286 (2011)
5. Candela, I., Bavota, G., Russo, B., Oliveto, R.: Using cohesion and coupling for software remodularization: is it enough? ACM Trans. Softw. Eng. Methodol. (TOSEM) **25**(3), 24 (2016)
6. Shatnawi, A., Seriai, A.D., Sahraoui, H., Alshara, Z.: Reverse engineering reusable software components from object-oriented APIs. J. Syst. Soft. **131**, 442–460 (2017)
7. Balalaie, A., Heydarnoori, A., Jamshidi, P.: Migrating to cloud-native architectures using microservices: an experience report. In: Celesti, A., Leitner, P. (eds.) ESOCC Workshops 2015. CCIS, vol. 567, pp. 201–215. Springer, Cham (2016). https://doi.org/10.1007/978-3-319-33313-7_15
8. Microservices a definition of this new architectural term. https://martinfowler.com/articles/microservices.html. Accessed 3 May 2018
9. Evans, E.: Domain-Driven Design: Tackling Complexity in the Heart of Software, 1st edn. Addison-Wesley Professional, Hoboken (2003)
10. Nooijen, E.H.J., van Dongen, B.F., Fahland, D.: Automatic discovery of data-centric and artifact-centric processes. In: La Rosa, M., Soffer, P. (eds.) BPM 2012. LNBIP, vol. 132, pp. 316–327. Springer, Heidelberg (2013). https://doi.org/10.1007/978-3-642-36285-9_36
11. Lu, X., Nagelkerke, M., van de Wiel, D., Fahland, D.: Discovering interacting artifacts from ERP systems. IEEE Trans. Serv. Comput. **8**(6), 861–873 (2015)
12. Wei, F., Ouyang, C., Barros, A.: Discovering behavioural interfaces for overloaded web services. In: 2015 IEEE World Congress on Services (SERVICES), pp. 286–293 (2015)
13. PrinciplesOfOod. http://www.butunclebob.com/ArticleS.UncleBob. Accessed 7 May 2018
14. De Alwis, A.A.C., Barros, A., Fidge, C., Polyvyanyy, A.: Discovering microservices in enterprise systems using a business object containment heuristic. In: Panetto, H., et al. (eds.) OTM 2018. LNCS, vol. 11230. Springer, Cham (2018). https://doi.org/10.1007/978-3-030-02671-4_4
15. De Alwis, A.A.C., Barros, A., Polyvyanyy, A., Fidge, C.: Function-splitting heuristics for discovery of microservices in enterprise systems. In: Pahl, C., Vukovic, M., Yin, J., Yu, Q. (eds.) ICSOC 2018. LNCS, vol. 11236, pp. 37–53. Springer, Cham (2018). https://doi.org/10.1007/978-3-030-03596-9_3
16. Salah, K., Calyam, P., Boutaba, R.: Analytical model for elastic scaling of cloud-based firewalls. Trans. Netw. Serv. Manage. **14**(1), 136–146 (2017)
17. Klock, S., Van Der Werf, J.M.E., Guelen, J.P., Jansen, S.: Workload-based clustering of coherent feature sets in microservice architectures. In: 2017 IEEE International Conference on Software Architecture (ICSA), pp. 11–20. IEEE (2017)
18. Patidar, K., Gupta, R., Chandel, G.S.: Coupling and cohesion measures in object oriented programming. Int. J. Adv. Res. Comput. Sci. Soft. Eng. (2013)
19. Bauer, E., Adams, R.: Reliability and Availability of Cloud Computing. Wiley, Hoboken (2012)
20. Bailis, P., Venkataraman, S., Franklin, M.J., Hellerstein, J.M., Stoica, I.: Quantifying eventual consistency with PBS. VLDB J. **23**(2), 279–302 (2014)

21. Khazaei, H., Barna, C., Beigi-Mohammadi, N., Litoiu, M.: Efficiency analysis of provisioning microservices. In: IEEE International Conference on Cloud Computing Technology and Science, pp. 261–268. IEEE (2016)
22. Levy, R., Nagarajarao, J., Pacifici, G., Spreitzer, M., Tantawi, A., Youssef, A.: Performance management for cluster based web services. In: Goldszmidt, G., Schönwälder, J. (eds.) Integrated Network Management VIII. ITIFIP, vol. 118, pp. 247–261. Springer, Boston, MA (2003). https://doi.org/10.1007/978-0-387-35674-7_29
23. Amaral, M., Polo, J., Carrera, D., Mohomed, I., Unuvar, M., Steinder, M.: Performance evaluation of microservices architectures using containers. In: Network Computing and Applications (NCA), pp. 27–34. IEEE (2015)
24. Felter, W., Ferreira, A., Rajamony, R., Rubio, J.: An updated performance comparison of virtual machines and Linux containers. In: Performance Analysis of Systems and Software, pp. 171–172. IEEE (2015)
25. Huber, N., von Quast, M., Hauck, M., Kounev, S.: Evaluating and modeling virtualization performance overhead for cloud environments. In: CLOSER, pp. 563–573 (2011)
26. Lehrig, S., Eikerling, H., Becker, S.: Scalability, elasticity, and efficiency in cloud computing: a systematic literature review of definitions and metrics. In: Proceedings of the 11th International ACM SIGSOFT Conference on Quality of Software Architectures, pp. 83–92. ACM (2015)
27. Herbst, N.R., Kounev, S., Reussner, R.H.: Elasticity in cloud computing: what it is, and what it is not. In: ICAC, pp. 23–27 (2013)
28. Deb, K., Pratap, A., Agarwal, S., Meyarivan, T.A.M.T.: A fast and elitist multi-objective genetic algorithm: NSGA-II. IEEE Trans. Evol. Comput. 6(2), 182–197 (2002)
29. Estrada, Z.J., Stephens, Z., Pham, C., Kalbarczyk, Z., Iyer, R.K.: A performance evaluation of sequence alignment software in virtualized environments. In: Cluster, Cloud and Grid Computing (CCGrid), pp. 730–737. IEEE (2014)
30. Tsai, W.T., Huang, Y., Shao, Q.: Testing the scalability of SaaS applications. In: IEEE International Conference on Service-Oriented Computing and Applications (SOCA), pp. 1–4 (2011)
31. Bauer, E., Adams, R.: Reliability and Availability of Cloud Computing, 1st edn. Wiley, Hoboken (2012)

Discovering Crossing-Workflow Fragments Based on Activity Knowledge Graph

Jinfeng Wen[1], Zhangbing Zhou[1,3(✉)], Yasha Wang[2], Walid Gaaloul[3],
and Yucong Duan[4]

[1] China University of Geosciences (Beijing), Beijing, China
wenjinfeng.cugb@gmail.com, zhangbing.zhou@gmail.com
[2] Peking University, Beijing, China
[3] TELECOM SudParis, Evry, France
[4] Hainan University, Haikou, China

Abstract. This paper proposes a novel crossing-workflow fragment discovery mechanism, where an activity knowledge graph (AKG) is constructed to capture partial-ordering relations between activities in scientific workflows, and parent-child relations specified upon sub-workflows and their corresponding activities. The biterm topic model is adopted to generate topics and quantify the semantic relevance of activities and sub-workflows. Given a requirement specified in terms of a workflow template, individual candidate activities or sub-workflows are discovered leveraging their semantic relevance and text description in short documents. Candidate fragments are generated through exploring the relations in AKG specified upon candidate activities or sub-workflows, and these fragments are evaluated through balancing their structural and semantic similarities. Evaluation results demonstrate that this technique is accurate and efficient on discovering and recommending appropriate crossing-workflow fragments in comparison with the state of art's techniques.

Keywords: Crossing-workflow fragments · Activity knowledge graph · Topic discovery

1 Introduction

Considering the fact that developing a scientific workflow from scratch is typically a knowledge- and effort-intensive, and error-prone mission, reusing and repurposing the best-practices which have been evidenced by legacy scientific workflows in the repository is considered as a cost-effective and risk-avoiding strategy. Techniques have been proposed to facilitate the reuse and repurposing of workflows. The similarity of workflows (or business processes) can be assessed to evaluate whether a workflow can be replaced (or reused) by another one, and they can be categorized into annotation-based, structure-based, and data-driven mechanisms. A layer-hierarchial technique is developed to compute the similarity of scientific workflows in the *myExperiment* repository, where a layer

© Springer Nature Switzerland AG 2019
H. Panetto et al. (Eds.): OTM 2019, LNCS 11877, pp. 515–532, 2019.
https://doi.org/10.1007/978-3-030-33246-4_32

hierarchy represents the relations between a workflow, its sub-workflows and activities [8]. Generally, these techniques aim to calculate the similarity for pairs of workflows, and they can promote the reuse or repurposing of workflows as the whole. It is worth emphasizing that a novel requirement may be relevant with multiple workflows. In this setting, this requirement should be achieved through discovering appropriate fragments contained in corresponding workflows, and assembling these crossing-workflow fragments accordingly. A crossing-workflow fragments discovery mechanism is developed in [6], which aims to discover fragments whose activities may be contained in various workflows. Note that parent-child relations, besides invocation ones, may exist between workflows, their sub-workflows and activities, and they have not been considered in this technique. Consequently, the discovery of crossing-workflow fragments containing activities in various granularities can hardly be implemented.

To address this challenge, we propose a novel crossing-workflow fragments discovery mechanism as follows:

- An activity knowledge graph (denoted AKG) is constructed, where edges represent partial-ordering relations between activities in workflows, and parent-child relations specified upon sub-workflows and corresponding activities.
- After transferring the name and text description of activities and sub-workflows into short documents, the semantic relevance of these activities and sub-workflows is quantified by their *representative* topics, where topics are generated by biterm topic model [7].
- Given an activity description in the requirement as represented in terms of a workflow fragment, candidate activities or sub-workflows are discovered independently w.r.t. their semantic relevance, and then, are selected according to their short documents. Candidate crossing-workflow fragments are generated by instantiating relations in AKG specified upon candidate activities or sub-workflows, and these fragments are evaluated through balancing their structural and semantic similarities.

Experimental evaluation is conducted, and the results demonstrate that this technique is accurate and efficient on discovering and recommending appropriate crossing-workflow fragments in comparison with the state of art's techniques.

The rest of this paper is organized as follows. Section 2 presents the technique for constructing activity-based knowledge graph. Section 3 explores the topic relevance of activities and sub-workflows. Section 4 discovers fragments crossing scientific workflows. Section 5 presents experimental setting, and Sect. 6 compares the evaluation results of this technique with the state of arts. Section 7 discusses related techniques, and Sect. 8 concludes this paper.

2   Activity Knowledge Graph Construction

As presented in our previous work [8], a scientific workflow represents invocation and parent-child relations upon sub-workflows and activities. Specifically,

Definition 1 (*Scientific Workflow*). *A scientific workflow swf is a tuple (tl, dsc, SWF$_{sub}$, ACT, LNK), where: (i) tl is the title of swf, (ii) dsc is the text description of swf, (iii) SWF$_{sub}$ is a set of sub-workflows contained in swf, (iv) ACT is a set of activities contained in swf, and (v) LNK = {LNK$_{inv}$, LNK$_{pch}$} is a set of links, where LNK$_{inv}$ specifies invocation relations upon SWF$_{sub}$ and ACT, and LNK$_{pch}$ specifies parent-child relations upon sub-workflows in SWF$_{sub}$ and their corresponding activities in ACT.*

Note that a sub-workflow can be regarded as an activity with relatively *coarse* granularity. A sample scientific workflow is from *Taverna 2* of *myExperiment* repository with the title "*PubMed Search*" as shown in Fig. 1, and its corresponding layer hierarchy is shown at Fig. 2(a), respectively.

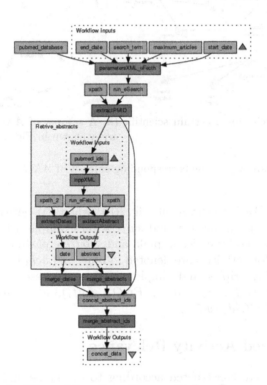

Fig. 1. A sample scientific workflow from *Taverna 2* of *myExperiment* repository with the title "*PubMed Search*".

To facilitate the discovery of crossing-workflow fragments, we construct an *AKG* to represent workflows, and their sub-workflows and activities. For a set of scientific workflows {*swf*}, *AKG* is defined as follows:

Definition 2 (*Activity Knowledge Graph*). *An activity knowledge graph is a tuple (E, R, S), where: (i) E is a set of entities, which includes workflows, their sub-workflows and activities in {swf}, (ii) R is a set of relation types including*

PrtOf *to specify that a sub-workflow or activity belongs to a workflow*, Invok *to specify an invocation relation between a pair of sub-workflows or activities, and* PrtCld *to specify a parent-child relation for a sub-workflow with its corresponding set of activities, and (iii)* $S \subset E \times R \times E$ *is a set of triples, which specify relations prescribed upon entities.*

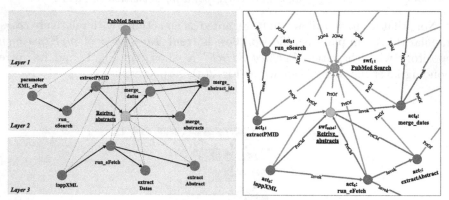

(a) Layer hierarchy for a certain scientific workflow.

(b) A snippet of AKG for layer hierarchy shown in Fig. 2(a).

Fig. 2. Layer hierarchy and the corresponding snippet of AKG. (Color figure online)

A snippet of AKG is shown at Fig. 2(b), where (i) entities for workflows are denoted by nodes in orange, and swf_1 is an example, (ii) entities for sub-workflows are denoted by nodes in pink, and "*Retrive_abstracts*" is an example, and (iii) entities for activities are denoted in blue, and act_3 is an example. Relations are denoted as triples, and sample relations are presented as follows: $s_1 = (swf_{sub4}, PrtOf, swf_1)$, $s_2 = (act_5, PrtOf, swf_1)$, $s_3 = (act_5, Invok, act_6)$, and $s_4 = (act_5, PrtCld, swf_{sub4})$.

3   Topic-Based Activity Relevance

Short documents are constructed according to the name and text description of activities and sub-workflows in order to generate their topics. Due to the briefness of the name which may hardly convey complete knowledge, words in the text description are evaluated and combined with the name to form short documents as the representation of activities or sub-workflows. A word in text description is considered as relevant when this word is (i) semantically similar with a word in the name by word similarity calculation (i.e., *semantic* relevance), or (ii) it co-occurs frequently with a word which is semantically equivalent or similar with a word in the name through word co-occurrence evaluation (i.e., *co-occurrence* relevance). Representative words are selected and appended to enhance their names, and short documents are generated accordingly.

3.1   Topic Discovery Using BTM

Leveraging short documents generated for activities and sub-workflows, this section aims to discover topics, where biterm topic model (*BTM*) [7] is assumed as the most suitable for handling the above constructed short documents. Generally, topics are represented as groups of correlated words in topic models like *BTM*. Topics are learnt by modeling the generation of word co-occurrence patterns (i.e. biterms) in our Short Document-based corpus, where the problem of sparse word co-occurrence patterns can be addressed at the document-level. The procedure of topic discovery includes the following steps:

Biterm Extraction. Based to the principle of *BTM*, a short text in short documents can be treated as a separate text fragment. Any pair of distinct words is extracted as a biterm, and these biterms are treated as the training data set of topic probability distribution.

BTM Training. The corpus of short documents can be regarded as a mixture of topics, where each biterm is drawn from a specific topic independently. The probability that a biterm drawn from a specific topic is further captured by the chances that both words in the biterm are drawn from the topic. The generative procedure is presented as follows, where α and β are *Dirichlet* priors.

- **Step 1:** For each topic z, draw a topic-specific word distribution $\phi_z \sim \mathrm{Dir}(\beta)$;
- **Step 2:** Draw a topic distribution $\theta \sim \mathrm{Dir}(\alpha)$ for the whole corpus of short documents;
- **Step 3:** For each biterm b in the set of biterms B, draw a topic assignment $z \sim \mathrm{Multi}(\theta)$, and draw two words: $w_i, w_j \sim \mathrm{Multi}(\phi_z)$.

The joint probability of a biterm $b = (w_i, w_j)$ according to the above procedure can be calculated as follows:

$$P(b) = \sum_z P(z)P(w_i|z)P(w_j|z) = \sum_z \theta_z \phi_{i|z} \phi_{j|z} \tag{1}$$

Therefore, the likelihood for the corpus of short documents is calculated:

$$P(B) = \prod_{(i,j)} \sum_z \theta_z \phi_{i|z} \phi_{j|z} \tag{2}$$

Inferring Topics of Activities and Sub-workflows. Since *BTM* does not model the document generation process, topic proportions for activities and sub-workflows cannot be discovered directly during the topic learning process. To infer topics for each short document d, the expectation of topic proportions of biterms generated from d is calculated as follows:

$$P(z|d) = \sum_b P(z|b)P(b|d). \tag{3}$$

Based on the parameters estimated by BTM, $P(z|b)$ is obtained using Bayes' formula while $P(b|d)$ is nearly a uniform distribution over all biterms in d.

3.2 Determination of an Optional Topic Number K

The topic identification and topic similarity are closely related. The lower the topic similarity and the higher the topic identification, K should be determined.

Perplexity. The perplexity is often used to evaluate the quality of the probabilistic language model. Generally, the perplexity decreases along with the increase of the number of topics. A small value of perplexity is supposed to generate a better predictive effect on testing text corpus. In a topic model, the perplexity is calculated as follows:

$$Per = \exp\{-\frac{\sum_{d=1}^M \log p(w_d)}{\sum_{d=1}^M N_d}\} \tag{4}$$

where M represents the number of short documents, and N_d is the number of words contained in a certain document d. The parameter w_d denotes the word in d, while $p(w_d)$ is the probability produced by w_d leveraging the document-topic and topic-word distributions. When Per approaches to 0, a better generalization ability is assumed to be achieved.

Topic Similarity. Topic similarity is calculated through adopting Jenson-Shannon (JS) divergence. We introduce the variance of random variables into the potential topic space, which can measure the overall difference of a topic space.

$$Var = \sum_{i=1}^K [D_{JS}(T_i, \bar{\xi})]^2 \div K \tag{5}$$

where $\bar{\xi}$ is the mean probability distribution of different words obtained by the topic-word probability distribution T. K represents the number of topics, and D_{JS} denotes the JS divergence. When Var is large, the difference between topics is greater, and thus, the distinction between topics is higher and the topic structure is more stable.

Table 1. Per, Var and Per_Var when K is set to various values.

K	80	120	160	260	350	360	**370**	380	400
Per	23.840	19.179	16.809	13.145	11.765	11.384	**11.288**	11.555	11.776
Var	0.264	0.289	0.296	0.311	0.314	0.313	**0.315**	0.312	0.310
Per_Var	90.007	66.268	56.657	42.225	37.380	36.302	**35.801**	36.993	37.012

Topic Number K Determination. Based on the perplexity and topic similarity afore-calculated, the factor Per_Var is calculated as follows:

$$Per\_Var = Per \div Var \tag{6}$$

When Per_Var is small in value, the corresponding topic model is optimal. The range for an optimal K can be determined by testing candidate K. As an example, values for Per, Var, and Per_Var are presented at Table 1. An optimal K as 370 is determined when Per_Var is the smallest in value as 35.801, while Per is the smallest as 11.288 and Var is the largest as 0.315.

3.3 Representative Topics Discovery

In most scenarios, a small number of topics can have a large probability score for each activity or sub-workflow, and these topics are assumed as *representative* to represent latent semantic information of activities or sub-workflows. The procedure of determining representative topics is presented as follows. For a certain topic, the average of probability is calculated w.r.t. all activities and sub-workflows. A threshold thd_{tp}, which is usually set to several times of this probability average, is determined to specify the significance of this topic. When the value is larger than thd_{tp}, this topic is assumed as significant. Consequently, the probability of this topic is reserved, and this topic is assumed as *representative* for a certain activity or sub-workflow. Since the probability for non-representative topics is set to zero, a probability normalization procedure is conducted for the topics of activities and sub-workflows.

4 Crossing-Workflow Fragments Discovery

This section presents our crossing-workflow fragments discovery mechanism leveraging the relevance of representative topics for activities and sub-workflows and the query processing upon AKG constructed in Sect. 2.

4.1 Candidate Activity and Sub-workflow Discovery

A requirement is shown at Fig. 3(a), and this requirement is assumed to be satisfied by the composition of activities act_4, act_5, act_6 and act_7, and sub-workflows swf_{sub3} from swf_1, and activities act_5, act_6, act_7 and act_8, and sub-workflows

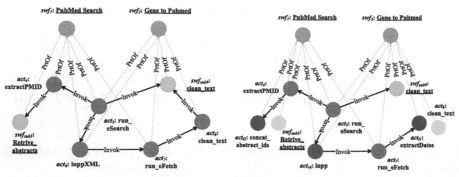

(a) A certain sample requirement.   (b) The testing requirement is developed from Fig. 3(a).

Fig. 3. A certain requirement and a testing requirement that have changed.

swf_{sub9} from swf_2. A scientific workflow fragment specified in the requirement may be similar to an existing one in the repository. Therefore, activities or sub-workflows are discovered and optimally composed accordingly.

It is worth emphasizing that topics can be regarded as a high-level categorization somehow. When two activities (or sub-workflows) are highly relevant in their topics, this fact can hardly specify that they are equivalent or highly similar. Taking this into concern, the semantic similarity between short documents is adopted to improve the accuracy of the discovery for activities or sub-workflows. Consequently, the relevance of a candidate activity or sub-workflow act_{cnd} and an activity stub in the requirement act_{rq} is calculated as follows:

$$relevance(act_{cnd}, act_{rq}) = \alpha \times sim_T(act_{cnd}, act_{rq})$$
$$+ (1 - \alpha) \times sim_S(act_{cnd}, act_{rq}) \tag{7}$$

where sim_T represents the similarity for representative topics, which is calculated through adopting *European Distance*. sim_T returns a value between 0 and 1, where 1 means the equivalent. sim_S represents the semantic similarity between short documents, which is calculated through adopting the minimum cost and maximum flow algorithm, while *WordNet* is used to calculate the semantic similarity for words. The calculation method of sim_S refers to the part of semantic similarity for activity name in our previous work [6]. sim_S returns a value between 0 and 1, where 0 means totally different while 1 means the equivalent. The factor $\alpha \in [0, 1]$ reflects the relative importance of sim_T w.r.t. sim_S. For instance, α is set to 0.7 in this paper to obtain the optimal efficiency, which is determined through experiments where α is set from 0.1 to 0.9 with an increment of 0.1. When candidate activities and sub-workflows are determined according to their relevance, top *K1* candidates should be recommended for a certain activity stub. It is proved that *K1* is set to 7 as an optimal value according to our experiments.

4.2   Crossing-Workflow Fragments Discovery

This section aims to discover crossing-workflow fragments, where relations pre-scribed by AKG are obtained to connect activities or sub-workflows for respective activity stubs in the requirement specification. This procedure is presented by Algorithm 1, where the requirement $RQ = \{ACT_{rq}, LNK_{rq}\}$ presents a cer-tain requirement, where rq refers the parts of the requirement to be involved. ACT_{rq} represents the set of activity stubs, and LNK_{rq} represents links connect-ing activity stubs in RQ. $|ACT_{rq}|$ and $|LNK_{rq}|$ refer to the number of activity stubs or links in ACT_{rq} or LNK_{rq}. Without loss of generality, RQ is assumed to have a single initial activity stub act_{int}. To facilitate the fragment discovery, activity stubs are numbered in an incremental manner by adopting the breadth-first search on RQ starting at act_{int}. Given an activity stub $act_{rq}^i \in ACT_{rq}$, $ACT_{cnd}^i \in ACT_{cnd}$ represents the set of candidate activities and sub-workflows generated in Sect. 4.1. Algorithm 1 is presented as follows:

Step 1: *Instantiated relations are examined whether they exist in AKG. (lines 1–10).* For a link given in the requirement, the sets of candidate activities and sub-workflows are obtained w.r.t. its source and sink activity stubs (line 2). For an activity stub act_{rq}^i in ACT_{rq}, $ACT_{cnd}^i \in ACT_{cnd}$ represents the set of candidate activities and sub-workflows generated in Sect. 4.1. Candidate activities or sub-workflows in ACT_{cnd}^{src} compose as a series of relations rl with those in ACT_{cnd}^{snk}. rl is represented as $(act_{cnd}^{src}, r, act_{cnd}^{snk})$, where r refers to an invocation relation upon activities or sub-workflows evidenced in legacy scientific workflows. Note that rl is verified through a query function $QryAKG$ upon AKG (line 4), and this query statement is presented as follows:

– **MATCH** $(e_1 : E\{act_{cnd}^{src}\})$ - $[r_1 : R\{r\}]$ -> $(e_2 : E\{act_{cnd}^{snk}\})$
   RETURN e_1 as *Source*, r_1 as *Rel*, e_2 as *Sink*

where the **MATCH** clause specifies the relation as constraints. Entities are written inside "( )" brackets (e.g., $(e_1 : E\{act_{cnd}^{src}\})$ and edges inside "[ ]" brackets (e.g., $[r_1 : R\{r\}]$). Filters for labels is written following the node separated with the symbol ":", such that $(e_1 : E)$ represents a node e_1 that must match to certain entity label in E. Certain values for properties can be specified within "{ }" (e.g., $\{act_{cnd}^{src}\}$). The **RETURN** clause aims to project the output variables. If rl exits in AKG, the triple (*Source*, *Rel*, *Sink*) is set to $(act_{cnd}^{src}, r, act_{cnd}^{snk})$, and to *null* otherwise. rl is inserted into the candidate relation set as the corresponding link (line 7). To reduce unnecessary combinations, unrelated activities or sub-workflows are removed. Source and sink activities of rl, i.e., act_{cnd}^{src} and act_{cnd}^{snk}, are inserted into new candidate sets $NACT_{cnd}^{src}$ and $NACT_{cnd}^{snk}$ w.r.t. corresponding activity stubs in ACT_{rq} (line 8).

Step 2: *Crossing-workflow fragments are generated (lines 11–37).* Fragments are initially constructed through the inclusion of a certain activity or sub-workflow (lines 12–17). Given a fragment frg in FRG, we examine each candidate activ-ity or sub-workflow act_{cnd}^k for the activity stub act_{rq}^i, and its related relations, to evaluate whether frg can be extended to generate new fragments. A tag is

Algorithm 1. Crossing-Workflow Fragments Discovery

Require:
- $RQ = \{ACT_{rq}, LNK_{rq}\}$: a certain requirement specification
- $ACT_{cnd} = \{ACT_{cnd}^i\}$: a set of candidate activities or sub-workflows for each $act_{rq}^i \in ACT_{rq}$ where $i \in [1, |ACT_{rq}|]$

Ensure:
- $FRG = \{frg\}$: a set of top $K2$ fragments where $frg = \{ACT, RL, sim\}$

1: **for all** $lnk_i \in LNK_{rq}$ **do**
2:     $ACT_{cnd}^{src} \in ACT_{cnd}$, $ACT_{cnd}^{snk} \in ACT_{cnd} \leftarrow$ get the sets of candidate activities and sub-workflows for source $lnk_i.act_{rq}^{src}$ or sink activity stub $lnk_i.act_{rq}^{snk} \in ACT_{rq}$
3:     **for** $\forall\, act_{cnd}^{src} \in ACT_{cnd}^{src}$ **and** $\forall\, act_{cnd}^{snk} \in ACT_{cnd}^{snk}$ **do**
4:         **if** $QryAKG(rl \leftarrow (act_{cnd}^{src}, r, act_{cnd}^{snk}), AKG) = null$ **then**
5:             **continue**
6:         **end if**
7:         $lnk_i.RL \leftarrow lnk_i.RL \cup \{rl\}$;
8:         $NACT_{cnd}^{src} \leftarrow NACT_{cnd}^{src} \cup \{act_{cnd}^{src}\}$; $NACT_{cnd}^{snk} \leftarrow NACT_{cnd}^{snk} \cup \{act_{cnd}^{snk}\}$
9:     **end for**
10: **end for**
11: **for all** $act_{rq}^i \in ACT_{rq}$ where $NACT_{cnd}^i \neq \emptyset$ **do**
12:     **if** $FRG = \emptyset$ **then**
13:         **for all** $act_{cnd}^k \in NACT_{cnd}^i$ **do**
14:             $frg.ACT \leftarrow \{act_{cnd}^j\}$; $FRG \leftarrow FRG \cup \{frg\}$
15:         **end for**
16:         **continue**
17:     **end if**
18:     **for all** $frg \in FRG$ **do**
19:         **for all** $act_{cnd}^k \in NACT_{cnd}^i$ **do**
20:             $tag_{cnd}^k \leftarrow$ **false**; $IDX \leftarrow$ get indexes for links in LNK_{rq}
21:             **for all** $idx \in IDX$ **do**
22:                 **for all** $rl \in lnk_{idx}.RL$ **do**
23:                     $idx_1, idx_2 \leftarrow$ indexes of activities in frg related to $rl.act_{cnd}^{src}$ or $rl.act_{cnd}^{snk}$
24:                     **if** $(rl.act_{cnd}^{src} = act_{frg}^{idx_1}$ **and** $rl.act_{cnd}^{snk} = act_{cnd}^k)$ **or** $(rl.act_{cnd}^{src} = act_{cnd}^k$ **and** $rl.act_{cnd}^{snk} = act_{frg}^{idx_2})$ **then**
25:                         $frg_n \leftarrow frg$; $tag_{cnd}^k \leftarrow$ **true**; $frg_n.ACT \leftarrow frg_n.ACT \cup \{act_{cnd}^k\}$
26:                         $frg_n.RL \leftarrow frg_n.RL \cup \{rl\}$; $FRG \leftarrow FRG \cup \{frg_n\}$; **break**
27:                     **end if**
28:                 **end for**
29:             **end for**
30:             **if** $tag_{cnd}^k =$ **false then**
31:                 $frg_n \leftarrow frg$; $frg_n.ACT \leftarrow frg_n.ACT \cup \{act_{cnd}^k\}$
32:                 $FRG \leftarrow FRG \cup \{frg_n\}$
33:             **end if**
34:         **end for**
35:         $FRG \leftarrow FRG - \{frg\}$
36:     **end for**
37: **end for**
38: **for all** $frg \in FRG$ **do**
39:     $frg.ACT \leftarrow$ remove activities irrelevant to $\forall rl \in frg.RL$
40:     **for all** $act \in frg.ACT$ **do**
41:         $act_{rq} \leftarrow$ get the activity stub in ACT_{rq} w.r.t. act
42:         $sim_{sm} \leftarrow sim_{sm} + SimCal(act_{rq}, act)$
43:     **end for**
44:     $sim_{st} \leftarrow |frg.RL|/|LNK_{rq}|$; $sim_{sm} \leftarrow sim_{sm}/|frg.ACT|$
45:     $frg.sim \leftarrow \beta * sim_{st} + (1 - \beta) * sim_{sm}$
46: **end for**
47: $FRG \leftarrow$ get $\{frg\}$ where $frq.sim$ is among the top $K2$

adopted to specify whether act^k_{cnd} has extended certain relations to produce new fragments (line 20). The set of indexes for links in LNK_{rq} are obtained associated with act^i_{rq} being processed and those activity stubs that have already been processed, where each index will be handled (lines 20–22). Involved candidate relations are decomposed into source and sink activities, which allows the indexes of their source and sink activity stubs, i.e., idx_1 and idx_2, to be determined for promoting the selection of extended relations (line 23).

When source and sink activities of a candidate relation are equal to (i) the activity for the corresponding index idx_1 of frg and the candidate activity being processed act^k_{cnd}, respectively, or (ii) act^k_{cnd} and the activity at the corresponding index idx_2 of frg (line 24), it indicates that a satisfied relation is found, and the tag can be updated as *true* (line 25). In this setting, the growth procedure for new fragments is executed on frg. In particular, act^k_{cnd} is inserted into the activity set of this new fragment while the satisfied relation is supplemented to the corresponding relation set (lines 25–26). Since act^k_{cnd} and the associated activity in frg are deterministic, there is at most one satisfied relation in the corresponding candidate relation set. Once this relation is discovered, the loop about its candidate relation set terminates (line 26). On the other hand, when no suitable relations are considered, i.e., the tag is *false*, we need to simply insert act^k_{cnd} into a new fragment without corresponding relations (lines 30–33), which contributes to the fragment discovery for the following phase act^{i+1}_{rq}. When the extension generation task of frg is complete, frg is removed from FRG.

Step 3: *Candidate fragments are discovered and recommended (lines 38–46).* The activity set of afore-generated fragments may contain irrelevant activities. Therefore, the activity set needs to be updated according to activities related to the relation set (line 39). Meanwhile, the fragment similarity $frg.sim$ is calculated as two parts, e.g., structural similarity sim_{st} and semantic similarity sim_{sm}(line 45), where $\beta \in [0, 1]$ reflects the importance of sim_{st} w.r.t. sim_{sm}. Note that sim_{st} refers to the structural similarity between frg and RQ, which is the relation ratio of the number of relations in $frg.RL$ to the number of total relations in LNK_{rq} (line 44). Besides, sim_{sm} represents the average semantic similarity between frg and RQ, which is calculated leveraging similarities between each activity in frg and the corresponding activity stub, and the number of activities in $frg.ACT$. Their similarities are obtained through the similarity calculation function $SimCal$ (line 42).

Generally, fragments with high structural similarity should be more appropriate to be recommended. In this setting, sim_{st} is assigned a high weight than sim_{sm} (i.e., β is set to 0.7). The similarity of each fragment returns a value between 0 and 1, where 1 means the equivalent. Consequently, top $K2$ (like 10) fragments $\{frg\}$ are selected and recommended according to their ranked fragment similarities (line 47).

5   Experimental Setting

5.1   Data Cleaning and Experimental Setup

We have collected 1573 scientific workflows in the category of *Taverna 2* of the *myExperiment* repository. Scientific workflows are cleansed as follows: (i) the titles or text descriptions of scientific workflows lacks specification. In this case, similarity computation for activities cannot be conducted, and the topic discovery is inaccurate, and (ii) activities corresponding to slim services are mostly the *glue* code, and they don't capture invocation relations between functionalities.

The semantic similarity between words is computed by *WordNet*. However, improper words which are not recognized by *WordNet* are contained in names or text descriptions of activities and sub-workflows, and they are handled case-by-case as mentioned in our previous work [8]. Besides, stopwords such as *can*, *of*, and *and*, are removed. Words like *accessed*, *accesses*, and *accessing* have a common word root *access*. Affixes are removed to keep the root only. This is important for topic model algorithms. Otherwise, these words are treated as different word entities, and thus, their topic relevance is not well-recognized. Therefore, the lemmatization technology is applied.

In order to ensure the rationality and universality of our technique, we have carefully selected samples from fragments which cross multiple scientific workflows in the activity knowledge graph, and modified them as novel requirements according to certain principles. These samples should cover most scale levels of crossing-workflow fragments to satisfy various complexity requirements. By observing scientific workflows in AKG, fragments span $2 \sim 4$ mostly, or even cross 5 or 6 scientific workflows. We select 20 samples among fragments crossing different scales of workflows, e.g., $1 \sim 6$, and samples across 2 to 4 are chosen at a high ratio. Particularly, we can simulate that the requirement is completely satisfied by a scientific workflow when the scale of is 1 in terms of the number of crossing-workflow fragments. Experiments are conducted when these sample fragments are remained as they are, or to be changed according to certain principles.

5.2   No Changes Applied to Sample Fragments

Experiments are conducted when sample fragments are remained as they are retrieved from the dataset. An expected result should be an exact matched fragments compared with the requirement fragment. Experiments for 20 sample crossing-workflow fragments return the *right* recommendations, which contain original sample fragments, and they are ranked as the first in terms of similarities. For instance, given the sample fragment swf_{smpl4}, which spans 3 scientific workflows (e.g., swf_{1687}, swf_{1768} and swf_{1757}). The representation of swf_{smpl4} based on AKG is transferred as follows:

- $E = \{act_0, act_2, act_3, act_6, act_7\}$
- $R = \{Invok\}$

- $S = \{(act_2, \text{ } Invok, \text{ } act_7), \text{ } (act_7, \text{ } Invok, \text{ } act_0), \text{ } (act_0, \text{ } Invok, \text{ } act_3), \text{ } (act_6, Invok, \text{ } act_3), \text{ } (act_6, \text{ } Invok, \text{ } act_0)\}$

where 5 relation triples are contained, and the fifth candidate crossing-workflow fragment is shown according to ranked similarity values:

- Candidate 5 $= \{frg.ACT = (act_0, \text{ } act_{866}, \text{ } act_3, \text{ } act_6, \text{ } act_7), \text{ } frg.RL = ((act_{866}, \text{ } Invok, \text{ } act_7), \text{ } (act_7, \text{ } Invok, \text{ } act_0), \text{ } (act_0, \text{ } Invok, \text{ } act_3), \text{ } (act_6, \text{ } Invok, act_3), \text{ } (act_6, \text{ } Invok, \text{ } act_0)), \text{ } frg.sim = 0.853\}$

This sample shows that most of the same or similar relations can be discovered, and most suitable candidate fragments can be recommended.

5.3   Changes Applied to Sample Fragments

Novel requirements may not be exactly the same as crossing-workflow fragments in the repository. In this case, sample fragments are changed to generate novel requirements. Changing operations include *insertion, deletion* and *replacement*. Besides, some novel activities or sub-workflows are constructed in sample fragments, which reflects new features in novel requirements. Consequently, 10 fragments are generated to conduct novel experiments. An example is shown in Fig. 3(b), where activity act_{i1} named *"extractDates"* is inserted into act_7 to build a new relation triple $(act_7, \text{ } Invok, \text{ } act_{i1})$. A new relation triple $(act_4, \text{ } Invok, act_{i2})$ is generated, where an inserted activity act_{i2} named *"concat_abstract_ids"* is reconnected to act_4. Sub-workflow swf_{sub3} and activity act_8 are deleted, and activity act_6 is replaced by a newly constructed activity act_{r6}. Results for 4 testing fragments return the *right* recommendations that contain sample fragments.

Since 6 experiments (e.g., swf_{tst21}, swf_{tst22}, swf_{tst28} and so on), which cannot recommend exact fragments w.r.t. their requirements, are set to add newly constructed activities, e.g., act_{r6} in Fig. 3(b). Their results can only discover relatively similar crossing-workflow fragments existed in AKG. Note that swf_{tst} refers to the testing requirements that have been changed on the basis of original samples. An example is swf_{tst28}, which spans 4 scientific workflows (e.g., swf_{1702}, swf_{1687}, swf_{1598}, and swf_{1754}), whose representation based on AKG is shown as follows:

- $E = \{act_{new}, \text{ } act_7, \text{ } act_{69}, \text{ } act_{201}, \text{ } act_{732}, \text{ } act_{738}, \text{ } act_{740}\}$
- $R = \{Invok\}$
- $S = \{(act_{69}, \text{ } Invok, \text{ } act_{new}), \text{ } (act_{new}, \text{ } Invok, \text{ } act_7), \text{ } (act_{201}, \text{ } Invok, \text{ } act_7), (act_{201}, \text{ } Invok, \text{ } act_{732}), \text{ } (act_{740}, \text{ } Invok, \text{ } act_{732}), \text{ } (act_{738}, \text{ } Invok, \text{ } act_{740})\}$

where act_{new} is a newly constructed activity and swf_{tst28} is changed through the operation of *insertion, deletion* and *replacement*. The fifth recommended crossing-workflow fragment is presented according to ranked similarity values:

- Candidate 5 $= \{frg.ACT = (act_2, \text{ } act_7, \text{ } act_{511}, \text{ } act_{201}, \text{ } act_{732}, \text{ } act_{738}, \text{ } act_{740}), frg.RL = ((act_{511}, \text{ } Invok, \text{ } act_2), \text{ } (act_2, \text{ } Invok, \text{ } act_7), \text{ } (act_{201}, \text{ } Invok, \text{ } act_7), (act_{201}, \text{ } Invok, \text{ } act_{732}), \text{ } (act_{740}, \text{ } Invok, \text{ } act_{732}), \text{ } (act_{738}, \text{ } Invok, \text{ } act_{740})), frg.sim = 0.976\}$

Generally, when changes are applied upon sample fragments, our technique can discover appropriate crossing-workflow fragments in most scenarios.

6   Experimental Evaluation

6.1   Performance Metrics

Precision and *recall* are adopted for the evaluation purpose. Given a testing fragment swf_{tst}, a reusable fragment swf_{ept} contained in the repository is assumed to be included in the *expected* list of recommendation (denoted SWF_{ept}) when the similarity between swf_{tst} and swf_{ept} is no less than a pre-specified threshold $thrd_{ept}$. In our experiments, each activity stubs in swf_{tst} is replaced by all activities and sub-workflows in dataset, to obtain a series of expected crossing-workflow fragments, where links on activities and sub-workflows are checked whether they are retained leveraging the relations specified upon scientific workflows in the repository. Importantly, similarities of fragments are calculated through line 45 in Algorithm 1 through balancing their structural and semantic similarity w.r.t. swf_{tst}. We use the notation SWF_{rec} to denote the set of workflow fragments, which are actually recommended. Precision and recall are computed:

$$precision = (|SWF_{ept} \cap SWF_{rec}|) \div |SWF_{rec}| \tag{8}$$

$$recall = (|SWF_{ept} \cap SWF_{rec}|) \div |SWF_{ept}| \tag{9}$$

where "$|SWF_{rec}|$" refers to the number of fragments in the set SWF_{rec} while "$|SWF_{ept}|$" specifies the number of elements in the set SWF_{ept}. "$|SWF_{ept} \cap SWF_{rec}|$" returns the number of fragments in SWF_{ept} in SWF_{rec}.

6.2   Baseline Methods

The following methods are chosen as the baseline:

- *Sub-graphRec:* The sub-graph matching algorithm [5,6] is adopted to discover and recommend fragments w.r.t. certain requirements. The sub-graph matching algorithm is applied to discover candidate fragments in a constructed activity network model, where edges reflect invocation relations between activities. Top $K2$ fragments are selected according to fragment similarities.
- *ClusteringRec:* Clustering has demonstrated its performance in [2,6]. We adopt a modularity-based clustering algorithm to generate activity clusters. When a certain requirement is to be satisfied, the target cluster is determined with respect to each activity stub, and candidate activities or sub-workflows are discovered to construct a series of crossing-workflow fragments. Top $K2$ fragments are selected according to fragment similarities.

Below, we present experimental results of our technique (denoted *AKGRec*), *Sub-graphRec*, and *ClusteringRec* w.r.t. the following three parameters: (i) $thrd_{ept}$: the pre-specified threshold of the similarity when generating SWF_{ept},

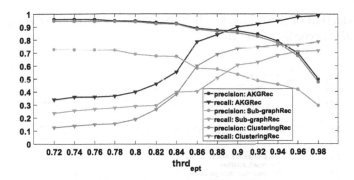

Fig. 4. *Precision* and *recall* for *AKGRec*, *Sub-graphRec* and *ClusteringRec* when $K2$ is set to 10, β is set to 0.7, and $thrd_{ept}$ is set from 0.72 to 0.98 with an increment of 0.02.

(ii) $K2$: the number of recommended fragments, and (iii) β: the relative importance of the structural similarity w.r.t. the semantic similarity for the calculation of fragment similarity.

Impact of $thrd_{ept}$. To explore the impact of $thrd_{ept}$ to *precision* and *recall*, we set $K2$ as 10, β as 0.7, and $thrd_{ept}$ as a value from 0.72 to 0.98 with an increment of 0.02. Figure 4 shows that precision drops and recall increases along with the increasing of $thrd_{ept}$, and *AKGRec* performs better than *Sub-graphRec* and *ClusteringRec* in precision and recall. Specifically, the majority of recommended fragments of *Sub-graphRec* are not expected somehow. In fact, *Sub-graphRec* guarantees the *structural* similarity of recommended fragments w.r.t. the requirement, but the semantically matching of activities is not the focus. Therefore, the precision and recall are relatively lower for *Sub-graphRec* than *AKGRec* and *ClusteringRec*. The precision of *ClusteringRec* is quite high, since recommended fragments are mostly included in SWF_{ept}. However, the recall of *ClusteringRec* is relatively low. After carefully analyzing the experiments, it is observed that activities are unevenly assigned to various clusters, and some clusters may contain quite a few candidate activities or sub-workflows. Consequently, there may have no enough fragments generated by *ClusteringRec* to be recommended.

Figure 4 shows that precision decreases, and recall increases, along with the increasing of $thrd_{ept}$ for *AKGRec*, *Sub-graphRec*, and *ClusteringRec*. In fact, SWF_{rec} does not change when $K2$ is set to a certain value. Fragments in SWF_{ept} may be less in number when $thrd_{ept}$ is set to a relatively large value. Consequently, more fragments in SWF_{rec} may be missed in SWF_{ept}, which makes the decreasing of the precision according to Formula 8. Figure 4 shows that precision for *AKGRec* and *ClusteringRec* is relatively stable when $thrd_{ept}$ changes from 0.72 to 0.84, since the similarity for the majority of expected fragments is within these two ranges. The number of fragments in SWF_{ept} decreases to an extent when $thrd_{ept}$ is set from 0.86 to 0.98, since expected workflows whose similarity is within this range is quite few. Leveraging the difference of $|SWF_{ept} \cap SWF_{rec}|$

and the reduction of $|SWF_{ept}|$, recall increases for *AKGRec*, *Sub-graphRec* and *ClusteringRec* according to Formula 9.

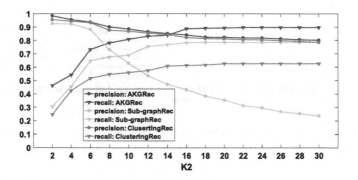

Fig. 5. *Precision* and *recall* for *AKGRec*, *Sub-graphRec* and *ClusteringRec* when $thrd_{ept}$ is set to 0.86, β is set to 0.7 and $K2$ is set from 2 to 30 with an increment of 2.

Impact of $K2$. To explore the impact of $K2$ to *precision* and *recall*, we set $thrd_{ept}$ as 0.86, β as 0.7 and $K2$ as a value from 2 to 30 with an increment of 2. As shown in Fig. 5, the precision and recall are larger for *AKGRec* than *Sub-graphRec* and *ClusteringRec*, due to the similar reason as presented in Fig. 4. In particular, when $K2$ is set to relatively large values, Fig. 5 shows that precision of all three technique begins to decrease, since more recommended fragments should be discovered, which are actually not that relevant and may not exist in SWF_{ept}. Note that the precision for *Sub-graphRec* does not perform well, since a large number of fragments are obtained by the sub-graph matching method. When $K2$ changes from 2 to 16, recall of all three technique increases to a large extent, since more expected fragments are recommended. Meanwhile, recall becomes relatively stable when $K2$ changes from 16 to 30, since most of expected workflows have been discovered and included in SWF_{ept}.

Impact of β. As discussed in Sect. 4.2, similarities of recommended fragments to a certain requirement are impacted by β. To explore this impact to *precision* and *recall*, we set $thrd_{ept}$ as 0.86, $K2$ as 10, and β as a value from 0.1 to 0.9 with an increment of 0.1. Due to the similar reason as presented in Figs. 4 and 5, *AKGRec* performs better in precision and recall than *Sub-graphRec* and *ClusteringRec*. Generally, precision and recall increase along with the increasing of β, which evidence the strong significance of structural relevance to recommended fragments. Concretely, SWF_{rec} does not change when $K1$ is a fix value, and precision increases when β changes from 0.1 to 0.6, since more recommended fragments are contained in SWF_{ept}. As to *Sub-graphRec*, the semantically matching is not considered in sub-graph matching algorithm. Therefore, most discovered fragments are not contained in SWF_{ept} and precision is relatively low. The importance of semantics is gradually decreased from the fragment similarity

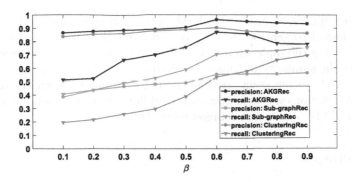

Fig. 6. *Precision* and *recall* for *AKGRec*, *Sub-graphRec* and *ClusteringRec* when $thrd_{ept}$ is set to 0.86, $K2$ is set to 10, and β is set from 0.1 to 0.9 with an increment of 0.1.

when β is set from 0.6 to 0.9, and results show that precision begins to decrease, since more recommended fragments are not contained in SWF_{ept}, in case the fragment similarity relies on structure while little regard to semantics. A high recall is got when β is set to 0.6. However, the recall of *ClusteringRec* is lowest. In fact, the number of recommended fragments is not enough compared with recommended fragments as explained for $K2$, which is affected by clustering effect and selection strategy of candidate activities or sub-workflows.

Results in Figs. 4 and 5 show that precision decreases, while recall increases, when $thrd_{ept}$ and $K2$ increase. Therefore, we suggest that $thrd_{ept}$ and $K2$ should not be set to relatively large values. Results in Fig. 6 show that the structure relevance should be considered as more important when discovering crossing-workflow fragments to achieve a promising result.

7   Related Work

Discovering crossing-workflow fragments is a promising research topic for supporting the reuse and repurposing of legacy scientific workflows when novel requirements are to be satisfied. The technique can discover fragments whose activities can be contained in various workflows [6]. However, besides invocation relations, hierarchical relations like parent-child ones may exist in workflows, their sub-workflows and activities, and they have not been considered when constructing an activity network. Hence, fragments containing activities in various granularities cannot be discovered. To capture more kinds of relations, besides *flat* invocation relations, in workflows, knowledge graph is adopted to encode service knowledge and relations manageable by computer systems [4]. Following this trend, this paper constructs AKG to capture various kinds of relations in a semantic fashion. Fragments discovery is reduced into a graph query upon AKG, which can be achieved through the path query [3], and a path reflects a sequence of relations. Topic models like LDA and BTM have been applied to promote the discovery of appropriate Web services w.r.t. user queries. In [1], web service structure is transferred into a weighted directed acyclic graph (*WDAG*), and *BTM* is adopted to generate topics upon *WDAG*. The similarity for the pairs of *WDAGs* takes the topic similarity into concern, where *JS* divergence is used to calculate the similarity of topics. Inspired by these methods, this paper constructs an *AKG* to represent partial-ordering relations between activities, and parent-child relations specified upon sub-workflows and corresponding activities, and adopts *BTM* to generate representative topis.

8   Conclusion

This paper proposes a novel crossing-workflow fragment discovery mechanism. Specifically, an *AKG* is constructed to represent partial-ordering relations between activities, and parent-child relations specified upon sub-workflows and corresponding activities. The semantic relevance of activities and sub-workflows is quantified by representative topics obtained by *BTM*. Given a requirement specified in terms of a workflow template, individual candidate activities or sub-workflows are discovered, and they are composed into fragments according to relations specified by *AKG*. Candidate fragments are evaluated through balancing their structural and semantic similarities. Evaluation results show that this technique is accurate and efficient on discovering appropriate crossing-workflow fragments in comparison with the state of arts.

References

1. Baskara, A.R., Sarno, R.: Web service discovery using combined bi-term topic model and WDAG similarity. In: International Conference on Information and Communication Technology and System, pp. 235–240 (2017)
2. Conforti, R., Dumas, M., García-Bañuelos, L., La Rosa, M.: BPMN miner: automated discovery of BPMN process models with hierarchical structure. Inf. Syst. **56**, 284–303 (2016)
3. Hong, S., Park, N., Chakraborty, T., Kang, H., Kwon, S.: Page: answering graph pattern queries via knowledge graph embedding. In: International Conference on Big Data, pp. 87–99 (2018)
4. Paulheim, H.: Knowledge graph refinement: a survey of approaches and evaluation methods. Semantic Web **8**(3), 489–508 (2017)
5. Theodorou, V., Abelló, A., Thiele, M., Lehner, W.: Frequent patterns in ETL workflows: an empirical approach. Data Knowl. Eng. **112**, 1–16 (2017)
6. Wen, J., Zhou, Z., Shi, Z., Wang, J., Duan, Y., Zhang, Y.: Crossing scientific workflow fragments discovery through activity abstraction in smart campus. IEEE Access **6**, 40530–40546 (2018)
7. Yan, X., Guo, J., Lan, Y., Cheng, X.: A biterm topic model for short texts. In: Proceedings of the 22nd International Conference on World Wide Web, pp. 1445–1456. ACM (2013)
8. Zhou, Z., Cheng, Z., Zhang, L.J., Gaaloul, W., Ning, K.: Scientific workflow clustering and recommendation leveraging layer hierarchical analysis. IEEE Trans. Serv. Comput. **11**(1), 169–183 (2018)

History-Aware Dynamic Process Fragmentation for Risk-Aware Resource Allocation

Giray Havur[1,2(✉)] and Cristina Cabanillas[1]

[1] Vienna University of Economics and Business, Vienna, Austria
{giray.havur,cristina.cabanillas}@wu.ac.at
[2] Siemens AG Österreich, Corporate Technology, Vienna, Austria
giray.havur@siemens.com

Abstract. Most Process-Aware Information Systems (PAIS) and resource allocation approaches do the selection of the resource to be allocated to a certain process activity at run time, when the activity must be executed. This results in cumulative (activity per activity) local optimal allocations for which assumptions (e.g. on loop repetitions) are not needed beforehand, but which altogether might incur in an increase of cycle time and/or cost. Global optimal allocation approaches take all the process-, organization- and time-related constraints into account at once before process execution, handling better the optimization objectives. However, a number of assumptions must be made upfront on the decisions made at run time. When an assumption does not hold at run time, a resource reallocation must be triggered. Aiming at achieving a compromise between the pros and cons of these two methods, in this paper we introduce a novel approach that fragments the process dynamically for the purpose of risk-aware resource allocation. Given historical execution data and a process fragmentation threshold, our method enhances the feasibility of the resource allocations by dynamically generating the process fragments (i.e. execution horizons) that satisfy the given probabilistic threshold. Our evaluation with simulations demonstrates the advantages in terms of reduction in reallocation efforts.

Keywords: Business process management · Dynamic process fragmentation · Quasi-online scheduling · Resource allocation · Process mining

1 Introduction

Resource allocation in business processes selects the resource(s) responsible for a process activity at run time among the suitable resources according to

Funded by the Austrian Science Fund (FWF) Elise Richter programme under agreement V 569-N31 (PRAIS).

predefined assignment criteria (e.g. based on roles or other organizational properties)[1]. Despite being a necessary functionality in any Process-Aware Information
System (PAIS), current systems provide limited support for resource allocation.
Generally, actual resource allocation is delegated to people to some extent, in the
best case by implementing Push/Pull patterns [1] (e.g. by offering the activity
to all the suitable resources and letting them decide who will become responsible for its execution – distribution by offer). This behavior tends to overlook
optimization functions regarding performance metrics such as process cycle time
or execution cost. On the other hand, when it is up to the process manager to
decide who to allocate to the next activities, they get no information about the
horizon until which the allocations will hold. When decision points are present
in the process, assumptions on the respective choices must be made beforehand.
The bigger the uncertainty in the process (i.e. the number of decisions), the
more critical this issue becomes. While taking a higher risk (i.e. allocating more
activities at once) may be beneficial as for process cycle time or cost, if the
assumptions made do not hold at run time the opposite effects may appear and
undesired reallocations may be necessary. On the contrary, a very conservative
(less risky) approach that allocates resources only when it is required (i.e. before
activity execution) avoids speculating about potential future behaviors of the
process but does not assure the most optimal (or even feasible) results at the
process level and can incur in non-anticipated delays or deadlocks. For instance,
if there is a binding of duties between A (executed first) and B, and at the
moment of allocating B the required resource is not available, the process will
be delayed.

In order to avoid manual resource allocation, several approaches propose
more advanced and automated techniques [2–5]. Some find out the most adequate resource at the moment of executing an activity, hence allocating the process *activity per activity* at run time to the "best" resource available [2,3] (also
known as *online scheduling* [6]). Others aim for a global optimal solution [4,5]
where the entire process is considered for allocation before it is started (also
known as *offline scheduling* [6]), so the resources for all the activity instances
are selected at once on the basis of the present process-, organization- and time-
related constraints. In terms of risk management, these techniques lie in the two
extremes of the spectrum, and to the best of our knowledge there is not yet an
approach handling risk and uncertainty in a more flexible way in this context.

In this paper we introduce a novel approach to dynamically create and allocate *process fragments* at run time being aware of the risks taken when making
resource allocation decisions. The novelties of the approach include: (i) the use
of historical execution data for making probabilistic decisions ahead of time; and
(ii) the dynamic fragmentation of the process based on a fragmentation threshold that provides flexibility in terms of risk management and helps to prevent
potential reallocations. We have implemented the approach using an encoding
based on Answer Set Programming (ASP) [7] that proved to produce good

---

[1] In this work we assume human resources but the concept could be adapted for
non-human resource allocation, too.

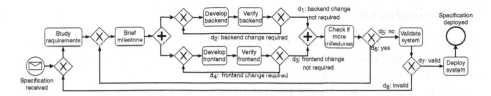

Fig. 1. BPMN model of the software development process

performance results in optimal resource allocation [5]. We have evaluated our fragmentation method with simulations aimed to assess its behaviour with respect to reallocation needs. The findings support our hypothesis that the feasibility of the resource allocations improves when the risk is kept low.

The paper is structured as follows. Section 2 describes an example scenario that illustrates the research problem. Section 3 defines concepts needed to understand our approach. Section 4 introduces our new process fragmentation method. Section 5 explains the implementation of the method and the evaluation performed. Section 6 provides a more detailed description of the state-of-the-art. Finally, Sect. 7 outlines the conclusions drawn from the work along with its limitations and potential future steps.

2 Motivating Scenario

A manager of a software development company would like to handle the allocation of their (human) resources to every new project. They developed and refined a business process model for the execution of software development projects as illustrated with Business Process Model and Notation (BPMN) [8] in Fig. 1. After a project specification is received, the requirements of the project are studied and a number of milestones are derived. Every milestone involves two separate development parts (frontend and backend) that are concurrently undertaken and which, in turn, may require one or more iterations depending on the respective verification results. Once all the milestones are fully achieved, the developed software needs to be validated against the requirements and specifications received at the beginning of the project. If the validation fails, the study of the requirements must be reinitiated and new milestones are developed.

The manager is aware of the fact that the process has multiple decision points (represented with XOR split gateways in BPMN) where their forecasting on the allocations of resources deviated many times in the past. This forced them to reallocate resources from scratch to the upcoming activities at each deviation. With the support of a PAIS, they keep track of previous executions of the software development process in event logs. This helps them to infer the duration of the activities depending on the resources allocated to them. However, they found the need for an automated mechanism that could perform their manual allocations in a more flexible and less risky way by leveraging the process-, organizational- and temporal-related data available, aiming to achieve time- and cost-effective executions and avoid the reallocations to a bigger extent.

3   Preliminaries

BPMN [8] is the de-facto standard process modeling notation due to its under-standability and ease of use. However, because of their well-defined semantics and their analysis capabilities, in this work we rely on Petri nets [9] satisfying the workflow properties [10] for process modeling. Nonetheless, note that many process modeling notations, including BPMN, can be automatically mapped to Petri nets [11].

A Petri net is a bipartite graph composed of *places* and *transitions*. The places might contain tokens, whose distribution might change over time.

Definition 1 (Petri net). A Petri net is a 4-tuple $PN = (P, T, F, \nu)$, where:

- $P = \{p_1, p_2, ..., p_n\}$ is the set of *places*, represented graphically as circles,
- $T = \{t_1, t_2, ..., t_n\}$ is the set of *transitions*, represented graphically as rectangles,
- $F \subseteq (P \times T) \bigcup (T \times P)$ is the set of *arcs* (flow relations), represented as arrows,
- $\nu : F \to \mathbb{Z}^+$ is the arc weight mapping indicating cardinality constraints on the movement of tokens throughout the net.

The *input places* and the *output places* of each transition $t \in T$ are $^\bullet t = \{p \in P \mid (p, t) \in F\}$ and $t^\bullet = \{p \in P \mid (t, p) \in F\}$, respectively. Similarly, the *input transitions* and the *output transitions* of each place $p \in P$ are $^\bullet p = \{t \in T \mid (t, p) \in F\}$ and $p^\bullet = \{t \in T \mid (p, t) \in F\}$, respectively. A *marking* (or state) $M = \{\mu(p_1), \mu(p_2), ..., \mu(p_{|P|})\}$, $\mu : P \to \mathbb{Z}_{\geq 0}$ represents the distribution of tokens over the set of places. When it assigns a non-negative integer k to place p, we say that p is marked with k tokens. Pictorially, we place k black dots in place p. A Petri net with an initial marking, which represents the initial distribution of tokens, is a *Petri net system*.

Definition 2 (Petri net system). A Petri net system is a tuple $PNS = (P, T, F, \nu, M_0)$, where (P, T, F, ν) is a Petri net, and M_0 is its *initial marking*.

The initial marking of the Petri net M_0 can change into successor markings. These changes are described as *firing rules*. Such rules introduce a dynamic aspect to the Petri net by modifying its state, giving rise to the net behavior. A transition t is *enabled* when there are at least as many tokens as $\nu(p, t)$ in each input place $p \in {}^\bullet t$. An enabled transition can therefore *fire*. The number of tokens that are added to each output place after firing of t is defined as $\nu(t, p)$. The firing of a transition changes the current marking by subtracting $\nu(t, p)$ amount of tokens from each input place $p \in {}^\bullet t$ and adding $\nu(p, t)$ amount of tokens to each output place $p \in t^\bullet$, and hence, it moves the net from a marking M_{k-1} to a new marking M_k denoted as $M_{k-1} \xrightarrow{t_k} M_k$. A *firing sequence* of transitions $\sigma = t_1, t_2, ..., t_n$ changes the state of the Petri net at each firing: $M_0 \xrightarrow{t_1} M_1 \xrightarrow{t_2} ... \xrightarrow{t_n} M_n$. A marking M_k is *reachable* if there is a sequence σ such that $M_0 \xrightarrow{\sigma} M_k$ (i.e. from the initial marking to M_k).

Petri nets are classified according to several criteria, including cardinality and behavioral constraints. The Petri nets that represent the business processes addressed in this work have the following properties:

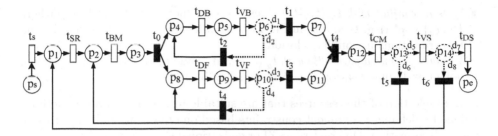

Fig. 2. Petri net model of the software development process

- They constitute a so-called *workflow net* [10], which means that they contain a starting place p_s such that $\bullet p_s = \emptyset$ and an ending place p_e such that $p_e^\bullet = \emptyset$; and they are *connected*, that is, every node in the Petri net is on the path from p_s to p_e.
- They are *1-safe*, which means that each place contains at most one token at any state (i.e. for any place $p \in P$, $0 \le \mu(p) \le 1$).
- They are *free-choice*, which implies that the choice between multiple transitions can never be influenced by the rest of the net (i.e. for any two different places $\{p_i, p_j\} \subseteq P$, $(p_i^\bullet \cap p_j^\bullet) = \emptyset$ or $p_i^\bullet = p_j^\bullet$),

Besides, the transitions of the Petri net represent process activities (tasks) and the places represent states of the business process. Some especial transitions, called *silent transitions* and colored in black, are incorporated for modeling specific process behavior. Therefore, to give more meaningful labels to the nodes of the Petri net, given the *alphabet* (set of labels) Σ, the function $\lambda : T \to \Sigma \cup \{\epsilon\}$ assigns to each transition $t \in T$ either a symbol from Σ or the empty string ϵ (for silent transitions). Figure 2 depicts the Petri net corresponding to the BPMN model in Fig. 1. For the purpose of this paper, dashed places denote *decision points*. A place p is a decision point if $|p^\bullet| > 1$. At run time, a non-deterministic decision is made on the output transitions $p^\bullet$ of a decision point p, and dashed arcs connected to these places denote different arcs that lead to different transitions (i.e. *decisions*) from which only one is to be fired during the execution of the system (e.g. decision d_1 in Fig. 1 corresponds to the flow arc (p_6, t_1) in Fig. 2).

Three types of ordering relations can be identified between transitions of a Petri net. Specifically, given two transitions $t_x, t_y \in T$ of a Petri net, then:

- t_x *directly precedes* t_y ($t_x \to t_y$) if the net contains a path with *exactly* two arcs (i.e. $(t_x, p_i) \cup (p_i, t_y) \subseteq F$) leading from t_x to t_y (e.g. t_{DB} and t_{VB} in Fig. 2). This precedence relation is reduced to cover activity transitions in the *direct activity precedence* relation ($t_x \xrightarrow{a} t_y$), such that $t_j \to t_{j+1} \to \dots \to t_n$, where only t_j and t_n are activity transitions (e.g. $t_{BM} \xrightarrow{a} t_{DB}$ and $t_{VB} \xrightarrow{a} t_{CM}$ in Fig. 2).

- t_x *is in conflict with* t_y $(t_x \# t_y)$ when the Petri net contains a place p where $\{t_x, t_y\} \subseteq p^\bullet$ (e.g. t_1 and t_2 in Fig. 2). A conflict-free Petri net system has no two transitions in conflict relation.
- t_x *can be executed parallelly with* t_y $(t_x \| t_y)$ if t_x and t_y are neither in preceding nor in excluding relation (e.g. t_{DB} and t_{DF} in Fig. 2).

The selection of the resources that are suitable to execute a process activity is done by defining assignment constraints based on organizational and process-related information. Different types of organizational structures lead to different organizational models [12]. In this work we assume an organizational structure based on roles following the Role-Based Access Control (RBAC) model [13].

Definition 3 (RBAC Model). An RBAC Model is a 6-tuple $O = (A, R, L, S_{AL}, S_{RL}, S_{LL})$, where:

- A is the set of *activities* that corresponds to the activity transitions in a $PNS = (P, T, F, \nu, M_0)$ that represents an executable business process, hence $A \subseteq T$,
- R is the set of *resources*,
- L is the set of *roles*,
- $S_{AL} \subseteq 2^{(A \times L)}$ is the set of activity-to-role assignment tuples specifying which activity can be executed by the resources associated with which role(s),
- $S_{RL} \subseteq 2^{(R \times L)}$ is the set of resource-to-role assignment tuples identifying the roles of a resource,

Table 1. RBAC model of the software company

$(a, l) \in S_{AL}$	$(r, l) \in S_{RL}$
{Study req., Manager}	{Amy, Manager}
{Study req., Coordinator}	{Oliver, Coordinator}
{Brief mile., Coordinator}	{Emma, Coordinator}
{Dev. backend, Coder}	{Glen, Software eng.}
{Dev. backend, Software eng.}	{Evan, Testing exp.}
{Verify backend, Testing exp.}	{Mia, Testing exp.}
{Verify backend, Software eng.}	{Drew, UI designer}
{Dev. frontend, UI designer}	{Ellen, UI designer}
{Dev. frontend, Coder}	{Jessie, Coder}
{Verify frontend, Testing exp.}	{Liam, Coder}
{Verify frontend, Software eng.}	{Alex, Coder}
{Check mile., Coordinator}	
{Validate syst., Manager}	
{Validate syst., Software eng.}	
{Deploy syst., Manager}	

- $S_{LL} \subseteq 2^{(L \times L)}$ is the set of role-to-role assignment tuples that creates a hierarchical structure. The symbol $\preceq$ indicates the ordering operator. If $l1 \preceq l2$, then $l1$ is referred to as the *senior* of $l2$ and therefore, the resources of $l1$ can also execute the activities assigned to $l2$. Conversely, $l2$ is the *junior* of $l1$. Note that for any $l_i \preceq l_{i+1} \preceq ... \preceq l_j$, $l_n \preceq l_m$ where $i \leq m \leq n \leq j$.

For example, given the RBAC model in Table 1 for our running example, the activity *Study requirements* must be performed by managers and/or coordinators. Therefore, Amy, Oliver and Emma might be involved in its execution. However, we also need to know how many resources of each type are required.

Definition 4 (Resource Requirement). A resource requirement $q \subseteq 2^{(L \times \mathbb{Z}_{\geq 0})}$ is a set of binary relations that represents the number of resources with role $l \in L$ required.

Definition 5 (Resource Requirement Set of an Activity). A resource requirement set of an activity $a \in A$ is $Q_a \subseteq 2^q$. Q_a contains all different resource requirement sets that allow the activity a to be executed.

For instance, given the requirements in Table 2, we now see that *Study requirements* can be executed by one manager *or* by a team of one manager and one coordinator.

On the other hand, data related to the execution of the process (e.g. when and by whom each activity instance is executed) is usually stored in event logs.

Definition 6 (Event Log). An event log is a 6-tuple $\mathcal{L} = (E, \varepsilon, \alpha, \varrho, \tau, \mathcal{T})$, where:

- $E = \{e_1, e_2, ..., e_n\}$ is the set of *events*,
- $\varepsilon : E \to \{start, complete\}$ assigns the event type to events,

Table 2. Activity and temporal requirement sets

a	q_a	$\delta(a, q_a)$
Study req.	$\{(Manager,1)\}$	20
Study req.	$\{(Manager,1),(Coordinator,1)\}$	15
Brief mile	$\{(Coordinator,1)\}$	1
Dev. backend	$\{(Software eng.,1),(Coder,2)\}$	10
Verify backend	$\{(Testing exp.,1),(Software eng.,1)\}$	4
Dev. frontend	$\{(UI designer,1),(Coder,1)\}$	12
Dev. frontend	$\{(UI designer,1),(Coder,2)\}$	8
Verify frontend	$\{(Testing exp.,1)\}$	2
Check mile	$\{(Coordinator,1)\}$	1
Validate syst.	$\{(Manager,1),(Software eng.,1)\}$	18
Deploy syst.	$\{(Manager,1)\}$	5

- $\varrho : E \to R$ assigns the resources to events,
- $\alpha : E \to A$ assigns the activities to events,
- $\tau : E \to \mathbb{Z}_{\geq 0}$ assigns a timestamp to events,
- $\mathcal{T} = \{\sigma_1, \sigma_2, ..., \sigma_n\}$ is the set of *traces* (i.e. process instances), where $\sigma_i \in E^*$ is a trace such that time is non-decreasing (i.e. $1 \leq j < k \leq |\sigma|$: $\tau(\sigma(j)) \leq \tau(\sigma(k))$).

The analysis of the event log can provide valuable information, such as the likelihood of different branches taken at the decision points.

Definition 7 (Temporal Requirement Function). The temporal requirement function of an activity requirement set $\delta : (A \times Q_a) \to \mathbb{Z}_{\geq 0}$ returns the duration required for an activity $a \in A$ to be executed with the requirement set $q_a \in Q_a$.

Table 2 indicates that the duration of *Study requirements* is 20 time units (TU) in case it is executed only by one manager, and 15 TU when it is allocated to a team with one manager and one coordinator. With this input data, resources can be allocated.

Definition 8 (Resource Allocation Problem). Given a conflict-free Petri net system PNS whose activities are in strict partial order (i.e. the precedence relation between activities is irreflexive, transitive and asymmetrical), an RBAC model O, an event log $\mathcal{L}$, one activity requirement set and an upper bound on the process makespan (or process cycle time) u, the computation of a feasible allocation of resources is $I \subseteq 2^{(2^R \times A \times U \times U)}$, where each activity $a \in A$ is assigned to several resources that comply with the activity's requirement set $\{r_1, r_2, ..., r_n\} \subseteq 2^R$, a start time $s_a \in U$ and a completion time $c_a \in U$.

Only one resource requirement set per activity needs to be satisfied for the execution of the activity. For the formal representation of the resource allocation problem in business processes, we define two binary variables o_{ras} and $o_{q_a a}$, and a starting time $s \in [0, u]$:

$$
o_{q_a a} = \begin{cases} 1, & \text{if the resource requirement set } q_a \in Q_a \text{ is selected for the execution} \\ & \text{of the activity } a, \\ 0, & \text{otherwise.} \end{cases}
$$

(1)

$$
o_{ras} = \begin{cases} 1, & \text{if the resource } r \text{ is allocated to the activity } a \text{ and } a \text{ starts at time } s, \\ 0, & \text{otherwise.} \end{cases}
$$

(2)

Note that if $o_{q_a a} = 1$, the completion of a occurs at time $s + \delta_{(a,q_a)}$. The objective function and the constraints of the model are as follows. For every $r_i, r_j \in R$; $a_m, a_n \in A$; $q_x \in Q_{a_m}$; $q_y \in Q_{a_n}$; $s_o, s_p \in U$; $U = \{0, 1, ..., u\}$; $u \in \mathbb{Z}_{>0}$ the objective is to

$$\text{minimize } max(\bigcup o_{q_{a_z} a_m} \cdot o_{r_i a_m s_o} \cdot (s_o + \delta_{(a_m, q_z)})) \qquad (3)$$

where

$$o_{q_x a_m} \cdot o_{q_y a_m} = 0 \qquad\qquad\qquad\qquad\qquad q_x \neq q_y \quad (4)$$

$$\sum o_{r_i a_m s_o} \cdot o_{q_x a_m} = n \cdot o_{q_x a_m} \quad (a_m, l) \in S_{AL}, \ (r_i, l) \in S_{RL}, \ (l, n) \in q_x \quad (5)$$

$$o_{r_i a_m s_o} . o_{r_j a_m s_p} = 0 \qquad\qquad\qquad\qquad\qquad s_o \neq s_p \quad (6)$$

$$o_{r_i a_m s_o} . (s_o + \delta_{(q_x, a_m)}) \leq o_{r_j a_n s_p} . (s_p) \qquad\qquad a_m \xrightarrow{a} a_n, \ o_{q_x a_m} = 1 \quad (7)$$

$$o_{r_i a_m s_o} . o_{r_i a_n s_p} = 0 \qquad\qquad a_m \| a_n, \ o_{q_x a_m} = 1, \ o_{q_y a_n} = 1,$$
$$[s_o, s_o + \delta_{(q_x, a_m)}] \cap [s_p, s_p + \delta_{(q_y, a_n)}] \neq \emptyset \quad (8)$$

As the set of activities that are not followed by another activity are the last activities to be executed, the objective function (3) minimizes the completion time of the activity that has the greatest value. Constraint (4) ensures there is only one activity requirement set selected for each activity. Constraint (5) indicates that an activity must be allocated as many resources as described in each of its potential activity requirement sets (i.e. roles of required resources and their cardinalities are satisfied). Constraint (6) restricts each activity to having only one start time. Constraint (7) secures that no activity is started until all its predecessors are completed. Constraint (8) enforces that no resource is allocated to any parallel pair of activities that have overlapping execution periods.

A *feasible allocation* occurs when I satisfies the constraints (4–8). By taking into account the minimization objective (3), the time optimal allocation I_{opt} is achieved.

4   History-Aware Dynamic Process Fragmentation

Our approach is based on two steps. First, we compute the probabilities of taking every single decision involved in the decision points of the process by analyzing previous executions stored in an event log. To do so, we define a decision probability function.

Definition 9 (Decision Probability Set Function). The decision probability set function $\Psi_{PN,\mathcal{L}} : (P \times T \times \mathbb{Z}_{>0}) \to 2^{\mathbb{R}_{[0,1]}}$ builds the set of probabilities of transition $t \in T$ (i.e. decision) being fired at a place $p \in P$ (i.e. decision point) for the nth time for each trace $\sigma \in \mathcal{T}$ in the event log $\mathcal{L}$, where $p \in P$, $n \in \mathbb{Z}_{>0}$, $P \in PNS$, $T \in PNS$ and $\mathcal{T} \in \mathcal{L}$. Let $\varphi : (\mathcal{T} \times T \times \mathbb{Z}_{\geq 1}) \to \mathbb{Z}_{\geq 0}$ be the function that returns the number of occurrences of $t \in T$ in $\sigma \in \mathcal{T}$ at its first i position, where:

$$\varphi(\sigma, t, i) = \sum_{j \in \{1..|\sigma|\}} \begin{cases} 1 & \text{for } \alpha(\sigma(j)) = t, \ j \leq i, \\ 0 & \text{otherwise.} \end{cases} \qquad (9)$$

then the decision probability set is calculated as follows:

$$\Psi_{PN,\mathcal{L}}(p,t,n) = \bigcup_{\sigma \in \mathcal{T}} \frac{\sum_{i \in \{1...|\sigma|\}} \begin{cases} 1 & \text{for } \alpha(\sigma(i)) = t', \ t' \in {}^{\bullet}p, \\ \phi(\sigma,t',i) = n, \ \alpha(\sigma(i+1)) = t, \\ 0 & \text{otherwise.} \end{cases}}{\sum_{i \in \{1...|\sigma|\}} \begin{cases} 1 & \text{for } \alpha(\sigma(i)) = t', \ t' \in {}^{\bullet}p, \\ \phi(\sigma,t',i) = n, \\ 0 & \text{otherwise.} \end{cases}} \tag{10}$$

Definition 10 (Decision Probability Function). The decision probability function $\psi_{PN,\mathcal{L}} : (P \times T \times \mathbb{Z}_{>0}) \to \mathbb{R}_{[0,1]}$ calculates the mean probability of a decision $t \in T$ being made at a decision point $p \in P$ for the nth time via returning the mean value of elements in the set that the function $\Psi_{PN,\mathcal{L}}$ builds.

$$\psi_{PN,\mathcal{L}}(p,t,n) = \frac{\sum_{x \in \Psi_{PN,\mathcal{L}}(p,t,n)} x}{|\Psi_{PN,\mathcal{L}}(p,t,n)|} \tag{11}$$

For instance, in our running example the option d_1: *backend change not required* (i.e. (p_6,t_1)) is selected in 20% of the cases and d_2: *backend change required* (i.e. (p_6,t_2)) in 80% of the cases at their first run. Table 3 shows the probabilities computed from the event log over the Petri net in Fig. 2.

Second and lastly, we select a fragment of the business process for resource allocation. The selection of the fragment depends on a *fragmentation threshold* and the computed decision probabilities. The higher the fragmentation threshold, the smaller the fragment of the process selected for allocation (thus hypothetically the lower the risk of an unfeasible allocation). A process fragment either starts at the starting place of the process and ends at a decision point, or starts at a decision point and ends at another decision point, or starts at a decision point and ends at the end of the process.

Table 3. Decision probabilities

Decision	(p,t)	$\psi_{PN,\mathcal{L}}(p,t,1)$	$\psi_{PN,\mathcal{L}}(p,t,2)$	$\psi_{PN,\mathcal{L}}(p,t,3)$
d_1	(p_6,t_1)	0.20	0.90	0.80
d_2	(p_6,t_2)	0.80	0.10	0.20
d_3	(p_{10},t_3)	0.55	0.40	0.70
d_4	(p_{10},t_4)	0.45	0.60	0.30
d_5	(p_{13},t_{VS})	0.80	0.50	0.80
d_6	(p_{13},t_5)	0.20	0.50	0.20
d_7	(p_{14},t_{DS})	0.90	0.55	n/a
d_8	(p_{14},t_6)	0.10	0.45	n/a

Definition 11 (Dynamic Process Fragmentation (DPF)). Given a Petri net system $PNS = (P, T, F, \nu, M_0)$ representing a business process, and a fragmentation threshold $\chi \in \mathbb{R}_{[0,1]}$, we generate a process fragment $\phi = (P', T', F', \Sigma, \lambda')$. The process fragmentation function $\gamma_{PN} : (M \times \chi \times \epsilon_f) \to 2^{F'}$ generates all the arcs of the process fragment ϕ with the help of the decision probability function $\psi_{PN,\mathcal{L}}$ and the state transition function Ω_{PN}. The initial value of the input ϵ_f is always 1 because the starting arc must be in ϕ. γ_{PN} copies the outgoing arcs at places where the given marking indicates a token while checking for the halting condition, which is bound to decision probability values computed by $\psi_{PN,\mathcal{L}}$, arc probability value ϵ_f, and the fragmentation threshold χ. Ω_{PN} copies the outgoing arcs at transitions while updating the marking M of the Petri net with respect to a given enabled transition $t \in T$ and returning the updated marking back to γ_{PN}. The copy function $\kappa : (P \cup T) \to (P' \cup T')$ copies the nodes of Petri net. The counting function $\theta : (T \times \Sigma) \to \mathbb{Z}_{\geq 0}$ counts the occurrences of a transition $t \in T$ in a firing sequence $\sigma \in \Sigma$.

$$\gamma_{PN}(M, \chi, \epsilon_f)$$
$$= \bigcup \begin{cases} (\kappa(p), \kappa(t)) \cup \Omega(t, M, \epsilon_f) & \mu(p) = 1, \ |p^\bullet| = 1, \ t \in p^\bullet, \\ (\kappa(p), \kappa(t)) \cup \Omega(t, M, \epsilon_f \cdot \psi_{PN,\mathcal{L}}(p, t, j)) & \mu(p) = 1, \ |p^\bullet| > 1, \ t \in p^\bullet, \\ & \theta(t, \sigma) = i, \ j = i + 1, \\ & \epsilon_f \cdot \psi_{PN,\mathcal{L}}(p, t, j) \geq \chi, \\ \emptyset & \text{otherwise.} \end{cases}$$

$$(12)$$

$$\Omega_{PN}(t, M, \epsilon_f) = \begin{cases} \bigcup_{p \in t^\bullet} (\kappa(t), \kappa(p)) \cup \gamma_{PN}(M', \epsilon_f) & \forall p' \in {}^\bullet t, \mu(p') = 1, \\ & M \xrightarrow{t} M', \\ \emptyset & \text{otherwise.} \end{cases}$$

$$(13)$$

P', T' and F' are defined as follows:

- $F' \subseteq (P' \times T') \cup (T' \times P')$, $\kappa(p) \in P'$, $\kappa(t) \in T'$,
- $P \subseteq P'$ and $T \subseteq T'$,
- $\forall p' \in P'$, $|p'^\bullet| = 1$ and ϕ is acyclic.

ϕ may contain multiple copies of the nodes (places and transitions) in the original Petri net system PNS when χ has a value closer to the lower limit 0 and the given PNS contains loops. In such a scenario, the fragmentation may include the same looping decision multiple times. Figure 3 shows resource allocations with DPF on the software development process (cf. Fig. 2) using the resources described in Tables 1 and 2 at run time with $\chi = 0.65$. After the process fragment ϕ_1 is generated and the resources are allocated, the process execution starts. In ϕ_1 the looping decision d_2 is taken once and the fragment ends at p_7 and p_{10}. This indicates that two informed assumptions are made at the decision point p_6 (i.e. $\psi_{PN,\mathcal{L}}(p_6, t_2, 1) \cdot \psi_{PN,\mathcal{L}}(p_6, t_1, 2) \geq \chi$). At the first ending place p_{10}, neither of the decision probabilities is higher than χ (i.e. $\psi_{PN,\mathcal{L}}(p_{10}, t_3, 1)$

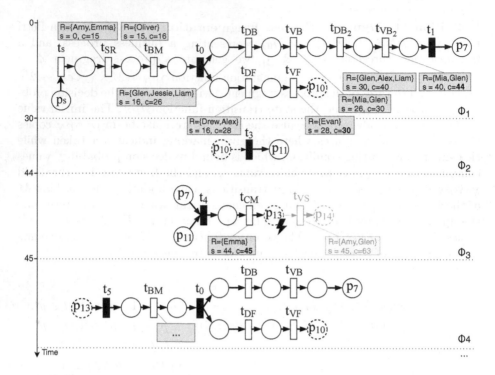

Fig. 3. Process fragments in run-time with a fragmentation threshold of 0.65

is 0.55 and $\psi_{PN,\mathcal{L}}(p_{10}, t_4, 1)$ is 0.45), hence this branch ends there. The DPF also ends at p_7 owing to the fact that the execution of the other parallel branch has not finished and thus t_4 cannot be enabled at 30 TU. When *Evan* finishes executing *Verify frontend* at 30 TU, the decision d_3 is adopted and the DPF generates the second process fragment ϕ_2. This fragment ends at p_{11} due to the same reason of p_7. At 44 TU, the execution of both parallel branches is finished and the DPF generates the third process fragment ϕ_3, which ends at p_{14}. After the activity *Check Milestone* is executed by *Emma*, d_6 is adopted at run time instead of the assumed decision d_5 during the DPF. This disruption causes the DPF to generate ϕ_4 starting from the decision point p_{13} towards the adopted decision d_6. This procedure continues until the process execution ends.

5   Evaluation

To test the effectiveness of our approach, we have developed a proof-of-concept implementation that lies on the system architecture illustrated in Fig. 4[2]. The components providing input data for our approach are a *Data Repository*, which

---

[2] With the Fundamental Modeling Concepts (FMC) notation (www.fmc-modeling. org/).

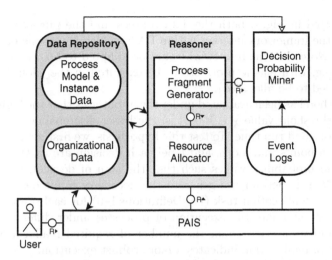

Fig. 4. History-aware Dynamic Process Fragmentation framework

contains design-time process and organizational data; and *Event logs*, which store traces of past process executions. The other components address the process fragmentation and resource allocation problems and have been implemented as explained next.

Decision Probability Miner. This component takes over the implementation of the decision probability function ψ (cf. Eq. 11 in Definition 10). It receives a request from the Process Fragment Generator specifying the decision points for which the probability values need to be computed. It takes the process model and the event log as input to derive probability values at these decision points.

Process Fragment Generator. This component is the implementation of the κ, Ω and γ functions described in Definition 11. It receives from the PAIS a request describing the current marking of the Petri net system and the fragmentation threshold value χ, selects an appropriate process fragment ϕ and sends a request to the Resource Allocator for performing the allocation of resources on it. Once receiving the response back from the allocator, it returns the optimal allocation I_{opt} back to the PAIS.

Resource Allocator. This component performs the resource allocation mechanism as described in Definition 8. It receives a request from the Process Fragment Generator with the process fragment to which the resources are to be allocated. All the other necessary knowledge is retrieved from the Data Repository.

The Resource Allocator and Process Fragment Generator components have been implemented using ASP [7], a declarative (logic-programming-style) paradigm for solving combinatorial search problems. We omit details here due to space limitations but refer to [14] for a brief introduction to ASP and a description of how to encode the resource allocation problem.

As depicted in Fig. 4, both the data sources and the purpose-specific components of the framework interact with a PAIS, which is responsible for process enactment. Note that the framework could be adapted to be used in other environments (e.g. with elastic processes to be executed in the Cloud where cloud resources need to be allocated).

Our method has been evaluated under the hypothesis that the higher the fragmentation threshold value $\chi \in \mathbb{R}_{[0,1]}$ is, the lesser discrepancy occurs between the allocations and run time. To test this hypothesis, we first generate Petri nets with decision points and loops, and label each decision arc (p, t) where $|p^\bullet| > 1$ with random probability values such that the sum of decision probabilities of every $p \in {}^\bullet t$ is 1. Second, we generate the necessary input data for performing the resource allocation task (i.e. Definitions 1–6) for each Petri net system. Afterwards, we simulate the execution of processes under different fragmentation threshold values and count the number of required reallocations where a low number of reallocation indicates a more robust execution.

We generate the Petri nets using the *Generate block-structured stochastic Petri net* plug-in [15] of the process mining tool ProM [16]. This generator performs a series of random structured insertion operations of new control-flow constructs resulting in a random Petri net given a number of transitions and a degree of parallelism, exclusiveness and cyclicity between the integer values 0 and

Table 4. Properties of Petri net instances

id_{PN}	deg_{par}	deg_{exc}	deg_{cyc}	sym	id_{PN}	deg_{par}	deg_{exc}	deg_{cyc}	sym
1	45	45	45	×	1	75	45	45	λ
2	45	75	45	+	1	75	75	45	≺
3	45	45	75	•	1	75	45	75	≻
4	45	75	75	⅄	1	75	75	75	★

Table 5. Properties of problem instances

id_i	id_{PN}	χ	id_i	id_{PN}	χ	id_i	id_{PN}	χ	id_i	id_{PN}	χ
1	1	0.1	11	3	0.1	21	5	0.1	31	7	0.1
2	1	0.25	12	3	0.25	22	5	0.25	32	7	0.25
3	1	0.5	13	3	0.5	23	5	0.5	33	7	0.5
4	1	0.75	14	3	0.75	24	5	0.75	34	7	0.75
5	1	0.9	15	3	0.9	25	5	0.9	35	7	0.9
6	2	0.1	16	4	0.1	26	6	0.1	36	8	0.1
7	2	0.25	17	4	0.25	27	6	0.25	37	8	0.25
8	2	0.5	18	4	0.5	28	6	0.5	38	8	0.5
9	2	0.75	19	4	0.75	29	6	0.75	39	8	0.75
10	2	0.9	20	4	0.9	30	6	0.9	40	8	0.9

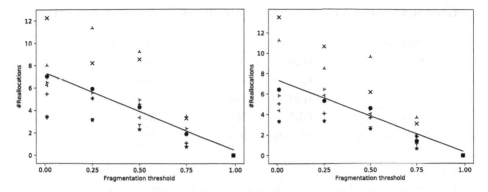

Fig. 5. The fragmentation threshold χ versus the runtime feasibility of allocations in two different runs

100. For our evaluation, we generated 8 Petri nets with 30 activity transitions using this Petri net generator and the properties of the problem instances created are summarized in Table 4. In this table, id_{PN} is the identifier of each different Petri net; deg_{par}, deg_{exc} and deg_{cyc} are the input parameters for adjusting the level of parallelism, exclusiveness and cyclicity; and sym is the symbol we use to depict the simulation behavior of Petri nets in Fig. 5. We summarize the properties of problem instances in Table 3 where id_i is the problem instance identifier; id_{PN} is the identifier of the Petri net used (cf. Table 4); and χ is the fragmentation threshold value used in the simulation environment while dynamically fragmenting the nets and performing the allocation of resources (cf. Table 5).

Figure 5 illustrates two similar results from different simulation runs. The x axis is the fragmentation threshold and the y axis is the number of calls for the resource reallocation mechanism during simulation to be able to repair the existing allocations due to a different decision path is taken at run time than assumed at DPF. The trend lines are almost parallel and they support our hypothesis.

Our DPF implementation has been run on an Ubuntu Linux server (64 bit) with a 16 core 2.40 GHz Intel Xeon Processor and 64 GB of RAM. DPF calls consistently took less than a minute and consumed less than 1 GB of memory given Petri nets in Table 4. Our ASP encoding (accompanied with a description) of the Process Fragment Generator, the simulation environment (with visualizations as in Fig. 5) in Python and the problem instances are available at https:// urban.ai.wu.ac.at/~havur/dpf/.

6   Related Work

We next summarize the most representative approaches related to resource allocation in several domains. The evaluation criteria used to compare the approaches include: (i) the risk taken for resource allocation; (ii) whether historical data from event logs is used to more accurately deal with uncertainty;

Table 6. Characteristics of current resource allocation and scheduling methods

Approach	Risk taken	History-aware?	Optimal solution?
[17]	High	N.A.	No
[2,3]	Low	N.A.	Yes
[4,18]	High	No	No
[5,14]	High	No	Yes
DPF (our approach)	Flexible	Yes	Yes

and (iii) whether optimization functions for performance metrics are aimed for or, on the contrary, finding a feasible allocation for the entire process suffices. The results are collected in Table 6, where *N.A.* indicates that the criterion is non-applicable due to the characteristics of the approach.

Scheduling is concerned with the optimal allocation of scarce resources to tasks over time [19]. The problem has been addressed in several domains, especially in Operations Research, where tasks are typically referred to as "operations" or "steps of a job". In such a domain, surgery scheduling problems, and more specifically the operating room scheduling problem, have been extensively investigated. The most expressive approach in this domain was recently developed by Riise et al. [17]. They propose a model for a "generalised operational surgery scheduling problem" (GOSSP) that can express a wide range of real world surgery scheduling problems as an extension of the multi-mode resource-constrained project scheduling problem with generalized precedence relations (MRCPSP-GPR). Similarly to other approaches in that field, resource allocation is addressed as a two-step problem (assignment and scheduling), and the objective is to minimize the makespan when scheduling several projects (which can contain parallelism but no decision points) at the same time. As an outcome, oftentimes only some projects might be scheduled: those for which all tasks can be allocated. Consequently, feasibility is actually pursued. Besides the surgery scheduling problems, project scheduling in general has been widely investigated [20,21]. However, due to the inherent differences between projects and business processes (e.g. projects are typically defined to be executed only once and decision points are missing), the problem is approached differently.

In the Business Process Management (BPM) domain, the state-of-the-art on resource allocation does not reach the maturity level of other domains despite the acknowledged importance of the problem [22]. Due to the computational cost that it entails, the existing techniques tend to search either for a feasible solution without applying optimizations [4], or for a local optimal using a greedy approach that might find a feasible but not necessarily a global optimal solution [2]. A framework is proposed in [23] to specify resource requirements where allocation services are independent of respective process models. Otherwise, the existing work has mostly relied on Petri nets. Van der Aalst [2] introduced a timed Petri net based scheduling approach considering activities, resources and temporal constraints. However, modeling this information for multiple process instances leads to very large Petri nets. Rozinat et al. [3] used Coloured Petri nets (CPNs) to overcome the problems encountered in timed Petri nets. In CPNs, classes and guards can be specified to define any kind of constraint. However, the approach is greedy such that resources are allocated to activities as soon as they are available. This may make the allocation problem unsatisfiable or incur in a longer makespan and cost. Several attempts have also been done to implement the problem as a constraint satisfaction problem, considering the business process as a whole for the allocation. For instance, Senkul and Toroslu [4] developed an architecture to specify resource allocation constraints and a Constraint Programming (CP) approach to schedule a workflow according to the constraints defined for the tasks. They aimed at obtaining a feasible rather than an optimal solution, and historical data from previous executions was disregarded. Later on, Heinz and Beck [18] demonstrated that models such as Constraint Integer Programming (CIP) outperform the standard CP formulations. Loops were disregarded in all these approaches. Global optimization is possible at a reasonable computational cost even with complex settings (including loops) using ASP [5,14]. However, the approaches developed with this formalism had no far considered historical data in the allocations. The dynamic process fragmentation (DPF) approach presented in this paper bridges the gap currently existing in the BPM domain and advances the state-of-the-art towards more realistic resource allocations.

7   Conclusions and Future Work

From this work we conclude that it is possible to allocate resources to process activities taking into account past execution data and the influence of uncertainty in the degree of risk taken when making decisions. Our approach for dynamic process fragmentation allows for a higher flexibility that helps to reduce the reallocation efforts. Furthermore, note that depending on the characteristics of the business process as well as the specific historical values available, the approach can behave as an offline, an online or a *quasi-online* scheduling approach [6]. Future work involves the implementation and testing of the approach in a real setting in connection with a PAIS.

References

1. Russell, N., van der Aalst, W.M.P., ter Hofstede, A.H.M., Edmond, D.: Workflow resource patterns: identification, representation and tool support. In: Pastor, O., Falcão e Cunha, J. (eds.) CAiSE 2005. LNCS, vol. 3520, pp. 216–232. Springer, Heidelberg (2005). https://doi.org/10.1007/11431855_16
2. van der Aalst, W.: Petri net based scheduling. Oper. Res. Spektrum 18(4), 219–229 (1996)
3. Rozinat, A., Mans, R.S.: Mining CPN models: discovering process models with data from event logs. In: Workshop and Tutorial on Practical Use of Coloured Petri Nets and the CPN, pp. 57–76 (2006)

4. Senkul, P., Toroslu, I.H.: An architecture for workflow scheduling under resource allocation constraints. Inf. Syst. **30**, 399–422 (2005)
5. Havur, G., Cabanillas, C., Mendling, J., Polleres, A.: Automated resource allocation in business processes with answer set programming. In: Reichert, M., Reijers, H.A. (eds.) BPM 2015. LNBIP, vol. 256, pp. 191–203. Springer, Cham (2016). https://doi.org/10.1007/978-3-319-42887-1_16
6. Sabuncuoglu, I., Goren, S.: Hedging production schedules against uncertainty in manufacturing environment with a review of robustness and stability research. Int. J. Comput. Integr. Manuf. **22**(2), 138–157 (2009)
7. Gebser, M., Kaminski, R., Kaufmann, B., Schaub, T.: Answer Set Solving in Practice. Synthesis Lectures on Artificial Intelligence and Machine Learning. Morgan & Claypool Publishers, san Rafael (2012)
8. OMG: BPMN 2.0. Recommendation, OMG (2011)
9. Popova-Zeugmann, L.: Time Petri nets. In: Popova-Zeugmann, L. (ed.) Time and Petri Nets, pp. 139–140. Springer, Heidelberg (2013). https://doi.org/10.1007/978-3-642-41115-1_4
10. van der Aalst, W.: Structural characterizations of sound workflow nets. Department of Mathematics & Computing Science, Eindhoven University of Technology (1996)
11. Lohmann, N., Verbeek, E., Dijkman, R.: Petri net transformations for business processes – a survey. In: Jensen, K., van der Aalst, W.M.P. (eds.) Transactions on Petri Nets and Other Models of Concurrency II. LNCS, vol. 5460, pp. 46–63. Springer, Heidelberg (2009). https://doi.org/10.1007/978-3-642-00899-3_3
12. Horling, B., Lesser, V.: A survey of multi-agent organizational paradigms. Knowl. Eng. Rev. **19**(4), 281–316 (2004)
13. Colantonio, A., Di Pietro, R., Ocello, A., Verde, N.V.: A formal framework to elicit roles with business meaning in RBAC systems. In: ACM Symposium on Access Control Models and Technologies (SACMAT), pp. 85–94. ACM (2009)
14. Havur, G., Cabanillas, C., Mendling, J., Polleres, A.: Resource allocation with dependencies in business process management systems. In: La Rosa, M., Loos, P., Pastor, O. (eds.) BPM 2016. LNBIP, vol. 260, pp. 3–19. Springer, Cham (2016). https://doi.org/10.1007/978-3-319-45468-9_1
15. Rogge-Solti, A.: Block-structured stochastic Petri net generator (ProM plug-in) (2014). http://www.promtools.org/. Accessed 01 Jan 2019
16. van der Aalst, W.M.P.: Process Mining - Data Science in Action. Springer, Heidelberg (2016). https://doi.org/10.1007/978-3-662-49851-4
17. Riise, A., Mannino, C., Burke, E.K.: Modelling and solving generalised operational surgery scheduling problems. Comput. Oper. Res. **66**, 1–11 (2016)
18. Heinz, S., Beck, C.: Solving resource allocation/scheduling problems with constraint integer programming. In: Constraint Satisfaction Techniques for Planning and Scheduling Problems (COPLAS), pp. 23–30 (2011)
19. Lawler, E.L., Lenstra, J.K., Kan, A.H.R., Shmoys, D.B.: Sequencing and scheduling: algorithms and complexity. In: Logistics of Production and Inventory. Handbooks in Operations Research and Management Science, vol. 4, pp. 445–522. Elsevier (1993)
20. Weglarz, J.: Project scheduling with continuously-divisible, doubly constrained resources. Manag. Sci. **27**(9), 1040–1053 (1981)
21. Hendriks, M., Voeten, B., Kroep, L.: Human resource allocation in a multi-project R&D environment: resource capacity allocation and project portfolio planning in practice. Int. J. Proj. Manag. **17**(3), 181–188 (1999)

22. Arias, M., Rojas, E., Munoz-Gama, J., Sepúlveda, M.: A framework for recommending resource allocation based on process mining. In: Reichert, M., Reijers, H.A. (eds.) BPM 2015. LNBIP, vol. 256, pp. 458–470. Springer, Cham (2016). https://doi.org/10.1007/978-3-319-42887-1_37

23. Ihde, S., Pufahl, L., Lin, M.-B., Goel, A., Weske, M.: Optimized resource allocations in business process models. In: Hildebrandt, T., van Dongen, B., Röglinger, M., Mendling, J. (eds.) Business Process Management Forum, pp. 55–71. Springer, Cham (2019). https://doi.org/10.1007/978-3-030-26643-1_4

Modeling Conversational Agents for Service Systems

Renuka Sindhgatta[✉], Alistair Barros, and Alireza Nili

Queensland University of Technology, Brisbane, Australia
{renuka.sr,alistair.barros,a.nili}@qut.edu.au

Abstract. Service providers are increasingly exploring the use of conversational agents (CA) or dialogue based systems to support end customers, as a CA promises natural method for users to interact and a convenient channel for customer service. Commercial CAs, excel in addressing specific tasks or functions such as searching for restaurants, providing location directions, or scheduling meetings, with small variations in the user request. Designing a CA for a more complex service system, requires sufficient knowledge of its services such as the service capabilities, their constraints, and effects, in addition to understanding user utterances. The design of a CA is typically an independent activity and its linkages to the service system it supports are left to the designers. In this paper, we study existing work with respect to text-based CAs and identify the conceptual elements of a CA. Further, a linkage between the model elements of a CA and service model of the service system it supports is established and presented. We show that interesting insights can be derived from the linkages, that can be useful to CA designers.

Keywords: Conversational agent · Services system ·
Unified service description language

1 Introduction

Conversational agent (CA) as the name suggests, is a software system that mimics human conversation and communicates with users in natural language. *Task-oriented dialogue system* is a type of CA that helps users accomplish tasks by supporting them with conversations (and is often referred to as chatbot). We focus on task-oriented dialogue systems in this work and refer to these systems as CAs in the rest of this paper. Recent success of commercial CAs, as personal assistants to accomplish small domain oriented tasks, has resulted in several organizations exploring use of CAs as one of their customer service support channels. Text-based CAs are being deployed by several service providers including public and government services[1]. The complementary benefit of cost effectiveness to service providers and accessibility to customers encourages the use of CAs for

---

[1] https://www.ava.gov.sg/, https://www.ato.gov.au/.

© Springer Nature Switzerland AG 2019
H. Panetto et al. (Eds.): OTM 2019, LNCS 11877, pp. 552–560, 2019.
https://doi.org/10.1007/978-3-030-33246-4_34

service support. However, there have been limited studies on designing CAs that provide customer support for these large service systems.

Existing research on CA, has focused on problems related to understanding natural language and orchestrating user conversations [1,2]. Studies on dialogue management focus on specific tasks or restricted topics such as flight reservation, restaurant reservation, scheduling meetings [3,4], or make no assumptions of the domain and use existing user dialogues for learning [5]. The design of a CA supporting a service system needs to be congruous with the multiple services and functions of the service system. State of the art approach to designing a CA focuses on identifying user intentions, user inputs, CA responses, and orchestration of the dialogue. The underlying linkage of the CA design with the service system is often handled by the developers of the CA [6] and has had limited attention. Nonetheless, modeling the CA with knowledge of service capabilities is crucial to improve its ability to provide information about service functions, and service inputs.

Unified service description language (USDL) [7,8] models business services of service systems, and covers human oriented services as well as automated services. There are multiple modules of USDL covering description of multiple facets of services such as service level agreements, pricing, and security. Much of the capabilities of services are captured by the functional and behavioral models. In this work, we use core elements of USDL that describe the operational aspects of a service system, and hence support USDL 3.0 and USDL 4.0. USDL is used as it describes the business and operational services of a service system.

The goal of this paper is to connect the conceptual model of a CA with the service model of the underlying service system it supports. First, we explore current literature on dialogue systems and capture the conceptual model of a CA. Next, we propose to capture the connection between the CA conceptual model and service model that helps provide novel insights, while keeping the original models independent. USDL is used to describe services. We show some interesting insights can be drawn of these connections that could be useful to the CA designers. In this work, we do not focus on challenges of understanding user utterances which is a run time challenge of developing a CA.

Table 1. Examples of types of questions to service agent on social support.

#	Questions posed by customers	Service system artefact
1	Is there any payment available for a [x] year old who is doing part-time [study] and part-time work?	Service input parameters
2	Can I receive study allowance while studying a major like master of arts?	Service input parameters
3	I'm on job seeker allowance. I'm going to study and apply for study allowance. Do I need to look for job?	Service dependencies and rules
4.	I cannot find [X] certificate on the website via my phone. How can I fill it?	IT application support

2   Motivating Example

Consider an e-government service system providing social support to its residents. Service system is a service oriented system with configurations of people, technologies, organizations, and information that creates and delivers services to its stakeholders [9]. The example is representative of a real-world public service support system. For the purpose of illustration, we consider the service system providing job seeker payment service and study payment service. Each service has eligibility criteria and payment entitlement (welfare amount) that depends on various factors related to customer circumstances. The CA for such a service system provides support to customer on queries associated to these services. In Table 1, user queries that initiate conversations are presented. These user queries reveal capabilities required by the CA: (i) access to knowledge of service system information or artefacts, (ii) support significantly distinct user tasks, and (iii) handle varying user inputs from being open ended with limited information to being specific.

For conducting a useful conversation, the CA requires knowledge of the service system and goes beyond understanding user responses in natural language. The knowledge of services comprises of information on service conditions, service inputs, the service outcome and service business rules. As design of the CA and service model describing the service system are conceived separately, to foster service system-aware CA modeling, it is necessary to capture the connection between the CA and the underlying service system it supports.

3   Conceptual Model

In this section, we introduce four core components of a text-based CA. One cycle through these components is one dialogue *turn*, i.e. an utterance from the user and the response from the CA:

Natural Language Understanding: parses the user's utterance as input and extracts (i) **user intent** reflecting the task (or goal) the user wants to accomplish using the CA, and (ii) the **slot** attributes and their values, that the user provides with respect to the intent [1]. A slot is an **informable slot**, if it is used to provide input information required for the task completion. A slot is a **requestable slot** when used as a response to give out information. The user intent is detected at each turn as the user could change the intent at any turn in the dialogue. All slots are by default requestable slots [10]. In addition, recent dialogue systems further identify the kind of action being performed by the user or **dialogue act**. A "dialogue act [is] a tag which represents the interactive function of the utterance" [6]. Examples of dialogue act are *confirming, informing, thanking, requesting* or others that could be task specific.

Definition 1 (Parsed Utterance). *Given a user utterance $\mathcal{U}_t$, at turn t, the NLU component generates a tuple $\mathcal{PU}_t$, containing zero or more user intents, one or more dialogue acts and zero or more slot attributes and values. The tuple*

$\mathcal{PU}_t$ *is defined as follows:*

$$\mathcal{PU}_t = \langle \mathcal{I}_t, \mathcal{DA}_t, \mathcal{A}_t \rangle,$$

where:

$\mathcal{I}_t$ is set of intents, $i \in \mathcal{I}$ or a $\emptyset$, $\mathcal{DA}_t$ consists one or more dialogue acts $d_{act} \in \mathcal{DA}$, and $\mathcal{A}_t$ is $\emptyset$ or has a set of slot, its value and type tuple $\langle attr, val, type \rangle \in \mathcal{A}$. These slots are required to fulfill the user intent.

Dialogue State Tracker (DST): stores the state of the dialogue that spans multiple turns. The input to the DST is $\mathcal{PU}_t$ and previous dialogue state $\mathcal{DST}_{t-1}$. The dialogue state $\mathcal{DST}_t$ at turn t would be a tuple of a set intents based on all intents so far $\mathcal{IS}_t$, one or more relevant dialogue acts processed through all the turns $\mathcal{DAS}_t$, and all slot values provided till the current turn $\mathcal{AS}_t$.

$$\mathcal{DST}_t = \langle \mathcal{IS}_t, \mathcal{DAS}_t, \mathcal{AS}_t \rangle$$

Dialogue Manager (DM): determines the action to be taken based on $\mathcal{DST}_t$ at turn t. It could determine the next informable slot that the user needs to provide, respond with a requestable slot value, or identify the end of the conversation and conclude.

Natural Language Generation (NLG): generates the response. A simple template-based generation is widely used in existing commercial dialogue systems.

3.1   Service Model

We discuss two core modules and the subset of the meta-models elements that are relevant for CA:

Functional Service Model: Service is a key concrete concept of the service system. Service has a set of capabilities that are provided to the customer. Service capabilities are exposed through one or more **Function(s)** which can be performed manually or in an automated manner. A Function may need one or more input **Parameters** and may result in some output Parameters. Functions comprise of pre-conditions and post-conditions (effects). A **Condition** pair indicates what must be true before the function is called and what will be true when the function finishes its work. Function can have **subFunctions**. A **Service-Bundle** provides parts (or grouping) of services based on one or more grouping constraints and there can be **Dependency** between services expressed by a dependency type such as requires, includes, enhances and so on.

Service Interaction Model: The interaction model captures the behavioral aspect of services. Service execution is broken down into a sequence of function executions. The interaction model can be described using Business Process Modeling Notation (BPMN) [7]. Hence, the service interaction model captures the dependencies between the service functions during the execution of the service.

4   Linking Service Model and CA Conceptual Model

In this section, we propose a binding or mapping that links the CA conceptual model and the service model. Two key conceptual model elements for a CA: intents and slots are linked to the service model. The links are established using an *Intent Map* and a *Slot Map* during the design of the CA.

Definition 2 (Intent Map). *Given a set of intents $\mathcal{I}$, and an intent, $i \in \mathcal{I}$, its Intent Map $IMap_i$ is a set of tuples $\{t_1, t_2, \ldots, t_n\}$, where each tuple t_k denotes the service, the service function, and service dependencies. The tuple t_k is defined as follows:*

$$t_k = \langle s_k, f_k, As_{set_k} \rangle,$$

where:

s_k is the service, f_k is the service capability or function associated to the service. A single CA intent can be linked to multiple services and functions and hence $IMap_i$ is a set of tuples. As an example, the intent *check_eligibility* can be supported by job seeker payment service as well as study allowance service.

Associated service $s_j \in As_{set_k}$ is a service that has an association relation with s_k and is necessary to accomplish the intent. $As_{set_k} = \emptyset$, if the intent or service function does not have any association. An association relation exists between services, when services are grouped together and offered as a part of the same service bundle. A service bundle could lead to an intent involving multiple services (example: user query 3 of Table 1). In the example scenario, "do I need to look for a job once I apply for study allowance", the function of 'job search' is associated to the job seeker payment service, while the user intent or query is related to the 'study payment service'. Intent map can be used to specify additional intents where the capabilities belong to the associated service $s_j \in As_{set_k}$, but need to be supported in the context of the service s_k.

Definition 3 (Slot Map). *Given an attribute attr of the slot slt $\in \mathcal{A}$, its Slot Map $SMap_j$ is a set of tuples $\{q_1, q_2, \ldots, q_m\}$, where each tuple q_k denotes a parameter, function and a set of pre-conditions or effects associated to the parameter. The tuple q_k is defined as follows:*

$$q_k = \langle p_k, f_k, \text{condition}_{set_k} \rangle,$$

where:

p_k is the input or output parameter, f_k is the function, and $condition_{set_k}$ is the set of conditions that correspond to the the function f_k, and the parameter p_k. A slot has multiple tuples as it can be mapped to multiple functions requiring the same input parameter or providing the same output. A parameter p_k can be of a primitive type or a custom data type with a set of attributes $\{attr_1, \ldots, attr_A\}$. If it is a primitive type then the slot attribute is mapped directly to the parameter. Instead, if a specific attribute of p_k is associated with the slot attribute, we explicitly specify it by $p_k(attr_l)$. The condition set, $condition_{set_k} = \emptyset$, if there are no function pre-conditions or effects corresponding to the slot.

Example: Figure 1 presents a graphical representation of the Intent Map and Slot Map. The example presents two services that have eligibility requirements: Study allowance service and Job seeker payment service. The services, functions, parameters and conditions are presented. The Intent Map for the intent 'check eligibility' is linked to two services and their functions. The Slot Map for the slot 'Age' is linked to the parameter age in multiple functions and their relevant conditions. Two example user utterances illustrate the use of Intent map and Slot map. In the *Utterance 1*, the service and the intent are specified by the user and hence, from the Intent map ($IMap_{chk\_eligibility}$), the tuple t_k corresponding to the service $s_{study\_allowance}$ is chosen and the service function $f_{assess\_eligibility}$ is available. The set of Slot Map(s) linked to the service function $\{q_{r,j}|f_{r,j} = f_{assess\_eligibility}\}$ provides the designer an indication of the number parameters (or slots) required to support the intent. The second example, *Utterance 2*, has the intent and slot as input with and no service information. The intersection of n functions linked to the Intent Map, $IMap_i$, and m functions linked to Slot Map $SMap_j$, ($\bigcup_{k=1,i}^{n} f_{k,i} \cap \bigcup_{l=1,j}^{m} f_{l,j}$), form the set of functions from which the CA needs to choose at run-time. The higher the cardinality of the set of functions, more turns would be required to identify the relevant service, and functions.

4.1   Insights from the Linkages

In this section, we discuss insights that can be identified using the Intent Map and the Slot Map, during the design of a CA.

Service Functions and Intents: Service functions are capabilities used by the end user and hence the conversations are focused on these functions. Not all service functions would be suitable for conversational support. The Intent

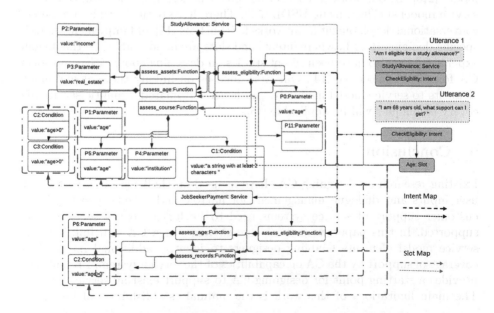

Fig. 1. Linking Service Model and CA Model elements

map allows the designers to specify service functions supported by the CA, thus drawing insight on the portion of services and capabilities with conversational support. An intent may be linked to different services, if similar tasks need to be accomplished by different services. The Intent Map allows designers to identify intents mapped to multiple service functions ($\bigcup_{k=1}^{n} f_{k,i}$).

Service Function Dependencies: The service interaction model of USDL describes sequences of service function execution. By linking the intents to service functions, an ordering of intents can be inferred. Existing models of CA do not consider ordering of intents. For example if 'booking flight' for corporate travel requires 'validation of visa', a user requesting a 'booking of flight' to a CA, will first need to be requested for inputs on 'validation of visa'. Intent dependencies can be identified using Intent Map.

Service Bundle Dependencies: Service bundles of USDL provide description of services grouped together. The As_{set} of the intent map captures services bundled together. The intents related to the service bundle may be requested in the context of the associated services. Additional intents would be added to services as illustrated in Sect. 4.

5   Related Work

Research efforts on building dialogue systems, have focused on tackling the problem of NLU components. Traditional approaches have been reliable for slot-filling [4]. Most of these research studies use a small hand-crafted ontology for defining slots and intents [3,10]. End-to-end dialogue systems, based on neural networks, use existing dialogue conversations and require no conceptual model [2,5]. In our work, a conceptual model is designed and is linked to the service model specified using USDL [7,8]. There have been multiple commercial conversational development frameworks for chatbots [11] and implementations in specific domains [12,13], where intents and slots are hand-crafted by the domain experts. There also have been recent studies on designing cooperative and social CA for customer service [14]. Our work focuses on linking the dialogue model elements to service model manually, and hence automated semantic service discovery techniques will be applicable [15].

6   Conclusion

Existing research on designing CAs have focused on challenges related to noisy user inputs and dialogue management for narrow and specific tasks. CAs for customer support of service systems need to be linked to the services being supported. In this paper we look at core elements of a CA and link it to the service model elements enabling designers to identify additional intents, and coverage of support by the CA on capabilities of the service system. Present work provides a starting point for designing CA to support existing service systems. The main limitations of this work is the manual establishment of linkage by the designer of the CA system. Automatically linking elements of CA model to the services and their functions using automated semantic service discovery techniques will be a future direction of our work. Further, we will focus on using cooperative principle [16] and use the social response theory [17], as it is suitable for the design of systems with human-like characteristics. We aim to evaluate the effectiveness of our approach using Intent and Slot Maps on a real-world service system supported by a CA in the context of a social welfare service system.

References

1. Mesnil, G., et al.: Using recurrent neural networks for slot filling in spoken language understanding. IEEE/ACM Trans. Audio Speech Lang. Process. **23**(3), 530–539 (2015)
2. Yang, X., et al.: End-to-end joint learning of natural language understanding and dialogue manager. In: IEEE ICASSP, pp. 5690–5694 (2017)
3. Bordes, A., Boureau, Y., Weston, J.: Learning end-to-end goal-oriented dialog. In: 5th ICLR, France, 24–26 April 2017
4. Gasic, M., et al.: POMDP-based dialogue manager adaptation to extended domains. In: Proceedings of the SIGDIAL 2013 Conference, France, 22–24 August 2013, pp. 214–222 (2013)
5. Dodge, J., et al.: Evaluating prerequisite qualities for learning end-to-end dialog systems. In: 4th ICLR, San Juan, 2–4 May 2016
6. Jurafsky, D., Martin, J.H.: Speech and Language Processing: An Introduction to Natural Language Processing, Computational Linguistics, and Speech Recognition, 1st edn. Prentice Hall PTR, Upper Saddle River (2000). ISBN 0130950696
7. Barros, A., Oberle, D., Kylau, U., Heinzl, S.: Design overview of USDL. In: Barros, A., Oberle, D. (eds.) Handbook of Service Description: USDL and Its Methods, pp. 187–225. Springer, Boston (2012). https://doi.org/10.1007/978-1-4614-1864-1_8
8. Cardoso, J., Pedrinaci, C.: Evolution and overview of linked USDL. In: Nóvoa, H., Drăgoicea, M. (eds.) IESS 2015. LNBIP, vol. 201, pp. 50–64. Springer, Cham (2015). https://doi.org/10.1007/978-3-319-14980-6_5. ISBN 978-3-319-14980-6
9. Maglio, P.P., Vargo, S.L., Caswell, N., Spohrer, J.: The service system is the basic abstraction of service science. Inf. Syst. E-Bus. Manag. **7**(4), 395–406 (2009)
10. Budzianowski, P., et al.: MultiWOZ - a large-scale multi-domain Wizard-of-Oz dataset for task-oriented dialogue modelling. In: Proceedings of EMNLP, pp. 5016–5026 (2018)
11. Daniel, G., Cabot, J., Deruelle, L., Derras, M.: Multi-platform chatbot modeling and deployment with the Jarvis framework. In: Giorgini, P., Weber, B. (eds.) CAiSE 2019. LNCS, vol. 11483, pp. 177–193. Springer, Cham (2019). https://doi.org/10.1007/978-3-030-21290-2_12
12. Afzal, S., et al.: Development and deployment of a large-scale dialog-based intelligent tutoring system. In: Proceedings of the 2019 NAACL-HLT (2019)
13. Nili, A., Barros, A., Tate, M.: The public sector can teach us a lot about digitizing customer service. MIT Sloan Manag. Rev. **60**(2), 84–87 (2019)
14. Gnewuch, U., Morana, S., Mädche, A.: Towards designing cooperative and social conversational agents for customer service. In: Proceedings of ICIS - Transforming Society with Digital Innovation (2017)

15. Paliwal, A.V., et al.: Semantics-based automated service discovery. IEEE Trans. Serv. Comput. **5**(2), 260–275 (2012)
16. Chapman, S.: Logic and conversation. Paul Grice, Philosopher and Linguist, pp. 85–113. Palgrave Macmillan, London (2005). https://doi.org/10.1057/9780230005853_5. ISBN 978-0-230-00585-3
17. Nass, C., Moon, Y.: Machines and mindlessness: social responses to computers. J. Soc. Issues **56**(1), 81–103 (2000)

Interactive Modification During the Merge of Graph-Based Business Process Models

Jürgen Krauß[(✉)] and Martin Schmollinger[(✉)]

Department of Computer Science, Reutlingen University,
Alteburgstr. 150, 72762 Reutlingen, Germany
{juergen.krauss,martin.schmollinger}@reutlingen-university.de

Abstract. Companies are constantly changing their business process models. In team environments, different versions of a process model are created at the same time. These versions of a process model need to be merged from time to time to consolidate changes and create a new common version.

In this short paper, we propose a solution for modifying a merge result. The goal is to create a meaningful merge result by adding connector nodes to the model at specific locations. This increases the amount of possible result models and reduces additional implementation effort.

Keywords: Business process model · Merging · Version management

1 Introduction

Companies represent their business processes as graph-based business process models [10]. These artefacts are used for automation and as a common base for discussions between business departments. During software development and business process management projects, process models change. Because of agile methods, changes are done collaborative and divided among many people working in parallel. Additionally, the changes in process models are often incremental. As a result, different versions of a process model exist. At some point, these versions have to be merged into one version. The goal is to create a correct and meaningful process model that is sound and contain all necessary parts from the input versions correctly integrated.

The creation of a result model by merging is limited to elements that exist in at least one of the input versions. However, it can be necessary to add additional elements to achieve a meaningful result model. An example is the joining or forking of control flows while none of the versions contain necessary connectors.

In this paper, we discuss this scenario in detail. We introduce a mechanism to modify a result model at connectors by adding generic connectors and move elements during a merge. This allows to modify the merge result during the merge process in order to create a more meaningful process model and to increase the

© Springer Nature Switzerland AG 2019
H. Panetto et al. (Eds.): OTM 2019, LNCS 11877, pp. 561–568, 2019.
https://doi.org/10.1007/978-3-030-33246-4_35

set of possible merge results. Afterwards, we discuss the modification of merge results as a more general approach.

In Sect. 2 we describe a typical merge scenario. Afterwards, we discuss in Sect. 3 our motivation with an example of a situation where a modification is necessary. In Sect. 4 we propose a solution for such situations. In Sect. 5, we give an overview on related work. Finally, in Sect. 6 we discuss a general approach on modification and conclude our work in Sect. 7.

2   Merge Scenario

For our scenario, we describe a three-way merge. The three-way merge considers a common ancestor version V. New versions are created by adding a specific delta to V. The delta are added, removed or updated elements. For a merge, there need to be at least two versions V1 and V2 with different deltas. The three-way merge consideres elements from V, V1 and V2 to create a result model VR [11]. In comparison, the two-way merge does not consider V and is solely based on the differencing between elements from V1 and V2. However, our solutions works also with a two-way merge.

Merging is a two step procedure. The first step is the detection of Δ V1 and Δ V2. This can be done by model differencing [2,5]. Differences can be expressed as change operations [5]. Change operations describe every change that needs to be done to create V1 or V2 from V. A change operation is for example the insertion, deletion, moving or update of an element [5,11]. If an element is equal in V, V1 and V2 it is unchanged.

In the second step, the result model can be created. Unchanged elements are automatically in the result model. Afterwards, it need to be decided which of the detected change operations are applied and which not.

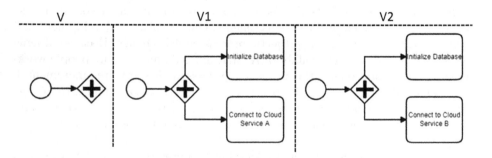

Fig. 1. Ancestor Process Model V and two Versions V1 and V2 for the merge example.

We want to demonstrate this with an example. In Fig. 1 we show three BPMN 2.0 process models V, V1 and V2. V contains a Start Event and a Parallel Gateway as connector. As a notation of change operations we use the work of [5]. The insertion of elements is an *InsertAction(V,x,a,b)*. It describes the insertion of an element x between a preceding element a and a succeeding element b in a process model V. Additional, it implicitly describes the connection of the edges between the elements. We detect the following change operations for V1 and V2:

- InsertAction(V1, "Initialize Database", Parallel Gateway, -)
- InsertAction(V1, "Connect to Cloud Service A", Parallel Gateway, -)
- InsertAction(V2, "Initialize Database", Parallel Gateway, -)
- InsertAction(V2, "Connect to Cloud Service B", Parallel Gateway, -)

The second step is the decision which of the change operations should be applied to create the result model. A possible result model is shown in Fig. 2 as VR1. For VR1, all change operations were applied. The amount of possible result models is limited by the amount of combinations of applying or ignoring detected change operations.

3   Motivation

Both versions, V1 and V2, implement a business process in which a database is initialized and a cloud service is connected. The Parallel Gateway causes a parallel execution of all activity nodes. In VR, all activity nodes got added to the Parallel Gateway. Therefore, all four activity nodes are executed in parallel. However, the business process model in reality could be different. A possible model is VR2 in Fig. 2. In comparison to VR1, there is a decision connector added, so that either the activity nodes from V1 or V2 are executed during runtime. Because of the incremental development, the decision connector is not necessary in V1 or V2. Both process models are valid incremental steps. However, for the combination of V1 and V2 into VR2 is a connector necessary that is not available in V1 or V2. VR2 represents only one possible alternative to VR1. The elements from V1 and V2 could be combined in other ways that could lead to necessary modifications because of missing elements.

Normally, the implementation of additional elements like the connector can be done in two ways. The first one is that at least one implementation of a version considers them already in advance. This assumes that the required elements are already known before the work on the versions begins. However, this has the disadvantage that there exists at least one version with elements, which are not required for the current incremental step. If the merge does not happen for any reason, this insertion needs to be undone. Second, the changes of the version are merged as shown in Fig. 2 as VR1 and the elements are added and changed afterwards. However, this would lead to a new step of implementation and increase the development effort. We introduce a controlled possibility to detect such situations and modify the merge result during the merge process to create a meaningful result model.

4   Solution Proposal

In this section, we propose a solution for modifying result models. As an example for the modification we use the described situation from Sect. 3. The situation

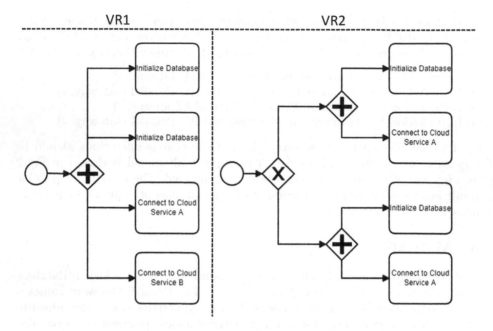

Fig. 2. VR1 and VR2 as possible result models for the merge example.

is that elements from different versions of a process model are merged adjacent to a connector node. We describe a set of conditions to detect these situation. Afterwards, we describe the modification.

4.1 Detection

We want to detect situations the modification can be applied. Therefore, we define conditions that are checked after each application of a change operation. If all conditions are true, the user can decide if a modification is necessary. During the merge, the detected situations can be signalled as merge warnings that are discussed by Langer [7] based on the ideas of Koegler et al. [4]. Based on merge warnings, it can be decided if a modification is necessary. A warning contains the original connector, the change operations that are applied and the direction of the change operations.

For our scenario, we want to modify merge results around connectors. Therefore, we define four conditions:

- The applied change operation was from type insertion or move.
- The inserted or moved element is adjacent to a connector.
- To the same side of the connector (incoming or outgoing), there was at least one other element applied during this merge by a change operation from type insertion or move and this operations is from a different version of the process model.

The first condition limits the observed operations during the merge. A deletion or update of an element can not lead to the situation we want detect. The second condition guarantees that the modification can just be done adjacent to an already existing connectors. The last condition guarantees that the modification is just possible if elements from both versions of the process model got combined. If there are change operations from only one version applied, the necessary modification should already be content of this version.

The conditions will detect the situation we described in Sect. 2. We detected four InsertAction operations which validates the first condition. Every InsertAction operation adds an element adjacent to a Parallel Gateway. The Parallel Gateway is a connector and therefore, the second condition is true. All InsertAction operations have the connector as preceding element. This means, all four elements are added on the same side of the connector. In addition, two actions each add an element from one of the two versions. Therefore, the third condition is true. With all three conditions true, the user can start the modification.

4.2   Modification

The modification is a three step procedure. It can be started when a warning exists and all necessary change operations are applied. First, we allow to add new connectors to the process model. The added connectors are generic. Generic connectors are based on configurable connectors from Rosemann and van der Aalst [8]. The idea of configurable connectors, is to be able to change the type of a connector to fit business requirements and to reuse process models. [8] describes a set of rules that limits the configuration. In this work, we want to achieve a flexible change of types. Therefore, the type of generic connectors can be set without restriction. Every connector that got inserted by modification is generic. Additionally, the original connector from the warning becomes generic. New generic connectors can only be added adjacent to the original connectors. The direction of such an insertion is defined by the detected warning.

As an example, we want to demonstrate the modification that leads from the result model VR1 in Fig. 2 to VR2. The insertion of new connectors can be expressed as change operations. VR indicates that the change operation is part of the modification and was not an element in V1 or V2.

- InsertAction(VR, "Generic Gateway 1", Parallel Gateway, -)
- InsertAction(VR, "Generic Gateway 2", Parallel Gateway, -)

The second step is the reordering of elements adjacent to the original connector. The precondition is that the change operations of the elements have already been applied and are in the correct direction. The reordering can also be expressed as change operations. In this case, we use $MoveActions(V,x,a,b)$ that describe the move of an element x between the succeeding elements a and b in process model V [5]. The connection of control flows is implicit. After the application of these change operations the result model is VR2 that is shown in Fig. 2 is finished:

- MoveAction(VR, "Initialize Database", Generic Gateway 1, -)
- MoveAction(VR, "Connect to Cloud Service A", Generic Gateway 1, -)
- MoveAction(VR, "Initialize Database", Generic Gateway 2, -)
- MoveAction(VR, "Connect to Cloud Service B", Generic Gateway 2, -)

The third step is the configuration of the connectors. The connector from the warning and all added connectors during the modification are generic. Therefore, the user can decide the type of the connector to create a specific merge result.

The example had only one warning at the connector. However, during a merge process, multiple situations can be detected and multiple warnings exist. The modification is a isolated operation during the merge process. The user can decide if and when to work on a warning and start the modification. After the modification, the user can continue the merge by applying further change operations from V1 or V2.

5   Related Work

The related work can be distinguished into merge algorithms for two use cases. The first use case is the combination of process variants. The goal of the merge is to create one process model that preserves all the functionality of the input process models. Rosa and Dumas et. al. [6] introduced an automatized merge algorithm. They combine fragments of process models by adding configurable connectors. Gottschalk et al. [3] introduce a merge algorithm that transforms Event Chain Models (ECM) into function graphs. The function graphs get merged and the result is transformed into ECM again. Derguech and Bhiri [1] extended the algorithm from [6] by allowing not only to merge pair of process models but a collection. Furthermore, they add configurable connectors [8] adjacent to certain elements to prevent an invalid amount of incoming or outgoing edges.

The second use case is the merge for design and development that was described in the introduction of this paper. In comparison to the combination of process variants, for this use case, the merge is a controlled process were a user solves conflicts by deciding about including or excluding changes from different versions of a process model. Küster et. al. [5] introduced an approach to detect and resolve model differences without an existing change log. They utilize Single-Entry-Single-Exit fragments to detect changes between two models. Sun et. al. [9] discussed fundamental concepts of pattern based merge operations and the detection of merge points.

In comparison to these papers, we do not introduce a new approach for merging but introduce an operation for merge algorithms for the second use case. Our approach is not relevant for merge algorithms that combine variants of process models. These merges are done automatically and there is no need for a manual modification.

The operation of [1] that prevents the invalid number of incoming and outgoing edges solves a problem of parallel modeling. The operation is similar to our solution because both add connectors to adjacent elements with multiple incoming or outgoing edges. In ECM it is not allowed to have multiple incoming or outgoing edges on certain elements. Therefore, [1] adds configurable connectors adjacent to such elements to protect them from having multiple edges. This guarantees that the merge result is a syntactical correct ECM. In comparison, we have another intention to add connectors to the merge result. We detect possibilities for modification and apply a rule set for adding connectors and move nodes to create a more meaningful result model.

6   Discussion

We introduced a merge operation to modify a merge result in the described scenario in Sect. 2. The conditions in this paper are defined to detect this specific scenario. Especially, the second condition limits the modification to cases where elements were added or moved adjacent to connectors. The conditions can be configured to adapt them to different scenarios. The conditions depend on the used merge algorithm and the goals that should be achieved. For example, we described the operation of Derguech and Bhiri [1] in Sect. 5 that adds connectors between elements to protect elements from having to much incoming or outgoing elements. With our approach, this operation can be added to other merge algorithm as for example Küster et. al. [5] by defining a condition that considers the amount of incoming or outgoing edges that are created by change operations.

The described steps of the modification is also a specific solution for our scenario. However, the change operations are a general approach that can be used for modification of other scenarios. Addtionally, the introduced generic connectors help to increase the flexibility and possibilities of the modification. For our scenario, we introduced three steps that add generic connectors, move existing elements to the new connector and determine the type of generic connectors. For the operation of Derguech and Bhiri [1] we would need two steps which add a new generic connector between existing elements and defining its type. For specific scenarios, a specific procedure can be defined that guides the user and helps to modify the result model.

7   Conclusion

We proposed a solution for modifying a process model during the merge. It contains a set of conditions for merge warnings and a possibility to add connectors and move nodes based on change operations. The modification increases the set of possible merge result and decreases the development effort. First, the conditions for the detection and the modification was described for a specific scenario. Afterwards, a more general approach for other situations was discussed.

As this is a short paper, there is further work to do. The detection and modification need to be formally expressed and evaluated. Furthermore, an implementation can proof the concept of modification and show the practicability. Additionally, the modification can be extended. For our specific scenario, it could be allowed to not only add connectors that are adjacent to an original connector, but to create complex structures of connectors. In addition, we want to discover more scenarios and define detection conditions and steps for modification. This could not only help to create more meaningful process models but support the user by preventing syntax errors and increase the practicability of existing merge algorithms for graph-based process models.

Acknowledgements. This research was partially funded by the Ministry of Science of Baden-Württemberg, Germany, for the Doctoral Program Services Computing.

References

1. Derguech, W., Bhiri, S.: An automation support for creating configurable process models. In: Bouguettaya, A., Hauswirth, M., Liu, L. (eds.) WISE 2011. LNCS, vol. 6997, pp. 199–212. Springer, Heidelberg (2011). https://doi.org/10.1007/978-3-642-24434-6_15
2. Dijkman, R.: A classification of differences between similar business processes. In: Proceedings of the 11th IEEE International Enterprise Distributed Object Computing Conference, EDOC 2007, p. 37. IEEE Computer Society, Washington, DC (2007). http://dl.acm.org/citation.cfm?id=1317532.1318035
3. Gottschalk, F., van der Aalst, W.M.P., Jansen-Vullers, M.H.: Merging event-driven process chains. In: Meersman, R., Tari, Z. (eds.) OTM 2008. LNCS, vol. 5331, pp. 418–426. Springer, Heidelberg (2008). https://doi.org/10.1007/978-3-540-88871-0_28
4. Koegel, M., Helming, J., Seyboth, S.: Operation-based conflict detection and resolution. In: Proceedings of the 2009 ICSE Workshop on Comparison and Versioning of Software Models, pp. 43–48. IEEE Computer Society, Washington, DC (2009)
5. Küster, J.M., Gerth, C., Förster, A., Engels, G.: Detecting and resolving process model differences in the absence of a change log. In: Dumas, M., Reichert, M., Shan, M.-C. (eds.) BPM 2008. LNCS, vol. 5240, pp. 244–260. Springer, Heidelberg (2008). https://doi.org/10.1007/978-3-540-85758-7_19
6. La Rosa, M., Dumas, M., Uba, R., Dijkman, R.: Business process model merging. ACM Trans. Softw. Eng. Methodol. **22**(2), 1–42 (2013). https://doi.org/10.1145/2430545.2430547
7. Langer, P.: Adaptable Model Versioning based on Model Transformation By Demonstration. Ph.D. thesis, University of Technology, Vienna (2011)
8. Rosemann, M., van der Aalst, W.M.P.: A configurable reference modelling language. Inf. Syst. **32**(1), 1–23 (2007). https://doi.org/10.1016/j.is.2005.05.003
9. Sun, S., Kumar, A., Yen, J.: merging workflows: a new perspective on connecting business processes. Decis. Support Syst. **42**(2), 844–858 (2006). https://doi.org/10.1016/j.dss.2005.07.001
10. Weske, M.: Business Process Management: Concepts, Languages, Architectures, 2nd edn. Springer, Heidelberg (2012). https://doi.org/10.1007/978-3-642-28616-2
11. Westfechtel, B.: Merging of EMF models. Softw. Syst. Model. **13**(2), 757–788 (2014). https://doi.org/10.1007/s10270-012-0279-3

International Conference on Ontologies, DataBases, and Applications of Semantics (ODBASE) 2019

ODBASE 2019 PC Co-chairs' Message

We are delighted to present the proceedings of the 18th International Conference on Ontologies, DataBases, and Applications of Semantics (ODBASE) which was held in Rhodes, Greece 22–23 October 2019. The ODBASE Conference series provides a forum for research and practitioners on the use of ontologies and data semantics in novel applications, and continues to draw a highly diverse body of researchers and practitioners. ODBASE is part of the OnTheMove (OTM 2019) federated event composed of three interrelated yet complementary scientific conferences that together attempt to span a relevant range of the advanced research on, and cutting-edge development and application of, information handling and systems in the wider current context of ubiquitous distributed computing. The other two co-located conferences are CoopIS'19 (Cooperative Information Systems) and C&TC'19 (Cloud and Trusted Computing). Of particular relevance to ODBASE 2019 were topics that bridge traditional boundaries between disciplines such as artificial intelligence and Semantic Web, databases, data analytics and machine learning, social networks, distributed and mobile systems, information retrieval, knowledge discovery, and computational linguistics.

This year, we received 27 paper submissions and had a program committee of dedicated researchers and practitioners from diverse research areas. Special arrangements were made during the review process to ensure that each paper was reviewed by approx. 3 members of different research areas. The result of this effort is the selection of 9 full papers. Their themes included studies and solutions to a number of modern challenges such as data governance, semantic enrichment, knowledge graphs, data transformation, semantic querying and search, linked data, and semantics-based applications to various domains.

We would like to thank all the members of the Program Committee for their hard work in selecting the papers and for helping to make this conference a success. Our special thanks go to Judie Attard, Jeremy Debattista, Xiao Guohui, Kris McGlinn, Harshwandir Pandit, Milan Dojchinovski and Gary Munnelly for taking on additional reviews. We would also like to thank all the researchers who submitted their work. Last but not least, special thanks go to the members of the OTM team for their support and guidance. In this regard we must specially thank Christophe Debruyne, the publication chair, for going beyond the call of duty in providing tireless support to us as chairs.

We hope that you enjoy ODBASE 2019 and have a wonderful time in Rhodes!

September 2019

Dave Lewis
Rob Brennan

Complex Query Augmentation for Question Answering over Knowledge Graphs

Abdelrahman Abdelkawi[1], Hamid Zafar[2(✉)], Maria Maleshkova[2], and Jens Lehmann[2,3]

[1] Computer Science Institute, RWTH Aachen University, Aachen, Germany
abdelrahman.abdelkawi@rwth-aachen.de
[2] Computer Science Institute, University of Bonn, Bonn, Germany
{hzafarta,maleshkova,jens.lehmann}@cs.uni-bonn.de
[3] Fraunhofer IAIS, Dresden, Germany
jens.lehmann@iais.fraunhofer.de

Abstract. Question answering systems have often a pipeline architecture that consists of multiple components. A key component in the pipeline is the query generator, which aims to generate a formal query that corresponds to the input natural language question. Even if the linked entities and relations to an underlying knowledge graph are given, finding the corresponding query that captures the true intention of the input question still remains a challenging task, due to the complexity of sentence structure or the features that need to be extracted. In this work, we focus on the query generation component and introduce techniques to support a wider range of questions that are currently less represented in the community of question answering.

Keywords: Question answering · Knowledge graphs · Query augmentation

1 Introduction

Question answering (QA) has been an active field of research for many decades in different areas such as information retrieval, natural language processing and machine learning. It provides users with a convenient interface to ask their question in a natural way.

As semantic web technologies developed in recent years, vast sources of structured data became available, for instance, domain-specific Knowledge Graphs (KGs) (such as UMLS [17], GeoNames [30], WordNet [20], etc.) and open-domain KGs (e.g. DBpedia [16], Freebase [5], etc.). Given these well-structured sources of information, QA over KG is able to provide concise answers not only to simple but also to more complicated questions, including the traversal of multiple relevant (triple) patterns in the KG.

© Springer Nature Switzerland AG 2019
H. Panetto et al. (Eds.): OTM 2019, LNCS 11877, pp. 571–587, 2019.
https://doi.org/10.1007/978-3-030-33246-4_36

Often *Semantic parsing* approaches are employed to build QA over KG, in which multiple components can be orchestrated in a pipeline architecture. This pipeline transfers the input question into a formal query representation of the question, which captures the intention of the user. As opposed to end-to-end methods [18] that work as a black-box, semantic parsing approaches provide a modular solution, which enables researchers to find out the reasons for the success and failure cases by investigating the components individually. Hence, it is also easier to improve and re-use the existing work as well. Furthermore, end-to-end methods, in general, are not applicable in cases where the training dataset is not large enough.

Semantic parsing approaches mostly consist of five components that are responsible for the following tasks [25]: *Shallow parsing* (a.k.a chunking), *Entity linking*, *Relation linking*, *Query generation* and *Ranking*. The first component analyzes the input question in order to partition it into entity and relation spans. These spans are the main clues for the entity and relation linking components to find the corresponding items in the knowledge graph. Given all the linked items, the query generator searches for the possible valid combinations of the linked items, which later would be compared to the input question in order to arrange them according to their similarity to the intention of the user.

Although these components are necessary to build a QA system, researchers mostly focus on earlier steps and limited attention is paid to the query generation and ranking modules, due to the fact that most of Question/Answering (Q/A) datasets contain mostly questions with a simple corresponding formal query. Therefore, most of the existing approaches fail to correctly comprehend the challenging questions, in which the query generation task is more demanding. The performance of the query generator depends on the complexity of the input question and the distinct features from the underlying formal query language, which should be supported by the query generator. Nevertheless, given the fact that it is burdensome to define a concrete metric to measure the level of complexity of a natural language question, we establish the complexity of a question based on two features from its corresponding formal query: Type of the formal query (enumerated in Table 1) and the number of linked items used in formal query, where the queries that use more linked items, correspond to more complex questions.

In the simplest case, a question can be answered using one entity and one relation from the underlying knowledge graph. In this case, the number of candidate formal queries are limited. For instance, consider the question `Who are the children of Barak Obama`, where the only entity is `Barak Obama` and the relation is `children`. In this example, there are just two possible formal queries that can be built: `SELECT ?c WHERE{?c dbo:Children dbr:Barak_Obama}` and `SELECT ?c WHERE{dbr:Barak_Obama dbp:children ?c}` where the first one is the latter interpretation of the question. However, as the number of linked items increases, the search space might explode and it would be challenging to explore the search space in order to find the candidate queries. SimpleQuestions [7] and WebQuestions [3] are the de facto standard Q/A datasets based on Freebase [5]

Table 1. Various types of queries and their corresponding sample question

Type	Description/Example/SPARQL
List	The question is a factoid question (single or multiple relations)
	Example: Who are the children of Barack Obama?
	SELECT ?child where {dbr:Barack_Obama dbp:children ?child}
Boolean	The question is a yes or no question
	Example: Is Paris the capital of France?
	ASK WHERE {dbr:France dbo:capital dbr:Paris; rdf:type dbo:Place}
Count	The intention of the question is to count the number of the possible results
	Example: How many cities are in Germany?
	SELECT COUNT(?city) WHERE {?city dbo:country dbr:Germany; rdf:type dbo:City}
Ordinal	The question requires ordering of the results over a certain criteria
	Example: What is the most populated city in Italy?
	SELECT ?city WHERE{?city dbo:country dbr:Italy; dbo:populationTotal ?population; rdf:type dbo:City} ORDER BY DESC(?population) LIMIT1
Filter	The question requires the results to be restricted using a certain criteria
	Example: List all cities with more than a million population in Egypt?
	SELECT ?city WHERE{?city dbo:country dbr:Egypt; dbo:populationTotal ?p; rdf:type dbo:City. FILTER (?p > 1000000)}

as they are used in many of QA over Freebase systems [4,6,31,32]. All the questions in SimpleQuestions and more than 80% of WebQuestions can be answered using a single relation in the underlying knowledge graph. Furthermore, there are only 3% *Ordinal* questions and no *Boolean* question in WebQuestions. Consequently, most of the introduced approaches mainly focus on the first type (see *List* in Table 1). However, LC-QuAD dataset filled the gap to some extent by providing 7% *Boolean* and 12% *Count* questions out of a total 5,000 questions. As a result, more researchers concentrate on these two types as well [8,19,33]. Yet, very limited effort has been spent on the last two categories, in spite of the fact that the number of *Ordinal/Filter* questions is increasing in QA datasets. Given that there are already advanced approaches to deal with the first three groups, we aim to enhance an existing query generator in order to not reinvent the wheel and benefit from the existing infrastructures. Among others, SQG [33] reports significantly better accuracy in comparison to other query generator components on various datasets. Thus, in this work we concentrate on extending SQG to support more complex queries, namely *Ordinal* and *Filter*.

The remainder of the paper is structured as follows: Sect. 2 briefly discusses the related works on various techniques, which have been employed to support complex features such as *Ordinal* and *Filter*. We then introduce the overall architecture as well as the details of the approach in Sect. 3 and present the evaluation results in Sect. 4. Section 5 concludes our findings.

2   Related Work

The main-stream question answering systems over knowledge graphs can be divided into two categories: Semantic parsing methods and End-to-end approaches. 62 semantic parsing question answering systems from 2010 till 2015 are analyzed Hoffner et al. [14]. They discuss the main challenges in question answering systems as well as the common solutions. Chakraborty et al. [22] provide a more recent overview of neural networks based question answering.

Although end-to-end QA system achieved state-of-the-art results, they mostly focus on simple/compound question, and either neglect other types [22] or use simple pattern matching techniques to address *Ordinal* or *Filter* types. Hence, we mostly study semantic parsing methods.

Walter et al. [29] introduce BELA - a QA system that consists of a 5-step pipeline: question parsing, template generation, string similarity computation, synonym-finding, and semantic similarity computation. The main idea of the system is that the system decides, which steps should be applied, depending on the complexity of the input question. The system is evaluated on QALD-2[1], however it is not capable of answering questions that require sorting or filtering of the results.

Unger et al. [28] propose TBSL, a QA system that parses the input question to extract syntactic information from the question using predefined lexicons, then it uses this information to generate a logical expression similar to the question. Using this expression, the system chooses the candidate query templates. Finally, TBNSL attempts to fill in the empty slots in the candidate templates through the entities and relations mentioned in the given question. Moreover, it uses ranking techniques to select the best candidate query. Considering that the query templates are manually created based on the dataset at hand, it is considered to be over-fitted for the dataset.

CASIA [26] and SINA [24] are two more examples of QA systems based on a pipeline architecture. The pipeline of such systems includes tasks such as question processing, entity and relation recognition and disambiguation, and SPARQL query generation. These systems are benchmarked on the QALD-3[2] challenge dataset. Similarly, there is no support for questions where complicated features such as *Filter*, *Ordinal*, etc. are required.

Hakimov et al. [12] develop a QA system that uses a semantic approach based on Zettlemoyer et al. [34]. They investigate the use of handcrafted lexicons to minimize the lexical gap between the vocabulary used in natural language questions and the one of the training data. The system is benchmarked on QALD-4[3], however, the systems has no support for *Ordinal* or *Filter* questions.

POMELO [13] is another pipelined QA system, which resembles the architecture of CASIA [26] and SINA [24]. In addition to the pre-processing steps in the pipeline, POMELO scans the question for certain terms such as numbers, mean,

---

[1] http://qald.aksw.org/index.php?x=task1&q=2.
[2] http://qald.aksw.org/index.php?x=task1&q=3.
[3] http://qald.aksw.org/index.php?x=task1&q=4.

higher, etc. in order to construct the SPARQL query. This step helps POMELO to support more query types than CASIA [26] and SINA [24]. However, it fails to handle compound questions. Moreover, its support for *Filter* and *Ordinal* types is limited due to the fact that it is based on a hand-crafted list of patterns.

The AskNow approach as described in [11] is a QA framework by M. Dubey et al. that takes a natural language question as its input, then transforms the question into an intermediate logical form called *Normalized Query Structure*, which later will be changed into a SPARQL query. AskNow defines three types of queries: Simple, complex and compound. As a result, it is able to support compound questions. Nevertheless, the support for *Filter* and *Ordinal* is limited to the pre-defined patterns. Much like the system proposed by Unger et al. [28], Abujabal et al. [1] use a similar approach with the main difference that the system is able to learn SPARQL templates from question-query pairs. Given a question, it tries to match the question to an empty candidate template(s) that corresponds to the given question. In addition, it benefits from ranking methodologies for selecting the best candidate queries.

The aforementioned QA systems are either based on templates/patterns or use and ad-hoc methods to support complex queries. While, we base our solution on extending a well structured, modular, standalone SPARQL query generator that is capable of generating target SPARQL queries for input questions, provided the entities and relations mentioned in the question.

3 Approach

Given a question in natural language and the correct linked items (entities and relations), SQG [33] goes into the details of generating a SPARQL query that corresponds to the input question. By using this generated SPARQL query and augmenting it with necessary constraints, we are able to obtain a SPARQL query that supports new, previously unsupported, types.

In order to extend SQG [33] to support the two new types, we model these types as extra constraints that need to be applied on the list of all possible answers. For the *Ordinal* class, to get the correct answer for the example question **Q1: "What is the most populated city in Italy?"**, we first need to get a list of all the cities in Italy, then sort them in descending order with respect to the population of each city and then return the top city as the most populated city in Italy. The same idea applies to the type *Filter*, where the list of possible answers should conform to a certain constraint. For example, given the question **Q2: "What are the cities with more than a million population in Egypt?"**, we need to get all the cities in Egypt and only return those with the population more than a million as the answer. This unified view of modeling the new types as constraints enables us to extend SQG by adding an extra layer over the existing architecture.

To support the aforementioned types, we divide the overall task into three sub-tasks. First, we need to classify the given questions in order to recognize those questions that belong to the new types. Second, we parse the given question to extract special keywords that would help us to select a KG property, which would act as the constraint for the intended SPARQL query. The last task is to set any parameters needed for the SPARQL query in order to capture the intention of the given question.

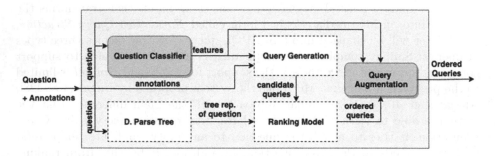

Fig. 1. Proposed ExSQG architecture. Components highlighted in red are modified/added components (Color figure online)

Figure 1 shows the architecture of ExSQG. It extends SQG [33] with two new components – *Question Classifier* and *Query Augmentation*. The new question classifier replaces the original question classifier from the SQG [33] as it does not support the new question types. The original question classifier is built as a flat classifier using Naive Bayes and SVM and supports only List, Boolean and Count questions.

In SQG [33], the ranking model was the last step in the query generation pipeline. However, in the ExSQG architecture, the query augmentation component resides at the end of the pipeline. The augmentation component is responsible for complementing the SPARQL query, which is selected by the ranking model, by adding the necessary constraints and parameters in order to generate the final query that corresponds to the input question.

Intuitively each question is of List, Boolean or Count type. However it may belong either to *Ordinal* or *Filter*, or both. We call the first three categories PRIMARY CLASSES and *Ordinal* and *Filter* secondary classes. Accordingly, we build a hierarchical question classifier, which consists of a multi-class classifier for primary classes and a binary classifier for each of the secondary classes. Figure 2 shows the architecture of the *Questions Classifier*. When a question is passed through the classifier module, it is first classified by the primary classifier to find out its primary class. Given the primary class, it passes through all the secondary binary classifiers to check if the question belongs to one or more of the secondary classes. As shown in Fig. 3, both **Q1** and **Q2** are identified as *List* by the primary classifier, however, **Q1** is classified as *Ordinal* as the secondary class, while the second class of **Q2** is established as *Filter*.

After the question is classified, it passes through the rest of the pipeline. If the question is classified to have only a primary class and no further secondary classes, then the query is returned by the ranking model as the result of

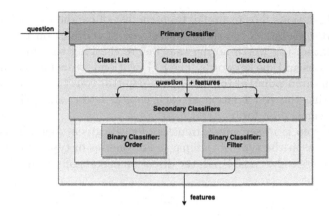

Fig. 2. Architecture of the hierarchical question classifier

SQG [33]. On the other hand, when the question is classified to be one of the secondary classes, it passes through the query augmentation component with its corresponding SPARQL query chosen by the ranking model.

The first task of the query augmentation is to select a KG property that acts as the constraint in the SPARQL query. First, the natural language question is cleaned by removing stop words and any entity mentions. The result of this process is called a *base-form* and is used in the *Parameters Settings* step. By parsing the base-form according to the class of the question provided by the question classifier, we are able to further clean it, which would result in having single or multiple words. This sequence of words is called *keyword* or *keywords*. For example, the base-form for the **Q1** is "most populated city" and the keywords are "most populated".

In parallel with the keyword extraction task, the SPARQL query provided by the ranking model is used to capture the list of KG relations in the one-hop distance of the subgraph containing the answer. Empirically, by analyzing Filter and Order questions and their corresponding gold SPARQL queries. We found that the relations used as constraints are always in the one-hop space distance from the subgraph that contains the answer. Thus, we operate under the assumption that the KG property that acts as the constraint is contained within this list. These extracted relations are then filtered retaining only those, which are comparable (e.g. Numbers, Dates, etc.). For instance, the candidate relations for **Q1** are dbo:areaTotal, dbo:Country, dbo:populationTotal, etc.

In order to select the correct KG relation from the list of possible relations, we capture the semantic closeness of the keywords and each of those relations by computing the cosine similarity between their word embeddings. The KG relation and keywords, which form the closest pair, are selected as the final KG relation, which acts as the constraint in the final SPARQL query. Note that since both the keywords and KG relations might consist of more than a single word, we use Word Mover Distance [15] to measure the similarity between the keywords and the KG relations. For example, from the list of candidate relations for **Q1**, `dbo:populationTotal` is the most similar one in comparison to the keywords `most populated`. It's worth noting that before checking the similarity between the KG relations and the keywords. The KG relation is transformed into a correct English form, from `populationTotal` into `population total`. This is done by simply splitting the KG relation at each capital letter, since they are always written in a camel case form.

The final step is to set any parameters for the given query. This parameter setting depends on the type of the query. For queries of type *Ordinal*, there are three parameters to be considered; the direction of sort, offset and limit. In order

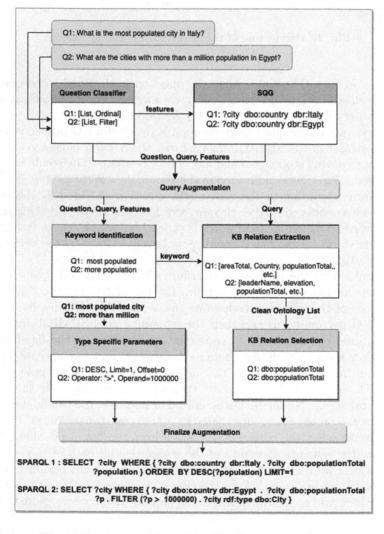

Fig. 3. ExSQG pipeline for Ordinal and Filter examples

to set the direction of sort, we train a classifier that predicts the sorting direction given the keywords. On the other hand, the offset is set by parsing the base-form provided by the components responsible for the keyword extraction. If the base-form contains an ordinal mention (e.g. first, second, third, etc.), it is used to set the offset in the SPARQL query. Otherwise, the offset is set to zero. The last parameter in the *Ordinal* queries is the limit. To set the limit of the query, we use Part Of Speech (POS) tags to check if the keyword or keywords refer to a singular or plural noun to set the limit accordingly. For our running example question **Q1**, the limit would be set to one as the keywords `most populated` refers to `city`, which is singular. Otherwise, it is set to negative one, which means all possible answers.

If the query belongs to the *Filter* class, there is only one parameter to be set, which is the comparison operator (e.g. less than, more than, same as, etc.). In order to be able to set the correct operator, we train a classifier that predicts the operator given the keyword. The keywords are prepared by running the keyword identification component on the training sets. The classifier is trained on such keywords and their corresponding operator extracted from each SPARQL query. For instance, the operator *greater* with operand `1000000` would be extracted for the example question **Q2**.

Finally, after the KG property is selected and the values of the parameters are set, these results are used to augment the SPARQL query provided by the ranking model. This augmentation is done as follows (i) first, we syntactically parse the query returned from the ranking model; (ii) we prepare the SPARQL equivalent for any of the parameters and/or constraints; (iii) we append these additions to the query returned by the ranking model.

Figure 3 illustrates the flow of ExSQG with the example questions **Q1** and **Q2**. It shows each component in the pipeline with its inputs and its output when the system is given an *Ordinal* or *Filter* question.

4   Empirical Study

In this section, we introduce the datasets used in this work and provide statistical information about them. In addition, we present the results of ExSQG on the benchmarking datasets.

4.1   Datasets

Q/A datasets commonly contain triples of (i) natural language question, (ii) the equivalent formal query, and (iii) the answer set. Since many of the Q/A datasets only contain *List* questions with no extra features such as *Ordinal* and *Filter*, we hand-picked the ones that include such questions from multiple datasets, so that we could build a robust and general query generator. In order to have a unified dataset, we aim to collect the datasets with the same underlying KG. Among others, DBpedia [2] is an ongoing community-based knowledge base that is in a constant process of development and we would use the datasets, which are based on DBpedia.

First, we use LC-QuAD [27], which contains 5,000 manually crafted questions and their corresponding SPARQL query. Although LC-QuAD does not contain any questions that belong to the new types, we include it in order to provide performance comparison with the baseline system (SQG). Second, we use all the datasets from the QALD[4] challenge (QALD 1–9). As these datasets where part of a Q/A campaign over multiple years, many of the questions are used more than once in these datasets (out of more than 5,000 questions in these datasets, only 1400 are unique). However, these datasets are particularly important since they contain all of the types of questions, and they are carefully designed to challenge different aspect of the QA systems. The last dataset we use is DBNQA [21], which is a template-based dataset containing about 800,000 automatically created question and SPARQL query pairs. This dataset is especially useful, since it provides a vast number of questions from the *Filter* and *Ordinal* types.

Although DBNQA contains the target question types, it is generated using a set of pre-defined templates. Thus, if we train the classifiers on DBNQA, it would be biased towards the underlying templates. On the other hand, considering the number of unique question/query pairs in the QALD 1–9 challenge, it is not sufficient to train the classifiers. Therefore, we combine training and testing sets from all the available datasets.

The idea behind these combinations is to compare the performance of the models trained on each of the combinations with each other. These combinations are as follows:

- LC-QuAD: Using only LC-QuAD
- LC-QuAD + QALD: Combined data from both datasets
- LC-Quad + QALD + DBNQA: Combined data from all the datasets

Since DBNQA has over 800,000 questions-query pairs, while LC-QuAD and QALD contain about 10,000 questions combined, we do not include DBNQA entirely but rather use a subset of the dataset in order to avoid the classifiers' overfitting over questions from DBNQA. We used random different subsets with different sizes that varied between **1%**, **5%**, **10%**, and **25%** from the available questions in the dataset.

Using these multiple subsets gives us a better idea when the model gives the best performance, while decreasing the chance of overfitting over DBNQA. The combined datasets are named as follows:

- LC-QuAD + QALD + 1% DBNQA: Combined 1
- LC-QuAD + QALD + 5% DBNQA: Combined 5
- LC-QuAD + QALD + 10% DBNQA: Combined 10
- LC-QuAD + QALD + 25% DBNQA: Combined 25

For the secondary classifiers, we prepare the training and testing sets using all the available data from all the available datasets. Since the amount of the

---

[4] http://qald.aksw.org/.

available data for the secondary classes is not as much as the data available for the primary classes.

Table 2. Datasets statistics

Dataset	# of Questions	Unique questions	List	Boolean	Count	Ordinal	Filter
QALD (1–9)	5,237	1,396	1,056	98	79	94	75
LC-QuAD	5,000	4,998	3,967	368	658	0	0
DBNQA	894,499	871,166	688,689	76,835	98,372	3,893	1,797

Table 2 shows the total number of question and query pairs per dataset. In addition, it shows the total number of questions available for each type per dataset.

4.2 Experiment Settings

For the training process for any of the aforementioned classifiers, we prepared a train/test set from all the available data. We split each dataset as 70% for the training set and 30% for the test set. Furthermore, we use 10-fold cross-validation during the evaluation process. In addition, we use *scikit-learn*[5] implementations for all the classifiers used.

Moreover, for the cleaning process of questions, we use Spacey[6] and NLTK[7]. Finally, to prepare the embedding matrix, which contains the vector representation for all the words in our vocabulary, we use the pre-trained word vectors by Global Vectors for Word Representation (GloVe)[8] [23].

4.3 Evaluation Metrics

Since the proposed system architecture consists of a pipeline of components, in order to evaluate the performance of such a system, we first evaluate the performance of each component individually. Then we assess the overall performance of the system.

We evaluate the performance of the classifiers trained in terms of *accuracy*. In addition, we use *precision, recall,* and *F1-score* to measure the performance of the KG property selection component.

4.4 Empirical Results

The selection process of the best classifier consists of two parts. First, we select the best classifier with the best set of features. Then, we experiment with the best performing classifier with the best set of features against different datasets with various sizes.

---

[5] https://scikit-learn.org/stable/.
[6] https://spacy.io/.
[7] https://www.nltk.org/.
[8] https://nlp.stanford.edu/projects/glove/.

Table 3. Accuracy for the question classifier under different features

Feature	NB	SVM	MaxEnt
1-gram	91.0%	96.7%	98.5%
(1+2)-grams	95.3%	96.9%	98.9%
(1+2+3)-grams	95.7%	96.7%	98.9%
+TF-IDF	94.5%	92.4%	99.0%
+Normalized Numbers	95.7%	96.9%	99.0%
+POS	95.9%	96.4%	99.1%
First N-words $N = 3$	93.6%	94.2%	96.2%
First Last N-words $N = 3$	93.3%	95.3%	97.4%

Table 3 shows the accuracy of the question classifier under a different set of features. This experiment is done on the **combined dataset 5**. In order to select the best set of features, we show the accuracy of the classifier at each row for the current feature, combined with the best set of features selected so far. As the table shows, we end up using the *MaxEnt* classifier as it out-performed the other classifiers.

Table 4. MaxEnt classifier performance against multiple datasets of different sizes

Dataset	MaxEnt
LC-QuAD	90.1%
LC-QuAD + QALD	89.7%
Combined_1	95.9%
Combined_5	99.3%
Combined_10	99.5%

Table 4 shows the performance of the classifier when it is trained on different datasets. In this experiment, we use the **combined dataset 25** as the test for all the classifiers. We can see from the table that the performance of the question classifier increases with the size of the dataset. However, this increase could also be due to the classifiers overfitting over questions from DBNQA.

For the following experiments, we mainly focus on the QALD datasets to show the performance of the system as they are very popular and used a lot in benchmarking QA over KG systems [9]. Thus, we are able to have a reference point to compare our approach with other systems.

Table 5 shows the accuracy of the hierarchical question classifier on QALD (4, 5, 6, 7). It also shows the total number of questions available per dataset. The accuracy of the proposed question classifier in Table 5 is less than the reported

Table 5. Accuracy of the question classifier on QALD (4, 5, 6, 7)

Dataset	No. questions	Accuracy
QALD-4	67	51 (76%)
QALD-5	33	28 (84%)
QALD-6	99	87 (87%)
QALD-7	30	25 (83%)

accuracy for the question classifier for SQG [33], because of the complex nature of the questions that belong to secondary classes.

Table 6 shows the precision, recall, and F1 score for ExSQG for questions of type *Ordinal*. A generated SPARQL query is considered correct if it yields the same answer as the target SPARQL query, this means that the system is able to correctly classify the question and successfully generate the correct SPARQL query. The performance of the ExSQG is lower than the performance on QALD-5, and 6 for two reasons. First, by inspecting the questions that lead to an incorrect answer, we found out that the number of miss-classified questions from QALD-4 is higher than those of QALD-5, and 6. Second, most of the questions that belong to the *Ordinal* class from QALD-4 were generally more complex than those that belonged to QALD-6. Not in terms of linked items, rather in the queries that correspond to the question and the constraints used in such queries. For example, some query constraints are not simply KG relations but a count over such relations.

Table 6. Performance of ordinal questions pipeline

Dataset	Precision	Recall	F1
QALD-4	0.40	0.33	0.36
QALD-5	0.83	0.83	0.66
QALD-6	0.80	0.66	0.72
QALD-7	0.33	0.50	0.40

Table 7 shows the precision, recall, and F1 score of ExSQG for questions of type *Filter*. It also shows that the ExSQG system does not provide the same performance as it does for questions of the type *Ordinal*. This is due to the fact that there are much fewer questions of the type *Filter* that we support in the datasets than questions of type *Ordinal*. The current system is able to correctly generate the SPARQL for questions that require filtration over the value of a KB Relation (e.g. *"Cities in Germany with area larger than 30000 KM"*), or questions that compare two KB resources over a certain KB relation (e.g. *"Does Game of Thrones have more episodes than Breaking Bad"*). In the first question the constraint is the `dbo:areaTotal` and in the second one – `dbo:numberOfEpisodes`.

Table 7. Performance of filter questions pipeline

Dataset	Precision	Recall	F1
QALD-4	0.11	1.00	0.20
QALD-6	0.14	0.33	0.20

On the other hand, questions that require a string matching filter query, date matching, or filtration based on a count are not yet supported. Therefore, any miss-classification or incorrect query generation would significantly impact the overall performance. The results for QALD-5, 7 are not shown as well in this table, because there were only 3 filter questions and our system was not successful to correctly predict and answer them.

Table 8. Absolute increase percentage in performance between the SQG [33] and ExSQG

Dataset	No. of questions	Performance increase
QALD 4	67	8.0%
QALD 5	33	18.0%
QALD 6	99	5.0%
QALD 7	30	3.0%

Table 8 shows the absolute difference in performance between SQG [33] and the ExSQG. For this experiment, we assume an ideal scenario for the question classifier for both systems – SQG [33] and ExSQG. We also assume that we always get an intermediate SPARQL query from the ranking model for questions that belong to the new types. These conditions are assumed to mitigate any error propagation from SQG [33] and to be able to measure the performance of the ExSQG on questions that belong to the new types. The variation of the performance of ExSQG on QALD (4, 5, 6 and 7) as shown in Table 8 is due to the fact that there is only a limited number of questions that belong to secondary classes in these datasets. However, there are more questions that have secondary classes in QALD-5 in comparison to the other datasets.

5   Conclusions

Encouraged by the existing efforts on query generation in the QA community, we presented ExSQG as an extension to an available query generator component (SQG [33]) in order to support *Filter* and *Ordinal* questions. We provided a hierarchical architecture for a question classifier, which yields high accuracy in different benchmarking datasets. Furthermore, ExSQG augments the query using identified keywords from the question and match them to the linked items from the KG based on word embedding techniques. Finally, we empirically showed that ExSQG achieves state-of-the-art accuracy on the benchmarking datasets.

Considering the upcoming Q/A datasets such as LC-QuAD 2.0 [10], which not only contains *Ordinal* and *Filter* in about 17% out of 50k questions, but also includes new types such as *aggregation*, which appears in more than 4% of all questions, we aim to expand our work to also cover aggregation.

Acknowledgments. This research was supported by the European Union H2020 project CLEOPATRA (ITN, GA. 812997) as well as by the German Federal Ministry of Education and Research (BMBF) funding for the project SOLIDE (no. 13N14456).

References

1. Abujabal, A., Yahya, M., Riedewald, M., Weikum, G.: Automated template generation for question answering over knowledge graphs. In: Proceedings of the 26th International Conference on World Wide Web, pp. 1191–1200. International World Wide Web Conferences Steering Committee (2017)
2. Auer, S., Bizer, C., Kobilarov, G., Lehmann, J., Cyganiak, R., Ives, Z.: DBpedia: a nucleus for a web of open data. In: Cudré-Mauroux, P., et al. (eds.) ASWC/ISWC -2007. LNCS, vol. 4825, pp. 722–735. Springer, Heidelberg (2007). https://doi.org/10.1007/978-3-540-76298-0_52
3. Berant, J., Chou, A., Frostig, R., Liang, P.: Semantic parsing on freebase from question-answer pairs. In: Proceedings of the 2013 Conference on Empirical Methods in Natural Language Processing, pp. 1533–1544 (2013)
4. Berant, J., Liang, P.: Semantic parsing via paraphrasing. In: Proceedings of the 52nd Annual Meeting of the Association for Computational Linguistics (Volume 1: Long Papers), pp. 1415–1425 (2014)
5. Bollacker, K., Evans, C., Paritosh, P., Sturge, T., Taylor, J.: Freebase: a collaboratively created graph database for structuring human knowledge. In: Proceedings of the 2008 ACM SIGMOD International Conference on Management of Data, pp. 1247–1250. ACM (2008)
6. Bordes, A., Chopra, S., Weston, J.: Question answering with subgraph embeddings. arXiv preprint arXiv:1406.3676 (2014)
7. Bordes, A., Usunier, N., Chopra, S., Weston, J.: Large-scale simple question answering with memory networks. arXiv preprint arXiv:1506.02075 (2015)
8. Diefenbach, D., Both, A., Singh, K., Maret, P.: Towards a question answering system over the semantic web. Semant. Web (Preprint) 1–19 (2018)
9. Diefenbach, D., Lopez, V., Singh, K., Maret, P.: Core techniques of question answering systems over knowledge bases: a survey. Knowl. Inf. Syst. **55**(3), 529–569 (2018)
10. Dubey, M., Banerjee, D., Abdelkawi, A., Lehmann, J.: Lc-quad 2.0: a large dataset for complex question answering over Wikidata and dbpedia. In: Proceedings of the 18th International Semantic Web Conference (ISWC). Springer (2019)
11. Dubey, M., Dasgupta, S., Sharma, A., Höffner, K., Lehmann, J.: AskNow: a framework for natural language query formalization in SPARQL. In: Sack, H., Blomqvist, E., d'Aquin, M., Ghidini, C., Ponzetto, S.P., Lange, C. (eds.) ESWC 2016. LNCS, vol. 9678, pp. 300–316. Springer, Cham (2016). https://doi.org/10.1007/978-3-319-34129-3_19

586   A. Abdelkawi et al.

12. Hakimov, S., Unger, C., Walter, S., Cimiano, P.: Applying semantic parsing to question answering over linked data: addressing the lexical gap. In: Biemann, C., Handschuh, S., Freitas, A., Meziane, F., Métais, E. (eds.) NLDB 2015. LNCS, vol. 9103, pp. 103–109. Springer, Cham (2015). https://doi.org/10.1007/978-3-319-19581-0_8
13. Hamon, T., Grabar, N., Mougin, F., Thiessard, F.: Description of the POMELO system for the task 2 of QALD-2014. In: CLEF (Working Notes), pp. 1212–1223 (2014)
14. Höffner, K., Walter, S., Marx, E., Usbeck, R., Lehmann, J., Ngonga Ngomo, A.C.: Survey on challenges of question answering in the semantic web. Semant. Web 8(6), 895–920 (2017)
15. Kusner, M., Sun, Y., Kolkin, N., Weinberger, K.: From word embeddings to document distances. In: International Conference on Machine Learning, pp. 957–966 (2015)
16. Lehmann, J., et al.: DBpedia - a large-scale, multilingual knowledge base extracted from wikipedia. Semant. Web J. 6(2), 167–195 (2015)
17. Lindberg, D.A., Humphreys, B.L., McCray, A.T.: The unified medical language system. Yearb. Med. Inf. 2(01), 41–51 (1993)
18. Lukovnikov, D., Fischer, A., Lehmann, J., Auer, S.: Neural network-based question answering over knowledge graphs on word and character level. In: Proceedings of the 26th International Conference on World Wide Web, pp. 1211–1220. International World Wide Web Conferences Steering Committee (2017)
19. Maheshwari, G., Trivedi, P., Lukovnikov, D., Chakraborty, N., Fischer, A., Lehmann, J.: Learning to rank query graphs for complex question answering over knowledge graphs. In: International Semantic Web Conference. Springer (2019)
20. Miller, G.A.: WordNet: a lexical database for English. Commun. ACM 38(11), 39–41 (1995)
21. Ngomo, N.: 9th challenge on question answering over linked data (QALD-9). language 7, 1
22. Chakraborty, N., Lukovnikov, D., Maheshwari, G., Trivedi, P., Lehmann, J., Fischer, A.: Introduction to neural network based approaches for question answering over knowledge graphs (2019)
23. Pennington, J., Socher, R., Manning, C.: Glove: global vectors for word representation. In: Proceedings of the 2014 Conference on Empirical Methods in Natural Language Processing (EMNLP), pp. 1532–1543 (2014)
24. Shekarpour, S., Marx, E., Ngomo, A.C.N., Auer, S.: Sina: Semantic interpretation of user queries for question answering on interlinked data. Web Semant.: Sci. Serv. Agents World Wide Web 30, 39–51 (2015)
25. Singh, K., et al.: Why reinvent the wheel: Let's build question answering systems together. In: Proceedings of the 2018 World Wide Web Conference on World Wide Web, pp. 1247–1256. International World Wide Web Conferences Steering Committee (2018)
26. SZ, H., et al.: Casia@ v2: A MLN-based question answering system over linked data (2014)
27. Trivedi, P., Maheshwari, G., Dubey, M., Lehmann, J.: LC-QuAD: a corpus for complex question answering over knowledge graphs. In: d'Amato, C., et al. (eds.) ISWC 2017. LNCS, vol. 10588, pp. 210–218. Springer, Cham (2017). https://doi.org/10.1007/978-3-319-68204-4_22
28. Unger, C., Bühmann, L., Lehmann, J., Ngonga Ngomo, A.C., Gerber, D., Cimiano, P.: Template-based question answering over RDF data. In: Proceedings of the 21st International Conference on World Wide Web, pp. 639–648. ACM (2012)

29. Walter, S., Unger, C., Cimiano, P., Bär, D.: Evaluation of a layered approach to question answering over linked data. In: Cudré-Mauroux, P., et al. (eds.) ISWC 2012. LNCS, vol. 7650, pp. 362–374. Springer, Heidelberg (2012). https://doi.org/10.1007/978-3-642-35173-0_25

30. Wick, M.: GeoNames. GeoNames (2006)

31. Yih, S.W.T., Chang, M.W., He, X., Gao, J.: Semantic parsing via staged query graph generation: question answering with knowledge base (2015)

32. Yin, W., Yu, M., Xiang, B., Zhou, B., Schütze, H.: Simple question answering by attentive convolutional neural network. arXiv preprint arXiv:1606.03391 (2016)

33. Zafar, H., Napolitano, G., Lehmann, J.: Formal query generation for question answering over knowledge bases. In: Gangemi, A., et al. (eds.) ESWC 2018. LNCS, vol. 10843, pp. 714–728. Springer, Cham (2018). https://doi.org/10.1007/978-3-319-93417-4_46

34. Zettlemoyer, L.S., Collins, M.: Learning to map sentences to logical form: structured classification with probabilistic categorial grammars. arXiv preprint arXiv:1207.1420 (2012)

A Subjective Logic Based Approach to Handling Inconsistencies in Ontology Merging

Samira Babalou[(✉)] and Birgitta König-Ries

Heinz-Nixdorf Chair for Distributed Information Systems, Institute for Computer
Science, Friedrich Schiller University, Jena, Germany
{samira.babalou,birgitta.koenig-ries}@uni-jena.de

Abstract. Ontologies reflect their creators' view of the domain at hand
and are thus subjective. For specific applications it may be necessary to
combine several of these ontologies into a more comprehensive domain
model by merging them. However, due to the subjective nature of
the source ontologies, this can result in inconsistencies. Handling these
inconsistencies is a challenging task even for modestly sized ontologies.
Therefore, in this paper, we propose a Subjective Logic based approach
to cope with inconsistencies originating in the ontology merging process.
We formulate subjective opinions about the inconsistency causing axioms
based on several pieces of evidence such as provenance information and
structural relevance by utilizing consensus and conditional deduction
operators. This allows creating an environment that supports handling
of these inconsistencies. It provides the necessary mechanisms to capture
the subjective opinion of different communities represented by the input
ontologies on the trustworthiness of each axiom in the merged ontology
and identifies the least trustworthy axioms. It suggests remedies of
the inconsistencies, e.g. deleting or rewriting axioms, to the user. Our
experimental results show that with this approach it is possible to
overcome the inconsistency problem in ontology merging and that the
approach is feasible and effective.

Keywords: Semantic Web · Ontology merging · Inconsistency ·
Subjective Logic · Trust model

1 Introduction

Ontologies are an important tool for capturing domain knowledge. They reflect
their creators' view on the domain and are thus somewhat subjective. For many
applications, it is necessary to combine several of these ontologies into a new
merged one. Even if the input ontologies are consistent, the resulting merged
ontology may be inconsistent due to differing world views encoded into the input
ontologies. These inconsistencies need to be resolved if one wants to make use
of the merged ontology. This resolution is, however, a challenging problem.

© Springer Nature Switzerland AG 2019
H. Panetto et al. (Eds.): OTM 2019, LNCS 11877, pp. 588–606, 2019.
https://doi.org/10.1007/978-3-030-33246-4_37

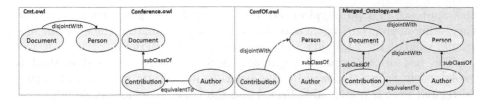

Fig. 1. Excerpt of three sample ontologies which are consistent themselves, but the merged ontology including the union of these axioms is inconsistent.

Existing approaches [8,15,17,24] only consider inconsistency in single ontology development environments and do not deal with the possibility of inconsistencies in the ontology merging domain, or they [21] heavily depend on the determination of a reference ontology. The main difference between the two is, that inconsistencies in single ontologies are typically the result of modeling errors (and thus relatively easy to correct) whereas inconsistencies in merged ontologies may stem from differing perspectives on the domain at hand, each of them correct in their own right. Resolving these inconsistencies is a lot harder and boils down to determining which of the sources is the most trustworthy one for the application at hand. This can be a considerable challenge even for experts in the face of modestly sized ontologies.

Let us illustrate this issue with an example to demonstrate how the merged ontology can become inconsistent relatively easily. Consider a few axioms in Fig. 1 from three sample ontologies of the OAEI conference benchmark[1]. The presented axioms in each input ontology themselves are consistent with the rest of the existing axioms in their respective ontologies. However, when the similar classes are merged, this results in an ontology that is inconsistent. The merged ontology including simultaneously the following axioms from the input ontologies is inconsistent (see Definition 2): {((Contribution ≡ Author) ⊑ Document), ((Author ≡ Contribution) ⊑ Person), (Document ⊑ ¬Person)}. In order to turn the merged ontology in a consistent one, one or several of these axioms need to be removed or altered. To decide upon which of these axioms are the least trustworthy, *Subjective Logic* theory [13] can be applied as it allows to reflect the subjective view of each input ontology.

In this paper, which extends, concretises and evaluates the idea we presented in [4], we propose a Subjective Logic-based approach to handling the inconsistency problem occurring while merging ontologies. Subjective logic captures opinions about the world in belief models and provides a set of operations for combining opinions. This provides an effective environment to manage and combine beliefs over a set of mutually exclusive assertions from multiple agents. It is applicable when the problem at the hand to be analyzed is characterized by considerable uncertainty and incomplete knowledge. We apply this logic to rank and estimate the trustworthiness of conflicting axioms that cause inconsistencies within a merged ontology. We have implemented

---

[1] http://oaei.ontologymatching.org/2018/conference/.

this approach in a prototypical tool that automatically generates repair plans suggesting appropriate axiom edits based on these estimates. The experimental results validate the feasibility and effectiveness of our method.

The rest of the paper is organized as follows: our proposed method is explained in Sect. 2, followed by the experimental results in Sect. 3. A survey on related work is presented in Sect. 4 and the paper concludes in Sect. 5.

2   Proposed Method

Before we introduce our method, we lay the foundation by outlining our assumptions about ontologies [7], inconsistent ontologies [2], and the merge process [22] as follows:

Definition 1. *An ontology $\mathcal{O} = (\mathcal{T}, \mathcal{A})$ is a formal explicit, description of a domain. It consists of a Tbox $\mathcal{T}$, a finite set of axioms describing constraints on the conceptual schema and an Abox $\mathcal{A}$, which contains assertions about individuals.*

Definition 2. *An ontology $\mathcal{O}$ is inconsistent iff there is no model of $\mathcal{O}$, i.e. $\mathcal{O}$ is unsatisfiable.*

Definition 3. *Given a set of input/source ontologies $\mathcal{O}_S = \{\mathcal{O}_1, \mathcal{O}_2, ..., \mathcal{O}_n\}$ ($n \geqslant 2$) and a set of mappings $\mathcal{M}$, an ontology merging process creates a new merged ontology $\mathcal{O}_M$. We denote an inconsistent result ontology by $\mathcal{O}_M$ while $\mathcal{O}'_M$ denotes a consistent one.*

Figure 2 provides an overview of our approach and shows how our proposed method can be used to repair inconsistent merged ontologies:

1. The merged ontology is evaluated using off-the-shelf reasoners such as Pellet [25].
2. For the inconsistent merged ontology, the sets of conflicting axioms that cause inconsistencies are identified using the reasoner.
3. Trustworthiness of each axiom is computed based on our Subjective Logic-based approach.
4. The axioms with the lowest trustworthiness are presented to the user.
5. A repair plan (revising the least trustworthy axioms) provided by the user or the system will be applied.

In this section, first the Subjective Logic theory briefly is described in Sect. 2.1. We then explain how we apply Subjective Logic to handle inconsistencies of the merged ontology in Sect. 2.2. We present our algorithm using this approach in Sect. 2.3 and provide some insights into the creation of a repair plan in Sect. 2.4. Finally, we provide an illustrative example in Sect. 2.5.

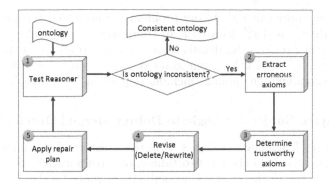

Fig. 2. An overview of our proposed method to handle ontology merging inconsistencies.

2.1   Subjective Logic

Subjective opinions express beliefs of agents about the truth of propositions with degrees of uncertainty [13]. This is a belief calculus that allows agents to express opinions with degrees of belief, disbelief, uncertainty and atomicity about propositions $\mathcal{P}$. In particular, *belief* is the belief that $\mathcal{P}$ is true, *disbelief* is the belief that $\mathcal{P}$ is false, *uncertainty* is the amount of uncommitted belief, and *atomicity* is the base rate (a priori probability in the absence of evidence).

Let $\mathcal{P}$ be a proposition such as "Axiom x is trustworthy in the context of merged ontology $\mathcal{O}_M$". Then, the binomial *opinion* w of agent[2] $\mathcal{O}_i \in \mathcal{O}_S$ about the proposition $\mathcal{P}$ is equivalent to a beta distribution for the information source x as the combination of belief $b_x^{\mathcal{O}_i}$, disbelief $d_x^{\mathcal{O}_i}$, uncertainty $u_x^{\mathcal{O}_i}$, and atomicity (a priori probability) $a_x^{\mathcal{O}_i}$ with a tuple given by Eq. 1 (as defined in [13]), where $b_x^{\mathcal{O}_i} + d_x^{\mathcal{O}_i} + u_x^{\mathcal{O}_i} = 1.0$ and $b_x^{\mathcal{O}_i}, d_x^{\mathcal{O}_i}, u_x^{\mathcal{O}_i}, a_x^{\mathcal{O}_i} \in [0,1]$.

$$w_x^{\mathcal{O}_i} = (b_x^{\mathcal{O}_i}, d_x^{\mathcal{O}_i}, u_x^{\mathcal{O}_i}, a_x^{\mathcal{O}_i}) \tag{1}$$

Opinions are formed on the basis of positive and negative evidence. Let r and s be the number of positive and negative past observations about x respectively by agent $\mathcal{O}_i$. Then, $b_x^{\mathcal{O}_i}, d_x^{\mathcal{O}_i}$, and $u_x^{\mathcal{O}_i}$ are defined as follows [13]:

$$b_x^{\mathcal{O}_i} = \frac{r_x^{\mathcal{O}_i}}{r_x^{\mathcal{O}_i} + s_x^{\mathcal{O}_i} + W}, \quad d_x^{\mathcal{O}_i} = \frac{s_x^{\mathcal{O}_i}}{r_x^{\mathcal{O}_i} + s_x^{\mathcal{O}_i} + W}, \quad u_x^{\mathcal{O}_i} = \frac{W}{r_x^{\mathcal{O}_i} + s_x^{\mathcal{O}_i} + W} \tag{2}$$

where, W is the default non-informative prior weight that in binomial opinions is defined as $W = 2$. Thus, the opinion's probability expectation value [13] is computed in Eq. 3 as the trustworthiness of x by agent $\mathcal{O}_i$ (for more details on Eqs. 2 and 3, see [13]):

$$t_x^{\mathcal{O}_i} = b_x^{\mathcal{O}_i} + a_x^{\mathcal{O}_i} \times u_x^{\mathcal{O}_i} \tag{3}$$

---

[2] In this work, we consider input ontologies as agents. see Sect. 2.2 for the rationale.

In order to apply this logic to our problem, we need to determine the agents and formulate $r_x^{\mathcal{O}_i}$ and $s_x^{\mathcal{O}_i}$ as a basis to computing $b_x^{\mathcal{O}_i}, d_x^{\mathcal{O}_i}, u_x^{\mathcal{O}_i}$ and $a_x^{\mathcal{O}_i}$. The next subsection provides the details about our contribution to this: First, we formulate $r_x^{\mathcal{O}_i}$, $s_x^{\mathcal{O}_i}$ and $a_x^{\mathcal{O}_i}$ in our context and second, we utilize consensus operators to combine the opinions includes dependencies across them.

2.2   Applying Subjective Logic to Debug Merged Ontologies

In the context of merging ontologies, it is the creators of the input ontologies that have opinions about the trustworthiness of certain axioms. Since we do not have direct access to the creators, we substitute them by the ontologies they created which reflect these subjective views. Thus for us, the input ontologies reflecting the creators believe play the agent role.

Negative Observation. Before determining the negative observation s, we first provide some basic definitions and notations:

Definition 4. *Unsatisfiable concepts[3] C_{un} are concepts which cannot have any individuals [2]. We denote them by $C_{un} = \{c_1, c_2, ..., c_u\}$.*

$Root(C_{un})$ returns the unsatisfiable root concepts[4] [15]. If there are a large number of unsatisfiable concepts in an inconsistent ontology, restricting the repair efforts to the root concepts may considerably reduce the necessary effort.

Definition 5. *Let $\mathcal{O}$ be an ontology entailing axiom x ($\mathcal{O} \models x$). $\mathcal{J}_d$ is a justification for x in $\mathcal{O}$ if $\mathcal{J}_d \subseteq \mathcal{O}$, and $\mathcal{J}_d \models x$, and for all $\mathcal{J}_d' \subsetneq \mathcal{J}_d$ $\mathcal{J}_d' \not\models x$ [10].*

Intuitively, a justification is a minimal subset of an ontology that causes it to be inconsistent. The ontology justification set $\mathcal{J}$ is the set of all justifications, $\mathcal{J} = \{\mathcal{J}_1, \mathcal{J}_2, ..., \mathcal{J}_l\}$ and $\mathcal{J}_d \in \mathcal{J}$, where there may be multiple, potentially overlapping justifications in $\mathcal{J}$. Each justification $\mathcal{J}_d \in \mathcal{J}$ includes several axioms, denoted by $\mathcal{J}_d = (x_1, x_2, ..., x_z)$. We represent all distinct axioms belonging to justification set $\mathcal{J}$ by X and call them the conflicting axioms set (a group of axioms that conflict with each other). We define the elements $\{e_1, e_2, ..., e_t\}$ of axiom $x_j \in X$ as those entities which are involved in x_j, e.g. A and B in the axiom $x_1 : A \sqsubseteq B$. Moreover, the trustworthiness of X is indicated by $\overline{X}$.

In the following, to determine the negative observation s, we use the axiom frequency for x_j (i.e. number of x_j) in the justification set $\mathcal{J}$ denoted by $\Psi_{x_j}(\mathcal{J})$, divided by the number of conflicting axiom sets $\Psi_{\mathcal{O}_i}(X)$ which belong to $\mathcal{O}_i$ in Eq. 4 (to reflect the view of $\mathcal{O}_i$). This idea is similar to the notion of *arity* of

---

[3] The term "concept" refers to the classes based on our given ontology definition. We keep the term here to be uniform with the unsatisfiable concept's definition in literature reviews.

[4] This is an unsatisfiable class in which a contradiction found in the class definition does not depend on the unsatisfiability of another class in the ontology.

the axiom as discussed in [23], and is already used in the [15] to accelerate the process of getting rid of unsatisfiable concepts.

$$s^{\mathcal{O}_i}_{x_j} = \frac{\Psi_{x_j}(\mathcal{J})}{\Psi_{\mathcal{O}_i}(X)} \tag{4}$$

Positive Observation. To determine the positive observations r of an axiom $x_j \in X$, we use its provenance information. Each axiom in $\mathcal{O}_M$ is derived from one or several input ontologies $\mathcal{O}_i$. Therefore, r for x_j from agents $\mathcal{O}_i$ is calculated as (i) the existence[5] of the axiom x_j in $\mathcal{O}_i$ (*provenance information*), and (ii) the impact of changes in the axiom x_j in $\mathcal{O}_M$ (*effect*). The metric in (ii) reflects how much the ontology gets affected, if the axiom x_j is removed or altered. To this end, we determine how often the elements e_{x_j} of axiom x_j have been referenced in other axioms in the ontology. Let $\Gamma(\mathcal{O}_i)$ be the total number of axioms in $\mathcal{O}_i$ and $\Gamma_{x_j}(\mathcal{O}_i)$ be the number of axioms in $\mathcal{O}_i$ that contains elements of x_j. Then $f_{x_j}(\mathcal{O}_i) = \frac{\Gamma_{x_j}(\mathcal{O}_i)}{\Gamma(\mathcal{O}_i)}$ is the fraction of axioms in $\mathcal{O}_i$ that contains elements of x_j. The significance of this strategy is based on the following intuition: if the elements in the axiom are used and referred too often in the remaining axioms, then changing or removing axioms related to these elements may be undesired. For example, if a certain class is heavily instantiated, or if a certain property is heavily used in the instance data, then altering the axiom definitions of that class or property is a change that the user needs to be aware of. Therefore, r is calculated as *provenance* × *effect* in Eq. 5. The provenance of the axioms is represented by the α and β parameters[6]; if $x_j \notin \mathcal{O}_i$, but at least one element of the axiom exist in $\mathcal{O}_i$, then $f_{x_j}(\mathcal{O}_i)$ is multiplied with β, otherwise, it is multiplied with α.

$$r^{\mathcal{O}_i}_{x_j} = \begin{cases} \alpha \times f_{x_j}(\mathcal{O}_i) & \text{if } x_j \in \mathcal{O}_i \\ \beta \times f_{x_j}(\mathcal{O}_i) & \text{if } x_j \notin \mathcal{O}_i \end{cases} \tag{5}$$

Atomicity. In the absence of evidence for belief, disbelief, and uncertainty, the atomicity metric plays an important role. It reflects prior knowledge about the phenomenon at hand. To determine this a priory probability in our context, we use the centrality measure as an available indicator based on ontology characteristics. We propose to use centrality measures to capture these characteristics. These measures are designed to rank the entities according to their positions in the graph and are interpreted as the prominence of entities embedded in an intended structure. In [1], centrality measures have been successfully utilized to rank the importance of ontology entities. Following this idea, we use them to express atomicity.

---

[5] In our prototype, the existence of an axiom in an input ontology is determined by searching their equivalent elements based on the given mapping assumptions $\mathcal{M}$. This could be extended to more powerful logic-based approaches.

[6] α and β parameters can be determined by the user.

This leads us to use degree centrality [18], which calculates the number of connections of a node. In a directed graph, there are an in-degree and an out-degree centrality that calculate the number of input and output links, respectively. In context of ontologies, we indicate the in-degree and out-degree with the number of super- and subclasses. Therefore, the base rate for axiom x_j with t elements $x_j = \{e_1, e_2, ..., e_t\}$ is given by Eq. 6, as the total number of super- and subclasses of the elements divided by the total number of elements $|e|$ in $\mathcal{O}_i$. It is evident that the atomicity value for an entity increases with its number of neighbors.

$$a^{\mathcal{O}_i}_{x_j} = \frac{1}{|e| \in \mathcal{O}_i} \times \sum_{g=1}^{t} |SubClass(e_g) \cup SuperClass(e_g)|, \quad e_g \in x_j \quad (6)$$

Combining Opinions. Up to now, we have been looking at opinions of individual agents. The combine operator of Subjective Logic computes (as its name suggests) the combination of opinions of different agents. In this way, the more trustworthy opinions will be those that are agreed upon by multiple agents. The consensus rule for combining opinions consists of combining two or more independent and possibly conflicting opinions about the same proposition into a single opinion that reflects both opinions in a fair and equal way. The Subjective Logic operator *consensus* ($\oplus$) [13] is used to achieve this.

Let $w^{\mathcal{O}_1}_x = (b^{\mathcal{O}_1}_x, d^{\mathcal{O}_1}_x, u^{\mathcal{O}_1}_x, a^{\mathcal{O}_1}_x)$ and $w^{\mathcal{O}_2}_x = (b^{\mathcal{O}_2}_x, d^{\mathcal{O}_2}_x, u^{\mathcal{O}_2}_x, a^{\mathcal{O}_2}_x)$ be opinions respectively held by $\mathcal{O}_1$ and $\mathcal{O}_2$ about the same proposition x. Then the consensus ($\oplus$) for these two opinions is calculated as follows [13]:

$$w^{\mathcal{O}_1\mathcal{O}_2}_x = w^{\mathcal{O}_1}_x \oplus w^{\mathcal{O}_2}_x = \left(\frac{b^{\mathcal{O}_1}_x u^{\mathcal{O}_2}_x + b^{\mathcal{O}_2}_x u^{\mathcal{O}_1}_x}{k}, \frac{d^{\mathcal{O}_1}_x u^{\mathcal{O}_2}_x + d^{\mathcal{O}_2}_x u^{\mathcal{O}_1}_x}{k}, \right.$$
$$\left. \frac{u^{\mathcal{O}_1}_x u^{\mathcal{O}_2}_x}{k}, \frac{a^{\mathcal{O}_1}_x u^{\mathcal{O}_2}_x + a^{\mathcal{O}_2}_x u^{\mathcal{O}_1}_x - (a^{\mathcal{O}_1}_x + a^{\mathcal{O}_2}_x)u^{\mathcal{O}_1}_x u^{\mathcal{O}_2}_x}{u^{\mathcal{O}_1}_x + u^{\mathcal{O}_2}_x - 2u^{\mathcal{O}_1}_x u^{\mathcal{O}_2}_x} \right) \quad (7)$$

where $k = u^{\mathcal{O}_1}_x + u^{\mathcal{O}_2}_x - u^{\mathcal{O}_1}_x u^{\mathcal{O}_2}_x$ such that $k \neq 0$ and $a^{\mathcal{O}_1\mathcal{O}_2}_x = (a^{\mathcal{O}_1}_x + a^{\mathcal{O}_2}_x)/2$ when $u^{\mathcal{O}_1}_x, u^{\mathcal{O}_2}_x = 1$. Further details on Eq. 7 can be found in [13].

Improving Our Method by Conditional Opinions. The described approach so far has a drawback: it does not consider the effect of the calculated ranked values for axioms in one $\mathcal{J}_d$ on the other $\mathcal{J}$s in justification set $\mathcal{J}$. To overcome this issue, we use conditional theory of Subjective Logic [13], which reflects the effect of dependent opinions.

Let us explain our intuition with an example: Suppose $\mathcal{J} = \{\mathcal{J}_1, \mathcal{J}_2, \mathcal{J}_3\}$ is a set of justifications, where axioms are repeated in multiple $\mathcal{J}$s, as $\mathcal{J} = \{(x^{\mathcal{J}_1}_1, x^{\mathcal{J}_1}_2, x^{\mathcal{J}_1}_3), (x^{\mathcal{J}_2}_4, x^{\mathcal{J}_2}_5, x^{\mathcal{J}_2}_6, x^{\mathcal{J}_2}_7), (x^{\mathcal{J}_3}_3, x^{\mathcal{J}_3}_4, x^{\mathcal{J}_3}_5, x^{\mathcal{J}_3}_7, x^{\mathcal{J}_3}_8)\}$. The opinions for $\mathcal{J}_1$ and $\mathcal{J}_2$'s axioms can be calculated as independent opinions using Eq. 1. However, some elements of $\mathcal{J}_3$ have already obtained some ranked values from $\mathcal{J}_1$ and $\mathcal{J}_2$, because, $\mathcal{J}_3 \cap (\mathcal{J}_1, \mathcal{J}_2) \neq \emptyset$. Here, we can use the previous ranked values from $\mathcal{J}_1$ and $\mathcal{J}_2$ for x_3, x_4, x_5, x_7 in $\mathcal{J}_3$, but it might happen that these axioms get differently ranked than the remaining axioms in $\mathcal{J}_3$. Therefore, in an incremental process, we calculate a new value in the each $\mathcal{J}$, but also we consider the effect of the previous ranked values for axioms in other $\mathcal{J}$s[7]. In this case, the proposition $\mathcal{P}$ for instance for axiom x_3 writes as "$x_3 \in \mathcal{J}_3$ is trustworthy if $x_3 \in \mathcal{J}_1$ already has trustworthiness of 0.3".

This idea translates to "IF x THEN y", which is equal to the probability of the proposition y given that the proposition x is TRUE. A more precise expression is therefore $p(\text{IF } x \text{ THEN } y) = p(y|x)$. This has been represented in [13] by $w_{y||x}$ with the following details.

Let $\mathbb{X} = \{x, \bar{x}\}$ and $\mathbb{Y} = \{y, \bar{y}\}$ be two binary frames where there is a degree of relevance between $\mathbb{X}$ and $\mathbb{Y}$. Let $w_x = (b_x, d_x, u_x, a_x)$, $w_{y|x} = (b_{y|x}, d_{y|x}, u_{y|x}, a_{y|x})$ and $w_{y|\bar{x}} = (b_{y|\bar{x}}, d_{y|\bar{x}}, u_{y|\bar{x}}, a_{y|\bar{x}})$ be an agent's respective opinions about x being true, y being true given that x is true, and y being true given that x is false, respectively. The conditional *deduction* operator $\odot$ is a ternary operator [13] (i.e. requires 3 input arguments) in Eq. 8.

$$w_{y||x} = w_x \odot (w_{y|x}, w_{y|\bar{x}}) \tag{8}$$

where the elements of $w_{y||x} = (b_{y||x}, d_{y||x}, u_{y||x}, a_{y||x})$ are specified in Eq. 9. Indicator K can be determined according to three different selection criteria detailed in [13], which are not repeated here due to space limitation.

$$\begin{aligned}
b_{y||x} &= (b_x b_{y|x} + d_x b_{y|\bar{x}} + u_x(b_{y|x}a_x + b_{y|\bar{x}}(1-a_x))) - a_y K \\
d_{y||x} &= (b_x d_{y|x} + d_x d_{y|\bar{x}} + u_x(d_{y|x}a_x + d_{y|\bar{x}}(1-a_x))) - (1-a_y)K \\
u_{y||x} &= (b_x u_{y|x} + d_x u_{y|\bar{x}} + u_x(u_{y|x}a_x + u_{y|\bar{x}}(1-a_x))) + K \\
a_{y||x} &= a_y
\end{aligned} \tag{9}$$

If y relates to multiple x variables, they are combined using the consensus operator as shown by Eq. 10. In our example, several axioms in $\mathcal{J}_3$ are already repeated in $\mathcal{J}_1$ and $\mathcal{J}_2$, i.e. $w_{y||(x_3, x_4, x_5, x_7)}$.

$$w_{y||(x_1, x_2, ... x_j)} = w_{y||x_1} \oplus w_{y||x_2} \oplus ... \oplus w_{y||x_j} \tag{10}$$

This deduction operator requires that $w_{y|x}$ and $w_{y|\bar{x}}$ be formulated in our context. Suppose $w_{x_j}^{\mathcal{J}_1} = (b_{x_j}^{\mathcal{J}_1}, d_{x_j}^{\mathcal{J}_1}, u_{x_j}^{\mathcal{J}_1}, a_{x_j}^{\mathcal{J}_1})$ and $w_{x_f}^{\mathcal{J}_2} = (b_{x_f}^{\mathcal{J}_2}, d_{x_f}^{\mathcal{J}_2}, u_{x_f}^{\mathcal{J}_2}, a_{x_f}^{\mathcal{J}_2})$ are already calculated by Eq. 1, and let for the sake of simplicity $y = x_f^{\mathcal{J}_2}$ and $x = x_j^{\mathcal{J}_1}$. Then, following the probabilistic conditional $p(y|x) = \frac{p(y \wedge x)}{p(x)}$, we re-write $p(y|x)$ as $w_{y|x} = \frac{w_{y \wedge x}}{w_x}$, where $w_{y \wedge x} = (b_{y \wedge x}, d_{y \wedge x}, u_{y \wedge x}, a_{y \wedge x})$ defined in [13] and is given by Eq. 11. We apply the same approach to $w_{y|\bar{x}}$, where $w_{\bar{x}} = (d_x, b_x, u_x, 1 - a_x)$ [13].

$$\begin{aligned}
b_{y \wedge x} &= b_y b_x, & d_{y \wedge x} &= d_y + d_x - d_y d_x, \\
u_{y \wedge x} &= b_y u_x + u_y b_x + u_y u_x, & a_{y \wedge x} &= \frac{b_y u_x a_x + u_y a_y b_x + u_y a_y u_x a_x}{b_y u_x + u_y b_x + u_y u_x}
\end{aligned} \tag{11}$$

---

[7] The justification set $\mathcal{J} = \{\mathcal{J}_1, \mathcal{J}_2, ..., \mathcal{J}_l\}$ is taken from the OWL-API explanation, which is already sorted by the axiom frequency in $\mathcal{J}$.

The division operation $\frac{w_y}{w_x}$ is defined in [13] as represented in Eq. 12.

$$b_{y\setminus x} = b_y - b_x, \qquad d_{y\setminus x} = \frac{a_y(d_y + b_x) - a_x(1 + b_x - b_y - u_x)}{a_y - a_x},$$

$$u_{y\setminus x} = \frac{a_y u_y - a_x u_x}{a_y - a_x}, \qquad a_{y\setminus x} = a_y - a_x \tag{12}$$

Further details on Eqs. 11 and 12 can be found in [13].

2.3   Algorithm

Algorithm 1 describes our proposed approach at a glance: The algorithm accepts an inconsistent merged ontology $\mathcal{O}_M$ with a set of input/source ontologies $\mathcal{O}_S$ and generates a consistent merged ontology $\mathcal{O}'_M$. At first, the justification set $\mathcal{J}$ for unsatisfiable concepts C_{un} is extracted (*lines 2–3*). For each justification $\mathcal{J}_d \in \mathcal{J}$, the algorithm checks whether it has some shared axioms with other $\mathcal{J}$s, i.e. $(\mathcal{J}_d \cap \{\mathcal{J}_1, \mathcal{J}_2, ..., \mathcal{J}_{d-1}\} \neq \emptyset)$ (*line 7*). If so, the opinion for $x_j \in \mathcal{J}_d$ is calculated as the conditional deduction in *line 8*, otherwise, it is calculated as *line 10*. Then, the opinion combination of all agents takes place *(line 13)*. The ranked value (trustworthiness) for each axiom $x_j \in \mathcal{J}_d$ is represented by $\bar{x}_j^{\mathcal{J}_d}$ and calculated in *lines 14–15* . Based on the ranked axioms, a repair plan is generated (*line 18*) and presented to the users. They can then apply our suggested plan directly or edit it. The produced plan will be applied on $\mathcal{O}_M$ (*line 19*) and if the merged ontology is still inconsistent, the whole process will be repeated, otherwise, $\mathcal{O}'_M$ will be returned as a consistent ontology.

2.4   Repair Plan

In the repair process, a plan should be generated whose primary goal is to suggest a solution for the least trustworthy axioms while preserving the remaining, more trustworthy axioms. To this end, a library of error patterns extracted from [15] has been embedded in our system. A set of candidate changes is presented to the user, in which the user can apply the repair plan on a particular or all proposed axiom(s). The customized generated plan will be applied to the inconsistent ontology and the consistency test will be repeated. It might happen that the user-selected plan cannot get rid of all inconsistency errors in one iteration in the ontology. Therefore, the mentioned procedures will be repeated until a consistent ontology will be achieved. The system, however, is able to apply the repair plan automatically without user intervention.

2.5   Example

Three sample ontologies $\mathcal{O}_1$: cmt, $\mathcal{O}_2$: conference, and $\mathcal{O}3$: confOf from the OAEI conference benchmark[8] have been merged in $\mathcal{O}_M$ as shown

---

[8] http://oaei.ontologymatching.org/2018/conference/.

Algorithm 1: The Subjective Logic-based algorithm for handling inconsistencies in ontology merging

---

Data: an inconsistent merged ontology $\mathcal{O}_M$, a set of source ontologies $\mathcal{O}_S$;

Result: a consistent merged ontology $\mathcal{O}'_M$;

1 **while** ($\mathcal{O}_M$ *is inconsistent*) **do**
2     $C_{un} \Leftarrow$ extract unsatisfiable concepts from $\mathcal{O}_M$;
3     $\mathcal{J} \Leftarrow$ extract justifications for C_{un};
4   **for** ($\forall \; \mathcal{J}_d \in \mathcal{J}$) **do**
5   **for** ($\forall \; x_j \in \mathcal{J}_d$) **do**
6   **for** ($\forall \; \mathcal{O}_i \in \mathcal{O}_S$) **do**
7   **if** ($\mathcal{J}_d \cap \{\mathcal{J}_1, \mathcal{J}_2, ..., \mathcal{J}_{d-1}\} \neq \emptyset$) **then**
8                 $w_{x_j}^{\mathcal{O}_i} \Leftarrow w_{y||(x_j)}^{\mathcal{O}_i}$ according to Eq. 8;
9   **else**
10                 $w_{x_j}^{\mathcal{O}_i} \Leftarrow (b_{x_j}^{\mathcal{O}_i}, d_{x_j}^{\mathcal{O}_i}, u_{x_j}^{\mathcal{O}_i}, a_{x_j}^{\mathcal{O}_i})$ according to Eq. 2 and 6;
11   **end**
12   **end**
13           $w_{x_j}^{\mathcal{O}} = w_{x_j}^{\mathcal{O}_1} \oplus ... \oplus w_{x_j}^{\mathcal{O}_n}$ according to Eq. 7;
14           $t_{x_j}^{\mathcal{O}} = b_{x_j}^{\mathcal{O}} + a_{x_j}^{\mathcal{O}} \times u_{x_j}^{\mathcal{O}}$ according to Eq. 3;
15           $\bar{x}_j^{\mathcal{J}_d} \Leftarrow t_{x_j}^{\mathcal{O}}$
16   **end**
17   **end**
18     $plan \Leftarrow GenerateRepairPlan(\overline{X})$;
19     $\mathcal{O}_M \Leftarrow ApplyPlan(\mathcal{O}_M, plan)$;
20 **end**
21 $\mathcal{O}'_M \Leftarrow \mathcal{O}_M$;
22 **return** $\mathcal{O}'_M$

---

in Fig. 3 (Merger component). The Pellet reasoner [25] component in Fig. 3 shows $\mathcal{O}_M$ is inconsistent and has two unsatisfiable root classes $C_{un}(c_1 = \text{Participant}$ and $c_2 = \text{Contribution})$. The justification of these two unsatisfiable classes returns 12 axioms[9] in 3 justification groups $\mathcal{J} = \{(x_1^{\mathcal{J}_1}, x_2^{\mathcal{J}_1}, x_3^{\mathcal{J}_1}), (x_4^{\mathcal{J}_2}, x_5^{\mathcal{J}_2}, x_6^{\mathcal{J}_2}, x_7^{\mathcal{J}_2}), (x_3^{\mathcal{J}_3}, x_4^{\mathcal{J}_3}, x_5^{\mathcal{J}_3}, x_7^{\mathcal{J}_3}, x_8^{\mathcal{J}_3})\}$, i.e. $\mathcal{J} = \{\mathcal{J}_1, \mathcal{J}_2, \mathcal{J}_3\}$. In order to make the ontology consistent, at least one axiom from each justification should be removed or rewritten. To compute which axioms should be revised, we follow the presented Subjective Logic-based approach.

Axioms in the first $\mathcal{J}$ are not dependent on previous justifications, so they follow the independent opinion process as it is shown in Fig. 3 (Ranker component). Proposition $\mathcal{P}$ for instance, for $x_1 \in \mathcal{J}_1$ is written as "the information source $x_1^{\mathcal{J}_1}$ is trustworthy in the merged ontology $\mathcal{O}_M$". Ontology agent $\mathcal{O}_1$ has the opinion $w_{x_1^{\mathcal{J}_1}}^{\mathcal{O}_1} = (b_{x_1^{\mathcal{J}_1}}^{\mathcal{O}_1}, d_{x_1^{\mathcal{J}_1}}^{\mathcal{O}_1}, u_{x_1^{\mathcal{J}_1}}^{\mathcal{O}_1}, a_{x_1^{\mathcal{J}_1}}^{\mathcal{O}_1}) = (0.3, 0.5, 0.2, 0.3)$, ontology $\mathcal{O}_2$ has the opinion $w_{x_1^{\mathcal{J}_1}}^{\mathcal{O}_2} = (b_{x_1^{\mathcal{J}_1}}^{\mathcal{O}_2}, d_{x_1^{\mathcal{J}_1}}^{\mathcal{O}_2}, u_{x_1^{\mathcal{J}_1}}^{\mathcal{O}_2}, a_{x_1^{\mathcal{J}_1}}^{\mathcal{O}_2}) = (0.7, 0.1, 0.2, 0.2)$,

---

[9] The axioms' details are represented in the orange boxes in Fig. 3.

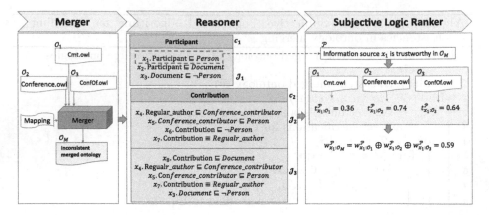

Fig. 3. An inconsistent merged ontology with three justifications $(\mathcal{J}_1, \mathcal{J}_2, \mathcal{J}_3)$ for two unsatisfiable root classes (c_1, c_2). Opinions from the three ontologies are combined by the Subjective Logic-based approach for one proposition. (Color figure online)

and agent $\mathcal{O}_3$'s opinion is $w^{\mathcal{O}_3}_{x_1^{\mathcal{J}_1}} = (b^{\mathcal{O}_3}_{x_1^{\mathcal{J}_1}}, d^{\mathcal{O}_3}_{x_1^{\mathcal{J}_1}}, u^{\mathcal{O}_3}_{x_1^{\mathcal{J}_1}}, a^{\mathcal{O}_3}_{x_1^{\mathcal{J}_1}}) = (0.4, 0.3, 0.3, 0.8)$. The combined opinion for $x_1^{\mathcal{J}_1}$ is calculated as $w^{\mathcal{O}}_{x_1^{\mathcal{J}_1}} = w^{\mathcal{O}_1}_{x_1^{\mathcal{J}_1}} \oplus w^{\mathcal{O}_2}_{x_1^{\mathcal{J}_1}} \oplus w^{\mathcal{O}_3}_{x_1^{\mathcal{J}_1}} = (0.56, 0.35, 0.09, 0.37)$. Thus, the opinion's probability exception value for axiom x_1 based on Eq. 3 is $t^{\mathcal{O}}_{x_1^{\mathcal{J}_1}} = b^{\mathcal{O}}_{x_1^{\mathcal{J}_1}} + a^{\mathcal{O}}_{x_1^{\mathcal{J}_1}} \times u^{\mathcal{O}}_{x_1^{\mathcal{J}_1}} = 0.59$. The opinions for $x_2, x_3 \in \mathcal{J}_1$ are calculated accordingly.

Axioms in $\mathcal{J}_2$ do not already have a value in $\mathcal{J}_1$, so they are calculated using the same procedure. However, for axioms in $\mathcal{J}_3$, we follow the conditional deduction, as they are dependent on the previous $\mathcal{J}s$. For instance, for axiom x_3 in $\mathcal{J}_3$, proposition $\mathcal{P}$ is written as "$x_3^{\mathcal{J}_3}$ is trustworthy iff $t^{\mathcal{O}}_{x_3^{\mathcal{J}_1}} = 0.63$, $t^{\mathcal{O}}_{x_4^{\mathcal{J}_2}} = 0.27, t^{\mathcal{O}}_{x_5^{\mathcal{J}_2}} = 0.32$, and $t^{\mathcal{O}}_{x_7^{\mathcal{J}_2}} = 0.58$". Then, the conditional opinion is $w_{x_3^{\mathcal{J}_3} || (x_3^{\mathcal{J}_1}, x_4^{\mathcal{J}_2}, x_5^{\mathcal{J}_2}, x_7^{\mathcal{J}_2})} = w_{x_3^{\mathcal{J}_3} || x_3^{\mathcal{J}_1}} \oplus w_{x_3^{\mathcal{J}_3} || x_4^{\mathcal{J}_2}} \oplus w_{x_3^{\mathcal{J}_3} || x_5^{\mathcal{J}_2}} \oplus w_{x_3^{\mathcal{J}_3} || x_7^{\mathcal{J}_2}} = 0.2$.

The remaining axioms follow the same processes. As a result, $x_1 \in \mathcal{J}_1$, $x_5 \in \mathcal{J}_2$, and $x_5 \in \mathcal{J}_3$ will be presented to the user for revision, as they are the least trustworthy in their respective justification sets.

3   Experimental Evaluation

To evaluate and validate the applicability of the proposed approach, we conducted a series of experiments utilizing different ontologies. In the following, we first present the used datasets, then we describe experimental environments, and finally, we report about experimental results.

3.1   Dataset

Our proposed method has been tested on a variety of ontologies (see Table 1). We selected sets of ontologies from the conference (*d1–d9*) and anatomy (*d10*) track

Table 1. Dataset statistics

id	Input ont. $\mathcal{O}_i$				$\mathcal{T} \in \mathcal{O}_i$				$\mathcal{A} \in \mathcal{O}_i$				$F_{\mathcal{M}_{non-perf.}}$	$\mathcal{T},\mathcal{A} \in \mathcal{O}_{M_{perf.}}$		$\mathcal{T},\mathcal{A} \in \mathcal{O}_{M_{non-perf.}}$	
d1	cmt	conference			226	272			0	0			0.55%	488	0	484	0
d2	edas	confOf			624	196			115	0			0.52%	777	115	777	115
d3	sigkdd	ekaw			116	225			0	0			0.70%	332	0	329	0
d4	confOf	conference			196	272			0	0			0.56%	434	0	437	0
d5	cmt	conference	confOf		226	272	196		0	0	0		0.52%	631	0	644	0
d6	confOf	sigdd	edas		196	116	624		0	0	115		0.60%	867	115	886	115
d7	cmt	ekaw	confOf		226	225	196		0	0	0		0.54%	562	0	593	0
d8	cmt	edas	ekaw	sigkdd	226	624	225	116	0	115	0	0	0.67%	1113	115	1137	115
d9	cmt	confOf	sigkdd	edas	226	196	116	624	0	0	0	115	0.63%	1051	115	1087	115
d10	human	mouse			5441		4493		6104	345			0.84%	6645	6449	6286	6449

of the OAEI benchmark[10], for which perfect mappings are available. We found that in the conference track, different variations of ontologies with high overlap exist, which easily causes the merged ontology to become inconsistent. In our tests, we selected those groups, whose consistency tests have failed. Moreover, we have fed the test with an existing non-perfect mapping, generated by the SeeCOnt [1] tool. The F-measure of this mapping is given by $F_{\mathcal{M}_{non-perf.}}$ in Table 1 (compared to the perfect mappings with 100% accuracy). Beside Tbox and Abox sizes of the input ontologies, the size information of the merged ontology is given for both cases: when created using the perfect mappings $\mathcal{O}_{M_{perf.}}$ and when using the non-perfect mappings $\mathcal{O}_{M_{non-perf.}}$. In our experimental tests, the merged ontologies have been created by a simple merge technique, where the equivalent entities from the mapping assumption are combined.

3.2 Implementation

The proposed approach has been implemented within our merge framework [3], a tool that is freely accessible through http://comerger.uni-jena.de/ and the source code is publicly available and distributed under an open-source license[11]. Pellet reasoner [25] and OWL-API explanation[12] have been embedded in the system. We used an Intel Core i7 with 12 GB internal memory on Windows 7 with Java compiler 1.8. Parameters can be determined by the users. In our experimental tests we determined them empirically, but we make no claim that these are optimal values. The maximum explanation for the reasoner has been adjusted to 5. Moreover, α and β parameters have been set to 1 and 0.5, respectively.

3.3 Experimental Results

This section is devoted to present experimental results with different experimental sets and scenarios. In the first test, we determine whether our approach is able to produce consistent merged ontologies and what the effect is of restricting the consideration to the root classes in the justification sets. In the

---

[10] http://oaei.ontologymatching.org/.

[11] https://github.com/fusion-jena/CoMerger.

[12] http://owl.cs.manchester.ac.uk/research/explanation/.

second and third test we investigate the quality of the resulting ontology while the final test examines performance and scalability issues.

First Test: Characteristics of Inconsistent Ontologies. We examined the characteristics of the inconsistency test in Table 2. In the first three columns, we show whether the merged ontology in each dataset ($d1$–$d10$) using perfect or non-perfect mappings is consistent (PASSED) or not (FAILED). For the ontologies that do not pass the consistency check, we then determine the number of unsatisfiable classes C_{un} and the size of the justification set $\mathcal{J}$. Afterwards, our method processes all axioms $\Psi(X)$ of the justification set and ranks them. The axioms with the lowest trustworthiness are presented to the user together with a suggested resolution. Furthermore, the table shows statistic values if we consider all unsatisfiable classes C_{un} (columns 4–7) or narrow it to the root classes $Root(C_{un})$ (columns 8–11). In both cases, we represented the size of $C_{un}, \mathcal{J}$ and $\Psi(X)$, and the number of iterations $iter$ needed to achieve a consistent ontology. The result shows that the number of iterations depends on how the justification set is narrowed. In some cases, once the inconsistency problem for all unsatisfiable classes is narrowed to the root classes (e.g. in $d10$ instead of processing 208 unsatisfiable classes, only 6 classes have been analyzed), more than one iteration is needed to get rid of inconsistencies.

Second Test: Answering Competency Questions. Competency Question (CQ)s are a list of questions used in the ontology development life cycle, which the ontology should answer. One of objectives of ontology merging is to provide more comprehensive knowledge, where each CQ is expected to have more complete answers using the merged ontology compared to the input ontologies. To this end, we used a set of CQs[13] in the conference domain. Each CQ converts to a SPARQL query and runs on the input ontologies and two versions of consistent merged ontologies created with the non-perfect mappings: $\mathcal{O}'_{M_2}$ the consistent merged ontology, which uses our ranking method and applies our proposed plan, and $\mathcal{O}'_{M_1}$, in which consistency was achieved by human intervention. We compare the CQ-results for each dataset with all possible answers from the input and merged ontologies on that dataset (see Fig. 4). The *complete* answer indicates a full answer. *Semi-complete* and *partial* answers respectively represent the answers which are nearly complete answers or at least parts of the answers. An answer is marked as a *wrong* answer if CQ returns false instead of true, or shows the wrong hierarchy. It happens that a CQ's elements exist in the ontology, but no further knowledge exists about them; in this case, we mark them by *null* answer. If the ontology does not have any knowledge about the CQ, we indicate this by an *unknown* answer.

As the results show, there is a large difference between input and merged ontologies answers. The merged ontologies in all cases provide more complete answers compared to the input ontologies. This is because of the nature of the

---

[13] http://comerger.uni-jena.de/cqCatalog.jsp.

Table 2. The characterization of inconsistency

id	$\mathcal{M}$ type	Test	All				Root only			
			$|C_{un}|$	$|\mathcal{J}|$	$\Psi(X)$	$|iter|$	$|Root(C_{un})|$	$|\mathcal{J}|$	$\Psi(X)$	$|iter|$
d1	*non_Perf.*	FAILED	21	79	622	1	1	1	5	2
	Perf.	FAILED	21	95	695	1	1	3	15	1
d2	*non_Perf.*	FAILED	11	24	122	1	1	2	8	1
	Perf.	FAILED	11	24	122	1	1	2	8	1
d3	*non_Perf.*	FAILED	5	14	113	1	1	2	13	1
	Perf.	PASSED	–	–	–	–	–	–	–	–
d4	*non_Perf.*	FAILED	21	71	484	1	1	1	4	1
	Perf.	FAILED	21	88	536	1	1	2	7	1
d5	*non_Perf.*	FAILED	25	99	679	2	2	3	12	1
	Perf.	FAILED	22	110	692	1	1	5	22	1
d6	*non_Perf.*	FAILED	13	65	371	1	1	5	24	1
	Perf.	FAILED	16	68	384	1	2	6	27	1
d7	*non_Perf.*	FAILED	3	4	17	1	3	4	17	1
	Perf.	PASSED	–	–	–	–	–	–	–	–
d8	*non_Perf.*	FAILED	33	165	1197	1	2	10	64	2
	Perf.	FAILED	32	148	946	1	2	6	30	1
d9	*non_Perf.*	FAILED	19	95	582	1	2	5	25	1
	Perf.	FAILED	23	103	569	1	2	6	38	1
d10	*non_Perf.*	FAILED	208	600	5168		4	6	38	2
	Perf.	PASSED	–	–	–	–	–	–	–	–

merge process, that aims to provide more comprehensive knowledge. Moreover, the ontologies in these datasets are small in size and lack of a complete knowledge modeling in the conference domain. This causes 100% complete answers hard to be achieved and included a large number of unknown answers. Last but not least, comparing the two versions of consistent merged ontologies indicates that the complete answer achieved by our method in most cases is the same or even better than the human-created ontology. This shows the feasibility and reliability of our method if applied on large-scale ontologies.

Third Test: Semantic Understanding. In this test, we aim to observe how the achieved consistent ontology can represent semantic understanding. Two groups of queries similar to [11] have been constructed: queries on the individuals and queries on the is-a relations. For each individual c of concept C in the tested ontology, we create a positive individual query like '*is c a C?*', and a negative individual query like '*is c a B?*', in which B is another concept selected randomly. In the relation-based queries, for each subclass-of relation like '$A \sqsubseteq B$', we make a positive query '$A \sqsubseteq B?$', and a negative query like '$A \sqsubseteq C$?', which '$B \not\sqsubseteq C$'. We compare two versions of the consistent merged ontology for the following two cases: *Case I*: in all datasets, the consistent ontology which is achieved by our

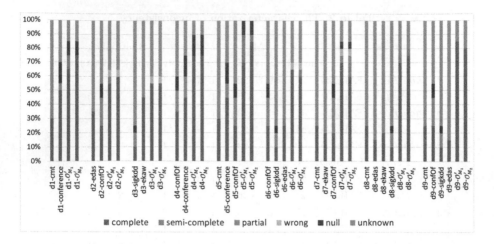

■ complete ■ semi-complete ■ partial ░ wrong ■ null ■ unknown

Fig. 4. Competency Question-based experimental tests

Table 3. The query-based experimental tests

id	$|Query|$	Correct Ans. $\mathcal{O}'_{M_1}$	Correct Ans. $\mathcal{O}'_{M_2}$	Accuracy $\mathcal{O}'_{M_1}$	Accuracy $\mathcal{O}'_{M_2}$
d1	24	24	24	100%	100%
d2	30	29	29	0.97%	0.97%
d3	22	22	22	100%	100%
d4	23	23	22	100%	0.96%
d5	34	34	33	100%	0.97%
d6	40	39	39	0.975%	0.975%
d7	33	30	30	0.91%	0.91%
d8	53	51	51	0.962%	0.962%
d9	51	50	48	0.98%	0.94%
d10$_{CaseI}$	80	80	80	100%	100%
d10$_{CaseII}$	80	80	80	100%	100%
Total	**470**	**462**	**458**	**0.98%**	**0.97%**

method $\mathcal{O}'_{M_2}$ and the one where an expert resolved the inconsistencies $\mathcal{O}'_{M_1}$. *Case II*: in *d10*, the merged ontology which used the perfect mappings is a consistent merged ontology $\mathcal{O}'_{M_1}$, while the merged ontology by the non-perfect mappings is an inconsistent one. We used our ranking method and applied the proposed plan and achieved a consistent merged ontology $\mathcal{O}'_{M_2}$. To measure the accuracy of the query results, we compare the achieved answers with the intuitive answers from the input ontologies. If the answer is the same as the intuitive answer, it is recorded as a correct answer. The accuracy of the result is determined by the number of correct answers divided by the total number of queries. As a whole, of the 470 query tests, 462 and 458 correct answers from $\mathcal{O}'_{M_1}$ and $\mathcal{O}'_{M_2}$ have been achieved, respectively (further details in Table 3). The results indicated

0.97% accuracy of our proposed method on solving inconsistency, and 0.98% accuracy for the human-created consistent ontology. This shows the usability and effectiveness of our method.

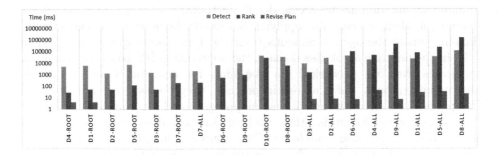

Fig. 5. The scalability test using the non-perfect mappings.

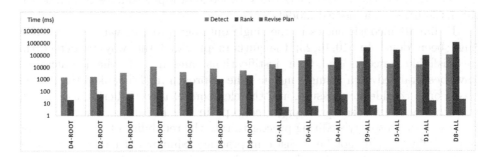

Fig. 6. The scalability test using the perfect mappings.

Fourth Test: Scalability. To evaluate the applicability of our approach in real life scenarios, we examine the aspect of scalability. To this end, we applied our algorithm on those datasets that failed the consistency tests (see Figs. 5 and 6). Each dataset has been tested in two scenarios: use all unsatisfiable classes or use only root classes. We present the runtime for detecting the inconsistencies (i.e. extracting C_{un}, $\mathcal{J}$ and $\Psi(X)$), ranking and generating the resolution plan, respectively. The datasets have been sorted and are ordered based on the number of conflicting axioms set (further details in Table 1). As the test demonstrated, mostly the time is increased by the number of conflicting axioms set. Given that ontology merging is a complex, time consuming task overall, they seem acceptable.

4   Literature Reviews

Over the last decade, the use of Subjective Logic in the Semantic Web has been increasing. It has been successfully applied on ontology alignments [9,14], annotation evaluation [5,6], recommendation systems [19], and inconsistency handling [24], to name only a few. In [24], Subjective Logic is used to solve ontology inconsistencies. However, the authors only utilized the atomicity value and omitted the belief, disbelief and uncertainty values. Moreover, no agent's opinion combination has been considered. Furthermore, this research considered a single ontology process, not applying Subjective Logic to ontologies merging domain, where the agent's opinions from the input ontologies play a serious role. In the multiple ontologies domain, the approach in [12] considered multiple ontologies that are networked via mappings for distributed and networked environments, only. For the repair process, they focused on repairing the mappings, and only axioms in the mappings could be removed to resolve the inconsistency. Moreover, their ranking function does not depend on the assumption of the input ontologies. The approach in [21] tried to build the consistent ontology in the ontology aggregation setting, which mostly depended on using a reference ontology result of the submitted preference profile by the agents. To the best of our knowledge, this is the first work that by using the Subjective Logic theory considers the knowledge of input sources to handle the inconsistencies on a merged model.

To handle inconsistencies in the single ontology process, various researches have been done. In [10,16,23] the authors provided the way to detect the unsatisfiable concepts and their justifications, and in [15], the justifications have been ranked with a single metric. The approach in [17] ranked the axioms based on a confidence measure, and the elements of the conflicting axioms are replaced by the weaker or stronger concept in the hierarchy. They used the history of the ontology's editing process to rate the reliability of the information source, which might not be realistic in practice. Similarly, there is a group of studies such as [8,20] on handling inconsistency in ontology evolution process. These approaches commonly keep different versions of the ontology to handle inconsistencies.

As a whole, we differ from the works above in three key respects: we solve inconsistencies in the ontology merging process; we combine several criteria to rank the conflicting axioms set by Subjective Logic theory with belief, disbelief and atomicity values; we consider the combination of agents' opinions and we employ conditional ranking when the conflicting axioms sets are dependent.

5   Conclusion

In this paper, we propose a novel approach to estimate the trustworthiness of conflicting axioms set that cause inconsistencies within a merged ontology using Subjective Logic. We use evidence such as provenance information and structural relevance to formulate the opinions of the input ontologies on the conflicting axioms set in the merged ontology. We use the consensus operators and conditional theory to combine opinions of different agents and to take into account dependencies across opinions. Our experimental results validate the feasibility and effectiveness of our method.

As our future work, we will study the exploitation of domain knowledge. We believe using more trustable background knowledge such as MeSH and SNOMED-CT (as domain-specific knowledge resources in the biomedical domain) or WordNet (as a generic knowledge resource) might significantly improve the opinion's probability expectation value as the trustworthiness of these rich agents on the conflicting axioms set.

Acknowledgments. S. Babalou is supported by a scholarship from German Academic Exchange Service (DAAD). We thank Sirko Schindler, Jan Martin Keil and Frank Löffler for their feedback on earlier versions of the manuscript.

References

1. Algergawy, A., Babalou, S., Kargar, M.J., Davarpanah, S.H.: SeeCOnt: a new seeding-based clustering approach for ontology matching. In: Morzy, T., Valduriez, P., Bellatreche, L. (eds.) ADBIS 2015. LNCS, vol. 9282, pp. 245–258. Springer, Cham (2015). https://doi.org/10.1007/978-3-319-23135-8_17
2. Baader, F., Calvanese, D., McGuinness, D., Patel-Schneider, P., Nardi, D.: The Description Logic Handbook: Theory, Implementation and Applications. Cambridge University Press, Cambridge (2003)
3. Babalou, S.: Holistic multiple ontologies merging. In: Proceedings of the EKAW2018 Co-located with the 21st (EKAW 2018) (2018)
4. Babalou, S., König-Ries, B.: On using subjective logic to build consistent merged ontologies. In: Proceedings of the SEMANTICS 2019 Poster and Demo Track (2019)
5. Ceolin, D., Nottamkandath, A., Fokkink, W.: Automated evaluation of annotators for museum collections using subjective logic. In: Dimitrakos, T., Moona, R., Patel, D., McKnight, D.H. (eds.) IFIPTM 2012. IAICT, vol. 374, pp. 232–239. Springer, Heidelberg (2012). https://doi.org/10.1007/978-3-642-29852-3_18
6. Ceolin, D., Van Hage, W.R., Fokkink, W.: A trust model to estimate the quality of annotations using the web. In: WebSci (2010)
7. Gruber, T.R., et al.: A translation approach to portable ontology specifications. Knowl. Acquis. **5**(2), 199–220 (1993)
8. Haase, P., van Harmelen, F., Huang, Z., Stuckenschmidt, H., Sure, Y.: A framework for handling inconsistency in changing ontologies. In: Gil, Y., Motta, E., Benjamins, V.R., Musen, M.A. (eds.) ISWC 2005. LNCS, vol. 3729, pp. 353–367. Springer, Heidelberg (2005). https://doi.org/10.1007/11574620_27
9. Hooijmaijers, D., Stumptner, M.: Improving integration with subjective combining of ontology mappings. In: An, A., Matwin, S., Raś, Z.W., Ślęzak, D. (eds.) ISMIS 2008. LNCS (LNAI), vol. 4994, pp. 552–562. Springer, Heidelberg (2008). https://doi.org/10.1007/978-3-540-68123-6_60
10. Horridge, M., Parsia, B., Sattler, U.: Explaining inconsistencies in OWL ontologies. In: Godo, L., Pugliese, A. (eds.) SUM 2009. LNCS (LNAI), vol. 5785, pp. 124–137. Springer, Heidelberg (2009). https://doi.org/10.1007/978-3-642-04388-8_11
11. Huang, Z., Van Harmelen, F., Ten Teije, A.: Reasoning with inconsistent ontologies. In: IJCAI, vol. 5, pp. 254–259 (2005)
12. Ji, Q., Haase, P., Qi, G., Hitzler, P., Stadtmüller, S.: RaDON — repair and diagnosis in ontology networks. In: Aroyo, L., et al. (eds.) ESWC 2009. LNCS, vol. 5554, pp. 863–867. Springer, Heidelberg (2009). https://doi.org/10.1007/978-3-642-02121-3_71

13. Jøsang, A.: Subjective Logic. Springer, Cham (2016). https://doi.org/10.1007/978-3-319-42337-1
14. Juszczyszyn, K.: A subjective logic-based framework for aligning multiple ontologies. In: Negoita, M.G., Howlett, R.J., Jain, L.C. (eds.) KES 2004. LNCS (LNAI), vol. 3214, pp. 1194–1200. Springer, Heidelberg (2004). https://doi.org/10.1007/978-3-540-30133-2_159
15. Kalyanpur, A., Parsia, B., Sirin, E., Cuenca-Grau, B.: Repairing unsatisfiable concepts in OWL ontologies. In: Sure, Y., Domingue, J. (eds.) ESWC 2006. LNCS, vol. 4011, pp. 170–184. Springer, Heidelberg (2006). https://doi.org/10.1007/11762256_15
16. Kalyanpur, A., Parsia, B., Sirin, E., Hendler, J.: Debugging unsatisfiable classes in OWL ontologies. J. Web Semant. **3**(4), 268–293 (2005)
17. Lam, J., Pan, J.Z., Sleeman, D., Vasconcelos, W.: Ontology inconsistency handling: ranking and rewriting axioms. Technical report aucs/tr0603, University of Aberdeen (2006)
18. Nieminen, J.: On the centrality in a graph. Scand. J. Psychol. **15**(1), 332–336 (1974)
19. Pitsilis, G., Knapskog, S.J.: Social trust as a solution to address sparsity-inherent problems of recommender systems. arXiv preprint arXiv:1208.1004 (2012)
20. Plessers, P., De Troyer, O.: Resolving inconsistencies in evolving ontologies. In: Sure, Y., Domingue, J. (eds.) ESWC 2006. LNCS, vol. 4011, pp. 200–214. Springer, Heidelberg (2006). https://doi.org/10.1007/11762256_17
21. Porello, D., Troquard, N., Penaloza, R., Confalonieri, R., Galliani, P., Kutz, O.: Two approaches to ontology aggregation based on axiom weakening. In: IJCAI (2018)
22. Pottinger, R.A., Bernstein, P.A.: Merging models based on given correspondences. In: Proceedings of the 29th International Conference on VeLDB-Volume 29, pp. 862–873 (2003)
23. Schlobach, S., Cornet, R., et al.: Non-standard reasoning services for the debugging of description logic terminologies. In: Ijcai, vol. 3, pp. 355–362 (2003)
24. Sensoy, M., Pan, J.Z., Fokoue, A., Srivatsa, M., Meneguzzi, F.: Using subjective logic to handle uncertainty and conflicts. In: TrustCom, pp. 1323–1326 (2012)
25. Sirin, E., Parsia, B., Grau, B.C., Kalyanpur, A., Katz, Y.: Pellet: a practical OWL-DL reasoner. J. Web Semant. **5**, 51–53 (2007)

VoIDext: Vocabulary and Patterns for Enhancing Interoperable Datasets with Virtual Links

Tarcisio Mendes de Farias[1,2](✉), Kurt Stockinger[4],
and Christophe Dessimoz[1,2,3]

[1] SIB Swiss Institute of Bioinformatics, Lausanne, Switzerland
[2] University of Lausanne, Lausanne, Switzerland
`tarcisio.mendesdefarias@unil.ch`
[3] University College London, London, UK
[4] Zurich University of Applied Sciences, Winterthur, Switzerland

Abstract. Semantic heterogeneity remains a problem when interoperating with data from sources of different scopes and knowledge domains. Causes for this challenge are context-specific requirements (i.e. no "one model fits all"), different data modelling decisions, domain-specific purposes, and technical constraints. Moreover, even if the problem of semantic heterogeneity among different RDF publishers and knowledge domains is solved, querying and accessing the data of distributed RDF datasets on the Web is not straightforward. This is because of the complex and fastidious process needed to understand how these datasets can be related or linked, and consequently, queried. To address this issue, we propose to extend the existing Vocabulary of Interlinked Datasets (VoID) by introducing new terms such as the *Virtual Link Set* concept and data model patterns. A virtual link is a connection between resources such as literals and IRIs (Internationalized Resource Identifier) with some commonality where each of these resources is from a different RDF dataset. The links are required in order to understand how to semantically relate datasets. In addition, we describe several benefits of using virtual links to improve interoperability between heterogenous and independent datasets. Finally, we exemplify and apply our approach to multiple world-wide used RDF datasets.

Keywords: Data interoperability · Virtual link · Vocabulary of Interlinked Datasets (VoID) · Federated query

1 Introduction

To achieve semantic and data interoperability, several data standards, ontologies, thesauri, controlled vocabularies, and taxonomies have been developed and adopted both by academia and industry. For example, the Industry Foundation Classes [7] is an ISO standard to exchange data among Building Information Modelling software tools [16]. In life sciences, we can mention the Gene Ontology (GO) among many other ontologies listed in repositories such as BioPortal

© Springer Nature Switzerland AG 2019
H. Panetto et al. (Eds.): OTM 2019, LNCS 11877, pp. 607–625, 2019.
https://doi.org/10.1007/978-3-030-33246-4_38

[31]. Yet, semantic heterogeneity remains a problem when interoperating with data from various sources which represent the same or related information in different ways [15]. This is mainly due to the lack or difficulty of a common consensus, different modelling decisions, domain scope and purpose, and constraints (e.g. storage, query performance, legacy and new systems).

Semantic reconciliation—i.e. the process of identifying and resolving semantic conflicts [29], for example, by matching concepts from heterogeneous data sources [18]—is recognized as a key process to address the semantic heterogeneity problem. To support this process, ontology matching approaches [26] have been proposed such as YAM++ [24]. Although semantic reconciliation enhances semantic interoperability, it is often not fully applicable or practical when considering distributed and independent RDF (Resource Description Framework) datasets of different domain scopes, knowledge domains, and autonomous publishers. In addition, even if the semantic reconciliation process among different RDF publishers and knowledge domains is complete and possible, querying and accessing the data of multiple distributed RDF datasets on the Web is not straightforward. This is because of the complex, time-consuming and fastidious process of having to understand how the data are structured and how these datasets can be related or linked, and consequently, queried.

To enhance interoperability and to facilitate the understanding of how multiple datasets can be related and queried, we propose to *extend and adapt the existing Vocabulary of Interlinked Datasets* (VoID) [2]. VoID is an RDF Schema vocabulary used to describe metadata about RDF datasets such as structural metadata, access metadata and links between datasets. However, VoID is limited regarding terms and design patterns to model the relationships between datasets in a less verbose, unambiguous and explicit way. To overcome this problem, we introduce the *concept of virtual link set* (VLS). A virtual link is an intersection data point between two RDF datasets. A data point is any node or resource in an RDF graph such as literals and IRIs (Internationalized Resource Identifier). An RDF dataset is a set of RDF triples that are published, maintained or aggregated by a single provider [2]. The links are required in order to comprehend how to semantically relate datasets. The major advantage of the VLS-concept is to facilitate the writing of federated SPARQL queries [19], by acting as joint points between the federated sources. We *exemplify and apply VoIDext to various world-wide used data sets* and discuss both the theoretical and practical implications of these new concepts with the goal of more easily querying heterogeneous and independent datasets.

This article is structured as follows: Sect. 2 presents the relevant related work. Section 3 details our approach to extend the VoID vocabulary. In Sect. 4, we describe the major benefits of using VoIDext, and we apply VoIDext to describe VLSs among three world-wide used bioinformatics RDF data stores. Finally, we conclude this article with future work and perspectives.

2   Related Work

Since the release of the SPARQL 1.1 Query Language [19] with federated query support in 2013, numerous federated approaches for data and semantic interoperability have recently been proposed [11,20,33], and [32]. However, to the best of our knowledge, none of them proposes a vocabulary and patterns to extensively, explicitly and formally describe how the data sources can be interlinked for the purpose of facilitating the writing of SPARQL 1.1 federated queries such as discussed in Sect. 3. In effect, existing approaches put the burden on the SPARQL users or systems to find out precisely *how* to write a conjunctive federated query. An emerging research direction entails automatically discovering links between datasets using Word Embeddings [17]. However, the current focus is mostly on relational data or unstructured data [6]. In addition, several link discovery frameworks such as in [25,28], and [21] rely on link specifications to define the conditions necessary for linking resources within datasets. With these specifications, these frameworks describe similarity measures or distance metrics (e.g. Levenshtein, Jaccard and Cosine) as part of conditions to determine, for example, whether two entities should be linked. The approaches of [17,25,28], and [21] are complementary to ours because they can aid in the process of defining virtual link sets—see Definition 2.

In the context of ontology alignment, the Expressive and Declarative Ontology Alignment Language (EDOAL) enables us to represent correspondences between heterogeneous ontological entities [9]. Although, transformations of property values can be specified with EDOAL, the current version of EDOAL solely supports a limited kind of transformations[1]. In [8] and [10], authors also recognize the limited support for data transformation in mapping languages. Moreover, since EDOAL does not focus on supporting the write of SPARQL 1.1 federated queries, the EDOAL data transformation specification requires an extra step to be converted into an equivalent one by using the SPARQL language. Applying data transformations during a federated query execution is often required to be able to link real-world independent and distributed datasets on the Web. As other related work in terms of RDF-based vocabularies, we can also mention VoID and SPARQL 1.1 Service Description (SD)[2]. Although the VoID RDF schema provides the *void:Linkset* term (Definition 1), this concept alone is not sufficient to precisely and explicitly define virtual links between the datasets (discussed in Sect. 3). By precisely, we mean to avoid multiple ways to represent (i.e. triple patterns) and to interpret interlinks. Moreover, by considering Definition 1 extracted from the VoID specification, this definition impedes the use of the *void:Linkset* concept to describe a link set between instances of the same class because both are triple subjects stored in different datasets.

Definition 1 (link set – *void:Linkset*[3]). *A collection of RDF links between two datasets. An RDF link is an RDF triple whose subject and object are described in different datasets [2].*

3   Contribution

To mitigate the impediments of interoperating with distributed and independent RDF datasets, we first propose design patterns of how to partially model

[1] http://alignapi.gforge.inria.fr/edoal.html.

[2] https://www.w3.org/TR/sparql11-service-description/.

[3] http://vocab.deri.ie/void#Linkset.

virtual links (see Definition 2) with the current VoID vocabulary and expose its drawbacks. To address these drawbacks, we then propose a new vocabulary (i.e. VoIDext) and demonstrate an unambiguous and unique way to extensively and explicitly describe various types of virtual links such as depicted in Subsect. 3.2. The VoIDext vocabulary is fully described in [14], that also includes examples of virtual link types.

Definition 2 (virtual link set). *A set of virtual links. A virtual link is a connection between common resources such as literals and instances from two different RDF datasets. Semantic relaxation (see Definition 3) is also considered when identifying common resources between datasets.*

Definition 3 (semantic relaxation). *It is the capacity of ignoring semantic and data heterogeneities for the sake of interoperability.*

In this article, the words *vocabulary* and *ontology* are used interchangeably. The methodology applied to develop VoIDext was inspired by the simplified agile methodology for ontology development (SAMOD) [27]. Indeed, the proposed VoID extension is a meta-ontology to explicitly describe interlinks between RDF datasets—virtual links. Further information about how VoIDext was built is given in the Supplementary Material in [13].

Figure 1 illustrates a complex virtual link about Swiss cantons between the LINDAS dataset (Linked Data Service[4]) of the Swiss Government administration and DBpedia [23]. To define this link, some semantic relaxation is applied. This is because heterogeneities are exacerbated when interoperating independent datasets. For example, what is considered a long name of a Swiss canton in LINDAS is actually a short name in DBpedia. In addition, the data types for the name of the canton are not the same in both datasets what impedes exact matching when performing a federated join query. Finally, LINDAS contains a few literals with different concatenated translations of the same canton's name such as "Graubünden / Grigioni / Grischun" that can be matched with the literal "Grisons" asserted as a canton's short name in DBpedia. Indeed, Grison is the French translation of Graubünden—German name. Nevertheless, both datasets share literals with some commonality. By exploring this commonality we are able to define a virtual link set between both datasets. Note that the Swiss cantons' resource IRIs in both datasets are not the same – otherwise defining a virtual link set would be simpler—i.e. a simple link set, see Definition 4. In the next subsections, we incrementally demonstrate with a running example how to model a complex link set (see Definition 6) with VoID and VoIDext terms. Table 1 shows other datasets and SPARQL endpoints considered in our examples in this article.

Definition 4 (simple link set). *A simple link set must be either a link set that does not target another link set (i.e. it has exactly one link predicate— Definition 5) or a set with exactly the same shared instances of the same type (i.e. class expression) in both datasets.*

---

[4] https://lindas-data.ch.

Table 1. SPARQL endpoints considered in this article.

RDF dataset	SPARQL endpoint
DBpedia [23]	http://dbpedia.org/sparql
LINDAS (see Footnote 4)	https://lindas-data.ch/sparql
OMA [3]	https://sparql.omabrowser.org/sparql
UniProtKB [30]	https://sparql.uniprot.org/sparql
Bgee [5]	http://biosoda.expasy.org/rdf4j-server/repositories/bgeelight
EBI RDF [22]	https://www.ebi.ac.uk/rdf/services/sparql

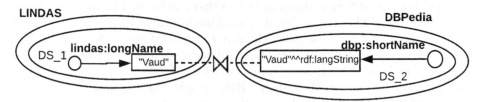

Fig. 1. An example of a virtual link between the LINDAS and DBpedia datasets where the DS_1 and DS_2 datasets are subsets of them, respectively. Circles: different resource IRIs; rectangles: literals; ⋈: virtual link; and edges: RDF predicates.

In practice, a simple link set allows us to model virtual links either between the subjects of two RDF triples in different datasets where their predicate is *rdf:type* with the same object or between link predicate assertions and *rdf:type* triples. Due to the space constraints, the patterns to model simple link sets with VoIDext are available in Supplementary Material Section 4 [13].

Definition 5 (link predicate). *According to the VoID specification, a link predicate is the RDF property of the triples in a void:Linkset [2].*

Definition 6 (complex link set). *It is a complex virtual link set. A complex link set is composed of exactly two link sets xor two shared instance sets (see Definition 7) where xor is the exclusive or.*

Definition 7 (shared instance set). *A shared instance set between exactly two datasets. For example, two datasets that contain the same OWL/RDFS class instances.*

3.1 Patterns to *partially* model complex link sets with VoID terms

Since our main goal is to facilitate the writing of federated queries by providing metadata of how the target datasets can be joined, let us suppose that we want to know how to relate Swiss cantons in LINDAS and DBpedia datasets as shown in Fig. 1. In other words, we want to find out the necessary and sufficient graph pattern in the context of Swiss cantons in each dataset to be able to relate and join them. Further triple patterns such as attributes (e.g. canton's population, cities, acronym) depend on the specificity of the requested information what goes beyond the task of joining the two datasets. Let us further assume a SPARQL user without any previous knowledge about these datasets. A possible workflow for this user to find out how to relate LINDAS and DBpedia in terms of Swiss cantons is described as follows:

(1) the user has to dig up the data schema and documentation, if any, looking for the abstract entity "Swiss canton". This task has to be done for both datasets.
(2) if (s)he is lucky, a concept is explicitly defined in the data schema. This is the case of the LINDAS dataset that contains the class *lindas:Canton*—prefixes such as *lindas:* are defined in Table 2. Otherwise the user has to initiate a fastidious quest for assertions and terms that can be used for modeling Swiss canton data. This is the situation of DBpedia where instances are defined as a Swiss canton by assigning the *dbrc:Cantons_of_Switzerland* instance of the *skos:Concept* to the *dct:subject* property such as the following triple (*dbr:Vaud, dct:subject, dbrc:Cantons_of_Switzerland*).
(3) The user has now to browse the RDF graph. For example, by performing additional queries, to be sure that the assertions to the *lindas:Canton* instances can be used as join points with assertions related to Swiss canton instances in DBpedia. Otherwise, the user has to repeat the previous steps.
(4) If data transformations are required because of data and semantic heterogeneities between the datasets, the user has to define data mappings to be able to effectively perform a federated conjunctive query.

Table 2. In this article, we assume the namespace prefix bindings in this table.

Prefix	Namespace Internationalized Resource Identifier (IRI)
rdfs:	http://www.w3.org/2000/01/rdf-schema#
rdf:	http://www.w3.org/1999/02/22-rdf-syntax-ns#
up:	http://purl.uniprot.org/core/
cco:	http://rdf.ebi.ac.uk/terms/chembl#
chembl:	http://rdf.ebi.ac.uk/resource/chembl/molecule/
ex:	http://example.org/voidext#
dbo:	http://dbpedia.org/ontology/
skos:	http://www.w3.org/2004/02/skos/core#
dbr:	http://dbpedia.org/resource/
dbrc:	http://dbpedia.org/resource/Category:
dbp:	http://dbpedia.org/property/
lindas:	https://gont.ch/
dcterms:	http://purl.org/dc/terms/
biopax:	http://www.biopax.org/release/biopax-level3.owl#
lscr:	http://purl.org/lscr#
void:	http://rdfs.org/ns/void#
voidext:	http://purl.org/query/voidext#
bioquery:	http://purl.org/query/bioquery#

```
SELECT * WHERE {
SERVICE <http://dbpedia.org/sparql>{
?dbp_inst dct:subject dbrc:Cantons_of_Switzerland.
?dbp_inst dbp:shortName ?dbp_name.
BIND(IF(STR(?dbp_name)="Grisons", "Graubünden / Grigioni / Grischun",
    IF(STR(?dbp_name)="Geneva", "Genève",
    IF(STR(?dbp_name)="Lucerne", "Luzern",
    IF(STR(?dbp_name)="Valais", "Valais / Wallis",
    IF(STR(?dbp_name)="Bern", "Bern / Berne",
    IF(STR(?dbp_name)="Fribourg", "Fribourg / Freiburg",
       STR(?dbp_name) )))))) AS ?lindas_name)}
SERVICE <https://lindas-data.ch/sparql>{
?lindas_inst a    lindas:Canton;
             lindas:longName ?lindas_name.}}
```

Listing 1. The initial basic graph patterns represented as a SPARQL federated query to perform join queries between Swiss cantons in the LINDAS and DBpedia datasets. Table 2 contains the IRI prefixes.

Finally, based on that workflow, a **SPARQL user** can draft the minimum set of triple patterns and data transformations to perform the virtual links concerning Swiss cantons between both datasets. This draft is represented as the SPARQL query in Listing 1. The link set built by intersecting the resources (i.e. the values of *lidas:longName* and *dbp:shortName* properties) can then be partially modelled with VoID terms. This enables **other SPARQL users or systems** to reuse this link set knowledge to write specialized queries over the two datasets starting from the Swiss canton context. In doing so, the second user avoid the fastidious, complex and time-consuming task of finding this link set. In addition, to the best of our knowledge there is no system capable of precisely establishing this virtual link set automatically because of the complexity and heterogeneities to be solved.

Listings 2 and 3 depict two different ways named VL_{m1} and VL_{m2} to model the virtual link set with VoID. Note that the examples of RDF graph patterns in this section are defined with the RDF 1.1 Turtle language[5]. On the one hand, VL_{m1} states that a given LS_1 link set targets another LS_2 link set that targets LS_1 back. On the other, VL_{m2} only states datasets as link set targets. By using the VL_{m1} model in Listing 2, the DS_2 instance asserts the DS_1 instance to its *void:objectsTarget* property. As a reminder, the *void:objectsTarget* value is the dataset describing the objects of the triples contained in the link set, in our example, the objects of *dbp:shortName*. This dataset must contain only the relevant triples to describe the virtual link set. In our example in Listing 2, we define the DS_1 dataset (i.e. a subset of LINDAS) as being also a *void:Linkset* that contains triples with the *lindas:longName* predicate. By using the VL_{m2} model in Listing 3, the objects' target dataset of the *dbp:shortName* link predicate is not a *void:Linkset* but a *void:Dataset* (i.e. superclass of *void:Linkset*). DS_2 in Listing 3 also contains triples with the *lindas:longName* predicate, however, this predicate is defined as part of a subset and partition of DS_2 by using the *void:propertyPartition* and *void:property* terms. Note that solely one

---

[5] https://www.w3.org/TR/turtle/.

void:propertyPartition should be directly assigned to DS_2 dataset, otherwise we are not able to know which predicate should be considered when stating the virtual links.

```
#DS_1 is a subset of LINDAS.                          #DS_2 is a subset of DBpedia.
ex:LINDAS_DBPEDIA_SWISSCANTON                         ex:DBPEDIA_LINDAS_SWISSCANTON
    rdf:type void:Linkset ;                               rdf:type void:Linkset ;
    void:linkPredicate lindas:longName ;                 void:linkPredicate dbp:shortName ;
    void:objectsTarget                                   void:objectsTarget
        ex:DBPEDIA_LINDAS_SWISSCANTON ;                      ex:LINDAS_DBPEDIA_SWISSCANTON ;
    void:subset _:DOMAIN_SET0 .                          void:subset _:DOMAIN_SET1 .
_:DOMAIN_SET0 void:propertyPartition _:b0 ;           _:RANGE_SET1 void:propertyPartition _:b2 ;
    void:classPartition _:b1 .                           void:classPartition _:b3 .
_:b0 void:property rdfs:domain .                      _:b2 void:property rdfs:range .
_:b1 void:class lindas:Canton .                       _:b3 void:class rdf:langString .
                    . . .                                                . . .
```

Listing 2. Patterns to model a complex virtual link set between the LINDAS Linked Data service and DBpedia relying on link sets as targets (e.g. *void:objectsTarget*). As a reminder, *void:Linkset* is a subclass of *void:Dataset*.

```
#DS_2 is a subset of DBpedia.
ex:DBPEDIA_LINDAS_SWISSCANTON rdf:type void:Linkset ;
    void:linkPredicate dbp:shortName ;
    void:objectsTarget _:b4 .
_:b4 rdf:type void:Dataset ;
    void:propertyPartition _:LINDAS_PROPERTY ;
    void:subset _:RANGE_SET2 .
_:LINDAS_PROPERTY void:property lindas:longName .
_:RANGE_SET2 void:propertyPartition _:b5.
_:RANGE_SET2 void:classPartition _:b6 .
    _:b5 void:property rdfs:range .        #it restricts lindas:longName
    _:b6 void:class rdfs:Literal .         #range to rdfs:Literal.
                    . . .
```

Listing 3. Patterns to model a complex virtual link set between the LINDAS Linked Data service and DBpedia relying on link sets and property partitions as targets (e.g. *void:objectsTarget*). For the sake of simplicity, only the link set in DBpedia is depicted because the link set in LINDAS containing the *lindas:longName* link predicate is similarly modelled as the one in DBpedia.

Yet, we also need to describe further information about the virtual link set such as the domain and range of the link predicates (e.g. *lindas:longName* and *dbp:shortName*). This information is used to restrict which resource type must be considered for a given triple that contains the link predicate (e.g. *lindas:longName rdfs:domain lindas:Canton*). By having this information in advance when writing and executing a federated query, we reduce the number of triples to match, if there are statements of the same predicate but with resources of other types. For example, the *lindas:longName* property is asserted to instances of *lindas:MunicipalityVersion, lindas:Canton* or *lindas:DistrictEntityVersion*. However, for the context of this virtual link set only *lindas:Canton* instances need to be considered. To restrict the resource types of a given link predicate with VoID, we can state subsets and partitions to a *void:Linkset* such as exemplified in Listing 2 by using VL_{m1}.

Note that for each link predicate's domain/range, we have to create one new subset to be sure that the class partitions of the subset correspond to the domain or range of the link predicate. In addition, if there are multiple resource types to be considered as the domain of a link predicate, we can state multiple class partitions to express the union of types—i.e. classes. Or, we can explicitly define it by using the OWL 2 Description Logic (DL) term *owl:unionOf* and related patterns to express class union. To express class intersection or other class expressions, we can rely on OWL 2 DL terms and state these class expressions as class partitions of the subset. Similarly, we can model the domain and range of predicates related to virtual links with VL_{m2} as described in Listing 3. For the sake of simplicity, we do not depict all predicate domains/ranges in Listings 2 and 3. However, there are several limitations when only considering VoID terms to model complex link sets:

(1) **Multiple representations.** The VoID vocabulary and documentation due to the lack of constraints and high generalization imply several ways to model virtual link sets such as VL_{m1} and VL_{m2} graph patterns to represent a complex link set. In addition, there are various ways to define the link predicate's domain and range. For example, class expressions can be defined by using either OWL 2 DL terms to express the union of classes or multiple class partitions (i.e. *void:classPartition* assertions), or by combining both of them. This multitude of graph patterns allowed by VoID makes interoperability more complex because we do not previously know how the virtual link set is modelled. Consequently, it requires to build complex parsers and queries to retrieve the virtual link set metadata.

(2) **Ambiguity.** With VoID, we cannot easily distinguish if a link set or dataset is being instantiated to define a virtual link set. For example, we do not know explicitly if two link sets compose a complex link set. Moreover, the use of property/class partitions to define domains and ranges of link predicates can be mixed with *void:class* assertions that are not part of a domain/range definition. Subsets can also be arbitrarily stated to any link set or dataset what increases the ambiguity to know if a given subset is actually part of a complex link set definition or not. With VL_{m1} and VL_{m2} models strictly based on VoID, we cannot explicitly state that the intersections between two link sets occur by matching the subjects-objects, objects-objects or subjects-subjects of link predicates in different link sets. Nevertheless, this information can be derived from the *void:objectsTarget* and *void:subjectsTarget* assertions, if any.

(3) **Description Logic (DL) compliance** [4]. By stating the domain and range of link predicates with class expressions based on OWL 2 DL (e.g. a range composed of multiple types/classes), we can take advantage of existing DL-parser and reasoner tools to infer instance types (e.g. http://owlcs.github.io/owlapi/). However, since we can mix DL-based class expressions

with *void:class* assertions, the resulting range/domain expressions are non-compliant with DL.

(4) **Verbosity**. The use of class and property partition partners considerably increases the number of triples to state for representing virtual links. This also increases the complexity of writing of queries to retrieve the virtual link set metadata.

(5) **Resource mapping**. VoID does not provide any explicit term and recommendation to state resource mappings. By doing so, we mitigate or even solve heterogeneities when matching resources with some commonality in different datasets.

In the next subsection, we show how to solve these issues with VoIDext terms and patterns.

3.2   Patterns to *fully* model complex link sets with VoIDext

To address the issues of modelling virtual link sets solely with VoID, we propose new terms and patterns in VoIDext. Listing 4 illustrates the main VoIDext terms (see terms with *voidext:* prefix) and design patterns to model complex link sets. To assert the range and domain of predicates with VoIDext, we can directly assign the *voidext:linkPredicateRange* and *voidext:linkPredicateDomain* properties to a link set, respectively (see Definitions 8 and 9). Complex link predicates' domains and ranges (e.g. multiple types—union/intersection of classes) must be stated as class expressions by using OWL 2 DL terms (e.g. *owl:unionOf*). To avoid ambiguities when interpreting link sets (i.e. a simple set *versus* a complex one), we can explicitly state that two link sets are indeed part of a complex link set. To do so, we must assign exactly two link sets to a complex link set with the *voidext:intersectAt* property (see Definition 10). In a complex link set, a link set must be connected to another link set by stating either *void:objectsTarget* or *void:subjectsTarget* properties. This allow us to precisely know where the intersection between RDF triples with predicates in different datasets occurs, in other words, the matched RDF resource nodes: object-object, subject-subject, and subject-object. For example, in Listing 4 with *void:objectsTarget* property, we state that the *lindas:longName* predicate's objects in LINDAS match the objects of the *dbp:shortName* link predicate in DBpedia, and *vice-versa*. To explicitly state the intersection type (e.g. object-object), we can assert the *voidext:intersectionType* property (see Definition 11) to a complex link set as shown in Listing 4.

Definition 8 (link predicate range).   *The link predicate's object type (i.e. class expression or literals), if any. Moreover, a link set (Definition 1) that is not part of a complex link set (see Definition 6) and connects two datasets through the link predicate's object must specify the link predicate range. Indeed, this object matches a second resource in another dataset. Therefore, the type of this second resource is asserted as the link predicate range.*

Definition 9 (link predicate domain). *The link predicate's subject type (i.e. class expression), if any.*

Definition 10 (intersects at). *It specifies the intersection of either exactly two shared instance sets (see Definition 7) or two link sets, that compose a complex link set.*

Definition 11 (intersection type). *It specifies the intersection type between two RDF triples in different datasets. In other words, if the intersection occurs at the subject xor the object node of a link predicate.*

Based on Definition 6, the *voidext:ComplexLinkSet* OWL class is defined with the following DL expression, IRI prefixes are ignored to improve readability:

$$ComplexLinkSet \equiv \neg SimpleLinkSet \sqcap$$
$$((\forall intersectAt.Linkset \sqcap \ = 2\ intersectAt) \sqcup$$
$$(\forall intersectAt.SharedInstanceSet \sqcap \ = 2\ intersectAt))$$

As a reminder, a *void:Dataset* is "a set of RDF triples that is published, maintained or aggregated by a single provider"[6]. However, a complex link set is composed of resources from two different datasets (e.g. two link predicates). Therefore, we define *voidext:ComplexLinkSet* as being disjoint with *void:Dataset* class. Consequently, a complex link set is not a *void:Dataset* and properties such as *void:propertyPartition* cannot be assigned to it.

To address data heterogeneities, we can implement semantic relaxation by stating the *voidext:resourceMapping* property (Definition 12) with a literal text based on SPARQL language. In Listing 4, DS_2 states a mapping in line 7 that converts *dbp:shortName* language-tagged string values into simple literals and maps the values to a corresponding one in LINDAS dataset. Thus, since this mapping is defined using SPARQL language, it can be directly used to build a SPARQL 1.1 federated query to perform the interlinks between datasets. In Listing 4, *voidext:recommendedMapping* (Definition 13) assigns the LINDAS DS_1 link set as the one containing the mapping to be considered when interlinking with DBpedia in the context of Swiss cantons.

Definition 12 (resource mapping). *It specifies the mapping function (f_m) to preprocess a resource (i.e. IRI or literal) in a source dataset in order to match another resource in the target dataset. The resource preprocessing (i.e. mapping) must be defined with the SPARQL language by mainly using SPARQL built-ins for assignments (e.g. BIND), and expression and testing values (e.g. IF and FILTER). The BIND built-in is used to assign the output of f_m, if any.*

Definition 13 (recommended resource mapping). *It specifies one recommended mapping function, if more than one mapping is defined in the different sets that are part of a complex link set.*

---

[6] http://vocab.deri.ie/void#Dataset.

```
                                         #DS_2 is a subset of DBpedia.                                    1
#DS_1 is a subset of LINDAS.             ex:DBPEDIA_LINDAS_SWISSCANTON                                     2
ex:LINDAS_DBPEDIA_SWISSCANTON              rdf:type void:Linkset ;                                         3
  rdf:type void:Linkset ;                  void:linkPredicate dbp:shortName ;                             4
  void:linkPredicate lindas:longName ;     voidext:isSubsetOf ex:DBPEDIA ;                                5
  voidext:linkPredicateRange               void:objectsTarget ex:LINDAS_DBPEDIA_SWISSCANTON ;             6
      rdfs:Literal ;                       voidext:resourceMapping                                         7
  voidext:linkPredicateDomain              "'?dbpedia_place dcterms:subject dbrc:Cantons_of_Switzerland.   8
      lindas:Canton ;                      ?dbpedia_place dbp:shortName ?c.                                9
  voidext:isSubsetOf ex:LINDAS;            BIND(                                                          10
  void:objectsTarget                         IF(STR(?c)="Grisons", "Graubünden / Grigioni / Grischun",   11
ex:DBPEDIA_LINDAS_SWISSCANTON ;              IF(STR(?c)="Geneva", "Genève",                              12
  voidext:resourceMapping                    IF(STR(?c)="Lucerne", "Luzern",                             13
      "'?x a <https://gont.ch/Canton>.       IF(STR(?c)="Valais", "Valais / Wallis",                     14
          ...'" ;                            IF(STR(?c)="Bern", "Bern / Berne",                           15
          ...                                IF(STR(?c)="Fribourg", "Fribourg / Freiburg", STR(?c)       16
                                             )))))) as ?lindas_objects)'" ; ...                          17
```

```
ex:DBPEDIA_LINDAS_SWISSCANTON_VL rdf:type voidext:ComplexLinkSet ;
  voidext:intersectionType voidext:OBJECT_OBJECT ;
  dcterms:issued "2019-06-30"^^xsd:date ;
  rdfs:label "A virtual link set for cantons in both DBpedia and LINDAS Swiss government datasets." ;
  voidext:intersectAt ex:LINDAS_DBPEDIA_SWISSCANTON ;
  voidext:intersectAt ex:DBPEDIA_LINDAS_SWISSCANTON ;
  voidext:recommendedMapping ex:LINDAS_DBPEDIA_SWISSCANTON ;    ...
```

Listing 4. VoIDext-based patterns to model a complex virtual link set between the LINDAS Linked Data service and DBpedia relying on link sets as targets. Dashed underlined: one of the two can be chosen as the *voidext:recommendedMapping*; and fully underlined: predicates used to connect the datasets by *void:objectsTarget* predicates.

To exemplify a complex link set composed of shared instance sets (Definition 7), let us consider the UniProt and European Bioinformatics Institute (EBI) RDF datasets (see Table 1). EBI and UniProt RDF data stores use different instance IRIs and classes to represent the organism species, and in a more general way, the taxonomic lineage for organisms. To exemplify this, let us consider the *<http://identifiers.org/taxonomy/9606>* instance of *biopax:BioSource* and the *<http://purl.uniprot.org/taxonomy/9606>* instance of *up:Taxon* in EBI and UniProt datasets, respectively. Although these instances are not exactly the same (i.e. distinct IRIs, property sets, and contexts), they refer to the same organism species at some extent, namely *homo sapiens*—human. By applying a semantic relaxation, we can state a virtual link between these two instances. To establish this link, we need to define a resource mapping function (i.e. $f_m(r)$) either to the EBI or UniProt species-related instances—either $f_m(<http://identifiers.org/taxonomy/9606>) \equiv <http://purl.uniprot.org/taxonomy/9606>$ or $f_m(<http://purl.uniprot.org/taxonomy/9606>) \equiv <http://identifiers.org/taxonomy/9606>$. Listing 5 depicts how this complex link set is modelled with VoIDext-based patterns. Note that it is not possible to define a shared instance set by only using VoID terms because there is no link predicate (Definition 5) associated with the interlinks that are different from *rdf:type*. To address this issue, we can assign a shared instance type (Definition 14) with the *voidext:sharedInstanceType* property for each *voidext:SharedInstanceSet* instance (Definition 7). Other examples of complex link sets are available in [13] and [14].

Definition 14 (shared instance type). *The type (i.e. class) of the shared instances in a given dataset. Shared instances imply equivalent or similar instance IRIs that belong to different datasets.*

4   VoIDext Benefits and Discussions

VoID instances ("assertion box"—ABox) are fully backward compatible with the VoIDext schema since we mainly add new terms. The only change performed in the VoID "terminological box" (TBox) concerns the *void:target*[7] property domain. In VoIDext, this domain is the union of the *void:Linkset* and *voidext:SharedInstanceSet* classes instead of solely *void:Linkset*, as stated in VoID. We did this to avoid the replication of a similar property to state target datasets to shared instance sets. Despite this modification, assertions of *void:target* based on VoID remain compatible with VoIDext.

4.1   Retrieving Virtual Link Sets

Once the virtual links are modelled with VoIDext as discussed in Subsect. 3.2 and Supplementary Material Section 4 [13], there may exist at most four kinds of virtual link sets as follows: (i) a *voidext:ComplexLinkSet* composed of *void:Linksets*—e.g. see Listing 4; (ii) a *voidext:ComplexLinkSet* composed of *voidext:SharedInstanceSets*—e.g. see Listing 5; (iii) a *void:Linkset* that is also

---

A) a subset of EBI
```
bioquery:EBI_UNIPROT_10
        rdf:type voidext:SharedInstanceSet ;
    voidext:isSubsetOf bioquery:EBI ;
    voidext:resourceMapping
    '''?IRI_EBI a biopax:BioSource.
BIND(IRI(CONCAT("http://purl.uniprot.org/taxonomy/"
    , STRAFTER(STR(?IRI_EBI),
    "http://identifiers.org/taxonomy/"))) as ?IRI_UNIPROT)
FILTER(STRSTARTS(STR(?IRI_EBI),
    "http://identifiers.org/taxonomy/"))''' ;
    voidext:sharedInstanceType biopax:BioSource ;  ...
```

B) a subset of UniProt
```
bioquery:EBI_UNIPROT_11
        rdf:type voidext:SharedInstanceSet ;
    voidext:isSubsetOf bioquery:UNIPROT ;
    voidext:resourceMapping
    '''?IRI_UNIPROT a up:Taxon.
BIND(IRI(CONCAT("http://identifiers.org/taxonomy/"
    , STRAFTER( STR(?IRI_UNIPROT),
    "http://purl.uniprot.org/taxonomy/" ) ) ) as ?IRI_EBI)
FILTER(STRSTARTS(STR(?IRI_UNIPROT),
    "http://purl.uniprot.org/taxonomy/"))''' ;
    voidext:sharedInstanceType up:Taxon ;  ...
```

```
bioquery:EBI_UNIPROT_12 rdf:type voidext:ComplexLinkSet ;
    voidext:intersectAt bioquery:EBI_UNIPROT_11 ;
    voidext:intersectAt bioquery:EBI_UNIPROT_10 ;
    voidext:recommendedMapping bioquery:EBI_UNIPROT_10 ;
rdfs:label "Links between EBI and UniProt considering shared similar instances of organism taxonomy"@en;  ...
```

Listing 5. VoIDext-based patterns to model a complex virtual link set between EBI and UniProt datasets modelled with shared instance sets (see fully underlined assertions). Dashed underlined: one of the two can be chosen as the *voidext:recommendedMapping*.

---

[7] https://www.w3.org/TR/void/#target.

a *voidext:SimpleLinkSet*; and (iv) a *voidext:SharedInstanceSet* that is also a *voidext:SimpleLinkSet*. Due to the page limit, the types (iii) and (iv) are exemplified in Fig. 7 and Listing 1.3 in Supplementary Material [13]. For each kind of virtual link set, a SPARQL query template to retrieve the essential information is asserted as an annotation of the *voidext:ComplexLinkSet* and *voidext:SimpleLinkSet* sub-classes of *voidext:VirtualLinkSet*. These annotations are done by asserting the *voidext:queryLinkset* and *voidext:querySharedInstanceSet* properties. Therefore, to retrieve virtual link sets of type (i) and (iii), we can execute the SPARQL queries assigned with *voidext:queryLinkset* to the *voidext:ComplexLinkSet* and *voidext:SimpleLinkSet* classes, respectively. Similarly, to retrieve virtual link sets of type (ii) and (iv), we can execute the SPARQL queries assigned with *voidext:querySharedInstanceSet* to the *voidext:ComplexLinkSet* and *voidext:SimpleLinkSet* classes, respectively. These queries are described in [14].

4.2 Writing a Federated SPARQL Query with VoIDext Metadata

To illustrate how VoIDext can facilitate the writing of federated SPARQL queries, let us consider that a SPARQL user wants to perform the Q_f query against the EBI dataset: *"Show me all assays in rodents for the drug Gleevec (i.e. CHEMBL941 identifier)"*. One possible way to write this query is to consider another dataset that contains organismal taxonomy information about rodents such as the UniProt dataset. To be able to write this federated conjunctive query over the EBI and UniProt datasets, the SPARQL user has to find out how to relate these datasets. To do so, the SPARQL user can query the metadata about virtual link sets modelled with VoIDext—see the template queries for this purpose in the VoIDext specification [14] and further details in Subsect. 4.1. Table 3 exemplifies a possible outcome of these queries containing virtual link set descriptions.

Based on the description of virtual link sets, users can select the link set that best fit their needs to write Q_f with SPARQL 1.1. In this example, a user can choose the complex link set *bioquery:EBI_UNIPROT_12* about organism taxonomy depicted in Listing 5 and defined as the query result over the

```
SELECT ?assay WHERE {
  ?activity a cco:Activity ;
           cco:hasMolecule chembl:CHEMBL941 ;
           cco:hasAssay ?assay .
  ?assay cco:taxonomy ?IRI_EBI.
  ?IRI_EBI a <http://www.biopax.org/release/biopax-level3.owl#BioSource> .
  BIND(IRI(CONCAT("http://purl.uniprot.org/taxonomy/",
    STRAFTER(STR(?IRI_EBI),"http://identifiers.org/taxonomy/"))) as ?IRI_UNIPROT)
  FILTER(STRSTARTS(STR(?IRI_EBI),"http://identifiers.org/taxonomy/"))
  SERVICE<https://sparql.uniprot.org/sparql>{
    ?IRI_UNIPROT a up:Taxon.
    ?IRI_UNIPROT rdfs:subClassOf ?taxon2 .
    ?taxon2 up:otherName "rodents". } }
```

Listing 6. A federated query between EBI and UniProt datasets to retrieve assays in rodents for the drug Gleevec (i.e. CHEMBL941). Table 2 contains the IRI prefixes.

VoIDext metadata in Table 3—i.e. the T_1 tuple. By considering T_1 in Table 3, the SPARQL user can draft Q_f starting with the interlink between EBI and UniProt as shown in bold in Listing 6. The user can now continue the writing of Q_f by solely focusing on each dataset separately—i.e. the non-bold part of the Q_f SPARQL query. Therefore, the fastidious process of finding out interlinks and data transformations between EBI and UniProt to perform a federated query is mitigated with the virtual link sets defined using the VoIDext vocabulary. The query in Listing 6 can be executed in the EBI SPARQL endpoint (see Table 1). Further examples of SPARQL federated queries that were written based on VoIDext metadata are available as part of an application described in Subsect. 4.4.

Table 3. The results of querying complex link sets composed of two shared instance sets between EBI and UniProt.

Outcome: A set of tuples $T = (V_L, ds_1, ds_2, I_{t1}, I_{t2}, A_{ds_1}, A_{ds_2}, f_m)$ where V_L is the virtual link set IRI; ds_1 and ds_2 are the names of the datasets that contain the instance IRIs; I_{t1} is the type (DL-class expression) of the instance in ds_1; I_{t2} is the type (DL-class expression) of the instance in ds_2; A_{ds_1} and A_{ds_2} are the access methods such as SPARQL endpoints to the ds_1 and ds_2 datasets, respectively; f_m is the recommended resource mapping procedure, if any, to be applied to instance IRIs of I_{t1} xor I_{t2} types, where xor is the exclusive or.
Example:
$T_1 = $ (bioquery:EBI_UNIPROT_12, "Linked Open Data platform for EBI data.","The Universal Protein Resource (UniProt)", biopax:BioSource, up:Taxon, <https://www.ebi.ac.uk/rdf/services/sparql>, <https://sparql.uniprot.org/sparql/>, $f_m^3(i)$))
where i is any instance of *biopax:BioSource* type and $f_m^3(i) \equiv$ "'?IRI_EBI a <http://www.biopax.org/release/biopax-level3.owl#BioSource>. BIND(IRI(CONCAT("http://purl.uniprot.org/taxonomy/", STRAFTER(STR(?IRI_EBI), "http://identifiers.org/taxonomy/"))) as ?IRI_UNIPROT) FILTER(STRSTARTS(STR(?IRI_EBI), "http://identifiers.org/taxonomy/"))"'

4.3   Virtual Link Set Maintenance

Although, to manage the virtual link set evolution is out of the scope of this article, we recommend to annotate the link sets with the issued and modified dates such as depicted in Listing 4. This date information helps with the maintenance of virtual link sets. For example, let us suppose the release of a new version of the DBpedia in August, 2019. By checking the difference between the DBpedia new release date and the complex link set issued/modified date (e.g. June 2019, see Listing 4), it might indicate a possible decrease in the virtual link set performance, or even, invalidity of the interlinks due to the fact of being outdated. In addition, for each virtual link set, we can state the performance in terms of precision, recall, true positives, and so on by asserting the *voidext:hasPerformanceMeasure* property. The range of this property is *mex-perf:PerformanceMeasure*[8]. Thus, we can rely on the Mex-perf ontology (see

---

[8] http://mex.aksw.org/mex-perf.

Footnote 8) to describe the virtual link set performances. The complex link set example about Swiss cantons in Listing 4 has a precision and recall of 100%. In this example, for every Swiss canton in LINDAS exists a corresponding one in DBpedia. Therefore, if this performance is deteriorated after the new release of one of the datasets involved, we should review this virtual link set. Further use cases are exemplified in Supplementary Material Section 5 available in [13].

4.4   Benefits and a SIB Swiss Institute of Bioinformatics' Application

Easing the Task of Writing SPARQL 1.1 Federated Queries. The formal description of virtual link sets among multiple RDF datasets on the Web facilitates the manually or (semi-)automatically writing of federated queries. This is because once the virtual link sets are defined between datasets with VoIDext, we can interlink different RDF datasets without requiring to mine this information again from the various ABoxes and TBoxes (including documentation, if any). The mining task becomes more and more complex and fastidious if the TBox is incomplete or missing when comparing with the ABox statements, for example, a triple predicate that is not defined in the TBox.

Applying Semantic Relaxation Rather than Semantic Reconciliation. The *virtual link* statements between datasets are more focused on the meaning of interlinking RDF graph nodes rather than the semantics of each node in the different datasets and knowledge domains. For example, let us consider the *virtual link* illustrated in Fig. 1. When considering solely the LINDAS dataset, the *lindas:longName* is a *rdf:Property* labelled as a "District name or official municipality name". In DBpedia, *dbp:shortName* is a *rdf:Property* labelled as "short name" and in principle can be applied to any instance. Hence, it is not restricted to district names. In addition, one property is about long names while the other one is about short names. However, they state similar literals in the context of Swiss cantons as discussed in Sect. 3. Therefore, although these properties are semantically different (hard to reconcile), we can still ignore heterogeneities for the sake of interlinking DBpedia and LINDAS.

Facilitating Knowledge Discovery. As noticed in [1], yet there are many challenges to address in the semantic web such as the previous knowledge of the existing RDF datasets and how to combine them to process a query. VoIDext mitigates these issues because RDF publishers (including third-party ones) are able to provide virtual link sets which explicitly describe how heterogeneous datasets of distinct domains are related. Without knowing these links, to potentially extract new knowledge that combines these datasets is harder or not even possible. The virtual link sets stated with VoIDext terms provide sufficient machine-readable information to relate the datasets. Nonetheless, the automatic generation of these link sets is out of the scope of this article.

A SIB Swiss Institute of Bioinformatics application. We applied the VoIDext vocabulary in the context of a real case application mainly involving three in production life-sciences datasets available on the Web, namely UniProtKB, OMA and Bgee RDF stores—see SPARQL endpoints in Table 1. The RDF serialization of virtual link sets among these three databases is available in [13] and it can be queried via the SPARQL endpoint in [12] with query templates defined in [14] as described in Subsect. 4.1. Based on these *virtual links*, a set of more than twelve specialized federated query templates over these data stores was defined and are available at https://github.com/biosoda/bioquery/tree/master/Queries. These templates are also available through a template-based search engine, see http://biosoda.expasy.org. Moreover, as an example of facilitating knowledge discovery, we can mention the virtual link sets between OMA and Bgee. These two distinct biological knowledge domains when combined enable to predict gene expression conservation for orthologous genes (i.e. corresponding genes in different species). Finally, new virtual link sets are being created to support other biological databases in the context of SIB—https://sib. swiss.

5 Conclusion

We successfully extended the VoID vocabulary (i.e. VoIDext) to be able to formally describe *virtual links* and we provided a set of SPARQL query templates to retrieve them. To do so, we applied an agile methodology based on the SAMOD approach. We described the benefits of defining *virtual links* with VoIDext RDF schema, notably to facilitate the writing of federated queries and knowledge discovery. In addition, with *virtual links* we can enable interoperability among different knowledge domains without imposing any changes in the original RDF datasets. In the future, we intend to use VoIDext to enhance keyword-search engines over multiple distributed and independent RDF datasets. We also envisage to propose tools to semi-automatically create VoIDext virtual link statements between RDF datasets. We believe these tools can leverage the adoption of VoIDext by other communities besides SIB, Quest for Orthologs consortium (https://questfororthologs.org), and Linked Building Data Community (https://www.w3.org/community/lbd) where the authors are involved. We also encourage other communities to collaborate on open issues in the public GitHub of VoIDext in [13] to refine this vocabulary for other use cases that have not been contemplated during this work. Finally, to support virtual link evolution, we aim to develop a tool to automatically detect broken virtual links because of either data schema changes or radical modifications of instances' IRIs and property assertions.

Acknowledgements. This work was funded by the Swiss National Research Programme 75 "Big Data" (Grant 167149) and a Swiss National Science Foundation Professorship grant to CD (Grant 150654).

References

1. Acosta, M., Hartig, O., Sequeda, J.: Federated RDF query processing. In: Sakr, S., Zomaya, A. (eds.) Encyclopedia of Big Data Technologies, pp. 1–10. Springer, Cham (2018). https://doi.org/10.1007/978-3-319-63962-8
2. Alexander, K., Cyganiak, R., Hausenblas, M., Zhao, J.: Describing linked datasets. In: Proceedings of the Linked Data on the Web Workshop (LDOW2009), Madrid, Spain, 20 April 2009. CEUR Workshop Proceedings (2009)
3. Altenhoff, A.M., Glover, N.M., Train, C.M., et al.: The OMA orthology database in 2018: retrieving evolutionary relationships among all domains of life through richer web and programmatic interfaces. Nucl. Acids Res. **46**(D1), D477–D485 (2018)
4. Baader, F., Calvanese, D., McGuinness, D., Patel-Schneider, P., Nardi, D.: The Description Logic Handbook: Theory, Implementation and Applications. Cambridge University Press, Cambridge (2003)
5. Bgee team: Bgee data sources (2019). https://bgee.org/?page=source. Accessed 25 Aug 2019
6. Brunner, U., Stockinger, K.: Entity matching on unstructured data: an active learning approach. In: 6th Swiss Conference on Data Science, Bern, 2019. IEEE (2019)
7. buildingSMART: IFC overview summary. http://www.buildingsmart-tech.org/specifications/ifc-overview. Accessed 25 Aug 2019
8. Crotti Junior, A., Debruyne, C., Brennan, R., O'Sullivan, D.: An evaluation of uplift mapping languages. Int. J. Web Inf. Syst. **13**(4), 405–424 (2017)
9. David, J., Euzenat, J., Scharffe, F., Trojahn dos Santos, C.: The alignment API 4.0. Semant. Web **2**(1), 3–10 (2011)
10. De Meester, B., Maroy, W., Dimou, A., Verborgh, R., Mannens, E.: Declarative data transformations for linked data generation: the case of DBpedia. In: Blomqvist, E., Maynard, D., Gangemi, A., Hoekstra, R., Hitzler, P., Hartig, O. (eds.) ESWC 2017. LNCS, vol. 10250, pp. 33–48. Springer, Cham (2017). https://doi.org/10.1007/978-3-319-58451-5_3
11. Djokic-Petrovic, M., Cvjetkovic, V., Yang, J., Zivanovic, M., Wild, D.J.: PIBAS FedSPARQL: a web-based platform for integration and exploration of bioinformatics datasets. J. Biomed. Semant. **8**(1), 42 (2017)
12. Farias, T.M.: The SPARQL endpoint of the SIB application and VoIDext specification examples. http://biosoda.expasy.org:8890/sparql. Accessed 25 Aug 2019
13. Farias, T.M.: VoIDext GitHub project repository. https://github.com/biosoda/voidext. Accessed 25 Aug 2019
14. Farias, T.M.: VoIDext vocabulary specification draft. https://biosoda.github.io/voidext/. Accessed 25 Aug 2019
15. Farias, T.M., Roxin, A., Nicolle, C.: FOWLA, a federated architecture for ontologies. In: Bassiliades, N., Gottlob, G., Sadri, F., Paschke, A., Roman, D. (eds.) RuleML 2015. LNCS, vol. 9202, pp. 97–111. Springer, Cham (2015). https://doi.org/10.1007/978-3-319-21542-6_7
16. de Farias, T.M., Roxin, A., Nicolle, C.: A rule-based methodology to extract building model views. Autom. Constr. **92**, 214–229 (2018)
17. Fernandez, R.C., Mansour, E., Qahtan, A.A., et al.: Seeping semantics: linking datasets using word embeddings for data discovery. In: 2018 IEEE 34th International Conference on Data Engineering (ICDE), pp. 989–1000. IEEE (2018)
18. Gal, A., Modica, G., Jamil, H., Eyal, A.: Automatic ontology matching using application semantics. AI Mag. **26**(1), 21 (2005)

19. Harris, S., Seaborne, A., Prud'hommeaux, E.: SPARQL 1.1 query language (2013). https://www.w3.org/TR/sparql11-federated-query/. Accessed 25 Aug 2019
20. Hasnain, A., Mehmood, Q., e Zainab, S.S., et al.: Biofed: federated query processing over life sciences linked open data. J. Biomed. Semant. **8**(1), 13 (2017)
21. Isele, R., Jentzsch, A., Bizer, C.: Efficient multidimensional blocking for link discovery without losing recall. In: WebDB (2011). https://dblp.org/rec/bibtex2/conf/webdb/IseleJB11
22. Jupp, S., Malone, J., Bolleman, J., et al.: The EBI RDF platform: linked open data for the life sciences. Bioinformatics **30**(9), 1338–1339 (2014)
23. Lehmann, J., Isele, R., Jakob, M., et al.: DBpedia-a large-scale, multilingual knowledge base extracted from wikipedia. Semant. Web **6**(2), 167–195 (2015)
24. Ngo, D., Bellahsene, Z.: Overview of YAM++–(not) yet another matcher for ontology alignment task. J. Web Semant. **41**, 30–49 (2016)
25. Ngomo, A.C.N., Auer, S.: LIMES–a time-efficient approach for large-scale link discovery on the web of data. In: Twenty-Second International Joint Conference on Artificial Intelligence (2011). aaai.org
26. Otero-Cerdeira, L., Rodríguez-Martínez, F.J., Gómez-Rodríguez, A.: Ontology-matching: a literature review. Expert. Syst. Appl. **42**(2), 949 – 971 (2015)
27. Peroni, S.: A simplified agile methodology for ontology development. In: Dragoni, M., Poveda-Villalón, M., Jimenez-Ruiz, E. (eds.) OWLED/ORE -2016. LNCS, vol. 10161, pp. 55–69. Springer, Cham (2017). https://doi.org/10.1007/978-3-319-54627-8_5
28. Sherif, M.A., Ngonga Ngomo, A.-C., Lehmann, J.: WOMBAT – a generalization approach for automatic link discovery. In: Blomqvist, E., Maynard, D., Gangemi, A., Hoekstra, R., Hitzler, P., Hartig, O. (eds.) ESWC 2017. LNCS, vol. 10249, pp. 103–119. Springer, Cham (2017). https://doi.org/10.1007/978-3-319-58068-5_7
29. Siegel, M.D., Madnick, S.E.: A metadata approach to resolving semantic conflicts (1991)
30. UniProt Consortium: UniProt: the universal protein knowledgebase. Nucl. Acids Res. **46**(5), 2699 (2018)
31. Whetzel, P.L., Noy, N.F., Shah, N.H., et al.: BioPortal: enhanced functionality via new web services from the national center for biomedical ontology to access and use ontologies in software applications. Nucl. Acids Res. **39**(Web Server issue), W541-5 (2011)
32. Wimalaratne, S.M., Bolleman, J., Juty, N., et al.: SPARQL-enabled identifier conversion with identifiers.org. Bioinformatics **31**(11), 1875–1877 (2015)
33. Živanovic, M.: SpecINT: a framework for data integration over cheminformatics and bioinformatics RDF repositories (2019). semantic-web-journal.net

NotaryPedia: A Knowledge Graph of Historical Notarial Manuscripts

Charlene Ellul[✉], Joel Azzopardi[✉], and Charlie Abela[✉]

University of Malta, Msida, Malta
{charlene.ellul,joel.azzopardi,charlie.abela}@um.edu.mt

Abstract. The Notarial Archives in Valletta, the capital city of Malta, houses a rich and valuable collection of around twenty thousand notarial manuscripts dating back to the 15th century. The Archive wants to make the contents of this collection easily accessible and searchable to researchers and the general public. Knowledge Graphs have been successfully used to represent similar historical content. Nevertheless, building a Knowledge Graph for the archives is challenging as these documents are written in medieval Latin and currently there is a lack of information extraction tools that recognise this language. This is, furthermore, compounded with a lack of medieval Latin corpora to train and evaluate machine learning algorithms, as well as a lack of an ontological representation for the contents of notarial manuscripts. In this paper, we present NotaryPedia, a Knowledge Graph for the Notarial Archives. We extend our previous work on entity and keyphrase extraction with relation extraction to populate the Knowledge Graph using an ontological vocabulary for notarial deeds. Furthermore, we perform Knowledge Graph completeness using link-prediction and inference. Our work was evaluated using different translational distance and semantic matching models to predict relations amongst literals by promoting them to entities and to infer new knowledge from existing entities. A 49% relation prediction accuracy using TransE was achieved.

Keywords: Knowledge Graph · Medieval latin text · Notarial Ontology · Relation extraction · Link prediction

1 Introduction

Archives around the world are a source of hidden information, which attract numerous researchers to dig out facts and stories that make up the jigsaw puzzle of the past. One of these archival gems is found at the Notarial Archives in Valletta, Malta and houses around 20,000 notarial manuscripts dating back to the 15th century. Most of the notarial deeds found in this archive fall under categories such as wills, receipts, dowries and transfer of land which are bound

This work is partially funded by project E-18LO28-01 as part of the collaboration between the Notarial Archives in Valletta and the University of Malta.

© Springer Nature Switzerland AG 2019
H. Panetto et al. (Eds.): OTM 2019, LNCS 11877, pp. 626–645, 2019.
https://doi.org/10.1007/978-3-030-33246-4_39

in registers or stored as fragments in boxes. They are often examined for their legal implications, historical research and tracing of inheritance.

The aim of any archive is the long-term preservation of historical documents and the dissemination of the collections for research. Traditionally, researchers had to spend hours flipping through these manuscripts in hope that they encounter some excerpt that would help them to get closer to answering their questions. However, today most archives have been digitised or are in the process of being digitised. This often results in high quality scanned images of the documents being made available online along with archival meta data. Exposing the content of notarial Latin documents is however no easy feat and requires the use of techniques including, information extraction [5,11] and knowledge representation, to extract, link and publish this content [22].

Recent efforts have focused on promoting a graph representation of knowledge through standards such as RDF[1] [4,9,16]. In such a graph-based knowledge representation or *Knowledge Graph* (KG), entities are represented as nodes, while relations are represented by the edges. One important step in the creation of a KG is deciding on the underlying model to use. When it comes to archiving in general, popular vocabularies include Dublin Core Terms[2] and LOCAH[3] amongst others. Nevertheless, a specialised vocabulary to represent notarial documents such as deeds is lacking.

Information extraction methods have been extensively used to extract entities and relations from unstructured historical text which can be used to populate KGs [6]. Extracting information from content written in medieval Latin, the predominant language used in these notarial transcribed documents [13], poses a number of challenges. These include the lack of readily available Named Entity Recognition (NER) tools and the lack of annotated corpora for training and testing. In [10], we used a combination of machine learning techniques to extract entities such as dates, people, places, deed types and keyphrases from a collection of transcribed notarial documents.

In this paper, we discuss how we used the same collection of Latin notarial transcribed manuscripts [13], to extend the work presented in [10] by focusing on relation extraction and the creation of the NotaryPedia Knowledge Graph (NKG). We treated relation extraction as a multi-class classification problem and managed to extract meaningful relations from these manuscripts such as *getty:ulan1512_parent_of*, *getty:ulan1511_child_of*, *schema:homeLocation*. Furthermore, since we are dealing with an information space that is continuously being rediscovered through research performed by historians, we cannot consider the NKG to be complete. For this reason we compliment the relation extraction method with link prediction using various translational embedding distance models and semantic matching models to discover new relations and enrich the graph as it is populated with newly found information. Although link prediction techniques have been used in different domains, as reported by [16], to our knowledge there is no research involving knowledge graphs for notarial documents.

---

[1] http://www.w3.org/RDF/.

[2] http://www.dublincore.org/specifications/dublin-core/dcmi-terms/.

[3] http://data.archiveshub.ac.uk/def/.

The rest of this paper is structured as follows. In Sect. 2 we discuss related research focusing on relation extraction, KG creation and link prediction. In Sect. 3 we discuss our approach to relation extraction from the notarial manuscripts and how we enrich the KG using link prediction techniques. Following is the evaluation section where we provide results for relation extraction, coreference resolution and comparisons between the different embedding techniques used. Finally we discuss future work and provide concluding remarks.

2   Related Work

One of the aims behind our research is to support historians while they are exploring connections amongst extracted entities found in notarial manuscripts. This is further enhanced by manually curated records that may be part of the digitisation process. The International Image Interoperability Framework (IIIF)[4] is a set of APIs which provide an easy way to share digital image data whereby associated manifests can include data related to provenance, attribution and licensing. In this section we discuss related research that focuses on the creation of KGs, relation extraction and how link prediction is used to complete KGs.

2.1   Knowledge Graph Creation

Although there exists an effort to represent archives as Linked Open Data (LOD), projects such as SAWS[5] focus on representing the physical dimension of their manuscripts by annotating them using the Text-Encoding Initiative (TEI) and providing an OWL ontology. According to Debruyne et al. [4] the content of a document can be represented by an ontology as a non tampered representation which is a transcription and quality control of the original document. This can be reused for different purposes and interpreted in a number of different ways. An interpretation ontology can be created to emphasise the separation of concerns and is used to answer specific questions that a historian might need to pose.

The Linked Open Copac and Archives Hub (LOCAH)[6] is a project aimed at representing archival and bibliographic data as LOD [19]. The scope behind LOCAH was to allow different archival content to be linked and thus enable researchers to learn more about history and society by freely navigating through the data and making new connections between different entities. The ontology reuses a number of established ontologies and standards, including EAD (Encoded Archival Description) which is used for data exchange, intereoperability and digital preservation and is used as the underlying model for the Archives-Hub of the Jisc organisation[7]. Although LOCAH allows for the representation of a number of repositories and related resources, it is mainly intended for cataloguing purposes and does not cater for the concepts and relations found within

---

[4] http://iiif.io.
[5] http://www.ancientwisdoms.ac.uk/.
[6] http://data.archiveshub.ac.uk/.
[7] https://www.jisc.ac.uk/archives-hub.

these collections. Nonetheless, LOCAH can be reused from within other vocabularies that are specific to particular collections. For instance through LOCAH it is possible to represent a repository and its associated archival resources using levels to indicate a group of documents (such as a registry) or subsections of it (such as a deed).

The collections used to populate the previously mentioned Archival-Hub are English texts, where there is a level of standardisation in language and thus contain fewer disambiguation than medieval Latin. [2] discuss the challenges of publishing historical texts, including the automatic processing of old languages, old expressions, grammatical forms and obsolete names. Furthermore, proper vocabulary that provides semantic markup and clear definitions is vital to avoid misinterpretation of concepts.

Knowledge graph building can leverage on both entity and relation extraction techniques. Relations in a KG provide a way to link concepts and traverse the graph to gain further insights on the data represented. Since entities have already been extracted in our previous work [10], we present research that focuses on relation extraction from historical notarial documents. A survey [18] focuses on binary relations that occur in the same sentence and the challenges that occur from one domain to another. It states how relation extraction is language dependent and how existing methodologies are not easy to be applied to non-English texts. Experiments have been conducted on Dutch historical notary deeds with a focus on extracting family relations [6]. The aim of this research was to discover social patterns such as household structure and family size along with family tree reconstruction. The authors discuss the challenges they encountered which include lack of training data, an imbalanced dataset and the lack of people's names standardisation leading to coreference resolution techniques. They used an annotated dataset and applied Support Vector Machine and a combination of bi-grams and tri-grams of words to identify genealogical relations between previously extracted person candidate pairs.

2.2 Knowledge Graph Prediction

A Knowledge Graph is not complete upon construction, with the two major flaws being that it can never reach full coverage and be fully correct [17]. Knowledge refinement is applied on machine interpreted ontologies [4] and aims to minimise these flaws by applying techniques on already constructed graphs to add, amend or delete knowledge with the aim of making the graph more complete and/or correct.

Some relations can be discovered by leveraging on the schema knowledge and applying inference, for example *getty:ulan1531_nephew-niece_of* can be inferred if *getty:ulan1532_uncle-aunt_of* is known. Paulheim et al. [17] discuss classification methods, where a tensor neural network is trained on the chains of other relations, for instance if a person is born in Germany than there is a high probability that he has a German nationality. The performance of such approaches relies on schema knowledge. When there is a lack of ontological knowledge, it is however possible to use a probabilistic approach such as link prediction to infer missing relationships. Learning joint embeddings of subject and object entities and thus sharing left and right embedding factors, can aid in solving the link prediction problem [3]. Data sparsity involving missing data and relationships makes it harder for link prediction to work effectively [21]. Furthermore, result metrics such as accuracy, precision and recall are highly influenced by the class imbalance of relations in the training data, where correct link prediction of rare triples might be more interesting than frequently represented triples [25].

Link prediction [3] is considered to be a refinement technique that is applied over existing entities and relations in a graph. Thus given a triple (h, r, t) where h represents the *head*, t represents the *tail* and r represents a *relation*, it is possible to either predict h, given $(?, r, t)$ or to predict t, given $(h, r, ?)$. Link prediction works by expanding a relation model, based on the structure/pattern of a graph, and then through descriptive analysis of the data, make simple model assumptions. Modelling multi-relational data involves the locality of existing relations and entities of different types at the same time [3].

Link prediction can be solved by embedding pairwise entities and relations in a lower dimensional continuous vector space to predict the existence of relations [17,23]. Entities and relations can be represented in a low dimensional continuous vector where entities are represented as deterministic points while relations are taken as operations on the vector space usually represented by vectors, matrices, tensors or Gaussian distributions. Through the use of a scoring function, it is possible to measure how plausible a triple *(h, r, t)* is by assuming graph triples as facts. Since a KG usually contains only true triples, corrupted triplets (negative sampling) have to be introduced by replacing either the head or tail entity by a random entity during the training phase [15].

3   Methodology

In this section we present NotaryPedia[8], a Knowledge Graph that represents an interpretation of the content of historical notarial manuscripts found in the Notarial Archives. These archives are visited by numerous researchers interested typically in finding information about inheritance, but also about traditional customs and other mundane topics such as music and fashion. To address these needs we extended our previous work on extracting entities and keyphrases [10] by providing a schema for the NKG. We furthermore describe how we performed relation extraction on the same collection of notarial manuscripts [13] and how link prediction was used to complete the KG.

3.1   Knowledge Graph Creation Pipeline

The aim of NotaryPedia is to have a scalable approach for storing and interlink data to provide further insight about the social and business interactions of our ancestors. A knowledge graph is ideal as it provides the flexibility required

---

[8] The prototype can be accessed from: https://notarypedia.opendatamalta.com/.

to maintain and incrementally add or discover new information. NotaryPedia's pipeline is shown in Fig. 1 and consists of a number of processes inline with existing research [22].

This pipeline starts with a Notarial Archives' team of volunteers which was involved in identifying the **specifications** related to NKG. Their input during this process proved to be important to determine which data should ideally be **mined** from the manuscripts. In this step, shown in Fig. 1, as part of the data acquistion stage, we used NER and rule based methods to extract important entities including dates, people and places [10]. These provide the fundamental data for commencing research on a number of areas such as genealogy and geography. Data acquisition also involved the extraction of a number of keyphrases which represent the content of a deed, thus allowing a topic search. Deed classification enables the categorisation of deeds in distinct categories such as *debitum - debt* indicating that some sort of transaction has been recorded in the deed. This was the work presented in [10]. A KG is able to present extracted data in an exciting and more human intuitive manner by interlinking its data. Thus we extended our previous work by using relation extraction techniques, where the extracted entities are linked to each other and therefore establish a path that the user can traverse to gain further insight on the data represented.

A **URI** was defined to represent the resources uniquely. This paved the way for the **data modelling** task whereby all the **data acquired** from the the the **mining** stage using NER, keyphrase extraction, text classification and relation extraction techniques, was mapped to a specific vocabulary and transformed into RDF during the **data lifting** stage. The vocabulary is chosen depending on which data is acquired. We explain this in Sect. 3.2.

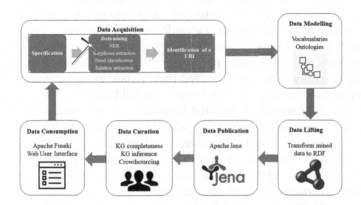

Fig. 1. NotaryPedia Knowledge Graph creation pipeline

We used the Apache Jena[9] framework together with the Fuseki[10] server to manage, store and query the knowledge graph. This is represented in Fig. 1 as

---

[9] https://jena.apache.org/.
[10] https://jena.apache.org/documentation/fuseki2/.

the **data publication** stage. **Data curation** was performed to clean, maintain and preserve the data within this structure. Knowledge Graph completeness methods and inference were performed to fill out missing relations which were not explicitly stated or could not be caught during the data acquisition stage. We are aware that the relation extraction technique in the **data acquisition** stage relies on entity extraction. A curation process similar to Feeney et al. [12] whereby domain experts verify the data acquired before publishing to users, may uncover new information that is present in a deed but that was not extracted, and therefore is not yet linked to other previously extracted entities. Although the curation pipeline is not yet fully implemented, we provide a prototype for data crowd sourcing, in hope that domain experts can clean the data and enrich it. We focused on completion techniques to increase coverage. A Web User interface is part of the **data consumption layer**, which was created to provide a visualisation of the Knowledge Graph through the traversal of hyperlinks. This will aid users in semantic search and question answering from the collection. This cycle can be repeated a number of times if new requirements are specified by the client in which case is the Notarial Archives.

3.2 Notarial Ontology

Since there is no readily available vocabulary representing the content of notarial manuscripts, we had to design our own ontology. We however kept in line with the LOD philosophy and reused as much as possible existing vocabularies. Having an ontological representation, which allows the semantic modelling of the NotaryPedia Knowledge Graph[11], can facilitate the derivation of conclusions from known facts for reasoning purposes. Its purpose is to provide a model of the Notarial Archives reality, including concepts that are present in the real world. An ontology has to have enough information to answer questions, which a user of the ontology might have. Thus, prior to designing the Notarial Ontology, its concepts were identified after a consultation with the Notarial Archives team of expert volunteers, who provided their expertise in creating an ontology which models the collection accurately and can aid historical research questions. Although we are presenting a Notarial Ontology, we are aware that the design of any ontology is an iterative process, where after designing the initial version, this has to be evaluated for its application and problem solving suitability. This is further defined as future work in the Conclusion Sect. 5.

We leverage on the LOCAH vocabulary and extend it to represent the relationship between deeds that are *ore:aggregates* in a register. A register is then *locah:associatedWith* a number of deeds and a collection of registers is associated with a repository such as the Notarial Archives. A deed representation in the **Notarial Ontology** (NO) is shown in Fig. 2.

Deeds are associated with a number of entities including Person, Item and Place. The Level of a deed indicates the part of an archival collection in which

---

[11] The current Knowledge Graph is found here: https://notarypedia.opendatamalta. com/graph/notarypedia.ttl.

the deed is located. It defines whether it is part of a whole collection or a sub-collection, in which case a deed is considered to be an item[12] in a file[13]. Each deed has an associated date and can also be associated with set of keyphrases (extracted from the deed). These are represented as literals, for example *hannacam* (in Latin) which means *necklace*. We chose to initially represent them as such because within the deed itself there might not be other properties associated with them. A deed has a type, for instance *apoca - receipt* or *dos - dowry* and an identifier that is used to facilitate deed identification. We had to furthermore extend NO to also represent relations such as *associated keyphrase, debtor of, creditor of* and *barteredWith* that are specific to deeds. A deed can be linked to another deed if it is *associatedWith* the same Person, Place or Item.

3.3   The Role of the Notarial Archives' Volunteers

Throughout this research we were supported by a number of individuals that do voluntary work at the Notarial Archives. Most of the volunteers at the Archives are historians who visit the Archives for personal research and thus became familiar with the collection and the language used.

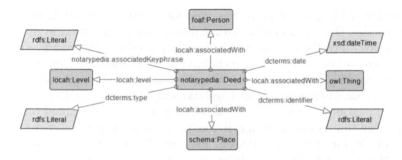

Fig. 2. Deed representation in the Knowledge Graph

They participated in the creation of a crowdtruth for relationship extraction, where they were asked to label the proper relation between two entities referred to as the Relation_Type dataset. The dataset was used to train and test models to extract genealogical and other relations such as *schema:homeLocation* from text prior to KG creation as discussed in Sects. 3.4 and 4.1 where we show our results using precision, recall and F1 score. A pre-process for such extraction, required us to disambiguate names prior to applying a multi class classification model, where volunteers tagged a list of disambiguated names described in Sect. 3.4 and created a crowdtruth referred to as the Disambiguation dataset, which was used to compare the precision, recall and F1 score of similarity metrics with a rule based approach. We also experiment with KG completion and link prediction

---

[12] The smallest unit of a description in an archival collection, for example a report. [1].
[13] An organized unit of documents grouped together either for current use by the creator or in the process of archival arrangement. In our case this is a register [1].

discussed in Sects. 3.6 and 4.2, which also required volunteers to tag appropriate relations between entities and literals and compiled a crowdtruth with entity and relation mapping ids (Table 1(right)) that were successfully utilised in training and testing translation distance models. This is referred to as the Link_Prediction dataset. These labels enabled us to compare the accuracy results of various low-dimensional representational models.

For each task, three Notarial Archives volunteers were appointed to perform tagging. The volunteers were presented with all the records of the dataset separately and resulted in three complete tagged datasets. For each task a majority poll was taken to establish a crowdtruth. Although this was time consuming, we could get the independent opinion of the volunteers. We are aware that it is not ideal to have such a small number of participants in the construction of a crowdtruth, as usually this relies on the observations of disagreements between annotators to eliminate ambiguity. Given that there were few people available at the Notarial Archives who are knowledgeable in reading medieval Latin documents and willing to provide their services in creating a crowdtruth, we opted to involve an odd number of volunteers to take a majority poll of their results.

3.4 Relation Extraction

In Gonzalez et al. [14] clustering was used for relation extraction, however, to our knowledge, there is no research that focused on medieval Latin documents. Furthermore, since the average word count per deed was 289 words, clustering was deemed to not be the ideal technique as this usually results in a sparse feature vector [20]. Efremova et al. [7] applied a supervised approach on Dutch Notarial documents to extract family relationships. This research enables explicitly stated relations in text to be extracted from the same domain as our corpus. We extended that research so that it was possible to identify relations between entities of the form: Person - Person, Person - Place, Place - Place. We then applied this on our Latin corpus from the transcriptions [13].

For this experiment we identified 14 different relations, the majority being genealogical relations such as *getty:ulan1501_sibling_of*, *getty:ulan1511_child_of* and other relations such as *foaf:nick*, *schema:containsPlace*, *schema:home Location*. Using the extracted persons and places from our previous work [10], deeds were annotated. Notarial Archives volunteers were involved in tagging the type of relation between two entities forming a candidate pair shown in Fig. 3 (left). This tagging process created the crowdtruth data referred to as the Relation_Type dataset which was later used for training and evaluation. The Relation_Type dataset had the format *(Person1, Person2, rel)*, where the candidate pair were the names of the persons which are related to each other and *rel* was the type of relation, such as *getty:ulan1512_parent_of*. Before tagging was performed, a coreference resolution technique was applied as it is very common to find variants of the same name and referring to the same individual, within the same deed, for example *Antonij, Antonium, Antonius*. There was no need for place name coreference resolution within the same deed as it was the norm for a scribe to write the whole deed, thus writing a place name consistently the same.

A standardised name had to be chosen to replace all the disambiguated names in the text. Most of the name variations were due to declensions. The character based similarity algorithm Jaro-Winkler [24], a token based cosine similarity function and a rule-based approach were compared for coreference resolution effectiveness. For Jaro-Winkler and cosine similarity, a list of the extracted names from each deed, both full and first names, were expanded in all possible pair combinations. A similarity score was computed depending on the similarity function used. A threshold of 0.8 was used to create a list of same names including full and first names, for example the name *Bernardus Curmj* had the coreferences *Bernardum Curmi, Bernardus, Bernardo, Bernardum.*

The rule based function leverages on the idea that most of the variances of the names are found in the ending (suffix), thus comparing the first few letters. An abbreviation of the full name was then created by considering the first 3 letters, for instance *Laurencio de Falsono* becomes *Lau Fal*. Grouping by abbreviations, created a list of disambiguated names. The list of first names and full names were processed separately and then joined together, giving priority to a full name being the name to replace all coreferences in the text. After each experiment, our team of three volunteers from the Notarial Archives was asked to separately label the True Positives and False Negatives for the records of the whole dataset, for each pair of disambiguated names using an interface shown in Fig. 3 (right). This process created the crowdtruth referred to as the Disambiguation dataset, that allowed us to calculate the precision, recall and F1 score of each method in the evaluation section. In Sect. 4.1 we present the results from the rule based approach which had the highest F1 score and was thus used to replace all instances of the disambiguated name with a standard name.

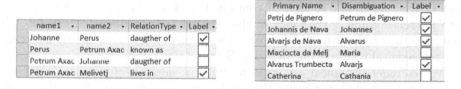

name1	name2	RelationType	Label
Johanne	Perus	daugther of	☑
Perus	Petrum Axac	known as	☐
Petrum Axac	Johanne	daugther of	☐
Petrum Axac	Melivetj	lives in	☑

Primary Name	Disambiguation	Label
Petrj de Pignero	Petrum de Pignero	☑
Johannis de Nava	Johannes	☑
Alvarjs de Nava	Alvarus	☑
Maciocta da Melj	Maria	☐
Alvarus Trumbecta	Alvarjs	☑
Catherina	Cathania	☐

Fig. 3. Relation and Coreference resolution tagging process UI

Using the disambiguated pairs of people and the extracted places, a bag of words was created consisting of words that reside between the entities and two words before and after the first and last entity. These are all lemmatised using Schmidt's treetager[14]. The number of words in-between were also extracted in an attempt to improve classification. The bag of words is grouped if the disambiguated candidate pair is the same. The same three volunteers associated candidate pairs with the relevant relationship in the document. Candidate pairs were tagged by the three different volunteers to take a majority poll of the designated relation label. An interface shown in Fig. 3 (left) was distributed

---

[14] http://www.cis.uni-muenchen.de/~schmid/tools/TreeTagger/.

to each volunteer where each volunteer had the option to label, change the relationship type or choose from other non suggested candidate pairs. To make the tagging process less tedious, a list of suggested relationships was provided. These suggestions consisted of set of words that might be in the bag of words of a candidate pair for example, if the word *filius* was in the bag of words of a particular candidate pair there was a likelihood that a *getty:ulan1511_child_of* relationship is present for that candidate pair. A total of 950 deeds were tagged with a total of 1738 relationships. The dataset was highly imbalanced as most candidate pairs had no relationships between them. Such candidate pairs were down-sampled to the mean of the other relationship counts (124 samples).

3.5   Knowledge Inference

In knowledge graphs it is typically the case that logical inference is performed using deductive reasoning over concepts and relations, to be able to infer additional facts. In our completion efforts over NotaryPedia we performed such an inference task through which we managed to identify a number of relations with the majority of these being genealogical relations.

Apache Jena allows inference engines/reasoners to be plugged into Jena. There are four available reasoners in the Jena distribution - Transitive reasoner, RDFS rule reasoner, OWL reasoner and Generic rule reasoner. Since we wanted control over which axioms should be inferred, we chose to use a Generic rule reasoner which supports rule based inference over RDF graphs.

An inference model from the original Knowledge Graph model was created. Rule sets were defined using a list of premises and a list of conclusions. Using the forward chaining engine, the inference model was queried and all relevant data was sent to the rule engine. Any new triples that are triggered from the rule set, could trigger additional rules. This continued until no more rules were triggered. The inference graph is the union of the original and the deducted graphs. We managed to complete the family tree down to three level hierarchy by inferring the genealogical relations mentioned in Sect. 3.4.

We consider a typical use case whereby a number of genealogical relations were extracted regarding the family of the nobleman *Bartholomei de Bernardo* from the 15th century, see Fig. 4. Through the extraction process discussed in Sect. 3.4 it was possible to identify that *Amate, Ylagie* and *Chuse* were *Bartholomei's* daughters. However, the fact that *Chuse* was also the *getty:ulan1501_sibling_of Amate* and *Ylagie* was inferred later and shown in blue in the figure.

3.6   Knowledge Graph: Link Prediction

The information space that NotaryPedia covers, forms part of the 20,000 manuscripts in the notarial collection which is still being rediscovered offering a mine of untapped information. Whenever new research is conducted, we want this information to be linked within the knowledge graph. Furthermore, relation extraction (discussed in Sect. 3.4), relies on entity extraction, and any verification

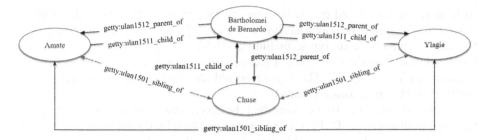

Fig. 4. Genealogical relationships for Nobleman Bartholomei de Bernardo. (Color figure online)

process conducted by researchers may uncover new information that is present in a deed but that was not extracted, and therefore is not yet linked to other previously extracted entities. Thus, if a historical researcher provides further data about a deed, we would like that meaningful relations are discovered, that relate the current and newly inputted data. For this reason we were motivated to research completion techniques to increase coverage in NotaryPedia.

Our research experiments with both *translational distance models* and *semantic matching models*. A TensorFlow implementation for knowledge representation learning was adopted using the open source library OpenKE [15]. This library also allows the embedding of large scale KGs, which NotaryPedia should become once more of the Archive collection is included. Although this library can be used to predict the subject, object and relation, we adopted the models for relation prediction between two entities. These entities could be people, places or a keyphrase that has been elevated from a literal to an entity. A keyphrase for which no further information is yet available, is initially represented by a literal. When and if, new information is found that enriches a keyphrase, this is redefined as a resource with associated properties.

We experimented with various classic knowledge embedding models which according to [23] and [15] have achieved great performance on benchmark datasets, including FB15K[15] and WN18[16]. TransE, TransH, TransD, RESCAL, DistMult, HolE, Analogy and ComplEx are used from the OpenKE library. Data from NotaryPedia was fed into OpenKE models to get the rank of the Top-1 relationship as this should be the most likely relation that exists between two entities.

To execute these models a dataset was created by querying NotaryPedia. First, a list of tuples with all the existing (and potential) entities in the knowledge graph and their unique IDs, was generated through a SPARQL query executed over all unique entities (people, places) and literals (keyphrases). Using Apache Fuseki, we were able to successfully query the knowledge graph and produce this list. The query relied on the ontological fact representation where

---

[15] https://github.com/thunlp/OpenKE/tree/master/benchmarks/FB15K.
[16] https://github.com/thunlp/OpenKE/tree/master/benchmarks/WN18.

each deed can be related to any of these entities through the *associatedWith* or *associatedKeyphrase* relations as shown in Fig. 2 These tuples are filtered to get the most common deeds types, including: *Debitum - debt, Vendicio - business transaction* or *Locacio - contract*. A sample with three such tuples from this list is shown in Table 1 (left). The keyphrase *abbatia melite* can be elevated to an entity if further relations are found.

A list of relations to be identified between two entities, were compiled together with a unique ID. 11 relations were identified by the archives' volunteers, that could provide further insights into the data. Their choice was motivated by ongoing research at the archives and we initially focused on these. Some of these relations are Person-Person relations, such as *notarypedia:debtorOf, frapo:sellsTo* and *getty:ulan1217_employee_of*, other relations are Person-literal such as *dbpedia:nationality, dbpedia:religion, frapo:purchases* and *dbpedia:occupation*. There are other relations that link a literal to a Place such as *dbpedia:locatedInArea* and relations between two literals such as *schema:colour, schema:containsPlace* and *notarypedia:barteredWith*, with both relation types requiring an elevation of the subject to an entity before proceeding with the algorithm.

Next we performed an exercise with the same team of expert archive volunteers to create a crowdtruth that was used for evaluation referred to as the Link_Prediction dataset. These experts were familiar with the collection and proficient in medieval Latin. Given a deed with related entities and relations (from the lists mentioned earlier), their task was to annotate any relation that existed between any two entities. There were 1014 unique relations identified and these were saved using OpenKEs format where each triple $(e1, e2, rel)$, refers to the subject, object and relation, as can be seen in Table 1(right). The annotated Link_Prediction dataset shown in Table 1(right) and was divided into training, testing and validation datasets using a ratio of 8 : 1 : 1. A big chunk of the data was used for training since the data collected was not large. This training dataset included 811 relations which were imbalanced as can be seen from the frequency distribution in Fig. 5. The most common types of identified relations include the *frapo:purchases, notarypedia:debtorOf* and *frapo:sellsTo*, which given the nature of the documents, was to be expected. We discuss the details and results from the application of the different models on this dataset in Sect. 4.2.

Table 1. Sample of Entity/Literal-ID List (left) and Link_Prediction dataset (right)

Entity/Literal	ID
http://natarchives.com.mt/person/person12386	5601
http://natarchives.com.mt/place/place24	5602
abbatia melite	5603

e1	e2	rel
3884	3883	1
3883	7852	2
7852	3899	4

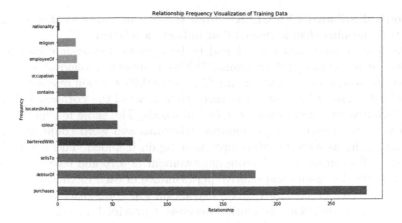

Fig. 5. Relation frequency of Training data

4 Results and Evaluation

In this section we discuss how we used the crowdtruth data referred to as *Relation_Type*, *Disambiguation* and *Link_Prediction* datasets to evaluate our work on relation extraction, coreference resolution as well as on link prediction. We also discuss the results obtained from these experiments.

4.1 Relation Extraction and Coreference Resolution Results

Finding relations between extracted data enables users to traverse a graph in a meaningful way. The problem was treated as a multi-class classification problem and a number of experiments were conducted with five different models - Naive Bayes Multinomial, Logistic Regression, SVM, Random Forest and KNN. Naive Bayes and SVM were both used by [8] in their approach for automatically retrieving family relationships from Dutch historical notary acts. On the other hand, Logistic Regression, SVM and KNN can also be used for multi-class classification, hence we decided to experiment with them.

Using the crowdtruth referred to as the Relation_Type dataset, whose collection process is discussed in Sect. 3.4, we were able to train and evaluate each model. We calculated the True/False Positives and Negatives and presented our results using the metrics precision, recall and F1 score.

Our approach followed a similar methodology as [8], where a bag of words was compiled using different set of features including uni-grams, bi-grams, tri-grams and their combinations. Using bi-grams and tri-gram features will also allow us to discover patterns in the deeds' text which will also take into account the sequences of words in contrast to just using singular words (uni-grams). Therefore if we want to discover if a person lives in a certain village, it is more likely that the bag of words will contain words such as *habitator - lives* or *habitator casalis - lives in village*. We also experimented with removing the list of stopwords distributed with CLTK[17] from the bag of words as they carry less important meaning than keywords that indicate a relation.

The best trained model was found to be Logistic Regression with a combination of uni-grams and tri-grams. Without stopword removal this model resulted in an accuracy of 0.68 and an F1 score of 0.66. Certain relations, such as *getty:ulan1512_parent_of* were more correctly extracted than others. This result was attributed to a more consistent bag of words. The same machine learning model was then tested using uni-grams, tri-grams and word count in between candidate pairs as features. Stopwords were again included. This resulted in a slight overall accuracy and F1 score improvement of 0.70 and 0.68 respectively. Table 2 shows the results and relative performance of each method tested.

A preliminary process for relation extraction was coreference resolution. We had to perform coreference resolution because it provided a single name to the same individual. As discussed in Sect. 3.4, each person is represented with multiple variations of his name. We explained that this was due to the use of declensions in the Latin language.

Table 2. Accuracy results of models including between word count - (SW - Stopwords)

	Unigrams		Unigrams & Bigrams		Unigrams & Trigrams		Bigrams & Trigrams	
	SW included	SW removed	SW included	SW removed	SW included	SW removed	SW included	SW removed
KNN	0.53	0.54	0.41	0.42	0.37	0.37	0.29	0.29
NB	0.56	0.57	0.59	0.61	0.61	0.62	0.56	0.54
LR	0.67	0.64	0.68	0.68	**0.70**	0.67	0.56	0.51
SVM	0.25	0.25	0.24	0.24	0.24	0.24	0.24	0.24
RF	0.63	0.61	0.62	0.63	0.62	0.61	0.51	0.50

We experimented with the Jaro-Winkler [24] and cosine similarity distance measures. We also experimented with a rule-based approach that we created, which favours a match of the first three letters in a name. The Python *strsim*[18] library was used for the implementation of Jaro-Winkler and cosine similarity. After each experiment, our team of three volunteers from the Notarial Archives was asked to label the True Positives and False Negatives using a developed interface as shown in Fig. 3 (right). This process created the crowdtruth referred to as the Disambiguation dataset, that allowed us to calculate the precision, recall and F1 score of each method.

Cosine similarity resulted in the highest precision but had the lowest recall. This means that fewer name similarities were being identified, but that these were mostly correct. However, a lot of name similarities that should have been identified as correct were not, resulting in a number of false negatives. Although the

---

[17] http://docs.cltk.org/en/latest/index.html.
[18] https://github.com/luozhouyang/python-string-similarity#jaro-winkler.

Jaro-Winkler metric gave similar results to the rule-based method (the method of choice), the precision of the latter outperformed that of the former and resulted in an F1 score of 0.96, as opposed to the Jaro-Winkler that resulted in an F1 score of 0.87. This result was interesting as the Jaro-Winkler also takes into account the similarity of the first few letters.

4.2   Evaluation Results for Link Prediction

As explained in Sect. 3.6 we experimented with a number of low-dimensional representation models to achieve knowledge graph refinement. Our refinement target is completion, that is often addressed through link prediction, where given a head (subject) and a tail (object), a relationship is predicted. We used classic translational distance models and semantic matching models, including TransE, TransH, TransD, Analogy, ComplEx, DistMult, HolE and RESCAL and compared their accuracy in finding missing links between a head and a tail in a triple. These models are chosen as according to [23] they proved to be effective on benchmark datasets. The open library OpenKE[19] developed by [15] implements TensorFlow and PyTorch, and allows the models to be executed on GPU models. [15] also adapted models for parallel learning on a single CPU. This splits up training triples and trains each part of triples in a corresponding thread. Since our dataset was small, we decided to implement CPU parallel learning, keeping our options open to GPU training, when more data is available. According to [15] OpenKE achieved comparable accuracies to the original papers where these models were introduced and it significantly accelerated the training process of the models trained both on CPU and GPU improving overall efficiency.

All models were initially trained with a set of initial parameters including number of epochs, learning rate, batch size, implementation of negative sampling and the choice of an optimisation algorithm. Models are set to traverse all training triples for 1000 epochs and training triples were split into several batches, whereby each batch contained 100 triples that were allocated to a separate thread. The learning rate was set at 0.001 alpha, which is the default parameter in OpenKE. This allowed us to control how much the weights are adjusted with respect to gradient loss in the optimisation algorithm.

Initially we set the optimisation algorithm as Stochastic Gradient Descent (SGD), however later on we tried out other optimisation algorithms, including Adadelta, Adagrad and Adam to monitor their effect. OpenKE also implements negative sampling which is used to corrupt entities and relations to construct negative triples. [15] emphasise the importance of corrupted triples as they empirically found that they greatly influence the final performance.

Although in the evaluation of OpenKE, [15] use the top-N ranked relations to calculate accuracy such as Hit@10, Hit@20 and Hit@50, we only take top-1 ranked relationship as this should be the most likely predicted relation that exists between a subject and an object. This approach was adopted as our aim was not to rank the proportion of correct relations, but rather to predict a relation

---

[19] https://github.com/thunlp/OpenKE.

between two entities. The overall accuracy of each model, implementing SGD as an optimisation algorithm is shown in Fig. 6.

Translation Distance Models that exploit the distance-based score functions performed the best with TransE resulting in 49% relation-prediction accuracy. This was followed by TransE extensions TransD and TransH. All the other models that we used performed much worse. Since the crowdtruth referred to as the Link_Prediction dataset was highly skewed (shown in Fig. 5), applying sampling techniques to balance the skewness of the classes, such as oversampling or SMOTE, and then retraining the models might improve the overall accuracy.

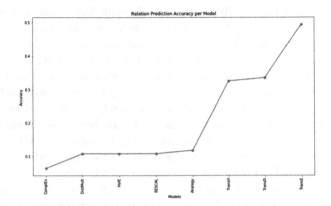

Fig. 6. Accuracy per embedding model

In an attempt to improve the results for TransE, different optimisation algorithms were tested out. In this experiment we changed the optimisation algorithm for the TransE model. We tried out different optimisation algorithms including Adagrad, Adadelta (modify the learning rate) and Adam (modifies both the learning rate and the gradient component) to monitor their effect on the accuracy of the model. The accuracy results that we obtained from this experiment are shown in Table 3, with Stochastic Gradient Descent (SGD) still performing better than the others.

Table 3. Accuracy of TransE model with different optimisation algorithms

Optimisation algorithm	Accuracy (%)
SGD	49%
Adagrad	38%
Adadelta	7%
Adam	42%

Referring to Fig. 7, although relations such as *purchases* and *debtorOf* were more common in the training data than for instance *nationality* and *religion*, this aspect did not directly effect the results. This might be due to the sparsity of, and variations within, this rather small dataset. Furthermore, although a TensorFlow approach is not recommended in general for a small amount of data, we wanted to lay down the foundations of a scalable approach that will eventually need to deal with many more manuscripts in the near future.

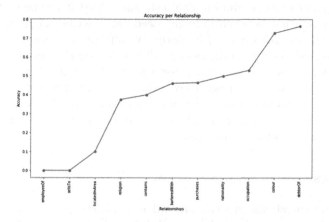

Fig. 7. Accuracy per relation TransE with SGD optimisation algorithm

5   Conclusion and Future Work

In this paper we presented NotaryPedia which is a knowledge graph for notarial heritage, Latin texts. We discussed how we were able to represent dates, people, places, deed types and keyphrases, as well as archiving metadata through the definition of the Notarial ontology. We furthermore compliment relation extraction with embeddings for link prediction. We consider the results from the initial evaluation to be encouraging (since work in this domain is limited) but there is room for improvement, especially if more data is available.

From our research we learnt that explicitly stated relations with a consistent bag of words are more easily extracted. Furthermore, although our rule based coreference resolution outperformed existing similarity metrics such as Jaro-Winkler, we did not exhaustively tested out all similarity metrics. Future tests may include Monge-Elkan where names are tokenised and average similarity is computed between tokens. We attribute the better results of the rule based approach compared to Jaro-Winkler as in latter the substitution of 2 close characters is considered less important than the substitution of 2 characters far from each other. We also concluded that semantic matching models (TransE and its extensions) perform much better than translational matching models in correctly identifying relations in medieval Latin RDF representations. The choice of optimisation algorithm, highly effects the accuracy results obtained, thus it is worth testing their effects on the other embedding models.

In our effort to consolidate the curation phase, we will be introducing a controlled crowd-sourcing service for researchers who would like to contribute to NotaryPedia's enrichment. Our goal is to expose the KG to more entities and relations while trying to achieve improved completion. We aim to conduct a user evaluation of the Notarial Ontology to assess its suitability to answer historical research questions and the proper representation of concepts. Although we did not perform coreference resolution within the same deed, it will be useful to apply coreference resolution between different deeds as a scribe might write a place name differently ex: *Bircarcara, Bircalcara*. We furthermore, want to experiment with the classification of *Item* entities into distinct categories such as *animals* and *agrarian items* to facilitate searching for a particular areas of study. Moreover, we hope to identify ways to enrich *Item* entities by using external sources such as DBpedia. Finally, there is a plan to publish our evaluation datasets and enhance the user interface to officially launch it as part of the Archive's effort to make the information accessible to everyone.

References

1. ISAD(G): General international standard archival description 2000, 2 edn. (2000)
2. Ahonen, E., Hyvonen, E.: Publishing Historical Texts on the Semantic Web –A Case Study, pp. 167–173. IEEE (2009)
3. Bordes, A., Usunier, N., Garcia-Duran, A., Weston, J., Yakhnenko, O.: Translating Embeddings for Modeling Multi-relational Data, pp. 2787–2795 (2013)
4. Debruyne, C., Beyan, O.D., Grant, R., Collins, S., Decker, S., Harrower, N.: A semantic architecture for preserving and interpreting the information contained in irish historical vital records. Int. J. Digit. Libr. **17**(3), 159–174 (2016)
5. Efremova, J., Montes García, A., Calders, T.: Classification of historical notary acts with noisy labels. In: Hanbury, A., Kazai, G., Rauber, A., Fuhr, N. (eds.) ECIR 2015. LNCS, vol. 9022, pp. 49–54. Springer, Cham (2015). https://doi.org/10.1007/978-3-319-16354-3_6
6. Efremova, J., García, A.M., Iriondo, A.B., Calders, T.: Who are my ancestors? Retrieving family relationships from historical texts. In: Braslavski, P., et al. (eds.) RuSSIR 2015. CCIS, vol. 573, pp. 121–129. Springer, Cham (2016). https://doi.org/10.1007/978-3-319-41718-9_6
7. Efremova, J., Montes Garcia, A., Calders, T., Zhang, J.: Towards population reconstruction: extraction of family relationships from historical documents (2015)
8. Efremova, J., et al.: Multi-source entity resolution for genealogical data. In: Bloothooft, G., Christen, P., Mandemakers, K., Schraagen, M. (eds.) Population Reconstruction, pp. 129–154. Springer, Cham (2015). https://doi.org/10.1007/978-3-319-19884-2_7
9. Ehrlinger, L., Wob, W.: Towards a Definition of Knowledge Graphs (2016)
10. Ellul, C., Abela, C., Azzopardi, J.: Extracting Information from Medieval Notarial deeds, pp. 25–28. EKAW (2018)
11. Erdmann, A., et al.: Challenges and solutions for latin named entity recognition. In: The COLING 2016 Organizing Committee, pp. 85–93 (2016)
12. Feeney, K.C., O'Sullivan, D., Tai, W., Brennan, R.: Improving curated web-data quality with structured harvesting and assessment. Int. J. Semant. Web Inf. Syst. **10**(2), 35–62 (2014)

13. Fiorini, S.: Documentary Sources of Maltese History Part I Notarial Documents No 1 Notary Giacomo Zabbara. University of Malta, 1 edn. (1996)
14. Gonzalez, E.: Unsupervised Relation Extraction by Massive Clustering (2009)
15. Han, X., et al.: Openke: an open toolkit for knowledge embedding. In: Proceedings of EMNLP (2018)
16. Monti, M., et al.: Construction of enterprise knowledge graphs. In: Pan, J.Z., Vetere, G., Gomez-Perez, J.M., Wu, H. (eds.) Exploiting Linked Data and Knowledge Graphs in Large Organisations. Springer, Cham (2017). chap 8
17. Paulheim, H.: Knowledge graph refinement: a survey of approaches and evaluation methods. Semant. Web **8**(3), 489–508 (2016)
18. Pawar, S., Palshikar, G., Bhattacharyya, P.: Relation Extraction: A Survey (2017)
19. Ruddock, B.: Linked data and the locah project. Bus. Inf. Rev. **28**(2), 105–111 (2011)
20. Siddiqui, T., Aalam, P.: Short text clustering; challenges & solutions: a literature review. Int. J. Math. Comput. Res. **3**(6), 1025–1031 (2015)
21. Srinivas, V.: Link Prediction in Social Networks, 1st edn. Springer, Cham (2016). https://doi.org/10.1007/978-3-319-28922-9
22. Villazon-Terrazas, B., Garcia-Santa, N., Ren, Y., Srinivas, K., Rodriguez-Muro, M., Alexopoulos, P., Pan, J.Z.: Construction of enterprise knowledge graphs (I). Exploiting Linked Data and Knowledge Graphs in Large Organisations, pp. 87–116. Springer, Cham (2017). https://doi.org/10.1007/978-3-319-45654-6_4
23. Wang, Q., Mao, Z., Wang, B., Guo, L.: Knowledge graph embedding: a survey of approaches and applications. IEEE Trans. Knowl. Data Eng. **29**(12), 2724–2743 (2017)
24. Winkler, W.: String comparator metrics and enhanced decision rules in the fellegisunter model of record linkage. In: Proceedings of the Section on Survey Research Methods (1990)
25. Yang, Y., Lichtenwalter, R.N., Chawla, N.V.: Evaluating link prediction methods. Knowl. Inf. Syst. **45**(3), 751–782 (2014)

Applying a Model-Driven Approach
for UML/OCL Constraints: Application
to NoSQL Databases

Fatma Abdelhadi[2], Amal Ait Brahim[1(✉)], and Gilles Zurfluh[1]

[1] Toulouse Institute of Computer Science Research (IRIT),
Toulouse Capitole University, Toulouse, France
{amal.ait-brahim,gilles.zurfluh}@irit.fr
[2] CBI2 – TRIMANE, Paris, France

Abstract. Big Data have received a great deal of attention in recent years. Not only the amount of data is on a completely different level than before, but also we have different type of data including factors such as format, structure, and sources. This has definitely changed the tools we need to handle Big Data, giving rise to NoSQL systems. While NoSQL systems have proven their efficiency to handle Big Data, it's still an unsolved problem how the automatic storage of Big Data in NoSQL systems could be done. This paper proposes an automatic approach for implementing UML conceptual models in NoSQL systems, including the mapping of the associated OCL constraints to the code required for checking them. In order to demonstrate the practical applicability of our work, we have realized it in a tool supporting four fundamental OCL expressions: Iterate-based expressions, OCL predefined operations, If expression and Let expression.

Keywords: UML · OCL · NoSQL · Big data · MDA · QVT

1 Introduction

Big data have received a great deal of attention in recent years. Not only the amount of data is on a completely different level than before, but also we have different type of data including factors such as format, structure, and sources. In addition, the speed at which these data must be collected and analyzed is increasing. This has definitely impacted the tools required to store Big Data, and new kinds of data management tools i.e. NoSQL systems have arisen [8]. Compared to existing systems, NoSQL systems are commonly accepted to support larger volume of data, provide faster data access, better scalability and higher flexibility [2].

One of the NoSQL key features is that databases can be schema-less. This means, in a table, meanwhile the row is inserted, the attributes names and types are specified. Unlike relational systems - where first, the user defines the schema and creates the tables, second he inserts data -, the schema-less property offers undeniable flexibility that facilitates the physical schema evolution. End-users are able to add information without the need of database administrator. For instance, in the medical program that

© Springer Nature Switzerland AG 2019
H. Panetto et al. (Eds.): OTM 2019, LNCS 11877, pp. 646–660, 2019.
https://doi.org/10.1007/978-3-030-33246-4_40

follows-up patients suffering from a chronic pathology – case of study detailed in Sect. 2 – one of the benefits of using NoSQL databases is that the evolution of the data (and schema) is fluent. In order to follow the evolution of the pathology, information is entered regularly for a cohort of patients. But the situation of a patient can evolve rapidly which needs the recording of new information. Thus, few months later, each patient will have his own information, and that's how data will evolve over time. Therefore, the data model (i) differs from one patient to another and (ii) evolves in unpredictable way over time. We should highlight that this flexibility concerns the physical level i.e. the stored database exclusively [10].

In information systems, the importance and the necessity of conceptual models are widely recognized. The conceptual model provides a high level of abstraction and a semantic knowledge element close to human comprehension, which guarantees efficient data management [1]. Furthermore, this model is a document of interchange between end-users and designers, and between designers and developers. Also, the conceptual model is used for system maintenance and evolution that can affect business needs and/or deployment platform. The Unified Modeling Language (UML) is widely accepted as the standard of information system modeling.

On the one hand, NoSQL systems have proven their efficiency to handle Big Data. On the other hand, the needs of a conceptual modeling and design approach remain up-to-date. Therefore, we are convinced that it's important to provide a precise and automatic approach that guides and facilitates the Big Database implementation task within NoSQL systems. This approach will assist the developers to map Big Database UML conceptual model into NoSQL physical models. It's also required to have a tool to maintain data consistency since most of the NoSQL systems lacks of constraint checking and enforcement mechanism.

For this, we propose the "Object2NoSQL" MDA-based approach. The Model Driven Architecture (MDA) is well-known as a framework for models automatic transformations. The Object2NoSQL approach starts from a conceptual model (PIM) (UML class diagram and OCL constraints) and transforms it into a unified logical model compatible with the three types of NoSQL database (column, document and graph). The conceptual model is automatically transformed into a logical model using QVT rules. Then, logical model is transformed into a physical model (PSM after choosing one of the three platforms: Cassandra, MongoDB or Neo4j). In this paper, we focus on how to automatically transform UML/OCL conceptual model into NoSQL physical level. As discussed in the related work, few solutions have dealt with the NoSQL databases conceptual modeling. To the best of our knowledge, none of the existing contribution has treated the OCL constraints and their implementation into NoSQL databases.

The remainder of the paper is structured as follows. Section 2 motivates our work using a case of study in the healthcare field. Section 3 defines our models transformation approach. Section 4 introduces our OCL constraints transformation approach and shows two transformation processes. The first one creates a logical model starting from an OCL conceptual model, and the second one generates the java code required to check the constraints within NoSQL database. Section 5 reviews previous work. Finally, Sect. 6 concludes the paper and announces future work.

2 Illustrative Example

To motivate and illustrate our work, we present a case study in the healthcare field. This case study concerns international scientific programs for monitoring patients suffering from serious diseases. The main goal of this program is (1) to collect data about diseases development over time, (2) to study interactions between different diseases and (3) to evaluate the short and medium-term effects of their treatments. The medical program can last up to 3 years. Data collected from establishments involved in this kind of program have the features of Big Data (the 3 V):

Volume: the amount of data collected from all the establishments in three years can reach several terabytes.

Variety: data created while monitoring patients come in different types; it could be (1) structured as the patient's vital signs (respiratory rate, blood pressure, etc.), (2) semi-structured document such as the package leaflets of medicinal products, (3) unstructured such as consultation summaries, paper prescriptions and radiology reports.

Velocity: some data are produced in continuous way by sensors; it needs a [near] real time process because it could be integrated into a time-sensitive processes (for example, some measurements, like temperature, require an emergency medical treatment if they cross a given threshold).

This is a typical example in which the use of a NoSQL system is suitable. As mentioned before, this kind of systems operate on schema-less data model enabling developers to quickly and easily incorporate new data into their applications without rewriting tables. Nevertheless, there is still a need for a semantic model to know how data is structured and related in the database; this is particularly necessary to write declarative queries where tables and columns names are specified [4]. UML is widely accepted as a standard modelling language for describing complex data [1]. In the medical application, briefly presented above, the database contains structured data, data of various types and formats (explanatory texts, medical records, x-rays, etc.), and big tables (records of variables produced by sensors). Therefore, we choose a UML class diagram to describe the medical data.

3 Object2NoSQL Approach

This article focuses on the automatic translation of constraints associated to the conceptual description of data. To properly define this process, it is necessary to know the framework in which it will fit. It's about our approach Object2NoSQL developed in previous work [12]. This section outlines this models transformation approach.

Object2NoSQL is a MDA-based approach that provides a set of transformations to automatically generate several NoSQL physical models starting from a conceptual model expressed using the Unified Modeling Language (UML). Our approach relies on a new generic logical model as an intermediate representation that facilitates the integration of several types of NoSQL systems (column, document and graph). This model exhibits a sufficient degree of platform-independency making possible its mapping to one or more NoSQL platforms.

Object2NoSQL approach is composed of two steps: (1) Object2GenericModel is the first transformation that converts the input UML class diagram into the proposed generic logical model; (2) GenericModel2PhysicalModel is the second step that generates NoSQL physical models starting from the generic logical model. This is illustrated in Fig. 1.

In [12], we have only considered some constraints such as data type and the uniqueness constraint for identifiers. In this article, we aim to complete our approach taking into account other additional constraints, defined using the Object Constraint Language (OCL), that require writing code (Sect. 4).

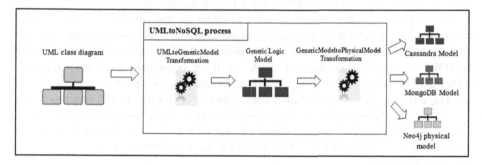

Fig. 1. Overview of Object2NoSQL process

4   OCL2JAVA Approach

An important part of UML is the Object Constraint Language (OCL), a textual language that allows to specify additional constraints on models in a more declarative and precise way than it is possible to do with diagrams only. This section gives a brief overview of OCL; the background information on OCL is presented, and the need for mapping OCL expressions to java is motivated.

4.1   Motivation and Contribution

A constraint refines a model element by expressing a condition to which this element must conform. While UML offers a rich set of graphical notation to define constraints, additional constraints are required to further refine the semantics of UML model elements; these constraints are generally expressed using OCL.

OCL is a widely accepted standard allowing the formal specification of constraints on models as context conditions. For example, in the class diagram of the medical program (Fig. 1), we have an attribute age of type Integer in the class Patient. Without further constraint, a patient may have negative values for the age attribute. The following constraint refers to class Patient and restricts the allowed range of age values to positive integers.

context Patient **inv** ValidAge:
self.age > 0

Checking OCL constraints within a NoSQL system is a real challenge, since most of these systems lack any mechanism of constraint checking and enforcement. Considering this limitation, we propose in this paper the OCL2Java approach that generates java programs starting from OCL constraints defined at the conceptual level. These programs enable the constraints checking at the physical level.

Once the NoSQL physical model is created by Object2NoSQL process (Sect. 3), another transformation (OCL2Java) must be performed to translate the OCL expressions associated to the UML conceptual model into java programs. Like Object2NoSQL process, OCL2Java is based on three-tier architecture: (1) conceptual level where the OCL constraint is defined and associated to a UML class diagram element, (2) logical level where a java logical model is created; this model exhibits a sufficient degree of platform-independency making possible its use on one or more NoSQL platforms, (3) physical level in which java programs are generated starting from the java logical model; each program will be used to check the constraints on a specific NoSQL system. To illustrate our work we have considered Cassandra (column-oriented), MongoDB (document-oriented) and Neo4j (graph-oriented) systems.

The advantage of using a unified logical model is that this model remains stable, even though the NoSQL system evolves over time or the developer wants to change the system used. In these two cases, it would be enough to evolve the physical level, and of course adapt the mapping rules; this simplifies the transformation process and saves time for developers.

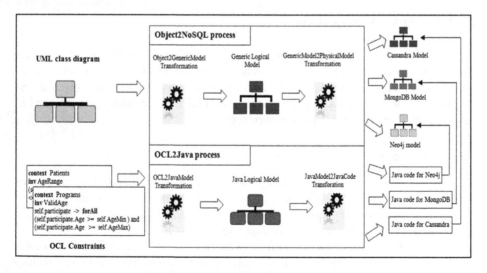

Fig. 2. Overview of OCL2Java process

Figure 2 shows the different component of OCL2Java process. This process is composed of two steps: OCL2JavaModel (1) is the first transformation that converts the input OCL constraint into the proposed java logical model (2); this model is conform to the java metamodel presented in the next section. JavaModel2JavaCode (3) is the second step that generates java programs starting from the java logical model.

4.2   OCL2JavaModel Transformation

In this section we present the OCL2Java transformation, which is the first step in our approach shown in Fig. 2. We first introduce the structure of the OCL metamodel and then, we describe a mapping between OCL and java expressions.

Metamodel for OCL Expressions

The purpose of this work is to complete the Object2NoSQL process by taking into account more constraints defined using OCL. To achieve this goal, we propose an OCL metamodel with reference to OCL documentation provided by OMG [5]. The benefit of this metamodel is that it defines the syntax of different OCL expressions like iterate-based expressions, OCL predefined-operations, If expression, etc. Thus, several kinds of OCL expressions will be considered in our transformation process. The class diagram in Fig. 3 illustrates an excerpt of the OCL metamodel.

Constraints are primarily used to express invariants on classes and pre-/post-conditions on operations. Therefore, we have specialized the class Constraint into three subclasses: Invariant, Pre-Condition and Post-Condition. In this paper, we focus only on class invariants mapping. Thus, only classes and relationships defining this concept are illustrated in the metamodel.

Invariants are conditions that must be true for all objects of a given class. The condition is specified as an OCL expression that forms the body of the invariant.

The class *OclExpression* defines a set of available expressions in OCL. In the OCL documentation [5], the concept of OCL expression is used and defined informally in different contexts; thus, it is difficult to propose an exhaustive metamodel for OCL and define precisely what constitutes all possible kinds of OCL expressions. The proposed metamodel in Fig. 3 contains the core elements necessary to describe the most frequently used OCL expressions.

All OCL expressions require a *Context* and have a *Type*. The *Context* is given by the name of a class; it specifies the class to which the invariant is applied. The *Type* indicates the result type of the OCL expression. The available types in OCL are: (1) Basic types: Integer, Real, String and Boolean, (2) Collection: Set, Bag and Sequence, (3) Enumeration: are defined by a list of distinct data like Color: {red, green, blue}, and (4) Object: used to refer to classes defined by users in the UML model. These four types are modeled as subclasses of the class *Type*.

Example of class invariant:
The attribute age of the class Patient must be restricted to hold only positive values. This may be achieved by attaching the OCL expression self.age >0 of type Boolean to a specific context that correspond in this example to the class Patient.

context Patient **inv** ValidAge:

self.age > 0 – *The age attribute of patients must be greater than zero*

The class OclExpression can be specialized into four fundamental expressions: Iterate-based expressions, OCL predefined-operations, If expression and Let-In expression. In the following, we describe each of these expressions and we give examples to illustrate their different components.

A *Let-In* expression allows to declare and initialize a variable which will be used in another OCL expression that forms its body (In).

An *If* expression comprises three parts: a *condition-expression* to be tested followed by a *then-expression* to be evaluated if the condition is true and an *else-expression* for evaluation if the condition is false.

Example of Let and If expressions

The following invariant verifies that an ongoing program has at least one involved hospital.

context Program **inv** MinInvolvedHospital:

<u>**let** NumberHospital: Integer</u> = <u>self.Hospital->count()</u> **in**

        Declaration   Initialization

if isOngoing=true **then**

NumberHospital >= 1

else

NumberHospital = 0

Endif

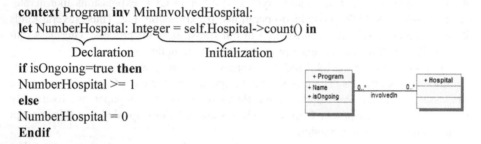

The invariant *MinInvolvedHospital* uses the Let expression to declare and initialize the variable *NumberHospital* whose type is *Integer*. This variable contain the number of hospital involved in a given medical program, and is used in the If expression to check that each ongoing program has at least one involved hospital.

The class *Iterate* represents the common properties of the iterate-based OCL expressions: Select, Reject, Iterate, forAll, isUnique, Exists and Collect. Each of these expressions has (1) a *Source* expression, also called the *Input* expression, resulting in a collection, and (2) an *Argument* expression which is evaluated for each of the input collection's elements. Furthermore, an iterate-based expression may contain a declaration expression and, in case of *Iterate*, an initialization expression of variables that will be used in its argument expression.

Example of iterate-based expression

The following expression selects from the set of doctors participating in the medical program those who are specialist in Hepatology. The result of this selection is a collection of doctors (set (Doctor)) that initialize the variable specialist. For each element of the input collection (self.participate), the argument expression (specialty = 'rheumatology') is evaluated. Note that in this select expression, a variable d of type Doctor is declared to be used in the argument expression; this is optional.

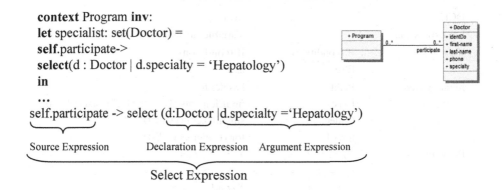

context Program **inv**:
let specialist: set(Doctor) =
self.participate->
select(d : Doctor | d.specialty = 'Hepatology')
in
...

self.participate -> select (d:Doctor |d.specialty ='Hepatology')

Source Expression   Declaration Expression   Argument Expression

Select Expression

OCL predefined-operations is another type of OCL expressions supported by our approach. A large number of expressions can be classified as OCL operations. In this work, only predefined OCL operations, like +, −, *, < , > , size(), etc., are considered. These are modeled by the class Operation. All predefined OCL operation has (1) a name, and (2) a list of arguments. Generally, the argument list consists of class attributes and constant values.

<u>**Example of OCL operation:**</u>

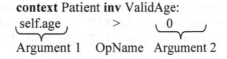

context Patient **inv** ValidAge:
self.age   >   0

Argument 1   OpName   Argument 2

Mapping OCL Expressions to Java Model
Before generating the code required to check the constraints on a specific NoSQL database, we first transform each OCL expression associated to our input class diagram into a java model as depicted in Fig. 2. As mentioned before (Sect. 4.1), this model exhibits a sufficient degree of platform-independency making possible its use on one or more NoSQL platforms. This simplifies not only the translation into java code but more importantly facilitates the integration of several kinds of NoSQL databases in our approach since the mapping of OCL constraints to Java expressions is performed in this step regardless of the technical properties of NoSQL systems.

The java model is conform to the java metamodel illustrated in Fig. 4. This metamodel is adapted from the one proposed in Eclipse Documentation [13], and limited to the elements necessary for mapping the OCL expressions supported by our approach.

In order to perform the OCL2JavaModel transformation, it is necessary to establish a mapping between OCL and java expressions. As presented before, supported OCL expressions are divided into four types: iterate-based expressions, OCL predefined-operations, Let expression and If expression. Due to lack of place, we only present in Table 1 a subset of OCL expressions and their corresponding in java.

Table 1. OCL2Java mapping

OCL		Java
Let expression		Variable declaration initialization
If expression	If (condition)	If (condition)
	Else	Else
Iterate-based	Iterate	hasNext()
	Exists	findElements(By.id("value")).size() ! = 0
	Collect	stream().collect(List)
	forAll	for (E element : list)
Predefined Operation	+, −, *, /	+, −, *, /, =
	<, <=, > ,> = , =, <>	<, <=, > ,> = , =, !=
	and,or,not	&&,‖,!
	size()	arrlist.size()
	isEmpty()	list.size() == 0

We have formalized this mapping using the QVT (Query/View/Transformation) language, which is the OMG standard for models transformation. We carry out the experimental assessment using a model transformation environment called Eclipse Modeling Framework (EMF). It's a set of plugins which can be used to create a model and to generate other output based on this model. Among the tools provided by EMF we use: (1) Ecore: the metamodeling language that we used to create our metamodels. (2) XML Metadata Interchange (XMI): the XML based standard that we use to create models. (3) Query/View/Transformation (QVT): the OMG language for specifying model transformations.

OCL2JavaModel transformation is expressed as a sequence of elementary steps that builds the resulting model (java logical model) step by step from the source model (OCL model):

Step 1: we create Ecore metamodels corresponding to the source (Fig. 3) and the target (Fig. 4).

Step 2: we build an instance of the source metamodel. For this, we use the standard-based XML Metadata Interchange (XMI) format (Fig. 5a).

Step 3: we implement the mapping by means of the QVT plugin provided within EMF. An excerpt from the QVT script is shown in Fig. 5c.

Step 4: we test the transformation by running the QVT script created in step 3. This script takes as input the source model builded in step 2 and returns as output the logical model. The result is provided in the form of XMI file as shown in Fig. 5b.

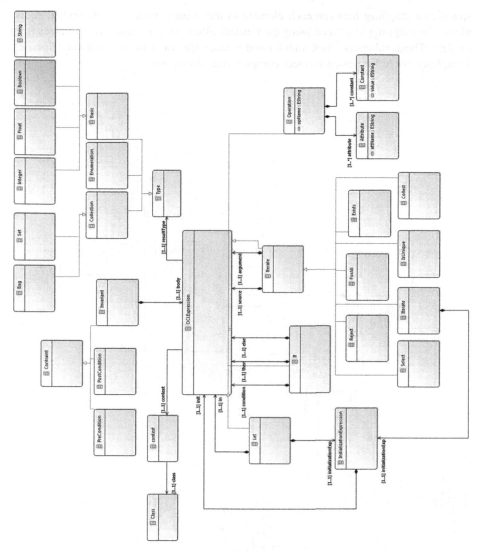

Fig. 3. Excerpt of OCL metamodel

Code Generation

To generate the code required to check the constraints, it was necessary to apply a mapping on the java model created in the previous step (OCL2JavaModel). We have performed this mapping using the automated tool MOFScript [14]. It is an Eclipse plugin that provides an environment for transforming models to text. MOFScript uses a templates-based approach in which the text generated from a model is specified as a set of text templates that is parameterized with the input model elements. A template specifies a mapping between each element in the source model and its textual equivalent. The mapping is defined using queries that allow to select and extract values from models. These values are then transformed to code fragment using predefined libraries. Templates could be nested to meet complex transformations.

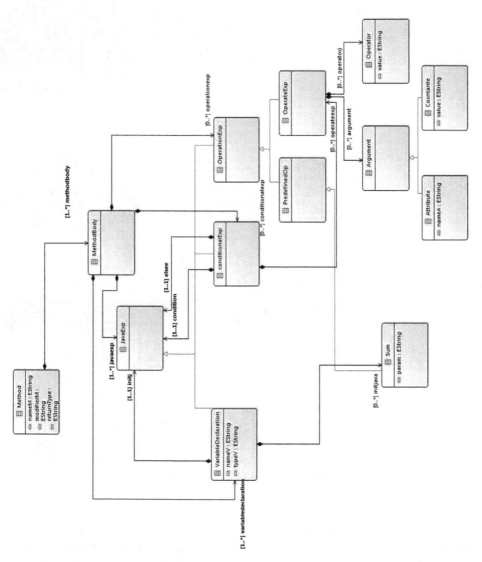

Fig. 4. Excerpt of java metamodel

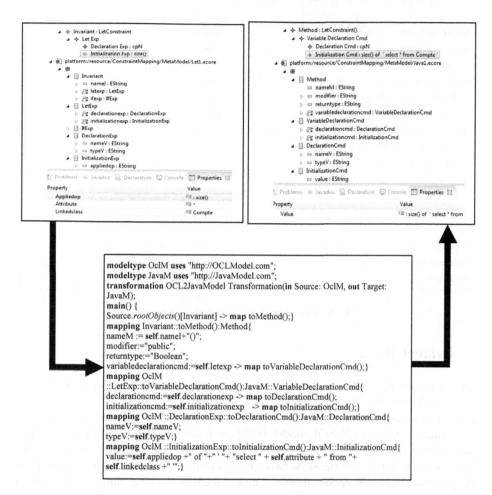

```
modeltype OclM uses "http://OCLModel.com";
modeltype JavaM uses "http://JavaModel.com";
transformation OCL2JavaModel Transformation(in Source: OclM, out Target:
JavaM);
main() {
Source.rootObjects()[Invariant] -> map toMethod();}
mapping Invariant::toMethod():Method{
nameM := self.nameI+"()";
modifier:="public";
returntype:="Boolean";
variabledeclarationcmd:=self.letexp -> map toVariableDeclarationCmd();}
mapping OclM
::LetExp::toVariableDeclarationCmd():JavaM::VariableDeclarationCmd{
declarationcmd:=self.declarationexp -> map toDeclarationCmd();
initializationcmd:=self.initializationexp  -> map toInitializationCmd();}
mapping OclM ::DeclarationExp::toDeclarationCmd():JavaM::DeclarationCmd{
nameV:=self.nameV;
typeV:=self.typeV;}
mapping OclM ::InitializationExp::toInitializationCmd():JavaM::InitializationCmd{
value:=self.appliedop +" of "+" ' "+ "select " + self.attribute + " from "+
self.linkedclass +" '";}
```

Fig. 5. (a) Source model, (b) Target model, (c) QVT mapping

In our scenario, the MOFScript tool takes as input the java logical model, and returns code files; one file for each NoSQL system (Cassandra, MongoDB and Neo4j). Figure 6 presents an excerpt of code files generated from our java model.

import com.datastax.driver.core.Cluster;	**import** com.mongodb.DB;
import com.datastax.driver.core.ResultSet;;	**import** com.mongodb.DBCollection;
import com.datastax.driver.core.Session;	**import** com.mongodb.Mongo;
public class CassandraFile {	**import** com.mongodb.BasicDBObject;
public static void connector(){	**public** class MongoDBFile {
Cluster cluster; Session session;	**public** static void connector(){
cluster = Cluter.builder().addContactPoint("127.0.0.1").build();	DBCollection db=null;
session = cluster.connect("keyspace1");}	**try**{
Public boolean exists (list I){	mongo = new Mongo("localhost",27017);
for (Iterator i = I.iterator(); c.hasNext();){	}**catch** (UnknownHostException e){ e.printStackTrace(); }
ElementType element = i.next(); if (exInJava){	db=mongo.getDB("database1");}
return true;}} return false;}	**Public** Boolean forAll(Collection cll){
Public list select(Collection cll){ List result;	for (Iterator i = I.iterator(); c.hasNext();){
for (Iterator i = cll.iterator(); c.hasNext();){	if (!exInJava){ return false;}}
ElementType element = i.next();	return true;}
if (exInJava) {result.add(element);}} return result;}	**Public** void predefinedOp(){

Fig. 6. Constraint Code generation (excerpt)

5   Related Work

To our knowledge, only few solutions targets conceptual modeling for NoSQL databases, and even less focusing on the OCL constraints. For example, in the specific context of a data warehouse, both [7] and [6] have proposed to transform a multidimensional model into a NoSQL model. In [7] the authors defined a set of rules to map a star schema into two NoSQL models: column-oriented and document-oriented. The links between facts and dimensions have been converted using imbrications. Authors in [6] proposed three approaches to map a multidimensional model into a logical model adapted to column-oriented NoSQL systems. Other studies [3] and [9] have investigated the process of transforming relational databases into a NoSQL model. Li [3] have proposed an approach for transforming a relational database into HBase (column-oriented system). Vajk et al. [9] defined a mapping from a relational model to document-oriented model using MongoDB.

More specific to UML conceptual models and NoSQL systems, Li et al. [11] propose a MDA-based process to transform UML class diagram into column-oriented model specific to HBase. Starting from the UML class diagram and HBase meta-models, authors have proposed mapping rules between the conceptual level and the physical one. Obviously, the proposed approach is applicable to HBase only, and does not include OCL constraints. Gwendal et al. [4] describe the mapping between a UML/OCL conceptual models and graph databases via an intermediate graph meta-model. The transformation rules defined in this work are specific to graph databases used as a framework for managing complex data with many connections. Generally, this kind of NoSQL systems is used in social networks where data are highly connected.

Regarding the state of the art, some of existing works [3] and [9] focus on relational model that, unlike UML class diagram, lacks of semantic richness, especially through the several types of relationships that exist between classes. Other solutions, [7] and [6] have the advantage to start from the conceptual level. But, the proposed models are Domain-Specific (Data Warehouses system), so they consider fact, dimension, and typically one type of links only. The approach proposed in [11] is limited to only one column-oriented system (HBase) and does not take into account constraints defined in the input conceptual model. In [4] authors have presented a framework to implement UML conceptual schemas in graph databases. Once the graph-oriented model has been created, another transformation was performed to translate the OCL expressions defined in the conceptual schema into a gremlin query model; a query language for graph databases. While this solution is well suited for graph-oriented systems, it is not generic. For now, the UML/OCL transformation process is restricted to graph-oriented databases. However, it makes more sense to choose the target system according to the user's needs. For example, if processing operations requires access to hierarchically structured data, the document-oriented system proves to be the most adapted solution.

6   Conclusion

Big Data have received a great deal of attention in recent years. Not only the amount of data is on a completely different level than before, but also we have different type of data including factors such as format, structure, and sources. In addition, the speed at which these data must be collected and stored is increasing. This has definitely changed the tools we need to store Big Data, giving rise to NoSQL systems. While NoSQL systems have proven their efficiency to handle Big Data, it is still an unsolved problem how the automatic storage of Big Data in NoSQL systems could be done. One solution for addressing this problem is to model Big Data, and then define mapping rules towards the physical level. This article proposes an automatic approach that translates UML conceptual models into NoSQL physical models. Our approach relies on a pivotal model designed for NoSQL systems. Several instances of this model can be generated to target specific NoSQL system. Once the NoSQL physical model is created, another process has to be performed to check the OCL constraints defined in the conceptual model. Checking OCL constraints is a real challenge since the vast majority of NoSQL systems lack any advanced mechanism for integrity constraint checking.

Considering this limitation, we have presented a framework for mapping the OCL constraints defined at the conceptual level to the code required to check them at the physical level using two intermediate metamodels (OCL and Java). Our approach is specified as two successive transformations: OCL2JavaModel which is a Model2Model transformation and JavaModel2JavaCode, a Model2Text transformation.

In order to demonstrate the practical applicability of our work, we have realized it in a tool supporting the mapping of four fundamental OCL expressions: Iterate-based expressions, OCL predefined operations, If expression and Let expression.

As future work, we plan to complete our transformation process in order to (1) take into account other types of OCL constraints and (2) preserve the semantics when transforming the conceptual model to the logical one. Furthermore, we want to define the transformations rules of physical models into NoSQL scripts using model-to-text transformation (M2T).

References

1. Abelló, A.: Big data design. In: Proceedings of the ACM Eighteenth International Workshop on Data Warehousing and OLAP, (pp. 35–38). ACM (2015)
2. Angadi, A.B., Angadi, A.B., Gull, K.C.: Growth of new databases & analysis of NOSQL datastores. Int. J. Adv. Res. Comput. Sci. Software Eng. **3**, 1307–1319 (2013)
3. Li, C.: Transforming relational database into HBase: a case study. In: 2010 IEEE International Conference on Software Engineering and Service Sciences (ICSESS), pp. 683–687. IEEE, July 2010
4. Gwendal, D., Gerson, S., Jordi, C.: UMLtoGraphDB: mapping conceptual schemas to graph databases. In: The 35th International Conference on Conceptual Modeling (ER) (2016)
5. About the Unified Modeling Language Specification Version 2.5. http://www.omg.org/spec/UML/2.5/. Accessed: 09 Feb 2018
6. Dehdouh, K., Bentayeb, F., Boussaid, O., Kabachi, N.: Using the column oriented NoSQL model for implementing big data warehouses. In: Proceedings of the International Conference on Parallel and Distributed Processing Techniques and Applications (PDPTA), p. 469. The Steering Committee of The World Congress in Computer Science, Computer Engineering and Applied Computing (WorldComp), January 2015
7. Chevalier, M., El Malki, M., Kopliku, A., Teste, O., Tournier, R.: How can we implement a multidimensional data warehouse using NoSQL? In: Hammoudi, S., Maciaszek, L., Teniente, E., Camp, O., Cordeiro, J. (eds.) ICEIS 2015. LNBIP, vol. 241, pp. 108–130. Springer, Cham (2015). https://doi.org/10.1007/978-3-319-29133-8_6
8. Cattell, R.: Scalable SQL and NoSQL data stores. Acm Sigmod Record **39**(4), 12–27 (2011)
9. Vajk, T., Feher, P., Fekete, K., Charaf, H.: Denormalizing data into schema-free databases. In: 2013 IEEE 4th International Conference on Cognitive Infocommunications (CogInfoCom), pp. 747–752. IEEE, December 2013
10. Herrero, V., Abelló, A., Romero, O.: NOSQL design for analytical workloads: variability matters. In: Comyn-Wattiau, I., Tanaka, K., Song, I.-Y., Yamamoto, S., Saeki, M. (eds.) ER 2016. LNCS, vol. 9974, pp. 50–64. Springer, Cham (2016). https://doi.org/10.1007/978-3-319-46397-1_4
11. Li, Y., Gu, P., Zhang, C.: Transforming UML class diagrams into HBase based on metamodel. In: 2014 International Conference on Information Science, Electronics and Electrical Engineering (ISEEE), vol. 2, pp. 720–724. IEEE, April 2014
12. Abdelhedi, F., Ait Brahim, A., Atigui, F., Zurfluh, G.: MDA-Based Approach for NoSQL Databases Modelling. In: Bellatreche, L., Chakravarthy, S. (eds.) DaWaK 2017. LNCS, vol. 10440, pp. 88–102. Springer, Cham (2017). https://doi.org/10.1007/978-3-319-64283-3_7
13. https://help.eclipse.org/Javametamodel
14. Oldevik, J.: MOFScript eclipse plug-in: metamodel-based code generation. In: Eclipse Technology Workshop (EtX) at ECOOP, vol. 2006 (2006)

Manhattan Siamese LSTM for Question Retrieval in Community Question Answering

Nouha Othman[1]([✉]), Rim Faiz[2], and Kamel Smaïli[3]

[1] LARODEC, University of Tunis, Tunis, Tunisia
othmannouha@gmail.com
[2] LARODEC, University of Carthage, Carthage, Tunisia
rim.faiz@ihec.rnu.tn
[3] LORIA, University of Lorraine, Metz, France
kamel.smaili@loria.fr

Abstract. Community Question Answering (cQA) are platforms where users can post their questions, expecting for other users to provide them with answers. We focus on the task of question retrieval in cQA which aims to retrieve previous questions that are similar to new queries. The past answers related to the similar questions can be therefore used to respond to the new queries. The major challenges in this task are the shortness of the questions and the word mismatch problem as users can formulate the same query using different wording. Although question retrieval has been widely studied over the years, it has received less attention in Arabic and still requires a non trivial endeavour. In this paper, we focus on this task both in Arabic and English. We propose to use word embeddings, which can capture semantic and syntactic information from contexts, to vectorize the questions. In order to get longer sequences, questions are expanded with words having close word vectors. The embedding vectors are fed into the Siamese LSTM model to consider the global context of questions. The similarity between the questions is measured using the Manhattan distance. Experiments on real world Yahoo! Answers dataset show the efficiency of the method in Arabic and English.

Keywords: Community question answering · Question retrieval · Word embeddings · Siamese LSTM

1 Introduction

Community Question Answering (cQA) platforms such as Yahoo! Answers[1], Stackoverflow[2], WikiAnswers[3], Quora[4] and Google Ejabat[5] have become

---

[1] http://answers.yahoo.com/.
[2] http://stackoverflow.com/.
[3] https://wiki.answers.com/.
[4] https://fr.quora.com/.
[5] https://ejaaba.com/.

© Springer Nature Switzerland AG 2019
H. Panetto et al. (Eds.): OTM 2019, LNCS 11877, pp. 661–677, 2019.
https://doi.org/10.1007/978-3-030-33246-4_41

increasingly popular in recent years. Unlike traditional Question Answering (QA), users can interact and respond to other users' questions or post their own questions for other participants to answer. However, with the sharp increase of the cQA archives, numerous duplicated questions have been amassed. Retrieving relevant previous questions that best match a new user's query is a crucial task in cQA, known as question retrieval. If good matches are found, the answers to similar past questions can be used to answer the new query. This can avoid the lag time incurred by waiting for other users to respond, thus improving user satisfaction. The question retrieval task has recently sparked great interest [2, 3, 19, 21, 22, 24]. One big challenge for this task is the word mismatch between the queried questions and the existing ones in the archives [21]. Word mismatch means that similar questions can be phrased such that they have different, but related words. For example, the questions *How can we relieve stress naturally?* and *What are some home remedies to help reduce feelings of anxiety?* like in Arabic: كيف يمكننا تخفيف التوتر بشكل طبيعي؟ and ماهي العلاجات المنزلية التي تساعد على تقليل الشعور بالقلق؟ have nearly the same meaning but different words and then may be regarded as dissimilar. This constitutes a barricade to traditional Information Retrieval (IR) models since users can formulate the same question employing different wording. Moreover, community questions have variable lengths, mostly short and usually have sparse representations with little word overlap. While many attempts have been made to dodge this problem, most existing methods rely on the bag of-words (BOWs) representations which are constrained by their specificities that put aside the word order and ignore syntactic and semantic relationships. Recent successes in question retrieval have been obtained using Neural Networks (NNs) [5, 9, 12, 17] which use a deep analysis of words and questions to take into account the semantics as well as the structure of questions in order to predict the text similarity. Motivated by the tremendous success of these emerging models, in this paper, we propose an approach based on NNs to detect the semantic similarity between the questions. The community questions are expanded with words having close embedding vectors. We use a variation of Long Short-Term Memory (LSTM) called Manhattan LSTM (MaLSTM) to analyze the entire question based on its words and its local contexts and predict the similarity between questions. We tested the proposed method on a large-scale real data from Yahoo! Answers in Arabic and English.

The remainder of this paper is structured as follows: Section 2 reviews the main related work on question retrieval in cQA. Section 3 describes our proposed LSTM based approach. Section 4 presents our experimental settings and discusses the obtained results. Section 4.6 concludes the paper and outlines areas for future research.

2   Related Work

Recently, a whole host of methods have been proposed to address the question retrieval task.

Early works were based on the vector space model referred to as VSM to calculate the cosine similarity between a query and archived questions [3,6]. Nevertheless, the main limitation of VSM is that it favors short questions, while cQA services can handle a wide variety of questions not limited to factoïd questions. In order to overcome this shortcoming, Okapi BM stands for Best Matching (Okapi BM25) has been used by search 14 engines to estimate the relevance of questions to a given search query taking into account the question length [3]. Language Models (LM)s [4] have been also used to model queries as sequences of terms instead of sets of terms. LMs estimate the relative likelihood for each possible successor term taking into account relative positions of terms. However, such models might not be effective when there are few common words between the questions. In order to handle the vocabulary mismatch problem faced by LMs, a model based on the concept of machine translation, referred in the following as translation model, was employed to learn correlation between words based on parallel corpora and it has obtained significant performance for question retrieval. The intuition behind translation-based models is to consider question-answer pairs as parallel texts then, relationships of words can be built by learning word-to-word translation probabilities like in [2,21]. Within this context, Zhou et al. [26] attempted to enhance the word-based translation model by adding some contextual information when translating the phrases as a whole, instead of translating separate words. Singh et al. [19] extended the word-based translation model by integrating semantic information and explored strategies to learn the translation probabilities between words and concepts using the cQA archives and an entity catalog. Even though the above-mentioned basic models have yielded interesting results, questions and answers are not parallel in practice, rather they are different from the information they contain [24]. Further methods based on semantic similarity were proposed for question retrieval toward a deep understanding of short text to detect the equivalent questions. For instance, there have been a handful of works that have exploited the available category information for question retrieval such as in [3,4,27]. Although these attempts have proven to improve the performance of the language model for question retrieval, the use of category information was restricted to the language model. Wang et al [20] used a parser to build syntactic trees of questions, and rank them based on the similarity between their syntactic trees. Nonetheless, such an approach requires a lot of training data and existing parsers are still not well-trained to parse informally written questions. Latent Semantic Indexing (LSI) was also used to address the given task like in [16]. Although LSI has proven to be effective in addressing the polysemy and synonymy by mapping terms related to the same concept close to each other, the efficiency of LSI depends on the data structure and both its training and inference are computationally expensive on large vocabularies. Recent works focused on the representation learning for questions, relying on an emerging model for learning distributed representations of words in a low-dimensional vector space called Word Embedding. This latter has recently been subject of a burgeoning interest and has shown great promise in several NLP tasks, As we believe that the representation of words is crucial for retrieving similar questions, we rely on word embeddings to represent the community questions. Along with the popularization of word embeddings and its capacity to produce distributed representations of words, advanced NN architectures such as Convolutional Neural Networks (CNN), Recurrent Neural Networks (RNN) and LSTM have proven effectiveness in extracting higher-level features from constituting word embeddings. For instance, Dos Santos et al. [5] employed CNN and bag-of-words (BOW) representations of the questions to calculate the cosine similarity scores. Within the same context, Mohtarami et al. [12] developed a bag-of-vectors approach and used CNN and attention-based LSTMs to capture the semantic similarity between the community questions and rank them accordingly. LSTM model was also used in [17] with an attention mechanism for capturing long dependencies in questions. Interestingly, the weights learned by the attention model were exploited for selecting important segments and enhancing syntactic tree-kernel models. More recently, the question retrieval task was modeled as a binary classification problem in [9] using a combination of LSTM and a contrastive loss function to effectively memorize the long term dependencies. In our work, we use a siamese adaptation of LSTM [13] for pairs of variable-length sentences named MaLSTM. This latter has accomplished excellent outcomes in the semantic text similarity task and inspire us in our question retrieval problem.

It is worth noting that work on cQA has been mostly carried out for other languages than Arabic. The most promising approach [12] used text similarities at both sentence and word level based on word embeddings. The similarities were computed between new and previous question, and between the new question and the answer related to the previous question p. A tree-kernel-based classifier was employed in [1] where the authors used supervised and unsupervised models that operated both at sentence and chunk levels for parse tree based representations. A supervised learning approach was adopted in [10] where learning-to-rank models were trained over word2vec features and covariance word embedding features produced from the training data. More recently, the given task was investigated by Romeo et al. [18] using advanced Arabic text representations made by applying tree kernels to constituency parse trees along with word embeddings and textual similarities.

3   Description of LSTMQR

We propose an approach called LSTM based Question Retrieval (LSTMQR) to retrieve the semantically similar questions in cQA. As depicted in Fig. 1, our approach is composed of four main modules namely, question preprocessing, word embedding learning, question expansion and Manhattan LSTM (MaLSTM).

By and large, the basic intuition behind LSTMQR is to expand the filtered questions with words having close embedding vectors in order to have longer and richer word sequences. The word vectors of the expanded questions are fed to the Siamese LSTM to represent them in final hidden state encoding semantic meaning of the questions. Community questions are then ranked using the Manhattan similarity function based on the vector representation for each question.

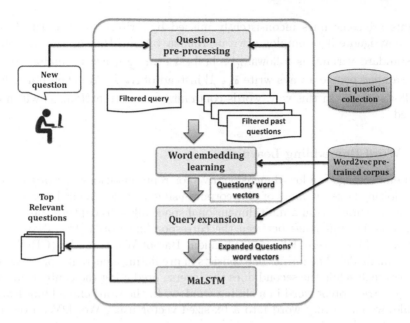

Fig. 1. LSTMQR pipeline for question retrieval in cQA

A previous posted question is considered to be semantically similar to a queried question if their corresponding LSTM representations lie close to each other according to the Manhattan similarity measure. The previous question with the highest Manhattan score will be returned as the most similar question to the new posted one. The components of LSTMQR are detailed below.

3.1   Question Preprocessing

Preprocessing is a crucial step in NLP tasks to assess and improve the quality of text data in order to ensure the reliability and validity of the statistical analysis. Our question preprocessing module intends to filter the natural language questions and extract the useful terms to represent them in a standard way. This module essentially encompasses text cleaning, tokenization, stopwords removal and stemming. We also remove punctuation marks, non letters, diacritics, and special characters such as &, #, $ and £. English letters are lowercased while dates are normalized to the token *date* and numerical digits are normalized to the token *num*. At the end of the question preprocessing module, we obtain a set of filtered queries, each of which is formally defined as follows: $q = \{t_1, t_2, ..., t_Q\}$ where t represents a separate term of the query q and Q denotes the number of query terms. As for the Arabic question collection, in addition to the aforementioned tasks, orthographic normalization is required to reduce noise and ambiguity in the Arabic text data. This task includes Tachkil removal (ignoring arabic short vowels), Tatweel removal (deleting stretching symbol), and Letter normalization (variant forms to one form conversion). Indeed, different spelling variants are sometimes inconsistently misued by writers, such as the Hamza; some may ignore it or employ a wrong Hamza variant. Hence, we normalize to one standard variant as follows: « أ ، إ ، آ ، ؤ ، ء ، ئ » are normalized to «ا». For example, people always write المروؤة instead of المروءة. We then normalize it as follows: المرواة. In this way, words containing miswritten Hamzas will not be ignored.

3.2 Word Embedding Learning

Word embeddings are low-dimensional vector representations of words, learned by exploiting large amounts of text corpora using a shallow neural network. The word representations in a multidimensional space allow to capture the semantic and syntactic similarities between the corresponding words [11]. Two types of word embeddings were defined; Continuous Bag-of-Words model (CBOW) and Skip-gram model. The former one consists in predicting a current word according to its context, while the second does the inverse predicting the contextual words given a current pivot word in a sliding window. In the word embedding learning module, we map every word into a fix-sized vector using Word2Vec pretrained on an external corpus.

3.3 Question Expansion

One of the most challenges in the question retrieval task is the shortness of the community questions which leads to the word mismatch problem. To over-come this and improve the retrieval performance, we propose to add terms to the community questions. The additional words are those having similar embedding vectors. The number of the additional similar words is set as a variable parameter Nsw. More precisely, for each distinct word in a given question, we look for the Nsw words that have similar word vectors from the vocabulary and we add them to the question in order to have an expanded one while maintaining the order of words in the sequences. For example, let's consider the original question *Do chocolate really kill my dog?* containing 3 distinct words and Nsw is set to 3, the expanded query after preprocessing will have 12 words as follows: ***chocolate kill dog*** *eat death bitch candy toxic puppy food sick animal.* Similarly, we give an example of an Arabic query: الشوكولاته تقتل الكلب and its corresponding expanded version:

الشوكولاته تقتل الكلب اكل موت كبة حلوى سامة جرو غذاء مريضة حيوان.

We assume that expanding queries with additional words used in similar contexts may increase the chances of detecting equivalent questions.

3.4 Manhattan LSTM

Long Short-Term Memory (LSTM)[8], which is a powerful type of RNN used in deep learning, has gained wide attention in recent years owing to its capacity to capture long-term dependencies and model sequential data. LSTM helps prevent the vanishing gradient problem [7] which is the main limitation of RNN. It is endowed with a memory to maintain its state over time, and internal mechanisms called gates which regulate the information flow. The main reason for choosing LSTM in our work is its proven performance in handling variable-length sequential data. Given input vector x_t, hidden sate h_t and memory state c_t, the updates in LSTM are performed as follows:

$$i_t = sigmoid(W_i x_t + U_i h_{t-1} + b_i) \tag{1}$$

$$f_t = sigmoid(W_f x_t + U_f h_{t-1} + b_f) \tag{2}$$

$$\tilde{c}_t = tanh(W_c x_t + U_c h_{t-1} + b_c) \tag{3}$$

$$c_t = i_t \odot \tilde{c}_t + f_t \odot c_{t-1} \tag{4}$$

$$o_t = sigmoid(W_o x_t + U_0 h_{t-1} + b_0) \tag{5}$$

$$h_t = o_t \odot \tanh(c_t) \tag{6}$$

where i_t, f_t, o_t are input, forget, and output gates at time t, respectively. W_k, U_k are LSTM parameterized weight matrices, b_k represents the bias vector for each k in $\{i, f, c, o\}$ and $\odot$ denotes an element-wise product of matrices, known as the Hadamard product which is simply an entrywise multiplication.

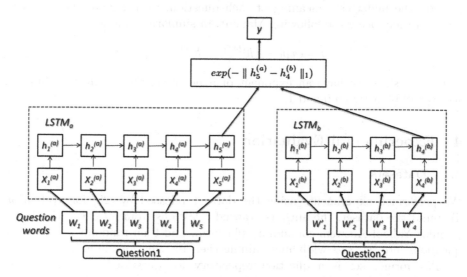

Fig. 2. General architecture of the MaLSTM model

The Manhattan LSTM (MaLSTM) refers to the fact that the Manhattan distance is used to compare the final hidden states of two standard LSTM layers instead of another distance such as Cosine and Euclidean distances. The overall aim of MaLSTM is to compare a pair of sentences to decide whether or not they are semantically equivalent. MaLSTM uses the Siamese network [13] architecture which is known to have identical sub-networks LSTMleft and LSTMright that are passed vector representations of two sentences and return a hidden state encoding semantic meaning of the sentences. These hidden states are then compared using a similarity metric to return a similarity score as depicted in Fig. 2. Note that we decided to use LSTM for each sub-network, but it is also possible to swap LSTM with GRU. In our work, MaLSTM was adapted to the context of question retrieval, that is to say, the sentence pairs become pairs of questions.

LSTM learns a mapping from the space of variable length sequences d_{in} and encode the input sequences into a fixed dimension hidden state representation d_{rep}. In other words, each question represented as a word vector sequence (e.g., Q_1 is represented by x_1, x_2, x_3) is fed into the LSTM, which updates, at each sequence-index, its hidden state. The final state of LSTM for each question is a d_{rep}-dimensional vector, denoted by h in Fig. 2, which holds the semantic meaning of the question.

Unlike other language modeling RNN architectures which predict next words, the given network rather computes the similarity between pairs of sequences. A main feature of the Siamese architecture is the shared weights across the sub-networks, which reduce not only the number of parameters but also the tendency of overfitting. MaLSTM uses the Siamese structure along with the Manhattan distance, hence the name MaLSTM model. Once we have the two vectors that capture the underlying meaning of each question, we calculate the similarity between them using the following Manhattan similarity function:

$$y = exp(- \parallel h^{(left)} - h^{(right)} \parallel_1) \tag{7}$$

Note that since we have an exponent of a negative, the Manhattan function scores will be between 0 and 1.

4   Experimental Evaluation

4.1   Datasets

We performed experiments using the dataset released by [25] for evaluation. To build the dataset, the authors crawled questions from all categories in the popular Yahoo! Answers community platform, and then randomly splitted the questions into two sets while maintaining their distributions in all categories.

The former set is a question repository for question search containing 1,123,034 questions, while the second is the test set containing 252 queries and 1624 manually annotated related questions. Note that the number of relevant questions related to each original query varies from 2 to 30.

The questions in the collection are of different lengths varying from 2 to 20 words, in various structures and belonging to diverse categories e.g., Computers and Internet, Health, Sports, Diet and Fitness, Pets, Yahoo! Products, Travel, Entertainment and Music, Education and Reference, Business and Finance, etc.

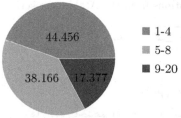
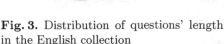
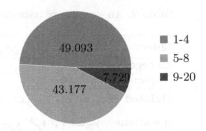

Fig. 3. Distribution of questions' length in the English collection

Fig. 4. Distribution of questions' length in the Arabic collection

Annotators were hired to annotate the questions with *relevant* if a candidate question is considered semantically equivalent to the original query or *irrelevant* otherwise. In case of conflict, a third annotator will make judgement for the final decision. As there is no Arabic Quora dataset available for the question retrieval task, for our experiments in Arabic we used the same English collection translated using Google Translation, the most widely used machine translation tool. The Arabic collection contains the same number of questions as the English set. To train word2vec for Arabic, we used a large-scale data set from cQA sites, namely the Yahoo!Webscope dataset[6], translated into Arabic including 1,256,173 questions with 1 2,512,034 distinct words. Note that the parameters of word2vec were fixed using a parallel dev set of 217 queries and 1317 annotated questions. Tables 1 and 2 give examples of queries and their corresponding related questions from the test sets in English and Arabic respectively.

Table 1. An example of community questions from the English test set.

Query:	I often feel restless, uneasy, loss memory, lack of concentration, lose my temper. Why?
Category:	Health care
Topic:	Memory loss
Related questions	– I get short memory loss what should I do? – What to do when you are restless? – How can I improve my concentration and my memory or any mental exercise? – What is the best way to sharpen my brain?

To train Siamese LSTM, we used the publicly available Quora Question Pairs dataset[7]. The collection contains 400,000 samples question duplicate pairs where each sample has a pair of questions along with ground truth about their similarity (1: similar, 0: dissimilar). A set of 40,000 pairs was used for validation. Our test

---

[6] The Yahoo! Webscope dataset Yahoo answers comprehensive questions and answers version 1.0.2, available at "http://research.yahoo.com/Academic_Relations".

[7] www.kaggle.com/quora/question-pairs-dataset.

Table 2. An example of community questions from the Arabic test set.

Query:	كيف أقوم بتدريب كلب بلدي بالغ من العمر سنة واحدة؟
Category:	Pets
Topic:	Puppy training
Related	- ما هي أفضل طريقة لتدريب جرو جديد؟
questions	- هل لدى أحدهم اقتراح حول كيفية إيواء جرو عمره ١٠ أسابيع؟
	- كيف تدرب كلبًا يبلغ من العمر عامًا؟
	- كيفية تدريب كلب صغير جداً؟

set was organized as pairs of questions to be directly fed into MaLSTM. Note that data preprocessing was done using Python NLTK.

4.2 Word Embedding Learning

For English word embedding training, we resorted to the publicly available word2vec vectors[8], with dimensionality of 300, that were trained on 100 billion words from Google News. As there is no Arabic version of Google News vectors, we train on the Yahoo!Webscope dataset using the CBOW model, since it has proven through experiments to be more efficient and performs better than Skip-gram with sizeable data. The training parameters of the Arabic CBOW model were set after several tests:

- Size = 300: feature vector dimension. We tested different values in the range [50, 500] but did not get significantly different precision values. The best precision was achieved with size=300.
- Sample = 1e-4: down sampling ratio for the words that are redundant a lot in the corpus.
- Negative samples = 25: number of noise words
- min-count = 1: minimum number of words which we set to 1 to make sure we do not throw away anything.
- Context window = 5: fixed window size. We tested different window sizes using the dev set. The best accuracy was obtained with window equals 5.

4.3 LSTM Training

For LSTM training, we applied the Adadelta method [23] for weights optimization to automatically decrease the learning rate. Gradient clipping was also used with a threshold value of 1.25 to avoid the exploding gradient problem [15]. Our LSTM layers' size is 50 and embedding layer's size is 300. We used the back propagation and small batches of size equals 64, to reduce the cross-entropy loss

---

[8] https://code.google.com/p/word2vec/.

and we resorted to the Mean Square Error (MSE) as a common regression loss function for prediction. We trained our model for several epochs to observe how the results varied with the epochs. We found out that the accuracy changed with changing the number of epochs but stabilized after epoch 25. Note that the given parameters were set based on empirical tests; each parameter was tuned separately on a development set to pick out the best one. For developing our model we used Keras[9] and Scikit-learn[10]. Note that we used the same LSTM configuration for both languages.

4.4 Evaluation Metrics

We used the Mean Average Precision (MAP), Precision@n (P@n) and Recall as they are the most widely used metrics for evaluating the performance of question retrieval in cQA. MAP assumes that the user is interested in finding many relevant questions for each query and then rewards methods that not only return relevant questions early, but also get good ranking of the results. Precision@n returns the proportion of the top-n retrieved questions that are relevant. Recall is the proportion of relevant similar questions that have been retrieved over the total number of relevant questions. Accuracy was also used which returns the proportion of correctly classified questions as relevant or irrelevant.

4.5 Main Results and Discussion

To evaluate the performance of LSTMQR, we compare against our previous approach called WEKOS as well as some competitive state-of-the-art question retrieval methods tested by Zhang et al. in [25] on the same dataset. The methods being compared are summarized below:

- **WEKOS** [14]: A word embedding based method which transforms words in each question into continuous vectors. The questions are clustered using Kmeans and the similarity between them was measured using the cosine similarity based on their weighted continuous valued vectors.
- **TLM** [21]: A translation based language model which combines a translation-based language model with a query likelihood approach for the language model for the question and the answer parts respectively. TLM integrates word-to-word translation probabilities learned by using different sources of information.
- **ETLM** [19]: An entity based translation language model, which is an extension of TLM where the main difference is the replacement of the word translation with entity translation in order to integrate semantic information within the entities.
- **PBTM** [26]: A phrase based translation model which uses machine translation probabilities assuming that question retrieval should be performed at

---

[9] https://keras.io/.
[10] https://scikit-learn.org.

the phrase level. PTLM learns the probability of translating a sequence of words in a historical question into another word sequence of words in a given query.

- **WKM** [29]: A world knowledge based model which integrates the knowledge of Wikipedia into the questions by deriving the concept relationships that allow to identify related topics between the queries and the previous questions. A concept thesaurus was built based on the semantic relations extracted from Wikipedia.
- **M-NET** [28]: A continuous word embedding based model, which incorporates the category information of the questions to get a category based word embedding, assuming that the representations of words belonging to the same category should be semantically equivalent.
- **ParaKCM** [25]: A key concept paraphrasing based approach which explores the translations of pivot languages and expands queries with the paraphrases. It assumes that paraphrases offer additional semantic connection between the key concepts in the queried question and those of the historical ones.

The results in Table 3, show that PBTM outperforms TLM which demonstrates that detecting contextual information in modeling the translation of entire phrases or consecutive word sequences is more effective than translating separate words, as there is a dependency between adjacent words in a phrase.

Table 3. Question retrieval performance comparison of different models in English.

	TLM	ETLM	PBTM	WKM	M-NET	ParaKCM	WEKOS	LSTMQR
P@5	0.3238	0.3314	0.3318	0.3413	0.3686	0.3722	0.4338	**0.5023**
P@10	0.2548	0.2603	0.2603	0.2715	0.2848	0.2889	0.3647	**0.4188**
MAP	0.3957	0.4073	0.4095	0.4116	0.4507	0.4578	0.5036	**0.5739**

ETLM performs as good as PBTM, which proves that replacing the word translation by entity translation for ranking improves the performance of the translation language model. The performance of WKM is limited by the low coverage of the concepts of Wikipedia on the diverse users' questions. ParaKCM achieves good precision by exploring the translations of pivot languages and expanding queries with the generated paraphrases for question retrieval. M-NET, based on word embeddings performs well owing to the use of metadata of category information to capture the properties of words. WEKOS also based on word embedding, TF-IDF weighting and kmeans achieves comparable results and further proves that the use of word embeddings get benefits from dense representation and reduce the negative impact of word mismatch by detecting semantic relations between words, while the other methods mostly do not capture enough information about semantic equivalence.

Our proposed approach LSTMQR outperforms in English all the compared methods on all criteria by returning a good number of relevant questions among the retrieved ones. This good performance indicates that the use of Siamese LSTM along with query expansion and Manhattan similarity is effective in the question retrieval task. Word embeddings help to obtain an efficient input representation for LSTM, capturing syntactic and semantic information in a word level. Interestingly, our approach does not require an extensive feature generation due to the use of a pre-trained model. The results show that our Siamese based approach performs better than translation and knowledge based methods, which demonstrates that the question representations produced by the Siamese LSTM sub-networks can learn the semantic relatedness between pairs of questions and then are more suitable for representing questions in the question retrieval task. The Siamese network was trained using backpropagation-through-time under the MSE loss function which compels the LSTM sub-networks to capture textual semantic difference during training. A main virtue of LSTM is that it can accept variable length sequences and map them into fixed length vector representations which can resolve the length and structure's problems in cQA.

In order to properly evaluate the MaLSTM model performance on our question similarity prediction problem, we plot training data vs validation data loss using the Matplotlib library. The loss is often computed on training and validation to diagnose its behavior and to check whether it is a good fit for the data or could perform better with a different configuration. It is a sum of the errors made for each instance in training or validation sets. From Figs. 5 and 6, we can see that for both English and Arabic there is no considerable difference between the training and validation loss. The training loss keeps decreasing after every epoch which means that the model is learning to recognize the specific patterns. Similarly, the validation loss continues to decrease reaching 0.132 and 0.129 for English and Arabic respectively, thus our model is generalizing well on the validation sets. We can say that we have a good fit since both the train and validation loss decreased and leveled off around the same points.

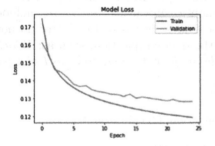
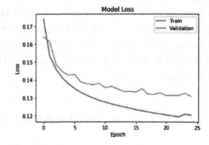

Fig. 5. Epochs vs loss of MaLSTM on the English dataset

Fig. 6. Epochs vs loss of MaLSTM on the Arabic dataset

We used the simple Manhattan similarity function which forces the LSTM to entirely capture the semantic differences during training. In practice, our results are fairly stable across different similarity functions namely cosine and Euclidean distances. We found out that Manhattan distance outperforms them as depicted in Tables 4 and 5 which proves that it is the most appropriate measure for the case of high dimensional text data.

Table 4. Comparison between similarity measures on the English dataset

	P@5	Recall
Manhattan	**0.5023**	**0.5385**
Cosine	**0.3883**	**0.4253**
Euclidean	**0.3383**	**0.3751**

Table 5. Comparison between similarity measures on the Arabic dataset

	P@5	Recall
Manhattan	**0.3692**	**0.4136**
Cosine	**0.2552**	**0.2997**
Euclidean	**0.2052**	**0.2496**

The cosine distance outperforms the Euclidean distance which demonstrates that it is better at catching the semantic of the questions, considering that the direction of the text points can be thought as its meaning, texts with similar meanings will have similar cosine score. Another reason is that Cosine distance is computed using the dot product and magnitude of each vector. So, it is only affected by the words the two vectors have in common, whereas the Euclidean measure has a term for every dimension which is non-zero in either vector. We can therefore say that the Cosine distance has meaningful semantics for ranking texts, based on mutual term frequency, whereas Euclidean distance does not.

Furthermore, we observed that LSTMQR could find the context mapping between certain expressions mostly used in the same context such as *bug* and *error message* or also *need help* and *suggestions*. In addition, LSTMQR was able to retrieve similar questions containing certain common misspelled terms like *recieve* instead of *receive* while it failed to detect other less common spelling mistakes like *relyable* or *realible* instead of *reliable*. Such cases show that our approach can address some lexical disagreement problems. Moreover, there are few cases where LSTMQR fails to detect semantic equivalence. Such cases include queries having only one similar question and most words of this latter do not appear in a similar context with those of the queried question, such as: *Which is better to aim my putter towards, the pole or the hole?* and *How do I aim for the target in golf?*.

Table 6. Question retrieval performance of LSTMQR in Arabic

	WEKOS	LSTMQR
P@5	0.3444	**0.3692**
P@10	0.2412	**0.2854**
MAP	0.4144	**0.4513**
Recall	0.3828	**0.4136**

Table 6 shows that our approach outperforms in Arabic the best compared system which gives evidence that it can perform well with complex languages.

However, our method ignores the morphological structure of Arabic words. Indeed, the Arabic language is an inflectional and a morphologically rich language with high character variation that has a significant impact on how influential a dataset is for producing good word embeddings. Therefore, exploiting the word internal structure is critical to detecting semantically similar words. For instance, the most similar words to «فعل» are all variants of the same word such as «نفعل، فعلنا، يفعلون ، سنفعل ، فاعل». Accordingly, endowing word embeddings with grammatical information (such as the person, gender, number, tense) could help to obtain more meaningful embeddings that capture morphological and semantic similarity. In terms of recall, LSTMQR reaches 0.4136 for Arabic which implies that the number of omitted similar questions is not big. We fine-tuned the parameter Nsw for the English and the Arabic corpora. We remarked that the query expansion has improved the results in terms of accuracy but also increases the execution time with the increase of the question size. With Nsw=5, the accuracy reaches 0.5377 and 0.3927 for English and Arabic respectively and then continues to slightly hover over this value but does not much increase. Thus, we set Nsw at 5 as an estimated value to avoid increasing the runtime. Interestingly, unlike traditional RNNs, Siamese LSTM can effectively handle the long questions and learn long range dependencies owing to its use of memory cell units that can store information across long input sequences. However, for very long sequences, LSTM may still fail to compress all information into its representation. Therefore, we envisage adding an attention mechanism to let the model attend to all past outputs and give different words different attention while modeling questions.

4.6 Conclusion

Work on cQA has been mostly carried out for English, resulting in a lack of resources available for other languages, mainly Arabic. Motivated by this aspect, we tackled in this paper the task of question retrieval which is of great importance in real-world community question answering, in both English and Arabic. For this purpose, we proposed to use word embeddings to expand the questions and MaLSTM to capture the semantic similarity between them. Experiments conducted on large scale Yahoo! Answers datasets show that our approach can greatly improve the question matching task in English and Arabic and outperform some competitive methods tested on the same dataset. Interestingly, we showed that MaLSTM is capable of modeling complex semantics and covering the context information of question pairs. The word embedding based query expansion helped to enrich the questions and improve the performance of the approach. In the future, we look forward to improving the siamese architecture by adding an attention layer to calculate a weight for each word annotation according to its importance which offers a more meaningful representation of the question. We also intend to enhance the Arabic word embedding by incorporating morphological features to the embedding model.

References

1. Barrón-Cedeno, A., Da San Martino, G., Romeo, S., Moschitti, A.: Selecting sentences versus selecting tree constituents for automatic question ranking. In: Proceedings of COLING, the 26th International Conference on Computational Linguistics, pp. 2515–2525 (2016)
2. Cai, L., Zhou, G., Liu, K., Zhao, J.: Learning the latent topics for question retrieval in community qa. In: Proceedings of 5th International Joint Conference on Natural Language Processing, pp. 273–281 (2011)
3. Cao, X., Cong, G., Cui, B., Jensen, C.S.: A generalized framework of exploring category information for question retrieval in community question answer archives. In: Proceedings of the 19th International Conference on WWW, pp. 201–210. ACM (2010)
4. Cao, X., Cong, G., Cui, B., Jensen, C.S., Zhang, C.: The use of categorization information in language models for question retrieval. In: Proceedings of the 18th ACM Conference on Information and Knowledge Management, pp. 265–274. ACM (2009)
5. Dos Santos, C., Barbosa, L., Bogdanova, D., Zadrozny, B.: Learning hybrid representations to retrieve semantically equivalent questions. In: Proceedings of ACL and the 7th International Joint Conference on NLP, vol. 2, pp. 694–699 (2015)
6. Duan, H., Cao, Y., Lin, C.Y., Yu, Y.: Searching questions by identifying question topic and question focus. In: ACL, vol. 8, pp. 156–164 (2008)
7. Hochreiter, S.: The vanishing gradient problem during learning recurrent neural nets and problem solutions. Int. J. Uncertainty Fuzziness Knowl. Based Syst. 6(02), 107–116 (1998)
8. Hochreiter, S., Schmidhuber, J.: Long short-term memory. Neural Comput. 9(8), 1735–1780 (1997)
9. Kamineni, A., Shrivastava, M., Yenala, H., Chinnakotla, M.: Siamese LSTM with convolutional similarity for similar question retrieval. In: 2018 International Joint Symposium on Artificial Intelligence and NLP (iSAI-NLP), pp. 1–7. IEEE (2019)
10. Malhas, R., Torki, M., Elsayed, T.: Qu-ir at semeval 2016 task 3: learning to rank on arabic community question answering forums with word embedding. In: Proceedings of SemEval, pp. 866–871 (2016)
11. Mikolov, T., Sutskever, I., Chen, K., Corrado, G.S., Dean, J.: Distributed representations of words and phrases and their compositionality. In: Advances in Neural Information Processing Systems, pp. 3111–3119 (2013)
12. Mohtarami, M., et al.: SLS at semeval-2016 task 3: neural-based approaches for ranking in community question answering. In: Proceedings of SemEval, pp. 828–835 (2016)
13. Mueller, J., Thyagarajan, A.: Siamese recurrent architectures for learning sentence similarity. In: Thirtieth AAAI Conference on Artificial Intelligence (2016)
14. Othman, N., Faiz, R., Smaïli, K.: Enhancing question retrieval in community question answering using word embeddings. In: proceedings of the 23rd International Conference on Knowledge-Based and Intelligent Information & Engineering Systems (KES) (2019)
15. Pascanu, R., Mikolov, T., Bengio, Y.: On the difficulty of training recurrent neural networks. In: International Conference on Machine Learning, pp. 1310–1318 (2013)
16. Qiu, X., Tian, L., Huang, X.: Latent semantic tensor indexing for community-based question answering. In: ACL, vol. 2, pp. 434–439 (2013)

17. Romeo, S., et al.: Neural attention for learning to rank questions in community question answering. In: Proceedings of COLING, pp. 1734–1745 (2016)
18. Romeo, S., et al.: Language processing and learning models for community question answering in arabic. In: IPM (2017)
19. Singh, A.: Entity based q&a retrieval. In: Proceedings of the 2012 Joint Conference on Empirical Methods in Natural Language Processing and Computational Natural Language Learning, pp. 1266–1277. ACL (2012)
20. Wang, K., Ming, Z., Chua, T.S.: A syntactic tree matching approach to finding similar questions in community-based qa services. In: Proceedings of the 32nd international ACM SIGIR conference on Research and development in information retrieval, pp. 187–194. ACM (2009)
21. Xue, X., Jeon, J., Croft, W.B.: Retrieval models for question and answer archives. In: Proceedings of the 31st Annual International ACM SIGIR Conference on Research and Development in Information Retrieval, pp. 475–482. ACM (2008)
22. Ye, B., Feng, G., Cui, A., Li, M.: Learning question similarity with recurrent neural networks. In: 2017 IEEE International Conference on Big Knowledge (ICBK), pp. 111–118. IEEE (2017)
23. Zeiler, M.D.: Adadelta: an adaptive learning rate method. arXiv preprint arXiv:1212.5701 (2012)
24. Zhang, K., Wu, W., Wu, H., Li, Z., Zhou, M.: Question retrieval with high quality answers in community question answering. In: Proceedings of the 23rd ACM International Conference on Conference on Information and Knowledge Management, pp. 371–380. ACM (2014)
25. Zhang, W.N., Ming, Z.Y., Zhang, Y., Liu, T., Chua, T.S.: Capturing the semantics of key phrases using multiple languages for question retrieval. IEEE Trans. Knowl. Data Eng. **28**(4), 888–900 (2016)
26. Zhou, G., Cai, L., Zhao, J., Liu, K.: Phrase-based translation model for question retrieval in community question answer archives. In: Proceedings of the 49th Annual Meeting of the ACL: Human Language Technologies-Volume 1, pp. 653–662. ACL (2011)
27. Zhou, G., Chen, Y., Zeng, D., Zhao, J.: Towards faster and better retrieval models for question search. In: Proceedings of the 22nd ACM International Conference on Conference on Information & Knowledge Management, pp. 2139–2148. ACM (2013)
28. Zhou, G., He, T., Zhao, J., Hu, P.: Learning continuous word embedding with metadata for question retrieval in community question answering. In: Proceedings of the 53rd Annual Meeting of the ACL and the 7th International Joint Conference on Natural Language Processing of the Asian Federation of Natural Language Processing, pp. 250–259 (2015)
29. Zhou, G., Liu, Y., Liu, F., Zeng, D., Zhao, J.: Improving question retrieval in community question answering using world knowledge. In: IJCAI, vol. 13, pp. 2239–2245 (2013)

A Formalisation and a Computational Characterisation of ORM Derivation Rules

Francesco Sportelli and Enrico Franconi[✉]

KRDB Research Centre, Free University of Bozen-Bolzano, Bolzano, Italy
{francesco.sportelli,franconi}@inf.unibz.it
http://www.inf.unibz.it/krdb/

Abstract. Object-Role Modelling (ORM) is a framework for modelling a domain using a rich set of constraints with an intuitive diagrammatic representation, not dissimilar to UML class diagrams. ORM is backed by Microsoft with Visual Studio, and it is used to support the design of large database schemas and/or complex software, easing the workflow for all stakeholders and bridging the gap among them, since every constraint of the diagram is encoded in a language which is understandable even by non-IT users. Besides the standard constraints, ORM also supports Derivation Rules that, in a way similar to UML/OCL constraints and SQL triggers, are able to express knowledge which is beyond standard graphic-based ORM capabilities. Despite ORM has its own formalisation in literature, Derivation Rules in ORM lack of this feature. The purpose of this paper is to provide a formalisation for ORM Derivation Rules in order to extend the automated reasoning on diagrams equipped with Derivation Rules. Automated reasoning is useful to check the consistency of diagrams, new inferred knowledge to validate the diagram or to avoid mistakes which could degrade the quality of the system. We provide the formalisation of Derivation Rules with a precise syntax and a semantics grounded on a precise and non-ambiguous encoding in first-order logic. Finally, we also detect an expressive decidable fragment of Derivation Rules by means of an encoding in an expressive Description Logic. A reasoner for this fragment has been implemented in a plugin for Microsoft Visual Studio.

1 Introduction

Conceptual modelling is a critical step during the development of a database system. It is the detailed description of the universe of discourse in a language that is understandable by users of the business domain. Object-Role Modelling (ORM) [13,16] is a conceptual language for modelling, like UML and ER, which includes a graphical and textual language for specifying models, a textual language for formulating queries, as well as procedures for constructing ORM models. ORM provides a general and intuitive idea of the concepts of the domain being modelled and the associations among them. It turns out that the ORM

H. Panetto et al. (Eds.): OTM 2019, LNCS 11877, pp. 678–694, 2019.
https://doi.org/10.1007/978-3-030-33246-4_42

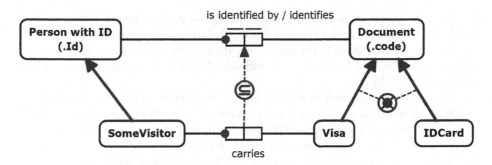

Fig. 1. An example ORM conceptual diagram.

standard graphical language alone is not expressive enough to allow defining all the relevant information of the domain.

For example, consider the ORM conceptual diagram in Fig. 1 about persons and their documents. The conceptual diagram captures all the necessary entities (*Person with ID*, *Visitor*, *Document*, etc.) together with their relationships (*carries*) and additional constraints (such as cardinalities, subtyping, uniqueness, etc.), thus providing a quite precise idea of the specified domain, where each *Person with ID* is identified by a document which can be either visa or id card. A *Person with ID* can be a citizen or visitor. In spite of that, the conceptual diagram is not expressive enough to encode further information, e.g., that all the visitors are exactly those who are identified by a visa or to capture all the people that have no documents.

For this reason, languages like UML and ORM are supported by some textual languages that allow defining such additional information in a precise and unambiguous way in the form of rules. *Derivation Rules* in ORM where introduced by [12], so to express additional knowledge and constraints over an ORM schema, similar in form to triggers or stored procedures and views in a relational DBMS, or OCL in UML, and equipped with a full logic based semantics. The expressed knowledge is beyond the ORM graphical language, thus leading to a further complexity of the reasoning.

For example, derivation rules are necessary to represent additional entities:

- Visitors are exactly the *Persons with ID* identified by a Visa;
- Citizens are exactly the *Persons with ID* identified by an IDCard;
- Stateless are exactly the *Persons with ID* neither identified by an IDCard nor by a VISA.

The goal of this paper is to provide a non-trivial decidable fragment for ORM derivation rules, by defining a precise and formal syntax and semantics. More precisely, the fragment covers *acyclic first-order subtype and facttype derivation rules*. The rules in this fragment are then encoded in a decidable description logic which has been specifically designed for n-ary relationships, namely $\mathcal{DLR}^{\pm}$ [1], in order to run reasoning procedures on conceptual diagrams with ORM derivation rules. The results presented in this paper can be reused to add rules to any conceptual modelling language encodable in description logics, such as UML class diagrams and Extended Entity Relationships diagrams.

Another contribution is the implementation of the above formalisation as an extension for NORMA, which is the official Microsoft Visual Studio tool which implements ORM [4].

The paper is organised as follows: after a Section on related works, we give a quick recall to ORM and its most relevant constraints. Then, we introduce ORM derivation rules and their semantics also by means of examples. The core part of the paper is the formalisation of ORM derivation rules, which are given an explicit syntax, semantics and encoding in $\mathcal{DLR}^{\pm}$. In the examples we also show the benefit of reasoning and how it can be helpful for a modeller during the early stages of software development. The present work is intended as an extension and a rework of [19], where only subtype derivation rules were formalised. Here, we take into account the Fact Type Derivation Rules as well, providing also a unified grammar and a new encoding to generalise ORM Derivation Rules formalisation. A complexity analysis about computational properties is provided as well.

2   Related Work

The ORM formalisation starts with Terry Halpin's PhD Thesis [11]. His thesis was the first attempt to formalise a database conceptual modelling language, providing a non-ambiguous meaning to conceptual schemas for making decision choices. After the spreading of ORM and its latest implementation in NORMA [4], ORM became more popular so the logicians' community took into account the possibility to formalise this very expressive language into description logics in order to provide automated reasoning over conceptual schemas (see, e.g., [6] also for a good survey on different description logics encodings). Eventually, a complete formalisation of ORM with the introduction of a linear syntax, a first-order logic semantics, and a provably correct complete encoding in OWL has been published in [7,8,10]. More recently, the n-ary description logics $\mathcal{DLR}^{+}$ designed to match more directly conceptual modelling languages such as ORM has been introduced in [1]. An implementation of a reasoning engine for ORM diagrams according to its formalisation in description logics is in the ORMiE tool [10], fully integrated with NORMA, the ORM extension of Microsoft Visual Studio [4]. There are also two tools similar to ORMie: ICOM [5] and DogmaModeler [18]. ICOM is an advanced conceptual modelling tool, which allows the user to design multiple class diagrams with in addition inter and intra-schema constraints expressed in a rich view relational algebra similar to OCL. ICOM implements logical reasoning in order to verify the specification, infer implicit facts, devise stricter constraints, and manifest any inconsistency, with a provably complete inference mechanism. DogmaModeler implements directly an earlier formalisation of ORM [17]: it is an ontology modelling tool based on ORM integrated with a description logic reasoning server which acts as a background reasoning engine.

This paper extends the first formalisation for ORM Derivation Rules in [19], where a limited form of subtype derivation rules only are formalised and mapped into OWL.

3   ORM

ORM stands for Object-Role Modelling. It is a language that allows users to model and query information at the conceptual level where the world is described in terms of *objects* (things) playing *roles* (parts in relationships). The idea behind ORM and its approach is that an object-role model avoids the need to write long documents in ambiguous natural language prose. It's easy for non-technical users to validate an object-role model because ORM tools can generate easy-to-understand sentences. After an object-role model has been validated by non-technical domain experts, the model can be used to generate a class model or a fully normalised database schema. ORM main features are:

- *fact-oriented*: the central syntactic categories are the *fact type* and the *entity type*, denoting typed *n*-ary predicates and classes, respectively; the arguments of predicates are called *roles* and are always *typed* by entity types; roles are represented by the name of the predicate followed by an integer index denoting the position of the role within the predicate arity;
- *expressive*: a powerful set of constraints on fact types makes ORM more expressive than UML and EER;
- *attribute-free*: unlike EER and UML attributes are always modelled as fact types; although this often leads to larger diagrams, an attribute-free approach has advantages for conceptual analysis, including simplicity, stability, and ease of validation;
- *graphical*: it has a graphical notation implemented by the software NORMA;
- *natural language-oriented*: all facts and rules can be modelled and verbalised in terms of a controlled natural language (FORML) sentences easy to understand even for non-technical users;
- *formalised*: it has a clear syntax and semantics, setting a sound ground for interoperability and reasoning.

Attribute-free models with an associated controlled natural language facilitate model validation by verbalisation and population. Model validation should be a collaborative process between the modeller and the business domain expert who best understands the business domain. All facts, fact types, constraints and derivation rules may be verbalised naturally in unambiguous language that is easily understood by domain experts who might not be experts in the software systems ultimately used for the physical implementation [15].

Let's quickly introduce the most important constructs of ORM by means of the example conceptual schema of Fig. 1. We make use of the FORML controlled natural language which provides the most intuitive way to understand the meaning of a diagram, since in ORM it is based on a precise mapping with the internal structure of the conceptual schema; we use the variant of FORML adopted by NORMA [14]. We then use first-order logic (FOL) formulae to state the exact semantics of the diagram.

With respect to Fig. 1, this diagram better specifies the concept of visitors. It says that each *Person with ID* has a unique document which can only be either a VISA or an IDCard, but not both. Each document is associated to at most one *Person with ID*. The entity SomeVisitor is a subtype of *Person with ID*, and each of its instances owns one VISA. The roles of the predicate "carries" are "carries.1" and "carries.2"; similarly for the predicate "is identified by". The diagram is verbalised in FORML as follows:

```
Person with ID is an entity type.
SomeVisitor is an entity type.
Document is an entity type.
VISA is an entity type.
IDCard is an entity type.
Person has Document.
SomeVisitor carries VISA.
Each SomeVisitor is an instance of Person with ID.
Each VISA is an instance of Document.
Each IDCard is an instance of Document.
Each Person has exactly one Document.
Each SomeVisitor carries exactly one VISA.
For each Document, at most one Person has that Document.
For each VISA, at most one SomeVisitor carries that VISA.
For each Document, exactly one of the following holds: that Document is
some VISA; that Document is some IDCard.
If some SomeVisitor carries some VISA then some Person with ID that is
SomeVisitor carries some Document that is that VISA.
```

The exact semantics of the conceptual schema is given as first-order logic statements, corresponding to the constraints in the schema:

FactType

$\forall x, y. isIdentifiedBy(x, y) \rightarrow PersonWithID(x) \wedge Document(y)$

$\forall x, y. carries(x, y) \rightarrow SomeVisitor(x) \wedge Visa(y)$

Subtype

$\forall x. SomeVisitor(x) \rightarrow PersonWithID(x)$

$\forall x. Visa(x) \rightarrow Document(x)$

$\forall x. IDcard(x) \rightarrow Document(x)$

Mandatory

$\forall x. PersonWithID(x) \rightarrow \exists y. isIdentifiedBy(x, y)$

$\forall x. SomeVisitor(x) \rightarrow \exists y. carries(x, y)$

Uniqueness

$\forall x, y. isIdentifiedBy(x, y) \rightarrow \exists^{\leq 1} z. isIdentifiedBy(x, z)$

$\forall x, y. isIdentifiedBy(x, y) \rightarrow \exists^{\leq 1} z. isIdentifiedBy(z, y)$

$\forall x, y. carries(x, y) \rightarrow \exists^{\leq 1} z. carries(x, z)$

$\forall x, y. carries(x, y) \rightarrow \exists^{\leq 1} z. carries(z, y)$

Exclusive

$\forall x. Visa(x) \rightarrow \neg IDCard(x)$

Exhaustive

$\forall x. Document(x) \rightarrow Visa(x) \vee IDCard(x)$

Subset

$\forall x, y. carries(x, y) \rightarrow isIdentifiedBy(x, y)$

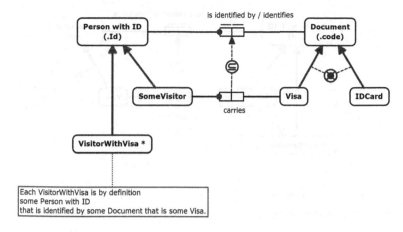

Fig. 2. Adding the entity type *Visitor With Visa*.

The first-order semantics specifies the exact meaning of the conceptual schema in a precise and non ambiguous way. Note that the ORM schema in Fig. 1 can be easily expressed both as a UML class diagram and an EER diagram.

4   Derivation Rules by Examples

This section shows by examples how derivation rules are used in ORM. We distinguish between Subtype and Fact Types Derivation Rules. The former define entity types as a specialisation of other entity types, the latter define fact types by means of more specific argument types. A derivation rule is a collection of restrictions defined along one or more paths in the ORM diagram. The entity or the fact type which is defined by a derivation rule, has its own values restricted according the the paths which are specified in the derivation rule.

The diagram described in the previous Section (Fig. 1), does not capture exactly the intended meaning for the Visitor entity. Observe, that there is no constraint stating that *all* VISA holders are visitors. How can we capture in the schema exactly all the visitors? We need to use a derivation rule stating the needed *exact* definition.

Let's add (Fig. 2) the new *Visitor With Visa* entity as a subtype of *Person-WithID* with an attached derivation rule as follows:

```
Each VisitorWithVisa is by definition some Person with ID
that is identified by some Document that is some Visa.
```

$$\forall x.\, VisitorWithVisa(x) \leftrightarrow PersonWithID(x) \wedge \exists y.\, isIdentifiedBy(x, y) \wedge Visa(y)$$

The derivation rule *defines* exactly what a visitor with VISA is, by means of an *if-and-only-if* statement.

684   F. Sportelli and E. Franconi

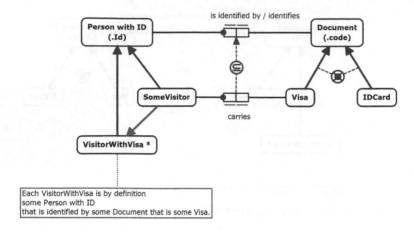

Fig. 3. Reasoning after adding the entity type *VisitorWithVisa*. (Color figure online)

Given the ORM conceptual schema with the derivation rule of Fig. 2, it is obvious that the entity *SomeVisitor* should turn out to be a subtype of *VisitorWithVisa*, as shown in green in Fig. 3. This inference can be automatically computed by a logic prover using the semantic translation of the ORM conceptual schema. As a matter of fact, the tools implementing an inference engine for ORM are all based on description logics provers, exploiting the conversion of the first-order semantics in some computable fragment of description logic (see Sect. 6). Figure 3 also shows another inference, namely the inheritance of the uniqueness constraints to the *carries* fact type.

Note that there is also an alternative way to express the same derivation rule, since documents can be either VISAs or IDCards but not both. Indeed, if we add the entity *VisitorWithoutIDCard* with the following derivation rule:

```
Each VisitorWithoutIDCard is by definition some Person with ID
that is identified by some Document
where that Document is no IDCard.
```

$\forall x.\,VisitorWithoutIDCard(x) \leftrightarrow PersonWithID(x) \wedge \exists y.isIdentifiedBy(x, y) \wedge \neg IDCard(y),$

it turns out that the new entity behaves exactly like the previous one, and indeed it can be derived that they are equivalent (see the new inferred links in green in Fig. 4).

Now, let's suppose that all the people with an IDCard are citizens and stateless people are exactly those without any document:

```
Each Citizen is by definition some Person with ID
that is identified by some Document that is some IDCard.
Each Stateless with ID is by definition some Person with ID
that is identified by some Document
where that document is no IDCard and that Document is no VISA.
```

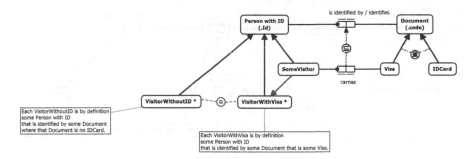

Fig. 4. Reasoning after adding the entity type *VisitorWithoutIDCard*. (Color figure online)

$$\forall x. Citizen(x) \leftrightarrow PersonWithID(x) \wedge \exists y.isIdentifiedBy(x,y) \wedge IDCard(y)$$
$$\forall x. StatelessWithID(x) \leftrightarrow PersonWithID(x) \wedge \exists y.(isIdentifiedBy(x,y) \wedge \neg IDCard(y)) \wedge$$
$$\exists z.(isIdentifiedBy(x,z) \wedge \neg Visa(z))$$

Note the complete outcome of the reasoning process in green and red in Fig. 5: among others, valid inferences according to this formalisation of the domain are that persons with ID are partitioned between citizens and visitors with VISA, and that there can't be any stateless person with ID. Indeed, stateless persons with ID are defined not to hold any VISA nor IDCard, but persons with ID are required to have exactly one document. The whole schema makes the *StatelessWithID* entity inconsistent (in red). Clearly, if persons were not obliged to have at least one document (i.e., via the mandatory participation constraint), the reasoning process would not derive the inconsistency of the *StatelessWithID* entity.

We now apply some changes to the previous diagram involving the usage of a fact type derivation rule. In order to clarify the distinction between the people

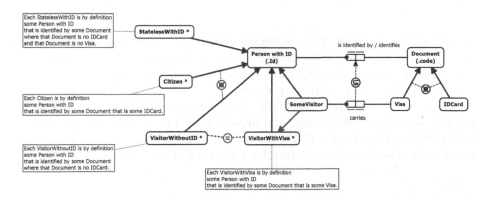

Fig. 5. Reasoning after adding the entity types *Citizen* and *StatelessWithID*. (Color figure online)

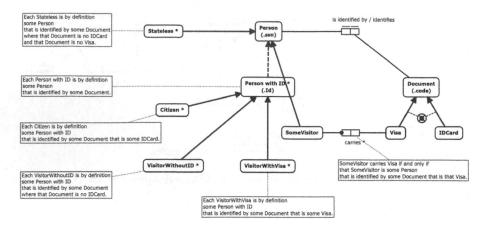

Fig. 6. Fact type Derivation Rule.

who possess a document and the others, in Fig. 6 we introduce a more generic entity named *Person*, supertype of *Person with ID*, with the associated fact type "*Person is identified by document*". *Stateless* is a subtype of *Person*, no more a subtype of *Person with ID*. Moreover, the fact type *SomeVisitor carries Visa* is not anymore an explicit subset of the fact type *Person is identified by document*; the subset constraint is implicitly stated in the *fact type derivation rule* associated to the fact type *SomeVisitor carries Visa*:

```
SomeVisitor carries Visa if and only if
that SomeVisitor is some Person
that is identified by some Document that is that Visa.
```

$$\forall x, y. carries(x, y) \leftrightarrow SomeVisitor(x) \wedge Person(x) \wedge isIdentifiedBy(x, y) \wedge$$
$$Document(y) \wedge Visa(y)$$

Indeed, the outcome of the reasoning depicted in green (Fig. 7) tells us that the the fact type *SomeVisitor carries Visa* is a subset of *Person is identified by document*, and that the entity *SomeVisitor* is a subtype of the entity *VisitorWithVisa*, as was before explicitly stated.

Moreover, as expected, the newly defined Stateless entity type, unlike the previous one, is now consistent, and disjoint from Person with ID. The reason behind this is the absence of the mandatory constraint on the entity Person, which states that is not mandatory for a person to have a document.

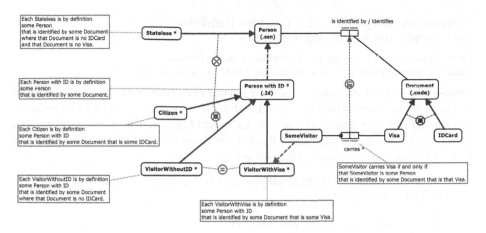

Fig. 7. Fact type Derivation Rule reasoning. (Color figure online)

5   Formal Syntax and Semantics

We now present the formalisation for the *first-order* fragment of the full ORM Derivation Rule language, namely we disregard all the second-order aggregation constructs in the ORM Derivation Rule language. In this fragment we consider both *subtype derivation rules* and *fact type derivation rules*.

An ORM signature includes:

- entity types denoted by the syntactic category T;
- predicates denoted by the syntactic category P;
- roles denoted by the syntactic category ROLE;
- data elements denoted by the syntactic category D.

We also introduce in the signature a syntactic category for *variables* (bound to roles) denoted by VAR, written as integers prefixed by a question mark (e.g., ?1, ?2, etc).

We do not introduce in this paper a specific syntax or semantics for the class diagram part of ORM, since we assume that it is well known from [7,8,10]. As a matter of fact, the definitions and the results about the derivation rule language introduced in this paper are applicable to any conceptual modelling language formalised in first-order logic, such a UML class diagrams [2] or EER diagrams [3]. In this case, entity types would correspond to classes (or entities), predicates to associations (or relationships), and roles to association ends. As we already mentioned, a fact type corresponds to a predicate with its arguments typed by entity types.

Derivation rules are based on *path expressions*. Intuitively, a path expression from a root role is inductively defined as a join of the predicate the root role belongs to with the root role of another path. A path defines the set of all instances at the root of the path which satisfy the conditions specified along the path expression. A derivation rule can be either a subtype derivation rule (defining an entity type), or a fact type derivation rule (defining a fact type). For example, the subtype derivation rule

```
Each VisitorWithVisa is by definition some Person
that is identified by some Document that is some Visa.
```

defines the set of the instances of `VisitorWithVisa` with the path rooted in the role `isIdentifiedBy.1` restricted to be a `Person` where the predicate `isIdentifiedBy` is joined at the role `isIdentifiedBy.2` with the empty path restricted to be a `Document` and a `Visa`. Indeed, as we have seen before form the first-order semantics of such rule, this set is:

$\{x \mid \text{Person}(x) \land \exists y.\text{isIdentifiedBy}(x, y) \land \text{Document}(y) \land \text{Visa}(y)\}.$

The fact type derivation rule

```
SomeVisitor carries Visa if and only if
that SomeVisitor is some Person
that is identified by some Document that is that Visa.
```

defines the set of pairs of instances of `carries`, with the first instance from the path rooted in the role `isIdentifiedBy.1` restricted to be a `Person` and a `SomeVisitor` where the predicate `isIdentifiedBy` is joined at the role `isIdentifiedBy.2` with the empty path restricted to be a `Document` and a `Visa` and being the second instance of the pair Indeed, as we have seen before form the first-order semantics of such rule, this set of pairs is:

$$\{< x, y > \mid \text{SomeVisitor}(x) \land \text{Person}(x) \land \text{isIdentifiedBy}(x, y) \land$$
$$\text{Document}(y) \land \text{Visa}(y)\}.$$

RULE	::= SRULE | FRULE
SRULE	::= T ("==" | ":=") PATH
FRULE	::= P ("==" | ":=") ("("VAR "=" PATH ")")+
PATH	::= T
	| ROLE "JOIN" ("(" ROLE PATH ")")+
	| PATH "OR" PATH
	| PATH "AND" PATH
	| PATH "MINUS" PATH
	| T ("=" | "≠" | "≤" | "≥") TERM
	| "{" D+ "}"
	| "(" PATH ")"
TERM	::= VAR | D | f "(" (TERM)+ ")"

Fig. 8. The syntax of ORM Derivation Rules.

Figure 8 defines the full syntax of both subtype and fact type derivation rules; rules can also include arbitrary functions f. We show below how the derivation rules taken from the examples above are encoded with this syntax:

```
Each VisitorWithVisa is by definition some Person that is identified by
some Document that is some Visa.
```

```
VisitorWithVisa == (Person AND
    isIdentifiedBy.1 JOIN (isIdentifiedBy.2 (Document AND Visa))
```

```
Each VisitorWithoutID is by definition some Person that has some Document
where that Document is no IDCard.
```

```
VisitorWithoutID == (Person AND
    isIdentifiedBy.1 JOIN (isIdentifiedBy.2
        (Document AND (Document MINUS IDCard)))
```

```
Each Citizen is by definition some Person that is identified by some
Document that is some IDCard.
```

```
Citizen == (Person AND
    isIdentifiedBy.1 JOIN (isIdentifiedBy.2 (Document AND IDCard))
```

```
Each Stateless is by definition some Person that is identified by some
Document where that Document is no IDCard and that Document is no Visa.
```

```
Stateless == (Person AND
    isIdentifiedBy.1 JOIN (.2 (Document AND
        ((Document MINUS IDCard) AND (Document MINUS Visa)))
```

```
SomeVisitor carries Visa if and only if that SomeVisitor is some Person
that is identified by some Document that is that Visa.
```

```
Carries ==
    (?1 = SomeVisitor AND Person AND isIdentifiedBy.1 JOIN
        (Document = ?2))
    (?2 = Visa)
```

Once the grammar has been formalised, we can now assign to this grammar a precise and not ambiguous semantics. As we stated before, the standard ORM language has its own formalisation and its encoding in first-order logic [8]. So we can extend the language using ORM Derivation Rules. As we already seen in

$$(T == PATH)^{\mathcal{I}} = \forall x. T(x) \leftrightarrow \exists VAR_1...VAR_m \ PATH^{\mathcal{I}}(x)$$

$$(P == (?1 = PATH_1)...(?n = PATH_n))^{\mathcal{I}} = \forall ?1...?n.P(?1...?n) \leftrightarrow$$
$$\exists VAR_1...VAR_m. \ PATH_1^{\mathcal{I}}(?1) \wedge ... \wedge PATH_n^{\mathcal{I}}(?n)$$

$$(T := PATH)^{\mathcal{I}} = \forall x. T(x) \leftarrow \exists VAR_1...VAR_m \ PATH^{\mathcal{I}}(x)$$

$$(P := (?1 = PATH_1)...(?n = PATH_n))^{\mathcal{I}} = \forall ?1...?n.P(?1...?n) \leftarrow$$
$$\exists VAR_1...VAR_m. \ PATH_1^{\mathcal{I}}(?1) \wedge ... \wedge PATH_n^{\mathcal{I}}(?n)$$

$$(T)^{\mathcal{I}} = \lambda x. T(x)$$

$$(P.i \ JOIN \ (P.i_{j_1} \ PATH_{j_1}) \ ... \ (P.i_{j_m} \ PATH_{j_m}) \ )^{\mathcal{I}} = \lambda x. \exists (x_1)...\exists (x_n).P(x_1...x_n) \wedge$$
$$PATH_{j_1}^{\mathcal{I}}(x_{j_1}) \wedge ... \wedge PATH_{j_m}^{\mathcal{I}}(x_{j_m}) \wedge x = x_i$$

$$(PATH_1 \ AND \ PATH_2)^{\mathcal{I}} = \lambda x. PATH_1^{\mathcal{I}}(x) \wedge PATH_2^{\mathcal{I}}(x)$$

$$(PATH_1 \ OR \ PATH_2)^{\mathcal{I}} = \lambda x. PATH_1^{\mathcal{I}}(x) \vee PATH_2^{\mathcal{I}}(x)$$

$$(PATH_1 \ MINUS \ PATH_2)^{\mathcal{I}} = \lambda x. PATH_1^{\mathcal{I}}(x) \wedge \neg PATH_2^{\mathcal{I}}(x)$$

$$(T=TERM)^{\mathcal{I}} = \lambda x. T(x) \wedge x = TERM^{\mathcal{I}}$$

$$(\{D_1...D_n\})^{\mathcal{I}} = \lambda x. x = D_1 \vee ... \vee x = D_n$$

$$(f(TERM_1...TERM_n))^{\mathcal{I}} = f(TERM_1^{\mathcal{I}}...TERM_n^{\mathcal{I}})$$

Fig. 9. The FOL semantics of ORM Derivation Rules.

Sect. 4, ORM Derivation Rules are encoded in first-order logic as well. For this reason, we can formally define the semantics at first-order consistent with the previously defined grammar.

The formal semantics of derivation rules is specified in Fig. 9 by a function $(\cdot^{\mathcal{I}})$ translating ORM derivation rules into First-Order Logic (FOL) formulas. It is easy to check that the given transformational semantic specification returns the above given FOL translation to the derivation rule examples previously presented in the paper.

It can also be proved that the language for derivation rules presented in this paper is expressively equivalent to relational algebra, and to the first-order fragment of OCL [9].

6 Computational Properties

We provide a mapping of the rules into the $\mathcal{DLR}^+$ language which belongs to the Description Logics family that has been specifically designed to deal with n-ary relationships [1]. $\mathcal{DLR}^+$ encodes directly some ORM constraints like subset, uniqueness key and external uniqueness. From [1] we know that fragments of languages like ORM, UML and ER, are in $\mathcal{DLR}^+$. We want to apply reasoning algorithms on those ORM diagrams equipped with ORM Derivation Rules, so we first need to detect a decidable fragment.

In order to perform a sound and complete reasoning procedure over those diagrams, we need to consider a decidable fragment of the language presented so far. Decidability is based on the expressivity power of Description Logics and in this specific case the $\mathcal{DLR}^{\pm}$ language, which is the decidable fragment of $\mathcal{DLR}^{+}$. From the grammar in Fig. 8, we have to discard the data elements and the variables, in order to avoid syntactic re-entrances; we call this fragment *acyclic*.

Thus, we consider only the fragment in Fig. 10, where also the transformation $(\cdot)^{\dagger}$ from derivation rules to $\mathcal{DLR}^{\pm}$ axioms is presented.

RULE	::= SRULE | FRULE
SRULE	::= T ("==" | ":=") PATH
FRULE	::= P ("==" | ":=") ("("VAR "=" PATH ")")+
PATH	::= T
	| ROLE "JOIN" ("(" ROLE PATH ")")+
	| PATH "OR" PATH
	| PATH "AND" PATH
	| PATH "MINUS" PATH
	| "(" PATH ")"

$$(T == \text{PATH})^{\dagger} = T \equiv \text{PATH}^{\dagger}$$
$$(P == (?1 = \text{PATH}_1)...(?n = \text{PATH}_n))^{\dagger} = P \equiv \sigma_{P.1=PATH_1}{}^{\dagger}.P \sqcap ... \sqcap \sigma_{P.n=PATH_n}{}^{\dagger}.P$$
$$(P.i \ JOIN \ (.i_{j_1} \ \text{PATH}_{j_1}) \ ... \ (.i_{j_n} \ \text{PATH}_{j_n}) \ )^{\dagger} = \exists [P.i].\sigma_{j_1=PATH_{j_1}}{}^{\dagger}.P \sqcap ... \sqcap \exists [P.i].\sigma_{j_n=PATH_{j_n}}{}^{\dagger}.P$$
$$(\text{PATH}_1 \ \text{AND} \ \text{PATH}_2)^{\dagger} = \text{PATH}_1^{\dagger} \sqcap ... \sqcap \text{PATH}_2^{\dagger}$$
$$(\text{PATH}_1 \ \text{OR} \ \text{PATH}_2)^{\dagger} = \text{PATH}_1^{\dagger} \sqcup ... \sqcup \text{PATH}_2^{\dagger}$$
$$(\text{PATH}_1 \ \text{MINUS} \ \text{PATH}_2)^{\dagger} = \text{PATH}_1^{\dagger} \sqcap \neg \text{PATH}_2^{\dagger}$$
$$(T)^{\dagger} = T^{\dagger}$$

Fig. 10. Decidable fragment of $\mathcal{ORM}$ Derivation Rules, and its translation into the $\mathcal{DLR}^{\pm}$ description logic.

We can prove a theorem stating that the translation into $\mathcal{DLR}^{\pm}$ preserves the models of the ORM schema, namely the models of the ORM schema as defined in the semantics in the previous Section are the the same as the models of the translated $\mathcal{DLR}^{\pm}$ knowledge base. Therefore the translation is correct. The complexity of reasoning is in EXPTIME, since reasoning in $\mathcal{DLR}^{\pm}$ is EXPTIME-complete; we conjecture that reasoning is EXPTIME-hard, but we haven't proved it yet. We also believe that by considering the fragment with also *data elements*, the language remains decidable; while we can prove that the addition of unrestricted variables to the fragment makes the language undecidable.

All the examples presented in this paper belong to the decidable fragment. An example of a *cyclic* derivation rule not in the decidable fragment is in Fig. 11.

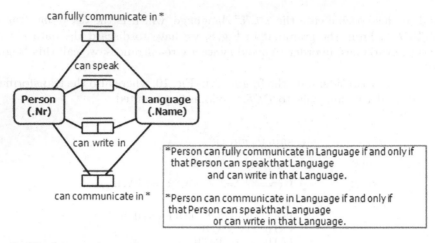

```
canFullyCommunicateIn ==
   (?1 = Person AND
       (speak.1 JOIN (speak.2 (Language = ?2))) AND
       (write.1 JOIN (write.2 (Language = ?2))))
   (?2 = Language)

canCommunicateIn ==
   (?1 = Person AND
       (speak.1 JOIN (.2 (Language = ?2))) OR
       (write.1 JOIN (.2 (Language = ?2))))
   (?2 = Language)
```

Fig. 11. A cyclic fact type Derivation Rule.

7   Conclusions and Acknowledgements

In this paper we have presented a formalisation for ORM Derivation Rules in ORM, which are rules represented by textual language which define additional constraints in a precise and unambiguous way in order to express knowledge that is beyond ORM capabilities. We have provided a precise and not ambiguous syntax and semantics, along with a provable correct encoding in Description Logics by the $\mathcal{DLR}^{\pm}$ language. Moreover, we have analysed some computational properties in order to detect a decidable fragment, useful to apply reasoning algorithms over those ORM diagrams equipped with ORM Derivation Rules.

A reasoner based on this formalisation as an extension to the ORM2 conceptual modelling tool NORMA for Microsoft Visual Studio is currently being implemented in the context of a project funded by the European Space Agency (ESA).

We thank the anonymous reviewers for the useful comments to the submitted version of this paper.

References

1. Artale, A., Franconi, E.: Extending DLR with labelled tuples, projections, functional dependencies and objectification. In: Proceedings of the 29th International Workshop on Description Logics (2016). http://ceur-ws.org/Vol-1577/paper_6.pdf
2. Berardi, D., Calvanese, D., De Giacomo, G.: Reasoning on UML class diagrams. Artif. Intell. **168**(1–2), 70–118 (2005). https://doi.org/10.1016/j.artint.2005.05.003
3. Borgida, A., Lenzerini, M., Rosati, R.: Description logics for databases. In: Baader, F., Calvanese, D., McGuinness, D.L., Nardi, D., Patel-Schneider, P.F. (eds.) The Description Logic Handbook, pp. 462–484. Cambridge University Press, New York (2003). http://dl.acm.org/citation.cfm?id=885746.885763
4. Curland, M., Halpin, T.A.: The NORMA software tool for ORM 2. In: Information Systems Evolution - CAiSE Forum 2010, pp. 190–204 (2010). https://doi.org/10.1007/978-3-642-17722-4_14
5. Fillottrani, P.R., Franconi, E., Tessaris, S.: The ICOM 3.0 intelligent conceptual modelling tool and methodology. Semantic Web **3**(3), 293–306 (2012). https://doi.org/10.3233/SW-2011-0038
6. Fillottrani, P.R., Keet, C.M., Toman, D.: Polynomial encoding of ORM conceptual models in *CFDI*. In: Proceedings of the 28th International Workshop on Description Logics (2015). http://ceur-ws.org/Vol-1350/paper-50.pdf
7. Franconi, E., Mosca, A., Solomakhin, D.: ORM2 encoding into description logics. In: 2012 International Description Logics Workshop (DL-2012) (2012)
8. Franconi, E., Mosca, A.: Towards a core ORM2 language (research note). In: Demey, Y.T., Panetto, H. (eds.) OTM 2013. LNCS, vol. 8186, pp. 448–456. Springer, Heidelberg (2013). https://doi.org/10.1007/978-3-642-41033-8_58
9. Franconi, E., Mosca, A., Oriol, X., Rull, G., Teniente, E.: OCL$_{FO}$: first-order expressive OCL constraints for efficient integrity checking. Softw. Syst. Model. **18**, 1–24 (2018). https://doi.org/10.1007/s10270-018-0688-z
10. Franconi, E., Mosca, A., Solomakhin, D.: The formalization of ORM2 and its encoding in OWL2. In: International Workshop on Fact-Oriented Modeling (ORM 2012) (2012)
11. Halpin, T.: A Logical analysis of information systems: static aspects of the data-oriented perspective. Ph.D. thesis, July 1989
12. Halpin, T.: Adding derivation rules and join paths in NORMA. Technical report, ORM Solutions, August 2013
13. Halpin, T.: Object-Role Modeling Fundamentals: A Practical Guide to Data Modeling with ORM, 1st edn. Technics Publications, Basking Ridge (2015)
14. Halpin, T., Wijbenga, J.P.: FORML 2. In: Bider, I., et al. (eds.) Enterprise, Business-Process and Information Systems Modeling, pp. 247–260. Springer, Berlin (2010)
15. Halpin, T.A.: Object-role modeling: principles and benefits. IJISMD **1**(1), 33–57 (2010). http://dx.doi.org/10.4018/jismd.2010092302
16. Halpin, T.A., Morgan, T.: Information Modeling and Relational Databases, 2nd edn. Morgan Kaufmann, San Francisco (2008)
17. Jarrar, M.: Towards automated reasoning on ORM schemes. In: ER 2007, 26th International Conference on Conceptual Modeling, pp. 181–197 (2007). https://doi.org/10.1007/978-3-540-75563-0_14

18. Jarrar, M., Meersman, R.: Ontology engineering - the DOGMA approach. In: Dillon, T.S., Chang, E., Meersman, R., Sycara, K. (eds.) Advances in Web Semantics I. LNCS, vol. 4891, chap. 3, pp. 7–34. Springer, Heidelberg (2008). http://Portal.acm.org/Citation.cfm?Id=1505684
19. Sportelli, F., Franconi, E.: Formalisation of ORM derivation rules and their mapping into OWL. In: On the Move to Meaningful Internet Systems: OTM 2016 Conferences - Confederated International Conferences: CoopIS, C&TC, and ODBASE 2016, Proceedings, Rhodes, Greece, 24–28 October 2016, pp. 827–843 (2016). https://doi.org/10.1007/978-3-319-48472-3_52

What Are the Parameters that Affect the Construction of a Knowledge Graph?

David Chaves-Fraga[1]([✉]), Kemele M. Endris[2,3], Enrique Iglesias[4],
Oscar Corcho[1], and Maria-Esther Vidal[2,3]

[1] Ontology Engineering Group, Universidad Politécnica de Madrid, Madrid, Spain
{dchaves,ocorcho}@fi.upm.es
[2] TIB Leibniz Information Centre for Science and Technology, Hanover, Germany
maria.vidal@tib.eu
[3] L3S Institute, Leibniz University of Hannover, Hannover, Germany
endris@l3s.de
[4] University of Bonn, Bonn, Germany
s6enrigle@uni-bonn.de

Abstract. A large number of datasets are made publicly available on a wide range of formats. Due to interoperability problems, the construction of RDF-based knowledge graphs (KG) using declarative mapping languages has emerged with the aim of integrating heterogeneous sources in a uniform way. Although the scientific community has actively contributed with several engines to solve the problem of knowledge graph construction, the lack of testbeds has prevented reproducible benchmarking of these engines. In this paper, we tackle the problem of evaluating knowledge graph creation, and analyze and empirically study a set of variables and configurations that impact on the behaviour of these engines (e.g. data size, data distribution, mapping complexity). The evaluation has been conducted on RMLMapper and the SDM-RDFizer, two state-of-the-art engines that interpret the RDF Mapping Language (RML) and transform (semi)-structured data into RDF knowledge graphs. The results allow us to discover unknown relations between these engines that cannot be observed in other configurations.

Keywords: Knowledge graph construction · RDFizers · Testbeds

1 Introduction

Following the FAIR principles [19] and Open data initiatives, the size of publicly available data has grown exponentially in the last decade, expecting a faster growth rate in the following years as a result of the advances in the technologies for data generation and ingestion. In order to extract values for existing datasets, several data integration approaches have been proposed in the literature [5]. The Semantic Web community has also proposed various approaches that enable the integration of data presented in diverse formats into a knowledge graph. Knowledge graphs comprise data and the knowledge that describe the main characteristics of the integrated data following a graph-based data model, e.g. RDF

© Springer Nature Switzerland AG 2019
H. Panetto et al. (Eds.): OTM 2019, LNCS 11877, pp. 695–713, 2019.
https://doi.org/10.1007/978-3-030-33246-4_43

[18]. With the aim of transforming structured data in tabular or nested formats like CSV, relational, JSON, and XML, into RDF knowledge graphs, diverse mapping languages have been proposed. Exemplary mapping languages include RDF Mapping Language (RML) [3], R2RDF [16], xR2RML [12], and R2RML [2], as well as tools like KARMA [4], SPARQL-Generate [11], and DIG [9]. Despite these developments, the absence of testbeds has prevented the community from conducting fair evaluations of the existing tools for knowledge graph creation. This testbed deficiency has also impeded for a holistic understanding about the pros and cons of the state of the art, as well as for clear directions to advance the area. Given the expected growth rate of available data, testbeds are demanded in order to devise the next generation of tools able to integrate data at scale.

Our Goals: We study the process of knowledge graph creation and analyze various variables and configurations that can impact on the performance of RDFizers – tools for transforming (semi)-structured data following mapping rules specified in the RDF Mapping Language (RML). The relevant parameters studied in this paper include selectivity of the joins between mapping rules, types of relations, and percentage of duplicates. We also present diverse examples that evidence the heterogeneous behaviour that each RDFizer may exhibit whenever small changes are conducted to the variables and the configurations of a testbed.

Our Approach: We devise a set of parameters involved in a knowledge graph construction process and we empirically show how they can impact on the behaviour of two existing RDFizers: RMLMapper[1] and SDM-RDFizer[2]; these engines are compliant with the RML specification according to a set of defined test-cases[3]. We develop a synthetic data generator for the generation of (semi)-structured data and RML mapping rules, that consider the identified set of parameters. The results of our empirical study provide evidence of the importance of the proposed set of variables and configurations during the evaluation of these tools. The testbeds used to conduct this evaluation are available online[4].

Contributions: Our main contribution includes the definition of various dimensions and set of variables to be considered during the creation of testbeds or to be measured while the evaluation of knowledge graph construction tools. Another contribution represents the empirical evaluation of the effects that the variables and configurations have on the tasks of knowledge graph creation. Furthermore, the results of the experimental study contribute to the understanding of the pros and cons of the studied RDFizers, and the directions that need to be followed in order to devise tools able to scale up to real-world scenarios.

The remainder of this article is structured as follows: Sect. 2 presents several examples where the evaluated tools exhibit unexpected behaviours. Section 3 analyses the variables and configurations that need to be considered in a testbed in order to ensure reproducibility and generality during benchmarking. Section 4

---

[1] https://github.com/RMLio/rmlmapper-java.
[2] https://github.com/SDM-TIB/SDM-RDFizer.
[3] http://rml.io/implementation-report/.
[4] https://github.com/SDM-TIB/KGC-Param-Eval.

```
<TripleMap1>
  a rr:TriplesMap;
  rml:logicalSource [
    rml:source "/home/data/Sensor.csv";
    rml:referenceFormulation ql:CSV];
  rr:subjectMap [
    rr:template "http://example.org/Sensor/{SensorID}";
    rr:class example:Sensor];
  rr:predicateObjectMap [
    rr:predicate example:isLocatedAt;        Two
    rr:objectMap [                           POMs
         rml:reference "SensorLocation"];
  rr:predicateObjectMap [
    rr:predicate example:device;
    rr:objectMap [
         rml:reference "TypeSensor"];]].
```

```
<TripleMap2>
  a rr:TriplesMap;
  rml:logicalSource [
    rml:source "/home/data/Observation.csv";
    rml:referenceFormulation ql:CSV];
  rr:subjectMap [
    rr:template "http://example.org/Observation/{ObservationID}";
    rr:class example:Observation]
  rr:predicateObjectMap [
    rr:predicate example:observationSensor;   Join Between
    rr:objectMap [                            TripleMap2 and
      rr:parentTriplesMap <TripleMap1>;       TripleMap1
      rr:joinCondition [
        rr:child "SensorLocation";
        rr:parent "ObservationLocation";]];].
```

Fig. 1. Motivating example. RML triple maps to transform two CSV files into RDF. TripleMap1 is composed of two predicate-object, i.e., Two POM. TripleMap2 has a join to TripleMap1; Observation.csv (outer relation) is joined to Sensor.csv (inner relation) and the result, SensorID, is used as an object value.

reports on the results of the empirical study where several parameters and configurations are evaluated. Related work is presented in Sect. 5, and finally, Sect. 6 concludes and give insights for future work.

2 Motivating Examples

We motivate our work by analysing different scenarios where the performance of RMLMapper and SDM-RDFizer may be affected by changing the configuration of the testbeds utilised for empirically evaluating these engines. We aim at remarking the importance of taking into account different parameters during the definition of a testbed. We first describe a scenario where naïve parameters (size and format) leads to wrong decisions during the comparing of SDM-RDFizer and RMLMapper. The testbeds include a data source with one thousand rows, different number of predicate-object (POM) in RML triple maps, and diverse configurations of selectivity of triple map joins.

RML expresses mappings to transform sources represented in (semi)-structured format, e.g. CSV or XML, into RDF. Each mapping rule in RML, named RML triple map, is represented in RDF and consists of the following parts [3]:

- A *Logical Source* that refers to a data source from where data is collected.
- A *Subject Map* that defines the subject of the generated RDF triples.
- *Predicate-Object Maps* (POM) that expresses the predicate and the object the RDF triple to be generated; a triple map can comprise several POMs.
- A *Referencing Object Map*, that indicates the reference or join condition to another triple map; the subject URL is the referenced triple map corresponds to the result of the evaluation of the join.

Figure 1 illustrates two RML triple maps. TripleMap1 is composed of two predicate-object maps, i.e. it is a Two POM mapping rule. TripleMap2 has a referencing object map that joins the records of file Observation.csv with the records of the file Sensor.csv on the attributes SensorLocation and

ObservationLocation. The result of executing the join between the two RML triple maps is the identifier of the sensor that collected the observation; this value is used as the object value of the predicate observationSensor.

2.1 Impact of Number of Predicates and Objects in Mapping Rules

In this example, we execute a testbed where three different configurations of an RML mapping rule: Two-POM, Five-POM, and Ten-POM, i.e. they correspond to three mapping rules with two, five, and ten Predicate-Object Maps, respectively. Both RDFizers exhibit a similar behaviour while the number of predicate-object maps varies from two to five POMs, as shown in Table 1. However, when more complex mapping rules with more POMs are considered, the behaviour of the SDM-RDFizer and RMLMapper is not impacted equally. Moreover, the results suggest that RMLMapper execution time increases with the number of POMs, while the SDM-RDFizer seems to be slightly affected.

Table 1. Impact of Number of Predicate-Object Maps. Various predicate object maps (POM) specified in the mapping rules. The behaviour of the two RDFizers is similar when the mapping rules are simple (less than 5 POM) but it is different when more complex mappings are running (10 POM).

Engine	Execution time (secs.)	Number of results
Two POM		
RMLMapper	0.92	2,000
SDM-RDFizer	1.72	2,000
Five POM		
RMLMapper	1.84	5,000
SDM-RDFizer	1.85	5,000
Ten POM		
RMLMapper	3.36	10,000
SDM-RDFizer	1.98	10,000

2.2 Impact of Join Selectivity

We consider the join selectivity, i.e. the cardinality of matching values from outer to the inner table (relation), in a referencing object map between two RML mapping rules; Fig. 1 depicts an example of a join between two RML triple maps. The join selectivity varies from **High Selectivity**, **Medium Selectivity**, and **Low Selectivity**, and Table 2 reports on the results of RMLMapper and SDM-RDFizer. First, it can be observed that the RMLMapper execution time increases by around 8 seconds, while the SDM-RDFizer behaviour is not equally affected by the selectivity of the join condition. As can be seen in Table 2, the SDM-RDFizer execution time (in seconds) increases from high to medium selectivity by 0.04 (from 2.16 to 2.20), then decreases from medium to low selectivity by 0.01 (from 2.20 to 2.19). On the other hand, the RMLMapper execution time increases by 1.83 (from 38.6 to 40.43), and 5.63 (from 40.43 to 46.06) seconds from high to medium, and medium to low selectivity, respectively. As in the previous example, both engines are not equally affected by the complexity of the testbed.

Table 2. Impact of Join Selectivity. Impact of the join selectivity variable over the RDFizers with high, medium and low percentage of selectivity. While RMLMapper engine behaviour increases in terms of execution time when the selectivity decreases, the SDM-RDFizer behaviour is maintained, i.e. this variable affects to the first engine but it does not impact equality to the second one.

Engine	Execution time (secs.)	Number of results
High Selectivity		
RMLMapper	38.6	2,100
SDM-RDFizer	2.16	2,100
Medium Selectivity		
RMLMapper	40.43	23,000
SDM-RDFizer	2.20	23,000
Low Selectivity		
RMLMapper	46.06	30,000
SDM-RDFizer	2.19	30,000

The uncorrelated behaviour of studied RDFizers shows clearly the need to considering diverse variables and configurations during the definition of testbeds, and thus, uncovering characteristics of these engines. In this paper, we analyze the parameters that might affect a knowledge graph construction process and evaluate some of the most problematic ones (e.g. partitioning, relation type) to remark the importance of setting them during testbed design.

3 Relevant Parameters for Testbed Design

In this section, we perform a study of the parameters that have impact on the knowledge graph construction engines. First, we identify the generic groups of parameters involved and the effect they produce in this process. Second, we provide a list of specific variables that influence the construction of knowledge graphs and determine the relationships among them. Finally, we describe each parameter in detail given the reasons why it might affect the performance of the engines. Together with these descriptions, we provide use cases over a set of parameters to illustrate the importance of involving them in a testbed definition.

As in every empirical study, we consider two groups of variables: independent and observed. The independent variables are those features that need to be specified in a benchmark to ensure that the performed evaluation is reproducible. These variables are grouped in five dimensions: mapping, data, platform, source, and output. On the other hand, observed variables correspond to those characteristics that are measured during the evaluation of the testbed and that may be influenced by independent variables. The observed variables are as follows:

- *Execution time:* The variable is in turn comprised of: *(i) Time for the first triple* (elapsed time between the engine starts and the first triple), *(ii) total execution time* required to produce all the triples of the knowledge graph.
- *Completeness:* Number of returned triples in relation to all the RDF triples that should be created according to the data and input mappings.

The relations among independent and observed variables are presented in Table 3. These variables are described in detail in the next section.

3.1 Mapping Dimension

This dimension involves the variables that characterise the mappings in terms of their structure and evaluation. Regarding the structure, there are various aspects

Table 3. Variables and Configurations. Set of variables and configurations that impact on the behaviour of the tools for knowledge graph creation. Independent variables are divided into five groups and the impact on the observed variables is depicted.

	Independent variables	Observed variables	
		Execution time	Completeness
Mapping	mapping order	✓	
	# triplesMap	✓	✓
	# predicateObjectMaps	✓	✓
	# predicates	✓	✓
	# objects	✓	✓
	# joins	✓	✓
	# named graphs	✓	✓
	join selectivity	✓	✓
	relation type	✓	✓
	object TermMap type	✓	
Data	dataset size	✓	
	data frequency distribution	✓	
	type of partitioning	✓	✓
	data format	✓	✓
Platform	cache on/off	✓	
	RAM available	✓	
	# processors	✓	
Source	distribution data transfer	✓	✓
	initial delay	✓	
	access limitation	✓	✓
Output	Serialization	✓	✓
	Duplicates	✓	✓
	Generation type	✓	✓

to be considered: mapping order, the complexity of the mapping in terms of number of predicates, objects, and the join type and selectivity.

Mapping Order. Although the mappings are usually defined using an RDF serialisation, where the order is not relevant, the features of each `rr:tripleMap` (e.g. joins) can affect the execution plan generated by each tool, having, thus, a potential negative impact on the total execution time.

Table 4. Impact of Relation Types. Various relation types in a join specified in the mapping rules. N corresponds to 15 values in the case of 1−N and N−1 relations, N and M has 10 values in the last case. RMLMapper execution time is not affected by 1−N and N−1 relation types while it is affected by N−M relations. SDM-RDFizer performs better in N−1 than 1−N but the time increases in N−M.

Engine	Execution time (secs.)	Number of results
1−1		
RMLMapper	42.86	25,000
SDM-RDFizer	2.19	25,000
1−N		
RMLMapper	43.34	22,490
SDM-RDFizer	2.19	22,490
N−1		
RMLMapper	43.26	22,490
SDM-RDFizer	2.15	22,490
N−M		
RMLMapper	78.64	25,200
SDM-RDFizer	2.33	25,200

Mapping Complexity. The number of properties defined in a rule mapping, e.g. number of predicates, objects, or named graphs may affect the observed variables because the number of triples to be generated, is related to what is specified in the mappings. Additionally, the `rr:termtype` of the `rr:objectMap` can affect the total execution time because the cost of generating a constant or a template is not the same. Finally, the join selectivity (as illustrated in Sect. 5) and types of relation have also impact on the performance of an RDFizer. In Table 4, we illustrate how the relation type affects the total execution time of the studied RDFizers. In this case, the behaviour of the RMLMapper only occurs when the relation type is N−M. However, the SDM-RDFizer behaviour is impacted during the evaluation of 1−N and N−M joins. Additionally, during the join evaluation, there are many cases when duplicates are generated, then the engines have to eliminate them. Table 5 reports on how the generation of the duplicates –during the join condition evaluation– affects the total execution time. RMLMapper decreases its performance while the percentage of duplicates increases. However, SDM-RDFizer implements optimised data structured that allow for efficiently eliminating duplicates, and seems not to be equally affected by the complexity of these configurations, e.g. number of duplicates.

3.2 Data Dimension

We describe the independent variables related with the original data that are required for the generation of a knowledge graph. Each dataset can be defined in terms of **size** and **total number of sources**. The first characteristic impacts on the number of triples that will be generated, affecting, thus, the total execution time. Additionally, the total number of sources that have to be processed to generate a knowledge graph may also affect the total execution time.

Table 5. Impact of duplicates generation during join evaluation. Various configurations of duplicates generated during the evaluation of a join between two triple maps. While the complexity of the configuration increases (more percentage of duplicates), the RMLmapper decreases its performance. Surprisingly, the SDM-RDFizer seems not to be affected by the complexity of the testbeds, and improves its performance even when the complexity of testbeds increases.

Engine	Execution time (secs.)	Number of results
Low percentage of duplicates		
RMLMapper	37.94	20,027
SDM-RDFizer	2.01	20,027
Medium percentage of duplicates		
RMLMapper	39.201	20,105
SDM-RDFizer	1.87	20,105
High percentage of duplicates		
RMLMapper	40.81	20,263
SDM-RDFizer	1.89	20,263

Partitioning and **distribution** are important variables considered in the generation of a knowledge graph. Partitioning refers to the way that a dataset is fragmented, and distribution is the format (e.g. CSV, JSON) of each partition. A dataset can be presented in only one format or in multiples formats, and this variable affects not only the total execution time but also the completeness of the results. A dataset may be fragmented into disjointed partitions; the partition may be horizontal, vertical or a combination of both. Horizontal partitioning fragments the dataset, so that, they represent different instances of the same resource (equal *TripleMaps* with different sources). Vertical partitioning produces fragments that contain at least one property of the same resources (*TriplesMaps* with *JoinCondition*). The horizontal partitioning may affect the completeness of a knowledge graph while the vertical partitioning has an influence on the execution time. Table 6 compares the behaviour of the RMLMapper and SDM-RDFizer with different configurations. The two engines increase their execution time when the horizontal partitioning is compared with and without including replication. However, RMLMapper decreases its execution time when the vertical partitions with and without replication are compared, while SDM-RDFizer execution time increases. Thus, even SDM-RDFizer is tailored towards efficient duplicate elimination, data partitioning– with and without replication – seems to affect the SDM-RDFizer performance.

Table 6. Impact of Partitioning: Various configurations of vertical and horizontal partitioning with and without duplicates. The two engines perform similar with the two cases of the horizontal partitioning but they have different behaviours in vertical partitioning.

Engine	Execution time (secs.)	Number of results
Horizontal partitioning without replication		
RMLMapper	1,904.31	310,000
SDM-RDFizer	4.84	310,000
Vertical partitioning without replication		
RMLMapper	2,067.77	310,000
SDM-RDFizer	4.73	310,000
Horizontal partitioning with replication		
RMLMapper	2,276.98	310,000
SDM-RDFizer	5.86	310,000
Vertical partitioning with replication		
RMLMapper	2,024.66	310,000
SDM-RDFizer	4.98	310,000

3.3 Platform Dimension

The platform dimension comprises variables related with the hardware used to create a knowledge graph. We include a set of variables related with the system cache, the available RAM memory for running the tool, and the number of processors of the machine. The **cache** and the **available RAM memory** may affect the total time execution. We recommend that other parameters, like the versions of operating system and processor, should be specified in the evaluation setup. To conclude, during testbed design, the platform and hardware specification requires attention and needs to be defined in detail.

3.4 Source Dimension

In this dimension, we consider different variables related with the original sources defined in the mapping rules. The **distribution data transfer**, which corresponds to the transfer time of a file by a Web service–in case the data is not in a local machine– will definitely influence the total execution time. Additionally, the **initial delay** of each engine to configure the corresponding wrappers for each data format and the **limit access** for example, a database, also strikes out the execution time and the completeness of the results.

3.5 Output Dimension

In this dimension, we consider the variables related with the output of the generation process. The **serialization** impacts on the total execution time; the effect will depend on the size of the output and the number of times the processor has to access the disk to store the output. **Generation type** represents how an RDFizer generates a knowledge graph. The generation can be continuous, e.g. the SDM-RDFizer stores each RDF triple in a file once it is generated. Contrary, the generation can be in-memory, e.g. RMLMapper stores the output when the knowledge graph is created completely. Finally, the RDFizers usually can have a flag for removing **duplicates**; this operation has to be specified in the setup because it strikes out the completeness and also the total execution time. The efficiency of the RDFizers components that eliminate duplicates, can be captured by observing the variables of this dimension.

Table 7. Datasets. Properties of datasets used in the empirical evaluations.

Dataset	#rows	#columns	#tables
1K	1,000	2	2
10K	10,000	2	2
50K	50,000	2	2

As can be observed in the results reported in this section, the behaviour of the studied engines is not equally affected by the different independent variables. Thus, benchmarks need to include all these variables in order to provide a holistic overview of the performance of the studied engines, and ensure general and reproducible evaluations.

4   Experimental Evaluation

The goal of our experiment is to assess the impact of the discussed variables and configurations during the evaluation of existing knowledge graph creation tools. We aim at answering the following research questions: **(RQ1)** What is the effect of mixing different variables in one testbed? **(RQ2)** What is the impact of considering configurations of different complexity of the same variable in one testbed? **(RQ3)** Do the different variables and configurations influence in the behaviour of existing knowledge graph creation tools? To answer these research questions, we set up the following experimental studies:

Datasets. For this evaluation, we generated three different datasets with 1,000 (1K), 10,000 (10K), and 50,000 (50K) rows, and various number of columns based on the tested parameters; Table 7 shows the properties of the datasets generated for `Relation Type`, `Join Duplicates`, and `Join Selectivity` evaluations. For the *Dataset Size (Naïve)* parameter, we generated the same number of rows as in Table 7, but with 30 columns. During the experiments, we only considered the CSV file format to represent the generated tables.

Configurations. We consider different configurations for the above-discussed variables in each dimension. `Dataset Size Configurations`: (1) SDM-RDFizer 1K; (2) SDM-RDFizer 10K; (3) SDM-RDFizer 50K; (4) RMLMapper

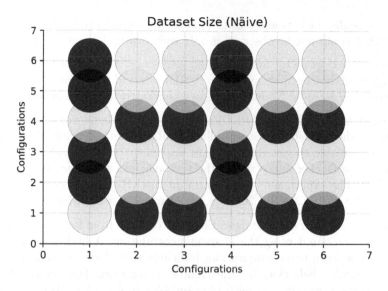

Fig. 2. Comparison of Knowledge Graph Creation Tool on Different Dataset Sizes (Naïve). The first three configurations, i.e. 1, 2, and 3 in x-axis and y-axis, correspond to SDM-RDFizer on datasets 1K, 10K, and 50K, respectively. The last three configurations, i.e. 4, 5, and 6 on x-axis and y-axis, correspond to RMLMapper 1K, 10K, and 50K, respectively. Grey bubbles correspond to correlation value of 1.0; blue bubbles show a positive correlation. The number of blue bubbles suggests that both systems exhibit similar behaviour. (Color figure online)

1K; (5) RMLMapper 10K; and (6) RMLMapper 50K. In each configuration of this parameter, we only use one data file. `Relation Type configurations:` (1) SDM-RDFizer 1-N; (2) SDM-RDFizer N−1; (3) SDM-RDFizer N−M; (4) SDM-RDFizer Combinations (all relation types); (5) RMLMapper 1−N; (6) RMLMapper N−1; (7) RMLMapper N−M; and (8) RMLMapper Combinations (all relation types). For relation cardinality, we evaluated $N = \{1, 5, 10, 15\}$ and $M = \{1, 3, 5, 10\}$. In addition, we set the percentage of rows that involve in those relation types to 25%, i.e. 25% of the overall rows from outer table have a matching join value to inner table, and 50%, respectively. `Join Duplicate configurations:` (1) SDM-RDFizer Low, (2) SDM-RDFizer High, (3) RMLMapper Low, (4) RMLMapper High. `Low` Join Duplicates refer to datasets with low percentage of duplicates, i.e. from 5% to 20% of data generated could have duplicates due to the join conditions, similarly `High` Join Duplicates refer to higher percentage of duplicates, i.e. from 30% to 50% of data generated could be duplicated. `Join Selectivity Configurations:` (1) SDM-RDFizer High; (2) SDM-RDFizer Low; (3) RMLMapper High; and (4) RMLMapper Low. In this case, the join selectivity `High` represents how many time the join condition matches the values in the inner join file from 5% to 20% of the overall rows, while `Low` means that the join condition matches range from 60% to 100% of the overall number of rows. As previously shown, we hypothesise that these configurations allow us to uncover patterns in the behaviour of these engines that could not be observed if only naïve variables were studied.

Metrics. We report on the following metrics or observed variables: **(a)** *Execution Time*: Elapsed time between execution of RDFizer and the delivery of the results. **(b)** *Number of Results*: Number of triples generated by the RDFizer.

Implementations. The SDM-RDFizer and the testbeds are implemented in Python 3.6; the SDM-RDFizer is publicly available[5]. Furthermore, Jupiter Notebooks are available to generate the data and plot the results. Additionally, we have created a Docker image to run the testbeds and reproduce the experimental results[6]. The experiments were run in an Intel(R) Xeon(R) equipped with a CPU E5-2603 v3 @ 1.60GHz 20 cores, 100G memory with Ubuntu 16.04LTS.

Testbeds. Results of each configurations are ordered from lower to higher complexity and compared using the Pearson's correlation. A high positive value of correlation between two configurations indicates that the corresponding RDFizers had a similar behavior, i.e. the trends of execution time of the tools are similar; they are represented with blue bubbles in our plots. When a configuration is compared to itself, the Pearson's correlation reaches the highest value (1.0), represented with grey bubbles in our plots. On the other hand, a negative value indicates that there is an inverse correlation between the RDFizers, i.e. they exhibit an opposite behaviour; they are represented with red bubbles.

Discussion of the Observed Results

We observe that the behaviour of the engines can be affected when multiple variables are involved in a testbed (e.g. size and relation type) or when different levels of complexity of a variables (e.g. low, high join selectivity). We discuss the obtained results during our evaluation over the different configurations and parameters involved in each experiment:

Dataset Size (Naïve): Figure 2 depicts the comparison of RDFizers when the dataset size is considered. When `configuration 1` is compared to itself, the Pearson's correlation value is 1.0; additionally, it is high and positive when it is compared to `configurations 2, 3, 5, and 6` (large blue bubbles). Using this parameter, the correlation analysis suggests that both RDFizers behave similarly in all configurations. Moreover, this indicates that only considering the data size is not enough to uncovered the properties of the studied engines.

Relation Types: Figure 3 reports on the correlation of different configurations for various join relation types. We can observe in Figs. 3a, b, and c several red bubbles, indicating a negative correlation in the behaviour of the compared configurations and RDFizers. Contrary, Fig. 3d does not depict any red bubble, suggesting thus, that the two RDFizers in all the configurations exhibit the same

---

[5] https://github.com/SDM-TIB/SDM-RDFizer.
[6] https://github.com/SDM-TIB/KGC-Param-Eval.

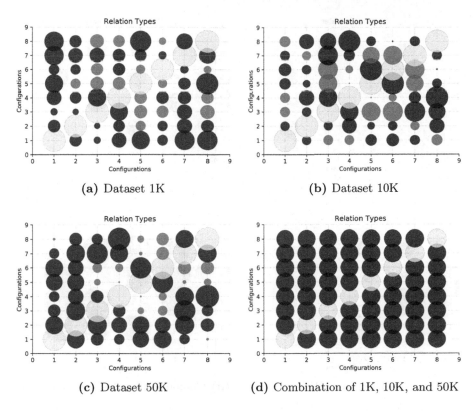

(a) Dataset 1K

(b) Dataset 10K

(c) Dataset 50K

(d) Combination of 1K, 10K, and 50K

Fig. 3. Comparison of Knowledge Graph Creation Tools on Different Types of Relations. The first four (4) configurations, i.e. 1–4 in both x-axis and y-axis, represent results of SDM-RDFizer on $1-N$, $N-1$, $N-M$, and combination of all relations types, respectively. The later configurations, 5–8 both in x-axis and y-axis, shows results of RMLMapper on $1-N$, $N-1$, $N-M$, and combination of all relations types, respectively. Grey bubbles correspond to correlation value of 1.0; blue bubbles show a positive correlation while red bubbles show a negative correlation. The plots reveal that both type of relations and size of the dataset need to be taken into account to uncover patterns in the behaviour of the engines. (Color figure online)

behaviour. These results clearly illustrate the need of considering different configurations and parameters in order to avoid drawing wrong conclusions about the main characteristics of existing tools.

Join Duplicates: Figure 4 depicts the correlation between different configurations when different setting of duplicates are produced during the execution of joins between triple maps. As can be observed, Figs. 4a, and c include several red bubbles that indicate an opposite behaviour of the RDFizers. Contrary, Figs. 4b, and d suggest that both engines behave similarly.

Join Selectivity: Figure 5 shows the correlation between different configurations for the selectivity of join conditions. Similarly, these testbeds reveal

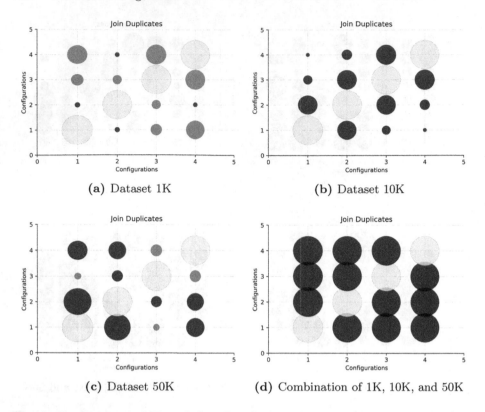

(a) Dataset 1K

(b) Dataset 10K

(c) Dataset 50K

(d) Combination of 1K, 10K, and 50K

Fig. 4. Comparison of Knowledge Graph Creation Tools on Duplicates during Join. The first two (2) configurations, i.e., 1–2 on x-axis and y-axis, represent results of SDM-RDFizer on datasets with *low* (5%–20% of data) number of duplicates and *high* (30%–50% of data) number of duplicates generated during joins, respectively. The last two configurations, i.e., 3–4 on x-axis and y-axis, represent results of RMLMapper on datasets with *low* number of duplicates and *high* number of duplicates generated during joins, respectively. Grey bubbles correspond to correlation value of 1.0; blue bubbles show a positive correlation while red bubbles show a negative correlation. Results evidence that both join duplicates and dataset size are needed for characterising an engine performance. (Color figure online)

contradicting patterns in the behaviours of the studied RDFizers. On the one hand, Figs. 5a, b, and c are composed of several red bubbles and indicate that these engines perform differently whenever the selectivity of the join condition is changed. Surprisingly, when the size of these datasets are also taken into account in the testbed (Fig. 5d), these patterns are hidden, and the results of the evaluation suggest that both RDFizers perform similarly whenever the selectivity of the join condition is changed.

The results reported in this experimental study provide clear evidence of the importance of the variables and configurations that composed the methodology devised in this work. Actually, in the four studied cases, they reveal important

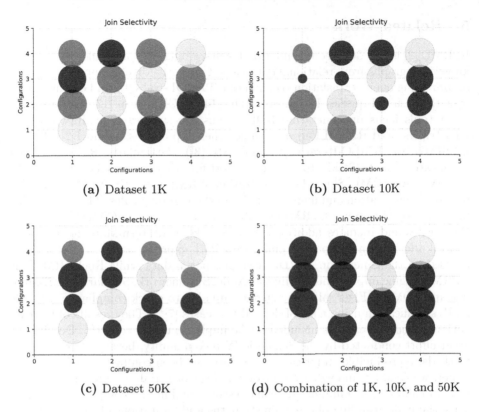

(a) Dataset 1K

(b) Dataset 10K

(c) Dataset 50K

(d) Combination of 1K, 10K, and 50K

Fig. 5. Comparison of Knowledge Graph Tools on Join Selectivity. The first two configurations, i.e., 1–2 on x- and y-axis represent SDM-RDFizer on joins with *high* selectivity (5%–20% of data) and joins with *low* selectivity (60%–100% of data), respectively. Configurations 3 and 4 represent RMLMapper on joins with *high* selectivity (5%–20% of data) and joins with *low* selectivity (60%–100% of data), respectively. Grey bubbles correspond to correlation value of 1.0; blue bubbles show a positive correlation while red bubbles show a negative correlation. Dataset size and join selectivity affect both engines differently. (Color figure online)

patterns that could not be observed whenever other parameters were studied simultaneously. Based on these observations, we can conclude that these variables and configurations should be included in the benchmarks in order to ensure that the characteristics of knowledge graph creation engines are uncovered. Thus, these observations allow us to answer our three research questions: **RQ1**, **RQ2**, and **RQ3**. We encourage developers and users of knowledge graph creation tools to bear in mind them during benchmarking in order to draw clear conclusions about the performance of their tools.

5   Related Work

R2RML [2] is a W3C recommendation for describing mapping rules to generate knowledge graphs from relational databases. Currently, diverse approaches focus on providing query-translation techniques (SPARQL-to-SQL) and optimisations over the resulted queries like morph-RDB [14] or Ultrawrap [17]. Additionally, other tools focus on generating RDF graphs are supported by R2RML (e.g. DB2Triples[7] and R2RMLParser[8]), while other approaches extend R2RML (e.g xR2RML [12], RMLC-Iterator [1], and RML [3]). Particularly, RML is defined as an extension of R2RML to provide support for other formats like JSON, XML or CSV. YARRRML [8] is other serialization of RML using the YAML format; it improves the creation and maintainability of the mapping rules. There are multiples tools that support the RML specification. For example, CARML[9] executes RML rules and includes additional features like MultiTermMap (to deal with arrays) and XML namespace (to improve XPath expressions). GeoTriples [10] is focused on the generation of RDF from geospatial data while RocketRML[10] is an RML engine implemented using the NodeJS framework. Similar to RMLMapper and SDM-RDFizer, all these engines are able to check compliance with the RML specification using a set of defined test-cases [7][11]. They results of the execution of the test-cases is included in the implementation report[12]. Despite the great effort conducted by the Semantic Web community, because of the lack of testbeds, reproducible empirical studies have not been conducted so far. In this paper, we conduct an evaluation involving a set of variables and configurations that will allow the community to define testbeds of different complexity, enabling thus, the understanding of the main strengths and limitations of the state of the art. Furthermore, the analysis of these variables and configurations will enable developers to better understand main features of their tools.

The Semantic Web community has also actively worked on the definition of several testbeds. As an example of the existing contributions, we can mention the work done in the area of federated query processing. Specifically in this area, FedBench [15] is an exemplar benchmark; it comprises three datasets, (i.e. cross-domain, life science and SP^{2}Bench), 25 queries, and two proposed metrics to measure a federated engine performance, (i.e. total execution time and number of requests to SPARQL endpoints). LSLOD is another benchmark [6] that consists of 20 queries –classified as simple and complex; it comprises ten real-world datasets from the Life Sciences domain. LSLOD proposes to measure the performance in terms of total triple pattern-wise sources selected (TTPWSS), the number of SPARQL queries ASK, the source selection time, the overall query execution time, and the result set completeness. Finally, Montoya et al. [13] identify a main drawback in existing benchmarks for SPARQL

---

[7] https://github.com/antidot/db2triples.

[8] https://github.com/nkons/r2rml-parser.

[9] https://github.com/carml/carml.

[10] https://github.com/semantifyit/RML-mapper.

[11] http://rml.io/test-cases/.

[12] http://rml.io/implementation-report/.

federated queries; particularly, Montoya et al. focus on the study of FedBench and illustrate how the lack of considering independent variables impact on the effectiveness of the benchmark, e.g. complexity of the queries, data used, platforms involved, and endpoints. They show the relevance of these variables in order to ensure reproducibility of the results observed during an empirical evaluation. In this paper, we build on the work conducted by Montoya et al. and present a similar evaluation composed of diverse variables and configurations that strike out the performance of the tools for knowledge graph creation. Our ambition is that the results of this work will facilitate the definition of suitable testbeds able to ensure reproducible experimental studies that evaluate solutions to the problem of knowledge graph creation.

6   Conclusions and Future Work

In this paper, we performed an in-depth analysis of the variables and configurations that impact on the behaviour of two RDFizers. The observation that existing RDFizers exhibit heterogeneous behaviours whenever small changes in the testbeds are conducted, motivated the need of conducting this study involving a set of parameters that can reveal patterns in the behaviour of the studied engines. Additionally, the lack of testbeds encouraged us to acquit the definition of variables and configurations that enable for the characterisation of the pitfalls of existing RDFizers and for identifying the list of challenges and research directions in the state of the art. With the proposed analysis and the results of the experimental study, we contribute with an empirical configuration that can be reused for the evaluation of other knowledge graph creation tools and mapping languages (e.g. SPARQL-Generate, TARQL, or R2RML). Furthermore, our set of variables and configurations can be utilised as a guideline during testing and benchmarking. One of the main lessons learned during the definition and evaluation of our approach, is that none of the evaluated RDFizers behaves consistently whenever the complexity of the testbeds increases. Our ambition is that the reported results inspire the community to define general testbeds that facilitate the understanding of the state of the art and the development of novel tools for the creation of knowledge graphs at large scale. In the future, we plan to define testbeds and conduct a more detailed analysis of other RDFizers and mapping languages. Moreover, we envision to motivate the community to conduct a joint effort in the definition of benchmarks that enable for fair evaluations of knowledge graph creation tools with replicable and generalizable results.

Acknowledgements. This work is partially supported by the EU H2020 RIA funded project iASiS with grant agreement No. 727658, by the Ministerio de Economía, Industria y Competitividad (Spain), by EU FEDER funds under DATOS 4.0: RETOS Y SOLUCIONES - UPM Spanish National Project (TIN2016-78011-C4-4-R), and by an FPI grant (BES-2017-082511).

References

1. Chaves-Fraga, D., Priyatna, F., Perez-Santana, I., Corcho, O.: Virtual statistics knowledge graph generation from CSV files. In: Emerging Topics in Semantic Technologies: ISWC 2018 Satellite Events, Studies on the Semantic Web, vol. 36, pp. 235–244. IOS Press, Amsterdam (2018)
2. Das, S., Sundara, S., Cyganiak, R.: R2RML: RDB to RDF mapping language, W3C recommendation, 27 September 2012. World Wide Web Consortium, Cambridge (W3C) (2012). www.w3.org/TR/r2rml
3. Dimou, A., Sande, M.V., Colpaert, P., Verborgh, R., Mannens, E., de Walle, R.V.: RML: a generic language for integrated RDF mappings of heterogeneous data. In: Proceedings of the Workshop on Linked Data on the Web Co-located with the 23rd International World Wide Web Conference (WWW 2014) (2014)
4. Gupta, S., Szekely, P.A., Knoblock, C.A., Goel, A., Taheriyan, M., Muslea, M.: Karma: a system for mapping structured sources into the semantic web. In: The Semantic Web: ESWC 2012 Satellite Events - ESWC 2012 Satellite Events, Heraklion, Crete, Greece, 27–31 May 2012. Revised Selected Papers, pp. 430–434 (2012)
5. Halevy, A.Y.: Information integration. In: Liu, L., Özsu, M.T. (eds.) Encyclopedia of Database Systems, 2nd edn. Springer, New York (2018)
6. Hasnain, A., et al.: BioFed: federated query processing over life sciences linked open data. J. Biomed. Semant. 8(1), 13 (2017)
7. Heyvaert, P., et al.: Conformance test cases for the RDF mapping language (RML). In: 1st Iberoamerican Knowledge Graphs and Semantic Web Conference (2019, to appear)
8. Heyvaert, P., De Meester, B., Dimou, A., Verborgh, R.: Declarative rules for linked data generation at your fingertips!. In: Gangemi, A., et al. (eds.) ESWC 2018. LNCS, vol. 11155, pp. 213–217. Springer, Cham (2018). https://doi.org/10.1007/978-3-319-98192-5_40
9. Knoblock, C.A., Szekely, P.A.: Exploiting semantics for big data integration. AI Mag. 36(1), 25–38 (2015)
10. Kyzirakos, K., et al.: GeoTriples: transforming geospatial data into RDF graphs using R2RML and RML mappings. J. Web Semant. 52, 16–32 (2018)
11. Lefrançois, M., Zimmermann, A., Bakerally, N.: Flexible RDF generation from RDF and heterogeneous data sources with SPARQL-generate. In: Ciancarini, P., et al. (eds.) EKAW 2016. LNCS (LNAI), vol. 10180, pp. 131–135. Springer, Cham (2017). https://doi.org/10.1007/978-3-319-58694-6_16
12. Michel, F., Djimenou, L., Zucker, C.F., Montagnat, J.: Translation of relational and non-relational databases into RDF with xR2RML. In: 11th International Conference on Web Information Systems and Technologies (WEBIST 2015), pp. 443–454 (2015)
13. Montoya, G., Vidal, M.-E., Corcho, O., Ruckhaus, E., Buil-Aranda, C.: Benchmarking federated SPARQL query engines: are existing testbeds enough? In: Cudré-Mauroux, P., et al. (eds.) ISWC 2012. LNCS, vol. 7650, pp. 313–324. Springer, Heidelberg (2012). https://doi.org/10.1007/978-3-642-35173-0_21
14. Priyatna, F., Corcho, Ó., Sequeda, J.F.: Formalisation and experiences of R2RML-based SPARQL to SQL query translation using morph. In: 23rd International World Wide Web Conference, WWW 2014, Seoul, Republic of Korea, 7–11 April 2014, pp. 479–490 (2014)

15. Schmidt, M., Görlitz, O., Haase, P., Ladwig, G., Schwarte, A., Tran, T.: FedBench: a benchmark suite for federated semantic data query processing. In: Aroyo, L., et al. (eds.) ISWC 2011. LNCS, vol. 7031, pp. 585–600. Springer, Heidelberg (2011). https://doi.org/10.1007/978-3-642-25073-6_37
16. Sequeda, J.F., Arenas, M., Miranker, D.P.: OBDA: query rewriting or materialization? in practice, both! In: The Semantic Web - ISWC 2014-13th International Semantic Web Conference, Riva del Garda, Italy, Proceedings, Part I, 19–23 October 2014, pp. 535–551 (2014)
17. Sequeda, J.F., Miranker, D.P.: Ultrawrap: SPARQL execution on relational data. J. Web Semant. **22**, 19–39 (2013)
18. Vidal, M., Endris, K.M., Jazashoori, S., Sakor, A., Rivas, A.: Transforming heterogeneous data into knowledge for personalized treatments - a use case. Datenbank-Spektrum **19**(2), 95–106 (2019)
19. Wilkinson, M.D., et al.: The FAIR guiding principles for scientific data management and stewardship. Sci. Data **3**, 160018 (2016)

Creating a Vocabulary for Data Privacy

The First-Year Report of Data Privacy Vocabularies and Controls Community Group (DPVCG)

Harshvardhan J. Pandit[1]([✉]), Axel Polleres[2]([✉]), Bert Bos[3], Rob Brennan[4],
Bud Bruegger[5], Fajar J. Ekaputra[6], Javier D. Fernández[2],
Roghaiyeh Gachpaz Hamed[1], Elmar Kiesling[6], Mark Lizar[7], Eva Schlehahn[5],
Simon Steyskal[8], and Rigo Wenning[3]

[1] Trinity College Dublin, Dublin, Ireland
pandith@tcd.ie
[2] Vienna University of Economics and Business, Vienna, Austria
axel.polleres@wu.ac.at
[3] W3C/ERCIM, Sophia Antipolis, France
[4] Dublin City University, Dublin, Ireland
[5] Unabhängiges Landeszentrum für Datenschutz Schleswig-Holstein, Kiel, Germany
[6] Vienna University of Technology, Vienna, Austria
[7] OpenConsent/Kantara Initiative, London, UK
[8] Siemens AG, Vienna, Austria

Abstract. Managing privacy and understanding handling of personal data has turned into a fundamental right, at least within the European Union, with the General Data Protection Regulation (GDPR) being enforced since May 25th 2018. This has led to tools and services that promise compliance to GDPR in terms of consent management and keeping track of personal data being processed. The information recorded within such tools, as well as that for compliance itself, needs to be interoperable to provide sufficient transparency in its usage. Additionally, interoperability is also necessary towards addressing the right to data portability under GDPR as well as creation of user-configurable and manageable privacy policies. We argue that such interoperability can be enabled through agreement over vocabularies using linked data principles. The W3C Data Privacy Vocabulary and Controls Community Group (DPVCG) was set up to jointly develop such vocabularies towards interoperability in the context of data privacy. This paper presents the

We thank all members of the W3C DPVCG for their feedback and input to this work: a preliminary outline of the goals of CG has been presented in ISWC2018's SWSG workshop [5] where we also gathered valuable feedback by the participants; this work is the first complete presentation of the resulting, proposed vocabulary elaborated by the DPVCG since. This work was supported by the European Union's Horizon 2020 research and innovation programme under grant 731601 (SPECIAL), by the Austrian Research Promotion Agency (FFG) under the projects "EXPEDiTE" and "CitySpin", by the ADAPT Centre for Digital Excellence funded by SFI Research Centres Programme (Grant 13/RC/2106), and co-funded by European Regional Development Fund.

© Springer Nature Switzerland AG 2019
H. Panetto et al. (Eds.): OTM 2019, LNCS 11877, pp. 714–730, 2019.
https://doi.org/10.1007/978-3-030-33246-4_44

resulting Data Privacy Vocabulary (DPV), along with a discussion on its potential uses, and an invitation for feedback and participation.

Keywords: Privacy · GDPR · Interoperability · Semantic web

1   Introduction

Concerns regarding privacy and trust have been raised to a point where regulators, citizens, and companies have started to take action. Services on the Web are often very complex orchestrations of co-operation between multiple actors, and the processing of personal data in Big Data environments is becoming more complex while being less transparent.

Yet, while from a legal point of view, the adoption of the General Data Protection Regulation (GDPR) [10] in April 2016, as well the California Consumer Privacy Act (CCPA) [1] of 2018 regulate processing of personal data, their technical implementation in operative IT systems is far from being standardised. While building privacy-by-design [7] into systems is a much wider scope, we lack the tools, standards, and best practices for those wanting to be good citizens of the Web to provide interoperable and understandable privacy controls, or to keep records of data processing in an accountable manner, with the possible exception of work on permissions [15] and tracking protection [12], but even those only cover partial aspects.

To this end, the work presented in this paper aims to set a basis for the establishment of *interoperable standards* in this domain. In particular, it addresses the following gaps by complementing existing (W3C) standards:

- There are no standard vocabularies to describe and interchange personal data. Such vocabularies are relevant, for instance, to support data subjects' right to data portability under Article 20 of the GDPR [10].
- There are no agreed upon vocabularies or taxonomies for describing *purposes* of personal data handling and *categories of processing*: the GDPR requires legal bases for data processing, including consent, be tied to the specific *purposes* and *processing* of personal data to justify their lawful use. Consequently personal data processing should be logged with a standard reference to a purpose which complies with the norms set by the legal bases - such as the individual's consent. The concrete taxonomies for representing this information in the context of personal data handling are not yet standardised.
- There are no agreed upon vocabularies or ontologies that align the *terminology of privacy legislations* - such as the GDPR, to allow organisations to claim compliance with such regulations using machine-readable information.

The herein presented Data Privacy Vocabulary (DPV) aims at addressing these challenges by providing a comprehensive, standardized way set of terms for annotating Privacy policies, consent receipts, and - in general - records of personal data handling. To this end, the rest of the paper is structured as follows: Sect. 2 explains the setup and governance of the DPV Community group within the World Wide Web Consortium (W3C) whereafter Sect. 3 summarizes pre-existing relevant vocabularies and standards that served as inputs. Section 4 describes the methodology that we applied in reconciling these towards the DPV vocabulary. The vocabulary itself and its modules are described in Sect. 5 (omitting detailed descriptions of all classes and properties, which can be found in the published W3C CG draft at https://www.w3.org/ns/dpv). We close with a discussion of applications and adoption (Sect. 6) followed by conclusions and a call for participation and feedback (Sect. 7).

2   DPVCG: Data Privacy Vocabularies and Controls CG

To address the gaps mentioned in Sect. 1, a W3C workshop was announced[1], which received 32 position statements and expressions of interest. These were used to create an agenda based on standards and solutions for interoperable privacy. The workshop took place on 17th and 18th April 2018 in Vienna and consisted of about 40 participants. Discussions and interactions were structured into sessions around the four themes of: (1) 'relevant vocabularies and initiatives', (2) 'industry perspective', (3) 'research topics', and (4) 'governmental side and initiatives'. The workshop concluded with a discussion of the next steps and priorities in terms of standardisation and interoperability. The identified goals were (from highest to lowest priority): taxonomies for regulatory privacy terms (including GDPR), personal data, purposes, disclosure and consent (as well as other legal bases), details of anonymisation (and measures taken to protect personal data), and for recording logs of personal data processing.

Following this, a W3C Community Group (CG) with the title 'Data Privacy Vocabularies and Controls CG' (DPVCG) was formally established on 25th May 2018 - the implementation date of the GDPR. The group has a total of 55 participants to date representing academia, industry, legal experts, and other stakeholders. Its discussions are open via the public mailing list[2], along with a wiki[3] documenting meetings, resources, general information.

The CG had its first face-to-face meeting on 30th August 2018 co-located with the MyData 2018[4] conference at Helsinki, Finland. The goal of this meeting was agreement on the first steps and deliverables of the CG as well as establishment of meeting and management procedures. The outcome of this meeting was agreement on working towards the following deliverables:

– **Use cases and requirements:** Collect and align common requirements from industry and stakeholders to identify areas where interoperability is needed in the handling of personal data. The outcome of this was a prioritised list of requirements to enable interoperability in the identified use-cases.

---

[1] https://www.w3.org/2018/vocabws/.
[2] https://lists.w3.org/Archives/Public/public-dpvcg/.
[3] https://www.w3.org/community/dpvcg/wiki/Main_Page.
[4] https://mydata2018.org/.

- **Alignment of vocabularies and identification of overlaps:** Collect existing vocabularies and standardisation efforts, and identify their overlaps and suitability for covering the requirements prioritised in step one. The identified vocabularies are presented in Sect. 3.
- **Glossary of GDPR terms:** An understandable and interoperable glossary of common terms from the GDPR and an analysis of how they are covered by the agreed vocabularies.
- **Vocabularies:** Based on the heterogeneity or homogeneity of identified use-cases and requirements, create a set of (modular) vocabularies for exchanging and representing information in an interoperable form for personal data, purposes, processing, consent, anonymisation, and transparency logs. The resulting vocabulary is presented in Sect. 5.

A second face-to-face meeting was conducted on 3rd and 4th December 2019 at Vienna, Austria. The goal of this meeting was to analyse the collected use-cases and vocabularies, to establish agreement on the requirements for vocabularies to be delivered, and to plan ahead towards their conception and completion. A third face-to-face was organised on 4th and 5th April 2019 in Vienna and Dublin to finalise the vocabulary and reach an agreement towards the first public draft. The outcome of the meeting was agreement of terms used and its expression using RDF and OWL. The meeting also provided agreement over the namespace of the vocabulary, its hosting, and documentation. After over a year of collaborative effort, the CG published the '*Data Privacy Vocabulary*' (DPV) on 26th July 2019. The CG is currently welcoming feedback for DPV from the community and stakeholders in terms of comments, suggestions, and contributions.

3 Existing and Relevant Vocabularies

Existing relevant use cases and vocabularies were collected and documented in the wiki[5] through individual submissions by CG members. The wiki page for each vocabulary presents a summary, its relevance, covered requirements, uptake, and applicable use-cases. Relevant terms were then identified from each vocabulary and categorised as per requirements. These were used as the basis for discussions regarding terms to be included and aligned in the DPV.

3.1 Existing Standards and Standardisation Efforts

The CG considered several web-relevant standards for terms relevant towards identified requirements: PROV-O [17] (and its extension P-Plan [13]) for provenance, ODRL [15] for expressing policies, vCard [14] for describing people and organisations, Activity Streams [27] for describing activities on the web, and Schema.org [26] for metadata used in description of web pages.

---

[5] https://www.w3.org/community/dpvcg/wiki/Use-Cases,_Requirements,
_Vocabularies.

The CG also considered standardisation efforts undertaken by bodies relevant to the areas of privacy and interoperability. Classification of Everyday Living (COEL) [8] describes a privacy-by-design framework for the collection and processing of behavioural data with a focus on transparency and pseudo-anonymisation. It was developed by OASIS, which is a non-profit organisation dedicated to the development of open standards.

The ISA[2] is a programme by the by the European Parliament and the Council of European Union for development of interoperable framework and solutions, which includes a set of vocabularies, termed 'Core Vocabularies' [2], for person, business, location, criterion and evidence, and public organisation. IEEE P7012 [20] is a work-in-progress effort to standardise privacy terms in a machine-readable manner for use and sharing on the web.

Consent Receipt [18] is an interoperable standard developed by the Kantara Initiative for capturing the consent given by a person regarding use of their personal data. The standard enables creation of receipts in human as well as machine readable formats for expressing information using pre-defined categories for personal data collection, purposes, and its use and disclosure. However, it does not address the requirements specified by the GDPR.

The Platform for Privacy Preferences Project (P3P) [19] is a (now-abandoned) protocol for websites to declare their intended use of personal data collection and usage with an emphasis on providing users with more control of their personal information when browsing the web. P3P provided a machine-readable vocabulary for websites and users to define their policies, which were then compared to determine privacy actions.

3.2 Vocabularies Addressing Privacy and GDPR

The Scalable Policy-aware Linked Data Architecture For Privacy, Transparency and Compliance (SPECIAL) is an European H2020 project that uses semantic-web technologies in the expression and evaluation of information for GDPR compliance. SPECIAL has developed vocabularies for expressing Usage Policy [6] and Policy Log [4] in order to evaluate whether the recorded use of personal data is compliant with a given consent.

Mining and Reasoning with Legal Texts (MIREL) is another European H2020 project that uses semantic-web technologies for GDPR compliance. It has developed PrOnto (Privacy Ontology for Legal Reasoning) [21] - a legal ontology of concepts consisting of privacy agents, personal data types, processing operations, rights and obligations.

GDPRtEXT [23] provides a linked data version of the text of the GDPR that makes it possible for links to be established between information and the text of the GDPR by using RDF and OWL. It also provides a thesauri or vocabulary of concepts defined or referred to within the GDPR in a machine-readable manner using SKOS.

GDPRov [24] is an ontology to represent processes and activities associated with the lifecycle of personal data and consent as an abstract model or plan indicating what is supposed to happen, as well as the corresponding activity logs indicating things that have happened. It extends PROV-O and P-Plan with GDPR-specific terminology. GConsent [22] is an ontology for expressing necessary information for management and evaluating compliance of consent as governed by the obligations and requirements of the GDPR.

Considered ontologies developed prior to implementation of GDPR also include an ontology to express privacy preferences [25], a data protection ontology based on the GDPR [3], and an ontology for expressing consent [11].

4   Methodology

The process of vocabulary development was largely shaped by discussions and interactions between CG members, and was (informally) based on NeOn methodology scenarios [28]. The CG decided to work towards creating a generic or top-level vocabulary rather than restricting it to a particular domain or use-case in order to facilitate universal application and adoption. For this, existing work and approaches were analysed to identify terms relevant for describing specific categories of information, such as purposes of processing and personal data.

The analysis of existing vocabularies revealed a lack of top-level or abstract concepts necessary to provide an extendable mechanism for representing information in a hierarchical structure. Therefore, the CG decided to work towards creating a vocabulary that provided the necessary top-level concepts and relationships in a hierarchical structure. Agreement over categories of terms to be included in the vocabulary and relevance of existing terms was carried out through discussions, and documented in the wiki[6].

While initially working towards a hierarchical taxonomy, the need for representing relationships and logic between terms led towards the creation of an ontology, with RDF/OWL being used to provide standardised serialisation. A base vocabulary was created based on the SPECIAL Usage Policy Language [6] to represent a policy, and additional terms were structured to extend them as modular (sub-)ontologies. Terms were then added in a top-down fashion, based on existing work or its identified absence.

Documentation of how terms were proposed, discussed, and added was recorded through a collaborative spreadsheet hosted on the Google Sheets platform[7]. The spreadsheet contained separate tabs for each 'modular' ontology and a base ontology representing combined their combined usage to represent personal data handling. The columns in the spreadsheet were mapped to semantic web representations, as depicted in Table 1. The vocabulary was created by using the Google Drive API in a script[8] that extracted terms to create documentation of the taxonomy. This was then modified to generate RDF serialisations using

---

[6] https://www.w3.org/community/dpvcg/wiki/Taxonomy.
[7] https://www.google.com/sheets/about/.
[8] https://github.com/dpvcg/extract-sheets/.

Table 1. Columns in spreadsheet for generating RDF serialisations and documentation

Column name	Description	Representation
Class/Property	If term is Class or Property	*rdfs:Class/rdfs:Property*
Term	The IRI of the term	as IRI
Description	Description or definition	*dct:description*
Domain	Domain if it is a property	*rdfs:domain*
Range	Range if it is a property	*rdfs:range*
Super classes/properties	Parent classes or properties	*rdfs:isSubClassOf*
Sub classes/properties	Child classes or properties	N/A
Related terms	Terms relevant to this	*rdfs:seeAlso*
How related?	Nature of relation	Use as is
Comments	Comments used for discussion	N/A
Source	The source of the term	*rdfs:isDefinedBy*
Date	Date of creation	*dct:created*
Status	Status e.g. accepted, proposed	*sw:term_status*
Comments	Comments to be recorded	*rdfs:comment*
Contributor	Dc:creator	*dct:creator*
Date-accepted	Date of acceptance	*dct:date-accepted*
Resolution	Record e.g. minutes of meeting	as IRI

rdflib[9] as RDF/OWL was later adopted[10] and documentation using ReSpec[11]. Plans for additions and changes to the vocabulary will follow a similar approach, where the proposal is documented and agreed upon through the public mailing list or CG meetings.

5   Data Privacy Vocabulary

As a result of the process above, the '*Data Privacy Vocabulary*' (DPV) has been published on 26th July 2019 at the namespace http://w3.org/ns/dpv (for which we will use the prefix dpv:) as a public draft for feedback. The current vocabulary provides terms (classes and properties) to annotate and categorise instances of *legally compliant personal data handling*. In particular, DPV provides extensible concepts and relationships to describe the following components (which are elaborated in further sections):

1. Personal Data Categories
2. Purposes

---

[9] https://github.com/RDFLib/rdflib.
[10] In hindsight, a better alternative was mapping languages such as R2RML https://www.w3.org/TR/r2rml/ for creating RDF data from spreadsheets.
[11] https://github.com/w3c/respec.

3. Processing Categories
4. Technical and Organisational Measures
5. Legal Basis
6. Consent
7. Recipients, Data Controllers, Data Subjects

These terms are intended to express *Personal Data Handling* in a machine-readable form by specifying the *personal data categories* undergoing some *processing*, for some *purpose*, by *data controller*, justified by *legal basis*, with specific *technical and organisational measures*, which may result in data being shared with some *recipient*. The vocabulary is built up in a modular fashion, where each 'module' covers one of the above listed aspects, and which is linked together using a core Base Vocabulary.

5.1 Base Ontology

The 'Base Ontology' describes the top-level classes defining a policy for legal personal data handling. Classes and properties for each top-level class are further elaborated using sub-vocabularies, which are available as separate modules and are outlined in subsequent sections. While all concepts in DPV share a single `dpv:` namespace, the modular approach of providing the base ontology as a separate module makes it possible to use sub-vocabularies without the `dpv:PersonalDataHandling` class, for example to refer only to purposes. Exceptions to this are the NACE purpose taxonomy (cf. details Sect. 5.3) extending the `dpv:Sector` concept in the *Purposes* vocabulary, and the GDPR legal bases taxonomy (cf. details in Sect. 5.6) extending the top-level `dpv:LegalBasis` class - which are provided under a separate namespaces to indicate their specialisation. The core concepts of the Base Ontology module and their relationships are depicted in Fig. 1.

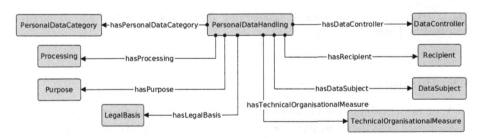

Fig. 1. DPV base ontology classes and properties

5.2 Personal Data Categories

DPV provides broad top-level personal data categories adapted from the taxonomy provided by EnterPrivacy [9]. The top-level concepts in this taxonomy refer to the nature of information (financial, social, tracking) and to its inherent source (internal, external). Each top-level concept is represented in the DPV as a class, and is further elaborated by subclasses for referring to specific categories of information - such as preferences or demographics.

Regulations such as the GDPR allow information about personal data used in processing to be provided either as specific instances of persona data (e.g., "John Doe") or as categories (e.g., name). Additionally, the class dpv:Special-CategoryOfPersonalData represents categories that are 'special' or 'sensitive' and require additional conditions as per GDPR's Article 9.

The categories defined in the personal data taxonomy can be used directly or further extended to refer to the scope of personal data used in processing. The taxonomy can be extended by subclassing the respective classes to depict specialised concepts, such as "likes regarding movies" or combined with classes to indicate specific contexts. The class dpv:DerivedPersonalData is one such context where information has been derived from existing information, e.g., inference of opinions from social media. Additional classes can be defined to specify contexts such as use of machine learning, accuracy, and source.

While the taxonomy is by no means exhaustive, the aim is to provide a sufficient coverage of abstract categories of personal data which can be extended using the subclass mechanism to represent concepts used in the real-world. For instance, Fig. 2 shows the hierarchy of concepts for classifying depictions of individuals in pictures.

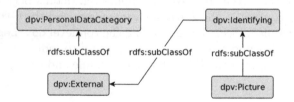

Fig. 2. Hierarchy of concepts for classifying depictions of individuals in pictures (inspired by EnterPrivacy [9])

5.3   Purposes

DPV at present defines a hierarchically (by subclassing) organized set of generic categories of data handling *purposes*, as depicted in Fig. 3. Overall, DPV provides a list of 31 suggested purposes as subclasses of these generic purposes which may be extended as shown in Listing 1 by further subclassing to create more specific ones. As regulations such as the GDPR generally require a specific purpose to be declared in an understandable manner, we suggest to such declare specific purposes as subclasses of one or several dpv:Purpose categories to make them as specific as possible, and to always annotate them with a human readable description (e.g., by using rdfs:label and rdfs:comment).

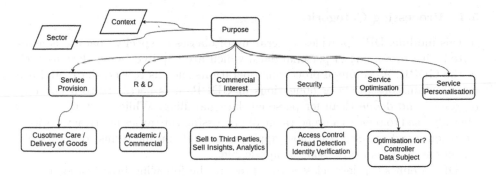

Fig. 3. Categories of purposes for data processing in DPV

```
1   :NewPurpose
2       rdfs:subClassOf dpv:DeliveryOfGoods, dpv:FraudPreventionAndDetection ;
3       rdfs:label "New Purpose" ;
4       rdfs:comment "Intended delivery of goods with fraud prevention" .
```

Listing 1: Extending pre-defined purposes with human-readable descriptions

Moreover, purposes can be further restricted to specific *contexts* using the class `dpv:Context` and the property `dpv:hasContext`. Similarly, DPVCG provides a way to restrict purposes to a specific *business sector*, i.e., allowing/restricting data handling to purposes related to particular business activities, using the class `dpv:Sector` and the property `dpv:hasSector`. Potential hierarchies for defining such business sectors include NACE[12] (EU), NAICS[13] (USA), ISIC[14] (UN), and GICS[15]. At the moment, we recommend to use NACE (EU) codes using `dpv-nace:NACE-CODE` as shown in Listing 2, where the prefix `dpv-nace:` represents the DPV defined namespace http://www.w3.org/ns/dpv-nace.

```
1   :SomePurpose a dpv:Purpose ;
2       rdfs:label "Some Purpose" ;
3       dpv:hasSector dpv-nace:M72 .
```

Listing 2: Creating a new purpose and restricting it to Scientific Research using the NACE sector code (M.72)

---

[12] https://ec.europa.eu/eurostat/ramon/nomenclatures/index.cfm? TargetUrl=LST_NOM_DTL&StrNom=NACE_REV2.
[13] https://www.census.gov/eos/www/naics/.
[14] https://unstats.un.org/unsd/classifications.
[15] https://en.wikipedia.org/wiki/Global_Industry_Classification_Standard#cite_note-mapbook-1.

5.4   Processing Categories

In this module, DPV provides a hierarchy of classes to specify operations associated with processing of personal data, which are required by regulations such as the GDPR. As common processing operations such as collect, share, and use have certain constraints or obligations in GDPR, it is necessary to accurately represent and define them for personal data handling. While the term 'use' is liberally used to refer to a broad range of processing categories in privacy notices, we recommend to select the most appropriate and specific terms to accurately reflect the nature of processing as applicable.

DPV defines top-level classes to represent the following broad categories of processing - Disclose, Copy, Obtain, Remove, Store, Transfer, Transform, and Use, as shown in Fig. 4. Each of these are then again further expanded using subclasses to provide 33 processing categories, which includes terms defined in the definition of processing in GDPR (Article 4-2).

The DPVCG taxonomy further provides properties with a boolean range to indicate the nature of processing regarding *Systematic Monitoring, Evaluation or Scoring, Automated Decision-Making, Matching or Combining, Large Scale processing,* and *Innovative use of new solutions,* as these are relevant towards assessment of processing for GDPR compliance.

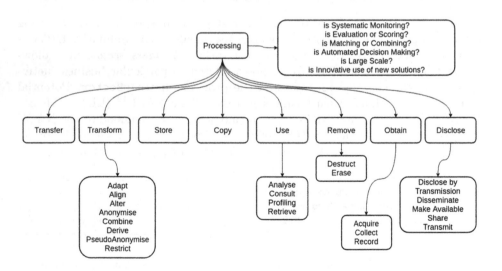

Fig. 4. Categories of data processing in DPV

5.5   Technical and Organisational Measures

Regulations require certain technical and organisational measures to be in place depending on the context of processing involving personal data. For example, GDPR (Article 32) states implementing appropriate measures by taking into account the state of the art, the costs of implementation and the nature, scope, context and purposes of processing, as well as risks, rights and freedoms. Examples of measures stated in the article states include:

- the pseudonymisation and encryption of personal data
- the ability to ensure the ongoing confidentiality, integrity, availability and resilience of processing systems and services
- the ability to restore the availability and access to personal data in a timely manner in the event of a physical or technical incident
- a process for regularly testing, assessing and evaluating the effectiveness of technical and organisational measures for ensuring the security of the processing

To address these requirements, DPV defines a module comprising of a hierarchical vocabulary for declaring such technical and organisational measures, as shown in Fig. 5.

For any of the DPV declared measures, we provide a generic ObjectProperty (`dpv:measureImplementedBy`), and for the values of this attribute, we either allow a blank node with a single `rdfs:comment` to describe the measure, or a URI to a standard or best practice followed, i.e. a well-known identifier for that standard or a URL where the respective document describes the standard. The class *StorageRestriction* represents the measures used for storage of data with two specific properties provided for storage location and duration restrictions. While at the moment, we do not yet refer to specific certifications or security standards, in the future, we plan to provide a collection of URIs for identifying recommended standards and best practices, as they further develop. Feedback on adding specific ones to future versions of the DPV specification is particularly welcome.

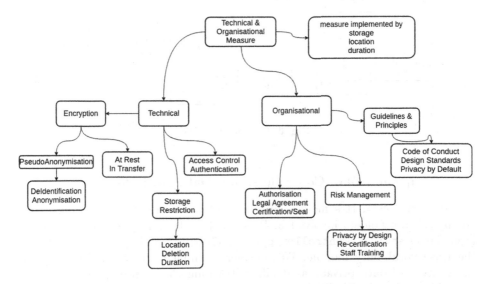

Fig. 5. Technical and organisational measures in DPV

5.6   Consent and Other Legal Bases

While the vocabulary provides dpv:LegalBasis as a top-level concept representing the various legal bases that can be used for justifying processing of personal data, such legal bases may be defined differently in different legislations within the scope of legal jurisdictions. For the particular case of GDPR, we therefore provide the legal bases specific to GDPR as a separate aligned vocabulary, under the https://www.w3.org/ns/dpv-gdpr namespace (prefix: dpv-gdpr:).

This vocabulary defines the legal bases defined by Articles 6 and 9 of the GDPR, including consent, along with their description and source within. For example, dpv-gdpr:A6-1-b denotes the legal basis provided by *fulfillement/performance of a contract*.

In addition to the legal bases, Consent is addressed with additional properties and classes within the core DPV vocabulary as it is a common form of legal justification across jurisdictions. The module describing consent, illustrated in Fig. 6, provides the necessary terms to describe consent provision, withdrawal, and expiry. This is based on an analysis of existing work in the form of Consent Receipt [18] and GConsent [22].

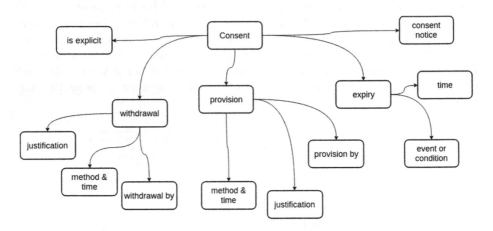

Fig. 6. Consent in DPV

5.7   Recipients, Data Controllers, and Data Subjects

Last but not least, this module of the ontology is meant for defining a taxonomy of stakeholders involved in Personal DataHandling, extending the top level classes dpv:DataController, dpv:DataSubject, and dpv:Recipient from the Base vocabulary module. We consider defining recipients is important in the context of data privacy as it allows tracking the entities personal data is shared/transferred with. Similarly, a categorisation of Data Controllers and Data Subjects has bearing on the privacy of personal data handling, especially when considering situations such as where data subjects are children. The vocabulary currently provides only a few top-level classes to describe such recipients and data subjects, with an invitation to suggest/provide more terms for future releases:

- dpv:Child as a subclass of dpv:DataSubject in order to capture policies and restrictions of data Handling related to children;
- dpv:Processor as a subclass of dpv:Recipient to denote natural or legal persons, public authorities, agencies or other bodies which *processes personal data on behalf of the controller*;
- dpv:ThirdParty as a subclass of dpv:Recipient to provide a generic class for third party recipients, i.e. natural or legal persons, public authorities, agencies or bodies *other than the data subject, controller, processor* and persons who, under the direct authority of the controller or processor, are authorised to process personal data.

6   Potential Adoption and Usage

The primary aim of DPV is to assist in the representation of information concerning privacy in the context of personal data processing. To this end, it models concepts at an abstract or top-level to cover a broad range of concepts. This shall enable the DPV to be used as an domain-independent vocabulary which can be extended or specialised for specific domains or use-cases. Though the DPV does not define or restrict how such extension should be created, this section highlights some suggested methods for its adoption and usage.

Firstly, the modular nature of DPV enables adoption of a selected subset of the vocabulary only to address a specific use-case. For example, an adopter may only wish to utilise the concepts under *Purpose* and *PersonalDataCategory* without using/describing all aspects of a particular *PersonalDataHandling* from the base vocabulary.

In addition, the use of RDFS and OWL enables extending the DPV in a compatible manner to define domain-specific use-cases. For example, an extension targeting the finance domain can define additional concepts by using RDFS' subclass mechanism. Such an extension, when represented as an ontology, will be compatible with the DPV, and will enable semantic interoperability of information, and ideally applications such as automated compliance checking for privacy policies and data handling records annotated with DPV and its extensions.

The DPV is intended to be used as an interoperable vocabulary where terms are structured in a hierarchy and have unambiguous definition to enable common agreement over their semantics. Such usage involves limiting the concepts to other pre-defined vocabulary, as seen in the case of Consent Receipts [18] and the SPECIAL vocabularies [4].

The SPECIAL project[16] actually has demonstrated how the above-mentioned use case of automated compliance checking can be implemented based modeling

---

[16] http://www.specialpricacy.eu.

privacy policies and log records of personal data handling in a manner compatible with DPV [16]. The SPECIAL project with its industry use case partners may also be viewed as a set of early adopters of the DPV, where currently further tools and a scalable architecture for transparent and accountable personal data processing in accordance with GDPR is being developed.

7 Conclusion

The Data Privacy Vocabulary is the outcome of cumulative effort of over a year in W3C's Data Privacy Vocabulary and Controls Community Group (DPVCG). It represents the first step towards an effort to provide a standardised vocabulary to represent instances of legally compliant personal data handling. To this end, it provides a modular vocabulary representing concepts of personal data categories, purposes of processing, categories of processing, technical and organisational measures, legal bases, recipients, and consent.

With the onset of regulations in the privacy domain, the DPV fills an important gap by providing the necessary terms in an interoperable and extendable format. It is, to the best of our knowledge, currently the most comprehensive vocabulary regarding definition of privacy-related terms in addition to being aligned with regulations such as the GDPR, and attempting to comprehensively cover the relevant aspects of personal data handling. For continued development of this work, the DPVCG is currently inviting participation in the form of comments, feedback, and suggestions. Specifically, the DPVCG kindly requests proposals to extend its initial taxonomies by additional terms, where these are missing or need refinements in order to describe specific use cases of personal data handling.

Future plans also include producing documented examples of how the DPV could be adopted for further specific use-cases. Examples include annotating privacy policies, documenting information for specific laws such as GDPR, and producing transparent, machine-readable processing logs (for instance by mapping the DPV to existing database schemas and thereby generating/aggregating machine-readable transparency records directly out of their logging.

References

1. Assembly Bill No. 375 Privacy: personal information: businesses. California State Legislature, June 2018. https://leginfo.legislature.ca.gov/faces/billTextClient.xhtml?bill_id=201720180AB375
2. Aleksandrova, Z.: Core Vocabularies, November 2016. https://ec.europa.eu/isa2/solutions/core-vocabularies_en
3. Bartolini, C., Muthuri, R.: Reconciling data protection rights and obligations: an ontology of the forthcoming EU regulation. In: Workshop on Language and Semantic Technology for Legal Domain, p. 8 (2015)
4. Bonatti, B.A., Dullaert, W., Fernandez, J.D., Kirrane, S., Milosevic, U., Polleres, A.: The SPECIAL policy log vocabulary, November 2018. https://aic.ai.wu.ac.at/qadlod/policyLog/

5. Bonatti, P., et al.: Data privacy vocabularies and controls: semantic web for transparency and privacy. In: Semantic Web for Social Good Workshop (SWSG) Co-located with ISWC2018. CEUR Workshop Proceedings, vol. 2182, October 2018. CEUR-WS.orghttp://ceur-ws.org/Vol-2182/paper_3.pdf

6. Bonatti, P.A., Kirrane, S., Petrova, I.M., Sauro, L., Schlehahn, E.: The SPECIAL usage policy language, V0.1. Technical report (2018). https://www.specialprivacy.eu/vocabs

7. Cavoukian, A., et al.: Privacy by design: the 7 foundational principles. Information and Privacy Commissioner of Ontario, Canada 5 (2009)

8. Classification of Everyday Living Version 1.0, January 2019. https://docs.oasis-open.org/coel/COEL/v1.0/os/COEL-v1.0-os.pdf

9. Cronk, R.J.: Categories of personal information, March 2017. Enterprivacy Consulting Group. https://enterprivacy.com/2017/03/01/categories-of-personal-information/

10. European Parliament and Council: Regulation (EU) 2016/679 of the European Parliament and of the Council of 27 April 2016 on the protection of natural persons with regard to the processing of personal data and on the free movement of such data, and repealing Directive 95/46/EC (General Data Protection Regulation), May 2016

11. Fatema, K., Hadziselimovic, E., Pandit, H.J., Debruyne, C., Lewis, D., O'Sullivan, D.: Compliance through informed consent: semantic based consent permission and data management model. In: Proceedings of the 5th Workshop on Society, Privacy and the Semantic Web - Policy and Technology (PrivOn2017) (PrivOn) (2017). http://ceur-ws.org/Vol-1951/PrivOn2017_paper_5.pdf

12. Fielding, R.T., Singer, D.: Tracking Preference Expression (DNT), January 2019. https://www.w3.org/TR/tracking-dnt/

13. Garijo, D., Gil, Y.: The P-PLAN ontology, March 2014. http://vocab.linkeddata.es/p-plan/

14. Iannella, R., McKinney, J.: vCard Ontology - for describing People and Organizations, May 2014. https://www.w3.org/TR/vcard-rdf/

15. Iannella, R., Villata, S.: ODRL Information Model 2.2, February 2018. https://www.w3.org/TR/odrl-model/

16. Kirrane, S., et al.: SPECIAL deliverable d2.8 - transparency and compliance algorithms v2, November 2018. https://www.specialprivacy.eu/images/documents/SPECIAL_D28_M23_V10.pdf

17. Lebo, T., et al.: PROV-O: The PROV Ontology (2013)

18. Lizar, M., Turner, D.: Consent Receipt Specification v1.1.0. Technical report, Kantara Initiative (2017). https://docs.kantarainitiative.org/cis/consent-receipt-specification-v1-1-0.pdf

19. P3p: The Platform for Privacy Preferences. https://www.w3.org/P3P/

20. P7012 - Standard for Machine Readable Personal Privacy Terms. https://standards.ieee.org/project/7012.html

21. Palmirani, M., Martoni, M., Rossi, A., Bartolini, C., Robaldo, L.: PrOnto: privacy ontology for legal reasoning. In: Kő, A., Francesconi, E. (eds.) EGOVIS 2018. LNCS, vol. 11032, pp. 139–152. Springer, Cham (2018). https://doi.org/10.1007/978-3-319-98349-3_11

22. Pandit, H.J., Debruyne, C., O'Sullivan, D., Lewis, D.: GConsent - a consent ontology based on the GDPR. In: Hitzler, P., et al. (eds.) ESWC 2019. LNCS, vol. 11503, pp. 270–282. Springer, Cham (2019). https://doi.org/10.1007/978-3-030-21348-0_18

730   H. J. Pandit et al.

23. Pandit, H.J., Fatema, K., O'Sullivan, D., Lewis, D.: GDPRtEXT - GDPR as a linked data resource. In: Gangemi, A., et al. (eds.) ESWC 2018. LNCS, vol. 10843, pp. 481–495. Springer, Cham (2018). https://doi.org/10.1007/978-3-319-93417-4_31

24. Pandit, H.J., Lewis, D.: Modelling provenance for GDPR compliance using linked open data vocabularies. In: Proceedings of the 5th Workshop on Society, Privacy and the Semantic Web - Policy and Technology (PrivOn2017) (PrivOn) (2017). http://ceur-ws.org/Vol-1951/PrivOn2017_paper_6.pdf

25. Sacco, O., Passant, A.: A Privacy Preference Ontology (PPO) for linked data. In: LDOW. Citeseer (2011). http://citeseerx.ist.psu.edu/viewdoc/download?doi=10.1.1.357.3591&rep=rep1&type=pdf

26. Schema.org. https://schema.org/

27. Snell, J.M., Prodromou, E.: Activity streams 2.0, May 2017. https://www.w3.org/TR/activitystreams-core/

28. Suárez-Figueroa, M.C., Gómez-Pérez, A., Fernández-López, M.: The NeOn methodology for ontology engineering. In: Suárez-Figueroa, M.C., Gómez-Pérez, A., Motta, E., Gangemi, A. (eds.) Ontology Engineering in a Networked World, pp. 9–34. Springer, Heidelberg (2012). https://doi.org/10.1007/978-3-642-24794-1_2

Cloud and Trusted Computing
(C&TC) 2019

C&TC 2019 PC Co-chairs' Message

Welcome to the Cloud and Trusted Computing 2019 (C&TC2019), the 9th International Symposium on Secure Virtual Infrastructures, held in Rhodes, Greece, as part of the OnTheMove Federated Conferences & Workshops 2019.

The conference solicited submissions from both academia and industry presenting novel research in the context of cloud and trusted computing. Theoretical and practical approaches for the following main areas have been called:

- Trust, security, privacy and risk management
- Data Management
- Infrastructures and architectures
- Applications

In this scope, specific challenges have been addressed by our authors, including risk optimization and decision support. All submitted papers passed through a rigorous selection process involving at least three reviews.

Organizing a conference like C&TC is a team effort, and many people need to be acknowledged. First, we would like to thank authors who submitted their contributions to this event for having chosen C&TC to present and discuss their work. Their contributions were the basis for the success of the conference.

Second, we would like to acknowledge the hard work of all our colleagues from the Program Committee, experts in the research domains of the conference, for performing the extremely valuable tasks of reviewing and discussing the contributions.

Finally, we would like to thank everyone at the OTM organizers team for their exceptional support and, in particular, the OTM Conferences & Workshops General Chairs Robert Meersman, Tharam Dillon, Hervé Panetto, and Ernesto Damiani, and the Publication Chair Christophe Debruyne.

All of these people contributed to the Proceedings of the 9th International Symposium on Cloud and Trusted Computing, and all of them deserve our highest gratitude. Thank you!

October 2019

C. A. Ardagna
E. Damiani
A. Vasilakos
C&TC2019 Co-chair

Multi-cloud Services Configuration Based on Risk Optimization

Oscar González-Rojas$^{(\boxtimes)}$ and Juan Tafurth

Systems and Computing Engineering Department, School of Engineering,
Universidad de los Andes, Bogotá, Colombia
{o-gonza1,jc.tafurth10}@uniandes.edu.co

Abstract. Nowadays risk analysis becomes critical in the Cloud Computing domain due to the increasing number of threats affecting applications running on cloud infrastructures. Multi-cloud environments allow connecting and migrating services from multiple cloud providers to manage risks. This paper addresses the question of how to model and configure multi-cloud services that can adapt to changes in user preferences and threats on individual and composite services. We propose an approach that combines Product Line (PL) and Machine Learning (ML) techniques to model and timely find optimal configurations of large adaptive systems such as multi-cloud services. A three-layer variability modeling on domain, user preferences, and adaptation constraints is proposed to configure multi-cloud solutions. ML regression algorithms are used to quantify the risk of resulting configurations by analyzing how a service was affected by incremental threats over time. An experimental evaluation on a real life electronic identification and trust multi-cloud service shows the applicability of the proposed approach to predict the risk for alternative re-configurations on autonomous and decentralized services that continuously change their availability and provision attributes.

Keywords: Multi-cloud services · Variability modeling · Product line configuration · Risk optimization · Machine learning

1 Introduction

A multi-cloud service is a business resource that offers a specific functionality within a cloud services catalog [5] from multiple providers. A multi-provider configuration requires the interoperability between autonomous and decentralized services that continuously change their availability and provision attributes due to threats materialized over time. These services can be analyzed as a dynamic PL in which a service is configured according to user specified requirements (*e.g.*, service level agreements), and is able to change according to contextual events (*e.g.*, service-component failures, threats) and new requirements. In this context, there is a need to adapt configured products as PLs and business' needs evolve (see a motivation case study in Sect. 2.1).

© Springer Nature Switzerland AG 2019
H. Panetto et al. (Eds.): OTM 2019, LNCS 11877, pp. 733–749, 2019.
https://doi.org/10.1007/978-3-030-33246-4_45

This paper addresses the question of how to model and configure multi-cloud services that can adapt to changes in user preferences and threats on individual and composite services. Existing approaches allow selecting cloud services at the design-time from a single provider. Some of them analyze static values for risk criteria [2,10], whereas others frame risk analysis as a supervised learning problem [1,9]. However, risk data is quantified by people but not by the actual performance information of services. Multi-cloud configuration approaches at deployment-time [7,8] lack of models that account for the variability of individual services, the risk of composite services, and user preferences (see Sect. 2.2).

The paper proposes combining PL and ML techniques to model and find optimal configurations of large adaptive systems such as multi-cloud services (see Sect. 3). A program synthesis named CoCo is used to manage three levels of variability modeling to configure multi-cloud solutions. Domain variability supports changes in the multi-cloud environment (*cf.* product family model) by describing non-functional properties of cloud services. Preferences variability describes changes in user preferences to configure cloud applications according to business restrictions on non-functional properties such as costs, quality attributes, or risks. Adaptation variability describes contextual events (*reconfiguration rules*) that change the configuration of a multi-cloud application (*i.e.,* a product). ML regression algorithms are used to quantify the risk of resulting configurations by analyzing how a service was affected by incremental threats over time. Resulting risk data is used for further analysis within an existing framework for impact and risk assessment of cloud services. This capability of services for learning about risk behavior allows adapting multi-cloud services according to user expectations.

We illustrate the applicability of our approach to configure and adapt a real life electronic identification and trust multi-cloud service. Several threats were simulated to quantify and predict the risk for alternative re-configurations on autonomous and decentralized cloud services. These prediction values had low error rates when comparing with actual values on services behaviors (see Sect. 4). Conclusions and future work are presented in Sect. 5.

2   Motivation Scenario and Related Work

2.1   Requirements for Modeling a Multi-cloud Service

A company operating identity services requires to build a cloud controller to govern an *online identity service application*, supporting international electronic transactions. Figure 1 illustrates a multi-cloud scenario composed of three services and the alternatives to deploy them by two different cloud providers. The identity application manages electronic documents (*e.g.,* certificates), of official use in different countries, emitted by organizations subscribed to the service.

The *authentication* service is replicated in multiple clouds to authenticate and authorize users and to handle their session during the entire process. The *signature* service is also replicated to increase trust (*i.e.,* with digital signs) in the authentication and storage services. The *storage* service handles all requests

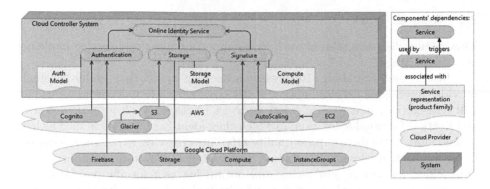

Fig. 1. Excerpt of an identity multi-cloud service configuration.

for file persistence in the file system or in external databases. Additionally, the service migrates clouds upon fail-over.

The underlying infrastructure must auto-scale to different country-based transaction rates, be highly available, and resilient, to comply with a high Service Level Agreement (SLA) enforced by governments. These continuous changes scope at least three challenges for variability modeling on multi-cloud services.

C1 *Domain Variability.* Information about cloud services is obtained directly from providers' public sites or APIs, which change without notice. Therefore, an approach to manage and evolve a cloud computing domain model, with its provider-specific models, is required.

C2 *Preferences Variability.* Searching configurations across multiple clouds must analyze particular attributes for each provider. Therefore, user preferences on business restrictions (*e.g.,* costs, quality attributes, risk) must be modeled and the searching process must be automated to find the optimal configurations for a cloud service. For instance, the following preferences are defined by multiple users to configure the cloud controller: (1) the three services are mandatory, (2) use the best data availability SLA for the storage service, and (3) use the highest scalability level for the signature service.

C3 *Adaptation Variability.* Federated multi-provider configuration requires interoperability between autonomous decentralized services that continuously change their availability and provision attributes. Therefore, the reconfiguration of products in multi-cloud environments is required to migrate clouds based on provision variability such as resilience to global SLAs, fails, and performance changes. In particular, risk analysis becomes critical due to the increasing number of threats affecting applications running on cloud infrastructures. Variation of services can be achieved by using (1) a multi-cloud deployment model that migrates applications to achieve fault tolerance, or (2) a multi-cloud replication model, in which several services replicate over multiple clouds to achieve high availability, or work together as a single solution.

2.2 Related Work

This section discusses related work that supports multi-cloud service modeling at a design stage.

Martens and Teuteberg [10] present a decision model that evaluates single provider inter-dependencies between static cost criteria (*e.g.*, coordination) and risk criteria (*i.e.*, integrity) to select a service. Assis *et al.* [2] propose a 4-layer architecture for cloud federation, in which they identify critical gaps such as lack of modelling methods to express quality attributes (service, experience, security) in service contract design. In contrast, our approach allows the configuration of multi-cloud services by evaluating and optimizing user-specific preferences on risks and non-functional properties of individual and composite services. Risk criteria is quantified by using statistical methods.

Ahmed and Abraham [1] test different ML algorithms to assess the risks involved when migrating to cloud services. Risk data is gathered from surveying the opinion of experts. In contrast, we provide a modelling approach to describe the main attributes and measures associated to cloud services, a ML method to quantify risks data, and a method to configure a multi-cloud service based on user preferences. The authors in [9] present a time series method to select cloud services by evaluating the performance–costs and potential risks resulting from fluctuating quality of service and flexible service pricing. They translate Service Measurement Index (SMI) attributes into quantitative definitions to rank cloud services. Despite the very high alignment with our approach, they do not take into account multi-cloud characteristics of how risk is affected by different clouds. We configure multi-cloud services by formulating the selection of services from multiple providers as a multi-criterion decision-making (MCDM) problem. We quantify the risks of services by using ML techniques whereas the optimal multi-cloud service configuration considering user-specific needs is solved by using constraint programming.

Despite the approach we present in this paper does not support deploying the related applications across the clouds, our approach can complement deployment approaches [7,8] with capabilities to search and select optimal resources by analyzing the variability of individual services, the risk of composite services, and user preferences on quality attributes.

3   Risk-Based Configuration of Multi-cloud Services

3.1 CoCo: A Program Synthesis for Managing Variability

A PL describes the set of *common* and *variable* characteristics a product family, in which valid products must be derived satisfying domain constraints to allow *mass customization* and development of unified *platforms* [3].

CoCo is a program synthesis tool that supports PL configuration by using a Model-Driven Engineering approach [11]. A PL is represented in CoCo by an Extended Feature Model (EFM), a tree-based structure where nodes represent product features, attributes represent non-functional properties on features (*e.g.*, costs, risks), and edges represent constraints. CoCo transforms systems' requirements specification into Constraint Programming (CP) programs executed by an off-the-shelf CSP solver (*e.g.*, Choco).

Modeling *domain variability* requires representing large and inter-dependent application domains (**C1** in Sect. 2). CoCo contains a composition metamodel representing variability in single or multi-PL environments [13], by including their related features, attributes, and three types of constraints. Tree Constraints (TCs) restrict children features of a parent: *(1) Mandatory*: all children must be selected; *(2) Optional*: children can be selected optionally; *(3) Or-group*: at least one child should be selected; and *(4) Alternative-group*, at most one child should be selected. Cross-Tree Constraints (CTCs) relate non-connected features: (1) *Requires:* selecting the antecedent feature demands the selection of the consequent feature; and (2) *Excludes:* deselects the consequent feature upon selection of the antecedent. Cross-Model Constraints (CMCs) inter-relate EFMs in multi-PL environments by using *forces* and *prohibits* constructs, which respectively carry the semantics of the *requires* and *excludes* CTCs constraints, combined with the groupings of TCs. Using multiple product lines is required to support the evolution, analysis, and reuse of independent product lines representing a particular domain (*cf.* cloud providers).

Modeling *preferences variability* must specify and compute user preferences (**C2** in Sect. 2). CoCo provides a Domain-Specific Language (DSL) to specify feature attributes (*e.g.*, costs), and Configuration Constraints (CCs) to define global decision rules to select preferred variants [12]. These correspond to *(1) Optimization:* applying a *minimization* or *maximization* function to the aggregation value of attributes; *(2) Hard-limit:* defining boundaries (*e.g.*, less than, greater than) over the aggregated value of an attribute type; *(3) Selection state:* forcing selection of a set of features over the product family; and *(4) Finite domain:* reducing the size of feature attribute's domain.

Modeling *adaptation variability* must allow representing contextual events of a given domain (**C3** in Sect. 2). These events are statically modeled in CoCo as on-demand user preferences applied on a new domain variability model containing the changes of cloud provision attributes. For instance, stakeholders may demand the selection of the cheapest configuration at the beginning of the system's operating life cycle. However, the system quality attributes may vary overtime (*i.e.*, if a service is unavailable, the value of its feature attribute becomes 0), requiring the new configuration discarding services and enforcing new ones.

3.2 Risk Quantification of Cloud Services

A cloud service risk is the scenario where a service is exposed to an external attack and has a probability of being affected by a threat. This is frequently given as a qualitative and subjective value, however it is possible to find a quantitative value if its described as a combination of threats affecting a service.

Any given service can be described as a combination of the following seven Service Measure Index (SMI) attribute groups [4]. *Accountability* contains attributes used to measure the properties related to the cloud service provider's organization. We measure the Compliance attribute which is the ability of the solution to commit to infrastructure best practices for quality, performance and resilience. *Agility* indicates the ability to change quickly to client's strategies and with minimal disruption. We measure the Scalability attribute which allows a cloud service provider to increase or decrease the amount of resources to meet client requirements and agreed SLAs. *Assurance* indicates how likely the service is available as specified. We measure the Availability attribute as the appropriateness of the service availability window, as well as the likelihood that the availability window will actually be provided to clients. *Financial* is the amount of money spent on the service by the client. We do not measure attributes in this category. *Performance* covers the features and functions of the provided services. We measure Accuracy and Service response time attributes. Accuracy is the extent to which a service adheres to its requirements. Service response time is the time between a service request and the availability of its response. *Security and privacy* indicates the effectiveness of a cloud service provider to ensure that only the personnel with granted privileges can use or modify data/work products. There are no attributes measured from this category. *Usability* is the simplicity with which a service can be used. We do not measure these attributes.

The risk for a pre-configured cloud service is quantified as follows.

Identify the threats of cloud services and relate them with SMI attributes (see Table 1). The affected SMI attributes are calculated using formulas derived from SMICloud [4], whereas threats are identified following the QUIRC quantitative risk and impact assessment framework [14].

Table 1. Threat specification for the illustrated multi-cloud scenario

Service	Threat	Affected SMI attribute
Authentication service	Insecure interfaces and API	Scalability, Availability, Accuracy
	Eavesdropping	Accuracy, Data privacy & Loss
Compute services	Shared services issues	Accuracy, Response time
	Shared performance degradation	Capacity, Elasticity, Data privacy & Loss
	Service injection attack	Compliance, Confidentiality, Availability, Data privacy & Loss
Storage services	Data loss	Availability, Accuracy
	Data leakage	Availability, Accuracy
	Remote data loss of control	Availability, Reliability
	Multilocation access	Location, Availability, Compliance

Calculate Threat Impact. In general, a risk is quantified as the product between the probability (P) and the impact (I) of a specific threat event $(_T)$ [15]. The overall risk for a given configuration (R_c) is quantified as the weighted average of the security risk for each threat. For example, if you have a configuration using the authentication service from GCP and AWS, but only the compute service from GCP, then threat calculation should only include those services.

Threat weight (W) sets a weight relative to client requirements by considering the total number of attributes (n), the value of a SMI attribute affected by threat i (A_f), and the rating given by the client to the attribute (R_a) according to metrics defined previously. The overall *impact* (I) of the system attributes is relative to the client requirements and it will change depending of the conditions of the system. The impact is computed for all possible configurations by adding all the weighted impacts and then diving the result by the number of impacts (see Eq. 1). This value must be feed into the regression model which contains all the information about past configurations.

$$R_c = \sum_{i=1}^{n} W_{T_i}(I_{T_i} * P_{T_i}); \quad W_T = \sum_{i=1}^{n} \frac{R_{a_i}}{\#A_f}; I_T = \sum_{i=1}^{n} \frac{A_f}{\#A_f} \tag{1}$$

According to this equation, the risk of a configuration is calculated as the weighted average of each individual risk associated with a specific threat (R_c). The weighting factor for a threat (W_T) is calculated as the average of the quantitative weights of each SMI attribute associated with the threat, represented as the rating given by an expert in the field (R_{a_i}). This helps to associate the factor in which an attribute affects the outcome of a threat materialization against a vulnerability. The impact is calculated as the average of the nominal values of each SMI attribute associated with the threat (A_f). This value is defined specifically for each attribute depending on its definition.

Calculate Probability and Risk. The *probability* value is quantified by using ML methods. These methods are effective in creating models based on organized quantitative data as presented in domains of cloud computing risk analysis [1] and software project risk management [6]. R_c in Eq. 1 can be associated with a linear regression equation from the ML domain. Linear regression is a model that assumes a linear relationship between the input variables and the single output variable. Specifically, in the risk quantification domain, the input variable is the impact of a given threat (X) and the output variable is the risk for that threat (Y). With these values it is possible to find the coefficients (β, α) of the linear equation (see Eq. 2), which define the probability values of a threat (P). This is done by leveraging a computational estimation of expert insights over risk on multicloud configurations and then solving the last variable on the risk calculation equation. After this is completed, the risk for future configurations could be calculated using preexisting data and new feedback given to the system to refined probability values based on experimental results.

$$Y = \beta X + \alpha, \quad \text{where} \quad \beta = P_i w_i \implies P_i = \frac{\beta}{w_i} \tag{2}$$

This equation of a linear regression has been selected due to its mathematical similarity to the analyzed risk model for multi-cloud services. This equation assumes that, for a limited number of cases, the risk analysis can be simplified enough as to be represented or at least accurately reduced to a linear behavior of interrelated facts. Hence the goal is to verify if the risk can be accurately modeled and optimized by reducing the complexity to the linear domain while still maintaining a reasonable certainty under strict configuration parameters.

Evaluate risk on different service configurations by including variations of threats. For example, the Storage service in the multicloud scenario contains four threats, data loss, data leakage, remote data loss of control and multi-location access. Each threat contains a defined set of attributes, but this service could have many more threats if a detailed analysis is performed. Increasing the threats does not add complexity to the calculation but requires more data to be collected so a reliable calculation of the SMI attributes can be performed.

4   Validation

This section illustrates the applicability of our approach to model and configure variability at different levels. Then, it evaluates the behavior of the risk quantification method for configuring a service in single and multiple cloud scenarios.

4.1   Configuring a Multi-cloud Service with CoCo

We use CoCo to generate the coordinator system required for the multi-cloud scenario described in Sect. 1. Figure 2 presents an excerpt of CoCo's capabilities to specify and process the variability of the analyzed cloud services.[1]

Domain variability in Fig. 2 includes TCs, CTCs, CMCs, features, and feature attributes. The *Multi-cloud* demands the selection of at least one of the four child features (*i.e., or-group* TC), while both *AWS* and *GCP* Feature Models (FMs) have *optional* TCs with all of their child features. There are three *requires* CTCs, the selection of the *Signature* feature demands the selection of the *Authentication, Compute*, and *ObjectStorage* features. Additionally, two CMCs exist, stating that if the *Authentication* feature is selected, the *AWS Cognito*, or the *GCP Firebase* features should be selected. The *SLA* attribute is specified and associated to the *EC2, S3, Compute Engine*, and *Object Storage* features to allow optimal product configurations.

Preferences variability includes three CCs specified with CoCo's DSL: two maximization functions over the aggregated values of the *Scalability* and *SLA* attribute types, and a selection state CC that forces the selection of the *Signature* feature in the *Multi-cloud* FM. CoCo found 17 PL configurations from these constraints, from which one was manually selected.

Adaptation variability is enforced with the definition of two *configuration constraints*. The first constraint discards the *EC2* service on the event that its

---

[1] The complete PL specification is available at: https://github.com/governit/MultiCloud/tree/master/MultiCloudPL/models.

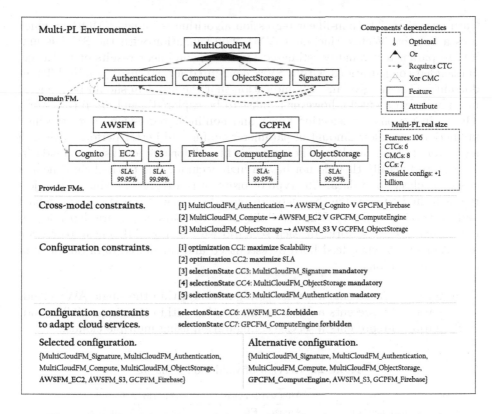

Fig. 2. Sample of CoCo's variability modeling for the multi-cloud scenario.

availability SLA is equal or less than 95%. CoCo reconfigured the multi-cloud environment by replacing the *EC2* service with the *CGP Compute Engine* service (*cf.* Alternative configuration), when the corresponding SLA was changed in the variability model.

The complete multi-cloud motivation scenario modeled in CoCo is composed of 106 features, one *mandatory* TC, 24 *optional* TCs, five *alternative-group* TCs, 20 *or-group* TCs, six CTCs in the *Multi-cloud* FM (both requires and excludes CTCs), and eight CMCs. From this specification, CoCo calculates over one billion valid configurations. When computing the three specified CCs, a total of 17 PL configurations are found in the Pareto front (*i.e.*, multi-objective optimization front) taking 0.211*s*. Similar performance results are obtained when calculating the alternative configuration.

4.2   Evaluation of the Risk Quantification Method

Configuration of Test Scenarios. The following scenarios were defined to test the behavior of including ML algorithms to quantify risks for product configurations. In particular, the behavior on linear and non-linear algorithms to analyze incremental threats on cloud services and the behavior of these algorithms to learn over time. The non-linear regression algorithm is named SMOReg, which uses a Support Vector Machine (SVM). The validation with the SVM is limited to parameters roughly estimated by taking non-linear results of Weka recommended configurations with a SVM configured for ML exercises in different domains. This can give an early indication that the problem should be modeled in a non-linear scenario, however it must to be explored deeply in future work. The main reasons for selecting linear and nonlinear regressions were the high prediction speed, low amount of parameter tuning and better performance with low amount of sample data. These reasons fit well for risk analysis on cloud services since typically they do not have a high accuracy due to the long time and costs to collect good data. The type of problem is a regression since the objective is to find a risk value that depends on independent parameters (see impact and probability in Eq. 1). The possibility that the parameters are dependent is not explored in this work. In each scenario we test how ML linear regression algorithms work when feed both by estimated and calculated data on different cloud configurations.

- Scenario #1 represents a service configuration within the single AWS cloud.
- Scenario #2 represents a service configuration within the single GCP cloud.
- Scenario #3 represents a service configuration using multiple clouds.

Table 2. Overview of validation scenarios

Threat	Affected service	Scenario	Affected attributes
Attack on virtualization	Amazon EC2	1,3	Availability
	Amazon S3	1,3	Accuracy
	Google Compute	2,3	Auditability
	Google Storage	2,3	Suitability
			Service response time
Abuse and nefarious use of cloud computing	Amazon EC2	1,3	Auditability
	Amazon S3	1,3	Suitability
	Google Compute	2,3	
	Google Storage	2,3	
Denial of service attack	Amazon EC2	1,3	Availability
	Amazon S3	1,3	Suitability
	Amazon Cognito	1,3	Auditability
	Google Compute	2,3	Scalability
	Google Storage	2,3	
	Google IAM	2,3	
Insecure interface and API	Amazon EC2	1,3	Suitability
	Amazon S3	1,3	Auditability
	Amazon Cognito	1,3	Service response time
	Google Compute	2,3	Accuracy
	Google Storage	2,3	
Malicious insiders	Amazon EC2	1,3	Auditability
	Amazon S3	1,3	Service response time
	Google Compute	2,3	Accuracy
	Google Storage	2,3	

Table 2 summarizes how the services of the three scenarios were configured in terms of threats and SMI attributes that affect each threat.

The selection of these attributes largely depend on the qualitative definition of the threat and its analysis. For example, the *attack on virtualization* threat exploits a virtual machine vulnerability to be accessed illegally via its hypervisor or surrounding network, causing that asset to be potentially cut off (availability) or compromised (accuracy, auditability) or bloated with malware that could affect its performance (suitability, service, response time).

Data Gathering. Every configuration consists on a key-value pair for each of the SMI attributes described in Subsect. 3.2. The values for this dataset correspond to real data collected from three different sources[2]. First, SMI attributes were obtained using the NewRelic infrastructure component[3]. We used the component called insights and the available dashboards (*i.e.*, Billing, EBS, EC2, ELB, IAM, Lambda) to collect information about the communication with specific AWS web services. Those dashboards were used to query average values of SMI attributes during two months to find the risk value of a given service in the configuration. Each set of exported values contains between 10 to 30 rows. Second, we gathered information from Service Status Web Pages from AWS[4] and GCP providers[5]. These pages provide information about service availability and the number of times the service has been down. This is useful to calculate attributes such as SLA and Accuracy. The dataset contains AWS information about service status up to 1 year, whereas GCP status page data correspond to a time frame, which is the time Google makes this data available. Finally, we used data found in cloud documentation to figure out some SMI attributes such as SLA, provider contract and cost. Values for these attributes were assumed based on public information found in the provider web page.

The dataset was stored in a non-relational database to be able to access them with ML ready to work utilities (*e.g.*, Weka) or by programming languages code. This database is formatted in JSON. These document-based collections allow fast access for different scenarios to be described with all the required information in a single document to be easily analyzed. Table 3 exemplifies client requirements, cloud services, and threats that are the characterized in the integrated dataset. The higher value in the client requirements section means that the attribute is more important to the client, this value needs to be normalized in the implementation. Values on service characterization represent SMI attributes normalized for each service. Finally, the values for the impact, probability and risk of each service for each threat are represented as an array.

Each configuration has its own resultant dataset expressed as a Weka ARFF (Attribute-Relation File Format) file that the program builds. This file contains

---

[2] Datasets are available at: https://github.com/governit/MultiCloud/tree/master/RiskQuantification.

[3] http://newrelic.com/.

[4] https://status.aws.amazon.com/.

[5] https://status.cloud.google.com/.

Table 3. Sample of the integrated dataset.

Client Requirements Characterization Example

Attribute	Solution #1	#2	#3	Authentication #1	#2	#3	Compute #1	#2	#3	Storage #1	#2	#3
Availability	0.9906	0.996	0.996	–	–	–	–	–	–	–	–	–
Capacity	3	4	3	–	–	–	–	–	–	–	–	–
Auditability	–	–	–	0	0	0	1	1	1	1	1	1
Portability	–	–	–	1	1	1	0	0	0	0	0	0
Accuracy	4	3	4	–	–	–	–	–	–	–	–	–
Scalability				1	1	1	2	3	3	3	2	1
High availability	0	0	1	0	0	1	0	0	1	0	0	1
Replication	0	0	1	0	0	1	0	0	1	0	0	1

Service Characterization Example

	AWS EC2	AWS EBS	AWS Glacier	GCP Compute	GCP Compute AppEngine	GCP Storage Object
	0.999606	0.999606	0.999999	0.988623	0.98	0.45
	1	1	1	1	0	0
	0.61	0.61	0.31	0.8	0.77	0.77
	0.8	0.8	0.2	0.8	–	–
	0.1	0.8	0.8	0.7	0.7	0.7
	1	1	1	1	1	1
	0.9995	0.9995	0.9995	0.89	0.89	0.89

Threat Characterization Example

Threat	Affected Attributes	Affected Service	Probability	Impact	Risk
Attack on virtualization	Availability Accuracy Auditability Suitability Service Response Time	AWS-EC2 AWS-S3 GCP-Compute GCP-Storage	[0.5,0.69,0.62 0,56,0.1,0.1,0. 0.2,0.25,0.26...]	[0.9.0.8,0.8,0.7 1,1,0.8,0.8,0.9, 1,1,1,0.9,0.5...]	[0.9,0.8,0.7, ,0.6,1,0.3,0.7, 0.4,0.8,0.5,1]
Abuse and nefarious use of cloud computing	Auditability Suitability	AWS-EC2 AWS-S3 AWS-Cognito GCP-Compute	[0.5,3,1,3.06, 2.97,2.89,2.81, 2.73...]	[0.1,0.4,0.8, 0.7,0.5,0.5, 0.9,1...]	[1,0.5,0.6, 0.7,0.7,0.8, 0.8,0.7,1...]

the type of the instance and its actual values. After each run of the program for a given instance the new calculated risk is inserted into the Dataset to create historical data. This means each time the program run for a given entity the risk is recalculated and inserted into the array of Risk, Impact and Probability as seen in Table 3. After the database was populated with the initial data, the risk was calculated by adding extra configurations to the model and let it feed and correct itself. This is done by calculating new values after each iteration with less variability depending on the quality of the data, and by running the Weka experimenter to make predictions for risk of a given configuration.

The expected behavior for new consistent information added to the model under multiple runs with the same configuration is a stabilization of calculated risk over time.

Experiments Scope. We defined two types of experiments to verify the accuracy of calculating risk for the aforementioned configuration scenarios.

The first experiment tests the three configuration scenarios under different conditions: incremental threats, use of historical data, and regressions. For every new threat the model calculated 100 times, after each result, the probability value by using the newly calculated model. After each 10 runs, a new threat is added to the model. Historical data corresponds to recalculated data generated from a new relic system that was monitoring ec2, ebs and s3 services.

The second experiment compares the results of the proposed approach and theoretical value estimated by different experts. An online survey was conducted by nine professionals working in the IT industry with the following years of experience: 0–5 (6.3%), 5–10 (37.5%), 10–15 (18.8%), 15–20 (12.5%), 20+ (25%). These professionals had the following profiles: Data Center consultant, Database administrator, Senior Risk Consultant, IT Director, General Manager, DevOps Engineer, Executive Director, Cloud Engineer, and Consultant. We asked them to estimate a risk and impact value for a set of threats of cloud computing found in literature: attack on virtualization, abuse and nefarious use of cloud computing, denial of service attack, insecure interface and API, malicious insiders, shared technology issues in multi-tenancy environment, data loss and leakage, service/account hijacking, identity theft, and unknown risk profile.

Results and Analysis for the First Experiment. Table 4 summarizes the results of comparing risks calculations under different conditions.

Table 4. Risk calculations under different test scenarios.

Test	Model	Correlation coefficient	Mean absolute error (AE)	Relative AE	Calculated risk
Incremental threats	0.6328 * I + 0.2408	0.6049	65.24	74.97	–
Multicloud	0.6528 * I + 0.0233	–	–	–	0.4564
Linear regression vs Non linear (SMOreg)	–	0.18 0.22	0.22 0.23	–	–

The test #1 shows that when doing 100 iterations and increasing the risk rating for the configuration on each 10 iterations, the model changes due to the new data from each set of results. However, the result stabilizes under the described condition. In this scenario and for each iteration, the risk is calculated using the abstracted model from the regression that contains information about all the previous tests and that can be used to predict values.

The test #2 shows how previous configuration can affect the risk rating, because each threat now has additional information about the calculated probabilities from the historic data. Including the data from Google cloud (*cf.* Multicloud test) has a slight impact on the model. We deduce from this behavior that adding a multicloud configuration works similar as adding a second configuration. However, as the parameters of the regression become related, the threats from one cloud can affect the other cloud. In contrast, for single configurations that do not correlate, it is possible that the model is no longer linear.

The test #3 shows that linear regressions have a lower correlation coefficient for data in the configuration #1 than the SMOreg algorithm (see Table 4). It indicates that the predictions made for nonlinear regression are more accurate from the correlation coefficient point of view. This could indicate that the actual model of risk vs impact for this configuration is nonlinear, or that the parameters from the function are not optimized. After gathering all this data, a set of predictions were run in the Weka experimenter, to see how accurate is the generated model for AWS using a linear regression (see Table 5).

Table 5. Comparing estimated and predicted risk on cloud services.

Estimated risk	Predicted risk	Error
0.267	0.317	0.05
0.346	0.346	0
0.289	0.289	0
0.346	0.346	0
0.37	0.316	0.054
0.339	0.347	0.007
0.351	0.343	0.008
0.267	0.318	0.05
0.37	0.317	0.054
0.351	0.346	0.004
0.289	0.289	0
0.267	0.318	0.05
Correlation coefficient	0.5442	
Mean absolute error	0.0231	
Root mean squared error	0.0335	
Relative absolute error	56.3148	
Root relative squared error	77.3123	

With the model created and validated, for the multicloud configuration, all the threat models were placed together to analyze how they correlate to each other. We found that if the perceived impact for a given configuration increases, the risk values will be calculated with the linear approximation. The intersect among threat models corresponds to a set of configurations where all threats have the same risk rating. This can be seen as an optimal risk minimization strategy. For nonlineal regressions there can be multiple intersection points.

Results and Analysis for the Second Experiment. Table 6 illustrates the risk values that were estimated by IT professionals for each threat vary from 0.6 to 0.8. The calculated risk value for a multicloud configuration that contains these threats is 0.456 when calculated using the proposed method. Therefore, the risk is lower when using a multicloud configuration than what people expect it to be.

Table 6. Overview of risk and impact estimated by experts.

Threat	Average estimated impact (normalized)	Average estimated risk (normalized)
Attack on virtualization	0.847	0,664
Abuse and nefarious use of cloud computing	0,847	0,735
Denial of service attack	0,770	0,717
Insecure interface and API	0,876	0,617
Malicious insiders	0,794	0,688
Shared technology issues in multi-tenancy environment	0,835	0,641
Data loss and leakage	0,8	0,717
Service/account hijacking	0,864	0,69
Identity theft	0,829	0,752
Unknown risk profile	0,733	0,68

4.3   Threats to Validity

This paper focuses on optimizing configurations of a multi-cloud self-adapting system. The experimental evaluation is restricted to the following assumptions that need to be tackled as future work to allow the approach generalization.

Our model compares directly SMI metrics of different cloud service providers. Therefore, normalization among these metrics for different providers must be further analyzed. Linearity between risk and threat impact is assumed, however different functions must be analyzed in terms of ML metrics that allow to assess the precision in estimating risk.

The approach presented in this paper focuses on optimizing the configuration of multi-cloud services by quantifying risk based on threats materialized over time. Additional analysis is required to quantify the risk when re-configuring multi-cloud architectures at runtime. For example, to quantify the impact on risk associated with the restrictions to migrate among cloud providers (*e.g.*, export private keys, transfer database users). CoCo can be used to model subtle capacity differences in cloud services as feature attributes (*e.g.*, for uploading multiparts, for tagging objects).

5   Conclusion and Future Work

The proposed approach allows modeling and configuring multi-cloud services that can adapt to changes in user preferences and threats on individual and composite services. CoCo allows modeling variability at different abstraction levels: at the domain level, at the user preferences level, and at the adaptation level. Thus, optimal alternatives that are statically configured allow a distributed system to adapt to provision degradation events and requirements given by systems or specified by users. These alternatives can be pre-calculated from different optimization constraints to allow the re-configuration of multi-cloud services. The proposed risk quantification method allows predicting risk values for alternative re-configurations on autonomous and decentralized cloud services. This enables searching and selecting optimal cloud resources for a multi-cloud services with lower error rates than risk values estimated by experts for individual services.

As primary future work, we see potential for integrating CoCo in continuous development processes. In the context of dynamic SPLs where product configurations change dynamically according to their variation constraints and requirements, CoCo requires analyzing functional (*e.g.*, discovery, configuration, monitoring) and non-functional (*e.g.*, interoperability) requirements of downwards and upwards interfaces of a cloud service. Additionally, gradual verification techniques should be included in CoCo so that changes evaluate part of the interrelated PLs, rather than its entirety. Other research path is to use neural networks to correlate the data for each threat event and to improve risk predictions.

References

1. Ahmed, N., Abraham, A.: Modeling cloud computing risk assessment using machine learning. In: Abraham, A., Krömer, P., Snasel, V. (eds.) Afro-European Conference for Industrial Advancement. AISC, vol. 334, pp. 315–325. Springer, Cham (2015). https://doi.org/10.1007/978-3-319-13572-4_26
2. Assis, M.R.M., Bittencourt, L.F., Tolosana-Calasanz, R.: Cloud federation: characterisation and conceptual model. In: 7th International Conference on Utility and Cloud Computing, pp. 585–590. IEEE (2014). https://doi.org/10.1109/UCC.2014.90
3. Böckle, G.: Introduction to software product line engineering. In: Pohl, K., Böckle, G., van der Linden, F. (eds.) Software Product Line Engineering, pp. 3–18. Springer, Heidelberg (2005). https://doi.org/10.1007/3-540-28901-1_1
4. Garg, S.K., Versteeg, S., Buyya, R.: SMICloud: a framework for comparing and ranking cloud services. In: 4th International Conference on Utility and Cloud Computing, pp. 210–218. IEEE (2011). https://doi.org/10.1109/UCC.2011.36
5. Grozev, N., Buyya, R.: Inter-cloud architectures and application brokering: taxonomy and survey. Softw. Pract. Exp. **44**(3), 369–390 (2014). https://doi.org/10.1002/spe.2168
6. Hu, Y., Huang, J., Chen, J., Liu, M., Xie, K., Yat-sen, S.: Software project risk management modeling with neural network and support vector machine approaches. In: Third International Conference on Natural Computation, vol. 3, pp. 358–362. IEEE (2007). https://doi.org/10.1109/ICNC.2007.672
7. Khorshed, M.T., Ali, A.S., Wasimi, S.A.: A survey on gaps, threat remediation challenges and some thoughts for proactive attack detection in cloud computing. Future Gener. Comput. Syst. **28**(6), 833–851 (2012). https://doi.org/10.1016/j.future.2012.01.006
8. Leite, A.F., Alves, V., Rodrigues, G.N., Tadonki, C., Eisenbeis, C., de Melo, A.C.M.A.: Automating resource selection and configuration in inter-clouds through a software product line method. In: International Conference on Cloud Computing, CC 2015, pp. 726–733. IEEE, Washington (2015). https://doi.org/10.1109/CLOUD.2015.101
9. Ma, H., Hu, Z., Li, K., Zhang, H.: Toward trustworthy cloud service selection: a time-aware approach using interval neutrosophic set. J. Parallel Distrib. Comput. **96**, 75–94 (2016). https://doi.org/10.1016/j.jpdc.2016.05.008
10. Martens, B., Teuteberg, F.: Decision-making in cloud computing environments: a cost and risk based approach. Inf. Syst. Front. **14**(4), 871–893 (2012). https://doi.org/10.1007/s10796-011-9317-x
11. Ochoa, L., González-Rojas, O.: Program synthesis for configuring collaborative solutions in feature models. In: Ciuciu, I., et al. (eds.) OTM 2016. LNCS, vol. 10034, pp. 98–108. Springer, Cham (2017). https://doi.org/10.1007/978-3-319-55961-2_10
12. Ochoa, L., González-Rojas, O., Thüm, T.: Using decision rules for solving conflicts in extended feature models. In: International Conference on Software Language Engineering, pp. 149–160. ACM, New York (2015). https://doi.org/10.1145/2814251.2814263
13. Ochoa, L., González-Rojas, O., Verano, M., Castro, H.: Searching for optimal configurations within large-scale models: a cloud computing domain. In: Link, S., Trujillo, J.C. (eds.) ER 2016. LNCS, vol. 9975, pp. 65–75. Springer, Cham (2016). https://doi.org/10.1007/978-3-319-47717-6_6

14. Saripalli, P., Walters, B.: QUIRC: a quantitative impact and risk assessment framework for cloud security. In: 3rd International Conference on Cloud Computing, pp. 280–288. IEEE (2010). https://doi.org/10.1109/CLOUD.2010.22
15. Stolen, K., et al.: Model-based risk assessment - the coras approach. In: iTrust Workshop (2002)

Modeling a Multi-agent Tourism Recommender System

Valerio Bellandi[1](✉), Paolo Ceravolo[1], and Eugenio Tacchini[2]

[1] Università degli Studi di Milano, Dipartimento di Informatica via Celoria 18,
Milan, Italy
{valerio.bellandi,paolo.ceravolo}@unimi.it
[2] Università Cattolica di Piacenza-Cremona, Via Emilia Parmense 84,
29122 Piacenza, Italy
eugenio.tacchini@unicatt.it

Abstract. Today's design of e-services for tourists means dealing with a big quantity of information and metadata that designers should be able to leverage to generate perceived values for users. In this paper we revise the design choices followed to implement a recommender system, highlighting the data processing and architectural point of view, and finally we propose a multi-agent recommender system.

Keywords: Recommender system · Big Data

1 The Tourism and the Big Data

Within this context, it arises that a new generation of tourism applications will be available. In the recent years, a constant trend has been established: users have evolved from simple observers to direct purchasers of tourist services, thanks to the direct accessibility offered by the Web and to the recommendations that can be provided by online marketplaces or sharing platforms. This constitutes a significant advantage for the consumer, to whom research is simplified and speeded up. Regarding the owners of tourist services, as hoteliers, owners of transport companies, etc., they must be able to emerge within a very wide and often very uniform commercial landscape. The new trend gets realization through four main steps: (i) *Inspiration:* recommendations play a key role in proposing destinations that might reflect a user's preferences. For instance, understanding the preference for maritime destinations, the scheme provides visitors with a number of places that are very popular at that moment of the year. (ii) *Research:* once the destination has been identified, a search method starts on all the required elements for the growth of the holiday, beginning with transport, lodging, and on-site operations. In this case, the proposals are sorted by a series of filters chosen by the user, such as the price or the review score, and, of course, by the availability during the selected period. (iii) *Booking:* once the most suitable solution has been identified, the system should support booking in brief and simple steps. Many consumers often prefer to contact the physical organizations for

© Springer Nature Switzerland AG 2019
H. Panetto et al. (Eds.): OTM 2019, LNCS 11877, pp. 750–757, 2019.
https://doi.org/10.1007/978-3-030-33246-4_46

saving after conducting informative studies or because a face-to-face interaction improves trust. (iv) *Sharing:* it concerns the sharing of views, ideas, pictures, videos or texts through social media. Friends of the user can get a lot of data or suggestions about a specific location that might be of concern to him in the nearby. A relevant role is also played by ratings, reviews and votes that the tourist makes through special sites consulted directly by other travelers who are looking for tourist experiences. In other words, this new way of handling and exchanging data about tourist facilities allows data from tour operators to be merged with user-generated data directly. This mainly improves the accessible information and opens the doors to a fresh Tourism Recommendation Systems generation.

2 Tourism Recommender Systems

Recommender Systems are "personalized information agents that provide recommendations: suggestions for items likely to be of use to a user" [5]. The "item" is the object of the recommendation, it can be, for example, a product to buy, a piece of content to consume or a person to get in touch with [7]. Recommender systems have been traditionally classified into three main categories, according to the technique used to provide recommendations: (i) Content-Based (CB) recommender systems base the suggestions on the analysis of the items: each item is analyzed and described using a set of features, (ii) Collaborative filtering (CF) is "the process of filtering or evaluating items through the opinions of other people" [8]: CF recommender systems don't require the analysis of the items' content, they use the feedback provided by users as the features of the item, and hybrids that merges the previous techniques [1]. While recommendation systems are implemented in many distinct domains, tourism is a domain where they can be especially helpful: considering the quantity of data accessible, consumers can use tourism recommendation systems to schedule a town visit or to obtain suggestions for operations, hotels, restaurants linked to a specific location [3]. At the same time, Tourism Recommender Systems impose novel functions and requirements [6]. In this paper, we are not focusing on a specific interface but we describe our engine that exposes API endpoints. They can be used by an end-user application to get recommendations. Considering the functionalities, four distinct kinds of functionality are typically supplied: travel location and tourist packs, ranked list of suggested attractions, route planning and social events [4]. While some systems only provide suggestions for a *destination* (according to user preferences), most systems recommend *attractions* (events, hotels, restaurants, activities, ...) once the user has chosen the destination of the trip.

3 A Multi-agent Tourism Recommender System

Our work was aimed at designing a multi-agent recommender that can provide suggestions for several types of tourism-related products: hotels, restaurants, activities and so on [2]. In our examples, we will concentrate on a particular category of items: *activities*. An activity is an experience that a tourist can have in a particular place, such as a guided tour of the Colosseum in Rome or weekend in the mountains to ski. We have a set of m registered users U and a set of n activities A, the goal of our recommendation engine is to suggest relevant activities to users when they ask for recommendations. Furthermore, the system should be able to suggest activities to users who are not registered and to groups. To achieve its goals, our system uses a combination of three different techniques: *collaborative filtering*, *content-based*, and *demographic*.

Collaborative Filtering. As said before the collaborative filtering approach is used to compute the similarities among activities based on the users who liked them. We have in input a matrix $F(m, n)$ containing, for each of the $m \times n$ combinations, the rating the user gave to the activity if the user consumed the activity and submitted feedback. We have a missing value for a specific combination of (users, activity) when the user didn't consume the activity or didn't submit feedback. The ratings are in a one-to-five range. To compute the similarities among activities, we consider each activity as a vector of user ratings and we compute the Pearson correlation between all the couples of activities, obtaining a similarity matrix $S_{cf}(n, n)$. Considering a couple of vectors X and Y, representing the ratings two activities have received by N users who rated both the activities, the Pearson correlation r is computed as follows:

$$r = \frac{N \sum XY - (\sum X \sum Y)}{\sqrt{[N \sum x^2 - (\sum x)^2][N \sum y^2 - (\sum y)^2]}} \tag{1}$$

The similarity matrix S_{cf} allows us to provide relevant suggestions for users if we know their history: we consider the activity the user liked the most in the past and we provide as a suggestion the fifty most similar activities the user has not consumed yet. The collaborative filtering strategy assumes a wealthy history of consumption and feedback. This is not always the case, particularly in a cold-start situation; when the system has just been implemented, the F matrix could be very sparse, so the Person correlation is calculated on small sample size, not capturing the underlying similarity between the activities, at least for some activity couples.

Content-Based. We use a content-based approach to calculate the similarities between activities (as we did for filtering collaboration), but in this case, the similarity is based on a set of features describing the activities and not on feedback from the users. Since these characteristics are something we can always provide, even without any activity consumption or feedback information, we can create a similar matrix Scb.

Our content model defines operations using categorical data; each characteristic may have a finite set of values: some characteristics are binary, e.g. "Children's Activity" may be true or incorrect, other characteristics may have a number of possible values higher than two, e.g. "geographic region". All the values assigned to the features are an integer: For binary functionality, we use

0 to indicate false and 1to denote true; for non-binary functionality, we use a finite set of integer values representing each category.

In specific, a subset of characteristics is used to categorize the tourist's real experience using binary tasks, some characteristics might be: "Sport", "Museums and Arts" and so on. This permits to model an activity based on multiple categories: for example, a Gallery tour that combines Wine tasting will have both the "Museums and Arts" and "Food and Wine" features set to 1.

We have this way, in input a matrix $AF(m, k)$ where, for each activity m, we describe the activity assigning a value to each of the k features. To compute the similarities among activities, we consider each activity as a vector of features values and we compute a similarity matrix $S_{cb}(m, m)$ based on the Jaccard index, which measures, for each couple of activities, the proportion of feature whose values differ[1].

Since we are using categorical data, the Jaccard index captures better than the Pearson correlation the distance (similarities) between items: if two activities are described, for a specific feature, by values 1 and 10 respectively, they differ exactly as two activities that for the same feature have values 1 and 2.

Once we have the similarity matrix S_{cb} we can use the same approach we used for the collaborative filtering technique: to suggest relevant recommendations to a user: we select the activity they like more in the past and we suggest the fifty most similar activities according to S_{cb}, excluding the activities the user already consumed.

Note that, even if the computation of the similarity matrix does not suffer from the *cold-start* problem, we are still unable to provide meaningful suggestions to users we do not have relevant information about their history.

Demographic Approach. To solve the *cold-start* problem, we mentioned in the previous section, we use demographic data. The idea is to compute the similarities among users and to suggest to a user U_i activities based on what the user's neighbors (the users most similar to U_i) liked. The approach is similar to a classic collaborative filtering user-based approach, but instead of using consumption/feedback data we used demographic data, assuming we can always have access to some demographic data about the user. Some of the features we use are, for example: "Age class", "Gender", "Has children", "Speaks English". The representation level is an input matrix $UD(n, z)$, where, for each user n, we describe the user assigning a value to each of the z demographic features. To compute the similarities between a user and all the others, we consider each user as a vector of demographic feature values and we compute the Jaccard index between them; we can then suggest to a user U_i the activities most liked by their neighbors: the users most similar to U_i. Please, note that features do not need to be strictly demographic: we can use any kind of categorical feature including user preferences, if available; for example "Interested in watching

---

[1] This represents the distance between two activities, not the similarity, but we can still easily get, for each activity, the most similar ones by sorting according to the distance, ascending.

sports". This allows mitigating the cold start problem using information that can be extracted from social media: for example, using Facebook login[2] it would be possible to get the pages liked by a user. The model used to represent a user can be extended adding or removing features without any impact on the implementation. This approach has been introduced, in particular, to suggest relevant activities to *prospects*, i.e. users who browse the Website but are not customers yet, and want instant recommendations. Since the process of computing similarities among users can take time if the number of users is very high, we implemented a model based on*fingerprints*, representing, the feature values of each user, allowing the fast computation of the neighbours and therefore the generation of a list of favourites activities for a typical customer having the same characteristics of the prospect who is querying the Recommender System.

Groups. All the algorithms we have just explained are intended to serve a client or prospect individually. We also have a particular module that offers group suggestions, i.e. two or more individuals who want to consume an activity together, e.g. a group of friends or a family. This modular application is very comparable to the one we used for prospects: we model distinct groups based on an extensible set of characteristics, e.g. group average age, group with kids, etc. Then we propose the operations most liked by organizations with comparable features to a prospect group.

3.1   RS Architecture

Our proposal consists of two key elements: the recommendation engine, which pre-calculates the recommendations, and the API, which offers, among other things, the suggestions for a customer, a prospect, or a group that has been requested.

The input data consist of the following collections:

```
activities (id, val_feat_1, val_feat_2,...val_feat_n),
customers (id, val_feat_1, val_feat_2,...val_feat_n, fingerprint),
customers_activities (id_customer, id_activity, rating, date).
```

These collections represent the information related to the activities, the customers and the consumption/feedback history of the customers; in particular, the `customers_activities` set represents, for each customer, the activities they consumed, the date of consumption and the rating.

It is worth to describe how the fingerprint field works: it is a list whose elements contain (one element for each feature) the code of the feature and the feature's value, for a customer. For example, let's assume that in our model we only have two features for customers: "Age class" (possible values: 1, 2, 3, 4) and "Country" (possible values: 1 to 206, each value represents a specific country); let's also assume that we denote "Age class" with the feature code

---

[2] https://developers.facebook.com/docs/facebook-login.

"001" and "Country" with the feature code "002"; for an Italian customer, 25 years old, the fingerprint will be ["001002", "002034"], assuming that 2 is the value corresponding to the 18–25 age class and that Italy is the country 34.

The fingerprint field allows the computation of the neighbors of a prospect in one MongoDB query; for example, to get the neighbors of an Italian prospect, 25 years old, we can execute the following query:

```
neighbors = db.customers.aggregate([{ "$project":
{"id": 1, "count": { '$size':
{'$setIntersection': ["$features",['001002','002034']]},
"_id": 0 } },{ "$sort" : { "count" : -1} },
{ "$limit" : 50 }]).
```

Which returns the 50 most similar neighbors. This approach also allows to change the model without changing the Python implementation code of the demographic technique: if you add or remove a customer's feature from the model you just need to update the schema of the customers' collection and the related records.

The information represented in the field *fingerprint* is redundant: the same information, in fact, is represented through the value_feature_1, value_feature_2, ... value_feature_n fields; however, we are keeping those fields in the schema because they work as fast middleware between the recommendation engine and other systems which might expect a schema where each field is represented by a feature.

Some additional collections are used to represent information related to groups:

```
groups (id, val_feat_1, val_feat_2,...val_feat_n, fingerprint),
group_activities (id_group, id_activity, rating, date).
```

The first collection, group, represents the information related to each group, the second one is similar to customers_activities and represents the consumption/feedback history of a group. Note that a record of the collection groups represents all the groups having the same characteristics while in customers the corresponding collection represents a single customer.

Output Data. Once the recommendations are computed, they are stored in some MongoDB collections. In particular, for each recommendation technique we explained in the previous chapter, we have a collection that stores the IDs of the activities suggested for a particular target, i.e., a customer, a prospect, or a group.

For each row, we store the id of the customer and an array containing the list of 50 activity IDs to suggest to the user, sorted by relevance. Storing the precomputed recommendations as an array in MongoDB, one per user, is a very fast and computationally inexpensive way to provide recommendations, even in a Big Data context, where both the total number of users n and the total number of items m (activities, hotels, or any other kind of item that needs to be recommended) are very high and also the recommendation requests concurrency is high. A typical Tourism Recommender System may expect to operate with millions of users and items, largely below the volumes addressed by Big Data applications in other domains.

3.2 Multi-agent Approach

While we have discussed in detail about the recommendation of *activities*, adding the support for a new typology of the item is straightforward. Most of the work consists of modeling a new set of features for this new type of item, in order to use the content-based technique. We also need additional data structures (MongoDB collections) to store all the data related to the new category of items. For example, to add support for hotels, we could describe each hotel using some categorical features such as the hotel luxury rating, the suitability for families or the price category. We also need to add all the MongoDB collections needed to represent the information related to hotels and to the ratings the hotels can receive by customers. While *hotels* and *activities* will have a different feature sets, customers_hotels and customers_activities will have the same structure. The collaborative filtering approach normally does not need changes: a user can, in fact, rate an activity, a hotel, a restaurant or any other kind of item and we always store just the rating and the date (if available). The demographic approach also does not need change: for both customers and groups, we still need to compute their neighbors (according to their features) and then the suggestions (according to the hotels most liked by the neighborhood). For each type of item we can use a different recommendation technique, according to the specific needs and data availability: for example if we have a rich consumption/feedback dataset for hotels but we don't have much data for activities, we could use a collaborative filtering approach for hotels and a content-based one for activities.

3.3 Conclusions and Future Work

The recommendation engine proposed is a work-in-progress project and we have planned several improvements. First, we want to work on cross-domain recommendations: our engine can recommend different types of items, belonging to different domains (e.g. activities and hotels); we might know very well the preferences of a user for a particular domain but not for *all* the domains. The adoption of a cross-domain strategy allows to exploit the knowledge available in a domain to recommend items belonging to another domain, for example, we could recommend, to a user that normally books luxury hotels, activities in the same price range, even if we do not have any consumption history, for that user, in the *activities* domain. This can be implemented in several ways, for example by defining a subset of features that work for all the domains or by exploiting, in order to suggest items to a user for a domain, the knowledge we have on that domain for the user's neighbors.

Acknowledgements. This work was partly supported by the "eTravel project" funded by the "Provincia di Trento", and by the program "Piano sostegno alla ricerca 2018" funded by Università degli Studi di Milano.

References

1. Adomavicius, G., Tuzhilin, A.: Toward the next generation of recommender systems: a survey of the state-of-the-art and possible extensions. IEEE Trans. Knowl. Data Eng. **17**(6), 734–749 (2005)
2. Ardagna, C.A., Bellandi, V., Bezzi, M., Ceravolo, P., Damiani, E., Hebert, C.: Model-based big data analytics-as-a-service: take big data to the next level. IEEE Trans. Serv. Comput. **PP**, 1 (2018)
3. Bahramian, Z., Ali Abbaspour, R., Claramunt, C.: A context-aware tourism recommender system based on a spreading activation method. Int. Arch. Photogramm. Remote Sens. Spat. Inf. Sci. **42**, 333–339 (2017)
4. Borràs, J., Moreno, A., Valls, A.: Intelligent tourism recommender systems: a survey. Expert Syst. Appl. **41**(16), 7370–7389 (2014)
5. Burke, R.: Hybrid web recommender systems. In: Brusilovsky, P., Kobsa, A., Nejdl, W. (eds.) The Adaptive Web. LNCS, vol. 4321, pp. 377–408. Springer, Heidelberg (2007). https://doi.org/10.1007/978-3-540-72079-9_12
6. Christensen, I., Schiaffino, S., Armentano, M.: Social group recommendation in the tourism domain. J. Intell. Inf. Syst. **47**(2), 209–231 (2016). https://doi.org/10.1007/s10844-016-0400-0
7. Damiani, E., et al.: Applying recommender systems in collaboration environments. Comput. Hum. Behav. **51**, 1124–1133 (2015)
8. Schafer, J.B., Frankowski, D., Herlocker, J., Sen, S.: Collaborative filtering recommender systems. In: Brusilovsky, P., Kobsa, A., Nejdl, W. (eds.) The Adaptive Web. LNCS, vol. 4321, pp. 291–324. Springer, Heidelberg (2007). https://doi.org/10.1007/978-3-540-72079-9_9

Author Index

Printed in the United States
By Bookmasters